Return to an Address of the Honourable the
House of Commons dated 15th February 2000 for the

Report of the Tribunal of Inquiry into the abuse of children in care in the former county council areas of Gwynedd and Clwyd since 1974

Lost in Care

Ordered by The House of Commons *to be printed*
15th February 2000

HC 201   LONDON: THE STATIONERY OFFICE   £76

TRIBUNAL OF INQUIRY INTO CHILD ABUSE IN NORTH WALES

The Rt Hon Paul Murphy MP
Secretary of State for Wales
Gwydyr House
Whitehall
London
SW1A 2ER

30 September 1999

Dear Secretary of State

On 20 June 1996 it was resolved by both Houses of Parliament that it was expedient that a Tribunal be established for inquiring into the abuse of children in care in the former county council areas of Gwynedd and Clwyd since 1974.

On 30 August 1996 your predecessor, the Rt Hon William Hague MP, appointed us, by a Warrant of Appointment, to be a Tribunal for the purpose of this Inquiry and declared that the Tribunals of Inquiry (Evidence) Act 1921 should apply to the Tribunal, which was constituted as a Tribunal within the meaning of section 1 of that Act.

We have carried out the Inquiry and now have the honour to submit our report.

We acknowledge and express our gratitude to the many persons who have helped us in this very wide-ranging investigation in Appendix 1 to the report. Here, however, we wish to mention particularly Sir Ronald Hadfield QPM, DL, who was appointed by your predecessor as an assessor to the Tribunal to advise us in respect of police matters and whose assistance has been invaluable.

Sir Ronald Waterhouse

Margaret Clough

Morris le Fleming

Outline of the Report

Table of Contents

Please note:

Complainants and some others are identified in this report by a capital letter instead of by name. The identification by letter is consistent within individual chapters but has no application outside that chapter unless expressly stated.

PART I

INTRODUCTION

The appointment of the Tribunal and a brief account of its work

1.01 On 17 June 1996 the Secretary of State for Wales, the Rt Hon William Hague MP, informed the House of Commons of the Government's decision, subject to the approval of both Houses of Parliament, that there should be a judicial inquiry, with the powers conferred by the Tribunals of Inquiry (Evidence) Act 1921, into the alleged abuse of children in care in the former county council areas of Gwynedd and Clwyd since 1974.

1.02 The Secretary of State announced also that the terms of reference of the Inquiry would be as follows:

(a) to inquire into the abuse of children in care in the former county council areas of Gwynedd and Clwyd since 1974;

(b) to examine whether the agencies and authorities responsible for such care, through the placement of the children or through the regulation or management of the facilities, could have prevented the abuse or detected its occurrence at an earlier stage;

(c) to examine the response of the relevant authorities and agencies to allegations and complaints of abuse made either by children in care, children formerly in care or any other persons, excluding scrutiny of decisions whether to prosecute named individuals;

(d) in the light of this examination, to consider whether the relevant caring and investigative agencies discharged their functions appropriately and, in the case of the caring agencies, whether they are doing so now; and to report its findings and to make recommendations to him.

1.03 On the same occasion the Secretary of State for Wales announced that the Secretary of State for Health, the Rt Hon Stephen Dorrell MP, had arranged for a further review of the safeguards against the abuse of children living away from home in England and Wales to be conducted by Sir William Utting, the former Chief Social Services Inspector at the Department of Health. That review was completed in July 1997 and Sir William's published report of his review, entitled "People Like Us", has been of great assistance to us in our own task.

1.04 On 20 June 1996 resolutions were passed in both Houses of Parliament declaring that it was expedient that a tribunal be established for inquiring into a definite matter of public importance, namely, the abuse of children in care in the former county council areas of Gwynedd and Clwyd; and on 30 August 1996, by warrant, the Secretary of State for Wales appointed the three of us to be a Tribunal for the purposes of the inquiry. He decided also to appoint an assessor to the Tribunal to advise us in respect of police matters and Sir Ronald Hadfield QPM, DL, a former Chief Constable successively of Nottinghamshire and the West Midlands, was appointed in this capacity.

1.05 Having regard to the scope of the inquiry and the length of the period under investigation, an immense amount of preliminary work had to be undertaken before we could begin to hear oral evidence. We are grateful to the Treasury Solicitor for providing the services of a team of lawyers under Brian McHenry, who was appointed Solicitor to the Tribunal, to direct and conduct this preliminary work and to assist the Tribunal generally in the course of its hearings. In addition, three counsel, namely Gerard Elias QC, a former leader of the Wales and Chester Circuit, Gregory Treverton-Jones and Ernest Ryder, who was appointed QC at Easter 1997, were nominated by the Attorney-General to act as Counsel to the Tribunal. They began work as soon as the Tribunal was appointed and were assisted by a team of para-legals and appropriate administrative staff provided by the Welsh Office.

1.06 Additional detail about the work of the Tribunal and its procedure is provided in Appendix 4 to this report. It is appropriate to emphasise here, however, the scale of the preparatory work involved. It included consideration of about 9,500 social services files made available to us, perusal of some 3,500 statements to the police made in the course of their own investigations together with many associated documents and the tracing and interviewing of potential witnesses, including those who responded to our public advertisements addressed to everyone who might be able to give relevant evidence. This task of gathering and assimilating the potential evidence could not have been accomplished without the full hearted and enthusiastic effort and support of the Tribunal's staff, to whom we pay warm tribute.

1.07 It was necessary for us to hold four preliminary hearings to deal with such matters as legal representation, recommendations as to costs and procedure generally. These took place on 10 September, 15 October and 26 November 1996 and on 3 January 1997. We are grateful to counsel, solicitors and the witnesses themselves for their outstanding co-operation in enabling us to deal with these matters expeditiously and with proper regard for the saving of costs whenever this was both fair and practicable.

1.08 Without going into unnecessary detail, it is appropriate to mention that two decisions of considerable importance to our deliberations were made at an early stage. Firstly, the Attorney-General authorised the Tribunal to say that anything that any witness said in evidence before the Inquiry would not be used in evidence against him or her in any criminal proceedings, except in relation to any offence of perjury or perverting the course of justice. Secondly, bearing in mind (amongst other things) the wide terms of sections 1 and 2 of the Sexual Offences (Amendment) Act 1992, which prohibit identification, in any written publication or broadcast programme to be published in England and Wales, of a complainant who alleges that a sexual offence has been committed against him or her, we decided to issue the following information for the assistance of the press and media:

> "The Tribunal wishes to indicate that it will regard the following as prima facie evidence of a contempt of court:
>
> publication of any material in a written publication (as defined in section 6(1) of the 1992 Act) available to the public (whether on paper or in

electronic form), or in a television or radio programme for reception in England and Wales, which is likely to identify any living person as a person by whom or against whom an allegation of physical or sexual abuse has been or is likely to be made in proceedings before the Tribunal, with the exception of those who have been convicted of criminal offences of physical or sexual abuse of children in care."

We said also that this was a general intimation but that it was open to the Tribunal to give a different ruling in relation to any specific witness.

1.09 Our main reason for issuing this notice was that we considered that there was a substantial risk that the course of justice in our proceedings would be seriously prejudiced or impeded in the event of such publication, not least because potential witnesses might be deterred from testifying, or from testifying fully, to the Tribunal. The guidance was particularly necessary because it was impracticable for us to grant anonymity in the actual hearing itself to witnesses giving evidence to the Tribunal, whether as complainants or as alleged abusers, having regard to the numbers of persons involved on either side. Any form of index by letter or number would have been both intolerably time consuming and potentially confusing. Nevertheless, for both complainants and alleged abusers, the giving of oral evidence about events alleged to have occurred many years earlier was a very painful experience, involving discussion of matters and their surrounding circumstances of which probably very few within their present social circle were aware. It was clear to us, therefore, that witnesses who were prepared to speak of these matters within the comparative privacy of the Tribunal hearings would be significantly deterred if they were to be identified in the press or otherwise publicly and might be tempted to trim their evidence to avoid recrimination or other adverse consequences.

1.10 We are grateful to the press and broadcasting authorities for following this guidance and for seeking clarification from the Tribunal whenever it was thought to be needed. In the event it did not prove necessary for the Tribunal Chairman to certify to the High Court as contempt of the Tribunal's proceedings any publication or broadcast. An adverse consequence of our ruling may have been that the evidence heard by the Tribunal was less widely reported in the national press than it would otherwise have been but we believe firmly that it did have the effect of encouraging witnesses to come forward and there were comparatively few who declined to give oral evidence once they had made a written statement to a member of the Tribunal's interviewing team.

1.11 We were told at the outset that our hearings were likely to last at least a year because of the breadth of the Inquiry and our initial target was to begin in mid-January 1997. In the event we sat for three days, beginning on 21 January 1997, to hear opening statements and were able to start hearing oral evidence on 3 February 1997. In all we sat on 201 days (excluding the four preliminary hearings) to hear evidence and submissions, ending on 7 April 1998. In that period the Tribunal heard the oral evidence of 264 witnesses. For a variety of reasons it was agreed also that we should receive in evidence the written statements of a further 311 witnesses, which were incorporated in the transcript, either in full or in summary form, but this was done on the footing that the contents of the statements were not agreed by all the parties and that counsel were at liberty to comment critically on the statements. Strenuous efforts were made to limit the almost intolerably voluminous documentary evidence by a strict application of the test of relevance to our terms of reference and all the documents admitted were scanned and filed on the Tribunal's computer for ease of reference. In the end 12,000 documents, some of which ran to many pages, were dealt with in this way.

1.12 Finally, we arranged a seminar, which was held at Ewloe on 6 and 7 May 1998, after the hearings of evidence and submissions had been concluded. The purpose of this seminar was to enable the Tribunal itself and the parties to the Inquiry to put to a selected panel of experts for their comment possible recommendations for the future designed to strengthen existing safeguards for the protection from abuse of looked after children. We invited Sir William Utting CB, Sir Ronald Hadfield QPM, DL, Adrianne Jones CBE, Brian Briscoe, Secretary of the Local Government Association and Dr Anthony Baker[1], a Consultant in Psychiatry with a special interest in the needs of children in care, to form our panel. We are very grateful to them for agreeing to take part and for the very helpful discussion that ensued.

---

[1] Nominated by Counsel for the complainants.

The general background to the Inquiry

2.01 When announcing the Government's decision to appoint this Tribunal, the Secretary of State for Wales referred to the fact that it had been known for several years that serious sexual and physical abuse of children had taken place in homes managed by the former Clwyd County Council in the 1970s and 1980s. The Secretary of State mentioned, in particular, an intensive investigation by North Wales Police begun in 1991, in which about 2,600 statements had been obtained from individuals and which had resulted in eight prosecutions and seven convictions of former care workers, but he said that, nevertheless, speculation had continued in North Wales that the actual abuse was on a much greater scale than the convictions themselves suggested.

The independent investigation commissioned by Clwyd County Council: the Jillings Report

2.02 One of the matters that had given rise to particular disquiet was that the Social Services Committee of Clwyd County Council had, in January 1994, commissioned an investigation by an independent panel of three experts, presided over by John Jillings, a former Director of Social Services for Derbyshire and ex President of the Association of Directors of Social Services, but the Panel's report, ultimately presented in March 1996, had not been published. The Panel had carried out its investigation between March 1994 and December 1995, initially with draft terms of reference but, from December 1994, with the following terms of reference set out in a letter from the County Council dated 30 November 1994:

> "The County Council has appointed John Jillings as Chairman of an independent panel to conduct an internal investigation for the County Council into the management of its Social Services Department from 1974 to date with particular reference to and emphasis upon what went wrong with child care in Clwyd in the light of a number of incidents and convictions culminating in the conviction of Stephen Norris in November 1993 of further offences committed against children in the care of the County Council."

The Panel were required to "inquire into, consider and report to the County Council upon (1) what went wrong and (2) why did this happen and how this position could have continued undetected for so long" and their attention was specifically directed to such matters as recruitment and selection of staff, management and training, suspension, complaints procedures etc.

2.03 The misfortune was that, in the view of leading lawyers who were instructed to advise Clwyd County Council, the report could not be published because to do so would expose the Council to actions for defamation in the absence of any relevant absolute or even qualified privilege and because publication would probably constitute a fundamental breach of the Council's contract of insurance, entitling the insurers to refuse to indemnify the Council in respect of outstanding and potential claims against the Council by children formerly in its care who alleged that they had been abused whilst in care. The Council's insurers had warned against publishing the report on the latter ground and leading members of the Council felt obliged to accept the County Solicitor's advice that they should not do so, having regard to Counsel's opinion. This part of the history is dealt with in more detail in Chapter 32 of this report: it is sufficient to say here that neither the Welsh Office nor the County Councils nor the successor authorities that took over administrative responsibility from the County Councils on 1 April 1996, only days after the presentation of the report, were willing to undertake its publication. Meanwhile, speculation in the press and other media about its contents fermented and a notice of motion signed by six Members of Parliament, tabled on 27 March 1996, deplored the actions of the insurance company in (allegedly) attempting to suppress the report.

The Report of the Examination Team on Child Care Procedures and Practice in North Wales

2.04 Another factor in the Government's decision to establish this Tribunal, and one that led to the inclusion of the administrative area of the former Gwynedd County Council within the scope of its inquiry, was that the Secretary of State for Wales had, in December 1995, accepted the recommendation of Nicola Davies QC that there should be a detailed examination of the child care procedures and practices of both Clwyd and Gwynedd County Councils since 1991. Adrianne Jones CBE, a former Director of Social Services for Birmingham City Council, was appointed under section 80 of the Children Act 1989 to carry out the examination: she was assisted by an independent team of three, and she presented her report to the Secretary of State in May 1996.

2.05 The report contained some 41 recommendations, aimed mainly at improving the planning, management and monitoring of children's services, and the Secretary of State told the House of Commons:

> "Adrianne Jones' report will make a substantial contribution towards achieving my objective of securing the safety and well-being of children in care in North Wales, but it also reveals that, despite the Children Act, the Warner report and all the other actions that the Government have taken in recent years to protect children, serious shortcomings remained up until the abolition of the Clwyd and Gwynedd County Councils earlier this year. This is a disturbing conclusion, which has to be coupled with continuing public concern about the full extent of what happened and how it could apparently have continued undetected for so long.
>
> The Government are determined that there should be no cover-up of events in the past, and that every possible step is taken to protect children in care in the future. In the light of these developments, we have decided that further initiatives need to be undertaken."

2.06 Whilst the account in the preceding paragraphs of this chapter[1] adequately indicates the most proximate reasons for the appointment of this Tribunal, a more extended outline of the chronology of events is necessary to explain the conflicts and mounting concern about the welfare of children in care in North Wales in the years preceding 1996.

Criminal proceedings prior to 1991

2.07 Before the major police investigation began in 1991 the following were convicted of relevant offences within the administrative areas of Clwyd and Gwynedd:

(1) 1976 **Anthony David Taylor** was convicted on 6 January at Talgarth Magistrates' Court of two offences of indecent assault upon boys staying with the Bryn Alyn Community, the owner of private residential establishments for children in the vicinity of Wrexham. He was fined £20 for each offence[2].

(2) 1977 **Leslie Wilson**, a house father at Little Acton Assessment Centre, Wrexham[3], who had been suspended on 15 July, was convicted on 22 December in Chester Crown Court of indecent assault, gross indecency and attempted buggery and sentenced to 15 months' imprisonment.

(3) 1978 **Bryan Davies**, Warden of a residential unit at Ystrad Hall School, Llangollen[4], who had been suspended on 25 May was convicted on 4 September at Llangollen Magistrates' Court of three offences of indecent assault involving two pupils at the school, for which he was placed on probation for 12 months, with a condition of hospital treatment, and ordered to perform 160 hours' community service.

(4) 1980 **Reginald Gareth Cooke**, known also by a number of different aliases but hereafter referred to as Gary Cooke[5], pleaded guilty on 30 June 1980 in the Crown Court at Mold to two offences of buggery, one of indecent assault and one of taking an indecent photograph. He was sentenced to a total of five years of imprisonment, from which he was released on parole on 23 November 1981. Cooke had been employed for two weeks only in a Clwyd children's home, Bersham Hall, probably in or about 1972. Later, he had been employed as a care worker for over a year by the Bryn Alyn Community in their children's homes, firstly at Marton's Camp, Winsford, Cheshire and then at Cotsbrook Hall, Higford; and he had then been Assistant

---

[1] See paras 2.01 to 2.05.
[2] See paras 4.10, 4.11, 21.48 and 21.49.
[3] See paras 12.10, 12.25 and 12.26.
[4] See paras 22.10 to 22.14.
[5] See paras 52.30, 52.34 to 52.51 and 52.59 to 52.70.

Warden of a probation hostel in Ruabon, near Wrexham, for six months. None of the victims named in the 1980 convictions had been in care at the time when the offences against them were committed but they were all young persons, some of whom had been or were about to be children in care, and Cooke was known to have ready access to children in residential care in the Wrexham area. An associate of Cooke and a known paedophile, **(Arthur) Graham Stephens**, was a co-defendant in the proceedings. He pleaded guilty to an offence of buggery and one of indecent assault and was sentenced to three years' imprisonment.

(5) 1986   In July 1986 at Mold Crown Court **Iain Muir**, a deputy head of the Bryn Alyn Community[6], was convicted of an offence of unlawful sexual intercourse with a female resident at Bryn Alyn and was sentenced to six months' imprisonment. The following month, on 5 August 1986, at Wrexham Magistrates' Court, a full time residential child care worker, **Jacqueline Elizabeth Thomas**, who had been employed in another Clwyd children's home, Chevet Hey[7], and suspended on 3 January, received a three months' suspended sentence of imprisonment for indecent assault on a 15 years old boy resident at Chevet Hey.

(6) 1987   On 16 January 1987, in the Crown Court at Mold, **David John Gillison**, linked with Jacqueline Thomas by family friendship, pleaded guilty to two offences of gross indecency with a male resident of Bersham Hall, aged 16 years[8]. He was sentenced to three and a quarter years' imprisonment and was dismissed by Clwyd County Council from his employment as a social worker for the physically handicapped in the Rhuddlan area office (but it was not alleged that the offences had been committed on Council premises). Gillison's co-defendant on this occasion, **William Gerry**, a former resident of Bryn Estyn, was sentenced to two years' imprisonment for an offence of buggery with the 16 years old boy and four offences of gross indecency involving both the latter and the 15 years old boy referred to in (5) above. Gerry committed suicide on 1 December 1997. On 29 April 1987 **Gary Cooke** appeared again in the Crown Court, this time at Chester, and was sentenced to a total of seven years' imprisonment for four offences of buggery, three of indecent assault on a male person and one offence of taking an indecent photograph. These offences involved boys and young persons between the ages of 12 and 18 years, who had been taken by Cooke to his home in Wrexham. Two of the victims were in care at the time of the offences and the 18 year old, who was the victim of buggery, had been in care for over three years between 1980 and 1983. Cooke was not released on parole until 19 June 1991.

---

[6] See paras 21.50 and 21.51.
[7] See paras 14.32 to 14.45.
[8] See paras 14.38 to 14.43.

(7) 1990 On 5 October 1990, in the Crown Court at Chester, **Stephen Roderick Norris**, who had been Officer-in-Charge of Cartrefle children's home at Broughton in Clwyd from 1 December 1984[9] and, earlier, a housemaster at Bryn Estyn children's home[10], pleaded guilty to five specimen charges of indecent assault involving three boys who had been the victims successively of his indecent conduct almost throughout his period in charge until his arrest in June 1990. He received a concurrent sentence of three and a half years' imprisonment for each of the offences.

(8) 1991 On 30 July 1991, **Frederick Rutter**, a former police officer for a short period, who had been employed as a care worker by Clwyd County Council successively in two children's homes and then a hostel between 1982 and 1988[11] and who was an approved foster parent with his wife[12], was convicted in Chester Crown Court of four offences of rape and two offences of indecent assault, for which he received a total of 12 years' imprisonment. The Rutters had provided approved lodgings for a young girl at their home from 1986 and had been approved as foster parents for another girl in May 1988. Then in September 1988 Rutter had become Warden of Pen-y-Lan Hostel at Connah's Quay, a private hostel owned by a housing association and catering for young homeless persons aged between 16 and 25 years. Two of the rape victims were the girl in care who lodged with him and his wife from the age of 17 years and the girl fostered by them, who was 16 years old when she was raped by him. The other victims named in the offences were all residents at the hostel, three of them being aged 17 and 18 years and the last 20 or 21 years.

The complaints of Alison Taylor

2.08 It will have been observed that none of the offences listed in the previous paragraph had been committed within the administrative area of Gwynedd. However, the North Wales Police investigated a number of other alleged criminal offences against children in care in the period between April 1974 and July 1991, although these investigations did not result in successful criminal proceedings. Several of them involved staff at private children's homes in Gwynedd and others related to Gwynedd County Council children's homes at Tŷ'r Felin, Bangor, Y Gwyngyll at Llanfair PG and Queen's Park Close, Holyhead. It is only necessary here to refer to the investigation undertaken in 1986 and 1987, following representations to the Chief Constable by a Gwynedd county councillor and university lecturer, Councillor Keith Marshall, to whom Alison Taylor had made a number of complaints. Taylor was then Officer-in-Charge of the local authority's children's home Tŷ Newydd at Bangor and she

---

[9] See Chapter 15.
[10] See paras 8.23 to 8.34.
[11] See paras 8.41, 8.42 and 10.151 to 10.156.
[12] See Chapter 26.

held that position from 16 August 1982 until she was suspended from duty on 1 December 1986. She had served earlier as Deputy Officer-in-Charge and then Acting Officer-in-Charge at Tŷ'r Felin, Bangor, from September 1976 until 1 January 1978, when Joseph Nefyn Dodd had become Officer-in-Charge. Taylor had then served for about two and three quarter years as Deputy Officer-in-Charge under Dodd until she left to undergo further training at the North East Wales Institute from the autumn of 1980 until 1982.

2.09 By the time that Alison Taylor made her complaints to Councillor Marshall she had tried to raise them with a number of her superiors. This part of the history is dealt with in detail in Chapters 34 and 45 of this report. In her view, other channels of complaint had been effectively blocked. Nefyn Dodd had been given additional duties from about October 1978, being charged with the responsibility of visiting other Gwynedd homes to give support to staff and to report problems to an Assistant Director. It is not clear whether he was relieved of these additional duties for a period from March 1979 (except in respect of Y Gwyngyll) but, from 1982, he was said to have undertaken responsibility for all aspects of work relating to the residential care of children in the county, with the title (from 1983) of Co-ordinator/Supervisor Community Homes, whilst retaining his post as Officer-in-Charge of Tŷ'r Felin. Thus, he acted as line manager to the other three homes then existing in the county. Finally, the County Council confirmed his appointment as Principal Officer (Residential Care - Children), coupled with his Tŷ'r Felin appointment, from 1 October 1985. Taylor's own views on the conduct and management of children's homes differed radically from those of Dodd so that a clash was inevitable. She could not be expected to direct her complaints to Dodd himself alone but she was unable to obtain any favourable response from line managers above him, including the Director of Social Services, Lucille Hughes.

2.10 The dossier of complaints presented by Alison Taylor to Councillor Marshall was wide ranging. He sought the advice of a senior fellow Councillor, W R Pierce, who was then Vice-Chairman of the North Wales Police Authority and who advised that the police should be informed. The upshot was that the head of the force's Criminal Investigation Department (CID), Detective Chief Superintendent Gwynne Owen, met Councillor Marshall at his home in Bangor with Taylor on 20 February 1986 and a criminal investigation, which lasted, in the end, until May 1988, began.

2.11 Taylor's complaints included criticism of Nefyn Dodd's dual role as Officer-in-Charge of Tŷ'r Felin and Supervisor of all the children's homes in the county, of his wife June's appointment as deputy to him at Tŷ'r Felin, and of lack of support that she (Alison Taylor) had received from senior officers. She also complained of matters relating to herself involving breaches of confidentiality and alleged thefts of documents. Most relevantly, however, she listed a series of alleged assaults upon seven children in residential care, six at Tŷ'r Felin and one at Tŷ Newydd and suggested that there had been a homosexual relationship between a boy at Tŷ Newydd and a member of staff. Her general allegation was that none of the offences had been investigated adequately or properly dealt with. Detective Chief Superintendent Owen reported these matters to the Assistant Chief Constable and he was instructed early in March 1986 to investigate the allegation that criminal offences had been committed.

The 1986/1987 police investigation

2.12 This investigation, referred to hereafter as the 1986/1987 investigation, is discussed fully in Chapter 51 of this report. There were two features of it that must be mentioned here. Firstly, the investigation was carried out by Detective Chief Superintendent Owen, the head of the CID, himself and was not delegated to a less senior member of his department. Secondly, no approach was made to any officer of the county Social Services Department in connection with the allegations. The reason for this given by Detective Chief Superintendent Owen was "the need to conduct a thorough 'independent' investigation to avoid any suggestion of collusion, bearing in mind that the Social Services Officers have a 'vested interest' in concealing any allegations of abuse". By May 1986, however, both the Chairman of the Social Services Committee and the Director of Social Services, were aware of the fact that an investigation was taking place and of its general nature.

2.13 The result of the investigation was that the Crown Prosecution Service advised that no criminal proceedings would be justified. This advice was given initially, by letter dated 14 October 1986, in respect of 12 of the 13 cases that had been reported upon. Additional statements were asked for in the other case but the same advice was given in this case when they had been obtained.

2.14 The Director of Social Services for Gwynedd was told of the decision not to prosecute as early as 17 October 1986. A letter followed three days later and Alison Taylor was informed by letter of the outcome at the same time. There followed meetings between Lucille Hughes and Detective Chief Superintendent Gwynne Owen which are narrated in Chapter 51 of this report and in which the police findings were discussed, including (it is said) criticisms of Nefyn Dodd's manner and actions. Nevertheless, the Chief Executive of Gwynedd, Ioan Bowen Rees, who had not apparently been informed of the police investigation until September 1986, felt able to say to the press early in November 1986:

> "The police report completely vindicates the decision taken by the County Council not to suspend any officer during the course of the investigations. We believed the allegations to be unfounded, but unfortunately there was some extremely irresponsible reporting of the affair by some sections of the media. I very much hope that these sections will give equal prominence to putting people's minds at rest."

2.15 The police investigation did not, however, come to rest at that point because, in December 1986, a former resident at Tŷ'r Felin told a police officer of other alleged assaults on children by Nefyn Dodd that she said that she had witnessed at the home. These alleged assaults involved six children born between 1966 and 1973, only two of whom were thought to be living in North Wales by the end of 1986. Investigations were, therefore, pursued by Detective Chief Superintendent Gwynne Owen, making use of other police forces where the potential complainants were resident outside North Wales. The file was submitted to the Crown Prosecution Service in October 1987 but the latter advised once more on 5 January and 21 April 1988, after another statement had been obtained, that the available evidence did not merit criminal proceedings.

Alison Taylor's further representations and her dismissal

2.16 Meanwhile, Alison Taylor had become increasingly dissatisfied with the response to her complaints and had written to the Chief Executive on 1 July 1986 making a further complaint about Dodd's behaviour the previous day. Her letter concluded "We are instructed by the Social Services Department that Mr Dodd is the only person with whom we are permitted to discuss the management of Tŷ Newydd" (of which Taylor was Officer-in-Charge) "and its children, and to whom all written communications must be sent. His actions place me in a completely untenable position, and I must request your urgent intervention in this matter".

2.17 It is astonishing that Bowen Rees did not learn immediately of the police investigation as a result of this letter. He does not appear to have replied to it. Some matters were raised by the Assistant Director (Children) with Taylor on 10 July 1986 and she was seen at Tŷ Newydd on 2 October 1986 by the Chairman of the Social Services Committee, by which time plans were evolving for the closure of Tŷ Newydd. The Chairman, Councillor Eric Davies, had not met Taylor previously but he formed a very unfavourable view of her at this meeting, describing her thus in a memorandum dated 5 October 1986:

> "Finally, having interviewed this person, at length, I am of the opinion that she is a most unfit person to be in charge of a children's home, and that she is a blatant trouble maker, with a most devious personality, and one in my estimation who is very much involved with the anonymous letters which have been circulating. I would very humbly suggest that Tŷ Newydd be closed as soon as possible, and that this lady's services be dispensed with at the earliest possible time."

2.18 The result was that Taylor was informed by a letter from the Director of Social Services dated 1 December 1986 that she was suspended from duty until further notice, pending investigation, on the ground that "the spirit of professional trust and co-operation between you and your colleagues in the residential child care sector, which is so necessary for the efficient running of that service, has broken down". On 13 January 1987, Lucille Hughes, who had met Taylor on 16 December 1986 in the course of the investigation, told her in a further letter that the enquiry had been completed and that Hughes' conclusion was that "the breakdown in professional relationships is a real one, and is the direct result of your work performance and attitudes over a considerable period". Taylor's suspension on full pay was confirmed and disciplinary proceedings were to ensue.

2.19 A list of matters allegedly illustrating Taylor's failings was sent to her union representative in a letter dated 4 February 1987 and the Council's Disciplinary Panel ultimately met on 2 November 1987 in her absence to consider the case against her. The relevant part of the County Personnel Officer's letter, dated 5 November 1987, informing Taylor of the Panel's decision read as follows:

> "The Panel was most concerned at your unexplained absence from the hearing, but bearing in mind the inordinate delays that have dogged this matter from the beginning, partly caused by your non-attendance at two previous meetings with your Director, and your refusal to attend medical interviews arranged by the Council, and noting the explicit terms of the County Secretary's letter to you dated 9th October 1987, as well as the terms of your letter dated 28th October 1987, it was decided to proceed with the hearing. . .
>
> Before coming to a decision the Panel adjourned overnight in order to read and consider your letter dated 28th October 1987 addressed to the County Secretary and the papers enclosed with that letter. The Panel was satisfied that there had been a breach in the professional relationships between yourself and other staff of the children's section; that this breach was most detrimental to the interests of children in the Council's care and that this breach was the direct result of your work performance and attitude over a period of time. The members of the Panel were of the unanimous opinion that this amounted to gross misconduct on your part and they decided that you be dismissed from the service of the Council as from 3rd November 1987."

2.20 Taylor consulted solicitors and notified an internal appeal to the Council's Appeals Committee. A claim of unfair dismissal was also submitted to the Industrial Tribunal. The proceedings dragged on, however, and an attempt was eventually made to fix the internal appeal for hearing in May or June 1989 but a compromise was then negotiated under which Taylor agreed on 25 August 1989 to accept voluntary redundancy from her post as Officer-in-Charge of Tŷ Newydd Children's Home with effect from 30 November 1987 and receive financial compensation and costs in full and final settlement of her claim.

2.21 Meanwhile, Alison Taylor had pursued an energetic campaign to draw attention to her allegations against Nefyn Dodd and her criticisms of Gwynedd County Council's Social Services Department. She addressed letters to the Prime Minister, the Welsh Office, the Secretary of State for Health and the Local Government Ombudsman amongst others and, in 1989, she was approached by Yorkshire Television through the Children's Legal Centre. Over this period she became aware of many more complaints, a significant number of which involved children's homes in the Wrexham area, namely, Bryn Estyn, a Clwyd County Council home designated as part of the regional plan for Wales[13] and Bryn Alyn Community homes, which were private homes, owned by the Community of that name, which had been founded by John Allen[14]. These were homes to which

---

[13] See para 7.10.
[14] See paras 4.10, 4.11 and 4.22 to 4.27.

a number of Gwynedd children in care had been sent from time to time and Alison Taylor herself had been attached to Bryn Estyn for three months as part of her training course for the CQSW[15] between 1980 and 1982 at the North East Wales Institute at Cartrefle, Wrexham.

2.22 In the end Taylor compiled a voluminous document that she called "GCC Analysis"[16], in which she gave details of all the complaints of which she had heard relating to children in care and the staff responsible for them, including many rumours and a great deal of hearsay. It seems that the document was revised from time to time: the 129 page edition put before the Tribunal is dated 1991 and refers to events that occurred as late as December 1991. It was with most of this information that Taylor met at her home in Bangor, Councillor Dennis Parry, the newly elected leader of Clwyd County Council and a member of the North Wales Police Authority, on 10 June 1991. This meeting took place almost exactly a year after Stephen Norris had pleaded guilty to serious sexual offences committed at Cartrefle children's home in Clwyd and shortly before the trial of Frederick Rutter for serious sexual offences against young women in his care. Councillor Parry was, therefore, particularly perturbed by Taylor's allegations of further offences against children who had been in care in Clwyd. At a subsequent meeting that he held with the new Chairman of Clwyd's Social Services Committee, Councillor Malcolm King, the newly appointed Director of Social Services, John Jevons, and the Assistant County Secretary (Legal), Andrew Loveridge, it was decided that the North Wales Police Authority should be requested to carry out an investigation.

The setting up of the 1991/1993 police investigation

2.23 The letter to the Chief Constable of the North Wales Police requesting an investigation was dated 17 July 1991 and signed by the County Secretary, Roger Davies. It gave a comprehensive account of the Council's concerns following the investigations into Norris, Gillison and Rutter and included the following passage:

> "From the lists that I have enclosed you will observe that there is, in my view, an unusually high level of convictions and admissions and the level of suspicion and query is such that the County Council cannot but be gravely concerned as to any possible explanation for those suspicions and queries. I understand that when your officers investigated the case against Mr Rutter they were, at one stage, concerned as to the question of the existence of a paedophile ring in North Wales.
>
> This question exercises my mind greatly and I believe it will be a matter of equal concern to you. A perusal of the contents of the list of individuals will immediately demonstrate that there are an overwhelming number of links back to the former approved school, later residential care home at Bryn Estyn which has now closed. It may, of

---

[15] Certificate of Qualification in Social Work.
[16] Gwynedd County Council Analysis.

course, be nothing more than coincidence but if it is coincidence then it appears to be an extremely high level of coincidence."

2.24 The Chief Constable agreed to carry out the proposed investigation and it was then extended to cover the Gwynedd children's homes by the end of 1991. The history was that, following her earlier contact with Yorkshire Television, Taylor was able to interest HTV in allegations of child abuse in Gwynedd with the result that, on 26 September 1991, HTV's "Wales this Week" programme broadcast allegations by four former residents at Tŷ'r Felin, of physical abuse, mainly by Nefyn Dodd, and allegations by two others of abuse at Queen's Park children's home, Holyhead, Gwynfa residential clinic, Colwyn Bay and Ysgol Talfryn residential school near Holywell. This led immediately to a request by Lucille Hughes, Gwynedd's Director of Social Services, by letter dated 30 September 1991, to the Chief Constable for the Tŷ'r Felin allegations to be investigated. Then, on 1 December 1991, the *Independent on Sunday* published, as its lead story, a long article, under the heading "New child abuse scandal", in which allegations of widespread abuse in North Wales children's homes were made and the police investigations that have been referred to were severely criticised. Thus, between 2 and 4 December 1991 decisions were taken to amalgamate the police investigations in the two counties and on 9 December 1991 Taylor supplied Detective Superintendent Peter Ackerley of the North Wales Police, the senior investigating officer heading them, with a copy of her "GCC" analysis.

The article in the *Independent on Sunday*

2.25 The *Independent on Sunday* article had been written by a free-lance journalist, Dean Nelson, assisted by two others. Nelson had previously written an article in May 1991 about allegations of abuse at Tŷ Mawr children's home, Abergavenny, and he went to North Wales at the suggestion of an *Independent on Sunday* staff member. In the course of his visit he saw Taylor, Councillor Dennis Parry, various former residents of North Wales children's homes, three former members of staff at Bryn Estyn and Clwyd's Director of Social Services. The article itself contained criticisms of the earlier police investigations and references to allegations by Councillor Parry of a police cover up to conceal the failure of senior police officers and social services' executives to reveal the extent of abuse in the children's homes. The article contained also allegations of sexual abuse by the deputy headmaster of Bryn Estyn and reference to allegations of physical assaults by Dodd against "dozens of children" at Tŷ'r Felin. In a separate report by the same authors on another page, more specific details were given of these allegations. It concluded:

> "Clwyd County Council will look sympathetically on claims for compensation from those who suffered abuse but the council leader, Dennis Parry, said no amount of money could make good the damage caused.
>
> Lives have been ruined by this. God help us how many young people with drugs and sexual problems have come from those kinds of establishments? It's frightening because it's a microcosm of what's going on around the country."

2.26 The article on the front page of the *Independent on Sunday* of 1 December 1991 also contained the following reference to former Police Superintendent Gordon Anglesea[17]:

> "According to former residents at Bryn Estyn, Gordon Anglesea, a former senior North Wales police officer, was a regular visitor there. He recently retired suddenly without explanation. Another serving officer has been accused of assaulting a child at Tŷ'r Felin."

Anglesea consulted solicitors immediately and they wrote to the newspaper describing the passage quoted as the grossest libel on Anglesea and demanded publication of an equally prominent agreed statement of rebuttal and apology in the next edition of the newspaper together with damages and costs.

Other published allegations against Gordon Anglesea

2.27 No apology was forthcoming, however, and on 13 September 1992 the *Observer* newspaper wrote:

> "A former police chief has been named as a prime suspect in the North Wales child sexual abuse scandal, police sources in the region confirmed last night. . . The ex-police chief is due to be questioned this week as evidence emerges that staff in some children's homes 'lent' children to convicted paedophiles for week-ends."

Similar references followed in the next two issues of the *Observer* and on 17 September 1992 HTV's "Wales this Week" again broadcast allegations of sexual abuse on the part of Anglesea against two former residents of Bryn Estyn, both of whom appeared in the broadcast.

2.28 Finally, on 27 January 1993, *Private Eye* magazine published an article about the North Wales investigations criticising what it regarded as the apparent reluctance of the North Wales Police to prosecute "no fewer than 12 serving and former colleagues" for sexual offences involving young boys who had been in care over a 20 year period. The article continued:

> "The reluctance has nothing to do with the involvement of a number of the local great and good as members of a paedophile ring, which regularly used homes, like the now-closed Bryn Estyn near Wrexham, to supply boys for sex to local celebrities.
>
> In the late 1970s, Superintendent Anglesea of the North Wales Police was appointed to investigate an allegation of buggery made by X against the son of a then member of the North Wales police authority. The Superintendent found there was no case to answer. Coincidentally the police authority member and Superintendent Anglesea were prominent masons."

---

[17] See Chapter 9: The case of Gordon Anglesea.

Gordon Anglesea's libel actions

2.29 Anglesea brought proceedings for libel in respect of each of these publications and his actions against Newspaper Publishing plc (the publisher of the *Independent on Sunday*), The Observer Ltd, HTV Ltd and Pressdram Ltd (the publisher of *Private Eye*) were then consolidated into one action, which was heard in London before the Honourable Mr Justice Drake, a senior judge of the Queen's Bench Division, who was in charge of the civil jury list, and a jury between 14 November and 7 December 1994. Each of the defendants had pleaded justification, namely, that the words complained of by Anglesea were true in substance and in fact.

2.30 At the trial Anglesea gave evidence and three members of his family, namely, his second wife, a son and a step-son were called as witnesses on his behalf. In addition, Gladys Green, who had been secretary to the headmaster of Bryn Estyn and a senior administrator at the school for nearly 12 years, gave evidence for Anglesea. The defendants relied upon the evidence of three former Bryn Estyn residents, two of whom alleged that Anglesea had both indecently assaulted and buggered them and the third of whom, who had not emerged as a potential witness until shortly before the trial, gave evidence of a joint indecent assault by Anglesea and Howarth. Two other witnesses, a housemother at Bryn Estyn, who was also a policeman's wife, and a probation officer who had been attached to the staff of the home for three months whilst on a training course gave evidence of having seen Anglesea there. Dean Nelson, the author of the first article in the *Independent on Sunday*, was not called as a witness but it was reasonably clear from the evidence that he had not been in possession of any actual evidence of child abuse by Anglesea at the time when his article appeared.

2.31 It is clear from the trial judge's summing up that the central issue that the jury had to decide was "Have the Defendants satisfied you that Mr Anglesea was guilty of very serious sexual misconduct at Bryn Estyn?" The Defendants had to prove the main "sting" of the charge, that is, that Gordon Anglesea did commit some serious offence at Bryn Estyn against the boys who were there, although they did not have to prove every detail alleged. Moreover, the judge told the jury "Because in this case the charges made by the Defendants are so very grave, the Defendants must prove them to a high standard so that you, the jury become satisfied that the Plaintiff did commit these serious assaults". Having spoken of the balance of probabilities test in civil cases and the tilting of the scales, he concluded:

> "The more serious the charge, the further down the scales have to go. So in this case, where the charge against Gordon Anglesea is just about as serious as you could consider, the evidence required to prove the Defendants' case must be that much stronger."

2.32 In the event, on 6 December 1994, the jury found in favour of Anglesea by a majority of 10 to 2, after a retirement of about nine hours. The following day it was agreed between the parties that he should receive total damages of £375,000 by way of compensation, together with appropriate undertakings about non-repetition of the libels and payment of his legal costs.

The course of the 1991/1993 police investigation

2.33 Meanwhile, the major investigation by the North Wales Police had proceeded a long way with the full co-operation of senior officers of both County Councils. The waters had been muddied to an uncertain and indeterminable extent by the intervention of Nelson because he had returned to North Wales to seek evidence against Anglesea in support of the *Independent on Sunday's* defence to the libel action. He was in North Wales in February, May, June, August and September 1992 before leaving the UK in December 1992 for Hong Kong to re-launch a news magazine. In the course of his 1992 visits he sought out two former children in care, who both eventually alleged that they had been sexually abused by Gordon Anglesea, but other potential witnesses approached by him denied that Anglesea had abused them. He did, however, obtain statements from some witnesses in support of the assertion that there had been a period when Anglesea had been a frequent visitor to Bryn Estyn.

2.34 By September 1993, when the main part of the police investigation was nearing completion, the police had taken about 3,500 statements from about 2,500 potential witnesses, of whom not less than 500 who had been in residential establishments, complained that they had suffered sexual or physical abuse. The number of those who complained of sexual abuse was about 150. The Crown Prosecution Service had assigned a special case work lawyer from an early stage to consider all the files submitted by the North Wales Police in the course of the investigation and John Lord performed this task throughout. The upshot was that by the end of 1993 the North Wales Police had recommended that 20 suspects should be prosecuted, of whom 19 were alleged abusers; but between 1993 and 1995 criminal proceedings were taken against only eight individuals, of whom six were ultimately convicted. One of the two acquitted had not been one of the 20 recommended by the police for prosecution.

Criminal proceedings following the 1991/1993 police investigation

2.35 The relevant proceedings[18] were as follows:

(1) 1 July 1993, Mold Crown Court

Norman Brade Roberts was convicted of an assault occasioning actual body harm on his foster child. He was acquitted of cruelty to the same child and he received a conditional discharge for a period of two years in respect of the assault. Norman Roberts' son, **Ian Malcolm Roberts** received the same order for a common assault on the same foster child. Both offences had been committed between 1980 and 1985. **Evelyn May Roberts**, Norman's wife, was acquitted of a charge of cruelty towards the child[19].

---

[18] The list does not include the conviction of Malcolm Ian Scrugham, a foster father, on 23 April 1993, which is particularised in para 42.09 because it did not arise from the major police investigation.

[19] See Chapter 41.

(2) 11 November 1993, Knutsford Crown Court

Stephen Roderick Norris, who had been released at the end of his 1990 sentences[20] on 2 February 1993 to a bail hostel at Warrington on various conditions, pleaded guilty to three offences of buggery, one of attempted buggery and three of indecent assault committed between 1980 and 1984 against six boys, each of whom had been resident at Bryn Estyn at the time of the offence. All these offences had occurred when Norris was the Housemaster of Clwyd House at Bryn Estyn[21]. Two other counts of buggery, seven of indecent assault and one of assault occasioning actual bodily harm were ordered to remain on the Court file, as was another indictment alleging six further offences of buggery. All 16 counts left on the file referred to offences alleged to have been committed at Bryn Estyn against other boys in the same period. The total sentence imposed on Norris was 7 years' imprisonment.

(3) 8 July 1994, Chester Crown Court

Peter Norman Howarth, a former Deputy Principal at Bryn Estyn, was convicted of an offence of buggery and seven offences of indecent assault committed between 1974 and 1984 against seven boys who were resident at Bryn Estyn at the time[22]. One of the victims of indecent assault took his own life on 21 May 1995 by hanging himself from a tree. Howarth was acquitted of two other counts of buggery and two of indecent assault involving three other Bryn Estyn residents. He was sentenced to ten years' imprisonment in all for the eight offences of which he was convicted but he died of a heart attack in Pinderfield Hospital, to which he had been moved from Wakefield Prison, on 24 April 1997, **Paul Bicker Wilson**, a former Residential Child Care Officer at Bryn Estyn, was acquitted in the same trial of three alleged offences of indecent assault involving two Bryn Estyn boys, one of which offences was alleged to have been committed jointly with Howarth. Wilson faced a second trial, however, in November 1994[23].

(4) 28 November 1994, Knutsford Crown Court

Paul Bicker Wilson pleaded guilty to three offences of assault occasioning actual bodily harm and one of common assault committed between July 1980 and March 1984 on young male residents at Bryn Estyn, for which he received a total sentence of 15 months' imprisonment, suspended for two years. A not guilty verdict was entered in respect of another count because the complainant in respect of that alleged common assault in 1984, Y, had committed suicide on 6 January 1994, when he had been found

---

[20] See para 2.07(7).
[21] See paras 8.29 to 8.34.
[22] See paras 8.04 to 8.10.
[23] See paras 8.39 and 8.40.

hanging from a door at his home. One other count of assault occasioning actual bodily harm and two alleging cruelty to a child, involving three other Bryn Estyn boys, were ordered to lie on the Court file[24].

(5) 12 January 1995, Knutsford Crown Court

David Gwyn Birch, another former Residential Child Care Officer for six years at Bryn Estyn and subsequently for four years at Chevet Hey, was acquitted of an alleged offence of buggery against a complainant X and of an alleged indecent assault against another boy[25]. X's evidence against Howarth of indecent assault on him by the latter alone had been accepted by a different jury but had not been accepted by that jury in respect of a joint charge of indecent assault on him by Howarth and Wilson and a separate charge of indecent assault on him by Wilson alone. In the light of the jury's verdicts in respect of Birch, the prosecution decided not to offer any evidence against him in respect of another count of buggery on X, alleged to have been committed in the same period between 1981 and 1982, four counts of alleged cruelty to children and one of assault occasioning actual bodily harm, two of which involved Y, who had died a year earlier[26].

(6) 9 February 1995, Chester Crown Court

John Ernest Allen, the founder of the Bryn Alyn Community residential schools[27], was convicted of six offences of indecent assault against six young male residents at the schools between 1972 and 1983. He was acquitted of four other counts of indecent assault involving four different residents. Allen received a total sentence of six years' imprisonment.

Further events leading to the Jillings inquiry

2.36 Whilst these investigations and prosecutions were taking place there was continuing public interest in the subject and Alison Taylor pursued her campaign for a public inquiry. Questions were asked in the House of Commons on a number of occasions. An Assistant Chief Constable of the North Wales Police, Mr Richard Heseltine, appeared in a television programme calling, on behalf of the police, for a public inquiry. This call was subsequently reiterated by the Chief Constable himself. On 7 September 1992, the Parliamentary Secretary to the Welsh Office, Gwilym R Jones, announced that a public inquiry into allegations of abuse in North Wales would take place when the North Wales Police had completed their enquiries. He did not indicate,

---

[24] See paras 10.09 to 10.12, 10.26 and 10.27.
[25] See paras 8.37 and 8.38.
[26] See para 2.35(4).
[27] See paras 21.24 to 21.44, 21.59 and 21.60.

however, the form that the inquiry would or might take and it was clear that the police investigation would continue for a substantial period because new allegations of abuse were continuing to be made.

2.37 It was against this background that in January 1994 Clwyd County Council set in train the private inquiry by an independent panel under John Jillings[28]. There was continuing discussion within the Welsh Office meanwhile about the form any public inquiry might take, if there was still need for one, and it was on these points that Nicola Davies QC was asked to advise in 1995[29]. Ultimately, the existence of the unpublished Jillings report led to further allegations of a cover up and widespread speculation, fanning public disquiet, with the result that the Government decided that the present Public Inquiry under the Tribunals of Inquiry (Evidence) Act 1921 was necessary to deal with the situation.

---

[28] See paras 2.02 and 2.03.
[29] See para 2.04.

The legislative[1] and administrative background in 1974

3.01 It is no exaggeration to say that the Social Services Departments of the new Clwyd and Gwynedd County Councils were in a state of turmoil when they took over responsibility for the former five county areas on 1 April 1974 under the provisions of the Local Government Act 1972. The main factors relevant to the welfare of children contributing to this turmoil were:

(1) The recommendations of the Seebohm Committee on Local Authority and Allied Personal Social Services (1968) as implemented in the Local Authority Social Services Act 1970;

(2) The proposals set out in the Government's White Paper, entitled Children in Trouble (1968) as enacted in the Children and Young Persons Act 1969; and

(3) The re-organisation of local government and administrative areas throughout North Wales pursuant to the Act of 1972.

Report of the Seebohm Committee on Local Authority and Allied Personal Social Services

3.02 The Seebohm Committee's report was presented shortly after the publication of Children in Trouble so that the Committee were able to comment upon the Government's proposals in the White Paper and to take into account, for example, the likely demise of approved schools in the near future. The report covered the whole field of social services and the Committee's conclusions were set out in 206 numbered paragraphs, many of which are not directly relevant for our purposes. Overall, however, the recommendations involved radical changes in the administration of social services, including social services for children. At their centre was the proposal that there should be a new local government department, to be called the social services department, providing "a community based and family oriented service, which will be available to all"[2]. This new department was to take over the services then provided by children's departments, welfare services under the National Assistance Act 1948, the home help service, mental health social work services, other social work services provided by health departments, day nurseries and certain social welfare work then undertaken by some housing departments. Its responsibilities were, however, to go beyond those of existing local authority

---

[1] See Appendix 6: Main statutory regulation from 1974 until the Children Act 1989 came into force on 14 October 1991, for a summary of the provisions relevant to the terms of reference of the Tribunal of Inquiry.

[2] Report of The Committee on Local Authority and Allied Personal Social Services, July 1968, Cmnd 3703, HMSO, para 2.

departments: local authorities were to be required to review needs and services in their own areas to determine priorities; and it was envisaged that most authorities would be likely to feel that children under five and very old people called for special attention. It was recommended also that there should be one government department responsible for the relationship between central government and the social services departments and for the overall national planning of social services, social intelligence and social research.

3.03 The Seebohm Committee's proposals involved radical alterations to the structure established by the Children Act 1948, following many of the recommendations of the Curtis Committee. There was no longer to be a children's department headed by a children's officer in each local authority; and child care services were no longer to be the responsibility of the Home Office. Instead, the head of all social services for a local authority area (usually a county or county borough) was to be a newly appointed Director of Social Services, acting with the Social Services Committee; and responsibility for child care services was to move, in Wales, from the Home Office to the Welsh Office, the transfer taking effect on 1 January 1971 (responsibility for other social services in Wales having been transferred from the Department of Health and Social Security to the Welsh Office in March 1969).

3.04 It is relevant to refer briefly to a number of other specific recommendations made by the Seebohm Committee because of their significance in relation to the events that we have to review. Thus:

    (1) The Committee considered that central government had three essential functions to perform in relation to local government social services, namely:

        (i) It must in planning for the future decide what the aims of the service are, and make sure that local authorities understand those decisions.

        (ii) It must set and ensure minimum levels of service over the country as a whole.

        (iii) It must collect and disseminate relevant and useful information about the services and the needs they ought to be trying to meet[3].

    (2) The Committee did not attempt to explore in detail the way in which the relationship between central and local government should develop in the running of the social services but they did emphasise that, in prescribing aims and standards for the personal services, the central government must also "take the primary responsibility for making sure that resources, and in particular trained manpower, will be available on a scale and timetable which will make the aims and standards realistic"[4].

---

[3] Ibid, para 646.
[4] Ibid, para 647(a).

(3) The central government department must have "a strong, accessible and well-respected inspectorate, to advise local authorities, to promote the achievement of aims and the maintenance of standards, and to act as two-way channels for information and consultation between central and local government. The role of the inspectorate would be not so much regulatory as promotional, educational and consultative. Its help would be particularly valuable in the early stages of the new service, and for that reason it is vital that early action be taken to set it up"[5].

(4) They emphasised the high qualities required of a suitable Director of Social Services, the heavy responsibilities that would fall upon that person and the wisdom of considering the widest possible field of recruitment[6].

(5) The committee envisaged that a single social worker with a comprehensive approach would be responsible for a family or an individual's needs and thought that narrow specialisation could have a detrimental effect on professional judgement. They proposed therefore that the pattern of specialisation should be radically altered and that social workers should be expected to undertake wider responsibilities at an early stage[7].

(6) They considered it essential that the central government department responsible for personal social services, in co-operation with a proposed central advisory council, should be responsible for making estimates of the numbers of workers likely to be required by social services departments, for keeping them under continuous review and for planning training resources[8].

(7) The Committee referred to the report of the Williams Committee on Staffing of Residential Homes (1967) and drew attention to the fact that the proportion of staff with no training designed to prepare them to have charge of a home varied from about 98 per cent in old people's homes to 82 per cent in children's homes. They endorsed the Williams Committee's proposals for training for such work and suggested that they deserved urgent consideration by government. They added "It seems to us essential that training for residential care should lead to a nationally recognised qualification and that in-service training should be developed rapidly, especially for those members of staff now in post who are unlikely to be released for full training"[9].

---

[5] Ibid, paras 647 and 649.
[6] Ibid, paras 618 to 620.
[7] Ibid, paras 516 to 521.
[8] Ibid, para 551.
[9] Ibid, paras 563 to 565.

Local Authority Social Services Act 1970

3.05 The main structural recommendations of the Seebohm Committee were embodied in the Local Authority Social Services Act 1970, which came into effect in the main on 1 January 1971. Having dealt in earlier sections with the establishment of social services committees and the appointment of directors of social services (with the demise of children's officers), section 7(1) of the Act provided that "Local authorities shall, in the exercise of their social services functions, including the exercise of any discretion conferred by any relevant enactment, act under the general guidance of the Secretary of State". This was made subject to certain specified exceptions listed in section 7, none of which are relevant for our purposes.

"Children in Trouble"

3.06 As we have said earlier, the Government's White Paper, Children in Trouble, had been published shortly before the Seebohm Committee reported and its main proposals were embodied in the Children and Young Persons Act 1969. The White Paper's main proposals were based upon the view that child neglect and juvenile delinquency ought not to be dealt with differently because they were both symptoms of deprivation, which led to many children being received into care. At paragraph six of the document it was said "Juvenile delinquency has no single cause, manifestation or cure. Its origins are many, and the range of behaviour which it covers is equally wide. At some points it merges almost imperceptibly with behaviour which does not contravene the law. A child's behaviour is influenced by genetic, emotional and intellectual factors, his maturity and his family, school, neighbourhood and wider social setting. It is probably a minority of children who grow up without ever misbehaving in ways which may be contrary to the law".

3.07 It was proposed, therefore, that the commission of an offence by a child aged between 10 and 14 years should cease to be, by itself, a sufficient ground for bringing him before a court. Instead, where proceedings were necessary, they were to be brought under the care, protection and control procedure by appropriate amendment of section 2 of the Children and Young Person Act 1963. Restrictions were also to be imposed on the prosecution of offenders aged between 14 and 17 years and care, protection and control proceedings considered as a potential alternative. Three main changes were to be made in the powers of the juvenile court, namely:

    (a) the approved school order was to be abolished;

    (b) new forms of treatment, between supervision in the home and committal to care, were to be developed; and

    (c) all supervision of children under 14 years was to be by the local authority.

3.08 On the subject of residential care the White Paper said that local authorities would be responsible for developing a comprehensive system of residential care and treatment for the children received or committed into their care who were not boarded out with foster parents; and a considerable variety of provision was envisaged. Their basic duty towards the children would remain that of providing the care, protection and guidance or treatment which they considered appropriate in the interests of each child and that duty would include restoring the child to his home as soon as practicable and desirable, "having regard to the need to protect society while children and young persons whose behaviour is difficult to control are undergoing treatment". It was stated further that "The needs of the great majority of children will be met by homes which, as now, will care for them as nearly as possible in the same way as a good family, making use of the education, health and other services which are generally available". There would nevertheless be a continuing need for some establishments providing education and treatment on the premises and all the existing approved schools, including the senior schools, would probably be required for the accommodation of children and young persons in care: the schools would retain an important role in continuing to provide for the needs of both offenders and non-offenders.

3.09 The White Paper outlined a proposed integrated system of community homes embracing existing local authority children's homes and hostels, remand homes, reception and remand centres, local authority and voluntary approved schools and some voluntary children's homes which regularly accommodated children in care. It recognised the importance of providing homes on a genuinely local basis to preserve links with each child's family and environment but proposed that specialist facilities should be planned nationally. Local authorities were to participate in joint planning committees covering areas approved by the Secretary of State in order to draw up comprehensive plans for developing the full range of residential, observation and assessment and intermediate treatment facilities required. Voluntary approved schools and voluntary children's homes on which local authorities relied were to be included within the public system (as local authority or controlled or assisted voluntary community homes) if and when agreement about the future role of the establishment was reached with the planning committee and the area plan had been approved by the Secretary of State. Moreover, voluntary organisations wishing to continue, or to establish children's homes operating outside the public system would remain free to do so, subject to existing statutory requirements as to registration, inspection etc. and would be known as registered voluntary children's homes.

Children and Young Persons Act 1969

3.10 Detailed provisions implementing these proposals were enacted in the Children and Young Persons Act 1969 but responsibility for approved schools and remand homes was not transferred to the Secretary of State for Wales until 1973. In the interim period from 1 January 1971, when other child care responsibilities in Wales apart from adoption had been transferred from the Home Office to the Welsh Office, the Secretary of State for Social Services had borne the responsibility of overseeing the integration of approved schools and remand homes into the system of community homes throughout England and Wales; and it was in October 1973 that Bryn Estyn, in particular, became a community home with education on the premises instead of an approved school.

Community Homes Regulations 1972

3.11 Regulations made under the Act of 1969 and governing the conduct of community homes, namely, the Community Homes Regulations 1972, came into effect on 1 April 1972. They did not apply to voluntary or private children's homes or to independent residential schools. The responsibility for arranging that proper provision was made in each local authority home for the care, treatment and control of the children accommodated therein was placed on the local authority and, in the case of controlled or assisted community homes, on the managers. The regulations also contained provisions for such matters as health, safety and religious observance. Regulation 3(2) required each home to be visited at least once a month and a report to be provided by the visitor: local authority homes were to be visited by such persons as the local authority considered appropriate whereas the visits to controlled or assisted homes were to be by a manager. Suitable facilities were to be provided also for visits by parents, guardians, relatives and friends of children accommodated. Section 24(5) of the Act of 1969 already required local authorities to appoint an "independent person" to be a visitor to a child accommodated in a home who had infrequent contact with his parent or guardian or none at all in the preceding 12 months and who did not leave the home to attend school or work: the duty of the independent person was to visit, advise and befriend the child.

3.12 The regime of control of a community home was dealt with in Regulation 10 in the following way:

> "(1) The control of a community home shall be maintained on the basis of good personal and professional relationships between the staff and the children resident therein.
>
> (2) The responsible body in respect of a local authority home or controlled community home and the local authority specified in the instrument of management for an assisted community home may approve in respect of each home such additional measures as they consider necessary for the maintenance of control in the home, and the conditions under which such measures may be taken, and in approving such measures and conditions they shall have regard to the purpose and character of the home and the categories of children for which it is provided.
>
> (3) Any approval mentioned in the preceding paragraph shall be given in writing to the person in charge of the home, save that in the case of an assisted home the approval shall be given to the responsible organisation, and shall be reviewed every 12 months.

(4) Full particulars of any of the measures mentioned in paragraph (2) of this regulation which are used and of the circumstances in which they are used shall be recorded in permanent form by the person in charge of the home and the record shall be kept in the home."

3.13 The guidance issued by the Welsh Office with the Regulations pointed out that the precise type and degree of control which might normally be exercised through good personal and professional relationships could not easily be defined without reference to the circumstances of each individual case and that it would "invariably require the careful and sensitive consideration of the staff directly involved"[10]. The hope was expressed that in the great majority of community homes the need to have recourse to additional measures under Regulation 10(2) would rarely arise but, the guidance continued, "in any home where formal punishments are thought to be necessary for the maintenance of control it will plainly be desirable that advance approval should be sought for whatever measures are required so that they are available when needed".

3.14 Commenting on corporal punishment under the heading of "Additional Measures" the guidance stated this:

"Regulation 10 differs most markedly from the previous regulations in making no mention of corporal punishment. There has in recent years been a marked decline in the use of corporal punishment in all types of children's establishments including approved schools for boys (in approved schools for girls it has disappeared entirely) and it is hoped that this trend will continue. At the same time, however, it is recognised that it would be impracticable at this stage to prohibit the use of all forms of corporal punishment in every home. The regulations thus formally leave the matter to the discretion of the parties directly concerned. For all practical purposes, the use of corporal punishment will be confined to the circumstances envisaged in regulation 10(2) that is, the measures and the conditions under which they are employed must be approved in advance for each home by the local authority (acting either as the responsible body or, in the case of an assisted home, as the authority principally responsible for the well-being of the children in the home) who will thus be publicly accountable both for the measures approved by them and for the conditions of their use. It is hoped that they will authorise the use of corporal punishment sparingly and as a last resort and will consider at each annual review, in the light of experience, whether it is still needed."[11]

3.15 Stringent conditions were also imposed by Regulation 11 in respect of the provision and use of secure accommodation. Such accommodation could only be provided and used in a community home with the approval of the Secretary of State, who was empowered to attach to it such terms and conditions as he thought fit. Moreover, even when such approval had been given, detention on the authority of the person in charge of the home was limited to one maximum

---

[10] Para 11 of the Memorandum of Guidance on the Community Homes Regulations 1972.
[11] Para 13 of the Memorandum of Guidance on the Community Homes Regulations 1972.

continuous period of 24 hours or 48 hours in any consecutive period of seven days if there was more than one period of admission.

The Children's Regional Planning Committee for Wales

3.16 The Secretary of State for the Home Office issued a direction on 12 August 1970 that regional plans for community homes under the Children and Young Persons Act 1969 were to be submitted on or before 31 December 1971[12]. The Children's Regional Planning Committee for Wales (Region 12) (CRPC), set up under section 35 of the Act of 1969, met for the first time on 24 June 1970 and it continued in existence until early in 1984. Its initial plan was submitted to the Secretary of State for Wales on 31 December 1971 and came into operation on 1 April 1973. A revised plan requested by the Secretary of State was submitted in September 1979 and it was subsequently revised further at three yearly intervals until the statutory requirements for the committees and the production of plans were abolished on 1 January 1984[13]. The CRPC had been responsible also for the preparation of plans for intermediate treatment in Wales.

3.17 This is not the place for a lengthy account of the work of the CRPC for Wales or of its successive regional plans. From 1974 onwards its membership was drawn mainly from the eight new county councils. The committee, its sub-committees and working groups met frequently and they did some useful work. They drew attention from time to time to such matters as the shortage of training facilities for social workers in North and West Wales and the poor educational facilities in the community homes with education on the premises. In England and Wales as a whole, however, the committees were soon thought to have outlived their usefulness because the number of children in residential care had declined appreciably and there was increasing emphasis on the desirability of local placements. Local authorities were opting increasingly for foster care and felt able to make their own arrangements for residential care in smaller units. As early as 1979, the Government announced, in a White Paper, "Central Government Controls over Local Authorities", its intention to remove the statutory basis of Children's Regional Planning as part of a policy of placing greater responsibility for local matters on local authorities and of increasing their freedom of action. Thus, after January 1984, a local authority could act on its own or could agree with other local authorities to form a group for planning purposes but there was no requirement to form a group or to submit plans to the Secretary of State.

Local Government Act 1972

3.18 Whilst all these developments were taking place in the field of social services, and particularly in relation to the welfare of children in care, substantial reorganisation of the local authority administrative areas was also in train. The Local Government Act 1972 was to establish a radically altered structure in

---

[12] See para 3.03.

[13] Section 4 of the Health and Social Services and Social Security Adjudications Act 1983.

Wales for 22 years from 1 April 1974. The number of Welsh Counties was reduced from 13 to eight, despite the division of the former county of Glamorgan into three; and in North Wales the reduction was from five to two. Thus Gwynedd emerged to replace the previous administrative county areas of Anglesey, Caernarvon, Merioneth (less a former rural district) and a small part of Denbighshire, whilst Clwyd replaced Flintshire, most of Denbighshire and a former rural district of Merionethshire.

Appointment of senior officials to the Social Services Department of Clwyd County Council

3.19 This reorganisation of local government areas following closely upon the establishment of new structures for the provision of social services, including responsibility for children in care, inevitably led to much disruption of newly established working teams, working practices and administrative systems. Inevitably also there was a scramble for appointments. The senior positions went, in the main, to former employees of the extinguished local authorities rather than to men and women from further afield who might have been expected to bring with them fresh ideas.

3.20 Thus, Clwyd County Council appointed as its first Director of Social Services, (Joseph) Emlyn Evans, who was in his mid-fifties on 1 April 1974 and who remained in post until the end of 1979. His speciality was in mental health and he had become Chief Mental Welfare Officer for Denbighshire, after many years experience in that field, before being appointed Director of Social Services for Denbighshire in 1971. Dennis Hughes was appointed to the parallel post in Flintshire but he went off to Suffolk in 1973, whereupon Evans took over responsibility for Flintshire as well and in addition became "shadow" Director of Social Services for the emerging Clwyd.

3.21 Under him, as Deputy Director of Social Services for Clwyd, was (Daniel) Gledwyn Jones, who was appointed on 1 December 1973, at the age of 47 years. He was an outside figure from South Wales with a dozen years experience of social services but mainly in a county welfare department and then as an Assistant Director for Community Services in Pembrokeshire. He had no specific experience in child care. Unusually, in Clwyd, no one in the senior management team had a specialist background in child care.

Appointment of senior officials to the Social Services Department of Gwynedd County Council

3.22 In Gwynedd T E Jones was appointed Director of Social Services designate for Caernarvonshire with effect from 1 January 1971, after serving for over 18 years as County Welfare Officer of Merionethshire County Council. He was 48 years old at the date of his appointment and he graduated to the same post with Gwynedd with effect from 6 July 1973, remaining until 6 September 1982, when he retired on the ground of ill health, after being on sick leave for three months. He had no specific experience of child care work except as clerk to a county council committee in 1951/1952.

3.23 His deputy was D A Parry, 14 years younger than him, who had been Deputy Children's Officer and then Children's Officer for Anglesey before being appointed Director of Social Services for that county from 1971. He was nominally Deputy Director for Gwynedd from 1974 until 1983 but he was then, in effect, demoted to the post of Assistant Director (Special Duties), in which he remained for four years before accepting voluntary redundancy on 31 March 1987, on the eve of his 51st birthday.

A summary of residential care provision for children in Clwyd between 1974 and 1996

The overall position in 1974

4.01 On 1 April 1974 the new Clwyd County Council assumed responsibility for a resident population of about 378,000, of whom 105,350 were aged under 18 years. The total number of children in care was 542, of whom 451 were the subject of care orders, either full or interim, and the rest in voluntary care. There were 203 children in residential care and a similar number, 212, were in foster care.

Local authority community homes in Clwyd in 1974

4.02 The local authority community homes then available within Clwyd were:

Name of home   *Designation in the Regional Plan of 31 December 1971*

In the Wrexham area of the former Denbighshire

(1) Bersham Hall   A new home to be adapted by August 1972 and to be used by six North Wales Counties and (Radnorshire ad hoc) for a maximum of 12 boys at a time for observation and assessment. Under the 1979 Plan there were to be 13 assessment places, including four secure places, for boys aged ten and over, available to the whole of Wales.

(2) Little Acton   A new home to be completed by March 1973 and
     Assessment Centre,   to be used by Flintshire, Montgomeryshire and
     Box Lane   Radnorshire for children needing open assessment (category C) and by all six North Wales counties for children needing semi-secure assessment (category B). Maximum of 15 to be accommodated (12 category C, three category B). Under the 1979 Plan there were to be five assessment places (three regional, two local) for girls aged ten and over. Up to 12 reception beds were also to be provided.

(3) Bryn Estyn,   A former approved school to be a special home,
     Bryn Estyn Lane   the responsibility of the local authority and used by the North Wales counties, for the accommodation of up to 49 boys in the intermediate and senior age ranges. It was proposed in the Regional Plan that there should be secure provision for two boys. In the 1979 Plan it was shown as having 61 places, to be reduced to 49 from 1980/1981, including eight secure places.

(4)	Little Acton Nursery	To provide accommodation for up to 21 children aged 0 to ten years. Available for Radnorshire, Montgomeryshire and East Monmouthshire. Latterly (to 1978) it provided 12 day care places for young children up to seven years.
(5)	Chevet Hey, Price's Lane	To provide accommodation for up to 18 children of school age and over. Available for Radnorshire, Anglesey and Montgomeryshire. The provision was said to be mainly for older children in the 1979 Plan and other local authorities were not referred to.
(6)	Cherry Hill, Borras Road	To provide accommodation for up to 11 children of school age and over (increased to 12 children in the 1979 Plan).
(7)	Heulfre, Horsley Drive	To provide accommodation for up to eight children of school age and over.
(8)	7 Tan-y-Dre	To provide accommodation for up to eight children of school age and over.
(9)	Coppenhall, 188 Centenary Road, Bryn Offa Estate	To provide accommodation for up to eight children of school age and over.
(10)	45 Tapley Avenue	Opened in 1971 to provide accommodation for up to six children from 0 to 19 years with severe learning difficulties (apparently identified as a Home for Mentally Handicapped at page 25 of the 1971 Plan).

Elsewhere in the former Denbighshire

(11)	15 Llwyn Onn, Elwy Road, Rhos-on-Sea	To provide accommodation for up to nine children (eight in 1979) of school age and over.

In the former Flintshire

(12)	Rhiwlas, Northop Road, Flint	After 1973 to provide accommodation for up to ten children under school age.
(13)	Cartrefle, 155 Main Road, Broughton	To provide accommodation for up to eight children. This was increased to ten in the 1979 Plan and the provision was said to be mainly for older children.
(14)	Y Nyth, Park Avenue, Mold	After 1973 to provide accommodation for up to ten girls over school age. Available to the North Wales counties.

(15) South Meadow,
Ffordd Ffrith,
Prestatyn

To provide accommodation for up to 12 children.

(16) Upper Downing,
Whitford

To provide accommodation for up to 24 children. But it was envisaged in the 1971 Regional Plan that this home would be replaced in 1973 by homes in St. Asaph and Prestatyn.

(17) Park House,
Nant Hall Road,
Prestatyn

Opened in 1973 to provide accommodation for up to 16 children.

4.03 We have not received any complaints about (4), (7), (9), (10) (11) and (14) in this list and they are not referred to hereafter in this report in that context. The only complaint about (8) related to two incidents in 1972, outside the period of our review, and was levelled by one child against another. It has not, therefore been investigated. One witness only complained about (12), where he said that he was "belted". He left there, however, on 29 April 1974 and the home closed on 31 December 1982 so that it does not call for separate consideration.

Controlled community homes in Clwyd in 1974

4.04 There was one controlled community home, namely, (18) Llanelwy in Holt Road, Wrexham. This had been opened in 1945 by the St Asaph Diocesan Board for Moral Welfare to give shelter to homeless girls. It provided accommodation for up to 16 girls. Then, in 1970, the Home Office recognised it as a voluntary children's home, at which places were established for six girls on remand. From 1973 it became a controlled community home managed by the Board (later the St Asaph Diocesan Association for Social Work) and Denbighshire County Council, in accordance with an instrument of management, providing 12 places for girls, of which three places were for girls on remand, as part of the Welsh Regional Plan. Education was provided in local schools and the residents had access to a child guidance clinic. In the Regional Plan (1971) it was envisaged that Little Acton would replace it in March 1973 as a placement for three girls on remand. The home was closed in 1978 and we know of no complaints about it.

Assisted community homes in Clwyd in 1974

4.05 There was also an assisted community home, (19), Tanllwyfan, at 510 Abergele Road, Colwyn Bay. This had been opened in 1916 and was operated by the Boys and Girls Welfare Society. Under the Act of 1969 it became an assisted community home and it was designated as a special home for boys and girls in the junior age range, available to the North Wales counties, in the 1971 Regional Plan for Wales. The home was managed by the Society and Denbighshire (later Clwyd) County Council. In the 1971 Plan it had been designated to provide accommodation for 16 younger children but eventually it provided for up to 20 mainly older boys and girls as residents (18 in the 1979

Regional Plan). Education was available on the premises as well as at local schools, and child guidance and medical services were available. A note in the 1979 Plan stated that this home was to close as a community home with education in 1980/1981 and it eventually did so on 31 December 1984.

Other non-private residential establishments for children in Clwyd in 1974

4.06 Another establishment having much of the character, but not the status, of a community home was administered latterly by the Clwydian Community Care NHS Trust. This was Gwynfa Residential Unit (or Clinic) (20), Pen-y-Bryn Road, Colwyn Bay. It was opened in 1961, for up to 16 children of both sexes from two to 13 years of age; and it was to serve as a centre for the investigation, assessment and treatment of children, from North Wales or elsewhere, showing severe emotional maladjustment, difficulties or abnormalities in personality development, or psychiatric disorder. As a rule, children who were considered capable of a definite degree of improvement were admitted on a short term basis for up to one year. At some stage the Unit accommodated up to 25 children and young persons and the age range was extended to 17 years. Until 1974 there was no consultant psychiatrist and the medical management of a child resident remained the responsibility of the child psychiatrist who referred the child. In April 1974, however, the Gwynedd child psychiatrist was designated as the co-ordinating consultant, providing two sessions per week; and a resident child psychiatrist was employed from 1981. The Unit was managed initially by the Clwyd and Deeside Hospital Management Committee but there were several changes of management structure in the following 30 years until the present NHS Trust took over the responsibility for the clinic on 1 April 1993. Gwynfa's functions were transferred to a new unit at the edge of Colwyn Bay (Cedar Court) in March 1997.

4.07 It is necessary to mention here one other local authority establishment that did not open until April 1978. This is Ysgol Talfryn (21) at Brynford, near Holywell, which opened as a day school for a limited number of pupils with emotional and behavioural disorders. A residential unit opened in April 1980, however, and three similar units were added in quick succession to September 1982. The school could provide residential accommodation for up to 40 children and for an additional 25 to 30 day pupils, the age range being six to 16 years. But it was not listed as a community home in the 1979 Regional Plan. It remains open for day pupils only but its future is uncertain.

4.08 The only other voluntary establishment in Clwyd listed in the 1971 Regional Plan was St Clare's Convent, Pantasaph, near Holywell, which remained registered as a voluntary children's home until 1976. It provided accommodation for six children but was closed in 1976, probably as the result of the disastrous fire at the nearby monastery. It had been managed by the Sisters of Charity of Our Lady of Mercy and its role was taken over by Petit House, Albert Avenue, Flint, and our Lady of the Taper home, owned and operated by the Catholic Children's Society (Wales) and the Menevia Family Social Service. Petit House was registered with the Secretary of State for Wales in September 1977 and provided accommodation for 18 children between the ages of one and 16 years until it closed in October 1985. We have not received any complaint about either St. Clare's Convent or Petit House.

Private children's homes and schools in Clwyd in 1974

4.09 There were quite a number of private children's establishments for varying purposes within the administrative county of Clwyd during the period under review but comparatively few were registered because there was no requirement at that time for private children's homes to register. In the course of our Inquiry our attention has been focussed on the private residential establishments owned by three separate organisations, namely, the Bryn Alyn Community, Care Concern and Clwyd Hall for Child Welfare, because it is about these that most complaints in the private sector have been made.

Bryn Alyn Community

4.10 In this group of three, the Bryn Alyn Community stands out because of the large volume of complaints covering almost the whole period of our review. This private organisation was incorporated by John Allen as a limited company in 1972. He had acquired in 1968 the lease for 21 years of Bryn Alyn Hall, a substantial property in Llay New Road on the outskirts of Wrexham, with 50 acres of land and, although he had had no formal training of any kind, he had opened Bryn Alyn Hall as a children's home for up to 20 boys in the age range of 11 to 16 years. He had started with three boys from north east England and one from Liverpool and had circulated a booklet about his project to most of the local authority children's departments in England and Wales.

4.11 The history of the Community is dealt with in detail later in this report, in Chapter 21, and it need only be summarised here. By 1974 Bryn Alyn Community Ltd had acquired the freehold of Bryn Alyn Hall, which was eventually divided and extended into three "houses", called Askew House, Blackley House and Lindisfarne, and the company had acquired three other properties. The first of these additional properties, 26 Talbot Road, Wrexham, was bought by Allen in about 1970 to provide hostel accommodation for about ten working adolescents. The second property was Pentre Saeson Hall, a more modest country house than Bryn Alyn Hall, at Bwlchgwyn, in the same general area, which opened on 27 September 1970 and was intended to provide accommodation for up to 20 boys between the ages of 11 and 13 years, that is, for rather younger boys than most of those at Bryn Alyn Hall. Finally in this particular list, John Allen had purchased in 1972, in his own name but on trust for the Bryn Alyn Community, Bryntirion Hall in Mold Road, Caergwrle, with which he intended to provide hostel accommodation for 15 boys in the range of 16 to 18 years. In his oral evidence Allen said that three local authorities in particular Manchester, Newcastle and Wirral, placed substantial numbers of boys with the Community with the result that, by 1975, over 70 were being accommodated.

Care Concern

4.12 Care Concern was the idea of David Rattray, a former Deputy Director of Social Services for Denbighshire, who owned a property called Ystrad Hall on the A5 road near Llangollen in the direction of Corwen. The property comprised Ystrad Hall itself, an hotel run by Rattray as a business and known as Eirianfa Hotel, together with 14 acres of land. Rattray recruited the Officer-in-Charge or Superintendent of Bersham Hall, Richard Ernest Leake, who had been in post for about two years, to establish a residential school for emotionally disturbed boys aged 11 to 16 years at Ystrad Hall. Leake was appointed Principal of the school and a number of staff, including David White, the senior teacher (later headmaster), were also recruited from Bersham Hall.

4.13 The new school was opened in 1974 and provisionally registered in September that year as an independent school. Separate from the school were two residential units for a total of 55 boys, called Eirianfa (for boys between 11 and 14 years) and Ystrad Hall (14 to 16 years). Full registration was granted in October 1975 and the school remained registered until May 1981, when it closed mainly because of declining numbers. When the school was first registered the proprietors spoke of an intention to move it to a site near Conway but this did not take place. In late 1976, however, the project was expanded when another school, Cartref Melys, (in the Sychnant Pass) near Conway, became available. Care Concern acquired this and it provided accommodation for 25 emotionally disturbed boys in the same age range as Ystrad Hall. It was at this time that the name Care Concern was adopted by the organisation and Leake became Assistant Director of Professional Services.

4.14 The residential accommodation at Ystrad Hall was damaged by fire at the end of 1979 or early 1980 where upon the pupils were moved temporarily to another school nearby, recently acquired by Care Concern. This was St David's College, Carrog, about two miles from Corwen. On their return to Ystrad Hall the school closed as a home for boys as already stated, as did Cartref Melys five years later in 1986. It appears, however, that Care Concern had started to provide education for girls at St David's College and, after Ystrad Hall closed to boys, it was re-opened by Care Concern as Berwyn College, a residential home for girls with learning difficulties, replacing St David's College. Berwyn College was registered from 13 August 1981 to 31 March 1985 and it did admit some boys during the period of industrial action by residential care staff.

4.15 There was a further acquisition by Care Concern when Hengwrt Hall at Rhydymain, five miles from Dolgellau in the Bala direction, was purchased in or about 1976. It was provisionally registered as an independent school on 12 August 1976 and its subsequent history is summarised in paragraph 5.09.

4.16 Care Concern's operations also embraced Westminster House, Chester (a halfway house), Firs Mount, Colwyn Bay (a home for severely mentally handicapped adults) and The Village, Llangwyfan (previously a tuberculosis sanatorium and used by Care Concern as a home for adults but catering for some teenagers).

Clwyd Hall for Child Welfare

4.17 Clwyd Hall was another residential school that accepted children from a range of local authorities in England and Wales. The company that ran the school was called Clwyd Hall for Child Welfare Limited but the effective owners until 1982 were Mr and Mrs William Carman. Clwyd Hall stood in its own substantial grounds at Llanychan, near Ruthin, and it apparently opened as a school in or about 1958. Mr and Mrs Carman lived on the estate and one of their daughters ran an equestrian centre there. The school itself provided accommodation for 50 to 60 children of deprived backgrounds, in the age range seven to 16 years, and about 70 per cent of the residents were boys. Girls slept separately in a building called 'The Paddock'. Many children stayed at the school for a substantial period until school leaving age. The ownership of the school changed in or about July 1982, although Mr Carman retained a financial interest, but subsequent efforts to re-finance the school, which required substantial capital investment, failed and it closed on 27 July 1984.

Local authority community homes in Clwyd in 1985

4.18 It is convenient next to summarise the position in Clwyd as at 1 April 1985 because it is the halfway point in the period of our review, the Regional Plan was dead and important changes had by then occurred. In the 11 year period the total number of children in care in Clwyd had diminished from 542 to 381 (in Wales as a whole from 4,551 to 3,756). Moreover, the ratio between children in residential care and those fostered/boarded out had altered quite dramatically from 203 : 212 to 107 : 199.

4.19 By this time the following local authorities community homes had closed:

In the Wrexham area of the former Denbighshire

(1)	Bersham Hall	This had been closed, in its previous guise, in 1980 and its functions transferred to Bryn Estyn. It had re-opened however, in May 1980 as a multi-purpose centre for up to 21 boys and girls aged between ten and 17 years on the closure of Little Acton Assessment Centre. Its name was changed to Bersham Hall Children's Centre and it took over (inter alia) Little Acton's role as an assessment centre for girls.
(2)	Little Acton Assessment Centre	Closed in or about May 1980.
(3)	Bryn Estyn	Closed on 30 September 1984.
(4)	Little Acton Nursery	Closed on 31 March 1978, when the remaining children were transferred to Heulfre.

(7)	Heulfre	It closed initially on 31 March 1978 but re-opened briefly as a nursery to accommodate children from Little Acton Nursery under five years old. It closed finally in 1980.
(8)	7 Tan-y-Dre	Closed on 29 June 1984.
(9)	Coppenhall	Closed on 31 March 1977.

Thus, only (1) the new Bersham Hall, (5) Chevet Hey, (6) Cherry Hill and (8) 45 Tapley Avenue remained open in the Wrexham area in April 1985. (1) closed at the end of 1993 and (5) in June 1990. The latter's functions were transferred in 1990 to (22) Gladwyn, formerly a residential home for the elderly at Gresford, near Wrexham, with 13 places and an independence training unit in the grounds, but Gladwyn too closed in 1995. We know of only one complaint about (22), which is dealt with in paragraph 14.76.

4.20 In the former Flintshire area, the picture was similar because the following homes had closed:

| (12) | Rhiwlas | Closed on 31 December 1982. |
| (16) | Upper Downing | Closed on 31 January 1977. |

The date of closure of (14) Y Nyth is not known. These closures left only (13) Cartrefle, (15) South Meadow and (17) Park House in the former Flintshire and (11) Llwyn Onn at Rhos-on-Sea. South Meadow closed in 1990 followed by Park House in August 1991. Their functions were taken over by Cefndy Hostel, the amalgamated unit being called (23) New South Meadow. The amalgamated unit closed in October 1993 and we have not received any complaint about it. Cartrefle also closed in 1993.

Other community homes in Clwyd in 1985

4.21 By April 1985 both (18) Llanelwy and (19) Tanllwyfan had closed[1].

Private children's homes and schools in Clwyd in 1985

4.22 The private organisations discussed earlier in this chapter were continuing to provide residential accommodation in Clwyd for children placed by a wide range of local authorities. The Bryn Alyn Community, in particular, had expanded its operations and had acquired properties additional to those listed in paragraphs 4.10 and 4.11.

Expansion of the Bryn Alyn Community

4.23 The first two additional properties acquired by the Bryn Alyn Community were outside Clwyd. Marton's Camp, near Bunbury in Cheshire, was bought in or about 1976 and retained for about two years only as a residential school, providing also 'outward bound' facilities, for up to 40 children between 11 and

---

[1] See paras 4.04 and 4.05.

16 years. At about the same time Cotsbrook Hall, Higford, (near Shifnal) in Shropshire was purchased with the intention that it should be a similar school to Bryn Alyn Hall, catering for 20 (later 40) children, again in the age range 11 to 16 years. In or about 1976 also premises in Poyser Street, Wrexham, were purchased to provide some classroom or play facilities and a gymnasium; but the use of the premises was changed quite soon to a film and theatre studio.

4.24 The following year, on 11 July 1977, the Community bought another large Wrexham house, Gwastad Hall, which was used as offices and also to provide accommodation for some younger children. At about that time Gwersyllt Hall Farm was bought as a working farm to provide vocational training and also to serve as the company's head office, but it was sold in April 1978 and was in effect, replaced by Wilderness Mill Farm, in the same area, which the Community operated as a halfway house towards independent living until 1980, when it was destroyed by fire. The farm was sold in 1984 to a member of Bryn Alyn staff but the Community continued to use the outbuildings for trade activities until 1990. Part of it is now registered as a small children's home. On 1 April 1983, Bryn Alyn Community opened yet another substantial property, Gatewen Hall in Berse Road, New Broughton, Wrexham which had been a residential school, to provide accommodation (according to John Allen) for up to 14 boys and girls, aged 14 to 18 years, in order to prepare them for independence. Finally, 92 Erddig Road, Wrexham, was opened in 1988 as an unregistered children's home for three children or fewer. Allen estimated that at one time the Community was accommodating a total of 200 children.

4.25 The affairs of the Bryn Alyn Community appear to have occupied a considerable amount of Welsh Office attention from 1975 onwards and some 37 pages of the written statement of the main Welsh Office witness before us, John Lloyd, were devoted to it. It is only necessary here to refer to the status of the various components in relation to registration from time to time. Bryn Alyn Hall itself was provisionally registered as an independent school in July 1977 and received final registration on 30 April 1980. On 8 March 1985 it was approved under section 11(3)(a) of the Education Act 1981 to take children with statements of special education need. Neither Bryntirion Hall nor Pentre Saeson Hall purported to provide educational facilities on the premises at that stage although in 1989 the latter was doing so and the Welsh Office drew attention to the need for separate registration. It appears that Pentre Saeson was subsequently inspected as a children's home by Clwyd County Council under the provisions of Children Act 1989 and registration as a children's home was refused by the council in 1992.

4.26 Despite continuing difficulties about the standards achieved at the school, which will be referred to later in this report, the Welsh Office did not withdraw SEN[2] approval for the Bryn Alyn Hall school before Bryn Alyn Community Ltd went into voluntary liquidation on 6 March 1997, after which, following unanswered letters, the Welsh Office informed the company, by letter dated 20 May 1997, that the school was assumed to be closed and that it would be removed from the register of independent schools in Wales.

---

[2] Special Educational Needs.

4.27 There was also confusion about the use and status of Gatewen Hall after it had been purchased by the Community. On the assumption that it had ceased to be a school, it was inspected by the Welsh Office as a children's home in February 1984 under its general powers but it was found that eight pupils were being educated full time there. The Welsh Office was subsequently informed by the Community that it wished to maintain Gatewen Hall's status as a school (having been registered finally under its previous ownership on 9 August 1978). The status of the premises remained uncertain until 22 August 1986 when the Community was informed of the Secretary of State's decision to remove Gatewen Hall from the register of independent schools, the prime consideration being that fewer than five children were attending the school. It appears to have operated as a children's home only from that date.

Other private residential establishments for children in 1985

4.28 By 1 April 1985 the other private residential schools and children's homes within Clwyd that have been discussed earlier in this chapter had all closed. Care Concern's last school on the Ystrad Hall site, Berwyn College, had just closed[3] and the organisation's North Wales activities were focussed in Gwynedd on Cartref Melys near Conway (for one more year) and Hengwrt Hall School at Rhydymain (until November 1991). Clwyd Hall had closed in 1984 and no other establishment had replaced it.

Decline of number of children in residential care by 1996

4.29 Considerable further changes had occurred by 31 March 1996, the date when Clwyd County Council ceased to exist. The population of the county was 411,000 (1991 Census updated) and its children's services budget for 1994/1995 had been £8,897 million (17 per cent of the Social Services Committee's gross expenditure), a higher percentage than any other Welsh local authority. Nevertheless, the number of children being looked after had fallen by 31 March 1994 to 218, of whom only 17 were in residential care (just under eight per cent). A year later the number in foster care had risen from 151 to 203 and the number of children being looked after by about the same amount (49) but by 1996, according to Adrianne Jones' evidence, only four per cent of children being looked after in Clwyd were in residential care.

Local authority community homes in Clwyd in 1996

4.30 At the end of the period of existence of Clwyd County Council it seems that there were eight local authority community homes left within its area, namely:

In the Wrexham area

(6)   Cherry Hill   This was said by Adrianne Jones in her report to provide six places (formerly up to 12).

---

[3] See para 4.14.

| (10) 45 Tapley Avenue | Said by Adrianne Jones to provide two places plus respite care but it closed as a children's home in June 1996, its functions being transferred to Daleside and Norfolk Road. |

Elsewhere in the former Denbighshire

(11) 15 Llwyn Onn, Elwy Road, Rhos-on-Sea	Said by Adrianne Jones to provide three places (formerly eight).
(24) 3 Belgrave Road, Colwyn Bay	A home opened latterly by Clwyd County Council and providing semi-independent accommodation for three young people who were being trained towards independence and leaving care.
(25) 8 Llys Garmon, Llanarmon-yn-Ial, Nr Ruthin	This is a house rented in or about 1994 to provide accommodation for a specific local family of four children. The arrangement is likely to end soon because it is intended that the children will move to live with an uncle in Anglesey.

We have not received a complaint about any of these three homes.

In the former Flintshire

(26) Medea Drive, Rhyl	This was opened in 1988 in a detached house in a residential area to provide for three children who had been resident in (15) South Meadow. Later the number of children was increased to four but more recently it has provided two places.
(27) Cornel Clyd, The Broadway, Brookdale Avenue, Shotton	This home provides two places for children with substantial disabilities plus respite care. It was run by Clwyd County Council in conjunction with an Housing Association and an NHS Trust.
(28) Clivedon Road, Connah's Quay	This is to provide two places for "difficult to manage" young persons and outreach work is also carried out from the premises.

We have not received a complaint about any of these last three homes.

Private children's homes and schools in Clwyd in 1996

4.31 We have received complaints about incidents in the Bryn Alyn children's homes that are alleged to have occurred as late as 1994, most of the later complaints referring to Gatewen and Pentre Saeson, but there have been no complaints to us of physical or sexual assaults in any other private children's home within Clwyd after 1985.

The scope of our account of alleged abuse in Clwyd

4.32 Part II of this report deals in detail with the history of alleged abuse in the local authority community homes within Clwyd between 1974 and 1996. We deal firstly with (3) Bryn Estyn[4], then the other four relevant homes ((2), (1), (5) and (6)) in the Wrexham area[5] and lastly the four local authority homes in the former Flintshire ((13), (15), (16) and (17))[6]. In Part III of the report we deal also with the three separate residential establishments in Clwyd: (19) Tanllwyfan[7], (21) Ysgol Talfryn[8] and (20) Gwynfa Residential Unit[9]. In Part IV of this report we deal with the allegations of abuse in the private residential schools and children's homes in Clwyd identified in this chapter, namely, the Bryn Alyn Community homes[10]; Care Concern's schools: Ystrad Hall, St David's College and Berwyn College[11]; and Clwyd Hall School[12]. Alleged abuse of foster children in Clwyd is dealt with in Part V.

---

[4] See Chapters 8 to 11.
[5] See Chapters 12 to 14 and 16.
[6] See Chapters 15 and 17.
[7] See Chapter 18.
[8] See Chapter 19.
[9] See Chapter 20.
[10] See Chapter 21.
[11] See Chapter 22.
[12] See Chapter 23.

A summary of residential care provision for children in Gwynedd between 1974 and 1996

The overall position in 1974

5.01 The resident population of the new administrative county of Gwynedd on 1 April 1974 was about 226,500, of whom 60,152 were aged under 18 years. The total number of children in care was 290, of whom 189 were the subject of care orders. The total number of children in residential care was then about 80 as against 122 who were in foster care[1].

Local authority community homes in Gwynedd in 1974

5.02 There were six local authority community homes within Gwynedd at that time, namely:

Name of home	*Designation in the Regional Plan of 31 December 1971*

In the former Anglesey area

(1)	5 Queen's Park Close, Holyhead	Opened in 1960 as a family group home, it was designated in 1971 as providing accommodation for up to eight boys and girls. It was similarly designated in 1979 for boys and girls aged 0 to 18 years and it remains open.
(2)	43/44 Ucheldre, Llangefni	Shown with the same designation as (1) in the 1971 Plan. It was closed in 1979 when the staff and residents were transferred to Y Gwyngyll. The one complaint that we received about it related to events prior to 31 December 1968, outside our terms of reference.

In the former Caernarvonshire area

(3)	Eryl Wen, Eryl Place, Llandudno	This was opened in the mid 1960s and was designated to provide accommodation for four boys and girls of school age in the 1971 Plan. It closed in 1976. We have not received any complaints about it.
(4)	Roslin Nursery, Nant y Gamar Road, Craig-y-Don, Llandudno	This was opened by Caernarvonshire County Council as a community home for four children but it was designated in the 1971 Plan as a residential nursery for up to 14 boys and girls aged 0 to eight years. It closed in 1979. No complaint has been made to us about it.

---

[1] Children in Care in England and Wales, March 1974, Cmnd 6147. Caernarvonshire (79) and Merionethshire (30) both relied heavily on foster care. The percentage of children in care in community homes was only 29 in both counties.

(5) Tŷ'r Felin, Maesgeirchen, Bangor

Named as Lon-y-Felin in the 1971 Plan, this was shown as a projected observation and assessment facility to be completed at a cost of £48,000 and to be occupied by the end of 1973. It was to provide for a maximum of five children for assessment plus seven for short stays. North Wales Child Guidance were to provide an educational psychologist service and the facility was to be available to Anglesey and Merionethshire as well. The categories of children to be received were said to be A (needing secure assessment) and B (needing semi-secure assessment) but no reference was made to the provision of such facilities. In 1979 it was shown simply as one of the "other homes" for boys and girls between three and 17 years providing up to six residential places and six for local assessment. It was said to have one classroom and one teacher: psychiatric and psychological input were available on request only. It closed eventually in the autumn of 1995 and was demolished in March 1997.

In the former Merionethshire area

(6) Cilan, 59/61 Hoel y Llan, Barmouth

To provide for up to nine children. It closed in 1979 and we have not received any complaint about it.

Voluntary homes in Gwynedd in 1974

5.03 The only two registered voluntary homes in Gwynedd shown in the 1971 Regional Plan were Bontnewydd and Benarth, both stated to be in Caernarvon. Neither was described as controlled or assisted. The former was a children's home built in 1907 and known as Cartref Bontnewydd. It was established by a Methodist body of trustees with the object of providing a service for orphaned children and for those who could not be cared for within their own families; and it remained open as a children's home until 1983, being categorised as "other residential arrangements for children outside the community home system" in the 1979 Plan. Benarth was, in fact, at Llanfairfechan and was listed in the same way as Cartref Bontnewydd in both the 1971 and 1979 Plans. We have no information as to when it opened and closed or about the voluntary organisation that managed it but it has been unnecessary to pursue the details because we have not received any complaints about it.

5.04 In the 1979 Regional Plan a third registered voluntary children's home in Gwynedd was listed under "other residential arrangements", namely, Arne Hall (Dr Barnardo's), Llandudno. Again, we have not been given any information about its relevant dates but the only complaint about it made to us was of a physical assault prior to 1 January 1970 and thus outside our terms of reference.

Other residential establishments for children in 1974

5.05 The only unregistered private residential home for children listed in the 1971 Plan as being used by a Gwynedd local authority was Bryn Alyn, Wrexham said to be used by Anglesey County Council. Caernarvonshire County Council was said to have two places at a home for the mentally handicapped with the address Social Services Department, Maes Imclay, Caernarvon, about which we have not had any complaint. Finally Merionethshire was said to have residential accommodation available at Gwynfa Residential Unit.

The overall change in the placement of children in care by 1985

5.06 By April 1985, midway through the period under review, the total number of children in care in Gwynedd (280) was almost the same as it had been in April 1974 but the number in residential care had declined from 80 to 23, whereas the total of children fostered/boarded out had risen from 122 (approx 42%) to 176 (approx 63%). For Wales as a whole the comparable percentage of children fostered/boarded out at that date was about 48.

Local authority community homes in Gwynedd in 1985

5.07 The number of local authority community homes within Gwynedd had by then been reduced to five. (1) 5 Queen's Park Close at Holyhead and (5) Tŷ'r Felin remained and three new homes had been established, namely:

Name of Home   *Designation in the 1979 Regional Plan*

In the former Anglesey area

(7) Y Gwyngyll,
Ffordd Tŷ Groes,
Llanfair P G

This had been opened in January 1979. As we have said earlier staff and residents from Ucheldre were transferred to it in 1979. It was shown in the 1979 Regional Plan as providing accommodation for 16 boys and girls aged 0 to 18 years plus two school leavers (sic), who had bed-sitting accommodation. "Handicapped children" were accepted. Its life was comparatively short, however, because it closed in 1986.

In the former Merionethshire area

(8) Pant yr Eithin,
     Morfa Road,
     Harlech

This too had been opened during the 1970s and was shown in the 1979 Plan as providing accommodation for up to 14 boys and girls aged 0 to 18 years. This home also accepted "handicapped children". It closed as a community home in 1982, when it became a hostel for adults with learning difficulties. We have received only one "complaint" in relation to this home made by a man who was 12 years old at the time of his stay in the home in 1980 but he says that he does not blame the person who slapped him twice to calm him down.

In the former Caernarvonshire area

(9) Tŷ Newydd
     Hostel,
     Llandegai,
     Near Bangor

This was opened in 1978 as a hostel for up to ten boys aged 16 to 21 years and was so described in the 1979 Plan. It closed in 1981 but re-opened the next year to provide accommodation for up to 12 boys and girls, closing again in 1987. It is now a bail hostel.

Private residential homes and schools for children in Gwynedd in 1985

5.08 In the 1979 Regional Plan, two private residential establishments for children in Clwyd were named as being used by Gwynedd. They were the Bryn Alyn Community at Wrexham and Care Concern's school at Ystrad Hall, Llangollen[2]. Nothing further need be said here about the former but by 1985 Care Concern had opened two residential schools within Gwynedd itself. The first of these was Cartref Melys in the Sychnant Pass near Conway, which was provisionally registered as a residential school on 1 October 1975, in view of the demand for places at Ystrad Hall School. It was granted full registration as a residential special school on 23 December 1976 for up to 20 emotionally disturbed children aged 11 to 17 years. The permitted number of children was increased progressively to 28 by 1981 and the school was given SEN approval[3] for that number of children on 12 December 1983 but we have been told that it closed in or about July 1986. We are aware of two complaints only in respect of this school, one of which was against an unidentified member of staff. Neither complainant has provided evidence to the Tribunal and we do not discuss the school further in this report.

5.09 The second Care Concern school to open in Gwynedd was Hengwrt Hall School at Rhydymain, between Dolgellau and Bala (not to be confused with Hengwrt House, which became registered as Ysgol Hengwrt[4]). This was provisionally registered on 12 August 1976 and achieved full registration on

---

[2] See paras 4.10 to 4.14 and 4.23 to 4.28.
[3] See Appendix 6, paras 38 and 39.
[4] See paras 5.10, 5.11 and 5.13.

24 January 1977 as a residential special school for up to 25 physically and mentally handicapped children, categorised at the time as ESN(S)[5]. The permitted number of children was increased in July 1980 to 35 and the school was granted SEN approval on 12 December 1983 for up to 35 boys and girls aged five to 16 years with severe learning difficulties. That approval was ultimately withdrawn on 3 April 1989 and the school was sold to new proprietors in November 1991. This history and the restoration of SEN approval to the school on 15 July 1996 under its new name of Aran Hall School are dealt with later, in Part VIII of this report.

Residential homes and schools run by Paul Hett

5.10　The other private residential schools and children's homes about which we have received complaints are: Ynys Fechan Hall at Arthog, eight miles from Dolgellau on the coast; Dôl Rhyd School, Barmouth Road, Dolgellau; and (confusingly) Hengwrt House at Llanelltyd, near Dolgellau. All three of these establishments were run by Paul Hett. The first of these was found by the Welsh Office to be operating as an unregistered school for about a dozen pupils in 1974. According to Hett the property was acquired with the aid of a large mortgage in 1974 and he started the school with three pupils. He was suddenly inundated with applications with the result that he took holiday placements immediately, mainly from Gloucestershire, and he began the academic year with 12 pupils. All the children came from local authorities (primarily in Lancashire initially) and included those subject to care orders, children on remand and emergency placements. Registration as a school was granted by the Welsh Office in 1975 but this was subsequently transferred to Dôl Rhyd School in 1976 as provisional registration. This house, which had formerly been the senior girls' house at the well known Dr Williams' School for Girls, was acquired on 1 December 1975 and, by February 1976, 30 boys were enrolled there, including three of primary school age. It appears that Dôl Rhyd took over from Ynys Fechan Hall as the school and the latter became merely a residential annexe until it was destroyed by fire in September 1981; but it was not until 15 February 1979 that the Welsh Office agreed to give Dôl Rhyd final registration for up to 34 emotionally and behaviourally disturbed boys in the age range of 11 to 16 years.

5.11　Hengwrt House was acquired by Hett in October 1980, according to his own evidence. It was ten minutes' walk from Dôl Rhyd and he had already discussed with the Welsh Office his intention to establish there a junior section of his school for 15 pupils. Thus, he intended to raise the full establishment to about 50 pupils and also to include girls. In the event Hengwrt House appears to have been treated as part of Dôl Rhyd until April 1986.

5.12　Various concerns about the running of Dôl Rhyd were expressed to the Welsh Office during the 1980s, including anxieties about harsh treatment of pupils. At this time Ynys Fechan Hall re-opened briefly in October 1984, after re-building at a cost of £350,000, as a school for dyslexic children but it closed in May 1985,

---

[5] Educationally Sub-normal (Severe).

when its pupils were transferred to Dôl Rhyd. It was sold in September 1986 to Barry Young and was registered by the latter with Gwynedd County Council in 1992 as a private children's home for up to 11 boys and girls. It remains open and we have not received any complaints about it during Young's regime. Hett's aim for Dôl Rhyd from 1983 onwards had been to secure approval to admit pupils with statements of SEN under section 11(3)(a) of the Education Act 1981 but this was refused by the Secretary of State in April 1984 and again in April 1987. In the interim period Dôl Rhyd had accommodated a reducing number of dyslexic pupils. By July 1987 the school had been discontinued and it was removed from the Register of Independent Schools on 12 August 1987. It was then re-opened by Hett's former wife and her sister as a unit (called Cerrig Camau) for young adults with learning difficulties and registered as such by Gwynedd County Council.

5.13   As for Hengwrt House, Hett applied for it to be registered separately from Dôl Rhyd and it was provisionally registered in the name of Ysgol Hengwrt on 14 April 1986 as an independent residential school. The application was for up to 20 boys and girls aged 11 to 18 years and Hett had in mind a small, family orientated special school for disadvantaged teenagers, concentrating on vocational courses for the 14 to 16 age range. The school had a very unhappy history, however, because successive inspectors were critical and there were a number of allegations of sexual abuse that were not satisfactorily resolved. The number of pupils on the roll fluctuated at a very low level and fell to two in January 1990 after Brent London Borough Council removed their six placements at the school. It was then removed from the register in March 1990, restored provisionally in September 1990 and again removed on 9 December 1991. Registration as a children's home was refused by Gwynedd County Council in October 1992 and the Registered Homes Tribunal dismissed Hett's appeal in April 1993. In his evidence to the Tribunal on 20 January 1998 Hett described Ysgol Hengwrt as "an empty school with a dream" and himself as "headmaster of a residential special school with no pupils since 1993".

Further change in the placement of children by 1996

5.14   When Gwynedd County Council ceased to exist the number of children in residential care within the county had been reduced further to 18 (from the starting point of 80 in 1974) and there were 139 children in foster care (122 in 1974). The figures given are those as at 31 July 1995 in the report of Adrianne Jones, which are the latest for that county before us. The total given for the number of children looked after was the sum of the two figures, 157.

Local authority community homes in Gwynedd in 1996

5.15   Tŷ'r Felin (with nine places then) had closed in November 1995 and only two local authority community homes remained open. These were (1) 5 Queen's Park Close (five places) and:

(10) Cartref Bontnewydd,
Bontnewydd,
Near Caernarvon

We have already outlined the earlier history of this former private children's home[6]. Since 11 October 1984 part of the building has been used by the same trustees as a family placement centre operating in partnership with Gwynedd County Council (now Gwynedd Council and Anglesey County Council under a joint agency agreement) as a fostering service. The rest of the building was re-opened in April 1988 as a local authority community home for up to seven children, following the closure of (9) Tŷ Newydd. It remains open.

Bryn Melyn (Farm) Community

5.16 It is necessary to mention one new private children's home established in Gwynedd after 1985 because it has attracted public attention from time to time. That is the Bryn Melyn (Farm) Community established at Llandderfel, near Bala by Brendan McNutt in 1986. It began then as a private children's home for young people in the age range of 15 to 18 years and was later registered under the Children Act 1989 for up to ten children. It now has a number of units accommodating one child at a time across North Wales which are open to children from both inside and outside the United Kingdom. The main criticism that has appeared in the press has been that allegedly extravagant amounts have been spent providing placements or holidays abroad for residents and accompanying staff at the expense of local authorities but this is not a criticism that has been made to us. We have not received any complaint of abuse of children in the care of the Community but we are aware that the Welsh Office was informed in 1994 that an unstable woman from outside the home had had sexual intercourse with a 15 year old resident there and had been successfully prosecuted subsequently for indecent assault. This incident had occurred prior to registration of the home and a collateral allegation about drugs had been found to be unsupported by any acceptable evidence.

The scope of our account of alleged abuse in Gwynedd

5.17 In the light of this summary we discuss in Part VII of this report the detailed history of alleged abuse in the local authority children's homes within Gwynedd between 1974 and 1996. We deal firstly with the homes in the Bangor area, (5) Tŷ'r Felin and (9) Tŷ Newydd; then with the Anglesey homes (7) Y Gwyngyll at Llanfair P G and (1) 5 Queen's Park Close, Holyhead; and lastly with (10) Cartref Bontnewydd. We continue in Part VIII of this report with the allegations that have been made in respect of Hett's three schools/children's homes in the Dolgellau area and with the history of Hengwrt Hall (later Aran Hall School). Complaints in relation to foster care in Gwynedd are dealt with in Part IX.

---

[6] See para 5.03.

The Tribunal's approach to the evidence

6.01 The nature and scope of the Tribunal's inquiry have given rise to a number of special, but not unique, evidential problems. One obvious difficulty is that most of the witnesses have given evidence to us about events that occurred many years ago. Thus, the majority of the complainants of abuse are now in the age range of 25 to 35 years and gave evidence about events that occurred in the first half of their teens or earlier. Moreover, all but a few of them had not made any complaint of abuse before the major police investigation began in 1991 and some had not complained until later than that. In these circumstances any documentary or other supporting evidence of incidents to which they referred was likely to be difficult to trace and patchy at best. As for members of the care and teaching staffs at the children's homes and social workers involved in the complainants' care, against whom allegations of abuse or neglect have been made, they have had to reach back in their memories far in time and have been in equally obvious difficulty in seeking oral or documentary evidence to support what they have had to say.

6.02 Having regard to these difficulties and the scale of the alleged physical and sexual abuse that has emerged in the evidence we do not consider that it would be either practicable or appropriate for us to attempt to reach firm conclusions on each specific allegation that has been made to us. We made it clear at the outset of the hearings that we did not propose to conduct a series of criminal or quasi-criminal trials of individual allegations, not least because the format and procedure of a tribunal of inquiry are unsuitable for such a purpose. The range of matters to be covered in the course of the Tribunal's hearings has been such that it would have been impracticable and wastefully expensive to undertake a detailed examination of each specific incident, bearing in mind the overall objectives of the Inquiry underlying our terms of reference. The first requirement of those terms of reference is that we should "inquire into the abuse of children in care in the former county council areas of Gwynedd and Clwyd since 1974" and we interpret that as a requirement that we should hear the available evidence of the alleged abuse and reach such conclusions as we feel properly able to as to its scale and when and where it occurred as a necessary preliminary to examining the other matters specified in the terms of reference and to formulating relevant recommendations.

6.03 At the conclusion of the hearings of evidence before us, Counsel on behalf of Salmon letter recipients (SLRs), ie those who are alleged to have committed acts of abuse against individual complainants, made a number of submissions to us about the nature of the findings that we should make and our approach to the evidence of abuse. In particular, it was submitted that we should not make any findings of fact implicating individuals in our report because the full evidence in relation to specific allegations that would be available at a criminal trial, including character evidence, has not been heard and because some allegations emerged very late in the proceedings so that the alleged abuser was at a disadvantage in dealing with them. It was pointed out that Anna Pauffley QC and Rachel Langdale represented more than 100 different SLRs so that attention to each individual's case was inevitably restricted and it was suggested that, in any event, it was unnecessary to make findings against specific individuals in order to make final recommendations.

6.04 A further submission on behalf of the SLRs was that, before making any general finding about the level and nature of abuse in any particular home, the Tribunal needed to be sure about it and about any comment upon it. In support of this proposition Counsel cited the following passage from the report of the Royal Commission on Tribunals of Inquiry 1966, which appears in that report under the heading "Should there be an appeal from the findings of the Tribunal?":

> "These Tribunals have no questions of law to decide. It is true that whether or not there is any evidence to support a finding is a question of law. Having regard, however, to the experience and high standing of the members appointed to these Tribunals and their natural reluctance to make any finding reflecting on any person unless it is established beyond doubt by the most cogent evidence, it seems highly unlikely that any such finding would ever be made without any evidence to support it."[1]

6.05 It would be inappropriate for us to become involved in an argument about legal semantics and, in the end, these legal points made on behalf of the SLRs are of academic significance only because we are sure of the correctness of the findings of fact that we make in our report. In our judgment, however, the proceedings before the Tribunal have been civil proceedings rather than criminal proceedings and the standard of proof to be applied is that applicable to the former. Since the Royal Commission reported in 1966, the courts have had to consider quite frequently the standard of proof applicable to civil proceedings in which grave allegations are made, including many cases in the Family Division in which the allegation has been of sexual abuse of a child. We take the correct approach, therefore, to be that enunciated by Lord Nicholls of Birkenhead in his speech in In *re H (minors)* (1996) AC 563 with which the majority of the House of Lords agreed. At page 586 D to G, Lord Nicholls said:

> "The balance of probability standard means that a court is satisfied an event occurred if the court considers that, on the evidence, the occurrence of the event was more likely than not. When assessing the probabilities the court will have in mind as a factor, to whatever extent is appropriate in the particular case, that the more serious the allegation the less likely it is that the event occurred and, hence, the stronger should be the evidence before the court concludes that the allegation is established on the balance of probability. Fraud is usually less likely than negligence. Deliberate physical injury is usually less likely than accidental physical injury. A stepfather is usually less likely to have repeatedly raped and had non-consensual oral sex with his under-age

---

[1] See para 134 of the report of the Royal Commission on Tribunals of Inquiry 1966, November 1966, Cmnd 3121.

stepdaughter than on some occasion to have lost his temper and slapped her. Built into the preponderance of probability standard is a generous degree of flexibility in respect of the seriousness of the allegation. Although the result is much the same, this does not mean that where a serious allegation is in issue the standard of proof required is higher. It means only that the inherent probability or improbability of an event is itself a matter to be taken into account when weighing the probabilities and deciding whether, on balance the event occurred. The more improbable the event, the stronger must be the evidence that it did occur before, on the balance of probability, its occurrence will be established."

6.06 In the present proceedings before us the nature and volume of evidence from former children in care have been such as to enable us to reach firm conclusions about the pattern of behaviour of the more prominent SLRs and we state those findings in our report. In reaching those conclusions we have had fully in mind the many criticisms that have been levelled against the complainants both generally and individually. Thus, it has been suggested that their complaints have been made belatedly because they have become aware of the possibility of compensation[2] comparatively recently and that there has been collusion between them to fabricate similar complaints against particular individuals. The length of the delay in making complaints has been stressed and it has been suggested that investigating police officers encouraged the complainants to make allegations by telling them of their right to claim compensation. Reliance has been placed by the SLRs also on the disturbed backgrounds of most of the complainants, their failure to respond co-operatively to residential care, their bitterness about their subsequent failures in life, which they attribute to their time in care, and, in very many cases, their long criminal records, involving petty dishonesty and, in some cases, serious crime resulting in long sentences of imprisonment.

6.07 Despite these substantial criticisms and other allied attacks upon the credibility of individual witnesses, including the paucity of direct corroboration in relation to most specific incidents, we have been impressed generally by the sincerity of the overwhelming majority of the complainants that we have heard and their own conviction that they are telling the truth about what occurred to them in care. Indeed, no one who has sat through the Tribunal's hearings and listened to their evidence impartially can have failed to have been impressed by what they have said and their stated motivation now in coming forward to give evidence. That is not to say that the evidence has always been accurate. Inaccuracies have been demonstrated from time to time in cross-examination on the basis of contemporary documents, including statements taken from others, and some of these inaccuracies may be the result of deliberate exaggeration or innocent embellishment in retrospect due to the lapse of time. We have in mind also that many alleged assaults occurred in circumstances in which a member of staff had been provoked by the victim or had to deal with an

---

[2] The Tribunal was provided, by Counsel to the insurers, with a table listing those individuals who as at 10 March 1998, had instituted civil proceedings against Clwyd County Council, Gwynedd County Council or those two former authorities jointly. The table shows that a total of 104 claims had been made as of that date, 60 of which were notified to the insurers after 16 June 1998.

eruption of violence that had already occurred. What has been most striking, however, is the similarity in the accounts of conditions in particular homes given by former children in care from widely separate areas of the country and between whom there was no contact when they were in the home or afterwards.

6.08 We have been urged, by Counsel on behalf of the SLRs already referred to, not to name in our report any alleged "perpetrator of child abuse" against whom we feel able to make a finding. The grounds of this are, firstly, that the individuals concerned have not had the same opportunity to challenge the case against them as they would have done in criminal or inter-party civil proceedings; secondly, that the consequences of naming a perpetrator of child abuse in a public report would have many of the consequences of a criminal conviction and would be likely to attract even greater publicity; and, thirdly, the paramount importance of protecting a specific child, which is the governing principle in family or child care proceedings, does not apply to the proceedings before this Tribunal.

6.09 We should say at once that we accept without reservation the gravity of a finding of sexual abuse and it will be apparent from our report that there are very few such findings in our report except those that we make in respect of persons who have already been convicted of sexual offences against children in care. The reasons for this are that the allegations against other specific individuals have in general, been very few in number, have not been corroborated and are so distant in time that, in our view, no one could safely conclude that the abuse had occurred without the risk of grave injustice to the alleged perpetrator. In respect of those individuals who have already been convicted of relevant offences against children in care, however, our approach has been that, in the absence of a successful appeal, the convictions are evidence that the offences were committed and that it has not been within our jurisdiction to question the correctness of those convictions, unless (possibly) fresh evidence were to be tendered going to the root of the convictions.

6.10 In the event no such fresh evidence has been submitted and none of the convicted persons referred to in Chapter 2 has appealed against conviction successfully. We have, however, heard evidence from additional witnesses not named in the specific charges before the courts that dealt with the principal offenders and we have evaluated this additional evidence in reaching our conclusions about the scale of the abuse that occurred. Similarly, we have heard evidence from witnesses in support of charges that were ordered by the relevant court to remain upon the court's file and have assessed that evidence for the same purpose.

6.11 Conversely, we have not deemed it appropriate to question the correctness of verdicts of juries in respect of those SLRs who have been acquitted of all or some of the charges laid against them in the absence of compelling fresh evidence in support of those allegations. We have not considered ourselves to be bound by any 'res judicata' principle in this respect but we acknowledge the force of the 'double jeopardy' objection to re-investigation of these cases. Again, however, we have not been faced with any practical difficulty because no fresh evidence of substance has been put before us in those cases.

6.12 A similar potential problem has presented itself in respect of the allegations of sexual abuse made against Gordon Anglesea, a former superintendent in the North Wales Police. As we have recounted at paragraphs 2.24 to 2.32, Anglesea brought libel proceedings against the *Independent on Sunday*, the *Observer*, HTV Ltd and *Private Eye* in respect of allegations that he had been guilty of very serious sexual misconduct at Bryn Estyn and on 6 December 1994 the jury found in his favour. This verdict was, of course, given in civil rather than criminal proceedings but, having regard to the way in which the central issue in the case was put to the jury by the trial judge, we can see no reason in principle for distinguishing the verdict from an acquittal. In considering the allegations against Anglesea, therefore, we have looked carefully for any compelling fresh evidence that would drive us to a conclusion contrary to that of the civil jury. The case against Anglesea is considered in detail in Chapter 9, because it has formed an important part of the inquiry, but in the end we have been unable to accept that it would be right for us to find against Mr Anglesea on the evidence presented to us.

6.13 The question of "naming names" has been a problem throughout our inquiry. We have explained in paragraphs 1.08 and 1.09 of this report the ruling that we made at the outset in relation to the reporting of the names of complainants and alleged abusers as the inquiry proceeded and our reasons for it. As far as the complainants of sexual abuse are concerned, it appears to us that section 1 of the Sexual Offences (Amendment) Act 1992 will apply to our report and it is not lawfully open to us to name them, whether or not one or two of them may have been identified in the past in the press or on television with or without their written consent[3]. This statutory embargo does not apply to complaints of physical abuse but one practical difficulty is that a substantial number of complainants have alleged both physical and sexual abuse and our account of the history might well appear to be distorted if we were to name those complainants in respect of part only of their overall allegations. Quite apart from this technical problem, we have to remember that all these witnesses have come forward in adulthood to reveal circumstances of their childhood that still cause them pain in recollection and which may well be unknown to members of their present families and close associates. We have decided, therefore, in the general public interest, to preserve in our report the anonymity of all the complainants and we are satisfied that the impact of what we have to say will not be significantly diminished by this decision.

6.14 Similar reasoning does not apply to the alleged abusers. In the first place, they do not have any statutory right to anonymity. Secondly, many of them have already been named in widely reported court proceedings so that no proper purpose would be served by not identifying them in our report. Thirdly, the essential purpose of our anonymity ruling in respect of them, namely, to encourage witnesses to come forward and to give evidence as freely as possible, has now been served. Fourthly, the potential injustice that could have arisen because of the inevitable delay between the reporting of the allegations in evidence and the Tribunal's findings about them does not now arise.

---

[3] Section 5(2) of the Sexual Offences (Amendment) Act 1992.

6.15 Nevertheless, we consider that we should exercise a restrictive discretion in naming alleged abusers in our report. We have, for example, been able to give assurances in advance to a substantial number of persons in this broad category because of the comparative triviality of the allegations against them or the very limited number of minor allegations made against them over a long period. In other cases no assurance has been given but we do not consider that the evidence against particular individuals has been such as to warrant naming them, bearing in mind the climate in which they were working.

6.16 In our judgment, however, we would be failing in our duty if we did not identify in our report:

> (a) those persons who have already been the subject of relevant court proceedings;
>
> (b) individuals against whom a significant number of complaints have been made, with our assessment of them;
>
> (c) other persons who have figured prominently in the evidence, whether or not they have been the subject of substantial complaints;
>
> (d) a limited number of persons who should be identified in the public interest in order to deal with current rumours; and
>
> (e) persons who have not been the subject of allegations of abuse but who were in positions of responsibility and whose acts and omissions are relevant to our full terms of reference, including council officials and police officers, but who have not had the benefit of any anonymity ruling by the Tribunal.

Such identification is, in our view, essential to enable us to report coherently and fully upon the evidence that we have heard and as a basis for our recommendations. This paragraph must be read, however, subject to the caveat that we are unable to report at all upon some allegations because they are the subject of ongoing police investigations or proceedings: a summary of the latest developments in respect of these is given in paragraphs 50.29 to 50.32.

6.17 The general approach of the Tribunal to the gathering of evidence from complainants was that each potential witness would be interviewed by a member of the Tribunal's investigating team and would be required to confirm or comment upon any earlier statements made by that witness to the police. Any complainant thus interviewed who was available and willing to give relevant evidence would then be called to give oral evidence and subjected to cross-examination. This procedure was followed in respect of most of the complainant witnesses. However, one witness, who is discussed fully in Chapter 9[4], insisted on preparing his own statement with the assistance of his solicitors and was permitted to do so. Some complainants could not be traced after they had been interviewed and others were unwilling to give oral evidence. In those cases it was agreed that their written evidence including any earlier statements to the police should be incorporated in the transcript but on the

---

[4] See paras 9.32 to 9.34.

footing that the contents of the statements were not agreed. In a small number of cases potential witnesses were not called or written statements were excluded because there were clear pointers to their unreliability.

6.18 Written statements were also admitted for a variety of other reasons. Some related to incidents that had already been the subject of court proceedings. Others were read because they dealt with relatively minor matters, by way of corroboration or otherwise, or contained complaints at the bottom end of the scale. In a limited number of cases statements to the police were read because the witness had not been found or could not be interviewed for another substantial reason. On behalf of staff in the homes, social workers, local authority officials and the North Wales Police numerous other written statements were admitted because their contents were not in substantial dispute (eg general character evidence or accounts of procedure or conditions in particular homes) or because they dealt with issues in respect of which it was unnecessary for the Tribunal to reach a concluded view. In several cases also the statements of potential witnesses who had died, including that of Peter Norman Howarth, were read.

6.19 On behalf of the SLRs implicated in allegations of abuse it has been submitted boldly that it would be inappropriate for the Tribunal to place any reliance upon the contents of statements that were read but this is obviously much too wide a proposition. We have assessed the written statements before us in the appropriate conventional way, having firmly in mind that they have not been subject to cross-examination. The evidence in them has been very useful in filling out the general picture before us and in giving us a much wider cross-section of views about the relevant issues but we have not based any of our findings adverse to individuals upon the contents of the written statements, except in the very small number of cases in which the facts were admitted or virtually indisputable. In the result overall the Tribunal has had an unusually full opportunity to assess the evidence of the many witnesses who gave evidence orally, not only on the basis of their recent statements to the Tribunal but also in the light of their earlier successive statements to the police, in some cases their statements to care workers at the time when incidents occurred and often statements to the police or to others by witnesses alleged to have been present at the time.

6.20 The findings of fact and expressions of view in this report are those of the full Tribunal.

PART II

ALLEGED ABUSE OF CHILDREN IN CARE
IN LOCAL AUTHORITY HOMES IN CLWYD
BETWEEN 1974 AND 1996

Bryn Estyn, 1974 to 1984

Background

7.01 Bryn Estyn Hall is a large and rather forbidding mansion, which was built in 1904, in the style of an Elizabethan manor house, by a successful Wrexham brewer to replace a previous house. It lies in ample grounds, which earlier formed part of the large Erlas Hall estate on the outskirts of Wrexham, and which were landscaped when the new house was built but are now very neglected. The property probably remained in private hands until the second world war when, after a short period as an ordnance depot, it became, in 1942, an approved school for boys from Merseyside and further afield. Since 1989 it has been used for other educational and local government purposes and it is now known as Erlas Centre.

7.02 As an approved school, Bryn Estyn remained the responsibility of the Home Office until 1 October 1973, when it became a local authority community home with education on the premises. Responsibility for it passed to the former Denbighshire County Council until 1 April 1974 when the new Clwyd County Council took over. During its period as an approved school Bryn Estyn had a rather chequered history. According to Granville Bernard (Matt) Arnold, who became Headmaster of the school with effect from 1 May 1973, the first Headmaster, James Bennett, remained in the school until 1967 but the regime was criticised as rigid, authoritarian and punitive for both staff and boys.

7.03 His successor, David Ursell, had no formal qualifications in teaching or child care; he was a dynamic person but suffered from diabetes and associated depression. Members of staff complained eventually of Ursell's alleged excessive use of physical force to boys at the school in breach of Rule 38 of the Approved School Rules 1933, as amended in 1949, and the managers appointed a committee of inquiry to investigate the allegations. The upshot of the committee's hearings and a subsequent appeal to the managers in May 1971 was that Ursell resigned and an interregnum followed until his successor, Peter Burton, was appointed. The latter was a young man and, in the autumn of 1971, he set about reversing his predecessor's policies but he too antagonised members of the staff. He was anxious to establish a favourable reputation for Bryn Estyn and (according to Arnold) was prepared to admit "rejects" from anywhere, but he met an untimely death in October or November 1972, when he, his wife and child and his deputy were killed in a motor car accident.

7.04 Thus, Arnold took over as Headmaster[1] just five months before Bryn Estyn changed its status and after a further hiatus of seven months, during which Brynley Goldswain had acted as Headmaster. Arnold came to Bryn Estyn with excellent references. He was then nearly 44 years old (born on 14 June 1929)

---

[1] Subsequently the holder of the post became styled Principal - see para 7.07.

and had already held senior teaching positions in approved schools for almost 13 years, firstly as Deputy Headmaster of Carlton School, Bedford, for 22 months, and then successively as Headmaster of Richmond Hill School in Yorkshire and Axwell Park School in County Durham, at which latter school his wife had been Matron. He held a teacher's certificate from the University of Wales (1952), a certificate in religious knowledge from Westminster College, London (1953) and was to receive, in September 1973, from Newcastle University, the Senior Certificate in Residential Child Care and the Diploma in Advanced Educational Studies (Residential). In 1976 he was awarded the degree of Bachelor of Education but we do not know how this came about.

7.05 One Director of Social Services who supplied a reference in January 1973 for Arnold in connection with his Bryn Estyn application described him as "one of the finest Headmasters of approved schools I have come across" and another said this:

> "Mr Arnold is a voluble and excitable Welshman, but he has a capacity for deep and serious thought into the problems of boys as groups and individuals. He has a flair for casework and much experience of it. He has an ability to animate people to create loyalty from them and to push through new ideas. At the same time he is a most unstuffy person, he is informal in his relationships and prefers to build a very relaxed sort of atmosphere where people get on well with other people and the whole school really does allow good person to person influences."

7.06 There was, however, a warning note (as it now appears, with hindsight) in the last paragraph of the latter reference, which said:

> "Mr Arnold will explain to you his own feelings that he should now leave Tyneside and if possible return to an environment nearer his home. We have discussed this at great length and I fully understand his feelings that he should return. He has had family difficulties over the past few years and he is conscious that this has temporarily drained him of some of his tremendous energy and positive outlook. I am absolutely confident that when the health of his wife is improved and he is back nearer home he will again demonstrate that he has the ideas, the drive and the methods that make any Community School into a thoroughly outward looking and therapeutic environment."

7.07 In the event Arnold remained Principal (as he became styled) of Bryn Estyn until almost the end of its days as a community home, although he did apply in 1977 for an appointment as Social Work Education Adviser to the Central Council for Education and Training in Social Work. He retired at the end of July 1984 because of the impending closure but was appointed to the Clwyd Panel of Guardian Ad Litem and Reporting Officers in January 1985. To our regret, Arnold, who was still alive when the major police investigation took place, died on 9 June 1994 and had only been asked to make a short statement to the police. We have not, therefore, had the benefit of any evidence from him about his period as Principal of Bryn Estyn, except that contained in his regular reports to Clwyd County Council's Management Committee for the community homes of Bryn Estyn, Little Acton and Bersham Hall[2], which met quarterly and for which we have copies of the agendas, minutes and accompanying reports from 10 December 1975 to 20 July 1984.

7.08 Arnold's widow survives but her health did not improve significantly at Bryn Estyn; she has been in poor health for many years and she did not play any active role in the affairs of the community home. We have received in evidence, however, a short statement from their son, Matthew Arnold, who was born in or about 1963, and lived at Bryn Estyn until about the end of the 1970s. In that statement he describes his happy recollections of participating in activities with Bryn Estyn residents and says that he never saw any boys being hit or abused.

7.09 The reports that Arnold submitted to the Management Committee were quite full and have provided helpful background for us. As one would expect, they presented an optimistic picture, at least until the closure of the home loomed, and they contained few hints of allegations against staff. In the first of those reports[3] before us Arnold defined the school's philosophy thus:

"1. Each child has a right to be different.

2. Each child has the right to hope for tolerant forgiveness, or overlooking of past foolishness, errors, humiliations or minor sins - in short, the Christian notion of the possibility of redemption.

3. Each child has the right to make a fresh start."

Very sadly, however, the evidence before us has disclosed that for many children who were consigned to Bryn Estyn, in the ten or so years of its existence as a community home, it was a form of purgatory or worse from which they emerged more damaged than when they had entered and for whom the future had become even more bleak[4].

Organisation and structure as a community home with education on the premises

7.10 As we have indicated in paragraph 4.02(3), Bryn Estyn was intended, according to the 1971 Regional Plan, to accommodate up to 49 boys in the intermediate and senior age ranges (13 to 17 years). When Arnold arrived in May 1973 there were about 30 resident boys. By late 1975, when he presented his first report to the new Management Committee, the number had increased to about 60 and the average length of stay was said to be 13 months. The capacity of the home was then considered to be 64, of whom 15 were to be accommodated in Cedar House, a unit for boys of working age, and the rest in the main building. It was administered by Clwyd County Council in accordance with the Regional Plan for Wales and the accommodation was available to all the new Welsh and some neighbouring English local authorities. On 8 November 1975 only 23 boys from Clwyd were in residence.

---

[2] Terms of reference of Committee (see minutes of the meeting on 20 October 1976).
[3] Report to Management Committee for the meeting on 10 December 1975.
[4] See paras 11.49 to 11.58.

The others were made up of 21 from South Wales, seven from Mid Wales, six from Gwynedd, two from Cheshire and one from Merseyside. This pattern continued until a late stage in the community home's existence.

7.11 The establishment of Bryn Estyn at that time in 1975 comprised 44 members of staff led by the Principal, a Deputy Principal and an Assistant Principal. They included eight teachers, 18 houseparents (of whom seven were senior housemasters) and two nightcare officers. The Deputy Principal and Head of Education was Brynley Goldswain, who had been at the approved school since 1969, but he left on 30 April 1976 to take an appointment at Red Bank, another former approved school. He was succeeded as Deputy Principal but not as Head of Education in July 1976 by Peter Howarth, who had followed Arnold from Axwell Park School to Bryn Estyn in November 1973 to take up the post of Assistant Principal. He remained Deputy Principal until he retired at the same time as Arnold on 31 July 1984. From the summer of 1976 Arnold left much of the day to day responsibility for running Bryn Estyn to Howarth, except during two periods when the latter was incapacitated, firstly, from about August 1978 to about May 1979 and, secondly, from December 1981 to July 1982. Arnold himself was ill and unable to work from the summer of 1979 until late March 1980. A second Deputy Principal (Education), Maurice Matthews, was appointed with effect from 1 June 1977 and he remained responsible for education at Bryn Estyn until 16 September 1984, a fortnight before it closed.

7.12 During the remainder of the 1970s the number of boys accommodated at Bryn Estyn gradually diminished and its role changed, in part, because it took over some of the assessment functions of Little Acton and also received boys on remand; from 1980 it took over all the assessment functions in respect of boys (girls were assessed at Bersham Hall) and some staff were transferred from Bersham Hall to Bryn Estyn[5]. On 26 January 1980, there were only 33 boys in residence at Bryn Estyn, including one on remand, but the average number in residence for the preceding three months was said to have been 41.8. From June 1979 to May 1980 throughput figures were 75 admissions, and 91 discharges or transfers on a mean population of 42.6 boys. At about this time the longest period of residence was reported as 21 months.

7.13 The working boys' unit in Cedar House withered quite soon. A major reason for this was the difficulty of finding suitable employment during a period of recession and economic stringency. In April 1977 the function of Cedar House was changed to that of a unit for immature younger boys and then in or about September 1978 this unit was transferred to a new 12 bed purpose built house, near the main building, which was named Clwyd House and retained its function, with a reducing number of residents, until the last year of Bryn Estyn's existence. Cedar House was subsequently used in part as a library. Bryn Estyn's functions, however, still included a responsibility to provide appropriate work experience for those resident boys who were past school leaving age.

[5] See paras 12.45, 13.02 and 13.09.

7.14 Various methods of organising the boys resident in the main building into units with which they could identify were tried. In his first report to the Management Committee at the end of 1975 Arnold said that there was no formal house structure within the school. Each residential social worker had responsibility for a group of boys. The aim was to match a child to a person rather than try to create 'emotional units'; and each social worker had, for each child in his care, a responsibility for fostering the child's welfare in many areas. By the late 1970s, however, it seems that a house system was put into operation in the main building. At one point there was an attempt to operate four houses but in the end there were two houses, Caradog and Glyndwr, the older boys being assigned to the latter. The house system appears to have continued until a late stage, when reducing numbers rendered it obsolete.

7.15 The Secure Unit at Bryn Estyn was an eight-bedded unit, which had been planned as part of a more extensive development programme for the home approved in 1975 but only implemented to a small extent. It was intended to be under the direction of Arnold and Howarth but with a staff of its own of 12, including a warden. After some delays it was eventually ready for opening in November 1979 and Howarth (in Arnold's absence whilst sick) reported that the Welsh Office had granted permission for this[6]. For a time four members of the care staff under Leonard Stritch shared their working periods between the unit and the main school and it appears to have been used intermittently to restrict or restrain recalcitrant residents, particularly glue sniffers, for short periods with, at best, dubious legal authority. Arnold's view was that, despite many seminars and courses, secure units, in general, had "grown without an initial philosophy"[7]. In May 1980 he said rather enigmatically "The Secure Unit is being used on a very limited level: but this has already taught us that what is easy in conceptual thought is entirely different in practice"[8].

7.16 The teaching staff at Bryn Estyn had a formidable and largely thankless task, bearing in mind the continuous flow of pupils in and out of their classes. A substantial proportion of the residents were in need of remedial education (in 1975[9] Arnold estimated the average retardation to be three years at the age of 13 years) and many of the students with brighter potential were quite severely disturbed. Discipline was difficult to maintain; there were few clear guidelines; and most teachers put in extra hours acting as substitute care workers because of staff shortages. There were further difficulties because of the lack of basic equipment and books and the unwillingness of Clwyd's Education Authority to assume responsibility for education in the community home. The shortcomings in the provision of education were so grave that we deal with them separately in Chapter 11[10]. In the circumstances considerable emphasis was placed at Bryn Estyn on outdoor activities, in which some members of staff played a very active role.

---

[6] See paras 11.07 to 11.25.
[7] Report to Management Committee for the meeting on 11 May 1979.
[8] Report to Management Committee for the meeting on 16 May 1980.
[9] Report to Management Committee for the meeting on 10 December 1975.
[10] See paras 11.26 to 11.41 and 11.47.

7.17 Arnold's periodic reports to the Management Committee recorded the success of these outdoor activities whenever possible. Understandably, they were much more successful in the 1970s than later, when the future of the home became uncertain. The five-a-side football team, for example, won a *Liverpool Daily Post* competition in 1975 and a football XI had, at one time, a regular programme of fixtures. Boys were permitted to attend local youth clubs, leisure centres and a boxing club regularly and their table tennis team played in a youth club league when a youth club was established in Bryn Estyn itself.

7.18 The sports field was used for cricket, baseball and athletics, for which there was an annual sports day. There was an outdoor swimming pool and a gymnasium in the main building; a number of boys gained certificates and badges in gymnastics. Emphasis was laid also on 'outward bound' activities in the form of week-end trips for camping, hiking, rock-climbing and canoeing. A Christmas fair and concert were held and if talent permitted an eisteddfod on St David's Day. Members of the youth club also achieved success in various art competitions.

7.19 All this involved considerable dedication on the part of some members of the staff and Arnold reported in September 1978[11] that the staff generally had raised £800 for the welfare of the boys: it was used to buy a new electric organ and table tennis table and also to fund outings and extra pocket money for the boys.

7.20 Whilst Arnold's reports generally were quite bland in tone, they did contain some pointers to the underlying disciplinary and other difficulties at Bryn Estyn. In his first report[12] he referred to the problem of "long term" children faced with the certainty of change of field social worker: a family of three brothers, who could not have any home leave, had known seven social workers in three years and a recent resident of Cedar House had known 11 different placements in 15 years. Glue sniffing and drinking were recurring causes for concern, particularly during travel when beginning or returning from leave. The rate of absconding was perturbingly and persistently high, although there were fewer references to this as Arnold's tenure continued. He did complain, however, that children were being detained unnecessarily long at Bryn Estyn because of the reluctance of social workers to permit them to return to the community. In October 1976 and on several subsequent occasions, Arnold drew attention to a growing group of 'hard core homeless' within the school, who had lost hope for themselves and seemed unable to re-create any thoughts for their future or plans towards adulthood: it was from this group that sheer self-destruction emerged, infecting others[13].

7.21 As early as April 1976 Arnold drew attention to what he called "the increasing number of threats of violence issued to the staff members by boys"[14]. In February 1979 came the first reference to an allegation by a boy against a member of staff, neither of whom was named. Arnold's comment was "the

[11] Report to Management Committee for the meeting on 8 September 1978.
[12] Report to Management Committee for the meeting on 10 December 1975.
[13] Report to Management Committee for the meeting on 20 October 1976.
[14] Report to Management Committee for the meeting on 14 April 1976.

70

complaint is of the common assault nature and if proven, will not provide dramatic headlines. One is constantly aware of the vulnerability of staff working in Social Services, both within an establishment and in the field. It requires firm decision and a willingness to gamble to survive"[15]. This rather enigmatic comment did not, however, provoke any recorded response by the Management Committee in their minutes.

7.22   In October 1981 Arnold said "We are going through a particularly bad period at the moment: some of the older boys are testing the limits of tolerance to the utmost, staff are reacting with commendable restraint but there must be a break somewhere soon. It is not therefore surprising that I am finding myself dealing with a stream of complaints against staff from ill-disposed children, who seek to create dissension by allegation. We have a group of some four older boys attempting to create their own hierarchy, bullying smaller boys and threatening staff. . . I imagine it will be some months yet before we settle to a more responsive climate"[16].

7.23   In July 1982 Arnold reported increased anxiety caused by the considerable amount of internal damage within the campus caused by younger residents, contrasting with the earlier 1970–1974 period when boys had caused considerable damage in the local community whilst Bryn Estyn itself had remained untouched[17]. To illustrate the staff's disciplinary problems he presented a striking account of a particular week-end at Bryn Estyn entitled "Anatomy of a weekend". It is reproduced as Appendix 10 to this report with letters of the alphabet substituted for the names of children identified in the original document.

7.24   From 1982 onwards Bryn Estyn was overshadowed by uncertainty about its future role. The number of residents had declined to an average of under 30, although this was augmented by a fluctuating number of boys on remand or for assessment. On 15 November 1983 Clwyd House was amalgamated with the main school. By January 1984, the year that saw the demise of the regional planning arrangements, the average total number of placements was down to 22.6 and the average number of boys on remand or for assessment was 5.1. At that point the Social Services Committee resolved that the number of places should be further reduced to match local needs by 1 October 1984 with a view to moving the "unit" off site as soon as suitable accommodation could be found. Finally, following the retirements of Arnold and Howarth on 31 July 1984, Clwyd House only, with Stritch in charge, was used to house the remaining residents for the last three months of Bryn Estyn's existence as a community home.

---

[15] Report to Management Committee for the meeting on 16 February 1979.
[16] Report to Management Committee for the meeting on 19 October 1981.
[17] Report to Management Committee for the meeting on 30 July 1982.

The allegations of sexual abuse at Bryn Estyn

8.01 In the course of our inquiry we ascertained that about 140 former residents of Bryn Estyn between 1974 and 1984 were known to have made allegations that physical and/or sexual abuse upon them had occurred whilst they had been resident there. About one half of this number complained of sexual abuse and ultimately we received in evidence the testimony of 48 of them, 25 of whom gave oral evidence before us and were subjected to cross-examination. Of the 21 other potential witnesses, many were untraceable and several were unwilling to give evidence before the Tribunal for a variety of reasons. We are aware, however, of the identities of the persons against whom their complaints were directed and we are satisfied that the evidence that we received from 48 witnesses was fairly representative of the whole spectrum of alleged sexual abuse at Bryn Estyn during the relevant ten years.

8.02 The overwhelming majority of these complaints were against Peter Howarth, the Deputy Principal, and Stephen Norris, the Senior Housemaster in charge of Clwyd House from its opening in or about September 1978. Of the total of 48 sexual abuse complainants, who gave evidence to the Tribunal, 26 alleged actual sexual offences by Howarth; and 13 alleged actual sexual offences by Norris but five of them are included in both figures because they complained of actual sexual offences by both of them.

Peter Norman Howarth

8.03 As we have said earlier[1], Peter Howarth followed Arnold from Axwell Park Approved School to Bryn Estyn in November 1973 on his appointment to the post of Assistant Principal. Howarth was then about 42 years old and had been a housemaster in special and approved schools since 1962, following earlier employment in the accounts department of a construction firm on leaving school at the age of 15 years. His professional qualification was a Certificate in the Residential Care of Children obtained in 1965 at Ruskin College, Oxford, where he met Arnold, who was a visiting tutor there at that time. During the course he was placed for a period at Richmond Hill Approved School in Yorkshire, of which Arnold was then Headmaster. The latter appears to have formed a friendship with, or at least a high opinion of, Howarth because he subsequently invited him to apply successively for posts at Axwell Park Approved School and Bryn Estyn. The result was that Howarth served as a housemaster at Axwell Park from 1966 to 1971 and then as third-in-charge there under Arnold before moving to Bryn Estyn as Assistant Principal until July 1976, when he was promoted to Deputy Principal.

---

[1] See para 7.11.

8.04 The allegations of sexual abuse by Howarth span the whole period of his stay at Bryn Estyn from November 1973 to July 1984 and are centred mainly upon the flat that he occupied there throughout. He was a bachelor and he was allocated a flat on the first floor of the building in a fairly discreet position, next to the sick bay and reached directly by a flight of stairs. It was Howarth's daily practice to invite resident boys, usually from the main building, to his flat in the late evening for drinks (including some alcohol) and light food and for the privilege of watching television and other recreation such as playing cards, board games etc. Invitation to these sessions was by a "flat list", as it was known, which was compiled by Howarth or made up on his instructions. It was then posted up on his door or delivered by one of his favourites. Attendance was part of the agreed programme of activities available to boys in the evening and the names of those attending would be entered in the activities log. The sessions would begin at about 8.30 pm and the boys attending, usually five or six or even more at a time, were required to dress in their pyjamas without any underwear. If they were wearing underpants under their pyjamas, they were ordered to remove them. The gathering would last until 11 pm or 11.30 pm, depending often on the programme on television, and the boys would then disperse to their dormitories.

8.05 According to Howarth's own statement, the idea behind this practice was to provide some sort of ordinary domestic experience in the evening for the boys selected, who were otherwise deprived of normal family life. He justified the practice also as providing an opportunity for "counselling" the boys when that was needed. Other evidence before us indicates that Howarth had begun the flat list system when he was still at Axwell Park Approved School and that, both then and at Bryn Estyn, Arnold knew that he was holding these gatherings in his flat.

8.06 As we have said earlier[2], Howarth was tried in July 1994 in the Chester Crown Court on 12 charges, three of which alleged buggery and nine indecent assaults (one of the indecent assaults being alleged to have been committed with Paul Wilson). The total period spanned by the charges was just over ten years, that is, from 1 January 1974 to 11 May 1984, and the number of former boy residents of Bryn Estyn named in the counts was nine. Howarth denied at his trial that any sexual impropriety had occurred and he persisted in this denial until his death in April 1997, before he was due to give evidence to us. He was convicted on 8 July 1994 of one offence of buggery and seven indecent assaults, for which he received a total of ten years' imprisonment. He was acquitted of the other four alleged offences, including the alleged joint offence with Wilson. There was no appeal by him against his convictions but we were told in the course of the Tribunal's hearings prior to his death that he was still considering an application for leave to appeal. We have heard compelling evidence, however, in support of the offences of which he was convicted and of other like offences committed by him against other residents of Bryn Estyn. Although some of the evidence was of much lesser quality, nothing that we have heard has led us to doubt the correctness of those convictions and we are satisfied that

[2] See para 2.35(3).

they were merely representative of a pattern of conduct by Howarth throughout the time that he lived at Bryn Estyn. In our judgment, the jury's differing verdicts on individual counts in July 1994 fairly reflect the variable quality of the wider evidence that we ourselves have heard.

8.07 A succession of former boy residents gave evidence about Howarth's activities in the flat and it was largely to similar effect. He had in turn a number of favourites, who were well known as such to other residents, and who were often referred to scurrilously as "bum boys". Although Howarth was a man of reclusive temperament, he did leave Bryn Estyn regularly to play golf, mainly at Wrexham Golf Club, and it was his habit to take one of his favourites to caddy for him. The flat lists were not limited to favourites but they figured prominently in the lists and it was they who were the main victims of Howarth's sexual assaults: they would be detained on some pretext when others were leaving, at which point, buggery or other indecency would occur. Quite often, however, similar conduct would occur in the kitchen of the flat, for example, whilst others were still present in another room watching television.

8.08 It is unnecessary for the purposes of this report to elaborate in detail the forms of sexual abuse perpetrated by Howarth. They were of an all too familiar type, progressing from masturbation to oral sex and in many cases to actual anal penetration. The processes by which these acts were achieved were variable but were also within a familiar pattern. A boy's confidence was gained by selection for the flat list, a form of favouritism, and often by personal comforting in the flat. A victim would be made to feel that he was an accomplice in the act and sworn to secrecy. The boys were very much alone at Bryn Estyn and rarely had anyone they trusted within easy access. A few were threatened by Howarth but many participated in fear of reprisals without any express threats; others were willing to comply simply to retain the privilege of inclusion from time to time in the flat list. For all there was the over-riding difficulty that Howarth appeared to be in *de facto* control of Bryn Estyn, the dispenser of discipline against whom no complaint could be made.

8.09 A few more resolute boys did refuse to participate. They tended to be the more self-confident and mature boys, able to look after themselves physically. On the whole they were left alone by Howarth after they had made their response clear: they were simply excluded from the flat list from then on. But one such boy did tell us that, within a couple of days, he was accused by Howarth of stealing a golf ball on the football field and was then told to look for it there until he found it; he was left on his own for six or seven hours until Stritch "came and got me off the field".

8.10 The allegations of sexual abuse by Howarth were not limited to his activities in his own flat. We heard other evidence of visits by him to dormitories when he is alleged to have fondled boys, who usually pretended to be asleep, and of infrequent incidents in his office, when he touched boys in the genital area over their clothes. It was alleged also that he was frequently present in the communal shower blocks, observing boys taking their shower. It seems, however, that he would be legitimately on duty in the showers as a supervisor and we do not consider that it would be safe to make any adverse finding against him under this head. As for the other isolated incidents, it may be that he betrayed his instincts outside his flat on some occasions and he may have tested some boys as potential victims before they were invited to his flat but we do not consider the evidence before us sufficiently strong to make specific findings, bearing in mind the lapse of time that has occurred.

The attitude of other members of the staff to Howarth's activities

8.11 We are fully satisfied that all the senior members of the staff at Bryn Estyn and most of the junior staff were aware of the flat list procedure and that favoured boys were regularly spending the evening until a late hour in Howarth's flat. It is equally clear that a substantial number of the staff, probably a majority, viewed the practice with disfavour. They objected, for example, to the principle of selecting boys for special favours and the impact of such favouritism on discipline generally. Members of the teaching staff found difficulty in dealing in class with sleepy boys who had been up to a late hour the previous night. Some of them spoke themselves of these boys in derogatory terms and many were aware that the boys were called "bum boys" or the like by their fellows. Many thought it highly unwise of Howarth to place himself in such a vulnerable position, open to allegations by the boys of sexual misconduct. Only two members of staff, however, admitted that they suspected Howarth of actual sexual impropriety and none said that they ever actually knew that it was occurring.

8.12 Arnold himself must have known of the flat list practice before he invited Howarth to apply for appointment as Assistant Principal because the latter had initiated it at Axwell Park Approved School, when he was a housemaster and, again, living in the main building and even then the boys had been required to wear pyjamas. We have not received any evidence, however, of any complaint or allegation of sexual or other misconduct by Howarth at Axwell Park Approved School and former colleagues there expressed shock when told of his convictions in 1994. The minutes of the meetings of the school's managers do contain an unexplained entry on 18 September 1969, which reads: "The Headmaster gave details of certain malicious rumours that had been circulating concerning the School. Mrs A confirmed the sympathy and backing of the Managers". We have been unable, however, to trace anyone who recalls these rumours and there is no evidence to link them with any actions of either Arnold or Howarth.

8.13 In our view Arnold must be criticised strongly for permitting the flat list practice to continue for almost the whole period during which he was Principal of Bryn Estyn. As an experienced and intelligent man he must have been aware of the obvious criticisms that we have summarised in the preceding paragraphs, whether or not they were raised with him by individual members of the staff, but he failed to intervene and took no steps to stop or even to modify what was happening. Quite apart from the sexual implications of the flat list, its impact on the conduct of the community home generally was such that he clearly ought to have intervened. Unfortunately, we have not been able to question either Arnold or Howarth about what passed between them on this subject.

In his statement for the Tribunal, drafted on the basis of his instructions to his Counsel and solicitors, Howarth described how he started inviting boys to his flat six or seven months after he arrived and he continues "There were never any allegations whatsoever concerning my behaviour and I had the full support of Matt Arnold. There were regulars on the flat list because those boys responded well and seemed to profit from being allowed the privilege".

8.14 We have no doubt that Arnold was wrong to give his support and that he should have intervened as Principal, without prompting by members of the staff, despite Howarth's attempted justifications of his practice. In this context we heard telling evidence from a witness who worked as a secretary at Bryn Estyn between February 1978 and June 1979. She said that one day during this period Arnold called a meeting in the general office of all the staff. He told them that there were a lot of rumours circulating with regard to Howarth and some of the boys and that they must be stopped straightaway. Anybody circulating more rumours or discussing the matter would be dismissed instantly. Arnold said that Howarth was taking a special interest in some of the boys but that there was nothing in the rumours and that they could obviously lead to other rumours going round.

8.15 Of all the other members of staff who gave evidence before us only Paul Bicker Wilson remembered such a meeting. He remembered a meeting being called on a Friday afternoon, mainly of care and teaching staff, in the board room but he thought it was because teachers were concerned that some boys were falling asleep in the classroom. John Ilton[3], on the other hand, remembers a meeting called by the teachers' union representative, and attended by teachers only, soon after Howarth's appointment, at which various concerns about the flat list were voiced. Arnold was "quite angry" with the suggestions made about Howarth at the meeting.

8.16 Despite the lack of support for her evidence we have no doubt that the secretary is correct in her recollection of the meeting called by Arnold and that this shows that he was aware of the adverse impact of the flat list on Howarth's reputation and that of the school. Despite this he continued to hold a protective umbrella over Howarth with the result that the latter was able to persist in his course of abuse whilst adverse comment on the flat list was suppressed.

8.17 Members of the staff generally were obviously in some difficulty in these circumstances if they wished to voice complaints or suspicions about Howarth. He had been placed in a dominant position by Arnold and the latter was manifestly unsympathetic to any criticism of him. According to many witnesses, Arnold was rarely seen about the school; he was usually in his office and was concerned mainly with administration. Howarth was responsible for all day to day decisions and appeared to be a lonely, isolated figure, who was nevertheless autocratic professionally. To a teacher, for example, he seemed to get on better with the care staff but they were over-awed by him and many of them, including Stephen Norris, did not like him at all.

---

[3] See para 10.85.

8.18 One member of the staff, Paul Bicker Wilson, told us that, when he was elected as a union representative (apparently in February 1984), he told the Clwyd Social Services Officer regarded as having direct responsibility for Bryn Estyn, namely Geoffrey Wyatt, of his suspicions about Howarth. Wyatt's response was to ask him whether he was making a formal complaint and to warn him that the repercussions could be quite serious. This is a subject to which we revert in Chapters 29 and 30.

8.19 In the event there was no investigation of Howarth's activities until the allegations against him came to light in the major police investigation that began in 1991 and in the course of which attempts were made to interview as many as possible former Bryn Estyn residents who had been there for any length of time between 1974 and 1984. Despite the weight of evidence that has now emerged against Howarth and the transparent sincerity of many of the witnesses a small number of former members of Bryn Estyn staff still refuse to believe that Howarth was guilty of any sexual misconduct. Some of them gave evidence on his behalf at his trial and they remain wedded to the idea that there has been a giant conspiracy against him and indeed against all or the vast majority of persons against whom other allegations before this Tribunal have been directed.

8.20 This view of the evidence has been represented to the Tribunal by, in particular, the loosely formed association calling itself the Bryn Estyn Staff Support Group, which apparently came into existence as the result of the arrests of various members of the staff in the course of the major police investigation. Many of the former residents of Bryn Estyn spoke very favourably in their evidence about the Chairperson of the group, Gwen Hurst, and its Secretary, John Rayfield, formerly a staff union official. Nevertheless, Hurst told us that she is quite certain that the majority of the allegations now being made by former pupils are fabricated. Rayfield, in similar vein, voiced the opinion that they may well have been "carefully trained", ignoring the detailed chronology of the police investigation and the impracticability of such training. He believes that the complainants' motive generally is to secure compensation. Whilst loyalty by former colleagues is readily understandable, we are unable to sympathise with the persistent ostrich-like response of these two witnesses (and some others) to the very substantial body of evidence placed before the Tribunal, much of which was heard by both of them for the first time.

8.21 We have not heard any acceptable evidence of complaints about Howarth's sexual offences made by victims to individual members of the staff at Bryn Estyn at any time before the police investigation. Nevertheless, the staff collectively must, in our view, share a degree of the blame for failure to stop his activities. There were clear grounds for grave suspicion and we believe that actual suspicion was felt by many more members of the staff than have admitted it. There were, however, mitigating factors such as the Arnold/Howarth relationship and the latter's dominance in running the home, which rendered effective action of individuals particularly difficult. We have in mind also the absence of any suitable forum for complaints of the staff generally. The evidence before us indicates, for example, that whereas the small body of teachers did meet regularly to discuss education matters, there were no meetings between them and care staff and the latter very rarely (if at all) met together as a body.

8.22 The consequences of the abuse by Howarth on his victims were immeasurable and remain so. The lives of these already disturbed children were grossly poisoned by a leading authority figure in whom they should have been able to place their trust. They felt soiled, guilty and embarrassed and some of them were led to question their own sexual orientation. Most of them have experienced difficulties in their sexual relationships and their relationships with children ever since and many have continued to rebel against authority. Even more seriously, their self-respect and ability to look forward to the future have been shattered.

Stephen Roderick Norris

8.23 Stephen Norris was born on 25 February 1936 so that he was 38 years old when he became a joint houseparent with his wife June on 1 March 1974 at Cedar House, Bryn Estyn. After national service followed by a decade of employment in such jobs as labourer, coach driver and insurance agent, he had become, in January 1970, a houseparent at Greystone Heath Approved School, Penketh, near Warrington. His wife, who was seven years younger than him, had been employed with him as a joint houseparent from January 1970, following their marriage in the 1960s, and both underwent a nationally recognised pre-qualifying course of training in residential work whilst they were at Greystone Heath. Their applications, which were supported by good references, were dated 12 December 1973 and they were interviewed at Bryn Estyn, by a panel (which included an Assistant Director of Social Services) on 16 January 1974, when they were offered the joint post.

8.24 There is a slight mystery about the circumstances of the appointment. Norris recollects being invited to visit Bryn Estyn, where he and his wife stayed the night, from Greystone Heath. They were shown around and then introduced to Arnold, whereupon Arnold told them that a full meeting of the planning committee was taking place in the board room and that he wondered if they would agree to be interviewed for a job at Bryn Estyn, which he would make beneficial for them (it involved an increase in salary of about £300 per annum). This may well be correct because a letter to their referees dated 18 January 1974 stated that they had already been offered "an informal interview" and it is quite possible that their application forms were back-dated. However, we have not received any evidence of prior knowledge by Arnold or Howarth of either Norris. Moreover, although no check was made at the time of Mr Norris' police records, such a check would not have revealed anything because he did not have any convictions, as far as we are aware, until October 1990[4]. No evidence has been submitted to the Tribunal to suggest that he had been guilty

---

[4] See paras 2.07(7) and 2.35(2).

of misconduct at Greystone Heath, although he knew there some colleagues, such as Jack Bennett[5] and Alan Langshaw[6], who were later convicted of sexual offences.

8.25 Margaret Norris was not implicated in any way in her husband's subsequent offences and we have not received any complaint about her. She served as a joint houseparent with her husband at Cedar House, living in flat No 1, until April 1977, when Cedar House ceased to be a working boys' unit and became a unit for younger boys. Mr Norris had meanwhile obtained the CRCCYP qualification in December 1976, after a year's course at Salford College of Technology. From September 1977 to June 1979 Margaret Norris trained successfully for the CQSW at the North East Wales Institute for Higher Education (Cartrefle College). She was then appointed to one of three senior RCCO posts at Bryn Estyn, at the same time as John Rayfield and Robert Jones, a post which she held until 26 February 1984, when she was appointed a social worker in the Clwyd Social Services Department working from Mold (after serving temporarily in 1983 as a study supervisor for CSS students). She continued to be employed by Clwyd as a social worker in various capacities until she retired on health grounds on 31 March 1993, six months before her 50th birthday, and she died in November 1996.

8.26 Norris himself was appointed a senior houseparent at Bryn Estyn, replacing Nefyn Dodd, following an interview on 21 December 1977 by a panel comprising Arnold, Howarth and Geoffrey Wyatt, Principal Officer, Residential and Day Care Services. He had previously made an unsuccessful application for an equivalent post in February that year. It seems that he remained in the flat at Cedar House with his wife and their two children until they moved to Clwyd House in or about September 1978 on his appointment as head of that unit without further interview. Mrs Norris was not, however, employed at Clwyd House. She and her husband lived at Clwyd House until 31 March 1981, when they moved to a house of their own in Wrexham. Norris had already acquired a smallholding, known as Talwrn Farm, Moel-y-Parc, Afonwen, which he was engaged in restoring and they moved finally to that address in or about September 1982. He remained in charge of Clwyd House until it was amalgamated with the main school in November 1983. He continued at Bryn Estyn then, more or less in limbo, until 8 July 1984, when he was redeployed as a supernumerary RCCO to Cartrefle Community Home, Broughton, in anticipation of the early retirement of the Officer-in-Charge there, Olivia Browell.

8.27 The history of Stephen Norris at Cartrefle and afterwards is related in Chapter 15 of this report. It was his sexual offences there that first came to light. He was suspended from duty on 18 June 1990 and convicted, on his own pleas of guilty, on 5 October 1990 when he was sentenced in the Crown Court at Chester by

---

[5] Convicted at Liverpool Crown Court on 26 November 1984 of five counts of indecent assaults on boys under 16 years for which he received nine months' imprisonment suspended for two years.

[6] Convicted at Chester Crown Court on 25 November 1994 of nine offences of buggery, 18 of indecent assault, two of gross indecency and two of assault occasioning actual bodily harm for which he received a total of ten years' imprisonment.

the Honourable Mr Justice Pill to a total of three and a half years' imprisonment[7]. The major police investigation then ensued and, before he had served fully his Cartrefle sentences, Norris was charged with numerous offences committed at Bryn Estyn. As we have said in paragraph 8.02, 13 of the sexual abuse complainants whose testimony was received in evidence by us alleged actual sexual offences by him against them at Bryn Estyn. All of these allegations related to the period when Norris was in charge of Clwyd House but many of the offences were alleged to have been committed at his smallholding.

8.28 Norris pleaded guilty on 11 November 1993 in the Crown Court at Knutsford to three offences of buggery, one of attempted buggery and three indecent assaults involving six former Bryn Estyn boys. The Bryn Estyn indictment against Norris contained ten other counts, to which Norris pleaded not guilty. They contained two allegations of buggery, seven of indecent assault and one of assault occasioning actual bodily harm involving nine boys, three of whom were named in the counts to which he had pleaded guilty. Norris was sentenced to a total of seven years' imprisonment and the Court ordered that the other ten counts should remain on the Court file on the usual terms[8].

8.29 We heard the evidence of a representative selection of the victims named in the indictment (nine in all, eight of sexual abuse) and from three other former residents of Bryn Estyn who alleged sexual offences against them by Norris. The evidence before us indicates that Norris was a coarse man of poor general education who should never have been placed in charge of a unit providing for the needs of immature and disturbed young boys. At least eight of them and some of the members of staff spoke of his apparent obsession with sexual matters and his habitual practice of making inappropriate sexual comments about, for example, the size of boys' genitalia and their potential sexual capacity. A recurring complaint was that Norris would be present in the shower block precincts when boys were taking a shower; he would observe them, comment upon them as already said, and would frequently wash boys' private parts on the pretext that the state of their foreskins required this. Subsequently graver forms of assault would occur there and elsewhere. The offences of indecent assault were committed in the shower blocks, often in bedrooms at Clwyd House and at Norris' smallholding where and when the opportunity occurred.

8.30 Norris' technique generally was to befriend selected boys by offering sympathy and understanding. One victim of Norris' admitted buggery offences described how, after a few months' residence in Clwyd House, when the victim was just 13 years old, he was invited to visit Norris' 'farm'. En route he was bought alcohol at a public house. On leaving there he was taken to a cottage near the smallholding, which was being looked after by Norris for the owners, and there his jeans were removed. Norris touched him all over his body, oral sex took place and he was buggered. Norris told him to keep his mouth shut and that no one would have any reason to believe him if he did complain. On other occasions buggery occurred at the smallholding. Norris would make a bed up

[7] See para 2.07(7).
[8] See para 2.35(2).

downstairs for the boy if his wife was away and would then visit him during the night; if she was there, the witness would be put to sleep in a caravan and Norris would visit him there.

8.31 When he gave evidence to the Tribunal, Norris admitted committing offences at Bryn Estyn from 1980 onwards but his admissions did not go beyond what was implicit in his pleas of guilty in the Crown Court. He denied threatening any child but he said that he did require a "101 per cent assurance" from a child that he would not tell anyone. The offences occurred in the shower or bathroom and in a child's bedroom on occasions. Another member of staff was very seldom on the premises at the time because he chose occasions when he was the only member of staff on duty. One boy victim would not know that any other was being abused. Norris disliked Howarth and had as little as possible to do with him but he was "totally and utterly" unaware that Howarth was sexually abusing children, although he was aware of the flat list, on which residents of Clwyd House were rarely included.

8.32 One recent statement by an alleged victim that was read to us did contain allegations that Norris took him twice to a large house near Chester where he was buggered by both Norris and the occupier and shown pornographic films involving children. This witness alleged also that Norris had arranged for him to be picked up by a man and taken to a house in Chirk where he was sexually assaulted: he resisted the attack and his assailant gave up eventually, after which he was driven home by the driver who had taken him there. This statement included an allegation that both Howarth and Norris tried to get him to recruit boys for sexual purposes. These allegations are, however, unique to the witness, who is now under psychiatric care, and we have not received any supporting evidence or additional detail to enable us to pursue further enquiries. We are unable, therefore, to find that there is any adequate evidence to support the allegations.

8.33 We are sure that Norris' sexual abuse of residents of Clwyd House went well beyond his own admissions and, subject to the qualification in the preceding paragraph, we have no reason to doubt the veracity of the evidence of most of the witnesses who alleged abuse by him. The abuse certainly began soon after he became responsible for Clwyd House and continued throughout the period during which he retained that responsibility. Nevertheless, we have not received any evidence of contemporary complaints by victims or witnesses of Norris' sexual abuse and there is no basis for a finding that other members of the staff at Bryn Estyn knew about it during the period when it was occurring.

8.34 Although some members of the staff were less than frank in their evidence about their attitude to Stephen Norris when he was their colleague, we are satisfied that many of them disliked him because of the coarseness of his thoughts and conversation and regarded him as unsuitable for the appointment that he held, having regard to his lack of education and insensitivity. Like Howarth, he was a solitary man and, like Howarth also, he bears an overwhelming responsibility for disfiguring the lives of so many children in his care in pursuit of his own sexual gratification.

Allegations of sexual abuse against other members of the staff

8.35 We are aware of sexual complaints against 14 other members of the staff at Bryn Estyn during the period under review but, in our judgment, they do not add significantly to the general picture of sexual abuse at Bryn Estyn for reasons that we explain here.

8.36 The complaints were made by one complainant only against one member of the staff only except in respect of David Gwyn Birch, Paul Bicker Wilson and Frederick Rutter.

8.37 In the case of **David Gwyn Birch** there were two complainants. He was employed as an RCCO at Bryn Estyn from 21 May 1979 until June 1984, after which he was employed in 1984 on a supply basis mainly at Park House, Prestatyn, before returning to work in the Wrexham area at Chevet Hey from 1 November 1984 until 1988. He was only 21 years old when he was appointed to Bryn Estyn but he had worked as a youth leader in the Holywell area and in camps in the USA and he had a distinguished record as a swimmer and as a junior rugby football player, both at international level.

8.38 As we have said in paragraph 2.35(5), David Birch was acquitted on 12 January 1995 of the sexual offences alleged against him by those two complainants and we have neither heard any additional evidence nor received any additional complaint to cast doubt upon the correctness of those verdicts.

8.39 The position in relation to **Paul Bicker Wilson** is slightly more complicated but the result for our purposes is the same. His detailed history is dealt with more appropriately later in the next chapter[9]. The main sexual complaints against Wilson were made by two alleged victims and were the subject of three counts of indecent assault on which Wilson was tried in the Crown Court at Chester and acquitted by the jury on 8 July 1994[10]. One of the counts was laid against Wilson jointly with Howarth, who was tried at the same time on that and other counts against him alone; and Howarth too was acquitted of the joint charge. We heard the evidence of both alleged Wilson victims but no additional evidence that would justify us in disagreeing with the jury's verdict has been produced.

8.40 The three counts on which Wilson was tried were based upon the stronger evidence against him of sexual misconduct and we do not consider that anything of substance could be added by five other complainants under this head who referred to other alleged incidents. Two of them spoke only of physical rather than sexual assaults and another two described acts intended to humiliate them rather than with a sexual motive. Finally, another potential witness, who had made a complaint against Wilson in 1978, could not now be traced and had been uncertain in later statements to the police about important detail. In the absence of any corroboration of this last incident, therefore, no jury would have been likely to convict Wilson in respect of it.

[9] See paras 10.04 to 10.39.
[10] See para 2.35(3).

8.41 **Frederick Rutter**, who is currently serving sentences totalling 12 years' imprisonment imposed on 30 July 1991[11], was employed at Bryn Estyn as a temporary RCCO from 5 July 1982 to 19 November 1983, before moving on to other work as a care assistant in Clwyd. He was in his middle 30s when at Bryn Estyn and had earlier served in the army for seven years, for two years as a probationer constable in the North Wales Police and as a storekeeper at a steel works before becoming a housefather at Gatewen Hall School, prior to its acquisition by the Bryn Alyn Community[12]. His later convictions all related to a period long after he left Bryn Estyn and were of heterosexual offences of rape and indecent assault whereas the two sexual complaints against him were of minor indecent assaults on separate isolated occasions.

8.42 The first of these complainants alleged that on an occasion in the laundry room, Rutter had put him over his legs and slapped him for denying knowledge of something (the witness could not specify what). The witness' allegation was that, in the course of the slapping, Rutter paused several times with his hand on the boy's bottom and gripped his buttocks. Another non-sexual allegation by this witness against Rutter was, however, demonstrated to be very unreliable because of its alleged date and, in any event, his account of the laundry room incident as an assault with an indecent motive was not persuasive. As for the other sexual complainant against Rutter, his known statements to the police and the Tribunal were read but only the latter referred to sexual abuse by Rutter without specifying its nature. That abuse was alleged to have been spelt out in a statement to the police made by the witness when he was in Swansea prison, of which the police say that they have no record. Moreover, the witness alleged that the sexual abuse occurred in 1977/1978, long before Rutter joined the staff of Bryn Estyn. In these circumstances we have no acceptable evidence that Rutter sexually abused any of the Bryn Estyn resident children.

8.43 The remaining sexual complaints are isolated single complaints against ten other members of the Bryn Estyn staff, all of which have been denied vigorously. They vary in nature from grave to comparatively minor and in likelihood from quite possible to highly unlikely. They are not to be dismissed out of hand; a small number were complaints of heterosexual abuse; and two involved a known and a probable homosexual acting independently of each other. However, they were not the subject of complaint at the time and we have not found any contemporary documentation or other corroboration to support them. Moreover, there is no pattern underlying them to suggest systematic abuse: in general, they are alleged to have been isolated incidents. It is, of course, exceedingly difficult for an individual to defend himself or herself now against single allegations of misconduct after the lapse of many years and criminal proceedings in respect of any of them would almost certainly be held to be an abuse of process now.

---

[11] See para 2.07(8).
[12] See para 4.24.

8.44 We have looked also for evidence of sexual abuse by resident boys upon each other, bearing in mind that an abused person may himself become an abuser. There has been a small amount of evidence of this but the complaints about it that have reached us have been remarkably few, having regard to the long period at Bryn Estyn that we have reviewed and the nature of the institution. Moreover, in most of the complaints of this kind the perpetrator has not been identified. We would not be justified, therefore, in finding that the scale of inter-resident sexual abuse at Bryn Estyn was greater than in other residential establishments in which pubescent boys are segregated.

Conclusions

8.45 It follows that, in our judgment, the scale of sexual abuse at Bryn Estyn and its highly damaging impact on the resident boys should be assessed mainly on the basis of what has been comprehensively proved against Howarth and Norris. The allegations against Gordon Anglesea, which centre upon Bryn Estyn, are dealt with separately in the next chapter, because he was neither resident there nor a member of the staff.

8.46 The picture that we have given of a community home with education on the premises in which two of the most senior members of staff were habitually engaged in major sexual abuse of many of the young residents without detection is truly appalling and no further words from us are needed to underline the gravity of our findings. Unhappily, however, it is not the complete picture because we heard other evidence suggesting that there was a pervasive culture at Bryn Estyn of immature and unhealthy attitudes to sexuality, which were very unhelpful to teenage boys whose developing sexuality needed handling with sensitivity.

8.47 This lesser form of abuse obviously does not command the same critical attention as the direct physical activities of Howarth and Norris but we have no doubt that its effect was insidious. We heard repeatedly, for example, of the use of foul language with sexual connotations by Norris and, to a lesser extent, by Wilson. There was evidence also of the availability of pornographic videos held by one or two members of the staff: videos that were shown to a small selection of boys in staff accommodation (portrayed as "fun") and on one admitted occasion to a wider audience of boys in the main building itself. Similarly, we heard of pornographic magazines and other sexual material kept in staff accommodation.

8.48 There is no sharp distinction between personal and professional behaviour when some staff live on site in a community home; and staff have to be aware of the importance of providing appropriate role models for the children in their care when they are, in effect, in *loco parentis*. Thus, in the environment that we have described, it is not surprising that some of the admitted bullying amongst boys had sexual overtones and that some boys emerged with wholly inappropriate attitudes to their sexuality.

The case of Gordon Anglesea

Background

9.01 We have already recounted in some detail in Chapter 2[1] the history of the libel action brought by Gordon Anglesea against four defendants in respect of the allegation or suggestion that he had been guilty of serious sexual misconduct at Bryn Estyn because it formed an important part of the background to the appointment of the Tribunal. The defendants failed to prove this to the jury's satisfaction and they found in Anglesea's favour by a majority of 10 to 2, whereupon his award of damages was agreed in the sum of £375,000.

9.02 There has been no appeal from this decision in December 1994 but the complaints against Anglesea have been repeated to this Tribunal and we have investigated them as fully as possible. Before summarising the results of our investigation, however, it is necessary to repeat that the trial of the libel action in the High Court occupied about a fortnight before a very experienced judge and that all the parties were represented by eminent Counsel so that the central issue was very fully examined.

9.03 The defendants in the action relied mainly upon the evidence of three witnesses, who we will identify only as A, B and C. Each of them alleged that he had been sexually abused by Anglesea at Bryn Estyn and gave evidence to that effect to the jury.

Witness A

9.04 Witness A, who appears from the records before the Tribunal to have been at Bryn Estyn from 13 May 1980 to 11 July 1981, was unable to read or write and attended a special school before he entered Bryn Estyn. There was some confusion in the evidence before the jury about the precise period when he had been resident there. He alleged that he had been buggered frequently by Howarth in the latter's flat and also in the sick bay, which was not far from the flat. He said that he had seen Anglesea at Bryn Estyn on "loads of occasions", coming in and out during the day and night-time, and had thought that he was a security guard; and that he had seen him in Howarth's company a large number of times. He had also seen Anglesea and Norris together but not so many times. He said that he had been sexually assaulted by Anglesea twice, on both occasions when he was sleeping in Clwyd House over a holiday period. The first attack had been an indecent assault when Anglesea had entered A's bedroom wearing a raincoat and had touched A's private parts. On the second occasion, about two days later, Anglesea had buggered him forcibly in the same bedroom. He was, however, effectively cross-examined about earlier

---

[1] See paras 2.24 to 2.32.

statements that he had made and the many inconsistent details in them, including a wide disparity in his estimates of the number of times that he had seen Anglesea at Bryn Estyn and his accounts of the actual offences.

Witness B

9.05 Witness B, who was born on Christmas Day 1962, told the jury of his most unhappy childhood before he was received into care. According to the Tribunal's records he was at Bersham Hall from 2 August to 27 September 1977 and then at Bryn Estyn from the latter date until 22 May 1979. Again, there was some confusion about the period when he was at Bryn Estyn because he was sure that he had been there two years and one month. He recounted being sexually abused by Howarth initially in the sick bay and later in Howarth's flat on occasions when he was on to the flat list. He had been buggered by Howarth perhaps a dozen, perhaps two dozen times and also regularly assaulted and buggered by Norris. Witness B claimed that he had seen Anglesea at Bryn Estyn dozens of times, in uniform and out of uniform, and had seen Anglesea in the company of Howarth eight or nine times. He alleged that oral and anal sex had occurred between Anglesea and himself in an outbuilding at Bryn Estyn, probably the cadet hut. In the course of giving this evidence the witness collapsed ("passed out in the witness box" as the judge described it) and he gave further detail the next day of what had occurred in the outbuilding, including payment to him by Anglesea of 50 pence or a pound. On another earlier occasion he had been made to perform oral sex for Anglesea in an outbuilding. Witness B spoke also of four further occasions when oral and anal sex had been performed with Anglesea in the cadet hut or an outbuilding. The main other assault that he remembered was in a lay-by or the like a couple of miles from Bryn Estyn, after Anglesea had stopped his car and told him to get in. On one other occasion he had been picked up by Anglesea outside Bryn Estyn and driven up a few lanes before oral sex had again taken place. Like witness A, he was cross-examined about inconsistencies in his previous statements, including his earlier denial, to the police that he had been abused by Anglesea, and also about his insistence that he should be paid an agreed sum of £4,500 by *Private Eye*, in respect of an earlier libel on him, before he gave evidence, which he described as perfectly good tactics of the kind employed by lawyers to ensure payment.

Witness C

9.06 Finally, witness C was recorded as having been at Bryn Estyn from 10 March 1981 to 18 October 1982 from the age of 14½ years until just after his 16th birthday. His recollection, however, was that he had been there for two and a half to three years from September 1979 (when his records indicated that he was in care in South Wales). He gave evidence of being indecently assaulted by Howarth, under the threat of an unruly order, but he denied that Howarth had buggered him. He had caddied for Howarth on about half a dozen occasions and had been introduced to Anglesea when he had appeared on the golf course in ordinary clothes. All three then went to Bryn Estyn, where the witnesses went to Howarth's flat to be paid £2 for caddying. Howarth and Anglesea then entered the flat and Howarth threatened him again with an unruly order. The two men pulled down his trousers and pants and one began playing with his private parts whilst the other was playing with his backside. That continued for about five minutes before the witness began crying and stormed out, pulling up his pants and trousers as he ran out to the dormitory.

9.07 Anglesea approached him subsequently on two occasions, once when he was either washing cars or sweeping the courtyard and once when he was listening to records by the staircase in the main building, inviting him to go up to Howarth's flat but on both occasions he had told Anglesea to "fuck off". He had not spoken to Anglesea on any other occasion but had seen him on about four or five other occasions. Unhappily, this witness had a history, after Bryn Estyn, of excessive drinking and drug dependence and he was cross-examined strenuously also about his failure to make any allegation against Anglesea before he was interviewed by a BBC representative prior to appearing on a BBC programme in January 1993. He denied, however, that his recollection had been affected by drink or drugs and said that the police had not put any question to him about Anglesea earlier: he had not mentioned Anglesea because he was scared of him, he was scared of power.

Further witnesses for the Defendants

9.08 The Defendants in the libel action relied upon two other witnesses in their case against Anglesea. One was a senior probation officer, well known in the courts of North Wales, who had been placed at Bryn Estyn for three months in the late summer of 1980 whilst undertaking a two year course at Cartrefle College. During his placement he was required to spend one night at Bryn Estyn and had to put the boys in the main building to bed at about 9 pm. He described how, after he had heard a door clicking when he was in a downstairs room, Howarth and Anglesea had entered the building and Howarth had introduced Anglesea as a policeman who had been a good friend to Bryn Estyn and to the lads. After they had passed, Howarth had said "Come along" or "Come on Gordon" and they had moved towards the stairs. The witness did not know at the time that the visitor was Inspector Anglesea (as Anglesea then was) but he had seen him on television subsequently and he remained convinced that the person whom he saw was Gordon Anglesea.

9.09 The other witness called for the defendants was Joyce Bailey, the wife of a police constable who had served under Anglesea at Wrexham. She had been a part-time housemother at Bryn Estyn between 1981 and 1984, according to her own recollection. She said that Anglesea was a regular visitor to Bryn Estyn in a professional capacity; she had seen him there on, perhaps, half a dozen occasions and he was usually wearing uniform. She remembered seeing him once in casual clothes on a sunny afternoon in the forecourt at Bryn Estyn. Bailey was with a group of boys and saw him arrive in his own car. He alighted, took some golf clubs out of the back of his car and gave them to Howarth. She was unable, however, to say what Howarth did with the golf clubs.

Anglesea's evidence at the libel trial

9.10 Anglesea himself gave evidence at the trial of his libel action, denying that he had sexually abused anyone. He gave the jury details of his long police career from 1957 to March 1991, after earlier service as a police cadet and then in the Royal Air Force. He had been promoted to the rank of uniformed police inspector in 1972, which he retained until his further promotion to chief inspector in 1985. He had married for a second time on 26 March 1977, immediately following his divorce from his first wife, by whom he had had two children. There were also three children of his second wife's first marriage. They had had a daughter together but she had died in May 1983; he had then had his vasectomy reversed and a further child had been born and had fortunately survived.

9.11 Anglesea said that his contact with Bryn Estyn had begun in September 1979 when he had been asked to set up an attendance centre at Wrexham, where juvenile offenders could be required to attend for two hours at a time up to a maximum of 24 hours as a form of punishment. From time to time individual Bryn Estyn boys had been required to attend the centre but he did not think that he ever went to Bryn Estyn before 1980. Later, from September 1980, he became the Operational Inspector at Wrexham and Bryn Estyn was within his section so that he did go there from time to time to administer cautions (seven such visits within a period of about three months were recorded in his own notebook). Overall, he estimated the total number of his visits to be about 11, including attendance at Christmas lunches twice in his official capacity as the person running the attendance centre and a visit to serve a notice upon Arnold about a boy's failure to attend the centre. He had given up golf in 1969 and had sold his clubs, which his wife confirmed; he had been on official business to Wrexham Golf Club but only to check their gaming machines. He had dealt with Arnold at Bryn Estyn and did not know Howarth.

Evidence heard by the Tribunal of Inquiry

9.12 This brief summary of the evidence heard in the libel action (apart from evidence from a Bryn Estyn administrator about the witnesses' periods at Bryn Estyn and from two of Anglesea's sons) is a necessary preliminary to an outline of the evidence that we ourselves have heard on the same factual issues. We have been at a disadvantage, in comparison with the jury, because, very sadly, witness A died on 2 February 1995, within two months of the jury's verdict, having been found hanging in his bed-sitting room. We have, therefore, been limited to reading his written statements and the transcript of his evidence in the libel action. We are aware that he appeared on a television programme alleging that he had been abused whilst he was at Bryn Estyn and that his mother later appeared in another programme, asserting that he had lied about the matter. Witness A was undoubtedly estranged from his mother from time to time and we have had no means of testing the veracity of either. However, we did admit the mother's undated statement to a solicitor in evidence although it consists almost entirely of hearsay. In it she said that her son had never complained to her or to his brothers and sisters that he had been abused at Bryn

Estyn and had never said that other boys were being abused. She says that witness A was happy at Bryn Estyn and she believes that, if he had been abused, he would have told her at the time. She does not think that he was telling the truth about being abused and believes that he made his allegations to gain compensation. She casts doubt also upon the veracity of another Bryn Estyn complainant, who is not connected, however, with the case of Gordon Anglesea.

9.13 We have heard oral evidence from all the other witnesses who gave relevant factual evidence in the libel action. In particular, we heard very full evidence from witnesses B and C and from Anglesea himself and their evidence followed closely what they had told the jury in the libel action. Moreover, the cross-examination of these witnesses inevitably followed a similar pattern to that heard by the jury. We have looked carefully, therefore, for any additional evidence that might indicate the truth or falsity of the allegations against Anglesea.

Witness D

9.14 We heard oral evidence from two new witnesses who complained of sexual abuse by Anglesea. Witness D (as we will identify him), was at Bryn Estyn from about September 1972 until March or April 1974. This period was immediately before the date when the period of our review began and at the time and, throughout the period that the witness refers to, Gordon Anglesea was a police inspector at Colwyn Bay, having been promoted to that rank from Deeside on 10 April 1972. Nevertheless, the witness alleges that he was sexually abused at Bryn Estyn by Anglesea, Howarth (who did not arrive there until 1 November 1973 by which time Arnold was already "Headmaster"), Norris (who arrived on 1 March 1974) and another member of the staff. The allegations against Anglesea are that he buggered the witness twice in the kitchen of Howarth's flat, the witness having been sent there by Howarth on both occasions. On a third occasion he went to Howarth's flat to watch television. However, when he went into the kitchen, Anglesea ran after him with the result that the witness went to a knife drawer and shook the knives. Anglesea called Howarth in and the incident ended with the witness being made to stand outside the office of the headmaster whom he named as Goldswain. He recognised Anglesea later when he saw him in inspector's uniform at a fete and learnt who he was, still in Goldswain's time. These complaints were first made in a statement to the Tribunal dated 4 December 1996.

Witness E

9.15 The other new complainant against Anglesea, witness E, was born on 22 October 1959 and was resident at Bryn Estyn from 8 October 1973 to 14 February 1975, after which he attended at Bryn Estyn intermittently on a daily basis to attend classes (his IQ was then assessed at 71) until he was sentenced to borstal training on 22 November 1976. It is most regrettable to relate that he is now serving a sentence of life imprisonment imposed at Caernarfon Crown Court on 28 February 1995 for the manslaughter of his wife.

9.16 This witness' first complaint about Anglesea was made on 20 March 1997, in his second statement to the Tribunal. In that statement he referred to seeing Anglesea for the first time at Bryn Estyn in the vicinity of the showers after tea on an occasion when Howarth entered the showers and told the witness to get out. The next time that he saw Anglesea was in a police cell in Wrexham police station after he had been arrested. Anglesea came to the cell and accused him of stealing matches. Anglesea told him to strip naked and then to turn round and bend down so that he could look into the witness's backside for matches, whereupon Anglesea touched his private parts and indecently assaulted him. He saw Anglesea at Bryn Estyn on other occasions in the daytime in the company of Howarth. In his evidence to the Tribunal this witness gave evidence about Anglesea to like effect but said that he had seen Anglesea at Bryn Estyn only once, that is, in the vicinity of the showers; when he had seen him on other occasions it had been at Wrexham police station. He said that he had learnt Anglesea's name whilst he was at Bryn Estyn but later said he had only learnt it from his social worker some time after he had made a statement to the police in September 1995 in Wakefield prison, where Howarth also was detained.

Witness F

9.17 The only other fresh evidence about Anglesea directly relevant to the issue of sexual abuse is a statement to the Tribunal made by witness F in prison on 30 December 1996. He was in Bryn Estyn for only three weeks in 1977 and then for about 12 months in 1978/1979. In his last statement he alleged that Howarth used to line up children in the hallway at Bryn Estyn and would pick "kids who were fragile and small" to carry his golf clubs for him. On one occasion Howarth lined up boys, including the witness, when he brought a Chief Superintendent, with a big birth mark on his face and neck, to the home. "The Chief Superintendent picked boys and they went away to Howarth's flat on the grounds or into a big car and away".

Anglesea's visits to Bryn Estyn

9.18 The other evidence that we have heard about Anglesea has been directed mainly to sightings of him on visits to Bryn Estyn. On this we have heard fuller evidence than was called in the libel trial. His own evidence then was that he had visited Bryn Estyn about 11 times[2]. This figure had grown from two (to the Christmas dinners) when he was spoken to, without prior warning, by Dean Nelson, who wrote the *Independent on Sunday* article, and three, in his solicitors' letter to the *Independent on Sunday* after the article appeared.

9.19 Documents before the Tribunal (principally Bryn Estyn logs and Anglesea's notebook) indicate that Anglesea was present at Bryn Estyn on 13 occasions between November 1979 and April 1984 in addition to the Christmas lunches

[2] See para 9.11.

in 1982 and 1983. On 17 November 1979 he returned absconders. On 7 August 1981 he took a boy to the surgery. There were six visits in 1982 before the Christmas lunch in connection with a fire on 15 January 1982, four later cautions and service of a summons. In 1983 there were four visits before the lunch, three of which were to administer cautions and the last in connection with an absconder. The last recorded visit was on 4 April 1984 to administer a caution to a boy who has since died in circumstances similar to witness A's death.

9.20 It will be remembered that boys began to be received at the Wrexham attendance centre from September 1979 and that Arnold was off duty because of illness from the summer of 1979 until late March 1980. On 28 March 1980 Arnold wrote to Inspector Anglesea as he then was:

"Dear Inspector Anglesea,

I received a letter today from the assistant director of Social Services regarding the late attendance of boys at the attendance centre. I have only just returned to work from a period of sick leave, so I'm not aware on a personal basis of all the discussions that have gone on between you and Mr Howarth."

9.21 These documentary records form a background to the oral evidence that we have heard about Anglesea's visits to Bryn Estyn. We heard evidence from four former members of the staff of Bryn Estyn, including Norris, that was broadly consistent with Anglesea's own account. On the other hand, in addition to the two witnesses referred to in paragraphs 9.08 and 9.09, who gave evidence in the libel trial and the witnesses who claimed to have been abused by Anglesea, we heard evidence from seven other witnesses, including four former members of staff who spoke of seeing Anglesea at Bryn Estyn, and most of them spoke of seeing him there in the presence of Howarth. Paul Wilson, for example, said that he had seen Anglesea at Bryn Estyn on at least 12 occasions, in uniform and in plain clothes. He had seen him once sitting in Howarth's flat and on another occasion on a staircase at or shortly before midnight.

9.22 Anglesea himself, however, in his evidence to the Tribunal, repeated his denial of any friendship with Howarth and said that he did not recollect any dealings with him. He had served as a police officer in Wrexham area from July 1976 to May 1987, latterly as Chief Inspector at Ruabon from 1 January 1985, and had left on promotion to Superintendent at Colwyn Bay. His visits to Bryn Estyn had always been in the daytime and always in uniform (except the two lunches), mainly to administer cautions. He recalled also the specific incident of the fire. When he attended at Bryn Estyn he would be taken by a member of staff to the office and he remained always on the ground floor. His earlier underestimates of the number of his visits had been made early on before he had had an opportunity to work out the number, when he had not had access to his pocket books and when he was distressed about what was being alleged against him. The allegations of abuse by him were all denied and the evidence of witnesses such as Paul Wilson was also a fabrication.

Golfing activities

9.23 Anglesea dealt again also with his history as a golf player. He had played the game for only a short period, starting in 1967 (1964 in his Tribunal statement) in the Flintshire Constabulary when he took advantage of a special reduced rate for 24 police officers at Padeswood and Buckley Golf Clubs. In the event he had played only five or six times and never in the United Kingdom after the Llanfairfechan murder, which he believes was in or about 1968. He had visited Wrexham Golf Club only three times, twice in connection with its gaming licence and a third time with his wife on a social occasion at the invitation of the captain. He believed that he had left his small set of golf clubs (only five or six) at the matrimonial home when he left his first wife in 1976 and the woods were broken. He had been mistaken in an earlier statement when he spoke of disposing of them but he had possibly sold a couple of irons to another policeman. He had given a junior set of clubs to his eldest son at Christmas in about 1984 but that was not of any relevance. The evidence to the effect that he had been seen at Wrexham Golf Club in the company of Howarth or alone there and the allegations that he had been seen handling golf clubs from or into cars at Bryn Estyn, including evidence by Joyce Bailey to that effect, were all untrue.

Freemasonry[3]

9.24 Anglesea was questioned also about his connection with freemasonry because of an underlying suggestion that there had been a "cover up" in his case. He disclosed that he had become a full member of Berwyn Lodge in Wrexham, in 1982, after being a probationer in a lodge at Colwyn Bay from about 1976. He had then transferred to a new Wrexham lodge, Pegasus Lodge, in 1984 after a gap from April to September, because it offered an opportunity for swifter advance in freemasonry. He did not know of any police officer member of either lodge and he had joined Berwyn Lodge initially because a particular social friend was a member. He was aware now from records that one member of the staff at Bryn Estyn had become a member of Berwyn Lodge in April 1984 when he himself was leaving it but he had not known that person before inquiries were made on his behalf in connection with the libel action. He had remained a member of the Pegasus Lodge since despite a directive from the Chief Constable of the North Wales Police, David Owen, in September 1984, which ended with the following paragraph:

> "We must be seen to be even-handed in the discharge of our office and my policy will be to say that if you have considered joining the Masons, think carefully about how that application might interfere with your primary duty. To those who are Masons I would say that you should consider carefully how right it is to continue such membership. In the open society in which we live that openness must be seen by all and must not be an openness partially crowded by a secrecy where people could question true motivation."

---

[3] See also paras 50.47 to 50.53.

Conclusions in respect of the allegations of sexual abuse made against Anglesea

9.25 Having considered all this evidence with very great care we are unable to find that the allegations of sexual abuse made against Gordon Anglesea have been proved to our satisfaction or that the trial jury in the libel action would have been likely to have reached a different conclusion if they had heard the fuller evidence that has been placed before us. Moreover, we have reached this conclusion without giving any weight to the statement of the mother of witness A, in effect seeking to negative A's evidence, because in our judgment, it would be improper to do so.

9.26 Having regard to the verdict of the jury in the libel action, major reliance has understandably been placed by those impugning Anglesea on the "fresh evidence" of witnesses D and E but, in our view, neither was a credible witness on the relevant issue. Without going into unnecessary detail, there is no reason to believe that witness D had any contact with Anglesea because he left Bryn Estyn soon after it ceased to be an approved school and long before Anglesea had any known dealings with Bryn Estyn. At that time Anglesea was serving as an Inspector at Colwyn Bay. Witness D's allegations against Howarth and Norris are also highly dubious for similar reasons: witness D only coincided with Norris for a very short period because Norris did not arrive at Bryn Estyn until 1 March 1974 and witness D's references in evidence to incidents in Howarth's flat before a summer fete must be incorrect because Howarth did not begin work at Bryn Estyn until November 1973.

9.27 There are similar difficulties about the evidence of witness E, who left Bryn Estyn on 14 February 1975, over four years before there was any established contact with the home by Anglesea. He was also inconsistent about the number of times when he had seen Anglesea at Bryn Estyn and at the police station and as to when he had learnt Anglesea's identity. Moreover, the circumstances in which this witness's allegation came to be made leave many lingering doubts, about his motivation.

9.28 Finally on this aspect of the additional evidence before us, we do not consider that we can attach any weight to the statement of witness F. We have neither heard nor read any evidence to similar effect. Again, there is difficulty about the periods when he was at Bryn Estyn, largely before there is any documentary record of regular visits by Anglesea and at a time when the latter was merely an inspector rather than a "chief superintendent". Furthermore, the statement contains speculation rather than direct evidence of any actual abuse by Anglesea.

9.29 A major, although not necessarily fatal, difficulty facing the Defendants in the libel action was the fact that the journalist who wrote the article published in the *Independent on Sunday* on 1 December 1991 had no evidence at the time of publication that Anglesea had been involved in child abuse. The journalist, Dean Nelson, was not called as a witness in the libel trial but we have heard full evidence from him about the course of his investigation. His main inquiries had been made in mid-November 1991 but he had met both Councillor Dennis Parry and Alison Taylor before that and he spoke to Anglesea himself by telephone on 30 November 1991. Nelson had been told of visits by Anglesea to Bryn Estyn but he had not received any direct allegation of sexual abuse by Anglesea. It was not until he revisited North Wales in 1992 that he obtained statements implicating Anglesea from witnesses A and B: the former made disclosures between 18 and 29 June 1992 and witness B between 4 and 11 September 1992, after complaining to the police earlier that he was being "hassled" by Nelson. As for witness C, he did not emerge as a complainant of abuse by Anglesea, as we have said earlier in this chapter[4], until about January 1993 when he was interviewed by a BBC representative. This sequence of events certainly left open an inference that the imputation against Anglesea in the December 1991 article had been an unfortunate error and that it was remarkably fortuitous that evidence to support the imputation was discovered several months later.

9.30 There are other more difficult problems for us about the direct evidence of sexual abuse by Anglesea presented to the libel jury and subsequently to us. One obvious difficulty is that witness A has died so that we have not been able to make any realistic assessment of his credibility, although we have seen his statements and a transcript of his evidence at the libel trial, including his cross-examination.

9.31 There are also grave difficulties about the evidence of witnesses B and C, quite apart from the late disclosure of their complaints against Anglesea. Both of them have complex, although quite different, characters and assessment of their evidence on specific detailed issues is a particularly hazardous task.

Assessment of the evidence of witness B

9.32 It would be inappropriate to prolong this report by a detailed analysis of the credibility of each of these witnesses but it is necessary to deal specifically with B and C. We are satisfied that B has suffered a long history of sexual abuse before, during and after his period in care and, to a significant extent until he left care, of physical abuse. As a result he has been, and remains, severely damaged psychologically; he has been greatly affected also by the sudden death of his young wife in very sad circumstances on 1 April 1992, leaving B with a very young child to bring up. A major problem is that the damage is reflected in B's personality in such a way that he presents himself as an unreliable witness by the standards that an ordinary member of a jury is likely to apply. Thus, he is highly sensitive to any criticism and explosive in his reactions, particularly to any suggestion of sexual deviation on his part, although he told us frankly that there was a period in his youth when, because of the persistent sexual abuse to which he had been subjected, he began to question his own sexuality. He has been described also as manipulative and there are many matters on which he is particularly vulnerable in cross-examination.

9.33 One of these matters, which inevitably leads to prolonged cross-examination, is the sequence in which his complaints of abuse have emerged. It is not unusual for a complainant of sexual abuse or a child complainant generally to deny at first that any abuse has occurred but in B's case we have had before us a

---

[4] See para 9.07.

plethora of statements. These included eight main statements made to the police between 30 March 1992 and 8 February 1993 but B alleges that the police have failed to produce six other statements that he made to them. Rightly or wrongly, he complains also of insensitive behaviour, and in some cases, downright misconduct on the part of a small number of officers involved in interviewing him. In view of the potential difficulties, B was permitted exceptionally to draft his own statement to the Tribunal rather than be interviewed by a member of the Tribunal's team. The statement runs to 48 pages, in the course of which B alleges that he has been sexually abused by 32 persons (eight of whom are not named) and otherwise physically abused by 22. It is not surprising in the circumstances that B's recollection, in a limited number of instances, was shown by contemporary documents to be incorrect.

9.34 In the light of these and similar difficulties it was decided in March 1993 by the Crown Prosecution Service, in consultation with counsel, that reliance ought not to be placed on the evidence of witness B for the purpose of prosecuting any alleged abuser. However, this decision did not deter the police from further investigating after that date allegations that had been made by him; and it seems likely that he was required to attend at some stage for the trial of Howarth in 1994 as a potential witness, although he was not called to give evidence. It must be said also that his claim to the Criminal Injuries Compensation Board in respect of the abuse that he suffered at the hands of Howarth, Norris and one other person dealt with later in this report has been settled for a proper sum; and he had no pending civil claim in respect of these matters when he gave evidence to the Tribunal. His libel action against *Private Eye* in respect of a collateral matter was also settled for proper sums in respect of damages and costs shortly before he gave evidence in the Anglesea libel action.

Assessment of the evidence of witness C

9.35 The difficulties in relation to the evidence of witness C are simpler but more acute. He became involved with drugs at the age of 15 years in 1986: he has been having treatment for his drug dependency since November 1987 but he still uses drugs. He is also an alcoholic now, in his own words, and he told the Tribunal that at the time of the libel trial he was drinking 15 pints daily as well as ingesting speed and morphine, which he takes orally and by injection. In consequence, he suffers from shakes in the morning and also experiences blackouts. He alleges that his memory is nevertheless unaffected but his history and demeanour are such that no jury would be likely to accept his evidence on an important disputed matter without independent evidence to confirm it.

9.36 We should add that strenuous efforts have been made on behalf of the Tribunal in the course of our inquiry to find independent evidence of Anglesea's golfing activities and his presence at, or membership of, local golf clubs but no evidence has been forthcoming to rebut his own account of these matters. In the end we have been left with a feeling of considerable disquiet about Anglesea's repeated denials of any recollection of Peter Howarth and the way in which his evidence of his own presence at Bryn Estyn has emerged. We agree with the trial judge in the libel action, however, that such disquiet or even disbelief of this part of Anglesea's evidence would not justify a finding that he has committed sexual abuse in the absence of reliable positive proof.

Approach taken to the case of Gordon Anglesea by the North Wales Police

9.37   We have dealt very fully with the allegations against Gordon Anglesea because they are obviously a proper matter of great public concern and formed part of the background to our appointment. A part of that concern was the suggestion that there had been a 'cover up' and that it was linked to membership of the freemasons. We must say, therefore, that we are fully satisfied that there has been no such cover up. We deal with the police investigations in a later chapter but it is appropriate to state here our findings that the potential evidence against Anglesea was investigated very thoroughly by the North Wales Police and that they recommended in February 1993 to the Crown Prosecution Service that he should be prosecuted on the basis of evidence that was available then. That advice was not accepted by the Crown Prosecution Service but the relevant issues came before a jury later by a different route and it is expressly outside our terms of reference to scrutinise decisions whether to prosecute named individuals.

9.38   In relation to membership of the freemasons we have already cited at paragraph 9.24 part of the guidance on the subject given to members of the North Wales Police as long ago as September 1984. At the outset of the Inquiry, Counsel for the North Wales Police, Mr Andrew Moran QC, made a statement on the instructions of the current Chief Constable that neither he nor the former Chief Constable is or was a freemason and the same is said of the former and current Deputy and Assistant Chief Constables. This disavowal applies also to the relevant Detective Chief Superintendents. There is no basis, therefore, for any suggestion of favour being shown to Gordon Anglesea by senior police officers or of any Masonic influence in the investigation of and decision making in his case.

The allegations of physical abuse at Bryn Estyn

10.01 As we say elsewhere[1], the establishment of Bryn Estyn in 1975, at or about its peak, comprised about 20 care staff and eight teachers together with the three senior officers. There were, however, quite frequent changes of staff so that the number of persons involved in the education and care of children there between 1974 and 1984 was considerably higher. From the incomplete records available to us it appears that not less than 80 persons were involved as members of the care or teaching staff for at least six months in this overall period and it is desirable to have this minimum figure in mind when considering the volume of complaints of physical abuse.

10.02 In the course of our Inquiry we became aware of complaints of physical abuse made against one or more members of the Bryn Estyn staff by 113 former residents who had been at the home between 1974 and 1984. Of these, however, 17 referred only to unidentified assailants. We heard the evidence of 64 complainants of physical abuse; 35 were called to give oral evidence and the statements of the other 29 were read to us. We received, therefore, a very representative account of the scale of the alleged abuse by identified abusers covering the full relevant period. Over half of the complainants of sexual abuse complained also of physical abuse. However, in all but a small number of cases they named different members of staff in respect of the alleged physical abuse. Thus, only six complained of physical abuse by Peter Howarth (mainly of a comparatively minor nature), and the number in respect of Norris was four.

10.03 The principal target of complaint by an overwhelming margin was Paul Wilson, against whom 53 former residents are known to have made complaints of physical abuse. Complaints against most other members of the staff were very thinly spread. In all about 30 of the staff were named by one or more of these complainants but it is necessary and appropriate to refer to only a small number by name. We will deal with the history of Paul Wilson and the other members of staff to be named before making more general observations on the incidence of violence at Bryn Estyn.

Paul Bicker Wilson

10.04 This member of the care staff has already been referred to in paragraphs 2.35(3), 2.35(4), 8.39 and 8.40. He came to Bryn Estyn as a temporary RCCO on 27 May 1974 at the age of 34 years and was very soon promoted to senior RCCO with effect from 1 July 1974, following an interview on 19 June 1974. He remained at Bryn Estyn until it was closed in September 1984 and then accepted employment as a supernumerary RCCO at Chevet Hey, with which we deal fully in Chapter 14.

---

[1] See paras 7.11 and 11.26.

10.05 Before his appointment to Bryn Estyn Wilson had quite varied experience. After working as a press photographer for six years and then in linen and shoe factories in Northern Ireland for another five years, he had been employed at Gwynfa Residential Unit, dealing with maladjusted children from three to 18 years, from 1 September 1970 to 30 April 1972, then at a reception centre in Southwark, where he had lived in as a houseparent, for about ten months, and latterly at a remand home for adolescents in Leicester. The remand home was, however, extremely disciplined and he left it for tree felling in Scotland before deciding that he wished to return to North Wales, where he learnt of a vacancy at Bryn Estyn.

10.06 The Director of Social Services for Clwyd, Emlyn Evans, was aware by the time that Wilson was appointed a senior RCCO that he had resigned from his post at Leicester following his conviction for an offence of stealing property from a house in Coalville, for which he had received a conditional discharge in the magistrates' court. This was referred to in a reference supplied by the Superintendent of the Remand Home but the latter added:

> "I found Mr Wilson to be an energetic young man who would adapt himself quite well particularly in the sporting field. He was a keen hockey player and represented Leicestershire in county matches. He was able to report quite well on boys, both verbally and in writing. I thought the future looked quite good for this young man until he committed the stealing offence.
>
> I sincerely hope that this applicant will eventually be successful in his search for a social worker's post, but one wonders how sincere he really is."

10.07 Despite, or perhaps partly because of, this qualified reference, Wilson seems to have enjoyed a rather protected existence at Bryn Estyn. During his probationary period he was under the supervision of Howarth and we have seen Arnold's monthly reports about him, which Emlyn Evans required to see. It soon became apparent that his written work was not up to standard and Arnold referred more than once to his immaturity and his tendency to give vent to frustration but the reports did suggest that he was maturing progressively and getting to grips better with his work. It was obvious that he was no thinker and that his preference was for outdoor activities. He was therefore relieved eventually of any responsibility for writing reports about the resident boys and permitted to concentrate mainly on "outward bound" type activities. He said in his own evidence that he took over outdoor pursuits from a member of staff who had left plus the usual daily routine responsibilities for getting the boys up, showering and feeding them but he was not involved in the "house" teams. Towards the end of his time at Bryn Estyn the head gardener retired and he was asked to take on a group of boys to look after the garden. He lived at first in the main building next to, or in part of, Howarth's flat, then elsewhere in the building and in a gardener's cottage before moving out to Llangollen and finally Chirk in April 1976 when he married.

10.08   The allegations of physical abuse by Wilson span virtually the whole period of his employment at Bryn Estyn. We heard the evidence of 39 complainants dealing with these allegations, 26 of whom gave oral evidence. All these gave evidence that they had been physically assaulted by Wilson and many said that they had witnessed assaults by him on others. Seven members of staff admitted in evidence that they regarded Wilson as a violent bully and two described assaults by him that they had seen. Other witnesses described incidents of random cruelty by Wilson, such as kicking a boy's crutches away from him, capsizing canoes and holding boys under water, deliberately exposing rock climbers to risk by, for example, dropping the rope or leaving a fearful climber dangling on a rope, and removing the steering wheel of a minibus whilst driving it in order to terrify the occupants.

10.09   There was no specific discernible pattern to Wilson's physical assaults and it would be oppressive to give a comprehensive account of them. Instead, it will be sufficient to summarise a few of them that are adequately illustrative beginning with three of the four assaults to which Wilson pleaded in November 1994[2].

10.10   Victim A, who admitted that he might have been cheeky to Wilson, described how Wilson came from behind the counter of the clothing store and punched him to the ground. When he stood up, Wilson punched him to the ground again, continuing to punch him when he remained on the ground. This was but one of many occasions when he was punched forcefully by Wilson to the face or to the ribs or back.

10.11   Victim B said in evidence that Wilson seemed to enjoy losing his temper and bullying and belittling people. He remembered running away from Wilson on one occasion and then returning five or ten minutes later via a back door, whereupon Wilson head-butted him on his nose, causing it to bleed. Wilson then goaded the victim to retaliate but he did not and ran off. The witness's worst "crime" at Bryn Estyn during the two and a half years that he spent there had been to break a store room window.

10.12   The assault on victim C was described by a member of the Bryn Estyn care staff who said in evidence that there had been an occasion when Wilson had pressed himself against her, to her distaste, outside the kitchen. Victim C had then come along and had told Wilson not to do it. Wilson's response was to punch the boy so hard in the face that his nose was broken. There was a lot of blood and the staff member had taken the boy to the surgery and on to hospital, where butterfly stitches had been inserted.

10.13   Numerous other witnesses spoke of frequent and varied assaults by Wilson, describing him as a bully. They spoke of being struck by him with keys, of being gripped in a headlock whilst he rubbed his knuckles against the victim's head, of being hit on the head regularly and of habitual backhanders. One of them told how he had been caught tattooing himself with Indian ink and a needle, against the rules, when he was outside near the school building. Wilson's

---

[2] See para 2.35(4). The circumstances of the fourth offence to which Wilson pleaded guilty are dealt with in paras 10.26 and 10.27.

reaction was to "boot him up the backside and legs" and to slap him across the face. He then threw the rest of the ink over the boy's head. The boy went straight to the showers and was told to keep the incident quiet.

10.14 In view of the volume and nature of the complaints about Wilson, the fact that he was rather a "loner" at Bryn Estyn and the attitude of many members of the staff towards him it is not surprising that some contemporary complaints were recorded. The surprise is that there were not more of them. As far as we have been able to ascertain there were only six in all whilst Wilson remained at Bryn Estyn.

10.15 The first related to a boy whose own evidence has not been before the Tribunal because he cannot now be traced. The relevant incident was alleged to have occurred late in 1978 when the boy said that he had been knocked around by Wilson and most recently knocked to the ground. The boy's social worker wrote a memo:

> "D often presents as a boy who is somewhat used to being able to fantasise with his elders . . . It is possible that he has a tendency to enlarge upon the truth."

10.16 The allegation was, however, reported to the police and on 19 December 1978 Arnold wrote to the Director of Social Services:

> "I gathered in conversation from the detective constable that the claims made by the boy did not seem to carry much substance, though obviously the matter had to be processed in the usual way . . . I have this morning spoken to the boy's social worker and we have agreed that the boy should remain at home on trial until the completion of the Christmas and New Year leave. We will then discuss whether the boy should return to Bryn Estyn or a placement sought for him in another community home."

10.17 Wilson's trade union, NALGO, had been brought into the matter and a hand-written memo in Clwyd's Social Services Department about a call from John Cooke, the union's branch organiser for Clwyd, recorded:

> "Following discussion with Mr Arnold, Bryn Estyn, it was felt that it would not be in Mr Paul Wilson's best interests to be suspended as it was highly unlikely that there was any substance in the complaint made against him. In the circumstances it was agreed that Mr Gordon Ramsay should arrange for the boy to be transferred as a matter of urgency (transfer arranged for 17 January 1979)."

D was transferred to Neath Farm School, a placement widely feared by boys in care at Bryn Estyn and often threatened as a punishment for misbehaviour.

10.18 On 17 January 1979 Arnold wrote to the Director of Social Services:

> "The allegation . . . is currently being investigated by Detective Sergeant Parry of the Wrexham CID office. He has interviewed the boy who made the allegations, he has also interviewed E and F who are both pupils at this school . . .

I have considered it wise to examine closely Mr Wilson's duty rota, and where he was on duty in a vulnerable position, ie taking a meal, collecting boys early in the morning and like situations, made readjustment so that at no time is he on duty with boys without another responsible and senior member of staff being present . . . It does not seem necessary at this stage to recommend to you that Wilson be suspended from duty, though any advice you would offer on this matter I would gladly accept."

10.19 One of the perturbing aspects of these events is that Robert Jones, a member of the care staff, to whom further reference will be made later in this chapter[3], said in evidence that he intervened twice during or after assaults by Wilson on boys. On the second occasion he had seen Wilson punch a boy and he asked the boy if he wanted to make a complaint. Robert Jones passed the matter on to both Arnold and Howarth: he believed that Wilson was asked to go home (Wilson himself said in evidence that he was asked by the Director of Social Services to take two days holiday whilst the D incident was sorted out and that the boy was moved to Neath Farm School). Robert Jones said that he had been dissatisfied with this outcome and had written to Geoffrey Wyatt in the Social Services Department at Shire Hall, who told him later that the matter was not being pursued. In the event the North Wales Police wrote to the boy's mother on 13 February 1979 informing her that the matter "has been thoroughly investigated with the result that no evidence has been obtained which would justify . . . instituting criminal proceedings".

10.20 There was another complaint by the mother of an unidentified boy about Wilson of which Arnold was aware in 1980. On 18 March 1980 Arnold wrote to the Director of Social Services:

"I am led to believe that the boy's mother has made a complaint to the social worker concerned, accordingly until this complaint is received I do not intend to take any further action."

To which Geoffrey Wyatt on behalf of the Director replied on 31 March 1980:

"I am happy to leave the matter with you as there has been no official complaint. However, as this is the second occasion when Mr Wilson's "play fighting" has led to a child being aggrieved, he may require some advice from you on his close contact re supervision of boys."

10.21 There were two further complaints about Wilson in 1982 of which we know. Witness G, whose home was in Bristol, told us of an incident that occurred when he was nearly 15 years old. At tea-time Wilson threw a plate across the dining room floor and then ordered G to pick it up. Instead G kicked the plate and ran out and up the stairs to the television room. He was pursued by Wilson, who slapped him and punched him to the floor until another boy, H, entered the room. Wilson told the latter to get out and then got hold of G's hair, dragging him down the main staircase, whilst G tried to cling to the banisters. He managed to get away at about the half landing level and shortly afterwards

---

[3] See paras 10.29, 10.36, 10.66, 10.67 and 10.75 to 10.77.

encountered Howarth near the main doors. Howarth told him to clean himself up and then to meet Howarth in the main conference room. In that room he saw Howarth, Wilson and H. G was prevented from telephoning his father, who was in Eire, and Howarth told him that it was a very serious matter to make an allegation against a member of the staff: it was unlikely he would get anywhere with it and that he would be "shipped out".

10.22 This appears to be G's version of an incident reported upon by Howarth to Arnold as follows:

"On the evening of the 10 May 1982, Mr Matthews (acting senior officer of the day) approached me at approximately 9 pm to inform me that G was making allegations that Mr P B Wilson had manhandled him during the evening. I advised Mr Matthews of the procedures and also informed him that I would make myself available at any time if he needed further support.

The following morning I requested Mr Matthews and Mr Stritch to see the boy in respect of his complaint.

I informed Mr R Powell and also Mr Pook Social Worker of the situation and promised to phone them again as soon as the complaint had been investigated.

At 10.30 Mr Matthews and Mr Stritch advised me that G had discussed the situation with them and that he was not prepared to make any charge of assault against Mr Wilson. He admitted that he had followed Mr Wilson around the building, verbally abusing him and also throwing implements at him.

I saw G with Mr Stritch and questioned him regarding the fairness of the enquiry proceedings, he stated he was happy with the situation and confirmed that he did not wish to make any complaint about Mr Wilson's behaviour.

I then saw Mr Wilson, together with his union representative Mr J Rayfield, and advised him that in our opinion he had acted in the best interests of the boy and the school and that the matter was closed.

I phoned Mr R Powell and Mr Pook and advised them of the situation."

10.23 G appears to have been transferred to Neath Farm in 1983 but he was fined in Wrexham in November 1982 and received custodial sentences on two occasions at Bristol in 1983 so that it is not possible to infer any causal link between the events of 10 or 11 May 1982 and his subsequent transfer.

10.24 The second incident in 1982 involved a boy who has not given evidence to the Tribunal. The Director of Social Services, however, by then Gledwyn Jones, noted in a memo dated 10 September 1982:

"Mr Wilson informed me with regard to the incident on the 16 August 1982 when he was alleged to have hit a boy named J at Bryn Estyn and (sic) that Sgt Williams of the Police had informed him that no further action was being taken by the Police. Mr Wilson indicated that he was anxious that after 3 such incidents, some day he was afraid that such an allegation would "stick". . . Mr Wilson appreciates the problems that could occur if such allegations were made again as had previously happened on the last three occasions."

At that time the unease of the Social Services Department about Wilson may have been the reason why the Director was discussing with him a possible transfer to Intermediate Treatment work. Nevertheless, J was removed from Bryn Estyn on 19 August 1982.

10.25 Difficulty in relation to the boy J surfaced again in April 1984 because he was re-admitted to Bryn Estyn and objection was taken to this by Wilson's NALGO branch organiser, John Cooke. Arnold discussed the matter with Wyatt, the Assistant Director, Residential and Day Care and the latter then met Cooke but Wyatt's decision was that J should not be removed from Bryn Estyn. This decision was made, however, in the knowledge that Bryn Estyn was soon to close and on 21 September 1984 Wilson was offered alternative employment at Chevet Hey community home as a supernumerary RCCO, which he accepted ultimately on 29 January 1985 after his application for redeployment to an Intermediate Treatment post had been rejected. The Tribunal has been unable to trace J, who had changed his name by 1992, and we are unable to say how long he remained at Bryn Estyn in 1984, on what was his third stay there.

10.26 Despite the interchange with Wilson in 1982 about J, there was soon afterwards another complaint about him. It reached the ears of the Principal, who asked Norris to see the complainant. In his memo of 27 January 1983 Norris reported:

"M was seen by SRN [Norris] at the request of GBA [Arnold] ref M's complaint to the SMO [Senior Medical Officer] of being kicked by Mr P B Wilson.

On the 25 Jan it was at break time on the morning Mr Wilson picked me up by the neck and top of my leg. He then started to swing me about into other people, like he usually does, then he put me down and started to annoy me by pushing me about. It drives me daft so I hit him on the leg with a stick. He then chased after me and kicked me on the left knee cap. I was laying on the floor crying. I don't think it was in fun or a game. Mr Curran wanted to take me to the matron but I would not go. Later in the day I went in to see the doctor and told him about it. I would like to complain about being kicked by Mr Wilson."

Wilson pleaded guilty on 28 November 1994 to an offence of assault occasioning actual bodily harm in respect of M.

10.27 Norris' evidence was that he wrote down the full words of the boy in that memo and is clear that the boy signed it. Norris gave it to Stritch, who was acting head on duty at the time. Two or three days later Stritch told him that M had dropped the allegations in view of the fact that he had been told that, if he continued with the allegation, which was his right, he would have to be moved because they could not afford to move a highly paid houseparent like Wilson: it was cheaper to move the boy.

10.28 Apart from this largely documentary evidence of how complaints about Wilson were dealt with at Bryn Estyn, we heard evidence from one member of the care staff, in particular, that she had witnessed two assaults by him, to one of which he later pleaded guilty. Although she took the boy involved in the latter incident to hospital[4] she never reported the matter to her superiors and was never asked for a report. By way of explanation she said that to record such an incident was "not the done thing". She had learnt by seeing what had been written earlier: if a boy had suffered an injury, you just put "sustained an injury". She said also that she did not report the other serious assault by Wilson on another boy because she was frightened of Wilson: she logged it simply as an injury. After she had left Bryn Estyn, however, this witness did report child abuse by others.

10.29 This last witness was obviously not the only member of the staff who witnessed assaults by Wilson. Robert Jones was one who did report at least two incidents involving Wilson but no effective action ensued. Nicholls[5] also said in evidence that, after he had rescued a boy from an assault by Wilson, he reported the fact to Stritch, who told Arnold. Nicholls does not recall anything being done about the assault but Wilson was later moved to largely garden work rather than normal care work. Other members of staff did not report Wilson's conduct because, for example, they considered themselves to be too junior to make a complaint or did not know how to pursue the matter beyond their immediate line manager. On the other hand, the Deputy Principal in charge of education, Maurice Matthews, said that he did speak privately to Wilson about his treatment of children although he never spoke to him officially and did not feel it necessary to tell Arnold.

10.30 Wilson himself said in evidence that he quite enjoyed his time at Bryn Estyn because he was involved in outside pursuits. There were quite a few hard "knocks" (the witness meant "nuts") there but there were also some really nice lads who he did not think should have been there. When he first joined the staff it was clear that the boys in Bryn Estyn were coming from the courts but as time went on more and more young people with family problems were being admitted. There used to be comments such as "you come in as a child maybe with no criminal background but you will go out as a thief".

10.31 Wilson said that he had never read a memorandum from Clwyd about corporal punishment[6] and he was not aware of any written rulings on the subject. He learned the ropes about discipline from colleagues who worked with him. He had come from disciplined areas before so he just carried on in the same way. They had to deal, for example, with boys running away, severe fighting in the dining room and boys under the influence of glue and petrol, which was quite widespread and a regular occurrence. By way of restraint he would clamp a boy severely round the waist, locking his arms, to protect the boy or himself; and sometimes the boy's legs too had to be locked. He said also that he had never

---

[4] See para 10.12. Wilson pleaded guilty on 28 November 1994 to an offence of assault occasioning actual bodily harm in respect of this incident.

[5] See para 10.63.

[6] See paras 30.04 and 30.05.

denied that he had clipped boys on the ear or back of the head or punched an arm to remind them to stay in line and that he was there, seeing what they were doing. He was aware that complaints were being made against him because he was interviewed by the police on one occasion and by the Officer-in-Charge on maybe a few occasions, but it was an everyday occurrence, not just with him. With 40 to 50 young people there, who did not want to be, the staff were "going to get a little bit of resentment, so complaints were part of the system".

10.32 Wilson accepted that the "most criticism" that was made of him was that he was a bully but denied that this description of him was justified: he was a disciplinarian who was firm in his job and believed in discipline. He admitted that he had lost his temper at times and become angry but he denied that he had ever gone beyond "a clip or a slap" in anger. He was asked about most of the incidents to which we have specifically referred but he could not now recollect even incidents in respect of which the police and/or his union branch organiser had become involved. In general, the allegations were totally untrue and the most that he might have done by way of punching or the like was to thump or punch a boy on the arm sufficiently hard to cause a bruise, which he had seen other named members of the staff do, including Arnold on one occasion.

10.33 This witness agreed that, when interviewed by the journalist, Dean Nelson, and asked about physical punishment, he had said:

> "If you are asking me if young people were thumped by members of the staff, it has been, I'd be lying if I said some kids didn't receive physical punishment. But this was always something which was talked about in a quiet, subdued manner. No one boasted that a kid had been knocked about. There were occasions where certain young people were hard to control and certain members of staff would be asked to go and sort it out."

When he was asked by Leading Counsel to the Tribunal whether that statement was true, he said that it was and he agreed also his later answer to the journalist:

> "There was no guideline to say if a child steps out of line you must go and batter that child. Certain members of the staff who felt threatened by a group of young people would possibly sort out the troublemaker and deal with him privately away from any form of supervision or where they could be seen."

10.34 We have no doubt that Wilson was rightly convicted of the offences to which he pleaded guilty in November 1994 and that they represented only a very small sample of a long catalogue of similar offences that he committed during his period of ten years at Bryn Estyn. What is both dismaying and astonishing is that he was allowed to survive as a Residential Child Care Officer for so long and then to move on to similar employment in another community home, despite his reputation and the number of occasions when he was the subject of complaint.

10.35 The history of Wilson at Bryn Estyn that we have summarised underlines the absence of any realistic complaints or whistleblowing procedure. Equally lamentable was the failure of Clwyd's Social Services Department to carry out any adequate investigation of the few complaints that did get beyond the walls of Bryn Estyn. If the police or the Crown Prosecution Service decided not to prosecute, the decision was regarded as absolving the alleged abuser and in no case was the complainant given a proper opportunity to be heard. It is readily understandable, therefore, that any potential complainant, whether a resident or a member of staff who disapproved of a colleague's conduct, was discouraged from proceeding with an "official" complaint.

10.36   In our judgment a substantial share of the blame for this failure to act in respect of Wilson must be borne by Arnold and Howarth, who threw a protective cloak over Wilson and also gave the firm impression to other members of the staff that they were ready to shield him for reasons that will never now be known. This does not wholly exculpate the staff generally from blame for failing to take effective action to have Wilson removed. Matthews, for example, as a Deputy Principal, clearly ought to have gone beyond speaking unofficially to Wilson himself on a couple of occasions, and more junior members of staff might have been more effective, despite Robert Jones' experience, if they had protested collectively, even though they lacked the forum for doing so that regular meetings of the care staff would have provided.

10.37   We deal with the responsibility of Clwyd's field social workers and higher officials in a later chapter[7] but we must say at once that the Social Services Department was greatly at fault in failing to respond appropriately to the complaints of Wilson's bullying behaviour. If they had investigated them conscientiously, they would have found evidence to support them and would have been driven to the conclusion that Wilson was not a fit person to be employed as an RCCO.

10.38   That is our own conclusion on the evidence that we have heard. It would not be unfair to say that Wilson should never have been appointed to the post at Bryn Estyn and that there was inadequate consideration of his references and record. Even if one condones his appointment because of the exigencies of the time, however, subsequent monitoring and supervision of his performance and consideration of the complaints about him ought to have demonstrated starkly his unfitness for the work that he was given. No doubt he had a degree of charm, which was discernible when he gave evidence, and probably he could get on with a proportion of the boys who were sufficiently robust to withstand his eccentric behaviour. But for very many residents he caused or contributed to substantial distress and unhappiness that have lingered, in some cases, for as long as two decades.

10.39   In fairness to Wilson it should be said finally, however, that when he was sentenced on 28 November 1994 to a total of 15 months' imprisonment, the sentencing judge, His Honour Judge Gareth Edwards QC, decided to suspend the sentences for a period of two years. The judge made that decision not only because of Wilson's pleas of guilty and the time that had elapsed since the assaults had been committed but also because of the good character that Wilson had established in the intervening years. After referring to the positive aspects of Wilson's work on outside activities at Bryn Estyn, he said "I also

[7] See Chapter 30.

take into account that since you have become a mature man you have done much on a voluntary basis for youngsters in the Chirk area, giving up many hours, indeed many days, of your time to work with them, with the result that you have fully earned the warm testimonials which have been presented to the Court by parents, and by persons in responsible positions in North Wales, who know of the work you have done".

David Gwyn Birch

10.40 David Birch has already been referred to briefly in Chapter 8[8] of this report because he was acquitted on 12 January 1995 of two counts alleging serious sexual offences by him. Those two counts had been severed for separate trial from six other counts. The latter alleged four offences of assault occasioning actual bodily harm (two of which involved an alleged victim who had died) and two offences of cruelty to a child. In respect of these other counts the prosecution decided to offer no evidence and verdicts of "not guilty" were accordingly registered in respect of each of them, but the Court record is confused and appears to be incorrect as a result of the re-numbering of the two counts tried by the jury.

10.41 The decision by the prosecution not to offer any evidence against Birch on the non-sexual charges was based partly on the death of the complainant referred to and publicity given to another complainant. It was said also by Leading Counsel for the prosecution that the offences did not involve the "more serious variety of violence" and that only two witnesses (victims) were available to be called.

10.42 We have some sympathy with Birch's protest now that he has had to face a form of "double jeopardy" in the proceedings before the Tribunal. Although he was never tried by a jury in the conventional sense in respect of non-sexual matters he was acquitted of all the charges laid against him and, it is said on his behalf, he should not be "re-tried" on any of them now. However, the Tribunal is aware that 17 former residents of Bryn Estyn, including the four named in the six non-sexual charges in the indictment, have complained of physical assaults by Birch during the period of five years when he was working as an RCCO at Bryn Estyn and we have received the evidence of 13 of these complainants, seven of whom gave oral evidence to us. It is necessary, therefore, that we should at least reach some conclusions about the evidence of 11 of them who were not named in the Birch indictment when assessing the scale of abuse at Bryn Estyn.

10.43 Before dealing with these allegations it is necessary to add a little to what has been said about Birch in paragraph 8.37. He had left school after O levels at the age of 16 years and had then taken a two year course in physical education before working for two years or so as a labourer. His contact with Bryn Estyn was through rugby football because he knew both David Cheesbrough[9] and Robert Jones of Wrexham RFC and it was through them that he applied for

---

[8] See paras 8.37 and 8.38.
[9] See para 10.87.

a post at Bryn Estyn. After an interview with Howarth and then with Arnold he was taken on as a temporary houseparent on 21 May 1979 at the age of 21 years, and he was appointed as an established RCCO with effect from 1 August 1979, following a formal interview on 9 July 1979. He remained an RCCO at Bryn Estyn until he was offered employment as a supernumerary RCCO at Park House Community Home on 22 June 1984, in anticipation of the closure of Bryn Estyn. He continued to live in a flat at Bryn Estyn until 31 October 1984, the day before he became an RCCO at Chevet Hey; and his post June 1984 history is dealt with later in this report[10]. It will have been noted that he had not received any social work training before his appointment to Bryn Estyn. Whilst he was there he was offered secondment on an In-Service Course in Social Care (ISCSC) starting in September 1980 at Cartrefle College but he did not take this up because of "ill health at the beginning of the course".

10.44 When assessing Birch's conduct at Bryn Estyn it is necessary to remember that he was very young, inexperienced and without any formal training throughout his period there. He was assigned to a team, working at various times under Phillip Murray[11] and Len Stritch and for substantial periods with Margaret Elizabeth (Liz) Evans[12], who said in evidence that she had good memories of him and that he got on well with the boys, like an older brother to them. He gravitated naturally to the "rugby set" of mainly care staff who all played for Wrexham at various levels whilst they were at Bryn Estyn. This set included Phillip Murray, Robert Jones, Anthony Nicholls and the teacher David Cheesbrough (who played elsewhere between 1981 and 1985) as well as David Birch himself; Liz Evans was also a member and supporter of the rugby club.

10.45 Probably the most serious allegation made against Birch was that on one occasion, after the deceased complainant named in the indictment had broken a light bulb, Birch rubbed his face in the remnants of the bulb. A log entry about the complainant dated 22 March 1984 but only recently found (and therefore not put to Birch) reads:

> "Refused to wash his hands for Mr Birch at tea time. He was told he'd have his tea as soon as he did, but he still refused. Peter said he didn't want any tea and went out of D/room. I found him later in the kitchen waiting for Cook to make him some toast. When he was told he couldn't have any he stormed back into the D/room and smashed a light bulb, which he refused to sweep up."

10.46 Having regard to this contemporary record, we are fully satisfied that there was an incident involving the complainant and Birch and a broken light bulb. We do not think that it would be right to make an adverse finding against Birch in respect of the matter in view of the verdict recorded at his trial and the fact that he did not have an opportunity before the Tribunal to refresh his memory from the log entry (Birch said in evidence to us that he had no recollection of the incident). Another difficulty is that the deceased complainant gave a different

---

[10] See paras 14.63 to 14.73.
[11] See para 10.59.
[12] See para 10.68.

version of how the light bulb breaking had occurred. In two of his ten statements to the police he gave quite detailed accounts of how another resident, who was a bully, had been calling him names when they were in the dining room. He had picked up a chair with which to hit the bully but, as he had swung it over his head, the chair had caught a chandelier, smashing all three light bulbs in it. It was then that he had refused to sweep up the bits because he considered the incident to be the bully's fault. After his face had been rubbed in the broken glass of the bulb he was so angry that he smashed six or eight small panes of glass in the sliding door of the dining room with his fists. This was the only incident involving light bulbs that he recalled.

10.47 Other allegations made against Birch are rather diffuse and, in the main, comparatively minor. Two matters do, however, call for specific mention. The first is a complaint by one witness, P, whose evidence was read to us, that Birch and Nicholls had forcibly removed a ring from his nose, cut off his "mohican" hair and made him run the gauntlet. Nicholls had grabbed hold of his hair and Birch had grabbed his legs whilst he was lying on his bed. Nicholls had then placed his forearm across the victim's throat whilst Birch "pulled" the ring out of P's nose with the result that "It hurt a lot and was bleeding". P had been kicking and shouting whilst this was happening and he was then told to go downstairs, where he was made to sit on a chair, Birch then pulled his head back whilst Nicholls cut his "mohican" hair off with a pair of scissors and then handed the cut hair to him. P complained also that, later that day, he was forced to "run the gauntlet" in the television room, that is, to run between two lines of about 20 boys in all and Birch and Nicholls, whilst he was punched about the body by the boys as he ran between them and then punched once more by Nicholls (but not by Birch).

10.48 According to P this was the second occasion when he had been required to run the gauntlet by Nicholls. On the previous occasion he and another boy had absconded and on returning both had been made to run the gauntlet in a similar manner in turn and he and the other boy had both been punched by Nicholls about the body and face at the end of the run.

10.49 P said that he complained to both his social worker and to his mother after each of these two incidents of running the gauntlet; and after the second time, ie the hair occasion, he complained to Arnold the next day in the latter's office about the way in which the ring had been pulled out and his hair cut. Arnold told him, however, that it was his own fault and that standards had to be maintained. He did not seek any treatment for his injuries.

10.50 When Nicholls gave evidence to us he said that he and Birch had taken part in removing the nose ring but had done so on the instructions of Arnold: Nicholls had held P in a bear hug whilst Birch had removed the attachment to the nose ring. The boy himself had removed the actual prong and they had refused to do that. The boy, who was an early "punk rocker" had not consented. Nicholls said also that they had joked about the colour of P's hair but he denied cutting it: the boy would wash out the colours himself. The practice of running the gauntlet was known to the staff and he assumed that they approved it. He had witnessed it only once, however, and he denied punching any boy who had had to undergo it. Nicholls accepted a police caution in respect of P but he said that it was for tipping P out of bed and not in respect of the nose ring incident.

10.51 David Birch himself was an unimpressive and unhelpful witness. He denied taking part in the removal of P's nose ring when he gave evidence to us and, when Nicholls' evidence about it was put to him, he said that he remembered P returning to Bryn Estyn with a ring in his nose and the staff being concerned about it but he did not witness its removal. His memory of the mohican hair was of seeing it sellotaped to P's bed.

10.52 This summary of the evidence about the nose ring and hair incident illustrates the difficulties of reaching firm findings about specific incidents over 15 years after the event (P spent about four months at Bryn Estyn in 1982). We are sure, however, that at least part of P's nose ring was forcibly removed by Birch and we see no sensible reason to doubt that his hair was cut against his will and that he had to run the gauntlet after that.

10.53 The other specific matter that calls for comment in relation to Birch is an allegation made by two former residents that Birch forcibly removed their new tattoos by scraping them with the abrasive side of a matchbox. This is an allegation that has been made against Nicholls and Wilson also but all three of them deny it and there was some confusion and hesitation in the evidence about the identity of the member of staff doing the scraping. It is clear that tattooing was against the rules at Bryn Estyn but that some boys experimented from time to time in tattooing themselves with Indian ink. In a letter to the Tribunal written after she had given evidence, because she had not been asked about the matter in the course of her evidence, the former Matron (Isabel Williams) said:

> "It was said in the newspaper (regarding the boys' self inflicted tattoos) that staff rubbed them off with matchboxes. This is quite wrong. The boys themselves rubbed them off when they tired of the poorly executed tattoos, leaving a weeping site which I or a housemaster treated. Seldom was it necessary to refer these to Dr Wilkinson."

10.54 Williams may well be correct in her recollection, in general terms, even though she is unlikely to have witnessed herself any scraping of tattoos. That does not necessarily discredit the evidence of the witnesses who allege that two boys had it done to them. It may well be that one or both of the complainants was or were punished, in effect, by removal of the tattoos as described but we cannot be sure on the evidence that Birch did so.

10.55 The other allegations against Birch at Bryn Estyn have been largely of random assaults, usually under provocation. The general tenor of most of the complaints has been of over-reaction by Birch to incidents in the course of which he punched or slapped or sometimes kicked a boy. One witness, almost uniquely, did allege that he complained to Birch that Howarth had interfered with him sexually, whereupon Birch called him a liar, slapped him and threw him into a pond. These complaints cannot be dismissed lightly on the ground that, individually, they are not corroborated. In our judgment there is a discernible pattern to them and the evidence is credible because most of the relevant complainants admitted provocative behaviour and did not try to exaggerate the effect upon them of Birch's response.

10.56 It follows that, in our view, David Birch was at fault from time to time in using physical force to boys when he should not have done and on other occasions in using excessive force when some physical action by way of restraint was permissible. It would be wrong to be very harsh in one's strictures upon him personally, however, bearing in mind the matters that we have already referred to[13] and the general climate of violence in which he was working. We shall say more about this climate in the next section of this chapter. Birch was the youngest member of the rugby set and he said in his own evidence that he received no instruction in how to restrain boys physically and that he learnt from older care workers. We deal briefly in Chapter 14 with Birch's subsequent record over a period of five years at Chevet Hey but it is noteworthy that only five complainants have alleged physical abuse by him there. One of them, for example, said of Birch that he was a decent bloke; his trouble was that he was a big man who did not know his own strength. There were, however, other criticisms of Birch at Chevet Hey, notably by Michael Barnes when Acting Officer-in-Charge.

10.57 In the event Birch has suffered substantially as a result of his employment at Bryn Estyn. He had to endure a long wait before his trial on charges of which he was acquitted and, since then, he has felt unable to work with children, which was work that he loved according to his own evidence, and there was some adverse publicity about him prior to the setting up of this Tribunal.

The other members of the rugby set[14]

10.58 It is convenient to deal here with these members of the staff for a number of reasons. One is that they were regarded by some other members of the staff and many residents as a rather elite group who tended to keep together and were sympathetic to each other. Secondly, although the complaints made against them are not very numerous, they are of a rather similar kind. Thirdly, unlike Birch, who was a taciturn witness, the other male members of the set all gave helpful general evidence about conditions at Bryn Estyn as they saw them, which has assisted us significantly in assessing the overall picture.

10.59 The senior man in this group in terms of experience and training was **Phillip Murray**, who began work at Bryn Estyn on 1 May 1978, just before his 28th birthday, and who remained there as a senior houseparent until 30 September 1984, when he began a two year course for the CQSW at Cartrefle College, as a prelude to field social work. When he applied for a post at Bryn Estyn, in response to an advertisement published nationally, he already possessed the CRCCYP as a result of training at Salford College of Technology and he had served at an observation and assessment centre for 11 to 16 year olds in the Wigan area. His appointment at Bryn Estyn was to replace David Cheesbrough, who had been transferred from the care staff to the teaching staff with effect from February 1978; and Murray thereafter lived with his wife and two young children in a tied cottage 100 yards from the entrance.

---

[13] See paras 10.43 and 10.44.
[14] See para 10.44.

10.60 Murray was critical of aspects of the Bryn Estyn regime but said that he never felt that he was facing a nightmare there, whereas he had hated his earlier posting because of the very strict regime. Amongst his criticisms of Bryn Estyn were that Howarth had a very autocratic style; quite a few staff were taken on at very short notice; there was no in-service training; they never had any staff meetings; and there was friction between teaching and care staff. Murray complained also that there was a lack of support and monitoring by County Hall: he was not sure who was responsible for this and he thought that Arnold felt frustrated about it. The relationship with the Wrexham Area Office was also not good and field social workers very rarely visited the premises, except for statutory reviews.

10.61 Murray said that broadly speaking, there were three types of children in the mixture of boys from North and South Wales at Bryn Estyn in his time, namely:-

> "(i) Delinquent children with a range of behavioural problems;
>
> (ii) A small group of 5 or 6 boys with behavioural problems, dumped at Bryn Estyn because there was nowhere else for them . . .
>
> (iii) A small group of non-school attenders who should not have been at Bryn Estyn."

Commenting on (ii), he added that, with the experience that he had subsequently gained as a specialist mental health worker, he would consider that those boys had a potential for mental illness/mental health problems in adulthood.

10.62 Despite this motley collection of different types of children, Murray described the atmosphere at Bryn Estyn as relaxed and informal and he denied that there was any "culture of fear". He accepted that a "pecking order" was part of the culture but said that it did not involve preferential treatment and that too much should not be read into it. Nicholls, however, was more realistic in his evidence when he said that there was a "top lad" system. In his time it was Q, who controlled the other boys in very loose terms and who used his size and influence to do so. Other boys saw Q as their mentor.

10.63 **Anthony Nicholls** is three years older than Murray but he did not have any experience of or training in care work before he took up employment at Bryn Estyn on 21 March 1981. The circumstances were that the company for which he had worked for 16 years, starting as an apprentice toolmaker, went into liquidation in 1979 and he learnt of possible employment at Bryn Estyn, like Birch, from David Cheesbrough. Nicholls had by then risen to a managerial post with his former company and this seems to have been regarded as a sufficient qualification because he was invited by Arnold by telephone, without any interview, to start work the next day. In the event he remained at Bryn Estyn as a Residential Child Care Officer until 30 April 1982, when he resigned because of disillusionment. He has now been manufacturing manager for a US pharmaceutical company for many years.

10.64 Nicholls formed a fairly poor view of the way in which Bryn Estyn was run early on. There appeared to be no structure and poor managerial skills were evident. Arnold seemed to be counting the days until his retirement whilst Howarth was bullish and aggressive and Nicholls regarded Wilson as an out and out bully. The witness believed that the aim of Bryn Estyn was to rehabilitate and assist those boys who were in care, with a view to making a better future for them. Regrettably, however, owing to the lack of leadership and direction from the top, he felt that this aim was not achieved. There was a lack of proper organisation and there appeared to be no basic strategy on how the place should be run.

10.65 Nicholls worked throughout in the main building at Bryn Estyn and lived out. He had married in 1967 and lived with his wife and two young children. For the latter part of his period at Bryn Estyn, Howarth was away with ankle trouble and Nicholls reported to Len Stritch, the Third-in-Charge. His team leader at first was Robert Jones, until September 1981, when the latter started a two year CQSW course at Cartrefle College; and Nicholls then worked under John Rayfield.

10.66 The third member of this trio of rugby playing care staff was **Robert Jones,** who was only 24 years old when he began work at Bryn Estyn on 1 May 1978. His own recollection is that he began work there as an assistant houseparent in 1976 and this may be correct but the records before the Tribunal show that he was appointed as a houseparent from 1 May 1978 and promoted to senior houseparent from 1 June 1979. He had qualified as a physical education teacher in 1975 but had then worked on an oil rig in Scotland before being told of the Bryn Estyn vacancy, again by Cheesbrough. He saw Howarth for an hour and was telephoned two hours later with an invitation to start work the following week, initially in a temporary capacity for two weeks. As will be apparent, he had no prior experience, or training in child care work but he was seconded eventually from September 1981 to July 1983 to Cartrefle College for the CQSW course. On completion of that course he returned to Bryn Estyn until the end of 1983, when he was transferred to field social work for Clwyd County Council. He remained with Clwyd until 1987 and then secured employment in a higher grade in Shropshire.

10.67 Robert Jones also was critical of the Bryn Estyn regime. He thought that it was very restrictive and that the home was run like an approved school. Placements there seemed to be made with little consideration of the needs of the particular child or the character of the residents already there. They often involved children being far from their homes and were frequently made at very short notice with minimal warning. The result was that the residents of Bryn Estyn were an inappropriate mix of boys and adolescents with differing and conflicting problems. Bullying by boys varied but was endemic. A pecking order was part of the regime and it was seen as an overall means of control.

10.68 Whilst he was at Bryn Estyn, Robert Jones became particularly friendly with another member of the care staff, **Elizabeth (Liz) Evans,** with whom he shared a flat on the campus for a time. She had undergone teacher training at Cartrefle College with the intention of becoming a primary school teacher. Whilst there she had met Robert Jones and had visited him several times at Bryn Estyn with the result that she had become interested in care work. After working as a supply teacher in her home area of Mid Glamorgan she began work at Bryn Estyn as a temporary houseparent on 30 April 1979, when she was about to be 23 years old, and she became an established RCCO Grade 2 from 1 August 1979. Liz Evans remained at Bryn Estyn until late September 1984, when she was redeployed to a day care centre in Wrexham briefly before being transferred to Bersham Hall with effect from 15 October 1984. She remained there until September 1987, when she was seconded to Cartrefle College for a CQSW course; and, on completion of that course, she secured an appointment as a social worker from 4 September 1989 in Clwyd's Delyn area. She remained in the employ of Clwyd County Council until it ceased to exist and is now a senior social worker for Flintshire County Council.

10.69 Evans, who was rather less frank than her colleagues most recently named, accepts that Bryn Estyn may have been a frightening experience for some of the more vulnerable young people who were placed there but she does not remember an atmosphere of intimidation and was not aware of a regime of physical violence or a climate of fear. She was not given any training or specific instructions or any job description but she realised what was expected of her from her earlier visits. Her own method was to treat the boys with respect and she expected the same treatment in return. In some ways she found tasks were easier for her than for some men: for example, if there was a physical confrontation, she would call in a man.

10.70 In the context of the Bryn Estyn history as a whole, we have heard relatively few complaints of physical abuse by the four members of the rugby set discussed in this section. The other member, apart from David Birch who has already been discussed in detail, was David Cheesbrough and he is more appropriately discussed with the other teaching staff because virtually all the complaints about him refer to events after February 1978, when he transferred to that part of the staff.

10.71 In all, 15 of the witnesses whose evidence we heard (ten gave oral evidence) alleged some form of physical abuse by one or more of the four members of the rugby set discussed in this section, but we have not been persuaded that severe criticism of them would be justified. The overall tenor of the evidence has been that each one of them was essentially a decent person, who established a good relationship with the boys. If, on occasions, they over-reacted to a situation, the reaction was momentary and no physical harm was done. None of them, therefore, can properly be categorised as an abuser.

10.72 Only three witnesses made allegations against **Phillip Murray,** despite the fact that he was at Bryn Estyn for over six years. One alleged that Murray spanked him for throwing knives but he did not blame Murray for doing so. The latter's own recollection is that this was the only occasion when he smacked a child: the boy had thrown milk bottles at people during the dinner time so Murray had chased and caught him and then smacked him once over his trousers. They had got on "brilliantly" after this and the boy had visited him for many years after he had left Bryn Estyn. The other witness alleged that Murray had punched and kicked and jumped up and down on him in his dormitory probably after a bed-wetting incident when the witness had been verbally abusive to Murray, but he added "but strange thing is, he wasn't you know, he wasn't a bad guy really". He agreed also that he got on well with Murray: Murray just had bad teachers really and went with the flow. Moreover, the witness had given a different venue for the incident when talking to Dean Nelson, the journalist, so that his recollection of it appears to be faulty. Murray, on the other hand, denies that he ever assaulted the witness. Finally, the third witness spoke only in general terms in his written evidence of being punched and kicked by Murray and three others at Bryn Estyn (apart from Wilson) but he did not refer to any specific incident involving Murray.

10.73 Six witnesses complained of incidents in which **Anthony Nicholls** was involved and we heard oral evidence from three of them. One of the witnesses whose evidence was read was the victim of the forcible removal of a nose ring described in paragraph 10.47, said by Nicholls to have been carried out on Arnold's instructions and no further comment is needed on that. The first of the oral witnesses complained about being tipped out of bed by Nicholls and of having his head put into a lavatory bowl and flushed; he alleged also that Nicholls had incited him to fight the "top dog" of the time. But this witness commented "If you didn't cross him, he was a fair, decent man", and he said also that, despite his complaints he liked Nicholls because "he treated us like grown ups generally". As for the "top dog", who also gave oral evidence, his only complaint was that he had been grabbed by Nicholls after giving Murray "a load of verbal". Nicholls said in evidence that the "top dog" had thrown a knife at Murray and he had merely done what was necessary. He admitted also that it was a practice of his (known as "flying lessons") to tip recalcitrant risers from their beds but boys were not injured by this; on one occasion only a boy's pyjamas had been torn. He accepted a caution from the police in respect of the admissions that he had made to them about the bed tipping and his involvement in the nose ring incident.

10.74 We have no doubt that Nicholls did from time to time have difficulty in controlling boys when they were all assembled in the dining room because of his lack of training and experience, and this was confirmed by Murray, who was sometimes called in to help. Nicholls himself said that on one occasion he smashed a plate in order to regain control in the dining room. One witness alleged that on one occasion in the dining room, when a boy refused or failed to stop talking when ordered to do so, Nicholls threw a plastic topped chair across the room which struck the boy on the back of his head (the only other person who spoke of this in a statement to the police said that it was the previous witness himself who was talking and that he was struck by the chair on the shoulder). It may well be that an incident of this kind did take place, even though it is denied by Nicholls; if it did, it is regrettable, but we cannot be sure about the detail on the limited evidence before us. In any event there is no evidence that the victim, whoever he was, sustained any significant injury.

10.75 The number of complaints that we heard about **Robert Jones** was rather larger but the favourable comment about him was at least as strong as that in relation to Murray and Nicholls. It must be remembered also that it was Robert Jones who intervened twice in relation to assaults by Wilson and who pursued his complaint about the second incident as far as Geoffrey Wyatt[15].

10.76 Robert Jones enjoyed participating in outdoor activities with the boys and one or two of the complaints relate to minor incidents that occurred in the course of these. It is clear, for example, that on one occasion he was struck on the head by a paddle when canoeing and that he responded by ducking the boy who had wielded the paddle but he said that this was good natured and that there was mutual ducking. Other witnesses referred to occasions when Jones is alleged to have punched a boy in the stomach or on the arm or clipped him on the head and one referred to him breaking up a fight by "slamming" one of the combatant's head on the floor. The total number of these allegations, however, is very few and all appear to have happened either in horseplay or by way of fairly mild punishment. Thus, a witness who made many serious allegations about other members of staff at Bryn Estyn said only of Jones that he remembered being punched and kicked by him in the showers but that he, the witness, treated the incident as quite minor.

10.77 Robert Jones himself denied mis-treating any boy when he gave evidence and we have not been persuaded that he consciously did so. It is notable that, despite Wilson's allegation that certain members of staff would "sort out" a troublemaker privately[16], no former resident has made a complaint to the Tribunal that a member of the rugby set acted individually or with others in that way.

10.78 **Elizabeth Evans** would not require separate comment in this context but for the fact that her name was linked in the evidence with the rugby set and that she herself said that, if she was faced with a confrontation, she would call one of the men on the staff to deal with it. However, only one witness complained to the Tribunal of being dealt with in this way (he said he was given "a good smacking" and told "less of your lip to Liz") and only four witnesses mentioned Evans' name in the context of physical abuse. On the contrary, most of the witnesses who referred to her described her as a kind, caring and sympathetic member of the staff.

10.79 Of the complainants, one said that Elizabeth Evans had kneed him between his legs when trying to prevent him from going up to his dormitory, after he had been told not to do so; and another said that she slapped him when he had been smoking in class. The worst allegation, made in a statement by a witness who could not be traced when he was due to give evidence, was that she had once spat on him, on being called names by him, when she was helping Norris and others to place him in the secure unit after absconding. Finally, one other boy, who described her as a good care officer, merely said that she was one of the members of staff who had seen him being assaulted by Wilson.

10.80 In her evidence Elizabeth Evans made it clear that she disapproved of Wilson's conduct and said she thought that boys had reported him for it. She knew that Howarth was aware of his behaviour: there was a feeling that Wilson "led a

---

[15] See paras 10.19 and 10.29.
[16] See para 10.33.

charmed life" and she did not feel that she could report him above Howarth because she was too young and lacking in confidence. She had not actually witnessed any assault by Wilson. As for the other allegations, she denied slapping or spitting and did not think that her knee had made contact with the boy who was trying to go upstairs, but she probably had lost her temper with him.

10.81 We do not consider that there is any acceptable evidence of physical abuse by Elizabeth Evans and we accept that she was regarded generally as a sympathetic and caring member of the staff.

The teaching staff

10.82 We have already referred briefly to the teaching staff in describing the organisation of Bryn Estyn[17] and we deal with the failings of the educational regime in the next chapter. Some of the allegations of physical abuse, however, were directed at teachers and it is necessary to deal with them here.

10.83 The head of the teaching section from 1 June 1977 was **Maurice (Matt) Matthews**, who was appointed to the new post of second Deputy Principal (Education) from that date. It seems that, in effect, he replaced Brynley Goldswain[18], who had left the previous year. Matthews was 43 years old and had spent 13 years in the Royal Navy on leaving school. He obtained his Certificate in Education in 1970 and his most recent experience had been as a teacher of general subjects for three years at a community home with education on the premises (Danesbury) in Hertfordshire, which was a former approved school. Prior to that he had been employed for two years on educational assessment, with some teaching, in a remand home at Enfield. Whilst at Bryn Estyn he took a three year part-time course at Bangor University leading to a CSS, for which he qualified in 1982. On the closure of Bryn Estyn he was redeployed briefly as a supernumerary until his appointment as Officer-in-Charge of Cherry Hill community home from 1 November 1984; but he retired early on 31 March 1986, giving as his reason "certain inflexibility in the staff I inherited, which has made it impossible to carry out my duties in the way I would wish".

10.84 The most senior members of the teaching staff in post when Matthews arrived and who remained for a substantial period at Bryn Estyn afterwards were Norman Green, John Ilton and Gwen Hurst. **Norman Green** had been there from 1965 as the building instructor and he was in charge of an army cadet detachment at Bryn Estyn, ultimately in the rank of Captain, until he retired from the cadets on 24 September 1974. He remained at Bryn Estyn until the end of 1983 when he was redeployed to Clwyd's Shire Hall as a Residential and Day Care Officer.

10.85 **John Ilton** also joined the staff when Bryn Estyn was still an approved school; he was there from September 1972 until 31 August 1984, after which he moved to Bersham Hall. He had had a varied career in factory and office work before

---

[17] See paras 7.11 and 7.16.
[18] See paras 7.04 and 7.11.

obtaining his teachers' certificate at Cartrefle College at the age of 31 years in July 1971 after a three year course. He then had six months teaching experience at a secondary modern school. At Bryn Estyn he taught mainly english and mathematics to the older boys (15 and 16 years old) but occasionally taught other subjects including geography and art. In the mid 1970s he took a course in mountain leadership and between 1981 and 1983 a part-time course that led to an advanced diploma in the education of children with special needs.

10.86 **Gwen (Gwyneria) Hurst** had joined the teaching staff at the age of 32 years on 1 September 1975 and she remained until the end of 1983, when she too was redeployed to Shire Hall as a Residential and Day Care Officer and then as Under 8s Officer for the South Division at Wrexham, before retiring in March 1995 because of disability in her back. She had gained a teachers' diploma in speech and drama and a general teachers' certificate and had then taught in junior and secondary schools in the Wrexham area. She was employed initially at Bryn Estyn to teach art, craft and drama but from 1977 she began to teach residents who were in need of remedial education. She was also involved in assessment work from about 1979 when and as Bryn Estyn took over this role from Bersham Hall.

10.87 Members of the teaching staff who joined after Matthews and who figured quite prominently in the evidence before us were David Cheesbrough and Justin Soper. **David Cheesbrough** had been recruited as a temporary senior housemaster at Bryn Estyn from 13 October 1975 and had become established in the post from 31 January 1976; he lived in a cottage close to the premises from the end of that year. It was his first appointment on completion of his teacher training course at Bangor Normal College and he was then 22 years old. He transferred to the teaching staff on 4 January 1978, following an interview by a panel of five, when other short-listed candidates were interviewed; and he remained in that post until Bryn Estyn closed, whereupon he underwent further training before taking up an appointment at a Clwyd school for children with moderate learning difficulties, becoming Deputy Head of the junior school in September 1991. Cheesbrough told us that he taught general science at Bryn Estyn, emphasis being placed on basic skills but the notes that he produced show that he covered quite a wide range of subjects, including english and arithmetic. He was also much involved in outside activities, teaching physical education, running youth rugby activities and, for example, organising the annual sports day from 1978 to 1981 (if the notes of this are complete).

10.88 **Justin Soper**, who was interviewed by the same panel as Cheesbrough, was also a newly qualified teacher, having gained a Bachelor of Education degree and teachers' certificate after four years at Cartrefle College; and before that he had taken a two year course at Shrewsbury School of Art. He began work at Bryn Estyn on 1 June 1978 at the age of 26 years, after a successful second interview, and by that time he had worked for nine months as a temporary senior housemaster at a Dr Barnardo's voluntary home for children near Oswestry. Soper remained at Bryn Estyn until it closed in September 1984. His appointment was to teach his main subject, namely, art and craft, up to CSE[19]

---

[19] Certificate in Secondary Education.

level but, after about three years, he agreed to join Hurst in her assessment work, replacing a part-time teacher who had left. From then on Hurst and Soper operated as a virtually separate unit in Cedar House dealing with boys who were at Bryn Estyn for assessment or on remand and also teaching younger, smaller and less able boys who would have had difficulties in other classes. Soper puts the average number of boys in the unit at about 14 until the last 12 months, when it declined to about seven.

10.89 We should say at once that there is no basis for any finding that Goldswain, Green, Hurst or Soper were involved in the physical abuse of residents at Bryn Estyn during the period under review.

10.90 Although a small number of serious allegations of abuse were levelled against **Brynley Goldswain** in respect of the period before 1 April 1974, only minor complaints were made by two witnesses in relation to the following two years during which he remained at Bryn Estyn. One of these complaints was of slapping by Goldswain but no specific incident of this was mentioned. The other was that Goldswain had a practice of making boys run around the gymnasium in the evenings whilst he swung a bamboo cane around, catching unwary boys painfully on the legs, but other evidence suggests that quite a few of them enjoyed this activity.

10.91 The evidence about **Norman Green** was generally favourable: he was regarded by most boys as a good member of staff. We are aware of only one complaint against him, despite the fact that he was at Bryn Estyn for 19 years. That complaint was made by a witness who was at Bryn Estyn between 1977 and 1979 and who said that he did not attend Green's classes in bricklaying etc. because he did not like getting his hands dirty. Nevertheless, or perhaps because of this, he had the "odd tiff" with Green, who once threw a half brick at him. This is an allegation that must, at best, be dubious because it is common ground that Green took the witness to Matthews there and then and complained to Matthews that the witness had thrown a half brick at Green. The upshot was that the witness was not required to attend Green's classes and was transferred to work in the kitchen.

10.92 The strong general tenor of the evidence about **Gwen Hurst** was that she was a much liked and respected member of the teaching staff, who went out of her way to help the boys that she taught and who would invite some of them to her home when it was appropriate to do so. She was also heavily involved, outside her working hours, in youth club activities for the benefit of the residents and other local young people. The only complaints of physical abuse that we heard against her were (a) that she dragged a witness by his hair after he had misbehaved "in some way" and (b) that she had given another boy some "whacks on the head with a brush" one bonfire night. The witness to (a) said, however, that Hurst was "not a bad person" and it is clear that the alleged victim in (b) had been drinking and was giggling with girls whom he had persuaded to accompany him to the bonfire so that Hurst was apprehensive about what they might do. Hurst denies using any physical force and specifically remembers what happened on the relevant bonfire night. Accurate recall at this distance of time, however, is unlikely. We are satisfied that both alleged incidents were minor and that they do not detract from the overall high esteem in which Hurst was held.

10.93   We are not aware of any allegation of abuse against **Justin Soper**. He, too, was much involved in extra mural activities with Bryn Estyn boys, certainly in his first three years there. When he left he was given a memorable testimonial by Arnold, who said:

> "He is truly an individual person, he was the only member of the teaching staff who managed to cope with very unhappy children on a continuing basis. He rarely lost hope, and when others would be rejective, he could still see possibilities."

10.94   The main target of criticism amongst the teaching staff has been **John Ilton.** Many witnesses have given evidence of his excellent general character but there has been compelling evidence too that he was unsuitable for the work that he was undertaking in teaching mainly disturbed and recalcitrant pupils. In all, we are aware of 14 complainants who alleged assaults by him at Bryn Estyn: ten of them gave oral evidence before us and the statements of two others, now dead, were read. This is not a formidable body of evidence by itself, bearing in mind the length of the period under review, but we heard substantial evidence also from many other witnesses, including members of the staff that Ilton was, throughout his period at Bryn Estyn, a man with a "low fuse" who was liable to explode out of control when he was provoked.

10.95   Two recurring themes in the evidence have been, firstly, that it was Ilton's practice to throw the blackboard dusters or rubbers (of a conventional solid type) at any boy who was misbehaving and, secondly, that he would also throw objects used in his body building exercises. His hobby was weight lifting, which he would practice from time to time with weights kept in the next door classroom and the objects referred to were dumb-bells and weights. In his own evidence Ilton said that he would put on an act of temper, shouting, banging and throwing books off his desk. He would bawl out children, hold and restrain them and he threw chalk but he did not recollect throwing board dusters. He added that you could not throw a dumb-bell weighing 15 pounds or a weight ranging from two and a half to 20 pounds. Whilst recognising the difficult conditions in which Ilton often had to teach we were unimpressed by his account of how he sought to maintain order in his class. He certainly had a very loud voice, to which many witnesses referred, but we are satisfied that he went beyond use of this and flinging pieces of chalk as his daily practice. The volume of complaint about his use of blackboard dusters and weights has compelled us to the view that his disciplinary methods were unacceptable by civilised standards. He ruled his classroom by fear and his methods were unlikely to benefit rebellious and disturbed adolescents.

10.96   Unhappily, the allegations against Ilton have not been limited to shouting and throwing objects at his pupils. At least eight of the witnesses who gave oral evidence to the Tribunal described serious assaults by him on them and Matthews himself admitted that he had seen Ilton "clack" a boy on the head on two occasions. Matthews had said in a statement to the police that Ilton was a strict man, who was not afraid to "clack" a boy who was out of line. Matthews' view of the prohibition of corporal punishment was that it applied to the use of the "cane, taws, belt, strap" but not to "clacking"; and, until he was reminded of a 1974 Clwyd memorandum on the subject, Ilton's recollection (according to his statement) seems to have been that corporal punishment was available until 1987.

10.97 The general picture of the alleged assaults by Ilton was that he would lose his temper when provoked and then lose all control of himself so that he, rather than the provoker, had to be restrained. One former resident, for example, who had already lived in the Far East for five years before his admission to Bryn Estyn, said in a geography class that Ilton had been incorrect in some information that he had given about Malaysia or Singapore and had laughed at him. Ilton started hitting the witness with his fists and later kicked and chased him to (what appears to have been) Cedar House, where the witness took refuge in an office whilst two members of the care staff restrained Ilton. The witness said that he still had a scar on his lip from the attack and at the time had bruises on his back, legs and hands as well as blood on his face. Ilton had gone berserk and the witness never attended his class again. Another witness spoke of Ilton going mad with him because of something he had done in the classroom (in a portakabin): the witness tried to get out but he just remembers being on the floor and being unable to breathe because he was being throttled until Green pulled Ilton off. A third witness described a prolonged attack on him which began with Ilton pulling the witness' scarf around his throat tightly and ended up with him having a swollen jaw and loosened teeth.

10.98 Ilton, in his evidence to the Tribunal, denied all these allegations. Rather remarkably, he described his period at Bryn Estyn as marvellously happy and he had no criticism of any member of the staff there. Bullying was not prevalent. He regarded himself as very even tempered but he had the reputation of being a strict disciplinarian and he did not doubt that he had had confrontations with a lot of boys. It was not his practice to slap boys but he had slapped two in the face, one at Bryn Estyn and one at Bersham Hall, because both had been hysterical at the time. He distinguished "clipping" from slapping and accepted that he had clipped boys on occasions. More revealingly he said, "The boys at Bryn Estyn had been sent by the Court, they were anti-authoritarian, anti-school, disaffected, amoral". He could not recall any children being sent to Bryn Estyn who had not committed criminal offences and he regarded all of them as problem children sent by the courts; but he could not remember any of the boys being deeply disturbed emotionally.

10.99 It would be wrong to be too harsh in criticising John Ilton bearing in mind his lack of prior training in dealing with children with special needs and the absence of firm guidance and supervision at Bryn Estyn itself. Moreover, we do not discount his positive contribution in, for example, playing an active role in accompanying residents during the week and at week-ends on outside trips that they enjoyed. Ilton did, however, contribute significantly, by his lack of self-control, to the damaging effect for many of incarceration at Bryn Estyn.

We must infer also that some educational opportunities were missed for boys about to emerge from care because of his narrow, disciplinarian approach to his duties and his generalised assessment of the boys in his care.

10.100 **David Cheesbrough** has already been referred to as a member of the care staff until February 1978 and as an active member of the rugby set[20], who recruited some of them to Bryn Estyn. When playing for Wrexham he was scrum half in the 1st XV. In his case too we have read impressive evidence of his general good character and, in particular, his notable work for rugby in North Wales and as a teacher since he left Bryn Estyn. There has been favourable evidence also about him at Bryn Estyn. Various former residents said of him, for example, "He treated me well", "I got on really well with him. He was a fair chap" and (from one complainant about him) "He was one of the fairer teachers there"; and a teacher, who left Bryn Estyn whilst Cheesbrough was still on the care staff, described him as "quiet, mild mannered and mild tempered".

10.101 Nevertheless, we have heard some evidence of the use of manifestly excessive force on occasions by Cheesbrough and he was described by one complainant as "a big, violent bully". Furthermore, Matthews told the police in a statement that Cheesbrough (unlike Ilton) had a short fuse: "he would go all red and I would worry that he might have a heart attack", although he (Matthews) had no knowledge of Cheesbrough assaulting anyone. Matthews' office was next to the latter's classroom and he said in his oral evidence that Cheesbrough would lose his temper about twice a week: he would hear Cheesbrough shouting. But Cheesbrough himself said that he would lose his temper in "a controlled manner". To complicate the picture further, it appears that there was a period in the early 1980s when Cheesbrough and Ilton taught together in a team teaching experiment until the decline in numbers rendered the scheme unviable. In this experiment two classes, totalling between 16 and 20 boys, were combined under two teachers; one of the latter would teach and the other would go round the pupils helping with problems. Thus, both Ilton and Cheesbrough were involved in some of the incidents about which complaint is made.

10.102 In all we are aware of eight residents who complained in their statements of physical abuse by Cheesbrough, of whom four gave oral evidence to the Tribunal and the evidence of one, now deceased, was read. Two other witnesses made complaints about him that were not in their statements. The most specific of all the allegations related to an incident on 19 April 1983, which, unusually, was dealt with quite fully in contemporary documents.

10.103 The complainant (Z) in respect of this incident was then a youth aged 16 years, who had been admitted to Bryn Estyn on remand in October 1982 and whose stay was ultimately prolonged until 26 May 1983, when he was sentenced to a period of 63 days in a detention centre. The incident on 19 April 1983 occurred at about 1.30 pm and his signed account an hour later was as follows:

---

[20] See paras 10.43, 10.59 and 10.87.

"I was walking down by a surgery door, before I got their" (sic) "I saw a member of staff and called her a nickname known to the boys. Which she either took no notice of or didn't hear me; but Mr Cheesbrough did. He then came towards me and grabbed me by the neck of me and started to throw me around the corridors. I banged my head on the surgery door knob and on one of the pillars. He then grabbed me and threw me on to the baskets which started to slide back and then I fell down the two sides, he then threw me to the right hand side of the corridor, then Mr Arnold came along, and Mr Cheesbrough walked on taking his group to the gym. I went into surgery after I felt a bit better and Mr Arnold put some ice and cream on my head and neck. Then the doctor had a look and took my blood-pressure."

10.104   It appears that this statement was written by Z at the invitation of John Rayfield, the senior housemaster of the unit in which Z was placed, who acted on Arnold's instructions. Rayfield reported that Z did not wish to make an official complaint: Z was happy that the Director of Social Services and Arnold would receive his and Arnold's written statements. Z was seen the next day by Len Stritch and was reported to have stressed that he did not wish to make a complaint. In his oral evidence to the Tribunal Z confirmed the accuracy of his written account, subject to the qualification that he did not think that Arnold had come on the scene. Z said that Arnold was always in his office and that Z did not remember seeing him until the following day in that office. Z did add in his oral evidence that Cheesbrough's ring or a finger nail had caught him between the eyebrows, leaving a permanent mark, but this had happened as Cheesbrough had gone to grab him and was not the result of a deliberate punch.

10.105   Despite the qualification by Z, we are sure that Arnold did come upon the scene. In his own statement dated 19 April 1983 Arnold said:

"I was walking down the corridor past the kitchens when I noticed a boy lying against the corridor wall. Preceding me were Mr Rutter and Mr Cheesbrough. Mr Rutter followed a group of boys who were going to the gym. I asked Mr Cheesbrough what had happened and he said there had been an upset I assumed this meant that some boys had had an argument and possibly a fight. I therefore instructed Mr Cheesbrough to carry on with his group of boys, and helped Z to his feet and into the Surgery. He did not appear very upset, but rather dizzy. I laid him on the Surgery couch and examined him, and found that there were some mild abrasions round his throat and that there was a perceptible lump behind his left ear over the mastoid area. I bathed his face and neck and applied a cold water compress to the lump . . . I asked Z what had happened and he told me that he had been walking down the corridor, had referred to Mr Cheesbrough by a nickname and that Mr Cheesbrough grabbed him and threw him around."

10.106   It is clear that Arnold misunderstood what Z had said about the nickname, which was "sweaty Betty" and referred to a member of the domestic staff. Otherwise, Arnold's account appears to be reasonably accurate. The Bryn Estyn doctor was visiting that afternoon and made a note of his examination of

Z, who was referred to him on Arnold's instructions. Dr Wilkinson examined Z at 1.45 pm and found a haematoma half an inch in diameter immediately behind Z's ear and contusions on his neck and round the whole of his neck consistent with firm pressure from a twisted T-shirt. There were similar contusions also on both axillae (armpits).

10.107 Cheesbrough's own typed and signed account of the incident was forwarded to the Social Services Department a few days later, after he had consulted his union representative. That statement, which cannot fairly be summarised, read:

> "Whilst taking a small group of boys to the Gym, some group members began shouting vulgar remarks when passing through an area attended by female domestic staff. The boys involved were reminded of where they were, reprimanded and asked to keep quiet. As the group made its way to the Gym one of the boys shouted a rather crude nickname at a particular member of the domestic staff.
>
> Having just told the boys about their use of foul comments, I took the boy concerned, Z , to one side in order to give him a further reprimand. As I was doing this the boy continually tried to move away treating the whole episode as a huge joke. In order to make the boy realise that I was serious and since Z persisted in moving away, I was forced to try and make him stand still and accept my reprimand. I was forced to grab at his sweatshirt in order to keep him in the vicinity of the incident. The ensuing pulling and tugging as the boy tried to avoid a severe verbal reprimand resulted in Z's sweatshirt neck being pulled up and over his head. As the boy was obviously taking little notice and I could see some damage was being done to the boy's sweatshirt, I released my grip on it.
>
> As I turned to retrieve a ball I had been carrying, Z deliberately overthrew a kitchen trolley, knocking two wheels off it. When told to replace the wheels, he point blankly refused with a mouthful of verbal abuse directly outside an office used by female personnel. For the third time in a matter of minutes I reminded him of his use of language and repeated that I wanted the trolley picking up and the wheels replacing. Z was ranting on about his rights and what I could and could not make him do, affirming that the only way to make him do as he was told was to hit him.
>
> I pushed Z away from me against a pile of potatoes from which he rolled off and onto the floor. I then pulled him up from the floor and restrained the boy who was now acting hysterically and continually shouting abuse at me. As I continued to restrain him, Z threw himself onto the floor and remained there motionless. Suspecting the boy may have been feigning injury I pulled Z from the floor and placed him on a laundry basket in order to look him over. Within seconds Z rolled off the basket and back onto the floor.
>
> At this point I noticed Mr Rutter standing by, he asked if I needed any assistance with the supervision of the rest of my group, having said 'Yes'

I accompanied Mr Rutter to the back door in order to inform him who the rest of the group were. As I returned to attend to Z I met Mr Arnold who asked me what had happened, I told him there had been an upset, Mr Arnold went over to Z telling me he would take charge of the situation and said it was all right for me to join the rest of the group.

At the end of my supervision period I made a point of going to see Mr Arnold to find out what had ensued. He told me that Z had been examined by a Doctor and had abrasions around his neck and a bump on his head. He then told me that Z was now making a statement with Mr Rayfield and that he would give me a copy along with a copy of his own report later that afternoon. With that I returned to my class.

I tried to reprimand Z for his persistent anti-social behaviour and despite being severely provoked I did not throughout the incident hit Z with my fist or inflict actual bodily harm.

N.B. Earlier that day in a P.E. lesson in the gym, Z severely banged his head directly behind his left ear on a door jamb made of concrete, whilst trying to stop a goal. The boy seemed quite shaken and needed a few minutes rest before he could carry on with a lighter activity."

10.108 In his oral evidence to the Tribunal Z described Cheesbrough's explanation of what had occurred as "rubbish". He denied throwing a trolley or knocking wheels off it and repudiated the suggestion that the bump on his head was due to an accident in the gymnasium. Z said also that he had not wanted to make a complaint because Cheesbrough had to teach him. He added "I would like to state he didn't speak to me for about three days after that incident and I ended up apologising to him. I was stupid you know. I felt I had done something wrong".

10.109 Rutter's statement about the incident, made on 27 April 1983, did not throw any real light on the conflicting accounts because he merely said "As I approached I saw Z roll on to the floor". Len Stritch, however, made a statement that he had interviewed Z on 20 April 1983 "about the incident he had during P E on Tuesday morning 19 April 1983". Stritch said that Z had confirmed that he had knocked his head on the corner of the wall but had claimed that it was not the same bump that he had received later. Z had gone on to say that he had two lumps on his head. Stritch added that he had examined Z's head and had found it difficult to define two lumps behind his ear but had not pursued the matter because he knew that the doctor had examined Z after lunch the day before.

10.110 On the evidence about this incident itself and evidence that we have heard about a small number of other incidents at Bryn Estyn, we have very grave misgivings about the way in which the suggestion that Z had sustained a bump on his head during P E in the morning of 19 April 1983 emerged. Moreover, our misgivings are not allayed by examination of the daily log in which a senior RCCO had made a later entry referring to a bump in the gym, which followed a note by the Matron on her examination of the boy, which made no reference to the gym. The upshot of the matter was that Geoffrey Wyatt interviewed

Cheesbrough in the presence of Arnold on 9 May 1983 at Bryn Estyn. According to Wyatt's belated file note of this interview, he thanked Cheesbrough for his report and informed him that Wyatt accepted his explanation of the events and that "the matter was now closed".

10.111 Whilst we are fully aware of the difficulty of reaching firm conclusions about specific incidents that occurred many years ago, this is one instance in which we are able to do so. We are satisfied that Cheesbrough did react excessively to Z's insolence and that he seized Z and threw him around with the result that he sustained the injuries that the doctor noted. Moreover, there followed an attempt to cover the matter up with Arnold's complicity: the alleged bump in the gymnasium was much too convenient a coincidence and ought not to have been accepted by Wyatt without further reference to Z. In any event the nature of Cheesbrough's reaction had been such that, at the very least, a formal warning should have been given to him and appropriate guidance for the future.

10.112 The other allegations against Cheesbrough that we heard in evidence were much more general. Thus, one witness said that he had been punched, kicked and sworn at by Cheesbrough and others and that Cheesbrough and Ilton had once grabbed him by the arms and kicked him on either side of the chest but another witness, who alleged similar conduct by the two men towards him, said that it was only done in play and that he was never hurt. Moreover, the former witness said of Cheesbrough generally that "he was alright in the main but he could be heavy handed". Finally, a third witness said of him "He wasn't a bad guy. I was hit and kicked by him. Nothing drastic" and the deceased witness told of being chased by Cheesbrough with a cricket bat but described the incident as "horseplay".

10.113 These allegations do not provide the basis for a finding that Cheesbrough was guilty of deliberate or habitual physical abuse of residents at Bryn Estyn. He was young, large, fit and strong and we have no doubt that he was heavy handed from time to time. He was also, in our judgment, prone to losing his temper from time to time, on which occasions his reactions to misbehaviour tended to be excessive but these failings could and should have been eradicated by firm and sensible leadership; and we are not aware of any similar complaints against him after he left Bryn Estyn.

10.114 **Maurice Matthews** was a somewhat remote figure in the eyes of most residents at Bryn Estyn. His model railway hobby earned him the nickname "Choochoo". He spent much of his time in his office and taught only occasionally residents with special needs. At first he did all the educational assessments but Gwen Hurst took over some of this work and later it was done by individual teachers. It must be remembered also that between 1979 and 1982 he was taking the part-time CSS course[21]. He applied for another post in Nottinghamshire in 1980 and Arnold wrote of him then (on 19 May 1980):

"Mr Matthews has suffered somewhat at Bryn Estyn in that there are a number of very dominant and capable staff, both in care and education. This has made his task difficult, particularly in asserting his rightful

---

[21] See para 10.83.

position as Deputy Principal. His overall control of large groups of children, particularly when faced with a long spell of duty on his own, is not always of the highest, but he copes reasonably."

10.115 We heard evidence of three main allegations of the use of force by Matthews to residents. To his credit, and in marked contrast to other witnesses, he admitted each of them. The allegation by the witness involved in the half brick incident with Norman Green[22] was that Matthews slapped him when Green reported the incident and told him to go to work in the kitchen. Matthews' own recollection of the matter appears to be patchy but he spoke in evidence of talking the matter through with the witness, who showed some remorse. Matthews admitted slapping boys on the head from time to time and that he did so on this occasion.

10.116 Matthews admitted also grabbing another boy by the scruff of the neck in an incident that occurred on 7 November 1977, which was the subject of a report by Arnold to the Director of Social Services three days later. Arnold reported the matter because the incident had been observed by Clwyd County Council workmen and he thought that they might make a complaint about what they had seen. It is unnecessary to go into great detail about what happened. The boy involved, now deceased, whose statements to the police made in December 1992 were read to us, was a Howarth victim and did not mention Matthews. However, according to Arnold, the boy was upset about having to change from one teacher to another in the mid-morning and he became abusive and threatening, with the result that Matthews, in his office, heard the noise. When Matthews went out to investigate the boy started to run away towards the playing fields, whereupon Matthews "caught hold of his jersey to restrain and the boy voluntarily collapsed on to the ground, continuing to threaten and shout. Matthews restrained him, though in the ensuing scuffle he would be uncertain as to how he held or controlled the boy . . . As far as the boy and Matthews were concerned the incident rests there". In his evidence, however, Matthews accepted that his conduct had been "plainly over the top".

10.117 The third incident occurred much later and was also the subject of a report by Arnold to the Director of Social Services, by now, (Daniel) Gledwyn Jones, which was dated 6 December 1983. A former resident of Bryn Estyn who witnessed the incident told the Tribunal that a boy called Matthews "Chooch" at tea-time as he entered the dining room through the double doors. Matthews then went straight to the boy, who was sitting at a table, and punched him four or five times directly in the face. The witness alleged also that Matthews brought the boy's head down on to his knee and then pushed the boy back in the chair. Arnold, however, wrote of "some sort of physical confrontation with Mr Matthews". The matter had been reported first by Howarth, who had come across the boy wandering over the playing fields to cool off. He was subsequently interviewed by Rayfield and alleged that Matthews had "banged his nose" but had said that he had no grudge against Matthews and that he did not wish to make any complaint against him. Arnold's recommendation to the

---

[22] See para 10.91.

Director of Social Services was that the matter should be left lying with no blame attached to either party and that recommendation was accepted ten days' later.

10.118 We did not have the benefit of any evidence from the victim himself but Matthews admitted in his oral evidence that he had lost his temper, grabbed the boy and pulled him away from a table. He admitted also causing the boy's nose to bleed because it had hit a chair (in some unexplained way). It was put to him that he had committed an assault on the boy and that his behaviour amounted to "an excessive use of force" and he accepted both propositions.

10.119 The only other complaints against Matthews before us are (a) by a deceased former resident that he was "laid into" and punched all over by Matthews after breaking into the latter's classroom in order to get petrol to sniff and being found in the classroom doing so and (b) by another former resident, who was unwilling to give oral evidence, that Matthews was one of several members of staff who had punched or kicked him in unspecified circumstances. Matthews denies (a), however, and has no clear recollection of the complainant in (b) so that neither of the allegations can be regarded as proved.

10.120 We do not think that it would be right to characterise Matthews as an abuser of children on the basis of the three isolated incidents and in which it has been proved to our satisfaction that he used unjustified force. However, the fact that he felt able to do so when holding a very senior position at Bryn Estyn is a serious reflection on the general climate of the home. It supports the view that there was a grave lack of direction from the top and a regrettable lack of self discipline at times by some members of the staff.

The night care staff

10.121 We are aware of 15 former residents of Bryn Estyn who have complained of the activities of one or other member of the night staff at Bryn Estyn, who seemed to be largely a law unto themselves, working as they did alone, subject only to intervention by Howarth, if he was called upon. The evidence before us about the arrangements for the night care officers has been patchy but it appears that one only would be on duty at any one time. The night shift would usually last from 8 pm to 8 am and each night care officer was expected to work three shifts per week. Other care staff would go off duty at 10.30 pm and would not be on duty until 7 am or 7.30 am so that there was a long period each night when the night care officer was on duty alone.

10.122 The two night care officers employed at Bryn Estyn for most of the period under review were Arthur Stanley (Stan) Fletcher and Thomas (Tom) George Davies. However, a third man, John Ellis Cunningham, who had been employed as a temporary RCCO at Bryn Estyn from 13 June 1983 to 31 January 1984, was re-employed there as a night care officer from 22 March to 30 June 1984, due to absences of the other two on sick leave; and he then remained as an RCCO until 15 September 1984.

10.123 We have comparatively little information about **Stan Fletcher** because he died on 24 December 1992. He was thought by some residents to have been a policeman formerly and he was employed as a night care officer at Bryn Estyn from 22 April 1974 to 30 September 1984 but it seems that he was probably absent because of sickness for about the last six months of this period. Only three of the witnesses who gave oral evidence to us made complaint about Fletcher. The earliest in time, who was at Bryn Estyn for 20 months from September 1977, said that Fletcher "would not think twice about hitting you" and complained of being hit with Fletcher's torch and punched when caught by him with another boy in the foodstore. The second and third, who were contemporaries at Bryn Estyn about four years later, also complained of Fletcher's use of force. One said that he would "give you the torch over your head" and the other said that he was given "a good hiding" by Fletcher on returning after running away. The latter witness said that he could not avoid Fletcher because Fletcher opened the door for him and, as the witness got upstairs, Fletcher hit him all over the face and head with fist and open hand. We do not know, however, what Fletcher would have said about these allegations, except that we do know that he told the police in March 1992 that during the whole of his ten year period at Bryn Estyn he had never once taken part in nor witnessed any acts of violence upon any of the boys at the home.

10.124 **Tom Davies** was employed as a night care officer from 21 December 1976 to 25 October 1985 but was absent sick from 10 June 1984 continuously until his contract was terminated (he was awarded a life disablement gratuity by the DHSS from 22 September 1985 on the basis of 5% loss of faculty). The volume of complaints about Davies is greater than in respect of Fletcher but Davies in turn alleged that he himself was the victim of serious assaults by the residents[23]. In particular, he described a serious assault upon him by a deceased witness, including head-butting, on 9 June 1984, which (he says) was the direct and immediate cause of his inability to work and permanent disablement.

10.125 Tom Davies was taken on initially as a temporary relief night care officer, after being interviewed by Howarth and Nefyn Dodd, and his appointment was made permanent from 31 August 1978. When he started the work he was nearly 47 years old and he had had varied experience as a regular army corporal in the King's Royal Hussars followed by 23 years as a fitter for an aircraft company; but he had no experience of dealing with children in care. Tiresomely, he regards himself as something of "a card" and this does not help assessment of his credibility. He described himself, for example, as the "George Best of the competition in the angling world" and as "God on The Flash" and he said of his first night on duty at Bryn Estyn "All I could see was 54 Clint Eastwoods looking at me". Davies' manner may be a reason, at least in part, why two witnesses described him as a "nutter".

10.126 Davies' duties from 8 pm to 10 pm appear to have been rather ill-defined but 10 pm was bed-time and the residents were expected to settle down by 10.30 pm. They could go to their dormitories from 8 pm but Davies would on

---

[23] See para 10.128.

occasions play football with them. At 9 pm they were expected to change into pyjamas and were required to hand in their cigarettes and tobacco. Davies regarded it as one of his duties to prevent "kangaroo courts" being held in this period as a prelude to bullying but his principal and later duty was the counting of heads to ensure, as far as possible, that no one was missing. For this purpose he had to tour many dormitories, looking at each bed and ensuring that there really was a boy in it, unless his absence was for a known reason such as inclusion on Howarth's "flat list"[24].

10.127 It is in connection with Davies' counting of heads and his later duty to ensure that silence reigned that many of the complaints about him have been made. We are aware that there were 12 complainants about him of whom six gave oral evidence before us and the statements of two were read; and six of these referred to Davies hitting them, or seeing him hit others, with a torch. Davies himself denied these allegations, saying that a victim would be decapitated if struck with the torch that he carried, which had a 12 volt battery and a handle and torch front, "which drops on to the battery" and is then screwed in place.

10.128 The torch complaint is not one of the more serious complaints before us but it has been made repetitively against Davies and has been mentioned also against the two other night care officers, most seriously against Cunningham. We are satisfied that, in Davies' case, he did not wield it with the intention of causing any injury but we do accept that he used it, unwisely and misguidedly, to cause some pain in the course of his rounds, when he saw fit to do so. We reject the suggestion that this evidence has been manufactured by witnesses acting in collusion. In our view the strong probability is that Davies used the torch as the weapon in his hand to cause minor pain, usually in the victim's back. This was a means of reprisal to make a boy feigning sleep realise that his minor misdeed was known; and, on other occasions, the torch was used in rather foolish "horseplay", as one witness described it, or as a prank. It was said, for example, that he would crawl into the dormitory at night, thinking he was a commando.

10.129 We have heard more serious allegations against Davies to the effect that he punched one boy in the face three times, knocking the boy unconscious, and that he had no fear at all of "punching lads in the face, nose, whatever". It was alleged also by two of the witnesses that Davies was frequently drunk on duty, one describing him as an alcoholic and alleging that he had put a fire hose in the witness' bed. On the other hand, Davies described serious attacks that he himself had experienced. He said that he had been threatened by a boy with a knife during his first week at Bryn Estyn. He was convinced that on another occasion a boy had attempted to poison him. Most seriously, in the early hours of 9 June 1984 he had been subjected to a vicious series of assaults by a now deceased complainant, involving head butts and punches with both hands to his face with the result that he himself was unable to work for at least 16 months[25]. Davies also denied the allegations that he himself had used violence to residents of Bryn Estyn and that he had been drunk on duty. He

[24] See para 8.04.
[25] See para 10.124.

said that he was not a drinking man: he limited himself to two pints of mild beer when he did have a drink. Several members of staff gave evidence that Davies never came on duty drunk and some former residents also spoke well of him in their evidence, saying that they had never seen him assault anyone. Finally, even the witness who alleged that Davies had knocked him out described him as "a good bloke".

10.130 We have not been able to find any contemporary documents that throw light on these allegations and counter-allegations but it is clear that Tom Davies did cease work on 9 June 1984 in the general circumstances that he alleges. The account of that incident given by his alleged assailant to the police on 8 January 1993 was as follows:

> "Basically Tom Davies was alright but there was one occasion when I had a fight with him. This was when one evening we had gone to bed or at least were in our dormitories when he had gone off on his rounds and for his cup of tea. At the time I was in the dormitories known as Caradog. Since Tom Davies had gone off myself and the other boys had barricaded ourselves in our dormitory and had taken the handle off the front of the door so that he wouldn't be able to come in. When he eventually came back to our dormitory he couldn't get in but we subsequently allowed him in. The door was opened from the inside and because I was the nearest one to him he just picked on me and punched me to the head and face causing me to have slight bruising to my left eye and a cut to my nose. These injuries caused me some pain. I hit him back and I think he also had a bruised eye and a split lip. After this had happened he took me to the night office and we both got cleaned up and had a cup of tea when he just spoke to me as if nothing had happened. I am almost sure that Tom Davies would have entered this incident in the Daily Log Book. At this time I would have been about 15/16 years of age and it was about two weeks before I left Bryn Estyn . . . I cannot recall any occasion when Tom Davies would hit any of us with his torch."

10.131 That witness now deceased left Bryn Estyn on 12 June 1984 after being there for three and three quarter years continuously. In an earlier statement to the police, made on 14 April 1992, he had referred to seeing Davies in a corridor on another occasion when Davies was bleeding from the nose and mouth and there was blood running down the front of his clothing. It seems to be likely that this was immediately after the incident in which Davies is alleged to have punched a boy three times in the face and the suggested inference is that the boy had reacted by attacking Davies.

10.132 Our overall conclusion about Davies is that, over the relevant period of seven and a half years, he probably did succeed in establishing a reasonable working relationship with most of the residents in his care at night. He had no training, however, in how to deal with the more rebellious boys, of whom there were a significant number, and it was virtually inevitable that he should become involved in confrontations with them from time to time. Without a close supervisor to guide him it is not surprising that he became involved in some fights and that he was sometimes worsted by the older and fitter boys. The reality of the matter is that he should never have been employed as a night care officer in the circumstances that prevailed at Bryn Estyn. As it was, he used physical force inappropriately from time to time. Most of these violent incidents would have been avoided by an experienced, trained man but we do not underestimate the difficulties of his job.

10.133 **John Cunningham** was 35 years old when he first became a temporary houseparent at Bersham Hall in September 1981, after nearly 20 years' experience in heavy industry and a short period as a child supervisor at a Liverpool Education Committee boarding school near Mold. He served in all for about 21 months at Bersham Hall on successive short term contracts and then at Bryn Estyn from 13 June 1983 on a similar basis until 15 September 1984. As we have said earlier, he performed the duties of night care officer from 22 March to 30 June 1984, following a break from 31 January 1984 in his employment, and after his spell as night care officer he reverted to the work of an RCCO at Bryn Estyn. In the following years he was employed in varying grades as an RCCO at Chevet Hey, South Meadow and then Cartrefle until about September 1991.

10.134 Two complaints were made about Cunningham at Bryn Estyn and the first, by one of the deceased complainants, was about an incident in the early autumn of 1983, before he took over night care duties. In short, the complainant (X) and others were taken by Rayfield and Cunningham on a trip to Blackpool, where X and another obtained a tin of glue to sniff. They sniffed the glue at the pier and continued to do so when they rejoined the bus. When told by Rayfield to get rid of the tin, X said that he would do so in a minute, whereupon Cunningham told Rayfield to pull off the main street and stop the bus in a minor road. Cunningham then went to the back of the bus, opened the door, grabbed the complainant by the neck and head-butted him in the face, causing his nose to bleed. His fellow glue-sniffer, who admitted being extremely difficult at Bryn Estyn, confirmed this incident in his oral evidence but Cunningham denied assaulting X. His account of the matter was that X had been kicked out of the minibus by the other boys in order to prevent Cunningham getting at the glue. Rayfield told the police in April/May 1992 that he had no recollection of this incident but he identified an entry in the main school log dated 23 October 1983, which fixes the date of the incident but does not throw any light on it.

10.135 The other complainant (Y) gave oral evidence of an assault by Cunningham on 30 April 1984, about which we heard and read a great deal of evidence. Y (who had recently returned to Bryn Estyn) said that it was the first night that he had actually seen Cunningham, who came into the dormitory and charged him, grabbing hold of him and "whacking" him on the bridge of the nose, which started bleeding. Y picked up a butter knife and "stabbed" Cunningham twice but it just bounced off his belly.

10.136 This assault was witnessed by at least three other boys whose evidence was put before us. One, who gave oral evidence, said that Cunningham hit Y in the face with a torch and also saw him fighting with Y on the landing outside the dormitory. Another, whose evidence was read, also alleged that Cunningham hit Y in the face with a torch and that "his nose exploded, there was blood everywhere", whilst the third, whose evidence also was read, said that Cunningham punched Y in the face and that his nose was bleeding.

10.137 It is relevant to mention that this incident, which occurred at about 10.30 pm, followed a series of incidents the previous night and through the day in all of which Y was involved and "playing up". They included an incident involving Liz Evans when Y wanted to go upstairs, which has been referred to earlier[26]. Cunningham's own account of what happened at about 10.30 pm, as given in an undated statement made shortly afterwards, was that he had gone into the working boys' dormitory to check that they were all present. As he left he was abused verbally by Y, who came towards him with clenched fists and a glazed look in his eyes. Cunningham pushed Y back onto his bed, Cunningham having his torch in his right hand and a rolled newspaper in the other. He then left the dormitory and made his way onto the landing, closing the firedoor and dragging a chair to a position at which he intended to sit. He next heard the fire door open and saw Y advancing and shouting abuse, with a shelf board and a coat hanger, which Y threw at him. Cunningham managed to dodge these objects but Y picked up the shelf and tried to ram him with it, all the while mouthing abuse. Cunningham grappled with him to "physically restrain him" but Y's force as he lunged at Cunningham caused Y to go to the floor with his head between Cunningham's knees and with Cunningham's arms around his waist, and Cunningham's chin in the small of his back. Another resident called for Y to restrain himself, whilst other boys urged Y to overcome Cunningham. Y then stopped struggling, Cunningham released him and they both stood up. Matthews, who had been on the scene, had the shelf in his hands and urged the boys back into the dormitory. Wilson appeared on the scene and Y returned to his dormitory, not showing any sign of injury at that point.

10.138 Cunningham went on to say that after the corridor had been cleared and Wilson had put the shelf in a bathroom, Y had reappeared with a knife in his hand and blood coming from his nose. Cunningham had backed against a wall and Y had stood with the knife in his right hand, urging Cunningham to try and take it from him and shouting threats. However, Matthews and Wilson had come down the corridor, telling Y to drop the knife. At the second time of asking, Y had flung the knife at Cunningham's feet and had then swung a punch at him, which landed on his left check, before storming back to the dormitory. At Matthews' suggestion Cunningham had then gone to the night duty office whilst Matthews and Wilson patrolled.

10.139 When he gave oral evidence to the Tribunal, Cunningham said that he took full responsibility for the injury to Y's nose, but denied Y's account of how it had occurred. He said that he still could not remember the order of events. He had pushed Y's head down to the floor to restrain him but had not hit him with the torch: the sheer weight of it would have caused more severe injuries. Cunningham understood that Y's nose had been broken but it seems that it remained straight so that surgical intervention was not required.

---

[26] See paras 10.79 and 10.80.

10.140 We are anxious not to give undue prominence to this single incident but a number of further comments are necessary about it. Firstly, the police became involved and attended because Matthews telephoned them. Secondly, Matthews made a log entry about the incident which broadly tallied with Cunningham's account: it referred to Y's bleeding nose but did not explain it. Thirdly, Matthews stated in his log entry that, when he telephoned the police, his intention was that they should remove Y. As Arnold pointed out in his own report of the matter[27], however, the police would not have been likely to take into custody overnight in a police cell an already injured youth and it was Arnold himself who took Y to hospital for an examination. Fourthly, we are satisfied that Matthews was determined not to have Y back at Bryn Estyn and told Y's social worker that: Y was due to appear the next day at Abergele Juvenile Court and was remanded further for a fortnight to an assessment centre at Swansea, after which he was sentenced to a total of six months' youth custody for six offences. His social worker reported that, in the course of the journeys to and from court on 1 May 1984, Y had admitted threatening a night care officer with a plank of wood and a knife but had said that he had only done so after provocation by the officer, who had attacked him. Fifthly, Cunningham accepted in cross-examination that Matthews had probably told him that he would be sacked if he admitted hitting Y. It is to be noted that his statement shortly after the incident did not explain or account for Y's injury. He said that Matthews told him to write a report to "cover himself".

10.141 Arnold had been called to the scene soon after the fracas between Y and Cunningham and he wrote a very detailed report over three typed A4 sheets in length about the matter and the report makes disturbing reading. It was dated 8 May 1984 and it did reach the Department of Social Services, although not addressed, because it was referred to in correspondence much later. Arnold did not witness any part of the incident but he said "From my perfunctory review of the drama when I arrived at the School, there did not appear to be an 'open and shut' case where Y was totally to blame and Mr Cunningham totally in innocence". But he stressed that that was "an immediate on the spot decision" and "not a judgment made in reflective retrospect".

10.142 When Arnold saw him, Y was lying on his bed with a bloodied face and there were three other boys in the dormitory. Y said that he had been attacked by Cunningham and that he had retaliated and lost his temper. The other boys confirmed this broadly and one said that Cunningham ought to be charged. Arnold bathed Y's face and it became clear to him that Y's nose had been damaged, "largely across the upper bridge".

10.143 The police were in attendance but Arnold did not wish them to take Y away because he did not expect Y to be placed in a cell overnight in his injured state. Arnold feared that Y would lay a charge against Cunningham and that non-accidental injuries investigations would be begun by the police. According to Arnold, he had a good relationship with Y and it was agreed that he would take Y to the hospital casualty department. He said further in his note:

---

[27] See paras 10.141 to 10.143.

"When I took Y to Casualty we discussed that until the circumstances could be looked at by me, we would not tell the Doctor how the injury had happened. Thus the duty doctor accepted our story of a 'swinging door'. Unfortunately I was not able to proceed further as Y was removed from Bryn Estyn. When Joan Thomas informed me of Y's removal at the request of the Magistrates, our submission to the Doctor did not seem so sensible."

Later in the note Arnold suggested that Y's removal had been at the request of Y's father and his solicitor but, it is likely that Matthews' opposition to his return was at least as influential with the magistrates.

10.144 In the event Y did not lay any charge and Cunningham heard nothing more about the matter until 16 March 1992 when he was suspended from duty following his arrest by the police during their major investigation. Cunningham was then undergoing a training programme to enable him to help people with special learning difficulties. His suspension lasted over two and a half years (his status in 1995 is unclear) and he was not informed that a decision had been made to invoke the formal disciplinary procedure until a letter signed by the Director of Social Services (John Jevons) was sent to him on 25 March 1994. This prompted a protest by John Cooke, the branch organiser of UNISON, on Cunningham's behalf on a number of grounds, including an assertion that the Social Services Department had known as early as August 1992 that the Crown Prosecution Service (CPS) had decided not to prosecute Cunningham (the assertion was that the CPS had "agreed" with the police).

10.145 At that time in the Spring of 1994 statements were obtained from Y, Matthews and Arnold and statements by three other Bryn Estyn residents were seen. Eventually, Cunningham was seen with Cooke on 2 December 1994 by two officers on behalf of Clwyd County Council, who questioned him about the events of 30 April 1984. The outcome was that Cunningham accepted by letter dated 9 July 1995 a relegation under the Disciplinary Code on the footing:

(a) that an act of gross misconduct had been committed by him and that he had given conflicting accounts suggesting an attempt by him (and possibly others) to conceal such misconduct;

(b) that this was, on his own account, a single incident that had occurred ten years ago because of extreme provocation and was the only stain on an otherwise unblemished record.

Part of the agreed relegation decision was that Cunningham would not work in children's services nor would he have unsupervised access to clients of the Social Services Department. It was not until December 1995 or January 1996 that Cunningham was found suitable work, however, and he has worked since August 1996 as a route inspector for the Highways and Transportation Directorate.

10.146 Our conclusion is that both complaints against Cunningham were justified in the sense that he used excessive force to both X and Y on separate occasions in provocative circumstances. His explanation of the incident on 23 October 1983 is unacceptable and he has virtually admitted using excessive force on

30 April 1984. He was not a man who regularly resorted to force but he was ill-suited to work with difficult adolescent children as his later career at three children's homes confirmed. If either incident at Bryn Estyn had been investigated as it should have been, regardless of a complaint by X or Y, it is likely that Cunningham would have been redeployed, at least, to other work then. As it was, he underwent a needlessly long period of suspension and probably suffered more than he would have done if effective reporting and disciplinary procedures had been in place.

Other members of the care staff

10.147 The limited number of allegations against other members of the care staff can be dealt with more generally but it is necessary to mention two other residential care officers, Joseph Nefyn Dodd and Frederick Rutter[28], because they are prominent in later parts of this report.

10.148 **(Joseph) Nefyn Dodd** became a care assistant at an assessment centre for the physically handicapped at the age of 36 years, after working as a wireman, then for ten years as an operating theatre technician and two years as a foreman in a plastic raincoat factory. After ten months at the assessment centre he moved to Bersham Hall for nine months before being appointed a housemaster at Bryn Estyn from 1 August 1974. He remained at Bryn Estyn until 31 October 1977 but his stay there was interrupted by a year's course in 1975 at Salford College of Technology, at the end of which he received the CRCCYP and was promoted to senior housemaster. Dodd left Bryn Estyn on his appointment as Officer-in-Charge of Tŷ'r Felin and spent two months undergoing "induction" training before taking up his post at Tŷ'r Felin from 1 January 1978[29].

10.149 Whilst he was at Bryn Estyn Dodd earned favourable comment, in particular, for conducting Welsh classes as an adjunct to the teaching programme and also voluntary classes in musical appreciation. He was brought up near Wrexham in the mining village of Rhosllanerchrugog, renowned for its male voice choir, of which Dodd was a member; and he was also a Sunday school teacher. Two or three former residents spoke well in their evidence of him but six alleged physical ill-treatment by him of varying gravity, one of whom described him as "a right evil bastard". The forms of assault included a heavy slap across the face to a boy who had bowled a "bouncer" at him, allegedly unintendingly, narrowly missing his head; a blow on the back of the head for smoking whilst cleaning a staircase; repeatedly ducking a boy's head in a cold bath for bed-wetting; and giving a boy a severe "one off" beating with punches and slaps in the board room, throwing chairs at him and trying to kick him when he took refuge under a table possibly because the boy's parents from South Wales had complained of bullying. Paul Wilson[30] alleged that he witnessed Dodd on more than one occasion adopting behaviour that was either "cussed" or violent (throwing punches, using his fists) to residents of Bryn Estyn. Two residents complained also that, on being first introduced to Dodd quite separately, he

---

[28] See paras 2.07(8), 8.41 and 8.42.

[29] See paras 33.05 and 33.22 to 33.28.

[30] See para 10.32.

said intimidating words to the effect, "If you play ball with me I will play ball with you. But if not . . ." showing his fist or otherwise threatening physical retribution.

10.150 Dodd himself denied all these allegations but, in the light of all the evidence we have heard about him, we have no reason to doubt that he did introduce himself to the two witnesses in the manner they allege. He was indeed an intimidating figure then and he said later in his evidence, when speaking of the regime at Tŷ'r Felin[31], that he thought it only fair to explain to new entrants the consequences of any transgression. We are satisfied also that he did on occasions administer physical punishment to residents at Bryn Estyn with his fists and by slaps although the description of the "one-off" beating in the board room may have grown somewhat with the passage of time. These incidents certainly ought not to have occurred but it is even more regrettable that Dodd was to take with him to Gwynedd generally and to Tŷ'r Felin, in particular, his experience of Bryn Estyn as a mode of disciplining young people. He said rather revealingly in cross-examination that, when he was at Bersham Hall, he was told by staff there that there was a lot of physical abuse at Bryn Estyn, that staff continually struck children, and that he was surprised when he went to Bryn Estyn that he did not see evidence of that.

10.151 **Frederick Rutter's** earlier history has been summarised in Chapter 8[32]. At Bryn Estyn Rutter worked in the main building with the older boys under the leadership of Robert Jones and (in his absence) John Rayfield. He told us that he had no qualifications other than some training by Norman Green. In his own evidence Rutter acknowledged that two of his nicknames by the boys were "Butch" and "Nutter", which perhaps give a flavour of the man. One former resident described him as "a heavy drinking, hard hitting man". Nevertheless, the evidence before us about him at Bryn Estyn is rather tenuous and vague.

10.152 Quite early on Rutter suffered a set back because he was suspended from 12 January to 8 February 1983 on full pay pending investigation of an allegation by a 14 year old resident that Rutter had punched him on 5 January 1983. The suspension was imposed by Geoffrey Wyatt and on this occasion the police investigated the matter. However, the decision of the police when the investigation was completed was that no further action should be taken, "mainly due to the direct conflict of evidence"[33]. Rutter's suspension was lifted by Wyatt as soon as the police decision was known and in advance of formal notification. There was no separate investigation by the Department of Social Services of the "conflict of evidence" and the complainant had been transferred to Neath Farm shortly after making his complaint. When interviewed by the police on 22 January 1992 the complainant said that he had no complaints about the way he was treated by any of the staff at Bryn Estyn and that he had not witnessed any assaults on other residents at the home. He has not come forward as a complainant or witness before the Tribunal.

---

[31] See para 33.31.
[32] See para 8.41.
[33] Letter from the Chief Superintendent of North Wales Police to the Director of Social Services dated 14 February 1983.

10.153 Two witnesses gave oral evidence that they were physically abused by Rutter but there are difficulties about both of them. The first spoke only generally of being hit by several members of the staff on different occasions but he did not pinpoint any specific occasion when Rutter was involved and there is some doubt about the length of the period or periods when they coincided at Bryn Estyn. Moreover, he did concede that Rutter had reprimanded him for bullying another resident. As for the second witness, his most serious allegation was that Rutter kicked the plaster cast on the witness's leg, cracking the plaster, because he refused to play football. The witness said also that Rutter forced him to play football in the plaster to make the numbers up. But he arrived at Bryn Estyn on remand on 10 May 1982 and, according to his own evidence, was taken to Maelor Hospital within two days of his arrival because he had had an accident playing football before his admission to Bryn Estyn: the leg was then in plaster for six to eight weeks because a fracture had to be re-set. However, his log entries show that the leg was X-rayed on 12 May 1982 when a partially healed fracture was observed and the leg was then in plaster until 10 June, when the plaster was replaced by a tubigrip. Moreover, he was examined on 24 June 1982, by which time almost full movement had been recovered, all before Rutter's arrival at Bryn Estyn on 5 July 1982.

10.154 This last witness alleged also that on another occasion[34] Rutter put him over his legs in the laundry room, pulled his pants down and started smacking him, gripping his bottom, when he did so because someone had complained about being "picked on" by the witness but, in view of what has been said in the preceding paragraphs, we cannot be confident that this complaint is accurate or that the identification of Rutter is correct.

10.155 Even more surprisingly, another witness, whose evidence was read and who referred to "Rutter the Nutter" as violent and sadistic making numerous allegations against him, was at Bryn Estyn from 8 June 1979 to 14 June 1980, so that he left two years before Rutter arrived.

10.156 The limited other evidence about Rutter was general and to the effect that he would clip or punch boys on the head; one former resident said that he used force or violence on numerous occasions. We do not consider, however, that the evidence before us is sufficiently clear and specific to justify an adverse finding against him in relation to his conduct at Bryn Estyn. Arnold, in an otherwise complimentary appraisal of him dated 11 March 1983, wrote:

> "Initially he had difficulty in understanding that what could be done in a private establishment was vastly different. He is a man with great enthusiasm and found it difficult to accept that there were statutory rules and obligations which could not be contravened. Once we had passed through this initial period of uncertainty, and clear definitions had been given to him of the conditions under which he worked, he was able to realign himself in a positive approach."

---

[34] See para 8.42 for earlier reference to this allegation.

This commentary, in our judgment, does provide an insight into Rutter's conduct during the earlier part of his stay at Bryn Estyn prior to his suspension.

10.157 The allegations of physical "abuse" by **Howarth** and **Norris** were limited to two witnesses in respect of each and their complaints do not call for separate comment because they do not affect the general picture significantly and are trivial in comparison with the allegations of sexual abuse made against these two members of the staff. As for **Arnold**, one of the witnesses who gave oral evidence, had told the police of being smacked by Arnold on the back of the head on one occasion but he did not recall this when he gave evidence to the Tribunal and it is clear that the incident was trivial, if it occurred. Otherwise the Tribunal has not received any evidence of alleged physical abuse by Arnold.

10.158 We are aware that 12 other former members of the staff were named in statements to the police, in 11 cases by a single individual and in one case by two brothers. At least one of these complaints related to an incident outside our period of review; another failed to identify the alleged abuser except by a common surname, which was inadequate for the purpose; and all the allegations were such they did not require separate analysis, bearing in mind the overall scale of this inquiry and its terms of reference. In the event we heard evidence, live or read, from about half of these complainants but it is not appropriate for us to attempt to make individual findings about them.

Conclusions

10.159 Although we have been restrained in our criticisms of inexperienced and untrained individual members of the staff, the overall picture of physical abuse at Bryn Estyn is bleak. Paul Wilson was obviously a rogue elephant on the staff, as we have found, and he should have been identified as such and removed early on. But it would be quite wrong to heap all the blame upon him. Our general finding is that there was an excessive use of force in day to day contact between the staff and residents of Bryn Estyn as well as in disciplining the residents. Bullying by peers was also commonplace and was accepted by staff, at least to an inappropriate extent, as part of a means of control, based on recognition of successive "top dogs". Thus, violence was endemic in the system and it persisted, whether or not it was inherited initially from the approved school regime. Moreover, its continuance was encouraged by (a) the reluctance of residents to complain because they did not believe that anything would be done about it and fear of reprisals, including the likelihood of a worse placement if the matter was pursued; (b) the equal reluctance of staff to complain about each other; (c) the cult of silence, with which we deal in the next chapter, and the positive covering up of unpleasant incidents when they occurred and (d) the readiness of Arnold (and those above him, as we discuss later[35]) to adopt the least embarrassing action in respect of staff about whom complaints were made and the apparent indifference to the best interests of the child.

---

[35] See paras 29.49, 29.50 and 30.15 to 30.30.

10.160 The broad picture that we have received is that there was a regrettable and alarming lack of effective leadership by Arnold throughout. Similarly, there was grave fault on the part of Howarth because he accepted (readily, as we understand it) responsibility for the day to day running of the home throughout the ten-year period, except during the months when he was disabled. Matthews also bore substantial responsibility from 1977 and must shoulder part of the blame. In the absence of clear directions and guidance, and without meaningful discussion of disciplinary and allied issues at staff meetings, members of the care and teaching staff were left to make up their own rules to an impermissible extent. We are very fully aware of the problems that they faced in looking after and controlling a substantial number of rebellious boys and adolescents in unsuitable premises that could not readily be adapted to cater for smaller and more manageable groups. But the obvious existence of these problems underlined the need for effective management and close supervision within Bryn Estyn itself of the largely untrained staff. Instead, a policy of drift appears to have been adopted, accompanied by increasing disillusion as numbers declined, and Arnold's reports to the Management Committee gave only occasional hints of the unsolved problems that he faced.

10.161 If the required leadership had been given and appropriate disciplinary action taken against any member of staff who transgressed, we believe that physical abuse of residents at Bryn Estyn could have been eliminated quite quickly. Similarly, bullying by residents could have been reduced substantially. Whilst both persisted, however, the regime was a travesty of what the care system should have provided and there could be little recognition of the needs of the resident boys as individuals, even though many of them may have considered that they were able to survive relatively unscathed.

Other aspects of the Bryn Estyn regime

11.01 Earlier in this report we have concentrated upon the evidence of sexual and other physical abuse but before leaving the subject of Bryn Estyn, it is necessary for us to comment upon certain other aspects of the regime there, which, in our judgment contributed to the abuse of residents there in a wider sense. The first of these is the cult of silence or cover up, to which we have referred earlier but which needs to be underlined further because of its importance for the future. Secondly, we need to deal briefly with the use of the secure unit. Thirdly, we must comment upon the educational aspects of the regime. Fourthly, there are the twin problems of recruitment and training of staff. Fifthly, we must consider more generally the extent to which the arrangements at Bryn Estyn failed to meet the needs of a child in care as described in the White Paper "Children in Trouble"[1] before making some concluding observations.

The cult of silence

11.02 It will be apparent from what we have said already in Chapters 8 and 10 that there was no recognisable complaints procedure at Bryn Estyn throughout the period under review. Many residents no doubt understood that they could complain, for example, to a parent or their field social worker or an approachable member of the staff, but the perceived disincentives for doing so were numerous and substantial and none of the residents that we have heard thought that anything positive to their benefit would result from a complaint. Despite this some complaints were made and we have sought to illustrate in the preceding narrative how these were suppressed in some instances[2] or dealt with ineffectually on the few occasions when a complaint was brought to the attention of headquarters[3]. Moreover, similar results ensued when a member of the staff made a complaint or witnessed an assault on a resident[4].

11.03 The most usual way in which potential complaints were suppressed was by an interview with the complainant, often on the direct instructions of Arnold, in which the complainant would be asked if he wished to pursue an official complaint and told of the likely adverse consequences for himself and the relevant member of staff if he did so. This was generally sufficient to persuade the complainant to withdraw. The procedure is well exemplified in a document dated 3 September 1981, signed by a complainant, which reads as follows:

> "3-9-81
>
> 'A'
>
> In the presence of Mr Norris and Miss Jones, A, who had initially made a complaint, regarding a member of staff, the previous evening was

---

[1] See paras 3.06 to 3.10.
[2] See paras 10.21 to 10.23, 10.26, 10.27 and 10.47 to 10.49.
[3] See paras 10.15 to 10.18, 10.20, 10.24, 10.116, 10.117.
[4] See paras 10.19, 10.28, 10.29, 10.75, 10.97, 10.103 to 10.111, 10.134, 10.135 to 10.144, 10.149.

asked to consider all aspects, before he made an official complaint, after due consideration A stated he knew exactly what he was doing and proceeded to make the following statement.

'While on a van ride with Mr Wilson, A with B and C took a short cut back to the van, they joked that they that (sic) beaten him back. Someone (A stated not himself) had been throwing stones at Mr Wilson and he proceeded to kick A in the leg. When in the van with all the boys, D was blamed for the throwing the stones, and "thumped" by Mr Wilson. A added that E was also hit.'

(signed) A"

A's evidence to the Tribunal, was that, despite his decision to proceed with the complaint, he heard nothing more about it.

11.04 It is, of course, understandable that Arnold should have wished to avoid official complaints against members of his staff unless they were soundly based but the means that he adopted to this end were, in our judgment, thoroughly discreditable. If the validity of a complaint was to be discussed before it was made official, he should have undertaken the task himself. Instead, he chose to delegate it to others when he must or should have known that the effect upon a child complainant was likely to be intimidatory.

11.05 It is clear that suppression of complaints did not end there. Thus, Arnold himself, on the evidence before the Tribunal:

(a) threatened staff with dismissal if rumours about Howarth's conduct in relation to the flat list were spread or fostered, without apparently making any investigation of them himself[5];

(b) protected Wilson from effective disciplinary action despite repeated complaints about him[6];

(c) condoned the practice of making neutral, uninformative entries in log books when injuries occurred[7];

(d) provided false information to a casualty department when a violent incident in which Cunningham was involved occurred and sought to avoid any investigation of the incident by the police[8]; and

(e) accepted any decision by the police or the CPS not to prosecute a member of staff as conclusive without making his own investigation or considering what remedial action might be needed in relation to that member of staff or more generally.

11.06 It is not surprising in these circumstances that there was no discernible improvement in the Bryn Estyn regime during Arnold's tenure of the headship and that the complaints that have now been made to the Tribunal span the full

---

[5] See paras 8.13 and 8.14.
[6] See paras 10.26 and 10.27.
[7] See para 10.28.
[8] See para 10.143.

period from 1974 until Bryn Estyn closed. There was little that visitors could learn about the real quality of life there from reading log books or talking to staff or even talking to residents; and no lessons were learnt from the very high level of absconsions because the reasons for them were not investigated in depth. Without open and genuine complaints and "whistleblowing" procedures accompanied by continuous monitoring and reappraisal of the community home's organisation and regime, it was always unlikely that such an institution would achieve the objectives that Parliament had in mind when it enacted the Children and Young Persons Act 1969.

The use of the secure unit

11.07 This unit did not figure prominently in the lives of residents at Bryn Estyn but there were quite frequent references to it in the evidence before us and a few complaints about its use so that some comment about it is necessary.

11.08 As we have said in paragraph 7.15 of this report, the unit was ready for opening in November 1979, seven months later than had been envisaged. At that time Arnold was on sick leave and it was Howarth who reported correctly to the Management Committee on 16 November 1979 that the Welsh Office had granted permission for the unit to be opened. The permission had been granted in a letter dated 26 September 1979 from T G Davies on behalf of the Secretary of State to the Chief Executive of Clwyd. The letter approved the use of the secure units at both Bryn Estyn and Bersham Hall and the only conditions imposed in relation to the former were:

> "a. the secure accommodation was only to be used in accordance with Regulation 11 of Community Homes Regulations 1972;
>
> . . .
>
> c. the maximum number of residents to be accommodated at any one time at Bryn Estyn is 8."

Attention was drawn in the letter, however, to Welsh Office Circular 39/75, which discussed secure accommodation in community homes generally in the context of Regulations 11 and 12 of the 1972 Regulations. The restrictions imposed on admissions to a secure unit and the periods during which a child in care might be detained in the unit were not spelt out but there was a short section on admission in which reference was made to Regulations 11 and 12 as the governing provisions.

11.09 It has been suggested in the evidence before us that some further approval of the Secretary of State was required before the secure unit could be opened and that such further approval was never given so that the unit was never put into operation as a secure unit. But no satisfactory explanation of this has been given to us by the Welsh Office or anyone else. The Welsh Office witness, David Evans, until recently Chief Inspector of the Social Services Inspectorate for Wales, said in evidence that the further approval was needed on confirming that the stated conditions had been fulfilled but we are unable to reconcile this with the terms of the letter dated 26 September 1979.

11.10 The policy of the Welsh Office from 1 April 1973 was to give general, rather than individual, approval to existing secure accommodation already in use, for a period of 12 months[9]. This was extended for a further 12 months from 1 April 1974[10] and again from 1 April 1975. It appears from Circular 39/75, however, that the process of giving individual approvals for pre-1973 accommodation was to be completed by 1 April 1976 and thereafter individual approvals were to be needed for all secure accommodation. None of these documents, however, suggest that the grant of approval was being effected in two stages.

11.11 When Howarth reported to the Management Committee in November 1979, he presented a paper outlining the proposed use of the secure unit. Under the direction of Arnold and Howarth there were to be 12 staff, comprising a Warden, seven Grade V houseparents, three Grade II houseparents and one full time domestic. It seems also that Len Stritch had been appointed as Warden and had attended a one week course for that purpose; and three other volunteer members of staff had been allocated to the unit for part of their working hours. Howarth's paper, however, envisaged a much wider use of the secure unit than was permitted by the Regulations and, remarkably, there was no discussion of this point by the Management Committee or of its own duties and powers in relation to the unit.

11.12 Subsequent developments in the unit remain something of a mystery. The "official view" seems to be that it was never put formally into operation because the financial resources to employ the additional staff envisaged were not forthcoming. But we have not discovered any documents to throw further light on the matter. Moreover, contrary to the official view just quoted, Arnold appears to have thought that the unit was in operation, at least for some months, because he reported to the Management Committee on 16 May 1980 that the unit was being used on a very limited level[11].

11.13 There has been conflicting evidence before us of the actual use of the secure unit from November 1979 onwards. The evidence of the members of staff has been that it was never used as such but that it was used, unlocked, for a variety of convenient purposes from time to time. It was used for dining, for example, when the usual dining room was being re-decorated and at Christmas to provide a better atmosphere for the small number of residents who were not able to have home leave. It is probably conceded also that it was used to detain more conveniently for short periods, measured in hours, some persistent absconders and glue sniffers who were out of control.

11.14 Seven of the complainants whose evidence is before us said that they had been locked in a room in the secure unit. One of them, whose evidence was read, was at Bryn Estyn from June 1981 to August 1982 and claimed that he had been locked in for 12 days on Arnold's instructions, and allowed only one piece of bread and one glass of water daily, because he had been overheard by a housemaster discussing running away with another boy. He said that he was

---

[9] Letter dated 15 March 1973 from P J Hosegood to the Clerks of Counties and County Boroughs (Wales), Circular 69/73 dated 15 March 1973.

[10] Circular 55/74 dated 13 March 1974.

[11] See para 7.15.

passed some school work whilst he was in there but that he was not allowed out. One other witness said that he had been detained for five days for absconding and, on another occasion, for one or two days for glue sniffing; a deceased former resident alleged that he had been locked in the secure unit for a couple of days after living rough for two or three months; and a live witness spoke of detention for two days for a similar reason. The remaining complainants about this spoke mainly of detention for hours, for example, when drunk and after petrol sniffing or of being threatened with the secure unit. But a number of these did complain also of being struck when in the unit by the person who had taken them there.

11.15 We think that the claim to have been detained for 12 days on bread and water is probably exaggerated, although we did not have an opportunity to assess the witness in person. The other evidence on this topic was, however, reasonably credible in the main. We accept that residents were on a few occasions locked in a room and, regrettably, that a small number were physically chastised there. On the footing that the secure accommodation had been approved by the Secretary of State there were probably very few breaches of Regulation 11(2) of the Community Homes Regulations 1972 and those that did occur were marginal; but we do not condone the physical chastisement that accompanied it on occasions.

11.16 In the event approval of the secure units at both Bryn Estyn and Bersham Hall was withdrawn by the Secretary of State by a letter dated 1 July 1983, the material part of which read as follows:

> "Recent discussions with representatives of Clwyd Social Services Department have indicated that the approved secure suites at Bersham Hall and Bryn Estyn Community Homes are not in use, and that there are no plans to bring them into use in the foreseeable future. As you will appreciate it is not possible to continue with their registration as secure accommodation in the absence of a staff and management policy. In the circumstances, with effect from the date of this letter the Secretary of State withdraws his approval given in our letter of 26 September 1979."

11.17 There are a number of disturbing features about this history. Thus:

(a) The persisting confusion as to whether or not the secure unit had been approved is astonishing.

(b) The Management Committee appear to have failed throughout to consider the status of the secure unit, its proper use and, most importantly, their own powers and duties in relation to it.

(c) It is not at all clear whether members of staff thought that they were acting lawfully in making use of the secure unit as they did (and, if so, under what powers); and it is equally unclear whether or not Arnold himself expressly authorised each admission.

(d) No guidance appears to have been given by Arnold about the use of the secure unit and it seems that he did not consider it to be necessary to consult the Management Committee or to ask for legal advice.

11.18 This type of confusion was by no means unique to Bryn Estyn. In February 1981, the report of a DHSS internal working party entitled "Legal and Professional Aspects of the Use of Secure Accommodation for Children in Care" was published. In that report the working party discussed the many ambiguities in the legislation and uncertainties in the profession about the proper use of secure accommodation; and it drew attention to some of the many changes that had occurred since the Children and Young Persons Act 1969 and the Community Homes Regulations 1972 had come into force.

11.19 Whereas there had been approximately 150 secure places within the child care system in 1971, mainly in three large regional units, it was expected that the number would exceed 500 by the end of 1981; and new units were being built in observation and assessment centres rather than community homes with education on the premises because of the phasing out of remands of juveniles to prison establishments. There was considerable variation in the way community homes made use of their "secure units" and the working party commented:

> "Persistent absconders may be contained in a secure unit on the principle that 'you cannot treat them if they are not there'. Some research[12] has shown, though, that children who abscond are frequently running away from unsatisfactory institutions, and it may be appropriate to review the system of care in the open unit rather than relying heavily on secure accommodation for absconders. The use of secure units must therefore be in the context of sound child care practice elsewhere in the community home system."

11.20 Much of the report was devoted to technical legal discussion of the extent of a local authority's powers at that time to restrict the liberty of a child in care and the limited legal safeguards available to such a child. It is unnecessary to repeat the discussion here because the report led to radical revision of the statutory provisions. A new section 21A of the Child Care Act was introduced by section 25 of the Criminal Justice Act 1982 and then quickly replaced with effect from 1 January 1984[13]. Concurrently the Secure Accommodation Regulations 1983 were just brought into force and then replaced from 1 January 1984 by the Secure Accommodation (No 2) Regulations 1983.

11.21 The effect of the new provisions in broad terms was that from 1 January 1984 the criteria which had to apply before a child in a community home might have his liberty restricted were that:

(a)(i) he had a history of absconding and was likely to abscond from any other description of accommodation; and

(ii) if he absconded it was likely that his physical, mental or moral welfare would be at risk; or

(b) that if he was kept in any other description of accommodation he was likely to injure himself or other persons.

---

[12] Locking Children Up-Milham *et al* – Saxon House 1978.
[13] By Schedule 2 para 50 of the Health and Social Services and Social Security Adjudications Act 1983.

Moreover, it was expressly stated to be unlawful for the liberty of a child in a community home to be restricted, no matter how short the period in security, unless the criteria were met. This last general provision was made subject only to limited exceptions in respect of children charged with or convicted of certain serious offences or previously convicted of an offence of violence, to whom modified criteria applied, and children detained or accommodated under the legislation specified in Regulation 6.

11.22 In general also, no child to whom the new section 21A of the Child Care Act 1980 applied was to have his liberty restricted for longer than 72 hours consecutively or in aggregate in any consecutive period of 28 days (subject to minor extension in specified circumstances). Thereafter any extension of the period had to be authorised by a juvenile court, which might authorise extension of the period by a maximum of three months on a first application (and further periods up to six months on subsequent re-application).

11.23 A final word needs to be said in this section about the further confusion introduced by the concept of "semi-secure accommodation," referred to by David Evans[14] as anathema to him. The term "semi-secure" was used in the Regional Plan for Wales in the context of the provision to be made for children requiring assessment. One of the categories, B, was stated to comprise "children needing semi-secure assessment" and they were defined as "children who are malfunctioning in some but not all aspects of their lives, and whose environmental circumstances are such that this malfunctioning aspect precludes assessment unless the child is removed from her/his environment". This was further explained at an early meeting of the Children's Regional Planning Committee for Wales[15] on the footing that "If we accept that secure conditions depend on high staff ratio, then semi-secure can be defined in terms of lower staff ratio and all that this implies - greater degree of individual freedom, more use of outside facilities etc. Physical restraints would be non-existent or minimal".

11.24 Unfortunately, the term came to be used loosely in a wholly different context and without any official definition. It came to be regarded at Bryn Estyn as a description of the secure unit on the assumption, some time after May 1980, that its use as a secure unit had not been approved by the Secretary of State. Thus, on this view, the secure unit could be used for restricting a resident's liberty if it was used as "semi-secure accommodation" with or without an individual's room being locked, provided that the unit as a whole was not locked. In our judgment this was erroneous thinking, undermining the safeguards intended to be provided by the legislation and exemplifying the lack of appropriate and coherent control over disciplinary matters at Bryn Estyn. For the future, it is to be hoped that the terminology will be shunned because of the confusion that it may cause. Furthermore experience of its use and the practice at Bryn Estyn underlines yet again the need for a clear code of practice governing the punishment and physical restraint of residents in community homes.

[14] See para 11.09.
[15] Minutes of the Children's Regional Planning Committee for Wales for 1970/1971.

11.25 Annex B to Welsh Office Circular 63/83, which gave guidance on the application of the new statutory provisions taking effect on 1 January 1984, stated[16]:

> "The following forms of the restriction of the liberty of children in care will not be permitted except in accommodation approved for use as secure accommodation by the Secretary of State:
>
> a. The locking of a child or children in a single room at any time, even when accompanied by a responsible adult or adults;
>
> b. The locking of internal doors to confine a child or children in a certain section of a home, even when accompanied by a responsible adult or adults."

The quality of education

11.26 Teachers at Bryn Estyn estimate that between 500 and 600 boys passed through their hands between 1974 and 1984 and this may well be an under-estimate. But we know of only one who has expressed a degree of satisfaction with the educational arrangements; he said that the education was not too bad; it was of a fairly good standard but he dealt with only one teacher, namely, Gwen Hurst. All the other complainants who were asked about the matter were severely critical. They said, for example:

> "all I was doing was reading a book and colouring in";
>
> "received no education other than painting and decoration";
>
> "didn't learn at all";
>
> "used to ask to go to school but no notice taken";
>
> "attended a minimal number of classes - after a couple of months put to work in the gardens";
>
> "learned nothing";
>
> "attempted to attend local school in order to take GCE but was not allowed to";
>
> "lack of education was part of the culture at Bryn Estyn - working in the gardens was part of the education."

11.27 This dismal picture did not apply to all the children who passed through Bryn Estyn. It is likely, for example, that a significant number of children who needed remedial education received substantial help from Gwen Hurst and Justin Soper. But very many others, particularly those who were emotionally disturbed at the time, some of whom gave live evidence to us, received virtually no educational benefit from their stay at Bryn Estyn and had to make up for lost opportunities in later years, if they had sufficient character to do so. It seems that, during the period of our review, only one Bryn Estyn resident,

---

[16] At Para 2.

a Howarth victim, was permitted to attend a local school because of his potential; but the boy cited above who was not allowed to attend a local school has since obtained a university degree in his mid-thirties.

11.28 According to Matthews, who became head of the education department from 1 June 1977, there was no curriculum at the school before 1978. He described it as a trade department establishment for painting, decorating, building, carpentry and gardening. Fortunately, however, the Parliamentary Under Secretary of State for Wales, Barry Jones, who is and was Member of Parliament for a Clwyd constituency, had visited Bryn Estyn on 9 January 1976 accompanied by the Director of Social Services and two Welsh Office SWSOs[17]. Whereas the SWSOs who had made the three previous inspections[18] had expressed concern about the washing and lavatory facilities at Bryn Estyn, Barry Jones drew attention to the fact that "full advantage was not (being) taken of the educational provisions at the home", although he did note that "Social Work Service Officers believe the Headmaster and staff are doing a fine job". The result was that Jones asked for a joint visit by the Social Work Service and HMI[19] to be arranged urgently. This request seems to have highlighted the need for a survey of CHEs[20] in Wales "to assess the organisation and effectiveness of the education provided in relation to the total living situation".

11.29 The joint visit to Bryn Estyn by an HMI and an SWSO took place on 30 March 1976. The SWSO noted "that staff/boy relationships as observed were friendly and the climate of the school was relaxed and without tension". However, the joint recommendation was that the Directors of Social Services and Education should consult together to ensure that teachers were given guidance and advice about the curriculum and to ensure that teachers in the CHEs, under the Social Services Departments, were not deprived of the opportunity to attend courses arranged by the Local Education Authority (LEA). They further recommended that young teachers in their first years of teaching, should not be appointed to these schools.

11.30 The document presented by David Evans containing this information[21] makes the comment, "There is nothing in these papers to suggest that these recommendations were followed". The SWSO, G W Smith, did follow the matters up, however, and it was noted that the Education/Social Services Liaison Group was to press for teaching staff at Bryn Estyn to have the opportunity to attend LEA courses. It was stated also that, on the departure of Goldswain, Arnold had become more actively involved in the operation of the school curriculum; there had also been some re-planning of the time table to include more general subjects.

11.31 A follow-up visit by Smith and the same HMI, John Garrett, took place a year later on 24 March 1977. On this occasion they spent some time talking to Arnold, when they considered the educational and daily programme for the

---

[17] Social Work Service Officers.
[18] On 14 May 1974, 17 July and 18 November 1975.
[19] Her Majesty's Inspectors of Schools.
[20] Community Homes with Education on the premises.
[21] Summary of Relevant Inspections and Visits of Community Homes made by the Social Work Service 1974–1985.

boys and they noted that Arnold was in very low spirits. Smith commented that there had been an improvement in the educational standards at the school. He said "The work in the classrooms seen, appears to be of a much higher standard than on our previous visit. The classrooms appear to be more organised, the work more purposeful and the boys seem to be more interested in what they are doing". The stated conclusion was that no action was called for on this report.

11.32 Garrett, however, remained critical. Following another joint inspection with Smith on 12 June 1978 he recommended that a team of educational advisers should be put into the school, and that a more balanced curriculum should be offered; for example, there were no music or science options. Barry Jones was shown that note and called for action on it but, despite discussions with Gledwyn Jones, Geoffrey Wyatt and Matthews in October 1978 and a further visit by Barry Jones on 2 February 1979, very little positive action ensued. This result is all the more remarkable because Clwyd County Council had set up a working party to consider support by the Education Department to social services establishments providing education, which had made the following recommendations in or about June 1978:

"i. That a Senior Adviser in Special Education, in consultation with Social Services personnel, devise an education programme for

    a. Bryn Estyn Community Home

    b. Bersham Hall and Little Acton Assessment Centres.

ii. That an Adviser in Special Education will be necessary to monitor and modify the programme.

iii. That an Educational Psychologist provide the essential services of,

    a. Assessments in individual children.

    b. Monitoring and assessment programme and advising the Officer-in-Charge and Teaching staff.

    c. Attending Case Conferences.

iv. That the Education Department make available to the teaching staff of Social Services establishments, information and advice on 'In-Service' training opportunities and consideration be given as to how staff can be funded to attend these courses.

v. That a representative of the Education Department shall attend at the appointment of all teachers to Social Services establishments.

vi. That the Education Department should provide a representative to the Social Services Management (as a consultant on professional matters) in their negotiations with Teaching Unions."

11.33 Before 1978 there was no structure to the educational provision at Bryn Estyn. Christina Lyndon, for example, who taught there between September 1975 and June of 1977, said that the age span of boys being educated was roughly 11 to 16 years and they were split roughly according to their abilities. At that time David Massey, who left four months after the witness, taught the brightest children; the middle range were taken by John Ilton and Gwen Hurst, the latter dealing also with some of the more difficult children. At 15 years boys could go into workshops and they would return to the classroom for one day a week. Each teacher would devise his or her own curriculum as far as possible. But Matthews said "There was more or less what I must call an entertainment of the boys. In other words the child would go into the classroom and he would then go at a project of his own choosing. There would possibly be a little teaching in the sense of showing him where he might find information or assisting with spelling. But I saw no actual curriculum".

11.34 Matthews told us that from 1978 the WJEC[22] syllabus was adopted at Bryn Estyn for those boys who were thought to be capable of, and willing to, sit the CSE examination in a particular subject within a limited range. He said that this was at Welsh Office insistence and that Garrett had facilitated his attendance at a seminar or course at Oxford Polytechnic at which widening the curriculum of CHEs was the subject of discussion between teachers and officials. In consequence, between 1978 and 1984, 37 residents at Bryn Estyn took CSE examinations in one or more subjects (an average of just over five per year). The most taken by any one candidate was five but the grades awarded were usually 4 or 5. However, there was some talent in art and design: three boys gained grade 1 in this subject and one of them staged an exhibition of his work. A team from Bryn Estyn also won two art competitions. Other successes, in Grades 2 or 3, were mainly in english, arithmetic and craft and design.

11.35 These boys were clearly exceptions to the mainstream of pupils and it has been extremely difficult to obtain a clear picture of how the latter was dealt with. The picture is also complicated by the decline in numbers from about 1980: Matthews' opinion was that Bryn Estyn was being used as a dustbin. It seems that, after the WJEC syllabus had been adopted, it was Matthews who made assessments for the purpose of allocating new entrants to an appropriate class (not to be confused with the assessment centre function carried out by Hurst and Soper) and he used mainly a simple test of reading and comprehension. The pupil was then assigned to a class but it appears that there was more movement from one teacher to another for different subjects after 1978: earlier each teacher had kept the same class throughout the day, changing subjects more or less hourly.

11.36 The clearest picture of the teaching arrangements then in place was given by Arnold in his report to the Management Committee in April 1982. There were five class or group teachers (Hurst, Soper, McLeod[23], Ilton, Cheesbrough) who were responsible for the english and mathematics teaching of their groups. Hurst, Soper and McLeod were also responsible for some general studies with their own groups. Soper taught art to the first three groups and to CSE students taking the subject. Hurst taught social studies to the oldest group (5). Ilton was responsible for geography in the CSE groups and group 3. Cheesbrough was responsible for PE and games throughout the school and human biology for the CSE group. Green offered a course for those electing building studies

[22] Welsh Joint Education Committee.
[23] James McLeod, at Bryn Estyn from 1 September 1978 to 31 August 1982.

153

leading to CSE brickwork and a remedial course for older boys. G P Jones[24] took woodwork for CSE and as therapy for less able and younger boys. As for working boys and work experience, there were two 16 year old boys in receipt of supplementary benefit and several above the age of 15.6 years, who were given odd days of work experience, if any was available. Older boys worked with senior care staff on the grounds, gardening or work experience. The whole of Cedar House was then a teaching unit housing the remedial (group 1) assessment and remand groups.

11.37 A recurring complaint from the teachers who gave evidence to the Tribunal was of their continuing isolation from the Local Education Authority and the lack of support from that authority, despite what has already been said[25] and the fact that Arnold raised the matter from time to time with the Management Committee. As late as 29 January 1982 Arnold reported to them:

> "We are looking for ways to develop the educational programme, I personally wonder if struggling along with a few candidates for doubtful CSE results is worthwhile when we have little enthusiasm from children, and perhaps an education geared more to their possible lifestyles would be more easily achieved. We would value support from the County Education Department, members who have been on the Management Committee for some time will remember that this is a perennial complaint, but the isolation of Bryn Estyn is still evident."

11.38 The minutes of the meeting of 29 January 1982 when this report was discussed are missing but the subject was raised again by Arnold at the next meeting on 23 April 1982, the minutes of which record:

> "Mr Arnold expressed his concern at the fact that the assistance and advice which the Education Department had promised to the home had not materialised. This was particularly disappointing as he considered that a degree of liaison with the Education Department would be of benefit to both parties. Members supported the view expressed by Mr Arnold regarding this matter and it was agreed that the question of providing support to the Education unit at Bryn Estyn be once again taken up with the Director of Education."

There is no evidence before us, however, that this evoked any positive response.

11.39 It is lamentable that little, if anything, had been achieved by way of LEA support, despite the intervention of the Parliamentary Under Secretary of State for Wales in 1976. It is all the more remarkable because the subject of education in CHEs was addressed by the Welsh Office together with the Department of Education and Science and the Department of Health and Social Security in Welsh Office Circular 194/73, dated 31 August 1973, in the following terms[26]:

> "Where an authority have placed a child in their care in one of these homes, it seems reasonable that the authority should not seek to recover

---

[24] Glyn Price Jones, at Bryn Estyn from 1 January 1963 to 31 March 1984.
[25] See paras 11.28 to 11.32.
[26] Paras 6 to 9 inclusive.

from the education account any part of the cost of the child's maintenance, although that cost will include an element in respect of the education provided. These establishments are not schools within the meaning of the Education Acts and any education provided in them should be regarded as provided otherwise than at school for the purposes of those Acts. Notwithstanding this, local authorities responsible in their social services capacity for approved schools and remand homes have rightly sought to ensure that the education in these establishments, whether situated inside or outside their area, benefits fully from the services they have developed as education authorities. Co-operation with the education service should be based on the following principles:

(a) It is essential to the concept of integrated treatment that overall control should be unitary and should accordingly be exercised by the "responsible body" as defined in the Community Homes Regulations, 1972. The local authority in their social services capacity are the responsible body for a local authority home or "controlled" home; for an "assisted" home, the voluntary organisation providing the home are the responsible body. Their responsibility for the home thus includes the provision of teaching rooms and equipment, and the recruitment, payment and superannuation of teachers. In some instances however, possibly to meet a special need, the education authority may be willing, on request, to second teachers for specified periods to work operationally under the direction of the head of the community home.

(b) The responsible body, however, should seek to avail themselves of all advice and assistance which the local education authority may be able to offer. For instance, its organisers should visit the home and the authority's advice should be sought in the appointment of teachers. So should its assistance in providing opportunities for teachers to move into and out of the community homes system and to develop their professional resources through participation in the work of local teachers' centres and attendance at conferences and training courses.

(c) The Secretary of State for Education and Science will have no statutory obligation to cause inspections to be made of any community home, but it is hoped that responsible bodies will continue to avail themselves freely of the advice of H M Inspectors, on which the highest value has long been placed by the managers of approved schools and remand homes.

The preceding paragraph does not, of course, attempt to enumerate exhaustively the fields in which close co-operation between local education authorities and local authorities in their social services capacity may be fruitful. The provision of facilities for observation and assessment (whether within residential community homes or on a day attendance basis) is another field where it may well be to the benefit of both to pool their skills and resources."

11.40 The problem of educational support, like other matters such as the provision of an educational psychologist for assessment purposes and staff reorganisation, was said to be insoluble, certainly in later years, because of lack of financial resources; and this became more acute as the future of Bryn Estyn came to be questioned. CHEs were a regional, rather than a local, provision so that a provider local authority such as Clwyd would instinctively look to the Children's Regional Planning Committee (CRPC) for Wales to provide additional resources when needed. But the CRPC did not appear to have had resources of its own for this purpose and additional cost could only have been funded by an agreed increase in the *per capita* charge made to user authorities by the provider authority. It is not clear that the CRPC ever was asked by Clwyd to agree an additional charge and the latter simply averted its eyes from the problem until both the CRPC and Bryn Estyn expired.

11.41 Similar problems may well arise in the future, particularly in Wales, where the former counties have now been divided into smaller administrative units so that collective action is likely to become increasingly necessary. In our judgment, therefore, it is essential that clear express directions should be given identifying the resources likely to be required, where the financial responsibility for providing them lies and whence that finance is to be obtained.

Recruitment and training of the staff

11.42 We deal in the next part of this chapter with the more general shortcomings of the Bryn Estyn regime, viewed in the light of the "Utting principles" enunciated in 1981[27], but it is appropriate here to focus particularly upon the inadequate arrangements for recruitment and training of staff in the period from 1974 to 1984.

11.43 It is, of course, notorious that, throughout the period of our review, the recruitment of suitable residential staff for community homes was exceptionally difficult due partly, at least, to the comparatively low status of the work, reflected in poor pay and career structures. What is remarkable, however, is that the problems of recruitment and possible initiatives in that field were never discussed by the Management Committee in any depth throughout the period of its existence. Instead, Arnold seems to have been left substantially to his own devices as recruiting master. Even though he was regarded as a very experienced and competent approved school Headmaster, this should not have been permitted.

11.44 In fairness to the Management Committee it must be said that Matt Arnold (May 1973), Peter Howarth (November 1973), Stephen Norris (March 1974), Paul Wilson (27 May 1974) and John Ilton (September 1972), had all been appointed before the committee held its first meeting (according to the available documents) on 10 December 1975. Looking at the history of

---

[27] Control and Discipline in Community Homes - Report of a Working Party (W B Utting), January 1981, DHSS.

recruitment generally, however, with particular reference to the members of the care and teaching staff whom we have named, it appears that the process was very haphazard and that few of them, received any training in the specific problems that they would meet in a large CHE successor to an approved school either before or after they joined the staff.

11.45 As far as the care staff are concerned, Peter Howarth, although experienced, was the personal choice of Arnold, which proved to be a disaster. Stephen Norris had some relevant experience and had undergone a pre-qualifying course but he also appears to have been the personal choice of Arnold, if Norris' evidence is correct. In any event he was manifestly unsuitable for care work and should never have been given the responsibility of Clwyd House; and he did not undergo any further training. Paul Wilson was formally interviewed but it is questionable whether he should have been appointed once his reference had been seen and his conviction disclosed. More certainly, he should not have survived his probationary period, when his failings were known. He had some limited experience as a houseparent but he was unsuitable for further training and his employment should have been ended long before Bryn Estyn itself closed.

11.46 The other members of the care staff named in Chapter 10 were all taken on when they had no training in residential care work and no experience of it, except for Phillip Murray and John Cunningham. Murray had qualified for the CRCCYP and had served at an observation and assessment centre, and he applied for a post as senior houseparent in response to an advertisement published nationally. Cunningham, on the other hand, was merely a temporary houseparent on contract, with very brief previous experience at a boarding school. The others appear to have heard of the possibility of employment at Bryn Estyn locally by word of mouth and to have been interviewed mainly by Arnold and/or Howarth before starting work. Four of them had undergone teachers' training (two in physical education) but only one of them, Robert Jones, underwent further relevant training whilst he was at Bryn Estyn.

11.47 The picture in relation to the teaching staff was broadly similar, although they all possessed general teaching qualifications. In addition to their difficult teaching and assessment duties, they were expected to perform the duties of care staff for at least 15 additional hours each week, but none of them had received any training in residential care work[28]. The evidence before the Tribunal has been that a degree of hostility between care staff and teaching staff persisted throughout the period of Bryn Estyn's existence as a CHE and the lack of any provision for joint staff meetings further militated against the exchange of information and discussion of practice.

11.48 Norman Green[29] did apparently arrange some seminars for the staff at Bryn Estyn during the winter of 1979/1980 at which a range of topics relevant to CHEs were covered[30]. The object was to cover subjects not always covered in

[28] See para 10.83 for particulars of Matthews' course whilst at Bryn Estyn.
[29] See paras 10.84 and 10.91.
[30] Reports of Arnold and others to Management Committee for the meeting on 16 May 1980, page 5.

depth by training courses and a number of "observational" visits were made to other establishments. It seems, however, that the staff were divided into two separate groups, ie residential staff and teaching staff, for the seminars, so that the opportunity for a full exchange was missed, despite the good intentions of the organisers. It was hoped to resume the seminars in September 1980 but staff morale was low by then and there is no further information about them in the reports.

The quality of care generally

11.49 Finally in relation to Bryn Estyn, we must express our grave dismay at the lack of individual care of the children who were resident at Bryn Estyn between 1974 and 1984 that has been demonstrated by the evidence before us. Arnold undoubtedly started with high principles, as he expressed them, for example, in his first report to the Management Committee[31], but the subsequent practice at Bryn Estyn failed, disastrously for many, to implement those principles and the aspirations.

11.50 Arnold had begun with the intention that every resident at Bryn Estyn would have a "key worker" on the premises to whom he could turn for advice and consolation, etc: to achieve this, appropriate members of the care staff would have a small number of residents attached to him or her so that a meaningful and caring relationship could be built up. None of the witnesses who gave evidence to us were able to recollect this arrangement in actual practice; in particular, none of the complainants whom we have heard were able to identify a member of the staff to whom they had been assigned.

11.51 It seems likely that Arnold abandoned the "key worker" idea at an early stage in favour of organising residents on a "house" basis but this did not provide the kind of personal, confiding relationship that he must have had in mind originally. Before Clwyd House was opened, there may have been as many as four "houses" in the main building but from late 1979 there were probably only three: two in the main building (one for younger, and the other for older, boys) plus the separate Clwyd House (for 12 or so boys with disturbed behaviour patterns).

11.52 There was also a blatant lack of close personal relationships between residents and their field social workers. This lack of contact was particularly felt by the many residents from areas outside Clwyd, particularly South Wales, who had limited contact with their families. They might see their social worker occasionally when on weekend or other leaves but, otherwise, contact was limited to case conferences at Bryn Estyn, when the field worker was able to attend. There was a better prospect for a Clwyd child of a visit by his field social worker in terms of practicality but, even so, the overwhelming majority of residents complained of lack of contact with, and inability to confide in, their

---

[31] See para 7.09.

assigned social worker. The problem was often aggravated by frequent changes of social worker. The result was that we heard evidence from only two complainants that they had made a specific complaint about abuse at Bryn Estyn to their social worker and in both cases, their evidence was that nothing was done about it.

11.53 A weakness of our Inquiry has been that it has not been possible to undertake a comprehensive review of field social workers' practice because of the passage of time and the patchy documentation now available. In order to obtain as full a picture as possible in the circumstances we commissioned Elaine Baxter, an independent consultant in child care matters, to analyse the available evidence from social work staff and records in Clwyd. We refer to this in more detail hereafter in Chapter 31 but it is appropriate to say here that Baxter's evidence indicated that there were wide variations in practice. In the absence of established practice and procedure manuals, Area Officers and Team Leaders developed their own working practices.

11.54 The only planning mechanism was the statutory review. Many practitioners applied the Boarding Out Regulations 1955 to visiting children in residential care, even though the Regulations applied only to foster children. There were heavy case loads and, due to time constraints, some would get in touch with children when they were in the local area visiting the family: contact with children in residential homes would then be by telephone and a child might not be seen for three to four months at the home (but some social workers claimed that they visited every three to six weeks). The analysis as a whole is dispiriting. In general terms the standard of record keeping overall was of a very poor level and Baxter commented:

> "One other very significant omission from almost every file was any evidence of a long term planning or review system. Thus young people had numerous changes of placement without any apparent consideration of the fact, or the implications it might have on their ability to develop into adults with any sense of identity."

11.55 Two aspects of the placement system are of particular concern in relation to Bryn Estyn. Firstly, it will be apparent from what we have said in Chapter 10 that it was customary for a resident who pursued a complaint against a member of staff to be transferred summarily to another establishment, usually to one perceived to have a harsher regime and in South Wales. Moreover, the threat of such a transfer was used from time to time to dissuade intending complainants from making a formal complaint. These decisions were made without any regard to the best interests of the child concerned, without any proper investigation of the complaint beforehand and without any case conference or the like. They appear to have been made solely in the interests of the member of staff pointed at, disregarding the paramount duty of the local authority towards a child in its care and without reference to appropriate senior officers.

11.56 Secondly, it will be recalled that Arnold complained to the Management Committee[32] about children being detained unnecessarily long at Bryn Estyn because of the reluctance of social workers to permit them to return to the community. This was a serious consequence of the lack of planning of individual carers referred to by Baxter. This was exemplified by the evidence of a witness brought up in Gwynedd, who had been resident at Bryn Estyn from 14 February 1977 (his date of birth was 13 November 1962) until 24 May 1979. It seems that his departure was very long delayed whilst a placement at Tŷ Newydd was awaited. His six monthly review in March 1979 disclosed that his progress since the previous review had been disappointing and that his behaviour at Bryn Estyn had deteriorated considerably in the past six months, particularly following his 16th birthday. The boy felt strongly that he had been allowed to "vegetate" in Bryn Estyn: the continued delays in opening Tŷ Newydd hostel, which he was to enter, had had a marked effect on him.

11.57 This criticism of the delays in moving residents on is linked with the lack of adequate preparation of residents for discharge from care or other developments in their lives as they approached the age of majority. The blame for this fault does not rest upon Bryn Estyn alone because we have not found any evidence of guidance given on this matter by Clwyd Social Services Department or of active field social worker involvement in the process. Bryn Estyn itself appears to have done what it could in a difficult employment situation, despite the demise of the working hostel in Cedar House, to provide job opportunities for residents when they could be found. Arnold reported late on for example[33] that they had a "leaving group" of older boys, well past the age of normal education, who were "used in a variety of tasks around the grounds and in a Careers Development Programme". The group was largely responsible to Matthews but it was "subsidised and supplemented" by Norman Green and Robert Jones. There was also a vocational group for boys interested in building and allied trades, largely taught by Green, with some trade training, career training and "thoughts to a future in a world where employment might not be possible".

11.58 There was a striking absence, however, of preparation of the residents to be self-sufficient in the outside world despite the fact that most of them had spent many years in care and were wholly untrained in basic domestic requirements and skills. This was understandably outside the agenda of Bryn Estyn as an approved school but very different considerations applied once it became part of the care system. Yet, the only hint we found of this type of training was contained in the following comment by the HMI, Garrett, on his visit to Bryn Estyn on 7 November 1980, "Mr D Cheesborough (sic) is also responsible for an activity called "Living Today" which attempt(s) to help the older boys look after and cater for themselves in one of the hostel kitchens for a day. They purchase their own food, under the supervision of Mr Cheesborough and cook and clean for themselves".

---

[32] See para 7.20.
[33] Report to the Management Committee for the meeting on 29 April 1983.

Some concluding observations

11.59 The transfer of direct responsibility for approved schools to local authorities at the same time as these establishments changed both their status and their purpose posed particular problems that were never satisfactorily solved at Bryn Estyn. It does not appear that Arnold received any substantial guidance or training to prepare for the change in his responsibilities: it was assumed that he was an expert in his field and he was left to run Bryn Estyn largely as his own fiefdom without close monitoring and control. The Welsh Office had not previously had any direct responsibility for such an establishment and control by the new local authority was to some extent weakened because of the community home's role and status in the Regional Plan as a facility available to the whole of Wales with consequential special arrangements for its funding.

11.60 The Children and Young Persons Act 1969 demanded a significant change in thinking and approach, involving treatment rather than punishment, but Bryn Estyn continued to be regarded as a place catering essentially for aggressive and disturbed boys with a strong criminal element and the approved school culture continued untouched to a large extent, despite Arnold's early aspirations. The result was that there was an institutional, regimented regime in which, for many, there was a heavy atmosphere of fear; and little consideration was given to the needs of individual boys, including the most vulnerable, and the problems that gave rise to their admission to care.

Little Acton Assessment Centre, 1974 to 1980

12.01 This community home was purpose built and was handed over by the builders to Clwyd County Council on 1 April 1974. The site in Box Lane, Wrexham housed the assessment centre itself, a residential nursery[1] and a hostel building with a day nursery on the ground floor. However, the rest of the hostel building was never opened because of financial constraints. Behind the assessment centre was a large field that had been grassed over and could be used for games and there was a tarmacadammed area between the centre and the hostel that could be used as a playground. The centre had three separate units within the same building: one was designed as a semi-secure unit and the other two as open units. Each unit was a self-contained flat to accommodate five children with a sitting room and a kitchen with facilities for preparing breakfast, tea and supper snacks, plus a bed-sitting room for sleeping-in staff. There was also a school attached to the building, providing 30 places for assessment of 15 residents and 15 others attending daily. Residential accommodation in four flats was provided for the Officer-in-Charge, his deputy and two senior houseparents; and there was a substantial service area for the whole building, comprising a main kitchen, a dining area, a laundry, administrative offices, a medical room, lavatories and a staff room etc.

The senior staff to 1978

12.02 Difficulties in securing the services of suitable senior staff were experienced from the outset. After advertising the post of Superintendent twice, it was thought that candidates of appropriate calibre had not applied. Nevertheless a third advertisement was not authorised and **Peter John Bird**, one of the existing candidates who was then 32 years old and had obtained the CRCCYP at Salford College of Technology in 1971, was appointed with effect from 1 December 1973. He had been brought up in Stockport and trained as a painter and decorator until he became a regional organising secretary for the Church of England Children's Society in 1962. His subsequent experience was of work in a probation hostel, then a remand home and finally successive appointments as Warden and Deputy Superintendent of children's homes in the London area. He remained in post at Little Acton until 20 April 1978, when he was suspended for nearly six months and then re-employed as a craft instructor at Marchwiel Adult Training Centre, having admitted eight specific allegations (of a total of 19) of failure to carry out his duty.

12.03 The response to advertisements for other senior posts was said to have been equally disappointing. The Deputy Officer-in-Charge, **Huw Meurig Jones**, did not take up his post until 21 July 1974 and remained only until 31 March 1976, when he resigned. On his appointment he was 25 years old, and like Bird, he

---

[1] See paras 4.02(4) and 4.03.

had obtained the CRCCYP at Salford (in 1973). He had become a houseparent, employed by the City of Liverpool, at the age of 18 years and he had served as an RCCO at Chevet Hey from 1 February 1972 and then briefly as Deputy Officer-in-Charge there after his course at Salford. Following his resignation from Little Acton, he became an unqualified social worker for Clwyd County Council at Wrexham and then Colwyn Bay. He failed the first year part of the course for the CQSW at Cartrefle College in July 1980 and ultimately resigned from Clwyd's employ on 28 July 1981, following periods of suspension from 19 December 1980 onwards, during successive investigations by the police of allegations of sexual abuse that had been made against him.

12.04 The appointment of a Deputy Officer-in-Charge to replace Huw Meurig Jones was equally unfortunate. His successor was **Carl Johnson Evans**, whose employment in that capacity lasted from 1 May 1976 until 8 October 1978 but who was suspended from duty from 13 January 1978, following an allegation of rape made by a girl resident against him on 8 January 1978 and during the subsequent investigation by Clwyd County Council of other allegations of misconduct on his part. It appears that Evans was the less favoured of the two candidates who were "pre-interviewed" for the post on 2 April 1976 and it is unclear whether the panel saw any (and if so, which) references before making a recommendation. However, they reported to the Personnel Committee (Appointments) that Evans appeared to have the necessary qualities and experience for the post but that they doubted his ability to relate well to staff and children in difficult situations. They assessed him accurately as an "over-confident type of person who might cause friction in difficult circumstances". They doubted also his sincerity and drew attention to the fact that he had no experience in dealing with girls.

12.05 Carl Evans' background was that he had left school at the age of 15 years and had then had varied employment, as a trainee forester, salesman, army musician and assistant manager of a finance company, for 14 years before starting residential care work. By the date of his appointment to Little Acton he was 40 years old and his experience of residential care had been at two approved schools and then as Third-in-Charge of an assessment centre for just over two years to February 1976. He had obtained the CRCCYP in 1967, having taken the housemasters' course at Lemorby Park. Immediately prior to his appointment at Little Acton he had been employed briefly by Care Concern at Ystrad Hall[2], Llangollen, where he had received an official warning for criticising the standard of the home in the presence of a new student. He had also secured an appointment as First Deputy at a remand home in Manchester but had been unable to take this up because of the needs of his foster child.

The 1978 investigation

12.06 In the event there were major difficulties at Little Acton throughout the first four years of its existence as an assessment centre with the result that the Chief Executive of Clwyd County Council requested the Director of Social Services

---

[2] See paras 4.12 to 4.13.

to conduct an investigation into the establishment. The Director of Social Services appointed a team of four (a training officer and two homes inspectors from the Social Services Department plus the social services group auditor from the Treasurer's Department) to conduct the investigation in January 1978. They were required to enquire into the conduct, administration and management of the assessment centre with particular regard to the circumstances leading to the disciplinary measures taken against Valerie Halliwell (Matron), Leslie Wilson (Senior Houseparent), and matters relating to the Deputy Superintendent.

12.07 The investigating team produced an exhaustive report running to 369 paragraphs, with eight appendices, by 6 July 1978. Much of it is not directly material to our own terms of reference but a substantial number of points made in the report need to be noted here, starting with the following summary of comments on the administrative and organisational difficulties encountered at Little Acton:

   (a) Unqualified staff had been appointed to the posts of Matron and senior houseparents (three) to enable the assessment centre to function because of the dearth of suitable candidates.

   (b) There had only been a period of three weeks when all three senior houseparents were in post and on duty.

   (c) A contributory difficulty was the County Council's policy of not filling vacant posts unless written justification for a replacement was produced and written approval subsequently given.

   (d) Other factors prohibiting the filling of senior posts at Little Acton were the suspension of a senior houseparent (Leslie Wilson) in July 1977 and his dismissal on 28 February 1978 and the absence of the Matron (Valerie Halliwell) on sick leave from March 1977 (except for about a month), followed by her suspension and then her resignation on 9 December 1977.

   (e) Between 1 April 1974 and 1 April 1977 there was only a period of two months, from 1 January 1975, when a Residential and Day Care Officer (RDCO) at Headquarters had specific responsibility for the community homes. Moreover, the Principal Officer (Residential Services) resigned on 30 April 1976 and the Assistant Director (Residential Services) retired on 31 August 1976.

   (f) A round table conference to discuss rota difficulties did not take place because of the Assistant Director's failure to take action, despite repeated requests by the Principal Officer and the fact that the Superintendent and his Deputy claimed to be working 70 hours per week each without overtime payment.

   (g) In February 1977 the Area Officer, Janet Handley, was requested by the Director of Social Services to chair a working party to investigate the assessment process at Little Acton and collateral matters but she was too busy to undertake the task.

(h) From 1 April 1977 the responsibility for Little Acton and 26 other residential and day care establishments in the Wrexham area was delegated to the Area Officer. On that date only one out of three required RDCOs was in post and she was soon absent for two and a half months because of illness. The third officer, with specific responsibility for children's establishments, Hannah Taylor, did not take up her appointment until 1 September 1977.

(i) Neither the Area Officer nor any of the newly appointed RDCOs had any previous experience of managerial responsibility for residential establishments.

(j) The Area Officer did not consider that the RDCOs were sufficiently experienced to write reports on their visits to establishments that could be seen by Officers-in-Charge without a breakdown in their relationship.

12.08 Against this chaotic background there was considerable staff unrest because of their dissatisfaction with proposals by the Social Services (General Purposes) Committee for the closure and redesignation of some of the children's establishments in the Wrexham area. There had also been a deterioration in staff relations prior to this, reflected in complaints by the Matron, a senior houseparent (not Wilson) and the senior teacher about difficulties that they were experiencing with Carl Evans. Despite these problems no official staff meeting had been held in 1977.

Valerie Halliwell

12.09 The section of the report dealing with Halliwell can be dealt with briefly. She had worked as a housemother at Chevet Hey for just over a year before taking up a similar post at Little Acton on 4 December 1973; and she was appointed Matron from 1 March 1975. Both Bird and Evans became suspicious of her activities by Christmas 1976 and began to carry out spot checks. Bird made a report to the Director of Social Services on 3 June 1977 and the matter was reported to the police. On 2 December 1977 Halliwell pleaded guilty at Wrexham Maelor Magistrates' Court to offences of theft, obtaining money by deception and falsification of records and was fined a total of £80.00. She resigned with effect from 9 December 1977, having been absent on sick leave almost continuously from 21 March 1977 and suspended without pay from 15 November 1977.

Leslie Wilson

12.10 The prosecution of **Leslie Wilson** resulted from a report initially by Arnold to Bird in a letter dated 27 May 1977. Wilson had been appointed a housefather at Little Acton on 1 August 1974 and then a senior housefather from 19 April 1976. He was also secretary of the Clwyd Residential Care Association. Arnold had become concerned that Wilson was visiting at Bryn Estyn a boy who had previously been at Little Acton for assessment between December 1976 and April 1977. The visits appeared to be upsetting the boy and Arnold asked Bird for his confidential opinion as to whether Wilson was a suitable person to continue visiting the boy. According to Bird's statements to the police, he warned Wilson to leave the boy alone on receiving this letter, but a month later the boy absconded from Bryn Estyn and was found on 5 July 1977 in Wilson's flat at Little Acton. Bird and Evans then returned the boy to Bryn Estyn and three days later Wilson confessed to two members of staff that he had "slept" with the boy. The facts were reported to Geoffrey Wyatt, who referred the matter to the police. Wilson meanwhile had left, pleading sickness, never to return to Little Acton. He was suspended without pay from 15 July 1977 and was charged with buggery a month later. Ultimately, Wilson pleaded guilty on 22 December 1977 in Chester Crown Court[3] to offences of indecent assault, gross indecency and attempted buggery, for which he was sentenced to 15 months' imprisonment; and he was dismissed by Clwyd County Council on 28 February 1978.

Carl Evans

12.11 The evidence before the investigating team indicated that there had been continuous friction between Bird and Evans from the date of the latter's appointment as Deputy Officer-in-Charge onwards. Soon after **Carl Evans** took up his post members of staff asked for a staff meeting because they considered that Evans had made their position intolerable by disregarding accepted policies and undermining staff but Evans monopolised that meeting. Further complaints to the RDCO at the time (Veronica Pares) resulted in another staff meeting on 23 November 1976, arranged by Wyatt and Pares. This did result in a number of agreed policy decisions, which were minuted, but the conclusion of the investigating team was that each decision had subsequently been broken or ignored by Evans and that, in consequence, many of the staff had felt seriously undermined.

12.12 Apart from this general case against Evans, there were allegations against him by the staff that he had given children alcohol, sent staff off duty when they were rostered to be on duty and nevertheless authorised payment to them, put "staff and children's heads down the toilet" and flushed it, and had physical contact with adolescent girls in care exceeding the staff's own self-imposed limits. By way of example of the last allegation, it was said that Evans had encouraged girls to sit on his lap and had encouraged other male members of staff to follow his example and reference was made to alleged specific incidents on 21 and 22 December 1977. It was alleged also that Evans spent far too much time allegedly "counselling" girls, on occasions disturbing the running of both the school and the centre, and without any productive feedback to other members of the staff.

12.13 A very serious weakness of the investigation in relation to Evans was that he was not interviewed. The explanation for this seems to be that he was being investigated by the police until 20 March 1978 and that the investigating team completed interviews at Little Acton four days earlier, but this does not appear

---

[3] See para 2.07(2).

to us to be a sufficient reason for not re-convening to hear him after 20 March. However, we have seen a typed but unsigned ten page statement headed in handwriting "Written by Carl Evans", which is annexed to the team's report and which stated that it was for the information of the Director of Social Services. The document contains many allegations against Mr and Mrs Bird and other members of the staff at Little Acton. In effect, Evans denied the allegations against him and said:

> "When the auditors were investigating the Matron episode they told me that due to the mis-management by Mr Bird a full inquiry into the running of the Centre would be held. I made the fatal mistake then of discussing this with a member of staff whom I felt I could trust and I said I would tell the inquiry the true facts of Mr Bird's pathetic show in running the establishment. Shortly after this that information was passed to Mr Bird and I would suggest from then he and his close associates were out to 'sink' me at any price."

12.14 The report of the investigating team contained a damning indictment[4] of Evans' performance and conduct as Deputy Office-in-Charge and it led to disciplinary proceedings against him on the basis of 17 particularised allegations set out in letters dated 18 April and 16 and 29 June 1978. The hearing took place eventually on 3 October 1978 before the Director of Social Services (Emlyn Evans) and the Director of Administration and Legal Services (E R Ll Davies). Evans, who was legally represented, admitted four allegations, namely, failure to keep records over the Christmas period, failure to comply with the policies and procedures laid down by the County Council, making unauthorised fieldwork visits to an adolescent girl in care and supporting that girl's application for housing without notifying the Officer-in-Charge of his (Evans') actions and involvement. No evidence was put forward on the 13 other allegations, which were dismissed. A formal written warning was issued to Evans in respect of the four matters admitted by him and it was agreed that it would be inappropriate for him to return to Little Acton. Instead, he was seconded to Clwyd Voluntary Services at Ruthin from 9 October 1978 to 30 April 1979, when he took up an appointment as Deputy Superintendent of an assessment centre in Islington.

12.15 The London Borough of Islington Council sought a reference from Clwyd County Council in respect of Evans' application for this appointment, which was supplied by the Director of Social Services by letter dated 21 March 1979. In that letter the only hint about the recent disciplinary proceedings was contained in the following paragraph:

> "From time to time he chaired case conferences and staff meetings and he was responsible for the semi-secure unit which accommodated difficult adolescent girls. Mr Evans' enthusiasm and close involved relationship with children resulted in an overdependency developing with children which led to some conflict with his employing authority

---

[4] At paras 317 to 338 of the "Report of investigation into L.A.A.C. January to March 1978".

which, as you are aware, is not conducive for the management of an assessment centre and made it difficult for other staff to establish their own role with children."

References in similar terms were supplied to four other local authorities by the Director of Social Services between January and April 1979 in connection with applications by Evans for senior posts in residential care, although the last of these did add:

"Mr Evans holds strong convictions regarding child care standards and the assessment processes and he will contend for these views to prevail. The philosophy of the unit would have to accord with his views or this could lead to conflict with the Management Team."

12.16 The terms in which these favourable references were written illustrate and underline the problems that arise if disciplinary proceedings are compromised in the way that they were in Evans' case. There were 17 allegations against him, some of them plainly amounting to gross misconduct if proved, and it was envisaged that "20 or 30" witnesses would be called. Moreover, the report of the investigating team indicated that there was compelling evidence to support its findings. Yet, the result of the agreement between the parties was that 13 allegations were dismissed without being tested and the four allegations that were admitted were dealt with by a written warning only, despite the fact that one of them, the failure to comply with County Council policies and procedures, was described in the formal note of the proceedings as "the main one".

12.17 We are forced to the conclusion that this agreement was made on behalf of Clwyd County Council without paying proper regard to their overall duty to safeguard children generally. The transcript of the disciplinary proceedings discloses that part of the overall agreement was that Evans would resign from the Council's employ by 30 June 1979 and that he undertook to attend, meanwhile, a training course in London beginning on 15 January 1979. This was a six month course at the Tavistock Centre on management and social planning, which Evans did apparently attend, at least until he secured his appointment at Islington. The references supplied for him between January and April 1979 were undoubtedly intended to facilitate his departure. In writing to them on behalf of the Director of Social Services Geoffrey Wyatt no doubt felt inhibited by the agreed dismissal of 13 of the allegations against Carl Evans but the recipient Councils were clearly not given an accurate picture of his short record of service at Little Acton and it is not unduly harsh to say that they were misled.

Peter Bird

12.18 The findings of the investigating team in respect of **Peter Bird** were also highly critical. Evaluating his management of the home as Officer-in-Charge, they said[5]:

---

[5] At para 339 of the "Report of investigation into L.A.A.C. January to March 1978".

"The impression that Mr Bird left on the Team was of a man totally ambivalent, unable to identify the source of his problems and lacking the insight as to what would happen if he failed to take action on a whole multitude of matters: a man who had no real concept of what was required of a manager and of a leader of staff. Despite this he had an inflated idea of his own ability. It became apparent, in the opinion of the Team in the course of the many interviews, that this attitude appeared to be a cover for a very insecure man with very little real knowledge of what the job was all about."

12.19 Without going into unnecessary detail about the team's findings in respect of Bird's failure as a manager, the following matters directly relevant to the quality of care at Little Acton are to be noted[6]:

(a) The centre gave the impression that it was run primarily for the convenience of staff rather than to provide good child care and genuine assessment.

(b) Emphasis on commercial outings (ie to commercial leisure facilities) made it easy for staff to control children and reduced their personal involvement with the children (to the detriment of the assessment process).

(c) Bird only reported incidents once it was inevitable that they would become general knowledge.

(d) Despite the fact that most of the staff were untrained there was no discussion of problems to enable the staff to learn from them.

(e) The staff had either no knowledge, or only the haziest notion, of the Community Homes Regulations, County Council policy on corporal punishment and the County's legal responsibilities for children in care in residential establishments.

(f) Discipline wavered between control (Bird) and leniency (Evans); staff sought the easy way out to keep children occupied (eg by watching television rather than involving themselves); and there had been no attempt to make the children's living units homely.

(g) The process of assessment required closer investigation by the Principal Social Worker (Children) (Ramsay) having regard to 16 matters of concern, including:

(i) Only 5% of the content of the assessment dossier presented to Case Conferences contained information not known to the Department when the child was admitted for assessment.

(ii) The majority of assessment reports were compiled by unqualified staff with little or no discussion with senior qualified staff about the particular child.

---

[6] At paras 340 to 356 and 365 of the "Report of investigation into L.A.A.C. January to March 1978".

(iii) No attempt appeared to have been made to arrange for psychiatric assessment of the child and the family at the assessment centre.

12.20 The disciplinary proceedings against Peter Bird followed a similar course to those against Carl Evans. Bird was informed by letter dated 18 April 1978 from the Director of Administration and Legal Services that there were 19 matters that the author of the letter and the Director of Social Services wished to discuss with him on 20 April 1978 and that these matters might result in disciplinary proceedings against him. Bird attended with John Cooke, the NALGO branch organiser, and he was suspended on full pay from that date. Eventually, the proceedings were concluded on the basis that he admitted eight of the allegations and that the other 11 were dismissed. These admissions related essentially to administrative matters, and like Evans, Bird received a written warning, in his case dated 3 October 1978. It was agreed that he should not return to Little Acton Assessment Centre nor take any post with Clwyd County Council involving financial administration. Instead, he was transferred, with effect from 9 October 1978, to Marchwiel Adult Training Centre as a craft instructor at a protected salary, and he remains in that employment, now with Wrexham County Borough Council.

The regime from 1978 to 1980

12.21 Bird's successor as Superintendent of Little Acton Assessment Centre was **Michael Barnes**, who had been in a senior position at Bersham Hall from September 1972 and who was asked to take over at Little Acton from 21 April 1978 in the difficult circumstances surrounding Bird's suspension from duty. He did so initially as Acting Officer-in-Charge until 31 December 1978, whilst remaining Officer-in-Charge of Bersham Hall. From 1 January 1979, however, he became Officer-in-Charge of Little Acton and gave up his Bersham Hall responsibility. He too had begun work in residential care at an approved school. That was at the age of 19 years in 1967, when he was appointed a houseparent. Thus, he was still only 24 years old when he went to Bersham Hall, having served at a reception centre and then a school for maladjusted children after the approved school. He had also obtained the CRCCYP at Portsmouth Polytechnic in 1972, together with the college's diploma in residential social work. At Bersham Hall he had progressed from Third-in-Charge to Deputy Superintendent in September 1973, on the resignation of Michael Taylor, and then to Officer-in-Charge from 15 February 1976 (in an acting capacity for the first three and a half months). When Little Acton closed in May 1980 Barnes returned to Bersham Hall as Centre Manager for seven years interrupted by a two year course at Keele University for the CQSW, which he gained with a university commendation in 1984. His subsequent career as Officer-in-Charge at Chevet Hey and then at higher levels is dealt with later in this report.

12.22 Carl Evans' successor as Deputy Superintendent at Little Acton Assessment Centre was **Christopher Ian Thomas**, who also came from Bersham Hall. He was three years younger than Michael Barnes and had intended to become a teacher when he attended Bangor Normal College between 1970 and 1972 but had then changed direction in favour of social work. He was employed as a medical emergency driver and then as a trainee residential social worker at Ealing before becoming a supervisor at Bersham Hall in September 1974. He progressed to Acting Deputy Superintendent in April 1978, having obtained the CRCCYP at Salford College of Technology in December 1976 and his appointment as Deputy at Little Acton was from 1 February 1979 until it closed on 21 May 1980. Like Barnes, he then returned to Bersham Hall, becoming Deputy Officer-in-Charge and ultimately Centre Manager from 1 January 1988 to 22 March 1994, when he resigned. He had also been Acting Officer-in- Charge of Bersham Hall from 1 October 1982 to 31 July 1984 whilst Barnes was attending Keele University.

Complaints to the Tribunal

12.23 We have not received any evidence of alleged abuse by Michael Barnes in the period from April 1978 to May 1980 or by Christopher Thomas between February 1979 and May 1980, that is, when they were respectively employed at Little Acton. In the case of Thomas we are not even aware that any such complaint was made about him as Deputy Officer-in-Charge there. As for Barnes, we do know that there were six complainants at one time or another but none have come forward to give oral evidence to the Tribunal or even to provide written statements. It must be said also that at least two of these complainants were not at Little Acton during the period when Barnes was there. Finally in relation to this period, we do not know of any allegation of abuse against any other identified member of the staff at Little Acton whilst Barnes was in charge.

12.24 Having regard to the findings of the investigation team in 1978, it is perhaps surprising that we have not received more complaints than we have about the earlier "Bird" period from 1974 to early 1978. Our estimate is that there were about 275 admissions to Little Acton during that period but we are aware of only 15 residents who have made complaints against members of the staff and four of them were unable or unwilling to identify the member of staff concerned. The complaints by the other 11 involved only seven members of the staff and we received evidence from nine of these complainants. We have not been given full details of the intended staff establishment and there were difficulties in recruitment throughout. However, there were 13 care staff in post in December 1975 and three teachers in addition to a full complement of nine domestic staff and there were frequent staff changes thereafter. It follows that complaints have been made against only a small proportion of the total number of staff employed at Little Acton from time to time.

12.25 We have already dealt with the major complaint against **Leslie Wilson** in respect of which he received a custodial sentence[7]. The only other allegation against him before us was made by a witness whose evidence was read because she is currently undergoing psychiatric treatment, allegedly because of her

---

[7] See para 12.10.

experiences at Little Acton in the summer of 1977. Her allegation was that Leslie Wilson actively condoned the actions of two fellow girl residents who ill-treated her when she returned after absconding. Wilson told her that she was going to get what she deserved and that there would be no point in complaining to the Officer-in-Charge; she was then dragged by the two girls to a bathroom, where she was forced to sit in cold water in her clothes, and subsequently had her shoulder length hair cut by the same girls in the presence of Wilson, who laughed.

12.26 This last witness alleged also that she had been raped by another named member of the staff at Little Acton with the result that she had to have an abortion in a South Wales hospital later. This allegation was apparently first made 19 years later in a psychiatric unit but the police have been able to find a record of the abortion which was carried out at East Glamorgan Hospital on 29 December 1977. The medical evidence suggests that the conception occurred after the witness left Little Acton in August 1977 and it is to be noted that the witness made a statement for the North Wales Police in August 1992 to the effect that she had not been physically or sexually abused by any member of the staff at Little Acton. In these circumstances it is clear that this witness has not substantiated her allegations of rape satisfactorily and her evidence about other matters has to be approached with caution. We have received persuasive evidence from other witnesses, however, that bullying by residents was rife at Little Acton and that staff turned a blind eye to it. We accept, therefore, that bullying by residents was condoned by staff far too often, although it would be inappropriate to single out Leslie Wilson for blame in this respect.

Peter Bird

12.27 Three complainants, each of whom gave oral evidence before us, alleged that they had suffered physical assaults on them by **Peter Bird.** The first of these, who was a ten year old boy at the time, in late 1974 and early 1975, said that he spent a lot of time in the "lock-up" because he kept running away. He recalled a specific incident when, after he had tried to "sneak out" of the unit, Bird behaved like a lunatic and slapped him across the face and all over the room. The other two complainants were girls who were both 14 years old when they were at Little Acton, the first in the Spring of 1976 and the second almost exactly two years later. The former alleged that residents would run upstairs after school to have a smoke in the bathroom. On a particular occasion when this happened, Bird picked her up and threw her into the bath with the result that she cracked her head and suffered bruising. Finally, the other girl complained of being falsely accused by Bird of stealing a purse (it was recovered later from an older boy) and of being made to search for it fruitlessly in the grounds whilst Bird watched her. On another occasion he lifted her by her hair with the result that her head was tender for a week and, at least twice, he flung himself against a door as she was going through a doorway after an argument, causing painful bruises.

12.28 Bird himself denied these allegations and said that the semi-secure unit was only used for disciplinary purposes on three or four occasions: it was normally occupied by girls (who were mainly from South Wales) and a resident would not be locked in her room. There was no corporal punishment and he believed that was one of the standing orders of the County Council but he did not recall a memorandum to that effect circulated in June 1974. He said also that the girl questioned about the purse had insisted on searching for it and had found it. However, we are satisfied that these three complainants have not invented these allegations and that Bird did use violence of the kind that they have described on occasions. He believed in a strict regime and neither he nor the staff under him had any clear understanding that corporal punishment was prohibited or of the proper boundaries of restraint.

Huw Meurig Jones

12.29   We heard perturbing complaints also about the conduct of **Huw Meurig Jones** from three witnesses. The former boy resident who alleged that he had been slapped across the face by Bird claimed also that a member of the staff called "Hugh" had made advances to him immediately after the Bird incident, when he was in "the secure unit" sitting on his bed. "Hugh" had kissed him on the neck and "tried to have sex" with him after removing his pyjamas. He had not succeeded but afterwards he had bathed the witness for no apparent reason. On another occasion the same man had driven the witness home and had tried to make the witness masturbate him in the car outside the house, threatening the boy that he would not go home again if he told anyone. The witness had not mentioned these allegations to the police in 1992 because he had not wanted to get involved. Another witness, who was at Little Acton about a year later described Jones as a "pure faggot" who used to walk around the units blowing kisses and nipping backsides. He said that Jones had frequented a cafe and public lavatories in King Street, Wrexham, "hanging around with all the kids" after the witness had left care.

12.30   Counsel on behalf of Jones questioned the identification of him by the first of these witnesses because (a) he thought that "Hugh" was about 40 years old and (b) Jones was known as "Hughie/Huwie" or "Mr Jones" and not as "Hugh/Huw". We are not aware of any other member of the staff with the name Hugh/Huw at the time[8], however, and we are satisfied that the witness was referring to Huw Meurig Jones, who was in charge of the semi-secure unit in his capacity as Deputy Superintendent.

12.31   Another witness who made a complaint about Jones, whom she referred to as the Deputy Superintendent, thought that he was in his late 40s. She described him as swarthy, with a big face and a beer belly and also losing his hair (a description largely confirmed by Peter Bird in cross-examination). This witness was 14 years old when she was at Box Lane from January to April 1996. She knew Jones as "Hughie" and she had discussed her position with him and another male member of the staff when she thought that she might have become pregnant as a result of sexual intercourse with boys in the open unit in

---

[8] See, for example, Bird's report to the Management Committee in December 1975. Bird said in evidence that Little Acton Assessment Centre was not fully staffed until late 1975.

which she was then housed. In consequence, she was transferred to the semi-secure unit, which was occupied by girls only. Her complaint against Jones was that, after an occasion when she had absconded with another girl and they had been returned to Little Acton by the police, they were taken into an office by Jones with another man and Jones shouted that they were going to be made to pay for what they had done. Jones then pushed her against a large central heating pipe and punched her heavily in the stomach. The other girl was then taken down by the two men to the recreation room and was seen by the witness the following day to have "one or two black eyes" and bruises.

12.32 When he gave evidence to the Tribunal, Huw Meurig Jones denied all these allegations but he was an unimpressive and uninformative witness. It must be stressed that the only allegation of physical abuse made against him of which we are aware is that summarised in the preceding paragraph and we are unable to make any confident finding about it at this distance of time in the absence of any corroboration. The perturbing aspect of Jones' case is the history of sexual complaints against him in the period of his employment in residential care and then as a social worker in Clwyd.

12.33 Jones' history during this period between 1 February 1972 and his resignation on 29 July 1981 has already been summarised briefly in paragraph 12.03. He was first suspended on 19 December 1980 in connection with sexual allegations made by two former Bryn Estyn residents (one of whom is now dead); and he was suspended for a second time on 12 June 1981 in connection with a police investigation of sexual complaints by another former Bryn Estyn resident. In respect of both investigations files were submitted to the Director of Public Prosecutions and we have been told that charges were preferred in respect of the second investigation, but in neither case was a prosecution pursued (findings of not guilty were recorded in the Wrexham Magistrates' Court in respect of the latter). A further complaint of sexual abuse by Jones was made in evidence to us by a fourth former Bryn Estyn resident[9]. It is apparent also that Jones was interviewed very extensively by police officers in the course of the major police investigation in 1992 about at least one additional sexual complaint.

12.34 It is obvious that we are unable to make findings in relation to police investigations in respect of which we have not heard the primary evidence; and we do not consider that it would be justifiable to make adverse findings against Jones on the two sexual complaints that have been made before us, coupled with the more general evidence of a third witness. These complaints were made very belatedly, about 20 years after the event, and there is no corroboration in law of either of them. Nevertheless, having studied the full record of Jones' interviews with the police in 1992 and heard his own evidence, we are fully satisfied that he is not a suitable person to be employed in residential care or more generally in social service work involving children. We have reached that conclusion having regard to his admissions about his own sexual orientation, his associations, particularly during the period when he was at Cartrefle

---

[9] It is one of those referred to in general terms in para 8.43.

College and later when taking a "skills course", and his activities generally outside working hours. In our judgment it would be impossible for the public, with knowledge of the facts, to have the degree of confidence in his judgment and probity that is essential for employment in social work involving the care of children.

12.35 It has been important for us to face this issue because, despite his resignation in July 1981, Jones was subsequently involved in residential care work, although he was not given any helpful reference by Clwyd County Council. He was unemployed for substantial periods following his resignation but he did serve briefly as Deputy Officer-in-Charge of a private holiday home in Talacre and then for some months as senior care officer at Clwyd Hall School[10]. There followed an appointment as head of care for about two years at a private school in Powys until it closed down. Since then Jones has been employed in quite different work in the London area but he did apply unsuccessfully for an appointment as Officer-in-Charge of Chevet Hey Children's Centre in November 1986 when, according to the particulars that he supplied, he was still employed at the private school in Powys.

Carl Evans

12.36 We have already referred in paragraph 12.12 to the allegations by fellow members of the staff about Evans' allegedly inappropriate behaviour towards girl adolescents who were resident at Little Acton. Major complaints were that he spent long periods of time alone with some girls (when he claimed to be "counselling" them) and that there was excessive physical contact between him and some of the girls. It was alleged, for example, that he had spent the whole evening at a Christmas party in 1977 dancing closely with one girl. That girl (R) subsequently made an allegation on 8 January 1978 that Evans had had sexual intercourse with her at Little Acton during the Christmas period. When interviewed by two members of the staff on 9 January 1978 R wrote a letter withdrawing the complaint but later in the afternoon she told a member of the staff that the complaint was true and it was referred to the police. This was the police investigation referred to in paragraph 12.13, which led to Evans' suspension from duty from 13 January 1978. On 20 March 1978 the Chief Superintendent of the North Wales Police wrote to the Director of Social Services informing him that the Director of Public Prosecutions had advised that no Court action should be taken but Evans' suspension continued to 9 October 1978 during and after the inquiry by the social services investigating team[11].

12.37 The investigating team did formulate charges against Evans in respect of R on the basis that he had behaved unprofessionally towards her and, specifically, that his behaviour towards her at the disco party on 21 December 1977 had amounted to misconduct but no evidence in support of these charges was put forward at the disciplinary hearing and they were dismissed.

[10] See para 4.17.
[11] See para 12.14.

12.38 R repeated her allegations against Evans in the course of the police investigation in 1992 and renewed them to the Tribunal in a written statement, which we have received in evidence. Evans, on the other hand, denied them when he gave oral evidence before us. There was some evidence, not now available, to suggest that R had been infatuated with Evans at the relevant time and two love letters that she had written to him were found in her room. Moreover, she was unwilling to give oral evidence to the Tribunal because of her present domestic responsibilities. There is no basis, therefore, on which we could properly find that her complaint to the Tribunal has been proved.

12.39 We must, however, record our view that Carl Evans was very unsuitable for the responsibilities that he undertook as Deputy Superintendent of Little Acton Assessment Centre. His conduct in relation to other staff and discipline generally, coupled with his behaviour towards resident adolescent girls, demonstrated that he was temperamentally unfitted for the work; and he had no relevant experience in dealing with adolescent girls. He showed an alarming lack of judgment in many areas, most notably, by placing himself in a highly vulnerable position and it is not at all surprising that he became the target of allegations. In these circumstances we do not consider that he is a suitable person to be employed in the residential care of children.

Other members of staff

12.40 Only two other identified members of the staff at Little Acton Assessment Centre were alleged, in the evidence before us, to have used physical (but not sexual) force to individual residents. One former girl resident, who described Little Acton as a "tense, pretty violent place", alleged that a male member of the care staff flew into a temper and assaulted her after she had spilt milk at breakfast but a general description of him was "aggressive but friendly" and "quite teasing, provocative, tormenting". The other complainant alleged that a woman houseparent, in the presence of Bird, singled him out as ringleader when he and others were "messing about" in their living unit: she dragged him into the bath room, swearing at him, and then pulled his hair, forcing him to the ground, whilst she slapped his face.

12.41 Both the alleged perpetrators denied these assaults, as did Bird in respect of the latter and we have no satisfactory means of testing where the truth lies at this late stage. In any event we do not think that it would be appropriate, in general, to make findings against individual members of staff in respect of isolated complaints of this kind. The reality of the matter, in our judgment, is that Bird and those members of the staff who thought like him regarded the use of physical force, quite apart from restraint, as permissible and we accept that it was often used despite the County Council's prohibition of corporal punishment.

Other aspects of the regime at Little Acton Assessment Centre

The assessment process

12.42 It seems clear on the evidence before us that Little Acton failed in its primary role as an assessment centre. The assessment process, such as it was, was carried out by largely untrained staff and the investigation team found in 1978 that it added little to the information already known about the individuals who were subjected to it. Moreover, the staff as a whole were insufficiently involved with the children to take full advantage of getting to know the children; and the centre suffered from lack of consultation with professionals with special skills, such as educational psychologists, psychiatrists etc.

12.43 Another weakness of the system was that some children were left at Little Acton far too long. The period necessary for assessment was six to eight weeks and it was intended that residents would usually stay there no longer than ten to 12 weeks but there were frequent delays in making subsequent placements and the regime was not designed to cater for longer stays. There was too little effort to make the living units as homely as possible and children were likely to deteriorate if they were detained beyond the three months in such an institution.

12.44 As we indicated in paragraph 12.01, it was originally envisaged that Little Acton would provide places for the assessment of 15 children attending daily as well as 15 residents but the demand for this facility proved to be far below expectations and there are very few references to daily attenders in the quarterly reports to the Management Committee. By 1978 the teaching staff had been reduced to two and a change of role from assessment centre to assessment/reception centre had been decided. This was reflected in a change of name to Little Acton Reception and Assessment Centre from about April 1978 onwards, shortly after Michael Barnes had become Acting Officer-in-Charge.

12.45 This change of role, which may not have been implemented until about a year after the change of name, resulted in a significant rise in occupancy rates with the emphasis on reception. Thus, in the period from April to October 1979 there were only nine referrals for assessment (two of whom were originally admitted for reception) and 37 admissions on a reception basis; and over a longer period, approximately one third of the admissions were for assessment. The multi-purpose role intended for Little Acton by Barnes was not to be, however, and on 21 May 1980 it closed, following the transfer of its assessment functions to Bersham Hall for girls and to Bryn Estyn for boys[12].

Education at Little Acton Assessment Centre

12.46 Educational facilities were of considerable importance at Little Acton, even though the intended duration of stay was short, and the teaching staff were expected to take part in the assessment process. The teaching function was

---

[12] See paras 7.12, 13.02 and 13.09.

particularly difficult for the staff because of the very varied levels of ability of the children admitted, some with long records of truancy, and the limited facilities and time available. The teaching staff did not participate in decisions about children admitted on a reception basis.

12.47 Between 1974 and 1980 there were seven visits by Welsh Office SWSOs, all but one prior to October 1976. The summaries of these inspections before us are not very informative but the following points from them, with wider relevance than education only, are worth noting here:

(a) On 13 February 1975 when SWSO Smith inspected on notice, Bird was absent. Smith noted that the centre had no access to an educational psychologist. He recommended that the SSD and LEA should co-ordinate on providing this service and also on support for teaching generally.

(b) On 29 March 1976 Smith visited Little Acton with HMI Garrett. They were favourably impressed, in general, but questioned the wisdom of developing a post-assessment holding unit. They recommended training for the teaching staff but noted that the quality of work done in the classroom was "especially pleasing". Bird's attention was drawn to the need to support the teaching staff, the importance of adding "homely touches" in the children's bedrooms and the need to involve parents in the conferencing process.

(c) On 26 September 1979 SWSO Myra Copleston found (amongst other things) that children could go for as long as six weeks after admission before being visited by a social worker. No information was available on additional measures of controlling residents. Admission documentation was often inadequate. Staffing levels in the educational unit were inadequate. Her conclusion was that "the experience of the first six months of operation as a reception unit suggests to me that a re-appraisal of various aspects of Clwyd's child care service is needed and that further thought needs to be given to the optimum use which can be made of the Centre's staff and facilities".

12.48 We have not received any formal complaints about the quality of education at Little Acton, although several former residents, when asked in the course of their oral evidence about it, made critical comments to the effect that they had learnt nothing or had merely been given a book to read. The balance of the evidence before us, however, points to the conclusion that the teaching staff were dedicated in the work that they did with little support, no opportunities for special training and very limited facilities.

The semi-secure unit

12.49 Little comment is necessary about this because it was neither designed nor intended to be used as a secure unit and we have commented earlier about the confusion arising from the use of the term "semi-secure"[13]. The unit at Little Acton was initially intended to house three girls on remand from the courts, but before Clwyd County Council assumed responsibility for Little Acton, it had been designated as an all-Wales regional facility for girls[14]. We have not received any complaints from former girl residents about its use as such. It appears that it was used mainly by South Wales counties to accommodate girls who were for the time being difficult to control but the unit was not locked. When it was not occupied by girls it was probably used on odd occasions to confine, for short periods, boy absconders or boys who were otherwise causing difficulty, but they have not complained that the use of the unit as such amounted to excessive restraint or physical abuse.

12.50 It is clear, however, that the use of the two open units as mixed accommodation and the persistent difficulty in recruiting adequate night staff did give rise to problems of the kind indicated by the evidence of the witness referred to in paragraph 12.31.

Conclusions

12.51 The brief and unfortunate history of Little Acton Assessment Centre underlines the paramount importance of the senior staff of community homes. If unsuitable officers are appointed, the consequences for resident children in their care are likely to be very grave. At Little Acton none of the persons initially selected for the senior posts had the necessary character, temperament, skills and experience to enable them to fulfil their responsibilities adequately and the quality of care between 1974 and 1978 was far below an acceptable standard. It is to the credit of Clwyd County Council that they appointed a team to investigate the home quite promptly when they became aware of some of the matters that were going wrong; and it is to be noted that two complaints of alleged sexual misconduct were referred to the police for investigation but the disciplinary proceedings that ensued in relation to Carl Evans were not concluded satisfactorily.

12.52 The community home was conducted in a more satisfactory way in the last two years of its existence but the uncertainty about its future seriously weakened its effectiveness both as an assessment centre and a reception centre; and during this period neither the Welsh Office nor senior officials of the Social Services Department nor the Management Committee appears to have made any significant contribution to planning its future. It is regrettable that a purpose built institution with an important primary function should have remained in use so briefly and unsuccessfully.

---

[13] See para 11.23.
[14] Extending (in area) the more limited use set out in para 4.02(2).

Bersham Hall, 1974 to 1993

13.01　Bersham Hall is a large red brick house set in just over an acre of land in a small village about one and a half miles from the centre of Wrexham, and, within its grounds, is a small three bedroom cottage with its own garden. It is believed that the house was occupied as a family residence until it was acquired by Denbighshire County Council with the intention of providing an observation and assessment centre for up to 12 boys to be used by the six North Wales counties (and Radnorshire) under the 1971 Regional Plan. It was to be a community home with education, described as a secure/semi-secure observation and assessment centre, and was to be available for use from August 1972.

13.02　It is convenient to consider the history of Bersham Hall in two distinct phases, namely, from 1974 to 1980 and from 1980 to 1993, because its function changed in 1980 and it closed for a short period at that time. It re-opened as an assessment and reception centre for up to 21 boys and girls, taking over many of the functions performed until then by Little Acton Assessment and Reception Centre. As we understand it, however, the assessment process was limited to girls[1]. At this time the cottage began to be used as an independent training facility for children of school leaving age. Education continued to be provided on the premises until 1990, by which time the majority of residents had been provided with school places locally. The teaching staff at Bersham Hall, however, were employed by Clwyd Social Services Department until 1987, when they were transferred to the Education Authority.

13.03　The community home closed in September 1993 but it was re-opened the following year as a private (registered) children's home called Prospects, which we visited on 19 March 1997, when we met its co-director, Stephen Elliott.

The Observation and Assessment Centre, 1974 to 1980

13.04　It seems that comparatively few alterations were carried out to Bersham Hall before it was opened as a community home in August 1972. In a report to the first meeting, on 10 December 1975, of the Management Committee established by Clwyd County Council for Bryn Estyn, Bersham Hall and Little Acton Assessment Centre it was stated that it was obvious that the washing and cooking facilities, cloakrooms, dormitories, dining and education facilities and staff rooms were all "much below" the required standard. Building work was, therefore, to begin in March 1976 with intended completion in September 1977, and would provide a new block containing dormitory and ancillary accommodation for 16 boys, a staff flat and a duty officer's flat and, on the ground floor, the Superintendent's office, a new dining room and kitchen and

---

[1] See paras 7.12 and 12.45.

secure accommodation. The existing house was also to be adapted and up-graded to provide improved educational facilities, domestic facilities, a library and lounge, a conference room and additional staff and student accommodation.

13.05 The remodelling of Bersham Hall was virtually complete by January 1978, apart from some outside work and the extended educational unit was opened in April 1978. It had been hoped that the secure unit would be put into operation then but, as in the case of Bryn Estyn, the official view was that the unit was never approved for actual use because the required staffing level was never achieved. The Officer-in-Charge, William Tunnah, reported to the Management Committee on 16 November 1979 that Welsh Office SWSO Smith, had visited the centre on 14 September 1979 and had approved the use of the unit "when the staffing levels are correct". However, the Secretary of State's approval was given by letter dated 26 September 1979 without any express mention of this condition[2]. The letter stated that the maximum number of residents to be accommodated in the unit at Bersham Hall was two.

13.06 The reports to the Management Committee by successive officers-in-charge indicate that the need for the secure unit was felt by staff to be urgent because of the difficulty of dealing with some of the more disturbed residents. A report by the Teacher-in- Charge, John Morris, in January 1979, for example, showed that, of 27 boys admitted in the preceding five months, 19 were said to be maladjusted, ten psychotic/needing isolation, 20 violent or extremely disruptive and 22 had learning difficulties. The delay of nearly 18 months in completing the secure unit was due to physical defects or omissions in the work carried out. The 1979 Regional Plan envisaged 13 assessment places at Bersham Hall, including four secure places, available to the whole of Wales[3]. But there does not appear to have been any impetus after 1979 to provide the staff necessary to man the secure unit. The reference to accommodation for two residents in the Secretary of State's letter is also mystifying because our understanding is that the unit provided one secure room (in the sense of a cell) and three other rooms suitable for intensive care as planned originally. The subsequent use of the unit between 1980 and 1993 is dealt with later in this chapter[4].

13.07 It was unfortunate that there were frequent changes of senior staff at Bersham Hall between 1974 and 1980. In that period there were no less than six different Officers-in-Charge successively and five Deputies. One Deputy was promoted to Officer-in-Charge and one Officer-in-Charge for a short period was then downgraded to Deputy so that there were nine senior officers in the period of six years. It is only necessary, however, to name three for the purpose of our narrative. **Richard Ernest Leake** was Officer-in-Charge when Clwyd County Council assumed responsibility on 1 April 1974 and had held that position from the opening of Bersham Hall in August 1972 but he departed in June 1974 to

[2] See paras 11.08 and 11.09.
[3] See para 4.02(1).
[4] See paras 13.60 to 13.65.

take an appointment with Care Concern[5]. **Michael Barnes,** who had been Third-in-Charge from September 1972 and then Deputy Officer-in-Charge from 1 August 1973, became Acting Officer-in-Charge for six months from June 1974, reverting to Deputy until he became Acting Officer-in-Charge again from 15 February 1976. He was made substantive Officer-in-Charge from 1 June 1976 and he remained in that post until the end of 1978 when he took over at Little Acton as previously related, having been responsible for both homes from 21 April 1978[6]. For the last 12 months of its existence as an assessment centre for boys the Officer-in-Charge of Bersham Hall was **William (Bill)Tunnah**, now deceased, who had served blamelessly on the care staff at Bryn Estyn for eight years and who had been intended to have immediate charge of the secure unit there.

13.08   There is one other senior officer to whom reference must be made, namely, **Michael Taylor**, the predecessor as Deputy of Michael Barnes. He was Deputy Officer-in-Charge for ten months, from 26 September 1972 to 31 July 1973, before Clwyd County Council took over the home. He was nearly 31 years old when he was appointed and had been an Anglican Franciscan friar for four years before starting residential care work in 1965. Between 1965 and 1969 he had worked as a houseparent, latterly as a senior housefather in Warwickshire, before taking a two year course in residential care work at Enfield College of Technology. At the time of his appointment to Bersham Hall, he had been employed for just over a year as Deputy Superintendent of a reception centre for children in Islington and he received fulsome testimonials in respect of that work. He left Bersham Hall because he had been offered an appointment as a lecturer at South Cheshire Central College of further education but he stayed at Chevet Hey Children's Home for a short period until his college accommodation became available.

13.09   Bersham Hall suffered from chronic staff shortages at lower levels throughout this period and the absence of staff on courses further complicated the picture. It is not possible, therefore, to give a realistic estimate of the number of staff, including temporary and part-time staff, who were involved in the care of the children between 1974 and 1980. Morris did, however, remain the Teacher-in-Charge of the education unit from 1 September 1975 until about the end of April 1980, when admissions to Bersham Hall ceased for a period and he transferred to the assessment unit within Bryn Estyn at Cedar House for a few months before being appointed Teacher-in-Charge of the Hawarden Educational Centre in July 1980. The establishment for the education unit appears to have been only one teacher throughout, despite persistent representations to Clwyd County Council and to the Regional Planning Committee; and Morris was refused permission to attend Cardiff University in order to qualify for a Master's degree. The pressure for an increase was exerted most forcefully when refurbished accommodation was opened for use in April 1978 but Morris was provided with only part-time help by firstly, Jane Pearce,

[5] See paras 4.12 to 4.16.
[6] See para 12.21.

now deceased, and then Jim West, who transferred from Bryn Estyn. Pearce went on to Cedar House, Bryn Estyn with Morris when Bersham Hall closed in 1980.

13.10 We estimate that about 375 boys were admitted to Bersham Hall between April 1974 and the end of April 1980. This figure is based on the details supplied to the Management Committee for periods from 1 April 1975 to 31 January 1980. Admissions were at a higher rate up to about the spring of 1977 but building work intervened at about that time and the average occupancy dropped from the range of nine to 14 to six to eight thereafter, remaining fairly level at about nine in the final year. It was intended that children should stay as residents at the centre for only eight weeks but many stayed longer (one for as long as 174 days), usually because of difficulties in obtaining placements.

13.11 Observation and Assessment Centres have to deal with a high turnover of children, many of whom are offenders referred by the courts following stressful proceedings whilst others are transferred from equally stressful home or care placements that have failed; and the actual observation and assessment processes involve psychiatric and other interviews and tests which may well put pressure on those undergoing them. Children at such centres are likely therefore to be both damaged and in an emotional state, uncertain about their future. Potentially explosive situations between such children and between children and staff are to be expected and there is a need for stricter rules and a more controlling regime than would be appropriate in other community homes. Nevertheless, SWSO Smith was able to record in his report of visits to Bersham Hall in April and May 1978, "The visit to Bersham gave a favourable impression of staff relationships and team work approach under good leadership".

13.12 One of the weaknesses of Bersham Hall to which Morris drew attention was the lack of facilities for training adolescents who had already left school (in 1977/1978, 20% were in this category) and it does not appear that the cottage was utilised for this purpose before 1980[7]. Until late 1976 a majority of the children admitted were on remand to the courts but the proportion fell progressively and children who were the subject of care orders became equally prominent.

Complaints against members of the staff

13.13 We are aware of 19 complainants who have made complaints of abuse suffered prior to May 1980 at Bersham Hall. However, seven of these referred only to incidents before Clwyd County Council came into existence and another referred partly to incidents in that earlier period.

Michael Taylor

13.14 The main subject of these eight complaints was the conduct of **Michael Taylor**, the Deputy Officer-in-Charge from 26 September 1972 to 31 July 1973. There were three complainants who alleged sexual abuse by Taylor and all of them

---

[7] See para 13.02.

gave oral evidence before us. There was a complaint also by a former resident of Chevet Hey Children's Home that Taylor had indecently assaulted him when Taylor was staying there briefly in the summer of 1973 whilst waiting for his college accommodation to become available; and that witness too gave oral evidence before us. All the allegations were of indecent assaults, usually committed in the witness' bedroom, involving masturbation of the witness under the bedclothes and mutual masturbation, and often in circumstances in which Taylor was purporting to comfort the witness; and we are fully satisfied that the complaints are true.

13.15 One of these witnesses was heard complaining about what Taylor had done by a member of staff at Bersham Hall, who reported the matter to the Officer-in-Charge, Richard Leake. The latter interviewed the boy but requested the Matron to be present, to the boy's embarrassment. In consequence, the boy did not disclose the full details of the assault and wrongly admitted lying to other boys about the extent of the assault. Taylor made a signed statement saying that he had merely tidied up the boy's disarranged bed clothes. Leake reported the matter by letter dated 2 July 1973 to the Director of Social Services for Denbighshire, Emlyn Evans, and stated that both he and the Matron were of the opinion that there was no substance in the allegations. However, the Principal Social Worker (Residential Services), R W Dixon, did interview Leake three days later and his subsequent memorandum of 10 July 1973 to the Senior Assistant Director (Residential Services) is revealing about the attitudes of both Leake and Dixon to the matter. The relevant parts read:

> "Mr Leake was adamant from the outset of our discussion that the reason he conducted interviews with those concerned was to <u>clear up any suspicions created</u> by a conversation between boys, which was overheard by a member of staff, Mr J Blackman. Mr Leake stated that he did not consider the accusation being true even before he began his interview . . . and was convinced the incidents had been exaggerated when he completed his investigations. Mr Leake mentioned that the importance of his investigations was due to the constant vulnerability of staff working with disturbed children and therefore it was his intention to prove to staff and resident boys alike that suspicions of any kind within the Unit tended to cause anxieties which, by some discussion between the parties involved would help in the restoring of confidences. In discussing the report with Mr Leake certain irregularities came to light regarding lines of communication, procedures of administration etc. We fully discussed the report and its shortcomings and I issued appropriate directives and suggestions to the Superintendent for further reference.

> The points which were particularly relevant included the fact that Mr Leake had interviewed the boys and member of his staff without another senior member of the Department being present and committed the error of having a junior member of his staff as his witness throughout the interview. Secondly his lines of communication were at fault. Thirdly, his report would seem to have been written in haste and over dramatised thereby conjuring up some unintended suspicions.

In closing the interview both Mr Grant and I felt confident that the Superintendent had acted in good faith."

13.16 Leake's comment about this in his oral evidence to the Tribunal was that he remembered that meeting with considerable difficulty. The only thing that he remembered about it was that it was rather heated and that he came away from it with the belief that both Dixon and Grant were annoyed that he had not contacted them but had sent his correspondence to the Director of Social Services. Leake thought that the criticism was more political than professional.

13.17 Dixon did, however, receive direct a report from the Officer-in-Charge of Chevet Hey about the incident there that occurred two months later. Dixon's note of the report, dated 10 September 1973, reads as follows (the errors in it are reproduced):

> "Mr M J A Taylor Mr Ellis Edwards reported to me that a boy resident in Chevet Hey, "A", had made an accusation against Mr Mike Taylor, referring that Mr Taylor had interferred with him whilst lying in bed. On my instructions, Mr Edwards made enquiries of the accused and asked him to leave the premises.
>
> Mr Edwards reported that Mr Taylor left remarking that he denied the accusation; in his opinion, by leaving, he was at least ceasing to be an embarrassment to the Home."

13.18 No further action was taken in respect of either of the reported complaints.

13.19 Taylor was later convicted on 26 June 1980 in the Wrexham Magistrates' Court of two offences of indecent assault on a male under 16 years of age and asked for two similar offences to be taken into consideration. He was placed on probation for two years. The offences were committed in Shropshire and were wholly unconnected with the matters that we have related in the preceding paragraphs.

13.20 In the course of the major police investigation in 1991/1993 into the matters with which we are concerned, Taylor was interviewed extensively on 13 August 1993 and made very full admissions about the four complaints to which we have referred, all of which had by then been particularised in statements by the complainants to the police. The file was referred to the Crown Prosecution Service both before and after the interview with Taylor. The decision of the Crown Prosecution Service was that Taylor should be cautioned rather than prosecuted and on 24 September 1993, he accepted cautions in respect of offences of indecent assault against four named former residents of Bersham Hall, Chevet Hey and two un-named victims.

Other allegations of abuse

13.21 The other allegations of abuse at Bersham Hall prior to 1980 are more difficult to deal with because they are much more diffuse and consist mainly of complaints by single individuals against single members of the staff. Moreover, seven of the 19 complainants were unable to identify the member or members of staff against whom complaints were made and another three were unable to do so in part. Of the rest, it is sufficient to say that there were four who alleged physical assaults by **Michael Barnes,** (one of these complainants was in Bersham Hall before 1974) and two alleged physical assaults by **Nefyn Dodd**[8] (again, one before 1974). One complainant, for example, who was there in mid-1974, alleged that he had been punched by Barnes on three or four occasions and had seen him assault other boys. The same witness said that he had been physically assaulted by Nefyn Dodd on many occasions but the word "many" is of uncertain meaning in this context. A pre-1974 witness claimed to have been punched in the stomach, thrown to the floor and spat on by Barnes and yet another, at Bersham Hall in 1975, said that he had been picked up by the scruff of the neck, kneed in the back and thus thrown into a corridor by Barnes, after fighting with another boy. He complained also that he had been put into ill-fitting clothes by Barnes after absconding.

13.22 We will defer comment upon these allegations against Barnes until later in this chapter when we will deal with the full picture of the allegations made against him in his senior posts at Bersham Hall. As for the limited allegations against Dodd in the short period of nine months to 1 August 1974, before he moved to Bryn Estyn, it is sufficient for us to say that, in our view, the evidence does not add anything of substance to the later picture that we have given of him during his period at Bryn Estyn[9].

13.23 The individual allegations of physical abuse against other members of the staff, named and un-named, were of a similar character but they do not suggest that violence by members of the staff was characteristic of the regime at Bersham Hall prior to 1980. We should add also that we were not persuaded by the evidence of one complainant about a single incident in the baby pool of a swimming bath that he had been intentionally indecently assaulted by a member of the staff who was giving him a swimming lesson. The most serious allegation of physical violence during this period was made against a field social worker rather than a member of the residential staff and was to the effect that his nose was fractured by a punch on the face when he tried to run away on being delivered by the social worker to Bersham Hall; the boy himself, however, had physically attacked a teacher at his day school and was being admitted to Bersham Hall for that reason. His allegation is categorically denied by the social worker and by the two staff witnesses alleged to have been present.

The Children's Centre, 1980 to 1993

13.24 The re-naming of Bersham Hall as a Children's Centre was adopted by the Social Services Committee in or about May 1980 on the initiative of Barnes, who became its Officer-in-Charge again at the same time. He envisaged the future role of Bersham Hall as that of a multi-purpose unit, specialising in short term care and offering some assessment facilities[10]. In 1984 Barnes gave a "pen picture" of the scope of the centre's operations. It was then, essentially, a centre for boys and girls in the age range of 13 to 16 years who had more complex

---

[8] See para 10.148.
[9] See paras 10.149 and 10.150.
[10] See minutes of the Management Committee meeting on 16 May 1980, para 4.

needs or were otherwise more difficult to place. The Centre had to cope also with emergency admissions and the assessment of children involved in current court proceedings. In addition to catering for residents it had to provide also day care as a prelude to admission or as part of a rehabilitation scheme. Its educational facility was available for residents but was also offered on a day basis as a support service to other residential establishments and to the Local Education Authority. This diversity of roles reinforced the need to which we have referred earlier for a more controlling regime[11].

13.25　As we have said earlier[12], **Michael Barnes** returned to Bersham Hall as Officer-in-Charge in May 1980. He remained in that post from 21 May 1980 to 31 December 1987 but there was an interruption from 1 October 1982 to 31 July 1984 whilst he took the CQSW course at Keele University. To complete the picture further he was also Acting Officer-in-Charge of Chevet Hey from 1 April 1986 to 31 December 1987. **Christopher Thomas**[13] went with Barnes from Little Acton to Bersham Hall as Deputy Officer-in-Charge and remained there until it closed. He acted as Officer-in-Charge during Mr Barnes' absence at Keele University and then succeeded him in the senior post from 1 January 1988 to 22 March 1994, when he resigned because of allegations that he had misappropriated some of the Centre's funds. On 25 October 1995 in Wrexham Maelor Magistrates' Court, he pleaded guilty to theft and was ordered to undertake community service for 120 hours in addition to paying £1,500 by way of compensation. The Centre had closed in September 1993 but Thomas appears to have retained his post for six months longer because he was on prolonged sick leave and/or because of the police investigation into the misappropriations.

13.26　The Third Officer-in-Charge from 21 May 1980 was Angela Pritchard, who acted as Deputy Officer-in-Charge during the period when Christopher Thomas was Acting Officer-in-Charge. She left on 31 July 1989 and was replaced from 1 October 1989 until 30 June 1990 by **Frederick Marshall Jones**, of whom a full account will more conveniently be given in the next chapter[14].

13.27　We have seen the reports on Bersham Hall that were submitted to the Management Committee between September 1980 and July 1984 but it seems that the Management Committee ceased to exist on the demise of Bryn Estyn. From these reports it can be seen that about 220 children were admitted to Bersham Hall between April 1980 and April 1984 but the admission rates were affected, for example, by prolonged industrial action between September 1983 and January 1984. From the second half of 1982 the cottage or lodge in the grounds was used as a hostel for up to three girls, to prepare them for independent living, and the normal occupancy of the main unit was regarded as 18. Provision was made also for individual children housed elsewhere to attend on a daily basis at the education unit for day care but the maximum number of "day care days" in any quarter recorded in the period was only 36.

---

[11] See para 13.11.
[12] See para 12.21.
[13] See para 12.22.
[14] See paras 14.12 to 14.19 and 14.57 to 14.62.

It is difficult, on the basis of these limited figures, to estimate the total number of children admitted to Bersham Hall between 1980 and 1993 but it is unlikely to have exceeded about 600, bearing in mind the progressive trend towards fostering in the second half of the period and the overall reduction in the number of children in care. Throughout the period the overwhelming majority of children admitted were from Clwyd.

13.28 The staff establishment was gradually increased in the early 1980s so that by May 1985, when Barnes wrote an up-dated pen picture of the community home, there were the three managerial staff already named, two senior houseparents and ten houseparents, who, between them, provided "twenty four hour cover for 365 days per year". In addition, there were two teachers assigned to the education unit, who were employed by the Social Services Department until 1987, when they were transferred to the Education Department. The provision of education on the premises ended in 1990, after which the children were allocated to local schools (a policy that had earlier been pursued with some, but not all, of the children).

13.29 Changes in staff were much less frequent from 1980 onwards than they had been earlier. Nevertheless, there were continuing staff problems. Barnes' own training course and his subsequent additional responsibilities for Chevet Hey interrupted continuity and the Teacher-in-Charge was absent for a year, whilst undergoing training at Cartrefle College, at the same time as Barnes. The second teacher was absent also during pregnancy and then maternity leave, after which she worked for only a short period before leaving. Thus, heavy reliance had to be placed on supply teachers. More generally, the incidence of sickness and injuries seems to have been above normal and there were prolonged absences by some members of staff with important responsibilities.

Complaints against members of staff, 1980 to 1993

13.30 Although the period under review here was twice as long as the earlier period and the total number of children admitted was similarly larger, we have not received evidence of a similar increase in the number of complaints. We are aware of 24 former residents who have made complaints but 13 of these have not come forward to renew these complaints to the Tribunal and another gave oral evidence to us without renewing her allegation against a named member of staff. It must be said also that some of the allegations that have not been renewed were made against unidentified members of the staff.

Contemporaneous complaints

13.31 It is convenient to refer firstly to the few complaints of which we know that were made contemporaneously, that is, at the time of or shortly after the alleged incidents. The first of these occurred on 27 September 1988 and involved a boy resident, one of the 13 referred to in the preceding paragraph, who is said to have been in a disturbed state at the time. The material events began at lunch time when a woman member of the care staff had agreed to play badminton with the boy. She alleged that, as she had leant forward to retrieve the shuttlecock, the boy had touched her indecently and that she had responded spontaneously by slapping his face. The boy had continued to be attention seeking in the course of the afternoon, brandishing a large tree branch, threatening to damage cars and eventually smashing two windows in a store room. The boy was taken to an office by a male member of staff to be dealt with by the Third Officer-in-Charge (in the temporary absence of her seniors) and the member of staff who had slapped his face. Another male member of staff, **John Ilton**[15], who had been re-deployed from Bryn Estyn to Bersham Hall from 1 September 1984 as a teacher, was asked to be present in the office because it was thought that the boy might become violent. When Ilton entered the room he found that the boy was in a agitated state and becoming aggressive towards Angela Pritchard. In a statement made the same day, Ilton said that the boy rose to his feet and advanced towards Pritchard in a threatening manner, whereupon he (Ilton) stepped between them and pushed the boy back into his chair. The latter then became abusive and threatening to Ilton, who felt that he was beyond reasoning with and slapped him once across the face.

13.32 The incidents were fully investigated by Michael Barnes, who was by then Principal Social Worker (Child and Family Services) and who interviewed the boy personally at Bersham Hall in the presence of Christopher Thomas and his deputy. The facts were reported to the Assistant Director of Social Services, Raymond Powell, and instructions were given that the woman member of staff should be informed that "slapping children is not an acceptable means of control".

13.33 When interviewed by the police on 7 September 1992 the boy said, "I do recall being slapped by John Ilton. However, as far as I am concerned, I probably deserved to get a slap as I could be very abusive. I have no complaint to make against John Ilton". Ilton was employed by the Education Department in 1988 and the incident was reported to that department. According to Ilton, he was visited by an education official, Alan Williams, who concluded that it had been "regrettable but understandable in the circumstances" and that no official action was necessary.

13.34 We are aware of only two other complainants who made relatively minor allegations of physical abuse by Ilton during the period of eight years when he was teaching at Bersham Hall. The first of these was of pushing a boy with the result that he stumbled back and fell onto the floor. However, the boy admitted that he had been deliberately provoking Ilton and he said to the police in August 1992 "I don't actually blame Ilton for pushing me because, if I was in his position, I would have done the same. However, thinking back I think he should have just chucked me out of the classroom instead". As for the other "complainant", he did not allege that he had been assaulted himself and no evidence has been forthcoming from the two boys alleged by him to have been assaulted.

---

[15] See paras 10.85 and 10.94 to 10.99.

13.35 John Ilton remained at Bersham Hall until March 1992, when he was arrested by the police in the course of their major investigation. After the decision not to prosecute him had been made by the Crown Prosecution Service in or about May 1992, he was on sick leave until he returned to teaching later that year at a day school for problem children known as Wrexham Unit. Finally, he was employed from 1 January 1993 at a special school in the Wrexham area, St Christopher's, until he was suspended again from 13 December 1993, as a result of further allegations about his conduct at Bryn Estyn. Although he returned to teaching at St Christopher's briefly early in 1994, the strain caused by the allegations against him and the surrounding local publicity had affected his health and he took early retirement on 31 March 1994, at the age of 54 years.

13.36 Another incident that was contemporaneously investigated occurred on 20 November 1988 and involved a girl resident (S), who had very recently learnt that she was pregnant after absconding for several weeks. Most unusually for the time of year, there had been quite a heavy fall of snow, leading to a snowball fight outside amongst the boys, in the course of which some snow had been carried into the building. A male care worker dealt with this appropriately but a woman member of the care staff (T) came on the scene and was told by some of the boys that S had been responsible for some of the mess. There followed an unwise and unnecessary confrontation in S's bedroom between T and S, during which they fought on the bed and bit each other. Fortunately, another woman member of the care staff intervened and managed to separate the combatants, whereupon T left the bedroom and the intervener stayed to counsel S. Both S and T subsequently attended hospital separately: S had large bruising to the right wrist and a minor cut to the skin.

13.37 The incident was not reported to Christopher Thomas, the Officer-in-Charge, until about 30 hours after it occurred but he then made full inquiries and wrote an undated memorandum on the subject, probably for Barnes. In the memorandum he referred to the fact that he had spoken to the Area Officer to advise the latter that he was extremely concerned about the incident and that he wished to discuss it further but that the Area Officer did not share his level of concern and had merely noted his observations. We are not aware of any disciplinary action taken against T but she ceased to be employed at Bersham Hall on 31 July 1989. In her statement to the police made in June 1992, S said that she had been treated well in care in the five children's homes in which she had lived during nine years from the age of seven years and that she had no complaint to make.

13.38 A further incident investigated at the time occurred on 15 November 1989 and involved **Frederick Marshall Jones**. A disturbed boy resident (X) sustained an injury to his right thigh that day, in the early evening, whilst "play fighting" with Marshall Jones. The boy had called Marshall Jones "slap head" and had tapped him on the head, eventually causing some annoyance by his behaviour. Subsequently, when the boy was playing table tennis Marshall Jones kneed him (gave him a "dead leg"), causing him to sit down in tears. Christopher Thomas became aware that the boy's right leg had been injured two days later and the injury persisted, necessitating visits to a doctor on 22 and 29 November 1989 (visible symptoms were a swelling above the right knee and "massive bruising", according to one doctor). The boy was ambivalent initially about pursuing a complaint, because he did not want to get Marshall Jones into trouble, and there was evidence of varying unsatisfactory responses by Marshall Jones, including threats of another dead leg, telling the boy that he had hit the other leg and cajoling him generally.

13.39　There were a number of unsatisfactory features about the handling of this incident: delay in arranging for the boy to see a doctor; failure to complete log and accident reports; the fact that Marshall Jones was not interviewed until 30 November. Finally, Thomas's detailed report of his investigation was not sent to Barnes until 11 December, almost a month after the incident. That report ended:

> "In conclusion, I believe this is a most worrying incident which should now be handed over to a more senior officer for further investigation. X's parents are aware of the incident and the complaint and have been assured that it will be properly investigated. I have not been able to properly follow up with Mr Jones as he is currently on sick leave. It is essential that X, his parents and the staff group see that the complaint has been taken seriously."

13.40　The subsequent investigation was hampered by the fact X was moved to Hindley Remand Centre and then to a psychiatric hospital for reasons unconnected with the incident and Barnes was advised that he should not be interviewed. Barnes did interview both Thomas and Marshall Jones and then drafted a memorandum to the Area Officer. This memorandum dated 26 January 1990, which was signed by Geoffrey Wyatt, stated (correctly), "More recently, X has re-asserted his original view that the injuries were caused accidentally and that he does not wish to pursue a complaint". It set out Marshall Jones' version of the incident, referred to the absence of contemporary records and listed X's concerns about Marshall Jones' behaviour towards him in the days following the incident. The conclusion read as follows:

> "It is clear that X experienced injuries to his right thigh which have yet to be fully explained. Whilst it is possible that they were caused in the collision between X and Mr F M Jones, Mr Jones denies causing the injury in the manner stated. It is not therefore possible to conclude beyond reasonable doubt that the injuries were caused in anything but an accidental fashion."

13.41　The action in relation to Marshall Jones was recorded as follows:

> "Mr Jones has been made aware of the risks of engaging in physical play and of the need to immediately report and log details of collisions with clients (however caused) and of the need to ensure that where as a result, injuries are caused they are reported on an accident form even if as in this case they only become apparent some days later."

Other complaints of abuse received by the Tribunal

Sexual abuse

13.42 Turning to the complaints of abuse made in the evidence received by the Tribunal, only nine complainants referred to identified members of the staff. Allegations of sexual abuse were made by three women witnesses, only one of whom gave oral evidence. She alleged that, when she was at Bersham Hall for about seven months from 1 June 1980, a male member of staff (identified only by his first name), who otherwise treated her well and was "very charismatic", touched her and tried to kiss her, but she fought him off and he apologised, saying that he had been unable to resist her. She referred also, however, to "a snippet of memory of being behind a wall that was at the side of the building and having sex with him against a tree"; and she added that it was very vague, a snatch of memory, "and then walking up the stairs feeling like he had spoilt it". She did not complain to anyone because the man was her friend and she did not want to lose him because he was kind to her.

13.43 The second witness, whose evidence was read because she was not prepared to give oral evidence, said in her Tribunal statement that she awoke in bed one night and felt a hand on her leg under the blanket. She screamed and ran out of the room, opening the alarmed door, which triggered the emergency lights so that she saw the male member of staff responsible and he told her not to tell anyone on pain of not being allowed home. This would have been during 1981, when she was at Bersham Hall from 20 January to 31 August. She did not mention the incident when she was seen by the police in September 1992 but did so in her Tribunal statement made in November 1996.

13.44 Finally, the third witness, who appeared at the Tribunal but felt unable to give oral evidence when she did so, made allegations of sexual misconduct by several members of the staff. She was at Bersham Hall for the first three months of 1988 and then for two years from March 1989. Her first statement to the police, made in March 1992, contained a long account of her relationship the previous month away from Bersham Hall with a member of staff there. She was then 18 years old and no longer in care. In her second statement to the police made in January 1993 this witness recounted an occasion when sexual intercourse occurred at Bersham Hall between two residents under 16 years of age allegedly to the knowledge of a member of the ancillary staff; she gave some account also of her non-sexual friendship at Bersham Hall with the member of staff referred to in her first statement; and she said that another member of the care staff had once touched her with his hand on her breast over her clothes but that she was not sure whether it had been accidental or intentional. Finally, in her third statement to the police made six months later, she complained that a third member of the care staff, when drunk, had touched her indecently with his hand and had lain upon her when she was in a sleeping bag in her tent on a camping trip with other residents and five members of staff from Bersham Hall. This was alleged to have occurred in the presence of another girl resident, who shared the tent with the complainant and to whom the member of staff exposed himself, according to the complainant. That girl denied to the police, however, that any of the incidents described by the complainant had occurred.

13.45 These brief details illustrate the difficulty of making positive findings about any of the sexual complaints. Some, at least, of the incidents may well have occurred but all were denied and it is impossible to investigate them satisfactorily many years afterwards. Only one of the members of staff, namely, the first referred to in the preceding paragraph was subjected to disciplinary proceedings: he was suspended on 3 March 1992 and then dismissed after disciplinary hearings on 7 and 13 October 1992, but it does not appear that any of the charges against him were based directly on the allegations contained in the third complainant's first statement. Eight charges were found to have been proved and it was decided that the residential worker's name should be referred to the Department of Health Consultancy Service for registration on the Index. We heard evidence from Christopher Thomas that he had spoken to that staff member on three occasions and then written to him about the unwisdom of being alone with the third complainant, who had also been warned about the matter; and Thomas had also requested the relevant line manager to see the member of staff in that connection.

13.46 We have no doubt that sexual intercourse between residents did occur at Bersham Hall from time to time and that there was some inappropriate conduct on the part of individual members of the care staff. The favourable side of the picture, however, is that the volume of complaints over the 13 year period has been very small and that no one has alleged persistent or habitual abuse of successive residents by any individual member of staff. Indeed, the only allegations of sexual incidents after 1981 are those referred to in paragraph 13.44.

Physical abuse

Christopher Thomas' view

13.47 Rather similar comments are appropriate about the level of physical violence at Bersham Hall in the second period. Christopher Thomas was quite a frank witness about this. He said of the earlier period between 1974 and 1980 that children were treated firmly at the assessment centre and that there were aggressive undertones but that he never saw a child assaulted. There was a lot of physical horseplay with an element of the staff showing their power. He himself had reservations about this but he took part on occasions to let off steam. There was quite a "delinquent culture" the children were not as "streetwise" as their London counterparts would be but they included more serious offenders, who could be more difficult to control.

13.48 Thomas described the environment at Bersham Hall after 1980 as a hotch potch, because of the Children's Centre's variety of functions, including the assessment of girls. The latter should not have been held for more than three months but, for some, their stay could be extended indefinitely. As for boys, it was intended to be a short term holding centre, pending further placement, but some were held for substantially longer periods. Barnes thought that six to nine months ought to be the longest period to avoid disruption. Other complicating factors were the alternating reigns of Barnes and Thomas as Officer-in-Charge, and Barnes' later additional responsibility for Chevet Hey; and the transfer to Bersham Hall from Bryn Estyn, when the latter closed, of several members of Bryn Estyn staff with their different views on and experience of discipline.

13.49 Thomas, according to his own evidence, favoured a more relaxed regime, Barnes was, in his view, an odd mixture of permissiveness and authority: his attitude to residents was "You'll do what we say. It is not up for discussion". He could be physically intimidating also, scaring, and had an aggressive manner of speaking. More seriously, he permitted excessive forms of restraint to be employed. Thomas said that he would see with his own eyes two or three members of staff sitting on an individual child, residents joining in, and the restraint lasting for perhaps an hour. Thomas admitted that he himself may have behaved inappropriately in his early days: he had not targeted anyone deliberately but he had used excessive restraint on occasions after allowing a confrontation to occur.

13.50 Thomas said also that there was "an element" of avoiding facing up to allegations: superficially they were taken seriously but the subsequent action taken did not do justice to the allegations (he cited particularly the incidents that we have described in paragraphs 13.36 and 13.38).

Michael Barnes

13.51 Barnes did not accept the picture given by Thomas and said that the latter was relatively inexperienced on his arrival at Bersham Hall in 1974. Barnes himself could not think of anything that he had done that he would not have liked a police officer, parent or superior to see. He disagreed with the criticisms of one former member of the care staff that the children were not treated like individuals and he would not accept that the atmosphere of the place was oppressive. There were occasions when children were physically restrained: incidents might occur three or four times per month, averaged out, but he would be very surprised if the restraint exceeded a quarter of an hour in the worst case.

13.52 Of the ten complainants who were at Bersham Hall between 1980 and 1993 and whose evidence we received, four complained of physical abuse by Michael Barnes in varying degrees. All these complaints, except one, refer to events alleged to have occurred within a year or so of his return as Officer-in-Charge in May 1980. The earliest in time of these was by a boy who alleged that, after absconding when he was 11 years old, he was taken into Barnes' office and asked why he had absconded. The boy raised his voice and shouted that he hated it, whereupon Barnes came round the desk and pushed him to the floor. He was then taken to the secure unit by Thomas, where they were joined by Barnes, who punched him on his arms and body. He was locked in that unit for three to four weeks in a cell like room with a mattress and blanket.

13.53 The other complainant who gave oral evidence alleged that he was verbally abused by Barnes many times and physically abused by him a few times when he was at Bersham Hall in the latter part of 1980, at the age of about 12 years. He was a Wrexham boy who absconded several times when he first arrived and he alleged that on one occasion, after being returned by the police, Barnes grabbed him round the throat and chest and threw him into the office, where Barnes threatened to take him to "a semi-secure unit in South Wales". A similar incident occurred when he had absconded on another occasion but one of the care staff was also present on that occasion.

13.54 The two witnesses whose evidence was read were former girl residents. The first, who was at Bersham Hall in 1981 just before and after her 12th birthday, also complained of being grabbed by the throat by Barnes during her initial interview in his office, when she denied that she had been stealing from her grandmother. On that or another occasion she ended up on the floor with Barnes pushing her arms up behind her back. She was shouting but she was not hitting out at him in any way. Finally, the other witness was a frequent absconder from Bersham Hall in the second half of the 1980s. She complained of physical abuse throughout the period when she was in care from the age of 13 years onwards and before she was admitted into care, but in her statement to the police in September 1992 she said that she had never been physically or sexually assaulted and had not seen any person assaulted. In her Tribunal statements made in April and August 1997, however, she alleged that Barnes used to push her into the wall and bang her head. He had also tied her hand and foot on a bed and had beaten her up in the secure unit once.

13.55 Barnes denied all these allegations and those that we have summarised in paragraph 13.21. We referred earlier to his general rebuttal of the criticism of his regime at Bersham Hall and, in his evidence to the Tribunal, he dealt with all the allegations against him chronologically, repeating his denial that he had ever used violence towards any resident except in necessary restraint. In reviewing the various criticisms of him we have had to consider not only his record at Bersham Hall but also the evidence about him at Little Acton Assessment Centre[16] and Chevet Hey[17] and his subsequent activities in more senior posts from 1988 onwards, which are described later in this report[18]. As we shall explain later, Barnes was a good communicator and he did provide intelligent ideas, for example, about the respective roles of the community homes for which he was responsible from time to time. His reports to the Management Committee were helpful and thoughtful and he produced to the Tribunal a wide selection of documents that he had written or helped to draft on a range of problems involving the welfare of children in care.

13.56 It is noteworthy that Barnes' main involvement was with children who were being held on a short term basis for assessment or otherwise pending placement and it is reasonably clear that a high proportion of the children at Bersham Hall were seriously disturbed in one way or another. It may be for these reasons that Barnes did not attempt to develop close relationships with the children in his care and saw himself as a disciplinarian. Whatever may have been the reason, however, we are satisfied that Barnes was viewed

---

[16] See para 12.23.
[17] See paras 14.49 to 14.54.
[18] See paras 28.27, 28.31 and 28.44.

by some of the residents as a remote, unfriendly and arrogant figure and that he was responsible for instituting, or at least maintaining, what they saw as an oppressive and authoritarian regime at Bersham Hall. One former resident did say that the place had a friendly atmosphere and that he was treated really well there and another said that the level of care was very good but the majority of those whose evidence we received were very critical. Thus, one referred to "a very hostile environment" and others described it as "strict and regimented" and "institutionalised". Three members of staff who had been transferred there from Bryn Estyn in or about 1984 were similarly critical, describing the regime as oppressive and John Cunningham described it as more so than Bryn Estyn.

13.57   There does not appear to have been any significant softening in Barnes' general approach as a result of his CQSW course between 1982 and 1984 but it is right to say that the main allegations against him of personal violence pre-date that course. Although we regarded some of the comparatively small number of witnesses who complained of physical assaults by him as unreliable, we do not think that all the allegations have been invented and we are satisfied that he did, on occasions, use excessive force against residents both by way of restraint and in response to impertinence or indiscipline by them.

Allegations against Christopher Thomas

13.58   Only three complainants gave live evidence of alleged physical assaults on them by Christopher Thomas. One of these was a former girl resident who alleged that, when she refused repeatedly to go to her room, Thomas dragged her there, shook her and threw her on the bed. The second alleged that he had been punched, kicked and sat on by Thomas as a punishment for smoking. The third witness claimed, that after he (the witness) had an altercation with a teacher who had attacked him, Thomas had intervened and dragged him away; Thomas had gone on to strike him and had then locked him in his bedroom for 40 minutes. Finally, a fourth complainant whose evidence was read, alleged that, after she had "accidentally spat" on Thomas' car, he had twisted or pushed up her arm behind her back, and "nearly broke" her arm. One other former girl resident said that she had seen Thomas assault a boy by punching and kneeing him in the back and that other members of the staff had then kicked the boy after he had set fire to a wardrobe in his room.

13.59   Bearing in mind that Thomas was at Bersham Hall for nearly 20 years, apart from absence at Salford for the CRCCYP course and later for 15 months at Little Acton Assessment Centre, the volume of complaints against him is small. Although he was an advocate for a more relaxed regime than that imposed by Barnes, he admitted that, in the climate that obtained at Bersham Hall, he had on occasions used excessive force in restraining residents. Without accepting every detail of the allegations that we have just summarised, we have no reason to doubt their general tenor. There were, in our view, a small number of occasions when Thomas used excessive force in restraint and others when he responded with force to provocation, as when the girl spat on his car, but he was not an abuser of the children in his care.

Other allegations of abuse and the use of the secure unit

13.60 The other allegations of physical abuse at Bersham Hall in this second phase of 13 years do not require separate discussion and do not affect the general picture that we have given. We are aware that about 12 other members of the staff were mentioned in such complaints at one time or another but only eight of them were referred to in the evidence before us, of whom only one was the subject of more than one complaint (in his case, two).

13.61 Several of these complaints arose out of the alleged use of the secure unit at Bersham Hall[19]. Michael Barnes' evidence was that the secure cell was never used but that the remainder of the unit was used on about three occasions because of concern about the safety of a resident. He recalled that a girl suffering from anorexia nervosa had been placed there because a consultant psychiatrist had so advised on the ground that, if she ran away, she might die. For similar reasons, a girl suffering from a respiratory complaint requiring steroid treatment had been dealt with in the same way. Christopher Thomas remembered another occasion when a girl had been brought under police escort to Bersham Hall to be locked up overnight, on the instructions of Geoffrey Wyatt, because she had misbehaved on an aeroplane that was to fly her from Hawarden to South Wales and the pilot had refused to fly with her.

13.62 Thomas accepted also that it was not unusual for frequent absconders to be placed in the secure unit, as he told the police in 1992, although they were not locked in. Two witnesses, in particular, complained about their treatment there. A former girl resident, who was at Bersham Hall for the second half of 1980 and who had originally asked to be taken into care when 14 years old the previous year, said that she was placed in the secure unit twice: on the first occasion, in August 1980, it was for absconding and she was there for three days; and on the second occasion, about nine days later, she was kept there for two weeks. On the first occasion she was not told how long she would be there and, on the second, she was told she would be there for two weeks but was not told the reason, although she inferred that it was because she had sworn at a secretary. She alleged also that she had been placed in the "cell" on both occasions - for the whole period of three days in August and for the first week of her detention in September.

13.63 The second complainant about the secure unit was the witness who said that he told Barnes that he hated Bersham Hall[20]. He was sick of being in care and absconded from Bersham Hall three times. The interview with Barnes took place on his return from the third absconding and he was taken from Barnes' office to the secure unit by Thomas, where he claimed to have remained for three to four weeks, as we have said earlier, in a cell like room with a mattress and blanket; and he alleged that he was locked in.

13.64 We are satisfied on the evidence before us that the secure part of the secure unit was used thus on a few occasions to contain absconders, although the other part of the secure unit (the semi-secure part) was also used for this purpose. Its

[19] See para 13.06.
[20] See para 13.52.

use as such probably occurred before 1983 when the formal approval of its use was expressly revoked. The reports on inspections by Welsh Office SWSO Copleston in November 1981 and May 1983 do not appear to have commented upon the use or non-use of the unit but a letter from the Welsh Office to the Chief Executive of Clwyd County Council dated 1 July 1983 stated that, as the unit was not in use and there were no plans to bring it into use, the Secretary of State was withdrawing approval for it to be registered as secure accommodation.

13.65   The use of the secure unit in the manner that we have indicated was plainly contrary to law and the periods of detention referred to by the two complainants were certainly excessive. Moreover, the use of the woolly term "semi-secure accommodation" led to important infringements of liberty that ought not to have been tolerated. We do not minimise the problems facing those responsible for residential care when dealing with violent children or persistent absconders but it is essential that their powers and the limits of their discretion should be clearly defined and made known to all residential staff in order that breaches of this kind are avoided.

Conclusions

13.66   Bersham Hall undoubtedly faced many problems during its comparatively short life as a community home. In the first period, between 1974 and 1980, there were too many changes of senior staff to enable it to settle down and the gradual withdrawal of its assessment function for boys was a further cause of unease. Then, in the second period there was continuing uncertainty about its role beyond the assessment of girls and as a short term holding centre for both sexes. In the event some children remained there for much longer periods than had been envisaged in 1980, although the regime generally was not suitable for long term care. Other disturbing factors in the later period were the influx of staff from Bryn Estyn in or about 1984, with a very different background of experience, and the differing outlooks of Barnes and Thomas, who alternated as de facto Officer-in-Charge for most of the decade from 1980. Overall also, there was no sufficiently clear policy from 1980 onwards governing admissions to the home with the result that much too wide a spectrum of children with problems had to be accommodated.

13.67   We are not in a position to comment authoritatively on the adequacy of the assessment and educational facilities provided at Bersham Hall. Our remit has been to inquire into the abuse of children and we have not received any suggestion that children were abused at Bersham Hall in the context of education or assessment. Some former residents were critical, saying (for example) that there was only very poor basic education or that the schoolwork was too easy, whilst others complained that there were no classes for them or that they spent only odd days at school and the rest of the time gardening or making wooden pallets. The reports by successive Teachers-in-Charge to the Management Committee, whilst it continued, show however, that the teaching was designed essentially for children who were to stay for six to eight weeks only and much of it was remedial in character because a high proportion of the children were behindhand in the basic skills[21]. The Teachers-in-Charge were conscious of the need to widen the curriculum, as were the SWSOs who inspected on behalf of the Welsh Office, but with only two full time teachers and no prospect of increased resources little more could be achieved. Our judgment is that the teachers at Bersham Hall were fully dedicated to their work and did the best that they could in the prevailing circumstances. Moreover, it was a sensible policy to arrange for the admission of longer term residents to local schools as far as possible. In the event, after the Education Department had assumed responsibility for the education unit from January 1988, it survived for only two more years, after which all residents were assigned to local schools, whenever it was practicable to do so.

13.68 The teachers were anxious as far as possible to participate in the assessment process but there were obvious difficulties about this when the establishment was limited to one full time teacher. When the establishment had been increased to two, some progress was made in teacher participation but we doubt whether the assessment process at Bersham Hall ever achieved a significantly higher standard than that at Little Acton Assessment Centre before it closed.

13.69 In our judgment the quality of care generally at Bersham Hall fell below an acceptable standard. Sexual abuse was not prevalent, bearing in mind that the activities of Michael Taylor, in particular, occurred before the period under consideration. But, on occasions, there was an unacceptable reliance upon physical force for the purposes of discipline and restraint, attributable in part at least to the lack of a coherent admissions policy, and the County's prohibition on corporal punishment was frequently flouted. The controlled regime of Bersham Hall geared to short stays and a constantly changing population was not suitable for those children who remained there for long periods. For them the experience was damaging and the home failed to provide them with the quality of care essential to young teenagers. It is right to say however, that some former residents in the short stay category compared it favourably with other homes in which they had been placed, such as Bryn Estyn.

---

[21] See eg para 13.06.

Chevet Hey, 1974 to 1990

14.01 Chevet Hey is a large house set in its own grounds in the centre of a residential community in Price's Lane, Wrexham, within walking distance of the town centre. It was opened as a children's home by Denbighshire County Council (we know of it as early as 1966) and it was designated in the 1971 Regional Plan as a community home to provide accommodation for up to 18 children of school age and over. It was a facility to be available for Radnorshire, Anglesey and Montgomeryshire as well as Denbighshire[1]. By 1979 its role had been modified because it was said (in the Regional Plan of that year) to be mainly for older children and there was no reference to any local authority other than Clwyd County Council.

14.02 Further changes were, in effect, forced upon Chevet Hey when Bryn Estyn closed because a number of Bryn Estyn residents were transferred to Chevet Hey together with several members of the Bryn Estyn staff, at which point it became a Group 2 home[2]. Its main function in its later years was to provide accommodation for troubled teenagers and those of school age attended local schools. It was re-classified as a Group 1 home on 1 January 1988 and closed in June 1990 when its functions were transferred to Gladwyn Children's Centre, Gresford[3].

14.03 The Officer-in-Charge of Chevet Hey for almost the whole of the period with which we are concerned was **Enoch Ellis Edwards**, who was appointed to the post by Denbighshire County Council with effect from 1 August 1972. He was then nearly 45 years old and had about five years' experience of residential care, starting as assistant houseparent at an approved school in Congleton run by the National Children's Home in September 1967. After obtaining the CRCCYP at Salford College of Technology in 1969, Edwards had served for about two years as Officer-in-Charge of a Cheshire County Council children's home at Sandbach for 15 boys and girls in the age range of 12 to 15 years. He remained at Chevet Hey until 8 March 1986, when he was transferred to Cherry Hill as Officer-in-Charge until 30 November 1987, when he retired at the age of 60 years.

14.04 With Edwards to Chevet Hey as Matron came his wife, **Irene Edwards,** who was 18 months younger than him and who had worked with him in joint appointments at Congleton and Sandbach. Their reference from the National Children's Home stated that "Mrs Edwards was good at the domestic skills and was a willing and thorough worker. She was the dominant partner and her husband lacked initiative". She was promoted to Deputy Officer-in-Charge of

---

[1] See para 4.02(5).

[2] To enable local authorities to determine the appropriate salary scales for Officers-in-Charge of community homes it was considered necessary to distinguish and recognise homes with specialised functions by dividing homes into three main groups according to the difficulty of the tasks undertaken by them (in descending order of difficulty from 1 to 3).

[3] See para 4.19.

Chevet Hey from 1 July 1979 and she remained in that post after her husband's transfer to Cherry Hill until she retired with him about 21 months later but it seems that she was on sick leave for a substantial part of the latter period[4]. The only complaint made against her by any former resident of Chevet Hey is dealt with in paragraphs 14.47 and 14.48.

14.05 Before Irene Edwards' appointment as Deputy three other Deputies had served under him in the space of less than seven years. The only one who need be mentioned, however, was **Huw Meurig Jones** with whom we have dealt quite fully already in Chapter 12[5]. He served as an RCCO at Chevet Hey for about seven months from 1 February 1972 before taking the CRCCYP course at Salford and then returned as Deputy Officer-in-Charge from about September 1973 to 20 July 1974. We are not aware of any complaint made against Huw Meurig Jones in respect of either of these periods when he was at Chevet Hey.

The history to August 1979

14.06 We deal with this period separately first because the main target of complaint at Chevet Hey was Frederick Marshall Jones[6], who began his employment there as a temporary RCCO on 2 September 1979. We are not aware of any complaint of abuse at Chevet Hey prior to the latter date save for the allegation made against Michael Taylor in respect of his short stay there in the late summer of 1973[7] and the evidence of one complainant about disciplinary action taken by Ellis Edwards in May 1973[8], also outside the period of our review.

14.07 Ellis Edwards said that he found Chevet Hey to be in a terrible state when he arrived there in August 1972. He described it as filthy dirty, unpainted, dark, dismal and dreary but it was painted within two years by men and youths undergoing community service. During his first four years there Chevet Hey acted as a reception centre for boys and girls in the age range of about six to 12 or 14 years, with a normal complement of about 21 children, and the staff establishment, including Mr and Mrs Edwards grew from five or six initially to ten to 12.

14.08 Chevet Hey then began to change in character, apparently more by force of circumstances than by a deliberate policy decision, to a community home providing long term care. Ellis Edwards spoke in his evidence of "a gridlock of children" developing because there was nowhere else to put the children, "the little homes were full". Chevet Hey was always full and on occasions they had as many as 21 children, with some children on mattresses on the floor. However, the usual arrangement was that there were three or four boys' bedrooms accommodating up to four to five boys in each and three or four girls' double bedrooms. Some members of staff stayed for a long period but the average length of stay of residential care staff nationally at that time was about

---

[4] See para 14.13.
[5] See paras 12.03 and 12.29 to 12.35.
[6] Previously mentioned in paras 13.38 to 13.41.
[7] See para 13.14.
[8] See para 14.10.

six months. The work was hard and poorly paid for long hours and women staff, in particular, found that the filthy and abusive language of the children was difficult to bear. He said also that there was too wide a mix of children at the centre: most of them arrived via the courts by one route or another without an assessment process.

14.09 Despite the rather depressing picture given by Ellis Edwards and the physical shortcomings of the building itself as a comparatively large children's home, many of the former residents who gave oral evidence before us spoke quite warmly of it, subject only, in the later years, to a qualification about the presence there of Marshall Jones. One witness described it in her Tribunal statement as "like home from home"; another said that it was "a happy place"; others spoke of it as being friendlier and more relaxed than Bryn Estyn and Bersham Hall; and a former girl resident who had been in five children's homes in all, said that the staff listened to, and were interested in, the children more than in any other home in which she had stayed.

14.10 The only complaint against Ellis Edwards himself by a former resident of Chevet Hey that we heard in evidence came from one of two boys who had been caught smoking, which was prohibited, in May 1973, before the period of our review. The complaint was that Ellis Edwards made the two boys eat "just a little bit" of soap to deter them from doing so again. The complainant alleged also that he was made to stand in his pyjamas on a landing outside Edwards' bedroom for a long time (it seemed "like for ever") until he was allowed to retire to bed. But this witness said also that he "got on alright" with Mr and Mrs Edwards during his three weeks' stay at Chevet Hey.

The period from September 1979 to March 1986

14.11 The last six years of Ellis Edwards' tenure of the senior post were undoubtedly affected adversely, firstly, by the arrival in September 1979 of Frederick Marshall Jones, who survived him at Chevet Hey for another three and a half years, and, secondly, by an influx of staff and residents from Bryn Estyn at the time, or in anticipation, of the latter's closure. Among the staff transferred was Paul Wilson, with whom we have dealt very fully in previous chapters[9]. Complaints by Wilson that he was in difficulties with his relationship with Ellis Edwards led to an internal investigation early in 1986 by Geoffrey Wyatt, who concluded 'inter alia' that it would be better for Edwards to be redeployed to a less demanding post or offered early retirement; and Edwards' transfer to Cherry Hill followed swiftly.

Frederick Marshall Jones

14.12 It is appropriate to begin this section with an account of **Frederick Marshall Jones** because 21 of the total of 33 complaints about identified members of the staff at Chevet Hey between 1974 and 1990 referred to him. He was 39 years

---

[9] See paras 8.39, 8.40 and 10.04 to 10.39.

old when he was appointed as a temporary RCCO at Chevet Hey from 2 September 1979, by which time he had about five years' experience of child care, dating back to November 1974, when he had become a care assistant at Ystrad Hall[10] for a year. He had then served briefly as a temporary houseparent at Little Acton Assessment Centre in 1977 before becoming youth warden at Maelor Youth Club for two years. His accounts of his earlier years varied a little but he had left school at 15 years and had worked as an engine driver for four years, a security officer for three years and then in commerce as a buyer and as a goods supervisor.

14.13 At Chevet Hey Marshall Jones advanced to a permanent appointment as RCCO from 17 February 1980 and he became Third Officer-in-Charge from 1 November 1981. Due to the sickness of Irene Edwards he became Acting Deputy Officer-in-Charge from 11 October 1986 until he advanced to Acting Officer-in-Charge from 1 February 1988 for five months on Michael Barnes' promotion to Principal Officer. He reverted to the status of Third Officer-in-Charge or Assistant Centre Manager (as the office had now become), under Michael Nelson and Christine Chapman, until he was transferred to the post of Assistant Centre Manager at Bersham Hall from 1 October 1989[11]. Marshall Jones' final move was to Cartrefle Community Home, where he was appointed Temporary Officer-in-Charge from 8 July 1990 on the suspension of Stephen Norris[12]. This appointment was made permanent from 1 December 1990 but the Divisional Director of Social Services, John Llewellyn Thomas, admitted in a letter to a potential applicant for the post dated 19 February 1991, that a mistake had been made in failing to advertise the vacancy: he said "We were in the process of advertising the post when it was offered through the Personnel Department and accepted by the Officer-in-Charge". Marshall Jones remained in the post until he was suspended on full pay with effect from 17 September 1992 whilst allegations of assaults by him on children were investigated. The suspension continued beyond the closure of Cartrefle in September 1993 but his employment by Clwyd County Council was ended on 30 November 1994, when he was 54 years old, on the ground of redundancy; and he died on 23 December 1998.

14.14 We received evidence from eight complainants who alleged physical abuse by Marshall Jones in the period between 1979 and 1986, of whom seven gave oral evidence before us; and there was a striking degree of consistency in their descriptions of his general conduct and behaviour. Six of them complained of his habit of striking them on the knuckles or fingers with the large bunch of keys that he carried around with him; or throwing the keys at them; and most of them alleged that they had been the victims of serious assaults by him in other ways. One witness spoke of being grabbed and shaken and thrown to the floor; another alleged that he had been punched and knocked to the floor; and others alleged generalised assaults by him on frequent occasions.

---

[10] See paras 4.12 to 4.14.
[11] See paras 13.26 and 13.38 to 13.41.
[12] See para 8.27.

14.15 All these complainants singled out Marshall Jones as a particular cause of unhappiness at Chevet Hey and the causes of complaint appear to have increased rather than decreased after he became Third Officer-in-Charge in November 1981. His general manner was also the subject of complaint by most of them: he was described as robust, loud and verbally aggressive to the children by one member of staff and "brusque and sergeant-majorish" by another, whilst former residents spoke of him shouting regularly.

14.16 Marshall Jones did have some defenders. One former resident who criticised his manner said nevertheless that his bark was worse than his bite and one of the two members of staff quoted in the preceding paragraph said that he was quite good and patient with the children. As for Ellis Edwards, the Officer-in-Charge at this time, he said that there was a lot of rough and tumble when Marshall Jones was around but there was no clash between them about the way the home was run. Marshall Jones and his wife would run the home when Ellis Edwards and his wife were absent and they never worked together but Ellis Edwards was not aware that Marshall Jones regarded himself as a disciplinarian. They had lots of talks and Marshall Jones knew what Ellis Edwards wanted when the latter was away. Ellis Edwards received only one complaint from a boy that Marshall Jones had thrown his bunch of keys at the boy, breaking the glass of the boy's watch. Ellis Edwards had responded to this by telling Marshall Jones that he could not do that and warning him that he would be dismissed if he did it again. Ellis Edwards had also taken Marshall Jones' bunch of keys and given him one key to the cupboard where the keys were kept in return; but he had not reported the matter to his superiors.

14.17 In his own evidence Marshall Jones said that he was dedicated to child care in Clwyd and had put more into his work than was required of him: he would listen to young people and help and advise them. He would do a lot of shouting but would sit down with them to discuss their problems at a difficult stage in their lives. He had never hit or kicked a boy (or girl) and was bewildered by the allegations against him. Horseplay had certainly occurred but it had been very much two way (as between a father and a boisterous son). From time to time he had also merely restrained residents, for example, when a boy had assaulted a member of staff. He had thrown his keys on occasions but he had never assaulted anyone with them; boys would generally throw the keys back at him and no one ever got hurt. He would rattle the keys from time to time at residents but he would never use them as a weapon or maliciously. He remembered discussing the throwing of the keys with Ellis Edwards and he readily accepted his advice that he should stop doing so because of the potential for injury; but he did not receive any formal warning.

14.18 Speaking more generally, Marshall Jones said that Ellis Edwards ran too lax a regime at Chevet Hey. He, Marshall Jones, sought to impose discipline where none had existed and Mr and Mrs Edwards had been happy that he should do so. They had not had a break previously and, after his arrival, they would go off from Thursday to Sunday afternoon, leaving him in charge. There was no assistance from senior management about how to run the home. The line manager, apparently, was Geoffrey Wyatt, who visited the home every Christmas morning, but otherwise they only saw him when he attended for appointment interviews or in connection with disciplinary matters.

14.19   In assessing Marshall Jones we have to take into account not only the evidence about his conduct between 1979 and 1986, under Ellis Edwards, but also the evidence about his later career at Chevet Hey, Bersham Hall and Cartrefle until his suspension from duty in September 1992, to which we will refer hereafter[13]. Viewing all this evidence we are compelled to the conclusion that his disciplinary attitude and methods were very seriously flawed throughout and that he was unfitted for all the posts, particularly the senior positions, to which he was appointed. In personal mitigation it can be said for him that he was untrained for child care work, apart from a youth leadership certificate obtained from Clwyd County Council in 1978 and a later three months Open University course (P653) in caring for children and young persons; and that he received virtually no effective guidance from above throughout the period of his employment as a care officer. We recognise also that many of the children in his care from time to time were seriously disturbed, some with delinquent tendencies. In our judgment, however, his own common sense and day to day experience ought to have taught him that his methods were inappropriate and that he was inflicting significant emotional damage on the children in his care. It appears that, instead, he was determined to pursue his own course according to his own lights, even when it brought him into conflict with other members of the staff.

Paul Bicker Wilson

14.20   We have already dealt very fully in Chapter 10 with the record of Paul Wilson at Bryn Estyn between 1974 and 1984[14]. He was transferred to Chevet Hey with four other Bryn Estyn staff as a senior RCCO with effect from 15 October 1984 and accepted the posting reluctantly because he had expressed interest from 1982 in doing Intermediate Treatment work but was regarded as unqualified for such work. In the event he remained less than a year at Chevet Hey because he was suspended from duty with effect from 15 August 1985 pending a police investigation into alleged assaults by him on two resident youths. The North Wales Police reported on 2 October 1985 that it had been decided that no further police action was to be taken in the matter but there were problems about Wilson's return to duty because (a) the Social Services Department wished to continue to place one of the two complainant youths at Chevet Hey, (b) Ellis Edwards and some other members of the staff were opposed to Wilson resuming work there and (c) Wilson had himself complained by letter dated 18 June 1985 to John Llewellyn Thomas of difficulties in his relationship with Ellis Edwards.

[13] See paras 13.38 to 13.41, 14.57 to 14.62 and 15.51 to 15.61.
[14] See paras 10.04 to 10.39.

14.21 The outcome of these difficulties was that an internal investigation was carried out by Geoffrey Wyatt into the various allegations and counter-allegations and it was ultimately agreed with Wilson and his NALGO branch organiser that he should be placed from 6 January 1986 as an instructor/supervisor at a day centre for the mentally handicapped, whilst remaining on the establishment of Chevet Hey. He retired on health grounds on 31 December 1987.

14.22 There were further complaints of physical abuse by **Paul Wilson** in the comparatively short period of his service at Chevet Hey before the incident in August 1985. One witness gave oral evidence to the Tribunal that, after he had complained to Marshall Jones that Wilson had been abusive to him, Wilson "flipped" him round the head and threatened to kill him. As a result the boy ran away with a friend, who alleged that he had also been threatened by Wilson, and they were returned by the police the next day. He was discharged from care on his 18th birthday on 20 March 1985 to his mother and step-father without any significant preparation after many years in care.

14.23 The incidents that led to Wilson's suspension occurred in the early hours of 14 August 1985 and one of the two complainants was the friend referred to in the preceding paragraph, who had already handed to Ellis Edwards on 19 March 1985 a note complaining about Wilson's threats. The short facts of what occurred on 14 August were that two residents who had absconded were returned to Chevet Hey, having been found in possession of two knives when picked up. Wilson was on night duty and learnt from the absconders that the knives had been lent to them by the two complainants, who were then roused from their respective beds by Wilson at about 3 am. Both alleged that they had been physically abused by Wilson. One said that he had been kicked in the back in bed and ordered out on to a hallway or landing, where he had been elbowed in the chest and kicked on the knee. In the struggle that had ensued Wilson had broken the complainant's watch. The second complainant alleged similar treatment, stating that Wilson had kicked him in the shin and elbowed him in the stomach. He was also told later that he could not leave the premises to go to the library and Wilson refused to give him a reason for his confinement.

14.24 These events seem to have been quite fully and promptly investigated at the home by Ellis Edwards. It seems also that the two headquarters Residential and Day Care Officers, Norman Green and Gwen Hurst, involved themselves by taking statements from three witnesses, including the two absconders. Neither of the two complainants could be called to give oral evidence but we received in evidence the statement of the boy who said that he had been kicked in bed made to the police on 6 November 1992 in which he said that Ellis Edwards arranged for a doctor to examine him. The police also were called in and the boy made a formal complaint to them. He consulted solicitors after the incident but was refused legal aid and he made an unsuccessful application for compensation to the Criminal Injuries Compensation Board. Ellis Edwards resisted the suggestion that the boy should be moved from Chevet Hey and he himself felt that he could only trust Mr and Mrs Edwards. Eventually, he was moved on to bed-sitting room accommodation.

14.25 For the purposes of his limited investigation, Geoffrey Wyatt interviewed only Ellis Edwards and Paul Wilson of the staff at Chevet Hey but he did interview also "several of the residents of Chevet Hey who asked to see us". His other interviews were with two police officers, the Area Officer, Norman Green (RDCO) and, above him, Gordon Ramsay and John Llewellyn Thomas. The matters under investigation were the complaint by Wilson that he was in difficulties in his relationship with Ellis Edwards[15], Wilson's suitability to continue to work with young people in a residential setting and the effectiveness and efficiency of Ellis Edwards' management of Chevet Hey.

14.26 In his conclusions Wyatt expressed dismay at what he had discovered but stated surprisingly, "We discovered nothing in our enquiries to prevent Wilson immediately returning to his duties at Chevet Hey". However, it is difficult to reconcile the latter statement with any other comment in the section of Wyatt's report in which he dealt with Wilson's position because he referred to:

(a) the opposition of senior staff and some other members of staff and residents to Wilson's return;

(b) the need for very careful handling of one of the complainants if both he and Wilson were to remain at Chevet Hey;

(c) the fact that Wilson had been the subject of investigations on six previous occasions in connection with allegations by boys of physical or verbal abuse; and

(d) Wilson's failure to avail himself of professional training during his 13 years of employment in child care.

Although Wyatt expressed the opinion 'inter alia' that Wilson would need "to adopt a far less assertive and confrontational style in future" he gave no indication as to how this transformation was to be achieved.

14.27 As we have already said, Wilson did not return to Chevet Hey, despite what Wyatt said in his report, so that it is unnecessary to prolong discussion of it. Wilson's behaviour at Chevet Hey was broadly in line with his earlier conduct at Bryn Estyn, although there were fewer complaints about him at Chevet Hey, and we have no reason therefore to qualify the views that we expressed about him in Chapter 10[16].

Enoch Ellis Edwards

14.28 It is convenient to deal with **Ellis Edwards** here in the context of Wyatt's report, because the latter dealt with his relations with Wilson and came at the end of his period as Officer-in-Charge at Chevet Hey. The main critics of the Edwards regime at Chevet Hey were Marshall Jones, whose views we have already summarised[17], and Paul Wilson. The latter's main complaint seems to have been that he understood from hearsay that a child who was to accompany him

[15] See para 14.20.
[16] See in particular, paras 10.37 and 10.38.
[17] See para 14.18.

on a Pennine Walk had been asked by Ellis Edwards to report on his conduct (to spy on him, in Wilson's view). Ellis Edwards' explanation of this was that the boys who were to accompany Wilson had expressed concern about the way in which he would or might supervise them, to which Ellis Edwards had replied "You will have to see that he does his job properly, won't you". This was said to illustrate the way in which both Ellis Edwards and Wilson tried to get boys "on their side" in disputes between them.

14.29 Other criticisms of Ellis Edwards were rather less clear. Reference was made by Wyatt to his "depressive moods" and "his ambivalence to both staff and children's situations". It was said that relationships in the home were not managed in a professional way and that Ellis Edwards believed that everyone should like him, respect him and carry out his wishes just because he was Officer-in-Charge. He was accused also of taking sides with the boys in disputes and of openly declaring himself as opposed to members of staff. Finally, he was accused of confusing his role as a senior shop steward of NALGO and his duties as Officer-in-Charge, particularly during the period of Wilson's suspension.

14.30 It is rather striking that Wyatt did not allege that Ellis Edwards had imposed a lax regime at Chevet Hey. However, in his conclusions, Wyatt emphasised that Chevet Hey was a costly resource and said that he did not believe that the existing management could provide the professional and management skills that were necessary to achieve clarity in its function and excellence in its performance. Part of the blame was to be attributed to management at Shire Hall for failure to monitor Chevet Hey adequately, and he mentioned the Principal Officer (John Llewellyn Thomas) and the RDCO (Norman Green) in this context but his main strictures were upon Ellis Edwards, for whom he recommended redeployment to a less demanding post or an offer of early retirement.

14.31 We do not have sufficient evidence to comment authoritatively upon Wyatt's conclusions in respect of Ellis Edwards' general performance as Officer-in-Charge of Chevet Hey because our inquiry, within our terms of reference, has been directed to the scale of abuse on children there. In those terms Chevet Hey would scarcely have merited separate consideration in the period 1972 to 1986 but for the activities of Marshall Jones. Ellis Edwards was clearly not a strong leader and the warning in his reference that he lacked initiative was plainly justified. His major fault that is relevant to our inquiry was his failure to control the activities of Marshall Jones and to report upon him appropriately to his superiors. He was probably less to blame in relation to Wilson and it is to his credit that he refused eventually to agree to Wilson returning to Chevet Hey. More generally, it is very questionable whether Ellis Edwards ever possessed the necessary attributes to be a successful Officer-in-Charge in the full sense, but he and his wife did at least provide a setting that most residents recognised as a home, which was a paramount need for children in care.

Jacqueline Elizabeth Thomas

14.32 It is necessary to deal with **Jacqueline Thomas** here because her conviction on 5 August 1986[18] related to events that occurred when she was employed as an RCCO at Chevet Hey. She was only 20 years old when she was appointed from a short list of four with effect from 26 February 1979. She had left school at 16 years with eight CSEs and two O levels and had about 18 months' experience of residential care after working initially with persons with learning difficulties for a short period.

14.33 Two former residents of Chevet Hey complained in their evidence to the Tribunal of sexual abuse by Jacqueline Thomas. The first, who was a 16 years old boy when he was at Chevet Hey for just over seven weeks in the late summer and early autumn of 1979, alleged that Thomas indulged in sexual play with him a few times in his bedroom, the bathroom and her motor car. In his bedroom, she came in and ended up on top of him. He alleged that sexual intercourse had occurred and oral sex once. This witness alleged also that he had sexual intercourse at Chevet Hey with two other members of the women care staff there, who were both in their 20s, and earlier with a woman care officer at Bryn Estyn.

14.34 The other complainant was a later girl resident of Chevet Hey, who was there from 15 August 1982 for over three years, initially because her brother, who was three years older than her, was also there. She described how the atmosphere was completely different from Bersham Hall and that she was happier at Chevet Hey but she complained 'inter alia' about Thomas displaying herself when they were on a camping holiday at Harlech, referring particularly to her scant night clothing and posture at breakfast time in mixed company in a tent.

14.35 Thomas denied these allegations but admitted having sexual relations with two young boys, one of whom was in care at the time. She formed a friendship with the first (G) when she used to take him from Chevet Hey to a youth club. Ultimately, she did have sexual intercourse with G on two occasions but not until he had moved on to Bersham Hall and was 16 years old. The other boy (S) was not in care and she had become romantically involved with him only after she had stopped him committing suicide. Sexual intercourse with him had occurred only once, in the late summer of 1985, when she thought that he was 19 years old, although his actual age was 16 years (in fact, he was then 15 years old); and this preceded the other sexual relationship.

14.36 Thomas' conviction was for an indecent assault on a male person aged under 16 years, namely, S, in August 1985, for which she received a suspended sentence of three months' imprisonment on pleading guilty in Wrexham Maelor Magistrates' Court. The police investigation had been triggered, however, by disclosures made by G (rather than S) on his return to Bersham Hall following Christmas leave in December 1985.

[18] See para 2.07(5).

14.37 Without going into unnecessary detail, G had been required to return early because of increasing concern about his behaviour during home leave. He was interviewed at length during the evening of 27 December 1985 by Michael Barnes, the Officer-in-Charge of Bersham Hall, in part with a houseparent present, and one of the matters of concern was a report that G had sold a gold bracelet to a local jeweller. G admitted eventually that he had obtained the bracelet from Thomas' flat at Gwersyllt, to which he had ready access. This led on to admissions about his relationship with Thomas, including sexual intercourse with her and staying overnight at her flat. Geoffrey Wyatt was informed and visited Bersham Hall with the Area Officer the following morning; the police were informed and G was interviewed by them that afternoon with the result that David Gillison became involved in the police investigation.

14.38 **David John Gillison**[19] is a long standing family friend of Thomas and was then employed by Clwyd County Council as a social worker for the physically handicapped at the Rhuddlan area office. The allegation that emerged was that he had stayed the night of 24 December 1985 at Thomas' flat in the company of G and S and a former resident of four Wrexham community homes, William Gerry, then aged 20 years; and that homosexual activity of various kinds had occurred between them that night and during the following two days. It was alleged also that Thomas had been present on the Christmas Eve and had taken part in "group sex" with G and S and Gerry.

14.39 Thomas, who had been on duty at Chevet Hey on Christmas Eve and had slept the night there, strongly denied the allegations against her that are summarised in the preceding paragraph. However, there was evidence that she had been absent from Chevet Hey for two substantial periods in the course of the evening and ultimately to 1 am; and she had been visited at Chevet Hey by Gillison and G earlier on.

14.40 In the event the prosecution did not proceed with any charge against Thomas in respect of her alleged participation in group sex on 24 December 1985. Instead, she pleaded guilty to taking part in a more limited form of group sex at her flat in August 1985 involving only herself, G and S.

14.41 Gillison and Gerry appeared at the Magistrates' Court on the same date as Thomas, Gerry being charged with offences of buggery and gross indecency and Gillison with gross indecency. They were later committed for trial at Mold Crown Court, where Gillison pleaded guilty on 16 January 1987 to two offences of gross indecency against G, for which he received three years and three months' imprisonment. Gerry, who had never been employed by the Social Services Department, was sentenced at the same time to two years' imprisonment for buggery with G and four offences of gross indecency involving both G and S.

14.42 Thomas had been warned earlier by Ellis and Irene Edwards, and probably by other members of the Chevet Hey staff, about the developing relationship with G. She was suspended from duty on 3 January 1986 and she resigned on 6

---

[19] See para 2.07(6).

August 1986. Gillison, who is discussed further in Chapter 52, was also suspended on 3 January 1986 and he was dismissed on 19 January 1987. Gerry, as stated earlier[20], committed suicide on 1 December 1997.

14.43 The sentencing judge at Mold Crown Court on 16 January 1987, the Honourable Mr Justice Mars-Jones, requested that an investigation should be carried out by the Social Services Department of Clwyd County Council into the circumstances in which Thomas and Gillison had come to occupy the positions that they held. This task was undertaken by the County Secretary, Roger Davies, but it was not until October 1990 that his report was presented to the Social Services (Child and Family Services) Sub-Committee of the County Council. Davies' only explanation for this extraordinary delay was that the investigation had been carried out quickly to the final draft stage but that the report had not been presented then due to an oversight: it was not signed until 8 October 1990. Davies' conclusion was as follows:

> "I have concluded that the appointments. . .were made in the normal way by experienced officers. In fact neither was appointed to a permanent post until there had been practical experience of temporary short term appointments. References were called for and read satisfactorily.
>
> The procedures of Circular 86(44) were not available at the time of the appointments. If they had been, they would have disclosed no criminal convictions.
>
> No officers interviewed said they were aware of any improper conduct by either."

Davies did, however, add that some officers interviewed had said that they would appreciate clearer guidelines on "befriending, complaints procedures and staff assessment procedures, particularly in the residential field". He said also that correct professional relationships between residential and field staff also caused concern through lack of clarity.

14.44 Although Davies' report did address the precise question formulated by the judge, the investigation was, in our judgment, superficial because it did not probe the many closely related questions that the judge must have had in mind and the underlying problems raised by the requests of some officers for greater clarity in their instructions. The documents before us suggest, in particular, that several members of the staff at Chevet Hey (and possibly some at Bersham Hall) were aware of and concerned about the relationship between Thomas and G as it developed but were unsure about how they ought properly to respond to it when initial warnings were ignored.

14.45 There are strong grounds for believing that Thomas' misconduct went well beyond the limited admissions that she made in her evidence to the Tribunal and it is notable that she does not even accept now the facts relied upon by the prosecution on the charge to which she pleaded guilty, saying that, at the time, she had been through "near enough a nervous breakdown" and that all she

---

[20] See para 2.07(6).

wanted to do was to plead guilty. With hindsight it is clear that more effective steps should have been taken earlier to terminate her relationship with G but there is no evidence that members of the staff knew of her friendship with S. It is to the credit of Mr and Mrs Edwards and other members of the staff that Thomas was warned about consorting with G and the history illustrates well the need for (a) vigilance in monitoring relationships of this kind and (b) clear guidelines about "whistleblowing" and allied procedures to enable members of staff to act confidently when presented with similar problems. We accept also that continuing and periodical staff assessments would be helpful as part of the monitoring process.

Other allegations of abuse during this period

14.46 We heard evidence from only four complainants of alleged abuse by four other members of the staff who have not been named in this section. These allegations do not, however, affect the general picture that we have given of Chevet Hey between 1979 and 1986 and do not call for separate discussion. We should, however, record that there was one other instance of a sexual relationship developing between a boy resident at Chevet Hey and a female care officer employed there. This occurred in 1982 and the boy involved, who had left school and was going out to work, had his 17th birthday in July that year. The care officer was interviewed by Geoffrey Wyatt, then Assistant Director (Residential), and another headquarters officer in the presence of Marshall Jones on 13 September 1982. The boy, who was the subject of a care order had admitted having an affair with the woman and having spent the night with her at her flat and there was other evidence of their association together. When interviewed she declined to comment on the allegations and was told that she would be suspended pending an investigation of the matter but she resigned the following day.

14.47 We did not receive any complaints about illicit sexual relationships between residents at Chevet Hey but one former girl resident did make a complaint that arose from such an association. She had been in and out of care from the age of 13 years because of family difficulties and was placed finally at Chevet Hey from 10 March 1978 to 31 December 1979, when she was discharged from care because she had attained the age of 18 years. Whilst at Chevet Hey she formed a relationship with a boy resident from Sierra Leone, who used to visit her in the girls' quarters, contrary to the rules. In consequence she became pregnant at the age of 17 years. Her complaint was that, when she told Irene Edwards, who already knew of the relationship, that she was pregnant, Irene Edwards ultimately advised her that she must have an abortion, arguing that, if she gave birth to the child, it would affect the putative father's appeal against deportation (he was subsequently deported) and threatening that the girl would be sent to a secure unit in South Wales and locked up until she reached the age of 21 years. The complainant said that, because she had been brought up as a Roman Catholic, she did not think that it would be right to undergo an abortion. Nevertheless, when examined by a doctor and asked if that was what she really wanted, she replied "Yes" because she felt that there was nothing else that she could do; and the abortion took place on 12 February 1979.

14.48 Irene Edwards was not called to give evidence because this was the only criticism of her by any resident of Chevet Hey so that we do not have her version of the advice that she gave. We refer to the matter in order to emphasise the importance of making independent counselling and advice available to children in care in circumstances of this kind. The complainant was a girl who presented quite severe behavioural problems at the time and there was a background of some earlier promiscuity (her main complaints related to Little Acton Assessment Centre) but she was of above average intelligence and clearly needed careful and sensitive handling; her religion was an additional very important factor.

The period from April 1986 to June 1990

14.49 This period can be dealt with quite shortly because the main persons about whom complaints are made have already been discussed quite fully and the volume of complaints was reduced as they left. On the departure of Ellis Edwards to Cherry Hill **Michael Barnes** was asked to fill the role of Acting Officer-in-Charge and he did so until 31 December 1987, when he was promoted to the rank of Principal Social Worker. His Deputy at Chevet Hey was still Irene Edwards until 30 November 1987 but she was on sick leave for much of Barnes' time there so that **Frederick Marshall Jones** was effectively his Deputy for substantial periods.

14.50 Barnes was not replaced as Officer-in-Charge until 27 June 1988, when **Michael Nelson** succeeded him for the last two years of Chevet Hey's existence. Thus, Marshall Jones appears to have been left in charge for the first six months of 1988 and he then reverted to Acting Deputy until **Christine Chapman** was appointed Deputy from 1 October 1988, a year before Marshall Jones left, during which time he reverted to his established position as Third Officer-in-Charge.

14.51 Michael Barnes said in evidence that he found the staff at Chevet Hey fragmented and the children disruptive and unsettled when he took over. He was not shown Wyatt's report or informed of Wyatt's conclusions but he wrote a report in November 1986, intended for the Director's eyes, in which he painted a very gloomy picture of the standard of child care at Chevet Hey. Having dealt in brief with various administrative deficiencies, including poor record keeping, he continued:

> "Within weeks of my arrival my concern shifted away from administrative routines to staffing matters. I was struck by the staff's lack of cohesion and lack of commitment. There was considerable evidence of poor skills and a noticeable poverty in training. It was very apparent that the Home had failed to adjust to an influx of redeployed staff and that there were serious differences within and between the various staff factions. At a senior level there were serious gaps in communication and open conflict over management styles and leaders' roles, At least three factions of staff were identified - staff indigenous to Chevet Hey, ex-Bersham staff, and ex-Bryn Estyn staff. Conflict within and between these groups was also compounded by major differences between senior staff. There was a noticeable lack of leadership.

Seemingly, under threat from increased staff numbers and a more militant element (ex-Bryn Estyn) senior staff had basically opted out leaving care staff to do almost as they pleased. Only the Third in Charge offered any resistance and aimed at the prospect of uniting the staff."

14.52 Barnes went on to deal specifically with child-care and supervision in the following passage:

"Throughout my stay I have been particularly concerned about standards of child-care and supervision. Delinquency has become institutionalised and staff attitudes to sexuality are poor. Parenting is weak and there is little commitment to social work practice. Despite low numbers and, for the most part, good staff ratios the majority of staff have been very unwilling to exercise proper supervision of and/or to work therapeutically with children. Relationships between some staff members and children are non-existent and with others quite rejecting. Only a minority of staff have pleasing relationships with the residents. I have been appalled by the rejecting nature of some staff and by the way the majority opt out of child-care contact and control - a trait which has bedevilled Chevet Hey for many years."

14.53 The immediate fate of this report is not known but it is noteworthy that Barnes followed it up with a letter to the Director two months later, after Mr Justice Mars-Jones had dealt with Gillison and Gerry. In his letter of 28 January 1987 he said 'inter alia':

". . .As the person mainly responsible for bringing these matters to light and seeing at first hand their impact on the clients and staff caring for them I must say that I share the judge's view that these matters call for a thorough investigation.

. . .

There are, I believe, a number of lessons to be learned from these events. It is of vital importance, especially in residential care where the capacity to damage is very much greater than in field work that we face up to the need to learn from past mistakes.

I very much hope that the Department will take up the judge's recommendation and will not only consider why the staff members came to be employed by the Social Services Department but will also examine why cases of this sort are becoming such a common feature of local residential provision."

This letter makes it all the more remarkable that the investigation at the judge's request was so superficial and the report upon it so long delayed. Barnes was seen later by Roger Davies, the author of the report, and Raymond Powell, Assistant Director (Children and Family Services), in the course (it seems) of the investigation but was severely reproved by Powell when he said that, unless something was done, the problem would recur.

14.54 No specific action appears to have been taken by senior management in response to Barnes' report but he recollects that he had a meeting with John Llewellyn Thomas, the Principal Officer (Children) at the time, at which it was "recognised" that there should be a planned closure of Chevet Hey, that a new home should be opened in its place and that the home required a permanent Officer-in-Charge.

Further complaints of abuse

14.55 The formerly "lax" regime of Ellis Edwards was replaced by stricter discipline under Barnes, with the co-operation of Marshall Jones, but we have not received any complaint about Barnes' behaviour at Chevet Hey save for one witness, who said in his oral evidence that **Barnes** had once thrown him on to a couch and then pushed him after which Marshall Jones had put his knee into the boy's chest; he recalled seeing Barnes give slaps across the ears also; and he expressed the view that Barnes turned a blind eye to Marshall Jones' abuse: Barnes was two-faced and lied.

14.56 These allegations were put to Barnes in cross-examination and he denied emphatically that he had ever manhandled the particular complainant or cuffed him. He denied also turning a blind eye to abuse by Marshall Jones, saying that the record would show that when concerns were brought to him, by staff or by children, he acted upon them. Bearing in mind that the complainant himself agreed in cross-examination that he had no real cause for complaint against Barnes and that he is the only witness who has alleged such misconduct by Barnes at Chevet Hey, we do not consider it likely that Barnes used excessive physical force against this complainant[21].

Frederick Marshall Jones

14.57 The complaints against **Marshall Jones** in respect of his conduct from April 1986 until his departure from Chevet Hey on 30 September 1989 followed a similar pattern to those made in respect of the preceding six and a half years. We are aware of six complainants about him who were at Chevet Hey in the later period, of whom three gave oral evidence to the Tribunal. Assaults with the bunch of keys continued and all three complained about them. One of the witnesses said that he was given 'dead arms' and 'dead legs' by Marshall Jones with the latter's fists and that he was also hit on the forehead by fist: sometimes there was a reason for it and sometimes it was supposed to be in jest. The witness said of himself that he was a 16 year old with a 'severe chip on his shoulder' and agreed that he could be "quite a handful"; he received sporadic violence and sometimes it went too far. As for the other two complainants who gave evidence, they complained of bullying generally by Marshall Jones; they too described how they were given 'dead legs' and 'dead arms' countless times. It was not a joke: it was just Marshall Jones' way of showing that he was "the boss".

---

[21] See, however, paras 12.23 and 13.52 to 13.57 for our earlier comments upon Barnes.

14.58 On 21 August 1987 a member of the staff at Chevet Hey reported to Michael Barnes that reports were circulating amongst the residents that Marshall Jones had been treating individual boys in a rough and physical manner. She said that she had no direct evidence of the alleged rough handling but that she, with another member of the care staff, had listened to a group discussing a number of grievances in a sensible and serious way. The general complaint was of an over-zealous approach to discipline but one boy alleged that his shoulder had been injured by Marshall Jones. Barnes carried out a series of interviews in the presence of the Acting Third Officer-in-Charge, Raymond Bew, as a result of this report and two of the residents whom he interviewed were witnesses referred to in the preceding paragraph. One of the two told Barnes that he had no complaints against staff but the other did complain that, after he had broken into a nearby school, Marshall Jones had pulled his hair and squashed his neck. This boy told Barnes that he was satisfied with his treatment in care and that he had no complaints about Marshall Jones, although the latter did get "a bit rough" in the incident that he described.

14.59 Other boys interviewed by Barnes described incidents of rough handling by Marshall Jones but Barnes' view was that they all did so "in the context of an otherwise positive relationship with him" (ie Marshall Jones). The boys were told by Barnes to report any future incidents that concerned them to senior staff and to discuss the matter with their respective social workers if they thought that would help.

14.60 The report by Barnes did not deal with Marshall Jones' version of these events because he had not been asked for it up to then. He had, however, questioned the motive of the care officer because he himself had earlier reported a staff member for slapping a child across the face. Barnes concluded his report with the following comment, after noting Marshall Jones' positive relationship with the boys:

> "There is clear evidence that the group merely wanted note taken of their concern rather than direct action against the staff member. Clearly this matter will need to be discussed with Mr Jones and until then no further action is intended. Regardless of any subsequent findings, Mr Jones will need to be advised that conducting disciplinary interviews with children alone is not to be recommended."

14.61 It does not appear that any formal disciplinary action was taken against Marshall Jones as a result of this report by Barnes. The report was addressed to the Social Services Department but we do not have any evidence as to when it was received or what was done about it but it did not impede Marshall Jones' promotion to the post of Assistant General Manager at Bersham Hall from 1 October 1989. Before then there was a further complaint about him by a woman member of the care staff at Chevet Hey, who had served for substantial periods at Bryn Estyn and Bersham Hall before starting work at Chevet Hey in January 1988. This staff member saw an incident on 23 December 1988 between a boy resident and Marshall Jones in which the latter appeared to handle the boy roughly. She made an appropriate entry in the incident report book and the boy subsequently made a complaint after she had counselled him to do so. The incident was fully investigated by Michael Nelson, who interviewed several witnesses and concluded that there had merely been inappropriate horseplay. He subsequently warned Marshall Jones of the dangers of horseplay with children and the need to be aware of the views of other members of staff about it. This investigation and an incident between Marshall Jones and another member of the staff on 23 February 1989 suggest that a marked deterioration was occurring in relations between him and his colleagues but he received a full testimonial from Nelson later that year in support of his application for the Bersham Hall post.

14.62 We have already summarised Marshall Jones' response to the allegations of physical abuse made against him[22]. Speaking of his later period at Chevet Hey, he said that he was given great support by Michael Barnes and he denied the allegations to which we have referred. In our view, however, the later evidence is consistent with the overall assessment of him that we have given in paragraph 14.19.

David Gwyn Birch

14.63 **David Birch** was transferred to Chevet Hey with effect from 1 November 1984, having worked briefly at South Meadow and Park House in Prestatyn as a supply officer on leaving Bryn Estyn in June 1984[23]. He remained at Chevet Hey until 14 January 1990 when his resignation took effect. It seems that he ranked immediately below Marshall Jones in seniority so that he was Acting Deputy Officer-in-Charge for a short period in 1988 after the departure of Michael Barnes until Michael Nelson became Officer-in-Charge on 27 June 1988. He was probably Acting Third Officer-in-Charge when Marshall Jones was Acting Deputy[24]. Nevertheless, he had a chequered career at Chevet Hey from 1986 onwards.

14.64 We are aware of five complainants who alleged physical abuse by Birch at Chevet Hey and three of them gave oral evidence before us. The first was the witness who agreed that he was "quite a handful" at the time[25] and he complained that Birch used excessive violence in restraining him on two occasions. The first of these incidents occurred in late January 1987, about six weeks after he arrived at Chevet Hey and he complained about it quite promptly to Marshall Jones and then to a woman member of the staff. It seems that there had been permitted bonfires that evening and the witness refused to co-operate in putting them out at the appropriate time. An argument or altercation with a male care officer ensued and in the end both Marshall Jones and Birch were involved in an exchange of blows with him in the office. His complaint against Birch was that Birch had then used an armhold around his neck to restrain him with the result that he was choking and passing out.

---

[22] See paras 14.17 and 14.18.
[23] His career at Bryn Estyn is dealt with in paras 8.37, 8.38 and 10.40 to 10.57.
[24] See paras 14.49 and 14.50.
[25] See para 14.57.

14.65 That incident was investigated by Barnes, who interviewed the witness in the presence of Birch, when his allegations against Birch were repeated and he accused Barnes of "mental harassment". This interview took place, however, against a background of further alleged misconduct by the witness and the dispute seems to have died down following a pre-arranged family meeting, despite the witness' threat to complain to the police.

14.66 The second incident occurred on 1 May 1987, when the witness was 17 years old, and was much more serious but his criticisms of Birch about this were comparatively mild. In short, the witness was involved in a further altercation with the same relief houseparent who had featured initially in the first incident and whom the witness claimed to despise. Angered by "a snide remark" by this houseparent, the witness, who had a leg in plaster at the time, punched him in the face, "jumped" and headbutted him with the result that his forehead was cut and his face and neck bruised. The witness then stormed into the office where he was restrained by Marshall Jones and Birch, who held him down on the ground so forcefully that he could not breathe, whilst he shouted "blue murder"; he was restrained thus until the police arrived. In his oral evidence the witness said that, with hindsight, he recognised that he would have hurt as many people as he could, if he had not been restrained. He said also that Birch was "a decent bloke" generally, echoing his earlier statement to the police in which he had said of Birch that "he was really a sound bloke but he was too strong and I don't think he really understood his own strength".

14.67 This witness did not return to Chevet Hey after his arrest on 1 May 1987. He was charged with unlawfully wounding the relief houseparent and was bailed to his parents' home. On 23 July 1987 at Wrexham Maelor Magistrates' Court he was convicted of the charge after contesting it. Sentence was deferred for six months and on 20 January 1988 he was ordered to perform 40 hours' community service.

14.68 The second complainant who gave evidence was at Chevet Hey for 18 months from April 1987 to October 1988 and reached the age of 16 years in the middle of that period. He spoke favourably of Michael Barnes, whom he described as "quite calm", and said of the staff generally, "we all seemed to get on quite well together". His complaint against Birch was based on one incident towards the end of his stay when he returned to the home late after seeing his girl friend. Birch answered the door and then kicked his legs from under him, kneed him in the back and punched him on the back of his head. Birch then asked him why he was late and laughed before telling him to go to bed: he was in quite a lot of pain. The witness admitted that he had returned late on many occasions but said that he was only a couple of minutes late on the relevant occasion. In general, however, he did "get on" with Birch.

14.69 The third witness, a girl who was at Chevet Hey for about three and a half years and left in or about March 1986, when she reached the age of 18 years, was critical of five members of the staff there in her time. She said that she got on reasonably well with Birch but that he had a habit of slapping children across the head with his hand. He did this to her once but she saw it happen also to others and it was a whack rather than a tap.

14.70 None of these alleged incidents at Chevet Hey was the subject of a criminal charge against Birch subsequently. We do not think that any substantial criticism can be made of him in respect of the restraint incidents but he was clearly at fault, in our view, in the other matters. Birch told us that he had no recollection of the incident described in paragraph 14.68 and he was not asked specifically about the third witness but we have no reason to doubt the two witnesses' broad accounts of their dealings with him; and this conclusion accords with our wider assessment of Birch's record at Bryn Estyn[26].

14.71 A notable feature of Birch's career at Chevet Hey, only indirectly relevant to the scale of abuse there, was persistent conflict between him and Michael Barnes, who was critical of his performance of his duties from 1986 onwards. It is unnecessary to go into great detail about these criticisms but they began with criticism of Birch's role in permitting Jacqueline Thomas to absent herself from Chevet Hey at Christmas 1985 for periods when she was supposed to be on duty. This criticism was associated with lingering doubts about Birch's veracity on the subject, to the extent that he provided an alibi for Thomas in respect of certain allegations of sexual abuse made against her[27].

14.72 Other criticisms of Birch were pursued in 1986. They included allegations that he had taken a girl friend with him on a summer caravan holiday financed by the Social Services Department and on a day trip to Blackpool with residents of Chevet Hey; allegations of inadequate accounting for monies spent on the Blackpool trip; and alleged pressure on three residents to tell lies in relation to the costs incurred on the trip. In consequence, Birch was suspended for a short period in October 1986. On 24 November 1986, as we have already stated[28], Barnes wrote a long memorandum setting out his assessment of Chevet Hey, of which he was highly (and in our view, justifiably) critical. Paragraph 3 of that report dealt in detail with outstanding complaints against Birch, including absenteeism, poor timekeeping and disregard of procedures. On 29 January 1987 an inconclusive meeting to discuss the issues raised by the report and attended by Raymond Powell, John Llewellyn Thomas and six others, including Michael Barnes, took place at Shire Hall. No disciplinary action appears to have been taken and further complaints about Birch's timekeeping and absenteeism, including allegations that he played rugby for his club whilst on sick leave, were still being pursued in late 1987. Eventually, on 7 December 1987 the Director of Social Services, Gledwyn Jones, conducted a managerial interview with Birch, in the presence of the Deputy County Personnel Officer and trades union representatives, when Birch was informed by the Director that "under no circumstances would he entertain any further complaints such as the one that was made that he had been playing rugby whilst on sick leave from Chevet Hey and unable to attend work during September 1987".

14.73 This was not an end of the matter because Barnes wrote to the Director on 4 January 1988 requesting confirmation that the many other complaints against Birch particularised in his six memoranda written between April and

[26] See para 10.56.
[27] See paras 14.37 to 14.42.
[28] See paras 14.51 and 14.52.

September 1987 had been dealt with. The Director was also informed subsequently of further absences by Birch between 22 December 1987 and 5 January 1988 and there were fresh complaints of a similar kind by Marshall Jones but Birch continued to survive in post until his appointment by the Metropolitan Borough of Sefton from January 1990 as Deputy Officer-in-Charge of a community home or homes in Aintree Lane and Cherry Road, for which he received a favourable reference, apparently written by Raymond Powell and signed in the name of the Director of Social Services, dated 12 September 1989, in which the only mildly adverse comment was "He has some difficulty with administration but is able to cope quite adequately with this if he sets his mind to it".

Another example of disciplinary action

14.74 One other example of the response of senior management to a complaint of abuse during Barnes' period as Acting Officer-in-Charge was brought to our attention. The relevant incident occurred on 15 July 1987 when a member of the care staff slapped a 16 year old boy resident across the face. The boy then complained to Marshall Jones, who reported the complaint to Michael Barnes. When the care worker was seen she admitted the slap but alleged that she had been provoked by the way in which the boy had demanded a drink of water and the exchange of words between them that had ensued. A meeting was arranged between the two, in the presence of Marshall Jones and with Barnes' approval, when mutual apologies were made but some differences of opinion remained. The care worker was then seen by John Llewellyn Thomas (Principal Officer, Children and Family Services) and Barnes on 23 July 1987, after which a formal warning letter dated 30 July 1987 was sent to her in the name of the Director of Social Services. After acknowledging that she bitterly regretted her action, the letter concluded:

> "It was noted that this resulted from provocation but this cannot be an excuse for striking a child in our care which is a matter of the gravest concern. I am satisfied that you will have learnt from this experience but nevertheless I must warn you that any repetition of such behaviour will result in disciplinary action."

The Nelson regime

14.75 **Michael Nelson** took over as Officer-in-Charge of Chevet Hey, which had become a Group 1 community home[29] on 1 January 1988, from 27 June 1988 until it closed in June 1990, when he became Centre Manager of Gladwyn Children's Centre, Gresford, until 1993. He was 41 years old when he took on the Chevet Hey appointment and had nearly 20 years varied experience in residential child care, most recently as a team manager for Liverpool Social Services Department working in the secure unit at Dyson Hall. He had attended a full time one year course in residential child care in 1971 and had subsequently attended conferences and seminars on case management and

---

[29] See footnote 2 to this chapter.

sexual abuse as well as a short course on restraint provided by the prison service prior to his employment in the secure unit. He is now a group manager in residential services for children employed by Wrexham County Borough Council.

14.76 Nelson said in his written statement to the Tribunal that he never witnessed any physical assault upon a child at Chevet Hey (or subsequently at Gladwyn). We are aware of only one complaint against him at Chevet Hey but that was made by a boy who admitted to a member of the staff that he had fabricated a complaint against Marshall Jones and he did not pursue his complaint against Nelson by providing evidence to the Tribunal. The only incident involving Nelson directly of which we have evidence occurred when he was at Gladwyn and on an occasion when he had to restrain a violent boy. The boy sustained a bruised shoulder but the incident was fully investigated at the time and the boy told the police in June 1993 that he accepted that there had been a full internal investigation after he had reported the matter to his social worker and that the injury had been accidental as concluded by a case conference. Although that witness ran amok with a knife at the end of his stay at Gladwyn, he told the police that he had been treated fairly there.

14.77 One or two of the complaints against **Marshall Jones** related to events between June 1988 and September 1989[30]. It is necessary to mention also one other member of the residential staff during Nelson's period, namely, **Andrew Humphriss**, who served as a residential care worker at Chevet Hey from 1 May 1988 to 25 September 1989, interrupted early on by four weeks' detachment to Bersham Hall to replace a member of the care staff who was on sick leave and later by his suspension from 25 April 1989 onwards. He was 27 years old when he was appointed and had served for about six years in the Metropolitan Police, as a cadet and then constable, after leaving school at 15 years old. He had then become a residential social worker for the London Borough of Newham in 1982 and had obtained the CSS qualification. However, he became disillusioned with his work at Chevet Hey and resigned in late September 1989, after which he took a degree course in Education at Cartrefle College, graduating in 1993. For the past four years he has been a teacher in Cheshire.

14.78 There were a number of problems in the course of the 11 months or so that Humphriss actually spent at Chevet Hey. Although he did well at his appointment interview with Barnes, Marshall Jones and one other in March 1988, his staff appraisal in December 1988 showed that reports on his progress had been mixed and Barnes, who conducted the appraisal with Nelson and Humphriss himself, wrote "If Mr Humphriss was subject to a probationary period aspects of his work would be earmarked for improvement". Then in January 1989 several allegations of physical abuse by Humphriss were made by the first of the two boys referred to in paragraph 14.76. These allegations involved not only the boy himself but also his brother and another boy. On investigation by Nelson, however, these complaints were not substantiated and the boy, who was causing problems because of his unruliness, asked to

---

[30] See, in particular, para 14.61.

withdraw his complaints. On 23 February 1989 Humphriss had a serious altercation with Marshall Jones about the content of a report written by Humphriss to which Marshall Jones objected and it is clear from Humphriss' evidence to us that he disapproved of Marshall Jones' methods: he described the latter's general approach to children as robust, loud and verbally aggressive and he alleged that it was Marshall Jones' practice to amend reports after they had been written, including reports written by others, to put himself in a favourable light. On the other hand, Marshall Jones was equally critical of Humphriss, alleging that he had lied and had also tried to head butt Marshall Jones.

14.79　Finally, on 24 April 1989, a local councillor and postmaster reported to Barnes that he had witnessed Humphriss physically assaulting one of the Chevet Hey residents outside Gwersyllt Swimming Baths. Barnes interviewed Humphriss promptly the next day in the presence of Nelson and suspended him on full pay pending an investigation of the councillor's complaint, in the course of which the clinical medical officer's staff were involved. A disciplinary hearing was ultimately fixed for 16 August 1989 but either it did not take place or no decision was reached at it because Humphriss' resignation with effect from 25 September 1989 was accepted without any adverse finding being recorded against him. In his evidence before us Humphriss strenuously denied any assault upon the boy at Gwersyllt Swimming Baths. We did not hear any oral evidence in support of the allegation so that we do not express any opinion about it.

Conclusions

14.80　The level of complaints and the evidence of abuse at Chevet Hey have been significantly less than at the other Wrexham community homes that we have discussed in detail; and the general picture that has emerged is that the atmosphere of the home was much better from the children's point of view. Most of the former residents there would probably say that they did not suffer any appreciable damage from their detention there. Nevertheless, there are many disquieting features about the history that we have related.

14.81　Although the Ellis Edwards regime may have been acceptable to most of the residents at the time, it is clear that Wyatt's criticisms in 1985 were fully justified[31] and they were re-inforced by Barnes' broader survey in November 1986 of the shortcomings of Chevet Hey when he had taken over Ellis Edwards' responsibilities earlier that year[32]. There had been a general failure on the part of the staff to relate to the children in their care in a meaningful way, an absence of guidance and lack of parental concern; and no adequate steps had been taken to face the problems that arose from the demise of Bryn Estyn and the transfer of staff and residents from there to Chevet Hey. A fair share of the blame for these failures must be attributed to Ellis Edwards himself but he appears to have been given little support and guidance from senior

[31] See paras 14.29 and 14.30.
[32] See paras 14.51 and 14.52.

management; and the weakness of the headquarters' leadership is well illustrated by their successive failures to discipline Wilson and by their later impotence in dealing with Marshall Jones and David Birch.

14.82 Some improvements in child care practice were achieved under Michael Barnes and we accept that he did have a coherent vision of what a community home should try to achieve. We accept also that he had to face some intractable problems because of the wide range of difficult children of both sexes who were being admitted to Chevet Hey. But, in our judgment, he was better on paper than in practice. He had some defects of personality, which were counter-productive in his relationships with staff and children, and he appeared to condone the activities of Marshall Jones to some extent during his period in charge. We recognise, however, that he had great difficulties in securing an adequate response from headquarters when he sought assistance in dealing with his problems.

14.83 In the end the most successful period was probably the final two years under Michael Nelson. Certainly, the level of complaints of abuse was by then much reduced and it is noteworthy that they appear to have been dealt with quite promptly because they were being made to the care staff (or in one case to a social worker) and investigated by Nelson himself. It was difficult by then to achieve more on the positive side because it had been decided, or at least "recognised", as early as 1987 that Chevet Hey would close and be replaced by another home.

Cartrefle Community Home, 1974 to 1993

15.01 Cartrefle is quite a small house standing in its own grounds on a main road next door to a police station at Broughton, east of Hawarden. It has the appearance of a council house but has its own garage and outbuildings. It was opened by Flintshire County Council in 1966 as a home for up to eight children aged between ten and 16 years and it was so described in the 1971 Regional Plan. In the 1979 Plan the number was increased to ten and the provision was said to be mainly for older children[1]. It appears, however, that it was used mainly as a resource for boys until the early 1990s, when a small number of girls were admitted, and it closed in 1993. There was accommodation for one physically disabled resident in a downstairs bedroom and the resident children usually attended local schools.

15.02 It is convenient to deal with Cartrefle here because the vast majority of complaints at this community home were levelled against **Stephen Norris**, whose career at Bryn Estyn has already been fully discussed[2], and because **Frederick Marshall Jones,** who figured prominently in the preceding chapter, moved on to Cartrefle, after nine months as Assistant Centre Manager (Third Officer-in-Charge) at Bersham Hall, with effect from 8 July 1990, succeeding Norris three months later, after the latter's conviction.

15.03 Before Norris took over as Officer-in-Charge of Cartrefle on 1 December 1984, there had been two heads of the home since Clwyd County Council had assumed responsibility for it on 1 April 1974. The first was Eleanor Forshaw, who was there (with her husband) for nearly four years to 31 August 1977, and the second was Olivia Browell (formerly Lewis), who was in charge from 7 November 1977 until 30 November 1984. We are not aware of any complaint against any identified member of staff in respect of the period from 1974 until Norris' arrival. On the contrary, the one former girl resident of those days who gave evidence, who was at Cartrefle in late 1975 and early 1976, said that Mr and Mrs Forshaw were really nice people. At that time there were five or six boys and girls in residence, who all got on with each other, and the house was in good shape.

15.04 Unfortunately, however, the official view was less complimentary about Mrs Forshaw. A Welsh Office SWSO, Mr F Beatty, inspected the home on 27 April 1977 on notice, four months before Forshaw retired and was accompanied by Veronica Pares, one of two residential and day care establishment inspectors appointed by the Social Services Department of Clwyd in 1977. Beatty's report noted that concern had been expressed about a lack of communication between staff and management and doubts raised about the ability of Forshaw to maintain control of the residents. He recommended that male staff should be

---

[1] See para 4.02(13).
[2] See, in particular, paras 8.23 to 8.34, 10.02 and 10.157.

employed at the home and that regular staff meetings should be held to improve communication. Other criticisms in the report were that there were no copies of review reports on the resident children's files and that social workers visits were said to be irregular and infrequent.

The Norris period, 1 December 1984 to 18 June 1990

15.05 Stephen Norris was transferred from Bryn Estyn to Cartrefle with effect from 9 July 1984 as a supernumerary RCCO, about two months before Bryn Estyn closed. According to his own evidence, he was off sick for three to four months after serving for only two or three days at Cartrefle. This did not, however, prejudice his appointment as Officer-in-Charge from 1 December 1984. The decision to appoint him was apparently made at the time of his transfer. The post was not advertised and it does not appear that Norris was interviewed. In a memorandum (to the County Personnel and Management Services Officer) dated 20 July 1984, which was signed by the Director of Social Services (D Gledwyn Jones) it was said that "Following recent discussions between Mr G Wyatt, Assistant Director (Residential and Day Care) and Mr J Thomas, Principal Officer (Child Care) it is recommended that "Norris" be redeployed to the above post, subject to the approval of the Chairman of the Personnel Sub-committee".

Complaints against Stephen Norris

15.06 We are aware of 24 complainants in this period of whom all but one complain of abuse by **Stephen Norris** himself. The average stay of the ten or so residents at any one time was about 18 months so that the number of complainants represents rather more than half the boys who came under his care at Cartrefle.

Allegations of sexual abuse by Norris

15.07 The pattern of Norris' conduct at Cartrefle was, unsurprisingly, closely similar to his behaviour at Clwyd House, Bryn Estyn. Of the 23 complainants against him, 20 complained of sexual abuse and only seven of physical abuse. We heard oral evidence from six of those who complained of sexual abuse and we received the statements of a further six in evidence. Norris' activities in the showers, watching boys and indecently handling some there, continued as before. On occasions he washed boys when they took a bath or a shower and masturbated them on one pretext or another. There were also indecent assaults in the boys' bedrooms, involving masturbation and sometimes oral sex. One boy alleged also that Norris incited him to masturbate another boy whilst Norris watched.

15.08 When he appeared at Chester Crown Court on 5 October 1990 Norris pleaded guilty to five offences of indecent assault, involving three boy residents at Cartrefle, which were all committed in this period; and he was sentenced to a total of three and a half years' imprisonment. No evidence was offered by the Prosecution in support of a charge of buggery involving one of those boys and a similar procedure was adopted in respect of two charges of indecent assault involving two other boys so that verdicts of not guilty were entered by the Court in respect of those three additional charges. Finally, a ninth count, of indecent assault in respect of a sixth boy, was ordered to be left on the file on the usual terms[3].

15.09 We heard oral evidence from three of these former residents and the statements of the other three were received in evidence. Their evidence fully substantiated all the charges laid against Norris in that first indictment. The witness who alleged that he had been buggered by Norris said that this had occurred at a number of different places: it had occurred, for example, in and out of Norris' Land Rover near Buckley water towers and during about four visits to Norris' smallholding, where he had slept in a caravan[4]. This witness said also that he had gone to the police station next door to Cartrefle in or about the late Spring of 1985, after he had been at the home for about six months, to complain that the children were being interfered with but had received the response that the police could not do anything without evidence and nothing further had been done about it.

15.10 The allegations of buggery by Norris during this period were not confined to the last mentioned witness. In all six other former residents of Cartrefle alleged that they had been buggered by Norris; and five of them, together with the witness whose allegation included in the first indictment had not been proceeded with, were named as victims in a new indictment containing six counts of buggery, which was preferred against Norris in 1993 following the major police investigation. That third indictment was before the Crown Court at Knutsford on 11 November 1993 when Norris pleaded guilty to a second indictment, which dealt with his offences whilst at Bryn Estyn, for which he received seven years' imprisonment[5]. The order of the Court in respect of the third indictment was that it should lie on the file on the usual terms[6].

15.11 We received the evidence of four of these six others who alleged that they had been buggered by Norris whilst at Cartrefle. Two of them gave persuasive oral evidence before us. One of them had been assaulted thus in his bedroom and had suffered a further attempt to bugger him about six months later. The other had suffered repeated assaults and buggery during a short stay at Cartrefle of less than three months in 1987. Oral sex and buggery had occurred on numerous occasions in his bedroom, after he had gone to bed, and assaults had occurred in the showers also from his first day at the home. This witness said that Norris was wrecking his life psychologically.

15.12 The two witnesses whose evidence was read shared a room for a period in late 1989 and early 1990 and one of them was the boy who complained eventually to a member of the staff, Henry Morton Stanley, as a result of which a police investigation began and Norris was suspended from duty on 18 June 1990. The boy who reported the matter was at Cartrefle for about four years in all and alleged that he had been subjected to indecent assaults and buggery by Norris

---

[3] ie not to be proceeded with unless with the leave of the Court of Appeal (Criminal Division) or the Crown Court itself.

[4] See para 8.30 for an earlier reference to this caravan.

[5] See para 8.28.

[6] See footnote 3 to this chapter.

for about two years from 1988 onwards. Indecent assaults had started in the showers and had continued there until May 1990, when Norris had left for Greece on holiday; they had occurred also in Norris' office and in the boy's bedroom; the assaults involved mutual masturbation on frequent occasions; and buggery had occurred in the bedroom during daytime. Norris had also forced him to "do things" with his room-mate, "have sex with each other", whilst Norris watched, "playing with his own penis". The room-mate's statements were to similar effect. In his case too the assaults began in the showers, where Norris would wash him all over on the pretext that he was not washing himself properly. Masturbation occurred there and in a staff bedroom to which Norris would take him. Buggery took place in that bedroom and in the boy's own bedroom during the night time when the other boy was there. This boy referred also to buggery with the latter in their bedroom, but he did not say that Norris was present when it occurred, saying rather that he thought that the reason why they did it was "because of what Steve Norris was doing to us I used to think that was the way I should behave".

15.13 When Norris himself gave evidence he did not make any detailed admissions but said that he had taken advantage of boys in a sexual way[7]. He denied that he was obsessed with sex and asserted in cross-examination that he had not regarded himself as doing wrong to the boys at the time when he was committing his offences. He was still, however, requiring "trust" from the boys, that is, an undertaking from them that they would not tell anyone, although he told the boy who eventually reported him that he had a right to do so when the boy said he would "tell". He accepted that he had abused children disastrously but he attributed the boys' failure to complain at the time to his relationship with them rather than to his position of power; and he denied developing the boys' trust for the purpose of abusing them.

15.14 We are satisfied that the evidence that we have summarised of Norris' sexual exploitation of boy residents at Cartrefle between 1984 and 1990 is substantially true. We have no reason to doubt the veracity on this subject of the many witnesses who described in detail Norris' methods of approach and his subsequent systematic corruption of youth after youth in his care at Cartrefle. We believe, moreover, that it would have continued unchecked for a further lengthy period but for the unusual courage of the 14 year old boy who spoke up about it in June 1990 and Stanley's sensitivity in facilitating the gradual disclosure to him. The result of Norris' activities was the complete negation of the concept of care for a wide range of boys in need who should have been able to rely upon the local authority for a safe refuge; and the wider long term social consequences for those children and their families of his breaches of trust are incalculable.

The response to Norris' sexual abuse

15.15 A further perturbing aspect of this lamentable history of sexual abuse by Norris at Cartrefle was the response of the Clwyd Social Services Department

---

[7] See para 8.31 for his evidence about Bryn Estyn.

in dealing with the children who remained in their care at Cartrefle after Norris' arrest. An immediate cause of concern to us was the lack of any specialist input to the counselling of the children still in care who had been affected by Norris' conduct. From the limited evidence before us it appears that there was little or no discussion at an appropriate level of the future placement of the children who had been direct victims of Norris either in their own best interests or in the best interests of children with whom they might be placed. In particular, we are not aware that any discussion took place of the risk that those who had been abused might become abusers in another community home and how best this risk could be minimised. This is a subject to which we will return in the next chapter. Equally importantly, no appropriate guidance was sought about how the affected children, whether direct victims or merely residents at Cartrefle in the relevant period, could best be helped to overcome the impact of Norris' arrest, the ensuing disclosures about his conduct and the adverse publicity generally accompanying them.

15.16 Very little specific counselling seems to have been arranged for the children and such counselling as was attempted seems to us to have been both amateur and seriously misguided. In particular, we have seen notes of three "informal meetings" (described as "sharing of information") held at Cartrefle Children's Centre, as it had become, on 12 and 19 December 1990 and 9 January 1991. Attending all the meetings were two representatives of the Hawarden Area Office and the five boys who had remained in residence at Cartrefle; and they were joined at each by one or two members of the residential care staff.

15.17 There are obvious and stringent criticisms that must be made of these meetings because:

(a) the delay of several months in providing counselling was inexcusable (the Court proceedings against Norris cannot be regarded as a proper excuse);

(b) broaching such a sensitive subject in group meetings of young children requires a high level of skill and preparation and is no substitute for individual counselling and risk assessment; and

(c) the conduct of the meetings was even more inappropriate.

To illustrate (c), the second meeting began with the question whether the children were prepared to meet Norris, Stanley and the member of the staff who had resigned and went on to discuss whether the boy who had reported Norris had been right or wrong to do so and what they felt about him. The third meeting began with the group being introduced to a glossary of "terms concerned with sex education" by questioning as to the meaning of "group sex", "oral sex", "masturbation", "fetishism", "masochism", "indecent exposure", "bestiality" etc. According to the notes, "The group's response to this newly acquired knowledge was one of incredibility (sic) and in some cases - disgust!".

15.18 We deal later in this chapter with other aspects of the response by the Social Services Department to the disclosures of Norris' sexual abuse. Before doing so it is necessary to complete the picture of abuse during Norris' period as Officer-in-Charge and the final three years until Cartrefle closed.

Allegations of physical abuse by Norris

15.19 The allegations of physical (other than sexual) abuse by Norris at Cartrefle were much more limited and were made in the main by former residents who complained also of sexual assaults by him. It appears that seven former residents alleged at some time that Norris had struck them but one of these had no recollection of being assaulted when he gave oral evidence to us. Three other witnesses gave oral evidence before us and the statements of one other were read. The most serious allegation, made by two of them, was of being beaten by Norris with a belt, said by one to have been studded; and one alleged that he had been threatened by Norris with a shotgun (kept in Norris' office) in order to scare him. The other allegations were of being slapped across the bottom or, in one case, across the head for fighting and of cold water being thrown over the witness by Norris when the witness was taking a shower.

15.20 Although Norris has denied these allegations we are satisfied that he did on occasions strike boy residents at Cartrefle with his hands and on rare occasions with a belt, but, in our judgment, the level of physical abuse by him was almost insignificant in comparison with the gravity of his persistent sexual abuse and his more general inadequacy as the Officer-in-Charge, to which we will revert later in this chapter.

Other allegations of abuse during this period

15.21 The Deputy Officer-in-Charge of Cartrefle from 1 December 1980 to 14 September 1990 was **Heather Patricia Lynn**, who was 29 years old at the date of her appointment. She had previously been employed by Clwyd County Council as an RCCO at Upper Downing Children's Home from 1 October 1975[8] and then at Cartrefle from 20 December 1976. She was appointed to the post of Deputy after an interview by a panel of three, presided over by Geoffrey Wyatt, following advertisement of the post externally and internally. She was, however, largely untrained and comparatively inexperienced. After clerical work, she had been employed as a residential nursery assistant at a Leonard Cheshire home, working with handicapped children, for 12 months before going to Upper Downing. At that time she attended a brief introduction course and she later followed, in her own time, an Open University course on the care of children but she had no formal qualifications.

15.22 Heather Lynn had to resign from her post with effect from 14 September 1990 following her admission that she had had a sexual relationship with a boy resident at Cartrefle. That boy (W), who was born on 6 April 1973, was resident at Cartrefle for six months from about January 1986 and then from January

---

[8] See paras 17.08 to 17.14 for an account of the complaint about her at Upper Downing.

1987 to 6 April 1990, when he moved to approved lodgings with Henry Morton Stanley, who had been an RCCO at Cartrefle since December 1985, and his wife Jane.

15.23 According to W, he was sexually abused by Norris persistently up to February 1990, although he was never buggered. His sexual relationship with Heather Lynn began when he was helping her to decorate her own house and intercourse occurred between them on seven or eight occasions in the staff room at Cartrefle and at her home over a period of about six months. It ended, said W, when Heather Lynn was "becoming serious".

15.24 The precise circumstances in which this liaison came to be disclosed are unclear. Lynn said in a written statement to the Tribunal that she told the police about it when she was interviewed in the course of their first Norris investigation and the Social Services Department was then informed. The admission was not included in her statements to the police but this may be because it was not relevant to the Norris investigation. What is clear is that she made a written statement to Geoffrey Wyatt in the presence of others on 8 August 1990, at the Shire Hall, Mold, in which she admitted having sexual intercourse with W three or four times at her home in April and May 1989, "just after his" (16th) "birthday". She attributed her conduct to her low emotional state on the ending of an 11 years relationship but added "I knew that W was in care and that it should not have happened, it was my fault not W's". She alleged, however, that both Stanley and Norris were aware of the affair and that Stanley had told her he knew. W confirmed in his own statement that he told Stanley about it.

15.25 Following the making of this statement, a disciplinary hearing was arranged for 17 August 1990 but had to be adjourned to 14 September 1990 because Lynn was unwell. She then sent her letter of resignation the day before the hearing was to take place. It is to be noted that in a statement made to the Tribunal on 17 March 1997 Lynn disclosed that she had an affair with another former resident of Cartrefle, who came to her as a lodger on his discharge from care at the age of 18 years. The dates when this occurred are not stated but she alleged that she made enquiries of the Officer-in-Charge of Cartrefle who confirmed that she did not need any authority to take the man as a lodger because he had been discharged from care. W subsequently lodged with her on and off between 1993 and 1996 but the sexual relationship was not resumed.

15.26 W's relationship with another member of the Cartrefle staff, namely, **Henry Morton Stanley**, was yet another cause for concern. There has not been any allegation by W against Stanley but a number of members of staff were concerned that Stanley had become unhealthily emotionally involved with W. Stanley was still a young man when he was at Cartrefle, having been born on 7 January 1963. He had entered social service young, at the age of 19 years, and had initially served for three years at children's homes in Prestatyn before moving to Cartrefle in December 1985. Throughout the period from 1982 he was employed as a temporary RCCO and member of the Temporary Relief

Pool but he was appointed to a permanent post as RCCO at Cartrefle from 24 April 1988. He held a Preliminary Certificate in Social Care which he had obtained in July 1982 but he said in evidence that he has more recently obtained a degree in youth and community education.

15.27 He remained at Cartrefle until about 12 July 1990, when he began sick leave, which was extended as special leave to December 1990. From 5 December 1990 he was redeployed as a temporary social worker attached to the East Division, subject to review after six months, but he resigned on 30 May 1991, saying that he felt that he had no alternative "under the circumstances of the pending conclusion of the review"[9]. However, in accepting the resignation the following day, the Director of Social Services, John Jevons, said "I am not aware of any reason why you should feel that the Review of Cartrefle Children's Home should cause you to resign".

15.28 The immediate reason for Stanley's earlier departure from Cartrefle on sick leave was that he felt himself to be on the verge of a breakdown. The causes of his condition were, however, complex and may never be fully disclosed. He had himself been abused as a child so that the disclosures of abuse by Norris were likely to have had a particularly severe impact on him. He denied in evidence that he had been obsessed with W but the fact remains that he did obtain approval for W to lodge with him and his wife on leaving Cartrefle with the result that W stayed with them from 6 April 1990; and some time after 17 June 1990, when Stanley was told by the first complainant of Norris' sexual abuse, W also confided in Stanley that Norris had abused him similarly.

15.29 Another factor in Stanley's overall state was his allegedly poor relationship with other members of the residential care staff. He had reported Heather Lynn's association with W to Norris in 1989 after W had told him about it and had said that he (W) wanted it to stop. Stanley had assumed that Norris would report the matter to his line manager but Norris had not done so: a serious disciplinary matter, therefore, remained unresolved. There was also wider tension because other members of the residential staff did not believe the boys' allegations against Norris, whereas Stanley firmly did; and had been instrumental in bringing them to official notice and some may have resented Stanley's assumption of some administrative responsibilities, outside his actual duties, due to Norris' failings.

15.30 Stanley initially expressed his willingness to return to Cartrefle after his sick leave because the counselling that he had received had been very supportive and he was prepared to try to work through any problems arising from the feelings of other members of the staff towards him. A meeting with the other members of staff was then held at Cartrefle on 14 November 1990, when all of them expressed their willingness to work with Stanley but he said that, on balance, he did not wish to return to Cartrefle because to do so would probably affect the stability of the staff and children built up over many months.

[9] See para 15.42 et seq.

15.31 A further perturbing development was that, shortly before Stanley resigned, he discovered that W was having an affair with his wife, then aged 32 years and employed as a cook and care assistant at Park House Children's Home. W thereupon ceased to lodge with the Stanleys and Mrs Stanley resigned her employment.

15.32 Only one former resident of Cartrefle has alleged sexual abuse by Stanley and the circumstances of that isolated and uncorroborated allegation are such that we are unable to regard it as reliable. The witness's main complaints were of frequent abuse by Norris and he did not make any allegations against Stanley to the police or to anyone else until January 1992. Since then his allegations against Stanley have varied and his oral evidence, alleging buggery by Stanley in the vicinity of water towers, (misplaced by him as near Buckley when they are near Broughton airfield), mirrored unconvincingly one of his allegations against Norris. This witness alleged also that Stanley, on a different occasion, slashed the witness's left thigh when they were in a wood together as a warning to him not to tell anyone what had happened, but Stanley refuted this and the primary allegation of sexual abuse vehemently, stressing his own response to the disclosures of Norris' abuse. For similar reasons we were unimpressed by the suggestion by another witness, who was unwilling to give oral evidence, that Stanley must have observed Norris abusing him in his bedroom on one occasion in or about 1987.

15.33 Our conclusion about Stanley is that there is no acceptable evidence that he was guilty of sexual or other abuse of children during his period as a residential care worker. However, in the light of the events that had happened and his own vulnerability, we think that his decision not to return to Cartrefle was wise, in his own best interests and those of the children.

15.34 The one Cartrefle complainant of this period who did not complain of abuse by Norris singled out a long standing woman member of the residential care staff, **Paula Dean**, for criticism; and it was his complaint that led to her dismissal. He alleged that, at teatime on 19 July 1988, she had become angry when he was unable ("too full") to eat a barbecue rib that she had provided for him. In her anger she "ripped his T-shirt off his back" and hit him once with the back of her left hand, which was in plaster. The boy had run out of the house and stayed out an hour. On his return, according to his oral evidence, Paula Dean behaved as if nothing had happened and he reported the matter to his "carer", another member of the staff, the next day. However, a note of what the boy said on August 1988 reads:

> "After lunch or about 1 pm.
>
> I refused to eat king ribs, if you don't eat them, then you go to bed.
>
> I ran out through the door. David told me to come in as Paula wanted me. I said 'no'. David pushed me towards her and she caught hold of my tee-shirt.
>
> She pushed me outside by the caravan. She told me to get my shirt off. I said 'no' so she tore it off. She pushed me into the kitchen and told me to take my trousers off. I said 'no'. So she got hold of my arm and pushed

it up my back, doing this her nails scratched my back. She then pushed me upstairs and told me to get my pants off then into bed. I did it. The bruise was when she pushed me onto the radiator in my bedroom."

15.35 It appears that the boy complained to his parents as well as his "carer" and the upshot was a formal complaint to the Director of Social Services by solicitors acting for the parents. Paula Dean was suspended from 12 August 1988 and a disciplinary hearing took place in November 1988. She denied then and in her evidence to us that she had caused any injury to the boy. She had written an account of the incident in the occurrence file describing the boy's misbehaviour, starting with a tantrum over a toy car, and his clothes had been taken from him only because he had said that "he was doing a runner".

15.36 In the event no finding was made that Dean had assaulted the boy. The decision to dismiss her was based on a finding that she had caused him undue distress by requiring him to undress and remain in his bedroom when she knew or should have known from the background to his entry into care that the effect of her action would be much more disturbing to him than to other boys. This finding of misconduct, following an earlier final written warning of 11 May 1988, was regarded as sufficient to justify Dean's dismissal and an appeal against the decision was dismissed on 16 December 1988. She then made an application to an industrial tribunal on the ground of unfair dismissal but her claim was settled on terms that have not been disclosed to us. From Cartrefle she went to work at a home for the elderly.

15.37 The only other complaint that we heard against Paula Dean was that she struck another boy resident several times after he had made a particularly obscene suggestion to her. He alleged that the blows were backhanders and that a permanent slight indentation on his right cheek had been caused by one of the large rings on her fingers. It was not this incident, however, that led to Dean's final warning. Stanley's evidence was that she was disciplined for throwing a chair at a child following a complaint by him about her action and that this was a factor in staff hostility towards him.

15.38 We are aware of significant complaints of abuse against only one other identified person (X) who was a member of the staff at Cartrefle during Norris' period. The allegations by a witness who gave oral evidence to the Tribunal are that X repeatedly abused him sexually on visits to a sauna bath on Deeside and that X assaulted him physically also on one occasion at Cartrefle with the result that he needed treatment to his neck at a Chester hospital. It was not possible to serve a 'Salmon Letter' on X, however, and the allegations were not made until the witness was interviewed by Tribunal staff in January 1997 so that it would be inappropriate for us to comment further.

The regime generally during Norris' period

15.39 It would be misleading to conclude the account of Cartrefle during this period without reference to severe wider criticisms that we heard in evidence of the regime and conditions at Cartrefle. Raymond Bew, for example, who had been a colleague (but not a friend) of Norris at Bryn Estyn, described the home as "a Mickey Mouse operation": it was neglected and rundown. There was no direction for the children and nothing to do other than watch television; they did not do what normal children of their age did but just lounged about and they were not encouraged to mix with the local community. This witness was also sufficiently concerned about the level of violence in the home to make a log entry to that effect.

15.40 Stanley was equally trenchant in his observations. He said that the home was like a zoo, chaotic. The children, the staff, nobody knew what anybody was doing or where anybody was because that was the way it functioned. There were no policies, no protocols, no staff meetings, no liaison, no recommendations, no constructive criticism. Other staff members regarded Norris as a joke and field workers regarded him as an idiot but he seemed to be held in high regard by more senior officials for his unorthodox approach. Stanley's view, which we accept, is that Norris was incapable of running the home administratively. He was almost illiterate and unable to deal with the routine paperwork in an acceptable manner. As for the physical condition of the home, the picture given by Stanley was bleak and depressing. He said:

> "It was threadbare carpets and three-piece suites that came from somebody else's skip or other home that had closed. The curtains were poor, the beds were poor, they were soiled. The decor was dismal and it was atrocious really. Sorry, but it was."

15.41 In the light of these views of two former members of the staff, it is not surprising that a disabled former resident said in his oral evidence to the Tribunal that he hated Cartrefle. He had been in a wheelchair all his life and he wondered why he had been put there (initially for short periods of respite care but later for months at a time) with offenders, when he had no criminal record. He was picked on a lot by the other boys, who used to call him "spastic" and things like that, and he got blamed for things that he did not do. He felt frustrated. This witness was one of Norris' many sexual victims and his opinion was that Norris could not run the place: it was out of control.

The Cartrefle Inquiry

15.42 In November 1990, after Norris' conviction and sentence on the first indictment brought against him[10], Clwyd County Council instructed John F Banham, a retired senior officer of Cheshire Social Services Department, to act as an independent reviewing officer on its behalf and to present a report into the events at and around Cartrefle Children's Home when residents were victims of sexual abuse. The Clwyd Area Child Protection Committee was informed of this initiative and decided to call for agency case reviews from the Health Authority and the Education Department in an attempt to conform with procedures recommended in Part Nine of Working Together (1988)[11]. The review on behalf of the Health Authority was carried

---

[10] See para 15.08.
[11] At pages 44 to 49 of Working Together: A guide to arrangements for inter-agency co-operation for the protection of children from abuse. (Department of Health and the Welsh Office, HMSO).

out by Dr Kathleen Dalzell and that on behalf of the Education Department by David Lund, Co-ordinator of Support Services. The three reports were presented by June 1991 and the Clwyd ACPC then appointed an independent panel of inquiry of five senior professionals to provide an overview, envisaging that four days at the beginning of July would be required to carry out their terms of reference. A robust response was given to this time estimate and the panel's own report was presented in February 1992 or soon thereafter.

15.43 The Banham report and the panel's own report of its overview of the three reports that it considered together form a strong indictment of the regime at Cartrefle and of its management, both internally and externally. The panel's report extended to 39 pages, excluding its appendices, and the Banham report to 32 pages so that it is impracticable here even to summarise them in great detail. It is, however, necessary to refer to the most striking and relevant points that emerged from them.

15.44 Banham's findings in relation to the internal management of the home included the following:

(a) Norris failed to manage the home in any acceptable way.

(b) He hated administration and the state of the paperwork was chaotic.

(c) Stanley's status within the home appeared to be inappropriate having regard to his seniority and caused resentment.

(d) The staff group under Norris were largely recruited from a pool and untrained.

(e) Norris failed to give any induction training to new staff and left them to operate as they pleased.

(f) The sickness records of Norris and Heather Lynn were appalling, showing a pattern of absences.

(g) The staff at Cartrefle were frequently required to run the home without their supervisors and there was no practice of staff supervision. There was no set work programme; no clear role definition was given or agreed; no planned or progressive approach was made to help with the considerable range of problems presented by the boys in residence; and no staff meetings were held.

(h) The home was used for cases outside its brief, purpose and resources. Placed under emergency, the boys' needs were not assessed and they seemed to have emotional and psychological problems that called for skilled and expert handling unavailable at Cartrefle.

(i) Prior to the discovery of Norris' abuse the ambience of the home and physical facilities had been described as "run down, poor, unhomely and uninviting".

(j) There was no evidence that anyone read the log books, other than members of staff on hand over from one shift to another.

(k) Norris discouraged any close involvement by staff as 'key workers' and there were few actual case reviews within the home.

15.45 Banham identified three members of the headquarters staff as responsible externally for the management of Cartrefle at the time when Norris' abuse was disclosed and before a major departmental re-structuring was put into effect in October 1990. The first line manager was Michael Barnes as Principal Social Worker from 1988 onwards; and he had as his assistant a Residential and Day Care Officer - Child Care (Norman Green). Barnes, in turn, was responsible to the Principal Officer (Children and Family Services), who was John Llewellyn Thomas.

15.46 Commenting upon the responsibilities of this trio of officers, Banham said "There is no doubt that theirs was a heavy workload, which was added to when certain duties from the retired Assistant Director were devolved. The Residential and Day Care Officer focussed more onto the "commendable effort" to extend training to residential staff....... The Principal Officer took on responsibility for the Children Act 1989 implementation, whilst the Principal Social Worker faced demands which often had him work long and tiring hours". Nevertheless, Banham's conclusion was that many specific duties resting with the management team had not been fulfilled: in his opinion, if they had been met, the climate of sexuality could not have matured and the inhibitions to abuse would have been greater. Discovery too should have been made possible earlier and easier.

15.47 This report contained an account also of how Barnes' early intention to make monthly visits to Cartrefle had waned because of his disapproval of Norris and his inability to get through to him. Barnes reprimanded Norris about his use of foul and sexual language and raised various concerns about the running of Cartrefle without any positive response, with the result that Barnes made fewer visits than he had planned. Banham commented "This type of situation has classic elements and symptoms to it, which any manager must guard against and overcome" and he stressed Clwyd's need for a training programme to enable their managers to develop the skills needed in middle ranking and senior posts.

15.48 Both the panel and Banham discussed also the response of Clwyd Social Services Department to the disclosures of Norris' abuse when they were eventually made in June 1990. Major criticisms were of (a) the failure to implement properly the Child Protection procedures because of confusion or at least uncertainty about the applicability of those procedures to children in care, attributable possibly to an assumption that such children were "safe", (b) the arrangements for the disposal of some of the victims without adequate case conferences, exchanges of information and counselling for residents and staff and (c) inexcusable delay of five months in setting up an inquiry into what had occurred.

15.49 Other points emerging from the conclusions and recommendations of these reports were:

(i) The need for a full rigorous interview of candidates for appointment to key child care posts, over-riding any redeployment agreement with trades unions.

(ii) External advertisement and open competition should be automatic when filling all middle and senior manager posts and rigorous attempts should be made to recruit women into such posts.

(iii) It was a sad indictment of the child care service in Clwyd that not one of the children at Cartrefle had a written assessment or care plan. Amongst the contributory factors to this were an unintegrated fieldwork and residential structure leading to lack of co-ordination and communication on assessment, planning and review matters; and the failure of managers to set a clear expectation of the standards to be maintained in this area and to monitor performance.

(iv) There was poor liaison with the Health Authority and Education Departments.

(v) The evidence suggested that it was not established practice to involve the child, parents, residential staff and other interested persons in the review process. Senior managers (it was suggested) were more concerned to have the reviews carried out in time than that they should be comprehensive and purposeful.

(vi) Managers and senior managers in Clwyd must ensure that programmes using the Central Government specific grant and internal training budgets reflected the essential priority of relevant training of residential care staff, including such matters as communicating with children, awareness of child abuse, awareness of child protection procedures, the management of disruptive and aggressive behaviour.

(vii) A practice manual was needed for residential care workers.

(viii) Children should have access to information and procedures by which they might express their anxieties/dissatisfactions about their care, make a complaint or challenge decisions about them. They should also have an A - Z guide containing all relevant information about their position etc.

(ix) Clwyd Social Services Department should review its policy in respect of staff becoming foster parents, providing lodging for young people in care and, generally, taking children in care into their private homes.

(x) Written guidance for staff should make clear their duty to report abusive behaviour to the line manager (or above, if the line manager is involved or condones the behaviour or fails to take appropriate action about it).

15.50 There were many other excellent detailed recommendations in these reports to which it is not necessary to refer at this stage. They dealt, for example, with the need to create a senior post with lead responsibility for Child Care Services; the evaluation, monitoring and inspection of residential care services; the role of councillors; and various inter-agency issues. We will comment on most of these matters in a later part of this report and will refer again to the Cartrefle Inquiry in that context.

The final period, 8 July 1990 to 12 March 1993

15.51 **Frederick Marshall Jones** took over as Temporary or Acting Officer-in-Charge of Cartrefle with effect from 8 July 1990[12]. It does not appear that he was interviewed for the post formally but he had been interviewed by a panel of four, including John Llewellyn Thomas, Michael Barnes and Norman Green, as recently as 19 September 1989, when it was decided to appoint him as Assistant Centre Manager of Bersham Hall. His temporary appointment at Cartrefle was made permanent early in December 1990, probably from 1 December 1990, but John Llewellyn Thomas admitted two months later that the Council's failure to advertise the post had been a mistake.

15.52 Marshall Jones was suspended from duty with effect from 17 September 1992 as the result of a preliminary investigation carried out the previous day by Karen Anne Reilly, the Deputy Service Manager, Children's Services, for the East Division. This investigation had, in turn, been triggered by reports from the NUPE representative, Kevin Mallon, who had relayed to the Staffing Officer the concerns and anxieties of the staff at Cartrefle about Marshall Jones' conduct towards the children. Heather Lynn and Henry Morton Stanley had departed shortly after Marshall Jones had arrived and the new Deputy Officer-in-Charge from 22 April 1991 was Paul Arthur Kenyon so that it was he and five RCCOs employed at Cartrefle who were interviewed by Reilly.

15.53 The general tenor of the complaints by these members of the staff about Marshall Jones was that his behaviour towards the resident children was threatening and intimidating and that, on occasions, he would use physical force towards them. Both the children and some members of the staff were frightened of him. Particular reference was made to Marshall Jones' conduct when four of the children had barricaded themselves in the bedroom of one of them shortly after Christmas 1991 and had placed furniture against the door. It was alleged that one boy had been dragged by the hair downstairs despite already having stitches in his head, and later held in a stranglehold as well as by the hair. Another boy had been grabbed and pushed downstairs. The staff spoke also of incidents that had occurred on 10 or 11 August 1992, the morning of the children's departure to France on holiday with Marshall Jones and some other members of the staff, when another boy had been held by the throat and punched. It was said also by most of the staff interviewed that they suspected that Marshall Jones was being forced to bribe some of the boys not to complain about him.

15.54 It was on the basis of these disclosures that Marshall Jones was suspended from duty the following day by Graham Harper, the Divisional Director (East), in the presence of his NALGO representative: in a letter dated 21 September 1992 it was stated that the allegations against him were that from December 1991 he

---

[12] For a summary of his full employment history, see paras 14.12 and 14.13.

had assaulted three of the child residents at Cartrefle. The allegations were passed on to the North Wales Police and Marshall Jones was interviewed in February 1993 about these and many other allegations, arising mainly from his employment at Chevet Hey[13]. The papers were passed to the Crown Prosecution Service in June 1993 but we do not know when the decision not to prosecute him was taken. He remained on full pay, despite the closure of Cartrefle in March 1993, until his employment was terminated (as we understand it, by agreement) on the ground of redundancy on 30 November 1994, following discussions with his union representative.

15.55 Apart from the three boys referred to in the letter confirming Marshall Jones' suspension, we are aware of two other former residents of Cartrefle who allege that they were assaulted by him; and we received in evidence the statements of two of these five complainants, who gave a sufficient account of the main incidents.

15.56 One of these two witnesses was the boy who was pushed downstairs following the barricading incident. He alleged a deliberate push that caused him to slide down about seven steps but he was not hurt in any way. He did not allege any other violence by Marshall Jones on that occasion but he was threatened and he cried. The barricading had been a spur of the moment prank at about 12.30 am by four of the six boys in the home at the time. Of Marshall Jones generally, he said "Marshall wasn't liked by the staff and lots of the kids. They didn't like his attitude and some of the grudges he used to have. I did like him sometimes and he did a lot for me, he sorted out a lot of my problems"[14]. This witness did not want to pursue any charges against him.

15.57 The other witness, who was not admitted to Cartrefle until 12 March 1992, when he was 14 years old, was more critical and said that Marshall Jones was one of the worst people he had ever met. Both witnesses referred to the incidents that occurred in August 1992 just before the departure for France and during the holiday there. There is no doubt that two of the residents behaved provocatively on the morning of the departure by demanding to go to Chester before they left in a minibus. Marshall Jones suspected that they wanted to buy alcohol and was understandably annoyed. The result was that there was some physical interplay and shouting between him and one of the boys and he was called an offensive name. The allegation is that Marshall Jones grabbed the boy by the collar and either threw him across the room or back on to the sofa on which he had been sitting.

15.58 As for the main alleged incident during the holiday, it appears that an argument flared up at a camp site because Marshall Jones thought (wrongly) that the boys had been sniggering at a suggestion that he was "fiddling" the petty cash. On failing to obtain an answer about what had been said from one of the boys, Marshall Jones is alleged to have taken his revenge by squashing

---

[13] See paras 14.12 to 14.19 and 14.57 to 14.62.
[14] Statement made to the police on 15 October 1992.

the boy's neck with his forearm in a wrestling hold, punching the boy in the chest and pushing him into a prickly hedge, after which Marshall Jones invited the boy to play 'crazy golf' with him by way of amends.

15.59 Marshall Jones denied using any violence on these occasions although he admitted gently pushing the first of the two witnesses by his back through the door of the barricaded room and ushering him to his own dormitory. One member of the staff under him also gave him some support in her evidence. She worked at Cartrefle from March 1990 for about three years as an unqualified care worker, during the evenings and at week-ends. She thought that Marshall Jones had been given a very difficult job, bearing in mind the attention being given to the home by newspapers and other media: the staff had been told that they could not afford another scandal and that the place had to be "squeaky clean". Nevertheless, there was often a near riot at Cartrefle. Marshall Jones was quite patient and would spend long periods trying to communicate with the boys even though he came across as brusque and as a sergeant-major type. In her experience his bark was worse than his bite and she never saw him use excessive force against a child, nor did she ever receive a complaint to that effect.

15.60 This last witness spoke also of a conversation that she had had with two of the complainants in which they had said that they had made false allegations to the police about the barricaded room incident in order to have Marshall Jones prosecuted, because they did not like him. On another occasion they had said that they were going to get a woman member of the staff the sack; and one of the two had cut his forearms after another incident involving a male member of the staff. However, the witness who alleged that he was pushed downstairs was one of those two complainants and his statements to the police coupled with the accounts given by members of the staff when interviewed by Reilly do not bear out the suggestion that false or exaggerated allegations were made. If the conversations took place, the boys may simply have been bragging mischievously.

15.61 Our conclusion about this period is that Marshall Jones was very ill-suited to the particularly difficult task that he had been set as Officer-in-Charge in succession to Norris. He continued to rule by intimidation, which affected other members of the staff as well as the resident children, and he resorted to violence on some occasions when dealing with provocative and difficult boys. We are not satisfied, however, that he regularly used excessive force during this period and there were some positive aspects to his regime. He did, for example, introduce a complaints box for the children to use and he did make some successful efforts to involve himself in the problems of the children under his care. Overall, however, the many failings of this community home identified in the reports that we have summarised remained largely unremedied because the inquiry came too late for effective remedial action to be taken at Cartrefle.

Other allegations of abuse during this period

15.62 As far as we are aware only three other members of the staff at Cartrefle during this last period have been named by complainants and each of these staff members was named by only one complainant. In the event we received evidence from only one of the complainants who described a minimal incident in which he was grabbed by the hand, after taking a male staff member's cigarette lighter as a joke, and suffered no injury. It is sufficient to say that the boy himself said that he did not wish any police action to be taken against the member of staff and asked "that no further interest be taken by any agency into this incident".

General conclusions about Cartrefle

15.63 Despite the fact that Cartrefle was a purpose built community home caring for quite a small number of children, its history from 1984 onwards was disastrous. We consider later in this report the failures of higher management that contributed to this lamentable result but the reports of the Cartrefle Inquiry gave clear pointers to the scale of the shortcomings of Clwyd Social Services Department generally in relation to this home. At the root of the problem was unsuitable staffing: in particular, Norris, Lynn and Marshall Jones, in varying degrees, were manifestly unsuitable for the senior posts to which they were appointed and this should have been known to the Department in the light of their respective records of employment and the information that ought to have been available. But there was a wide spectrum of other failures embracing such matters as the placement policy for children in care, the recruitment of untrained staff and use of a reserve pool to fill vacancies, the absence of training opportunities, the lack of adequate supervision and monitoring procedures, inadequate documentation and liaison with field staff and failure to prepare and implement proper plans for each child in care. The consequences of all these failings were highly damaging to the individual children, many with serious problems, who were placed at Cartrefle; and there was a signal failure in 1990 to tackle effectively and promptly the special problems of each of the children who had been affected, directly or indirectly, by Norris' persistent abuse.

Cherry Hill Community Home

Introduction

16.01 Cherry Hill is a large house, standing in its own grounds in Borras Park Road, a well established residential area on the outskirts of Wrexham. It was opened by Denbighshire County Council on 1 January 1971 as a community home for up to 11 children of school age and over (usually teenagers). It came under the aegis of Clwyd County Council from 1 April 1974 and its capacity was said to be for up to 12 children in the 1979 Regional Plan. Later, the age range of children accommodated was widened to include youngsters from seven years old but the number of children there declined to eight. Residents in the home attended local schools (but the home was able to accommodate children with learning difficulties) and were encouraged to play a part in the local community.

16.02 This community home remains open and it is now managed by the Children Looked After Team Manager of Wrexham County Borough Council, which took over responsibility for the home on 1 April 1996. It is now described as a six bedded unit for young people between the ages of 14 and 17 years, most of whom present different forms of challenges. According to the Council, it placed particular emphasis during 1997 on developing and strengthening its services at Cherry Hill: an outside consultant has been engaged and "a dedicated programme of training for staff" provided.

16.03 We have not received directly any complaints of child abuse at Cherry Hill and it would not have been necessary to devote a separate chapter to it but for events that occurred there in the aftermath of the disclosures of Norris' abuse at Cartrefle. These events have not been the subject of oral evidence before us, because of their nature, but the documentary evidence has been sufficient to enable us to summarise what occurred and to draw attention to the defects in the procedures that were followed.

16.04 According to a police report dated 24 July 1990, there were nine boys, in the age range of nine to 16 years, resident at Cartrefle at the time of Norris' suspension. Of these, two disclosed that they had been sexually abused by Norris and were transferred immediately, on 20 June 1990, one to Cherry Hill and the other to Gladwyn. Two other boys, who were brothers, were transferred shortly afterwards to Llwyn Onn[1]. One of them alleged much later that he had been raped by Norris and the other said for the first time in 1992 that he had witnessed sexual abuse at Cartrefle. The other five Cartrefle residents, one of whom subsequently, in 1996, alleged that he had been sexually abused by Norris, remained at Cartrefle and received the limited "counselling" that we have referred to in paragraphs 15.15 to 15.17.

---

[1] See para 4.02(11).

16.05 Without going into unnecessary detail about the subsequent movements of the four boys transferred from Cartrefle, the evidence indicates that two of them were at Cherry Hill in 1992. One of the two brothers arrived there on 8 January 1992 (probably from Llwyn Onn); the other boy had gone to Cherry Hill in 1990 for only five days, then to Tapley Avenue for a month, followed by Pentre Saeson (part of the Bryn Alyn Community) for nearly two years before returning to Cherry Hill in May 1992. Whilst at Pentre Saeson the other brother had been co-resident with this last mentioned boy from 11 September 1991.

The nature of the problem

16.06 It seems that a child protection conference on 5 November 1992 recorded that an investigation was taking place into a boy's admission that he had "done things" with other boys at Cherry Hill; and the minutes of a meeting held at Cherry Hill on 25 March 1993 disclosed the outcome of that investigation. It revealed that three boys (A, B and C) at the Children's Centre (as it was now known) were actively engaged in sexual activity between each other and that one of the trio (B) was the ex-Cartrefle boy who had returned to Cherry Hill in May 1992. Moreover, another member of the trio (A) had disclosed sexual involvement with a fourth and a fifth boy (D and E), who had both left Cherry Hill. A had also been seen touching a boy's penis in the public swimming baths and had received a caution for exposing himself to B. D was known to have a history of sexual abuse and had been "linked with a local paedophile ring". C had made allegations of sexual involvement with two males but there was uncertainty about his credibility on the subject.

The process of investigation and the lack of remedial action

16.07 Very little progress had been made in dealing with this problem or series of problems by the date of the meeting in March 1993 and the decisions taken then lacked any sense of urgency. Further information was to be sought; "Longer term aims and goals regarding specific work with the boys would be open for further discussion"; and the staff group were to start to work immediately with Linda Butler, described as "Principal Child Therapist", who was attached to the Division's Child and Family Services. She provided on 17 June 1993 a report in which she outlined possible treatment needs for A, B and C and training for the Cherry Hill staff but pointed out that it was important to remember the needs of the other young people involved in the situation. She warned also of the high cost in terms of time and resources of the work that she recommended but emphasised that the costs of not doing it would be "higher in terms of future life for the young people, the level of risk they present to others, the increased difficulty in breaking patterns of behaviour the more established they became and costs to future victims".

16.08 Meanwhile, the Officers-in-Charge of Cherry Hill and Gladwyn had expressed to the Director of Social Services, John Jevons, their grave concern about the procedure that was being adopted to investigate the allegations. They thought that the Department's Child Protection procedures were not being followed and that insufficient urgency was being shown. On 25 May 1993, therefore, Jevons wrote a memorandum to the Child Protection Co-ordinator (David H Davies) and the Assistant Child Protection Officer (Paul Richards) requesting them to carry out an investigation into the history of the alleged incidents going back to November 1992 and how they were dealt with within the home, within the child protection team and amongst departmental managers. The Director required advice also as to whether there were grounds for concern about how the matters had been handled, whether other action was necessary to protect children and whether there were lessons for all to be learnt from what had happened; and the Director stressed the urgency of the second matter on which he sought advice.

16.09 Unhappily, the response to this memorandum was far from satisfactory. On 18 June 1993 Paul Richards replied to the effect that certain practical matters had been recommended to secure the protection of the children but that finance was required and the cost was being investigated. Richards did not feel that any further investigation by him would provide further useful information: in his view the matter ought to be dealt with within the Division. Richards had two concerns that, he thought, should be addressed. The first was the perceived lack of communication between teams and of feedback to the home. The second was that the investigation had taken too long. Other comments by him were that a strategy meeting (including the police) should have been held at the very beginning and that it would be prudent for case conferences to be held so that any decisions as to abuse and protection would be the responsibility of an inter-agency group and not just the Social Services Department.

16.10 David Davies, who had left the investigations to Paul Richards, followed up ten days later with a memorandum of his own to the Director, in which he made a number of indecisive comments and posed a number of questions, not all of which were very pertinent to the particular problem that was being investigated. Examples are:

(i) Providing treatment is difficult and the outcome is uncertain.

(ii) The emphasis on containment and vigilance, with limited therapy, may place staff in increasingly confrontational roles.

(iii) There had been six child protection conferences arising from Cherry Hill children complaining about physical restraint between October 1989 and June 1993.

(iv) Is there a case for a policy that allegations against staff should always be independently investigated by another division?

(v) I am not clear whether the current enquiry is an assessment of the problems in order to plan therapeutic service or is social services carrying out its duty to investigate under Section 47 of the Children Act 1989?

16.11 The Director's response to Paul Richards' memorandum preceded this last memorandum and made no comment on the finance required for therapeutic treatment of the children involved. The Director said, in his own memorandum of 25 June 1993 to the Divisional Director (South), that he accepted the advice that there was little point in continuing to investigate the matter from the centre. He said also that he had been unable to discuss with Paul Richards the latter's view as to the wisdom of sharing his report in full with the individuals whom he had interviewed because of Richards' absence on leave. The Divisional Director (South) was left to address the two concerns identified in Paul Richards' report, namely, communication between teams and the delay in progressing the investigation after the initial report coupled with the failure to convene case conferences.

16.12 The Divisional Director (South), Glynn Ridge, was "bemused" about the communication issues because he thought that there had not been any failures in this area. By 3 August 1993 he understood that case conferences had been convened and that they would ensure that the up-to-date information would be received and that the need for any protection measures or further investigation would be identified. However, the Division's Team Manager for Child Protection, John Roberts, was much less sanguine. In his response to the Divisional Director dated 11 August 1993, Roberts made the following points about communication between teams:

> "There have been problems of communication in the way this matter was initially handled which subsequently developed into problems of interpretation and unwillingness to reach any consensus view on resolving issues raised. Strategy meetings which have taken place have been plagued by polarised views which, not having been clearly resolved, have been perpetuated outside of the meetings. I have no doubt that practitioners involved in work with the boys concerned have been "caught in the cross fire" and their effectiveness lessened as a result."

16.13 Roberts accepted that case conferences for each child involved should have been held at an early stage and that the reasons why this had not been achieved needed to be closely examined. But he added:

> "As matters have evolved, I am not unhappy that conferences were delayed on these particular boys for there was/is a real danger that arbitrary decisions may be made in distinguishing between 'victim' and 'perpetrator'. Even now, with conflicting statements the matter is still open to professional interpretation and far from being clear cut, with no obvious criteria such as the use of 'force', 'coercion' or 'inducements' we are left with subjective interpretation of the individual's power of influence over others.

> Regardless of any conference decision, we are still left with a serious problem in Cherryhill (sic). The sexual activity which has come to light is both totally inappropriate and illegal and all of the boys concerned need extensive input to reduce future risk to themselves and others. The major decision ought to be whether this is done on a group basis within Cherryhill or whether they should be split-up in an attempt to break the pattern and treated as individuals. If they remain at Cherryhill equally attention should be given to functioning and culture of Cherryhill as well as individual work with these boys. If they are split-up, intensive preparation would be required to ensure that similar patterns do not emerge in that placement."

16.14 That memorandum indicates that much remained to be done in August 1993, nine months after the problem had first been recognised. In our judgment Roberts summarised clearly the issues that had to be addressed but we do not have any direct evidence as to how matters progressed thereafter. This history was the subject of critical comment by the Jillings Independent Panel, which carried out its own investigations between March 1994 and December 1995, and we have before us a copy of a memorandum from Brian Stickels, Children's Services Manager for the South Division dated 5 January 1996, in which he provides responses to some of the Panel's criticisms. It is sufficient for our purposes to quote his response to the second criticism with which he dealt, namely, "Given past experiences of abuses within the children's residential sector in Clwyd, the Independent Panel feels that the organisational response to this situation was less than satisfactory".

16.15 Stickels wrote:

"The 'abuses' involved inappropriate sexual activity between male residents at Cherry Hill, no adults were involved or implicated. The disclosure of information was piecemeal and over a six to nine month period before the pattern and extent of behaviour began to emerge. From February '93 it became clear that it was a major group management issue, involving a significant number of previous and existing residents, from that point the following action was taken:

(i) Multi-Agency Planning Group established, Chaired by the Child and Family Social Work Manager (South Division), which included membership from NW Police and Health. Met throughout 1993 - completed its work January 1994.

(ii) All matters thoroughly investigated and Child Protection Conferences convened. Police involved and consulted throughout and decided with CPS against prosecutions.

(iii) Assessment of risk and intervention plans for all children carried out with the assistance of an independent Consultant with many years experience of work with young people who are sexually aggressive.

. . .

(v) Staffing levels enhanced and support provided to Care Staff to increase levels of awareness and vigilance.

(vi) A block imposed on all male admissions to Cherry Hill from March '93 to October '94.

(vii) All parents kept fully informed of concerns, information shared and joint action agreed.

(viii) All children offered health counselling and support."

16.16 In our judgment, however, this response obscures Clwyd's failure to tackle the central problems referred to in the Roberts' memorandum of August 1993. Moreover, it was merely a repetition of what the Independent Panel had already been told. Thus, (iii) corresponds with what Jevons described as the situation "as of February 1993". On (v), the Panel had already commented, "We have been told that this support, provided by two specialist workers, was considered by residential staff to be the most useful input of all that was offered. It was, however, time limited due to financial constraints. The input of one of these workers was withdrawn after two sessions, the reason for which is unclear". As to (vi), as the Panel pointed out, Paul Richards said in his June 1993 memorandum that the block on admissions would not have provided any respite because Cherry Hill was full. The Panel had already criticised (vii) and (viii) also, saying that staff had told them of delays of up to six weeks in informing some parents and commenting on the counselling "Health counselling is indeed vitally important for all young people in residential care. However, it cannot be considered sufficient to impact on sexual offending behaviour".

Conclusions

16.17 Although we have some sympathy with Clwyd Social Services Department because nationally there was little by way of professional experience or practice guidance to assist in addressing such a situation, there were serious deficiencies in the Department's response to the serious problem that had arisen at Cherry Hill. In the end, technical procedural considerations are far less important than the actual effectiveness of the steps taken to protect from further harm the children involved and from future harm other children who might subsequently be affected.

16.18 In our judgment the main relevant breaches of good practice were the failures of the local authority:

(a) to arrange a speedy independent investigation of the facts as soon as the existence of the problem became known, in conjunction with North Wales Police and an independent social services representative;

(b) to hold immediate case conferences in respect of each of the children involved as soon as the basic facts had been determined;

(c) to make firm decisions about the disposal and treatment of these children promptly in consultation with their parents;

(d) to implement appropriate treatment of the children affected;

(e) to provide necessary training and guidance for the residential care staff dealing with the children, wherever they were placed; and

(f) to keep the parents, residential care staff and field staff fully informed about what was happening.

16.19 The consequences of these breaches of good practice were that senior managers failed to tackle the central issues affecting the welfare of the children involved and became preoccupied with procedural matters of marginal relevance. The residential care staff were given limited assistance. Discussion was bedevilled by misguided emphasis on the question whether the boys' conduct had been "consensual" and they did not receive any professional treatment despite the advice that was received from Linda Butler.

Three community homes in north Clwyd

17.01 We complete this history of the relevant community homes in Clwyd with an account of three that were located in the former parliamentary constituency of West Flintshire and linked in the sense that they catered for similar children in the same broad geographical area. They were Upper Downing in the village of Whitford, about three miles north-west of Holywell, South Meadow and Park House, both in Prestatyn.

Upper Downing Community Home

17.02 Upper Downing or Downing Ucha' was a very large old country mansion[1] set in secluded grounds and approached by a long drive. It was opened in 1948 as a home registered under section 37 of the National Assistance Act 1948 for 48 older boys and girls. The home was administered by the former Flintshire County Council and in the 1971 Regional Plan it was described as providing accommodation for up to 24 children but the intention then was that it should be replaced in 1973 by homes in St Asaph and Prestatyn. In the event it survived the transfer of responsibility to Clwyd County Council for nearly three years until 31 January 1977 and it was described latterly as a reception centre. The resident children attended local schools.

17.03 We are aware of only five complainants who were resident at Upper Downing after 1 April 1974. Of these, three complained of sexual abuse by a gardener/driver at the home, who is now dead. A graphic account was given to the police in July 1992 by one of the three, who had been taken into care at the age of 15 years in 1974, following disagreements between her and her mother, of the circumstances in which she came to be abused. Whilst at Upper Downing between 2 March and November 1976 and aged 17 years (after placements at Cartrefle and Rhiwlas) she was permitted to work at a cafe in Holywell, travelling to and fro by minibus. On Saturday 6 March 1976 the driver took her to a public house to watch a darts match on the pretext that other girls and a female member of staff would be there. She drank seven or eight cherry brandies at the public house and was then taken to the house of a friend of the driver, where she passed out after a couple of further drinks. She came to on the floor, finding the gardener performing oral sex upon her whilst his friend fondled her upper body. She then ran from the house and was seen at 2.35 am by a policeman crying and apparently drunk. She told him briefly what had happened and was taken to the police station, where she answered further questions, alleging that the gardener had had intercourse with her, but she did not make a written statement at that point. She was later taken to Rhiwlas before being returned to Upper Downing.

---

[1] It was mentioned by Thomas Pennant of Downing Hall, a noted historian, in his History of the Parishes of Whitford and Holywell (1796) as the home in 1749, at the time of her marriage, of Mary Lloyd, an heiress and descendant of Edwyn, prince or lord of Tegengl.

17.04 We have seen numerous documents recording subsequent developments in the matter. The girl declined to lay a complaint if it would involve her appearing in court as a witness but she did not want the gardener to "get away with it". He denied any form of sexual assault or other impropriety, claiming that the girl had had permission to go to the public house with him and that she had behaved bizarrely later because she had made herself drunk. The Deputy Director of Social Services (Gledwyn Jones) and the Principal Social Worker (Children) (Gordon Ramsay) both attended at Upper Downing on 7 March 1976 and statements were provided by the relevant social services staff. Prosecution of the gardener was not considered to be appropriate but he was suspended from duty without pay on 8 March 1976 at a meeting that day with the Director of Social Services (Emlyn Evans) and others. The following day the Personnel Sub-Committee accepted a recommendation to dismiss him for gross misconduct in: (1) taking the girl out of Upper Downing without the consent of the Officer-in-Charge or his Deputy; (2) using a County Council vehicle without authority; (3) taking the girl to two public houses, where she had consumed intoxicating liquor; and (4) his subsequent behaviour in relation to the girl.

17.05 There followed an appeal to the appeals committee, which was dismissed on 16 June 1976. The gardener, who was a shop steward of NUPE, then applied to an industrial tribunal for compensation on the ground of wrongful dismissal. After a hearing lasting several days, at which the girl complainant failed to appear to give evidence, the Industrial Tribunal ruled in the applicant's favour on 9 December 1976 on the grounds that (a) the allegation of sexual interference had been excluded on 8 March but had still been put before the Personnel Sub-Committee on 9 March and (b) other procedural unfairness. The Industrial Tribunal found also, however, that the applicant had contributed to his dismissal and reduced the assessment of his loss by 50 per cent on that ground. Thus, the actual award to the applicant, who was then 56 years old, was only £507.20. He was not re-employed by Clwyd County Council.

17.06 We are not in a position to reach any conclusion about the veracity of this complainant's allegations of sexual abuse by the deceased gardener in March 1976. It is right to record, however, that there were two other girl residents who complained of less serious sexual interference by him in April 1975 but who were not believed by the woman officer then in charge, who left in November 1975. By the time these complainants were interviewed by the police in the course of the major police investigation the man in question had died.

17.07 As a result of the publicity associated with the Industrial Tribunal hearing the Chairman of an organisation called "Clwyd Watchdogs" wrote on 31 December 1976 to the Chairman of Clwyd Social Services Committee suggesting that the "affair" had revealed a number of very grave weaknesses in the running of community homes, notably: (a) the lack of clear, written instructions to staff (it seemed that there was only one slim document, which (he said) provided "the very minimum of enlightenment"); (b) inadequate provision for in-service training; and (c) no guidelines for staff with respect to children leaving the premises.

17.08 The other major complaint during the Clwyd period also came to light in March 1976, at least partly. The dismissed gardener had reported to Geoffrey Wyatt that **Heather Lynn,** then aged 24 years, who was serving a probationary period as a housemother at Upper Downing that started in October 1975, had been allowing a boy resident (K), aged 15 years to spend a lot of time in her bedroom and that K had been seen leaving her bedroom on one occasion at 7 am. It was alleged also that Lynn had begun drinking heavily. By the time of this report K had been transferred to Little Acton Assessment Centre but concern had been expressed by the staff there and a social worker that K was receiving frequent letters from Lynn, some with sexual connotations, and that their relationship "appeared to be very involved".

17.09 It was decided to treat the report as an official complaint and an investigation ensued, in the course of which both K and Lynn were interviewed. They both denied that there had been anything improper in their relationship. K said that he never went alone to Lynn's bedroom but that he sometimes took her tea in the morning at 7 am or knocked on her door in case she had overslept. Lynn confirmed that boys did go into her bedroom. She said also that she was inexperienced in child care, admitting that she had become "over involved" with K, which might have been avoided if she had had more guidance.

17.10 None of the letters referred to were available except for an unsigned note in code. Lynn admitted writing letters to K, including the note, but could not remember the circumstances in which she had written the coded note and "was unable to explain its contents", according to Wyatt's subsequent memorandum to the Director of Administration dated 22 March 1976. K, on the other hand, strenuously denied that the note was from Lynn and alleged that it was from a girl in Rhyl; but Wyatt formed the opinion that he was "covering up".

17.11 Wyatt concluded that the lack of any substantial information to corroborate the complaints made it difficult to pursue the matter further but he recommended that Lynn's probationary period should be extended by six months on the ground that her first period of employment had not been entirely satisfactory. This recommendation[2] appears to have been agreed earlier with Emlyn Evans and Peter Gibson of the Legal and Administration staff who, jointly with Wyatt, interviewed Lynn on 11 March 1976 in the presence of a NUPE representative.

17.12 In her written evidence Lynn maintained her denial of any improper association with K. He, however, gave oral evidence before us, confirming his earlier statements, beginning in May 1993, in which he had given a very detailed account of how sexual intercourse between him and Lynn had begun in her bedroom at Upper Downing and had developed quickly, at Lynn's instigation, into a very regular occurrence. He had been at Upper Downing for only a short period from 20 October 1975 to 12 January 1976, when there were about 16 children at the home, of whom half were very young. Subsequently, when he had been interviewed whilst at Little Acton, he had not told the

---

[2] For Lynn's subsequent career at Cartrefle, see paras 15.21 to 15.25.

interviewers what had occurred because he had thought that he would not be believed and that he would get into trouble. Later, he had been at Cartrefle from 4 June 1976 to 5 July 1977 and Lynn had been transferred there from 20 December 1976: he alleged that she had tried then to renew the relationship but that he had avoided her, staying out of her way, except on two occasions when she had taken him out in her parents' car and he had had sex with her.

17.13 In the course of his oral evidence the coded note was produced to K, to his manifest surprise. He explained the childishly simple numerical code that had been adopted and translated the note as follows:

> "A is 1   Superman
>
> Dear (K)
>
> I love you more than anything in the world and if that is what you want it's okay by me.
>
> I'm not free and easy so you must realise how special you are to me.
>
> We must be very careful tonight though.
>
> Encyclopaedias
>
> Forever
>
> XX."

17.14 In the light of all the evidence before us we are fully satisfied that K has given us an essentially truthful account of his relationship with Lynn. We accept that he had no previous experience of sexual intercourse at the time and, in our judgment, her conduct did amount to serious sexual abuse of him.

17.15 The only other relevant complaint of which we are aware was made by a former girl resident who was at Upper Downing for about seven weeks in the summer of 1976. Her allegation was that she was punched in the face by a young male member of the staff, with the result that she knocked over a settee, sustaining a black eye and a very swollen finger. Her injuries were seen by a social worker and a woman member of the residential staff but she did not wish to make a formal complaint. The man who struck her was not regarded as a suitable residential care worker. He was employed at Upper Downing for a comparatively short period and left to work as a postman.

Conclusions

17.16 As far as we have been able to ascertain, there were few complaints about Upper Downing in relation to the period when Clwyd County Council managed it (and before). The former residents whose evidence we have seen have, in general, described their time in the home as happy: it seems that a genuine effort was made to create a homely atmosphere, even though most of the residential care staff were untrained. The two serious matters that did arise in 1976 came to light quite quickly and were then investigated with a proper sense of urgency at a high level within the Social Services Department. We do not think that it would be appropriate to criticise the procedural steps then taken because these were the early days of implementation of the provisions of the new employment legislation beginning with the Employment Act 1972. The failure to dismiss Heather Lynn then was however highly questionable, despite K's denials of any improper association with her; the coded note could have been deciphered by anyone with an elementary knowledge of the subject and would thus have thrown a clear light upon the truth. As it was Lynn survived and failed to learn from the experience, as her eventual conduct at Cartrefle demonstrated.

South Meadow Community Home

17.17 South Meadow, in Ffordd Ffrith, Prestatyn, was also quite a long established children's home. It was a large house in the centre of a residential area and it was opened by Flintshire County Council, probably on 1 January 1967, as a home for up to 12 children. In its grounds was a cottage providing accommodation for some of the staff but latterly this was used to provide residents with training for independence. The resident children of appropriate age attended local schools.

17.18 South Meadow survived for 16 years from 1974 under the management of Clwyd County Council until its functions were transferred on 14 September 1990 to Cefndy Hostel, Rhyl, formerly an adult hostel for the physically handicapped, which became known thereafter as New South Meadow. Similarly, Park House, which is dealt with in the next section of this chapter, closed in August 1991, when its functions were transferred to New South Meadow. The new amalgamated unit then lasted only two years before closing in October 1993.

17.19 As we have said earlier[3], we have not received any complaint about New South Meadow and we deal here, therefore, with the history of South Meadow itself as a community home in the 16 years period referred to in the preceding paragraph. We know of five complainants who were resident there before 1974 and who complain of being abused there by one or both of a married couple then on the staff but these complaints refer to alleged incidents long before the take-over by Clwyd and therefore outside our terms of reference.

1974 to 1981: the regime of Joan Glover

17.20 The Officer-in-Charge of South Meadow for about the first half of the relevant period was **Joan Glover** and she has been the main target of the complaints of which we are aware. She had become a housemother at South Meadow on 1 October 1969, at the age of 22 years. She remained there until the end of 1972 and up to that point she had not received any training: she had lived in Staffordshire previously, working in the packing department of a Royal Doulton factory, teaching at Sunday School and doing voluntary work in youth clubs. However, in 1973 she took a year's course for RCCOs (the CRCCYP) at Salford Institute of Technology before returning to South Meadow as senior housemother or Officer-in-Charge from 1 January 1974.

---

[3] See para 4.20.

17.21 Although Joan Glover had apparently had an unblemished record as a housemother at South Meadow and had received a letter from Flintshire's Director of Social Services thanking her warmly for her service in that capacity (when she left in 1973 for her training course), there were difficulties soon after she returned and became Officer-in-Charge. She received a copy of a memorandum from the Director of Social Services (Emlyn Evans) dated 20 June 1974 and addressed to "Staff in Residential Establishments for Children and Young People". This read:

> "Corporal Punishment in Residential Establishments for Children and Young People
>
> 1. Revised Community Home Regulations are to be published at an early date. These regulations follow the policy of both former Authorities that no member of staff will inflict corporal punishment on any child or young person in any circumstances (Corporal punishment to include striking, slapping, pushing etc.).
>
> 2. The Children & Young Persons Act (Community Home Regulations) 1972 states that 'The control of a Community Home shall be maintained on the basis of good personal and professional relationships between staff and the children resident therein'.
>
> 3. The above Clwyd County Council policy decision is drawn to the attention of all staff employed in the appropriate Homes in order that there can be no unfortunate misunderstanding or misconduct, and any infringement of this policy will be viewed with the utmost gravity. Please ensure that every member of your staff is aware of this regulation."

17.22 Despite this clear instruction, Glover was involved in an incident on 26 August 1975 with a girl resident, then aged 13 years, in the course of which Glover caught hold of the girl from behind, turned her round and slapped her across the face. The girl in question (M), who had been at South Meadow for only about seven weeks, had undoubtedly proved to be particularly difficult and had been bullying other girls persistently; on the occasion when she was slapped, she had herself just slapped an eight year old girl across the face, knocking her over. Moreover, there had followed further difficulties with M, which had been resolved in the course of the next day or so. Nevertheless, a serious view of the matter was taken and it was investigated by Veronica Pares, then Principal Residential and Day Care Officer, at least to the extent of a full discussion with Glover.

17.23 In her oral evidence to the Tribunal, Glover admitted "losing her rag" with M because the latter had been very troublesome. The upshot of the matter was that she was required to meet formally with the Deputy Director and Pares on 29 September 1975, following which she received a written warning and reprimand by letter dated 3 October 1975 from the Director.

17.24 We do not know of any further reports or complaints about Joan Glover until 1979 but by that time the other members of the staff at South Meadow had become very restive about her conduct towards the children and her temperament generally. Geoffrey Wyatt (Principal Officer), W P Grant (Staffing Officer) and the Area Officer (Mrs E G Griffiths) all became involved in the matter and a number of meetings took place between officials, with the staff and with Glover herself. The matter came to light when, on 21 June 1979, members of the residential care staff at South Meadow told the Area Officer of their concern about Glover's behaviour, which (they said) had become more noticeable over the past few months. They reported that Glover was shouting at the children, extremely irritable and very tense, impatient and intolerant; and their concern was said to be for the children, who were becoming frightened by this behaviour. It was said also that the RDCO had commented on this behaviour pattern. The Area Officer commented on this report that, to her knowledge, Glover had no outside interests and was very insular. She said also that Glover was not delegating work to her staff and that communication and staff relationships were breaking down.

17.25 There was no improvement in the following month, although Glover was undergoing treatment from her own doctor and the County's Occupational Medical Officer was consulted. She claimed to have been unaware of anything amiss until she learnt from her doctor of the Occupational Medical Officer's interest in her condition. Eventually, however, one of the housemothers, on behalf of the staff and children, confronted her with these anxieties and advised her to seek medical help.

17.26 The result of these developments was that on 14 August 1979 Wyatt and Grant held meetings, firstly with the staff and then with Glover and six days later it was agreed that she would take four weeks leave from 1 September 1979. It seems to have been agreed also that she would become non-resident Officer-in-Charge, initially for a two months' trial period; and she lived out from 1 September 1979, at Meliden, for the last 18 months of her period as Officer-in-Charge.

17.27 Unfortunately, there was little, if any, improvement in Glover's behaviour when she resumed her work at South Meadow after her holiday. Anxiety was being expressed again by the staff at the home in November 1979 and was being repeated in the following two months. The main problem was that Glover was said to be hitting children still and subjecting them to harsh treatment; she was said to be quite paranoid and it was alleged that she had not really changed since her holiday. There was also confusion for the resident children because Glover's attitude contrasted strongly with that of another member of the staff when left in charge, who was so kindly that the children were sometimes uncontrollable in the evening.

17.28 We are not aware of any steps taken to remedy the situation in the following 12 months but it then resolved itself because in February 1981 Glover applied successfully for a post as a housemother with the Pentecostal Child Care Association. She left South Meadow to take up this new appointment on 27 March 1981[4]. It lasted for about two years, until she was made redundant, and she has been employed as a family support worker since then.

---

[4] See para 17.33.

17.29 Two former child residents of South Meadow confirmed the general picture that we have given of Glover's behaviour during her period as Officer-in-Charge. The witness (X) who gave oral evidence about her was particularly clear and impressive. He was there from the age of five to 14 years, that is, from December 1968 until 1977; and he was there with two brothers because their parents' marriage had broken down. He described Glover as a "Jekyll and Hyde" character, a split personality. He was bedwetting about twice a week for a time and he alleged that Glover "took against him" for this reason and would push his face into the wet bedclothes. Assaults on one or other of the children by Glover were a daily occurrence. X himself was smacked on the head or legs; she would grab him by the back of his hair; and she would crack him with her "clogs or Scholls" (which she always used to wear). He referred also to a particular girl resident, who suffered this kind of treatment every couple of days but who, on other occasions, would be hugged by Glover and praised as if she were Glover's own child. His older brother, who was more interested in football than in schoolwork, was also, for example, "whacked" on the back of his head with a shoe because he had not done his homework.

17.30 In more general evidence about South Meadow X said that he had respect for the way in which it was run but the children were not treated with respect by Glover specifically. There were other members of the staff who sympathised and were approachable and he mentioned particularly a part-time member of the staff who used to take children to tea at her house for a break. She would also stay around if there was "an atmosphere" in order to protect the children. Most of the staff would have seen what was happening but only a couple of them would stand up to Glover. Other members of the staff did on occasions slap children but they did so very rarely.

17.31 X was also asked about his relationship with his social worker. In response, he said that he had mainly one social worker, who was "useless". He saw his social worker very rarely, just once every couple of months: he would speak in confidence to this social worker, who would then disclose what had been said. X made a plea for much stricter confidentiality because a child's social worker should be a proper lifeline and should have greater influence on how the child is treated.

17.32 The other former resident whose evidence we heard was the girl (M) mentioned in paragraph 17.22 as "an eight year old girl", for whom Glover had special affection. In her statement M said that Glover treated her like her own child but became ever stricter with her, spanking her (for example) on the bottom with hand and slipper. She had been in care with her two sisters from the age of two years and was at South Meadow from 1969, when she was three years old, until 1982; and the result was that she thought that being smacked all the time was natural. But Glover was the only member of the staff who struck her. Glover was obsessed with her and she said, "Although I loved her and was loved by her, I was very frightened of her". In the course of her statement to the police in September 1992, M described numerous specific incidents of abuse by Glover, which continued until she was 14 years old, and she said that they were usually followed by apologies. She said also that she had often run away from South Meadow to the local police station and told them what was going on but they had done nothing to help and would merely telephone the home for someone to collect her.

17.33 It is right to record that M did go on, at her own request, in 1982 to live at a hostel in Clevedon, Avon, run by the Pentecostal Child Care Association, of which Glover was then Officer-in-Charge. M's explanation was that she had visited Glover there in the interim and thought that Glover had changed. The move was not successful, however, and she considered that she was mentally abused by Glover with the result that she took an overdose of tablets; a week later she was moved to Park House, with which we deal next, and later to Bersham Hall until she was discharged from care.

17.34 In her oral evidence, Joan Glover accepted that she had "lost her rag" from time to time. She had usually shouted on those occasions and had sometimes slapped children but only one across the face (in the 1975 incident). In her view slapping had been permitted until 1974. Her explanation for slapping after the prohibition was that sometimes she did not know what else to do and she added that it had not happened on more than two or three occasions when she had been very stressed. She had not had as much time off as she should have had. She accepted that by 1979 her relations with some other members of staff were strained and she was shouting a lot: she was aware that things were not right, that she was not feeling well and that she was not coping. She denied, however, ill-treating X: she said that he was not a difficult child and she did not remember ever having to discipline him. His bed wetting was not a disciplinary matter: everything was tried and eventually it just stopped suddenly. As for M, the latter had serious behavioural problems and would go into uncontrollable rages with the result that she had to undergo therapy for several months.

17.35 Our conclusion is that the staff concerns about Joan Glover's behaviour towards the children at South Meadow were fully justified and that the account of her conduct that we have summarised, in terms of comment at the time and the evidence to the Tribunal of two complainants, gives a fair picture of the extent to which she abused children. We accept that her aspirations for the children in her care were high and that she retained strong fundamental religious beliefs but she had serious temperamental or character defects, which disabled her from carrying out her work as Officer-in-Charge in an appropriate manner.

17.36 The Social Services Department acted promptly in 1975 by issuing a written warning and it is to the credit of the residential care staff that they made their concern known in 1979. But, in our judgment, there should have been closer monitoring of Glover's performance in the intervening period. It is unlikely that there was a sudden lapse in her performance at about Easter 1979 and it is highly probable that there ought to have been intervention by the Department before then. Moreover, the response by the Department in 1979 was unsatisfactory when measured against the evidence available then and the fact of the earlier written warning. There is no persuasive evidence of any immediate improvement in Glover's behaviour on her return from her break. On the contrary, the anxieties of the staff survived, at least between October

1979 and January 1980, although David Nicholas Evans, who was appointed Deputy Officer-in-Charge from 1 November 1980, did say in evidence that he could not think of any criticism of Glover and that he overlapped with her on duty often. In our judgment, it is regrettable that the problem caused by Glover's behaviour was not tackled more boldly and that the situation was left to fester for another year (a significant period in a young child's experience). We have noted also with disquiet that in February 1981 Glover was provided with a reference, in the name of the Director of Social Services, to her prospective new employers in which no explicit mention was made of her serious shortcomings as Officer-in-Charge of South Meadow.

1981 to 1990: the regime of Glyn Williams

17.37 Other relevant matters in relation to South Meadow can be dealt with quite briefly. Following Joan Glover's departure it seems that David Evans took over from her in an acting capacity for about four months until **Glyn Williams** was appointed Officer-in-Charge with effect from 3 August 1981. The latter remained in post until September 1990, when South Meadow closed, and he then moved to New South Meadow as Officer-in-Charge until the end of February 1992. Before starting to work in child care with Liverpool Social Services in 1970 he had been employed in the prison service for six years. His later experience had been as a housefather for five years in a family group home run by his wife and then a further five years at an approved school, rising from housefather to housemaster; and from 1980 he had been Deputy Officer-in-Charge of a children's home adolescent unit run by Wirral Social Services. He had completed the In-Service Certificate of Attendance course from a college in Liverpool in 1976 and obtained the CRCCYP from Salford College of Technology in 1977.

17.38 The role of South Meadow changed more than once during the 1980s. In the latter part of Joan Glover's period, and possibly earlier, it was being described as a family group home (a Group 3 community home), taking in young children (mainly eight to 14 years) from quite a wide area. In or about 1981, however, six wards of court from the same family were moved in and became the only residents. There followed a period of uncertainty when the future of the home was uncertain but in 1985 South Meadow's function was changed to that of an adolescent unit and it was re-categorised as a Group 1 community home. The three older children of the family of six stayed on and other boys and girls in the age range of 12 to 18 years were admitted, some for remand and assessment. Numbers rose to about 15; the staff were increased substantially also, providing effective 24 hour cover; and the residents tended to be more turbulent. However, the home appears to have generated some loyalty because it was the residents who insisted on retaining the name South Meadow when the move to Rhyl took place.

17.39 We must stress that there has been no suggestion of any sexual abuse at South Meadow, as far as we are aware, throughout the period under review. As for other complainants of physical abuse, that is, other than those made against Joan Glover, we know of only four potential complainants against identified members of the staff and none of those complainants has provided statements to the Tribunal. All were at South Meadow in the last few years before the move to Rhyl and their complaints, apart from one admittedly false allegation that was withdrawn, were of comparatively minor "excessive restraint" on occasions when disorder had occurred.

Conclusions

17.40 There was no Welsh Office inspection of South Meadow during the period under review and we have not received any independent appraisal of the success of this community home. It is difficult for us to comment confidently, therefore, on the positive aspects of the successive regimes there. It appears to have provided a home atmosphere, however, for the children there, subject only to the erratic and oppressive conduct of Joan Glover, which we have discussed fully and who, in our judgment, was an unsuitable Officer-in-Charge. Bearing in mind the early written warning that she had received, it is probable that she should have been removed from her post before 1979. Whether or not there is an element of hindsight in this view, she should have been dismissed in 1979 when the staff voiced their great concern about her conduct. Conditions in the home became more difficult in the late 1980s because older residents with varied behavioural problems were admitted but it is to be noted that there have been no allegations of substantial physical abuse by other members of the staff even in this later period and no allegations of sexual abuse throughout the period under review.

Park House Community Home

17.41 Park House was a large old two storey building in Nant Hall Road. Like South Meadow, there was a cottage in its grounds that was used as staff accommodation initially and latterly for training for independence. It had been used formerly as an old people's home but was opened by Flintshire County Council in 1972 as a home for up to 12 boys and girls in the age range of ten to 17 years. Education was provided at local schools and the home remained open until 31 July 1991, when the remaining residents moved to Cefndy Hostel, Rhyl[5].

1974 to 1981: the regime of Mary Ellis

17.42 The first Officer-in-Charge of Park House when Clwyd County Council took over responsibility for it in April 1974 was **Mary Philomena Ellis**, who had been appointed to that position by Flintshire County Council with effect from 1 September 1973. She was then nearly 46 years old with children of her own and had had other previous child care experience at St Clare's Convent, Pantasaph and Cartrefle. She had also obtained the CRCCYP at Salford in December 1972 and had then worked from January 1973 in a nursery for

---

[5] See para 17.18.

babies at Mold, whilst awaiting a more suitable opening. Mary Ellis remained at Park House until 31 March 1981, when she took early retirement. She had become non-resident from 1 January 1980, at her own request.

17.43 It seems that all the residential care staff were women until the arrival of **David Evans** as Deputy Officer-in-Charge with effect from 6 February 1979. He was then 39 years old and he remained at Park House until 31 October 1980, when he moved to South Meadow as Deputy there[6]. He had been employed in child care from 1963 and had obtained the CRCC at Selly Oak College, Birmingham, in 1965 before being appointed housemaster at an approved school and then superintendent of a children's home; but he had then worked in commerce and for the Ministry of Defence for nine years, returning to child care as a senior housemaster at Red Bank Community Home in 1978.

17.44 The role of Park House in the Ellis period was similar to that of South Meadow at that time but it was classified as a Group 2 community home. It was a family group home accommodating up to 15 children and very young children were admitted with older brothers and sisters.

17.45 There was a campaign in 1974 and 1975 by a local Prestatyn resident, whose true motivation is not known to us, to secure the closure of Park House, ostensibly on the ground that children were being ill-treated there. He wrote to the Welsh Office in that vein and he instigated letters to the press. In particular, on 1 September 1975 he invited a girl resident (L) aged 14 years, to his house and drafted a letter in her name to the *News of the World*. This letter listed the 12 children and seven staff, including two domestic staff, then at the home and alleged that the following punishments were being imposed at the home:

"(a) Sent to bed immediately after ten with no supper.

(b) No pocket money.

(c) Cleaning 12 pairs of shoes for a week.

(d) Cleaning the boot room for a week.

(e) No Girl Guides.

(f) No Youth Club.

(g) No privileges.

(h) Everyone, even the little ones, have to make their bed before breakfast in Hospital style daily. This is not a punishment but it is our duty."

The letter claimed also that the children had to peel vegetables when ordered to do so, and do all the internal cleaning on Saturday and it alleged that mail was held up, giving rise to the suspicion that it was being steamed open and "censured".

---

[6] See paras 17.36 and 17.37.

17.46 *News of the* World reporters met L, who ran away from Park House, the following day and an investigation was carried out by Gledwyn Jones (Deputy Director) and Geoffrey Wyatt (Principal Social Worker) following the ensuing publicity given to the matter. The investigation into the circumstances appears to have been quite thorough; L was interviewed by them in the presence of her mother and signed statements were obtained from all the staff except the cook. The findings of the two man panel were that there had been obvious collusion between the local resident and L, whose own motive was to secure a move. As for her complaints about punishments and chores, the panel made one or two criticisms and recommendations, saying, for example, that sending children to bed early was likely to create problems and that no child should be required to forfeit all his or her pocket money in any one week; but, otherwise, the complaints were, rightly in our view, dismissed. The panel did, however, state that there was a need for a less rigid regime.

17.47 The panel's report contained also a number of criticisms of the administration of Park House. They drew attention to the fact that, apart from Ellis, no member of the staff had read or was familiar with the Community Homes Regulations 1972, despite the fact that the Assistant Director (Residential and Day Care Services) had circulated copies of the regulations and a note of the Social Services Committee's interpretation of them to all Officers-in-Charge of Community Homes on 29 June 1975, with a request that they should ensure that all members of their staff were familiar with the contents of the documents. The panel said also that the Residential and Day Care Officer must give guidance and advice on methods of control and discipline (supplementing the prohibition of corporal punishment) rather than leave staff to do what seemed right to them in their own eyes. Finally, the panel expressed surprise that, with the exception of Ellis, none of the staff at Park House had access to the case histories of the children because she believed they constituted confidential information between the social workers and the Officer-in-Charge.

17.48 The report made reference to an allegation that on one occasion two women members of the staff had hit three girl residents, who were sisters, because they had not made their beds tidy in hospital style. They were not able to reach a conclusion about this but they commented that both the members of staff had left the Council's employ and had been generally regarded as "staff who were very young, untrained and very lax in their attitude and not very control minded". We received evidence from two of the sisters alleged to have been hit and neither made reference to this alleged incident.

17.49 A further investigation was carried out into the administration of Park House early in 1980 as a result of complaints made by staff at the home and pursued through NALGO. This investigation was carried out by a Clwyd inspector of Principal Social Worker rank, Ivor Hughes, who presented an interim report dated 9 April 1980, following meetings between personnel officers, union officials and staff from Park House and headquarters in February and March that year. It is unnecessary to go into great detail about these reports, which drew attention to many administrative failings at Park House, but they did show also that considerable indiscipline was occurring and that the attitudes of the staff to the resident children were unsatisfactory.

17.50 The inspector drew attention to the fact that the records indicated that children were:

    (a) disruptive at night;

    (b) making nuisances of themselves at local stores (two girls were currently in trouble for shoplifting);

    (c) smoking in the bedrooms;

    (d) piercing each other's ears;

    (e) playing on fire escapes;

    (f) absconding;

    (g) annoying neighbours by climbing walls, throwing things into their gardens and shouting abuse. There were also accusations by children that boys and girls were going to bed together.

17.51 Although these matters were apparent from the records, the inspector was critical also of aspects of the record keeping, including frequent gaps in the internal day book; and he made adverse comment on the administration of punishments. There was some evidence of staff not taking responsibility for the children and of chaos prevailing on occasions. The follow up report in August 1980 dealt with a wide range of staffing and disciplinary issues and the inspector concluded:

> "In general Park House was seen to be an establishment where there was considerable turmoil and unrest. In connection with aspects relating in this Report to staff ratios, sleeping-in and Food and Clothing, in particular, it is considered that the needs of the children in care are taken account of only after the demands and inclinations of staff have been met.
>
> Some of this originates from factors which have assumed a degree of permanency by 'custom and practice', but also valid is considered to be the lack of unified direction and guidance from the Officer-in-Charge and her Deputy."

17.52 As we have said earlier in this chapter, until the arrival of David Evans in February 1979 all the staff at Park House had been women. This had not prevented some discord arising between Ellis and her Deputy about access to records etc by the Deputy when Ellis was off duty but differences between the two senior officers became much more acute as soon as Evans took over as Deputy. Ellis was very critical of Evans in her reports on his probationary period, beginning within two months of his arrival; and by August 1980 the inspector's view was that the relationship between the two officers was beyond recall.

17.53 The inspector made a number of criticisms of Ellis' running of Park House that are not directly relevant to this report. In short, he said that she "presented as a somewhat over-conscientious, anxious person who was convinced that her approach to her work was appropriate and considered to be 'good child practice'". In her relationships with children, it was said that she was seen to issue punishments but not to carry them through and it was alleged that she had shown favouritism to some older children; but probably her major failings were that she spent a disproportionate part of her time in her office and would not share responsibility appropriately with her Deputy. Evans, on the other hand, was said to have a genuine concern for children that was, in part, misdirected. He performed his duties more at the level of a senior houseparent at a larger assessment centre rather than Deputy Officer-in-Charge of a community home for 15 children. It was thought that he had a good deal to offer elsewhere but was suffering frustration at Park House under Ellis.

17.54 Whilst this investigation was taking place the number of children at Park House diminished from 15 to ten and this led the inspector to question whether the community home was needed for the future in terms of residential child care provision. However, it survived for another ten years under changed regimes. Evans duly left to take up the post of Deputy at South Meadow on 1 November 1980 and Ellis, who had told the inspector that she was contemplating taking early retirement because of the stress and strain, did so on 31 March 1981.

17.55 One of the three sisters referred to in paragraph 17.48 (A) gave oral evidence before us of her experiences at Park House between August 1974 and August 1977 and again between September 1979 and May 1980 (she was born in September 1969). A said that she complained about the way that she was treated by staff and workmen whilst she was there. She said that one woman staff member had put her in a cupboard with cockroaches "hundreds of times" and that the woman had done the same to quite a few others. She alleged also that, after she returned to Park House, she was made to eat a sparrow by the same member of staff because she had tried to kill it with a catapult and it was limping. A's other complaint was that David Evans had pushed her on to a headboard with the result that the headboard injured her groin and she was detained in hospital for two nights.

17.56 None of these complaints, however, were made in A's earlier written statements to the police and the Tribunal, which contained many serious allegations against the couple who had fostered her between August 1977 and September 1979. Moreover, the second sister whose evidence was received by the Tribunal (B) made no complaint against the care staff at Park House. B said in her written statement that Ellis was strict and was not liked but that she had no complaint about Ellis and was treated well by the other care staff. Her one complaint was that she had been indecently interfered with there by a gardener, who had also exposed himself to her, when she was nine years old (that is, shortly before she was fostered). She had told Ellis about it later and the gardener had been dismissed.

17.57 David Evans was not asked about the alleged incident referred to in paragraph 17.55 because the allegation had not been made when he gave oral evidence to us. It was made so belatedly and A has such a disturbed recent history that we are unable to attach credence to it.

1981 to 1988: the interrupted regime of Jeffrey Douglas

17.58 David Evans' successor as Deputy Officer-in-Charge of Park House was **Jeffrey Douglas**, whose appointment was from 1 March 1981, his 39th birthday. On the departure of Ellis a month later, however, he became Acting Officer-in-Charge for three months before being confirmed as her successor with effect from 1 July 1981. He remained in that post until 31 October 1988, at which point he became a social worker for children and family services in the Alyn and Deeside area. His period at Park House was interrupted in 1986 by two years' training for the CQSW from September 1986 to July 1988 and he was only back at Park House effectively for about two months in 1988 before his new appointment.

17.59 During the period of Douglas' further training, **David Evans**[7] was appointed as Acting Officer-in-Charge. He then returned to South Meadow for a short period until he was appointed to succeed Douglas at Park House from 1 August 1989. He remained in that position until 31 July 1991, when the community home closed, and he then became Deputy Officer-in-Charge of New South Meadow at Rhyl until he retired on 31 December 1992. These moves by Evans between Park House and South Meadow complicate the history from 1979 onwards and it is further complicated by the fact that Evans was suspended from duty on 4 November 1989 pending the investigation of complaints by two female residents, which had been referred to the police the previous day. He was informed by the North Wales Police by letter dated 18 December 1989 that the Crown Prosecution Service was of the opinion that no proceedings should be instituted against him due to insufficient evidence and on 21 December 1989 he was told by Geoffrey Wyatt that he was to return to Park House. The complaints of the two residents are dealt with later in this chapter.

17.60 The background of Jeffrey Douglas was that he began work in child care at the age of 36 years in July 1978 after 21 years as a textile worker with Courtaulds. His first appointment in his new role was as a houseparent (supervisor) at Bersham Hall and whilst there he underwent in-service training for 12 months at Cartrefle College. He then served for nearly a year from April 1980 as a houseparent at Ysgol Talfryn, a residential school[8], with responsibility, shared by a housemother, for a group of ten children in a residential unit. After his period of seven (effectively five) years at Park House, he served as a field social worker for Clwyd County Council, at a substantially lower salary, for six years and was then seconded for two years to the NSPCC to work with children who had suffered abuse. He retired at the end of March 1997 after a short further period as a field social worker. He and his wife have fostered four children, including a brain damaged child.

17.61 The only complaint against Douglas of which we are aware was made by a former girl resident, who was at Park House for about a year from September 1981 and who was not prepared to give oral evidence to the Tribunal. She was

---

[7] See para 17.43.
[8] See para 4.07.

a very disturbed girl who had been admitted to Gwynfa Clinic for 12 months and then three community homes before she arrived at Park House at the age of 12 years. Her allegation was that she had returned to the home late one evening from a disco whereupon Douglas had got hold of her and shouted at her, saying that it was no use her explaining because he would not believe her. Douglas had pushed her against a door and she had grabbed his tie. The result of the exchange was that she had banged her head and back on the door and had a small bruise on her back. She alleged also that Douglas kicked her several times on the bottom as she went upstairs, having been ordered by him to go to bed. She had reported the incident to her mother two weeks later.

17.62 This allegation was put to Douglas by the police and he denied that he had ever kicked any youngster. He had no recollection of the specific incident but he accepted, in his oral evidence, that he would have shouted at the girl in the circumstances described. He said also that he had never kicked or pushed her so that she banged her head. He told the police that the girl was probably one of the most difficult that he and the staff had had to deal with; his recollection was that the doctor had had to put her on medication because of her violent outbursts.

17.63 The girl herself does not allege that Douglas pushed her in such a way that he intended to injure her and we are not at all satisfied that he did kick her as she alleges. There is no other suggestion that Douglas was a man who acted violently towards children or otherwise lost control of himself and we do not think that this allegation should reflect adversely on his generally good record.

17.64 There were comparatively few allegations of violence or other abuse against other members of the staff, during Douglas' effective period in charge between 1981 and 1986. He did have to deal with complaints against two members of the staff that were the subject of evidence before us. During this period there were no less than three Deputy Officers-in-Charge and the first was **David Bibby**, who held the post from 1 April 1981 to 31 August 1982 in a temporary capacity, following ten years service with the Bryn Alyn Community on leaving school at the age of 17 years. The allegation against him was that he "slippered" each of three girls who had run away and had been brought back by the police. One of these girls gave oral evidence before us and said that she was at Park House from the ages of six to 16 years. She said that "they" used to run away quite a lot to the houses of friends; the police would bring them back and it was a game. On one such occasion (when she was 14 or 15 years old) Bibby disciplined three of them by requiring them to bend over and slippering each once or twice. They were wearing jeans and it stung a bit; she thinks that she cried at the time but she says that she did not make any complaint. She said also that, apart from this, she "got on" with Bibby and that she had no serious complaints about Park House.

17.65 Douglas recalled that Bibby did report this incident to him and that he treated the matter as serious. His recollection is that the girls had been missing for 24 hours or more and they had returned when Douglas was off duty so that Bibby was in charge. Douglas said that he had a heated argument with Bibby, telling him that he could not condone physical punishment and that he would be reporting the incident to the Residential and Day Care Officer, which he did. Bibby's response was that he believed strongly in physically chastising children if they were naughty and that Douglas was a weak manager for not doing so, but he agreed reluctantly not to do so again. Bibby himself, however, in his written statement to the Tribunal denied that he had slippered any of the girls and said that two of the three did not support the allegation. There is no evidence that any disciplinary action was taken against Bibby.

17.66 It is unlikely, in our view, that Douglas has made up his account of the matter but the complainant's account of the actual slippering is not supported by any other evidence. The evidence about it is, therefore, unsatisfactory. In any event, if there was a lapse on Bibby's part, it was an isolated one towards the lower end of the scale of possible physical abuse.

17.67 **Frederick Rutter**[9] joined the staff of Park House in or about October 1984 after serving as a temporary RCCO at Bryn Estyn for 16 months and then as a care assistant at a hostel in Aston, Queensferry, for about ten months. His transfer to Park House was made initially on a temporary basis because of the staff shortages but he was appointed to fill a permanent vacancy as an RCCO from 1 November 1986. He remained at Park House until 28 August 1988, when he left to become Warden of Pen-y-Llan Hostel, which was operated by Clwyd Alyn Housing Association. The four offences of rape and the two indecent assaults of which Rutter was convicted on 30 July 1991 were all committed after 1 February 1988 at his home or the latter hostel against girls and young women in the age range of 15 to 21 years.

17.68 Rutter's activities as a foster-parent and owner of approved lodgings are dealt with separately in Chapter 26 but it should be mentioned here that he and his wife, who had two daughters of their own then aged 14 and 11 years, made their first application to foster, in respect of a 13 years old boy resident at Park House, on 28 December 1984. This was later withdrawn but the Rutters' home at Flint was approved as lodgings on 21 March 1986 for teenage children, although the particular lodging arrangement then in being broke down quite quickly. The Rutters then moved to Connah's Quay in 1987 and re-applied on 26 January 1988 to become foster-parents. This application was made in respect of a 15 years old girl resident at Park House (C) who had become a friend of the Rutter's younger daughter; and the boy referred to earlier in this paragraph was by then, at the age of 17 years, lodging with the Rutters together with another teenage boy lodger. The application was approved specifically for C in May 1988 and C was raped by Rutter when she was 16 years old, that is, fairly shortly after she left Park House.

17.69 One other former resident of Park House (D) alleged that she had been raped twice by Rutter but he was not charged with this in the indictment against him because, as far as we are aware, she made no complaint about the matter until she was interviewed on behalf of the Tribunal on 4 August 1997. D had previously made a statement to the police, in the presence of a psychiatric social worker, on 28 September 1992, when she had said that she had never been

[9] See paras 2.07(8), 8.41, 8.42 and 10.151 to 10.156.

physically or sexually assaulted in the children's homes that she named, including Park House, and had never seen any other person being assaulted in such a way. We received in evidence her typed statements, including a three page document headed "My Life Story", because she was not willing to give oral evidence. The essence of D's evidence was that she had been admitted into residential care and went to Park House at the suggestion of Rutter, who was a friend of her step-father. D said that Rutter and a friend had thought it a big joke to make girls bend down in their short skirts and pick up a dish cloth from the floor. They all had an idea why this was being done and, when she eventually refused, Rutter sent her to her bedroom. He then followed her up and raped her. She struggled and tried to shout but he put something over her mouth and threatened that, if she told anyone, he would kill her.

17.70 D alleged that the second rape occurred in Rutter's car. Her mother had sent her to Rutter's house in Flint to get something and he had insisted on giving her a lift home. He had then driven her to a place near the British Legion Club and had raped her. On that occasion he had said that he would get her, if she told anyone, and she would be transferred to a secure unit. However, these allegations set out in her "Life Story" are different in material respects from what was said in her statement to the Tribunal. In that statement she said that she had run away from her own home whilst on week-end leave and had gone to Rutter's house. He was to take her home but he stopped in a car park and started touching her up, whereupon she got out and ran home. She said also that this incident occurred before Rutter raped her in her bedroom at Park House.

17.71 Rather surprisingly, Rutter said in his oral evidence that he had no recollection of D at Park House. Nevertheless, the inconsistencies between her statements and her generally disturbed background are such that, in the absence of any corroboration, it is unlikely that a jury would feel able to convict him on her evidence, despite his subsequent record of sexual offences against young women well known to him.

17.72 The other sexual allegations against Rutter have been comparatively minor. One was that he had regularly kissed goodnight the sister of his prospective boy foster child[10], who was also resident at Park House. This witness had, however, made very serious allegations against a non-member of the staff, which had been carefully investigated by the Deputy Area Officer early in 1985 and not believed, and her mention of kissing by Rutter was in the nature of a boast rather than a complaint. There was also a complaint by another girl about Rutter's activities during a camping holiday in a holiday park at Caernarvon between 27 May and 2 June 1985, which was the subject of a detailed report by Jeffrey Douglas on 20 June 1985 to Norman Green, the Residential Day and Care Officer. The girl in question, who was 16 years old, alleged that during the week she had slept in the same half of a tent as Rutter without female supervision and that, on one occasion, Rutter had moved her night-gown to look at her legs and had made some remarks about her bikini or bathing costume.

---

[10] See para 17.68.

17.73 Douglas took up this matter as soon as he heard about it on 5 June 1985 from the girl's social worker, although the girl had said that she did not want to make a fuss about it. When taxed about it Rutter was quite upset and said that he could not recall making any remarks about swimwear other than to suggest to the girl that she should wear one of the other girls' bikinis if she wanted to get her back brown. He denied moving the night-gown and added that he had told the girl many times at Park House to sit properly and not to show her legs. He accepted that he had been very foolish to share the same part of a tent with a girl but attributed it to the need to avoid repetition of an incident that had occurred on the first night of the camp.

17.74 Green responded to the report with a number of further questions to be put to Rutter. There followed a meeting between John Llewellyn Thomas (Principal Officer Children), Green, Douglas and Rutter on 9 July 1985 at which it was pointed out that the preparations for and supervision of the camp had been far from satisfactory and it was stated that a circular regarding the planning of camps and holidays had been sent to Officers-in-Charge for future guidance. This circular dated 27 June 1985 required certain specified information, including details of staffing, to be given to Officers-in-Charge (with a copy to the Principal Officer Children) before holidays away from residential homes.

17.75 There was one more complaint about Rutter shortly before he left Park House, which was investigated by Douglas as soon as he returned from his CQSW course. This girl (E) complained to Douglas on 17 July 1988 that Rutter had hit her on the side of the face two days earlier as she left in the morning for the last day of the school term. She thought that she had been struck because (a) she had been smoking at the rear of the house and (b) she had had an argument with another member of the staff about taking her cassette/radio to school that day. E wished to keep her complaint confidential because she feared repercussions from Rutter and other members of the staff.

17.76 Douglas sent a report of this complaint to E's social worker after discussing it with Michael Barnes on 20 July 1988, when the latter paid a pre-arranged visit to Park House. He compiled also a rather fuller incident report, dated 22 July 1988. This report contained the following rather revealing passage:

> "I told E that no member of staff was allowed to hit any child, and that if this happened I would want to make sure it did not happen again. She then told me it could have been an accident, and that Mr Rutter may have just raised his hand, not really meaning to hit her. Again she told me she did not want me to talk to Mr Rutter about the incident, expressing concern that staff 'would have it in for me for telling tales' and claiming this happened to another girl in Park House who complained about the way she had been treated by a member of staff."

17.77 E's social worker complained of the delay in reporting this incident but the matter was investigated quite thoroughly. The social worker helped E to compile a statement in which she said "I don't think Fred meant to hit me. I think that he was trying to push me away. I walked into him. He was trying to stop me leaving. I was angry and swearing at the time". In the end a memorandum in the name of the Director (but drafted by Barnes) was sent to the Area Officer to whose area the social worker was attached on 24 August 1988 stating that there was clear evidence from E's statement that the incident might have been an accident and that, bearing in mind Rutter's resignation from his post at Park House, he did not propose to take any further action.

17.78　In his oral evidence to us Rutter did not dispute that it was his practice to kiss goodnight the girl mentioned in paragraph 17.72 but said that it was a practice of staff to do so to girl residents and that there was nothing improper about it. He was not asked about E's complaint at the time because he had gone on leave and the decision to take no further action had been made before he returned. He had decided to move to other employment when he learnt that Douglas was returning to Park House and E's complaint had nothing to do with his resignation. Douglas had provided him with a letter of reference on 6 August 1988 in connection with his application for a post at a hostel in Hurst Newton, with which Rutter presumably did not proceed. He received also a letter of reference from his "immediate supervisor" (un-named) in connection with his application for the post of Warden at Connah's Quay.

The 1988 Inquiry

17.79　Before Douglas returned to Park House from his training course, arrangements had been made to take a group of five resident boys and four resident girls, under the supervision of five members of staff to Butlins Holiday Camp at Pwllheli from 27 August to 3 September 1988. One of the group of children was E[11], who was 13 years old at that time. According to her written evidence, she fell in love during the holiday with a 19 years old Irishman staying at the camp. The result was that, on the last night of her holiday, she had sexual intercourse with this man, with her consent, near the car park in the camp, She told a friend what had happened and, on the group's return to Park House, that friend informed a member of staff.

17.80　Douglas had returned to Park House before this holiday took place. On learning of the arrangements that had been made for it, he expressed disapproval (according to his own evidence) but it was not thought practicable or appropriate to cancel the holiday. After it had taken place he saw E, who told him about the events of the last night. Her complaint is and was that there was a lack of supervision by the care staff during the holiday: nobody ever checked where she was and the children had too much freedom.

17.81　The police were informed about the matter and carried out an investigation but it seems that the Irishman could not be traced. Clwyd County Council, on its part, appointed a panel of inquiry "to enquire into and consider all aspects of the planning and execution" of the holiday "in the light of existing departmental policy, practice and guidance for the well-being of young people in Council care and to report the findings to the Director of Social Services". The panel of three comprised a senior officer of the National Children's Homes in the chair, the Assistant County Secretary of Clwyd (J A Loveridge) and the

---

[11] See para 17.75 et seq.

Area Social Services Officer for the Rhuddlan District (Margaret Clarke). It heard evidence over the course of three days at the end of November 1988 but the report itself is undated.

17.82 By the time that this inquiry had been set in train E's mother had expressed her grave concern about the incident and had instructed solicitors to advise her about possible legal proceedings against the Council. The report referred to this and said rather surprisingly:

> "The immediate purpose of the Inquiry was therefore to enable the Council to meet those proceedings in full possession of all relevant information and to draw the appropriate conclusions from that information."

In the event, however, the report did not contain such information: it did not even contain any account of what had actually occurred during the Butlins holiday. Instead the "Statement from the Review" included the following two paragraphs:

> "In receiving the evidence both oral and documentary, the Panel viewed with grave concern the consistent indications of unsatisfactory standards of care, low staff morale, distant and ineffective management.
>
> That grave concern is reflected in the recommendations which follow. Given the guarantees of confidentiality made to each witness, it is neither the Panel's wish nor indeed open to them to reproduce in any but the most general terms the matters which give rise to each of the individual recommendations. This in the Panel's view may most conveniently be done by setting out each of the recommendations and then briefly canvassing the reasons for them."

17.83 In the introduction section of the report, the panel pointed out that, on the figures available to 31 March 1987, Clwyd County Council relied more heavily than other counties in Wales upon "residential services" for children and young persons in its care (24% of all such in care in Clwyd as against 17% for the whole of Wales). It was the panel's view that, although their inquiry had been limited to the incident involving Park House, many of the concerns that they had identified would "in all probability, apply equally to other residential Child Care establishments within the County".

17.84 The panel's recommendations and the findings on which they were based together constituted scathing criticism of the state of residential child care in Clwyd at that time. A summary will inevitably dilute the impact of the document but the recommendations and some of the findings were as follows:

> "1. To immediately ensure that all staff involved in the Social Work task are familiar with and trained to operate the existing Clwyd County Council Child Protection procedures."

Witnesses displayed no knowledge of the procedures and relevant manuals were not available at Park House.

"2. To develop a County wide policy statement for residential care with appropriate guidelines and to ensure that these are made available and known and understood by all staff involved in the Social Work task."

There was lack of clarity and some conflict of views as to the purpose of residential care, which was a fundamental defect. This recommendation had wide management and training implications. Clear steps were needed to correct the impression that the managerial style within the residential service was "distant, impassive and inspectorial and re-active after the event rather than providing pro-active leadership".

"3. To agree and implement specific aims and objectives for each individual residential care establishment in accordance with the Countywide policy statement for residential care and guidelines made thereunder and to ensure all staff are familiar with those aims and objectives, understand them and are trained to implement them."

This was a corollary of recommendation 2. It was a matter of particular regret to the panel, but perhaps understandable in view of what they had said earlier, that "the aims and objectives of Park House, so far as they existed, appeared to be simply to feed, water and contain the clients".

"4. To establish, in conjunction with the field Social Worker, and all other interested parties/agencies implement, monitor and update when necessary a care plan for each child in every residential establishment."

There was no evidence of a care plan for E. Park House was perceived as a dumping ground for difficult children who could not be fostered and "for whom no light could be seen at the end of the tunnel". Too much reliance was placed on the key worker system within Park House and there was no evidence of regular staff meetings. Field workers were not involved in day to day planning and residential staff wrongly discouraged parental involvement.

"5. To ensure that all aspects of work involving holidays undertaken by Residential Care Homes conforms in all respects with the Countywide policy statement, the agreed aims and objectives of the Residential Care Home and facilitates the relevant individual child care plans."

No attempt had been made to address the problems of the individual children or to consider their suitability for any particular kind of holiday. There was also a clear need for a strong managerial line to be taken that each of the "constituent elements" of the holiday was fully discussed and agreed as suitable.

"6. To make and monitor a commitment to provide training, support, guidance and regular supervision so as to ensure that all staff involved in the social work task are equipped to implement:

(i) individual care plans;

(ii) the agreed aims and objectives of each Residential Care Home;

(iii) the County Residential Care policies.

To achieve this consideration needs to be given to the development of professional social work and managerial skills at all levels within the agency."

It was apparent that each residential care worker operated as a self-contained unit with little opportunity for support, guidance or regular supervision. There was no evidence of any attempt to monitor the actions of staff or to advise them of any new practices or desirable practices or even existing practices, far less to ensure that these were carried out.

"7. To develop a corporate management approach to support and enable all staff undertaking the residential social work task to help identify, develop and implement new thinking and initiatives . . ."

17.85 The panel's report was eventually sent to the Director of Social Services (Gledwyn Jones) on 11 September 1989 but it was seen by very few other eyes. Jones agreed in cross-examination that the report was a great shock but he was unclear about what was done in relation to its recommendations save to say, in effect, that its recommendations were intended to be incorporated in the Council's developing strategy for implementing the forthcoming Children Act 1989. His recollection was that copies were given to Geoffrey Wyatt, John Llewellyn Thomas and Michael Barnes as the relevant officers in the field but it was not shown to the Chief Executive (Mervyn Phillips) and he did not recall discussing it with his own Deputy (John Jevons). Gledwyn Jones was sure that he outlined to the Chairman of the Social Services Committee that there was concern and what was being done about the recommendations but he did not know whether the Chairman received a copy of the report. From the documents before us it appears that Barnes drafted a response to the criticisms in October 1989 but, as far as we are aware, it remained simply a draft. The matter was allowed to drift for some months and no countywide policy statement on residential child care was produced.

17.86 The report was never debated in either the Social Services Committee or the Council. Jones' explanation for this was that he regarded the inquiry as an internal one and that he wanted to "move quickly on doing something about the recommendations". What happened in fact was that approximately two years later, on 18 December 1990, he presented his own report on Group Care Holidays for Children in Community Homes, which had been previously circulated, to the Social Services (Children and Family Services) Sub-Committee. According to the minute, and to our surprise, he told the Sub-Committee that it was his Department's response to "national concerns that group holidays arranged by local authorities needed to be properly planned". At the same time a revised code of practice relating to such holidays, probably drafted by Barnes, was approved. The members expressed anxiety that personal accident cover was only provided on a limited basis and the County Secretary was asked to prepare a report on the subject.

17.87 Before the meeting referred to in the preceding paragraph Michael Barnes met the Park House staff with John Cooke of NALGO and Jean Brady of NUPE, probably on 12 September 1990, to give them "feedback" on the panel's report. They were told that the principal findings were that no one person or group was to blame, that there had been a system failure and that there were lessons to be learned at every operational level. The recommendations (but not the findings accompanying them) were listed in very summary form with the comment in respect of each that the matter was being attended to or that the necessary action had been taken. On the question of a countywide policy statement it was said that various reports eg control and discipline, had been put to committee and that further policy was being shaped by implementation of the Children Act 1989. The trades union representatives commented on the need to see the whole report but we have not seen any subsequent formal request for this.

1989 to 1991: the David Evans regime

17.88 It seems likely that Tim Hawes, who had been Deputy Officer-in-Charge of Park House from 1 November 1986, acted as Officer-in-Charge during the inter-regnum between Douglas' departure on 31 October 1988 and the return of David Evans on 1 August 1989[12]. The latter's period as Officer-in-Charge began inauspiciously because he was suspended from duty on 4 November 1989 but he was reinstated just before Christmas and he then remained in charge, with Tim Hawes as his Deputy until Park House closed on or about 31 July 1991.

17.89 The reason for Evans' suspension was that two girl residents (F and G) complained that Evans had "touched their bottoms". To be more precise it was probably F who made the complaint to one of the residential care staff on her own behalf and recounted also what G had told her. Both F and G gave oral evidence to the Tribunal and their complaints were of a relatively minor kind. F, who was 14 years old at the relevant time, said that when Evans returned to Park House he was stricter than he had been previously because there had been some unruliness. Her allegations were that Evans would touch her bottom when he was walking past her, a light slap or touch, which she regarded as perverted; and on one occasion he put his arm around her shoulder and licked the side of her face several times. Of this last occasion she said that Evans thought it funny but she told him that he stank. She said also that Evans would say stupid things when he passed her: she could not remember now what he said but "he was being like perverted". Her complaints were extracted from F reluctantly when a member of staff asked why she had groaned on being told that Evans would be on duty and had persisted in questioning her. Evans did not repeat his alleged conduct after his suspension.

17.90 G, who was also 14 years old in 1989, was more positive about Park House (and South Meadow). She had been happy at both places. She felt safe and cared for at Park House and she was helped a lot. As for Evans, she did not have much to do with him and she did not really have any nastiness from him. Her complaint was that on one occasion he had "touched her bottom": she was alone with

---

[12] See paras 17.43 and 17.59.

him, which did not usually happen, and he put his arm around her shoulder, after which his hand went down her back. She did not make an official complaint but she did tell F and she does not think that F told her of F's own experiences with Evans.

17.91 It seems that F was seen on 3 November 1989, very soon after her complaint, by two field social workers on the initiative of John Llewellyn Thomas and we have read the social workers' report on the matter dated 9 November 1989. Evans was seen on 4 November 1989 and vehemently denied any sexual misconduct: his explanation for F's allegation was that she had become very friendly with the leading Park House male resident bully, who was being disciplined by Evans, and that the allegation was a reprisal for this. A Child Protection conference was held in respect of F (but not G) on 21 November 1989 and reached the conclusion that abuse had not occurred. Meanwhile, a police investigation proceeded, in the course of which F, G, Evans and many others were interviewed and we have read the investigating officer's report dated 21 November 1989. The predictable outcome was that the Crown Prosecution Service advised that no proceedings should be taken against Evans because there was insufficient evidence to support a charge of indecent assault in respect of either F or G.

17.92 We are not aware of any other allegations of physical or sexual abuse during this last period of Park House's history as a community home.

17.93 David Evans was asked about the existence of any formal complaints procedure. He agreed that there had not been any such procedure in the early years but said that Michael Barnes had initiated one, which operated during Evans' last period at Park House. He did not remember it being in writing but all the resident children were told about it "a few times". The procedure was for them to make a complaint to the Officer-in-Charge or to his Deputy and it would then be taken up with Barnes.

Conclusions

17.94 Although Park House had quite a difficult role to play, particularly in the later part of its history because older and more troublesome adolescents were living there, comparatively few allegations of abuse have been made to this Tribunal. The presence of Rutter on the staff from 1984 to 1986 is troubling and gives rise to obvious questions but there is no compelling evidence that he was guilty of any sexual abuse at the community home or in that period. The other notable aspect of the account that we have given is that residents were prepared to complain to members of the staff even before a formal complaints procedure was initiated by Barnes. This was no doubt attributable, at least in part, to the fact that the children were, in general, long term residents, who were on closer terms with the staff than, for example, children in observation and assessment centres could be; but it is to the credit of the staff that complaints do not appear to have been actively discouraged and that, when they were made, they were passed on appropriately so that they could be investigated.

17.95 Nevertheless, wider shortcomings of Park House were disclosed by successive reports in 1975, 1980 and 1988 and little action appears to have been taken to address them. The criticisms in those reports reflected adversely upon the higher management and supervision of Park House and we discuss this aspect of them in a later section of this report. It must be said here, however, that they indicated grave deficiencies in the quality of care provided by Park House. The chairman of the 1988 panel of inquiry did say in his preface to its report that the panel recognised the energy and effort put into the residential care service by individual members of staff but that they (the panel) considered such energy and effort to be largely wasted without a clear central direction and purpose. It is probable that residents at Park House like G, who could withstand peer pressure and accommodate a degree of turbulence, did "feel safe" there but we have grave reservations about the extent to which the needs of individual children were met and the adequacy of the guidance and training for future independent living that was provided.

PART III

ALLEGED ABUSE OF CHILDREN IN CARE

IN OTHER NON-PRIVATE RESIDENTIAL

ESTABLISHMENTS IN CLWYD

BETWEEN 1974 AND 1996

Tanllwyfan

18.01 Tanllwyfan is a former farmhouse standing in five acres of land at Penmaen Head, Old Colwyn, with the formal address of 510 Abergele Road, Colwyn Bay. It was opened as a children's home in 1916 by the Boys and Girls Welfare Society, whose headquarters moved from Manchester to Cheadle during the period under review. Under the Children and Young Persons Act 1969 Tanllwyfan was categorised as an assisted community home with education on the premises (CHE) and it was operated by the Society with Denbighshire County Council and then Clwyd County Council under an instrument of management.

18.02 As we have said earlier[1], Tanllwyfan was designated in the 1971 Regional Plan as a special home for up to 16 boys and girls in the junior age range, available to the North Wales counties. Some children, however, were also admitted from English local authorities in the north-west. Denbighshire Education Committee at that time provided teaching facilities and premises (a portakabin classroom) but some children attended local schools. Psychiatric oversight and treatment were provided at a nearby child guidance clinic and a psychiatric social worker attended weekly.

18.03 In the 1979 Regional Plan the home was said to accommodate up to 18 boys and girls in the junior range, the facility being available to all local authorities within the Welsh region. The educational provision was one teacher and one classroom and there were re-stated provisions for psychiatric, psychological and medical services. However, the future of the home was not very clear from the document because a note stated that it was to close as a CHE in 1980–1981 whereas another section of the plan showed it as continuing to be a community home intended to accommodate up to 18 mainly older boys and girls with the same educational provision as before and available to Gwynedd as well as Clwyd. In the event it seems to have accommodated children in the age range of six to 16 years and it eventually closed on 31 December 1984.

18.04 Management of the day-to-day running of Tanllwyfan was vested in a local committee (managers), including three local authority (Clwyd) members, which met monthly at Tanllwyfan. A representative of Clwyd Social Services Department attended these meetings: Veronica Pares attended in the early years when she was Principal Residential and Day Care Officer and later Gordon Ramsay (Principal Social Worker Children) did so regularly. The General Secretary of the Boys and Girls Welfare Society also attended these meetings. The managers were responsible for the appointment of staff, including the Officer-in-Charge, and they reviewed admissions and discharges of children (it was usual for two or three members of the committee to attend case conferences). It was the practice for a member of the committee to make

[1] See para 4.05.

a separate visit to Tanllwyfan each month in accordance with a rota. There was also an independent visitor living locally, who was appointed by the General Secretary.

18.05 The Officer-in-Charge or Warden of Tanllwyfan when Clwyd County Council took over its part of the shared responsibility for the community home was Mr D Shepherd, whose wife was housekeeper contemporaneously. They resigned in July 1976 and were succeeded by Mr and Mrs Groome with effect from 7 August 1976.

18.06 **Richard Francis Groome** became 36 years old in the month when he took over as Warden of Tanllwyfan and he had four years' experience of full time social work. Before that he had served as a musician in the Royal Marines for 13 years and had then had varied commercial experience including a spell with the NAAFI in South America. He had done some part-time work with youth clubs before working as an RCCO for Northamptonshire County Council from June 1972 and served subsequently as manager of a children's home in Kingston-upon-Thames and then Team Leader for two years at an assessment centre in Hertfordshire. He had also attended the pre-qualifying In-Service training at Ewell College in 1973 and qualified for the CRCCYP in 1976 at Havering College. The Groomes remained at Tanllwyfan until 11 November 1982 and continued to live in Colwyn Bay until April 1984.

18.07 From Tanllwyfan Richard Groome went immediately[2] to Clwyd Hall School[3] as head of care and then principal but he left in or about April 1984. His next venture was to found a therapeutic community for young people called Milverton Court at Ludlow in Shropshire which occupied him for six years from 1984. Since 1990 he has been a volunteer worker for SSAFA[4] and director of a leisure company and he has also served as a member of the complaints committee of a regional health authority.

18.08 We have not investigated the short period of about two years following the Groomes' departure from Tanllwyfan until it closed because we have not received any complaint in respect of that period[5].

1974 to 1976

18.09 It seems that there was some anxiety on the part of Welsh Office inspectors about conditions at Tanllwyfan at the time when it became an assisted community home because there were three inspections between 17 September 1973 and 19 November 1975. The first inspection was triggered by a request by the Society for a grant towards the cost of work done on the home but SWSO O'Brien was critical of some of the toilet facilities and he thought that the ground floor accommodation and bedrooms "just about reached adequate

---

[2] He declined the Wardenship of a Berkshire hostel to which he had been appointed.

[3] See paras 4.17, 4.18, Chapter 23 and 50.31(7).

[4] Soldiers, Sailors and Air Force Association.

[5] This is subject, however, to what is said in paras 18.26 to 18.28.

standards of cleanliness and domestic good order". Other concerns were "breaches of the corporal punishment regulations" and the need to increase the number of care staff.

18.10 New staffing arrangements were implemented in 1974 and SWSO Smith noted the other previous recommendations had been dealt with by the time that he visited Tanllwyfan on 24 September 1974. But there had been considerable problems between the Shepherds and the rest of the staff, including a 'walk-out' because of Shepherd's "autocratic and rigid regime", as it was described by the staff. Smith, however, largely agreed with the staff arrangements that had been put in place and the 'walk-out' did not appear to have damaged the children. Smith's view was that domestic order was satisfactory and that the home provided a reasonable degree of comfort.

18.11 SWSO Smith made a further visit on 19 November 1975 to follow up matters raised on his previous visit. He was critical of the staffing structure because it left little room for manoeuvre in case of sickness etc and he regarded the day rooms as "bare and cheerless". But, otherwise, he was favourably impressed by the home and he noted that staff/children relationships were very good. He felt that the home was providing good care, more personalised than in the past, and operating effectively. It must also be said that he was informed by the General Secretary of the Society that new furnishings for the day rooms had been ordered and were delivered shortly after his visit.

18.12 Our major concern about this period is that we are aware that six former boy residents have complained since that they suffered sexual abuse by **Kenneth Andrew Scott** at Tanllwyfan, and the Tribunal received evidence from two of them to that effect. Kenneth Scott was a care assistant at Tanllwyfan from 1974 to 1976, rising to the position of Third-in-Charge. He was born on 2 July 1951 so that he was still a very young man whilst he worked at Tanllwyfan. He had left school at 16 years to work for the National Coal Board for two years and had then become an Assistant Warden for the Youth Hostels Association for a similar period. This was followed by two years as a barman and about one year as a care assistant for Wandsworth Borough Council before his appointment to Tanllwyfan. He had not received any formal training but he did attend a one year course at Bangor Technical College, gaining an In-Service Certificate of Attendance from the CCETSW, whilst he was at Tanllwyfan, and he says that he "did day release some week-ends".

18.13 Kenneth Scott appeared before the Crown Court at Leicester on 28 February 1986 when he was sentenced to a total of eight years' imprisonment, having pleaded guilty to two offences of buggery and three offences of gross indecency. The victims of these offences were three boys, aged between 14 and 16 years, and the offences had been committed between 1982 and 1985 at the children's home in Leicestershire of which Scott had been Officer-in-Charge from 1 May 1978 until his arrest on 29 July 1985, at his own home and on holiday[6]. His predecessor at the home, but only for a short period of less than three months

---

[6] See the Leicestershire Inquiry 1992 by Andrew Kirkwood QC (now the Hon Mr Justice Kirkwood), paras 45.1 to 45.11.

as Acting Officer-in-Charge, was Frank Beck[7]. After leaving Tanllwyfan, Scott had remained briefly in the employment of the Society as Deputy Warden of Belmont House, Cheadle, and had then served as a housemaster at a boarding school for children with special needs in Ipswich. We are perturbed to record also that, following his release from prison, he was employed between 1991 and 1993 as Warden at a youth hostel for the YHA, according to his written statement to the Tribunal. He says that they were unaware of his conviction but that "my work, in any event, was involved with adults in the main".

18.14 The complaints against Scott in respect of his conduct at Tanllwyfan were not made until the police investigation between 1991 and 1993. The first of the two relevant witnesses, who both gave oral evidence before us, said that Scott would examine his bare body when he returned from home visits, purportedly to check for any bruises or abrasions. Then, after he had sustained injuries requiring sutures in a go-kart accident and his dressings had to be changed periodically, Scott started to touch his private parts, apparently accidentally at first. This progressed to regular masturbation and on one occasion Scott inserted a finger in the boy's anus. As a result he started wetting the bed and developed a rash, to which Scott applied cream.

18.15 That witness was at Tanllwyfan from January 1975 to September 1976 whereas the second witness was there from October 1972 to June 1976. The latter said that Scott touched him indecently on one occasion only, on the last night of a week's camping holiday at Morecambe. About ten boys went on that trip with Scott and the witness was required to sleep near Scott in the centre of a bell tent on the last night as a punishment for talking. After he had been asleep for some time he awoke to find that Scott's hand was on his penis. The witness said that "he supposed it could be put down as masturbating him". He froze and kept still. Scott whispered his name twice but he did not reply: Scott was stroking his penis and whispering and he did not know how to handle the situation. He thinks that he made a waking up gesture, disturbing Scott, who took his (Scott's) hand away. The witness then pulled his sleeping bag tighter round him and feigned sleep. On his return to Tanllwyfan he wanted to tell Mrs Shepherd what had occurred but lacked the courage to do so. He was on his guard from that night onwards.

18.16 Scott denied the allegations of both these witnesses in his statement to the Tribunal made on 21 January 1997 and he had earlier (in 1993) denied to the police the allegations in relation to Tanllwyfan that had been made against him at that time. However, both the witnesses that we heard were very credible witnesses and, bearing in mind Scott's subsequent convictions, there is no sensible reason for doubting the truth of what they said. We should add that it became apparent during the first witness' evidence that he was not aware of Scott's later imprisonment until told about it in the course of his evidence. It must be stressed, however, that Scott did not have any criminal record before or during the period when he served at Tanllwyfan.

---

[7] Ibid, Chapter 18.

18.17 There have been very few other complaints relating to this period from former residents and three of the five of which we know were made against unidentified persons. We accept that Shepherd did impose a strict regime in the early part of the period giving rise to some anxiety in the Welsh Office but that had been ameliorated by 1975, when the third inspection to which we have referred took place.

1976 to 1982

18.18 There was one further Welsh Office inspection of Tanllwyfan during the period of Richard Groome's wardenship, again by SWSO Smith. This took place on 13 April 1978 when there were 14 boys and four girls in residence in the age range of eight to 15 years (mostly, ten to 13 years). Records showed that the school had been operating at close to maximum capacity for the preceding two and a half years. The living pattern was based on a "group system" approach of two (junior and senior) living units, but this was said to be "modified in the absence of purpose built accommodation". Lengths of stay varied between a few weeks and four and a half years.

18.19 There were 11 care staff in post, including a qualified teacher, and eight of them were resident on the premises. Five members of the staff had a professional qualification in working with children, another had a nursing qualification and all the rest had undertaken formal in-service training. There had been, however, a total turnover of staff, save for two, since the previous inspection in 1975. Support was provided by the equivalent of five full time domestic staff, including a gardener. No active night supervision was provided but two members of staff slept in to provide an 'on call' duty system. Five of the children presenting special difficulties and requiring intensive remedial teaching were being taught on the premises whilst the rest were attending one or other of five local schools.

18.20 SWSO Smith was impressed by what he saw. In his opinion the home "demonstrated further advance under the new leadership of Mr Groome and in all aspects of its operation Tanllwyfan was seen to be offering a good quality of care to the residents and a useful service to the local authorities using it" (Clwyd, Gwynedd, Liverpool, Stockport, Sefton and Trafford at that time). Rather remarkably, it was claimed that there had been no absconding for 18 months despite the fact that some of the resident children had long histories of truanting and absconding. Behavioural problems also were said to be rare and were dealt with by admonition, being sent early to bed or reduction of pocket money to no less than 50% of entitlement. The home looked well cared for and there were no signs of damage or neglect.

18.21 Of the eight known complainants who were at Tanllwyfan in this period five have made allegations against **Richard Groome** himself. In the event we received evidence from only two of the five and the evidence of both of them was read. The first of these (born in February 1965) was at Tanllwyfan from 7 August 1979 and 22 May 1981 and, when he was interviewed by the police in 1992, he said expressly that he had no complaints about the way he was treated at Tanllwyfan, although he made serious allegations about what had happened to him at Bersham Hall earlier. In his Tribunal statement dated 22 October 1996, however, he said that he wished to add the following:

> "I have never said this before but whilst I was at Tanllwyfan Richard Groom(e) who was a housemaster found out that a boy called "A" had been messing about with the younger boys and because of that he made myself and about seven other boys give "A" a hiding in the gym."

We know no more about the alleged incident than that.

18.22 The other witness, X, who was 12 years old when he began a three and a quarter years stay at Tanllwyfan on 8 September 1981, told the police in October 1992 that he had problems with Groome on a couple of occasions over small matters. He alleged that, in one incident, he told another boy that Groome's new leather jacket was PVC, whereupon Groome smacked him on the side of the head with the result that his head hit a door. On another occasion X was taken from the school on the premises by Groome to the latter's office because he had been blamed for something. When X told Groome that he had not done anything, Groome smacked him on the side of the head and told him to shut up. However, X added "Mr Groome when he was nice you couldn't wish for a better person but if he got upset you steered clear of him. The only injury I ever received from him was a slight bump when my head hit the door but I don't want to make a complaint about anything that went on while I was in Tanllwyfan".

18.23 X was more critical of the general regime at Tanllwyfan because he said also "The only thing I would like to say is that I don't think that they were very caring . . . at all and they just let the children run the place. They used to let the kids run riot at times and they never bothered to come around and check you at night or anything".

18.24 Most unfortunately, this last witness lost an eye as the result of an accident at Tanllwyfan. Two other boys were throwing darts at each other late at night as the witness made his way to the lavatory. On hearing one of the others call his name, he looked around a door and a dart hit his right eye. He recovered financial compensation for the loss of his eye subsequently. In his Tribunal statement he said that there should be better trained staff running the children's homes and that there should also be a way of helping children who come out of care, "as it appears they are just left to look after themselves and many can't do this".

18.25 Richard Groome's response to X's criticism about children running riot was to say that it was not a true description of Tanllwyfan during his period as Warden and that X's injury occurred after Groome had left and when he was working at Clwyd Hall School, that is, on 9 January 1983. He recalled that he and his wife provided meals, accommodation and transport for X's family to help them to visit him in hospital because the Groomes were still living in Colwyn Bay. As for the allegations of assault, Groome denied ever smacking X, which would have been contrary to his rules and he denied equally firmly setting boys upon A as the other witness alleged. In his oral evidence to the

Tribunal he said that there was a policy of encouraging residents to confront a resident whose behaviour was unacceptable but to do so in a non-violent way in the presence of a member of staff or with one nearby.

18.26 It is readily understandable that X should be critical of the supervision at Tanllwyfan in view of the injury that he sustained but it occurred after the Groomes' departure and the information before us indicates that X stayed on there for two years after they left. It may be, therefore, that his criticisms relate more accurately to that final period of Tanllwyfan's history, although we have not received any specific complaint about it. It is likely that there were some defects in the overnight supervision throughout on the basis of the arrangements explained in SWSO Smiths' 1978 report. As for the specific complaints against Groome, they were expressed in restrained terms and it would be surprising if he did not lapse on occasions from his own stated standards when dealing with turbulent children in provocative situations. We do not consider that the evidence that we have received is of sufficient weight to justify a finding that Richard Groome himself physically abused children at Tanllwyfan or that he encouraged such abuse. We should add that such evidence as we have received about Mrs Groome, who became known as the Domestic Bursar, has been positive and favourable.

18.27 One other former resident of Tanllwyfan gave oral evidence before us in support of his complaint that he was struck by a member of the care staff (Z). This witness (Y) had been in care for ten years when he arrived at Tanllwyfan in August 1980 at the age of 11 years; during his period in care he had been placed in three children's homes, including three months at Bersham Hall, and he had been fostered by the Saints[8]. His stay at Tanllwyfan lasted four years and his general description of it was "not too bad". Y's specific complaint is that he was punched in the face by Z with the result that he had a cut lip and bruising near his right eye (he referred only to a sore eye). This incident occurred on 16 November 1982, in the week following Groome's departure, and after it happened Y ran down to the latter's private house, from which he was collected by the Acting Officer-in-Charge. The background circumstances were that Y, who subsequently threw the dart that injured X, had attacked X and had been fighting with him. Z had intervened twice and, according to his own account, he thought that Y was about to strike him: he therefore struck out first to forestall Y and he thought that he had probably cut Y's lip. X confirmed that Z had struck Y but said that it was definitely Y's fault.

18.28 Z attended a disciplinary hearing at Tanllwyfan on 25 November 1982 before a panel of three, comprised of the Chairman of the Managers, the Acting Officer-in-Charge and the General Secretary. Z chose to represent himself and gave a full account of the incident. The unanimous decision of the panel was that he had been guilty of gross misconduct meriting dismissal but that he should be paid one month's salary in lieu of notice rather than summarily dismissed. There was no appeal from that decision and Z's contract of employment terminated on 31 December 1982.

---

[8] See paras 25.21 to 25.29.

Conclusions

18.29 The overall picture that we have received of Tanllwyfan is rather less favourable than that given by the Inspector in 1978 but it does appear that the Boys and Girls Welfare Society did achieve some success between 1974 and 1984 in caring for an appreciable number of quite disturbed children over long periods. With hindsight the presence of Kenneth Scott on the staff is a cause for grave concern but the Society did not have any information about him at the time to put them on their guard and no complaint was made about his activities whilst he was at Tanllwyfan. Other complaints against other identified members of the staff have been comparatively few and we accept that, in general, corporal punishment was effectively prohibited. On the few occasions when physical force was used it was usually in very provocative circumstances and the degree of force was moderate.

18.30 There have been a very small number of allegations of sexual abuse against individuals (apart from those against Scott) but we have not received any complaints to the Tribunal in respect of them. As we explain in paragraph 50.31(7), Richard Francis Groome is currently awaiting trial for a number of alleged sexual offences against boys one of whom was resident at Tanllwyfan at the time. In view of the continuing police investigation into Groome this former resident was not called to give evidence to the Tribunal.

18.31 It is, of course, much more difficult to assess the quality of care provided by this home more generally and we have not received a sufficiently wide range of evidence about it to reach any confident conclusion. Such pointers as we have do, however, suggest that the quality of care at Tanllwyfan compared favourably with that provided by local authority community homes of similar size and purpose in North Wales.

Ysgol Talfryn

19.01 Ysgol Talfryn was a Clwyd Education Authority day and residential school on the outskirts of the village of Brynford, one mile south of Holywell. Its purpose was to provide education for children, in the age range of six to 16 years, with emotional and behavioural difficulties, who generally had special educational needs (it was formerly described as a school for maladjusted children). The school was purpose-built and was designed to provide residential accommodation for 40 children in four house units of ten. It opened in April 1978 and the first of the residential units began to operate in April 1980 and all four were open by September 1982. In the summer of 1988 there were 63 pupils on the roll, of whom 31 were residents. The Headmaster throughout the 1980s and until 31 July 1992 was George Eric Austin, working with a Board of Governors. Numbers have declined in the 1990s and the latest information that we have is that only 22 day pupils remain (eight from outside Flintshire). The school will remain open until September 1999 but its future thereafter is problematic.

19.02 It is important to stress that many of the children attending Ysgol Talfryn were not in care. The school would not, therefore, have been within the ambit of our inquiry but for the fact that 18 former residents who had been at Ysgol Talfryn in the 1980s subsequently made complaints to the police of abuse in one form or another against one or more members of the staff; and some of these complainants had been in care at the time. None of these allegations were, however, directed against the Headmaster.

Allegations of sexual abuse

19.03 We are aware of only one complainant who alleged that he had been sexually abused by a member of the staff at Ysgol Talfryn. At the time when the complaint was made to the police in 1992 the complainant was himself serving a sentence of imprisonment for rape committed when he was still a minor and his allegation was uncorroborated. No prosecution ensued and the complainant has not provided any evidence to the Tribunal.

Allegations of physical abuse

19.04 The remaining allegations, all of physical abuse or complicity in such abuse, involved ten identified members of the staff and one who was unidentified but the majority of these members of staff were the subject of only one, or at the most two, allegations. Moreover, most of the complaints were of the use of excessive force in restraint, not causing any significant injury, in circumstances in which a degree of physical restraint appears to have been necessary on the complainant's own account of the matter. It must be said also that several of these complainants said that they had benefited from their stay at the school, the object of which was to fit them, if possible, for a return to mainstream education.

19.05 Against this background we heard oral evidence from three complainants who had all been in care at or about the time when they were resident at Ysgol Talfryn. The first of these chronologically, A, spent two years at the school from September 1981, starting when he was 13 years old, following a year at Gwynfa clinic. He is of above average intelligence but had serious emotional and behavioural problems at that time with the result that his mother and adoptive father regarded him as beyond their control. His behaviour had deteriorated at Gwynfa and it seems that he had been received into voluntary care by Gwynedd County Council in July 1981 to enable him to stay at Y Gwyngyll until he went to Ysgol Talfryn, at which point he was to be discharged from care until the following vacation. His later history is unclear but he said in evidence that, although his education suffered, for which he is paying now, he has obtained two A levels in media studies at a college in Rhos-on-Sea.

19.06 A was very critical in his evidence of Ysgol Talfryn. There was a far stricter regime than he had previously experienced ("much more like a prison or borstal") and some of the houseparents were very domineering and bullying. There was teaching to CSE level but he regarded it as very limited and craft orientated. However, A praised the outdoor activities, which he thoroughly enjoyed, and said that he got on very well with some of the teaching staff: one of them was particularly helpful, taking an active interest in him and making him feel positive (the Headmaster's view, according to A, was that he ought not to have been at the school). A's main allegation was that one member of the care staff, X, was a "vicious bully", who assaulted him (using just hands) many times. X would goad him with (or about) extracts from his personal file but he would not rise to the bait. A alleged also that he had witnessed far worse assaults upon other residents by X, including one with whom the latter had a fist fight on the day that A left.

19.07 The weakness of this witness' evidence is that he named the other residents who had been the victims of assaults by X but they did not support his allegations. One other witness, whose evidence was read, did make complaints about X: he said that X, had on one occasion, grabbed his hair and then dragged him through ground floor corridors, punching and kicking him. This witness alleged also that he had seen X assaulting another boy. We are left, however, in some doubt about the veracity of these allegations, bearing in mind how disturbed some of the children, including A, were at the time, although the number of allegations made against X is troubling. X himself strongly denied them in his written evidence and he alleged that A had telephoned him between 1992 and 1996 threatening that A was "going to have him".

19.08 The second oral witness (B) was at Ysgol Talfryn for about two years from 9 March 1987, when he was just 14 years old. He had been adopted three years earlier but his adoptive father had died. He had been attending Holywell High School but was transferred to Ysgol Talfryn following suspension from the former for disruptive misbehaviour. A serious breakdown in his relationship with his adoptive mother occurred in late 1987 with the result that he was received into voluntary care on 12 February 1988 and placed at Park House as his "home base" whilst continuing to attend Ysgol Talfryn. Thus, he continued to board at Ysgol Talfryn but spent week-ends and vacations at Park House. He remained at the school until the incident described in the next paragraph.

19.09 B's only complaint about Ysgol Talfryn is that he was assaulted by a teacher there at about 10.10 am on 22 February 1989. His account of this was that the teacher (Y) asked him, unusually, to read aloud, whereupon B told Y to "fuck off". Y then grabbed B by the collar and punched him on the chin. B gripped Y back but Y manhandled him out of the class and to a nearby lavatory, where Y pushed him around further whilst another teacher stood guard at the door. Eventually, B smashed a window with his fist and this brought the incident to an end. B had suffered a bang on the head from a wall or the floor (when he had slipped in the classroom); there were also scratches on his neck, where Y had gripped him, and his jaw was sore. His T-shirt was ripped and his coat was torn.

19.10 We have seen substantial documentary evidence relating to this incident, which was reported by B when he returned to Park House at about 4 pm; and a very full account of the matter was recorded by Kevin Bird, one of the residential care staff. That account was much fuller than the summary we have given based on B's oral evidence and it differs in many details but it is unnecessary to repeat it here because it does not affect the substance of the complaint or reflect adversely on B's veracity. Bird's record does indicate, however, that, according to B, Y admitted shortly afterwards that he had probably "gone over the top" and apologised to B at the end of the school day. Y had also offered to shake B's hand and had asked if they were still mates but B had merely said "OK" without shaking Y's hand.

19.11 B had not been offered any treatment or examination at Ysgol Talfryn but he was taken to see a local doctor at Prestatyn, who noted bruises on the back of his head and the left side of his neck. The doctor saw also a minor scratch on the boy's throat, adding (rightly or wrongly) "which apparently he had on a previous incident". A sketch made by Kevin Bird the same day suggests that the injuries were more extensive, albeit minor. A complicating factor was that B had been involved in an incident with the police two days earlier, in which he sustained injuries, some of which were rather similar, but we have been able to distinguish them broadly in the light of the police surgeon's report on the earlier injuries based on his examination of B at 11.40 pm on 20 February 1989.

19.12 It is unnecessary to go into great detail about subsequent events in relation to Y's assault. Michael Barnes was informed and the Child Protection procedure was set in train. A case conference was held on 1 March 1989 at which Barnes, the Assistant Child Protection Officer, various Delyn Area social workers, the police, the Area Health Authority and Park House were represented but Ysgol Talfryn and the NSPCC failed to send representatives. It was decided that the police should be requested to carry out a full investigation and that the Social

Services Department ought to discuss the implications of the incident with the Education Department. The view of the conference was that B had been abused and that his attendance at Ysgol Talfryn should be discontinued pending investigations.

19.13 A second case conference was held on 18 April 1989 at which the representation was similar but wider. The NSPCC was represented and George Austin attended. The purpose of the conference was said to be "to consider conclusions resulting from police interviews of abused child and alleged abuser and to receive representation of events related to the incident of alleged abuse from Education Department representatives". The rather surprising conclusion of the conference was that no child abuse had occurred. No legal proceedings were to be instituted and no further investigations were necessary. Dialogue was to be resumed with the Education Department about B's educational needs. B had a chequered career in 1989, however, including a number of court appearances. He was made the subject of supervision orders in June 1989 and again in December 1989. It seems that he moved to Chevet Hey in June 1989 and then to independent accommodation in Wrexham in December 1989 before being discharged from voluntary care on 17 September 1990.

19.14 Y who received excellent references about his rapport with children on his appointment to Ysgol Talfryn gave oral evidence to the Tribunal and provided a written statement. He said that B was an aggressive and unco-operative person whose usual reply when asked to do anything was "fuck off". He was frequently restrained because of his behavioural problems and complete lack of self-control (but Y's first training course in physical restraint was four years later, in 1993). Y recalled that there was an incident in February 1989, but not the details: Y could certainly have grabbed B's lapels to remove him from the class, because he was unlikely to go willingly and because of his conduct towards Y in front of the other children, and it was inevitable that B would have retaliated. In his oral evidence Y said that he might have held B down on the floor. But Y denied punching B or deliberately banging B's head or causing any scratches to his neck. Y took B to the toilet block so that B could wash his face but did not push him around. Y waited outside the wash room but went in when B broke a window out of frustration and temper. Y denied also that he said to anyone that he had gone over the top but it was not unusual to offer to shake hands after an incident to bring the matter to a close.

19.15 We have not seen the contemporary statements obtained by the police about this incident in 1989 but we have seen what was said by three fellow pupils in the course of the wider investigation in 1992. Our conclusion is that Y certainly did go "over the top" in provocative circumstances on this occasion and we believe that he admitted doing so shortly afterwards. It was not an occasion when physical restraint or any other use of force was called for and, on Y's own evidence, B's choice of offensive language was habitual. In our judgment Y was fortunate to escape disciplinary action for what he did on the basis of our findings and it would have been salutary if he had been given at least an official warning.

19.16 The third oral witness, (C), was also in voluntary care for part of the period during which he attended Ysgol Talfryn. He was a Shropshire boy who was admitted into care on 1 October 1987 and started attending Ysgol Talfryn as a boarder 16 days later, when he was just 14 years old, because he had been suspended from his last local school for unruly behaviour. He continued to attend Ysgol Talfryn until December 1989 or possibly April 1990 but was discharged from care on 4 February 1989. His reviews and reports referred to him as essentially a gentle person who needed tactful handling, despite his record of unruliness, but his home situation was a cause of recurrent stress. In his oral evidence C said that being at Ysgol Talfryn was better than being at home: the teaching was quite good and he achieved a GCSE[1] in woodwork. However, he did not get on with Y, who took physical education. There was mutual dislike and C complained that, on one occasion, Y pulled him by the hair down the football pitch, marched him into a building and prodded him around because he had responded with "fuck off" when told to play goalkeeper. On other occasions Y pushed him to the floor and jumped on his chest with both knees. But C said in his written statement and in his oral evidence that Y did not punch him in the football incident or on any other occasion.

19.17 C's other main complaint was against a careworker at the school who drove two staples into his head with a staple gun, apparently as a joke and without any provocation. C complained then to another member of the staff but nothing was done about it. More generally, C was critical of the methods of restraint used at the school, alleging that four or five men would hold one boy down and that there were always "kids being hit".

19.18 Y told us that he does not recollect B and has no memory of marching him off the football pitch. On the question of restraint generally, he said in his written statement that there were three occasions when children had to be restrained, namely, if they were hitting themselves, if they were hitting or hurting other people or if they were damaging property. If restraint had to be used, it would be the minimum necessary and consisted always of holding, never kicking or punching. The witness referred to in paragraph 19.07 whose evidence was read said that Y enjoyed throwing his weight round and would punch and kick boys for no apparent reason.

19.19 The evidence of one other former resident at Ysgol Talfryn not previously mentioned was read to the Tribunal. He was at the school at a much younger age than the other witnesses, that is, from about nine to 11 years (between 1983 and 1985), but it seems that he was not placed in voluntary care until the first half of 1988. His evidence was that he was treated fairly at the school and he had no complaints about it. He was occasionally slapped but he thinks that it was no more than he deserved.

---

[1] General Certificate in Secondary Education.

Welsh Office inspections

19.20 Ysgol Talfryn was visited by Her Majesty's Inspectors in the summer term of 1988 and we have seen a copy of the comprehensive report that they presented. Of the 63 pupils then on the roll, only seven were girls (five resident). Ten of the pupils had been placed there by authorities other than Clwyd. The report recorded that in its first ten years over 60 pupils had been re-integrated into other schools, of whom only six had gone to special schools; and only a few transfers had been unsuccessful.

19.21 The Headmaster was well qualified and experienced in teaching pupils with behavioural problems. However, none of the nine members of the teaching staff had received "appropriate post-initial qualification relating to work with pupils with emotional, behavioural disorders", although five of them were then studying to obtain such qualifications. The inspectors commented that the general level of experience and qualification was barely appropriate.

19.22 The care staff were headed by an SRCCO, who was responsible to the Headmaster for the residential provision. Under that officer were 14 leaders, 12 houseparents and two night attendants, one of whom was a qualified nurse. Some of these did not have relevant qualifications for the work and a significant number of the staff were recent appointments. Attempts were being made to provide appropriate in-service training.

19.23 The school was organised into nine classes on the basis of "age, ability and socio/emotional compatibility", producing classes of between five and eight pupils; and all classes were taught for varying amounts of time by teachers other than their class teachers. Through contacts established by the staff, work experience was available for pupils over 15 years of age.

19.24 The Inspectors' comments on the quality of care provided by the school were generally favourable but, on behaviour management, they noted that some groups were difficult to handle and some members of the staff showed the need for additional support and training in coping with unruly and disruptive behaviour. Their overall conclusion was that Ysgol Talfryn provided a good level of care and a wide range of opportunities for pupils, which could readily be consolidated to provide more effective education. They commended particularly the school's staff development programmes and its policy of planning for the re-integration of pupils into mainstream education.

19.25 Subsequent inspections by HMIs disclosed much less satisfactory teaching and care. By September 1993 the number of pupils had diminished to 32 boys (ten resident four nights a week). The complement of teachers remained as before but the number of care staff had been reduced to 11. There were six classes, most with no more than five pupils. The classrooms were described as dismal and bleak environments for learning. Aspects of the residential accommodation were better than this but the bedrooms were dismal, "unpersonalised" with much damaged furniture. Relationships between children and care staff seemed to be sound but the inspector described the overall situation as dire. The penultimate paragraph of his report read :

"Numbers on roll are falling (even though there is a national demand for places for pupils with EBD[2]), staffing levels are high, outcomes are poor, resources inadequate, accommodation and learning environments arid."

19.26 The most recent and very full inspection took place in September 1996 by a team of four inspectors over a period of two and a half days. The outcome of this inspection was much more favourable and the number of pupils had increased to 47. (Surprisingly the 25 page report did not disclose the number of resident pupils). Improvements had been made in most of the relevant areas and the school was said to provide good value for money within the available financial resources. A member of the teaching staff had been appointed the Child Protection Co-ordinator. The quality of teaching was assessed as satisfactory or better in 77% (56% good) of the 52 lessons observed, despite an increase to 12 in the average teaching group size and an increased pupil/teacher ratio of 7.6 : 1. The school was said also to function as an orderly community: the staff made every effort to promote a good quality of life and the majority of pupils felt safe and secure in its surroundings.

Conclusions

19.27 It is clear from the successive reports of HMI Inspectors that Ysgol Talfryn has had an up and down history in the 20 or so years that it has existed so far but it has met, at least in part, a widespread need. On the limited evidence that we have received about the school it would be wrong to conclude that there was regular physical abuse and there has been only one unproved complaint of sexual abuse. However, we are satisfied that in the 1980s there were occasions when excessive force was used in restraint of troublesome pupils and others when improper physical chastisement occurred. This underlines the importance of the criticism made in the first of the Inspector's reports (in 1988) that none of the teaching staff then had received any training in dealing with emotionally and behaviourally disturbed children. We regard such training as essential for teaching staff as well as care staff in any school catering for such children; and it is particularly necessary for teachers such as Y, of some physical prowess, who, without training, are likely to rely upon their strength inappropriately to maintain order and discipline.

19.28 Although the quality of care is said to have improved latterly, the history of this to 1993 is disappointing, particularly in the standard of residential accommodation. The school began with quite high aspirations in this respect but there seems to have been a progressive decline, mainly because of inadequate financial resources, and we regard this as a serious failing, bearing in mind the importance of the home environment to an already disturbed child in care.

---

[2] Emotional and behavioural difficulties.

Gwynfa Residential Unit

Brief history

20.01 This unit was established in 1961, as an NHS psychiatric hospital for children, in an Edwardian house with substantial grounds situated in Pen-y-Bryn Road in Upper Colwyn Bay; and there was a school on the site. The residential unit, also known as a clinic, was administered by the Clwyd and Deeside Hospital Management Committee and the school by Denbighshire County Council. The purpose of the facility was to provide residential assessment, investigation and treatment for up to 16 children between two and 13 years old showing evidence of severe emotional maladjustment, difficulties in personality development and psychiatric disorders. Those children thought capable of improvement and who could not be treated satisfactorily at home were admitted on a short term basis, usually for up to one year.

20.02 In 1974 Gwynfa became the responsibility of the new Clwyd Area (from 1982, District) Health Authority and the school that of Clwyd County Council. At the same time the newly designated child psychiatrist for Gwynedd became the co-ordinating consultant, providing two sessions per week, but the consultant admitting the child continued to advise upon and monitor treatment. By then the unit was providing accommodation for up to 25 emotionally disturbed and maladjusted children up to school leaving age and it was described as the residential extension of the North Wales Child Guidance Clinic Service, which was responsible for offering and monitoring all admissions. A League of Friends was attached to the unit.

20.03 In 1981 a child psychiatrist, Dr Barry Kiehn, was appointed specifically for Gwynfa and the concept of a therapeutic community was introduced. The object was to offer the patients opportunities to develop, and to bring about positive behavioural changes; and the emphasis shifted towards working with families. Group and individual psychotherapy were provided and clinical psychologist and social work posts were established, whereas previously such professionals had merely visited the unit from the Child Guidance Service in Old Colwyn.

20.04 From 1982 to 1993 Gwynfa was administered by the Mental Health Unit of Clwyd Health Authority, which became the Community and Mental Health Unit from 1991. The 18 bed unit (as it had become) was visited by the Hospital (later Health) Advisory Service (HAS) in 1987 in the course of its review of services for mentally ill people in Clwyd and found evidence of declining use, in conformity with a national tendency. However, referrals from Gwynedd were increasing and accounted for 50% of referrals. In 1987 as a whole there were 47 admissions and the average length of stay was 104.7 days. There were eight qualified nurses, six other nurses and four psychologists. The HAS recommended that, due to the high cost of the unit, the new clinical management team should evaluate the need for Gwynfa against the increased need for non-residential services.

20.05 In April 1993 the Clwydian Community Care NHS Trust took over the responsibility for administering Gwynfa, which continued to provide residential care for up to 18 youngsters, but in the older age range of 12 to 18 years (it was often referred to as an adolescent unit). It continued to serve Clwyd and Gwynedd with some referrals from Cheshire and northern Powys. About 40 of the larger number of children referred were being admitted annually and the average stay was five months.

20.06 In March 1996, at the end of the period under review by this Tribunal, Gwynfa had 12 in-patient places and six day places but it closed a year later, in March 1997, when the services it offered were transferred to a new unit with better facilities, called Cedar Court, on the outskirts of Colwyn Bay.

20.07 The local education authority (now Conwy) has continued throughout to provide education on the site.

20.08 The person with immediate overall management responsibility for Gwynfa was the (Principal) Nursing Officer, later called Senior Nurse for Child and Adolescent Services, who was responsible for the recruitment and selection of staff, even after the appointment of a full time child psychiatrist in 1981. This officer was also responsible for routine and discipline, subject to consultation with the psychiatrist about children. Prior to reorganisation in 1974 he reported to the consultant psychiatrist but thereafter he reported to the Divisional (later Unit) Nursing Officer, based at the North Wales Hospital in Denbigh, who visited Gwynfa monthly and who had to be consulted about any suspension or dismissal of a nurse. This officer was latterly known as Director of Nursing Services.

20.09 The holder of the senior nursing post at Gwynfa from November 1972 to March 1990 was **Nigel Mannering Berry**, who had already been employed there for nine years, successively as a staff nurse and then a charge nurse; and he had been Acting Nursing Officer for a year before he became established in the post. He was then 37 years old and had qualified as a registered mental nurse in or about 1959 after service in the RAMC between 1954 and 1956. Prior to his transfer to Gwynfa he had been employed at the North Wales Hospital but had been seconded to Clatterbridge Hospital for two years during his period of training. He does not appear to have had any specific training in dealing with disturbed children and adolescents but he had attended management courses at a technical college and Abergele Hospital before his appointment as Nursing Officer.

Previous investigations

20.10 During the period covered by our inquiry there were five internal investigations or reviews of the conduct of specific members of the nursing staff at Gwynfa.

20.11 The first investigation, in 1986, was into an allegation by a boy patient that he had been head-butted by a male staff nurse. The complainant was interviewed by the Divisional Nursing Officer and the outcome was that the nurse received a final warning. He was also transferred from Gwynfa to another hospital to perform services for adults.

20.12 In August 1991 the relationship between a 16 years old girl patient, P, and a 45 years old male nursing auxiliary was investigated following the discovery of a letter in an article of her clothing. This girl, who gave oral evidence to the Tribunal was not in care but was suffering at the time from a depressive disorder. Unfortunately, despite considerable efforts by the clinical staff, they were unable to obtain full details of what had occurred from the girl. The auxiliary, **Robert Martin Williams**, had previously been counselled about his behaviour towards other patients because of concerns expressed by other members of the Gwynfa staff. He denied committing any offence against the girl when interviewed under the Clwyd Health Authority's disciplinary procedure but then resigned before he could be dismissed.

20.13 It was not until January 1996 that P felt able to disclose to the police what had occurred (she had refused to do so when seen by them in September 1993) but a copy of the highly incriminating letter, which we have seen, was still available. According to P, Williams had befriended her at Gwynfa, which she had welcomed, but he had then had sexual intercourse with her against her will twice within the space of a few days. In the event Robert Williams was charged with two offences of rape upon P. He was tried in Mold Crown Court, when P gave evidence, and he was convicted on 14 March 1997 of both offences, for which he received concurrent sentences of six years imprisonment[1].

20.14 Following the appearance on television in September 1991 of a former Gwynfa patient[2], who is identified as A in the preceding chapter, a review of Gwynfa's records from 1975 to 1981 was undertaken by Irene Train, then the Divisional General Manager (North) of Clwyd's Community and Mental Health Unit. The major police investigation had begun and, when the Train report was written for the Health Authority Board, the police had asked for the addresses of 14 former patients and seven past and present members of the staff.

20.15 It became evident by July 1993, in the course of the police inquiries, that allegations of a more serious nature were being made against some members (again past and present) of the Gwynfa staff. A selected member of the NHS Trust that had by then become responsible for Gwynfa saw the relevant statements that had been obtained by the police; and by letter dated 26 July 1993 Detective Superintendent Ackerley was invited to conduct a fuller investigation into Gwynfa. Appropriate documentation and information were supplied to the police, which enabled them to carry out an investigation by sample of all admissions to Gwynfa in the period of our own review to 1993 (and of some earlier admissions).

---

[1] These convictions are referred to in para 50.31(2) because they occurred after the appointment of the Tribunal.
[2] See para 2.24.

20.16 At some stage the NHS Trust became aware that seven former patients of Gwynfa had made serious allegations to the police against a then current member of the staff (Z). The Trust therefore asked the North Wales Police to obtain permission from the authors of the relevant statements for their statements to be released to the NHS Trust for use in the latter's own inquiry and disciplinary procedures. Only four of the former patients gave that permission with the result that the NHS Trust had to investigate the matter on an incomplete basis. The legal advice that the NHS Trust's Board received was that the available evidence was insufficient to justify summary dismissal and it was decided, therefore, to transfer Z to a Psychiatric Day Hospital, where he would not be expected to nurse children. At that time a decision not to prosecute Z had been taken. Later, further allegations were made against Z and he was again suspended from duty in July 1997 pending a decision as to whether he was to be prosecuted. By March 1999, the Crown Prosecution Service had advised that a prosecution would not be justified but as far as we are aware he remained suspended at the time that this report was signed.

Allegations of abuse

20.17 By the end of the Tribunal's hearings, there were 27 complainants who were known to have alleged that they had been abused whilst they were at Gwynfa, but of these three left there before the period of our review began. The latest known date when any of the 24 other complainants left Gwynfa (except P who left on 27 August 1991) was 17 July 1987. Thus, a total of 23 former patients made complaints relating to the period 1974 to 1987; and the evidence is reasonably clear that 13 of these were in care at the time when they were resident in Gwynfa.

20.18 Seven of the relevant 24 complainants made allegations of physical aggression in varying degrees by unidentified members of staff; and one other former girl resident, who was in care, alleged that she had been indecently assaulted by an adolescent male fellow-patient. The remaining 16 made allegations against one or more of eight named members of the staff but ten of them named Z and only one other member of the staff (not Robert Williams) was the subject of allegations by more than two complainants.

20.19 In view of the continuing police investigation into allegations against Z whilst the Tribunal was sitting, we heard evidence from one complainant against him only (when his legal position was not clear to the Tribunal) and none from Z himself. It would be inappropriate, therefore, for us to make any further comment about the allegations save for the brief reference in the next paragraph and paragraph 20.23.

20.20 Allegations of sexual abuse have been made against four members of the staff, including Z and Robert Williams, but they do not suggest a pattern of such abuse amongst the staff, bearing in mind the length of the period under review. They are allegations of sexual abuse in different forms committed by individuals separately from one another. Half of the allegations against Z are of this type of misconduct and they remain to be adjudicated upon; and the only sexual allegations against Robert Williams are those of P, in respect of which he has been convicted. As for the other two members of staff, one is alleged to have been guilty of indecent "groping" in 1978/1979 by a girl patient then 13 years old, who did not report the matter; the other is alleged to have committed buggery with a 17 years old male patient in 1979/1980, but the allegation did not come to light until the complainant was interviewed by the police in August 1992. A decision not to prosecute the alleged offender was taken in the autumn of 1993.

20.21 The Tribunal received evidence in the end from 14 of the former patients of Gwynfa, of whom three gave oral evidence. These three were P, A and the witness who made allegations against Z so that not a great deal can be added here. None of them was in care at the time of his or her stay at Gwynfa but A was received into care later in his youth and the third was in and out of care. P did not make any other complaint about conditions at Gwynfa. She had been abused earlier by another man when she was ten years old and suffered from low self esteem; she had cut herself, made herself sick and taken overdoses before her admission to Gwynfa. However, she found the staff at Gwynfa approachable. There was a complaints system but she thought it was for more trivial things such as arguments and she did not feel able to resort to it in respect of Robert Williams' conduct.

20.22 A was more critical of Gwynfa. He had behaved disruptively as a day boy at a private school in Llandudno but he had thought that he was entering Gwynfa as a hospital for an investigation of a heart condition. He regards his year at Gwynfa as wasted and blames it for his subsequent inappropriate placement at Ysgol Talfryn. He did not receive the medical attention that he thinks he needed and he criticised the educational arrangements because they were not geared to meet the needs of patients staying longer then six weeks: after that period it was repetition. He was frightened initially, until he made some friends, and he had personality clashes with some of the staff. He complained, in particular, of two alleged assaults by male members of staff. The first occurred after a "bandage fight" when two of them made a harness with rubber rings and pulled him up on a door. It was very painful but he did not make a complaint: they said that he should learn to take it "in good spirit". On another occasion one of the two dropped him outside from a ground floor window after some play fighting. He landed on his back, which hurt a great deal. He was also wrongly blamed at Gwynfa for two incidents.

20.23 Finally, the third oral witness went to Gwynfa from her foster home when she was nearly 14 years old and in danger of being excluded from her school. She was at Gwynfa for four and a half months in 1975. She was assessed as of below average ability and was not thought to be bright enough to learn new behaviour patterns through the Gwynfa type of therapy. Later in the year she was admitted in care to Little Acton and Cartrefle successively and she had been in residential care or fostered from the age of three and a half years. She complained about the pyjama punishment (being required to wear pyjamas) then in use at Gwynfa but thought that the school there was very nice. She said also that she told her social worker that she did not like Z but her social worker (a woman) told her not to be silly, that he was nice. When she persisted the social worker said that she was just seeking attention.

20.24 Of seven other main complainants whose evidence was read, only one was able to identify the member of staff who was the alleged aggressor. That witness alleged one specific physical assault by Z and we say no more about it. Another complained of bullying by fellow residents rather than by staff. She was only eight years old when she was admitted to Gwynfa in 1977 and her complaints were that (a) members of staff saw her being bullied and (b) she reported other incidents of bullying to them but nothing was done to stop it. On one occasion she was pushed through a ground floor window by a named girl, who was much bigger then her, and she was taken to the local hospital by a staff member to have her left arm stitched. She was not, however, able to name any of the members of staff alleged to have been at fault.

20.25 The remaining five of these main complainants alleged various physical assaults by unidentified members of staff in the overall period from 1976 to 1984. One, for example, complained of being gagged on half a dozen occasions with elastoplast by a female member of the staff and he said that removal of the gag left him in considerable pain. Another complained of being put in a dog collar, when he was about seven years old, and led around with an attached piece of string for several days by an older resident because he had run away. The third complained of being grabbed and hung out of a window by a staff member who also hit him on the back of the head with a pool cue on another occasion and who used to assault him about twice a week for no reason. Finally, the other two complainants in this group complained respectively of open-handed slaps to one and clips around the ear to the other but the first said that, generally, Gwynfa was well run and the latter said that the clips were no more than he deserved at the time.

20.26 Four other witnesses whose evidence was read touched upon their stays at Gwynfa in statements mainly directed to other matters but they did not add anything of substance to the evidence given by other witnesses. Two of them were critical of the regime, one complaining of being bullied and also of being beaten up by one member of the staff and the other comparing it to a prison. But another, who had a drink problem at the age of about 15 years in 1981, said that his time at Gwynfa was good: he got on well with all the staff, he was not abused or assaulted in any way, and his drinking problem was sorted out.

20.27 The opening submission on behalf of the NHS Trust disclosed that two forms of punishment, known respectively as "pyjama therapy"[3] and "bed therapy" were discontinued on unspecified dates many years ago. The former involved putting children in pyjamas for a specified period following absconding or repeated aggressive behaviour towards other residents. The latter meant taking away the resident's pyjamas (and thus confining them to bed for practical purposes) but it was used only for repeated absconders for specified short periods and when a resident was considered to be significantly at risk of deliberate self harm. It is accepted by the NHS Trust that such practices would be questionable by today's standards although it suggests that "they were acceptable at the time".

[3] See para 20.23.

Conclusions

20.28 The picture that we have received of conditions at Gwynfa has been incomplete for a variety of reasons but most notably because we have not been able to investigate the activities of Z, who was on the staff of Gwynfa from April 1974 until he was suspended in July 1993, pending the outcome of an internal inquiry. We have not attempted therefore to reach detailed conclusions about the regime at Gwynfa. It is clear from what we have said, however, that sexual abuse did occur during the period under review. We accept also that on occasions unjustified physical force was used by staff members and sometimes inappropriate methods of punishment or restraint. The evidence that we have heard does underline the vulnerability of young children when they are living in a residential clinic like Gwynfa, whether or not they are formally in care at the time. The problem of protecting them from abuse is closely akin to that which arises in community homes and, in our judgment, similar measures to stamp out abuse and to prevent its recurrence are appropriate for both kinds of establishment.

20.29 In view of the similarities between a residential clinic for children who may be emotionally or behaviourally disturbed and some community homes there is a strong argument for greater social service involvement in the former, particularly when a substantial proportion of children admitted to the clinic are already in care. We are not persuaded that it is necessarily right to leave the care of such children over periods that may be a year or longer in the hands of nursing staff alone. The nursing staff at Gwynfa appear to have been recruited from mental nursing resources (often male) and many of them had little or no experience of dealing with disturbed children. It is strongly arguable, therefore, that some trained residential care staff ought to be introduced into the staff establishment and that the senior staff at the residential unit, whether or not they are nursing officers primarily, should have an appropriate qualification in residential child care.

20.30 It must be said, however, that, in her written evidence to the Tribunal, Irene Train said that there have been considerable developments at Gwynfa (and its successor). She referred specifically to an on-going programme to improve the training of individual members of staff and continuing efforts to increase the involvement of parents in the care of their children. For some years before its close children were being admitted to Gwynfa on a four day week basis, returning home at week-ends. As for child protection, confidential free telephone facilities have been provided for patients to obtain independent counselling and child advocacy services are being established. Moreover, child residents are now informed by means of a bi-lingual leaflet of their right to have complaints dealt with by the Chief Executive with a right of appeal to a non-executive director of the NHS Trust. It is said also that steps have been taken to strengthen staff recruitment procedures and to ensure that staff "are appropriately qualified to work with children".

PART IV

ALLEGED ABUSE OF CHILDREN IN CARE
IN PRIVATE RESIDENTIAL
ESTABLISHMENTS IN CLWYD
BETWEEN 1974 AND 1996

The Bryn Alyn Community

History and Organisation

21.01 We have set out in paragraphs 4.10 to 4.11 and 4.23 to 4.27 an outline of the foundation and subsequent expansion of this organisation and it is necessary to fill in some of the details here.

21.02 **John Ernest Allen** was born in Walsall on 22 July 1941 but his family subsequently moved to Gloucestershire, where he underwent training in hotel management after leaving school. He was later employed in the hotel trade in Oxfordshire and Worcestershire and became interested in residential care work in the course of conversations with care workers at a school. According to his own statement, he worked in various private sector children's residential homes in Gloucestershire over a period of about six years before he moved to Holywell in Flintshire in or about 1965 to work at the Talbot Hotel, which was being used by his then employers to train adolescents in the range of 15 to 18 years; and he became interested in making alternative provisions for children who, at that time, were being sent to approved schools.

21.03 In or before 1968 the owner of Bryn Alyn Hall offered to give the house to Dr Barnardo's Homes for use as a children's home but the offer was declined with the result that in 1968 John Allen was able to acquire a 21 years lease of the 50 acre property in Llay New Road on the outskirts of Wrexham on favourable terms with an option to purchase after seven years. In April 1969, in partnership with his wife-to-be, whom he married in 1970, his parents and an uncle, Thomas Askew, Allen opened a children's home at Bryn Alyn with 12 staff to provide for up to 20 boys in the age range of 11 to 16 years. None of the nine care staff, other than Allen and his future wife, had any previous experience of residential work with children and none of them had any formal qualifications for the work. There was one teacher who had experience in remedial teaching.

21.04 From 1968 until he retired in 1990, ostensibly on health grounds, Allen was, at least nominally, in charge of the affairs of the Bryn Alyn Community, including care issues, although it was said by one witness specifically that he had divested himself of day to day control by the mid-1980s. The private limited company, Bryn Alyn Community Ltd, was formed in 1972, on the advice of accountants, and it appears that Allen remained chief executive until 1990. The freehold of Bryn Alyn Hall was purchased with the aid of a mortgage when the company was formed. Norma Allen, his wife, occupied the post of Matron until late in the 1970s.

21.05 In this chapter we deal with complaints of abuse from former residents at four main establishments within the Bryn Alyn Community. These were as follows:

(a) **Bryn Alyn Hall**

The main house was enlarged and divided after the freehold had been acquired and an additional residential establishment was built near the house. The three parts of the property were then called Askew House, Blackley House and Lindisfarne.

(b) **Pentre Saeson Hall**

This smaller country house at Bwlchgwyn, near Wrexham, was acquired in 1970 and opened on 27 September that year as a children's home for children younger then those at Bryn Alyn Hall. The provision was intended to be for up to 20 boys between the ages of 11 and 13 years.

(c) **Bryntirion Hall**

This house in Mold Road, Caergwrle, was purchased by Allen in 1972 in trust for the Community and was intended to provide hostel accommodation for 15 working boys between 16 and 18 years.

(d) **Gatewen Hall**

This is in Berse Road, New Broughton, Wrexham, and had been a residential school prior to its purchase by the Community in or about 1982. It was opened on 1 April 1983 as a children's home to provide for 14 boys and girls in the age range of 14 to 18 years with a view to preparing them for independence.

21.06 In paragraphs 4.23 and 4.24 we have referred to some seven other properties owned by the Bryn Alyn Community from time to time, including one in Cheshire and one in Shropshire, but it is unnecessary to refer to them in greater detail here for the purpose of relating the alleged abuse within the Community in Clwyd. John Allen estimated that at its peak the Community was accommodating about 200 children and adolescents. At that time Marton's Camp in Cheshire and Cotsbrook Hall in Shropshire were still operating within the Community so that the figure for Clwyd would not have exceeded about 120 but other evidence suggests that the total occupancy in Clwyd alone exceeded 150 at times during the 1980s. It is important to stress, however, that only a small proportion of the children who went to the Bryn Alyn Community as a whole were placed there by either Clwyd County Council or Gwynedd County Council. The point is illustrated by analysis of the complainants known to the Tribunal who were formerly residents of one or more of the four homes listed in the preceding paragraph. The most accurate assessment that we can make is that, of a total of 172 complainants, only nine were placed by Clwyd and eight by Gwynedd (no information is available about three).

21.07 Reverting to the history of the company, we cannot be confident of the accuracy of some of the details that have emerged in the evidence, but the general picture is reasonably clear. The company was very much a family concern initially with Allen's father as chairman, Allen himself as chief executive and his uncle (Askew) the director responsible for estate management. Allen held a majority of the shares with the balance in the hands of his wife, Allen senior and Askew.

21.08 **Kenneth Henry White** (White senior) became involved in the affairs of the Community after selling his hotel to the company for £130,000 on 11 July 1977. He had run the large house at Cefn-y-Bedd, near Wrexham, as White Sands Hotel in the 1970s but it reverted to its former name of Gwastad Hall after acquisition by the Community and it was used principally as offices but also to provide accommodation for some children and the Allen family. The Allens had lived early on in their marriage in a bungalow three miles from Bryn Alyn Hall and later spent a period at Bryntirion Hall before moving into Gwastad Hall with Allen senior and Askew. White senior was suffering from ill health at about this time and was advised to take some work as a form of therapy with the result that he became, initially, a volunteer in overall charge of the Community's catering. He said in evidence that he did not have any involvement with child care matters, individual units, staff recruitment or the provision of education either then or later, but it is clear that he soon became increasingly involved in the financial affairs of the Community.

21.09 In or about 1980 White senior invested £300,000 in the company in return for a salary and an income on his investment. It seems that in November 1983 he accepted appointment as chief executive of the company but it is unlikely that this took effect because on 1 April 1984 he was appointed Business Administrator of the company for a period of five years at a salary of approximately £13,000 (and Allen was still on the scene). Then, on 14 August 1984, he was appointed finance director, his employment and salary continuing; and 2,000 shares were allocated to him in return for a payment of £3,000 and a loan to the company of £20,000.

21.10 The sketchy documentation available to us and the complications of the various property transactions make it impossible to trace accurately the financial dealings between White senior, Allen and the company. However, it seems reasonably clear that White senior made a number of subsequent loans to the company (mostly secured on the company's properties) and substantially increased his shareholding at the expense of Allen. By February 1990 his secured loans to the company amounted to £356,000 and there was also an unsecured loan to Allen himself of £20,000. Further transfers of shares followed and on 16 October 1991 Allen was "paid off", to use White senior's words.

21.11 It seems that by October 1991 Allen was indebted to the company in the sum of about £210,000 on his director's loan account. The agreement made with him was that he should receive the equivalent of £510,000 for his remaining 13,695 shares in the company, which were to be cancelled, and that an additional payment of £50,000 was to be made to him and his wife as compensation for loss of office. Of the £510,000, about £210,000 was to be in cash and was to be used to repay his loan account. The balance of £300,000 was represented by the release of a company car (£10,000) and of the company's interest in a Brighton property, a French villa and a boat (£200,000), similar release of the company's interest in a cottage in Gloucestershire (£80,000) and the transfer of the company's 100 per cent shareholding in Bryn Alyn Care Ltd (£10,000), which had been a subsidiary of the company for only seven weeks or so, that is, from 25 August 1991. There was a separate transaction also immediately before this in which Allen transferred 1,300 shares in the company to White senior. The price ultimately agreed for the latter shares was £26,000 but this probably took into account Allen's personal indebtedness to White senior.

21.12 Bryn Alyn Community Ltd continued to trade thereafter with White senior holding 17,995 of the 19,405 issued shares (including 3,100 new shares issued on 16 October 1991). There were protracted discussions with the banks in relation to their security for loans and about re-structuring the company. Eventually, probably in 1995, re-structuring was effected: the various properties were transferred to a new company[1], Bryn Alyn (Holdings) Ltd, whilst Bryn Alyn Community Ltd became the trading company, carrying on the care and educational activities. There were continuing registration difficulties, however, leading to voluntary liquidation of the trading company on 6 March 1997[2]. White senior gave evidence before the Tribunal on 15 July 1997 but he died at the end of the year.

21.13 Although the venture ended in financial failure, it enjoyed about 20 years of considerable success and, as late as 1990, it had about 150 employees. Allen claimed that, at the height of the company's trading, which he put in the mid-1980s, its annual turnover was about £2.6m and the profit of the order of £80,000 to £90,000. Accounts between 1977 and 1990 show that the total turnover, made up almost entirely of payments by local authorities, was £28.25m and that Allen's salary in 1988 was £204,894. However, by 1990 his salary was shown as £50,000 (and White senior's salary then was £28,000).

21.14 It has not been necessary for us to consider in depth the administrative structure of the Bryn Alyn Community and it would have been difficult to do so in view of the limited documentation available to us. It is necessary, however, to mention that some other directors joined the board from time to time. In particular, **Kenneth J White** (White junior), the son of White senior, assumed an increasingly prominent role from the early 1990s and he remains active in the affairs of Bryn Alyn (Holdings) Ltd. He became a shareholder (500 shares) in Bryn Alyn Community Ltd, when new shares were issued in 1991, and then joined the board. Similarly, **Stephen J Elliott**[3] became a shareholder at the same time as White junior and subsequently a director for a short period before moving on to run Prospects, the successor of Bersham Hall. He had been a co-ordinator of child care at Blackley before undertaking a university degree course, after which he became part of the Community's senior management on the child care side. The company secretary for many years was

---

[1] However, Pentre Saeson Hall, valued at £150,000, was transferred to White senior in lieu of a three year pension on 2 February 1995.
[2] See paras 4.25 to 4.27.
[3] See para 13.03.

D Russell Evans. He acted also as personnel officer and was director of administration from about 1987, succeeding **Frederick Streetly**, formerly a probation officer in Liverpool, who was the first holder of the latter position from 1982.

21.15 We were told there were a number of senior managers answerable to the board of directors. These included a financial manager, a liaison manager, an education manager and a divisional director of child care (North Wales). The role of the liaison manager, who was qualified and experienced in social work, was to be responsible for liaison with local authorities, to deal with referrals and to co-ordinate visits and inspections. This post was held successively by Norman Wainwright, a former Liverpool social worker who later became marketing director; John Dickinson; and Stephen Elliott. The education manager was head of the teaching unit and was probably Adrian Jarvis who became Headmaster at Bryn Alyn Hall after teaching at Marton's Camp.

21.16 According to Allen, his aim and that of the Community was for the regime to provide (in contrast to approved schools based on training and discipline) an environment that was as close as possible to that of a family: it was to be "stimulating and responsive, a therapeutic environment". His idea was to provide a wide spectrum of establishments for youngsters and adolescents, ranging from residential special schools to various types of homes for children and on to halfway houses preparing young people for independent living, with later after care support for the vulnerable. Moreover, each unit had to be flexible in order to cater for individual needs, with a variable balance between containment and instruction for the same reason.

21.17 Allen's scheme was to have each of these units run by a head or senior officer who would be professionally qualified and he claimed to have achieved this for all the units by 1990. Under the head there was to be a deputy and two teams, each with a team leader, working on a shift basis. There was also a night service of security staff, in effect, one being assigned to each unit on 'waking duty' from 11 pm to 7 am, complemented by sleeping in duty care staff.

The Community's intake

21.18 We do not know specifically of any children who were placed with the Community privately. The vast majority of the children were in care and were placed at Bryn Alyn by local authority Social Service Departments. However, analysis of the complainants' origins does not suggest any particular pattern in relation to these local authorities. We understand that initially placements by authorities in the north-east may have predominated but overall it seems that the Community attracted placements by authorities throughout England, from Newcastle and Durham in the north to Bromley in the south and from Blackpool in the west to Lincoln in the east. The London boroughs were prominent, as were Manchester and the West Midlands but there was no child from a South Wales authority on the list of complainants[4]. It was undoubtedly

---

[4] See para 21.06 for the Clwyd and Gwynedd numbers.

a deliberate policy of Allen to maximise the Community's intake and he said in evidence that he circularised no less than 38 local authorities with particulars of the facilities that he claimed to provide at an early stage.

21.19 The member of staff responsible for contact with local authorities was the liaison manager (and presumably later the marketing director also). According to Allen, all the placing authorities inspected the premises before any child or young person was admitted from that authority but this must, in our view, refer to a first placement only. The inspections were conducted by senior managers from each local authority who were responsible for 'out of authority' placements. Allen claimed also that senior management from 30 or more placing agencies using the Community, especially those with a number of residents on the premises contemporaneously, were accustomed to visit and inspect the facilities every six months or so. Each child's social worker also was expected to attend once every six months for the purpose of reviewing the child.

21.20 Assessment of children on their reception by the Community was the responsibility of the liaison manager, in conjunction with the head of the unit to which a child was intended to be assigned, and the head of education. The Community did not provide any formal observation and assessment facilities but it did have available the services of an educational psychologist and a child psychiatrist on a contractual basis.

21.21 Whilst Allen no doubt intended to describe in his evidence how his system was designed to work, we heard evidence from several members of the staff of the influence of commercial pressures. Thus, we were told that the Community was paid more to cope with difficult youngsters with the result that, when staff advised that the Community was not the right place for a particularly difficult or troubled child, they would nevertheless be encouraged to persevere: many (according to one member of staff), or at least some, children were retained when they ought to have been placed elsewhere. It appears also that many emergency placements were accepted without consideration by the placing authority or the Community of the suitability of the placement or preparation of the child. There would be phone calls from a local authority pleading that a child should be taken in overnight until a place for the child could be found and, once in, the child would remain with the Community for months. One former member of staff spoke of a policy of "packing them in" at Pentre Saeson (not at Gatewen) and we were told that during a period of industrial action by social workers there were as many as 35 children in Pentre Saeson (in contrast to an optimum number of 20). Again, we were told by a staff member that it was decided to admit girls to the Community because the charge for girls was twice that for boys.

21.22 Finally, the facilities provided by the Community were intended to be essentially for long term care. Of the 172 complainants known to the Tribunal, it appears that only six stayed for six months or less whilst the large majority were there for periods of two or three years and upwards, the longest for ten years.

Allegations of sexual abuse

John Ernest Allen

21.23   Any account of the alleged sexual abuse by Community staff must inevitably begin with the allegations against **John Allen** himself. We know of 28 former male residents who have alleged that they were sexually abused by Allen whilst they were placed with the Community and six have alleged that they were buggered by him. Of these potential witnesses, six gave oral evidence to the Tribunal and we received in evidence the written statements of six others.

21.24   As we said in Chapter 2[5] Allen was convicted on 9 February 1995 in the Crown Court at Chester of six offences of indecent assault committed on young male residents of the Community between 1972 and 1983. Each offence involved a different resident. Allen was acquitted of four other counts of indecent assault involving four separate former residents alleged to have been committed between 1979 and 1984. Four other former residents gave "similiar fact" evidence. He was sentenced to six years' imprisonment on each of the counts of which he was convicted, the sentences to run concurrently. Allen denied the offences and maintained his denial when he gave oral evidence to the Tribunal on 16 and 17 February 1998 but there has not been any appeal.

21.25   We heard evidence from five of the former residents who were witnesses in that trial (two in respect of whom a conviction was recorded, two who gave "similar fact" evidence and one in relation to whom there was an acquittal). The statements read to us included one by a witness in respect of whom Allen was convicted, but who died before the Tribunal's hearings began, in circumstances to which we will refer later. The statements included also the evidence of the third "similar fact" witness. It follows that, in all, 19 former residents have given evidence of sexual abuse by Allen either at the trial or to the Tribunal in oral or written form.

21.26   The first (A) of the two witnesses before the Tribunal in respect of whom Allen was convicted of indecent assault gave oral evidence to us that he lived with the Community between 1973 and 1975. He alleged that he was abused first by Allen after he had been at Bryn Alyn Hall a few months. A was then 13 years old and Allen went to A's bedroom and kissed A before making A masturbate him. Similar incidents occurred about 12 times at Bryn Alyn Hall but Allen did not go further there. When A moved to Bryntirion Hall after about 12 months, the sexual abuse by Allen continued and occurred "quite a few times" in the form of masturbation and then oral sex. A said that he was confused and did not complain. He was given a few presents, more than the others, such as shoes and clothes, cassettes, a record player, a guitar, vouchers and money. After he left at the age of 15 years he received a Yamaha 50cc motor cycle from Allen, just before his 16th birthday in December 1975.

21.27   The second witness in this category (B) was with the Community much longer, from July 1974, when he was ten years old; and he was there with three brothers. He was not indecently assaulted by Allen until he was 13 or 14 years

---

[5] See para 2.35(6).

old and had moved on from Pentre Saeson Hall and then Bryn Alyn Hall to Wilderness Mill Farm[6]. B was sharing a flat there with two other boys and became worried on one occasion that he had swallowed some glass whilst drinking milk. Allen turned up, which was not unusual, and took B to Gwastad Hall in his Range Rover to stay the night. Whilst there Allen took B to the lavatory, made B lie down there and asked B to touch him; he undid his trousers and asked B to masturbate him, which B did. B's explanation of this was that he was frightened of Allen because B had seen him lose his temper and knew that he could be violent. Allen asked B if he was worried and whether he was missing anything that would make him happy. B alleged also that Allen went further and forced himself into B, penetrating him: it was painful and B discovered later in his bedroom that he was bleeding. Allen was interrupted because his wife made a noise. Allen left the room briefly and then returned, telling B to go to his bedroom. B said also that he was too scared to tell anyone what had happened. A couple of days later Allen picked B up at his flat and took him to Wrexham, where Allen asked him if there was anything that he wanted. B pointed out a hi-fi system costing about £500 and Allen bought it for him.

21.28   Later on there was a fire at the Wilderness Mill flats with the result that B had to move back to the main building of Bryn Alyn Hall. He alleged that Allen then assaulted him in his dormitory in the same way as on the first occasion. There were three other beds in the dormitory but they were unoccupied at the time. Altogether there were about four occasions when indecent assaults occurred: the first two culminating in buggery have been described, and the others occurred respectively at Bryn Alyn Hall and at a flat in Rhos(llannerchrugog), bought by Allen, where B stayed. On the third and fourth occasions only touching occurred. This witness also referred to further presents that he received from Allen: he received a pedal cycle as a Christmas present on one occasion and later a new Suzuki 50cc motor cycle. Allen also helped B with loans to purchase two subsequent more powerful second hand motor cycles.

21.29   B gave a full account of the first incident, at Gwastad Hall, when he was first interviewed by the police in May 1993 but did not then allege that it had gone beyond mutual masturbation or that there had been subsequent incidents. He was not willing at that stage to give oral evidence against Allen but he agreed to do so later. In his written statement to the Tribunal in October 1996 he said that there had been five other occasions when Allen had assaulted him but it was not until he gave oral evidence to the Tribunal that he spoke of the alleged acts of buggery. His explanation for not telling the police or the Tribunal about these acts earlier was that he was concerned about the effect such disclosure might have on his small business and upon his intended move from Manchester, where he was when interviewed by the police, back to North Wales.

---

[6] See para 4.24.

21.30 This witness said also in evidence that, when he was 14 or 15 years old, he suffered from anal bleeding. A member of staff whom he told about it arranged an appointment for him at the Wrexham hospital but he was told at the hospital that it was caused by "piles". He did not tell the staff at the hospital what had happened nor did he tell the general practitioner whom he saw on another occasion.

21.31 One of the two "similar fact" witnesses at Allen's trial (C) was admitted to the Community at Cotsbrook Hall[7] initially in September 1982 but went on to Bryntirion Hall in October 1984 and then to Gatewen Hall in January 1985. C alleged that Allen sexually abused him when he was 16 years old and living at Bryntirion Hall. The first incident involved oral sex and occurred during what purported to be a counselling session at Gwastad Hall and subsequent incidents occurred there when Allen telephoned him to visit Gwastad Hall or there was a pre-arranged meeting. C alleged also that Allen buggered him once at the Poyser Street studio[8]. That was the only occasion when he was buggered but indecent assaults continued when he was at Gatewen Hall. In return Allen gave him presents of money from time to time such as £20 by way of pocket money and £45 to buy a jacket.

21.32 C said that, eventually, in or about 1986, he went to Brighton at Allen's suggestion after staying in three of Allen's halfway houses. Allen told him to get a rented flat in Brighton for which Allen would pay and Allen provided him with four weeks rent as a deposit. Allen told him that he had had a fragmented life and that Allen would be a father to him; but on other occasions he called C his boy friend. The sexual relationship continued and he received about £150 per week spending money in addition to having the bills paid. Allen visited him monthly and later fortnightly when he moved to another flat in Brighton. They met also in London and at Allen's home in Gloucestershire. The relationship continued until the early 1990s when C was 23 or 24 years but there were difficulties about terminating it because of the mortgage payments on a third flat into which C had moved.

21.33 C made several statements to the police covering a wide range of matters in the course of their overall investigation. It is clear, however, that he alleged that he had been buggered by Allen in his first statement made on 5 September 1993.

21.34 The second "similar fact" witness (D) gave a rather different picture of his relationship with Allen. D was one of the first three boys to enter Bryn Alyn Hall and his recollection is that he did so on 24 October 1968, his 16th birthday, which was six months before the home opened formally. D remained there for about 18 to 20 months, by which time there were 30 to 40 boys. He had met Allen earlier at a children's home in Gloucestershire and had been invited by Allen to move to Bryn Alyn Hall. D described a number of occasions when Allen had made sexual advances to him, which he had rejected, and he said that Allen had admitted several times to him that he (Allen) was a homosexual. After leaving Bryn Alyn Hall there was a period in 1971 when, according to D,

[7] See para 4.23.
[8] Ibid.

he looked after Gwersyllt Hall for Allen, whilst living at Brymbo. D wrote a poem called "The Ruin", which prompted Allen to suggest that D should be filmed reading it out as part of a documentary film. They went to the Poyser Street studio to collect equipment and then returned to Gwersyllt Hall. After D had read over the poem three or four times and some drink had been consumed Allen said that it would give it more poignancy if D were to take his clothes off and he did so. D was then filmed several times reading the poem whilst naked. Allen started touching D, saying that his skin was incredibly soft; D became aggravated and an altercation ensued, bringing the filming session to an end.

21.35 Many years later, in 1977 or 1978, this witness visited Allen at Bryntirion Hall to ask him for money to enable D to buy an amplifier. D's justification for doing this was that Allen had encouraged him to come back if he needed a bit of pocket money because they were all one big family. On this occasion Allen gave D a glass of brandy and then sat very close to him, putting an arm around him and trying to pull him closer but D pulled away, saying that if he were ever to want to do anything in that way it would not be because of money. The upshot was that Allen accepted the rejection and he still gave D a cheque, albeit post-dated by three weeks.

21.36 The third "similar fact" witness (E), whose evidence was read to us and who was unwilling to give oral evidence to the Tribunal, lived with the Community between 1973 and 1975, as far as we have been able to ascertain. E alleged that Allen first made an indecent approach to him when he was at a summer camp in the grounds of Bryn Alyn Hall. On that occasion Allen stroked his head, cheek and upper body. Later on Allen sexually abused him in his bedroom at Bryntirion Hall: Allen, who had alcohol on his breath, entered the room whilst E was asleep and put his hand down inside E's pyjamas. On another occasion, about three months later, E awoke to discover that Allen was fondling E's penis. E pushed him away and the boy in the next bed stirred, whereupon Allen left the room.

21.37 The evidence that we have so far summarised gives a broad picture of the sexual activities of Allen of which complaint has been made. We heard or read the evidence of six other witnesses who alleged sexual abuse by Allen. One of the two who gave oral evidence alleged that he had been indecently assaulted on about 12 occasions whilst he was asleep but he was not an impressive witness and the jury found Allen not guilty of the count relating to him.

21.38 The other live witness (F), who gave a better impression, was with the Community for nearly six years from March 1975 (two months or so before his tenth birthday). F said that he was very close to Allen, who seemed to take to him from the instant when Allen saw him. Allen spoilt him with presents, clothes and money and both staff and residents called him "John's boy". F alleged that Allen fondled F's private parts on many occasions from very early on mainly in F's bedroom: it happened in Bryn Alyn Hall, Pentre Saeson, Bryntirion Hall, Allen's house (Gwastad Hall, where F often slept), at the Poyser Street studio and on group holidays to the Bryn Alyn property in St Florien, near Bordeaux. Allen would also try and kiss F when he drank and F was very upset by it. The most severe assaults occurred when Allen was drunk and F would pretend that he was asleep. Despite all this, F continued to regard Allen as a father figure. F was nearly 16 years old when he was transferred to Tŷ'r Felin by Gwynedd Social Services Department on 6 January 1981[9]; and he was given a Kawasaki 50cc motor cycle by Allen after he left. F kept in touch with Allen for a couple of years and was in touch with him again at the time of the trial: he said in evidence that he was not going to claim anything from Allen.

21.39 It is necessary to mention specifically one other witness (G), whose evidence was read and in respect of whom Allen was convicted of indecent assault. G was the brother of D and he went to Bryn Alyn Hall at the age of 12 or 13 years in or about 1971, after D had left. G described how he was given special attention in the first six months of his stay by Allen, who bought him new clothes and gave him a pedal cycle at Christmas. He alleged that the first indecent assault on him occurred just before Christmas 1971 when Allen led him from Askew House to a staff bedroom in the main house and there undressed him on a bed, whereupon Allen fondled and kissed him. A similar incident then occurred on New Year's Eve, when mutual masturbation occurred. G said that Allen assaulted him after this in a similar manner at least once a month until he left Bryn Alyn at the age of 15 or 16 years. Oral sex occurred on one occasion only.

21.40 After G left Bryn Alyn he went to London and slept rough for about 12 months, earning money as a rent boy. He then moved to Amsterdam for 17 years, where he had occupations varying from rent boy to computer programmer, and he attempted to take his own life on several occasions. Allen got in touch with him there and sent him presents of money ranging between £250 and £1,000 from time to time. In 1992 G moved to Brighton, where a younger brother who had also been at Bryn Alyn was already living. He referred in his statement to the police made on 22 October 1992 to a visit paid by Allen to his brother's flat when G was present and said that two weeks later (on the 18 April 1992) this brother was killed in a fire in a flat in a converted house in Brighton. The verdict at the inquest was that the brother had been unlawfully killed[10]. G gave evidence at Allen's trial but was found dead on a mattress in his flat on 1 February 1995 before the trial was concluded. The inquest verdict in his case was that the cause of death was "non-dependent abuse of drugs".

21.41 Of the other four witnesses whose evidence was read to us, only one alleged that Allen had buggered him. This witness first met Allen in Gloucestershire and then moved to the Talbot Hotel at Holywell before becoming a resident with the Community. He was born in 1949 and his allegation is of a single incident at the Talbot Hotel; he does not allege any repetition when he was living with the Community and his evidence is not directly relevant to our terms of reference because he must have been discharged from care in or about 1968, if (as he says he did) he remained with the Community until he was 19 years old.

---

[9] For comment on this transfer see para 46.44.

[10] The investigation into this fire by Sussex Police was re-opened in the course of the Tribunal's hearings but no arrest has been made.

This witness did, however, make the allegation in his first statement to the police on 1 June 1995, which post-dated Allen's trial. Another witness alleged inexplicably that he was "groped" by Allen on the second day of the witness' three week stay at Bryn Alyn in 1979. The other two witnesses, however, gave more credible accounts of indecent assaults of a familiar pattern by Allen during their respective stays with the Community from 1971 to 1975 and from 1981 to 1982, the earlier resident alleging also four attempts at buggery.

21.42 The evidence that we have outlined highlights two particular aspects of Allen's alleged sexual activities, namely, his selection of individual boys for particular attention and favouritism and his practice of giving very valuable presents to those boys. Allen's own estimate of the amount of Community money that he spent on extra support to child residents, over and above pocket money and incidentals, was £180,000. This total represented the overall cost of presents of the kind we have referred to, including stereo equipment, bicycles and clothes, the cost of accommodation and help with rent, and financial support. Allen denied, however, that this money was spent in return for favours received and the evidence does not support the view that his generosity was confined to those residents with whom he had a sexual relationship. The impression given is that he was much more generous to those with whom he had such a relationship.

21.43 When Allen gave evidence to the Tribunal, he repeated his previous denials of any sexual activity with Community residents and said that all the complainants were lying about him. He explained his policy in giving presents, usually in the name of the Community rather than himself, and said that they were given mainly to boys rather than girls because of their particular needs: for example, hi-fi equipment was given to everyone who moved into flats and bicycles were given to residents in employment to enable them to travel to work etc. Financial support was provided also for those leaving care who needed it and he, Allen, contributed some of this personally. Allen referred particularly to £6,000 he had advanced to two former residents who were starting a catering firm and to sums provided for witnesses C, D and G. Allen estimated that between £7,000 and £8,000 had been provided to the family of D and G by the Community and himself and he said that it was he who went to Holland to get D to return to the UK. As for C, again money had been provided by the Community and himself: he estimated that C had received about £12,000 in all. He felt that C had been blackmailing him: C had been to a newspaper and his demand for money was a result of his drug taking. On the other hand, Allen denied that a particular demand for £500 that he received from another former resident, 12 years after the latter left the Community, was a form of blackmail. That former resident did not give evidence to the Tribunal but he was one of the six in respect of whom Allen was convicted of indecent assault and Allen agreed that the £500 was paid to him (part of about £2,000 in all that he received).

21.44 Despite Allen's continuing denials of improper conduct, we are fully satisfied that he was rightly convicted of indecent assaults on six former residents with the Community and that those offences were merely a sample of his overall offending in that respect, involving many more residents there between 1968 and about 1985. When Allen was tried early in 1995 he was not charged with any offence of buggery but we have heard evidence from three witnesses who alleged that they were buggered by him and another who said that he attempted to do so on four occasions. The fairest judgment that we can make upon this matter is that there is now credible evidence that Allen's offences went beyond indecent assaults on some occasions but that we cannot make a more decisive finding, bearing in mind the procedural limitations of an inquiry like this. We should add that the complaints of buggery and attempted buggery by three of the four witnesses whose evidence we have heard were not made until after Allen's trial, even though two of the three made the complaints in their first statements to the police.

21.45 We do not have adequate material on which to reach confident conclusions about Allen's overall motivation in his non-sexual activities but it is fair to say that his reputation was that of a caring and generous person. As one member of the Community staff, Keith Allan Evans, who was employed there for 23 years, put it, "he came across to me as a person, not just to me but to everyone else as well, (as) a very, very caring person who devoted a lot of his time and finances, you know, to the young people. I mean we have seen some extraordinary expenses that he spent on young people, not just individuals, I'm talking generally speaking, and we thought he was just an extremely generous person".

21.46 The evidence that we have heard indicates that from the late 1980s Allen became less involved with the Community as financial difficulties arose and White senior assumed the dominant role. Allen then turned his attention elsewhere, to London and Brighton particularly, where he and/or the company Bryn Alyn Care Ltd had acquired various properties; and Allen took over that company in the 1991 financial settlement[11]. It appears that these properties were used, probably mainly, to house young men who had been discharged from care but it has not been within the scope of our terms of reference to investigate these later activities of Allen. Such evidence as has been given about them to the Tribunal has been largely hearsay, although not remote hearsay, and it would be inappropriate to make any findings about them; but the evidence has given us some cause for concern and has underlined the vulnerability of many young persons on leaving care.

21.47 We are satisfied that there was some contemporaneous discussion or gossip about Allen's predilections amongst both staff and residents. Indeed, in view of his favouritism and distribution of presents, it would have been very surprising if there had not been such talk. There were rumours amongst the residents about his liking for particular boys and some talk of "Allen's bum boys" but it did not amount to a great deal. These rumours were known to some members of the staff but they do not appear to have taken them seriously. Keith Evans did, however, go somewhat further in the evidence. He said that when staff heard rumours about Allen being gay and interfering with young boys nothing was ever said to the effect that he was interfering with a particular boy: it was his general reputation with "the few" and the staff put it down to

---

[11] See para 21.11.

jealousy. There was an occasion in about 1981 or 1982 when he was asked to go to Llay police station and was there questioned by two police officers (one of whom he knew) about allegations by some boys that Allen was interfering with them and about a boy in custody in the north east who said that he had been receiving money from Allen to keep him quiet. Evans was told that an investigation was being carried out and that he must not discuss the matter with anyone but, as far as he is aware, nothing happened after that.

Anthony David Taylor

21.48 Another member of the Community staff who has been convicted of sexual offences against former residents is **Anthony David Taylor**[12], who appeared at Talgarth Magistrates' Court on 6 January 1976, when he was convicted of two offences of indecent assault and fined a total of £40. We do not have details of the circumstances of these offences but Anthony Taylor wrote to the Welsh Office in November 1975, when he was suspended from his employment pending his appearance in Court, describing offences that he had committed against boys from Newcastle upon Tyne when they attended a summer holiday scheme that he ran for the Community. He asked the Secretary of State whether something could be done to protect social workers from publicity when they committed offences, citing his own case as an example. He was dismissed after he had been convicted.

21.49 We know of four complainants who have more recently complained of sexual abuse by Anthony Taylor whilst they were with the Community and we received evidence from three of them. All four complainants were there at the same time and the longest resident of the four was with the Community for five years from about January 1971. The evidence that we received established that Taylor's sexual assaults were not confined to those with which he was charged but occurred also in dormitories at Bryntirion Hall (where he was on the staff) and extended to oral sex with one of the complainants. In his written evidence to the Tribunal Anthony Taylor denied the offences but we have no reason to doubt the truth of the complaints. He is now retired and ill and it is unnecessary to say anything further about him.

Iain Muir

21.50 The third member of the staff to be convicted was **Iain Muir**[13], who was Deputy Headteacher of the Community school in the mid 1980s. He was convicted on 22 July 1986 in the Crown Court at Mold of an offence of unlawful sexual intercourse with a girl under the age of 16 years, for which he received a sentence of six months' imprisonment, whereupon he was dismissed. The victim of this offence who gave oral evidence to the Tribunal, was resident at Bryn Alyn Hall for just over three years from October 1982 and attended school there. She was 15 years old when she left.

[12] See para 2.07(1).
[13] See para 2.07(5).

21.51 Muir, who was then 36 years old, committed the offence on 16 June 1985 at his flat in Wrexham at the conclusion of a weekend that the girl had spent with him and his family in Hertfordshire. It came to light in October 1985 when the girl confided in a fellow resident, who informed a Team Leader in Askew House. Muir, who could not be traced by the Tribunal, admitted the offence, which he said had occurred on one occasion only, and he tendered his resignation, which was accepted. The girl did not add much to this account in her evidence but she did say that there had been numerous occasions before the act of intercourse when there had been physical contact, including kissing, between them at Muir's flat and on the school premises, which she had "gone along with". She had been to his flat often and had been seeking affection from, and happiness with, him. This witness was a girl who alleged that she had suffered sexual abuse earlier in other children's homes and from two other members of the Community's staff.

Kenneth Taylor

21.52 We are aware of four complainants who allege that they were sexually abused by this former member of the Community staff and of 12 who complained of physical abuse by him. We did not hear any evidence in support of these allegations of varying gravity, however, because **Kenneth Taylor** was the subject of continuing police investigation in the course of the Tribunal's hearings. He died suddenly on 8 August 1998 of a heart attack, at a time when it was expected that he would be charged with some of the alleged offences.

21.53 Kenneth Taylor was, according to Allen, a fully qualified residential care worker. He worked for the Community for a substantial period from about 1977, starting at Marton's Camp and ending as Officer-in-Charge of Pentre Saeson Hall from about 1983. He was suspended from the latter position in or about April 1992 following allegations by children relating to possible sexual abuse of one resident by a Team Leader and a regime of excessive physical control exercised by him. The Crown Prosecution Service advised against a prosecution in relation to Pentre Saeson but Kenneth Taylor was dismissed in January 1993[14].

Other allegations of sexual abuse

21.54 It appears that about 28 former residents of the Community have made complaints of indecent assaults by other members of the staff. Most of these complainants, however, name different staff members; seven are unable to identify their assailants and four members of staff are named by two complainants so that 17 of the staff in all are named. Most of the allegations are of one form of indecent assault or another but three female former residents allege that they were raped (one by an unidentified person) and three of the men allege buggery (against one by an unidentified person). In these circumstances no pattern of alleged sexual misconduct by one of the accused members of staff has emerged and it has not been practicable to reach firm conclusions about

---

[14] See para 21.56 for the decision in relation to the Team Leader.

individual allegations relating to events said (with only three exceptions) to have occurred between ten and about 25 years ago. We did, however, hear the evidence of eight of these complainants, four of whom gave oral evidence before us.

21.55 The girl who was the complainant in respect of Muir told us that she was also seriously assaulted by her key worker on the Community staff in the course of a camping trip, when he attempted to have sexual intercourse with her; and an allegation by her of rape by another member of the staff is currently under investigation by the police. Other evidence before us has been of indecent assaults of varying gravity by male staff on boys, including oral sex in a caravan on a pony trekking expedition. Another male witness said that he saw a member of staff ripping the top off a girl resident, exposing her breasts, for which the member of staff was allegedly dismissed.

21.56 The principal witness on behalf of the Welsh Office, John Lloyd, told us of a number of allegations of physical and sexual abuse at the Community's various premises that were reported to the Welsh Office between 1989 and 1992. Thus, in July 1989 an allegation was made by a former resident that she had been sexually abused by a member of staff and this led to correspondence between Bryn Alyn and Clwyd Social Services Department, which we have not seen. We were told that the police were informed of the matter but no prosecution ensued and the member of staff was merely advised to have no further contact with the girl. Then in 1992 there was another investigation by Clwyd Social Services Department and the North Wales Police of serious allegations made by children about alleged sexual abuse of a girl resident by a Team Leader (and an alleged regime of excessive physical control at Pentre Saeson Hall[15]). Although no prosecution ensued a child protection conference concluded that the complainant girl had been abused by the Team Leader, who had been suspended meanwhile. The girl's name was put on the child protection register pending a full assessment but she then left the Community. The upshot was that the Team Leader was conditionally re-instated in December 1992.

21.57 Our conclusions are that (John Allen apart) sexual abuse by members of staff of the Community was not rife but that it did occur to a significant and disturbing extent. The comparatively few girl residents were specially vulnerable to this and, in our judgment, the organisation and structure of the Community and its premises were never suitably adapted for co-educational purposes. Paedophile activity in relation to boys was dominated by that of Allen himself. Otherwise it appears to have been sporadic and less likely to be detected for that reason. It is a cause for grave concern, however, that so many members of staff were named in the major police investigation, even though the allegations against particular individuals were limited in number.

---

[15] This was the investigation previously referred to in para 21.53.

Allegations of physical abuse

21.58 It appears that 139 former residents with the Community have complained of physical abuse during the period of their residence and 121 of them have named a total of 49 members of staff as alleged abusers in this respect (ten of whom are alleged to have been guilty also of sexual abuse). The other 18 former residents were unable to identify the alleged aggressor.

John Ernest Allen

21.59 **John Allen** himself was named by 14 of these former residents and we heard or read the evidence of seven of them. Most of them alleged that they had been punched by Allen. Witness E[16], for example, said that Allen punched and slapped him on three occasions but, after one of them, Allen gave him a leather jacket. Another witness complained that Allen punched and shouted at him twice. He said also that the home was "brutally run" and that there was a lot of violence between boys from different areas, which the staff chose to ignore. A third witness said that Allen assaulted him twice, once causing his nose to bleed and on the other occasion giving him two black-eyes. Witness B[17] said that Allen would lose his temper and throw people around: it happened to B once. Two other male witnesses made complaints of being punched or smacked in the face and a former girl resident said that Allen was very aggressive: he punished her on numerous occasions with a punch, a slap or a kick.

21.60 Allen denied these allegations but we are satisfied that he did punch and slap residents on occasions when he was angry about what they had said or done. It was undoubtedly improper of him to do so but, in mitigation, it may be said that many of the residents were difficult children and that he was often faced with provocative situations. We do not think that he was an habitually violent man: the complaints against him of using excessive physical force are heavily outweighed by the allegations against him of sexual misconduct.

Peter Steen

21.61 The other main alleged physical abuser was **Peter Steen**, who has been named by 19 complainants. He worked for the Community from about late 1976 until Gatewen Hall closed in or about 1993 with a break of about 12 months when Bryntirion Hall closed in or about 1986. Steen was about 36 years old when he joined the Community as a residential care worker at Bryn Alyn Hall. Earlier in his life he had been a self-employed building contractor but he had had to give this up because of an injury to his right arm, which ultimately required removal of the elbow joint and which necessitated five separate surgical operations over a period of four years, during which period he was unemployed. He had been involved, however, in running a five-a-side football team and this had led to voluntary youth work with the result that he had played a prominent role in establishing Plas Madoc Youth Association at

---

[16] See para 21.36.
[17] See paras 21.27 to 21.30.

Ruabon Leisure Centre. He had had no professional training in social work and he had been before criminal courts on seven occasions between 1955 and 1965, mainly for offences of dishonesty but on one occasion, when he was 23 years old, for two offences of assault occasioning actual bodily harm committed in Devizes when he was acting as a club "bouncer". In his oral evidence Steen said that he told the truth about his convictions when he was interviewed for the Bryn Alyn post by Streetly, who said that a check would be made with the police.

21.62 Steen was employed by the Community initially at Bryn Alyn Hall for about seven years (he thought that it was four), starting as a shift worker for 12 months and then becoming a Deputy Team Leader. He estimated the ratio of staff to children to be one to ten at that time. There were about 80 children in all: the youngest (about 20) were in Lindisfarne; new entrants and the more difficult children (about 40) were in Blackley; and the less difficult children or those about to leave (about 20) were in Askew. Whilst he was at Bryn Alyn Hall, Streetly, a former Liverpool probation officer who had been employed earlier to run Marton's Camp with Kenneth Taylor, was in charge and then Arwyn Thomas; and Keith Evans became Senior Team Leader and later Officer-in-Charge of Blackley House.

21.63 Steen was transferred to Bryntirion Hall when an allegation was made that he had assaulted two Blackley House boys. The allegation was made by a student residential care worker, Denis Finlay Williams, aged 34 years, who was sent to Blackley House as his final training placement in October 1983. The Tribunal's staff were unable to trace this potential witness but we have seen the report that he submitted to the Directors of Social Services of Clwyd and Manchester and Salford College of Technology and the two statements that he made to the police in September 1992. In view of what occurred Williams only worked three eight hour shifts beginning on 11 October 1983. He was assigned to the team led by Steen and on the third day a minor incident occurred in a dormitory when a number of boys became involved in mock kung-fu fighting. A staff member sent two of the boys down to the office and Williams accompanied them. In the office Steen asked the boys, who were wearing only trousers, what they had been doing and on being told that they had been fooling around or words to that effect, Steen punched one of them in the heart area of the chest, telling him not to fool about again. Steen then turned to the other boy and started punching him in the chest. When he doubled up in pain Steen kept on punching him on his shoulder blades and back. The boys were then sent up to bed and Williams observed that both were heavily bruised, or at least their skin was distinctly reddened, where they had been struck by Steen.

21.64 Williams described also an incident that had occurred the previous day when Steen had thrown two substantial pieces of wood at two boys (one of whom was punched the next day), who had been playing football and were running because they were late for their class. The piece of wood missed the boys by about six feet but Williams was sure that, if either piece had struck the boys, they would have been injured.

21.65 Williams alleged also that on 13 October 1983, Steen had instructed him to be hard on another boy whilst supervising the boy in the task of scrubbing the showers[18]. Steen said "if he stops for one minute, add another day to his punishment" and he added "I want to see really bad bruises on his knees when I come back" (caused by raised bumps on the tiles on which he was required to kneel). There were also bruises on the boys' legs.

21.66 Steen said in evidence that he was transferred to Bryntirion Hall after Williams had alleged that he had punched two lads in the chest but he denied punching them and said that he had merely pointed at them when saying to them "Don't you do this" when they were in the office with him. There was an internal inquiry and he was told by the head of Manchester Social Services Department that Williams had "overstepped the mark" and had been negligent in doing his (Williams') own work. Steen alleged also that he received a letter to that effect. He admitted (in a hand written statement) throwing a light piece of rotten wood towards the two boys who were late for class but said that it fell far short of them and broke.

21.67 We have not received any evidence from the four other known complainants about Steen during his seven years at Bryn Alyn Hall and there was only one complainant in respect of his next three years at Bryntirion Hall. There were, however, 12 former residents of Gatewen Hall between about 1987 and 1992 who alleged that he assaulted them and we heard the evidence of four of these potential witnesses.

21.68 Both witnesses who gave oral evidence to the Tribunal about Steen alleged that they had been struck by him in the office at Gatewen. The first of these, V, who had previously been at Cartrefle, Bersham Hall and Bryn Alyn, was at Gatewen Hall for about six months when he was 16 years old between July 1989 and February 1990. V said that Steen was not "all bad at all": it was possible to have something of a relationship with Steen, who would put himself out to help at times but, the witness complained of two specific incidents. The first of these occurred when he had returned late with another boy. Steen saw them both in the Gatewen office and Steen's wife, who was the Matron, was present. V alleged that Steen hit him around the head, although it did not "really hurt" him. The second incident was more serious and occurred during a camping holiday in Cornwall. One of the boys was thought to have hit another boy in Padstow with the result that the latter had been admitted to hospital; and on their return to camp, V and another boy were questioned by Steen about their knowledge of what had occurred. V alleged that, when they both denied any knowledge, Steen attacked them, punching him in the stomach and ribs and kicking him when he went to the floor. In consequence, he was bruised around the ribs and he thinks that he had a cut lip. He added that he would imagine that other members of the staff heard him screaming but nothing was done about it. Everyone knew that Steen behaved in this way and residents took it as punishment. Of his overall period in care, V said in his written statement to the Tribunal that "Generally it was alright, but Cartrefle was a nightmare, Gatewen was violent, Bersham and Bryn Alyn were OK".

---

[18] See para 21.83 for the prelude to this incident.

21.69 The second witness who gave oral evidence, X, was at Gatewen Hall for about 12 months and arrived there about mid-way through V's stay. X was a Plymouth boy who was placed at Gatewen Hall to prepare him for independence and because of family problems: he had been unable to cope with living in bed and breakfast accommodation. But he found that the staff were more violent then caring: they seemed to have been employed for their weight and strength rather than any professional qualifications. In his opinion Steen was one of four bad members of the staff and X complained of being dragged by Steen upstairs, where Steen pushed the back of his head against a wall three or four times. He was then taken by Steen into an office and lifted off the floor by his neck against a wall so that it felt as if he was being strangled. About six other members of staff were present, and one of them said "I saw you hit Pete Steen first", to which the witness responded that he was a liar. X was bleeding from his head and had a graze on the side of his face three to four inches long. He was then taken to his room where Steen refused his request to go to hospital and he was given no treatment. He apologised to Steen, who said that it was his fault but X told Steen that it was he (Steen) who had started it. The only person who helped when he was in care was White junior[19] (then Head of Gatewen Hall), who was one of the best and fair.

21.70 Steen appears to have made a near contemporary record (which he signed) of this incident at 8.50 am on 9 March 1990, relating that he had become aware that X was involved in an altercation with a girl resident and a member of staff and was refusing to collect his belongings and money, despite the fact that he had a bus to catch. The note continued:

> "I intervened telling X to go into the office. X absolutely refused. Holding his arm I tried to guide him up the stairs. X pulled his arm away and lay down on the stairs, refusing to move, still being abusive and threatening. Again I got hold of him. He started kicking; I lifted him on to his feet and took him upstairs. X now had an audience because of all the commotion. He stood back against the wall threatening to punch me if I held him again. Crying in rage X tried to punch and kick out at me I pushed X against the wall pinning him by the chest. His head went back, hitting the wall. This sent X into a frenzy, trying to thrash and kick. I held him in this position until he calmed down. Afterwards he was spoken to by myself and Steven Ford. X later apologised for his behaviour."

21.71 In X's case, and almost exceptionally in relation to former residents of the Bryn Alyn Community, we have seen copies of many social services records about him during his stay at Gatewen Hall, compiled by or supplied to Devon social workers. These show that X made complaints to the police in October 1989 and August 1990 about incidents involving members of the staff at Gatewen Hall and that a solicitor's letter was sent to his social worker at Plymouth on 15 June 1990 complaining of his treatment at Gatewen Hall. The relevant part of the letter read:

---

[19] See paras 21.14 and 21.101.

"X is, of course, a stranger to the writer" (the senior partner) "but gives the impression of being extremely nervous and shy, although he expresses himself very fluently. He complained to us that he is extremely unhappy at Gatewen Hall, principally because of bullying from members of the staff. He named four members of the staff and the Director as having acted towards him in a more or less bullying way and complained that in some cases physical force had been used towards him. His head has been banged against the wall and his face bruised. His face bore no indication of injury and he says that he has not received any medical treatment."

21.72 X's complaints were taken up by his Plymouth social worker with White junior, who wrote a long letter in reply dated 24 July 1990, in which he set out detailed accounts of the incident on 7 March and other incidents on 7, 22 and 24 June, involving three other members of the staff. It contained also the following passages:

"With regard to X's negative attitude towards Gatewen the positive response from the case review has continued throughout the week. X is keen to take on board the opportunities offered in terms of moving on to Cluster Flats etc . . . As far as staff at Gatewen are concerned there appears to be no core of negative feeling towards X. He himself, through my discussions with him, has quoted examples of staff support in a number of different situations. In general, I feel that there is a lot of positive support for him within the unit, however, X must realise that the support offered will sometimes take the form of facing him with the consequences of his own actions and his responsibility for them."[20]

21.73 This outline of events in 1990 in relation to X illustrates how difficult it is now to unravel quite complex incidents that occurred as long as eight years ago in a series of heated exchanges. Steen said in his evidence that, at first, X did not get on with him but later, on a camping holiday in Anglesey, he was the only person who would have anything to do with X. Steen denied banging X's head against a wall but recalled two other incidents in which he had had to restrain X. In the first, X had fixed wires on the doors of this room "to electrocute" anyone entering. Steen went in, whereupon X went berserk so that Steen had to sit on him. In the second, X took a knife in the kitchen and went for another member of staff with the result that Steen had to hold X by putting his arms around him. X was a "little bit schizophrenic" and would say that a voice (Steven) had made him do it when he was caught doing wrong.

21.74 Speaking more generally, Steen volunteered that he (Steen) was the so-called bastard of the unit and said that some of the boys did call him that. He was the "trouble-shooter" at Bryntirion and Gatewen but not at Bryn Alyn. He did become angry with boys from time to time. Of V, who alleged that he had been struck by Steen, the latter said that he was regarded as a loveable rogue and that Steen got on as well with him as anyone else did, although Steen did not have much to do with him. Steen recalled interrogating V in the main tent in

---

[20] See further in relation to this incident para 21.101.

the presence of the rest of the staff at the Cornwall camp after a boy had been taken to hospital and not believing what V said but he denied assaulting him. It was after midnight and he had thought that it would be better to deal with the whole incident the following morning.

21.75 Two former girl residents of Gatewen Hall whose evidence was read to the Tribunal also alleged that they had been assaulted by Steen. The first alleged that, after she had been tied up for about 20 minutes by a woman member of the staff for something that she had done wrong, she and another girl ran away. They were caught and taken back to Gatewen Hall, where they were seen by Steen, who was Team Leader that day. She said that everyone was scared of Steen because he had such a temper. She could see that he was in a temper on this occasion when she was left alone with him in his room and he hit her full in the face, causing her to fall back over the desk. He was shouting and banging the table and said "Get out before I fucking kill you". The second witness said that at Gatewen she would be slapped for not taking her medication and that she remembered Steen doing this to her. She said also that there was a room called "the palace" where people were taken to be assaulted and that Steen used to punch and kick her in the stomach. However, Steen said of the first of these two that she was a liar, who had made allegations against others that he did not believe; and the second was too disturbed emotionally to give oral evidence and be cross-examined.

21.76 Finally, two other witnesses whose evidence was read to us, claimed to have seen Steen assaulting a resident or inferred that he had just done so. The first, who was at Gatewen in the early summer of 1989, said that he saw Steen slapping a boy's face and kicking his backside. The other, who was a girl resident at Gatewen three years earlier, alleged that she saw a boy who had taken a staff member's car emerge from Steen's office with blood on his face and shirt. Steen, however, denied both these allegations and said that he did not deal with the latter incident.

21.77 It is not easy to assess the allegations against Steen on the limited evidence before us. It is fair to say that as "trouble-shooter" at Bryntirion Hall and then Gatewen Hall, he was likely to be involved in confrontations with troublesome residents and to attract criticism for what he did in those situations. What is mildly surprising is that there were more complaints about his conduct at Gatewen Hall than at Bryntirion Hall, where the more troublesome residents were said to have been housed. The correct view probably is that the later residents of Gatewen Hall were older than before and proved to be more difficult to control, as some witnesses indicated. Steen himself said that he made several requests for training in physical restraint but was told that none was available. Bearing in mind his admission that he did lose his temper from time to time and his complete lack of professional training, we have no doubt that he did use excessive force from time to time in restraining and in disciplining both boy and girl residents. The overall volume of complaints about him, however, is moderate (if that is an appropriate word in this context), having regard to the nature of his role in the last ten years of his employment by the Community and the absence of any guidance as to how to perform it. One member of the staff, Keith Evans, said of Steen that he had a reputation as a hard man but that it was grossly exaggerated by the young people: he was strong and a disciplinarian, but he was a fair person.

Other complaints of physical abuse

21.78 As we stated earlier[21], **Kenneth Taylor** was the subject of complaints of physical abuse by 12 complainants but we were not able to hear evidence about them because of the continuing police investigation during our hearings. All but two of these related to his regime at Pentre Saeson as Officer-in-Charge between 1983 and 1992.

21.79 The other complaints of physical abuse have been so diffuse that, in general, it would be invidious to single out individuals. Thus, of the 49 members of staff referred to in paragraph 21.58, 31 were named by only one complainant and a further nine by only two or three. An additional problem has been the absence of any Community records of most of their residents because we were told in the course of our preliminary hearing that these records were destroyed in a fire that occurred on 25 October 1996 at a Pickfords storage depot in Hoole, near Chester. The result has been that the Tribunal's ability to trace former Community residents from outside North Wales has been limited. In these circumstances the fairest course is to summarise the allegations that were made against some of the staff who held senior positions in the Community.

21.80 **Keith Allan Evans** was employed by the Community from April 1974, when he was nearly 30 years old until 30 June 1996. Before that he had served in the army for six years, driving armoured tanks reaching the rank of corporal, and then for seven years as a machine tool operator with a Wrexham firm. His introduction to the Community was through a former sergeant, who was already on the staff, and he understood that he was to organise and run outward bound type courses. Evans' work, however, was that of a Residential Child Care Officer during the week and he was only involved in outward bound activities at week-ends and during holidays. He had no professional qualifications. According to his written statement, he progressed after about three years to Deputy Team Leader at Bryn Alyn Hall and then to Team Leader in or about 1980. He remained at Bryn Alyn Hall thereafter, rising to Senior Principal Officer from 4 January 1982 and to Head of Care from 7 June 1989. He had to revert to Principal Officer in June 1994 because new regulations disqualified him from holding the higher appointment, although he had undertaken some in service training by then. Evans was suspended for six days in August 1995 as the result of a slapping incident for which he received a written warning and he left the Community ten months later after a protracted argument about working shifts, although his own view, according to his statement, was that he was on sick leave until the Community went into liquidation in March 1997.

---

[21] See para 21.52.

21.81 It appears that five complainants alleged subsequently that they had been physically abused by Evans at Bryn Alyn Hall and we received the evidence of one of them. The male former resident who gave oral evidence was with the Community for just over four years from November 1976, when he was approaching 12 years of age, after a rather turbulent history. His complaint about Evans, who was know as "Beef" or "Beefy", was that "he had the weight behind him and a lot of the time he would let you know". A warning was probably punching you in the chest or grabbing hold of your throat or shaking you. He never experienced a lot of physical conflict with Evans: he had never been actually assaulted, not beaten up badly, it was slaps and things like that. This witness alleged also that, after he and two or three others had run away to Chester, Evans and another member of staff had made them run all the way back and then around the grounds of the home for two or three hours as punishment for absconding.

21.82 It is noteworthy that all five complaints against Evans referred to a period before March 1983. The second witness about him, whose evidence was read, did not allege that she was struck by Evans. She said that after she had run away with two other girls and had been returned by the police about a week later, she was questioned by Evans and another member of the staff about the whereabouts of the other girls. Suddenly, the other member of staff smacked her across the mouth with the back of his hand, causing her lip to bleed. She was then allowed to go to bed.

21.83 Another person who made allegations against Keith Evans was the student, Denis Williams[22]. He said in his report that he had witnessed the boy referred to in paragraph 21.65 being returned to Bryn Alyn Hall on 13 October 1983 after running away. Evans took the boy into the television lounge and Williams heard Evans shouting at him, saying that he had caused the home a lot of embarrassment by telling the police that boys were beaten there and that Evans would make sure that the boy himself was caused a lot of embarrassment over the next three days. The boy emerged in tears from the lounge after about 20 minutes, no longer wearing shoes, socks or jeans and was then set about the task of scrubbing the floors under Steen's supervision. Williams alleged also, later in his report, that Evans presented himself as a bully. Williams regarded the punishment of "scrubs"[23], as it was known, as totally out of place.

21.84 In his own evidence to the Tribunal, Evans described himself as strict but fair and he said that Williams' report was wildly exaggerated. At the time of his visit there was a social worker's strike and the Community was having to deal with many difficult children, mostly on remand from courts; and there was an influx of youngsters on the closure of Marton's Camp in Cheshire. Evans had to make decisions but the sanctions imposed were not of his devising: they were

---

[22] See paras 21.63 and 21.64.
[23] "Scrubs," according to one witness, involved wearing a vest, shorts and black pumps, with no socks or shoe laces, and working at a variety of unpleasant menial tasks without gloves and often with inappropriate equipment such as a toothbrush.

laid down by the Community. Moreover, his nickname "Beef" was given to him many years before by the sergeant who recruited him for the Community and who had known him from childhood.

21.85 Evans said also that he was suspended in August 1995 on his own initiative after he had slapped a boy, who had come into his office after being restrained. The boy was in a foul temper and had grabbed the Bursar and threatened the Matron. Evans had got the boy on the floor and had slapped his face after being head-butted by him. He had reported the incident and had suggested that he should be suspended pending an inquiry.

21.86 In his written statement to the Tribunal Evans pointed out that for about ten years prior to the closure of the Community he was almost always the person who was called upon to deal with the very difficult situations in which children might attack staff or there were other "confrontational" problems. He dealt in detail also with the allegations of the two witnesses whose evidence has been outlined denying specifically that boys were made to run from Chester (eight absconders were made to walk three-quarters of a mile from Gresford) or that he was present when a girl resident was struck across the face.

21.87 The comparative sparseness of the allegations against Evans when measured against the length of his service with the Community, the number of children passing through his hands and the nature of his role does not suggest that he was guilty of physical abuse. Despite his lack of professional training, he was quite an impressive witness, who gave a helpful account of the Community's activities, and the evidence before us does not establish that he used excessive force towards the children for whom he was responsible or that he condoned such conduct by other members of the staff.

21.88 **David Alan Challinor** joined the Community on 24 June 1980 at the age of 19 years after taking a pre-qualification course in residential care (PCSC) for two years at Aston College, Wrexham, on leaving school. He was employed initially as a residential care worker at Cotsbrook Hall, where he received an official caution after only three months for throwing an object (a clipboard) in the direction of some boys, causing superficial injury to one of them. Challinor moved to Bryn Alyn Hall in the same capacity in 1980, becoming Deputy Team Leader there on 1 January 1985 and a Team Leader on 7 April 1987. He remained at Bryn Alyn Hall until September 1991 when he began the two year CQSW course at Cartrefle College and then Plas Coch. On completing that course successfully he was appointed Deputy Officer-in-Charge of Gatewen Hall from 13 July 1993 but he moved to Pentre Saeson Hall in May 1994 as Acting Unit Manager and became Manager 12 months later until it closed in March 1997 (like Evans his P45 showed his employment to have ended on 30 June 1996 for unexplained reasons).

21.89 It appears that seven complainants in all alleged physical abuse by Challinor in statements to the police and all of them referred to the period between 1980 and 1986 when he was at Bryn Alyn Hall. Only two of them, however, provided statements to the Tribunal and these were read to us. The first, who is now a patient in Broadmoor Hospital, complained that he was thrown around (but not punched) by Challinor, whom he referred to as "Tiny". He alleged also that, after he had reported to Challinor and another staff member that some boys had tied him to a tree with part of the rope around his neck, neither Challinor nor the other member of staff would let him report the matter to the police or tell anyone. The second witness, who was unwilling to give oral evidence, was a resident in Askew House in 1986. She alleged that after she had dyed her hair green Challinor and a woman member of the staff forcibly dyed her hair blonde after she had refused to do so: Challinor forced her to the bath room and held her in a chair whilst the woman member of staff poured hair bleach over her hair and rubbed it in with the result that her hair started to fall out when she washed it and she had to have it cut off by a hairdresser.

21.90 Challinor said in evidence that he did not remember any argument with the girl who made the hair-dying allegation and he denied that he was involved when interviewed by the police. There was no Community rule about hair-dying. He denied also that he had pushed the other witness around. Challinor conceded, however, that he had been at fault on another occasion when a boy reported that he had been struck across the ear by a member of staff: Challinor suspended the latter that evening and thinks that he reported the incident, which he had not witnessed to his line manager, but he recognises that he should have arranged medical attention for the boy immediately rather than later, when the ear became more inflamed.

21.91 To sum up, therefore, the evidence against Challinor is so limited that we have not been persuaded that he was a party to child abuse during his service with the Community.

21.92 **John Leslie Jeffreys** worked for the Community for nine or ten years between about 1974 and 1983, starting when he was nearly 40 years old. He had begun working with children five or six years earlier in Derbyshire after five years as a supervisor for Rolls Royce in Derby. He became a community youth worker, after some training from the local education authority and then a residential care worker at a children's home, where he received some training organised by Derbyshire Social Services Department. In 1974 Jeffreys responded to an advertisement placed by the Community in New Society and was appointed (after being interviewed by Allen and Wainwright) to work in the Talbot Road property, where two houses had been converted into one, and which was being used as a halfway house. From there he moved to Cotsbrook Hall, where there were about 50 boys in the age range of seven to18 years. At Cotsbrook Hall Jeffreys was appointed a Team Leader and his wife became Deputy Matron.

21.93 Jeffreys moved to Bryntirion Hall in 1978, where there were about 20 boys aged 14 and upwards and he was one of two Team Leaders under Russell Evans. Finally, he was Officer-in-Charge of Pentre Saeson for about 18 months, until Kenneth Taylor succeeded him. His wife ceased to be a matron on leaving Cotsbrook Hall and she then became one of the directors of the Community, working in its office.

21.94 Seven former residents alleged that Jeffreys had been physically violent to them and we received evidence from two of them. The witness who gave oral evidence went to Bryntirion Hall in May 1980 and was there for about two years. He alleged that he was given a hiding by Jeffreys during an annual holiday at John Allen's villa near Bordeaux. The background was that he had stolen a penknife from a shop and that a boy had told Jeffreys about the theft. Jeffreys asked him where he had obtained the knife and, when he admitted stealing it, Jeffreys gave him a good hiding in a bathroom, punching and kicking him. As a result his shoulder blade hurt and he claimed that he still gets pain in the shoulder blade but said that he was given so many hidings by boys at Bryntirion (the worst time in his life) that he did not know which attack was the cause of his recurring pain. He did not receive any other punishment for stealing the knife.

21.95 The witness whose evidence was read was a Newcastle upon Tyne boy, who was already at Bryntirion Hall when Jeffreys moved there from Cotsbrook Hall. This witness had a brother who was at Cotsbrook Hall and had heard from others that the brother had been regularly beaten up there by Jeffreys. The witness (who would have been about 17 years old then) decided, therefore, to put his accusation to Jeffreys. His statement to the Tribunal continued:

> "We went into the drying room, I locked the door behind me. We started to talk and I lost my temper and a fight ensued. It was a serious fight which involved punching and kicking.
>
> Jeffreys' spectacles were broken during the fight. Within seconds, members of staff broke the door in and pulled us apart. There were no serious injuries to Jeffreys and myself as a result of the fight. Russell Evans dealt with the incident. After this incident I had no problems with Jeffreys."

The brother of this witness has not supplied any evidence to the Tribunal that he was assaulted by Jeffreys at Cotsbrook Hall.

21.96 Jeffreys said in evidence that he had found the boys at Bryntirion Hall easy to work with and that there was no excessive fighting amongst them. He recalled the theft of a pocket knife in France but said that he had sent for Russell Evans, who was in charge of the camp, to deal with it: and he denied beating up the boy responsible, who had made a different false allegation against him in 1992. This counter-allegation is not borne out by the documents before us, which show that the complainant made the same allegation against Jeffreys in his first statement to the police dated 8 June 1993 and said in a further statement on 1 January 1994 that the incident occurred on the first of his two holidays in France with the Community.

21.97 In relation to the drying room allegation, Jeffreys said that he had very little to do with that witness, although he could have spoken to the boy about the latter's brother. Jeffreys said in his written statement that he remembered the brother at Cotsbrook Hall, with whom he had had no trouble; there was no substance whatsoever in the suggestion that he had been assaulting the brother. Moreover, the drying room at Bryntirion Hall was part of the laundry, which was kept locked when not being used: you could not simply enter the room and lock the door behind you as the witness suggested and he would not have put himself in a room with the boy as alleged.

21.98 Jeffreys gave too bland an account of his relations with residents during his employment by the Community and of the relations between boys and their peers to be a wholly credible witness. His evidence about this in respect of Bryntirion Hall is particularly difficult to accept having regard to the fact that the more troublesome boys were usually housed there. It is unlikely, in our view, that the bathroom incident in France has been completely invented and, although the other witness was somewhat vainglorious in his account of the alleged fight in the drying room, we accept that it did occur. Our conclusion is that Jeffreys did on occasions use physical force to residents when he should not have done so and allowed himself, for example, to be drawn into a confrontation that was not of his own making. The evidence before us does not, however, justify a finding that he resorted to force frequently or that he sought to rule by fear or intimidation.

Reports to the Welsh Office of alleged physical abuse

21.99 To complete the picture it is necessary to mention also that a number of allegations of alleged abuse were reported by the Community to the Welsh Office in the period between 1988 and 1993. Thus, in May 1988 there was an allegation of assault on a resident made against White junior[24], who was then apparently Director of Bryn Alyn Hall. The Solihull boy involved was 16 years old and was a resident at Gatewen Hall, whilst attending school at Bryn Alyn Hall. The incident was investigated quickly by the Community and Clwyd Social Services Department set in train Child Abuse procedures. The conclusion reached in the Community's internal investigation was that White junior had "acted excessively". He had been suspended from duty during the investigation and, after the North Wales Police had informed him that he would not be prosecuted, he was transferred to administrative duties within the Community. He did, however, act as Deputy Head of Gatewen Hall from the summer of 1991 to January 1993 following the resignation of Lynn Williams.

21.100 In June, August and October 1989 there were further allegations of physical abuse. The first and last of these involved the same member of staff on both occasions. On the first occasion he was alleged to have physically abused two boys and removed all their clothes, for which, after an investigation, he was given a formal warning. Then in October 1989 he was alleged to have abused a girl resident, for which he was dismissed. The complainant in August 1989 alleged that he had been struck and pushed on three occasions by different members of the staff, after which he had absconded to his home in Sandwell. The allegations were referred to the police for investigation but no support for them by other children named as victims or witnesses was forthcoming and no prosecution ensued.

21.101 The incident involving Peter Steen and a Plymouth boy[25] was also reported to the Welsh Office by Devon Social Services Department in October 1990. It appears from the correspondence that Steen was temporarily re-located whilst

---

[24] See para 21.14.
[25] See paras 21.69 to 21.72.

the matter was investigated but the police found no case to answer and warned the complainant about wasting police time: it was concluded that reasonable action had been taken by Steen. The internal inquiry concluded that the boy had misread what had happened and had "twisted it to suit his own needs": he had accepted the outcome[26].

21.102 The Welsh Office also received reports from the Community about allegations in relation to Kenneth Taylor and a Team Leader in 1992 and the outcome of those allegations[27].

21.103 There was a further complaint of physical abuse in March 1993, this time by a 15 year old girl who had been placed with the Community by Oxfordshire Social Services Department. She alleged that on 17/18 March 1993 she had been thrown across a room by a member of staff, suffering extensive bruising to her back. Ten days later she went to Clwyd Social Services Department (who were supervising her on behalf of Oxfordshire) to make her complaint and she refused to return to the Community with the result that she was placed with foster parents. She alleged also that she had suffered persistent physical and sexual harassment from fellow residents because of inadequate supervision. The girl, who had been with the Community since March 1991 went to Wrexham Police Station on 6 April 1993 and asked to withdraw her complaint. The police considered that their investigation should continue in the public interest but the Crown Prosecution Service returned the file and no further action was taken. The staff member was not suspended because the girl had left and she apparently acknowledged that she had otherwise had a very positive, caring and supportive relationship with him. By that time only four girl residents remained at Bryn Alyn Hall and there were none at Pentre Saeson or at Gatewen Hall, which had only two boy residents, who were both about to reach the age of 16 years.

21.104 In May 1993 two further matters were investigated and reported to the Welsh Office. The first involved a boy resident at Bryn Alyn Hall, who suffered some injury whilst being restrained but who did not make a complaint. Following investigation it was decided that no action should be taken and the boy has not made any complaint to this Tribunal. The second concerned a boy resident at Gatewen Hall who was reported to the police for an offence of criminal damage. At the police station he complained that he had been injured whilst being restrained. Slight injuries were found and a child protection conference was held but the boy was not put on the register: the conference was swayed by the boy's own view that he was not at risk at Gatewen Hall.

Deficiencies in the evidence about the use of physical force generally

21.105 We are very conscious of the fact that the evidence that we have heard and seen about the use of physical force in the Community has been patchy and that we have not received a complete picture. This weakness has been unavoidable because the residents were drawn mainly from all over England so that they have proved to be difficult to trace and the disincentive for them to relive the

---

[26] Letter from Devon Social Services Department to D Brushett SSI, Welsh Office, dated 29 May 1991.
[27] See paras 21.52, 21.53 and 21.56.

painful past by volunteering evidence to a tribunal sitting in North Wales must have been great. The evidence before us, therefore, has been no more than a sample of what might have been heard if all the former residents who were seen by the police could now be heard. An alarming statistic is that the police themselves justifiably complained of having to deal with 280 absconders from the Community in one short period alone, that is, between 1 January and 19 June 1991.

21.106 Analysis of the sources of the complaints within the Community proves to be quite revealing. Thus, there were very few complaints by residents of Bryn Alyn Hall against identified members of the staff after 1986 and none in respect of Bryntirion Hall after 1984 (it operated as a children's home until 1986 or 1987). On the other hand, most of the complaints emanating from Pentre Saeson related to the period from 1988 to 1992 and a very high proportion of these were levelled against Kenneth Taylor alone. As for Gatewen Hall, most of the complaints related to the same period but a wider range of staff was named: there were not less than 26 complainants who named 12 members of staff in all.

Other aspects of the Community regime

21.107 Rather surprisingly, comparatively few of the complainants who gave evidence to the Tribunal commented on the general quality of care provided by the Community but this was because they were pre-occupied with their allegations of physical and sexual abuse by members of the staff and, in some cases, of bullying by fellow residents. There were, however, many other causes for concern.

21.108 Allen himself, in his written statement to the Tribunal gave a rather complacent account of the organisation and development of the Community in accordance with his definition of its aims[28]. According to him a comprehensive training programme was provided, beginning with senior managers, three of whom obtained certificates in the residential care of children (presumably the CRCCYP) at Salford Polytechnic and two progressed to a higher qualification. Middle management training was in the charge of another qualified social worker and one staff member each year was permitted to take the CQSW course. Teachers were assisted to obtain qualifications in special educational needs at Chester College; and in-house training, run by Stephen Elliott, was provided for care staff and teachers generally in the 1980s and 1990s.

21.109 Allen gave a similarly favourable picture of the organisation of management, supervision of care staff and night security arrangements. Following the Barclay report a system of key workers was introduced. Case reviews were attended by field workers from the placement agencies, of which 30 sent children to the Community regularly. Full documentation was maintained in respect of each child and other documents dealt comprehensively with such matters as complaints by children, disciplinary and grievance procedures, child protection principles, liaison with field social workers etc. Children were issued

---

[28] See para 21.16.

with an information pack on admission to the Community and any incident affecting a child was entered on both the unit's daily log and the child's personal file.

21.110 The reality was, however, very different. The overall picture that we have received has been of an organisation that developed rapidly far beyond its capabilities. By 1976, for example, it seems that there were about 80 children in Bryn Alyn Hall alone and substantial numbers of them were being transported daily to Marton's Camp to be taught, a round journey of about 50 miles. Then, when Marton's Camp closed in 1977, the children who had lived there were moved to Bryn Alyn Hall, increasing the number in residence there to at least 100 and requiring classrooms to be turned into dormitories. The pressure at all times then was to increase numbers; staff/resident ratios were low, and staff were unlikely to be released for training purposes.

21.111 Against this background several former members of the staff gave evidence of the lack of training opportunities before Stephen Elliott became responsible from about 1986 until he left in 1993. Peter Steen, who had no relevant experience or qualification when he was appointed in late 1976, said that he expected to receive training but was refused permission to take the CQSW course three times. Keith Evans also said that the reference to training in his contract was "absolute rubbish" in the 1970s, although some training became available in about 1981. Evans' reference to 1981 was probably mistaken, however, because Patrick Bates, who was taken on in 1981 with no child care experience, said that he received no training until 1987. Elliott did encourage training and realistic staff appraisals; and a member of staff who benefited from this was David Challinor, who was seconded for the CQSW course from 1991 to 1993 but there were increasing financial constraints in the 1990s for obvious reasons before the Community went into liquidation.

21.112 Former members of the Community's staff were critical also of the overall management and supervision of the various units. Keith Evans said that very little support was given, until Elliott arrived, to those on the ground who were running the units. John Jeffreys and Patrick Bates were similarly critical: there was very little help from senior management and team leaders were left to get on with it. Corporal punishment was not permitted but Lynn Williams, who progressed from care worker in 1983 to Deputy Director at Gatewen Hall, from 1987 to 1991, said in evidence that there was no policy on punishments whatsoever. It is right to say, however, that the later contracts of employment that we have seen included reference to sexual misconduct and physical assault of pupils as examples of gross misconduct that could lead to dismissal.

21.113 The report by the mature student Denis Williams, to which we referred earlier[29], came approximately half way through the Community's history (October 1983) and would certainly have been an antidote to complacency if it had been circulated. Apart from the alleged physical abuse that he reported,

---

[29] See paras 21.63 to 21.66.

he made a number of strong criticisms of the regime at Bryn Alyn Hall and, in particular, the part of it known as Blackley House. The criticisms that he listed included the following:

(1) A boy who absconded was put on "scrubs" for three days. To Williams' knowledge, he was not allowed food for at least the first day. Williams regarded "scrubs" as totally out of place.

(2) There was a lack of healthy communication between the care staff and children in their care.

(3) No paperwork of any description was in evidence, other than a petty cash book.

(4) Boys were forced to sit or lie on the floor of the TV lounge (which was extremely cold) from 8.30 pm to 10 pm nightly, clad only in pyjamas (in some cases pyjama bottoms only).

(5) Coal or wood was burnt in the fireplaces as a means of heating and fires were only lit in the staff office or in the lounges for the benefit of staff after the boys had retired to bed.

(6) Clothing was taken from a boy's bedroom whilst he was in the bathroom to prevent him going home on a Friday, although the matter had not been discussed with him and staff subsequently denied all knowledge of where the clothing might be.

(7) A booklet found in the office, which explained how the home was run, was immediately said to be "years out of date".

Williams referred also to over-crowding at Blackley House. Some boys were sleeping out with staff. Sleeping in accommodation for staff was also being used to accommodate children, forcing staff to sleep on the floor of lounges.

21.114 One of Williams' conclusions was that emotional care was non-existent, although in some respects Bryn Alyn Hall did cater for the material things in children's lives there. He thought that standards of care were very poor, that physical and emotional abuse were standard practice and that all future operations of the Community should be looked into in some depth by "the relevant authorities".

21.115 On 20 October 1983 he visited Bryn Alyn Hall with his course tutor and met there John Allen and Stephen Elliott (then Director of Child Care), who assured them that Williams' concerns would be communicated to the social workers involved. Subsequently, on 7 November 1983 he was told by a senior officer of Manchester Social Services Department that his concerns had been fully investigated and that they were satisfied that the report was both unfounded and unprofessional. The officer warned Williams that he (Williams) could not distribute the report and that legal action would be considered by Allen. Williams did, however, raise the matter with the Home Office in June 1985 and with a number of newspapers and was interviewed on the subject by a representative of BBC television in September 1992.

Surveillance by the Welsh Office

21.116 We have already outlined briefly in Chapter 4[30] the steps taken by the Welsh Office in relation to registration of Bryn Alyn Hall as an independent school and the question of SEN approval; and we have referred to problems about the status of Pentre Saeson Hall and Gatewen Hall in respect of the provision of education. As we explain in Appendix 6 to the report, there was no requirement for a private children's home to be registered until Part VIII of the Children Act 1989 came into force[31] but the Secretary of State did have comprehensive powers of inspection of all forms of premises in which children in care were accommodated[32]. As for independent schools, the law governing registration and inspection during the relevant period is summarised in the same Appendix at paragraphs 36 to 42.

21.117 If we were to give an extended account of the inspections carried out on behalf of the Welsh Office by HMIs and SWSOs (SSIWs from about 1989) and the correspondence with the Community following up those inspections, a separate chapter would be necessary. Having regard to our terms of reference, however, a fairly detailed summary will suffice.

21.118 Bryn Alyn Hall opened in April 1969 with two units, Blackley and Lindisfarne, as a private children's home. Blackley then operated as a school from 1973 but the Welsh Office was told that it would close on 12 July 1976 and move to premises in Cheshire (presumably Marton's Camp which opened in July 1976). The first brief inspection, by an HMI and an SWSO, took place during this early period on short notice on 14 November 1975. They looked at occupancy and turnover and the educational services available but the residential provision was not inspected. Impressions were favourable: Blackley was thought to be an unusual enterprise providing a stimulating and comfortable environment for difficult boys. Concern was expressed, however, about the Community's "expansionist tendency" and the dangers attendant on size and dispersal.

21.119 A follow up visit by an HMI in April 1976 revealed that Blackley was having difficulty in providing a full secondary school curriculum and that local secondary schools were reluctant to accept Community pupils. The Welsh Office wrote to Allen informing him that, on the HMI's evidence, the conditions for full registration laid down in 1973 were not being met and that a formal inspection was proposed. This took place in June 1976 and the senior HMI who conducted it was critical of several aspects of the educational provision. It was shortly after this visit that the Head of the school wrote to the HMI about the proposed closure of the school.

21.120 On 10 May 1977 the Welsh Office received a letter from the Community stating that a school was again located at Bryn Alyn Hall. This letter followed an unannounced visit by HMI who had found a number of unsupervised pupils

[30] See paras 4.25 to 4.27.
[31] See Appendix 6, paras 15 and 18 to 20.
[32] Ibid, para 29.

apparently visiting from Marton's Camp. No letter or notice had been received by the Welsh Office but the position was then regularised and the school was provisionally registered on 18 July 1977.

21.121 Substantive registration of Bryn Alyn Hall as an independent school for 69 socially maladjusted boys was eventually granted on 30 April 1980. In the three years preceding that there had been about seven visits by Welsh Office Inspectors to the Community and substantive registration had earlier been refused on 1 June 1978, when concern had been expressed about the school's organisation on multiple sites, the standard of care and accommodation and the education provided. Amongst other matters that had caused disquiet were overcrowding, the admission of handicapped pupils contrary to statutory requirements and the provision of education on the premises at Pentre Saeson Hall. It had also been found in November 1977 that classrooms were badly underheated, in a very poor decorative condition and not thoroughly cleaned and that considerable improvements needed to be made in the educational provision itself. Inexperienced and, in some cases, unqualified teachers with no special training were trying to control difficult boys. By May 1979 improvements had been achieved but there was still uncertainty about the status ofPentre Saeson Hall. Registration of Bryn Alyn Hall followed further visits in December 1979 and April 1980 but the letter of 30 April 1980, stating that registration had been conferred, expressed the hope that there would be further development of the boys' educational programme; that efforts should be made to place boys in outside schools, where practicable; that the Community should work with placing authorities to ensure the return of pupils to their home areas as soon as possible; and that more consideration should be given to the curriculum for the abler, older boys.

21.122 It appears that at this point, or by July 1980, the Community had decided not to attempt to use Pentre Saeson Hall (or Bryntirion Hall) for teaching and its ambition to expand its educational provision was focussed on securing approval for the admission of children with special educational needs[33]. Exceptional permission for individual children was granted on occasions by the Secretary of State but it was not until 19 February 1985 that general approval was given to Bryn Alyn Hall only, under Section 11(3)(a) of the Education Act 1981, following a joint SWSO inspection in the autumn of 1984. However, the report of that inspection, which was the first of its kind by the Welsh Office under the Act of 1981 drew attention to the absence of any overall educational philosophy at the school. It noted also "barely acceptable" standards of educational performance and achievement and expressed misgivings about some aspects of the social provision. Despite these reservations there was only one HMI visit (in January 1986) before the next inspection three years later.

21.123 A major inspection by HMI with secondary subject specialists and experts in SEN took place in February 1988. Rather surprisingly the education provided and library records were described as excellent, but the organisation of the

---

[33] See Appendix 6, paras 38 and 39.

education programme and the standards achieved by pupils were held to be unsatisfactory in general. The domestic accommodation was also described as excellent and other aspects such as the care arrangements, staffing and staff development and arrangements for admission and leaving were all deemed to be at least satisfactory. The Welsh Office drew the attention of the Community, however, to the fact that (a) the school was admitting some pupils below 11 years of age without specific approval (b) Pentre Saeson was providing education and needed to be registered separately and (c) the person in overall charge of the school had to be a qualified teacher.

21.124 The summary of the report dated 29 November 1988 contained the following revealing paragraph:

> "4. Part of the problem of these establishments stems from the pupils catered for, largely young people with severe behavioural problems from the English inner-cities. In the case of Bryn Alyn School there are on the roll 50 boys and 15 girls but only three are from Welsh counties. The others are drawn from English counties and county boroughs, as far away as Newcastle and various London boroughs. A high proportion are from the NW of England. All but one of the pupils are subject to some form of care order. Many have only a tenuous contact with their homes or other permanent bases in the home area. Placements for far away from home are a concern to us and, with DES, we are proposing new Circular guidance on special educational needs, including an emphasis on the need for close co-operation between LEAs and Social Services Departments in placement decisions and for the whole needs of the child to be considered."

21.125 It would be unnecessarily tedious to recount in detail the subsequent exchanges between the Welsh Office and the Community that led ultimately to the removal of Bryn Alyn Hall from the register in May 1997, after the company had gone into voluntary liquidation on 6 March 1997. It is sufficient here to summarise the main events, as follows:

(a) In January 1989 the Community was requested to provide within three weeks a response to the 1988 inspectors' report setting out what was to be done to implement the report's findings.

(b) The Community's response in September 1989 was considered to be unsatisfactory.

(c) A further visit by HMIs took place in December 1991 and by letter dated 22 January 1992 the Welsh Office required urgent action (within six months) by the Community in relation to behaviour management, staff turnover and certain care practices, failing which withdrawal of SEN approval would be considered.

(d) Following further visits by HMIs in November 1992, June 1993 and February 1994, it was recommended to the Secretary of State that SEN approval should be withdrawn. The Secretary of State's intention to do this was communicated to the school's Director by letter dated 9 May 1994.

(e) SEN approval was not in fact withdrawn until 3 February 1997[34] following additional visits by HMIs in November 1994, October 1995 and May 1996 and a full inspection (under the five year cycle[35]) between 28 and 31 October 1996. Each of these visits and inspections had been followed by a recital to the Community of matters to be remedied.

(f) The letter of 3 February 1997 withdrawing SEN approval referred also to the fact that the Secretary of State was considering serving a Notice of Complaint (as a prelude to withdrawal of registration) but the liquidation of the company supervened a month later.

Action by Clwyd Social Services Department

21.126 Prior to the coming into force of the Children Act 1989 on 14 October 1991, Clwyd Social Services Department did not have any direct responsibility for the Community's various units. Its concern with the Community was limited to its role as a placement authority to the extent that children in the care of Clwyd were placed with the Community and its role as the local authority charged with the duty of child protection within its area. From 14 October 1991, however, Clwyd became responsible for the registration of private children's homes, including independent schools within the definition, and acquired powers of inspection[36].

21.127 We have already referred, in the context of Welsh Office inspections, to the doubts that had been expressed earlier about the status of Pentre Saeson because children were receiving education there. A similar problem arose in respect of Gatewen Hall because it had been registered as an independent school from 1978 under its previous ownership and the Community wished to maintain its registration after acquiring the premises in 1983. However, successive inspections in February 1984 and January and July 1986 confirmed that the premises were no longer being used as a school and Gatewen Hall was removed from the register in August 1986 despite Allen's plea to maintain its status as a school. In the same year or the following year Bryntirion Hall ceased to operate as a children's home.

21.128 Thus it was that Clwyd County Council received applications from the Community in or about October 1991 for the registration of Pentre Saeson Hall and Gatewen Hall as private children's homes. There was then rather protracted correspondence with the Welsh Office about Pentre Saeson's status and in the event, no decision was made in respect of either application within the statutorily prescribed period. The Community then appealed[37] against what were "deemed refusals" to register and the appeals were dismissed by a Registered Homes Tribunal in December 1993. At the hearings of the appeals in September 1993 Clwyd County Council opposed them, a members' panel having endorsed an officers' recommendation against registration. The two

---

[34] The procedure was by then governed by section 347(5)(a) of the Education Act 1996.

[35] See Appendix 6, para 40.

[36] See Appendix 6, paras 15, 18 to 20 and 42.

[37] Under section 63 of the Children Act 1989.

children's homes had been inspected by Clwyd in April 1993; and an investigation had been carried out by a team of three in May and June 1993 into certain complaints about Gatewen Hall. The appeal tribunal's decision was made on the grounds that the proprietor of the Community was not a fit person to run a children's home.

21.129 The question of registration of Bryn Alyn Hall as a children's home under Part VIII of the Children Act 1989 did not arise until the Welsh Office withdrew SEN approval on 3 February 1997[38]. It was then academic, however, because, in the letter of that date, the Welsh Office asked the Community "to liaise with placing authorities so that all pupils would be removed by 26 March 1997". This request was made in the context that the Secretary of State was considering, as a separate issue, serving a Notice of Complaint. Nevertheless, Clwyd Social Services Department did earlier inspect Bryn Alyn Hall, in September 1992 and April 1993.

Conclusions

21.130 It is readily understandable that public concern, on the limited information then available, should have focused on the sexual abuse that was perpetrated on residents of the Community and, in particular, the abuse committed by John Allen himself. Whatever may have been Allen's motives when he started the Bryn Alyn enterprise, his subsequent criminal conduct inflicted untold damage upon a large number of residents and, in many cases, distorted their subsequent lives. It is a cause for grave concern also that his influence extended for some beyond the period of their residence in care with the Community to later years when they should have been establishing themselves in normal patterns of life. Instead, it appears that they were encouraged to live in unfamiliar surroundings such as Brighton or London in accommodation (halfway houses or the like) provided or subsidised by Allen, without appropriate supervision or guidance, at a time when they were highly vulnerable and likely to fall prey to many temptations.

21.131 The evidence before us has, however, disclosed many other reasons for public anxiety. The heart of the matter is that a small group of unsuitable and ill-trained persons was able to establish, with official sanction, a mushrooming centre for the care and education of behaviourally disturbed children when they had virtually none of the resources necessary to cope adequately with the task. The dangers attendant upon Allen's "expansionist" ambitions were recognised by Welsh Office Inspectors as early as November 1975 but the basic problems were allowed to persist and, to some extent, proliferate for over 20 years, despite quite frequent further inspections and some reports of alleged abuse. Throughout that period local authorities from far afield were able to consign "difficult" children to the Community for long stays, cut off from their families and local environments, with little prospect that they would eventually return better equipped to take their place in society. Yet this very problem had been canvassed in November 1988 in a summary of an inspectors' report[39]. A

---

[38] See Appendix 6, paras 18 and 19, where the definition of "children's home" is explained.
[39] See para 21.124.

harsh but fair assessment would be that local authorities, acting in good faith, were persuaded by Allen's blandishments and the Community's advertising documents, to use the Community as an apparently safe dumping ground for children in care for whose needs they did not feel able to provide themselves.

21.132 On the basis of the evidence before us our findings are that:

(a) The Community's staff were largely untrained and very few indeed had any training or experience in dealing with the special problems and needs of disturbed children.

(b) Members of the staff were not given any clear explanation of what the Community sought to achieve with individual children.

(c) Until Stephen Elliott assumed senior responsibilities there was no adequate managerial or supervisory control and the separate units within the Community were largely self-governing.

(d) There were many periods during which accommodation was over-crowded and staff/resident ratios inadequate. Physical conditions for the residents were often poor.

(e) Many children were retained by the Community, despite the fact that the regime was unsuitable for them to the knowledge of members of the staff.

(f) Despite the establishment of a key worker system at some stage following the Barclay Report in 1982, it had little impact on the residents and there was throughout a lack of individual care and attention to individual needs, except possibly for a favoured few.

(g) There were genuine attempts in the later stages to improve the regime but these attempts were bedevilled by financial difficulties stemming from earlier over-expansion and dissipation of resources in the absence of adequate managerial and financial control.

21.133 It has been difficult to obtain an accurate picture of the extent of physical abuse of staff and peer bullying because the number of former residents who have provided evidence is small as a proportion of the total number of children and young persons who were admitted to the Community and of those who eventually made complaints to the police. The picture given by Denis Williams was truly alarming. We do not doubt his sincerity but he stayed for only three days and his strictures upon particular individuals were not mirrored by the volume of subsequent complaints about them, despite their long service with the Community. We are satisfied that excessive force was used by members of the staff quite frequently, particularly in the early years of the Community when staff were almost wholly untrained; and in that context it is likely that bullying was prevalent. But we do not consider that the use of force by staff or residents was ever on a similar scale to that used in Bryn Estyn and we believe that the level receded in later years as more staff were trained, they matured and the climate of opinion generally hardened against any form of corporal punishment.

Care Concern's schools in Clwyd

Introduction

22.01 As we have said in our earlier outline of private residential establishments for children in care[1], Care Concern was the name given in 1976 to an organisation conceived by David Rattray, a former Deputy Director of Social Services for Denbighshire, which opened a new independent private school for boys known as Ystrad Hall in 1974. This was the name of the property, owned by Rattray, on which the school was sited on the A5 road on the Corwen side of Llangollen; and it comprised two residential units, that is, the Hall itself and an hotel known as Eirianfa Hotel, which Rattray had run as a business, together with 14 acres of land.

22.02 Ystrad Hall was registered as a school provisionally in September 1974 and fully in October 1975. A fire damaged one of the two residential units (Eirianfa) at the end of the decade and the school ceased to be registered in May 1981, when it closed because of a substantial fall in the number of pupils. It was re-opened, however, as a residential school for girls on about half the site, called Berwyn College for Girls, almost immediately and Berwyn College was registered from 13 August 1981 to 31 March 1985. Although it was a school for girls, it did admit some boys during a period of industrial action by social workers.

22.03 The 20 to 22 senior boys who were living in Eirianfa at Ystrad Hall when the fire occurred were transferred to another residential establishment (previously occupied by priests) that had been acquired by Care Concern. This was St David's College at Carrog, near Corwen, which was a school for girls and which was provisionally registered as such. The boys' period of exile there lasted about eight months but Ystrad Hall school closed quite soon after their return. The 12 or so girls who were at St David's College transferred to the new Berwyn College and St David's College became a home for adults with learning disabilities. We have not received any complaints of physical or sexual abuse at St David's College.

22.04 The activities of Care Concern were not confined to the three schools that we have so far discussed in this chapter. They opened also in 1976 schools in Gwynedd known as Cartref Melys[2] near Conway and Hengwrt Hall at Rhydymain between Dolgellau and Bala. The latter will be dealt with in Part VIII of this Report. The boys left at Ystrad Hall on its closure were offered places at Cartref Melys. In addition, Care Concern ran a halfway house accommodating 13 boys at Chester, a residential home for adults with learning difficulties in Colwyn Bay and a residential home known as The Village at

---

[1] See paras 4.12 to 4.16.
[2] See para 5.08.

Llangwyfan in Clwyd. Although the latter was essentially a home for adults, it did cater for some teenagers and we will make brief reference to it again later in this chapter.

Ystrad Hall School

22.05 This school was registered as a school catering wholly or mainly for handicapped pupils in the socially maladjusted category. The age range was, in general, 11 to 16 years and the permitted number of pupils was not specified but there were usually 50 to 55 boys in residence. The school did not have general SEN approval but exceptional admissions of statemented pupils were authorised from time to time[3]. One of the recommendations made by the Registrar on granting final registration on 21 October 1975 was that "Greater care should be taken in the vetting of pupils to ensure that too many disruptive boys are not admitted at the same time".

22.06 The structure of the school was that there were two substantial residential blocks (the country house and the former hotel) and a separate free-standing demountable block of classrooms. The Principal was in day-to-day charge of both care and education and there were two Assistant Principals, one responsible for care, the other for education. The bulk of the teaching was undertaken by two senior teachers, a remedial specialist and six class teachers. On the care side, each residential unit had a House Warden, three Senior Care Officers and six Assistant Care Officers.

22.07 The person with the main administrative responsibility for Ystrad Hall School was **Richard Ernest Leake**, who was recruited by David Rattray from Bersham Hall, where Leake had been Officer-in-Charge or Superintendent from 4 August 1972[4]. He was 33 years old when he joined Rattray on 1 July 1974 and had about 16 years relevant experience, having worked in the administrative department of a local education authority and in a children's department before becoming a care worker in increasingly senior positions in a children's home and a variety of remand and assessment centres. He had also obtained in 1972 an advanced certificate in residential care from Bristol University. Leake was the first Principal of Ystrad Hall School but, when Care Concern acquired Cartref Melys in 1976, he became an administrator with the title of Assistant Director of Professional Services and two years later he was advanced to Director. He continued to carry the same responsibilities within the organisation (under the title Assistant Director from 1980 with Rattray as Director) until January 1986 when he became involved in preparations for extending the organisation to the south of England; but he left a year later to work in the private sector in Kent, caring for adults with learning difficulties.

22.08 Rattray advertised the school widely amongst local authorities in England and Wales and the lists of pupils that we have seen show that it was mainly used by distant English local authorities. A few were admitted from Gwynedd but there

---

[3] See Appendix 6, paras 38 and 39.
[4] See paras 13.07 and 50.31(6).

appears to have been a clash of personalities in relation to Clwyd, possibly stemming from the recruitment of both Leake and the Headteacher from Bersham Hall, and we are not aware of the admission of any Clwyd child. It was noted by HMI Stone, when reporting on a visit made on 17 May 1979 that:

> "Boys from this school very rarely return to their home community until they have attained school leaving age and a special dispensation has had to be granted for one or two boys for whom no suitable outlet was available at school leaving age . . . Although the aim of the school is to return boys to their home as soon as possible so far this has not happened to any extent. The proprietor was unable to quote exact numbers but said it would be in the order of ones or twos rather than any significant number."

22.09 Despite the comparatively short life of this school no less than 40 former residents made complaints of abuse subsequently to the police and about 20 members of staff in all were named in those complaints.

Allegations of sexual abuse

22.10 An early culprit was **Bryan Davies**, who was named as a sexual abuser by eight former residents. Davies had been appointed Deputy Principal or Warden of Eirianfa unit, which housed boys aged from 11 to 14 years, in or about 1975, having had some previous experience of residential care work with children. He was arrested on 25 May 1978, however, and subsequently convicted in Llangollen Magistrates' Court on 4 September 1978 of three offences of indecent assault upon two residents of the school, for which he was made subject to a probation order for 12 months, with a condition requiring him to undergo hospital treatment, and ordered to perform 160 hours community service[5]. He did not return to the school after his arrest.

22.11 We received the evidence of two of the eight complainants, neither of whom was the subject of the charges on which Davies was arrested. A, who gave oral evidence, was a boy from the Midlands who was a resident of Eirianfa for nearly a year at the age of 14 years. He said that he was taken to Davies' home on two occasions by another care worker when he thought that the purpose of the visit was preparation of a report for a case conference. On both occasions Davies made A fondle Davies' groin and did the same to him. He reported what had happened to Davies' Deputy, Christopher Williamson, four to six weeks later and thought that nothing had been done about it but he learnt later that Davies had subsequently been convicted of other similar offences. He said also that Davies would have known from his social services file that he had been sexually abused previously by his step-father.

22.12 Witness B said in his written statement that he went to the school when he was 12 years old (probably in 1977 when he was 13 years old). One day, when he was telephoning his mother, Davies came up behind him and started to rub his

---

[5] See para 2.07(3).

chest and the side of his leg; Davies then started to do something to B's penis so B turned around and kicked Davies.

22.13 Leake's evidence was that he was aware that some boys would stay from time to time with Davies and Davies' wife at their home. He was not suspicious because he knew Mrs Davies and the home. Leake learnt of a complaint by a boy resident (neither A nor B) when the Principal, Susan Hildred, telephoned him about it. He was horrified and informed the police immediately. Leake and Hildred then went to Davies' home and suspended him forthwith. They did not carry out an investigation themselves but Davies was dismissed following certain admissions that he made to the police.

22.14 It was not possible for the Tribunal to serve Davies with a Salmon letter and we have not received any statement from him. We do not know, therefore, the extent of his express admissions but we have no reason to doubt the correctness of his convictions or the evidence that we received of his additional indecent assault on B. There is difficulty, however, about A's evidence in relation to dates, which we explain in paragraphs 22.21 and 22.25.

22.15 We were not able to investigate allegations of sexual abuse made against Leake himself by former residents of Ystrad Hall School because they were the subject of continuing police investigation[6].

22.16 Four other members of the staff (one unidentified) and one resident were the subject of allegations of sexual abuse made by five different former residents, each of whom referred to only one abuser. As we understand the position, police officers investigated the allegations, which were not corroborated, and no prosecution ensued. The evidence of two of these complainants was read to us. In his first statement to the police, made in prison on 10 August 1992, this witness, C, described in detail how he had been indecently assaulted and later buggered by a named member of staff in a staff bedroom at Eirianfa. He alleged that the last occasion when buggery occurred was shortly before the fire at Eirianfa. He had not complained to any member of the staff about what had been done to him but he had confided in four named friends.

22.17 Although that statement reads quite straightforwardly, doubt about the general credibility of the witness C arises from two subsequent statements that he made. Shortly after his first statement a former resident told the police that he had seen C assaulted physically on two occasions by another member of the staff, Christopher (Chris) Williamson. C was seen, therefore, on 26 November 1992 by a police officer, who wished to ascertain whether C would confirm the allegation. In response, however, C denied that he had been assaulted by Williamson and said he recalled the latter only vaguely as a handyman who had never worked as a care assistant. C described Williamson as an elderly man with a grey beard who was cross-eyed.

22.18 C made his third statement on 16 January 1997 when he was seen by a representative of the Tribunal. In that statement he repudiated the second statement attributed to him, saying that he did not make it and that its contents

---

[6] See para 50.31(6) for the position in September 1999.

were not true. He went on to say (contrary to his first statement) that he had complained to Williamson in his office about the first act of buggery on the day after it had occurred, but that he did not recall anything being done about it. Later in the same statement to the Tribunal C gave a full description of Williamson, putting his age in the early forties, and alleged that Williamson had assaulted him twice physically: the first occasion was when he had complained of being buggered, whereupon Williamson had come around his desk, grabbed him by the shoulder and smacked him across the face and had then pushed him down on to an arm chair, shouting "No, he didn't do it"; and the second occasion was when he repeated the allegation of buggery by a member of the staff to Williamson after some discussion with a friend's father and Williamson had thumped him on the face and head and kicked him in the ribs when he went to the floor.

22.19 The internal conflicts between these three statements are such that we cannot be sure that any of them is correct. The other complainant whose evidence was read named another young boy as his abuser and it has not been appropriate to pursue that allegation.

Allegations of physical abuse

22.20 The main target of complaints about physical abuse was **Christopher Williamson**, to whom we referred in paragraph 22.17 and who was named by 12 complainants. Two of these, however, alleged only that he had failed to act upon complaints made to him. Williamson went to Ystrad Hall as a care officer in March 1976 at the age of 23 years, after working at a remand centre for two years. His only training was an in-service pre-qualifying course in residential care for children involving attendance at Cartrefle College once per week for a year. Nevertheless, he was promoted to Deputy Officer-in-Charge of the Eirianfa Unit, under Bryan Davies, after six months. Williamson remained at Eirianfa until 1981 and then worked successively at St David's College, Carrog[7], and The Village, Llangwyfan[8], mainly with adults. After leaving Care Concern's employ in 1986 he went to South Glamorgan as a senior RCCO.

22.21 We received evidence from three of the complainants against Williamson, two of whom were A[9] and C and the latter's complaints have already been dealt with[10]. A's complaint against Williamson was that the latter failed to pass on or act upon the complaint of A that Bryan Davies had sexually assaulted him. There is considerable confusion about this allegation, however, because A says that his complaint was made towards the end of his stay at Ystrad Hall, which was from 13 March 1978 to 5 February 1979, whereas Davies was arrested on 25 May 1978 and never returned after that date to Ystrad Hall. Williamson was firm in his own recollection that two other boys complained to him on 20 May 1978, in circumstances that he described in detail, of sexual assaults by Davies. These two boys were the victims named in the subsequent criminal charges

---

[7] See para 22.03.
[8] See para 22.04.
[9] See para 22.11.
[10] See paras 22.17 and 22.18.

against Davies and he (Williamson) believed their complaints. He reported the matter directly to Leake so that Leake could investigate and he did not tell Davies about the complaints, despite the fact that Davies was a friend of his. Williamson did not recall A's complaint.

22.22 The result of all this is that we cannot accept that there was any cover up or failure to report by Williamson. Moreover, A said in cross-examination that he trusted Williamson and thought that he was "a good bloke". The other "complainant" against Williamson made a written statement in which he merely said that Williamson had once dragged him downstairs: he added that Williamson had later apologised to him for doing so and that he did not wish to complain about the matter. Finally, another witness (not one of the 12 complainants referred to in paragraph 22.20) alleged that he was kicked across the boot room by another member of staff (thought now to be in Holland) and that he had complained to Bryan Davies. The witness said that he was about 15 years old at the time and that he was "on about going to the police about it" to "a couple of the lads" but Williamson warned them not to go to the police. Speaking generally of Ystrad Hall, however, this witness said that the regime was good.

22.23 It follows that there is no basis, on the evidence that we have received, for a finding that Williamson physically abused children at Ystrad Hall and we are not satisfied that he condoned such abuse. In his own evidence to us he denied any such behaviour.

22.24 Although 11 other former members of the staff were alleged by individual former residents (in statements to the police) to have committed physical assaults upon them of varying gravity, only one was named by as many as three former residents, most of them were named by only one and few of these complainants provided statements to the Tribunal. Witness A, for example, complained that **Bryan Davies** had assaulted him physically as well as sexually but there are difficulties about the dates when some of the physical assaults are alleged to have occurred, as in respect of the alleged sexual assaults.

22.25 A was a persistent offender who had been sent from Nottingham to Ystrad Hall for that reason. According to his oral evidence, he and two others burgled a factory next to the school six days after his arrival, when Davies was still in charge of Eirianfa. He said that the police were involved in investigating the burglary and, when the culprits returned to Eirianfa, they were put in the office before Davies, who punched A in the ribs and slapped him across the face (he was not able to say precisely what happened to the other two). On another occasion A crept out at night and drove the school's minibus around the compound but was caught by one of the night security staff with the result that he received similar punishment from Davies in the latter's office next day. His identification of Davies on another occasion must have been wrong because he said that he was struck by Davies in the same office early in October 1978 on his return to Eirianfa after he had absconded from a local judo club to London with two other boys.

22.26 Other allegations of physical abuse by staff members that we heard in evidence were of variable weight. One former resident whose evidence was read, for example, alleged generally that he had been hit by staff for no reason whilst another spoke (in his third statement to the police) of being punched in the face by a named member of staff, with a resulting nose bleed, after he had been cheeky to a woman dietician, who was checking the diet. This witness alleged also that he had seen the same male staff member punch and head-butt another boy without any provocation.

22.27 The treatment of the former resident who alleged that he had been buggered by another boy at Ystrad Hall[11] did give rise to anxiety for other reasons when he was resident there between September 1977 and April 1981. This witness, D, whose evidence was read to us, originated from Wiltshire and had been admitted to Gwynfa Residential Unit for about eight months before moving to Ystrad Hall. His hyperactive and intrusive behaviour antagonised both the staff and his fellow residents with the result that he was subjected to frequent bullying, and it seems that he may also have been accident prone. In May 1978, when D was 13 years old, Care Concern's Properties Manager and the Domestic Supervisor became concerned about D for differing reasons and the upshot was that Leake carried out an investigation, including a survey of D's recent injuries. The investigation disclosed that at least three members of the staff had physically chastised D and each of them was cautioned. The school's prohibition of corporal punishment was also re-affirmed to all members of the staff. Leake's view was that D had been suffering excessive physical abuse because of the inexperience of staff, who were unable to understand the depths of his problems, and the frustration of his peer group, who were unable to cope with him.

Welsh Office inspections

22.28 From the documents produced to us, it appears that Ystrad Hall School was visited by HMIs on five occasions, the last being a formal inspection.

22.29 The first two visits were made on 19 November 1974 and 26 February 1975 in connection with the school's application for full registration following its provisional registration in September 1974. The second of the visits was a follow up by an SWSO with two HMIs because, although the teaching arrangements had been found to be adequate on the first visit, subject to expansion of the provision for abler children, there had been some criticism of the care arrangements. In particular, it had been said that the dormitories were unheated and overcrowded and that additional spaces ought to be provided in the residential units for privacy. The report by the SWSO on the second visit emphasised that the nature of the visit allowed for only impressions of the quality of care provided and no recommendations were made. On a third visit by HMI a year later, however, when 54 boys were on the roll, the school made a satisfactory general impression.

---

[11] See para 22.19.

22.30 The fourth visit did not take place until 17 May 1979, when two HMIs (and another HMI as observer) called at the school. The report of this visit did not comment directly on the quality of care but the inspectors told Rattray that they considered that the residential care arrangements were very poor. They commented to him also upon "the poor standards of work and behaviour in the education block", which they attributed directly to inadequate supervision and implementation of organisational plans and schemes devised by the Head of the school (Susan Hildred). For these reasons they thought that a formal inspection ought to take place later in the year.

22.31 That inspection, by two HMIs, took place on 3 December 1979 and resulted in a favourable report, although time did not permit the inspectors to visit the residential part of the school. In relation to that, the inspectors appear to have accepted an assurance that considerable reorganisation had taken place and that the general standards were much improved. On the educational side they found that there had been complete reorganisation and a number of changes of staff. There were 53 boys attending the school, who were taught in eight groups of varying size, including a remedial group of four. All the classrooms were visited and the improvement in their layout and decor and in the display of children's work was said to be quite remarkable. The domestic subjects teacher's achievement in developing her work and the boys' involvement were also praised as "most remarkable". The reporting inspector concluded:

> "I do not think we would any longer have any justification for withholding placement, provided the overall number did not exceed 56[12]. I think, however, that these 2 visits illustrate the absolute necessity for regular and close monitoring of independent schools of this kind. With our present manpower we are unable to do this, and will therefore, always be to some extent 'at risk' with these establishments."

Conclusions

22.32 We have not been able to obtain a full picture of the alleged abuse at Ystrad Hall School and some serious matters remain unresolved. The fact that sexual abuse has been proved here too gives additional cause for substantial concern and adds to the gloomy history that we have narrated in earlier chapters. Sexual abuse apart, the record of the school was patchy. It is clear that other physical abuse did occur on quite frequent occasions early on and that the prohibition on corporal punishment was not fully observed but it is reasonable to infer from the dates before us that physical abuse became less frequent as time went on, probably after the investigation by Leake into D's treatment. The quality of care fluctuated but the school might have survived, bearing in mind the improvements noted on the inspection in December 1979, but for the fire in the Eirianfa unit that occurred very soon afterwards and the consequent disruption. We draw attention, however, to the passage from the inspector's report cited in the preceding paragraph in which he emphasised the need for regular inspections and monitoring of this type of school.

---

[12] This referred to a temporary suspension of further exceptional SEN approvals recommended by the same inspector in July 1979 following the fourth visit but not apparently implemented by the Welsh Office.

Berwyn College for Girls

22.33 We can deal with the history of this school over a period of about three and a half years from August 1981 to the end of March 1985 quite shortly. It was established in the Ystrad Hall unit of Ystrad Hall School when the latter closed. The Eirianfa unit was never part of the new school, which occupied seven or eight acres of the original 14 acre site on the banks of the River Dee. Ystrad Hall itself, the former country house, served as residential and recreational accommodation, with dormitories on the upper floors. There was also a demountable house with two bedrooms, living room, kitchen and bathroom, which was used as an independence unit for training in daily living routines; and the classrooms, which had been used by Ystrad Hall School, were in demountable single storey buildings about 200 yards from the main house.

22.34 The school does not appear to have achieved full registration before it closed. When it was provisionally registered on 13 August 1981 it was said that HMI would visit the school in the near future and that the Secretary of State would communicate his further decision about the school after that. In the event, however, the visit did not take place until 1 and 2 November 1984 and the Welsh Office was informed of the decision of Care Concern to close the school by letter dated 10 January 1985, when the inspector's report was about to be, or had only just been, signed. Nevertheless, the school was granted exceptional SEN approval for named pupils on at least seven occasions[13].

22.35 At the time when the school was provisionally registered there were 17 resident pupils in the age range of 13 to 16 years, including the 12 pupils who had been transferred from St David's College. The staffing establishment of the new school was said to be based on 24 beds. By November 1983 it had been agreed with the Welsh Office that up to 27 girls could be admitted but Care Concern then informed HMI that it was intended that the school should function on a co-educational basis with an additional 28 placements (presumably bringing the Eirianfa unit into use again), beginning the admission of additional pupils on and after 1 December 1983. This received the response in January 1984 that HMI were prepared to agree provisionally to an increase in numbers, provided that it was a gradual increase and that Care Concern was perfectly satisfied that the care and safety arrangements were adequate. Almost exactly a year later, however, there were only 12 resident pupils and Care Concern decided that the school would close on 31 March 1985.

22.36 From the few lists of pupils at Berwyn College that we have seen, it appears that they were drawn from quite a wide range of local authorities. London boroughs were particularly prominent and there were children from a number of southern English counties. We know of only one placement from Wales, by Gwent County Council.

22.37 The full inspection by two HMIs on 1 and 2 November 1984 was successful from the school's point of view. There were then 15 pupils at the school, aged between 14 and 16 years. They were divided into four classes, each of mixed ability. All the pupils were in the care of a local authority and about half of them had formal

---

[13] See Appendix 6, paras 38 and 39.

statements of special educational need. The majority were in care because they had been out of parental control or truanting from school or the subject of a place of safety order. They had all been referred by social services departments and the average length of stay was two years (a minimum of six months was expected), continuing usually to school leaving age. A prospective pupil was required to visit with her social worker before a place was offered to her and parents were encouraged to attend. The pupil was assessed over an eight week period on admission after which she was reviewed and subsequent reviews (involving the social worker, pupil and staff) were at six monthly intervals.

22.38 The inspectors found that the residential leisure facilities were adequate in size and reasonably well furnished and decorated: the dormitories were functional and orderly rather than homely. Their comments on the education programme and the quality of care were generally favourable and the conclusion of the inspector who signed the report was summarised as follows:

> "Berwyn College is well organised and supported by the Care Concern Organisation and provides a stable and supportive background for young girls with certain kinds of social, emotional and behavioural problems. The general arrangements and the care programme are vigorously implemented and supervised by the Principal[14] but there are some weaknesses in the provision of education, which could be overcome if the same degree of oversight were exercised in this sector. Despite these weaknesses, in some of the education provision, the overall standard of provision is such that it should be approved under the Education Act 1981 . . . I suggest that, without holding up approval, reference to the need to continue with the development of sound schemes of work and to ensure that they are fully implemented, should be made in the covering letter."

Allegations of abuse

22.39 Berwyn College attracted some unhelpful local publicity in September 1982 when two resident girls, aged 14 and 15 years respectively, pleaded guilty at Llangollen Juvenile Court to an offence of arson at the school. They had deliberately set a bed in a spare bedroom alight, causing damage estimated at £2,500. Fortunately, the local fire brigade had responded promptly to the alarm. The explanation given by one of the girls was that she hated the college to which she had been sent by a local authority; and it was said by a solicitor on behalf of one of the two that "she had been so upset that this week-end she had tried to take an overdose and to cut her throat". The girls were made subject to orders of conditional discharge for two years.

22.40 We are not aware of any complaint of sexual abuse at Berwyn College.

22.41 We received copies of statements made to the police by eight former residents of Berwyn College who alleged that they had been assaulted whilst they were there. One of these complained only about a fight that she had with another

---

[14] Shirley Smith-Jones.

resident on her arrival at the school, which she regarded as a form of initiation ceremony, connived at by the staff and intended to put her in her place. The other seven all complained of physical abuse by **David Trevor Tinniswood**, mainly in the form of excessive restraint. Only one of the seven, however, provided evidence to the Tribunal and he was the only male complainant who made allegations against Tinniswood.

22.42 David Tinniswood was employed by Care Concern for about seven years, starting in October 1979, when he was 31 years old. He had not had any previous training in or experience of residential child care work but he had been a certificated teacher for 12 months at the end of the 1960s before running the family hotel and a couple of shops at Corwen for most of the 1970s. He was taken on by Care Concern initially as a care officer at Ystrad Hall School, moving with the boys to St David's College after the fire and then back to the previous campus until the school closed. He then worked at Berwyn College before moving in 1984 or 1985 to Cartref Melys until June or July 1986, when the latter was due to close. After Care Concern he worked for seven years or so with adults with learning difficulties as an employee of Clwyd Social Services Department until he ceased work to look after his father. Tinniswood said that he did not receive any actual training whilst working for Care Concern, apart from staff development meetings: courses were available for some members of the staff but he was not selected for one.

22.43 During his period at Berwyn College, Tinniswood was listed initially as one of the assistant teachers but he was later shown as a Group Leader on the care staff. The former pupils remembered him as a member of staff who was mainly involved in outdoor activities. The male former resident who complained about him, E, was a Coventry boy who had been taken into care at the age of nine months and who was just 16 years old when he went to Berwyn College at the end of 1983 for about six months after being expelled from other schools. E said in his oral evidence to the Tribunal that he did not "get on" with any of the staff: he simply looked on in the classroom and did not learn very much. He had particular trouble with Tinniswood, who was then a Group Leader and who thought that he could make E do things that E did not want to do. E alleged that more than once Tinniswood slapped him in the face and kicked him on his legs. E added that he ran away every day but he would be taken to the police station, told off and then sent back to the school.

22.44 E said also that he was a regular glue sniffer and that on one occasion Tinniswood caught him doing this by the canal. Tinniswood punched and kicked him and then dragged him all the way to the college from the canal.

22.45 Tinniswood denied all the former girl residents' allegations when he was interviewed by the police and said that they were made by a certain type of girl within the school. In his oral evidence to the Tribunal and in his written statement he dealt specifically with E's allegations and denied that he ever punched or kicked E. Tinniswood explained that E was only admitted to Berwyn College because of the national industrial action by social workers until a placement could be found for him in his home area. It was necessary to restrain E or to remove him from situations on several occasions to prevent him from harming himself and others when he was intoxicated as a result of solvent abuse; one of his practices had been to stand motionless ("playing statues") on the A5 trunk road, which ran past the college. Tinniswood did not recall now the alleged incident by the canal but said that he would have had to drag E back to the school for his own protection in the circumstances described. Speaking more generally of E, Tinniswood described him as "a loner", who was a victim of the industrial action and who should not have been at Berwyn College. Despite several hiccups the school thought that progress had been made with him because it was agreed at one stage that, on leaving, he would go to live at Berwyn Station on the Llangollen Railway and become stationmaster there, subject to overcoming his solvent abuse.

22.46 The allegations against Tinniswood illustrate the problems that are likely to arise if an untrained care worker is placed in charge of disturbed children, who may have to be restrained physically from time to time. The dangers are aggravated if the children are girls and the care worker is a robust man. In the absence of any evidence to the Tribunal from the former girl residents, however, it would be inappropriate for us to make any finding about their complaints. In relation to E we suspect that he is more bitter now than he was at the time, even though he never wanted to be at Berwyn College. Such contemporary documents as we have seen confirm his problems and suggest that he was handled quite sensitively. They show also that work was arranged for him on the local railway (his major interest was in his model railway, which he had with him) and, in one review, reference was made to his "nice rapport" with Tinniswood, who had suggested the work on the railway. We are not satisfied therefore, that Tinniswood was guilty of slapping or kicking him habitually or of using excessive force in returning him from the canal to the school.

Conclusions

22.47 The evidence before us does not suggest that Berwyn College was a school in which physical or sexual abuse of children occurred. It took upon itself the difficult task of looking after emotionally disturbed girls far from their own homes and achieved a degree of success, despite the shortcomings in training of most of the staff. Tinniswood spoke feelingly, however, of "working in a dustbin" because members of the staff felt that they were taking on responsibilities that had been abandoned by the placement authorities. We do not endorse that view but we shall comment again later upon the undesirability of distant placements and the problems that arise when children who have been subject to them leave school. It must be added that, although the basic quality of care at Berwyn College was probably adequate, it was formal and rather rigid, lacking much of the quality of homeliness, which is an important aspect of a young girl's training for life.

The Village, Llangwyfan

22.48 A postscript about this establishment is necessary, although it was neither a children's home nor a residential school, because it was owned by Care Concern and was the subject of complaints by one witness who gave oral evidence to the Tribunal.

22.49 The Village occupied the site of a former purpose built sanatorium for tuberculosis patients established under the auspices of the King Edward VII Memorial Fund in a village near Ruthin. Care Concern opened its residential institution there in March 1983 with the object of providing training for persons of both sexes between the ages of 16 and 65 years with learning difficulties and it included workshops in which residents could learn a variety of appropriate trades.

22.50 We deal with this matter briefly because the witness, F, does not appear to have been in care when he went to live at The Village on 28 June 1983, at the age of 16 years 8 months. F's background was that he had been born prematurely and suffered from both cerebral palsy and epilepsy. After he had attended special schools, The Village was recommended to his mother and his social worker and others and he stayed there for just over five years. F's complaints came to light in June 1996 (the month when he made a statement to the police) after he had seen a television programme and had communicated with a television company, which led to appearances on television and radio and interviews with the press.

22.51 The allegations made by F in his oral evidence to the Tribunal, were that (a) he had been indecently assaulted and buggered by a member of the staff on one occasion before his 18th birthday at The Village in the latter's office behind a locked door in an incident that lasted 20 to 30 minutes; (b) he had also been indecently assaulted and buggered on numerous occasions by a fellow resident several years older then him (who was a known homosexual) from before his 18th birthday until he left; (c) he had been punched in the stomach by two members of the staff independently of each other on two separate occasions but that he had become quite good friends with one of the two later.

22.52 Whilst we have no specific reason to doubt the veracity of allegation (b), it is impossible for us to be satisfied that (a) and (c) are correct. We heard evidence from the staff member referred to in (a) and he denied the allegations vehemently, describing it as "absolute rubbish". Moreover, it is the only allegation of that kind that has been made against him in respect of a long period of service with Care Concern in various establishments. There is no evidence whatsoever tending to confirm the allegation and, like the allegations in (c), it is said to have been an isolated incident, which was never repeated.

22.53 In these circumstances it is not appropriate for us to comment further upon the regime at The Village.

Clwyd Hall School

Introduction

23.01 This residential school for children with behavioural and emotional problems at Llanychan, near Ruthin, was founded in 1958 by **William Carman** and his wife Edith, who were the joint Headteachers until they retired in or about January 1972. William Carman had previously been the head of a Liverpool school for the maladjusted and Edith Carman had been head of a school for the delicate in the same city. A company called Clwyd Hall for Child Welfare Limited was formed to own and run the school but the effective proprietors were the Carmans.

23.02 It appears that the school occupied a notable site because it was described in fulsome terms in an SI's[1] report in December 1977, as follows:

> "The main residential house is a delightful building of historical interest, aesthetically pleasing both inside and out, set in about 18 acres of grounds, including adequate hard-surfaced areas and playing pitches for football and net ball. The setting with lovely old trees, lawns and flower beds all meticulously cared for is a joy to the eye, and the views are breath-taking. Such a setting can do nothing but good to the children."

Boys were housed in the main building, in which there was a teaching wing with three classrooms. Girls lived in a separate house in the grounds partly occupied by the Carmans. There were also workshop facilities nearby with teaching space for older children above.

23.03 Carman appointed **Barry Wademan**, then 42 years old, to succeed him as Headteacher from January 1972, and Wademan's wife was appointed Matron from July 1972. They were both salaried but they invested £2,500 in the company and were allocated 25 per cent of the issued shares. All financial aspects of the business continued to be dealt with by the Carmans, who lived in the separate house just referred to, comprising converted outbuildings within the estate. From this part of the estate a daughter of the Carmans ran an equestrian centre, later known as the Claremont Equestrian Centre. Wademan ran the educational system of the school with his wife. He had been most recently Headteacher of an observation and assessment centre for boys in Hampshire (he was national secretary of the association of those centres at the time) and had 20 years experience of working for the Home Office in approved schools and remand homes.

23.04 The school was recognised as efficient under the former education legislation until that status ended in April 1978 and Wademan said that it was in fact a special needs school for maladjusted children. When Wademan became Headteacher there were about 24 resident pupils but by January 1975 there

---

[1] Senior HMI (Staff Inspector).

were 48 (39 boys and nine girls), aged between seven and 16 years. The school was listed in the Department of Education's Independent Schools Directory and the majority of pupils were referred to it by local authorities in the north west, although some came from as far as Gateshead and Folkestone. Some of these children were in care. We have no information as to the placement at the school of any children from Clwyd or Gwynedd or anywhere else in Wales.

23.05 The Wademans remained at Clwyd Hall School only until 1976 because they considered that the Carmans had reneged on an oral promise to them that they would have sole control of the school. The new Headteacher was **Colin Fleming Williams**, aged 53 years, who had been Deputy Head for two years or so and in charge of the leavers' class. He had taught at various schools and had worked latterly with the psychological service for schools in the Chester area before moving to Clwyd Hall School as Deputy Head. Williams continued as Headteacher until 1982 and, during this period, pupil numbers fluctuated between about 36 and 46.

23.06 In or about July 1982 Carman made a new agreement, in effect taking in three new "partners" to run the school. These were **David Neil Edge**, who was then working for Trafford Social Services Department in the child care field, another Trafford social worker, **Brian Chatburn,** and **Richard Francis Groome**, who was Officer-in-Charge of Tanllwyfan until 11 November 1982[2]. It is unnecessary to go into great detail about the various changes that occurred in the succeeding two years because the school closed finally on 27 July 1984 but a summary will complete the picture.

23.07 Until the agreement referred to in the preceding paragraph, Carman had remained Principal of Clwyd Hall School but Edge then became Principal from 13 October 1982 to 26 February 1983, when he left to become Operations Manager, responsible for all child care matters at Dôl Rhyd and Hengwrt schools in Dolgellau[3]. Groome, who had been Head of Care, then succeeded him as Principal and with Chatburn took a lease of the school. A new Headteacher was appointed from September 1983. Substantial further improvements were needed at the school, however, and the required finance could not be obtained. Groome left, therefore, in or about April 1984 to found a therapeutic community for young people at Ludlow and Chatburn later joined Edge in Dolgellau (Chatburn died on 10 August 1986).

Welsh Office inspections

23.08 The first recorded visit by inspectors during the period under review by this Tribunal took place on 30 November 1977, on only 24 hours notice, following a complaint by a senior teacher, who had left after only a few days, to a Minister of State at the Department of Education and Science. The senior teacher had been critical of his own accommodation and classroom stock and had said "Not one single member of staff had undergone any training in connection with maladjusted children and no system of secondment existed for

---

[2] See paras 18.06 and 50.31(7).
[3] See para 39.26.

this purpose". He complained also that there was "not one single trained member of the House staff" at the school, questioning whether the school still met with the requirements for being recognised.

23.09 The inspectors found that there were 44 resident pupils (32 boys, 12 girls). In addition to the Headteacher, there were four teachers (and a riding instructor at week-ends). The post of Deputy Head was vacant and difficulty was being experienced in finding a suitable replacement. None of the staff had a special education extra qualification although two had some previous relevant experience and one had taken a special education option in her initial course. There were five care staff in addition to a housekeeper and about six domestic staff. The five care staff were resident but only one of them had a child care qualification (another had been accepted for a course starting in January 1978).

23.10 Despite the limited training of the staff, the inspectors were complimentary about what they saw. The teachers were seen to handle the children firmly but tolerantly and work seen was said to be "purposeful, varied, well presented"; and relationships between Headteacher, staff and children appeared to be easy, relaxed and pleasant. The care arrangements were also thought to be of a high standard and the inspectors concluded:

> "We can only say that we saw or heard nothing which would make us anyway uneasy, or which indicated any kind of emergency situation, which might endanger either recognition or registration."

23.11 It is not clear from the documents before the Tribunal whether Clwyd Hall School was ever granted final registration after April 1978. It is clear, however, that it did not receive general SEN approval and it may have remained provisionally registered only, although Edge referred to it as "recognised by the Department of Education and Science" in a letter written in September 1982[4]. The school was visited by two HMIs in May 1982, who considered it to be far from satisfactory. Their findings were that the fabric of the building and furnishings had been allowed to deteriorate; the dormitory accommodation was unsatisfactory; schemes of work and educational programmes were limited; staffing was inadequate, both for care and teaching purposes; and the school generally seemed to be low in morale and deprived of resources. In these circumstances the inspectors thought that it might be necessary for HMI to recommend to the Welsh Office that it was no longer a school for which exceptional (SEN) admissions could be approved.

23.12 This adverse report was part of the background to Carman's negotiations to sell the school or at least to re-finance it by agreement with new "partners". A further Welsh Office inspection was deferred whilst these negotiations took place and then to give an opportunity for re-organisation. It was not, therefore, until October 1983 that a further visit to the school was made by three HMIs. The purpose of the visit was two-fold: to co-ordinate standards of approval of

---

[4] See Appendix 6, paras 37 to 39.

independent schools for statemented children with HMI in England and to assess whether Clwyd Hall School had developed sufficiently under new management to justify an approval inspection.

23.13 The inspectors found that the conditions generally had improved. A good deal of re-decoration and refurbishment had been carried out; the dormitory arrangements were more satisfactory; good educational programmes and care practices were being developed. Staffing standards had also been improved. But the new financial arrangements did not appear to cater for further necessary developments; Edge had already withdrawn and left; and the future remained uncertain.

23.14 It was envisaged by the reporting inspector, in a consolidating minute in May 1984, that a further visit to the school would be necessary as part of a project "to clear approval of all independent schools" then operating in Wales but written notice confirming the closure of the school was received before this could be arranged.

Complaints of abuse

23.15 One parent wrote to the Department of Education and Science in July 1978 complaining about the placement of his son at Clwyd Hall School by Stockport Education Authority. The son was said to be of above average intelligence but had made no progress in two years at the school. The parent complained about the teaching and the quality of care and of his son being beaten about the head and back with a wooden stick by a teacher who lost her temper, causing the boy to run away and become lost on a November night. The letter concluded "I must state that until the matter has been considered and a firm decision made I fully intend to keep (my son) at home and not to send him back to Clwyd Hall School next term, even if it means educating him myself".

23.16 The Welsh Office, to whom this complaint was referred, did not apparently think it necessary to investigate this complaint with the school. The response of the Department of Education and Science to the parent, dated 24 August 1978, was as follows:

> "You made reference in your letter to conditions at Clwyd Hall and I have consulted colleagues in the Welsh Office Education Department about this school. I understand that it is considered a well-run, caring establishment by Her Majesty's Inspectors who make periodic visits to the school. I hope you will feel reassured by this and encourage (your son) to resume his studies at Clwyd Hall as soon as possible."

23.17 We are aware of 13 former residents of Clwyd Hall School, all male, who have complained of abuse whilst they were there and all 13 of them named **Noel Ryan** as an abuser. Of these complainants, 12 alleged serious sexual abuse by Ryan and not less than four alleged physical abuse.

23.18 It was neither appropriate nor necessary for the Tribunal to investigate these allegations fully because they were being investigated by the North Wales Police concurrently. In the event Ryan appeared before the Crown Court at

Chester on 4 July 1997, during the Tribunal's sittings, when he pleaded guilty to 14 of 22 counts alleging sexual offences against ten male residents of Clwyd Hall School under the age of 16 years committed between 1 January 1970 and 30 June 1981 (three offences of buggery, one attempted buggery and ten indecent assaults). Ryan asked the Court to take into consideration also when sentencing him seven similar (specimen) offences of indecent assault committed within the same period, which he admitted. Thus, he confessed to serious offences against a total of 17 boys over a period of about ten years. His Honour Judge Morgan Hughes then sentenced Ryan to a total of 12 years' imprisonment and ordered that the eight counts to which he had pleaded not guilty should lie on the Court file on the usual terms[5]. The Judge ordered also that Ryan should register with his local police within 14 days of his release in accordance with the new requirements of the Sex Offenders Act 1997.

23.19 Ryan, who was 66 years old when he was sentenced, was employed at Clwyd Hall School as a houseparent from about 1968 until he resigned in 1981, occupying a bed sitting room above the staff room at the top of the main building. He was not called to give evidence to the Tribunal and we have not seen any staff file relating to him so that we know little of his background. It appears from what was said on his behalf at his trial that he was "untrained, unskilled and untutored" when he went to Clwyd Hall School at the age of 37 years: he was a naive individual, who himself had been the victim of abuse as a child, and he had no other sexual experience.

23.20 It is clear from the evidence relied upon by the prosecution that there was a pattern of conduct by Ryan for most of the period of his employment at Clwyd Hall School. He was attracted to some of the boy residents and would groom them for subsequent sexual misconduct. They would be shown favours and later touched intimately in the bathroom or showers. Ryan was able to take advantage both of his quasi-parental status and the location of his bed sitting room, near to the boys' dormitories. Touching the boys progressed quickly to masturbation, and with some boys to oral sex and simulated buggery. Ryan pleaded guilty also to three counts of buggery with one boy as well as an indecent assault upon him and to attempted buggery and indecent assault in respect of another boy as well as eight other indecent assaults on different boys.

23.21 We received evidence from four of the complainants against Ryan, including oral evidence from the victim of the three offences of buggery that he admitted. This witness, A, from Merseyside, was at Clwyd Hall School for about eight years from the age of seven years in 1969 and said that Ryan befriended him and treated him as a favourite from an early stage: Ryan seemed to be in love with him at times and would hug him. Ryan played on his naiveté and he woke up on one occasion to find that Ryan was masturbating him manually. Masturbation, oral sex and buggery on four occasions followed, mainly when he was away from Clwyd Hall with Ryan on trips of various kinds. The pattern of conduct continued until he went on a trip to Blackpool with Ryan, when he was ten or 11 years old: he told Ryan then that he would not put up with it

---

[5] Not to be proceeded without leave of the Crown Court or the Court of Appeal, Criminal Division.

anymore. He alleged also that Ryan physically abused him on other occasions, by, for example, rubbing soap in his mouth and whipping him with wet towels, and Ryan would also instruct older boys to bully him.

23.22 A was a talented footballer who played soccer for North Wales and who had hoped to make a career in soccer. He spent his last two years at Clwyd Hall playing soccer but he could not spell his own name when he left. He said that there was no real teacher there and he never saw a social worker. When he left eventually he was only told that he was leaving that same day, half an hour before he left, and he had to make his own way by walking to Wrexham and then hitchhiking to Liverpool.

23.23 The other oral witness, B, was also named in a count in the indictment to which Ryan pleaded guilty. B was at Clwyd Hall School for about five years from the age of eight or nine years in or about 1971. He said that he slept in a dormitory and was singled out by Ryan, who gave him a hug and kiss and told him that he would be all right, within a week of his arrival there. Sexual assaults by Ryan began with touching B's penis; masturbation, including mutual masturbation followed; and on occasions Ryan put two fingers into the boy's anus. But B was not subjected to oral sex or to buggery. Ryan threatened B that, if B told anyone about the abuse, he would not be allowed to go home on leave at all but, about a year before he left Clwyd Hall, the sexual assaults ended because B "stood up to" Ryan and threatened to tell B's mother and step-father. After Clwyd Hall this witness went to another school of a similar type called Rhyd-y-Gors, Carmarthen, where "the staff were marvellous and the Headmaster absolutely brilliant", and then served in the Army for five years but he suffered three breakdowns later and had tried to take his own life, all of which he attributed to Ryan's sexual abuse of him.

23.24 B complained also of persistent physical abuse by Ryan. The latter would punish B by making him stand on one leg with both his arms held aloft. When he failed to maintain this posture, Ryan would cane him on his legs and arms and B said that this happened every week, up to four times a week. He had tried to get to the Headteacher to complain but Ryan was always about when he was close.

23.25 The two complainants whose evidence was read to the Tribunal were not named in the indictment against Ryan but we do not know whether they were named in the list of seven offences taken into consideration when he was sentenced. C, from the Bebington area of the Wirral, was in care when he went to Clwyd Hall in 1980 and he remained there about 18 months. He alleged that he was indecently assaulted by Ryan on only two occasions; on both, C was "wound up" and Ryan restrained him and squeezed his genitals in the process. This witness alleged, however, that he was persistently masturbated, and on one occasion subjected to oral sex, by another named member of the care staff.

23.26 Witness D, however, alleged that he was buggered by Ryan in a narrow room down a corridor from D's dormitory on about 40 occasions. D was also in care when he was placed at Clwyd Hall School by Bolton Social Services Department at the age of ten years in or about 1976 and he remained there until he was about 13 years old. Ryan began his indecent conduct by going to D's bed in a dormitory frequently and masturbating him; this led to Ryan later taking D to the narrow room just referred to where D was made to perform oral sex on Ryan. Subsequently, mutual oral sex and buggery occurred on frequent occasions there. D said that he had found it extremely difficult to cope with adult life as a result of the way in which he had been treated as a child. He had at times been sexually confused and even today felt more comfortable in the company of gay men. He said also that nearly all the staff at Clwyd Hall School treated the children without respect or any care and alleged "their way of maintaining discipline was to put you in fear of being punched or slapped and if you stepped out of line they would punch or slap. They hit any part of the body they could get away with".

23.27 It seems that in April 1981 the Headteacher, Williams, received a complaint from a parent about Ryan hugging her son and from a boy about Ryan holding his hand. This was at least part of the background to Ryan's resignation, which was handed by the Headteacher to Carman on 27 May 1981, following which Ryan took employment with a friend in a restaurant.

23.28 Apart from Ryan, only four other members of the staff were named in complaints by former residents and none were named by more than two complainants. The only staff member other than Ryan alleged to have committed sexual abuse was the care worker referred to by witness C.

23.29 The Tribunal did not receive any complaints against Richard Francis Groome but his activities were being investigated at the time of our hearings. He now awaits trial for various alleged sexual offences against boys, as explained in paragraph 50.31(7) of this report, and four of the alleged victims named in the indictment were resident at Clwyd Hall School when the alleged offences occurred.

Conclusions

23.30 Clwyd Hall School was yet another residential establishment for children poisoned by the activities of at least one persistent sexual abuser on its staff. Yet again that abuser had no previous convictions and was not suspected of abuse, as far as we are aware, by colleagues for ten years or more. The result is that the lives of at least a score of children, already emotionally and behaviourally disturbed, have been seriously and permanently disfigured.

23.31 Other criticisms of the school pale in comparison with this central failure to provide a safe home for the children. The allegations of other physical abuse presented to us have been few and do not justify a finding against any specific member of the staff, other than Ryan, who did not give evidence to us and who was not legally represented before the trial. The short history of the school within our period of review does, however, again underline the need for frequent and effective independent inspection. The visits by inspectors that we have recorded were not full inspections and were much too infrequent to provide effective monitoring of the school's performance, bearing in mind how short is the span of the pupil's school life and the extent of the deterioration in the school that was noted five years after the inspector's visit in 1977. We are also dismayed by the Welsh Office's response to the parent's complaint referred to in paragraph 23.15, without (apparently) any investigation of it with the school.

PART V

ALLEGED ABUSE OF CHILDREN
IN FOSTER HOMES IN CLWYD
BETWEEN 1974 AND 1996

The overall provision of foster care in Clwyd, 1974 to 1996

24.01 We have referred briefly in Chapter 4 to the progressive change within Clwyd between 1974 and 1996 from substantial reliance on residential care for children to a dominating preference for foster care[1]. Table A shows how this developed in Clwyd between 1974 and 1992. Thus, in 1974, 34.1 per cent of children in care were boarded out (the technical term for fostering by local authorities and some voluntary organisations) but by 1992 the percentage had risen to 76.2. The comparable figures for all Welsh counties were 30.7 per cent in 1974 and 75 per cent in 1992. In the same period the number of children in care in Clwyd declined from 577 to 328 so that the actual number of children in foster care rose only from just under 200 to 250, whilst the increase in the whole of Wales was about 350 to just over 1,850.

Table A - Children in Care: Rates and Unit Costs - Clwyd (Source CIPFA)

	Population aged under 18	Children in Care	Rate per 1000 under 18	% in residential accommodation	% boarded out
1974–75	105,350	577	5.5	38.4	34.1
1975–76	105,622	565	5.3	35.4	39.1
1976–77	105,035	522	5.0	33.9	39.0
1977–78	104,392	530	5.1	35.8	38.9
1978–79	104,348	558	5.3	34.0	43.0
1979–80	103,647	563	5.4	29.0	50.5
1980–81	103,118	540	5.2	30.0	48.9
1981–82	102,812	525	5.1	29.3	49.9
1982–83	100,626	489	4.9	28.3	49.7
1983–84	98,391	418	4.2	30.1	52.9
1984–85	96,392	381	4.0	28.1	52.5
1985–86	95,223	400	4.2	27.5	56.8
1986–87	94,322	397	4.2	27.7	57.2
1987–88	93,714	400	4.3	27.8	72.3
1988–89	93,894	372	4.0	29.0	61.3
1989–90	93,793	384	4.1	27.9	61.5
1990–91	93,048	360	3.9	37.5	64.2
1991–92	94,198	328	3.5	23.8	76.2

[1] See paras 4.01, 4.18 and 4.29. For Wales as a whole see Table C, referred to in para 40.02.

24.02 Both the increased emphasis on foster care and the progressive reduction in the number of children in care in Clwyd were broadly in line with Wales as a whole and similar trends in England. They were driven partly by a loss of confidence by social services professionals in the benefits of residential care and in part also by the financial stringencies affecting local government in the late 1970s and throughout the 1980s. Institutional care came to be regarded as particularly unsuitable for young children who needed to experience family life and to form close personal attachments to one or two figures. The benefits of community based alternatives were stressed also for offenders, who formed a large part of the care population. Residential care was not only seen as ineffective in reducing offending but also inappropriate so that other forms of disposal were developed for offenders, including intermediate treatment and specialist fostering schemes. The pursuit of these policies meant that much of the burden of looking after the more challenging children and young persons living away from home passed to foster carers.

24.03 We do not have figures directly comparable with Table A to show the equivalents in the last four years of Clwyd's existence but we do have them expressed as a percentage of children looked after[2]. The percentage of these children in residential care in 1991/1992 was 26 but by 1993 it had declined to eight and by 1996 to only four per cent. On the other hand, by 31 March 1995, 77.6 per cent of the children were in foster care; and in 1995 Clwyd had access to 300 foster carers.

24.04 Responsibility for fostered children is often more diffuse than it is for most children in residential care. It is not uncommon for Social Services Departments to recruit foster carers and place children outside their own areas; and, if and when foster carers move home, foster children move with them. Furthermore, prior to the Children Act 1989 intending foster carers (or adoptive parents) could apply to and be approved by more than one placing authority. Supervision could be delegated to the authority in whose area a child lived, if that authority agreed, but the placing authority retained its statutory responsibilities and status as the authority to whose care the child had been committed.

24.05 As part of the overall endeavour to find suitable foster carers, placing agencies formed consortia to find families further afield and children needing homes were advertised in national newsletters that were circulated to member agencies. Adoption was usually seen as offering the prospect of a more secure and stable family situation but there were many circumstances in which adoption was not a viable proposition and fostering was the preferred alternative.

24.06 Boarding out was quite tightly regulated from early on because experience had already shown that children could be mistreated in foster care and in recognition of the inherent risks. The provisions of the Boarding Out Regulations 1955, which remained in force without substantial relevant

---

[2] Report of the Examination Team on Child Care Procedures and Practice in North Wales (1996) at paras 4.95 and 4.96.

amendment until 31 May 1989, are summarised in Appendix 6[3]. They provided a framework of basic safeguards for children boarded out, prescribing in detail the steps to be taken before a child was placed in a foster home and the nature and frequency of the subsequent supervision. In addition to the statutory reviews required in respect of all children in care, the regulations required specific periodic reviews of the welfare, health, conduct and progress of children boarded out.

Complaints of abuse in foster homes in Clwyd

24.07 Alleged abuse of children in foster homes in Clwyd did not play any significant part in the events that led to the appointment of this Tribunal, which have been recounted in Chapter 2. However, in the course of our hearings the case of a foster carer, **Roger Platres Saint**, attracted nationwide publicity. Saint pleaded guilty on 7 March 1997, in the Crown Court at Mold, to nine counts[4] (out of 16 counts in three indictments) alleging indecent assaults upon a step-son, two pupils, a foster child and five adopted children between March 1975 and December 1987; and he was subsequently sentenced, on 23 May 1997 in the same Court, by the Honourable Mr Justice Laws to concurrent sentences of six and a half years' imprisonment on all nine counts (the other counts were ordered to lie on the Court file on the usual terms[5]).

24.08 Saint had lived in Clwyd from December 1976 to September 1990, a period covering almost the full span of his offending and the aspects of his case that attracted most attention were: (a) the failure of Social Services Departments to elicit information that Saint had been convicted on 9 June 1972, in Neath Magistrates' Court of indecent assault on a boy before he was approved as a foster carer or as an adoptive parent; (b) the fact that children continued to be placed with him after his conviction in 1972 became known in February 1988; and (c) the fact that he had been permitted to continue to serve as a member of a Clwyd Adoption and Foster Care Panel until Clwyd ceased to exist on 31 March 1996. These matters were drawn to the attention of Mr Justice Laws, who refrained from commenting upon them himself as they were clearly within the scope of this Tribunal's inquiry.

24.09 Quite apart from the Saint case and the questions that it raised, it would have been necessary for us, within our terms of reference, to inquire into any evidence of the abuse of children in care who were in foster homes within Clwyd during the relevant period, whether or not Clwyd was the placing authority. In the event we are aware of seven foster homes in Clwyd in respect of which complaints of abuse have been made by foster children against foster carers and/or against members of the latter's family. We deal with these complaints in the succeeding chapters of this part of the report, beginning with separate chapters on the grave cases of Roger Saint and Frederick Rutter and

---

[3] See paras 31 to 33.

[4] The number of pleas of guilty was wrongly calculated at ten at the subsequent hearing, the error arising in relation to the first count on the third indictment.

[5] Not to be proceeded with without leave of the Crown Court or the Court of Appeal Criminal Division.

dealing with the other cases, some of which also involve serious sexual abuse, in the following chapter.

The case of Roger Saint

Background and history prior to fostering

25.01 **Roger Platres Saint** was born on 11 May 1947 in Somerset and educated in South Wales. He left school at the age of 15 years and first undertook residential care work six years later in 1968. In the intervening period he had been variously employed, firstly in his father's business and later as a laboratory assistant, in catering and then in the cinema business. His first work in residential care was as a supervisor at a boys' remand home at Winchester, where he remained for a year; and he then worked successively at a children's home in Wednesfield (becoming Officer-in-Charge for a short period), as a relief superintendent of children's homes in Wiltshire and as Deputy Superintendent of a children's home near Salisbury.

25.02 It was whilst he was in the latter employment that Saint was convicted, on his own plea of guilty, on 9 June 1972 at Neath Magistrates' Court, of an indecent assault upon a boy aged 12 years, who was a stranger to him. The police statement of the facts of that offence alleged that on 6 March 1972 the victim had been walking with his dog along a road in Neath when Saint drove past him in a motor car. The boy then walked into a field intending to return to his home. Saint stopped his motor car, walked back towards the boy and called to him on the pretence of asking for directions. The boy stopped and Saint then caught him around the waist and tried to open the boy's trouser band and place his hand on the boy's private parts. The boy struggled and Saint then released him, whereupon Saint returned to his motor car and drove off. Saint was interviewed later and admitted responsibility, making a statement under caution.

25.03 Despite his plea of guilty in June 1972 Saint has since persistently denied that there was any indecent intent or motivation on his part in the assault and he has sought to explain his plea at the Magistrates' Court by saying that he was not legally represented. The account that he has given, which he repeated in his evidence to the Tribunal, is that the incident occurred at a time when he was staying with friends in Neath following the breakdown of a long standing friendship with a girl, whom he had hoped to marry. During his stay he drove out into the country alone to revisit childhood haunts and, whilst he was walking, the boy approached him and asked the time, whereupon he attacked the boy unjustifiably for a mixture of reasons: he felt angry at being "invaded" and reminded of his work in a children's home. The boy ran away and police officers took him to a police station shortly afterwards, where he admitted pushing the boy but did not (to his knowledge) admit any sexual impropriety.

25.04 In the light of the police statement of facts, Saint's plea at the time and subsequent events in Saint's life we have no doubt that he was rightly convicted of indecent assault in June 1972. We were unimpressed by both his explanation for his plea and his account of what had occurred between him and the boy.

25.05 Saint was fined £15 for the offence and ordered to pay £8 advocates fee. He was ordered also to contribute £10 towards his legal aid, which is inconsistent with his allegation that he was not legally represented. The facts set out in paragraph 25.02 were reported to the Home Office Police Department (F 1 Division) by the Chief Constable by letter dated 19 June 1972, in which Saint's current appointment was specified.

25.06 Saint was initially suspended from his employment and he resigned just before his conviction, according to his statement to the Tribunal. Afterwards he worked for a time as a debt collector but it seems that he was appointed to another post of Deputy Warden, this time of a voluntary children's home with education in Manchester, within about a year. It must be assumed that he did not inform the Boys and Girls Welfare Society, who ran that children's home, of his conviction but his next employers, at a children's home in Barry, South Glamorgan, became aware of it two or three months after his appointment as Officer-in-Charge and he was asked to leave.

25.07 Saint's connection with Clwyd began in December 1976 when he purchased a house in Holywell with his wife Carol, whom he had met when he was working in Manchester and whom he married on 6 March 1976 at West Kirby. Following his departure from Barry and a short period of unemployment, Saint had secured an appointment in the Wirral from 1 March 1975 as "Officer-in-Charge of Childcare" (his description) at a residential establishment for children known as the Children's Convalescent Home and School (later called West Kirby Residential School). According to his statement to the Tribunal his work in this capacity involved management of the staff rather than the children, although he did have "some minor contact with the children", and he retained the post for ten years. However, in the documents before the Tribunal he was consistently described as an RCCO at the West Kirby home and school (it appears that there were 160 children and 40 staff).

25.08 Roger Saint pleaded guilty on 7 March 1997, in the Crown Court at Mold, to offences of indecent assault upon two pupils at the West Kirby home and school, the first between 31 March 1975 and 31 December 1978 and the second between 1 January 1976 and 31 December 1979. These offences did not come to light until May and June 1996. They involved masturbation (and forced mutual masturbation) of very young boys who had health problems such as asthma, eczema and epilepsy. One of the boys had been taken by Saint to his house at Holywell, where an indecent assault had occurred. Three other counts alleging offences against two other West Kirby pupils were not proceeded with on Saint's pleas of not guilty to them.

25.09 **Carol Ann Saint**, who is nearly six years older than Roger Saint and who had been married previously for 17 years, had five children of that earlier marriage, born between 1959 and 1965. Two of those children, a boy (A) born on 23 July 1963 and a girl (B) born on 25 March 1965, moved with their mother to form part of the initial Saint household from July 1975.

25.10 A was a child who was emotionally disturbed and who had attended the Manchester home where Saint worked in 1973/1974, which was the background to the Saints' first meeting. He moved from the Saint household to live with his natural father before July 1977. There is no record of any contemporary complaint by him against Roger Saint but in December 1996 he alleged that he had been indecently assaulted regularly by Saint. The latter pleaded guilty in March 1997 to a specimen count in respect of these assaults, alleged to have occurred in the boy's bedroom when he was living in the Saint household; and the assaults again involved masturbation of the boy, who was then a young teenager.

25.11 The girl B continued to live with her mother and Roger Saint, at least nominally, until about 1982. At some stage she had become a student nurse at a psychiatric hospital, where she lived in, returning home for days off and holidays. We are not aware of any complaint by her of ill-treatment by her mother or by her step-father and contemporary documents suggest that she enjoyed a good relationship with the latter.

The Saints' dealings with Clwyd Social Services Department and the latter's failure to acquire knowledge of Roger Saint's 1972 conviction

25.12 Carol Saint first approached Clwyd Social Services Department in June 1977 in response to an advertisement for foster parents for a family group of children. The enquiry was dealt with by a social worker in the Delyn Area Office and she advised the Saints that they should resolve a number of domestic issues before proceeding further. These related to behavioural problems of the children A and B, who had not decided at that time whether they wished to continue to live with their mother or move to live with their father. At this time the Saints had applied for two posts as houseparents but wished to foster also.

25.13 In April 1978 the Saints again approached Clwyd Social Services Department, wanting to adopt a baby or a very young child. They had also applied to Cheshire, to foster a young boy. An application to adopt through the Adoption Resource Exchange[1] was processed by the social worker who had dealt with them the previous year and she made a number of home visits (all documented) to discuss the application and to gather information about the Saints' background and motivation. The Saints provided the names of two personal referees. Roger Saint did not disclose his previous conviction but the Saints authorised Clwyd to approach the North Wales Police to check whether any convictions were recorded in respect of either of them. Medical reports were obtained and the standard application Form F, recommended by BAAF[2], was completed in October 1978. This showed that the Saints wished to adopt one, or preferably two, children of the same family up to eight years old. The social worker's report to the local authority's Adoption Panel was in positive terms and the Saints were approved as adoptive parents on 5 December 1978.

25.14 In the Form F no reference was made to Roger Saint's employment at Barry in or about 1974 that had been terminated because of his 1972 conviction and no period of unemployment was disclosed. The incorrect details given were that he had been Deputy Superintendent of a Wiltshire Children's Home from 1971 to 1973 and then Deputy Warden of the (Manchester) home for severely

---

[1] A family finding consortium of Social Services Departments and voluntary organisation adoption agencies.
[2] British Agencies for Adoption and Fostering.

emotionally disturbed children from 1973 to 1975 leading to his West Kirby appointment as "Deputy Superintendent". We have no doubt that these details were deliberately falsified by Roger Saint in order to reduce the risk that Clwyd might become aware of his previous conviction.

25.15   Before the Saints were approved as adoptive parents the Social Services Department had enquired of the North Wales Police on 18 August 1978 whether anything was known about them. The reply by letter stated incorrectly that nothing detrimental was known in respect of either. The explanation given by North Wales Police for this lapse is that "in 1978 there was no readily available facility to check a person against a national collection of persons with criminal records held at New Scotland Yard". The only check made by the police in 1978 was of the records held by them at their Colwyn Bay headquarters and, because Saint had had no connection with North Wales in 1972, his conviction at Neath had not been communicated to them.

25.16   The result of this failure to check national records of convictions was that Clwyd Social Services Department remained ignorant of Roger Saint's 1972 conviction for nearly ten years until 10 February 1988. At that point Devon Social Services Department became aware of it through a check that they made following an approach by the Saints to them to adopt two Devon children. The Director of Social Services for Devon so informed Clwyd, who asked the North Wales Police to make a further check, which confirmed the conviction. The national police computerised record of convictions had been established in 1981.

25.17   There was another unfortunate aspect of the inquiries made by Clwyd in 1978. Among the referees nominated by the Saints in support of their adoption application were a couple whose name and address in Neath suggest that they were the friends with whom Roger Saint had been staying at the time of his offence in March 1972. It is likely, therefore, that they were aware of the subsequent conviction. However, West Glamorgan County Council reported to Clwyd on 15 December 1978 that they had been unable to contact the Neath referees at the address given, despite repeated visits and letters. It is odd that they could not be tracked down, with or without the assistance of the Saints, but they were not apparently pursued further and Clwyd relied upon references from an Holywell neighbour of two years' standing and a senior physiotherapist who knew Roger Saint in his recent working capacity at West Kirby.

25.18   There was another missed opportunity to learn of Saint's conviction four years later. On 23 November 1982 Tower Hamlets Social Services Department informed Clwyd that it was presenting the Saints to an Adoption Panel on 3 December 1982 as prospective adoptive parents for two brothers aged 14 and 13 years; and Clwyd Social Services Department was asked to make a fresh check with the North Wales Police to ascertain whether either of the Saints had criminal convictions. The evidence before us indicates, however, that Clwyd failed to request the check by the police and that Tower Hamlets failed to pursue the matter.

25.19 In the event not less than 11 children were placed with the Saints in the period between December 1978 and February 1988, although only two of these were placed by Clwyd Social Services Department[3].

25.20 The first placement chronologically was arranged privately with a view to adoption and was made on 7 December 1978, only two days after Clwyd had approved the Saints as adoptive parents. The child in question was a boy, born on 23 November 1978 at the H M Stanley Hospital in St Asaph and diagnosed later as suffering from cystic fibrosis. He was adopted by the Saints on 13 July 1979. It is clear that the arrangement was made directly by the child's mother with the Saints but appropriate welfare supervision visits were made by the social worker referred to in paragraphs 25.12 and 25.13 between 15 December 1978 and 26 June 1979. We are not aware of any complaint made by this boy against either of the Saints and he was still living in the household in September 1997.

25.21 The two boys, C and D, placed by Clwyd with the Saints went to them on 20 April 1979. They were brothers born on 3 March 1969 and 6 March 1970 respectively and had been in the care of Clwyd for most of their lives. After an earlier failed attempt at fostering in 1974 they had been living at Llwyn Onn children's home at Rhos-on-Sea[4]. C remained with the Saints only until 23 March 1980 whilst D remained 16 months longer, until 27 July 1981.

25.22 There is evidence of some lack of effective liaison within Clwyd Social Services Department in relation to the placement of these two boys, who were under the aegis of the Wrexham Area Office, whereas the boy already placed with the Saints for adoption was the responsibility of Delyn Area. It is unnecessary to go into detail about this because it did not affect the ultimate outcome significantly. Wrexham appears to have pressed ahead with the placement with a view to long term fostering, whilst Delyn would have preferred it to have been delayed until the adoption of the other boy had been approved by the Court. There were, however, eight contacts between Clwyd's fostering officer and the Saints between 5 December 1978 and 5 March 1979 in relation to the latter's application to foster children before the Social Services Sub-Committee approved the application on or about 13 March 1979.

25.23 Both C and D were disturbed children who had suffered rejection in the past and the placement with the Saints was unsuccessful for both of them. Difficulties with the boys' behaviour, particularly with that of C, emerged early on. Roger Saint was not very sensitive and tended to talk above the boys' heads. The Wrexham Area social worker made regular visits and was aware of the situation.

25.24 On 14 October 1979 and 11 January 1980 both boys ran away. On the first occasion they were picked up by the police and taken to Holywell police station. They gave the police the impression of being unhappy and a Social Services Department Duty Officer was called. They complained of physical

---

[3] These figures do not include short term placements, of which there appear to have been at least five in 1979 and 1980. We have inadequate particulars of these but we are not aware of any complaint in respect of them.

[4] See paras 4.02(11) and 4.30(11).

abuse by both foster parents including smacking them across the face, pulling their hair and, on occasion, kicking them upstairs. The boys stayed for two nights at Little Acton Assessment Centre whilst the situation was investigated. Although the Saints denied their allegations, except that Roger Saint admitted spanking C the previous Sunday, the social worker was impressed by the ring of truth in the boys' complaints. In the end, however, D wanted to return to the foster home and C also wanted to do so if his preferred alternative of returning to Llwyn Onn was not possible.

25.25 When the boys ran away again in January 1980 they were found in St Asaph and by this time the Saints were doubtful whether they (the Saints) wanted them to remain. Roger Saint said he felt inhibited in dealing with their misbehaviour because he was not allowed to smack the boys and he complained also that he was not receiving realistic payment to meet the costs incurred as a result of their destructive behaviour. By this time the social worker had become very doubtful whether it was wise for C to remain with the Saints, bearing in mind that they were expressing dislike of him openly. On the other hand, the Saints were pressing Clwyd for a further placement.

25.26 Matters came to a head in relation to C by the beginning of March 1980. C was showing serious signs of disturbance and was "generally in a bad state". Saint thought that the placement of another child would make him feel more secure but three social workers thought that it would impose additional strain and would not provide a stable situation for a newly placed child. By 18 March, C was again wanting to leave and a social worker inferred that he was causing further damage to provoke his removal. She removed him eventually on 22 March 1980; he subsequently spent periods mainly at Bersham Hall, Tanllwyfan (for nearly four years)[5], Chevet Hey and Cartrefle community homes and nearly a year with other foster parents in Old Colwyn before his admission to Chevet Hey.

25.27 C gave oral evidence to the Tribunal about his experiences in community homes but his statement to the police made on 27 March 1996 about his life with the Saints was read to us later, after Roger Saint's appearance at Mold Crown Court on 7 March 1997. He said that he had not liked the placement from the beginning; he had been hit frequently by Roger Saint but never by Carol. He usually received a hard slap to the face but it never left a bruise. C referred to two specific incidents when he had been wrongly accused of misbehaviour and slapped about the head by Saint when he denied that he was to blame. Carol Saint had been present on some of the occasions when he had been slapped. Saint had also made him stand in a corner at times.

25.28 C did not complain, whilst he was with the Saints, of any indecent assault upon him but in the police statement referred to in the preceding paragraph he did allege that Roger Saint had handled his penis on one occasion. This incident had occurred in the bathroom at the Saints' Holywell home on an occasion when he was sitting on Roger Saint's knee. It was the subject of a count of

---

[5] C is the witness Y referred to in para 18.27.

indecent assault in one of the three indictments against Saint before the Crown Court at Mold to which the latter pleaded not guilty; and that count was ordered, with others, to remain on the Court file on the usual terms[6].

25.29 In his oral evidence to the Tribunal Saint denied any indecent assault upon C and also denied slapping C or smacking him as a matter of practice. He had no recollection of speaking to social workers about the matter but he did remember causing a bruise to C's leg when admonishing the latter for not doing his homework. He commented "I think I was a bit too strict".

25.30 As we have already said, D remained with the Saints until 27 July 1981. The social worker responsible for him remained watchful of the situation. For some time D seemed to be secure in the household although Roger Saint was hard to please and prone to exert pressure on him. On 24 April 1981, however, following a two day stay by D with his grandparents and complaints by him to them of being caned and smacked by Saint, the social worker was able to elicit fuller details from D of the pressure being exerted by Saint on the boy about his school work and of the persistent physical chastisement to which he was being subjected. D was worried about the repercussions of his discussion with the social worker and she agreed not to take up his complaint with the foster parents without telling him first.

25.31 Various appropriate steps were taken by the social worker following these disclosures, including a helpful discussion with D's headmaster, and on 13 July 1981 she learnt from D's grandparents that he wanted to leave the Saints but was afraid of them being told. D confirmed this when seen by the social worker at school and he was duly removed ten days later, without prior warning to the Saints, by the social worker and the Deputy Area Officer. Although the Saints were not confronted with details of the latest allegations, the social worker noted that they were unable to accept any responsibility themselves for D's attitude and suggested that D had been influenced by his grandparents.

25.32 D had been in care from the age of four months but, on leaving the Saints, he went to live with his grandparents in Wrexham for a short time and then with his mother for about two years in Shropshire. In his oral evidence to the Tribunal he said that he did not enjoy a minute of his time at home with his mother: there were difficulties at home and at school and he put himself in a children's home "with the help of a couple of black eyes from (his) mother". He remained in care until his 18th birthday and his further schooldays were spent mainly at Ysgol Talfryn, whilst living at Cartrefle at week-ends and then with a teacher at the school who fostered him for just over a year. When giving evidence he said "the social services need to start to know how to go about after care", which we take to be a reference to the need for more effective social work involvement with young persons who are or have been in care in the post-school period.

25.33 D's account to the Tribunal of physical punishment by Roger Saint confirmed the complaints that he had made to his social worker and his grandparents at the time and was similar to that given by his brother C. He referred to three

---

[6] Not to be proceeded with except with the leave of the Crown Court or the Court of Appeal, Criminal Division.

incidents when he and C had been wrongly accused of matters and C had taken the responsibility. D described also how he had been slapped by Saint about 20 times on the leg, on failing repeatedly to read or pronounce a word correctly, with the result that he had limped to bed and had a large bruise on his leg, which Saint bandaged in order to hide it. The bruise had been seen by his P E teacher when the bandage fell off but the teacher had not taken any action about it.

25.34 D did not complain at the time of sexual abuse by Roger Saint but he told the police about this in March 1996 and had told C the previous summer. In his oral evidence to the Tribunal D said that the sexual abuse began in the Saints' bathroom some weeks after C had left. Saint put D on his knee and masturbated him and this became a regular practice that continued until D himself left. It would occur in the bathroom as described or in his bedroom when he was lying down three or four times a week; and Saint would make a peculiar noise in his throat when it was happening. On one occasion Saint was interrupted in the bedroom by the girl B but her view of what was happening was obstructed and Saint told her to get out. On another occasion D had fallen asleep in his bedroom and awoke to find Saint "gobbling him off".

25.35 D agreed that his social worker had visited him about 20 times in a period of 22 months but said that he had not felt able to talk to her about the sexual abuse. Speaking more generally about potential complaints, he said that usually the social worker would be sitting there with his foster parents and himself. If there had been anything wrong he would not have been able to say anything; and, if he had said anything, he would have had to stay and face "the flak" once the social worker had left. He agreed, however, that he had seen his social worker alone on occasions whilst living with the Saints.

25.36 Roger Saint pleaded guilty in March 1997 to a specimen count alleging that he indecently assaulted D on a day between 20 April 1979 and 27 July 1981.

25.37 The social worker for D prepared an "End of Foster Placement Report" dated 9 October 1981 in respect of him, which was critical of the Saints' negative attitude towards contact between D and his grandparents and C. The report referred also to Roger Saint's very decided views and his limited understanding of the effect of constant pressure on a child. The writer thought that the Saints would do better with a very young child but would have problems with a child whose personality was already formed. In our judgment, however, this report was seriously defective because it contained only an indirect reference to the allegations of physical punishment, stating that the foster parents discussed problems openly but that, if D's allegations were true, they were not open about their own reactions. Moreover, the report did not provide a full relevant account (from the person with the fullest knowledge to judge) of Clwyd's experiences with these foster parents.

25.38 There is no documentary evidence to indicate that Clwyd Social Services Department had any further discussions, after D's removal, about the suitability of the Saints as foster parents (or adoptive parents). Moreover, bearing in mind the particular circumstances of D's removal, they should have discussed with the Saints D's further allegations of physical punishment and sought their response. The failure to confront the Saints weakened Clwyd's position in sharing information with others and, in effect, permitted the Saints to continue denying, not only to themselves but also to other agencies, that they had had difficulties in caring for C and D.

25.39 According to an unproved chronology in the documents before us the Delyn (Area) Office stated on 11 December 1981 that the Saints were "not on active list" of foster parents but we have not received any oral evidence to clarify their position. According to Roger Saint's statement to the Tribunal he and his wife did foster three brothers for Clwyd for a long week-end around the end of 1981 but the placement ended because of a health risk; and nothing of substance turns upon this. From the information available to us, it appears that there was no significant further placement (boarding out) by Clwyd of any child with the Saints after D's departure.

25.40 What is clear is that from 1981 onwards the Saints sought fostering and adoption opportunities further afield. According to Roger Saint, he and his wife did so at the suggestion of Clwyd's Adoptions Officer, who also introduced them to "Be My Parent", a publication produced by British Agencies for Adoption and Fostering and providing information about children in need of families, through which he made contact with the London Borough of Ealing. Saint also came across PPIAS[7], a national self-help group of mainly adoptive parents, through whom he approached other authorities, including the London Borough of Tower Hamlets.

25.41 Approaches of this kind to other local authorities were being made by the Saints at the time when D was removed from their care. In April 1981 they were in touch with the London Borough of Ealing about the placement of two teenage boys but this did not proceed because they failed to bond with the children. Ealing were warned orally by D's social worker about the Saint's high expectations of, and pressure upon, children (rather than physical danger) and an Ealing social worker noted that Roger Saint did not accept any responsibility for the breakdown of C's fostering. In July 1981 the London Borough of Greenwich also was considering a placement with the Saints and had at least two telephone conversations about the removal of D with D's social worker, in which mention was made of the alleged physical abuse. The latter, was however, more concerned about the emotional effects on the boy of the way in which he had been dealt with by the Saints: she did not think that the foster home should be proscribed altogether but that careful selection of any child to be placed there would be needed. In the event Greenwich decided by the end of August 1981 not to use the Saints as foster parents; and enquiries by the London Borough of Brent and Nottinghamshire in the following year led to the same result.

25.42 It is necessary to mention one other development at about this time in which Clwyd was directly involved. On 5 March 1982 Cheshire County Council placed a young boy, E, born on 14 July 1981, with the Saints with a view to adoption as their second adopted child. This placement was made through Clwyd's Adoption Agency, which was part of the local authority. An adoption

---

[7] Parent to Parent Information on Adoption Services.

order was duly made on or about 25 June 1982 by Holywell County Court and E, who has cerebral palsy and had special educational needs, remained with the Saints. We are not aware of any complaint by or in respect of him against either adoptive parent.

25.43 From 1982 until 1990 onwards the Saints' main involvement in respect of new placements was with the London Borough of Tower Hamlets and this is dealt with in the next section of this chapter. They continued to live in Holywell until 15 December 1984, when they completed the purchase of a larger house at Llanarmon-yn-Ial, a village between Mold and Ruthin. They remained there until September 1990, when they moved out of Clwyd to a village near Bala in Gwynedd, where they planned to develop their house and to farm.

25.44 In relation to Clwyd the main relevant development in the intervening period was the appointment of Roger Saint as a member of the statutory Adoption and Foster Care Panel for Clwyd South. This occurred on or about 26 October 1987, after the Director of Social Services, Gledwyn Jones, had approved on 2 September 1987 Saint's nomination for the appointment by Clwyd's Adoptions Officer and by another member of the headquarters fostering and adoption group. The Saints were described in the nomination form as full-time "foster parents for Tower Hamlets . . . now providing care for six children including their own". Roger Saint was also then the local representative of PPIAS[8].

25.45 Thus, Saint became a member of the panel less than four months before the Director of Social Services learned on or about 10 February 1988 of Saint's 1972 conviction. The Director rightly took the view that it would be unwise for Saint to continue to be a member of the panel and he wrote on 11 March 1988 to the County Secretary, Roger Davies, expressing that view and seeking the County Secretary's advice. Astonishingly, the County Secretary did not reply to that letter despite a belated reminder 19 months later, dated 18 October 1989[9]. A hand-written note, which we have not seen, indicated that someone advised at some time that the matter should be dealt with under a Home Office Circular No 250/1964, which related to appointments to employment involving the care of children and was only marginally relevant. In the event no action was taken and Saint remained on the panel until Clwyd County Council ceased to exist on 31 March 1996.

25.46 In his written statement to the Tribunal, Roger Davies said that he had no memory of any issue relating to Saint and that neither the original request nor the reminder was brought to his attention as far as he could recall. In cross examination he conceded that he must accept responsibility for the failure to reply before October 1989; but he remained County Secretary until 1 August 1992, when he was appointed Chief Executive. Gledwyn Jones said in evidence that he would have spoken to the County Secretary or the latter's Deputy about the matter but he had no recollection of what was actually said.

---

[8] See footnote to para 25.40.
[9] See also paras 14.43 and 14.44 for other contemporaneous delay by Roger Davies.

Placements with the Saints by Tower Hamlets

25.47 Between February 1983 and September 1985 seven children were placed with the Saints by the London Borough of Tower Hamlets, of whom five were adopted by the Saints. All five of these children who were adopted by them were boys in the age range of nine to 14 years at the time when they were first boarded out with the Saints and all these boys complained after they had left of sexual abuse by Roger Saint. Moreover, four of the boys, who were brothers, were adopted on 11 January 1989, after Roger Saint's 1972 conviction had come to light (confirmed to Tower Hamlets by the Metropolitan Police by letter dated 8 March 1988). He pleaded guilty at Mold Crown Court in March 1997 to indecent assaults upon each of the five boys.

25.48 It seems that the Saints first expressed interest in adopting Tower Hamlets boys in November 1981 but it was a year later when another application by them in respect of two brothers, F and G, proceeded. It was this application that gave rise to Tower Hamlets' request to Clwyd to check whether the Saints had any criminal convictions, to which Clwyd did not respond[10]. Tower Hamlets had received a copy of Clwyd's 1978 Form F, which did not contain any reference to the conviction and which gave incorrect details of Roger Saint's employment dates in the early 1970s. A new and full application Form F was completed by the Tower Hamlets social worker responsible and initialled in parts by the Saints; and the social worker made at least one visit to the Saints' home in Holywell. Roger Saint again failed to disclose his 1972 conviction and gave a similar account to that given previously of his employment record.

25.49 The Saints were formally approved as foster parents for F and G on 3 December 1982 without any fresh police check and F and G took up residence with the Saints on 16 February 1983. F was then aged 14½ and G was a year younger. There is no evidence that Clwyd warned against the placements, of which they were aware, although the Tower Hamlets social worker was in touch with Clwyd's Adoptions Officer.

25.50 We do not have any detailed record of the progress of these placements. F remained until about September 1985, when he was 17 years old; according to Roger Saint he then went off in search of his natural mother in London. He had not wished to be adopted and was not the subject of an adoption application. F had quite severe behavioural problems and had a chequered career on leaving school. He resumed contact with the Saints intermittently after he left but he complained to the police later that he had been sexually abused by Roger Saint and a count to that effect was included in the first of the three 1997 indictments. Saint pleaded not guilty to the count and the judge ordered that it should remain on the Court file on the usual terms[11].

25.51 G remained with the Saints for five years until Easter 1988, when he left as the result of a dispute over an alleged theft from their home. He had been adopted by the Saints on 23 June 1987, just before his 18th birthday, after a number of contested hearings in the High Court (the adoption was opposed by his natural

---

[10] See para 25.18.

[11] Not to be proceeded with except with the leave of the Crown Court or the Court of Appeal, Criminal Division.

mother until a late stage). G too complained later that he had been indecently assaulted by Roger Saint and the latter pleaded guilty in March 1997 to two specimen counts in respect of these assaults, one in respect of the period when the family were living at Holywell and another in respect of their home at Llanarmon-yn-Ial. According to G the assaults had occurred regularly. They began in Saint's bedroom when the latter complained of migraine attacks and G kept him company: Saint would masturbate G to the point of ejaculation on the pretext of teaching him the facts of life. Later, at Llanarmon-yn-Ial, the assaults had occurred in the bathroom when G was in the bath and they had continued until he was 16 years old.

25.52 The four brothers were placed with the Saints on 19 December 1984, immediately following the move to Llanarmon-yn-Ial. It does not seem that any new Form F was completed but the Saints were approved as foster parents for the children on 15 August 1984. By this time the previous Tower Hamlets social worker responsible for F and G had left and another social worker (W) had become responsible for the Saints. In her report on the Saints' application W did refer to the many problems that had been experienced with F and G but there was no discussion of how the needs of six very deprived boys could be met by the Saints or of the impact of the placements on the two other children already adopted by the Saints (all in a four bedroomed house). In recommending approval W said that there was no feeling of a mini children's home because the Saints were so parental and she referred to the Saints' very sound relationship with Tower Hamlets.

25.53 According to Roger Saint, Tower Hamlets stipulated that he should give up his job at West Kirby and he did so early in 1985, becoming a full time foster parent from then on. It was agreed also that double rates would be paid to the Saints until a professional foster parents' scheme was finalised. Later, Tower Hamlets also enlisted the aid of a private charity to finance in part the purchase of the small holding at Llanarmon-yn-Ial; and the Saints' remuneration was raised further to a special enhanced rate from about May 1986.

25.54 The four brothers, who will be referred to as the H children, had been received into care on 14 July 1978 and Tower Hamlets had assumed parental rights in respect of them a year later. After four years in a children's home they had been placed with foster parents near Welshpool on 10 July 1982 with a view to adoption but this had proved to be unsuccessful and Tower Hamlets had had to seek an alternative placement. By December 1984 their ages ranged from $13\frac{1}{2}$ to nine years.

25.55 Three of the H boys gave oral evidence to the Tribunal, but not the eldest. None of them had any complaint to make about their earlier foster placement and none of them alleged that they had been physically abused by either of the Saints. Each of the three, however, described similar forms of sexual abuse by Roger Saint. H3, who was born on 1 March 1974, said that the first indecent assault occurred in the bathroom about a year after his arrival, and that Saint told him that it was sex education. It happened again in the bathroom one Sunday night later but H3 told Saint that he did not want Saint to touch him. Saint responded "We'll see" but he did not enter the bathroom again when H3 was there. H2, who was born on 26 February 1973, also described assaults that occurred first in the bathroom, beginning after he had been with the Saints a few months. In his case they were repeated every Sunday and then occurred several times a week during motor car journeys with Saint. The latter continued to assault him after they moved to Bala, where Saint would masturbate him when he emerged from a shower. The youngest boy, H4, born on 11 October 1975, was also indecently assaulted in the bathroom and his bedroom, and it continued when they moved to Bala. It occurred more frequently after H3 had moved out of H4's bedroom but it stopped when he was 15 or 16 years old.

25.56 These boys did not disclose Saint's assaults upon them to the police until January 1997 although each of them made two police statements in 1996. Roger Saint had been arrested in March 1996 following allegations made by G and H1 to social workers in Wrexham the previous month but he had persistently denied abusing any of the children until Christmas 1996, when he made admissions about his conduct generally to (amongst others) H2, H3, H4 and Carol Saint by telephone to the Bala home.

25.57 According to one of the H boys, W visited them about once a month and this was Roger Saint's recollection also. However, two of the boys who gave evidence said that W did not see them individually or on their own. The few reports that we have seen on boarding out visits to the foster home were unstructured and extremely brief: they did not provide a basis for the required review of the children's welfare, health, conduct and progress.

25.58 The Saints deferred making adoption applications in respect of the H boys because they did not wish to proceed with them until the outcome of their contested application in respect of G was known. It was in these circumstances that the adoption applications for the H boys were still being processed when Roger Saint's 1972 conviction came to light in February 1988. W wrote about the matter on 22 February 1988 to the social worker who had dealt with the Saints in 1982 and 1983, who was by 1988 Director of Social Services for the London Borough of Brent. It is clear from that letter that W had become an advocate for the Saints rather than a dispassionate assessor of the children's best interests, despite Roger Saint's failure to disclose his conviction. She had not by then seen the police account of the offence but appears to have accepted Saint's lame explanation that the "bother" was the result of a broken engagement and that he did not recall that the incident had been a sexual assault.

25.59 The reply on 15 April 1988 to W's letter threw no further light upon the matter and probably only reiterated what had earlier been said to similar effect on the telephone. By that time W had prepared a second report for a meeting of the Tower Hamlets' Family Placement Panel on 12 April 1988 in which both the police statement and Roger Saint's explanation of the 1972 offence were set out. There was no analysis, however, of the striking differences between the two; and the remainder of the report was a very fulsome account of Roger Saint's "long and successful career" in residential work. W concluded that the 1972 offence seemed to have been totally out of character and she appears to have attributed Roger Saint's non-disclosure of the offence to naiveté on his part.

25.60 The Panel was not a decision making body. However, it asked for reviews to be conducted of each of the children who had been placed with the Saints and for the reviews to be brought to the Panel for a "decision to be made". The response to this request appears to have been unsatisfactory because the review forms that we have seen, each dated 5 May 1988, were very incomplete. In the event the Panel recommended that the adoptions should proceed. According to the statement to the Tribunal made by one of its members, they "questioned the social workers concerned and were assured that the children had been seen alone, and that all appeared well: and in the light of this recommended that the adoptions proceed". We have not seen any report by the social workers of any interviews with the Saints or any of the children.

25.61 To complete the picture the evidence indicates that there were two interviews with Roger Saint: the first by W and the social worker of J[12] took place in London fairly soon after the conviction became known and before the police account of the incident was received; and the second, in North Wales, involved both these social workers and the Team Manager. It is likely that both interviews preceded the completion of the reviews.

25.62 In sharp contrast to the highly favourable view of the Saints formed by W, social workers from the London Borough of Southall were highly critical of them at much the same time. The latter were considering in 1987 whether or not to place a child with the Saints and a Southall social worker visited them to make an assessment of their suitability. She conveyed her views to W by telephone on 13 July 1987 and was very critical, in particular, of the Saints' wish to increase the family for whom they were responsible when the children with them already were so needy. Accordingly, Southall decided not to use the Saints as foster parents.

25.63 Adoption orders were made in respect of the four H boys on 11 January 1989 in the Mold (or Holywell) County Court. Their mother had initially refused to consent to the adoption but intimated to the guardian ad litem in 1988 that she was willing to do so. The mother's consent was sent to the Court on 21 October 1988 by the guardian, who said that she did not therefore consider it appropriate to continue with a full guardian ad litem enquiry. In the event her report dealt only with the mother's position. It contained little information about the Saints and the children, and expressed no view as to whether the proposed adoptions would be in the children's best interests.

25.64 We are perturbed that the County Court may not have been informed of Roger Saint's 1972 conviction. Rule 22(1) of the Adoption Rules 1984 required Tower Hamlets, as the placing agency, to provide a written report to the Court covering the matters specified in Schedule 2 to the Rules. Paragraph 4 of this schedule sets out the particulars to be given of the prospective adopters: it does not make any express reference to previous convictions but sub-paragraph (x) requires the report to set out "any other relevant information" (about the adopters) "which might assist the court". W compiled and signed reports in respect of each of the relevant H boys in purported compliance with the

[12] See paras 25.66 and 25.67.

requirements of Rule 22(1) but there were no paragraph 4 particulars. Moreover, if reliance was placed upon earlier particulars supplied in connection with the adoption application in respect of G, they pre-dated Tower Hamlets' knowledge of Roger Saint's 1972 conviction.

25.65 In a brief statement to Tower Hamlets in January 1988 W said that she discussed with the guardian ad litem the details of Roger Saint's 1972 conviction and that she and the guardian were present at the adoption hearing. We have neither seen nor heard anything, however, that indicates that the County Court was informed of it.

25.66 To complete the history of Tower Hamlets' placements with the Saints it is necessary to mention one other child. This was a girl, J, born on 8 May 1973, who was boarded out with the Saints in July or September 1985 and who had a very disturbed history. She remained with the Saints until September 1989. The Form F in respect of this placement stated incorrectly that police enquiries had been completed before F, G and the H boys had been placed.

25.67 We heard evidence of one complaint by J during the period when she was living with the Saints. This was provided by the proprietor of a taxi company who transported J from Llanarmon-yn-Ial to Ysgol Talfryn each school day for just over a year in or about 1987/1988. According to this witness J was sometimes very calm and quiet but on other occasions she was agitated and very excited (he had been told by Roger Saint that she was schizophrenic). One morning J told him that her father kept wanting her to take her knickers off and to look at her and she denied the witness' suggestion that Saint was merely trying to give her a bath. Subsequently she made similar allegations on two or three occasions within a fortnight and the witness decided that he ought to report them to Clwyd's Head of School Transport, who said that she would notify the Social Services Department. Within an hour Roger Saint telephoned the witness threatening that he would seek retribution through his solicitors and alleging that it was J's condition that made her say such things. Saint, in his evidence, denied threatening anyone but we accept that he did and it would have been in character for him to do so.

25.68 There were no further developments in relation to the witness' report as far as he is aware. He was not approached by either Clwyd Education Department or the Social Services Department and nothing further was said between him and Roger Saint on the subject. The latter's evidence was that J left ultimately, after an incident when she had run down the drive at the Saints' home shouting that she had had sex with a man three times. J was interviewed by the police and Saint sat in at the interview, but the man referred to was never traced.

25.69 J was not called to give evidence to us and we are unable to say whether there was any truth in her allegations. On the basis of very limited information before us it seems quite possible that they were imagined by her and were attributable, as Saint said, to her condition.

Later placements with the Saints

25.70 It is convenient to deal here, and finally, with the later placement of children with the Saints, although these occurred after they moved from Clwyd to Bala in Gwynedd in September 1990. In that period of five and a half years prior to Roger Saint's arrest in March 1996 it seems that five further children were placed with the Saints by three different local authorities but we have not received any complaint against Roger Saint from any of them or in respect of them from any other source.

25.71 The first of these children, a boy born on 5 April 1978, was the only one of them to be adopted by the Saints subsequently, becoming their eighth adopted child. He was placed with them by North Yorkshire County Council in September 1991, before the Children Act 1989 and the first regulations made under it came into force, and he was adopted by the Saints in 1995.

25.72 North Yorkshire County Council placed two other boys with the Saints; one, aged 15 years at the time, was placed in December 1993 and remained for four months only; and the other aged $13\frac{1}{2}$ years then, was placed in April 1995 and remained with them to the end of that year.

25.73 The other two children were placed by North Tyneside Metropolitan Borough Council and the London Borough of Greenwich respectively and both remained until Roger Saint's arrest. North Tyneside placed a boy, whose age is not known to us, in May 1994 and Greenwich placed a girl, born on 20 January 1984, in August 1995.

25.74 In the absence of any complaints about these later placements by different English local authorities, we have not sought evidence from them and the particulars that we have given in the preceding three paragraphs are those contained in the documents before us. It was said at Saint's trial that North Tyneside received from him an exculpatory account of the 1972 offence: the judgment made by North Tyneside was "that the conviction was not so significant and that he had successfully cared for so many children in the past and no person had made a complaint against him".

Conclusions

25.75 The history that we have related shows how very grave consequences resulted from a catalogue of administrative failings and errors of judgment, beginning with the failure to elicit details of Saint's 1972 conviction in 1978. It is clear that Saint deliberately suppressed this information and gave misleading particulars of his employment record to assist in the cover up but the conviction ought to have been discovered when Clwyd made the appropriate enquiry of the North Wales Police. It is regrettable both that the enquiry by the police was limited to their local records and that this was not made clear to Clwyd Social Services Department. In the event the check was almost valueless because of the Saints' brief residence in North Wales up to that time; and, if Clwyd had been aware of this, they would at least have had the opportunity to seek information from other sources.

25.76 Clwyd Social Services Department subsequently monitored the placements of C and D satisfactorily. Clwyd had no reason to suspect that sexual abuse was occurring, and we do not criticise Clwyd for the delay in terminating the placements, bearing in mind what C and D said at the time. There were defects in the End of Placement report in respect of D as we have indicated but it does not appear that Clwyd made any further placements with the Saints after that date, apart from its role as agent in the placement and adoption of E. The omissions in the report may, however, have encouraged others in Clwyd and elsewhere to form a more favourable view of the Saints than was justified.

25.77 Clwyd's main shortcomings after 1981 were their failures (a) to respond to Tower Hamlets' request in 1982 for a further check of the Saints' record to be made with the police and (b) to terminate Roger Saint's membership of the Clwyd South Adoption and Foster Care Panel on learning in February 1988 of his 1972 conviction. Both Clwyd and Tower Hamlets were at fault in overlooking (a). If either had pursued the matter, the subsequent placement of the H boys with the Saints might have been avoided. As for (b), there is no evidence that any abuse to children resulted from Roger Saint's membership of the Panel but it was plainly inappropriate for him to continue as a member after February 1988 and it is inexcusable that he was permitted to remain a member for a further eight years.

25.78 The history generally illustrates the dangers and confusion that may arise when foster parents are permitted to apply for placements to a variety of local authorities or agencies in the absence of any central or unified control. Thus, for example, liaison between Tower Hamlets and Clwyd appears to have been defective and the former went ahead with placements without effective reference to Clwyd; and later placements were made by other local authorities similarly. These dangers should now, however, be lessened by the requirement that there shall be only one "approving authority"[13] (ie local authority or voluntary organisation) in respect of any specific foster parent, although others may place children with the foster parent with the approval of that authority, and by the limitation on the number of children who may be placed with one person[14].

25.79 The response of Tower Hamlets to the discovery in February 1988 of Roger Saint's 1972 conviction was highly unsatisfactory. Once the conviction became known it was plain that Roger Saint had seriously deceived both Clwyd and Tower Hamlets and it was most inappropriate to rely upon the assessment made by W of the veracity of Roger Saint's inadequate explanations of the conviction itself and his failure to reveal it. The decision by the Panel to recommend that the proposed adoptions of the H boys should proceed appears to have been based upon inadequate information; and, if the County Court was not informed of the conviction, the omission was lamentable.

---

[13] See Regulation 3 of the Foster Placement (Children) Regulations 1991.
[14] See Schedule 7 to the Children Act 1989. The "usual fostering limit" is three children.

25.80 Following widespread critical reporting of the Saint case, the Department of Health issued the Children (Protection from Offenders) (Miscellaneous Amendments) Regulations 1997[15], which came into force on 17 October 1997. These regulations prohibit (subject to very limited exceptions) the approval as a foster carer or adoptive parent by adoption agencies, local authorities or voluntary organisations of any person who is known to have been convicted of, or cautioned for, any one of a list of specified offences, including indecent assault. The prohibition applies also if any adult member of that person's household is known to have been so convicted or cautioned. There is a prohibition on placement even if approval has already been given and, if the placement has already been made, immediate steps must be taken to remove the child. If a child has already been adopted, however, it is the duty of the local authority for the area where the child lives to investigate the position in accordance with the provisions of section 47 of the Children Act 1989, which apply generally in respect of all children within its area, if the local authority "have reasonable cause to suspect that a child . . . is suffering, or is likely to suffer, significant harm".

25.81 By way of postscript it should be said that, in his plea in mitigation on behalf of Roger Saint before the latter was sentenced, Counsel told the judge that Saint had himself been the victim of abuse as a child and Counsel emphasised the positive aspects of Saint's record as a carer of children, including the continuing allegiance of many of the adopted children.

---

[15] SI 1997 No 2308.

Frederick Rutter

Background

26.01 **Frederick Rutter** has already figured in this report as a temporary RCCO at Bryn Estyn from 5 July 1982 to 19 November 1983[1] and at Park House, initially on a temporary basis but then as a permanent RCCO, between October 1984 and 28 August 1988[2], after a period of ten months in between as a care assistant at a hostel for the mentally handicapped; and his general history has been summarised in paragraph 8.41. On 28 August 1988 Rutter began employment with Clwyd Housing Association Ltd as Warden of their Pen-y-Llan hostel for young people in Connah's Quay and he remained in that employment until he was suspended from duty on 18 May 1990 and then resigned on 12 June 1990.

26.02 On 3 April 1990 an 18 years old woman resident at the hostel complained to the police that Rutter had behaved improperly towards her there. In the course of the ensuing enquiries by the police she and other young women residents of the hostel made more serious sexual complaints against him, as did two girls who were living with Rutter and his wife at the time of the offences against them. Rutter was arrested on 22 October 1990 and, when interviewed, he denied all the allegations.

26.03 In July 1991 Rutter was tried in the Crown Court at Chester[3] on an indictment alleging five offences of rape, one of buggery and three indecent assaults involving five residents at the hostel and the two girls who had lived with the Rutters. On 30 July 1991 he was found guilty of raping both these girls. He was convicted also of two rapes and two indecent assaults involving three of the hostel residents but he was acquitted of alleged offences against the two other complainant residents. Concurrent sentences of 12 years' imprisonment were imposed for each of the four offences of rape and of 12 months' imprisonment for the two indecent assaults.

26.04 In view of our terms of reference we deal in this chapter with the Rutters' fostering history and Frederick Rutter's offences against the two girls living with them. As far as we are aware the proved victims from the hostel were not in care when they were resident there and all but one of them stayed for only a short period.

The Rutters' fostering history

26.05 The Rutters' first application to foster was made to Clwyd County Council on 28 December 1984, very shortly after Frederick Rutter had moved to Park House[4]. This was in respect of a boy who was a resident at Park House.

---

[1] See paras 8.41, 8.42 and 10.151 to 10.156.
[2] See paras 17.68 to 17.79.
[3] See para 2.07(8).
[4] See para 17.69.

This boy had already spent week-ends with the Rutters and part of the Christmas holiday; and there was some tension between the Rutters and the boy's social worker, who wished to build up his relationship with his mother. The application to foster was discontinued by agreement in March 1985 because of the planned rehabilitation.

26.06 On 28 February 1986 the Director of Social Services approved the Rutters' home as lodgings for another boy in residential care, who had already spent many week-ends and the Christmas period there. The Director acted under delegated powers and the approval was endorsed by the Adoption Case and Foster Care Sub-Committee on 21 March 1986, after the police had confirmed that nothing to the detriment of the Rutters was known. The application had been handled by Robert Jones[5], a former colleague of Frederick Rutter at Bryn Estyn, who recommended approval. However, it seems that the placement had broken down by September 1986.

26.07 In 1987 the Rutters moved from their home in Flint to a five bedroomed house in Connah's Quay and they applied again on 8 January 1988 to become foster parents. This application was in respect of girl A, who was one of the two girls subsequently raped at the house by Rutter, and it was recommended for approval by South Clwyd Adoption and Foster Care Panel on 21 March 1988. Roger Saint attended as a member of the panel that day but no sinister significance can be attached to his presence. The actual approval was given by the Adoption Case and Foster Care Sub-Committee on 12 May 1988.

26.08 A was another resident at Park House, where Rutter was still employed, and there was already a close relationship between her and the Rutter family. The Rutters had two daughters and A was said to have been the "best friend" of the younger daughter when they attended the same school. A was 15 years old at the time of the application. Her mother had died when she was eight years old, after which she had lived with her father and his woman partner until she had been received into care in January 1988 and placed at Park House. Contact with the Rutter family had then resumed and A had begun to stay with them at week-ends. She wished to be fostered by the Rutters rather than to remain at Park House.

26.09 From the documents before the Tribunal, it appears that the correct assessment procedure was complied with, save that the senior officer's final report disclosed that he had not visited the Rutters' home for a number of reasons, including sickness there and the officer's leave arrangements. The latter did have personal knowledge of Rutter for a number of years and we do not regard the omission as material in the context of our inquiry. Appropriate references were provided and an enquiry of the police revealed that Rutter had been convicted of a drink/driving offence, resulting in 12 months' disqualification from driving, since the previous enquiry in March 1986.

26.10 It seems that two boys were already living at the Rutters' home as approved lodgings when the application to foster A was approved. One of these was the boy in respect of whom the earlier application to foster had been begun in

---

[5] See para 10.66.

December 1984. He had kept in touch with the Rutters and Wirral Social Services Department decided on 22 January 1988 (when he was $16\frac{1}{2}$ years old) at a Child Care Review that he should move from Parkside Children's Home in the Wirral to lodge with the Rutters prior to his discharge from care. The two Rutter daughters, aged 17 and $14\frac{1}{2}$ years respectively, were also living at their home.

26.11 A's evidence was read to the Tribunal. In it she described how she had been raped by Rutter when she was 16 years old (ie in or about 1989). The offence had occurred in the living room when the rest of the household had gone to bed. She had been watching a film, dressed in a night-dress and dressing gown, when he had forced himself upon her, eventually ejaculating on the floor. He had then switched off the television and told her to go to bed. She had been too embarrassed to tell anyone, except a close friend and her brother-in-law, before the police visited her unexpectedly. She had also been worried about being thrown out and having nowhere to live. Rutter had never had sex with her again and she had made sure that she was never on her own with him. She left the Rutters in 1989 when she had become pregnant by her boyfriend. Joan Rutter did not want her to remain after that and the Social Services Department found her a flat in Connah's Quay.

26.12 Girl B was also resident at Park House before she went to live with the Rutters. She was born in April 1971 and she said that she moved to the home of the Rutters as approved lodgings when she was 17 years old. She had been taken into care when she was 14 years old on the ground that she was beyond her mother's control and had then lived successively at Bersham Hall, with her father and at Park House, to which she had moved when she was 16 years old. According to her written statement, she was only at Park House for about a month before moving out to live with her sister. She had not wanted then to go to live with the Rutters because Frederick Rutter, whom she had known at Park House, gave her "the creeps", but she was told by the Social Services Department that she had to move to approved lodgings.

26.13 We have not seen the documents relating to these placements but a report on them was presented by the Director of Social Services, John Jevons, to the Clwyd Children and Families Sub-Committee on 21 October 1992 after Rutter's trial. This report was based upon an internal investigation carried out by an Assistant Director, Geoffrey Wyatt, in the course of which such matters as the provision of a reference for Rutter by Jeffrey Douglas, the conduct of a social worker responsible for supervising one of the girls in the hostel, the approval of the Rutters as foster parents and as providers of approved lodgings and the supervision of A and B when placed with the Rutters were all considered.

26.14 Part of this investigation was carried out by Elena Fowler, Clwyd's Child and Family Social Work Manager. She criticised the fact that approval of the Rutters' home as lodgings had been transferred to their new house without completion of a fresh assessment but she said that it was difficult to assess any deficiency in the role played by Clwyd because of the "extreme disorganisation" of the two relevant files. It is similarly difficult for the

Tribunal to make any pertinent criticism. However, Elena Fowler did say that the Boarding Out Regulations had been complied with in relation to the approval procedures and that the supervision had been adequate. She commented that Clwyd may have adopted a "more relaxed approach" to the Rutters' applications because Rutter was already in the employ of the Social Services Department in a responsible position with children and may have been influenced by the fact that the Rutter family had known A as a young child.

26.15 In her written evidence before the Tribunal B said that she remained with the Rutters for only a "couple of months" before she ran away because she could not take any more of him. She alleged that Rutter had sexual intercourse with her against her will about five times within one month and had oral sex also with her. These rapes and sexual assaults had all occurred in the television room or her bedroom when no one else was around and Rutter had begun making improper approaches to her the very night that she moved in.

Other allegations against Frederick Rutter

26.16 As we have said earlier in this chapter, Rutter was convicted of two offences of rape and two indecent assaults in respect of three young women who had been resident at the time at Pen-y-Llan Hostel. It is unnecessary for the purposes of this report to go into the details of these offences, save to say that they were committed between February 1989 and April 1990 and that the victims were in the age range of 17 to 21 years.

26.17 The complaints by D of rape by Rutter, which were not the subject of a prosecution are discussed in paragraphs 17.70 to 17.72 of this report.

Conclusions

26.18 The very serious offences against A and B would only have been avoided if the Rutters had not been approved as foster parents and their home had not been approved as lodgings. We do not think that Clwyd can be realistically criticised, however, for granting the approvals on the basis of the information about Frederick Rutter available at the time. With a degree of hindsight it can be said that if a full record had been kept (and entered in his personal file) of all the matters involving Rutter during his employment by Clwyd, a less favourable picture of him would have been available to senior officials and this might have led to the Rutters' applications being refused.

26.19 This history provides yet another example of the dangers that arise when children in residential care are permitted to visit and stay with care staff in the latter's homes, even when the proposed arrangement has been vetted by other professional staff. The same high standard of vigilance has to be applied to the vetting of residential staff as to other applicants who seek to provide a home for vulnerable children. The possibility of staff selecting children whose particular vulnerability is known to them has to be guarded against. Moreover, employees of Social Services Departments should not be assessed by social workers who have worked closely with them.

Allegations against other foster parents resident in Clwyd

Introduction

27.01 In this chapter we outline complaints made in respect of five other foster homes in Clwyd during the period of our review, which illustrate a variety of problems that may arise when children are boarded out by a local authority.

Foster home A

27.02 Two girls, A1 and A2, were placed by Clwyd with Mr and Mrs A on 19 August 1977, when A1 was almost 8 years old and A2 nine years old. Clwyd County Council assumed parental rights in respect of both girls on 25 January 1978. A2 remained with the As for two years, leaving on 6 August 1979. A1 left about a month later, on 11 September 1979.

27.03 These two girls were members of a group of eight siblings, five of whom, including A1 and A2, had been received into voluntary care on 18 July 1970, after their parents had separated on their father's release from prison. A1 and A2 were placed at Little Acton Residential Nursery for about four years and then moved to Park House in September 1974, where they joined their three older sisters and where they remained until they were boarded out with the As. The three older sisters returned at that time to live with their father.

27.04 On leaving the As both girls went back initially to Park House and then to live with their father. A1 remained at home for five years but then spent short periods in Chevet Hey (twice) and Bersham Hall (seven months) as well as a variety of foster placements. A2, however, remained with her father until she was discharged from care at the age of 16 years, apart from a period of four and a half months at Bersham Hall for assessment in the latter part of 1982.

27.05 There is a considerable conflict of evidence between Mr and Mrs A on the one hand and the two girls on the other about what happened in the foster home between 1977 and 1979, which we are not in a position to resolve satisfactorily at this remote time. A1 gave oral evidence to the Tribunal and the statements of A2, who was under psychiatric care and felt unable to give oral evidence, were read to us; we heard oral evidence from both Mr and Mrs A, who provided a joint written statement. According to the girls they were treated harshly and made to work as virtual slaves throughout. They complain also of indecent behaviour towards them by the As' two sons. Mr and Mrs A, however, denied all these allegations, although they admitted slapping the girls from time to time when they misbehaved and encouraging them to help in the house. They produced photographs depicting happy events that had occurred and said that difficulties often arose following intervention by the girls' sisters or a telephone call from their father. In the end the As could not cope with the girls' misbehaviour and they did not seek to foster any further children after their experiences with A1 and A2.

27.06 It is unnecessary for the purposes of this report to go into elaborate detail about the complaints of A1 and A2 and there were some divergences between them. The household chores that they referred to included scrubbing the floor with toothbrushes, cleaning paintwork all day with a rag, prolonged washing and ironing and picking leaves for the pet rabbit. The As' sons were not required to do similar work. If the girls did not do it, they were smacked with a belt, usually by Mr A but sometimes by Mrs A. There were complaints also by A1 of being locked in the attic bedroom for long periods without food or drink and made to stand before the mirror for hours: they were not allowed to go to the toilet but had a "potty" from which they had to drink their urine (and eat their own waste) because there was nothing else to eat or drink. This was a punishment for eating a piece of chocolate without permission. It was also a punishment for bed-wetting. A2, however, made no reference, for example, to the bedroom door being locked: they were allowed to go to the toilet and she made no mention of drinking urine.

27.07 One of the more remarkable allegations by A1 was that, on one occasion early on, she and A2 threw the family cat out of their attic window to see if it had nine lives. The cat landed on its legs (feet) and was "alright". By way of punishment Mr A hung A1 out of the window by her legs. She said that she was hysterical and that it seemed to her that Mr A did so for ages before pulling her in. A2 said that Mr and Mrs A caught them before the cat was thrown because it was clawing them and making a noise. The As burst into the room and Mr A dangled A1 out of the window, holding her by her feet, saying that it was "to see how she would like it". A1 was screaming and crying and they were both punished.

27.08 The sexual allegations were of varying gravity. Both girls alleged that they were fingered and touched indecently by the As' sons. A1 said that the boys used to take them into a cubby hole under the stairs for the purpose but A2 made no mention of that and said that the boys would come into the girls' bedroom and start touching and kissing them. A2 referred also to being touched indecently when the children were in the back seat of the car. The most serious allegation by A1 was that she had been buggered by one of the sons in a field when she was eight years old. A1 complained also of being watched in the bath by the As and their sons and of being required to watch the As together in the bath.

27.09 In one of her written statements A1 alleged that a social worker had witnessed Mr A biting A1 on the bare buttock (apparently as a punishment for bed-wetting) and that the same social worker often used to watch things, including sexual acts between the two girls and the sons of the family. She referred also to seeing Mr A hand over cash to the social worker "quite a few times". Mrs A used to say that the cash was for donations but A1 believed it was bribery to keep the social worker quiet about what she had seen; and she heard arguments between Mr A and the social worker in which the latter would ask for money. A1 later retracted her allegation that the social worker had witnessed sexual acts by As' sons with the girls. She was also inconsistent about whether she had reported these sexual acts, withdrawing an allegation that she had told another social worker about them on leaving the foster home and saying later that she had only told him about "the beatings".

27.10 It will be obvious from what we have said in summary that there are problems about the credibility of A1 and A2 and the evidence before us indicates that A1, in particular, was a severely disturbed girl, who prided herself on her ability to make difficulties for staff. A1 said or agreed (apparently incorrectly) that the main social worker involved with them made frequent visits to the foster home, weekly or fortnightly plus unscheduled visits, but the contemporary records rebut A1's suggestion that she was continuously unhappy whilst living with the As. Thus, on 6 September 1977 both girls were saying that they were very happy; a report in 1978 records that A1 had told the social worker that she loved being with the As; and in September 1978 both girls said that they considered their home to be with Mr and Mrs A, which they envisaged leaving only to marry or to work. Even as late as August 1979 A1 was again insisting that she wanted to stay.

27.11 The two social workers that we have referred to both denied that either A1 or A2 complained of sexual or physical abuse whilst they were living with Mr and Mrs A. According to the main social worker, there had been discussion with the As about the appropriateness of making A1 wash her bed clothes as a response to bed-wetting; the girls had also complained on one occasion about doing ironing and other household tasks; and there was a record that Mrs A admitted hitting the girls but she could not recall the circumstances now.

27.12 Mr and Mrs A had previously fostered six children, mainly on short term placements. They said that they had loved A1 and A2 and had tried to do their best for them. Mr A denied specifically that he had bitten A1 on the buttock or that he had dangled her from a bedroom window. He said that the bedroom windows had been screwed shut before the children were placed because the sills were low and a child could fall out. The police had confirmed this in 1995, when the only window that opened was a small fanlight, which opened about four inches. He denied also an allegation that the girls had been kept away from school to conceal bruising, saying that the police examined their attendance records, which showed that they had never missed a day.

27.13 The foster parents admitted slapping the girls on quite a few occasions but Mrs A said that it was a rare occurrence, usually when they were hysterical and fighting or when, for example, one of them threw a chair. Thus, on 3 May 1979 there was a record of a home visit when Mrs A told the social worker that her husband was at his wits end and had smacked the girls hard, causing bruising. Mr A said of this incident that he had chased the girls from the lounge and up the stairs after A2 had smashed a number of ornaments, including a cut-glass cakestand, and a chair had been smashed against a wall. He had slapped both girls on the legs.

27.14 Mr and Mrs A said also that they had encouraged A1 and A2 (and their own sons) to help with household chores in an attempt to teach them self-sufficiency and not by way of punishment. These chores never took more than ten minutes and A1 and A2 had exaggerated the facts to such an extent that they now bore no resemblance to reality (the report of an interview between A1 and a psychiatrist dated 18 May 1979 records A1 as having said that she was happier in the foster home than at Park House because she was given the opportunity to take part in chores).

27.15 We do not consider that we would be justified in accepting the allegations by A1 and A2 that they were physically and sexually abused in this foster home because we do not regard their evidence as reliable. There were many inconsistencies in it and a great deal of exaggeration; and some of it was plainly untrue. Moreover, contemporary records do not support their general case that they were consistently unhappy from the beginning of the placement; and A1 had a long record of emotional disturbance before and after she was placed with the As. It is probable that the As' way of life was, in the end, unsuitable for such damaged children and that their recourse to slapping, which has become increasingly highly controversial in the family context, was an aggravating factor, but we accept that the As' intentions were good and that they did attempt to provide a suitable home for A1 and A2.

27.16 As we have already said, Mr and Mrs A withdrew their services as foster parents after A1 and A2 had left them. On 31 January 1980 they wrote to the Social Services Department complaining about the lack of support that they had received. They were seen by one of the three social workers who had dealt with the placement, who reported that part of their complaint related to the non-payment of certain discretionary grants and of compensation for damage by A1 and A2 to their home. They complained also, however, of lack of communication between social workers and the family, that visits by social workers had been too infrequent and too brief in relation to the severe behavioural problems that they were experiencing, and that no action had been taken when the family routine had been upset by numerous threatening telephone calls from the father of A1 and A2.

27.17 A report on the As' complaint was commissioned by the Area Officer for the Wrexham-Maelor area, whose office had been responsible for supervising the placement. Three social workers in succession based in that area, none of whom was professionally qualified, had carried out the supervision, although the fostering application had been dealt with by the Delyn area office. Our comments on the records and the report are that:

(a) The records of preparatory discussion with the girls are very brief and suggest that there was little understanding of the problems likely to be faced in placing satisfactorily two children with little or no experience of normal family life.

(b) There were only five home visits between 15 December 1977 and 13 March 1979 with one gap of six months in that 15 months period, showing inadequate supervision and support.

(c) From the record of the visit on 24 August 1978 it appears that Mr A had been unemployed for 12 months, unbeknown to the Social Services Department, with the result that the family had been struggling financially. It was recorded also by the social worker that Mrs A had not been available for her to visit during "the past few months" because she and her mother had been seriously ill (Mrs A had been under investigation for cancer but it had proved to be a false alarm).

(d) A fortnight later a Delyn area social worker alerted the Wrexham-Maelor area to the risk of the placement breaking down, mainly (it was said) due to the girls' stubbornness and defiance. This led to an arrangement whereby a Delyn social worker took on a supportive role for the foster parents whilst the existing social worker became more involved with the children.

27.18 Our conclusion is that there is substance in Mrs A's complaint in her oral evidence that she felt the lack of support at times. The gaps in visiting were not justified by Mrs A's stated non-availability and there was insufficient social worker input into the placement, bearing in mind the girls' troubled upbringing, the As' financial difficulties and the potentially disrupting effect of the natural father's interventions from time to time. Clwyd Social Services Department, however, had real problems at the time in providing supervision; there was a shortage of social workers in the Wrexham-Maelor area and a lack of trained staff. Moreover, there was no pool of qualified social workers nationally from whom they could recruit.

27.19 We do not criticise the prolongation of the placements for about a year after September 1978, having regard to the reported wishes of both girls to remain with the As. If it is correct, however, that there was a gap in visiting between 18 September 1978 and 13 March 1979, the failure of supervision at that juncture was most regrettable but also a serious breach of the Boarding Out Regulations; but for it, the ultimate outcome might have been different.

Foster home B

27.20 Mr and Mrs B are the uncle and aunt of four children (a boy and three girls) who were boarded out with them on 4 December 1977. The background circumstances were that the children's mother had committed suicide in 1976, when the whereabouts of their father were unknown. The children had then gone to live with their paternal grandparents on 9 November 1976, the date when they were received into care, but the grandmother had died on 27 November 1977, whereupon they had been placed with Mr and Mrs B, who were formally approved as foster parents for the children on 10 January 1978. Clwyd County Council assumed parental rights in respect of all four children on 17 December 1980.

27.21 The second daughter, B2, by then nearly 28 years old, made a written statement to the Tribunal on 6 August 1997 and gave oral evidence to us on 16 September 1997. She alleged that Mr B had sexually abused her from the age of four years and had had sexual intercourse with her from the age of seven years for about ten years. B2's statement to the Tribunal was made just over ten years after Mr B had pleaded guilty, on 13 March 1987 in the Crown Court at Mold, to an attempted rape of B2's younger sister, B3, born a year after B2, for which he had been sentenced to 18 months' imprisonment, suspended for two years. B2's explanations for not disclosing Mr B's offences against her, despite B3's first complaint in August 1986, was that she had been threatened with "going into homes" and "because of Mrs B".

27.22 Mr B denied B2's allegations but he was ultimately charged with 14 offences including six rapes of B2, the first on 24 December 1978 and covering the period between then and 1 October 1985, and two indecent assaults upon her, the first between October 1975 and October 1976, before her mother died. There were also six charges (two rapes and four indecent assaults) in respect of B2's elder sister, B1, born on 19 October 1968, covering a period from October 1976 to October 1984. Eventually, Mr B pleaded guilty to three rapes and six indecent assaults in respect of B2 and four indecent assaults upon B1. He was sentenced on 9 September 1998, in the Crown Court at Chester, to concurrent terms of three years' imprisonment for the rapes and 12 months' imprisonment for the indecent assaults.

27.23 It is unnecessary for the purposes of this report to give details of the offences to which Mr B pleaded guilty and he did not give evidence to the Tribunal because he could not be traced at the relevant time. It must be said, however, that B2 was supportive of him in 1986, when B3 made her allegations, and denied that she had been abused by him at that time. B2 herself became pregnant by another person in the latter part of 1986 with the result that she gave birth to a child in July 1987. She moved to a council house four months later and she was discharged from care on 14 December 1987.

27.24 B2 complained also in 1997 that she had been neglected and physically abused whilst boarded out with Mr and Mrs B. Her main allegation was that Mr B would hit her with a strap and that she ran away on 14 June 1982 because of this. A social worker visited the foster home that day and his record shows that B2 did allege that she had been "frequently clouted, often with a belt (across backside)". She asserted then also that 18 months previously she had been marked quite badly on her buttocks and on the tops of her legs. B2 wanted at that time to move to live nearby with an 18 years old married woman, with whom she had made friends. According to the record, B2 accepted the social worker's advice that she could not do so and a temporary truce was called, but the social worker felt that B2's placement was "tenuous" and was not really sure whether Mrs B wanted B2 to stay.

27.25 There was continuing concern thereafter about B2's attitudes at home and at school but the later reviews in her case do not indicate that she complained again of being hit. There was recurring tension between Mr and Mrs B and at least one short period of separation but there is no evidence of later physical abuse of B2 except her own general statement in her oral evidence that things got worse as the years went on and that the beatings carried on. She did add, however, that she told a social worker who assumed responsibility for her in or about August 1984 that "we were getting hit", to which the response was "If you're naughty, you're supposed to be hit".

27.26 We do not think that Clwyd Social Services Department can be validly criticised for placing the four children with Mr and Mrs B or for failing to discover earlier the sexual abuse of which the three girls belatedly complained. The pattern of successive offences against sisters and of late disclosure is often found in closely similar cases of incest. Appropriate action was taken following the complaints of B3 and we do not have any evidence of further offences by Mr B after 1 October 1985. B3 was moved to Bersham Hall for a period following her disclosure and the family underwent therapy with two social workers, before Mr B himself returned home, which was part of the background to the imposition of a suspended sentence in 1987. There was limited contact between B2 and Mr B thereafter because she lived, at least partly, at the home of her boy friend's mother during her pregnancy and until she moved to her own council house.

27.27 It is clear that B2 did complain on occasions, whilst still living in the foster home, of being physically struck by way of punishment for various misdemeanours and we have no reason to doubt the truth of these complaints or her oral evidence that Mr B would "belt her" with a strap from time to time. The social worker responsible for her in the mid 1980s said in a written statement to Clwyd's Child Practice Manager that she knew that the B family believed in slapping children whereas she (the social worker) did not agree with it. No signs of physical abuse were ever observed, however, by social workers. It may well be that more strenuous representations ought to have been made to Mr and Mrs B about this but we think that it is unlikely that the scale of any physical abuse was severe and, in contrast to the very grave sexual abuse, it does not appear to have had an important lasting impact on the girls.

27.28 We did not receive sufficient evidence about the quality and frequency of visiting by social workers early on to make any assessment but the documents before us from 1984 onwards suggest that the quality of work done with the family then was quite high and that visiting was more frequent than the minimum required. There were no individual care plans for the children but the statutory reviews appear to have been carried out conscientiously and realistically. There is some evidence that the children were not often seen alone but we do not think that these particular children would have complained sooner of the sexual abuse if they had been seen alone more frequently.

Foster home C

27.29 Mr and Mrs C became foster parents of three children on 26 July 1978 under emergency arrangements following the request of their natural father, who had separated from their mother, that they should be received into care by Clwyd County Council. It was subsequently ordered on 10 May 1979 in the Chester County Court, in the matrimonial proceedings between their parents, that the children should remain in the care of the County Council. Mr and Mrs C had three children of their own and later fostered four others contemporaneously with the three with whom we are concerned.

27.30 C1 was one of the three children who began to live with Mr and Mrs C on 26 July 1978. She was born on 16 June 1971 and suffered from recurrent epilepsy as well as learning difficulties. Although the placement appeared to have been successful for many years, C1 complained in April 1991 that Mr C had abused her sexually over a long period beginning with gross indecency, involving masturbation, and progressing to regular indecent assaults and to full sexual intercourse.

27.31 On the strength of these complaints Mr C, who was then nearly 45 years old, was charged with one offence of rape and four offences of indecent assault. He was committed on 5 August 1991 to stand trial in the Crown Court at Mold but he was found dead on 27 August 1991, having hanged himself on discharging himself from a Chester psychiatric unit, where he had been a voluntary patient, six days earlier. C1 was rather uncertain about the dates when the offences had begun and ended but they were particularised in the indictment as having occurred between 18 July 1982 and 24 April 1991. When interviewed by the police Mr C had denied raping C1 but had admitted the other offences.

27.32 After the disclosure by C1, she was placed with new foster parents on 3 May 1991 but the placement proved to be unsuccessful. On 11 June 1991, just before her 20th birthday, she was moved to Petit House, Flint[1], which was no longer a children's home but which afforded her accommodation from which she was able to attend work. A report from a specialist social worker at that time indicated that she functioned at a much lower intellectual level than would be expected of a young woman of her age[2]; her comprehension of events was limited; her emotional development was delayed; and her experiences of care had led to her being over dependent. It is sad to record that she had been "living rough" for eight weeks when in May 1993 she called at the home of her second foster parents; the Social Services Department then helped her to find fresh accommodation.

27.33 The documents before us show that Mr and Mrs C were carefully vetted before becoming foster parents, in accordance with approved practice. The references provided were taken up and enquiries made of the police. Mr C was a school manager and served on various other local committees. The quality of the subsequent social work was higher than in other cases we have examined; supervision of the placement was assiduous, often weekly and well in excess of the minimum; and both reporting and reviews were regular and comprehensive.

27.34 Despite what has been said in the preceding paragraph, it is troubling to record that on 16 March 1982 a social worker received a referral from a local headmaster about a complaint made by a natural daughter of Mr C that he had

---

[1] See para 4.08.

[2] She had been statemented in 1986 under Section 7 of the Education Act 1981 and the Educational (Special Educational Needs) Regulations 1983.

made sexual advances to her leading to a fight in which both had been injured: she had sustained an injury to her right wrist and Mr C was limping after she had stamped on his foot. The daughter alleged also that there had been a number of similar advances by Mr C previously. The complaint was quite fully investigated by the social worker and the headmaster; the deputy head teacher and a nurse were involved in the investigation to a lesser extent. Both Mr and Mrs C were also seen by the social worker and they denied their daughter's allegations. The social worker thought that it was almost certain that Mr and Mrs C were telling the truth and the daughter withdrew her allegations the following day. The Area Officer then decided that no further action need be taken.

27.35 With the advantage of hindsight, it can be seen that a fuller investigation in 1982 might have led to a prosecution then and the date of the complaint is significant because the criminal charges against Mr C in respect of C1 all post-date it. If the Child Protection procedures that were formulated later had been in place in 1982, the police would have been involved in investigating the matter and the outcome might have been different, in which event C1 might have been spared much, if not all, the damage that she suffered from Mr C.

Foster home D

27.36 Mr and Mrs D, who have a small-holding with chickens, ducks and goats, were registered foster parents for Clwyd County Council from 1985 to 1996. It seems that, during that period they fostered at least half a dozen children and one of these children made complaints to the Tribunal of being physically abused by Mr and Mrs D whilst boarded out with them. This child, D1, born on 29 November 1978, was received into voluntary care on 7 May 1989 and placed with Mr and Mrs D on 24 July 1989 after brief spells with two other sets of foster parents. He remained with Mr and Mrs D for nearly two years, until 19 April 1991.

27.37 In order to set D1's complaints in context it is necessary to add that D1 was a very troubled youth. Before he was received into care, he was admitted to Gwynfa Residential Unit for a fortnight in 1986 because his behaviour had been worrying his mother. After he left Mr and Mrs D, he was placed unsuccessfully with four successive sets of foster parents in the following eight months before being admitted to Llwyn Onn on 13 September 1991 and then South Meadow on or before 12 January 1993; and he was repeatedly in trouble at both those children's homes.

27.38 D1 complained, in a statement made to the police on 2 December 1992, that Mr and Mrs D had assaulted him and other foster children with a wooden clothes brush for misbehaviour or failing to do work correctly. He alleged that he had been assaulted in this way by both foster parents on numerous occasions, sustaining injuries to his arms and legs, varying from bruises to soreness, although he could not recall specific instances. Other complaints made by him were that he and the other foster children were given second-hand clothes to wear; that they were not given enough to eat; that he did not receive his full pocket money; and that they were made to do the washing up on returning from school and to clean the chicken pens at the week-ends. D1 confirmed these allegations in a written statement to the Tribunal on 20 November 1996 but he could not be traced when he was due to give oral evidence.

27.39 The only contemporary record of a complaint by D1 of abuse was dated 3 May 1991, a fortnight after he left the foster home, when he made allegations of being hit with a belt by the Ds. He had complained earlier, however, on 16 August 1989, within three weeks of his placement there, to his mother and social worker that he was unhappy with his foster parents and had "had three or four nights where he was wetting the bed".

27.40 In their own statements Mr and Mrs D denied striking D1 or any of the foster children, save that Mrs D admitted smacking another foster child on her bottom over her clothing. The children were well fed and also helped themselves from time to time. Providing a mix of clothing made economic sense; pocket money was banked with a building society and distributed as it was needed; and all the children helped with the livestock.

27.41 The complaints made by D1 are not supported by any other evidence before us. Moreover, social service records indicate that, in the period between 24 December 1991 and 29 January 1993, D1 made complaints of assault on not less than five occasions and that he admitted that on three of these the allegations had been false. Other aspects of his behaviour during this period were also extremely erratic.

27.42 In these circumstances we cannot be sure that D1's allegations of physical abuse by Mr and Mrs D are true. However, the length of the placement, in comparison with the duration of other fostering attempts, suggests that Mr and Mrs D at least provided some necessary stability and security for this highly disturbed boy. We have insufficient documentary evidence before us to justify comment on the quality of the supervision by social workers responsible for visiting him.

Foster home E

27.43 In the course of the hearings before us the Tribunal received a copy of a Part 8 Management Case Review[3] touching upon one other fostering placement by Clwyd County Council that calls for comment.

27.44 The review related to a girl E1, born on 3 August 1978, who had been in conflict with her mother and step-father for some time. E1 was a girl who suffered from learning difficulties and whose behaviour at home and at school had given rise to considerable anxiety. The worries about her had increased in the early months of 1994 and her mother and step-father had been unable to cope with her behaviour. The causes for concern included running away from home, an overdose incident, the use of alcohol, rejection by her parents, poor school attendance and alleged sexual intercourse with several youths.

---

[3] Conducted in 1994/1995 under Part 8 of the Working Together guidance.

27.45 E1 was found on 27 April 1994 by her mother and step-father at the home of E, a woman friend of E1 of a few months' standing. This was an address that the police had visited on previous occasions with the result that they had sent several "children at risk" reports to the Social Services Department, some of which the latter acknowledged receiving. The police removed E1 from E's home on 27 April 1994 and she spent the night at a police station.

27.46 A planning meeting was held the next day, when it was decided by Clwyd Social Services Department that E1 should stay at home with her mother and step-father; but the latter were unhappy about this decision and the mother walked out of the meeting. They refused to allow E1 to return home and her natural father would not help. E1 refused the offer of a foster home placement and decided to stay with E.

27.47 On 29 April 1994 Clwyd County Council, acting under section 20(1)(c) of the Children Act 1989[4], placed E1 with E as an immediate placement with a friend pursuant to Regulation 11(3) of the Foster Placement (Children) Regulations 1991[5]. The Social Services Department paid E an allowance and began the process of approving her as a foster parent, which needed to be completed in six weeks if the placement was to continue after that period.

27.48 On 27 May 1994 E1 presented herself at the social services office at Buckley, where she was advised to talk to her mother and step-father. At 8 pm that evening a friend of E1 asked police to attend to her in the local shopping precinct: E1 was in a very distressed state and complained of rape and serious sexual assault whilst living at E's home. The Clwyd Child Protection Procedures were set in motion and a full joint investigation by the police and social workers followed.

27.49 As a result of the investigation four young men and E were charged with a series of offences involving E1 and appeared on 6 March 1995 at the Crown Court at Chester. E was convicted of permitting unlawful sexual intercourse with E1 and of keeping a disorderly house for which offences she was placed on probation for 12 months. Two of the young men were convicted of unlawful sexual intercourse with E1 for which they were conditionally discharged; another was placed on probation for 12 months for indecently assaulting E1; and no evidence was offered against the fourth young man.

27.50 E1 went to stay with the friend who had reported to the police on her behalf. Her name was placed on the child protection register on 3 June 1994. Thereafter, there was great difficulty in placing her satisfactorily. She moved to a third foster home (counting from 27 May 1994) on 17 August 1994 but the Review Sub-Committee was informed that the placement had broken down.

27.51 The Review Sub-Committee expressed serious concerns about the judgment of several senior officers of the Social Services Department in the management of this case in that "at no time was E1 seen as a child in need of protection". Amongst its many critical findings were the following:

---

[4] This requires a local authority to provide accommodation for any child in need in their area in defined circumstances.
[5] Regulation 11 makes provision for emergency and immediate placements by local authorities.

(a) Child Protection Procedures in respect of E1 should have been set in train by early 1994.

(b) The Department had failed to provide emergency accommodation on 27/28 April 1994, resulting in an inappropriate overnight stay in a police station.

(c) The subsequent placement with E had been wholly unsuitable and had resulted from either a serious lapse of judgment or failure to obtain adequate information.

(d) There had been breaches of the requirements of guidance and regulations under the Children Act 1989 in relation to that placement such as failure to inspect the premises beforehand (despite the presence on file of a damning report by a police officer who had visited in April 1994), lack of consultation with other agencies and the absence of medical examination and assessment, supervisory visits, a written care plan and a statutory review.

(e) The response to E1's call on 27 May 1994 at the Buckley office gave cause for concern. It seemed harsh to deny the Department's responsibility for her and to refer her to persons with whom her relationship had broken down.

27.52 A perturbing concluding comment by the Review Sub-Committee was that "from the evidence and submissions received, managers within the Social Services Department, East Division, even with the benefit of hindsight, still believe there to be no significant errors and lessons to be learned from the handling of this case".

Conclusions

27.53 The performance of Clwyd Social Services Department in the five fostering cases discussed in this chapter was very uneven, ranging from bad, as exemplified by the case of foster home E, to at least adequate in the case of foster home B. There were serious shortcomings also, however, in the failure to give necessary support to Mr and Mrs A and the long impermissible gaps in visiting them.

27.54 Overall the histories underline the need for vigilant monitoring of all placements. We emphasise also the need for social workers to see foster children on their own and individually when a foster home is visited. Unless this precept is observed, it is unlikely that an adequate picture of a child's response to a placement will be obtained. We recognise that sexual complaints are particularly difficult to elicit but, if a child is seen alone, the social worker is more likely to be able to discern symptoms of anxiety or unease.

PART VI

THE RESPONSIBILITY OF
HIGHER MANAGEMENT IN CLWYD

Management structures and responsibility for Clwyd Social Services from 1974 to 1996

Introduction

28.01 In considering the responsibility of higher management in Clwyd the Tribunal has had to have in mind a limited number of specific questions posed by the terms of reference of this inquiry. These questions may be re-stated for the purposes of this part of the report as follows:

> (1) Could Clwyd County Council through the placement of the children or through the regulation or management of the facilities have prevented the abuse or detected its occurrence at an earlier stage?

> (2) What was the response of Clwyd County Council to allegations and complaints of abuse made by children in care whilst they were in care or later or by any other persons, and to what extent was the response inadequate and how could it have been improved?

> (3) Did Clwyd County Council discharge its functions in respect of children in care appropriately?

28.02 One of the many difficulties facing the Tribunal in examining these questions, covering a long period of time, is that Clwyd County Council ceased to exist on 1 April 1996 and could not, therefore, be represented before us. The successor local authorities in North Wales were represented but they did not purport to present a case on behalf of Clwyd County Council. It was left to the Tribunal itself to conduct the investigation, with assistance from the successor authorities, and to seek out appropriate witnesses. Inevitably in this process the Tribunal has been encumbered with considerable detail about administrative structures and with immense documentation, much of which is only marginally relevant to the central questions that we have to consider.

28.03 In the context of the questions that we have re-stated in paragraph 28.01, the main thrust of this part of our inquiry has been into the following matters:

> (a) The purpose and suitability of the children's homes provided by Clwyd County Council.

> (b) The placement of children in those homes and the regimes to which they were subjected.

> (c) The recruitment of staff for the homes and the subsequent management of both.

> (d) The training of staff and guidance given to them.

> (e) The adequacy of individual care in the homes.

> (f) Monitoring and inspection of the homes.

> (g) Complaints procedures.

> (h) The response to such complaints as were made.

(i) Staff disciplinary procedures.

(j) The adequacy of field social worker visiting and of care planning for the children.

(k) Preparation for leaving care.

(l) The responsibilities of Clwyd County Council in respect of private and voluntary homes and other residential establishments within their area.

(m) Whether any fault is attributable to Clwyd County Council for the abuse in foster homes that has been disclosed.

28.04 It will be convenient to deal also in this part of the report with the Jillings inquiry and report[1] and the role of the Council's insurers in discussion about possible publication of that report.

28.05 In carrying out this part of our task we will try to avoid as far as possible unnecessary references to Clwyd's administrative structures but a preliminary account is necessary here to explain the assignment of responsibilities to individuals during the period under review. We have already given, in Chapter 3 of this report, a brief account of the legislative and administrative background to Clwyd's assumption of responsibility for its area on 1 April 1974 and we take this as read in order to avoid unnecessary repetition. In particular, we introduced in paragraphs 3.20 and 3.21 the first Director of Social Services for Clwyd, Emlyn Evans, and his Deputy, (Daniel) Gledwyn Jones; and we made the point that, unusually, no one in the initial senior management team in Clwyd had a specialist background in child care.

The Social Services Department under Emlyn Evans, 1974 to 1980

28.06 Joseph Emlyn Evans, the Director of Social Services for Denbighshire from January 1971 and for Flintshire from about April 1973, served as Director of Social Services for Clwyd from April 1974 to 31 January 1980, when he retired at the age of 60 years. Throughout his Clwyd period, his Deputy was (Daniel) Gledwyn Jones, who succeeded him as Director.

28.07 Evans' recollection is that, on his retirement, there were 1865 staff in the department, which was responsible then for between 90 and 100 establishments.

28.08 In the early days there were two relevant Assistant Directors (of a total of four), one responsible for residential and day care and the other for fieldwork. The former was Tudor O Jones and immediately under him was a Principal Officer (Residential and Day Care Services), Bryan Hughes. Under the latter, from September 1975, was a Principal RDCO, Veronica Pares. Neither T O Jones nor Bryan Hughes had any experience of child care but Veronica Pares,

---

[1] See paras 2.02, 2.03 and 2.37.

who joined the department as an RDCO in January 1975, had wide experience as Homes Supervisor in Berkshire Children's Department from 1965. According to her statement, her responsibility as Principal RDCO was to advise heads of homes; to be responsible for staff supervision by means of monthly visits to all the residential homes in her area; and to submit her findings in written reports. There were also about four RDCOs with responsibilities for such matters as staffing, supplies, children and the elderly.

28.09 The Assistant Director (Fieldwork) was Raymond Powell, who was responsible for a wide range of social services, including the work of six Area Offices (the areas corresponded to the new local government districts). Under him the person nominally responsible for children until 1984 was the Principal Officer (Fieldwork), Iorweth Thomas, but he was a mental health specialist. The person effectively responsible, although in theory reporting to Powell through Thomas, was the Principal Social Worker (Children), Gordon Ramsay, who, after service in Cheshire, had been a Senior Child Care Officer in Flintshire Children's Department and then a Senior Social Worker in the same county, managing a generic team. Ramsay's job description included advising on all aspects of child care and considering jointly residential and day care facilities. Although, he did not have direct responsibility for residential homes and the area offices did not come under him, Ramsay was given responsibility for the placement of all children in care from about mid-1975 and was required to visit all the Area Offices regularly to discuss review procedures and the maintenance of good practice in child care matters at area level. It appears that Ramsay retained substantially the same duties until he retired on 31 July 1987, shortly before he reached the age of 60 years.

28.10 Quite radical changes to this structure were made early on. In 1976 Geoffrey Wyatt replaced Bryan Hughes and became Principal Officer Residential Services. Wyatt was to remain a key figure thereafter in relation to residential care for children in Clwyd for the next 16 years (apart from the period 1986 to 1989), until he took early retirement on 30 September 1992 at the age of 54 years. He held a Home Office Certificate in Residential Child Care and had been involved in work with children since about 1962; he had worked as a Child Care Officer for Denbighshire County Council from March 1969; and his most recent work, from 1971, had been as Courts and Police Liaison Officer for Denbighshire and then Clwyd. In 1976 Wyatt was shown in the organisation chart as directly responsible for all residential and day care establishments, reporting to Raymond Powell.

28.11 By this time T O Jones had retired and the "groups" formerly headed by him and by Raymond Powell had been merged under the latter as Assistant Director Operational (Fieldwork Services). The former fieldwork hierarchy remained substantially unchanged but, on the residential and day care side, an important change was to follow on 1 April 1977. From that date immediate management responsibility for the residential homes was transferred to the six Area Officers, each with a small complement of RDCOs. The Area Officers, however, reported direct to Powell and not to Wyatt, who was nevertheless shown in the relevant organisation chart as having a Principal Social Worker and two RDCOs working to him. It appears that none of the Area Officers had any experience of the management of children's homes, although Emlyn Evans said that four of the six were "children trained". The most important area, Wrexham/Maelor, failed to fill its required establishment of three RDCOs.

28.12 Another development at this time was the appointment of two inspectors, whose roles were to inspect every social services establishment within the county. The inspectors appointed were Veronica Pares and Ivor Hughes (subsequently the Principal Social Worker working to Wyatt). Each inspector covered half the county, spending about half her/his working time outside their shared office, and they reported to the Assistant Director Management Services. They received a week's training at the Welsh Office. The posts lasted for three years until the inspectorate was discontinued on economy grounds; and Pares took early retirement in June 1980.

28.13 The Senior Management Team from 1976 onwards comprised the Director, the Deputy Director and three Assistant Directors, the third of whom was responsible for administration. Part of the background to the changes made from 1974 onwards was a Ten Year Plan that had been submitted by Emlyn Evans to the shadow Social Services Committee on 4 October 1973. This was said to have been drawn up in response to Welsh Office Circular 195/72 addressed to the predecessor authorities. It is unnecessary to repeat the details of the Plan but it envisaged three phases of development, the last beginning in April 1977, and one of its objectives was the development of a comprehensive range of services as near as possible to the client with the establishment of six Area Offices as social work bases.

28.14 The chain of command to the top was clear in theory but its practical day to day implications were much less clear. Emlyn Evans told the Tribunal that he believed in delegation and that he delegated responsibility for children's services to Gledwyn Jones because the latter had a background in child care. Gledwyn Jones, on the other hand, said that he was happy to accept the delegated responsibility but that he had no specific experience in child care: he had had some experience as a senior social worker in Pembrokeshire in working closely with the Children's Department but he was not "children trained" and had not been a Child Care Officer. He believed very strongly that the staff under him were carrying out their responsibilities and he trusted them.

28.15 The relevant senior officer under Gledwyn Jones from 1977 onwards, Raymond Powell, also lacked experience of statutory child care work. His experience, for about 13 years from the age of 24 years, had been in mental health, although he had had about six years experience of wider social work services by 1977. Moreover, he had little management training and his remit for that year embraced all services delivered to clients. Whilst Iorwerth Thomas concentrated his attention on his mental health duties, effective day to day responsibility for children's services fell upon Geoffrey Wyatt and Gordon Ramsay.

O & M Report, February 1980

28.16 In the course of the year before the retirement of Emlyn Evans, an investigation was carried out into the overall organisation and general management of the Social Services Department by the Organisation and Methods Department of Clwyd County Council (as part of its general remit) and it reported in February 1980. It found that there was a deficiency at senior and junior management levels; some officers at Assistant Director and Senior Social Worker level had more responsibility than they could be expected to discharge; there was inadequate support to management from specialist advisers in child care matters and there was also inadequate control, direction and co-ordination of fieldwork. The report stated that the deficiency in professional resources was particularly evident in the control of client cases where the Department was most vulnerable.

28.17 Contrary to the evidence to us to which we have referred in paragraph 28.14 the report stated that the Deputy Director did not have responsibility for any specific function. His main role was said to be that of general overseer of the whole Department and his duties were described as duplicating in the main those of the Director in the co-ordination, control and direction of the Department's services. A major recommendation was that the Deputy Director, whilst continuing to deputise for the Director, should be directly accountable for all client services provided by the Operational Services and Residential and Day Care Services. This was in part a consequence of the report's recommendation that responsibility for Residential and Day Care Services should revert to headquarters to which we refer later. The Deputy Director's role would essentially be of co-ordinating the two functions to form a totally integrated client service. It was envisaged that this would provide the necessary executive management of the service, ensuring that County Council policy and statutory requirements were being properly implemented; and a major function of the post would be the development of future policy and strategic planning.

28.18 Amongst the report's criticisms was that, whereas Wyatt (described as Principal Officer (Residential and Day Care)) was responsible to the Assistant Director (Powell), he reported in many instances direct to the Director of Social Services. Wyatt's main functions were identified as:

"a. Overall co-ordination of residential and day care services.

b. The formulation of the residential and day care budget.

c. Industrial relations in residential and day care establishments.

d. Departmental committee representation in all residential and day care activities."

The report went on to point out that, despite Wyatt's responsibility for residential and day care establishments, the latter were actually under the immediate control of Area Officers, who had the responsibility to oversee and maintain standards through Area RDCOs. The view expressed in the report was that Wyatt could not properly fulfil his co-ordinating role because of the division of responsibilities.

28.19 The report noted that, at that time, the Residential and Day Care Service comprised 65 establishments employing almost 1,000 staff. The running costs of the service amounted to £3½ million per year. In the light of its criticisms the report recommended that a new separate division should be created, headed by an Assistant Director, which would have responsibility for all non-social work functions relating to the management of residential and day care establishments. The Area Officers would, however, retain responsibility for the provision of a social work service to clients in residential establishments. The Area RDCOs would continue to be based in the Area Offices for administrative convenience, but would become accountable to the new Assistant Director of Residential and Day Care Services.

28.20 The report did not comment on the anomalous position of Ramsay but it made the further important recommendation that an Operational Support Division should be formed to provide the Department (and Committee) with a "totally integrated and much needed specialist advisory and support service" on defined matters, including the co-ordination and implementation of training policy.

28.21 One other aspect of the report requires mention. It recorded that, on average, there were 8.4 field workers in each team and that in one instance there were 13 officers reporting to one team leader, whereas (in the writers' view) it was an accepted and reasonable guideline that one team leader was capable of effective control of only five to six subordinates. It recommended, therefore, that eight Senior Social Workers should be appointed: it was considered that this recommendation could be implemented "without recourse to any new posts at this stage and without diminution of the service".

The Gledwyn Jones regime, 1980 to 1991

28.22 On Gledwyn Jones' promotion to Director of Social Services, he was succeeded as Deputy by John Hubert Coley, then aged 49 years, who held the office from about July 1980 to February 1984, when he left to become Senior Deputy Director of Social Work for Tayside Regional Council. John Coley had been Assistant Director of Social Services for Dorset since 1974, accountable for the management of residential and day care services and central advisory and monitoring staff for fieldwork and domiciliary services; and he had long and wide experience of operational management in all the relevant fields.

28.23 Coley's successor as Deputy Director of Social Services was John Christopher Jevons, who joined Clwyd Social Services Department on 9 January 1984 as Assistant Director (Policy and Resources). John Jevons, then 37 years old, had degrees in mathematics, social administration and social work and management science and had most recently served for ten years as Social Development Manager for Milton Keynes Development Corporation; but he did not have experience in child care matters. He remained with Clwyd County Council for 11 years, succeeding Coley as Deputy in October 1984 and becoming Director on 15 April 1991 on the retirement of Gledwyn Jones.

28.24 The recommendations of the O & M report were put before the Social Services (General Purposes) Sub-Committee in March 1980 but were not implemented until 1982, and then only in part. However, the transfer of management responsibility for residential and day care establishments from Area Offices back to headquarters had been effected in 1980 and the RDCOs had been similarly transferred. Wyatt's direct responsibilities as Principal Officer Residential Services became clearer and the range of those responsibilities was recognised in December 1982 by his promotion to the new post of Assistant Director (Residential). As such, Wyatt initially had only one Principal Social Worker (Ivor Hughes) working under him with various RDCOs but from 1984 there were three Principal Officers, one of whom, John Llewellyn Thomas, was specifically responsible for children. The line of command was then from the heads of children's homes through two RDCOs to Thomas and thence to Wyatt. However, in 1986 Wyatt became Assistant Director (Adult Services) and Raymond Powell became the Assistant Director responsible for children and family services with John Llewellyn Thomas under him as Principal Officer (Children). Powell retired in October 1989 and Wyatt then held a watching brief for children and family services until reorganisation in 1990.

28.25 John Llewellyn Thomas came to Clwyd in February 1984 from the post of Principal Assistant in the Regional Planning Unit for Wales. He was rising 38 years of age on joining Clwyd and had had about nine years experience, mainly in the unit, after six years service as a probation officer. Initially in Clwyd John Llewellyn Thomas was responsible for the residential homes for children with two RDCOs under him but in 1986 his responsibilities were widened to include day and residential establishments for children, fostering and adoption, child abuse and a number of other matters with several principal social workers or the equivalent under him. Thomas remained in Clwyd seven years before moving to Mid Glamorgan in April 1991 as Assistant Director Children and Family Services. He then became Director of Social Services for Torfaen on the reorganisation of local government.

28.26 Gordon Ramsay continued as Principal Social Worker (Children) or (Child Care) but his position in the structure altered in 1984 and again in 1986 before he retired in 1987. The first change was recognition of the factual position that had already existed for some time in that he became directly accountable to Powell (rather than theoretically through Iorwerth Thomas) with Intermediate Treatment, Adoption and Fostering under him. Then in 1986, after Iorwerth Thomas' retirement, he was placed under John Llewellyn Thomas and Raymond Powell; he continued to be responsible for child care placements and reviews but his other responsibilities included Family and Day Care Centres, Under Fives' work and statementing of children.

28.27 Newcomers in the post 1984 structure promoted from within the Department were Norman Green, Gwyneira Hurst and Michael Barnes, all three of whom have been referred to earlier in this report. Norman Green[2] and Gwen Hurst[3]

[2] See para 10.91.
[3] See para 10.92.

had both been teachers at Bryn Estyn and became RDCOs in 1984, based at headquarters, working under John Llewellyn Thomas (Hurst moved to registration work under Ramsay in 1986). Michael Barnes[4] moved from Chevet Hey to headquarters on 1 January 1988 to take up an appointment as Principal Social Worker (Child and Family Services). By this time Ramsay had retired and had been succeeded by David Palmer (previously County Fostering Officer). According to Barnes, his duty was to manage the remaining nine or ten children's homes, reporting to John Llewellyn Thomas and through him to Powell. Barnes was also given some responsibility for policy, the appointment of staff, training and support; and "gatekeeping", that is, examining the need for a child to be taken into care, was part of his role, although the main burden in relation to this was on Area Officers and the social worker teams.

28.28 Despite the recommendations of the O & M report the Deputy Directors in the 1980s were not closely involved in children's services. In the first four years of the decade Coley was much involved in other matters. He had to acquaint himself with his new department and then to play a leading role in the implementation of the report. At a later stage 30 per cent of his time was taken up by work on the All Wales Strategy for Mental Handicap and much of the rest was occupied by supporting the Director in the preparation and presentation of material for a variety of purposes. Coley's recollection is that he intervened specifically in two matters, namely, the delays in statutory reviews and failings in admission to care procedures, when he learned of them. He had a specific role to play too in the County Council's function as an adoption agency. However, although he had a general disciplinary and enforcement role also, he cannot recall any complaints or allegations of abuse in respect of children in care reaching him.

28.29 John Jevons' initial appointment in Clwyd as an Assistant Director placed him with responsibility for policy and resources and he retained this responsibility when he became Deputy Director in 1984 (he was not replaced as Assistant Director). As Assistant Director he had Training Officers under him, a Principal Officer (Policy and Resources) mainly concerned with buildings related developments, a research officer occupied with statistical data, and an administrative officer who serviced committees. Jevons' input into policy was mainly in respect of mental handicap and mental illness, on which he was asked to focus. As Deputy Director, he was required to retain these responsibilities and to take on also a number of others, including that of adjudicating officer in disciplinary hearings. Jevons told us in his oral evidence that Gledwyn Jones made it clear to him that he was to focus his energies upon planning services for the various adult client groups whilst he (Gledwyn Jones) would concentrate the bulk of his energies upon children's services. Jevons continued to be heavily involved in mental health strategy and from 1989 he led the Department's response to the Towyn flooding that year, which involved the evacuation and resettlement of over 5,000 people.

---

[4] See paras 12.21, 13.25 and 14.49.

28.30 According to Jevons the Senior Management Team met approximately monthly during his period as Deputy Director. The records of these meetings are incomplete but he was only able to find 27 recorded instances of an issue relating to children's services being discussed at a meeting by that team between 1984 and 1990; he had always assumed that they would have been discussed in individual discussions between the Assistant Director, Raymond Powell, and Gledwyn Jones. Jevons could not recall any matter of complaint relating to children's services being discussed at a meeting of the Senior Management Team and could find no record of any such matter being so discussed.

28.31 It will be seen that, despite the recurring changes in structure, effective responsibility in the 1980s for children in residential care at Assistant Director level and below remained with a comparatively small group of officers. Geoffrey Wyatt and Raymond Powell carried the responsibility in varying ways as Assistant Directors. John Llewellyn Thomas was the Principal Officer with specific responsibility for children from 1984. Then, of the Principal Social Workers, Ramsay remained the most prominent until 1987, with his responsibility for placements, and Michael Barnes assumed direct responsibility for children's homes from January 1988. The other Principal Social Workers mentioned, Ivor Hughes and David Palmer, were not closely involved with residential care in local authority homes in the 1980s. Hughes did work under Wyatt after ceasing in 1980 to be an inspector but from 1984 he was involved with the elderly and he became responsible for private and voluntary homes in that sector. Palmer was County Fostering Officer from 1982 to 1987; he then became a Principal Social Worker, in succession to Ramsay, but with different responsibilities (child guidance and under fives).

The Final Phase and the delegation to divisions (1990 to 1996)

28.32 There was renewed turmoil in Clwyd Social Services Department as the 1980s drew to a close. In relation to children, a major and necessary preoccupation was preparation for the implementation of the Children Act 1989 and the many regulations to be made under it, but all social services departments in England and Wales were faced with this task. Implementation of the National Health Service and Community Care Act 1990 also required radical changes. It was at this time that Clwyd set in train a major reorganisation scheme involving the delegation to three new divisions of many functions formerly performed by headquarters.

28.33 It has been unnecessary for us to probe in detail the genesis of this reorganisation. In his Ten Year Plan[5] Emlyn Evans had envisaged dividing Clwyd with two divisional offices, based at Rhyl and Wrexham, which would be interposed between the area offices and headquarters, but this had not been pursued in the late 1970s for financial reasons. The concept of bringing services as near as possible to the client was revived, however, in the late 1980s and it was resolved to divide Clwyd into three divisions, to be named North, South and East, each with a resident population of about 130,000.

---

[5] See para 28.13.

28.34 This phase of the history is much less important in relation to child abuse than the earlier years of Clwyd's existence and it is not, therefore, necessary to give an elaborate account of the new structure which was put in place in 1990. The proposals for change were set out more or less finally in a document entitled "Future Organisation" dated November 1989 but preliminary work had been carried out, for example, by Clwyd County Council's Systems and Efficiency Unit, which had advised on the proposed devolvement to divisions in March 1989.

28.35 The main relevant changes proposed were that:

(a) Responsibilities for operational services should be transferred from headquarters to three divisional offices, each with a divisional director.

(b) Within each division a service manager would head a team responsible for services to one client group (eg the elderly) except in respect of children.

(c) Child care work was so large in volume that it should be split between a child care social work manager and another manager responsible for the resources to assist and protect children.

(d) The remaining smaller headquarters team would be responsible for policy and resources matters plus the inspection and support of the services delivered from the divisions.

28.36 It was said also that the three new divisions would permit service boundaries to follow natural boundaries to a greater extent and would enable each division to be self-sufficient in most of the services covered. As for the size of the population in each division, it was said that the preferred divisional population size of other local authorities that had changed to a divisional structure was in the range of 100,000 to 150,000.

28.37 These changes were implemented in October 1990, six months before Gledwyn Jones retired (he viewed them without enthusiasm). When John Jevons succeeded him there was no appointment of a Deputy Director to replace Jevons: the three new Divisional Directors, in effect, replaced the former Deputy Director in the hierarchy. At headquarters there was an Assistant Director (Operational Support and Inspection) with a Child Protection Officer and assistant amongst others working under him. There were also three Principal Officers responsible for such matters as development, performance review and training.

28.38 Whilst Geoffrey Wyatt is not shown by name in the organisational plan for this period that was submitted to us, he told the Tribunal that he remained at headquarters in a non-operational role as the Assistant Director (Operational Support and Inspection) with responsibility for the registration and inspection of children's homes and of residential homes for adults. He had the responsibility also of setting up a complaints procedure. Wyatt retired on 30 September 1992 at the age of 54 years.

28.39 John Llewellyn Thomas did not remain part of the headquarters team. He remained with Clwyd County Council only until April 1991[6] and in his last six months he served as Children's Resources Manager in the East Division. He had, however, played a leading role in preparing for the Children Act 1989, which ultimately came into operation on 14 October 1991, and was chairman of the implementation group; he had also been a member of the relevant Welsh Office working party so that he was aware of both the national picture and what was required locally. In addition to his divisional function he was therefore given "lead" responsibility for children's services policy and development throughout the county.

28.40 In the event this arrangement proved to be unworkable in Thomas' view and he wrote a report about this for the Director on 20 March 1991, shortly before he left. Major criticisms by Thomas were that:

(a) Co-ordinating County policies, procedures, standards, budgets etc when the emphasis had been moved from headquarters to division had proved to be very difficult; and there had been "inadequate support at the centre".

(b) The divisional structure had not taken into consideration fully the requirements of the Children Act 1989 and responsibilities for children were fragmented across each division.

In Thomas' view Children and Family Services needed a recognised post centrally with adequate administrative and professional support and with sufficient status to give it credibility in relation to the Senior Management Team and others, including the Welsh Office.

28.41 At this point[7] Clwyd was still providing 103 residential places in eight children's homes and was said to have one of the highest proportions of children placed in residential care in Wales. During 1990/1991 average occupancy of the homes was 97%; and an average of 16 children were in agency placements outside the county.

28.42 The response to Thomas' criticisms was the appointment eventually of Jackie Thomas[8] as Principal Officer (Children) from January 1992. She was based at headquarters, accountable to the Assistant Director (Strategic Planning), and she chaired the Children Act Implementation Group. Before her appointment one of the Divisional Directors was given the temporary responsibility of co-ordinating children's services policy.

28.43 Unfortunately, Jackie Thomas was not successful in this new post and her tenure of it lasted only until April 1994. She was not immediately replaced: it seems that she was suffering from a long term illness. Moreover, a report by the Assistant Director (Strategic Planning) at or about this time recommended that the Children Act Implementation Group should be disbanded. Instead,

---

[6] See para 28.25.

[7] Report by Director of Social Services to Clwyd Social Services (Children & Family) Sub-Committee 13 February 1991.

[8] Not to be confused with the Jacqueline Thomas who is referred to in paras 14.32 to 14.45.

each division should establish its own Children's Services Development Group with a remit for forward planning on all children's services issues. There should, however, be a county-wide Children's Strategy Co-ordination Group charged with such matters as integrated career structures for residential and fieldwork staff, implementing the Criminal Justice Act and the Children's Rights Initiative etc. The Assistant Director (Strategic Planning) would chair this group and other members would be the chairs of the divisional development groups and two other officers, the Principal Officer (Children and Families) and the Development Officer (Children).

28.44 In the event it does not appear that a Principal Officer (Children and Families) was appointed. Instead Michael Barnes was invited by Jevons in December 1994 to accept secondment from the North Division, based at Prestatyn, in which he had been Children's Resources Manager from October 1990, to headquarters. The secondment was to the Strategic Planning Division and his tasks were expected[9] to include:

"(1) leading and co-ordinating the production of the Department's Childrens Service Development Plan 1995/6

(2) co-ordination and monitoring of the Divisional Development Plans for childrens services

(3) completion of the Department's Leaving Care Strategy

(4) policy work on a series of outstanding items including the role of the key worker, policy guidance on sexuality, disability and use of leisure

(5) monitoring of standards in lodgings/aftercare

(6) race issues and anti-discriminatory practice

(7) role of the key worker

(8) recording practice in residential care."

Barnes took up his duties at headquarters in January 1995 and remained there, assisting the Assistant Director (Strategic Planning) until the demise of Clwyd County Council.

The role of the Chief Executive

28.45 The Chief Executive of Clwyd County Council for most of the period under review was **Mervyn Hugh Phillips**, a law graduate of Liverpool University and solicitor, who succeeded his well known predecessor, **T M Haydn Rees** (now deceased), in 1977, after serving as the latter's Deputy in Clwyd from its creation and in Flintshire before that. Mervyn Phillips served as Chief Executive until he retired on 31 July 1992, at the age of 60 years. He was in turn succeeded by **(Edward) Roger (Llewellyn) Davies**[10], an Oxford law graduate and solicitor, who had been employed by Clwyd from 1977 as Director of Legal

---

[9] Letter from John Jevons to Michael Barnes dated 6 December 1994.
[10] See paras 14.43, 14.44, 25.45, 25.46 and 32.20 for other references to him.

Services, from 1980 as County Secretary, and from 1982 as Deputy Chief Executive, although he continued to be referred to usually as the County Secretary. He served as Chief Executive of Clwyd County Council from 1 August 1992 until its demise.

28.46 Mervyn Phillips produced to the Tribunal a job evaluation of his post as Chief Executive prepared by management consultants in 1985/1986. At that time the gross expenditure of Clwyd County Council was £199m and it had 15,200 employees, of whom 8,700 were full time. The Chief Executive had in his view, four main functions, namely:

(1) representing the Council on outside bodies and on formal occasions (he was, for example, Clerk to the North Wales Police Authority and Secretary of the Welsh Counties Committee);

(2) servicing the County Council and three of its central committees, dealing with policy, finance and culture, recreation and libraries;

(3) development and management of the Council's corporate structure;

(4) economic development, following the closure of major industrial enterprises on Deeside and in the Wrexham area.

He did not service or attend the Social Services Committee, which were tasks assigned to Roger Davies as County Secretary/Deputy Chief Executive.

28.47 The Chief Executive's relationship with other Chief Officers and associated matters, was set out in the job description in 1973: he was given authority over Chief Officers so far as necessary for the efficient management and execution of the Council's functions. The 1985/1986 job evaluation report stated:

"The Chief Executive is head of the Authority's paid service. The departmental Chief Officers report managerially to him, although for the detailed content of Departmental policy and programmes they look for guidance to their respective Committees.

The Chief Executive leads a Chief Officer's Management Team (COMT) consisting of himself and six senior chief officers. This considers matters of common managerial importance across the departments and is the major mechanism at senior officer level for corporate integration. It, for example, considers Departmental options during the planning cycle prior to their submission to members. He calls together other groupings of Chief Officers as needed.

Whilst the COMT meets without senior elected member involvement there is a Policy Liaison Committee which meets eight times per annum, consisting of the leaders of the three main political groups, the Chairman and Vice-Chairman of the Council, the Chief Executive, County Secretary and County Treasurer. This is used to consult with members on major or sensitive issues and is considered a valuable "sounding" stage in between the COMT and Committees. It is not a formal decision-making body. When particular topics require, it is extended to include the relevant Chairman and/or Chief Officer."

28.48 The report noted also that a Performance Review Panel of five senior members was of importance in the context of top management: it "triggered" projects of a "value for money" or "policy review" type, sometimes using O & M or Audit staff.

28.49 Mervyn Phillips told us that the only major change after this report was the formation of a new department dealing with both economic development and tourism with a Chief Officer, called the Director of Tourism and Development.

28.50 Phillips' view was that it was the Chief Executive's role to have oversight of what was happening in the corporate work of the council. In relation to the Social Services Department this was exercised primarily through an annual position statement by the Department, an annual review of its activities and objectives by members and the studies incidental to those procedures. It was the County Secretary's role to observe on behalf of the County Council what was happening in the relevant committees and to report to the Chief Executive any non-compliance with statutory duties not dealt with by a committee: the County Secretary was the monitoring and compliance officer.

28.51 It follows from what has been said that Phillips relied heavily upon the Director of Social Services and County Secretary and expected to be informed by one or both of them of any significant problems. He met Gledwyn Jones for a talk about twice a month, apart from formal meetings, and he met the County Secretary almost daily. Phillips said "it would be expected that a reference would be made to the Chief Executive if it was the sort of thing that might need the attention of the County Council as opposed to the Social Services Committee".

28.52 This last answer does reveal a flaw, or at least a potential gap, in the arrangements to enforce accountability of the Director of Social Services to the Chief Executive. The job evaluation report had been less than crystal clear on the subject but a limitation of matters to be reported to the Chief Executive to those that "might need the attention of the County Council as opposed to the Social Services Committee" could itself create uncertainty and confusion. In reality the Chief Executive did expect to be informed by the Director, or if not by him, by the County Secretary, of significant matters that he ought to know. He learned, for example, of the convictions of social services staff when they occurred through the Director or the County Secretary and similarly of the request made by Mr Justice Mars-Jones for an investigation[11]. He would have expected to have been told also, again by way of example, of the report on the Butlins Camp holiday from Park House[12] but that was not brought to his attention.

28.53 We discuss in Chapter 32 of this report the successive responses of the Social Services Department to the various investigations that took place during the period under review and the reports upon them. In the light of those responses it would appear that the failure to inform the Chief Executive of criticism of the management and practice of the Department was part of a pattern of

---

[11] See para 14.43.

[12] See paras 17.81 to 17.86. It is to be noted, however, that the Little Acton investigation took place at the request of the Chief Executive to the Director of Social Services: see para 12.06.

deliberate non-disclosure; and the result was that monitoring of the performance of the Department and its senior officers by the Chief Executive was ineffective.

28.54 As Deputy to Gledwyn Jones, John Jevons' understanding was that Mervyn Phillips as Chief Executive expected Chief Officers to manage their own departments and "consume their own smoke". However, when Gledwyn Jones was in hospital in 1987, Jevons did discuss the Mars-Jones request with Mervyn Phillips and it was the latter who decided that the investigation should be carried out by Roger Davies. Jevons did not become Director of Social Services until April 1991, only 15 months before Phillips' retirement and just before the major police investigation began. He said that he did not receive any guidance then from Phillips, or subsequently from Davies, about what he was expected to refer to the Chief Executive. Phillips did not offer regular discussion or supervision and did not expect to be informed of day to day issues.

Comment

28.55 This is not the place for a detailed critique of the many organisational changes made during the period under review and the failure on the part of senior management to ensure their effective implementation, but some comment relevant to the purposes of our inquiry must be made.

28.56 The first, and probably the most obvious, comment is that these frequent changes imposed additional burdens on hard pressed staff, who were already having to cope with the major changes in social services departments generally, which we have outlined in Chapter 3 of this report. Moreover, Clwyd had limited resources in child care expertise and experience in its higher administration throughout and the organisational changes tended to dissipate these resources or at least to diminish their impact on the delivery of operational services.

28.57 Secondly, there were striking anomalies in the various structures from time to time. Thus, Gordon Ramsay was shown as accountable to Iorwerth Thomas as Principal Officer for ten years from 1974 to 1984 (almost until the latter's retirement) but this was never effective. Thomas was experienced in mental health but had no experience of child care and, after some initial visits to children's establishments, he seems to have left Ramsay to get on with his duties without supervising or monitoring him. Iorwerth Thomas was a striking example of a person who never shouldered his assigned responsibilities for children's services and his lack of previous experience in the field was not an adequate excuse for his failure to do so in the course of the decade in which he had the opportunity to acquire the necessary expertise. Moreover, it is a strong criticism of the senior management that this unsatisfactory situation was allowed to continue for such a long time.

28.58 There were other quite obvious problems about the positions and responsibilities of both Ramsay and Wyatt. Ramsay was responsible for a range of matters in addition to the placement of children: he was, for example, responsible for monitoring the assessment of individuals, the formulation of a strategy for each child and statutory reviews but the residential homes and area officers were both outside his line of responsibility and he had no direct links in the structure with Wyatt. There were meetings in 1975, 1978 and 1983 (and probably more) at which definition or re-definition of Ramsay's roles was discussed but his position remained anomalous until he retired in 1987.

28.59 The transfer of responsibility for residential homes from headquarters to the areas from 1977 was both ill-timed and inadequately supported. The Area Officers had neither the experience nor the resources to take on the additional responsibility which was particularly onerous in the Wrexham/Maelor area at that time. The appointment of two inspectors at headquarters was no more than a palliative and they themselves were overburdened. Furthermore, the hierarchy of responsibility above the Area Officers became even more confused as the authors of the O & M report pointed out.

28.60 Some improvements were achieved when that report was implemented but they were comparatively short-lived, partly because of changes of personnel. Able men such as Coley, Jevons and John Llewellyn Thomas were appointed to senior positions but they became involved in future planning and other fields with the result that their abilities were not fully exploited at a practice level in the 1980s in relation to child care.

28.61 It was unfortunate also that the ultimate divisional structure was adopted at a time when other major changes were required by the provisions of the Children Act 1989 and the regulations under that Act, which came into operation just a year after the structural change. In mitigation it can be said that the changes in 1990 facilitated in the social services field the local government reorganisation that was to follow between 1994 and 1996. But it should have been clear that strong central co-ordination of policies and procedures would be necessary in the child care field and the new structure failed to provide this.

28.62 A last comment must be that delegation of responsibility without effective accountability and monitoring is likely to be a recipe for disaster. All the evidence that we have heard in the course of the Inquiry suggests that between 1974 and 1991, the period of major abuse, there was little effective accountability or monitoring of performance at the higher levels of Clwyd Social Services Department's administration and that too much responsibility was left in the hands of middle tier officers, with little guidance from above. Some of the problems were drawn to the attention of the Department initially as early as 1978 in the report on the inquiry into Little Acton but little was done before 1991 to resolve them and it seems that both the Chief Executive and the Council remained unaware of the detailed criticisms made in that report and subsequent reports.

The failure to prevent sexual abuse or to detect it earlier

Introduction

29.01 In the course of this report we have considered in detail complaints of sexual abuse made against former members of the staff in eight Clwyd community homes; and we have considered similarly, as far as it has been practicable to do so, the history of such complaints in six[1] other residential establishments in Clwyd providing substantially for children in care during the same period from 1974 to 1996. Our findings have been that serious sexual abuse was committed by not less than six (and quite possibly more) former members of staff in the Clwyd homes and that residents in five of these homes were victims of that abuse.

29.02 In relation to the other residential establishments our findings have been necessarily less clear because separate prosecution proceedings against two former members of staff have not yet reached trial, decisions by the Crown Prosecution Service in relation to three others are still pending, and one other died, after our hearings had ended, at a late stage of the police investigation in respect of him. Nevertheless, the general picture of sexual abuse is similar to that found in the local authority homes. The nature and volume of the complaints by residents were broadly comparable. Three of the named alleged abusers have already been convicted of offences in Clwyd and a fourth has been convicted of sexual abuse subsequent to his employment in Clwyd. Moreover, residents with all three private organisations that we have considered were affected by the abuse.

29.03 Public concern about these events has understandably focussed mainly on revelations about Bryn Estyn and Bryn Alyn because of the number of victims, the positions held by the abusers and the persistence of the abuse. For the purposes of comment in this report also, they provide helpful illustrative material. But they should not be regarded as unique or even special cases. The number of large children's homes has now diminished substantially but, in our view, the lessons to be drawn from the histories of both the establishments are of wide significance and apply to a broad range of institutions providing accommodation for children and young persons.

29.04 In relation to fostering the picture is quite different. Although we have given an account of three proved cases of grave sexual abuse in Clwyd that occurred in the course of fostering, the number of complaints has been very much less, despite the increasing emphasis that Clwyd placed on fostering during the period under review, which is outlined in Chapter 24. Nevertheless, the risk of

---

[1] The private residential establishments such as those in the Bryn Alyn Community have been counted as one for this purpose, although residents were dispersed on more than one site.

such abuse in foster care and the problem of detecting it combine to present social workers and senior officials with onerous responsibilities that are similar in kind to those that they carry in respect of children's homes but arguably more difficult to discharge successfully.

29.05 Two obvious questions that arise immediately are:

(a) Who, if anyone, was at fault in appointing the abusers to the positions they held?

(b) Were any complaints made at or near the time when the abuse occurred and, if not, why not?

We will deal with these questions at the outset and then deal with other actual and potential criticisms of Clwyd's administration and practice in the context of sexual abuse.

The appointment of staff

29.06 The two central figures in the sexual abuse at Bryn Estyn, Peter Howarth and Stephen Norris, were both appointed to the staff before Clwyd County Council assumed its responsibilities on 1 April 1974. Howarth moved from Axwell Park Approved School to Bryn Estyn in November 1973 on his appointment as Assistant Principal[2]. Stephen Norris was appointed in January 1974, as a joint houseparent with his wife, with effect from 1 March 1974, having served in the same capacity until then at Greystone Heath Approved School[3].

29.07 We have investigated as thoroughly as we can the background to these appointments but have not found any basis for criticising either Clwyd County Council (in shadow form) or its predecessor in respect of these initial appointments. Neither man had any previous conviction; there was no discernible blemish on the record of either; and they both had relevant approved school experience in the transitional phase of conversion to a community home. It may be said that Norris' illiteracy and general unsuitability should have been apparent to the appointing panel but we are too far away in time to endorse this as a valid criticism. The references provided by Norris were said to have been good and we do not know of anything to his detriment that might have been elicited by further probing. In particular, there is no evidence of which we are aware that Norris had associated specifically at Greystone Heath with any of the other members of the staff there who were subsequently convicted of sexual offences.

29.08 The striking fact is that Arnold appears to have had an important influence on both appointments and his death has prevented us from questioning him about his reasons. There is no evidence before us, however, to support a finding that he knew or even suspected that Howarth or Norris was a potential abuser. We think it is probable that Arnold knew from his Axwell Park days of Howarth's

---

[2] See para 8.03.
[3] See para 8.23.

"flat list" practice but the evidence suggests that he had previously accepted Howarth's own explanation for this[4]. We have to remember also that, although we have criticised Arnold's response to some incidents of physical abuse of which he was aware, he did react promptly when he suspected Leslie Wilson (of Little Acton) of inappropriate interest in a resident of Bryn Estyn or at least of upsetting the boy by his visits[5]. As for the initial appointment of Norris, we have only Norris' evidence that he and his wife were invited by Arnold to apply for vacant posts at Bryn Estyn when they visited the home from Greystone Heath[6]. Assuming that to be true, however, there is no evidence to suggest a sinister intent on Arnold's part and his action was consistent with a straightforward wish that the vacancies should be filled by a couple with experience in a former approved school.

29.09 Howarth was one of four candidates (out of 13) shortlisted for the post of Deputy Principal in July 1976 but one withdrew. The remaining candidates were interviewed by Clwyd's Staffing Officer, a Principal RDCO (Veronica Pares) and Arnold. Although Howarth did not interview well, it appears that the panel decided that the appointment should go to a residential care specialist rather than a teacher and this approach may have been influenced by Arnold. There is no reason, however, to question the good faith of the panel in recommending Howarth for appointment; and there is no evidence that any of them, other than Arnold, had reason to suspect Howarth of sexual misconduct at that time.

29.10 On the other hand, there is good reason to criticise Norris' later advancement and, in particular, his subsequent transfers to Clwyd House in 1978 and to Cartrefle in July 1984[7]. His first advancement to senior houseparent occurred in December 1977, following an interview by Arnold, Howarth and Geoffrey Wyatt (then Principal Officer, Residential and Day Care Services) but there was no further interview or selection process before he became head of Clwyd House or before his transfer to Cartrefle to become Officer-in-Charge there, which was treated as "redeployment".

29.11 Only one witness before the Tribunal gave evidence of sexual offences by Norris (at his smallholding) before he moved to Clwyd House and no one has suggested that there was any complaint of sexual abuse by him before then. Nevertheless, evidence from many witnesses satisfies us that, by the end of 1977, Norris' general coarseness, his pre-occupation in conversation with sexual matters and his insensitivity were well known to a substantial number of staff. Making appropriate allowance for the fact that suitable residential care staff were difficult to recruit, we remain highly critical of Norris' appointment as head of a unit caring for young damaged children. In our judgment the post should have been advertised if there was no more suitable

[4] See para 8.05.
[5] See para 12.10.
[6] See para 8.24.
[7] See para 8.26.

candidate in Bryn Estyn; and, if the net had been cast wider, much of the subsequent abuse by Norris might not have occurred. Indeed, there is a case for saying that by 1978 his services ought to have been dispensed with.

29.12 We acknowledge that there is a degree of hindsight in this conclusion because we do not suggest that the appointing panel in December 1977 could have foreseen then that Norris would commit sexual offences as a senior houseparent. It is right to make clear also that there is no evidence that Howarth knew of any sexual propensity of Norris or that he associated with Norris in any relevant way. On the contrary, the evidence suggests that there was a degree of hostility between them.

29.13 Although Arnold was only one member of the panel that appointed Norris as a senior houseparent in December 1977, letters written by Arnold in February and September that year show clearly that he already had in mind that Norris should become the head of Clwyd House when it opened. It is plain that his view about the appointment was decisive and his error of judgment was to have dire consequences. Moreover, the way in which the appointment was made is but one of many examples of the way in which Arnold was permitted to run Bryn Estyn without adequate external management or monitoring by the Social Services Department.

29.14 Norris' subsequent transfer to Cartrefle following the closure of Clwyd House and in anticipation of the retirement of the Officer-in-Charge at Cartrefle took place with effect from 9 July 1984. His appointment as Officer-in-Charge from 1 December 1984 was confirmed to him by letter dated 14 July 1984 but it was not until 20 July that the relevant recommendation was made by memorandum to the County Personnel and Management Services Officer. The appointment or redeployment was said to have been discussed between the Assistant Director (Residential and Day Care) (Geoffrey Wyatt) and the Principal Officer (Child Care) (John Llewellyn Thomas) but was said to be subject to the approval of the Chairman of the Personnel Sub-Committee. It was one of many transfers made on or before the closure of Bryn Estyn in pursuance of Clwyd County Council's policy to avoid redundancies wherever it was possible to do so under a "containment" agreement made with the trades unions, to which fuller reference will be made in the next chapter.

29.15 There is no evidence of any complaint of sexual misconduct by Norris before his transfer to Cartrefle but an efficient management ought clearly to have been aware by then of his general unsuitability for appointment as an Officer-in-Charge. The blame for Clwyd's failure to discover this cannot fairly be attributed to Arnold alone: Wyatt and Thomas (to a substantially lesser extent) must share some of the responsibility. Wyatt had been a principal link between headquarters and Bryn Estyn for much of the preceding ten years and he ought to have been able to make a realistic assessment of senior members of the staff there, even though a cult of silence prevailed amongst the staff generally[8].

---

[8] See paras 11.02 to 11.06.

29.16 The other four abusers of children in local authority community homes to whom we referred to paragraph 29.01 were Leslie Wilson[9], Michael Taylor[10], Jacqueline Thomas[11] and Heather Lynn[12]. None had any previous convictions and there was nothing to indicate that they might be potential abusers prior to their Clwyd appointments. Wilson, for example, was appointed to Little Acton as a houseparent after an interview by a panel of two (Peter Bird and Grant, the Homes Officer) and had good references covering his voluntary youth work and his employment as a housemaster at a children's home near Preston. He was interviewed similarly before being promoted to senior houseparent, when Veronica Pares was the second member of the panel, and Bird himself provided a favourable reference. Michael Taylor, the former Anglican Friar, was appointed Deputy Superintendent of Bersham Hall in September 1972, following interview by Denbighshire's Management Committee for that children's home. He too produced good references from his current employer (he was Deputy Superintendent of an Islington Reception Centre at Watford), his Superintendent and an Enfield course tutor. It is to be noted also that his sexual offences did not occur until after he had given notice on 10 June 1973 with a view to becoming a lecturer.

29.17 Jacqueline Thomas and Heather Lynn were in quite a different category because they were both comparatively immature young women when they were appointed. Jacqueline Thomas was 20 years old when she went to Chevet Hey as a RCCO from 1 March 1979, following interview by a panel of three (the Officer-in-Charge, Grant and an RDCO). She had good references and adequate experience; and the report in September 1979 on her probationary period was favourable. She undertook in-service training at Cartrefle College in 1982/1983; and there was no adverse report about her of any significance until the events in August and December 1985 that led to her conviction and her resignation. Nevertheless, one of the complaints that were made about her later referred to incidents alleged to have occurred much earlier, in 1979.

29.18 Heather Lynn was a little older (nearly 24 years) when she was appointed as a resident housemother at Upper Downing after interview by a panel of two (the Officer-in-Charge and an RDCO) on 29 August 1975 but she had only one year's experience as a nursery assistant at a Leonard Cheshire Home in Cheshire. In her case too, the references were good and the report late in January 1976 on her initial probationary period favourable, but this period was extended by six months because of the complaint by a dismissed gardener to Geoffrey Wyatt in March 1976 that Lynn had been permitting a boy resident to spend time in her bedroom. We have given a full account of that matter in Chapter 17, in which we criticised[13] the failure to dismiss Lynn then. Her subsequent history at Cartrefle, beginning on 20 December 1976 and culminating in her resignation taking effect on 14 September 1990, has been outlined in Chapter 15. The transfer to Cartrefle followed an interview by the

---

[9] See para 12.10.
[10] See paras 13.14 to 13.20.
[11] See paras 14.32 to 14.45.
[12] See paras 15.21 to 15.25, 17.08 to 17.14 and 17.16.
[13] See para 17.16.

Officer-in-Charge, Wyatt and Grant (described as Staffing Officer) and was to a non-resident post as houseparent. Four years later Lynn was one of two candidates for the post of Deputy Superintendent interviewed on 5 November 1980 by a panel of three (again Wyatt and Grant, with the new Officer-in-Charge). According to the notes of the interview prepared by Grant, the other candidate, Paula Dean[14], fared very badly whereas Lynn performed well; and there is no reference in the notes to the complaint made about her when she was at Upper Downing. Lynn was therefore recommended for appointment as Deputy Superintendent from 1 December 1980 and served as such for nearly ten years.

29.19 The history of Lynn should be regarded as a cautionary tale. Her misconduct at Upper Downing should have been found to have been proved on the evidence of the coded letter and the boy's visits to her bedroom, despite their denials of an affair. Dismissal should have followed and the fact that the misconduct had occurred during a probationary period should have facilitated that decision. The later decisions cannot be criticised forcefully in isolation from that earlier error but we do question (however difficult the recruitment problem was at the time) the wisdom of appointing, as Deputy Superintendent of a demanding children's home, a woman with comparatively brief experience and no recognised qualifications, who ought to have had at least a question mark registered against her in respect of her record as a carer.

29.20 Clwyd did not, for obvious reasons, play any part in the selection of staff in the private and voluntary homes or in any of the other residential establishments for children that we have discussed, except Ysgol Talfryn, but the same general lessons are to be drawn from the incidence of sexual abuse in those institutions. None of the proved abusers had previous convictions of any relevance, whether or not a check was made with the police at the time; and, more elaborate records held centrally, such as the Department of Health Consultancy Service Index, would not have disclosed at the relevant time anything adverse about these persons.

29.21 This is, of course, a dispiriting conclusion but it is far from our purpose to diminish the importance of central records of convicted and suspected abusers. We regard such records and the process of checking them before any residential care appointment is made as an essential precaution. A nil return, however, even in the case of a long established care worker, must not be regarded as a cause for complacency. The statutory responsibilities of those who look after children in care are such that ceaseless vigilance is necessary not only when initial appointments are made but also when subsequent transfers and promotions are considered. Moreover, the maintenance of full and accurate staff records is an important part of this process of vigilance because only thus can interviewing panels and some potential referees have access to reasonably full information.

---

[14] See paras 15.34 to 15.37.

29.22 The range of problems that arise in selecting foster parents is, of course, very different, having regard to the importance of matching the needs of individual children with the capabilities and attributes of the potential foster parents. Nevertheless, there are common factors, including the importance of checking the central records that are available and re-checking them when further placements are proposed or planned. The need for continuing vigilance is also the same.

29.23 In the Saint case we have seen the very serious consequences that followed from the failure to check central police records in 1978[15] and again to re-check them in 1982[16] (and indeed on later occasions). A lesson is to be learned also from the way in which Roger Saint covered up the fact of his conviction in 1972 by falsifying his employment history in and around that year. If he had set out the correct history in his application form it is probable that questions would have been asked about the reasons for his various moves then and it is at least possible that further enquiries would have revealed the conviction. We emphasise, therefore, the importance of scrutinising and checking such details vigorously and of pursuing enquiries with former and current employers. The Saint case illustrated also the need for careful investigation when referees proffered by would be employees or foster parents prove difficult to contact.

29.24 The other two cases of proved sexual abuse by foster parents were not ones in which there was any record of a previous relevant conviction or of suspected sexual misconduct. We do say, however, that a full record in his personal file of all the matters involving Rutter during his employment by Clwyd would have shown him in a less favourable light and might (it cannot be put higher) have led to refusal of the Rutters' applications to foster.

The incidence of, and response to, complaints

29.25 The most discouraging fact in relation to complaints of sexual abuse is that very few children in residential care in Clwyd complained to anyone in authority of being sexually abused at or about the time when that abuse was occurring. The evidence is clearest about the complaints made by three boys.

29.26 Two of these boys were resident in Cartrefle and both made their complaints to Henry Morton Stanley. The first of the complaints was by the boy identified as W in Chapter 15, who told Stanley in 1989 of his affair with Lynn, which he wanted to stop. Stanley reported the matter to Norris but the information was not passed on higher, as Stanley had assumed it would be, and no action was taken until the following year when the matter came to light in unclear circumstances[17].

29.27 The most important complaint, which led directly to the termination of Norris' abuse and indirectly to the later full scale police investigation in 1991/1993, was made to Stanley in June 1990 by the boy referred to in paragraph 15.12. Great credit should be given to that boy, who did not find it easy to make the

---

[15] See para 25.15.
[16] See para 25.18.
[17] See para 15.24.

disclosure, and to Stanley, who dealt with him very sensitively and gave him time to steel himself to make a full disclosure. Stanley then reported the matter immediately to Michael Barnes, who travelled to Cartrefle at about 11 pm at Stanley's request, and the matter was put in the hands of the police. W, who was lodging with the Stanleys by this time, also confided in Stanley later that Norris had sexually abused him[18].

29.28 The third boy to make a contemporary complaint did so much earlier at Chevet Hey in September 1973[19], before Clwyd County Council assumed its responsibilities. He is referred to as A in paragraph 13.17 and his complaint, relayed to the Officer-in-Charge (Ellis Edwards), was to the effect that Michael Taylor had interfered with him in bed. Taylor had been staying at Chevet Hey as a guest, awaiting accommodation as a lecturer in Cheshire after leaving Bersham Hall. He denied the accusation and was permitted to leave. Ellis Edwards reported the incident to the Principal Social Worker (Residential Services), commenting that, by leaving, Taylor "was at least ceasing to be an embarassment to the Home". No further action was taken.

29.29 That complaint about Taylor is of enhanced interest because two months earlier, on 2 July 1973 at Bersham Hall[20], a member of staff had overheard one boy resident telling another that Taylor had sexually assaulted him the previous night. The member of staff reported this to the Officer-in-Charge (Richard Leake) and we have recounted in paragraph 13.15 how unsatisfactorily that report was dealt with. The boy was seen in the embarrassing presence of the Matron and did not disclose the full truth, which led him to say untruthfully that he had lied to other boys by exaggerating what had occurred. No one believed the boy's allegation and no action was taken. One of the disbelievers, who interviewed Leake, was the Principal Social Worker referred to in the preceding paragraph. Yet when Taylor was interviewed by the police ten years later, 13 August 1993, he made full admissions in respect of A and the Bersham Hall boy as well as others[21].

29.30 Although these events in relation to Taylor occurred shortly before Clwyd County Council assumed responsibility, the negative response to them was to become typical in Clwyd during the following 15 years, especially in relation to reports of physical abuse, and justified the pervading cynicism of most residents in care about the likely outcome of any complaints that they might make.

29.31 The sexual misconduct of Leslie Wilson[22] and Jacqueline Thomas (coupled with that of David Gillison and William Gerry)[23] came to light quite shortly after it occurred but not as a result of complaints by the victims. Arnold sounded a helpful warning note about Wilson but the latter himself confessed to two members of staff shortly after an absconder from Bryn Estyn had been

---

[18] See para 15.28.
[19] See paras 13.17 to 13.19.
[20] See paras 13.15 and 13.16.
[21] See para 13.20.
[22] See para 12.10.
[23] See paras 14.32 to 14.42.

found in his flat at Little Acton. Jacqueline Thomas, on the other hand, was unmasked because a boy resident at Bersham Hall was found to be in possession of a bracelet that he had obtained from her flat and made admissions about his relationship with her.

29.32 There remain the problems that Peter Howarth was permitted to pursue a course of sexual abuse at Bryn Estyn for about ten years[24] and that Norris was permitted to act similarly for a like period at Clwyd House and then Cartrefle until a complaint was made to Stanley[25].

29.33 We should say at once that we are fully aware of the wide span of compelling reasons that restrain residents in care and others from complaining of sexual abuse when it occurs. Amongst them are embarrassment and shame and, quite often, lack of full awareness of the true nature of what has occurred. Fear of reprisals is common; and, if the fear is not of direct reprisals, it is frequently of adverse consequences for the complainant, particularly transfer to an even worse or more remote home. In some cases there may be reluctance to forfeit the benefits of preferential treatment linked with the abuse or a desperate need for attention felt by children deprived of parental care and affection. Above all, there is the justified cynicism of the child, to which we have already referred, taking shape in the conviction that he or she is surrounded by a wall of disbelief. If the abuse is by the man or woman effectively in charge, the difficulty of making an effective complaint is even greater.

29.34 It is not very surprising in these circumstances that we have received little evidence of alleged contemporary complaints against either Howarth or Norris of sexual abuse at Bryn Estyn. Five witnesses stated that they complained about Howarth; and one alleged that he complained about Howarth and (less clearly) about Norris.

29.35 Three of the five who said they complained of sexual abuse by Howarth gave oral evidence early in our hearings. They were not impressive witnesses on matters of detail and each of them had been at Bryn Estyn for only a short period (up to about three months). Probably the most credible of them said that he told a named member of the Bryn Estyn staff, who told him to stop telling lies and beat him up. Another, who was very confused about names, said that he told his (field) social worker but that no action was taken. Later, he told his mother, who informed the same social worker. The third of these witnesses did not allege that he made any complaint whilst he was still at Bryn Estyn: his evidence was that he told a member of staff at Eirianfa later[26].

29.36 Both the witnesses whose evidence was read are now deceased. The first said that he informed a woman trainee on placement at Bryn Estyn that he had been abused (not buggered) by Howarth on the one occasion when it had occurred but that he had been glue sniffing before making this (true) complaint.

---

[24] See paras 8.03 to 8.22.
[25] See paras 8.23 to 8.34 and 15.07 to 15.14.
[26] Part of Care Concern's school at Ystrad Hall, see paras 22.01 and 22.02.

Finally, the other deceased witness said in his written statement that he had informed his mother of being abused by Howarth and she had then told his social worker, but that there had not been any follow up action.

29.37 The witness who said that he complained about both Howarth and (less clearly) Norris whilst he was still at Bryn Estyn is referred to as witness B in Chapter 9[27]. The high point of B's oral testimony to the Tribunal about his Howarth complaint came on his second day in the witness box when he said that he had two or three conversations with Geoffrey Wyatt whilst he was at Bryn Estyn, once in the board room and once in the grounds. On the second ("main") occasion in the grounds he told Wyatt that he was fed up with being beaten up by Nefyn Dodd and abused sexually by Howarth but it was just like talking to a brick wall. B remembered getting hold of Wyatt's jacket lapels and that Peter Howarth and Paul Wilson dragged him off. The previous day, however, B had said twice in evidence that, although he had made complaints to Wyatt, he had never told Wyatt of what Howarth had been doing in a sexual way. B had said also that previous day that he had not told anybody about Howarth's sexual abuse when he was at Bryn Estyn.

29.38 This allegation appears to have originated in a different form in a statement to the police by B dated 23 April 1992 in which he said that he had approached Wyatt whilst he was walking the grounds at Bryn Estyn "and tried to tell him about being abused by Howarth and Norris". B said that he specifically remembered approaching Wyatt on two separate occasions: as B began to tell Wyatt, the latter told him to fuck off and was not prepared to listen.

29.39 In the summer of 1992 B requested a meeting with the Director of Social Services (John Jevons) and then told Jevons that he had informed Wyatt, on a visit by the latter to Bryn Estyn, that there were boys at the home who were being physically and sexually abused by members of the staff.

29.40 Then on 9 September 1992, in a further statement to the police, B said that he had spoken to Wyatt on at least three occasions at Bryn Estyn. On one of Wyatt's visits B had approached him in the grounds and told him that "we are all fed up of being beaten and fucked by members of staff" and B remembered mentioning Peter Howarth and Nefyn Dodd[28] to him. On that occasion B was very angry and was holding on to Wyatt, tugging his jacket; B was also being abusive to Wyatt, attempting to get his full attention, and Wilson and (B thought) Howarth came to Wyatt's assistance. Wyatt's response was to call B a liar and to tell him to "piss off".

29.41 In the same statement to the police B said that he had spoken to Wyatt on another occasion when the latter was making his way to the boardroom. On that occasion also he had said that "we are all fed up" with being sexually and physically abused. Wyatt had responded with words to the effect "leave it with me".

---

[27] See paras 9.05 and 9.32 to 9.34.

[28] B did not, however, suggest that he had been sexually assaulted by Dodd.

29.42 The inconsistencies in B's various accounts of what he said to Wyatt are such that we cannot be confident that he ever specifically said to Wyatt that he or others were being sexually abused by Howarth. He may have intended to do so but his evidence to the Tribunal about what was said, if anything, was unreliable. There has been some consistency in his references to approaching Wyatt in the grounds but, if he did so, the approach was made in such a manner that Wyatt was able to brush him aside. Wyatt himself told us that he has no recollection of any approach by B at Bryn Estyn.

29.43 The evidence of a complaint by B about Norris is even more nebulous. As we have indicated in paragraph 29.37, on his own statements B does not seem to have advanced beyond an intention to name Norris to Wyatt as an abuser and he has more frequently referred to Dodd as the person whom he named with Howarth. In other evidence B spoke of conversations with a police officer after he left Bryn Estyn in which he suggested or at least hinted that there were serious matters at Bryn Estyn that ought to be investigated but there is nothing to persuade us that Norris was named in that context.

29.44 In relation to Cartrefle the picture is similar. Only one former boy resident alleged that he had complained of Norris' sexual abuse before June 1990. He was at Cartrefle between October 1984 and April 1986 (from the age of ten years) and he said that he told a few of the "kids in the home" about it: they told each other and he saw Norris "doing it to other boys". This witness said that he could not complain to staff because Norris was Officer-in-Charge and he could not trust anyone but later in his evidence he said that he told Lynn, whose response was that he could not make allegations like that without evidence. The witness alleged also that he had gone to the police house next door to Cartrefle about six months after he had been admitted and had told a police officer that he and other children ("we") were being interfered with. The police officer had looked at him as if he was strange and (like Lynn) had said that the police could not do anything without evidence.

29.45 This witness has had a troubled history and he told us that one of his problems was that he could not communicate. His inconsistent answers about complaining to staff illustrate the difficulty of assessing his evidence on matters of detail and it is noteworthy that he says that the responses to both his complaints were virtually the same. We cannot be confident therefore that either complaint was made. The evidence (if true) does, however, underline the importance of listening to, recording and taking seriously complaints of this kind made by children.

29.46 The evidence before us about complaints of sexual abuse in other residential establishments in Clwyd followed the same general pattern. The sexual abuse by John Allen persisted over a long period[29] but he was, in effect, the head and major proprietor of the Bryn Alyn Community and we are not aware of any contemporary complaint about him to a member of the staff or to any other person in authority. One former resident of the Eirianfa unit of Ystrad Hall[30]

---

[29] See para 21.24.
[30] See paras 22.16 to 22.19.

alleged that he complained to a member of staff about being buggered by another member of staff there and was physically assaulted for his pains when he did so, but we have explained in paragraph 22.19 our reasons for doubting this evidence. As for the abuse by Noel Ryan at Clwyd Hall[31], this appears to have continued for over ten years without any complaint being made by a victim to a person in authority save for the lesser complaints referred to in paragraph 23.27.

29.47 The picture in relation to foster children is not dissimilar. The offences of Roger Saint did come to light as a result of complaints by two of his adopted children to social workers in February 1996 but by then the abuse in the foster home had been continuing for many years. Rutter's abuse was arrested earlier but the initial complaints were made by comparatively mature girls in the hostels rather than by the children in the foster home; and the sexual abuse in foster home B persisted for nearly eight years before one of the children first made allegations against Mr B.

29.48 The almost total absence of contemporary complaints of sexual abuse by the young victims of it in Clwyd is typical of many cases that come before courts throughout the United Kingdom but that fact does not exonerate from responsibility the staff and officers in Clwyd who were charged with the duty of looking after these children, who were all in care. Quite apart from the general constraints on making a complaint that we have referred to in paragraph 29.33 there were additional factors in Clwyd militating against the early discovery of sexual abuse when it occurred. We summarise these in the succeeding section of this chapter.

The absence of any complaints procedure

29.49 It was a serious defect nationally that complaints procedures were not introduced generally until well into the 1980s. In Clwyd itself there was no recognised complaints procedure from 1974 until about 1991. This meant that, during that period, there was no guidance to children on the subject, no instructions to staff about how to respond to complaints and no accepted procedure for dealing with allegations when they were made. Over and over again victims of abuse told the Tribunal that they did not know how to make a formal complaint against a member of staff; and both Emlyn Evans and Gledwyn Jones, whose terms of office successively as Director of Social Services spanned this period, conceded that no such procedures were laid down. The higher management of the Social Services Department simply did not recognise the existence of the problem.

29.50 The absence of a complaints procedure was one important factor in discouraging complaints of sexual abuse and confirmed, in effect, the general view of residents that it was pointless to complain. It did not, however, excuse the failures on the part of staff, Officers-in-Charge and senior management to react positively when complaints were made. More will be said about this in

---

[31] See paras 23.17 to 23.27.

the next chapter of this report because residents were readier to complain when they were assaulted physically than when they suffered sexual abuse. In practice, when a resident did pluck up the courage to complain:

(a) he/she was rarely believed;

(b) he/she was almost invariably asked whether he/she wished to make a "formal complaint" (and the seriousness of the matter for the member of staff impugned was stressed);

(c) if he/she proceeded with the matter, a written statement would be taken but the complainant would rarely be seen subsequently by anyone with disciplinary authority;

(d) in most cases the complainant would be transferred to another (usually less congenial) home.

The awareness of staff

29.51 We have had in mind throughout the Tribunal's hearings and the preparation of this report that general awareness of the danger of sexual abuse of children in care has been very different in the latter part of the 1990s from what it was in the mid 1970s. It may well be that there was little recognition of the potential problem in that earlier period and that it was generally assumed that children in care were safe. It is, perhaps, significant that the first (1988 version) of Working Together issued by the Department of Health and Welsh Office as guidance on inter-agency arrangements for the protection of children from abuse, made no reference to children in care[32].

29.52 Nevertheless, residential care staff (and teaching staff, where applicable) can reasonably have been expected to possess a degree of common-sense and worldliness throughout the period; and Bryn Estyn provides ample justification for this approach. Thus, the evidence has satisfied us that an overwhelming majority of the staff at Bryn Estyn were aware of Howarth's "flat list" practice, that is, of inviting favoured boys to his flat and permitting them to stay to a comparatively late hour. Moreover, a substantial number of the staff disapproved of the practice for a variety of reasons. We doubt whether any of them positively believed that Howarth was committing offences against the boys but some were suspicious themselves, many knew of the boys' gossip about Howarth to the effect that he was a homosexual and many disapproved of the "flat list" on the ground that Howarth was placing himself in a very vulnerable position, as well as tending to disrupt discipline.

29.53 As we have said earlier, Arnold too was well aware of the "flat list" and, in our judgment, he knew of the unease felt by many members of the Bryn Estyn staff about it. We have accepted also that he knew of the rumours about Howarth that were circulating in the community home and that he called a meeting of staff at which he threatened instant dismissal for anyone giving currency to or

[32] The omission was remedied in the edition circulated on 14 October 1991.

discussing them[33]. Arnold must, therefore, bear an important part of the blame for the failure to discover Howarth's abuse earlier or at least to arrest it wholly or in part.

29.54 Although Arnold did play a praiseworthy part in the unmasking of Leslie Wilson as a sexual abuser[34], a letter that he wrote on 9 July 1977, in the course of that investigation, throws a perturbing light on his general attitude to the disclosure of abuse. The letter was addressed personally to the Director of Social Services (Emlyn Evans) and was expressly intended to be delivered to him by hand, although neither Evans nor any other member of the senior or middle management admits that he saw it at the time. The letter (clearly signed by Arnold) described how a five page statement had been taken by the police from the boy complainant (who had been at Little Acton) at the request of a Chief Superintendent of police and in the presence of Mr and Mrs Arnold. In the course of summarising the boy's allegations in the statement, Arnold said in his letter that "The statement, damaging as it is, does not contain the boy's fuller comments, which suggest that there was considerable laxity in supervision of what was happening. I apologise for this statement but feel you should be aware that if this child were brought into Court and allowed to speak freely, much damaging material would be disclosed". Arnold also wrote of "a hope that a fuller investigation by the Police might be averted" and referred to "odd comments of snowballing effect" at the Police Station and "other aspects" which he was not prepared to commit to paper. The consistent tenor of the letter was his desire to protect the department from further disclosures and it is strongly indicative of his negative attitude of mind to thorough investigation of a particularly serious matter.

29.55 Earlier in this report[35] we expressed some sympathy with the Bryn Estyn staff who were faced with the threat by Arnold of dismissal referred to in paragraph 29.53, but they must share collectively some of the blame for the failure to discover Howarth's abuse earlier, having regard to the gravity of the issues at stake. Only one member of that staff claimed to have raised the matter at headquarters and that was Paul Wilson, who said that he spoke of his suspicions about Howarth to Geoffrey Wyatt after he (Wilson) had been elected as a union representative, apparently in February 1984[36]. That was very late on in Howarth's offending but we have no reason to doubt Wilson's evidence on this point. According to Wilson, Wyatt's response was to ask whether he was making a formal complaint and to warn him that the repercussions could be quite serious, which is consistent with other evidence that we have received of Wyatt's unresponsive and defensive attitude to complaints. We add that, if Wyatt was unaware of Howarth's "flat list" practice by that late date, it exemplifies the inadequate monitoring of Bryn Estyn by the Social Services Department.

---

[33] See paras 8.14 to 8.16.
[34] See para 12.10.
[35] At paras 8.17 and 8.21.
[36] See para 8.18.

29.56 What we have said on this subject is in line with our wider discussion of the cult of silence that prevailed at Bryn Estyn[37]. That attitude of mind was probably more marked there than elsewhere but it certainly existed at other community homes in Clwyd during the same period and later at Cartrefle. In respect of the latter home, for example, we heard persuasive evidence that members of the staff strongly disapproved and disliked Norris, regarding him as unfit to be Officer-in-Charge, but no complaints about him appear to have been made to higher authority until June 1990.

29.57 The gravity and potentially dangerous consequences of these attitudes cannot be over-emphasised when we are discussing child protection. The existence of "whistleblowers" and their willingness and freedom to make complaints without fear of retribution are crucial, as is their confidence that they will be listened to positively. All the inhibiting factors, such as loyalty to colleagues and the wish for a quiet life, cannot be eliminated but it is a paramount duty of management to make sure that adverse information reaches it. In Clwyd, however, the pervading climate was of disapproval of such reports and unwillingness to investigate them. In that climate it is not surprising that sexual abuse was allowed to fester and persist.

29.58 The final comment that needs to be made under this head is that awareness on the part of members of the staff depends not only upon observation of the behaviour of colleagues but also upon confiding relationships between staff and residents coupled with sensitive monitoring of the behaviour of individual residents. The circumstances in which a boy at Cartrefle came to confide in Stanley about Norris' misdeeds underlines the importance of each of these factors. Stanley had observed that the boy appeared to be upset and had already won his confidence, and the boy's complaint was elicited carefully without pressure on him to say more than he wished to in the early stages and without questioning the boy's motivation etc.

29.59 Of the many complainant witnesses that the Tribunal heard and saw very few had any recollection of a confiding relationship with a particular member of the residential care staff. Various former Officers-in-Charge spoke of introducing or attempting to introduce at one time or another a key worker system, under which members of the residential care staff would be required to assume responsibility individually for establishing a close relationship with a small number of specific residents. But these sporadic efforts appear to have had little impact on the residential care system in Clwyd as a whole and failed to establish even an embryo complaints procedure in the minds of residents. This failure is illustrated by the high level of absconsions from several of the Wrexham homes and, in particular, from Bryn Estyn. Despite general concern about this problem and frequent involvement of police officers and field social workers in returning the absconders, little attempt was made to ascertain the true reasons for the absconding: instead the absconders would be questioned about offences committed whilst they were "on the run" and then punished at the community home for the absconding without further discussion.

---

[37] See paras 11.02 to 11.06.

The role of field social workers

29.60 We deal with this topic more fully in Chapter 31, in which we consider the quality of care generally, but it is necessary to stress here the importance of the duty of field social workers to establish and maintain a close relationship with children in residential care and to listen to their worries and complaints. Although there were no statutory regulations specifying a required frequency of visits by field social workers to children for whom they were responsible who were in residential care, the evidence before the Tribunal indicates that in Clwyd, as in many other local authority areas, the provisions of the successive Boarding Out Regulations[38] governing *inter alia* visits to children in foster care were accepted as the appropriate standard to be followed.

29.61 For most of the period under review that standard was set by Regulation 21 of the Boarding Out of Children Regulations 1955, which provided in its original form:

"A local authority or voluntary organisation who have arranged the boarding-out of a child shall ensure that a visitor sees the child and visits the dwelling of the foster parents—

(a) within one month after the commencement of the boarding-out;

(b) thereafter as often as the welfare of the child requires, but not less often than—

(i) in the case of a child boarded out with foster parents in whose household he has been less than two years, if the child has not attained the age of five years, once in every six weeks, or, if he has attained that age, once in every two months, or

(ii) in the case of a child who has been in the household of the foster parents more than two years, once in every three months;

(c) within one month after any change of dwelling by the foster parents; and

(d) forthwith after the receipt of a complaint by or concerning the child, unless it appears that action thereon is unnecessary."

29.62 Despite these clear provisions none of the complainant witnesses who gave evidence to the Tribunal recalled a meaningful relationship with his/her social worker. Yet John Coley (Deputy Director of Social Services 1980–1984)[39], for example, said in his written statement:

"The frequency of visits and the quality of trust between the child and field social worker are crucial and cannot be built up without continuity of supervision and time being spent with the child."

---

[38] See generally Appendix 6, paras 31 to 35.
[39] See para 28.22.

29.63 It is unlikely that the overall record of visiting by field workers was as bad as most of the complainants now recall and, in some cases, the present recollection of individual witnesses was shown by contemporary records to be incorrect. Nevertheless, the true record overall was, at best, very patchy. Thus, Gordon Ramsay, the Principal Social Worker responsible for placements for most of the relevant period, told the Tribunal that social workers tended to visit more at the beginning and end of placements but that children did not receive a high level of support in between. Moreover, the note of a meeting of senior management in May 1980 to discuss child care policy and practice referred to "infrequent or sometimes non-existent contact by social worker and child during periods of residence" and to the "very little" (fieldwork) "time spent in practical work with children". Again, in June 1983 Ramsay drew up a list of concerns for discussion at a meeting with senior managers, one of which was "infrequent visiting to community homes by social workers and consequently they feel unsupported and children are somewhat cynical".

29.64 This problem was general in the sense that it affected most of the local authority homes in Clwyd but it was probably felt most acutely by residents in Bryn Estyn. The latter was a large community home with the reputation that it was a hard place; and its organisation and structure were such that any resident was likely to feel isolated unless he was particularly self-assured and gregarious. It has to be remembered also that a high proportion of residents (well in excess of 50 per cent for most of the period) were from counties other than Clwyd or Gwynedd so that visits from their field social workers at the community home were comparatively rare. It is very credible, therefore, that most of the residents felt that they were unsupported and largely forgotten unless they behaved in such a way that further local authority or police action was triggered.

Monitoring, inspection and rota visits

29.65 General monitoring and supervision of community homes by higher management and rota visits by councillors are unlikely to lead directly to the disclosure of sexual abuse because of the very private nature of such abuse but they may do so indirectly and they may also help to eliminate practices or routines that conduce to or provide a cover for it. It cannot be said that the quality of surveillance in Clwyd, however, was sufficient to provide any protection for children in residential care against such abuse.

29.66 A notable feature of the evidence before the Tribunal has been the lack of any personal contact between children in residential care in Clwyd and anyone from the outside world (using that expression in the broadest sense). It is necessary to explain this in a little detail but it is useful to begin by referring to the formal statutory provision governing visits to local authority children's homes by the administering authority which was contained in Regulation 2 of the Administration of Children's Homes Regulations 1951, made under section 15(4) of the Children Act 1948. Regulation 2 provided:

    (1) The administering authority shall make arrangements for the home to be visited at least once in every month by a person who shall satisfy himself whether the home is conducted in the interests of the

well-being of the children and shall report to the administering authority upon his visit and shall enter in the record book referred to in paragraph 3 of the Schedule hereto his name and the date of his visit.

(2) Where the administering authority is a local authority the arrangements shall secure that the person visiting is a member of the children's committee of the local authority, a member of a sub-committee established by that committee or such officer or one of such officers of the local authority as may be designated by the arrangements.

29.67 There was no equivalent provision in the Community Homes Regulations 1972 and no children's committee as such after the implementation of the Local Authority Social Services Act 1970. Under the latter Act, every relevant local authority was required to appoint a Social Services Committee but Sub-Committee structures under that committee varied. In Clwyd there was, as we have said earlier, a Management Committee for the Community Homes of Bryn Estyn, Little Acton and Bersham Hall from 1975 to about 1984, probably because of the roles of these homes in the Regional Plan for Wales, but there was no other management committee of which we are aware for any of the other local authority community homes in Clwyd (despite Raymond Powell's contrary assertion). Moreover, in Clwyd itself the sub-committee structure was altered quite radically from time to time so that there was little continuity. Initially there was a Residential Services Sub-Committee (with its counterpart an Adult Services Sub-Committee); then, with delegation to the Areas from 1975 to 1980, came Area Sub-Committees, which seem to have continued beyond the demise of area responsibility for the homes; and in 1989 a Children and Family Services Sub-Committee, with an adult counterpart, was established.

29.68 These changing structures did not encourage an individual councillor's sense of continuing personal responsibility for the welfare of the children in specific community homes. It must be said, however, that whilst it remained in existence the Management Committee for the three Wrexham homes did meet quarterly at each of the homes in turn and these meetings did provide an opportunity for contact. Unfortunately, however, none of the former residents of the homes recalls actual, meaningful contact with any councillor on these or any other occasions. Moreover, the format of the meetings was such that few welfare or disciplinary problems were discussed. The Officers-in-Charge dictated in effect, what the Management Committee discussed by the contents of their reports; and even the persistently high rates of absconsions were discussed only occasionally and superficially. The Management Committee were clearly on safer and more familiar ground when they discussed building alterations and other such items of expenditure.

29.69 Provision was made for members of the Social Services Committee to visit the community homes in accordance with a rota, and it appears that there was a similar system for visits by members of the Management Committee to visit the three Wrexham homes for which they were responsible, but it cannot be said that the arrangements made any substantial contribution to the welfare of the children. We have been left with a lasting impression of councillors' unease and uncertainty about their role as visitors. We accept that they were encouraged by senior officials to perform this duty: they were, for example, issued with guidance on what to do and with simple forms to complete by way of reports upon their visits but their unease persisted and their reports were almost invariably limited to matters of domestic physical detail, such as the state of the lavatories, or neighbourhood issues.

29.70 The unhappiness of councillors with their role as visitors was reflected in diminishing attendance. In one of his reports to the Management Committee, Arnold said "We are missing our Rota Visitors: absence does not necessarily make the heart grow fonder. Staff welcome these visits, it enables them to discuss their work intimately and face to face". Later on, in 1992, long after Bryn Estyn itself closed, David Palmer (then Children's Resources Manager for the South Division) reported to the Director of Social Services (John Jevons) that no Wrexham children's home had been visited by senior officers or senior elected members in the past 12 months. This is all the more surprising given that, by then, the abuse at Cartrefle and the major police investigation were common knowledge. In 1995 attendance at a training day for rota visitors was so bad that plans for further training were abandoned.

29.71 There was no formal structure for inspection of the local authority community homes except during the period of delegation to the areas from 1977 to 1980, when there were two inspectors based at headquarters[40]. Their remit, however, covered all 65 social services establishments in the county and their work load was too heavy to enable them effectively to monitor the many community homes still in existence. Veronica Pares, for example, said that the aim was to visit each residential establishment in turn and she could spend two or three days in one children's home but she was not able to visit every children's home in her half of the county in the three years that her post lasted. The other inspector, who was responsible for the other half of the county, had very little experience of children in residential care and he seems to have spent much of his time looking at residential places for the elderly and training programmes for people with learning difficulties.

29.72 Outside the period from 1977 to 1980 visits to the community homes by senior officials seem to have been largely random. Emlyn Evans, the first Director of Social Services, for example, said that he visited Bryn Estyn once or twice a year. He thought that Arnold was living up to his high commendation by the Home Office and that Bryn Estyn was well endowed with material things. The boys seemed to be happy and there was no feeling of unhappiness or restlessness of any kind. Gledwyn Jones, who explained that he too was not children trained and had no "hands on" experience with children in care, expressed similar opinions about Arnold. He visited children's homes occasionally, usually on pre-arranged visits, and his view was that monitoring was the responsibility of the relevant Principal Officer and Principal Social

---

[40] See para 28.12.

Workers, not the RDCOs. He was under the impression that middle management was giving the necessary guidance and leadership, thus echoing Emlyn Evans' belief in delegation[41].

29.73 The person under Gledwyn Jones with the longest continuous responsibility at Assistant Director level for children in residential care was Raymond Powell, who held that status from 1974 until his retirement in October 1989. We have explained in Chapter 28 how that responsibility took different guises from time to time but he had responsibility for residential care for at least six years, between 1977 and 1981 and again between 1987 and 1989; and Gordon Ramsay appears to have been accountable to him, whether or not through Iorwerth Thomas, throughout. Powell did not play any part in monitoring the community homes, however, and he seems to have interpreted his role as largely passive: he relied heavily for information upon Wyatt and Ramsay.

29.74 In his oral evidence Powell said that he visited all the "Flintshire" homes but that he did not make regular visits. As for Bryn Estyn, he made formal visits about four times a year (later he said perhaps five or six times) and would attend Christmas lunches there. His view of Arnold was the same as that of his Directors; he felt that the atmosphere at Bryn Estyn was always good and that the boys seemed to be happy. He did not recall any specific problems that were reported to him for attention except that there were complaints from the residential side that field social workers were not visiting the residents and these were taken up with the Area Officers.

29.75 The member of middle management who provided the longest continuous link between the community homes and senior management was undoubtedly Geoffrey Wyatt and he had responsibility for Bryn Estyn as Principal Officer Residential Services from 1976[42] and later as Assistant Director (Residential) until it closed in September 1984. Whatever his position may have been technically from time to time in the organisational structure, Wyatt was regarded by members of staff and residents in the community homes as the officer at headquarters responsible for residential care, apart from a comparatively short period between 1986 and 1989 when he was deflected to Adult Services.

29.76 Wyatt told the Tribunal that he visited Bryn Estyn once every six weeks or so but he did not regard it as appropriate for him to tour the premises on these occasions or to inspect children's files or even to speak to the residents. His contact appears to have been almost exclusively with Arnold and he did not find it easy to be Arnold's line manager: Arnold had a great deal of experience and was accustomed to independence, finding it difficult to come to terms with working within a local authority framework. It is of some relevance also that Arnold earned substantially more than Wyatt and felt able to approach the Director of Social Services direct when he chose to do so. In Wyatt's opinion, Arnold was selective in what he divulged to Wyatt.

[41] See para 28.14.
[42] See para 28.11 as to his position in relation to the Area Officers between 1977 and 1980.

29.77 It is not surprising in these circumstances that Wyatt's knowledge of what was actually happening at Bryn Estyn was very limited. We will revert to this theme in the next chapters of this report but here it is relevant to record that Wyatt told the Tribunal that he knew nothing of Howarth's "flat list" practice until the major police investigation and was amazed when he learned of it. He said also that, if he had been aware of it, alarm bells would have rung in his mind. He claimed also that he had no knowledge of any failings of Norris that might have pointed against his redeployment to Cartrefle in 1984.

29.78 Gordon Ramsay, as a Principal Social Worker from 1974 to 1987, was junior in status to Wyatt (his grading was a recurring cause of discontent) and had narrower responsibilities but he did visit the community homes regularly. He was required to attend "placement" reviews in the homes twice a year (he chaired them except those at Bryn Estyn, Bersham Hall and Little Acton) and he attended also many case conferences in his capacity of placement officer. It was not part of Ramsay's duties to inspect the community homes (in his written statement he said that he "had no responsibility for the inspecting and visiting of children's homes") but he needed to be conversant with them to carry out his placement duties. In his opinion Arnold ran a very good establishment at Bryn Estyn, a "tight ship" for children in need of control, and he knew individual boys, treating them all the same, despite the fact that there was a strong criminal element.

29.79 Ramsay said in his evidence that he would speak informally to boys when he visited Bryn Estyn. His assessment was that it was a rough unit with the strong discipline and respect for staff to be found in an approved school; but he had no cause for concern and did not himself witness rough handling or hear abusive language. He did, however, form the view that Norris was uncouth and crude and that he was not management material; he agreed in cross-examination that he ought to have passed on this view to senior management but said that they must have known this themselves.

29.80 John Llewellyn Thomas did not arrive in Clwyd until July 1984, just before Bryn Estyn was closed, and remained only until April 1991. During this period he was Principal Officer (Children), working under Wyatt until 1986, then under Powell until 1989 and again under Wyatt after that until the split into divisions was implemented in October 1990. Thomas' evidence was that he found operational standards in the community homes to be very poor and that he and his colleagues were engaged in "fire fighting", which took up a great deal of time, whilst he had to deal also with an accumulation of paper work on a variety of matters following the departure of Iorwerth Thomas.

29.81 After the closure in 1984 of Bryn Estyn and another Wrexham home, 7 Tan-y-Dre[43], there were eight local authority community homes in Clwyd still operating, with about 100 residents; and Thomas had only one RDCO (Norman Green) to assist him in monitoring them when Gwen Hurst became increasingly involved with services for young children. Green had a visiting programme providing for visits to each community home about once a month

---

[43] See paras 4.02(8) and 4.19(8).

but, according to Thomas, he or Green would visit more frequently than that to deal with problems. Thomas started holding monthly Heads of Homes meetings, at which he would preside, and he made a point of visiting each home personally at least once a quarter. It does not appear, however, that Thomas felt any particular concern about Norris' suitability to head Cartrefle.

29.82 Finally, Michael Barnes did not join the headquarters staff until January 1988 so that he had little opportunity to take effective action at that level during the period of major sexual abuse. As Principal Social Worker (Child and Family Services) his major duty was to manage the remaining children's homes (including a new home, Gladwyn), acting under Thomas and Powell (later Wyatt); and he did so until the reorganisation in October 1990, when he became Children's Resources Manager of the North Division[44]. One of his new responsibilities also was "gate keeping", namely, scrutinising potential admissions to residential care in order to avoid unnecessary admissions, which had formerly been part of Ramsay's duties.

29.83 Barnes undoubtedly applied himself with great energy to his new duties in 1988 and he had the advantage of considerable experience of working with children in care in Clwyd community homes. He made monthly managerial visits to each home (except when attending a managerial course) and met with managers, staff and the children; and there were other routine visits for various purposes, including the investigation of complaints. Amongst the steps that he took were initiatives to develop the role of the Heads of Homes meetings, to supervise those Heads more closely and attempts to improve rota visiting by councillors.

29.84 One of the Officers-in-Charge with whom Barnes had to deal was Norris at Cartrefle, who was previously known to him, although they had not been colleagues in the same community home. In Barnes' evidence to the Cartrefle inquiry[45], he said that he had had differences with Norris previously in his career over the latter's attitude and language; and he described his first supervisory meeting at Cartrefle with Norris as frank and abrasive. Barnes made it clear to Norris that the use of foul and sexual language, together with "derogatory labelling", would not be tolerated. Norris subsequently obeyed this edict, at least within earshot of his own managers, but in subsequent supervisory visits Barnes raised many matters of concern about the running of Cartrefle and Norris responded with complaints about the Department. Barnes formed the view that Norris was not capable of doing his job and that he should not have been appointed. As a result of the difficulties between them, fewer managerial visits were made to Cartrefle than had been planned or should have been made.

29.85 Barnes responded promptly, however, to Stanley's request that he should attend Cartrefle late at night in June 1990 in view of a resident's complaint that he had been sexually abused by Norris. Barnes saw the boy, whose complaint he believed, and there has been no criticism of his subsequent actions in

---

[44] See para 28.44.
[45] See para 15.47.

reporting to his Principal Officer and placing the matter in the hands of the police. He dealt appropriately also with the anxieties of some members of staff about Stanley himself at that time.

Conclusions

29.86 Although we recognise that the identification of potential sexual abusers often presents insurmountable difficulties and that young victims are usually extremely reluctant to complain about it when sexual abuse occurs, we are strongly critical of many aspects of the regimes that prevailed in community homes in Clwyd between 1974 and 1990. It is true that, in the earlier part of that period, ignorance of the risk of abuse by residential care staff or by others involved with children in care was widespread but that does not absolve Clwyd's Social Services Department from blame for their failure in many respects to take essential precautions for the safety of children in residential care within the county.

29.87 In this chapter we have highlighted what happened at Bryn Estyn and Cartrefle because those were the two homes in which the most prolonged abuse occurred but many of the criticisms and all the lessons to be drawn apply to the other community homes within the county.

29.88 A major and inescapable conclusion is that Arnold was wrongly permitted to run Bryn Estyn as his own fiefdom without any adequate direction, monitoring and supervision from management above and that, in doing so, he made grave errors. The most serious of those errors were his failures to prohibit Howarth's "flat list" practice and to investigate what was happening in that flat, despite the rumours of which he was aware. But his role in the advancement of Norris was also seriously mistaken, as was his espousal and encouragement of the cult of silence amongst members of the staff. All these matters should have been within the knowledge of an alert and effective higher management.

29.89 These particular failures occurred in one establishment inherited from the Home Office, in respect of which Clwyd managers appear to have regarded themselves as incapable of exercising control or insufficiently experienced to do so, but other criticisms that we have made are of general application. These include the absence of any complaints procedure or any effective key worker system; the lack of awareness of staff that children were being abused and their reluctance to report anxieties about the behaviour of colleagues; the corresponding reluctance of headquarters staff to respond to complaints with thorough investigation, on which we enlarge in the next chapter; the isolation of residents in care and their inadequate access to, and relationship with, field social workers; and the failure of headquarters for most of the period to provide any adequate system of supervising, monitoring and inspecting the community homes. Cumulatively these shortcomings must have played a part in the prolongation of the sexual abuse and may have encouraged the abusers before it began to think that they would escape detection.

29.90 Our discussion in this chapter has been focussed mainly on the community homes for which Clwyd County Council was directly responsible but our comments are relevant to the agencies responsible for other residential establishments for children within the county with which we have dealt earlier in this report. We stress, in particular, the need for clear complaints procedures in these establishments and for recognised "whistleblowing" procedures with appropriate protection for members of staff who make adverse reports on colleagues. There is also a need for the training of all residential care staff in likely symptoms of sexual abuse of which they should be aware; and regular independent monitoring of the homes is crucial. These matters are of particular importance in relation to private homes like the Bryn Alyn Community without any element of external management.

29.91 We have not found any specific breach of duty by Clwyd in respect of its own children in care placed in non-local authority establishments within the County but we cannot over-emphasise the importance of regular visiting by field staff workers of such children wherever they may be placed and the need to build up a relationship of trust and confidence. In more recent times the direct responsibilities of local authorities have been enlarged under the Children Act 1989 by the provisions in Part VIII of that Act for the registration of private children's homes. A wide duty to investigate and to take appropriate action is imposed by section 47 of the Act (replacing a provision in section 2 of the Children and Young Persons Act 1969) where a local authority has reasonable cause to suspect that a child who lives, or is found in, its area is suffering, or is likely to suffer, significant harm.

29.92 The issues that arise in relation to the avoidance or early elimination of sexual abuse in foster care are rather different from those that we have discussed in the context of community homes; and we have dealt with foster care in Clwyd as fully as possible in Part V of this report. Again, however, the quality of the relationship between field social worker and child, awareness on the part of the former, and regular monitoring of the placement are all of the utmost importance.

The failure to eliminate physical abuse

Introduction

30.01 Many of the criticisms that we have made in the preceding chapter are equally relevant to the prevalence of physical abuse in the community homes within Clwyd but this form of abuse raises some different issues from those that arise in relation to sexual abuse. Obvious distinctions are that physical abuse tends to be less furtive and that it is much more likely to be the subject of complaint because the circumstances in which it occurs are likely to be less embarrassing to the victim. Moreover, there is a greater range of possible responses to complaints about physical abuse than in cases of sexual abuse. It is necessary, therefore, to consider separately in this chapter the incidence of physical abuse and the adequacy of the measures taken by Clwyd Social Services Department to deal with it, whilst avoiding repetition as far as possible.

30.02 In Part II of this report we have given accounts of the complaints of physical abuse in nine local authority community homes in Clwyd and in Parts III and IV we have dealt similarly with six[1] other residential establishments for children in the county. On the evidence that has been presented to us we have found that physical abuse on a significant scale occurred in six of the local authority community homes and in four of the other establishments.

30.03 Two specific questions that necessarily arise in considering allegations of physical abuse during the period under review are:

    (a) To what extent was corporal punishment prohibited in these homes and establishments?

    (b) What rules, if any, governed staff in exercising necessary or reasonable physical restraint?

30.04 The permissibility of corporal punishment in educational and similar establishments has been a contentious subject for many years but Clwyd County Council issued a directive on the subject very early in its existence. The general legal background in relation to corporal punishment in community homes under the Administration of Homes Regulations 1951 and then the Community Homes Regulations 1972 is summarised in paragraphs 21 to 23 of Appendix 6. However, the Director of Social Services for Clwyd addressed a memorandum to staff in residential establishments for children and young people on 20 June 1974 in the following terms:

---

[1] The private residential establishments such as those in the Bryn Alyn Community have been counted as one for this purpose, although residents were dispersed on more than one site.

"Corporal Punishment in Residential Establishments for Children and Young People

1. Revised Community Home Regulations are to be published at an early date. These regulations follow the policy of both former Authorities that no member of staff will inflict corporal punishment on any child or young person in any circumstances (Corporal punishment to include striking, slapping, pushing etc).

2. The Children & Young Persons' Act (Community Home Regulations) 1972 states that 'The control of a Community Home shall be maintained on the basis of good personal and professional relationships between staff and the children resident therein'.

3. The above Clwyd County Council policy decision is drawn to the attention of all staff employed in the appropriate Homes in order that there can be no unfortunate misunderstanding or misconduct, and any infringement of this policy will be viewed with the utmost gravity. Please ensure that every member of your staff is aware of this regulation."

30.05 It was not until 1987 that corporal punishment was banned in state schools and the ban was not extended to community homes by statutory instrument until 1990 but we are satisfied that the staff in community homes in Clwyd, with few exceptions, knew from about mid 1974 that they were not permitted by their employing authority to inflict corporal punishment, even by slapping or pushing.

30.06 There was much less certainty about the degree of physical restraint that was permissible. We are not aware of any national or local guidance on the subject that was readily available to members of the staff during the period under review and none of them received any training directed to this problem. The foreseeable results were that there were wide variations in practice and that many of the complaints of physical abuse that we received related to alleged excesses by members of staff in restraining residents.

30.07 Corporal punishment in voluntary homes continued to be governed by Regulation 11 of the Administration of Homes Regulations 1951[2] until it ceased to be permissible in 1990. It remained permissible in private children's homes, to which the 1951 regulations did not apply, but the ban on it was extended to the registered category of such homes by Regulation 9 of the Children's Homes Regulations 1991, which also specified a number of other prohibited sanctions.

30.08 The failure of Clwyd Social Services Department to deal effectively with the problem of physical abuse in its community homes stemmed mainly from shortcomings in its recruitment policies, the absence of adequate complaints procedures, the failure of staff to record and report untoward incidents accurately and lack of appropriate training. We will deal with each of these matters in turn, although they inevitably overlap to some extent.

[2] See Appendix 6, para 22.

Recruitment of staff

30.09 Two aspects of Clwyd's recruiting procedures caused us particular concern. They were:

(a) the frequent appointment of unqualified staff without advertising vacancies and without other conventional procedures;

(b) the use of a pool of unqualified staff to fill casual vacancies.

30.10 The first of these defects was a particular feature of recruitment at Bryn Estyn and exemplifies the extent to which Arnold was permitted to run that major community home as he saw fit, with virtually no management from above. In the preceding chapter we have criticised the way in which Norris was appointed initially but the casual process of recruitment was more startling in respect of other members of the care staff. This is illustrated most clearly by the circumstances in which David Birch and other members of the rugby set[3] were appointed. Of the five men and one woman belonging to that loosely connected group, only Phillip Murray had received any preliminary training or gained any experience in child care. The others all learned of vacancies at Bryn Estyn through the rugby club and began work almost immediately after an interview with Arnold or Howarth or both (in the case of Elizabeth Evans a woman representative of the Area Office was present); and only Robert Jones underwent professional training before Bryn Estyn closed. Night care staff without any experience or training were recruited similarly. Despite the special problems arising at Bryn Estyn because of its transformation from approved school to community home with education on the premises and the wide range in many senses of its resident population, these newly appointed members of staff were expected to learn their difficult roles "on the job" without any structured guidance or induction.

30.11 This informal method of appointment of staff does not appear to have been adopted generally in Clwyd in the 1970s but the use of a pool system to fill vacancies gathered momentum from about 1976 onwards and remained in use until 1996. Several former members of staff gave evidence to us about the use of this system. One of them was a school dinner lady when she was asked whether she would like to work in the Social Services Department. She was then interviewed by an RDCO and her name was added to the pool although she had no qualifications. She was later telephoned by Leonard Stritch from Bryn Estyn and served there and at four other children's homes. That witness' experience was fairly typical of the recruitment and use of the pool and we heard particularly of its use to fill vacancies at Bersham Hall and at Cartrefle.

30.12 Janet Handley, who was Area Officer for the Wrexham Maelor area from 1974 to 1985, said that the community homes were left to get on with recruitment themselves when responsibility for the homes reverted to headquarters from the Area Officers in 1980. Officers-in-Charge were given responsibility for staff appointments from the pool without reference to headquarters. The appointees were vetted but only by the provision of two personal references

---

[3] See paras 10.43 and 10.44.

and a check with the police. Temporary appointments from the pool were regarded as a useful means of checking the suitability of the persons chosen and avoiding the need for formal dismissal procedures. In a review of staffing in community homes in the Spring of 1989, however, John Llewellyn Thomas and Michael Barnes wrote:

> "The relief pool is of limited value. It is very costly and labour intensive and fails to attract sufficient staff at times of absence. It does not provide any senior (management) cover and cannot be relied upon to meet essential skill/gender needs. Moreover, the use of multiple carers encourages poor child care and discourages skill development because it is virtually impossible to adequately supervise transient staff."

30.13 One of the objectives of this review was to reduce dependence on the pool by recruiting established care staff to provide cover for leave etc but this objective does not appear to have been achieved. John Jevons told the Tribunal that all the staff concerned were unhappy with the pool system. He wanted to replace it when resources would allow him to do so but it was not seen to be a high priority.

30.14 The link between poor recruiting procedures and physical abuse should not be over-simplified. Poor recruitment was part of a much wider picture of reliance upon staff untrained in residential care, working with limited professional guidance and few opportunities for appropriate training. We recognise also that throughout the period under review there were very real difficulties about recruitment. There was no national pool or reserve of trained and experienced care workers on which a county such as Clwyd could draw and conditions of service generally for residential care workers were so unfavourable that the response to advertising of vacant posts was poor even at times of high unemployment.

Complaints procedures and the response to complaints

30.15 Despite the absence of any formal complaints procedures, residents in community homes did complain from time to time of physical abuse and we have referred in Part II of this report to the more significant examples of the ways in which they were dealt with. It was comparatively rare for a complaint to reach a formal stage because the complainant would be discouraged with warnings about the potential consequences for him/her and the member of staff. The relevant incident would rarely be recorded in any log book in appropriate terms so that an uninformed reader would not surmise that an alleged assault had occurred. Moreover, if the complainant persisted to the point of signing a statement, he would probably not be interviewed again. The interview would be conducted by a comparatively junior member of staff and the likely consensus amongst senior staff at the home would be that the complainant (often seen as a troublemaker) was not to be believed. Even more perturbingly, on some occasions when the complaint was plainly true in substance, records would be distorted in order to nullify it or to minimise a serious incident. Finally, if a complaint did get through to headquarters, it would usually be dealt with by Geoffrey Wyatt: the complainant would usually be transferred elsewhere, if that action had not already been taken; and, at worst, the staff member would receive a mild reproof.

30.16 The inadequacies of the system are fully illustrated by the history of Paul Wilson, who was ultimately convicted of a number of assaults on residents at Bryn Estyn. We have set out Wilson's history at Bryn Estyn in some detail in Chapter 10[4] and his later brief record at Chevet Hey in Chapter 14[5] (none of the counts in the indictment against him related to his period at Chevet Hey). The two accounts need to be re-read to absorb the full impact of Clwyd's successive failures to deal appropriately with this member of the care staff. He was fortunate to be retained after failing to disclose his conviction for theft; he was equally fortunate to survive his probationary period, when his defects of temperament were becoming known and his inability to write reports had been recognised; and he led a charmed life thereafter for over ten years, despite repeated occasions on which his use of unacceptable physical force to residents had been called into question.

30.17 In the course of his period at Bryn Estyn there were not less than six serious complaints against Paul Wilson that came to the notice of headquarters. The first, which was also reported to the police, was not believed and the complainant was transferred to the much feared Neath Farm School in South Wales. Both Ramsay and Wyatt were involved, as well as Arnold, and it seems that Robert Jones was a known witness to the alleged assault, who was willing to attest to it. No action appears to have been taken on the second complaint, which was not pursued by the boy "officially", except that Wilson may have been given some advice by Arnold on Wyatt's initiative. In respect of the third, Arnold did see the complainant, who said that he did not wish to pursue the matter. On the fourth occasion the police were again involved. By this time Wilson was becoming anxious about his position but no action was taken against him and the boy was removed from Bryn Estyn (there was difficulty with Wilson when the boy returned 20 months later). The fifth complaint, about an incident on 25 January 1983 in respect of which Wilson pleaded guilty 11 years later to an assault occasioning actual bodily harm, was not pursued by the complainant beyond Arnold after the boy had been warned by Stritch that he would have to be moved, if he continued with his allegation[6].

30.18 The last complaint about Wilson to reach higher authority was about incidents that occurred in August 1985 at Chevet Hey, which have been recounted in paragraph 14.23. As we have related in the three following paragraphs, there was quite a wide investigation into those incidents and Wyatt expressed dismay at what had been disclosed; but his surprising conclusion was that "We discovered nothing in our enquiries to prevent Mr Wilson returning to his duties at Chevet Hey". In the event, however, there was staff opposition to Wilson's return and a threat of legal action by the boy with the result that

---

[4] See paras 10.04 to 10.39.
[5] See paras 14.20 to 14.27.
[6] For our earlier comments on this history, see paras 10.35 to 10.38.

Wilson was ultimately placed at a day centre as an instructor/supervisor from January 1986, where he remained until he retired at the end of the following year[7].

30.19 This summary of the outcome of some of the complaints made against Wilson that reached the notice of higher authority is by no means exhaustive but it suffices to illustrate the various ways in which the purpose of complaining was frustrated. Quite apart from the disinclination to believe complainants, at least three other factors had an important influence on the outcome of investigations. These were:

(a) reluctance to set in train formal disciplinary procedures and misunderstanding of what had to be proved to justify written warnings and/or dismissal;

(b) persistent weakness in dealing with trades union representations on behalf of individual members of staff;

(c) the impact (but not an unavoidable effect) of a "containment" agreement with the trades unions.

30.20 In the course of the evidence generally we have been told of quite a large number of complaints against individual members of the staff of the community homes which were reported to the police but which did not result in a prosecution. These complaints were investigated by the police and the decision not to prosecute was subsequently made by the police themselves or by the Crown Prosecution Service for a variety of reasons, usually encompassed within an explanation that there was insufficient evidence to justify a prosecution. Invariably, it seems, this decision was regarded by Clwyd Social Services Department as an end of the particular matter and no disciplinary investigation or similar action in relation to the relevant member of staff followed. The result was that the latter emerged unscathed, whatever the rights or wrongs of the matter might have been, and no remedial action was taken to deal with any underlying causes of conflict or unrest.

30.21 In our judgment this approach to disciplinary matters was fundamentally flawed. It was based on the mistaken belief that the standard of proof required in a criminal prosecution applied to all complaints of misconduct by staff and it ignored the duty of the Council, in its dual capacities of employer on the one hand, and more importantly as carer for the children on the other, to investigate complaints thoroughly. A further error by the Social Services Department was to adopt a rule (the origin of which we do not know) that complainants and witnesses in care, of whatever age or capability, should not be heard in disciplinary proceedings because it was contrary to the best interests of children to be called to do so. Thus, no discretion was applied to the matter and the individual complainant was not consulted about it. The result was that a complaint was unlikely to reach the stage of disciplinary proceedings and, even if it did so, was still likely to fail, unless there was compelling evidence from at least one member of staff to support it.

---

[7] See para 14.21.

30.22 We have not found anything in Clwyd County Council's disciplinary code to explain or justify these errors of approach and it was an abdication of the Council's duties to rely upon police investigations of matters that involved important employment and welfare issues. We were told that the Social Services Department worked in close consultation with the Council's Personnel Department and received legal advice from the County Solicitor and the County Secretary but we are forced to the conclusion that the issues that we have raised in the preceding paragraph were never grasped and openly discussed. Instead, confused misapprehensions were accepted as an excuse for inaction, particularly by Geoffrey Wyatt, but his seniors and members of the other Departments must also bear a substantial share of the blame (we received no evidence that elected members discouraged the taking of disciplinary action, or that they displayed bias in favour of staff at appeals). The only mitigating factor appears to be that an Industrial Tribunal's adverse decision in the case of the Upper Downing gardener[8] had a lowering effect on morale but it seems that that decision turned on procedural considerations (the failure of the complainant girl to appear to give evidence to the Tribunal may also have been a factor) and it did not excuse a subsequent timid approach to disciplinary matters generally.

30.23 This rule of practice that complainants should not be called to give evidence seems to have held sway throughout Clwyd County Council's existence, although (in its last few years) John Jevons would have been prepared to consider calling a child, if the occasion had arisen. Gledwyn Jones said that it had been custom and practice from the time when the local authority was first established and that it was designed to protect younger children from the ordeal of cross-examination but he conceded that the end result effectively was that no disciplinary action was taken to protect the child concerned or others.

30.24 The other two factors mentioned in paragraph 30.19 involved the Council's relations with trades unions representing members of its staff but we are not persuaded that those trades unions went beyond the legitimate bounds of their duties. Some of the witnesses who gave oral evidence before us were critical of them. Emlyn Evans, for example, said that NALGO would defend its members regardless of the justice of the case whereas NUPE could be worked with. Michael Barnes said that the unions were very powerful, exercising influence at all levels of management, including the Council itself, with the result that, on occasions, their influence did exceed proper bounds. But we have not been given any example of improper conduct by a trades union representative: it was his/her duty to press the member's case as effectively as he/she could and the duty of management to respond firmly and fairly in the light of all the facts available. Instead, the evidence suggests that both senior management and middle management adopted an unduly timorous approach to staff problems within the Social Services Department and were too ready to accept what appeared to be an "easy solution".

---

[8] In 1976, see paras 17.03 to 17.07.

30.25 Geoffrey Wyatt's own evidence was that disciplinary proceedings were greatly influenced by the trades union (presumably NALGO), which batted hard for members of staff. He said that he himself was not afraid of the union but that disciplinary proceedings were seriously adversarial. Whilst Wilson was at Bryn Estyn he had become a NALGO steward and, when he was finally transferred from Chevet Hey to a day care centre, Wyatt (according to his own evidence) expected a huge trades union backlash but it did not transpire. It must be said also that many of the staff at Chevet Hey were opposed to Wilson returning there.

30.26 The "containment" agreement to which we have referred was made between Clwyd County Council and the trades unions probably in October 1980. According to its preamble its objective was to achieve a rational process for a reduction in staff costs without compulsory redundancies and it contained details of an early retirement scheme for employees aged 50 years or over. The provisions in it that are of particular relevance to our inquiry were those dealing with "redeployment". They laid down the principles and procedures that were to govern transfers of employees from one post to another. Only one offer to an employee of a comparable post was required but an employee was entitled to refuse transfer to up to two non-comparable posts at a protected salary. Moreover, the Council undertook to endeavour to preserve the employee's status and to effect a further transfer to a post commensurate with the employee's original grade and the employee's ability to perform the duties of that post.

30.27 We do not consider that this agreement should have inhibited proper disciplinary action against an employee who misconducted himself or herself nor did it justify the transfer of unsuitable care staff to senior positions in community homes. We have already criticised in the preceding chapter of this report the inappropriate redeployment of Stephen Norris from Bryn Estyn to Cartrefle in pursuance of the containment agreement[9] and equally stringent criticism must be made of the later appointment of Frederick Marshall Jones in July 1990 to succeed Norris as Officer-in-Charge of Cartrefle[10]. That appointment does not appear to have been expressed to be a redeployment because Bersham Hall, of which Marshall Jones had been Assistant Centre Manager since September 1989, was not about to close. The post at Cartrefle was not advertised, however, and the number of community homes in Clwyd was being reduced so that it is reasonable to place Marshall Jones' transfer to Cartrefle within the framework, or at least the policy, of the containment agreement.

30.28 That transfer should never have been made and the appointment of Marshall Jones as Officer-in-Charge was inappropriate on a number of grounds. Although he had worked in residential child care since November 1974 (interrupted from 1977 to 1979), he had not received any professional training. Secondly, the post called for special sensitivity and understanding in the

---

[9] See paras 29.14 and 29.15.
[10] See para 15.51.

aftermath of the grave abuse of residents by Norris. Thirdly, Marshall Jones had a long record of physically abusive behaviour at Chevet Hey, of which headquarters knew or certainly should have known.

30.29 Marshall Jones' history at Chevet Hey from 1979 to 1989 has been chronicled in Chapter 14[11] and we need not repeat it here. Viewing all the evidence about him, including his later record at Cartrefle[12], we set out in paragraph 14.19 our conclusions that Marshall Jones' disciplinary attitude and methods were very seriously flawed throughout and that he was unfitted for all the posts, particularly the senior positions, to which he was appointed. We do not believe that, if there had been an adequate complaints procedure, including effective and appropriate responses to complaints, Marshall Jones could have advanced as he did without a radical alteration in his approach and conduct. Even without such a system, senior and middle management should have been aware, through Wyatt, Barnes and Ellis Edwards particularly, of Marshall Jones' shortcomings. In the event, complaints and unrest about Marshall Jones persisted at Cartrefle and he lasted there only for just over two years, until he was suspended from duty from 17 September 1992.

30.30 Other examples of inadequate responses to complaints of physical abuse are legion throughout this report and in our judgment they were probably the major factor in Clwyd's failure to eliminate such abuse in their community homes. In the end physical abuse could only have been swept aside if a new culture had been established through vigorous monitoring of both standards and practice, coupled with appropriate disciplinary action.

The inadequate recording of complaints and incidents

30.31 One of the difficulties of obtaining an accurate picture of the extent of physical abuse in the period under review, long after the material events, has been inadequate recording of incidents by staff of the community homes. The general standard of the records in the home logs and in personal files varied a great deal from time to time and from home to home. But the evidence before us points clearly to the conclusion that misleading recording and even, on occasions, falsification of records were part of a deliberate system intended to suppress the truth.

30.32 Once again Bryn Estyn provides examples of this malpractice but it was by no means confined to that community home. In its most prevalent form an injury sustained by a resident would not be specified except in the most general terms and the circumstances in which it occurred would be similarly described, without any incriminating detail, in bland language[13].

30.33 In paragraphs 10.103 to 10.111 of this report we have given a full account of an incident that occurred on 19 April 1983 at Bryn Estyn, following which there was, in our view, a deliberate cover up in which Arnold was implicated

---

[11] See paras 14.12 to 14.19 and 14.57 to 14.62.
[12] See paras 15.51 to 15.61.
[13] See, for example, para 10.28.

and in which a late entry was made in the daily log by a senior RCCO to support the cover up. The incident was reported to Wyatt but the cover up was successful because Wyatt accepted the untrue explanation of Z's head injury ("a bump in the gym") and adjudicated that "the matter was now closed" without further reference to Z. Thus, the member of staff involved, David Cheesbrough, escaped any disciplinary action.

30.34 Another example of suppression of the facts in which Arnold was directly involved is described in paragraphs 10.117 and 10.118. In reporting that incident in December 1983 to the Director of Social Services, Arnold described a severe assault by Maurice Matthews on a boy as "some sort of physical confrontation with Mr Matthews". Arnold's recommendation that the matter should be left lying with no blame attached to either party was accepted.

30.35 More seriously, we have given a very full account in paragraphs 10.135 to 10.146 of the way in which an incident on 30 April 1984 at Bryn Estyn between John Cunningham and Y was subsequently covered up on Arnold's initiative (the "swinging door" explanation). In paragraph 10.140 we have criticised also the role in the affair played by Matthews, who told Cunningham to write a report "to cover himself" and warned him that he would probably be sacked if he admitted hitting Y. The result of the suppression of the truth at the time was that disciplinary action was not begun against Cunningham until nearly eight years later and was not concluded until 9 July 1995.

30.36 If there had been adequate investigation of these complaints by headquarters instead of passive responses and, in particular, if the complainants had been interviewed fairly and independently, we believe that the true facts would have emerged and serious malpractice in recording would have been revealed. As it was, from the residents' point of view, the conspiracy to obstruct justice was allowed to continue and members of the staff were encouraged to think that they would be allowed to escape retribution for physical abuse.

The lack of training opportunities for residential child care staff

30.37 The inadequacy of the training of staff employed in residential child care establishments in Clwyd generally has been a recurring theme of this report but it requires special mention in the context of physical abuse. We have already referred specifically to the absence of any guidance or training in the exercise of physical restraint but, even more seriously, a large proportion of the staff, including both care workers and teachers, had received no training in child care whatsoever and were expected to learn by experience alone. It was almost inevitable, therefore, that bad practices would be perpetuated and that newcomers would absorb the existing customs and attitudes of the particular establishment to which they were first assigned. Thus, for example, bad habits such as the physical chastisement of children and lack of frankness in the recording of incidents were likely to be adopted by the newcomer unless very firm guidance was given by the Officer-in-Charge and other senior members of the staff.

30.38 Bad practices were by no means unique to Clwyd or to North Wales in the 1970s and 1980s and the need for appropriate training of residential child care staff was stressed in a number of reports commissioned by central government during that period. The impact of the problem was most severe, however, in residential establishments providing for a high proportion of severely disturbed or delinquent children, such as Bryn Estyn and (at times) Bersham Hall, and is reflected, therefore, in the number of allegations of physical abuse in community homes in Clwyd.

30.39 We have not been provided with any statistics about the training of residential child care staff in Clwyd during the period under review. Gledwyn Jones asserted in his evidence that Clwyd was "proactive" at the outset of its existence in securing the establishment of a CQSW course at Cartrefle College in Wrexham to cover both field work and residential care. He said also that there was a joint scheme, with Gwynedd, in the early 1980s to establish a CSS course at Wrexham. Other witnesses such as Raymond Powell, however, made it clear that the training of residential child care staff took second place to that of field work staff.

30.40 Whereas the percentage of qualified field social workers in Clwyd advanced from 48 to 89 between 1975 and 1985, there was no similar progress in respect of residential child care staff. Amongst the problems were shortages of such staff and their tendency to transfer to field work as soon as possible if they did receive training. After the arrival of John Llewellyn Thomas an attempt was made to redress the balance. A training strategy was formulated in 1984 and periodically reviewed but comparatively little was achieved in the training of residential child care staff. There was a Welsh Office Training Support Programme under an All Wales Strategy for the Mentally Handicapped but no equivalent in respect of residential child care. Thomas told the Tribunal, on the basis of his experience of regional planning for Wales, that it was known from the mid 1970s that only 10 to 15 per cent of residential child care staff for the whole of Wales were qualified: he added "For the small homes you would be lucky if it was just the Officer-in-Charge and possibly the deputy". In his opinion, the position in Clwyd could only have changed "around the margins" by the 1990s in view of national policy towards residential child care training, in contrast to the positive change of national policy in respect of field work training.

Other relevant factors

30.41 In the preceding chapter, from paragraph 29.51 onwards, we discussed the importance of awareness on the part of staff and their willingness to report abusive behaviour, the potential role of field social workers in the discovery of abuse, and the need for effective monitoring, supervision and visiting of all community homes. Our comments there were made in the context of preventing, or at least arresting, sexual abuse but they apply with even greater force to the elimination of physical abuse because the latter is usually more easily detectable.

30.42 The evidence that we have heard has demonstrated that Clwyd Social Services Department failed to discharge its duty to the children in its care to a substantial degree in all these respects in the period between 1974 and 1990. The result was that the community homes were left in the main to run themselves and that, where physical abuse was occurring, it was allowed to continue. The responsibility for these homes lay with senior management throughout, whatever organisational changes may have been made from time to time, and the blame for failure must rest there too.

Conclusions

30.43 Although our analysis of the failure to eliminate physical abuse in Clwyd's community homes has been somewhat different from that in Chapter 29 in relation to sexual abuse, our conclusions are essentially the same, with differences only of emphasis. The lessons to be learned in respect of other residential establishments for children are the same. Where children in care are placed in such establishments, even for comparatively short periods, it is essential that they should be visited regularly by persons they trust, that there should be an adequate complement of trained care staff and that the practices and performance of the establishments should be closely monitored. Without such safeguards there will always be a risk that physical abuse may occur and the children in care will be inadequately protected from harm.

30.44 In Clwyd there were a number of residential child care staff, whom we have identified, who persistently disregarded the County Council's prohibition of corporal punishment and who were allowed to continue to do so for long periods without disciplinary action being taken against them. One of the causes of this was the failure of management to communicate rules such as the prohibition of corporal punishment. Other contributory factors were the habitually inadequate responses to legitimate complaints and pervasive timidity in enforcing disciplinary procedures. These were faults of the staff of community homes and middle management throughout but there were many other underlying causes and senior management cannot escape its responsibility by reliance upon an ineffective, and often confused, system of delegation.

Basic failings in the quality of care

Introduction

31.01 The Tribunal's terms of reference do not refer specifically to this topic but the evidence that we have heard from complainants and others has demonstrated that, for many children in care in Clwyd during the period under review, the quality of care provided fell far below an acceptable standard. The cumulative effect of the Social Services Department's various failings in this respect amounted, in our judgment, to abuse of those children; and the lamentable result was that many of them emerged from care unfitted to meet the demands of adult life, without adequate continuing support and filled with resentment about their treatment in care.

31.02 It has not been the purpose of this Tribunal to carry out an audit of Clwyd Social Services Department's practice and procedures generally and the procedure of a Tribunal of Inquiry is not appropriate for such an investigation. Nevertheless, the evidence before us has pointed so clearly to basic failings in the quality of care provided by Clwyd that our report would be incomplete without reference to them.

31.03 The major failings that we have identified were:

(a) The lack of adequate planning of each child's period in care.

(b) The absence of any strategic framework for the placement of children in residential care.

(c) Ineffective reviewing processes and lack of consultation with the child.

(d) Intermittent and inadequate surveillance by field social workers.

(e) Failure to establish any co-ordinated system for preparing residents for their discharge from care.

The lack of adequate planning for each child in care

31.04 The need for individual child care plans was recognised generally as good social work practice throughout the period under review but we found little evidence of them in Clwyd and the practice in respect of them was at best patchy. On a different, but analogous, subject, Gordon Ramsay said that a social history proforma to be used for all children coming into care was drawn up in 1974 but was rarely completed properly; and available information was rarely put into reports or transfer summaries. Moreover, Janet Handley, the Area Officer for Wrexham Maelor, told us that the standard of maintaining case notes of a child in residential care, including admission documentation, "lapsed in practice" by some staff between 1971 and her retirement in 1985.

31.05 Elaine Baxter, who carried out a review of files and of interviews with social workers on behalf of the Tribunal, confirmed the lack of structured assessment and planning: the social workers interviewed commented that there was no structural proforma for individual care planning in the 1980s and that the only planning mechanism was the review, the form for which provided a space for future plans. None of the social workers interviewed could recall any specific training or guidance in care planning prior to the Children Act 1989. Furthermore, despite the statutory requirements that the local authority should, so far as was practicable, ascertain the wishes and feelings of a child regarding any decision and give due consideration to them having regard to the child's age and understanding[1], the social workers could not recall any training or guidance on that subject in the same period. The reality, as one quite senior officer put it, was that obtaining the views of the child did not happen in Clwyd in the 1980s in any formal sense before the Children Act 1989.

31.06 The result of all this was that many of the children in residential care had no coherent picture of their likely future in care and were not given any clear conception of how they might progress positively.

The absence of any strategic framework for placements

31.07 One of the reasons for the lack of individual care plans may have been the absence of any clear framework for the placement of children after their reception into care. Gordon Ramsay's role as Placement Officer was formalised in 1975 and he retained this responsibility until his retirement in 1987 but he seems to have had very limited effective discretion in the matter. The practice was to hold a case conference at a community home shortly after a child had been admitted there initially, except in the case of Bryn Estyn and the two assessment centres at Bersham Hall and Little Acton. Ramsay would preside at case conferences at the assessment centres, which would be multi-disciplinary, and the appropriateness of each placement would be reviewed together with future plans for the child. The latter would not be present at the discussion but might be invited in at the conclusion of it to be told the outcome. At Bryn Estyn a similar type of case conference would take place and would be chaired by Arnold.

31.08 This procedure was apparently designed initially for children who had been the subject of emergency placements but it became the practice in respect of all placements. The reality was that the number of available places in residential care in Clwyd was limited throughout and that, in many cases, admissions were treated as emergency cases when they need not have been. Thus, many (perhaps most) placements were decided on the basis of availability rather than suitability. Concern about unplanned admissions figured in management discussions in 1980 and 1981 and again in 1983. According to John Coley, the Deputy Director of Social Services from 1980 to 1984, unplanned admissions escaped the scrutiny and endorsement of supervising officers; they could

[1] Section 18(1) Child Care Act 1980.

involve the inappropriate reception of children into residential care as an easy short term solution but with the attendant danger that they might become institutionalised.

31.09 The other form of review in which Gordon Ramsay played a leading part was a six monthly review, called a placement review, at each community home, other than the three Wrexham homes mentioned in paragraph 31.07, of all the children in the home. The object was to consider the suitability of the placement of each child there and Ramsay went to the home on his own for that purpose. At Bryn Estyn, Arnold would chair reviews but they were not strictly parallel to Ramsay's placement reviews: a review there would take place as the need arose for a particular child or, for example, if there was a need to reduce numbers. Ramsay would attend, if he was available, and the review at Bryn Estyn might be multi-disciplinary. At the assessment centres also reviews would be held if there was a special reason, such as non-availability of a placement for a child, and the head of home would preside but Ramsay would attend.

31.10 Despite these procedures there was no underlying strategic planning. From the point of view of the child in care he/she was liable to be moved for reasons unconnected with his/her welfare or behaviour and might be placed far away from his/her home of origin and friends. Moreover, financial constraints became a factor in the reviews from 1980 onwards, particularly in relation to the impending closure of Bryn Estyn. Thus, it was difficult for many children in care to hold on to any coherent vision of their future or to retain any realistic immediate aims.

Ineffective reviewing processes and lack of consultation with the child

31.11 We have referred in the preceding section of this chapter to what were called placement reviews but there were statutory requirements governing a different type of review, known as a "statutory review", throughout the period. Section 27(4) of the Children and Young Persons Act 1969 required a local authority to review the case of every child in its care every six months and to consider upon the review whether to apply to discharge the care order. A parallel duty in respect of boarded out children under successive Boarding-Out Regulations was to review the child's welfare, health, conduct and progress, in the light of written reports about the child, at six monthly intervals, following an initial review within three months of the placement. In practice Clwyd, like many other authorities, integrated these two forms of review into a single system covering both requirements; but Clwyd went a step further by including in the system children in day care and children subject to supervision orders, neither category of whom were covered by a statutory requirement.

31.12 We received evidence of divergent practice in carrying out these reviews. Gordon Ramsay told us that they took place in the Area Office until he retired in 1987; they usually involved just the field social worker (who was expected to represent the views of the residential care workers involved with the child) and his/her line manager, although a health visitor or school welfare officer might attend. Neither Ramsay himself nor any representative of the residential sector would attend. Janet Handley, on the other hand, said that in the Wrexham Maelor area reviews of children in residential care were held in the community home so that the field social worker and residential care workers could review the case with an independent person. Another Area Officer said, however, that the only people involved in the early days were the social worker and the Area Officer (later the Deputy). Whichever procedure was followed, however, the direct contribution of the child was very limited in the 1970s and 1980s. It was not normal for the child to be consulted or directly involved in reviews.

31.13 It is difficult to see how a system of reviews without direct input from the residential care workers or the child could be effective, particularly when relations between field social workers and residential care workers were poor and there were criticisms of the visiting records of the former. Furthermore, parallel systems of separate placements and statutory reviews conducted by different personnel were most unsatisfactory and unlikely to result in coherent, positive planning for each child in the light of full information and understanding.

31.14 A further serious problem was the delay in carrying out the statutory reviews in some areas, which was all the more serious because these reviews were regarded as the main instrument of care planning. In November 1977 the Director of Social Services (Emlyn Evans) instructed Area Officers to certify to their Area Sub-Committee that statutory reviews had been completed but we heard evidence of subsequent long delays in completing reviews in both the Wrexham Maelor and Delyn areas. In 1980 Emlyn Evans and Ramsay visited the Wrexham office and found that there were serious delays; and in 1982 Janet Handley reported that 209 (including 80 supervision order cases) out of 267 reviews were overdue in that area. As for the Delyn area, a detailed report by Ramsay on 16 June 1981 showed that there had been many breaches of detailed requirements: 42 reviews had been missed, some reviews were 12 months late, and two of the teams had each been late in completing 35 reviews. In consequence, according to Ramsay, three persons in the Delyn area were disciplined: it appears that the Area Manager received a formal written warning and a Team Leader was given a final written warning.

31.15 We must emphasise finally on this subject that, in any event, the review process is not a substitute for a clear and recorded initial child care plan. Reviews should provide independent monitoring and evaluation of the assessment and planning processes but they should not be used as a substitute for those processes.

Intermittent and inadequate surveillance by field social workers

31.16 Field social workers provide the primary point of contact with families in difficulty and their work is crucial in determining whether children enter the care system or remain at home. Once a child is admitted into care, the field social worker carries the main responsibility for planning the future, including working with the child's family towards rehabilitation, where this is a possibility. In this context the development of a close and confiding relationship between social worker and child is of paramount importance and this, in turn, can only be established by regular visiting of both children in residential care and boarded out children.

31.17 Elaine Baxter's review of social work practice in Clwyd on the Tribunal's behalf confirmed the oral evidence that we heard to the effect that visiting patterns were extremely varied, with long gaps in reported visits to both community homes and foster homes. The account that we have given of this in paragraphs 29.60 to 29.64 of this report emphasises both the inadequacy of the contact between field social workers in Clwyd and children in residential care and the fact that this was known to senior management in the early 1980s. This serious breach of approved practices did not, however, provoke any effective managerial response.

31.18 Whilst we heard some evidence of good practice in visiting and of the general availability of social workers at, for example, Park House and South Meadow and early on at Bersham Hall, we have no doubt that for most children contact with social workers was insufficient to establish or maintain a level of confidence that would enable them to make complaints or indeed to preserve a significant relationship. Once children were placed in residential care, they became a low priority and field social workers tended to concentrate their efforts on work with their families; some saw children mainly when they were on home leave, thus missing the opportunity of observing and talking to them in their residential care situations. Moreover, even if the minimum frequency of visiting taken from the Boarding Out Regulations was complied with, this was insufficient to foster a confiding relationship with a child.

31.19 One of the consequences of (or reasons for) the infrequent contact between field social workers and some of the community homes was that there was considerable disaffection between them and residential care staff. Janet Handley described the relationships between them as "abysmal", although this varied from home to home. At Bryn Estyn, for example, social workers felt unwelcome. On the other hand, some senior residential care officers attributed delays in rehabilitating some children, after they had ceased to benefit from residential care, to inefficiency or indifference on the part of the field social workers after the initial placements had been made.

31.20 It would be wrong to infer that all the blame for the failure to establish appropriate relationships with the children rested upon fieldwork staff. Quite apart from the failure of senior management to monitor the performance of field social workers in this respect, there were other contributory factors. Some children did not have any social worker allocated to them. Some other children were placed far from their own homes, making visiting by social workers, who were limited at one stage to a monthly mileage allowance of 250 miles, difficult. In general also, case loads were high.

31.21 According to the Area Officers, inadequate staffing levels and the loss of qualified and experienced staff were major factors in the lack of support and supervision by fieldworkers from the beginning. In February 1976, the agreed field social work establishment was 58 (against a policy ideal of 76), but only

49 were in post, of whom 25 were qualified. Since 1974, 63 field staff had left, of whom 44 were qualified, and only 14 qualified social workers had been recruited. Thereafter, the lack of experience of the unqualified staff was a constant worry, according to Janet Handley, and professional training needs further reduced the number of staff available at any particular time. However, substantial progress was made in the following ten years. Whereas in 1975 only 48% of fieldworkers were qualified, the percentage of them who were qualified by 1985 was 89 (93% in 1994).

Failure to prepare residents for their discharge from care

31.22 A recurring criticism made by complainants who had been in care for substantial periods was that they were unprepared for their discharge from care when it occurred. They had not been given any adequate training specifically directed to the problems that they would face on discharge and received little support from social workers once they ceased to be in care.

31.23 From the evidence presented to us it would appear that greater sustained efforts to prepare young persons in care for discharge were made in the earlier part of the period under review than later, when the boarding out of children predominated. At Bryn Estyn, for example, Cedar House was used until about April 1977 as a working boys' unit[2]; and several other community homes, such as Bersham Hall, Park House and South Meadow, had a cottage in the grounds that was intended in the early years to be used as accommodation for small numbers of older residents, who would be taught some of the basic skills necessary for independent living. As unemployment increased, however, work training for residents seems to have faded from the picture and we heard very little of any positive training once residents had passed the compulsory school age limit.

31.24 In November 1984 the Director of Social Services (Gledwyn Jones) was invited to address a conference organised by the National Association for the Care and Rehabilitation of Offenders at Llandrindod Wells on the subject of housing homeless young people at risk. In preparing his own contribution to that conference, dealing with the responsibilities of Social Services Departments, the Director arranged for a survey to be carried out of young people in Clwyd who had left care during the period of 18 months between 1 April 1983 and 30 September 1984. The information was supplied by the social workers responsible for supervising the young persons and the aim was to achieve a "down to earth" evaluation of the results of the service provided for children in care with a view to improvement where necessary.

31.25 In the event 62 (37 boys, 25 girls) out of a total of 79 young persons who had been discharged in the prescribed period were covered by the answers to the questionnaire that was distributed; and 44 of them had been discharged from a community home against 18 from a foster home. On discharge only about 50% of them (32) went to accommodation in which they might expect to receive continuous support: 21 went to live with a parent or parents, four to relatives

---

[2] See paras 7.10 and 7.13.

and seven remained in their foster homes. The other 27 (excluding two serving custodial sentences and one absconder) had to survive independently in various types of accommodation (almost wholly temporary) as indicated by the following list:

Friends	2
Approved lodgings	7
Private house/flat/bed sit	1 (inherited)
Landlady/boarding house	1
Hostel	2

31.26 The report on the survey, written by John Llewellyn Thomas (Principal Officer (Children)) and David Davies (Child Abuse Co-ordinator) was prefaced with the following bleak quotation from Mia Kellmer Pringle on "The Needs of Children", "Not only does the child in long-term care have no reliable past; equally devastating, he has no predictable future except that he will come out of care at the age of eighteen". Amongst the report's findings were that only ten of those in temporary accommodation were receiving any planned follow up and 37 of the total of 62 were unemployed (11 others were on Youth Training Schemes). The authors commented:

> "Even by Clwyd's serious unemployment figures the 60 per cent of young people being without work when they leave care presents a very grim picture. In a general discussion with the Principal Careers Officer he suggested they often do not have the skills to compete in the jobs market and partly for this reason are placed on 'sheltered' Youth Training Schemes (eg cleaning railway lines, cemeteries etc). They are, therefore, not attached to potential employers (eg Boots, British Aerospace) where they could obtain a permanent post at the end of the scheme."

31.27 The report concluded also that, on the basis of the answers to the questionnaire, most children in care were offered few opportunities to learn basic 'survival' skills. The authors added:

> "We fully appreciate the difficulties, such as Health and Safety Regulations, the management of group-living and some adolescents might even reject adult standards. However, we would suggest that if offered a tangible task related programme, agreed with the teenager, (and parents where appropriate) most would respond rather than face an insecure future and self-doubts about surviving alone."

31.28 Follow up action was confined to distribution of this report to the Area Officers and other middle management staff involved with child care, including the heads of community homes, in June 1985 but it does not appear to have resulted in the formulation of any programme to prepare children for their discharge from care before the Children Act 1989.

31.29 That Act imposed a wide range of duties on local authorities in relation to young people leaving care and led to comparatively swift developments in Clwyd when it came into force in October 1991. These included presentation of a report on "Leaving Care", which was placed before the Children and Families Sub-Committee on 12 February 1992; the subsequent attendance of staff from the Social Services Department at a Welsh Office two day workshop on the same subject; and the formation in Clwyd of a steering group and working parties to examine issues relating to preparation for independence, housing and accommodation, support (emotional, financial and practical) and after care. The result was the formulation of a leaving care strategy embodying 11 policy statements, which was approved by committee on 3 May 1995.

31.30 Whilst these developments were taking place, the Welsh Office carried out an inspection in November and December 1992 of outcomes for children leaving care in three Welsh counties, one of which was Clwyd. The report extended to 64 pages, with annexes, and the overall picture presented was dismal, although Clwyd did not compare unfavourably with the other two counties. Nevertheless, the situation in Clwyd was still much as it had been eight years earlier, during the period surveyed by Thomas and Davies. Of eight young persons seen (in the South Division), who had all left care in the preceding 14 months, only one was undergoing training and the other seven were unemployed; and all were dependent on state benefits and top-up payments made by the Social Services Department. In the view of the inspectors, some of the young people had been well prepared for leaving care but there was no consistency of approach. Most had found reasonable accommodation, though choice was limited, and social workers had been very active in assisting them to find accommodation: all were continuing to receive support and advice from social workers and others. The inspectors stressed the need for Clwyd to produce a statement on leaving care policy and the high priority that should be given to education, training and employment in all reviews of children looked after. They urged the authority also to explore further ways of diversifying accommodation available to young people leaving care, in order to enhance choice.

Conclusions

31.31 We have highlighted in this chapter specific shortcomings in the quality of care provided by Clwyd County Council for children in residential care within the county but the list is by no means exhaustive. They underline the reasons why so many of the children felt deserted and purposeless whilst they were in care and were unable to cope with their problems when they left care. Elsewhere in this report we have drawn attention to other failings, particularly in the educational provision in the community homes with education on the premises, such as Bryn Estyn[3]. The overall effect was to leave many of the former residents with a lifelong resentment that precious years had been wasted and that they had emerged from care as damaged (if not worse) as they had been when they were admitted.

---

[3] See paras 11.26 to 11.41.

31.32 It is likely that many of the failings of the Clwyd care system were common to other local authorities at least until the requirements of the Children Act 1989 began to concentrate minds. Some officers in Clwyd were, however, aware of the need for action well before the Act of 1989 and the major fault in failing to respond to it lay with senior officers, most of whom had inadequate skill in management and who made little effort to overcome their initial lack of expertise in child care matters. It was they who should have given the necessary strategic impetus and directions for reform.

The response of higher management to investigations, including the Jillings inquiry

Introduction

32.01 It is of some relevance to the relationship between Clwyd county councillors and the Social Services Department that from 1974 until 1989 no political party had overall control and that until 1987 committee and sub-committee chairmanships were shared between groups, in which the group of independents was prominent. Emlyn Evans, the first Director of Social Services, found that the members were supportive but, apart from a small number of prominent figures, they had neither the inclination nor the ability or experience to give a firm lead; and this last comment applied to successive chairmen of the Social Services Committee. Members saw the Director of Social Services rather than themselves as the employer and the staff as his employees.

32.02 This relationship changed from 1989 when the Labour group became a majority of the elected members. From 1987 Labour members had conducted themselves as the opposition to a coalition of the other groups and, when they became the majority, conduct of the Council's affairs changed quite quickly. In particular, two relevant leading figures emerged. The first, Councillor Dennis Parry, a former Mayor of Holywell and of Delyn Borough, who had been a county councillor from 1981, became chairman of the Labour group in 1990 and its leader in 1991, whereupon he became Leader of the Council, with his own office at Shire Hall. The second leading figure was Councillor Malcolm King, who had been employed by the Council as Centre Manager/Area Organiser of an Intermediate Treatment Centre at Wrexham from 1977 to 1982 and had then become manager of a community project for children and families in Wrexham. Councillor King was elected to the County Council in May 1989 and became Chairman of its Social Services Committee from January 1990, after serving as Vice-Chairman for six months. The result was that these two men played leading roles with John Jevons in all major decision making in relation to the County's social services from 1990 onwards until the County Council ceased to exist on 1 April 1996.

32.03 By an unhappy coincidence for them the Norris scandal surfaced in June 1990 and major decisions had to be made in the aftermath of the police investigations into Norris' activities at Cartrefle. Up to that point only the prosecution of Thomas and Gillison in 1986 and 1987[1] had raised any public concern about possible abuse in Clwyd community homes (as distinct from private homes): we are not aware of any general public reaction in 1977 to the prosecution of Leslie Wilson[2], perhaps because it concerned his obsessive relationship with one boy only. From June 1990, however, there was persistent public discussion of alleged abuse in the community homes. It is convenient,

---

[1] See para 2.07(5) and (6).
[2] See para 2.07(2).

therefore, for a number of reasons to consider separately in this chapter (a) the response to internal investigations before 1990 and (b) action taken by the Council after 1990 in the light of successive further disclosures.

The response to internal investigations before 1990

32.04 In this period there were five internal investigations into the affairs of community homes but three of these were into Park House. The latter took place in 1975, 1978 and 1988 and the other two were into Little Acton in 1978 and Chevet Hey in 1986. A sixth inquiry, at the behest of Mr Justice Mars-Jones in 1987, was into the circumstances in which Gillison and Thomas had become employed by the Social Services Department. All these investigations have been outlined earlier in this report but it is necessary to emphasise here the ineffective response of higher management to all of them and the failure to report them promptly and adequately to members of the Council.

32.05 All three reports about Park House were highly critical. The first investigation was triggered by the actions of a local resident, who drafted a letter for a girl resident to send to the News of the World, in which she complained about her treatment[3]. It was carried out by Gledwyn Jones and Geoffrey Wyatt, who dismissed the girl's complaints but disclosed a number of matters of concern, including the unfamiliarity of staff with the Community Homes Regulations, the need for advice on control and discipline from the Residential and Day Care Officer, the need for a less rigid regime and the failure of the Officer-in-Charge to provide access to case records to residential care staff. This report does not appear to have led directly to any general administrative action. Veronica Pares (RDCO) did produce an undated discussion document entitled "A Guide to Good Practice in Community Homes" for distribution to residential and field staff, although it stated that "the views expressed are personal and must not be quoted as Clwyd policy".

32.06 The investigation in 1980 was into complaints made by NALGO and staff at the home about various working practices and also about the food and clothing supplied for residents. It was conducted by Pares' co-inspector, Ivor Hughes, who reported that he had found "turmoil and unrest" and that the demands and inclinations of the staff were being met first rather than the needs of the residents (the cook, for example, worked only from 9 am to 1 pm so that she served the staff rather than the children and she was unwilling to change). The relationship between the Officer-in-Charge and her Deputy was so strained that the Inspector regarded it as beyond recall. Two out of four rota visit reports by councillors had been adverse and there were deficiencies in the background information about residents supplied by their social workers[4]. Probable consequences of the report were that both the Officer-in-Charge and her Deputy left Park House by the end of March 1981. The remarkable fact is, however, that the new Officer-in-Charge was not shown a copy of the report

[3] See para 17.45.
[4] For further details, see paras 17.50 to 17.54.

nor told of its contents. As far as we are aware, the report did not go beyond senior and middle management and it was not thought necessary or appropriate to put it before councillors.

32.07 The third Park House report in 1988 contained severe criticisms. A panel of three, comprising a senior officer of the National Children's Homes, the Assistant County Secretary of Clwyd and the Area Social Services Officer for Rhuddlan, had been commissioned to enquire into and consider all aspects of the planning and execution of a holiday at a Butlin's holiday camp, arranged for a group of residents, in the course of which a 13 years old girl resident had had sexual intercourse with a young man staying at the camp[5]. The report, however, went much wider than the panel's terms of reference and set out what we have described as "scathing criticism of the state of residential care in Clwyd at the time". Our summary of the report's findings and recommendations at paragraph 17.84 needs to be re-read to gather their full range and impact. Together, they pointed to serious weaknesses in the management of the residential child care service in Clwyd and underline the validity of many of the criticisms that we ourselves have made.

32.08 That report was sent to the Director of Social Services on 11 September 1989, but, as we have explained in paragraphs 17.85 and 17.86, its subsequent distribution was very limited. On the evidence before us only Geoffrey Wyatt, John Llewellyn Thomas and Michael Barnes saw it, apart from Gledwyn Jones. It was not shown to the Chief Executive (Mervyn Phillips) and it was not even discussed with the Deputy Director of Social Services (John Jevons), who probably did not see it until he became Director in April 1991. Michael Barnes drafted an immediate response to the report's criticisms but that document appears to have remained a draft only.

32.09 The most serious aspect of the matter is that the members of the Social Services Committee were not given any adequate account of the circumstances that had given rise to the inquiry or of the report's findings and recommendations. Gledwyn Jones' surprising and lame explanation for this was that he regarded the inquiry as an internal one and that he wanted to "move quickly on to doing something about the recommendations". We are unable to accept this as correct. The truth of the matter is that the report was largely suppressed because it revealed such widespread failings in the administration of the children's services over the preceding 15 years. We think that it is unlikely that he discussed the contents of the report with the Chairman of the Social Services Committee (certainly not with Malcolm King[6]) and his own report to the Social Services (Children and Family Services) Sub-Committee a year later was seriously misleading: it purported to be a response to national concerns and avoided mention of the serious weaknesses identified in Clwyd's own management[7].

---

[5] See para 17.81 for the full terms of reference, which were apparently drafted and agreed by the panel itself.
[6] See para 32.02.
[7] See para 17.86.

32.10 The report on the Butlins holiday and the response to it are of particular significance in the overall history because they illustrate so clearly the stifling climate that pervaded the Social Services Department, from the Director downwards, until 1990. Self-protection was the dominant thought in any response to criticism or complaint and this was reflected in the Department's management of the business of its committees and sub-committees. It appears that councillors were only permitted to know what it was comfortable for them to hear, even when a claim by an understandably disgruntled mother on behalf of her daughter was threatened.

32.11 The responses to other inquiries before 1990 were no more satisfactory. We have summarised in paragraph 12.07 the relevant comments made in 1978 by the investigating team into Little Acton on the administrative and organisational difficulties there (apart from their findings in relation to the individuals identified in paragraph 12.06 and Peter Bird). Like the Park House report ten years later the Little Acton Inquiry had drawn attention to weaknesses in the overall management systems in respect of children's residential services. Both Emlyn Evans (Director) and Gledwyn Jones (Deputy Director) were interviewed extensively by the team: we have seen copies of the records of the questions put to them and their answers, from which it is clear that they were fully apprised of the team's concerns. Nevertheless, we have not received evidence of any general managerial response to the report. It was not put before the Management Committee for the three Community Homes in Wrexham. The minutes of that committee's meeting on 8 September 1978 include the following note under the heading of matters arising from the minutes of the previous meeting:

> "Reference was made to the problems which had been encountered recently at Little Acton and concern was expressed at the limited amount of information which the members had received. In the event of similar difficulties being encountered elsewhere in the County it was emphasised that a greater degree of liaison between officers and members take place."

32.12 There is nothing in the committee's minutes for 1978 and 1979 to suggest that its members were ever told the contents of the Little Acton report, save for bare details of the disciplinary action subsequently taken. The attitude of the senior officers seems to have been that it was intended to close Little Acton as soon as practicable and that no wider remedial action was necessary.

32.13 The investigation into Chevet Hey in 1986 by Geoffrey Wyatt was of a much more limited kind. The immediate problems were opposition by the Officer-in-Charge, Ellis Edwards, and other members of the staff to the return of Paul Wilson after suspension and complaints by Wilson of difficulties in his relationship with Ellis Edwards[8]. However, Wyatt heard evidence from quite a wide range of officers and some residents who asked to see him; and he expressed some views in his report on matters outside the problems linked with Wilson and Ellis Edwards. Thus, he said in his conclusions:

---

[8] See para 14.20.

"I was dismayed at what I discovered during my investigations. Chevet Hey is a costly resource and could serve a very important role in the provision of services to children in care but for this to happen its functions and purposes need to be clearly defined and we must have the necessary professional and management skills to promote a sense of excellence about the service that is delivered.

. . . Some of the blame for the state of affairs at Chevet Hey must rest with the management at Shire Hall and the direction, guidance and support they have given to this. There has been far too much activity and not enough action. Senior management have failed to critically examine what was going on at Chevet Hey and did not adequately monitor the standards of service. The general impression that is given is that things were left to drift."

These were remarkable comments from the person with line management responsibility himself.

32.14 At both Little Acton in 1978 and Chevet Hey in 1986 the Officer charged with putting the community home right was Michael Barnes, but he did not receive a copy of either report. His evidence to us was that he was made aware of the serious concerns of the department about both. At Chevet Hey he was apprised of the overall situation, much of which was apparent, and told to turn the place round. He was asked also to comment on whether Chevet Hey should be closed.

32.15 In the same year as the Chevet Hey report Michael Barnes and Christopher Thomas[9] presented an eight page document, dated 22 August 1986 and entitled "Report on Child Care – Draft Policies", which was, in effect, an indictment of the existing state of residential child care in the county. In the following quotations the description "Areas" has been substituted for "Districts" to avoid confusion. The authors said, for example, in the Introduction:

"Even though a lot of progress has recently been made in developing a child care strategy and in planning policy, it is still generally true that aims and objectives of the Department (which are not always clear and lack specificity) are weakened by uncertain management. I am not quite sure why this should be but we have noticed that Areas, and indeed residential establishments, have been more isolated and therefore independent from Headquarters. As a result the role of HQ in setting policy and in maintaining practice has become so blurred to the point that some Areas (and some residential settings) find it easy 'to do their own thing' regardless of policy. We are not quite sure whether this cavalier attitude is the cause or the effect of uncertain management."

32.16 Barnes and Thomas went on to draw attention to what they described as "a marked withdrawal of community based support to residential establishments" evidenced by such developments as the withdrawal of direct psychiatric support, increasing resistance by head teachers to permitting

---

[9] As Acting Officers-in-Charge of Chevet Hey and Bersham Hall respectively.

children in care to receive mainstream schooling and the failure of social workers to work with community homes and to use them to best effect. They added:

> "On a more practical level, community involvement is affected by failure to promote home contact. Placements out of the area weaken community ties. Frequently disrupted placements have a similar effect. Many social workers find it too easy to discard their clients out of the area and to abandon them 'in care'."

32.17 Finally, the document contained many helpful comments on the importance of placement policies and care planning. The authors' views were stated most succinctly in the following passage:

> "The placement of children needs improving professionally and managerially. Care planning is haphazard, open to abuse and lacks authority. Admission into and discharge from care requires careful monitoring and a very tight control if abuses are not to occur. The present system is arbitrary, dependent more on personal goodwill than a good professional practice and often not in the child's best interest."

We are not aware, however, of any coherent steps to overhaul Clwyd's procedures and practice before preparations for implementation of the Children Act 1989 began.

32.18 The other pre-1990 inquiry that needs to be mentioned briefly was the P and Q Inquiry, as it was called, at the request of Mr Justice Mars-Jones in 1987, following the prosecution of Gillison and Thomas. The request by the judge was that an investigation should be carried out by Clwyd's Social Services Department into the circumstances in which those two defendants had come to occupy the positions they held. There followed the most extraordinary delay despite the fact that Michael Barnes, who had been present in court for most of the trial, wrote to the Director of Social Services about the matter on 28 January 1987, only 12 days after the judge had made his request.

32.19 In that letter Barnes said that he shared the judge's view that there should be a thorough investigation and continued:

> "This is, I feel, particularly important since it is clear to me that there are a number of parallels in this case with previous similar incidents notably those occurring at Box Lane [Little Acton] some years ago. In addition there have been other isolated incidents involving actual and suspected sexual abuse by staff members as well as some more recent evidence suggesting that two former members of Care Staff (who, I understand are the subjects of unrelated court proceedings) have also been involved in sex crimes against young children who are in loco parentis with the local authority.

> I am sure you will agree that we must do all we can to protect children, especially those in care from this vile abuse.

There are, I believe, a number of lessons to be learned from these events. It is of vital importance, especially in residential care where the capacity to damage is very much greater than in field work that we face up to the need to learn from past mistakes.

I very much hope that the Department will take up the judge's recommendation and will not only consider why the staff members concerned came to be employed by the Social Services Department, but will also examine why cases of this sort are becoming such a common feature of local residential provision. For my part I will gladly provide any information or service which may assist in this process."

32.20 When the report by the County Secretary, Roger Davies, was eventually presented to the Social Services (Child and Family Services) Sub-Committee nearly four years later, on 16 October 1990, it dealt with the judge's request in the narrowest possible way and absolved the Council from any blame. Moreover, it gave a misleading account of the availability of police checks on prospective employees and made no reference at all to the Department of Health Consultancy Service Index or to the Department of Education's List 99 (the erroneous impression was given that vetting procedures had not been available before 1986). Thus, there was no informed discussion by the Sub-Committee or by officers of the adequacy of Clwyd's recruitment and vetting procedures and no wider consideration was given to the matters that Barnes had specifically raised.

32.21 The way in which the request by a senior High Court judge, who was himself a native of Clwyd, was dealt with reflects very badly on the administration of Clwyd County Council at the time. It is yet another example of the lack of frankness of its senior staff and their unwillingness to probe deeply. We do not believe that Davies' report would have gone beyond him (it was not signed until 8 October 1990) but for the prosecution of Stephen Norris[10] and a journalist's comment then that the response to Mr Justice Mars-Jones' request had not been made known.

Later investigations

32.22 There were four more investigations into specific homes or persons between 1990 and 1995 in addition to the overall Jillings inquiry. These investigations were into Cartrefle[11] (1990 to 1992), Frederick Rutter[12] (1992), Cherry Hill[13] (1994) and Foster home E[14] (1995). Of the four, the most important and wide-ranging was the investigation into Cartrefle and we will deal with this and the Jillings inquiry in succeeding sections of this report.

---

[10] He was sentenced on 5 October 1990 - see para 2.07(7).
[11] See paras 15.42 to 15.50.
[12] See paras 26.13 and 26.14.
[13] See paras 16.06 to 16.19.
[14] See paras 27.43 to 27.52.

32.23 The circumstances giving rise to the other three investigations and the relevant findings and recommendations that were made have been sufficiently summarised already in the passages cited below. It should be noted, however, that there were unsatisfactory aspects of all three. Both the Rutter and the Cherry Hill investigations were limited. The Rutter report, apparently drafted by Geoffrey Wyatt, was presented to the Social Services (Children and Family Services) Sub-Committee on 21 October 1992 and one member commented upon its inadequacy. It was far from thorough and the investigation of the supervision and support of children boarded out or in lodgings was little more than cursory. The Cherry Hill investigation, on the other hand, appears to have been quite inconclusive, as we have indicated in Chapter 16. The documents before us point to organisational disarray in dealing with the problem and, most importantly, the danger that victims of sexual abuse might become offenders does not appear to have been addressed adequately. Finally, despite the serious concerns and criticisms expressed by the Review Sub-Committee that considered the placement of E1 in Foster home E, it was their view that managers within the East Division still believed that there had been "no significant errors and lessons to be learnt from the handling of this case".

The Cartrefle Inquiry, 1990 to 1992

32.24 The investigation into events at Cartrefle leading to the conviction of Stephen Norris took place in two phases. After the Director of Social Services had consulted the Welsh Office and the Area Child Protection Committee had considered the position three management case reviews were established by the Social Services, Education and Health authorities. These reviews were commissioned in November 1990, after the conviction of Norris and some five months after the abuse came to light, and they were completed by June 1991. Clwyd ACPC then appointed a panel of inquiry comprising five members to provide an overview of the case reviews[15]. The panel's report was delivered in February 1992 and an edited version of its conclusions was ultimately presented to the Social Services Committee.

32.25 The procedure that Clwyd adopted was an attempt to follow the guidance on inter-agency working given in the Department of Health and Welsh Office document "Working Together"[16], at what was then Part Nine[17]. In our opinion, however, it was an error to try to adapt that guidance to circumstances to which it was not intended to apply. The problems that had arisen at Cartrefle were such that a quick and wide investigation within the Social Services Department was called for, embracing the question whether similar problems had arisen or were likely to arise in other community homes and the remedial action that was necessary. As it was, the process was set in train much later than it should have been and the unwieldy involvement of other agencies, followed by an overview, led to further unnecessary delay: it took 15 months to the presentation of the panel's report whereas Working Together envisages action within weeks of discovery of the problems that trigger the review.

---

[15] See paras 15.42 and 15.43 for further details.
[16] 1988, HMSO.
[17] Now Part Eight.

32.26 The key management review of social services was carried out by John Banham, a retired senior officer of Cheshire Social Services Department, who interviewed 60 members of staff. His report was highly commended by the panel and we have summarised some of his conclusions and those of the panel at paragraphs 15.44 to 15.49 of this report. They were, however, highly critical of the review or inquiry procedure adopted by Clwyd, in particular of the delay in putting the arrangements in hand, and commented that it had soon become apparent to them that the key focus of their own review would not be on inter-agency issues.

32.27 Before leaving this subject it is necessary to note that many of the criticisms by the panel and Banham were directed to the same matters that had been the subject of criticism four years earlier in the report on the Butlin's holiday from Park House and in the Little Acton report of 1978. They were highly critical of the lack of leadership and direction shown by senior management in Clwyd and its lack of awareness of the seriousness of its responsibility to safeguard and promote the welfare of the child: in their view, a change of style and culture was needed to develop an ethos which put the interests of the service user first. They criticised also aspects of the new divisional structure, whilst supporting it in principle. Amongst their criticisms were that the role of Divisional Child Care Managers needed to be defined and that there was a need for co-ordinated, consistent and integrated managerial arrangements across the Social Services Department. They recommended also the appointment of a new headquarters Officer-in-Charge of Child Care Services, equivalent in rank or senior to Divisional Directors, because they did not regard the newly created post of Principal Officer as sufficiently senior. Overall, the weakness of management arrangements was seen as a significant contributory factor to both the poor quality of care at Cartrefle and the failure to protect children living there from abuse.

32.28 Legal and administrative problems were by no means over when the panel presented its report in February 1992. It was not until 27 October 1992 that a report of the conclusions of the inquiry panel together with the response of the Director of Social Services were put before the Social Services Committee. In the meantime there had been discussions with the Council's insurers and the County Solicitor had been heavily involved in considering whether and, if so, to what extent the report could be published. By 1992 the major police investigation into allegations of abuse in many North Wales children's homes was fully under way and was thought to be giving rise to potential claims against the Council so that the County Solicitor was working closely with solicitors appointed by the insurers in preparation of the Council's defence.

32.29 The advice tendered by the County Solicitor to the Director of Social Services was that the panel's report was privileged from disclosure in legal proceedings: the Council's insurers were "most anxious therefore, that the report should remain confidential and that any publication, however limited, should be made on the basis that such publication (was) not to be construed as any waiver of public interest immunity in respect of either the document or any documents referred to in the publication". Discussions had taken place also with representatives of the Crown Prosecution Service, who had said that the report must not be published because its publication might prejudice forthcoming or contemplated criminal proceedings and would constitute contempt.

32.30 These difficulties were resolved by an agreement with the insurers that there should be limited publication of conclusions and recommendations extracted from the report. Discussion by members of the council was, however, to be confined to "the general principles disclosed" and "must not be related to individual circumstances which (might) be the subject of criminal proceedings or give rise to potential claims against the Council".

32.31 It is not surprising in these circumstances that the Social Services Committee (and the Area Child Protection Committee) received a much censored and anodyne version of the panel's findings and recommendations in preparation for its meeting on 27 October 1992, eight months after the report itself had been presented. Summarised recommendations were set out in one column and against them, in a parallel column, were set reassuring comments by the Director of Social Services (John Jevons) in very general terms about programmes for such matters as management development and training, the preparation of care plans and improvements in the process and practice of reviews. The recommendation that there should be a senior post at Assistant Director level or equivalent for child care services within headquarters was, however, rejected by the Director on the ground that it reflected "a centralist approach directly contrary to the aims of the new department structure (which the Panel supports)".

32.32 It appears that the summary of the Panel's conclusions and recommendations and the Director's responses were also put before a meeting of the county's community homes managers on 3 November 1992 (not 26 October 1992 as stated in the first draft of the minutes); and they were highly critical of the Director's responses. Michael Nelson, for example, commented that, on reading the Director's answers, he had queried whether they worked for the same organisation: staff felt that recent progress had been overstated, for example, on strategy, staff development and care planning.

32.33 To this Michael Barnes made the revealing reply that:

> "The Director had to take a global view and that comments meant for a wider audience would not appeal to everyone. Sometimes a balance had to be struck between the need to give a factual account (warts and all) and the need to reassure staff and talk up the service."

Barnes said he was concerned that a totally negative message was not in staff/ children's best interest. He felt that, if the service was to survive, it was important "to highlight glimmers of hope in what otherwise might seem to be a mass of darkness".

32.34 This meeting helped to emphasise the need for a positive response to the Cartrefle report. On 30 November 1992 the Social Services Management Team commissioned the Principal Officer Children (Jackie Thomas), with assistance from others, to produce by 26 February 1993 an implementation plan in relation to the panel's recommendations, following upon an audit of progress by each Division. According to Jevons, he was unhappy about the quality of Jackie Thomas' response, which disclosed considerable disarray. His evidence to the Tribunal was that a strategy had been formulated by October 1992 but that it was not at that time to be found in a single document. On 30 March 1993 a strategy paper entitled "A Framework for the Development of Services to Children and Families" was approved in committee and it was published the following month. Two years later final responses to the detailed recommendations of the Cartrefle panel were also circulated.

The Jillings inquiry and the Insurers' involvement

32.35　In paragraphs 2.36 and 2.37 of this report we have given a brief account of the background to this Inquiry, which was set in train when the main part of the major police investigation had been completed. The proposal to set it up was first discussed by the Leader of the Council (Dennis Parry) and the Chairman of the Social Services Committee (Malcolm King) with the Chief Executive (by then, Roger Davies), the Director of Social Services (John Jevons) and the County Solicitor (Andrew Loveridge); and it was approved by the Social Services Committee on 12 January 1994. The Council's insurers were not consulted about the proposal.

32.36　The stated reason for the inquiry was that the police investigations had been protracted and that considerable further time was likely to elapse before any public inquiry could start: it was felt that the Council needed to review the past more quickly than a public inquiry could in order to learn whether anything else needed to be done by the Council to ensure the proper care and protection of children. The panel of inquiry was instructed initially to conduct "an internal investigation for the County Council into the management of its Social Services child care services from 1974 to date with particular reference to those concerns which prompted the investigation by the North Wales Police". It was anticipated that the panel would complete its work by August 1994; its report would be submitted to Loveridge and Jevons and it was intended then to put it before the Council's Policy, Finance and Resources Committee.

32.37　John Jillings, a retired Director of Social Services for Derbyshire and former President of the Association of Directors of Social Services, agreed to act as chairman of the Panel of inquiry. The other two members were Gerrilyn Smith, a clinical psychologist, and Jane Tunstill, a social work academic, who was subsequently appointed Professor of Social Work at the University of Keele. Draft terms of reference were agreed with the County Council before the panel began its work in March 1994 and finalised in November 1994[18]. The investigation lasted 16 months longer than had been originally envisaged and the Panel's report was completed in February 1996.

32.38　In the course of its investigation the Panel interviewed a cross section of staff and former staff of the County Council and some other agencies with child protection responsibilities in Wales. They interviewed also some former

---

[18] See para 2.02.

residents of Clwyd community homes and foster homes: and they saw documents relating to events of the past 20 years. Finally, the Panel also visited a number of homes in Clwyd.

32.39 The Jillings report, covering the period from 1974 to 1995, ran to 254 pages (excluding six appendices). Its central core was a discussion of, and commentary upon, the investigations and reviews to which we have referred in this chapter coupled with an account of events at Bryn Estyn, including the earlier inquiry in 1971 into the conduct of the Principal at that time, David Ursell[19]. Other sections dealt with mainly administrative and organisational matters under the headings Organisational Overview, Policy and Practice at Divisional Level and Staff Issues; but there were sections also on specific issues for children and young people as service users and additional external influences on child protection.

32.40 This Tribunal decided at an early stage that the Jillings report should not be admitted in evidence before us. Major reasons for this decision were that the report consisted substantially of expressions of opinion on matters which we ourselves were required to investigate afresh and to reach our own conclusions and that it had been presented on 22 February 1996, less than two months before the demise of Clwyd County Council and too late for any response by that authority in terms of positive action. In saying that we do not intend any criticism of the report itself or of the time taken by the Panel to investigate and to formulate its report. Other important reasons for our decision were that, apart from expressions of the Panel's opinions, the contents of the report were largely hearsay in relation to the issues that we had to decide, on which we were to receive direct evidence. Moreover, the form of the report was such that it could not helpfully be used in cross-examination of individual witnesses.

32.41 The members of the Tribunal were, however, supplied with copies of the Jillings report to enable us to consider the action taken in respect of it after it had been presented to the Director of Social Services and the County Solicitor. It was helpful also to Counsel to the Tribunal in advising as to the evidence that ought to be placed before us.

32.42 For reasons similar to those set out in paragraph 32.40 we did not consider that it would be appropriate for John Jillings or the other members of the Panel to be called to give evidence before us.

32.43 Following the receipt of the Jillings report on 22 February 1996 by Andrew Loveridge, it was given very limited circulation. It was seen by the senior officials involved and by the Leader of the Council, who consulted other leading members of the Council nominated by their respective groups. According to Loveridge, "The initial reaction of the Council was one of amazement (at) the number of inaccuracies contained therein and the style and content of the Report". It appears that an effort was made to establish a list of the alleged factual inaccuracies with a view to concurrent publication with the Report and on 7 March 1996 instructions were sent to Leading and Junior Counsel to advise on the question of publication. Supplementary instructions

---

[19] See para 7.03.

were sent to them shortly afterwards in the light of representations by the North Wales Police and by the Council's insurers and by 20 March 1996 Loveridge had received a Preliminary Joint Opinion, a Joint Opinion and a Supplementary Joint Opinion from Counsel.

32.44 Counsel instructed were the Honourable Michael Beloff QC and Paul Stinchcombe and they had to consider three main primary problems, namely:

(1) whether publication of the report might avoid Clwyd's insurance policy, bearing in mind the large number of objections raised by the insurers to any publicity attaching to the report;

(2) the potential liability of Clwyd for publication of any defamatory comments contained within the report; and

(3) whether there was any risk to the proper administration of criminal justice through the impact upon any pending trials of publication of the report.

32.45 In relation to the first problem the view of Counsel was that (a) any formal adoption or approval of the report by Clwyd could be taken as an admission of liability in respect of any cases considered in it which might become the subject of claims by victims of child abuse when in Clwyd's care and (b) any publication of the report so as to bring into the public domain matters which would otherwise be confidential, privileged or protected by public interest immunity, could amount to a waiver of rights to assert the same. In either event there would be a grave risk that Clwyd would have acted in breach of an express condition of its insurance policy (and of a fundamental term), disentitling it from protection in respect of the claims referred to. Counsel advised also that publication to the wider public of even an abridged version of the report would be dangerous.

32.46 On the second problem, Counsel advised that:

(a) there was insufficient reciprocity of duty and interest between Clwyd and the public at large to enable the Council to argue that qualified privilege attached to the report if published at large;

(b) if the Court were to rule that disclosure to members did involve further publication rather than the mere reception of the report by those who had commissioned it, there was a legitimate interest in members in receiving it, even though the Council was about to dissolve, and that the Council could, therefore, invoke the defence of qualified privilege to any claim of libel in respect of that limited publication.

32.47 In the light of these conclusions Counsel advised that the report should only be made available to members under strictly controlled conditions, observing safeguards suggested by the Council's insurers. In short, each page of the report was to be numbered individually; the report was not to be circulated to members but elected members were to be invited to read it in an appropriate senior officer's room; and, when the report was received by the Policy, Finance and Resources Committee, it was to be dealt with under part 2 of the agenda so that it would be received in private in the absence of the press and public. Members of the Committee were to be instructed also not to discuss the report or its contents with members of the public, particularly representatives of media. On this basis Counsel advised also that there would not be any risk that the good administration of criminal justice would be prejudiced by the actions of Clwyd.

32.48 The Supplementary Advice of Counsel (identified as Joint Opinion 2) dealt with such matters as the retrieval of copies of the report that had already been distributed (all were to be returned) and the future custody of all copies, subject to the transfer provisions governing property on the demise of Clwyd County Council. Counsel advised that the report could be made available to members within the Council Chamber at the meeting at which it was discussed provided that all copies were returned at the conclusion of the meeting; and they dealt also with the liability of any member to surcharge, if he/she took any action contrary to the express instructions given that exposed Clwyd to liability.

32.49 The advice of Counsel was accepted and the Policy, Finance and Resources Committee duly received the report at its meeting on 22 March 1996, after earlier discussions between the leading members referred to earlier. The committee dealt with the matter by simply noting the report and agreeing to refer it to the Secretary of State for Wales to assist him in considering whether or not a public inquiry should be instituted. The procedure adopted is not clear but the evidence is that neither members of the committee nor other members of the council read the report. It may have been available in an office for them to read if they wished to do so. The decisions of the committee were approved by the Council at its last meeting on 26 March 1996.

32.50 The Welsh Office also had sought advice about the feasibility of publishing the Jillings Report and had consulted Treasury Counsel. We have not seen any written opinion given by the latter but in a letter to Loveridge (as Director of Legal and Administration for Flintshire County Council, the designated successor authority to Clwyd in respect of insurance matters), dated 14 May 1996, the Welsh Office did state:

> "It is not normal practice for Treasury Counsel's advice to be made available or divulged to third parties in the way that you have suggested. However, I can advise you that while in our discussions with Counsel he has generally endorsed Mr Beloff's opinion on this matter he has indicated that it should be possible to publish an edited version of the Report's recommendations. This could be accompanied by some newly-drafted contextual passages which would explain the basis on which the recommendations are made."

32.51 At this time the Welsh Office was encouraging the successor authorities to produce an edited version of the Jillings recommendations but was unwilling to publish such a document itself. The successor authorities did not, at first, reject the idea of publication and discussed with Jillings the possibility of preparing a "safe" version but they concluded by 6 June 1996 that they could not publish the report and the Secretary of State was so informed. The problem then receded, however, with the Prime Minister's preliminary announcement on 13 June 1996 of the Secretary of State's intention to institute a public inquiry.

32.52 In the months following the presentation of the Jillings report to Clwyd County Council, it was almost inevitable that there would be allegations of a "cover up" by Clwyd and (less forcefully) criticism of the Welsh Office and the successor authorities for failing to take on the burden of publishing the report after 31 March 1996. We do not accept, however, that these allegations and criticisms were justified. In our judgment leading members and senior officers of Clwyd County Council were bound, in the exercise of reasonable prudence, to accept the authoritative legal advice that they received very promptly and to act accordingly in the short space of time left to them. The Welsh Office was not under any duty to publish the report and the successor authorities were still grappling with the dubious possibility of preparing a "safe" version when the problem ceased to be of major importance with the announcement of this Tribunal of Inquiry.

32.53 The other target of criticism in this context has been the conduct of the insurers, who were represented by Counsel before this Tribunal. The nature of the criticism was that they had exceeded their proper role in demanding that neither the Cartrefle report nor the Jillings report should be made public. Underlying this criticism was the suggestion that they had improperly prevented elected councillors and local government officers from discharging properly their duty to electors in matters that had given rise to widespread concern.

32.54 The insurers waived their privilege in respect of their correspondence and discussions with Clwyd County Council about all relevant matters in relation to publication of the Cartrefle and Jillings reports and the conduct of the Jillings inquiry in order that the Tribunal should have a full picture. We have also been given full information (including documents) about the representations made by the Crown Prosecution Service and the North Wales Police. There is no dispute, therefore, about the relevant facts and it has been unnecessary for the insurers or the Crown Prosecution Service to give oral evidence to us.

32.55 It will be helpful to explain that Clwyd County Council's insurers were Municipal Mutual Insurance Ltd (MMI) until 1 April 1993. That company was formed in 1903 by a group of local authorities as a mutual company. It had no share capital and was limited by guarantee; its policy holders were mainly local authorities, who were its members. In 1990, having expanded and diversified, MMI suffered heavy losses with the ultimate result that it ceased to write new business or renew existing policies from the end of September 1992. On 9 March 1993 Zurich Insurance Company (Zurich) bought the right to seek renewal of most of MMI's insurance business, and thereafter Zurich operated that part of its business under the name Zurich Municipal (ZM).

32.56 Zurich did not assume any liability to creditors of MMI but there was a claims handling agreement under which Zurich provided MMI with claims processing and financial administration services in respect of most of the insurance business written by MMI prior to 30 September 1992. Thus, ZM processes, investigates and settles, on MMI's behalf, claims arising under former MMI policies; but the agreement provides for referral to MMI when, for example, claims based on sexual allegations are received. An experienced claims manager was transferred with other employees of MMI to ZM and he continued to deal with claims against MMI, acting on the advice of a solicitor in private practice with long experience of MMI's local authority business and who advised local authorities on a wide range of matters, not limited to the conduct of litigation in respect of which they were entitled to an indemnity from MMI or subsequently ZM.

32.57 In view of the way in which matters developed and in the light of our terms of reference, it is unnecessary to record here the details of the discussions and correspondence that took place between 1992 and 1996, which we have studied. One reason for this is that the Crown Prosecution Service vetoed, in effect, publication of the Cartrefle report in 1992 because the major police investigation, involving further allegations against Stephen Norris amongst others, was still being pursued. In our judgment that action by the Crown Prosecution Service, on the basis that contemplated criminal proceedings might be prejudiced, was fully justified and it was not until November 1993 that Norris was sentenced for his earlier offences at Bryn Estyn. We accept also that the insurers were prepared in 1992 (but for the CPS veto) to countenance presentation of the Cartrefle report to an appropriate committee, provided that its confidentiality to the relevant elected members and officers of the Council was preserved. A major concern of the insurers at that stage was that the Council should not be seen to waive public interest immunity that would otherwise attach to the report, or to important parts of it, and to many background documents.

32.58 The issues that arose in relation to publication of the Jillings report in 1996 were more complex but essentially similar to those that arose in 1992 in respect of the Cartrefle report. There was no statutory protection afforded to the Council in libel proceedings other than that provided by the Defamation Act 1952. Moreover, the form of the report was such that it contained a great deal of defamatory material based on hearsay and dealt with some matters that were not within the inquiry's terms of reference. In relation to the insurers' contractual position, apart from the Council's potential liability for defamation, there were further difficulties because of the wish of some councillors to make statements intended to appease public concern but which might be construed as admissions of liability or at least as encouraging further financial claims against the Council. Any public discussion by the Council was likely to give added fuel to potential claimants and to undermine to some extent arguments available to the Council on questions of privilege from disclosure.

32.59 An important distinction between the position in 1996 and that in 1992 was that neither the Crown Prosecution Service nor the North Wales Police objected to publication of the Jillings report on the ground that it might prejudice current or potential criminal proceedings. However, the Chief Constable, in a letter to Loveridge dated 12 March 1996, made substantial criticisms of factual statements in the report and comments in it about the level of co-operation by the police with the Panel; and he referred also to potential liability for defamation. In the first of his concluding paragraphs he said:

"I hope that the issues I have raised are sufficient in themselves to cause the County Council to reflect over the weight they place on some of the unsupported assertions made in the report, and to think very carefully over the potentially actionable consequences of publishing the report as it currently stands."

32.60 Looking at the part played by the insurers' representatives in this history as a whole, we accept that they acted throughout with the honourable intention of preventing Clwyd County Council, its officers and members from acting in such a way that the insurers would be compelled to repudiate liability for claims by victims of abuse or by persons who alleged that they had been libelled by either report. The insurers' representatives adopted an interventionist role with this objective so that Clwyd knew where it stood in the matter; and, in our judgment, that was strongly preferable to a passive role that might well have led to repudiation, with grave consequences for the Council and many others. In his submissions to the Tribunal Counsel for the insurers said that, in hindsight, they accept that, at times, the tone of the correspondence on their behalf was intemperate and went too far in the demands made of the Council. They accept also that their approach to the dilemma of striking a balance between the duty of a council to seek the truth and identify reforms on one hand and its duty to protect its financial interests on the other may be open to criticism. However, they have been in discussion with the Association of British Insurers and with the Local Government Association and its predecessor with the object of producing guidelines for authorities on the subject of inquiries where insurers may be involved.

32.61 For our part we do not think that it would be appropriate on the evidence before us to express any stronger criticism of the insurers' conduct in this matter than that indicated in the preceding paragraph. The legal and contractual issues that arise in relation to the conduct of inquiries of the kind that we have discussed and the publication of reports on them are matters of public concern that deserve further consideration at a high level. Those issues themselves involve different specialist questions in tort and contract. Firstly, in relation to the law of defamation, the following questions arise:

(1) Should there not be a general statutory provision enabling local authorities to institute inquiries into matters of wide public concern and to publish the reports of such inquiries to the public at large with the protection of qualified privilege, whether or not the public has a sufficient interest in receiving the report within the terms of present legislation?

(2) If not, should not the limits of legitimate publication of such reports be defined in order to safeguard the position of elected members and officers in discharging their public duty?

(3) If the issues are not considered suitable for legislation, should there not be central government guidance to local authorities on them, including guidance as to the format of inquiries and the content of reports?

(4) Is similar legislation or guidance desirable for other public authorities that may need to institute inquiries into matters of wide concern?

We consider that the problems underlying these issues are likely to recur quite frequently and that they are suitable for consideration by the Law Commission.

32.62 The contractual issues that arise are less suitable for legislation because insurers cannot be compelled to underwrite liabilities and will make their own assessments of risk when they do agree to provide cover. It is highly desirable, however, that there should be an agreed code of practice to guide local authorities in their response to situations of the kind that arose in Clwyd. The Jillings experience raised questions, amongst many others, about:

(1) The decision to institute an inquiry.

(2) The advertising of requests for witnesses to come forward to give evidence.

(3) Disclosure by the local authority of documents to assist the inquiry.

(4) Evidence to the inquiry by Council staff, particularly senior officers.

(5) References in the course of the inquiry and in any report to matters, including documents, which might be the subject of claims of privilege in subsequent litigation.

(6) The extent of circulation of any report and permissible comment by councillors and officers upon it.

These are all matters of pressing concern on which agreement should be sought and which may require intervention by central government to facilitate it.

32.63 In the context of these recommendations we draw attention to the report entitled "Ad Hoc Inquiries in Local Government" by a committee presided over by Sir Alan Marre KCB, which was commissioned by the Society of Local Authority Chief Executives and the Royal Institute of Public Administration and published in February 1978. Its recommendations included the suggestion that local authorities should, by a change in the law, be given the power to set up formal inquiries, empowered to summon witnesses, require the production of documents and take evidence on oath[20]. The committee proposed also that a code of practice and procedural rules to govern such inquiries would be necessary to ensure that they were both effective and fair[21]. In response to this report the Local Authorities Associations published in 1980 their own comments on the Marre committee's proposals. That response indicated that the Associations had decided not to pursue a request for statutory powers to

---

[20] See paras 4.13 and 4.14 of the report.
[21] Ibid, see para 4.15 and the following paragraphs of the same chapter.

hold inquiries at that stage; but they endorsed the call for a code of practice and procedural rules, putting forward their own suggested versions of such a code and rules[22]. In our judgment, however, the Associations' proposals on the reporting of inquiries[23] did not deal satisfactorily with the problems that subsequently arose in relation to the Jillings report and the time has come for further consideration to be given to those problems on the lines that we have suggested.

[22] See paras 12 to 16 and the Appendix to the report.
[23] Ibid, see the Appendix, paras 2.13 to 2.17.

PART VII

ALLEGED ABUSE OF CHILDREN IN CARE IN LOCAL AUTHORITY HOMES IN GWYNEDD BETWEEN 1974 AND 1996

Tŷ'r Felin, 1974 to 1995

Introduction

33.01 Tŷ'r Felin was a local authority community home in a large council estate on the northern outskirts of Bangor known as Maesgeirchen. The projected home was identified as Lon-y-Felin in the 1971 Regional Plan for Wales: it was then planned as an observation and assessment centre and was to be built, at a cost of £48,000, in time for occupation by the end of 1973. Up to 12 children were to be accommodated at a time, five for assessment and seven for short stays, and the facility was to be available for the whole of Gwynedd, as the county area became in April 1974. The categories of children to be received were those needing to be detained in secure or semi-secure accommodation but no special facilities of this kind appear to have been either planned or provided.

33.02 In the 1979 version of the Regional Plan Tŷ'r Felin was shown as one of the "other homes" but it was still to provide six places for local assessment, the other six being residential places. It was a community home for both boys and girls and the age span was said to be three to 17 years. Education was provided on the premises in one classroom and there was one teacher on the staff. The services of a psychiatrist and a psychologist were said to be available on request.

33.03 Tŷ'r Felin was a long two storey building designed to resemble, as far as possible, a small terrace of houses in the estate but the open plan front garden running the length of the home and the prominent front door made it an obvious institution. At the rear was a large grassed area forming the back garden, which was fenced. The design incorporated a separate living unit at each end, with its own outside entrance. One of these units was used by a staff member and the other could be used from time to time as an independent unit for a resident as preparation for discharge from care. The top floor comprised two identical landings, one used for boys and the other for girls. Most of the bedrooms were single but each landing had a double room.

33.04 Tŷ'r Felin remained open as a community home from about January 1974 until the autumn of 1995. It was demolished in March 1997 and we were able to inspect it as demolition began.

33.05 Most of the evidence that we heard about it related to the period between 1 January 1978 and 23 May 1990, when the Officer-in-Charge was **(Joseph) Nefyn Dodd**[1]. Throughout this period his wife, **June Dodd**, whom he married in 1961, was also employed at Tŷ'r Felin. She had worked part time as an assistant domestic supervisor at Bersham Hall between 1972 and 1977. After three months or so as a typist at Tŷ'r Felin she became a temporary assistant housemother there in April 1978, before being appointed a resident housemother from 22 August 1978. She undertook in-service training almost

---

[1] See paras 10.148 to 10.150, 13.21 and 13.22 for his earlier history at Bryn Estyn and Bersham Hall.

immediately at Gwynedd Technical College and then at Cartrefle College, Wrexham, from September 1979, obtaining the Certificate in Social Service at the end of the year's course. In due course she progressed to Senior RCCO from 1 August 1982, initially in a temporary capacity, and until 1988 she and her husband lived in a flat forming part of Tŷ'r Felin with their daughter, born in 1970.

33.06 June Dodd became Acting Officer-in-Charge on 1 December 1989 when her husband became ill and she succeeded him in a permanent capacity on his retirement from 1 September 1990. She herself then took early retirement on 31 December 1992. During the later part of the Dodds' regime, that is, from 1988, they lived in a house at Talybont, which they had acquired in 1979 and used initially at weekends and during holidays only.

33.07 The care staff establishment at Tŷ'r Felin consisted of the Officer-in-Charge, the Deputy and four houseparents at the time when June Dodd was appointed as a resident houseparent. In addition there were a full time teacher (provided by Gwynedd Education Department), two domestic staff, a cook and a gardener/handyman. When June Dodd became a temporary Senior RCCO in August 1982 she appears to have become effectively Deputy Officer-in-Charge because she was required by the terms on which she was appointed to deputise for the Officer-in-Charge in his absence. The post of Deputy Officer-in-Charge had been deleted at that time for community homes in Gwynedd and the establishment at Tŷ'r Felin provided for two Senior RCCOs under the Officer-in-Charge.

33.08 The extent to which the Dodds have dominated the evidence that we have heard about Tŷ'r Felin may be judged from the fact that, of the 84 former residents of the community home known to have complained of abuse there, 65 complained of abuse by one or both of the Dodds. In all, we heard oral evidence from 15 former residents and we received in evidence the written statements of 12 others; of these 27 witnesses, only three did not complain about one or both Dodds and one of these three left Tŷ'r Felin a year before the Dodds arrived there.

The pre-Dodd history (1974 to 1977)

33.09 The first Officer-in-Charge was **Haydn Jones** but we know little about him and have not been able to see any file relating to him. The complainant witness who left before the Dodds arrived, X, told us in her oral evidence that during her first period at Tŷ'r Felin, of just over four months ending in April 1976, the atmosphere was friendly and it was better than being at home. When she returned for three months from August to November 1976, however, Tŷ'r Felin was "dreadful". The girls were rougher and she was regularly beaten up by older girls, which the staff did not prevent. X complained also of being assaulted more than once by Haydn Jones and referred to him as a "horrible man". As for the education at Tŷ'r Felin, she described the classroom as a zoo; there were no books and the woman teacher had to concentrate on the younger children.

33.10 It is not appropriate to recount X's evidence in greater detail because we were not able to trace Haydn Jones and have not been able to hear or see his account of his period at Tŷ'r Felin. The complaints made against him by X are the only ones of which we are aware. The only other former resident who gave oral evidence about this period was at Tŷ'r Felin from October 1976 to February 1977 (coinciding in part with X) and he said that he had no problems there: like X during her first stay, he was happier than he had been at home.

33.11 It was during this early period that **Alison Taylor** arrived at Tŷ'r Felin, following her appointment as Deputy Officer-in-Charge with effect from 6 September 1976[2]. She was then aged 32 years, had undergone university training in various subjects during the 1960s, and had married in 1974, giving birth to a son in April 1976. After a period in 1969/1970 obtaining experience at Gwynfa Residential Clinic as a volunteer she had undertaken industrial training preparatory to taking up a post as an industrial therapist at a North Wales hospital. From 1973, she had been employed successively as Deputy Officer-in-Charge of a psychiatric rehabilitation unit in Stockport, as an occupational therapist/social worker in Wrexham and then as Deputy Warden of a large probation hostel in Sheffield. Whilst at Stockport she had undergone in-service training and she later obtained a Diploma in Social Work and the CQSW after a two year course at Cartrefle College, Wrexham, ending in July 1982.

33.12 Alison Taylor was at Tŷ'r Felin during an unsettled period and she remained there only until July 1980. About three months after her arrival Haydn Jones went off sick, never to return, and Taylor became Acting Officer-in-Charge for a year until Nefyn Dodd took up his appointment on 1 January 1978. Taylor then reverted to Deputy for two and a half years until she went to work briefly at the Area Office as a prelude to her CQSW course. On completing that course she was appointed as Officer-in-Charge of Tŷ Newydd from 16 August 1982[3].

33.13 According to Taylor, there was no Deputy whilst she was Acting Officer-in-Charge of Tŷ'r Felin but it appears that **David Bayley Hughes** was regarded as Temporary Deputy during that period and later when Taylor was off sick. He had arrived at Tŷ'r Felin on 18 May 1976 as an assistant houseparent on transfer from Eryl Wen Children's Home, Llandudno[4], on the latter's closure. Hughes was then 26 years old and did not have any professional qualification: he had failed to qualify as a teacher and had then worked as a shop manager before becoming a houseparent at a former approved school in Kent from 1 June 1975 for six months before he took up his post at Eryl Wen. Hughes remained at Tŷ'r Felin until July 1978, when he too went to the Area Office for two months before starting the CQSW course at Cartrefle College. On completion of that two year course, he served at Tŷ Newydd and then Pant yr Eithin[5] (at Harlech) before becoming Officer-in-Charge of Y Gwyngyll[6] from 14 September 1981.

[2] See Chapter 2 from para 2.08 for an account of her part in the background history to this inquiry.
[3] See Chapter 34.
[4] See para 5.02(3).
[5] See para 5.07(8).
[6] See Chapter 35.

33.14 As far as we are aware, there was only one allegation of abuse made by a resident of Tŷ'r Felin during the period when Taylor was Acting Officer-in-Charge. The allegation was made in March 1977 by a highly disturbed girl, who had been transferred from Tŷ'r Felin to Silverbrook Treatment Centre at Pontypridd, Mid Glamorgan the previous month. She alleged that she had had sexual intercourse with Hughes two or three times whilst she had been resident at Tŷ'r Felin and had become pregnant as a result. It appeared, however, that she had made similar allegations against a different person earlier. The matter was investigated by the Deputy Director of Social Services (David Alan Parry) and he was "completely satisfied that the relationship between (Hughes) and (the girl) was completely innocent in all respects and that the allegations made were completely unfounded". Mid Glamorgan and Hughes were so informed and no further action was deemed to be necessary. We have seen the background documentation and do not criticise this decision.

33.15 Whilst she was Acting Officer-in-Charge Taylor lived on the premises with her husband, son and adopted daughter. She told us that Tŷ'r Felin was geared then to only short term stays by residents of eight to 12 weeks and that 12 weeks was intended to be the maximum period for assessment. The home received also many emergency placements and some children on remand. Supply teachers were provided by the Education Department and the services of an educational psychologist were available. There was always a battle to obtain records of the children: the social worker involved would provide a summary of a child's history but, in respect of non-emergency placements, the Area Office would decide what documents the home should receive. Corporal punishment was permitted in Gwynedd, at the discretion of the Officer-in-Charge, until it was prohibited by the County Council on 8 February 1983[7], and she was told by Parry that a cane should be on display; but she never used the cane or permitted it to be used. Normal punishments were restitution by deductions from pocket money and deprival of outings. On one or two occasions she ordered residents to wear pyjamas as a punishment but then regarded it as futile and she disapproved of stopping home leave.

33.16 Alison Taylor applied for the post of Third-in-Charge at Silverbrook[8] in Mid Glamorgan in the summer of 1977. In the reference that he provided for her[9], Parry said that she had coped with her responsibilities despite being under considerable pressure for several months on her arrival at Tŷ'r Felin because of difficulties that had developed there, but he continued:

> "It is my view that she is a person unsuited to the post which she currently occupies. She is not happy working with the total responsibility of the establishment devolving upon her and her satisfactions from involvement with administrative and policy matters conflicts noticeably with her deeper interest in more direct contact with

---

[7] Approving a recommendation of the Social Services Committee on 19 October 1982, itself approving the Children's Sub-Committee's recommendation of 17 September 1982 that Gwynedd County Council should ban the use of physical punishment, as control should be based on good personal and professional relationships.

[8] See para 33.14.

[9] Letter dated 31 August 1977 to the Director of Social Services, Mid Glamorgan County Council.

her charges. This immediate link with the children is her essential forte and she copes adequately and responsibly though requiring support from Senior Personnel even in this area."

Mr Parry did explain, however, that in many respects Taylor was "learning on the job".

33.17 That letter tends to rebut any suggestion that Alison Taylor herself wished to become permanent Officer-in-Charge of Tŷ'r Felin and that she was antagonistic to Dodd from the moment when he was appointed for that reason. She told us that she did apply for the post but only under pressure from Parry to do so and that she had not wanted it. She was glad initially that Dodd had been appointed.

33.18 Nevertheless, it is clear that from a very early stage Nefyn Dodd and Taylor were in conflict. At best there was a conflict between their different approaches to residential child care. There was mutual disapproval, which developed into deep bitterness as the years went by, and the seeds of future conflict could be seen as early as 1 February 1978, when Taylor was sent what was described as an official reprimand relating to the performance of her duties at "both an administrative and managerial level" as Acting Officer-in-Charge at Tŷ'r Felin. This, rather bizarrely, followed swiftly on a letter of 20 January 1978, in which Parry had thanked Taylor for undertaking those duties in 1977.

33.19 The letter of 1 February 1978 was apparently drafted by Parry and signed by the Director of Social Services, Thomas Edward Jones (hereafter T E Jones). The main grounds of criticism of Taylor were that:

(a) she had responded inadequately to or ignored much of the guidance given to her;

(b) members of the staff at Tŷ'r Felin, including her Deputy, had not received adequate guidance from her in fulfilling their duties and had not been handled by her firmly and consistently; and

(c) documentary records were in an indefensible condition and slip-shod administrative work had resulted in accounting difficulties.

The Director stated that Parry and Nefyn Dodd would now agree with Taylor clear areas of responsibility in addition to clarifying her responsibilities as a Deputy in the absence of the Officer-in-Charge, adding:

"I think it is time to permanently erase from the circumstances at Tŷ'r Felin the recurrent bogey of the former Officer-in-Charge."

33.20 Finally, the letter alleged that there had been "problems of co-operation" between Taylor and Haydn Jones as well as with her recent Deputy, for which she had been partly to blame, and stressed the importance of her future co-operation with Nefyn Dodd. The only balm in the letter was the statement, "I do not wish to comment at all on the work you have done with the children as this gives the appearance of being satisfactory".

33.21 Alison Taylor said that she was not given any prior intimation that this letter was being sent to her or any opportunity to discuss the specific criticisms made of her; and she was furious when she received it. When she spoke to Nefyn Dodd about it, he told her that he had had to report to headquarters "what state the place was in" when he arrived and she inferred that his report had provoked the letter to her.

The Dodds' regime, 1978 to 1992

33.22 Although Nefyn Dodd remained Officer-in-Charge of Tŷ'r Felin for nearly 12 years of this period he was given additional responsibilities at an early stage. The Community Homes Officer for the County, Elizabeth Hughes, was on sick leave for a long period in 1978 and from 9 October 1978 it was agreed that Nefyn Dodd should be employed for 15 hours per week fulfilling part of her duties referable to children's homes until she returned to duty. Nefyn Dodd was to be employed thus at headquarters and visiting community homes for children and the remaining 25 hours of his working week were to be devoted to Tŷ'r Felin.

33.23 This arrangement was apparently ended on 28 February 1979 but any interruption in Nefyn Dodd's external responsibilities was of fairly short duration. His own recollection is that late in 1980 Parry asked him to assist by supervising the running of Y Gwyngyll[10], where there had been riots: he was to visit that home once per week and on other occasions when specifically requested to do so. When giving evidence to the Tribunal he was unable to recall how long that supervisory role continued but said that he was still doing it when an independent inquiry team investigated that community home in July and August 1981. Some months later Nefyn Dodd's responsibilities were extended to cover all the Gwynedd community homes. The extent of those responsibilities was clarified in a memorandum from Owain Gethin Evans, the Officer-in-Charge, Children's Section, to the Officer-in-Charge, Tŷ Newydd (the newly appointed Alison Taylor), dated 10 August 1982.

33.24 That memorandum read as follows:

["Role of Mr. Nefyn Dodd"]

"To clear up any ambiguity about Mr. Dodd's present responsibilities and duties can I please clarify the situation thus:

1. The Committee have asked Mr. Dodd to undertake full responsibility for <u>all</u> community homes on a temporary basis.

2. This means that all Officers in Charge are directly accountable to Mr. Dodd for the management and oversight of their establishment.

3. Mr. Dodd reports back to me on all matters concerning the homes, and I shall work through him when dealing with the children's residential sector.

---

[10] See Chapter 35.

4. Present arrangements will continue until the Committee has decided otherwise.

A final note, all placements in the homes will be decided by Mr. Dodd, and in his absence by myself.

If you have any queries please contact me."

33.25 In his new role Nefyn Dodd was given the title of Supervisor/Co-ordinator and Gethin Evans[11] confirmed, in a further memorandum dated 23 November 1983, that all Officers-in-Charge were directly answerable to Nefyn Dodd for all aspects of their duties. He was said to have "full operational control for the management and organisation of the four community homes in the county"[12] and was to advise on matters relating to the residential care of children. His duties entailed "responsibility for staff, finance, standards of care, admission placement of children, fabric of buildings and other related tasks".

33.26 The next change in Nefyn Dodd's status took effect from 1 October 1985 when he became Principal Officer (Residential Care–Children), whilst remaining Officer-in-Charge at Tŷ'r Felin. This was by resolution of the County Council's Staff Committee on 14 November 1985, which was confirmed by the County Council itself on 12 December 1985. The decision, on a recommendation from the Social Services Department, was made in recognition of the work that Nefyn Dodd had carried out from 1982 onwards: his new job description was broadly in line with the earlier definitions of his responsibilities.

33.27 Quite soon after Nefyn Dodd had become Principal Officer a police investigation into his conduct, instigated by Alison Taylor, began[13]. That investigation lasted eventually from February 1986 to April 1988 and is dealt with in detail in Chapter 51 of this report. Nefyn Dodd was not suspended from duty during the investigation and the decision of the Crown Prosecution Service, initially in October 1986 and again in April 1988, was that he should not be prosecuted.

33.28 Nefyn Dodd's health deteriorated in 1989. He had suffered from diabetes for a number of years and then in 1989 he was diagnosed as suffering from neuropathy, causing numbness and sensitivity of his lower legs and feet, and associated depression. He was unable to continue working after the end of November 1989 because of these disabilities and he retired on health grounds on 23 May 1990, at the age of 54 years.

33.29 It follows from what we have said that Nefyn Dodd became progressively less involved in the daily running of Tŷ'r Felin during the 1980s. June Dodd, for example, said that he did not have much to do with the children there from the mid 1980s. Nevertheless, Tŷ'r Felin remained his home during the week until 1988 and his wife was effectively his Deputy there from August 1982[14]. She said in evidence that, when he was not at headquarters or visiting other community

---

[11] See para 44.19.
[12] Tŷ'r Felin, Tŷ Newydd, Y Gwyngyll and Queens Park.
[13] See paras 2.08 to 2.15.
[14] See para 33.05.

homes, he would work in the office at Tŷ'r Felin from 9 am to 5 pm daily before retiring to their flat. Before August 1982, and following the departure of Alison Taylor, his Deputy or Acting Deputy was **Alison Mary Bradshaw**. She was not, however, the subject of any complaint by a former resident and she did not give evidence to the Tribunal.

The disciplinary climate at Tŷ'r Felin under Nefyn Dodd

33.30 It is necessary to describe quite fully the nature of the regime at Tŷ'r Felin under Nefyn Dodd as the background to the allegations of abuse made against him and other members of the staff; and this is particularly so because there has been a sharp conflict of evidence on the subject. On the one hand, Nefyn Dodd has been painted as an aggressive and dictatorial man, who did not hesitate to use physical force when dealing with children and who imposed a tyrannical and unreasonable regime upon child residents and the staff. In short, it is said that he ran Tŷ'r Felin as "a little Bryn Estyn" when it was very inappropriate to do so. On the other hand, it is suggested that he was a gentle giant, who believed in running "a tight ship" in the interests of the children themselves and who was able to establish good rapport with them. On this view, he was a "firm but fair" Officer-in-Charge, who was conscious of his duty to society to keep effective control of the disturbed children in his care.

33.31 When Nefyn Dodd arrived at Tŷ'r Felin, he did so with excellent references gained during his training course for the CRCCYP and from Arnold, the Principal of Bryn Estyn. The latter described him as "undoubtedly one of my most capable staff, both in the areas of child assessment and in general control throughout the school" and the college said that his practice of child care had been almost without fault (the only fault being a tendency to pack eight days into a week). Writing in January 1978 of Tŷ'r Felin's assessment role, Dodd himself said:

> "Tŷ'r Felin should be a place where a child should be able to feel secure (and therefore, safe). It should be clear that it understands why it is here and that it will be with us for a short time only. Our setting should not demand conformity, but there should be an <u>underlying sense</u> of control. The need for structure and control should not cut across the maintenance of a moderately permissive climate. A moderate amount of permissiveness, space and a sense of freedom are essential so that our children have an opportunity to behave in a characteristic way, and <u>within limits</u> give vent to their anxieties and feelings, otherwise observation of their behaviour would not be meaningful."

33.32 Comparatively few of the complaints of which we know relate to the earliest part of Nefyn Dodd's reign as Officer-in-Charge and there is evidence that he established a good image for himself and Tŷ'r Felin in the locality at that time. There was some favourable publicity in the local press. Bangor Round Table, for example, took an interest in the community home and presented it with a video recorder and Anglesey Aluminium Employees Charity Committee gave a large television set in July 1980, following earlier generous gifts. The Salvation Army and a group called Community Action were also actively involved with the home. Residents attended the Salvation Army service each Sunday and Community Action organised, amongst other things, a joint visit with staff and residents to Liverpool in December 1981 to see a pantomime. It is clear also that Nefyn Dodd impressed D A Parry, the Deputy Director of Social Services, with responsibility then for children's services, who was a regular visitor to Tŷ'r Felin, and Laurence (Larry) King, who was Senior Officer (Children) from 1 August 1975 and Principal Officer (Children) from 1 June 1979 to 14 May 1988.

33.33 A Welsh Office Inspector, SWSO Copleston, visited Tŷ'r Felin on 7 November 1978, shortly after Nefyn Dodd had begun to carry out his first additional duties elsewhere. The Inspector's report was favourable, although only seven children were in residence at the time. She recorded that corporal punishment in line with that permitted under the Children's Homes Regulations 1951 (sic) was allowed in Gwynedd community homes and that a cane was on display in Nefyn Dodd's office "as required by the Authority" but that he did not permit corporal punishment. Punishments recorded in the Punishment Book (five only from January to November 1978) seemed to the Inspector to be reasonable.

33.34 Of Nefyn Dodd himself, the Inspector wrote:

> "I found it difficult to assess Mr Dodd and I know that senior staff in the department are uncertain what to make of him but I finally concluded that he was a sincere person doing his best to provide a sound service and largely succeeding in doing so. Brought up in a small Welsh speaking community near Wrexham, it seems to have been important to him to overcome the variously potentially handicapping circumstances of his earlier years and achievement of all kinds is still very important to him . . . Mr Dodd has certainly introduced a number of new procedures and to use his own words again "generally tightened things up" but he appeared to have taken his staff along with him in the changes he had made, there seems to be a warm relationship between him and the children and his approach seems in no way authoritarian."

33.35 SWSO Copleston's report also highlighted a problem about Tŷ'r Felin's role, which was to persist. She said that the word "assessment" had been used very loosely for some time. Of the 27 admissions during the first half of 1978 only ten were listed as assessment/remand and 13 for short stay, ranging from a few days to seven months. The Inspector followed up the position in the five months following her visit and noted in April 1979 that there was a suggestion that Tŷ'r Felin should cease to operate as an Observation and Assessment Centre and become an ordinary community home for children from the Arfon area.

33.36 A very different view of Tŷ'r Felin under Nefyn Dodd was given by Dewi Evans, the present Director of Social Services for Carmarthen (and formerly for Dyfed), who gave oral evidence to the Tribunal about his visit to Tŷ'r Felin in August 1981. Evans (then Deputy Director for Dyfed) and two other members of the staff of Dyfed County Council were commissioned in 1981 (following a request to the Chief Executive of Dyfed) to investigate complaints made by current and former members of the staff of Gwynedd County Council into the running of Y Gwyngyll community home. In the course of that investigation the inquiry team visited the other community homes in Gwynedd, including Tŷ'r Felin. In their report they were critical of the appointment of Nefyn Dodd to a supervisory role in respect of Y Gwyngyll, which they regarded as an error of judgment.

33.37 Of Tŷ'r Felin itself, they said:

"Tŷ'r Felin is clearly the Establishment in the best state of physical repair and maintenance. We were interested to note the use of school uniforms and hope that this does not impair the integration of the children and the Establishment into the community. We consider that it would be wrong for the Authority to suppose that the management style adopted at Tŷ'r Felin is appropriate to any or all of the other Children's Establishments within Gwynedd."

33.38 The reference to "school uniforms" was to the requirement by Nefyn Dodd that all child residents at Tŷ'r Felin should wear the uniform that he had prescribed (blazer, pullover, badge, shirt, tie and trousers for boys in the photographs that we have seen and similar uniform for girls). Whilst this made the children presentable in appearance to older eyes, it marked them out from their peers as residents of Tŷ'r Felin when, for example, they were attending local schools or visiting Bangor.

33.39 Dewi Evans was more outspoken in his evidence to the Tribunal. He said that the inquiry team had been told that they should see Tŷ'r Felin as a model of good practice and they spent three to four hours there. They were concerned about Nefyn Dodd's style of management. Tŷ'r Felin had the atmosphere of an army camp for small soldiers: the kerbstones were all painted white, the youngsters were in uniform and were required to wear a tie with Tŷ'r Felin written on it, and every time they went to the shop for sweets they had to bring back a receipt. Dewi Evans referred also to an atmosphere of fear and compared the children to mice, "scurrying here and there when we visited"; and he added in cross-examination, when questioned about the atmosphere of fear:

"Yes, I stand by that. The children were so well controlled. There wasn't a relaxed homely atmosphere, which I would have thought would have been one of the main objectives of the home—children coming into care—it's difficult enough to be subjected to this, regimentation rather than fear is possibly a better description."

Moreover, Dodd was in the team's shadow throughout their visit.

33.40 Evidence in support of Nefyn Dodd and his regime at Tŷ'r Felin from four main sources was put before the Tribunal. It came, firstly, from senior officers of Gwynedd Social Services Department to whom he was responsible from time to time, such as D A Parry, Lucille Hughes[15] and Larry King, who each visited Tŷ'r Felin but with varying frequency. Secondly, there were neighbours

---

[15] See paras 44.18 and 44.25.

and other interested persons in the locality, such as Salvation Army officers and local councillors. Thirdly, there were some former members of staff and, finally, some former residents.

33.41 We have no reason to doubt the sincerity of the witnesses in the first two categories, who formed a high opinion of Nefyn Dodd. He was undoubtedly effective in presenting himself and was determined that Tŷ'r Felin should be seen by outsiders as a well conducted, disciplined home, in which residents did not answer back and did not cause trouble with the home's neighbours. He was anxious also that the physical appearance of the home should convey a similar impression. We have received persuasive evidence that, in his first years as Officer-in-Charge, Nefyn Dodd did effect improvements to the appearance of Tŷ'r Felin and involved himself with the children to the extent, for example, of eating with them. To many of the children, however, and at least some of the staff he was an intimidating figure and a bully. He was a large man with a powerful presence who frequently raised his voice to impose himself. Moreover, he was dictatorial to those under him, brooking no disagreement; and his approach to residential child care was no doubt influenced by his early experience at Bryn Estyn and Bersham Hall.

33.42 It may well be that in his first two years or so at Tŷ'r Felin the balance of achievement was in Nefyn Dodd's favour in the sense that, although he imposed an inappropriately repressive and regimented pattern of life upon residents, he did show interest in them and did provide a degree of security for children placed there. It can be said also that good order and discipline was of particular importance for most of the children, who were not intended to stay at Tŷ'r Felin for more than 12 weeks. As time passed, however, Nefyn Dodd's external duties grew as did his powers; he became more remote from the residents of Tŷ'r Felin, having little daily contact with them; and he became a more awesome figure, to whom June Dodd would report for punishment misdemeanours that had occurred during the day.

33.43 Nefyn Dodd's attitude to the staff of Tŷ'r Felin was highly authoritarian from the beginning. An unusual facet of this was that he would address numerous homilies and directions to them in a log book kept for the purpose of recording relevant matters for staff purposes. We have seen entries covering the period from 2 January 1978 to 29 March 1980 and some later entries but four citations will be sufficient to convey the general flavour of Nefyn Dodd's own comments:

> 3 July 1978
>
> > "This morning at 8.55 a.m. whilst in the boot room with DBH and the children, I was amazed to find an unofficial tea break going on. Mrs. Hughes, Mrs. Williams, Mrs Berthelemy were all in possession of tea. Why? I understand this has been going on for some time. As DOIC please ensure this does not happen again, if people don't like it send them to me. I don't mind staff taking up to 15 minutes to read the daily log. Unofficial breaks are not on. I know that ad lib smoking goes on but to push the boat out this far is bordering on anarchy."

3 February 1979 (extract)

"If I was responsible for a long term therapeutic unit then there would certainly be a different philosophy implemented. Due to the fact that this is an Assessment Centre and that I through necessity adhere to boundaries and constants which are clearly defined I expect a certain ADULT MATURE response from staff and do not expect people to encourage children to complain, rebel, vote with their feet and abscond, all to no avail. All that this irresponsible level of working proves to me as an experienced ASSESSMENT officer is that certain adults are totally irresponsible, immature and have far more personal conflicts than our clients?"

20 November 1979

"With reference to AGT's comments regarding X, which once again confirms my opinions, on no account is this young baby to be permitted to use the portable T.V. or given any perk more in keeping with his chronological age; treat at the stage of his present behaviour, still in nappies."

(X was aged 16 at the time that this was written)

14 January 1980

"There is a true saying 'To be continually admonished, is to be continually discouraged' so for God's sake and the children's give me an opportunity to express satisfaction of your work."

33.44 The log entries give an accurate picture of Nefyn Dodd's attitude to members of the staff and the child residents. All members of the staff, except June Dodd, were subjected to criticism, although Alison Taylor fared rather better than the others as Deputy Officer-in-Charge. There was an early passage of arms with her because of an allegation that she had claimed to have been offered the post of Officer-in-Charge before Nefyn Dodd was appointed but that dispute subsided quite quickly. The penultimate entry, on 29 March 1980, concluded:

"AGT has responded by doing that bit 'EXTRA' which separates the professional from the wage earner, I am sure she will be missed when she goes on C.Q.S.W, as JD [June Dodd] is in her capacity whilst undertaking C.S.S."

33.45 As for the children, it is clear from the log entries that, in Nefyn Dodd's view, every waking hour was to be organised. Even unsupervised football in the back garden, using a low goal provided by Nefyn Dodd, was discouraged, as were unsupervised visits to town. The withdrawal of "perks", such as use of a portable television, and deductions from pocket money (to be redeemed by extra work) were regular features of children's lives. Complaints were discouraged and dealt with by Nefyn Dodd alone; and visits by outsiders were treated rather like military inspections.

33.46 The evidence of two of the former members of the staff who gave oral evidence covered almost the full period of Nefyn Dodd's tenure as Officer-in-Charge after August 1980. Peter Michael Jones was at Tŷ'r Felin for just over a year to September 1981 as an unqualified RCCO. He described Nefyn Dodd as a martinet who ruled with a rod of iron. Early on, Nefyn Dodd was absent ill for six to eight weeks (probably when his diabetes was first diagnosed). On his return there was a honeymoon period whilst he eased himself back but slowly the atmosphere changed completely. According to this witness, the children were "absolutely" petrified: Nefyn Dodd had a loud voice and a large presence, he was manipulative and he made people dance to his tune. It was Dodd's view that familiarity with children bred contempt in them. Sometimes he would not be seen for days and June Dodd, who was quite good with children in comparison with him, would try to run the home in his absence, but would report every little thing, including anything said, to Nefyn Dodd. She came across as "a nice person" but the staff regarded her as the "poisoned arm" of Nefyn Dodd.

33.47 The second oral witness referred to was Peter Jones' successor, Mari Thomas (formerly Roberts Jones), who was employed as a RCCO at Tŷ'r Felin from 7 June 1981, after graduating that year at the University College of North Wales (Normal College) in Administration, until 1988. She did not have any professional qualification as a social worker at that time but she was promoted to Senior RCCO in 1984 and has since obtained the Diploma in Social Work at Bangor, after a full time two years course, and she was, at the time of giving evidence to us, Team Manager at Cartref Bontnewydd.

33.48 Mari Thomas described Nefyn Dodd as very autocratic. He imposed a very tight routine: every day was the same and you did not question what went on. She was very inexperienced when she went to Tŷ'r Felin and for a time she honestly thought that that was how things were done. The main emphasis was on keeping children quiet and ensuring that there was no running around. The children were not permitted any space or privacy and there was no one to one work with them. To this witness, Nefyn Dodd appeared to be modelling himself on Arnold of Bryn Estyn. There were newspaper cuttings in his office that supported this view. He was verbally aggressive and his loud voice could be heard telling people off from one office to the other at the opposite end of the building. Mari Thomas said that the staff were quite unhappy in their work, although they were supportive of each other. Many found it difficult to accept what Nefyn Dodd said to them and the messages that he put in the log book: there was a high turnover of staff and she was amazed how many young and inexperienced staff came to Tŷ'r Felin. Her compensation was that she enjoyed working with children but she agreed that both staff and children were frightened.

33.49 We heard oral evidence from six other members of the staff during the period 1978 to 1988, including June Dodd, Alison Taylor and the teacher from 1979 to 1985, John Roberts; and we received the written evidence of five other members of the staff, including a cook who was at Tŷ'r Felin between 1977 and 1980 and a houseparent, who was there during the same period but stayed until 1981. Having reviewed all the evidence, we are satisfied that the two witnesses whose evidence we have summarised in the preceding two paragraphs have given us a broadly accurate general picture of relationships between Nefyn Dodd and the staff and children and the role played by June Dodd.

33.50 When considering the general history of Tŷ'r Felin it is important to have in mind that it was early in 1986 that Alison Taylor's complaints against Nefyn Dodd first came to a head when she met Councillor Marshall and Detective Chief Superintendent Gwynne Owen at the former's home[16]. This meeting set in train a criminal investigation that lasted until May 1988, although the first decision not to prosecute Nefyn Dodd was taken as early as October 1986. Alison Taylor's complaints were wide ranging and included allegations of physical abuse by Nefyn Dodd at Tŷ'r Felin. It is a reasonable inference, therefore, that Nefyn Dodd's behaviour at Tŷ'r Felin was more circumspect from 1986 onwards[17]. He had become Principal Officer (Residential Care - Children) from 1 October 1985 and he ceased to live at Tŷ'r Felin in 1988, although he remained Officer-in-Charge until 1 December 1989, by which time his health had deteriorated severely.

33.51 One other factor of some importance in considering the general history of Tŷ'r Felin is that its role was ill-defined in the 1980s. The log entries indicate the importance that Nefyn Dodd attached to the function of Tŷ'r Felin as an Observation and Assessment Centre and a community home accommodating children for short stays in shaping the regime that he imposed. As early as 1980, however, he was saying that it was to be an Assessment Centre and Family Unit and that it would deal with disturbed families.

33.52 As far as we are aware this change of function was never formally recognised in Nefyn Dodd's time but it seems that the actual role of Tŷ'r Felin became indistinguishable from that of the small number of other community homes in Gwynedd. In the autumn of 1988 two representatives of the Social Work Service of the Welsh Office undertook an examination of the current care and care career of 12 children in residential care in Gwynedd on 19 September 1988, eight of whom were at Tŷ'r Felin and four at Queens Park, Holyhead. By that time Tŷ'r Felin's accommodation had been increased to 14 beds because the two flats were no longer being used as accommodation for staff living on the premises. The report by the Welsh Office representatives extended to 41 pages, with annexes totalling 26 pages, so that it cannot sensibly be summarised here.

33.53 We will revert to the subject of this report when we discuss the responsibility of higher management in Gwynedd in Chapter 46. Meanwhile, it is to be noted that, apart from the Dodds, the care establishment of Tŷ'r Felin was six RCCOs, of whom two were senior RCCOs. None of them had a recognised professional social work qualification. One of the care staff had worked for four years at Tŷ'r Felin but had been on sick leave for four months and all the others had begun work there in 1988. The accommodation and regimes in both

---

[16] See paras 2.09 to 2.15.

[17] He made statements to the North Wales Police on 10 September 1986 and 5 October 1987.

homes were described favourably but a comment made was that "Some of the few rules which did exist, especially in Tŷ'r Felin, were quite institutional and perhaps inconsistent".

33.54 Major criticisms in the report were of the assessment role of Tŷ'r Felin and the provision of education. The authors pointed to the staff's lack of appropriate qualifications and experience to carry out assessments. There was a lack of coherence about the purposes of assessment even in discussion and the authors were left in grave doubt as to whether the residential staff undertaking assessments were given clear guidance about what they were supposed to be assessing. They stressed the dangers of admitting children into open-ended care: children tended to stay in no-man's land between rehabilitation and permanence; at least six of the 12 children were in that situation and two were moving into it. Most revealingly, the authors pointed out that whereas the use of Tŷ'r Felin was described as "for assessment and remand" and that of Queens Park as "for continuing care and rehabilitation", the children actually in the two homes were "interchangeable with reference to their ages and the kinds of problems they presented". The stated objective of "assessment" in Tŷ'r Felin had little meaning without reference to purpose.

33.55 As for the education provision at Tŷ'r Felin, it was described as "basic in the extreme". Tŷ'r Felin itself merely provided a classroom and teaching staff were provided by the Education Department on secondment. The scale of the service provided depended on the number of children receiving education on the premises and was at the rate of two hours per child per week (three were receiving this at the time of the inspection). The education component of a child's care at Tŷ'r Felin was not formally integrated with any other part of it. The report continued:

> "A short discussion with the teacher revealed that he was on supply and not permanently on the staff of any teaching unit in the county. He appeared to have received no brief as to his role at Tŷ'r Felin either from the education department or the social services department and had not received supervision or professional support during the few weeks he had been at Tŷ'r Felin. His locus in relation to the head of the home had not been explained nor had he been given an understanding of the sort of support he may expect from that quarter."

Allegations of sexual abuse

33.56 Complaints of sexual abuse at Tŷ'r Felin did not figure prominently in statements made to the police or in evidence received by the Tribunal; and we are not aware of any suggestion that there was a persistent sexual aggressor on the staff of Tŷ'r Felin. Of the 84 complainants of whom we are aware, covering the full period of nearly 22 years when the community home was open, 12 alleged that they had been abused sexually and each of these made that allegation against only one member of the staff. We have already dealt with the allegations of one of these complainants[18]. The allegations by the others

---

[18] See para 33.14.

implicated five members of the staff, of whom David Bayley Hughes was not one.

33.57 In the event we heard evidence from four witnesses who alleged sexual abuse whilst they were at Tŷ'r Felin but the evidence of one of them, alleging abuse of a lesser kind within the possible scale of such an offence, was very unreliable. We are satisfied that the other potential witnesses, some of whom alleged only minor isolated incidents, would not have added anything substantial to the general picture before us.

33.58 It is necessary to mention **Nefyn Dodd** in this context because he was the subject of the largest number of complaints under this head. We are aware of five complainants (three female, two male) who alleged sexual abuse by him to the police and we heard oral evidence from three of them (two female, one male), who were the major complainants because the other two referred only to single incidents. However, there was no discernible pattern to the allegations by the five complainants (or to those of the three who gave evidence to us) about events said to have occurred between 1979 and 1985 ; none of the allegations were corroborated; there was no documentary record of the one alleged contemporary complaint, by a complainant's mother; and all the allegations have been vehemently denied by Nefyn Dodd throughout, with such limited support from his wife as she has been able to give.

33.59 In these circumstances we are unable to find that any sexual abuse has been proved to have occurred at Tŷ'r Felin. Without casting any reflection upon any particular individual we are bound to say that, in the nature of things, some incidents may have occurred; but we have not received any adequate evidence to justify a finding against any identified member of the staff.

Allegations of physical abuse against Nefyn Dodd

33.60 We received evidence from 17 former residents of Tŷ'r Felin alleging physical assaults of varying gravity by Nefyn Dodd whilst they were resident there. One witness who gave oral evidence seems to have been mistaken about the identity of her attacker. According to the documents before us, she was not admitted to Tŷ'r Felin until 21 November 1991, over a year after Nefyn Dodd's final retirement and two years after he became disabled from working: and her description of her attacker did not fit Nefyn Dodd at that time.

33.61 Another witness who gave oral evidence to us presented similar problems because most of his period in residential care was spent with the Bryn Alyn Community rather than in local authority community homes. According to social services records, he was at Tŷ'r Felin for only nine days in October 1976, over a year before Nefyn Dodd arrived there. He was at Tŷ Newydd later for 14 months between February 1981 and April 1982, that is, from just after his 16th birthday, but he said of his stay there that it was "like Butlins compared with other homes". Whilst he was at Tŷ Newydd he attended a catering course at an hotel in Bangor and he was also required by Nefyn Dodd to work at Tŷ'r Felin from time to time as cook and/or dishwasher; but the witness said that Nefyn Dodd was not capable then of physical violence against him, bearing in mind his age. It seems that this witness' memory was affected, at least for a period, by a breakdown later; and he told the Tribunal that he did not recover it until it flooded back at the age of 20/21 years when he was in the Army. This may account for some confusion on the witness' part but, in the light of the social services documents, we are not able to attach any weight to his allegations against Nefyn Dodd, such as they were.

33.62   The other 15 witnesses (eight of whom gave oral evidence to the Tribunal) were all at Tŷ'r Felin for varying lengths of time between 1978 and 1988, mainly in the earlier part of that period. Six of them were at Tŷ'r Felin for short stays not exceeding three months (one was there for two such periods) but the rest were there for appreciably longer periods ranging from six months to just over two years.

33.63   Ten of these witnesses complained of substantial assaults and threats by Nefyn Dodd. Witness A, for example, who was at Tŷ'r Felin for two and a half months from September 1982 and a similar period in 1983, referred to Nefyn Dodd as a bully and described being head-butted by him in his office for no apparent reason. A was told by Dodd not to tell anyone but no explanation was given for the assault. Witness B, who also gave oral evidence and was only at Tŷ'r Felin for just over a fortnight in 1980, said that Nefyn Dodd warned him that he would be thrashed if he did not behave. B avoided Dodd as much as he could but he used to get slapped by Dodd for smoking and was told that he was not fit to speak to the Dodds' daughter. On one occasion B had been fighting with witness C in the living room and had got the better of the exchange, whereupon Dodd dragged B into the hallway and put him against the wall. Dodd then told B that he had been waiting for this; referring to C as a "sheep shagger", Dodd said that, if C did it again, B was to slap him and then to report to Dodd.

33.64   Witness C was at Tŷ'r Felin for seven and a half months from 1 May 1980 and, like the fourth oral witness, claimed to have been caned by Nefyn Dodd. He described the latter as "a large fat bully". C's complaints were that Dodd had beaten him with a cane, punched and kicked him, made him lick Dodd's boots (or attempted to do so) and forced him to eat carbolic soap. The caning had been on his bare buttocks and it had occurred on three or four occasions in Dodd's office. He added that Alison Taylor had been present at the caning a couple of times. One of the canings was for allegedly stealing a gold necklace when he had bought it for a girl in the home with his own pocket money. Another was for losing a football match. C described also being struck from behind at the breakfast table by Dodd as a punishment for having run away (he had been returned the night before in Dodd's absence). As a result of the blow he fell to the floor and Dodd kicked him. He was made by Dodd to eat green carbolic soap at a wash basin as punishment for swearing and it caused ulcers and blisters in his mouth, for which he received no medical help. The licking of Dodd's boots was, in C's view, a "power trip": C was made to do it at least half a dozen times and Dodd made most of the children do it.

33.65   Alison Taylor did not confirm that she had been present when C was caned by Nefyn Dodd. She left Tŷ'r Felin in July 1980 so that she was only there for two to three months at the beginning of C's stay. In her evidence to the Tribunal she suggested that C, whom she remembered, might have confused her with Alison Bradshaw, her successor as Deputy Officer-in-Charge. Alison Taylor said that she did witness one assault on witness C, after he had absconded one week-end when his promised home leave had been stopped by Nefyn Dodd, but that was not the occasion when he alleges that he was struck by Nefyn Dodd at the breakfast table[19].

33.66 Taylor was cross-examined about an entry made by her in a Tŷ'r Felin log book on 3 May 1980, two days after C's arrival, which read:

> "C appears to me to be a very spoilt boy, used to having whatever he wants and giving people a hard time if he does not have it. Harsh though it may sound I think that unless he has a hard time here he is going to continue to find that offences have no nasty consequences for him."

The following day C absconded and was returned to Tŷ'r Felin by Taylor and Bradshaw, according to the log book. It would appear possible, therefore, that the alleged breakfast table incident occurred on 5 May 1980 when Dodd returned to duty. Other entries in the log suggest that C had absconded on 4 May 1980 at night time because he had been sent to bed for smoking and not because of any refusal of home leave; and he had been recovered from his home by Taylor and Bradshaw the same night. It is relevant also (as will become apparent) that 5 May 1980 was a Bank Holiday when the teacher, John Roberts, would not have been present at Tŷ'r Felin.

33.67 On 5 May 1980, Nefyn Dodd wrote in C's personal file:

> "This child is a classic case of over indulgence, and it would appear that he thinks that he can get away with almost anything. I think our advice should have been adhered to, and that he should have experienced a salutary imposition[20]. We are on a loser with this kid, because his Social Worker has also been conned by him. I am pleased that the old system of putting kids in absconding gear[21] has been again put into force. I want the pressure kept on this boy, as he seems to think he can do anything he wishes. THIS IS NARROW COLOQUIAL (sic) PAROCHIALISM AT ITS WORST, we have a responsibility to put the score right."

33.68 To complete the picture, Alison Taylor herself wrote in the log on 6 May 1980:

> "Would advise all staff to be very circumspect in handling of C. He is apparently prone to making accusations of assault, so do not take any risks, ie make sure you are not in a position where he can allege assault—see file."

---

[19] Alison Taylor's GCC Analysis p.76.
[20] C was made the subject of a care order by Bangor Juvenile Court on 1 May 1980, at the age of 13 years, for burglary and taking away a motor vehicle without lawful authority.
[21] Pyjamas.

The corresponding entry by Taylor in C's personal file the previous day read:

> "Informed by the other boys that C is saying either myself or CW hit him last night. As I have no intention of being alone with him, I have informed C that matters will be discussed on Thursday with Mr Dodd."

33.69 Alison Taylor's own account of the assault by Dodd on C that she witnessed was that it occurred early on during C's stay at Tŷ'r Felin after he had absconded during the day because of Dodd's refusal of home leave that had been previously promised. On Dodd's return to duty on Monday morning he took C into his office, where John Roberts was present. Taylor thought that Peter Jones may also have witnessed what occurred but this is unlikely because he was on the staff of Tŷ Newydd at the time. In the office Dodd began a tirade of verbal abuse directed at C and ordered him to lick Dodd's shoes, which C refused to do. Dodd then lashed out at the boy, whilst Roberts pushed him within Dodd's reach. Taylor dragged C out of the room and told both Dodd and Roberts that she would report any subsequent assault that she might witness to the police.

33.70 Witness D was a Holyhead boy who described himself as "difficult to handle" at the age when he was admitted to Tŷ'r Felin for assessment. The records are not clear but it seems that he went there for eight weeks assessment in or about December 1977. On 22 February 1978 he was made the subject of a care order[22] and, on completion of the assessment, he was transferred to Eryl Wen Community Home, where he remained for about 12 months before being discharged home. He was later in residential care for over three years from 23 July 1981, initially at Y Gwyngyll for about six weeks, then at Bryn Estyn for 21 months, where he was prominent, before returning to Y Gwyngyll for 15 months. From Y Gwyngyll he went to approved lodgings as a prelude to his discharge from care on 7 May 1985, three months before his 18th birthday. He presented a problem throughout because he was of above average ability and a natural athlete but his behaviour varied from apathetic and apparently conforming to highly disruptive and, at times, bullying; he was said to know how to work the system.

33.71 D described Nefyn Dodd as a tyrant, over-disciplined, overpowering: he controlled everything, everybody. To D he appeared to be massive and his voice and actions inspired fear. D alleged that Nefyn Dodd used force on many occasions. When asked what sort of force Dodd used, D replied "As much as was necessary, which could be defined as anything, slapping, kicking, punching". D alleged also that he was caned by Dodd. According to D, the assaults frequently occurred in the boot room at Tŷ'r Felin and he recalled a specific incident in that room when he was punished by Dodd after a cleaner had reported him for having a cigarette stump and a match under his pillow. Dodd pushed and shoved him and then grabbed him by the ears, pulling his face into Dodd's stomach. D became breathless, lost his temper and kicked himself free but Dodd then charged him with his stomach with the result that

---

[22] For burglary and theft from a meter (with 23 other offences taken into consideration).

D hit his head on a hanger and slid down the wall. The caning had been fierce and to his hands; it was inflicted because he had broken a window accidentally with a ball.

33.72 We have referred to the evidence of C and D in some detail because their credibility was attacked by Counsel for Nefyn Dodd with particular severity on the grounds, amongst others, that they had been part of an alleged conspiracy with Alison Taylor to blacken Nefyn Dodd and that both had appeared on television to do so. It should be said for clarification, however, that Taylor did not recall D's stay at Tŷ'r Felin and he said that she was not there then. A log entry on 10 January 1978 refers to her being "off on course" and it appears to be common ground between her and Dodd that she was absent due to sickness for some weeks at the beginning of 1978. The recollection of both Taylor and D was that they met first at Bryn Estyn in 1983 when she was placed there in the course of her training for the CQSW.

33.73 The other four "live" witnesses who gave evidence to the Tribunal of assaults upon them by Nefyn Dodd whilst they were at Tŷ'r Felin spoke in the main of lesser incidents. Witness E was there in October 1982 for only 11 days initially, when he was nearly 13 years old, but returned for four months in November 1983 and for two days on remand in May 1985 before being sent to a Detention Centre. He said that he was scared of Dodd, who would hit him across the face (he amended this to "pushed violently" when reminded of his statement to the police). He ran home out of fear and wept "loads of times" but Dodd would just shout more. In his view June Dodd was scared of Nefyn Dodd as well and he used to shout at her in front of others; but E got on well with the rest of the staff. A typed letter of dubious authenticity purporting to have been signed and sent by this witness to the Director of Social Services from H M Prison Risley in October 1991 in support of the Dodds was repudiated by him and we are unable to attach any weight to it for this and other reasons.

33.74 The witness who was at Tŷ'r Felin for the longest period, witness F, was there for two years from 17 February 1984, whilst awaiting a further foster placement. He was in care because of family circumstances and was on medication to control his epilepsy. F said that he was happy at first and that the Dodds made him quite welcome but "then things started spiralling and going downhill". He was overweight because of his steroid medication and was bullied by older boys. F's complaint was that Nefyn Dodd would lose his temper and "go ballistic" very often, on a regular basis. He would throw people around; if someone said something to Dodd, he would throw that person on the floor and F had seen Dodd throw somebody from the dining room area through to a toilet area, whilst the staff just stood around. In F's view, Dodd did not have the right temperament to be in that type of work and was very paranoid. The place was more like a military prison than a place of safety where you would be cared for; and if you tried to run away, you would have a beating for it from Dodd. F complained also of inappropriate responses by the Dodds on occasions to his grand mal seizures, grabbing hold of him and shaking him as he recovered consciousness, apparently in exasperated attempts to speed his return to normality. On these occasions Nefyn Dodd, but not his wife, would sometimes even slap him around the face.

33.75 One "live" witness complained of being pushed violently by Nefyn Dodd. Another woman former resident, who was at Tŷ'r Felin for seven months in 1985, when she was 12/13 years old, alleged that, although Dodd was nice to her at first, he later "picked on her" by slapping her with his hand or with a Hoover part across the back of her hand or her head, causing her to cry. She was also made to lick his shoes, even his bare feet some times, if she failed to carry out an errand properly.

33.76 The evidence that we received in written statements by seven other witnesses mirrored these allegations. Two of them wrote of being caned by Dodd. One of the two had been caned after climbing a tree to escape Dodd, who threw wood, stones and bricks at him when he was in the tree. The other had been caned for smoking. He said that on another occasion he had been punched twice by Dodd in his bedroom; he had also seen Dodd punch two other boys; and this witness had also seen the "tree assault". Another witness said that he was kneed and thrown into a chair by Dodd for being cheeky in class but that this was the only assault on him by Dodd during his eight months stay in 1981/1982. Yet another described being punched by Dodd on the face from behind when the witness was misbehaving at the tea table. Finally, there were two separate allegations that Dodd had thrown a boy over the "goal posts" (crossbar) at the rear of Tŷ'r Felin, one by the alleged victim and one by a witness who said that the victim on that different occasion was his brother.

33.77 These allegations of physical abuse have all been strenuously denied throughout by Nefyn Dodd, who has also denied ill-treatment of any child in his care. He said in his evidence to the Tribunal that he believed firmly that children learning to live away from home needed an ordered existence and that he had tried to provide a family home at Tŷ'r Felin that was a secure place for a child. He wanted the children to be proud of where they lived. His first impression had been that Tŷ'r Felin was run down, that there was quite a considerable amount of apathy about the establishment and that there was a lot of structural damage. In his view it looked pretty unkempt. Both staff and children had taken part in renovating the garden and painting, but not as a punishment; the reasoning behind this was that, if the children undertook the work themselves, they were more likely to look after it. He had been very much involved with the children daily and in the evenings, eating meals with them, until he had assumed additional responsibilities, which eventually required him to spend several days a week at other homes.

33.78 On the question of punishment, Nefyn Dodd told the Tribunal that he detested corporal punishment and had been horrified to learn that canes were on display in every home in Gwynedd when he had first arrived there. He considered that he had been instrumental in getting rid of them and he had been fully aware of the policy of Gwynedd County Council following the prohibition of physical punishment, approved by the full Council on 8 February 1983[23]. Nefyn Dodd did say, however, that before the prohibition he had made the children aware of the presence of the cane as a sanction of last resort. He agreed that shouting

---

[23] See footnote 7 to para 33.15.

at children had been part of his method of working and that it had had the
effect of intimidating them sometimes; and he regretted using bad language
from time to time. Most of the verbal abuse was to boys. He would say "You
could not lick my boots" in jest.

33.79 When interviewed by the police, Nefyn Dodd made only one admission about
the use of physical force. He said then that he recalled grabbing one named
resident (not a witness before the Tribunal) by the shoulders and pinning him
against the wall, when telling him not to do something again. When asked by
the police officer "Was that a regular thing?", he replied "Yes, I'm ashamed of
it now but it happened". He added that it was permissible to restrain a child
but that he did not think that violence achieved anything anyway. In answer
to questions by Counsel to the Tribunal about this admission, he accepted that
the effect of it was that he had agreed that he had "used force or violence
against a child in circumstances where (he) should not have used it".

33.80 June Dodd fully supported her husband in her evidence to the Tribunal,
describing him as "strict but fair": the regime was far stricter in the early 1980s
but it became much more relaxed towards the late 80s when she took over. In
an aide-memoire she wrote "In total we accepted children for all manner of
reasons irrespective of their needs because there was no alternative available at
that point in time"; and she did not feel that she was either trained or
sufficiently experienced to deal with such a broad mix of children. Nevertheless,
the children were always well treated and well cared for and the atmosphere in
the home was very relaxed. She had never physically abused a child, nor
witnessed such abuse, and she would not have condoned it. She said also that
Nefyn Dodd was very fair in his treatment of other staff at the home and very
supportive of them; the staff were a very happy group over the years.

33.81 On the subject of punishment, June Dodd said that she thought that in the
beginning the Officer-in-Charge or the Deputy was permitted to slap a child
with a bare hand but she did not see anyone do so, probably because the
occasion never arose. Punishments were reduction of pocket money (with the
chance to repay), deprivation or curtailment of outings (which caused
difficulties, however for others), pyjamas or other night attire for persistent
absconders, locking in a room for very short periods and domestic chores.

33.82 The other ten former members of the staff of Tŷ'r Felin who gave oral evidence
to the Tribunal or whose written evidence was admitted, excluding from this
number Alison Taylor, were mostly (six) critical of the regime under Nefyn
Dodd but only two of them said that they had witnessed physical abuse by him
or circumstances pointing to it. Both these witnesses gave oral evidence. One
of them was Peter Jones[24], who confirmed his earlier statement to the police
that on one occasion, when he was in the general office, he heard noises from
Dodd's office. He heard the raised voices of Dodd and John Roberts and he
thinks that the door of Dodd's office was partly open because he could see
inside partly when he walked past. What he saw was witness C on his hands
and knees with his head parallel to the ground and Dodd facing him, with John

---

[24] See paras 33.46 and 33.69.

Roberts on Dodd's right. Most of the words spoken were in Welsh, which the witness did not understand, and he did not allege that he saw any blow struck. He did add, however, that Roberts hated C and was being verbally abusive to C.

33.83 The other former staff member said that he had seen one of the complainants whose evidence we received being struck by Nefyn Dodd with a ring binder when they were in the dining room and that a struggle between them had followed.

33.84 Assessing the allegations of physical abuse made against Nefyn Dodd has been one of the more difficult tasks that we have had to face. We accept that some of his aspirations as Officer-in-Charge of Tŷ'r Felin were well meant. We are satisfied, however, that the regime that he imposed upon both children and staff was unduly oppressive and that many of his methods of working were inappropriate. Having gathered his experience mainly at Bryn Estyn, he ran Tŷ'r Felin in the manner that a harsh sergeant-major might run an army camp; and he was unduly preoccupied with both his own position and his ambitions, which involved demonstrating to the outside world that Tŷ'r Felin was (as he saw it) a model community home.

33.85 In reaching a conclusion about the allegations against Nefyn Dodd we have had to take into account the overall picture that we have received of him in relation to other community homes as well as Tŷ'r Felin. We have had in mind the fact that corporal punishment was not prohibited in Gwynedd officially until February 1983 and that over the years Tŷ'r Felin had to accommodate a wide range of children, some of whom were very unruly at times. We accept also that, after a long lapse of time, there has been an element of exaggeration in some of the evidence before us. Nevertheless, we are satisfied that Dodd did frequently use excessive force to the children in his care. Such conduct was not, in our view, habitual but it did reflect frailties in his temperament and his determination to stamp upon behaviour that cast a reflection upon the home or appeared to challenge his authority in any way. Thus, he would inflict inappropriate physical punishment upon absconders and was prone to do so for illicit smoking or other breaches of his rules that he regarded as flagrant or impertinent. For the most part, however, he relied upon his build, his voice and his personality to dominate the home.

Other allegations of physical abuse

33.86 The only other former members of the staff against whom many complaints of physical abuse have been made are June Dodd and the teacher, John Roberts.

33.87 We are aware that about ten former residents made such complaints against **June Dodd** and we received evidence from four of them, although only one (D[25]) gave oral evidence to us. D's complaint was that, in 1978, June Dodd used to inflict "Chinese burns" as a method of punishment[26], mostly for boys, and

---

[25] See paras 33.70 and 33.71.
[26] D described this as holding the forearm and the wrist of the victim with separate hands and then twisting the victim's skin in opposite directions.

that he suffered excruciating pain when she did this to him. It was a punishment for offences such as talking or giggling. The only witness to allege a serious assault by June Dodd said in his written statement that she kneed him in the groin when he was at Tŷ'r Felin for three months in the summer of 1991. Someone had "set light" to Nefyn Dodd's dog and a cleaner had told June Dodd that a friend of this witness had done it. When June Dodd confronted the friend in a corridor the witness butted in and told her that the friend could not have done it because he had been with the witness. She was very angry and kneed him in the groin, telling him to keep out of it and saying that she had flushed bigger things than him down the toilet. The witness was not bruised but was in pain for about ten minutes.

33.88 Both the other witnesses were former girl residents of Tŷ'r Felin who complained of punishments imposed by June Dodd rather than physical attacks. One of them was a resident who was sent to Tŷ'r Felin on remand towards the end of 1986; she said that she had no real complaints except that "we were being constantly locked in our rooms". She recalled one occasion when she was locked in the kitchen pantry by June Dodd for about half an hour after she had run away from the home because she had not been let out on her father's birthday. She was also required to wear her night dress and dressing gown "for most of the time" if she had run away or attempted to do so. The second of these witnesses was at Tŷ'r Felin three years later for eight and a half months, having been found to be beyond the control of her mother. In her statements to the Tribunal (but not in a 1992 statement to the police) this witness alleged that she had been abused by June Dodd in the sense that the latter had frequently made her wear pyjamas and had locked her and others in a room overnight from about 6 pm to 8 am. On one of these occasions the witness had escaped through a window in her pyjamas, had found a pair of shoes in a skip and had then obtained a lift to her home, about 20 miles away, from a passing motorist.

33.89 The main allegations were put to June Dodd when she gave her oral evidence but she denied them. She could not remember D being at Tŷ'r Felin. She recalled the dog incident, because the dog subsequently became incontinent and had to be put down, but she had not kneed anyone in the groin. As for punishments, she agreed that putting residents in nightwear and locking in a room for short periods were sanctions that were used, as we have already stated, but she denied locking girls in a room overnight. The only "physical incident" involving her that was recorded had occurred at Tŷ Newydd and had been the subject of a contemporary complaint by Alison Taylor, who had not been present when it happened.

33.90 It is convenient to deal with that incident here because there is no other allegation of abuse by June Dodd at that home. It appears that Gethin Evans[27] was telephoned by a temporary RCCO at Tŷ Newydd during the evening of Sunday 2 February 1986. The RCCO alleged that she had a riot on her hands and was unable to cope; she was not willing to sleep in and was threatening to

---

[27] Owain Gethin Evans was then Assistant Director (Children) and Head of Children's Services.

leave the home. Nefyn Dodd was unavailable and so June Dodd, who was about to go off duty at Tŷ'r Felin, was given authority to take any necessary action. In the event June Dodd had to go over to Tŷ Newydd in the early hours of the following morning because of continuing trouble there and an 11 year old boy alleged that June Dodd struck him ("thumped him on the shoulder") in the office at Tŷ Newydd with the result that he fell into a chair. The boy reported the matter the following day to Alison Taylor, the Officer-in-Charge at Tŷ Newydd, a police officer and another member of the care staff but he did not make a formal complaint: he mentioned the matter when refusing to go to school and there was no physical sign of the assault.

33.91 June Dodd denied any assault upon or physical contact with the boy when interviewed. She admitted shouting at him because he was impolite and refused to apologise for his actions; he fell over into the chair in fright. Gethin Evans, who investigated Alison Taylor's complaint, wrote a report on the matter and concluded that, although there was a divergence of opinion as to whether June Dodd had touched the boy, it did not merit attention because, if she had done so, it would have been a reasonable reaction to the situation. The boy involved, who would now be in his mid-twenties, did not give evidence to the Tribunal and June Dodd said that she cannot now recall the details of what happened.

33.92 In our judgment it would be quite inappropriate on this evidence to find that June Dodd was guilty of physically abusing children in her care either at Tŷ'r Felin or elsewhere. We have no doubt that her disciplinary approach, especially in the early years, was governed by Nefyn Dodd's attitudes but the balance of the evidence before us suggests that, in general, she adopted less harsh methods when she felt able to do so. Her position was inevitably difficult because she was employed as a care worker and then as Deputy in the community home of which her husband was Officer-in-Charge in contravention of generally approved good practice. One of the many adverse consequences of this was that she was distrusted by some as a spy for Nefyn Dodd; and nothing that we have heard in this inquiry has led us to doubt the soundness of the normal practice of not employing man and wife as residential care staff in the same community home or in any line management relationship.

33.93 The number of complainants of physical abuse by **John Roberts** was similar to that in respect of June Dodd but they alleged much severer abuse. In the event we heard oral evidence from six of these former residents and we received written evidence from two others, both of whom had been resident at Tŷ Newydd whilst attending school at Tŷ'r Felin.

33.94 John Roberts was 32 years old when he became teacher-in-charge at Tŷ'r Felin in September 1979. Up to that point his main experience had been of remedial teaching, after obtaining his teacher's certificate at the Normal College, Bangor, in 1968. He had been a remedial teacher at Llangefni Comprehensive School for four and a half years and had then served for a similar period as a peripatetic remedial teacher. Roberts' relocation to Tŷ'r Felin was stated to be temporary but he remained there for nearly six years until July 1985. He was then transferred to the special unit of a primary school from September 1985.

During his Tŷ'r Felin period he was absent for the academic year 1981/1982 whilst attending a full time course at Chester Training College for an advanced diploma in the education of children with special needs.

33.95 A principal critic of John Roberts was witness D[28], who described him as a "trainee Nefyn Dodd". D said Roberts had no self-control whatsoever. There were only three other pupils in the class at that time and, if D was to talk to one of them or giggle with them, Roberts would "lose it" and "go ballistic". Roberts would shake him by the head whilst slapping him violently; and five minutes later would give him a quick jab with a pencil in his ear or his back or his arm as a reminder that Roberts had not forgotten the earlier incident. D said also that, because he was only about four and a half feet tall, the revolving blackboard would connect with the top of his head as the bottom was swung upwards or downwards. He alleged that he and other pupils were deliberately struck in this way by the blackboard when Roberts revolved it and that on some occasions this was done as Nefyn Dodd watched through a window from the latter's office. D remembered also being caned by Roberts.

33.96 The difficulty about the allegations of D against John Roberts is that the documentary evidence before the Tribunal suggests that D was only at Tŷ'r Felin for eight days during Roberts' period there. As we have said earlier, D's major stay at Tŷ'r Felin was for about eight weeks at the beginning of 1978[29], over 18 months before Roberts was posted there. D's only other admission to Tŷ'r Felin was for about eight days at the beginning of June 1981, said to have been at his mother's request; and it seems clear that D's allegations relate essentially to the earlier and longer period in 1978. D remained adamant in cross-examination that John Roberts assaulted him as described and he complained of being slapped by Roberts in the first of his statements to the police before us, made as long ago as 8 August 1991. However, he did not suggest that he attended the educational unit at Tŷ'r Felin when resident elsewhere (for example, in Y Gwyngyll for six weeks in 1981 and 15 months in 1983/1984). In these circumstances there must be considerable doubt about the veracity of his allegations against Roberts.

33.97 The three other male former residents who gave oral evidence about physical abuse by John Roberts all alleged that they had been assaulted severely by him. Witness C[30], for example, said that he was always aggressive and nasty and that C learned nothing from him. C alleged that Roberts assaulted him three or four times: on one occasion Roberts hit him on the head with a snooker cue and on another threw a blackboard duster at him. C did not know of any resident who "got on" with Roberts. Witness A[31] also complained that he learned nothing: his recollection of class was of always watching stupid programmes on television. A alleged that, after he had made a silly remark, Roberts hit him in

---

[28] See paras 33.70, 33.71 and 33.87.
[29] See para 33.70.
[30] See paras 33.64 to 33.69.
[31] See para 33.63.

the face with the result that his nose exploded and bled. That was the only assault by Roberts upon him but, in his view, Roberts was a bad teacher and a "bully with the kids".

33.98 Witness E[32] also was very critical of Roberts' teaching and his use of children's programmes on television. He said that, to keep discipline, Roberts would "hit (you) across the head with his hand or throw things at you or shout at you". E spoke of a specific incident, outside class, when he had had a fight at dinner time with another resident who had spilled orange juice over him. Roberts, on seeing what was happening, chased and pursued E until he knocked E to the floor in the hallway and then kicked and punched him in the face, with the result that his eye or face was swollen. This assault was witnessed by June Dodd, according to E, but she did nothing about it.

33.99 The other complainant against Roberts to give oral evidence was at Tŷ'r Felin as a girl resident for seven months in 1985, in the course of which period Roberts left. Her recollection is that she was not taught by him for very long but she does remember that Roberts threw the blackboard duster at her a few times, although it only actually hit her once.

33.100 One other former girl resident, who was at Tŷ'r Felin for three months in 1983, gave evidence of seeing boys struck by Roberts, whom she described as very aggressive. She said that one of them, who used to pull faces and generally act silly to cheer the others up, was beaten daily by Roberts (and by Dodd). She also saw Roberts strike that boy on the head with the revolving blackboard. Another boy was struck by Roberts frequently and there was physical abuse every day.

33.101 The two witnesses who attended school at Tŷ'r Felin from Tŷ Newydd both complained of serious assaults by John Roberts. The first was there in 1981/1982 and he, like others, complained of being hit by the blackboard duster when Roberts threw it at him: the duster hit him on his head, which bled a little. Roberts, however, then walked up to him and slapped him across the head, knocking him to the floor or causing him to fall off his chair. Roberts then kicked him on his upper body as he lay on the floor. Roberts slapped him across the head on two further occasions without injuring him, and the witness saw Roberts hit several other boys (but not girls) during classes.

33.102 Finally, the other witness alleged that he was assaulted by Roberts on 24 May 1984. The witness had walked over to another pupil who was having trouble with his work, whereupon Roberts went over to him and smacked him very hard on the side of his face. The witness said in his statement that his face became very swollen and that he reported the incident to Alison Taylor on his return to Tŷ Newydd. She took him to the local hospital for an X-ray but there was no bone injury. This witness alleged also that Roberts slammed a desk down on his hand on another occasion.

---

[32] See para 33.73.

33.103 The incident on 24 May 1984 was taken up by Alison Taylor. It appears from contemporary documents that it was reported to her late the following day by the victim and another boy, who had witnessed it. The victim was taken to the hospital on 26 May 1984. His account that day of the incident was that he had gone to witness A's desk to borrow a book. When Roberts hit him, his forehead knocked against the desk and he felt dizzy. Alison Taylor observed swelling and bruising and she thought that the victim seemed to be "rather lethargic since the incident". She wrote a memorandum on 26 May 1984 to the Director of Social Services, Lucille Hughes, with a copy to Gethin Evans[33], reporting the incident. She informed also the Area Officer and the victim's social worker. The response of the Director on 30 May 1984 was to request Alison Taylor to supply a completed insurance form, which she did, but Taylor is not aware of any other action that was taken. She received a telephone call from June Dodd, who said, in effect "How could you let us down?".

33.104 John Roberts denied all these allegations of physical abuse by him. He said that discipline was not a problem at Tŷ'r Felin because of the small numbers, which usually varied between four and eight in the classroom. Roberts was the only teacher officially but there were three qualified teachers on the care staff, who helped from time to time with their own expertise. He was left by the Education Department to get on with the job and no one inspected the education unit at Tŷ'r Felin. The curriculum was devised by him and based on the needs of individuals. Pupils spent varying periods attending the unit, and from time to time pupils from Tŷ Newydd and Y Gwyngyll would attend, but it was not usual for any pupil to attend for a longer continuous period than two months at a time. Roberts estimated that about 100 children had passed through his hands whilst he was teaching at Tŷ'r Felin. An objective was that pupils should go on to attend local schools, if that was practicable.

33.105 Dealing with the specific allegations made against him, Roberts accepted that he had shouted at some pupils. When he was at Tŷ'r Felin he had believed that there was a place for corporal punishment, if all else failed, but he had never used it. He had never thrown a blackboard duster after an incident in Cheshire very early in his teaching career. In relation to the other allegations, Roberts said that:

(i) he had no recollection of D at Tŷ'r Felin;

(ii) C had been struck by the blackboard accidentally as Roberts swung it upwards, whilst C was standing nearby, sharpening a pencil;

(iii) A had been prone to suffer nose bleeds and had not been struck;

(iv) he had intervened in the fight between E and another boy and had escorted E away but E had then become hysterical and had fallen to the floor whilst struggling: Roberts had merely restrained him and E had calmed down after about five minutes;

---

[33] See footnote 27 to para 33.90.

(v) he had found that the best way of dealing with the joker had been to isolate him at the back of the class; on one occasion he did tap the boy on the side because he was pulling faces to amuse the class whilst having his book marked at Roberts' desk;

(vi) his recollection of the incident on 24 May 1984 was that the boy had been out of his place in the classroom disrupting others; Roberts asked the boy to sit down and put his hand on the boy's head and directed him towards his seat.

33.106 We did not hear any very persuasive evidence either way about John Roberts from former members of the care staff at Tŷ'r Felin. The Dodds were predictably supportive of him. On the other hand, Peter Jones, who gave evidence of the alleged incident in Nefyn Dodd's office at which (he said) John Roberts was present[34], said also that Roberts would haul children off by the ear and that on one occasion he saw Roberts punch C, who was a cheeky boy, on the ear. We did receive, however, written statements attesting to Roberts' general good character and his successful work with children from teachers and others who knew him as a remedial teacher and/or as secretary/leader of Llanfairpwll group of the Urdd Gobaith Cymru (Welsh League of Youth). In another statement David Alan Parry, who was Deputy Director of Social Services for Gwynedd with responsibility for children's services from 1976 to 1981, said that he paid regular visits to Tŷ'r Felin during that period and that he seldom did so without randomly looking into the classroom or having a discussion with Roberts. He found the atmosphere in the classroom "relaxed and committed". In his view the children appeared to be at ease with Roberts and he never heard Roberts reprimand a child without doing it in a humorous way. He found Roberts' relationship with children to be "humane, kindly and reasonable".

33.107 After leaving Tŷ'r Felin John Roberts taught in the Special Needs Unit at Ysgol Maesincla, a primary school in Caernarvon, until July 1992, when he was suspended from duty as a result of allegations made against him in the course of the major police investigation. He had earlier received an informal warning in April 1992 from the Assistant Director of Education (Personnel) as the result of complaints by the mother of a nine year old boy at the school arising out of incidents on 23 January and 6 April 1992. The decision not to prosecute Roberts in respect of the Tŷ'r Felin investigations was taken by early 1993 but he remained suspended until a disciplinary hearing took place on 9 November 1994. During the interim period Roberts had worked from January 1993 in the Area Office at Llangefni assisting the Youth and Community Service. The outcome of the disciplinary hearing was that Roberts was given a formal written warning "regarding (his) work as a teacher arising from the alleged incidents during (his) time at Tŷ'r Felin". He resigned from his teaching post and was appointed as an administrative officer with the pupils' service unit from 1 January 1995.

---

[34] See para 33.82.

33.108 Our firm conclusion is that Roberts did use inappropriate and excessive physical force to some of his pupils during his tenure of the teaching post at Tŷ'r Felin. The total volume of complaints against him has not been specially high and the proportion of his former pupils at Tŷ'r Felin who have come forward to give evidence against him is comparatively small, but we reject any suggestion that there has been an orchestrated conspiracy against him. In mitigation it can be said that he was greatly under the general influence of Nefyn Dodd, who had already established his own regime at Tŷ'r Felin by the time that Roberts took up his appointment there. It must be said also that Roberts did not receive any specific professional training or guidance in dealing with the wide range of disturbed children who attended his classroom at Tŷ'r Felin, other than his teachers' training in special needs and remedial work. These disadvantages do not, however, excuse his excesses or his failure to recognise and admit that he was at fault.

33.109 The only other member of the staff who it is necessary to identify as the target of complaints of physical abuse is **Mari Thomas**, formerly Roberts Jones, who was employed on the care staff at Tŷ'r Felin from 7 June 1981 until 9 April 1988, when she left to take up the post of Officer-in-Charge at Cartref Bontnewydd[35]. Thomas impressed Nefyn Dodd during her period of probation as a temporary RCCO and he described her as "a highly efficient dependable worker who at all times has given punctilious attention to the children in her care" in April 1982, when she applied successfully for a permanent appointment as an RCCO at Tŷ'r Felin from 1 May 1982. It seems that she became de facto Third-in-Charge and a temporary Senior RCCO on 1 August 1982 under Nefyn and June Dodd, when the person who had been Deputy following Alison Taylor's departure (Alison Bradshaw) left[36]. Thomas' promotion as a permanent Senior RCCO followed in 1984.

33.110 Four witnesses, of whom three gave oral evidence to us, made complaints about the conduct of Mari Thomas at Tŷ'r Felin. The first of the "live" witnesses described her as two-faced and said that she would lock you in your room until the next day for just messing about. His most serious complaint was that Thomas and another member of staff had sent him to his room for misbehaving in a minibus, on returning from a visit to a swimming bath, and that Thomas had then given him big slaps across the face whilst he was held by the other staff member. One other witness who alleged being assaulted by Thomas said that, after he had returned from a party by taxi at 3 am instead of by bus at 10.30 pm, Thomas attacked him next morning in his bedroom at 7.30 am, lashing out at him and dragging him out of bed by his hair.

33.111 The other two witnesses made lesser complaints. One (a woman) said that Thomas was one of Nefyn Dodd's henchwomen: she was very big and aggressive and used to push people around. The written evidence of the other was that on a number of occasions Thomas would come into the day room and

---

[35] See para 33.47.
[36] See paras 33.11, 33.12 and 33.29.

put her hand over his nose and mouth with the result that he felt that he was being suffocated. He did not know why she did this to him and he had not done anything wrong.

33.112 In her evidence to the Tribunal Mari Thomas denied each of these allegations except the last, which could have happened when playing around (but she did not recall it). She accepted that she had been strict but that had been expected of the staff. She had told off the boys referred to in paragraph 33.110 but she had not struck either of them. She agreed in cross-examination that she had been forced to follow the regime laid down by Nefyn Dodd and that there had not been any training in how to restrain children.

33.113 We accept that, for some, Mari Thomas was part of the overall oppressive atmosphere of Tŷ'r Felin in view of her close link with the Dodds and her status in the hierarchy. In our judgment, however, the evidence before us falls far short of establishing that she physically abused residents at Tŷ'r Felin.

33.114 It seems that about ten other former members of the staff from time to time during the Dodds' regime were the subject of allegations of physical abuse by individual complaints of varying gravity. It would be inappropriate to identify any of them, however, because only four complainants came forward with evidence in support of the allegations and one of them had withdrawn her complaint. It is fair to say also that another of the four had pleaded guilty in the Magistrates' Court to assaulting the member of staff blamed by him for the relevant incident. In these circumstances the evidence against other members of the staff has not added anything of substance to the general picture that we have given.

The quality of care generally

33.115 There is little that we need to add here under this heading for two reasons. Firstly, the most significant aspects of the quality of care at Tŷ'r Felin have already been described in the section of this chapter dealing with the disciplinary climate under Nefyn Dodd[37]. Secondly, many of the other relevant aspects of the quality of care were common to the other local authority community homes in Gwynedd and can be dealt with more conveniently in a later chapter. It is necessary, however, to make some additional points about Tŷ'r Felin briefly.

33.116 There was no complaints procedure until the late 1980s. A document entitled "Handbook for Children in Residential Care", drafted by Nefyn Dodd and approved by Gethin Evans was circulated to the heads of community homes in Gwynedd on or about 28 October 1988. This 15 page booklet contained useful information about being in care, the responsibility of social workers, the various statutory provisions governing committal to care, reviews, medicals, complaints, discipline, visits, leave, care planning and leaving care. According to the booklet, residents were free to complain and were invited to discuss their complaint with whoever was supervising them, which might be the area (field)

---

[37] See paras 33.30 to 33.55.

or residential social worker. If they were unwilling or unable to do so, they were advised to contact the Director of Social Services, whose address and telephone number were given (together with the name of the person acting on behalf of the Director in services for young people and children). The evidence of Nefyn Dodd was that this booklet was subsequently handed to each child but contrary evidence from some members of staff suggests that it was more usually retained by the head of home and (at best) available in his office.

33.117 The booklet made passing reference only to the residential key workers, without explaining who or what they were. The evidence before us is that a key worker system was introduced in or about 1985 but few of the witnesses referred to it and it does not appear to have had any significant impact upon the residents who were intended to benefit from it. The absence of any clear account of the role of a residential key worker in the booklet confirms our view that the system was not implemented in any detail and that it was of little practical benefit to residents during the period under review. Commenting upon it in relation to Tŷ'r Felin in the autumn of 1988, two Welsh Office inspectors said "The concept of key worker was an administrative method of nominal allocation rather than a social work method".

33.118 Nefyn Dodd's evidence was that, before this booklet was circulated, residents of Tŷ'r Felin were told that they could complain: there was a list of relevant telephone numbers posted in both offices at Tŷ'r Felin and residents had access to the telephone. There was also a written grievance procedure for members of the staff. A practical difficulty for most of the period to December 1989 was that Nefyn Dodd was not only the dominant Officer-in-Charge but also the line manager for other heads of home. This was certainly the position from the time when he became responsible for all the community homes in 1982[38] and he himself emphasised this in several memoranda. Mari Thomas said that it was difficult or impossible for a child's complaint to go higher due to Dodd's position in the Department.

33.119 Despite the difficulties a few complaints were made by residents. We have recounted in paragraphs 33.102 and 33.103 what happened when Alison Taylor took up one such complaint in 1984. Two other complaints that she passed on from Tŷ Newydd received a negative response. In respect of the incident involving June Dodd, outlined in paragraphs 33.90 and 33.91, Gethin Evans told her that she was making mountains out of molehills. Again, on 30 July 1985 she wrote a report to Nefyn Dodd on an allegation by a girl resident that she had been hit by a male member of the Tŷ Newydd staff and Taylor discussed this allegation with Gethin Evans. The latter did speak to the member of staff but then told Taylor that the man had been under stress and that nothing was to be done.

33.120 More seriously, another former member of the care staff at Tŷ'r Felin, who was there for 20 months in 1983 and 1984, told the Tribunal that in 1984 he received a complaint from a boy (not a witness before the Tribunal) that he had been struck by John Roberts and observed that the boy had a lump on his head. The

---

[38] See paras 33.23 to 33.25.

staff member wrote a report of this complaint in the boy's file but the next day he was called by Nefyn Dodd to the general office, where Roberts was already present, and he was told that the report had been deleted from the file (or he was told to remove it himself).

33.121 That staff member left Tŷ'r Felin in August 1984. Five months later he wrote to the new Deputy Director of Social Services for Gwynedd, (David) Glanville Owen, who had moved to Gwynedd on appointment to that office in April 1984, complaining about many aspects of Nefyn Dodd's management of Tŷ'r Felin, including his relationships with staff. Amongst the complaints directly affecting the residents that he made were allegations of favouritism, physical abuse, lack of food, inappropriate punishments and excessive control of children's free time. He gave, as examples of physical abuse, the incident referred to in paragraph 33.83, of which he was the witness, and that referred to in paragraph 33.120. The response four months later was in a letter in the name of the Director of Social Services (Lucille Hughes) but bearing Owen's reference. It stated that the complaints had been thoroughly investigated and continued:

> "Following the investigation, I am confident that the Home is managed in accordance with Departmental policy and procedure and that the care given to the young people resident there is of a high standard.
>
> I also retain full confidence in the ability of Mr N Dodd to successfully manage the home."

33.122 When asked about this in cross examination Glanville Owen said that he saw the former staff member and explained to him the seriousness of his complaints, asking him whether he wished to "stand by" them. Subsequently, some of the complaints had been withdrawn, but not those under the heading of physical abuse. The allegations were looked at as a whole rather than individually and Nefyn Dodd denied all of them. The witness added that, looking at the matter 12 years on, he was quite appalled by the allegations and the way that they were or were not investigated by himself: he could only say that, in the 12 years, things had moved along considerably and positively because there was no way now that he would have allowed the letter to stand in the way that it stood 12 years ago.

33.123 Another matter that needs to be highlighted is the absence of individual care plans for children in residential care before the end of the 1980s. The handbook that we referred to included three paragraphs under the heading "Planning/Contract" outlining the contents of care plans and explaining when and how they were formulated but they appear to have been statements of aspiration rather than fact. The Welsh Office SWSOs found in 1988 that written contracts between children in care and social workers were used extensively in Gwynedd and almost all the children in residential care had on file written statements signed both by the children and by representatives of the authority; but the inspectors were sharply critical of the contents of these contracts and aspects of the planning process, including reviews.

33.124 Having regard to our terms of reference, it would be inappropriate for us to attempt an overall audit of the shortcomings in social work practice at Tŷ'r Felin but it is desirable to set out briefly here the main defects affecting the quality of care that have been disclosed by the evidence before us. These were:

(1) The lack of adequate assessment prior to the admission of a child to care. There were too many emergency admissions and, even in non-emergency cases, the purpose of admission to care was ill-defined; often it was stated to be "for assessment" without further analysis of probable outcomes in terms of placement or time. Welsh Office inspectors in 1988 could find "no correlation between the statutory basis of care and either the precipitating reason for admission or the current reason for being in care".

(2) The assessment process in care was defective because there were insufficient trained and experienced staff at Tŷ'r Felin to carry it out and residential staff were not given clear guidance about what they were supposed to be assessing. Too many children were left to drift "in the no-mans land between rehabilitation and permanence".

(3) There was an unacceptably low level of fieldwork contact with children in residential care.

(4) It was the practice for Nefyn Dodd, who was responsible for all placements within the County, to preside over all case conferences and it was his view that prevailed. Responsibility and authority were confused and the individual social worker was marginalised once a child entered residential care.

(5) There was no effective county strategy nor monitoring system with the result that placements were haphazard and depended too often on availability rather than suitability. One result of this in a county covering a large geographical area was that many children were placed at great distances from their home communities.

(6) Successive teachers at Tŷ'r Felin appear to have received no briefing as to their role and to have been required to function, in general, without supervision or professional support.

33.125 It is fair to add, however, that by 1988 Welsh Office SWSOs did find that the general atmosphere at Tŷ'r Felin during their inspection was relaxed and friendly. It felt generally accepting and "there was evidence of good rapport with the young people", although they felt over-supervised outside the home. The inspectors noted also that there was no evidence of families being pushed aside and excluded once their children had been received into care.

The aftermath of the Dodds' regime (1993 to 1995)

33.126 Unhappily, the departure of the Dodds did not lead to a period of tranquillity at Tŷ'r Felin and within three years the home was closed. None of the complainants who gave evidence to the Tribunal was resident at Tŷ'r Felin during this last period but we received oral and written evidence about it from Dafydd Ifans, who was Principal Officer (Children and Adolescent Services) from 29 March 1993 and, as such, line manager responsible for the three remaining community homes for children in Gwynedd. We received also copies of a report on Tŷ'r Felin by O and K Associates, dated 14 February 1995, commissioned by the Director of Social Services in September 1994.

33.127 According to Ifans a number of improvements were instituted shortly after his arrival, some of which had already been set in hand. Thus, the first inspections by an independent Inspection Unit took place and the inspectors' reports were put before the Children's Sub-Committee; a staff counselling scheme was introduced; a training scheme for residential staff on topics more relevant to their work was organised; Officers-in-Charge were redesignated as Residential Team Managers; the role of the key worker within the home was re-defined; and an appropriate form of care plan was devised. At Tŷ'r Felin itself a number of important structural changes were also put in hand to improve the physical standards within the home.

33.128 Nevertheless, Ifans became aware within a very short time of his arrival that there were major difficulties at Tŷ'r Felin. The Residential Team Manager, although enthusiastic, was inexperienced. A Senior RCCO had to be suspended, then warned for misconduct and transferred to other duties. Other members of the staff misbehaved and there were divided loyalties. To make matters worse the Chairman of the Children's Sub-Committee was in the habit of making very frequent, unannounced visits to the home and intervening in its management inappropriately. Then in or about early March 1994 the personal diary of a young woman resident was reported to be missing but a month or so later a councillor and an ex-member of staff were said to have talked about the contents of the diary to others.

33.129 Without going into unnecessary detail, the outcome of these events was that O and K Associates, who were already advising the Social Services Department on other matters, were commissioned by the Director of Social Services on 6 September 1994 to investigate the circumstances surrounding the alleged theft of the diary and allegations contained in the diary. O and K Associates reported on 14 February 1995 after seeing more than 25 persons and their report was an important (probably crucial) factor in the decision of the Children's Sub-Committee in September 1995 to recommend the closure of Tŷ'r Felin.

33.130 The report found that three pages from the diary, covering the period 5 to 14 February 1994, in a brown envelope had been pushed through the door of the Chairman of the Social Services Committee and that she had passed them to the Director of Social Services on 25 April 1994; but the investigation did not reveal who had stolen the diary or who had passed the three pages to the Chairman. The allegations in the diary were that several television sets, two micro-wave ovens, a video-recorder and quantities of food had been stolen from the home over a period; that drugs and alcohol were being consumed by residents on the premises; that there had been several incidents of violence between residents; and that several of the residents were sexually active within the home during early 1994. The report referred also to the boredom of some of the residents, who were excluded from school for a variety of reasons but for whom no educational facilities were provided on the premises. Amongst the disturbing factors were the reaction following the departure of the Dodds and ensuing divided loyalties; the locating of the home within the Maesgeirchen Estate, resulting in ties with some "dubious and unsavoury elements who knew about drugs and how to dispose of stolen property"; and a sometimes disappointing level of partnership between the home and the fieldwork staff. The authors made numerous recommendations on the basis of their findings, including one directed to improving the quality of visits by councillors, but they were not implemented at Tŷ'r Felin because the home was closed.

Conclusions

33.131 There is no evidence that sexual abuse was prevalent at Tŷ'r Felin. Bearing in mind the length of the period under review, the number of allegations has been comparatively few and they do not suggest a pattern of habitual abuse by any member of the staff there. If sexual abuse did occur, it was on a few isolated occasions only and the evidence before us has not been sufficiently persuasive to justify a finding against any individual member of staff.

33.132 We are satisfied, however, that, during the Nefyn Dodd regime, he and the teacher, John Roberts, did use excessive physical force to residents and staff in care from time to time as we have indicated. Moreover, both of them enforced discipline in an inappropriately hectoring and authoritative manner with the result that the whole atmosphere of Tŷ'r Felin was unduly oppressive for many of its residents and staff over a period of several years. The impact of this was particularly severe on children who remained at the home beyond the "normal" maximum assessment period of 12 weeks and the proportion of these children appears to have risen in the 1980s as the distinctive role of Tŷ'r Felin as an observation and assessment centre became increasingly blurred. The atmosphere improved later, when John Roberts left the staff and as Nefyn Dodd became increasingly pre-occupied with other responsibilities. It is likely also that the police investigation in 1986 caused the latter to modify his conduct. But the aftermath of the Dodd's regime was a degree of anarchy and the home survived for only a short period, as we have explained.

33.133 We do not think that Nefyn Dodd's initial appointment as Officer-in-Charge of Tŷ'r Felin can fairly be criticised because it is likely that he presented himself well and he received a strongly favourable reference from Arnold of Bryn Estyn. It was a grave error, however, to give him additional and increasing responsibilities thereafter, despite the adverse independent Dyfed report in 1981, and his wife should not have been appointed to a senior position in the same community home. The combined effect of these actions was to facilitate the suppression of legitimate complaints about the regime at Tŷ'r Felin and to confer on Nefyn Dodd excessive powers and responsibilities beyond his capacity. These errors had direct impact on the quality of care generally at Tŷ'r Felin. In any event, however, effective monitoring and supervision of the community home ought to have revealed defects in Nefyn Dodd's attitudes and practices and to have led to a re-appraisal of him even before the police investigation in 1986.

33.134 Some of the wider failings in the quality of care generally were attributable to Nefyn Dodd's dominant role in assessment and placement decisions but much greater blame rests upon higher management for assigning that role to him, for failing to devise an effective county strategy for residential children's homes and for failing to ensure that appropriate care plans were formulated and implemented for the comparatively small number of children in residential care within Gwynedd. These are matters on which we will comment further when we deal with the responsibility of higher management in Gwynedd later in this report.

Tŷ Newydd, 1982 to 1987

Introduction

34.01 Tŷ Newydd at Llandegai is a rather forbidding stone building of the lodge type, which stands close to the A5122 road leading from the A5 and A55 trunk roads into Bangor; and it is about a mile south-east of the Maesgeirchen Estate, in which Tŷ'r Felin was located. It is now a bail hostel.

34.02 As we have said in paragraph 5.07(9), Tŷ Newydd was opened in 1978 as a hostel for up to ten boys aged 16 to 21 years and was so described in the 1979 Regional Plan for Wales. We have been told that it closed as a hostel in 1981 but it was visited in July or August 1981 by the Dyfed inquiry team, who commented:

> "At the time of our visit the Officer-in-Charge was away on an extended period of sick leave and the Home was staffed by one temporary Child Care Officer. We regret to record that we were appalled by the physical state of the Home, its furnishings, decoration and grounds. There is a serious failure on the part of management in allowing the placement of young people in the care of the County Council in such surroundings, and then to expect them to prepare themselves for life in the community."

However, we have not been informed of any complaint of abuse at the home prior to 1982.

34.03 Tŷ Newydd re-opened as a community home in 1982 to provide accommodation for up to 12 (but more usually nine) boys and girls in the age range from about five to 18 years, who attended local schools or Tŷ'r Felin for education. The home closed on 31 January 1987.

34.04 The number of complaints of abuse at Tŷ Newydd in the period from 1982 to 1987 would not justify a separate chapter on the home but it is necessary to give a brief account of it because the Officer-in-Charge from its reopening on 16 August 1982 until she was suspended from duty on 1 December 1986 was **Alison Taylor**[1]. Thus, she was in charge for very nearly the whole of the second phase of Tŷ Newydd's history as a community home. For the same period she held the post of Supervisor of an Intermediate Treatment Centre known as Canolfan, at Llanallgo, near Meolfre in Anglesey, about 15 miles from Tŷ Newydd.

34.05 We have not been given precise details of the staff establishment at Tŷ Newydd but it appears that the Deputy Officer-in-Charge from a date in 1982 or early 1983 until it closed was **Anna Rees Ashton,** who had been Officer-in-Charge of Pant yr Eithin Community Home at Harlech from October 1978 until that home closed in 1982. **Peter Gadd**, a former butcher and salesman, who was not

---

[1] See paras 2.08 to 2.22 and 33.11 to 33.21.

professionally trained, joined the staff as an RCCO in August 1979 and remained at Tŷ Newydd until 30 May 1984, when he transferred to Y Gwyngyll and then later to Queens Park and to Cartref Bontnewydd. It seems that he was effectively Third-in-Charge under Alison Taylor at Tŷ Newydd and that he acted as Deputy from 8 March 1984 to 22 May 1984, whilst Anna Ashton was absent sick.

34.06 According to Alison Taylor, Tŷ Newydd was in a state of considerable disrepair when she re-opened it; its quite extensive grounds were overgrown and the furniture and equipment inherited from the previous occupation were in "a disgraceful condition". Subsequently, she received "grudging sums" to spend on replacing broken beds and other essential items of furniture, but nothing else. She, some other members of the staff and the residents undertook decorating and general maintenance regularly and made periodic assaults on the grounds but, in her view, the physical conditions of Tŷ Newydd were barely fit to house children. It seemed to her that Tŷ Newydd was being deliberately run down in anticipation of its replacement by Cartref Bontnewydd, which opened as a community home in April 1988.

34.07 The history of Tŷ Newydd in its second phase is very much bound up with the complaints and allegations made by Alison Taylor leading ultimately to her dismissal. We have already outlined this part of the background to our inquiry in Chapter 2 of this report and it is not central to our terms of reference. It is necessary, however, to fill in some of the detail because it is relevant both to Alison Taylor's own motivation and by way of illustration of the response of higher management to complaints when they were made. We will deal with Alison Taylor's activities, therefore, after considering such evidence that we have received of complaints by residents of abuse at Tŷ Newydd.

Complaints by residents of abuse at Tŷ Newydd

34.08 We know of only one complaint by a resident of sexual abuse by a member of the staff at Tŷ Newydd. This was made by a former girl resident against a male member of the staff many years after the alleged event and related to one occasion only. There was no corroboration of the allegation and no evidence in support of it has been presented to the Tribunal.

34.09 Five other complainants are known to have alleged that they were struck by a member of staff at Tŷ Newydd. One man alleged that he had been slapped in a corridor by **Nefyn Dodd** when the latter was visiting Tŷ Newydd; and two former girl residents told the police that they had each been slapped once by **Alison Taylor,** but one of the two said that she had deserved it. A third former girl resident told the Tribunal that she had been struck across the head once by another (male) member of staff (X) on one occasion for refusing to join in football and that she reported this to Taylor. However, we received no evidence in support of their allegations.

34.10 The only Tŷ Newydd complainant who gave oral evidence to the Tribunal was there briefly in May 1984 and for just over three months a year later, when he was 15 years old. His allegations were directed against X, who (he said) liked to push people around and to abuse them vocally, but who was not physically threatening. However, the witness added that on one occasion X did grab him by the throat and pin him against the wall, apparently for giving cheek. In consequence, the witness stole a tin of petty cash and absconded to get away from X.

34.11 A log entry by Alison Taylor on 12 August 1985, the day of this incident (on which the witness was transferred to Queens Park), read:

> "Absconded 12.45 after argument with X over lunch. Bangor police informed immediately. Picked up on way to Bangor. Returned to Tŷ Newydd by 136 Rogers. Next hour spent in being extremely abusive, offensive and threatening to self (AGT) and X. Finally assaulted X and ran off. Bangor police informed. Arrangements made via O G Evans for transfer to Queen's Park Close."

When this entry was put to the witness, he said that it was completely inaccurate. It is to be noted also that a petty cash box was recorded as missing in the Tŷ Newydd log on 9 August 1985 and in the daily log on 10 August 1985. When it was recovered about £20 was said to be missing and PC Rogers took a statement from the complainant witness dealing with the amount that he said was in the box.

34.12 To sum up, we have not received any persuasive evidence of either sexual or other physical abuse at Tŷ Newydd. It appears that any use of physical force by staff rarely exceeded a slap in provocative circumstances. Whilst living conditions at Tŷ Newydd were far from ideal, the few witnesses who commented on the atmosphere there described it as relaxed and the female complainant against X told the police that Alison Taylor was very helpful.

Alison Taylor's complaints and the criticisms of her

34.13 It was probably inevitable that there would be conflict between Alison Taylor and Nefyn Dodd from the moment that she took up her appointment as Officer-in-Charge of Tŷ Newydd. Their views about how to run a residential home for children differed greatly and Taylor was placed in the unusual (and, in her view, inappropriate) position of reporting to Dodd, a fellow Officer-in-Charge, as her line manager. To underline the latter's dominant position, Gethin Evans sent a memorandum to Taylor on 10 August 1982, six days before she became Officer-in-Charge, outlining Dodd's duties and responsibilities[2].

34.14 A complicating factor in the Dodd/Taylor relationship was that Dodd's base was at Tŷ'r Felin but he was frequently elsewhere visiting other community homes or headquarters. He was not, therefore, readily available for discussion on many occasions. Dodd's instructions were that messages were to be left with

---

[2] See paras 33.23 and 33.24.

the senior person available on duty at Tŷ'r Felin but Alison Taylor was unwilling to relay sensitive information to persons whom she regarded as junior members of staff. Moreover, June Dodd effectively his Deputy during this period was quite often unavailable because Nefyn Dodd did not drive and she had to act as his chauffeur to and from other community homes. Thus, the seeds of persistent tension and irritation were well sown.

34.15 In the four years following Taylor's appointment to Tŷ Newydd there were two parallel developments of complaints and criticisms: on the one hand there were complaints to headquarters by Taylor about the system and about some individual cases of alleged maltreatment and, on the other hand, criticisms from headquarters of Taylor's own conduct, some of which she attributed to Dodd as instigator.

34.16 It would not be helpful to trace these developments in great detail. Alison Taylor's opinion, with which we agree, was that her line management arrangements were unworkable and she made her views known. It is also clear that she was reproved from time to time for approaching headquarters direct instead of through Nefyn Dodd. What is less clear from her own and other evidence is how her complaints of maltreatment of children in residential care developed.

34.17 On the basis of Taylor's own written statement to the Tribunal (called Statement Number One and undated but received in 1997), her history of relaying complaints by children in residential care whilst employed by Gwynedd County Council was as follows:

(1) In late 1976, whilst at Tŷ'r Felin, she reported to D A Parry, the Deputy Director of Social Services, that she had witnessed un-named girls being slapped across the face by the Officer-in-Charge, Haydn Jones. The latter went on extended sick leave and did not return.

(2) She reported to Dodd the complaint referred to in paragraph 33.14 but he said that he did not believe the allegations and instructed her to drop the matter. Taylor must be wrong about this, however, because Dodd arrived at Tŷ'r Felin nine months later.

(3) She did not report the incident in 1980 outlined in paragraph 33.69 but she warned Dodd and Roberts that she would report any subsequent assault to the police. It was an error of judgment by her, in her opinion, not to report it to the Deputy Director of Social Services.

(4) Whilst on attachment at Bryn Estyn she reported to her college supervisor a complaint by a boy resident, who later committed suicide, that he had been sexually abused by Peter Howarth (but it was ambiguous as to whether that boy or others had been abused). She had understood that Arnold was to be informed.

(5) She did not report similar complaints made by two boys to her on the day that she left Bryn Estyn because neither could face reporting the allegations and she respected their wishes.

(6) At Tŷ Newydd on 26 May 1984 she wrote a memorandum to the Director of Social Services, Lucille Hughes, about the alleged assault on a Tŷ Newydd resident by John Roberts, which is outlined in paragraphs 33.102 and 33.103, but the Director did not investigate the matter, as far as Taylor is aware.

(7) On 30 July 1985 she sent a written report to Dodd about an incident at Tŷ Newydd on 24 July 1985 referred to in paragraph 34.10 in which X was alleged to have slapped the third girl resident across the face. This followed a longer report, three days earlier, about inappropriate hostile behaviour on the part of X when the girl had been visited by her mother and brother on 14 July 1985. Taylor said that she had a telephone conversation about the matter with Gethin Evans, who interviewed X, but the former told her later that nothing was to be done about the complaint because X had been under stress. She had commented that it was a bad precedent.

(8) On 3 February 1986 she and her Deputy and a police officer were told by the complainant of the incident involving June Dodd that has been described in paragraphs 33.90 and 33.91. She made a complaint, which was dealt with by Gethin Evans, whose finding was that the boy had merely been pushed into a chair. She was told by Gethin Evans that she was creating trouble unnecessarily.

34.18 Alison Taylor did refer in her Statement Number One to the Tribunal to one other alleged incident that occurred before her suspension from duty. The alleged victim on this occasion was the first of the two witnesses referred to in paragraph 33.101, who attended a local school from Tŷ Newydd from mid 1982 until early 1984. According to Taylor, there was an occasion during this period when an altercation occurred at Tŷ Newydd between a local schoolmaster and Nefyn Dodd on the one hand and the boy (who was refusing to attend school) on the other in the course of which voices were raised and the boy was roughly handled in the hallway by the schoolmaster, who was abusing him vocally, encouraged by Dodd. Taylor said that the boy wanted to report the incident but saw no point in doing so because any complaint would have to be made through Dodd. She did not, however, report the incident herself and, in his statement to the police, made in 1992, the alleged victim, who was then 23 years old, said that he was not hit or otherwise ill treated by any of the staff at the school and that he could not recollect any relevant incident other than those that had occurred when he was attending school at Tŷ'r Felin.

34.19 It was early in 1986 when Alison Taylor approached Councillor Keith Marshall, a member of the Gwynedd Social Services Committee to complain of maladministration in the Social Services Department and violence by staff to children in residential care. She said in a subsequent letter to the Prime Minister (then the Rt Hon Margaret Thatcher MP) that "by late 1985 the burden of (her) knowledge was too great to ignore" and she had failed to get any positive response from the Social Services Department. Councillor Marshall consulted another councillor, who was then Vice-Chairman of the North Wales Police Authority and who advised that Taylor's allegations should be reported to the police. The result was that Detective Chief Superintendent Gwynne Owen, the head of the Criminal Investigation Department of the North Wales Police, met Taylor and Councillor Marshall at the latter's home in Bangor on 20 February 1986.

34.20 The subsequent history of Taylor's complaints and representations prior to the setting up of this Tribunal has been summarised in Chapter 2 and is dealt with more fully in Chapter 49. It is necessary to say here, however, that Detective Chief Superintendent Owen listed the complaints that she made to him under nine different heads of which a number were organisational or administrative and only four heads related directly to alleged abuse of children in care. Taylor referred to eight cases of alleged abuse at Tŷ'r Felin and Tŷ Newydd, including the incidents mentioned in sub-paragraphs (6), (7) and (8) of paragraph 34.17. Four of the other allegations related mainly to conduct of Nefyn Dodd at Tŷ'r Felin; and there was reference to suspected homosexual activity by a member of staff at another community home, which has not been supported by any evidence subsequently. Taylor did not allege, however, that these other allegations had been reported by her to higher authority before her meeting with Detective Chief Superintendent Owen.

34.21 In the event Taylor's allegations were investigated by the North Wales Police to the extent that the matters complained of constituted criminal offences and we deal with that investigation in Chapter 51 of this report. Councillor Marshall did not disclose to others the source of the allegations but it became widely known or believed that Taylor had instigated the investigation and her relationships with some colleagues deteriorated further.

34.22 Before this happened Alison Taylor had already been the subject of some criticism. We have recounted in paragraphs 33.18 and 33.19 how she received an official reprimand in February 1978 whilst still at Tŷ'r Felin. On 8 June 1984 she received a formal oral warning from Gethin Evans[3] for failing to meet a group of six magistrates on 4 May 1984 when they visited Tŷ Newydd, although she had been on the premises in her office at the time. Her explanations included confusion about the date of the visit and the after effects of influenza but they were not regarded as satisfactory. In March 1985 she was criticised by Nefyn Dodd for appearing at a Court hearing in respect of a resident without prior consultation with him and for consulting a higher officer without informing him. In May 1985 Taylor herself was complaining to the County Personnel Officer about various allegations said to have been made against her, including one that she was "never at work". There were also exchanges of correspondence about the needs of Tŷ Newydd, including repairs, with Dodd and headquarters, to which the reply (on 26 November 1985) was that the Director was most anxious that no great expense should be incurred at Tŷ Newydd "with its closure imminent". On 11 November 1985, in response to further criticisms by Taylor, Dodd wrote of her:

---

[3] The Head of Children's Services.

"In terms of progress/development it is <u>sincerely</u> felt that this worker remains the victim of her own folly, in that she fails miserably to exploit her own potential, and persists with her insatiable appetite for mayhem and conflict with management and area based child care worker teams, whilst less experienced O-i-Cs, potentially less capable, use their personal talents and attributes to the full, for the benefit of client children and the dept."

34.23 It seems likely that Alison Taylor had become increasingly isolated from management by 2 October 1986 when she was visited at Tŷ Newydd by the Chairman of the Social Services Committee, Councillor Eric Davies. A number of community workers were undertaking renovations, including painting, and Councillor Davies discussed with Taylor her various complaints and concerns. But his report three days later on the discussion concluded:

"Finally, having interviewed this person, at length, I am of the opinion that she is a most unfit person to be in charge of a children's home, and that she is a blatant trouble maker, with a most devious personality, and one in my estimation who is very much involved with the anonymous letters[4] which have been circulating.

I would very humbly suggest that Tŷ Newydd be closed as soon as possible, and that this lady's services be dispensed with at the earliest possible time."

34.24 In her letter of 1 December 1986, in which she instructed Taylor to remain off duty and away from Tŷ Newydd, the Director of Social Services (Lucille Hughes) said:

"I have become increasingly concerned that the spirit of professional trust and co-operation between you and your colleagues in the residential child care sector, which is so necessary for the efficient running of that service, has broken down."

Taylor was informed that the Director wished to investigate the situation and, in a further letter dated 13 January 1987, the Director said that she had concluded that the breakdown in professional relationships was a real one and was the direct result of Taylor's work performance and attitude over a considerable period. Taylor was formally suspended from the latter date on full pay pending consideration of the matter in accordance with the County Council's disciplinary procedures.

34.25 The Area Officer of NUPE was subsequently supplied, by letter dated 4 February 1987, with "examples of the kind of work performance and attitudes on Mrs Taylor's part which (had) led to the breakdown in professional relationships between members of the Residential Child Care section and Mrs Taylor". It was alleged that her behaviour and attitude had created insecurity, anxiety and mistrust of her amongst a substantial number of colleagues, undermining the effectiveness of the Department's services to children; that her management of Tŷ Newydd had been seriously deficient,

---

[4] We have received no evidence about these.

including failure to pull her weight in respect of time-keeping and duties; that she had consistently failed to co-operate with management and had ignored or undermined the administrative/managerial process; that she had not acted in an acceptable professional manner towards the children; and that she had attempted to create rifts and tensions between Nefyn Dodd and other colleagues by untruths and deceit.

34.26 Various members of the staff at Tŷ'r Felin and Tŷ Newydd, including Ashton and Gadd, supplied written statements to the County Council in support of these allegations. It is not within our remit, however, to adjudicate upon them. Although Taylor was summarily dismissed following a meeting of the County Council's Disciplinary Panel on 2 November 1987, which Taylor did not attend, she appealed against that decision and began proceedings for unfair dismissal. Before a hearing of either took place a compromise was agreed on 25 August 1989 under which Taylor accepted voluntary redundancy together with financial compensation and costs in full settlement of her claim.

Conclusions

34.27 We do not think that grave criticism would be justified of the manner in which the very limited number of contemporary complaints about abuse at Tŷ Newydd were dealt with. The most serious contemporary complaint emanating from there related to abuse at Tŷ'r Felin rather than Tŷ Newydd and is referred to in paragraph 34.17(6). There is no evidence before us of any effective response by headquarters to that complaint about John Roberts and, in our judgment, the failure to investigate it was a glaring omission. Less severely, we do criticise also the response to the complaint about X[5] because, in our view, on the limited evidence before us, a formal disciplinary investigation should have taken place, whether or not X was suffering from stress at the time.

34.28 It is clear that Alison Taylor was a thorn in the side of higher management from the moment when she returned to Gwynedd after professional training. In our view this was attributable to a substantial degree to the decisions to give Nefyn Dodd wide additional responsibilities and to retain him as Officer-in-Charge of Tŷ'r Felin. There were faults on both sides but Alison Taylor's complaints about Nefyn Dodd and John Roberts, although at times exaggerated, have been substantially vindicated by our own findings. In the event Dodd's position as her line manager placed her in great difficulty and she would have failed in her duty to the residents in care if she had remained silent.

34.29 It is more difficult to evaluate Taylor's own performance as Officer-in-Charge of Tŷ Newydd. There is no persuasive evidence that she acted contrary to the interests of the children in her care and there is some evidence that her relationship with them was good. It seems likely, however, that she had failings as a manager and leader of staff with the result that she did not endear herself to many of her colleagues, who were not prepared to support her when major disciplinary proceedings were taken against her.

---

[5] See para 34.17(7).

Y Gwyngyll, 1979 to 1986

Introduction

35.01 Y Gwyngyll was a purpose-built community home for children in a small private housing estate at Llanfairpwll (Llanfair PG) in Anglesey, about three miles from the suspension bridge over the Menai Straits. Although plans were submitted to the Welsh Office as early as 1974 and a cost limit approved, the building was not completed until 1978. It opened in January 1979 when the staff and five children who had been resident at 43/44 Ucheldre, Llangefni were transferred to Y Gwyngyll and the former closed as a children's home[1]. In the 1979 version of the Regional Plan for Wales Y Gwyngyll was shown as providing accommodation for 16 boys and girls aged 0 to 18 years plus bed-sitting accommodation for two school leavers.

35.02 We have been told that the building was selected for an architectural award when it was first constructed but successive professionally qualified and independent social service officers were critical of its appearance, lay-out and amenities. It was architecturally unconventional and lacked warmth and a homely feeling. For example, the interior walls were unplastered and painted white with a large green or red circle in the centre of some of the larger wall areas. Windows reached down to floor level in the bedrooms and living rooms and light wood panelling added to the home's ultra modern appearance. Accommodation was on two floors (there were also unused attic rooms) and there was a downstairs flat intended for the use of the Officer-in-Charge. The garden comprised small grassed areas to the rear and side of the building and adjoined the playing field of the local primary school.

35.03 The first Officer-in-Charge of Y Gwyngyll from 1 January 1979 was **R A Dyson,** a man in his early 50s, who had previously been in charge for 17 years of a voluntary children's home in Derbyshire, catering mainly for children with special educational needs. Dyson had obtained the CRCCYP at Northampton. He remained as Officer-in-Charge at Y Gwyngyll until the summer of 1981 but he was off sick for several months at the end of this period and the number of residents in mid-1981 was only six. Whilst he was ill in 1981 the Acting Officer-in-Charge was **Valmai Haf Morris**, who transferred from Queens Park to Y Gwyngyll on 6 April 1981[2]. When Dyson's successor was appointed to take over from 14 September 1981, Haf Morris reverted to Senior RCCO and she remained at Y Gwyngyll until it closed in 1986.

35.04 The first Deputy Officer-in-Charge was **Pamela Jones,** who had been Officer-in-Charge at 43/44 Ucheldre and who was transferred with a woman RCCO and the children to Y Gwyngyll from 19 January 1979. Pamela Jones' relationship with Dyson proved to be difficult, however, and she apparently left

[1] See para 5.02(2).
[2] See further para 36.04.

early in 1980 after starting a CSS course at Bangor, from which she had to withdraw because of illness. Her personal file was not available to us and we have no information about her subsequent history. It does not appear that any successor to Pamela Jones was appointed. However, two Senior RCCOs, **Ann Elizabeth Young** and **Maureen Theresa Bradley Ryan**, took up their appointments on 6 May 1980 and they worked under Dyson and latterly Morris for the next 12 months until Young left on 16 May 1981 and Ryan moved two months later to Queens Park as Acting Officer-in-Charge.

35.05   On 9 October 1979 Y Gwyngyll was visited by SWSO Copleston of the Welsh Office, whose criticisms of its structure are reflected in what we have said about it. At that time there were 12 children in residence and three other children, normally in other residential establishments during term time, were spending holidays and occasional week-ends there. There had been 24 admissions and nine discharges since the home opened; and there was a full staff establishment of three full time RCCOs, two part-time and one relief in addition to the Officer-in-Charge and his Deputy, together with four part-time ancillary domestic staff, which the Inspector regarded as adequate. The staff, other than Dyson, were not professionally qualified save that a senior RCCO held a Home Office Certificate in Residential Child Care.

35.06   SWSO Copleston's report on Y Gwyngyll was generally quite favourable, except for her criticisms of the premises and some of the furnishings. The atmosphere in the home seemed to be relaxed, with children clearly expecting staff to be interested in their activities. Amongst matters of concern raised by the Inspector, however, were:

> (a)   the extent of the involvement of D A Parry, the Deputy Director of Social Services, in running the home, thus fettering Dyson's discretion;
>
> (b)   the operation of the case conference/review system based at Tŷ'r Felin and Nefyn Dodd's dominance as chairman of all case conferences.

These matters were discussed with both Parry and the Director of Social Services, Thomas Edward Jones, but it was the latter who was more receptive to the criticisms.

35.07   The next "inspection" of Y Gwyngyll was made by the Dyfed inquiry team, at the invitation of the Chief Executive of Gwynedd County Council (Ioan Bowen Rees), in July and August 1981. By that time Dyson was described as retired and Haf Morris as Acting Officer-in-Charge. However, **David Bayley Hughes**[3] had joined the staff in May 1981, at the age of 31 years, and he was to become Officer-in-Charge (non-resident, as Dyson had been) from 14 September 1981; he retained that position until 27 January 1986 but was off sick from the second week in December 1985.

---

[3] See paras 33.13 and 33.14 for an earlier reference to this man and his history.

35.08 The Dyfed inquiry team comprised Dewi Evans, then Deputy Director of Social Services, but subsequently Director for Dyfed and latterly for Carmarthenshire, the Assistant Director of Personnel and Management Services (D G Llewellyn) and the Industrial Relations Officer (H Beynon). Their brief was to investigate complaints made by current and former members of the staff of Gwynedd County Council about the running of Y Gwyngyll and they were to consider:

> (i) staffing arrangements, management and supervisory controls over staff and residents;

> (ii) the level and quality of administrative arrangements in the children's section;

> (iii) the relationship between the headquarters staff of the children's section and the homes and also between the homes and the Area Offices, in particular the Area Offices at Ynys Mon and Dolgellau;

and to report their conclusions to the Chief Executive.

35.09 In brief the complaints referred to were that:

> (a) Children were inappropriately placed at Y Gwyngyll. Instead of being a Family Unit home it had become a home for children requiring specialist care. Admissions were unplanned and there were no individual plans for the resident children.

> (b) Managerial control was lacking and staffing arrangements were inappropriate and inadequate. The Officer-in-Charge had also failed to lay down clearly defined standards and procedures so that practice by staff was variable.

> (c) There was no co-ordinated policy for the management of children in care so that there were different standards in different homes as well as variations in practice within the same home.

> (d) Lack of qualified staff and failure to provide in-service training.

> (e) The involvement of Nefyn Dodd without explanation to Dyson or other members of the staff.

> (f) Noise and disturbance to neighbours late at night.

> (g) Poor design of the building and its physical state.

35.10 The result of the inquiry was a robust and critical report. It was noted that the County Council had defined the role of Y Gwyngyll as catering for "the more sophisticated needs of children of Primary School age and to late teen-age, including those with special and even of exceptional needs, together with adolescents who will occupy bed-sitter accommodation and require more relaxed management" but it criticised the lack of planning of admissions and the absence of individual care plans. Breakdowns in communications appeared to have occurred between area based social workers and the Children's Section at headquarters.

35.11 It is unnecessary to repeat other criticisms in detail because the team substantially endorsed the complaints that we have listed, even though they considered that the Department had adequate resources for in-service training and did participate in CSS training. It must be noted also, as we have said earlier[4], that the team considered the involvement of Nefyn Dodd in the running of Y Gwyngyll to be an error of judgment.

35.12 A conclusion drawn by the Dyfed team was that the Gwynedd Children's Section was poorly administered both at headquarters and within individual homes and that this was reflected in lower standards of provision for children. A specific recommendation was "that urgent attention needs to be given to the generally poor standard of administration within most of the homes and the poor standard of decoration and repair". The team commented also that it would be too simplistic and wrong to conclude that the fault lay entirely with the Deputy Director (D A Parry) because there was a more fundamental problem of poor personal relationships between particular individuals within the Children's Section at headquarters and between individuals at headquarters and others in particular homes. Other comments by the team will be more appropriately considered in a later chapter when we comment upon the responsibility of higher management.

35.13 This was the situation that faced **David Bayley Hughes** when he took over as Officer-in-Charge in September 1981, although he was not shown a copy of the Dyfed team's report. Hughes' own evidence about Y Gwyngyll was that it was in a mess when he arrived. The premises looked unfinished and it did not have the feel of a home. Most of the staff were quite junior and were in a state of despair, although there were only six residents when he arrived. Subsequently, the correct complement of 12 plus three was exceeded and, at times, they had 22 residents.

35.14 It is not clear that there was an officially recognised post of Deputy Officer-in-Charge of Y Gwyngyll whilst Hughes was Officer-in-Charge. Theresa Ryan was succeeded as a Senior RCCO at Y Gwyngyll by **John Patrick Harvey** from 12 October 1981. Harvey, who was then 30 years old, had served in the Royal Air Force for nine years before becoming a residential care worker in Scotland in mid 1978. He was not professionally qualified but he had received some in-service training during his three years in social work in Scotland and he passed Part I of a three part Social Services course, attending as a day release student, whilst he was at Y Gwyngyll. Funding was not available for him to take the next part of the course at John Moores University in Liverpool. Harvey remained at Y Gwyngyll for just over two and a half years, that is, until 30 May 1984, when he was replaced by Peter Gadd. He then served as a Senior RCCO at Tŷ Newydd until his employment was terminated by Gwynedd County Council, by notice dated 1 December 1986 taking effect on 21 March 1987, on the ground of ill health (Tŷ Newydd closed on 31 January 1987).

---

[4] See para 33.36.

35.15 **Peter Gadd**[5] was at Y Gwyngyll from 30 May 1984 until 21 July 1986. It seems that, like Harvey before him, he was a Senior RCCO but regarded as Deputy Officer-in-Charge, whilst Haf Morris continued to serve as a Senior RCCO. Gadd became Acting Officer-in-Charge at the time of Hughes' illness in late 1985 and then Temporary Officer-in-Charge on 27 January 1986, on Hughes' departure, pending further decisions about the future of the home. He reverted to Senior RCCO on 21 July 1986 and shortly afterwards moved to Queens Park, where he was initially Acting Officer-in-Charge for two and a half months whilst the Officer-in-Charge was away sick. He remained at Queens Park as a Senior RCCO until 1 July 1988 when he was transferred to Cartref Bontnewydd in the same rank for a year before becoming Assistant Warden of Tŷ Newydd in its new guise as a bail hostel.

35.16 On leaving Y Gwyngyll, Hughes became family placement officer at Cartref Bontnewydd, working for the independent agency there that provides a fostering service for the local authority[6], and he remains in that employment.

Complaints of abuse during the Dyson period

35.17 Only two complainants of whom we know have made allegations of abuse that occurred in this period and both complained of being punched by a member of staff, one when he swore in front of other children and the other when he opened some curtains and the curtain rail fell down. Neither alleged that he was injured by being punched and the one whose evidence was read to the Tribunal said that he was fairly treated at Y Gwyngyll.

Complaints of abuse during the Hughes' regime

35.18 It appears that 11 former residents of Y Gwyngyll between 1981 and 1986 made allegations to the police that they had been abused by identified members of the staff there or by Nefyn Dodd. Of these only two alleged that they had suffered sexual abuse and neither alleged that they had been abused in this way by Dodd. One was a former boy resident identified as D in paragraph 33.70 in the chapter on Tŷ'r Felin, who alleged that he was seduced when he was about 16 years old by a student member of the staff: she had been giving him the eye and making it obvious that she was attracted by him. Sexual intercourse occurred after he had gone downstairs to drink cider with her. On another occasion oral sex had occurred in a shower bath. He had bragged about it and the student had left shortly afterwards. D alleged also that he had sold a pornographic video that he had stolen to a male member of the staff.

35.19 The other allegation of sexual abuse was by a former girl resident against a male member of the staff. She alleged that sexual intercourse occurred on two occasions with this man when she was at Y Gwyngyll but she did not complain until about eight years later and there was no corroboration then of her allegation. She did not provide the Tribunal with any evidence in support of her allegations.

---

[5] See para 34.05.
[6] See para 37.02.

35.20 Of the remaining nine complainants who are former residents of Y Gwyngyll, all of whom alleged physical abuse of one kind or another, four gave oral evidence and we received written evidence from three of them. Each of the four claimed to have been struck by Nefyn Dodd. One, for example, who had been at Y Gwyngyll for nearly two years between 1983 and 1985, said that it was a bad experience because of Dodd. He said that Dodd used to smack him in the face and on the bottom for lying. He would be put over Dodd's knees with his trousers pulled down; the smacks would be quite hard and they made him cry. This happened on three or four occasions and he used to wet his bed in fear of Dodd. This witness alleged also that Hughes used to laugh when Dodd dealt with him. He did not get on with Hughes and did not like Hughes very much. Hughes "beat him up" a few times for being naughty but he did not see Hughes beat others up. There were some riots at Y Gwyngyll because residents were not being properly treated by staff.

35.21 Another witness (who apparently has an IQ of 133) described Dodd as extremely big and overbearing. He complained of being told by Dodd to paint the mortar between bricks with an artist's brush. When he feigned illness the next day he was not given any food: he went down to tea but Dodd then screamed and swore at him in Welsh. On another occasion the witness went to the boot room to have a smoke but he was seen by Dodd, who grabbed him around the neck, frogmarched him, "belted" him in the stomach and then threw him upstairs.

35.22 The other "live" witnesses complained respectively of being punched on the side of the face and to the floor by Dodd and of being hit by him over the head with a bunch of keys.

35.23 Nefyn Dodd denied all these allegations and they were not supported by Hughes or any other member of the staff at Y Gwyngyll. Hughes' evidence to the Tribunal was that he did not see Dodd use any physical force to residents and that he himself neither used nor condoned physical punishment. On the question of sanctions generally, Hughes said that he did not impose punishments because be believed in counselling and thought that it worked excellently.

35.24 Only two former residents of Y Gwyngyll alleged physical abuse by Hughes and both gave evidence to the Tribunal. One has been referred to already in paragraph 35.20. The other alleged that Hughes attacked him and threw him to the floor on one of the three or four occasions when the residents at Y Gwyngyll barricaded themselves in. This witness spent just over six months there in the first half of 1981 so that he was there when Hughes arrived and left before the latter became Officer-in-Charge. According to the witness, the residents were dissatisfied with conditions at the home and they protested also about the failure of the staff to take effective action against a particular bully, who was one of the residents at that time.

35.25 Other allegations of physical abuse during Hughes' period were few in number and did not suggest any habitual use of force by staff. About six other members of the residential care staff were named by individual complainants to the police but only one of these complainants provided a written statement to the Tribunal and unhappily that was confused because of his drug addiction. One other complainant was unable to identify his assailant but alleged that he was thrown over a low wall by a trainee student after he had been cheeky to the student: he was winded but not otherwise injured and the student was dismissed from Y Gwyngyll shortly afterwards by Hughes, following an inquiry.

35.26 It will be apparent from what we have said that we have not received any evidence of habitual or persistent abuse at Y Gwyngyll. Any incidents of sexual abuse that occurred were isolated and were not the subject of complaint (as distinct from bragging) until many years afterwards. As for the use of physical force, it is unlikely that most of the complaints would have surfaced but for the allegations against Nefyn Dodd. We accept that the latter did, on a limited number of occasions, use inappropriate and excessive physical force to residents at Y Gwyngyll but this was on a much lesser scale than at Tŷ'r Felin. In general, the residents were in awe of him because of his size, his personality and his loud voice; and he visited the home once a week usually. Other members of the staff rarely resorted to force and then only in provocative situations or when some form of physical restraint was necessary.

35.27 In reaching our conclusions about the nature and extent of any abuse that occurred at Y Gwyngyll we have taken into account the evidence of a majority of the complainants who were there at the time that the regime under Hughes was very relaxed. That was how D, for example, described it and he said that the staff barely had an input. Another witness said that it was great, like a holiday home and yet another that the children were allowed to do what they wanted. A more critical former resident said that it was "a shambles" and that everyone ran riot.

35.28 One of the curiosities of this history is that, although Dodd may have been critical of Hughes' outlook and methods, he does not appear to have interfered with the regime until (perhaps) a late stage. Harvey regarded himself as a strict disciplinarian, according to his own written statement, but he was replaced by Gadd, whose own account of the Hughes regime was that there were few rules and that sometimes you would think that the residents were running the home.

The quality of care generally

35.29 Although the level of any sexual or physical abuse by staff at Y Gwyngyll was low, the general quality of care provided there left much to be desired. We have already described in the introduction to this chapter how the first period of about two and a half years in the home's history culminated in the complaints investigated by the Dyfed team[7]. The report by that team was highly critical but it was not seen by Hughes when he took over as Officer-in-Charge, nor was he given a summary of its main relevant conclusions. D A Parry disappeared from the residential child care scene shortly afterwards and no one took over those responsibilities at such a high level. Day to day control and supervision were vested in Nefyn Dodd but there was little direction from above and no strategic planning.

---

[7] See para 35.09.

35.30 Hughes told the Tribunal in his evidence that, as Officer-in-Charge at Y Gwyngyll, he felt a lack of support from headquarters and professional supervision; he was conscious also of the lack of a corporate strategy. His impression was that he and the residential care staff were being left "to keep a lid on" the problems surrounding troublesome youngsters whilst higher management washed their hands of them.

35.31 Hughes voiced some of his dissatisfactions at the end of 1984 with the result that he had a number of meetings between January and early March 1985, mainly with Gethin Evans[8] but also involving the Deputy Director of Social Services (Glanville Owen) and Nefyn Dodd. Parts of the discussions related to Hughes' career wishes and need not be repeated here. His criticisms of the administration of residential care, however, were countered with criticisms of his own performance; and there were contemporaneous exchanges of memoranda and letters.

35.32 It appears from the correspondence that incidents of damage at Y Gwyngyll had occurred in the last two months of 1984 and that Hughes was feeling the strain of being called out to the home frequently; in his view, the situation had worsened after the arrival of Gadd, who "avoided contacts with residents and was over tired when he came on duty". Hughes wished to explore reasons why Y Gwyngyll had not been a success and suggested that folklore in the local community militated against it, that its location was unsuitable and created problems and that the design of the home did not allow for close supervision or experiment.

35.33 Nefyn Dodd himself produced a three page memorandum at this time, dated 21 January 1985, under the heading "Main Difficulties with the Management of Y Gwyngyll". In that memorandum he said, amongst other things, that:

(1) There had been no planned admissions to Y Gwyngyll or any other community home: such admissions as had occurred had been in response to emergencies.

(2) There were children at Y Gwyngyll who were potentially violent and destructive; due to their general demeanour and anti-authority levels of functioning they could not be considered for fostering or adoption.

(3) The lack of employment possibilities further complicated a difficult situation.

(4) The location of the home was not conducive to good neighbourly relations and a good community spirit.

(5) At one stage Hughes and four other full time staff were ill but Gadd and Haf Morris had saved the situation by their sterling efforts; and Gadd had been transferred to Y Gwyngyll at Hughes' request.

(6) A general lack of leadership by, and delegation from, Hughes had added greatly to the overall difficulties.

---

[8] Then Head of Children's Services.

Dodd added that his reservations and anxieties regarding Hughes had been communicated to Gethin Evans almost daily over a protracted period of time.

35.34 The outcome of the discussions was that Hughes was sent on 7 March 1985 a list of areas of concern and of the action to be taken to deal with them, with the intention that his progress would be reviewed periodically and in about six months' time. Many of the points made were administrative but emphasis was also laid on improving his relationships with staff. Weekly staff meetings were to be arranged; rules and regulations were to be written and developed; and movement of residents were to be more closely observed. Most relevantly, under the heading "Social Environment", the areas of concern were described as "Lack of purpose for residents" and "Individual and group programmes ill defined or non-existent". Hughes was required to:

> "Develop programmes/contracts and objectives for residents, individually and in groups. Evaluate these periodically and define a process which is understood by all staff and residents.
>
> Improve working agreements with area staff."

We do not know what progress was made in achieving these objectives in the following nine months. Hughes was seeking other job and training opportunities at the time and he succeeded in obtaining a transfer to other child related activity in January 1986[9].

35.35 The exchanges in early 1985 underline the lack of progress made at Y Gwyngyll in improving the quality of care following the adverse Dyfed team report in or about November 1981. Emergency admissions still predominated. There was no overall strategy for the remaining community homes for children and there were no individual care plans. Placements remained in the control of Nefyn Dodd and Y Gwyngyll appears to have become a form of refuge for disturbed adolescents, where (it was hoped) they would have the minimum opportunity to cause trouble to others. Those of school age attended local schools (including two catering for special needs) but there was no provision for children who were excluded from school, except the possibility of tuition by a visiting teacher for two hours per week; and there was no training for independence and little creative organised activity for residents beyond school age. Even the separate units provided in the original design as accommodation for residents who were being prepared for independent living were never used for that purpose.

Conclusions

35.36 Y Gwyngyll was planned with the best of intentions but it was probably doomed to failure from the moment when it eventually opened in January 1979. It was badly designed and unsuitably situated and, in the event, it was mis-used because of the lack of an overall county strategy for community homes in Gwynedd. Leadership within the home was defective throughout and the care staff were largely untrained for the work that they had to perform.

---

[9] See para 35.16.

Moreover, the introduction of Nefyn Dodd in a supervisory role should have been recognised as an error at the latest by the end of 1981. It is a relief to be able to find that the level of any sexual and physical abuse at the home was comparatively low but there were other grave shortcomings. The most serious of these were the lack of individual care planning and the failure to prepare residents for a meaningful future, including their discharge from care, with appropriate liaison with field social workers. In the end, a significant number of residents were left mouldering there and all too many of them went on to more rigorous forms of detention under the penal system.

5 Queen's Park Close, Holyhead

Introduction

36.01 This community home (hereafter "Queens Park") is situated in a fairly large council estate, near the centre of Holyhead. It was opened by the former Anglesey County Council in 1960 as a family group home and was designated in the 1971 Regional Plan for Wales as a community home providing accommodation for up to eight boys and girls. In the 1979 revision of the Plan the age range for those boys and girls was put at 0 to 18 years but only up to five children were accommodated after the Children Act 1989 came into operation. The home remains open and it has been run since 1 April 1996 by the new Anglesey County Council.

36.02 The council estate in which the home stands comprises terraced and semi-detached houses and small blocks of flats or maisonettes. There are broad grass verges, giving open play spaces, in the approach road. Queen's Park Close itself is a large cul-de-sac, which gives a large open space as the home's outlook and which is used mainly for parking.

36.03 Queens Park had, during the period under review, five quite spacious bedrooms for residents (three double, two single), all on the first floor. On the ground floor there was a sitting room and a dining room for residents; and at the front and rear of the building there was a small garden and a small yard respectively.

36.04 The evidence before us about the succession of Officers-in-Charge at Queens Park is incomplete but our attention has been focussed mainly on the period between 1984 and 1988 to which most of the complaints known to us relate. It is not necessary to go back beyond 1 January 1978, which was the date when **Valmai Haf Morris**[1] became Officer-in-Charge. She had been appointed as a houseparent at Queens Park in 1970 and remained in the employ of Gwynedd Social Services Department until 1986, when she left to seek work nearer her home because of her father's illness. Haf Morris was Officer-in-Charge of Queens Park until 6 April 1981 when she was transferred to Y Gwyngyll as a Senior RCCO and became Acting Officer-in-Charge there during Dyson's illness.

36.05 It seems that there was a gap of about three months before **Theresa Ryan**, then a Senior RCCO at Y Gwyngyll, moved to Queens Park as Acting Officer-in-Charge. She was then 24 years old and had been employed for about two years by Gwynedd Social Services Department, for about nine months as Deputy Officer-in-Charge at Tŷ Newydd in its first phase and then at Y Gwyngyll from

---

[1] See para 35.03.

6 May 1980. It follows that Theresa Ryan had only just taken over at Queens Park, on what was described as secondment from Y Gwyngyll, when the Dyfed inquiry team visited Queens Park in July or August 1981[2].

36.06 The Dyfed team were strongly critical of the condition of Queens Park at that time. They said:

"The physical state of the Home was deplorable. The playroom was a disgrace; the kitchen unkempt and disorderly; the downstairs toilet was dirty and out of use; the laundry room was unkempt; the inadequate grounds were unkempt and did not provide for outdoor recreation.

The personal files of the children and the other paper work within the Home was in a state of complete disarray. We would recommend that urgent steps be taken to improve record keeping at the Home and to standardise records throughout all the Children's Establishments and also to ensure that they are inspected regularly by an officer from headquarters."

36.07 Theresa Ryan remained at Queens Park until October 1982, when she left to gain experience as a field social worker before undertaking a CQSW course at Cardiff and she did not return to residential child care work. She made it clear that she was not prepared to work under Nefyn Dodd because she did not approve of his attitudes to staff and children and it appears that this was a factor in her transfer to Queens Park, for which he did not have responsibility at the time. Ryan's line manager there was Lucille Hughes, who was then Principal Assistant Director and who took over responsibility for children's services from the Deputy Director (D A Parry) from about July 1981.

36.08 The next Officer-in-Charge, from 11 October 1982 to 31 December 1984, was **Karen Olwen Owen**. She had begun work as a care assistant in Gwynedd in August 1980, when she was nearly 27 years old. After a brief placement at Tŷ Newydd, she had worked at Tŷ'r Felin until February 1982 and then, on promotion, at Pant yr Eithin. She resigned her post at Queens Park at the end of 1984 because she wanted a career change.

36.09 Owen's successor, **Beryl Anne Condra**, had been employed at Queens Park from 1981. She had been married twice and has now three grown up children and eight grandchildren. She was not professionally qualified but, before going to Queens Park, she had about six years experience of part-time work as a child care officer for Dr Barnardos in Derbyshire. She was made a permanent RCCO (non-residential) at Queens Park from January 1983 and then Acting Officer-in-Charge two years later for a period of two months before she was confirmed as permanent head of the home from 11 March 1985. Condra did not retire from that position until June 1997, but she was off sick from September 1996.

36.10 There was no Deputy Officer-in-Charge at Queens Park but there were occasions when Condra was ill and someone else had to act in her place. Thus, **Emma Rogers** (formerly O'Brien) performed this function between October 1985 and February 1986, when she was 19 years old, on secondment from Tŷ'r

---

[2] See para 35.07.

Felin. At that time there were about five children in residence. **Peter Gadd**[3] was another who performed this role but he did so after he had been transferred from Y Gwyngyll to Queens Park as Senior RCCO in the autumn of 1986. He was Acting Officer-in-Charge from 6 November 1986 to 22 January 1987 and then remained at Queens Park as a Senior RCCO until 1 July 1988.

36.11 The inspection by representatives of the Social Work Service of the Welsh Office referred to in paragraph 33.52 took place in the autumn of 1988, when there were four children in residence. At that time there were three care workers under Beryl Condra, one of whom was an acting Senior RCCO; and none had more than three years' experience. Condra had by then attended the national in-service pre-qualifying course in residential care but none of the other members of the staff had received any similar training. Condra had asked to be permitted to take a CSS course but had been told by Nefyn Dodd that "she had got there" without it. The report on the inspection stated that children were admitted to the home for the stated purpose of assessment but added that "this activity could not be carried out by this number of people even if all had been professionally qualified".

36.12 The SWSOs commented quite favourably, however, on the premises generally. The house was said to be pleasant and fairly large and indistinguishable as a children's home from other houses in the estate. The main criticisms of it were summarised as follows:

> "It would be somewhat cramped when at full occupancy and there was little provision for private leisure and study. The sleeping accommodation was pleasant and adequate but some of the furniture was in poor condition. The bedrooms had been personalised by the young people who had obviously made themselves at home. The washing and toilet facilities were not of the same standard as the other living quarters. There was a lack of imagination in the wall decoration."

Complaints of sexual abuse

36.13 Three former residents have complained to the police that they were sexually abused whilst they were at Queens Park. The first of these was there for a substantial period in the 1970s when he was very young and his allegation was that an older male fellow resident attempted to bugger him on two occasions. He was unable, however, to identify the culprit to the police, except by his Christian name, and he did not make a complaint about the assaults for many years, albeit for understandable reasons. He did not suggest that any member of the staff was aware of what occurred.

36.14 The second complainant (A) was at Queens Park much later, that is, from 12 August to 20 November 1985. It was during this period that Emma Rogers became Acting Officer-in-Charge from a date in October 1985, when she was seconded temporarily from Tŷ'r Felin. The subject matter of the complaint, which was that a woman member of the staff (X) had had sexual intercourse

---

[3] See paras 34.05 and 35.15.

with A, did not come to light, however, until Beryl Condra returned to work as Officer-in-Charge at the beginning of February 1986. By this time A had been transferred to Tŷ Mawr at Abergavenny, a community home with education that had formerly been an approved school.

36.15 A, who was nearly 16 years old at the time of the relevant events, told the Tribunal in his oral evidence that it was his habit at Queens Park to stay up talking to the staff on 'sleeping in' duty. He had spent the night with X on a couple of occasions when she had followed him into his bedroom at about 3 am, five minutes after he had gone up to bed. She had stayed with him until it was time for her to awaken the other children and sexual intercourse had occurred several times.

36.16 A was transferred to Tŷ Mawr on 20 November 1985 and remained there until 14 February 1986, apart from a visit to North Wales for Christmas. In his evidence to the Tribunal he said that his transfer there was "to try and keep (his) mouth shut about the fact that (he) was sleeping with (X)". However, A did not indicate how anyone with sufficient authority to arrange his transfer could have known of his alleged relationship with X by 20 November 1985. Moreover, he advanced a rather different explanation later in his evidence to the effect that he had been present when X was beating another boy resident's head against a bedroom wall. He continued:

> "I threw her off, I threw her across the room and told her to lay off him because there was no need for it, and I didn't talk to her after that. Within a fortnight I had been moved down to South Wales."

36.17 It was on 2 February 1986 that Beryl Condra was told by a girl resident that X had been having sex with A. Condra was told at the same time by a youth (B), who visited Queens Park quite frequently to see his brother, that the same thing had happened to him; and he agreed to put his allegation in writing, which he did, calling it "his confession". Condra was unable to speak to Nefyn Dodd that evening but she did so the following morning. She spoke also to the Deputy Director of Social Services because the Director was not available. Later that day X was interviewed by Larry King[4] and Nefyn Dodd at Queens Park in the presence of a representative of the Director. X denied the allegations and King wrote a long report based on his notes of the interview and what was said by Condra and the girl resident, who were also questioned.

36.18 King's comment on the interview with X was:

> "I was quite impressed by the open attitude of this young woman. She was obviously disturbed by the allegation and it is not possible to see how, in the absence of an eye witness or an admission on her part, that we shall be able to come to any conclusion other than on the balance of probabilities."

He was dubious about the timing and motivation of the girl resident's report to Condra and the way in which B had been brought into the matter.

---

[4] Lawrence Reginald King, then Principal Officer (Children).

36.19 It was clear that the investigation would have to be pursued but, according to King, he was by-passed thereafter by Dodd. Dodd's own evidence was that both he and King made a request by telephone to Tŷ Mawr early on 4 February 1986 that A should be "interviewed regarding the allegation that he had sexual intercourse with X, within the confines of his bedroom whilst he was a resident client at 5 Queen's Park Close". According to Dodd, this produced a response, at 11.38 am the same day, from the Deputy Headmaster of Tŷ Mawr at the time, one Phelan, who was said by Dodd to be well known to him.

36.20 Dodd's account of the oral report by Phelan was set out in a two page hand-written document, headed "Report of enquiry made on behalf of Gwynedd Social Services", bearing the date 4 February 1986 and signed by him as Principal Officer Residential Services Children. It read as follows:

"(1) The youth completely 'REFUTES' the allegation, and disclaims any knowledge of any illicit staff/client relationships whilst in residence at the Holyhead Community Home.

(2) A admits to a relationship with another client girl, but again he denies any sexual involvement with her, despite at one time absconding to London with her. In referring to (her), "I got fed up with her she was in the habit of fantasising and telling stories about anyone to get her own way".

(3) Mr Phelan then informed the boy "if you're still feeling bitter about the staff having had you sent to 'Tŷ Mawr' here is a good chance to right an injustice if you want to". A replied "I got on with all the staff ... and any way unlike Tŷ Mawr 5 Queens Park Close is only a couple of rooms and everyone would know if there was anything going on".

(4) When questioned regarding B, A it was claimed, said "Oh he is a daft old b----- always bragging about his affairs with girls, I can tell you now he hasn't had sex with anyone either, he only came to see his brother . . ."

(5) Mr Phelan stated "I am thoroughly convinced that A is telling the truth and that the whole affair is pure fabrication". The Deputy Officer then went on to relate to Mr Dodd, as to the very 'Positive' levels of functioning presented by A to date at 'Tŷ Mawr', and the very sound relationship that the boy had formed with himself.

(6) Mr Phelan was thanked on behalf of the Director for his 'punctilious' action on behalf of the Gwynedd Social Services Department."

36.21 It was not, in our judgment, appropriate to leave the questioning of A to a senior officer of a distant establishment, armed with only a telephone briefing about the allegation and the surrounding circumstances. More seriously, however, we are left in some doubt as to whether A was interviewed at all at Tŷ Mawr about the matter. Christopher Phelan, who gave oral evidence to the

Tribunal, was the Principal of Tŷ Mawr at the time (he had been from 1984) and not the Deputy Headmaster as Dodd recorded in his note. Furthermore, he remembers A and the circumstances in which A was admitted to Tŷ Mawr, about which a letter of complaint was sent by Tŷ Mawr. Phelan told us that he could state categorically that he had never discussed any allegations or any details of inappropriate behaviour with A; and it was absolutely false to state that he had "claimed to have thoroughly investigated the allegation with A over a protracted period of time". Dodd might have visited Tŷ Mawr when he (Phelan) was Deputy Headmaster but he could not recollect ever meeting Dodd and they were not well known to each other.

36.22 A also denied that he had been questioned by Phelan about his relationship with X or that he had discussed the matter with Phelan. He did say, however, in his oral evidence to the Tribunal that he was called to Phelan's office on one occasion and asked whether members of the staff at Queens Park had been having sex with each other but that was by way of casual conversation and Phelan "did not make a big deal of it".

36.23 A was interviewed by the North Wales Police in Caernarvon on 18 February 1986 and by the Arfon Area Officer and a Senior Social Worker on 21 February 1986. His statement then to the police is not now available but we have seen a memorandum, dated 26 February 1986, by the Area Officer in which A's up-to-date position was summarised. It seems clear that he was repeating his own allegations against X at that point and had no intention of retracting them. X was interviewed by the police then and again in 1992 but she denied the allegations and there was no prosecution.

36.24 The upshot of all this was that no other adverse action was taken against X, who repeated her denials of any improper behaviour with A or B when she gave oral evidence to the Tribunal. Dodd acted on the alleged retraction by A and reported it to Condra. Her recollection was that he showed her an A4 piece of paper and said that it was a statement by A that nothing had happened but that she never actually saw the statement. King did not apparently play any part in the subsequent events. As for the Director of Social Services (Lucille Hughes), her attitude appeared to be set out in a memorandum dated 27 February 1986 to the Arfon Area Officer in her name, in response to his report on his interview with A and his complaint that he had not otherwise been informed of the matter.

36.25 In that memorandum, apparently drafted by Gethin Evans, it was said:

> "When the rumour of events at 5 Queen's Park came to light I immediately decided to investigate, primarily because time was of the essence since a member of staff was involved. I had no wish to delay the matter and cause unnecessary grief to the staff member.
>
> This was done and I was satisfied that there were no grounds to the rumour. I did not therefore feel that there was any reason to widen knowledge within the department of the incident—this to include you at Area. Unfortunately the matter did not rest there as you now know."

The writer added that, although technically it could be argued that the matter should be considered under the Child Abuse procedure, "given the boy's age, behaviour and attitude I feel its the staff member who has been abused".

36.26 When she gave oral evidence to the Tribunal, Lucille Hughes said that she had never seen that memorandum at the time. She said also that she was not surprised to see now the highly critical comments made by the Area Officer (W Oswyn Rees) in his written response to the memorandum and, in particular, to the suggestion that it was X who had been abused. Gethin Evans appended the following note to the Area Officer's response in his own hand-writing:

> "Spoke to AO—no written reply to memo. Matter now closed so far as Area concerned apart from general supervision of (A). AO unhappy that they had not been informed of original accusation."

36.27 The history of this matter was further confused by Lucille Hughes' oral evidence to the effect that she oversaw the initial investigation. She said that it was she who instructed King and Dodd to interview X on 3 February 1986. She said also that she had regarded the matter as "very urgent"[5] and that it was she who had telephoned "Mr Davies" at Tŷ Mawr to ask him to interview A to see what had happened and to get information from A. She was adamant also that she had received a call back from Davies, who told her that the boy completely denied anything to do with it and withdrew the allegation completely. To add to the confusion, the Deputy Director (Glanville Owen), told us that it was he who asked King and Dodd to investigate the allegations although he did not receive any subsequent report back.

36.28 Our conclusion is that, although Phelan was an honest witness, the balance of probability is that he did speak to A at Tŷ Mawr about his relationship with X and that A may have denied to him that he had had sexual intercourse with her. We have however grave reservations about the way in which Phelan is alleged to have reported his conversation according to the note prepared by Dodd. We regard it as remarkable that no written statement was obtained from A and that Phelan was not asked to confirm in writing his oral report. Lucille Hughes is clearly mistaken in her recollection of her own role in the matter and there was no Davies in a senior position at Tŷ Mawr at the time. The method of dealing with the matter, however, was very inappropriate and motivated by an improper desire to bury the allegations as quickly as possible in the interests of X and no doubt the Social Services Department.

36.29 The fact that A may have repudiated the allegations when questioned by Phelan is not a weighty argument against their veracity, having regard to the surrounding circumstances, and it is clear that he repeated them very shortly afterwards, as he has done ever since when questioned. A dozen years later it is impossible for the Tribunal to reach a firm conclusion as to where the truth lies in the absence of any corroborative evidence either way. What is clear is that there should have been a full investigation of the allegations in the course of disciplinary proceedings by Gwynedd County Council as soon as they came to light and that questioning of A (and B) should not have been delegated in

---

[5] Cf. the memorandum of 29 February 1986.

the way that it was. In the event X remained in the employ of the Social Services Department for a substantial period but was not involved with children in care after 1987.

36.30 Before leaving this subject it is necessary for us to make two further comments. The first is that Phelan's protest about the way in which A was transferred from Queens Park to Tŷ Mawr was, in our view, fully justified. According to A, he was not given any prior warning of the move: he was simply told after finishing his tea that he was moving and must pack his belongings. He was then placed in a taxi without being told the reason for the move or where he was going (except that he was told "Abergavenny" by one of the two men in the taxi). On his arrival at Tŷ Mawr "he was locked in a cell overnight", and the next morning he was held in a chair whilst his hair (in Mohican style) was cut off. Phelan was not on duty when A arrived but he was aware that A was deposited at the door of Tŷ Mawr at 10.30 pm by two men, who said that they were taxi drivers and who handed over a large envelope. No social worker accompanied A. Phelan complained also that A was dressed in "punk" fashion with a lavatory chain and studded dog collar around his neck, two studded belts around his waist, obscene badges on his jacket and similar graffiti covering his jeans, all of which made him an immediate object of ridicule by residents. Phelan's letter stated that King had arranged with a Gwent Social Services Department officer for this transfer to be made and this is likely to be correct, although King told the Tribunal that he does not recollect doing so. We have not heard evidence that enables us to say who gave the instructions as to how the transfer was to be carried out.

36.31 The second comment is that, in our judgment, it was an error to appoint Emma Rogers as Acting Officer-in-Charge of Queens Park, even for a short period, bearing in mind her age, her lack of training and experience, the ages of the residents and staff for whom she was to be responsible and the geographical remoteness of Nefyn Dodd or any other supervisor. The appointment appears to have been made on the ground of expediency alone and was recognised by Gethin Evans subsequently to have been a mistake.

36.32 The other complaint of sexual abuse at Queens Park has an unhappy background on both sides. The complainant (C) was admitted to the home in August 1990, when she was just 14 years old, after a short period in foster care, and she remained as a resident of Queens Park until March 1994, attending school in Holyhead until she was 16 years old and later a college at Bangor. It is clear that during her stay she became particularly close to one member of the care staff (Y). C must, however, have been a particularly difficult child to deal with because she had already started drinking alcohol and smoking cannabis before she was admitted to care and her drink and drugs problems increased whilst she was at Queens Park. According to her oral evidence to the Tribunal and her written statement she took speed, gas, magic mushrooms and acid and was smoking heroin by the age of 15 years; and she developed an eating disorder. She drank also and was permitted in her last year to have vodka, gin and cider mixed with lager in her bedroom. Y discouraged her from drinking at first but later drank with her on occasions. C used to tell Y about her drug taking. If other members of the staff were present, Y would say that C should not do it but, if they were alone, Y would just laugh.

36.33 C did not apparently receive any treatment for her addictions whilst she was in care, apart from some consultations with a psychiatrist. There is abundant evidence of her drinking in such records of her as we have seen and some evidence also of her drug abuse. The first reference to her being drunk was on 31 August 1990 and numerous similar incidents were recorded up to 23 October 1992. The drug related entries are also clear but empty glass cylinders were found in her bedroom and C appeared to be "glassy-eyed" late in September 1990. On 3 November 1990 she was brought back by police after being caught sniffing lighter fuel. There were also sniffing incidents (of deodorant) in 1991 and there was concern by staff on 15 June 1992 that she was experimenting with drugs and not eating properly (being sick after "bingeing" on food late at night). On the latter occasion staff asked for a planning meeting to discuss how to manage the situation.

36.34 It appears also from the records that C was seen by a psychiatrist on six occasions between January 1991 and June 1992. She received other forms of medical treatment frequently between September 1990 and April 1993 and was admitted to hospital at Ysbyty Gwynedd on at least six occasions in that period. One of the admissions (on 28 December 1991) followed an overdose of 25 paracetamol tablets coupled with alcohol and there was a similar incident involving cider, temazapan, a throat spray and Tippex on 19 June 1992. Severe nose bleeds were a recurring problem and the record for 11 April read "Nose bleed—severe—fainted—convulsing. Dr suspects solvent abuse".

36.35 An unusual complicating factor in C's case was that she was the beneficiary of quite a substantial Trust Fund, representing compensation for the death of her father at sea, from which she received a significant monthly allowance, exceeding pocket money in the latter part of her period in care. She became entitled to the capital of the fund on her 18th birthday.

36.36 C acknowledged the closeness of her bond with Y and said that Y treated her as her favourite girl from an early stage of C's stay at Queens Park. C's main complaint against Y was that on occasions when both of them had been drinking, particularly at Christmas when the other residents were away, Y took her to a bedroom and lay with her, forcing her to touch Y indecently. This first occurred at Christmas in 1990 and there were four or five further occasions when it happened. On one occasion, at Christmas in 1993, a boy resident was present and lay across the front of the bed but did not take part in the indecency, of which he may have been unaware because he was soon told to leave the room for tickling C's feet. On two other occasions similar conduct by Y occurred at Y's home in 1994, after C had left Queens Park.

36.37 C's other major complaint against Y was that, after she had become entitled to the capital of her Trust Fund and had ceased to be in care, she was pressurised by Y into lending Y a sum of £2,000. Y repaid her ultimately but C had difficulty in obtaining the money from Y.

36.38 Y gave oral evidence to the Tribunal and denied that she had been involved in any indecent behaviour with C or that she had drunk alcohol with C. According to Y, C's self esteem was very low when she was admitted to Queens Park and Y, who was her key worker, was the first person she trusted. It had been good to see C doing well at school, after having been excluded previously. She had not treated C in a special way but C had been at Queens Park for a long time and wanted Y to be her mother so that they did become very close. Y said that she knew that C was abusing soft-drugs whilst C was resident at Queens Park. C was using cannabis and then speed and Y had tried to find out from C her source of supply. Y had also counselled C and had then referred her to a psychiatrist, although C had refused at first to see him. After C had left Queens Park, Y had taken her to a Drugs Advisory Unit. Y had also tried to re-kindle C's relationship with C's mother.

36.39 Y's explanation for borrowing £2,000 from C in 1994 was that she needed the money urgently to pay to her husband a capital sum in respect of his share in the former matrimonial home and to settle some other debts that she had incurred in the course of the break up of her marriage. It had been C who had offered to lend her £2,000 and the arrangement had been for Y to pay the money back when she cashed an insurance policy the following June or July. An additional influence on Y at that time was the fact that C was spending her capital on her boy friend and drugs.

36.40 C's complaints against Y did not come to light until she got in touch with this Tribunal in late 1996 and was referred to The Bridge for support. She made statements to the police in the period from January to March 1997 and an investigation ensued but the decision of the Crown Prosecution Service was that there was insufficient evidence of any criminal offence to justify a prosecution. By that time Y had left the employ of Gwynedd County Council. C then wrote to the Tribunal and her written statement to the Tribunal was signed on 6 January 1998.

36.41 We are not aware of any other allegation of sexual misconduct on the part of Y and, in the absence of any corroboration of C's allegations of indecency by Y, we think that it would be inappropriate to find against her on the evidence before us. The history that we have related does, however, illustrate the perils that may arise from too close a relationship between a member of staff and a child within a small children's home, which may be exacerbated if (as here) the staff member herself is suffering from emotional problems. Other aspects of C's evidence reflect on the quality of care generally at Queens Park during her stay and we will comment further upon them later in this chapter.

Allegations of physical abuse

36.42 Although Queens Park has been open as a children's residential home since 1960, we are aware of only seven former residents who have alleged that they were physically abused whilst staying there; and the complaints relate only to an overall period from 1 January 1984 to 16 October 1987, during most of which period Beryl Condra was Officer-in-Charge. We do not know of any allegation, however, that Condra herself was guilty of physical abuse on residents. On the contrary, most of the former residents of Queens Park who gave evidence to us spoke highly of her, referring to her as a very nice lady or in similar terms. Moreover, they described the regime there favourably. One, for example, said that it was brilliant and that all the staff were nice; and two others said that they enjoyed it as much as you could enjoy being in a care environment.

36.43 The allegations of physical abuse at Queens Park made to the police involved four members of the staff and only two of them were the subject of more than one allegation. The two were **Peter Gadd**[6] and X but the allegations against the latter were trivial. The one witness (D) who came forward to give evidence against Peter Gadd was at Queens Park for five months from February to July 1987 (he became 15 years old in June that year), when Gadd was a Senior RCCO there. D had just set fire to his foster parent's home and he left Queens Park when he was remanded in custody in relation to that offence. In his oral evidence D said that on one occasion, when Gadd was "fuming" following an argument with Gadd's wife, Gadd picked him up and put him against a wall. D swore at Gadd, telling Gadd to put him down, whereupon Gadd punched him "a couple of times" in the chest. He then ran away from the home but was picked up on the A5 road by Beryl Condra. D had not, however, referred to this incident in his earlier statements to the police and to the Tribunal. In those he had spoken at first of having enjoyed his stay at Queens Park on the whole and had later complained of being thumped by Gadd on three occasions when Gadd had caught him smoking.

36.44 Gadd denied striking D at any time and he told the Tribunal that he did not have problems with D, whom he used to take fishing in a group. D did have problems with some other residents and Gadd remembered telling him off about smoking.

36.45 The other complaints to the police about Gadd referred only to minor incidents of slaps or threats and one former girl resident alleged hairpulling. None of them wished to pursue allegations of assault against him and they spoke favourably, in general, of their periods in care at Queens Park.

36.46 It follows, in our judgment, that there is no evidence before us of persistent physical abuse by any member of the staff at Queens Park. No doubt there were occasions when a hand was raised by a member of staff but the regime was non-violent and corporal punishment was not resorted to. As for Gadd, he has been the subject of few allegations arising out of his ten years' service in residential child care in Gwynedd and we acquit him of any suggestion that he was guilty of physical abuse of residents in care.

The quality of care generally

36.47 Although the level of any abuse at Queens Park of which we have received evidence was comparatively low and most witnesses spoke favourably of the regime during the period when they were resident there, we have serious

---

[6] See para 36.10.

misgivings about the quality of care that was provided. Many of the deficiencies were common to other local authority community homes for children in Gwynedd and other failings were attributable to the absence of professionally qualified staff and of effective monitoring of the way in which this home was run.

36.48 Our overall picture of these deficiencies and failings has been obtained partly from the evidence presented to us directly and partly from the findings of the SWSOs who examined the care and career of four children in residence at Queens Park (and eight at Tŷ'r Felin) in the autumn of 1988. The major general deficiencies may by summarised as follows:

(1) The purpose of Queens Park was never properly defined within a county wide residential care strategy.

(2) Preventive measures to avoid admissions to care were inadequately developed and there were far too many emergency admissions.

(3) The ostensible purpose of admission for assessment was abused because the Queens Park establishment was incapable of carrying out assessments and the use of the expression masked the failure to prepare and implement individual care plans.

(4) Field social workers were side-lined in the planning and review processes and ceased generally to have meaningful continuing contact with the children in residential care for whom they were responsible.

(5) Many of the children placed in Queens Park and remaining there for long periods were far from their homes of origin with the result that field worker and family contacts were reduced; rehabilitation was thus rendered more difficult and children tended to linger in care for reasons (if any) unconnected with those that had led to them being admitted into care.

36.49 The result was that Queens Park became progressively a repository, in effect, for a small group of older children, frequently not exceeding five in number, who were in care for a wide variety of reasons and who led largely separate lives within the home. Their physical needs were met and there was a great deal of freedom but the staff were inadequately trained to provide the kind of guidance and framework of rules that they needed if the experience of being in care was to provide positive benefits for them and to equip them for independent living.

36.50 The particular failings of Queens Park were graphically illustrated by the history of C, who was admitted to care with alcohol and drug problems at the age of 14 years and who, according to Condra, began injecting herself with heroin on leaving care just before her 18th birthday. She undoubtedly presented great problems throughout her period in care but, if only a proportion of her evidence is true, there was considerable laxity in the regime at Queens Park and a culpable lack of professional rigour in tackling her difficulties, with distressing results. Part of the blame for them must rest upon

Condra as Officer-in-Charge but higher management should have been aware of the problems and should have intervened to ensure that appropriate remedial action was taken.

Conclusions

36.51 To sum up, we have been unable to find at this distance of time that the two major allegations of sexual abuse at Queens Park have been proved to our satisfaction but we are highly critical of the way in which the Social Services Department dealt with the allegations of A against X. This criticism does not apply to C's allegations against Y because they were made to this Tribunal initially and Y had left her employment before any disciplinary proceedings could reasonably have been taken.

36.52 Although we are aware of a small number of allegations of physical abuse by members of staff at Queens Park between 1984 and 1987 and heard oral evidence from one of the complainants, most of the allegations were minor in comparison with the allegations that we have heard in respect of other children's homes and we have not been persuaded that any identified member of staff was guilty of physical abuse during the period under review.

36.53 Most of the former residents of Queens Park who gave evidence to the Tribunal spoke well of the regime there and of their relationships with members of the staff, including (in particular) Beryl Condra, who was Officer-in-Charge effectively from January 1985 to September 1996. Nevertheless, there were important failings in the quality of care provided in this small community home, as we have explained in the preceding section of this chapter, and Condra must bear part of the responsibility for some of these failings, despite the fact that she was not professionally trained. Heavier blame, however, rests upon higher management for the deficiencies and failures generally and for failing to manage and monitor the home effectively.

Cartref Bontnewydd, 1988 to 1996

Introduction

37.01 Cartref Bontnewydd was established as an orphanage in 1907 in the village of Y Bontnewydd, about three miles south of Caernarvon, on the main A487 road to Porthmadog. It was administered by a Methodist Trust, inspired by the vision of Robert Bevan Ellis, and it remained open until 1983, operating latterly as a voluntary community home. According to the Trustees, over five hundred children were cared for at different times at Cartref Bontnewydd during this period of its history and we are not aware of any complaint in respect of it.

37.02 It is said that the reason for the closure of Cartref Bontnewydd as a voluntary community home was the emergence of fostering as the preferred method of providing for children in need. The Trust decided, therefore, to establish a Family Placement Centre at Cartref Bontnewydd and this fostering unit opened on 11 October 1984. In its new guise the agency entered into a partnership arrangement with Gwynedd County Council to provide fostering services and the arrangement continued until the demise of that County Council in March 1996. It is a non-profit making organisation employing a staff of four. One of its early employees was David Bayley Hughes[1], who was appointed as a family placement officer from 3 February 1986; and some later employees were seconded to the unit by Gwynedd County Council.

37.03 The fostering unit does not occupy the whole of the premises and in 1988 the rest of the building was re-opened as a community home for up to seven boys and girls, but this was managed and controlled by Gwynedd County Council, occupying it under licence from the Trust. The intention had been that it should replace Tŷ Newydd and open in 1987 but four of the residential care staff were to be transferred from Tŷ'r Felin and difficulty was experienced in replacing them there. In the event **Mari Thomas**[2] took up her appointment as Officer-in-Charge on 10 April 1988 and she held that position until early 1995, when she took maternity leave and then started a full-time two year course at the University of Wales, Bangor, for a Diploma in Social Work. The senior of the three other care workers who moved to Cartref Bontnewydd from Tŷ'r Felin on 10 April 1988 was **Anna Ashton**[3], who had served as a Senior RCCO with Mari Thomas under the Dodds at Tŷ'r Felin following the closure of Tŷ Newydd, and she remained at Cartref Bontnewydd until the end of the period under review. She became Temporary Residential Team Manager there for six months on 6 January 1995, when Mari Thomas left, and then became

---

[1] See paras 33.13, 33.14, 35.07, 35.16 and 35.18 to 35.34.
[2] See paras 33.109 to 33.113.
[3] See para 34.05.

Deputy Manager when another person replaced her as Temporary Manager. Finally, **Peter Gadd**[4] served as the other Senior RCCO from 1 July 1988 to 28 July 1989, when he left to work for the probation service.

37.04 Cartref Bontnewydd remains open as a community home and is managed jointly with Queens Park. This is the result of an agreement made recently between the new Gwynedd Council and Anglesey County Council. Cartref Bontnewydd is still a seven bedded unit and now provides accommodation for children and young people aged between 13 and 17 years. Mari Thomas is again Officer-in-Charge and Anna Ashton is her Deputy. Queens Park caters for the same age range and is a four bedded unit. The line manager for both is one of four Children's Services Managers appointed by Gwynedd Council.

Complaints of abuse

37.05 We are aware of only four complainants in relation to Cartref Bontnewydd and none have alleged that they were sexually abused there.

37.06 Three of the complainants alleged comparatively minor physical abuse by **Mari Thomas** and the evidence of two of them was read to us. The first of the two was at Cartref Bontnewydd between 11 April 1988 and 6 March 1991, with a gap of eight months or so in 1989. This witness had three complaints about his time there. Firstly, he alleged that he was required by Thomas to strip down to his shorts (worn instead of underpants) when he was rightly suspected by the police of being in possession of stolen money. Secondly that Thomas slapped him across the face with her left hand whilst she slapped the third complainant (whose evidence was not read to us) similarly with her right hand. This incident was said to have occurred after the two victims had absconded and had then been returned by the police (the third complainant confirmed being slapped but bore no grudge about it: for most of the time he was happy at Cartref Bontnewydd). Thirdly, the first complainant alleged also that he had been slapped by another member of the residential care staff after he had spat on the floor of his bedroom whilst talking to her.

37.07 The second complainant whose evidence was read also went to Cartref Bontnewydd immediately it re-opened and stayed there for just under six months, when she was 14 years old, having previously been at Tŷ'r Felin for 18 months. This witness, who was herself the target of some allegations of bullying elsewhere, alleged that she too was struck by Mari Thomas after absconding from Cartref Bontnewydd with another girl and being returned by the police. She said that she and the other girl were sent to their shared bedroom by Thomas and told to undress and hand over their clothes. When she refused to do so, Thomas grabbed her by the hair and deliberately knocked her head against the flat of the windowsill with the result that she had a headache but no other injury. In retaliation she kicked Thomas on the knee. This witness told the police that she did not wish to pursue any complaint about her treatment at Cartref Bontnewydd.

[4] See paras 34.05, 35.15, 36.10 and 36.43 to 36.46.

37.08 In her oral evidence to the Tribunal Mari Thomas denied that she had struck any of the complainants. She said that there was an element of truth in their allegations in the sense that, when residents had run away and then came back, she did give them a telling off but she had never hit or slapped them. In the course of her evidence, Thomas explained that Nefyn Dodd's practice at Tŷ'r Felin had been very autocratic and he had insisted on very high standards. She had probably communicated more with him than other members of the staff there and she was, in effect, forced into his ways and into following his routine. A result of this was that initially she was strict at Cartref Bontnewydd but subsequently she could not see the point of it.

37.09 The complainant who gave oral evidence to the Tribunal was, unhappily, a very unsatisfactory witness. She was anxious to give "live" evidence to us, although she was very nervous about doing so, but her recollection of events was confused and at times demonstrably false. She alleged that she had spent two short periods at Tŷ'r Felin and one at Cartref Bontnewydd but the only relevant records before the Tribunal indicated that she was a resident at Tŷ'r Felin only for a short period in 1991. Moreover, her allegation in relation to her period at Cartref Bontnewydd was directed against a member of staff called Mark, whom no one has been able to identify; and she had not been interviewed by the police in the course of the major investigation between 1991 and 1993 so that she was not identified as a complainant until she was visited in Yorkshire by the Tribunal's team as part of a general trawl in January 1997.

37.10 To sum up, therefore, we are not persuaded that any sexual or physical abuse by members of the residential care staff or anyone else occurred at Cartref Bontnewydd after it had re-opened as a community home. It may well be that Thomas did on one to two occasions in the early days use very limited force to absconders on their return in the circumstances that they have described but we are satisfied that she neither intended to nor did in fact cause any injury on those occasions.

The quality of care generally

37.11 The representatives of the Welsh Office who visited Tŷ'r Felin and Queens Park in the autumn of 1988 did not include Cartref Bontnewydd in their study because it had only recently opened as a local authority community home. We do not, therefore, have the benefit of any independent assessment of the quality of care there then and, as far as we are aware, there has not been any subsequent inspection.

37.12 The fact that the home has attracted so little criticism is obviously a pointer in its favour and the small amount of evidence that we received from former residents about conditions there generally was also favourable. It is clear, however, that some of the deficiencies that pervaded the residential care system in Gwynedd as a whole persisted at least for some time and Nefyn Dodd remained the line manager for residential homes until he took sick leave at the end of November 1989 before retiring on 23 May 1990.

37.13 Mari Thomas told the Tribunal that many improvements in practice were effected over the following seven years. There is now much closer scrutiny of admissions. No emergency admissions are accepted at Cartref Bontnewydd and there are planning meetings before placements are made. After an admission there is a further planning meeting to formulate a detailed plan for the child, over which the line manager (a children's services manager) presides; and the Independent Reviewing Officer in the Independent Inspection Unit presides over all statutory reviews. In the home itself six full time residential support workers are employed (in addition to a cook and a domestic worker) and some training is provided for them by way of seminars and day release schemes, although these do not provide professional qualifications. There are staff meetings fortnightly, at which specific children and their care plans are discussed. The complaints procedure is set out on a card for each resident; and there is a recognised "whistleblowing" system enabling members of the staff to report untoward incidents to Thomas. A daily log is kept at the home and there is a file for each child. Thomas' view is that residential carers need to move on now to doing more individual work with each child and that more research is needed into how that should be done most effectively.

Conclusions

37.14 The evidence before us does not justify any suggestion that sexual or physical abuse has occurred at Cartref Bontnewydd. We have included an account of the place in this report, however, partly because it has had a dual role since the 1980s as an independent fostering unit and a community home operating in different parts of the same premises and partly because Cartref Bontnewydd and Queens Park are the two community homes within the geographical area of the former Gwynedd County Council that survive. It has been helpful also to include a summary of Mari Thomas' account of the present regime at Cartref Bontnewydd because she has been Officer-in-Charge there both before and after the recent local government reorganisation.

PART VIII

ALLEGED ABUSE OF CHILDREN IN CARE
IN PRIVATE RESIDENTIAL
ESTABLISHMENTS IN GWYNEDD
BETWEEN 1974 AND 1996

Hengwrt Hall School and its successor, Aran Hall School

Introduction

38.01 Hengwrt Hall at Rhydymain, between Dolgellau and Bala, was built in or about 1870 as a large country house. It was opened as a residential school by Care Concern[1] in 1976 and it remained in that organisation's ownership until it was sold to new owners in 1991. The main hall, a three storey building, housed the residential part of the school, the main kitchen and offices. A separate school block was situated in the coachhouse to the rear of the main building and included two demountable classrooms. There were also hard and grass play areas and rooms for additional activities such as arts and crafts and domestic science.

38.02 The original proposal put to the Welsh Office was for a school taking 30 to 40 "mentally or physically handicapped" pupils aged five to 16 years. It was provisionally registered as an independent school on 12 August 1976 and granted full registration on 24 January 1977 as a residential special school for up to 25 "physically and mentally handicapped children categorised as ESN(S)". It was indicated that, if the school recruited further staff with specific qualifications, pupil admissions could be increased to 40 children but attention was drawn to a number of instances in which the school had admitted handicapped children without the placing local education authority obtaining specific consent as required under Ministry of Education Circular 4/61. We must stress, however, that only a proportion of these children (for example seven out of 19 in January 1990) were children in care.

38.03 In the event in July 1980 the Welsh Office increased the maximum permitted number of pupils to 35. Then, on 12 December 1983, under new legislation, the Welsh Office granted SEN approval[2] for up to 35 boys and girls aged five to 16 years with severe learning difficulties; and it appears that the upper limit of the permitted age range was later increased to 19 years.

38.04 On 6 March 1989 notice by letter was sent to Care Concern of the intention of the Secretary of State for Wales to withdraw the SEN approval under section 11(3)(a) of the Education Act 1981 granted on 12 December 1983, subject to any representations that might be made within 21 days. Concern was expressed about the poor physical condition of the building; the quality of life experienced by pupils with a lack of basic every day comforts; inadequate staffing levels, particularly care staff; the relative inexperience of some of the staff; underdeveloped and uncoordinated educational and care programmes; and the lack of a training programme for staff.

---

[1] See paras 4.12 to 4.16, 5.08, 5.09 and Chapter 22. It later became Care Concern International Ltd.
[2] See Appendix 6, paras 38 and 39.

38.05 Despite the extent of these concerns, it was said that the Secretary of State considered that the problems were remediable and that the immediate removal of all the children might well be against their interests. If section 11(3)(a) general approval was withdrawn, therefore, he would be prepared to grant individual consents under section 11(3)(b) to enable most of the existing pupils to remain, provided that certain specified requirements were fulfilled within four and nine months respectively.

38.06 Placing authorities were informed by letter dated 3 April 1989 that, 21 days having elapsed, the Secretary of State had decided formally to withdraw the school's section 11(3)(a) approval but that he was giving consent under section 11(3)(b) of the Act of 1981 for the existing placements to continue, with the proviso that he would wish to withdraw the consent if the requirements imposed were not complied with to his satisfaction.

38.07 The Secretary of State was still not satisfied that restoration of SEN approval under section 11(3)(a) was appropriate when the sale of the school was completed on 19 November 1991. At that time there were 18 pupils on the roll, two of whom were without consents and none placed by a Welsh local authority. Some new pupils had been admitted with consent despite what has been said in the preceding paragraph.

38.08 We have been given few details of the organisation of the school between 1976 and 1987. Care Concern's head office was at Sealand in Clwyd, near Chester. The Principal of the school itself from 1 October 1980 was Andrew D Britton, who had the degree of Bachelor of Education (Special Needs), and the teaching staff comprised four or five class teachers under a senior teacher, who was Sarah Britton. The care staff were headed by the Deputy Principal, Mrs M Griffiths, a State Registered Nurse, under whom there were three male Team Leaders (sometimes four). Each team had a senior care officer, one or two care officers and five to seven care assistants, working a rota system between 8 am and 10 pm. There were also up to ten night care assistants.

38.09 When the school changed hands in November 1991 its name was changed to Aran Hall School. The company formed to own, administer and run it was called Aran Hall School Ltd and its directors were Vernon Jones and Michael Jordan. Jones had been Chief Psychologist with Care Concern from 1987 whilst Jordan, a qualified psychiatric social worker, was a former Deputy Director of Social Services for Lancashire, with experience of special education, who had served as Director of Development and Training for Care Concern. The new Headteacher (instead of Principal) was the former senior teacher of Hengwrt Hall, Sarah Britton, who had been Acting Principal for the preceding 18 months.

38.10 The view of the Welsh Office at this time was that further work was needed at the school before general approval could be granted by the Secretary of State under section 11(3)(a) of the Education Act 1981. Accordingly, section 63 of the Children Act 1989 came into play because the school was an establishment providing boarding for fewer than 50 boarders and was not approved under section 11(3)(a) of the Act of 1981: it was thus a children's home, required to be registered with Gwynedd County Council under Part VIII of the Children Act 1989 and Schedule 6 to that Act[3].

38.11 Aran Hall School eventually applied to Gwynedd County Council to be registered as a children's home in May 1994 because the Secretary of State for Wales continued to withhold general approval under section 11(3)(a) of the Act of 1981. The application was granted on 1 September 1994, subject to a list of conditions, covering a wide range of matters such as staff supervision, staff training, complaints policy and procedure and the physical state of the premises.

38.12 On 15 July 1996 the school was informed by the Welsh Office that the Secretary of State had decided to grant general approval for the admission to Aran Hall School of statemented pupils under the new relevant statutory provision in section 189(5)(a) of the Education Act 1993. This approval followed an inspection by HMIs in February 1996. Sarah Britton had left in the autumn of 1994 and had been replaced as Headteacher by a member of the teaching staff after an interregnum during which a director had acted as Headteacher. The teaching staff comprised the equivalent of three full time teachers. A new head of residential care had been appointed in May 1992, following a national advertisement, and the residential care staff under him totalled 30.

38.13 The grant of general approval under section 189(5)(a) of the Act of 1993 was again made subject to conditions under which the school had to produce an action plan to address identified deficiencies and to improve certain identified aspects of its provision, including timescales.

Complaints of abuse

38.14 The Tribunal has not received directly any allegation of abuse at this school from a complainant and we have no evidence of any alleged abuse there since it became Aran Hall School. There was a complaint in 1988, however, by the mother of a pupil, about Hengwrt Hall School, which was taken up by the Spastics Society and by her Member of Parliament and which led ultimately to the withdrawal of general SEN approval for the school in 1989.

38.15 The Welsh Office first became aware of this complaint in October 1988 when a clinical psychologist employed by the Spastics Society telephoned the Welsh Office Education Department about it. Two days later the Society notified Care Concern that it was withdrawing its staff, who were giving outreach support to the pupil (A) pursuant to a tri-partite agreement between the Society, the school and Cheshire LEA. A report by the Society, dated 18 October 1988, was then sent to the Registrar of Independent Schools in the Welsh Office Education Department and to an SWSO.

38.16 That report, which was highly critical of Hengwrt Hall School, was prepared by staff of the Spastics Society's Beech Tree School (North) in Preston, which A had attended before his transfer to Hengwrt Hall School, and based on

---

[3] See section 63(6) of the Children Act 1989 before it was amended by section 292 of the Education Act 1993.

observations between 10 and 14 October 1988. They criticised the physical environment and many aspects of the quality of care provided by the school; they were critical also of the school's educational standards and provision; and they alleged physical and verbal mistreatment of pupils by members of staff, itemising 13 observed incidents. A had not been involved in any of these incidents but it was said of him that he had sustained unexplained bruises and marks on his arms and legs during the period and separate reference was made to an occasion on 13 October 1988 when a woman teacher had had to restrain A, according to her own account, by putting her knee on the back of his neck.

38.17 The report concluded:

> "We have attempted to present our observations in a factual and unemotional manner. We nevertheless feel bound to record the shock and anger we felt to see such vulnerable children mistreated and denied planned and effective education.
>
> We readily appreciate the stress involved in working with such demanding children and know all too well that staff can have bad days. However, what we observed was too all pervasive to be accounted for by such explanations. Nor can the incidents be explained as simply the malpractice of a few individuals—the ethos of Hengwrt Hall appeared to be repressive with a common feeling that the childrens' behaviour was the result of 'naughtiness'. This is a simplistic analysis which denies the complexity of the conditions which lead severely mentally handicapped children to produce challenging behaviour.
>
> Our concern in writing this report is not only for the welfare of A but for all the children presently attending Hengwrt Hall and for any children who might be enrolled in the future."

38.18 The complaint by the Spastics Society led to an inspection by Welsh Office HMIs and SWSOs in November 1988, at which time there were 31 pupils on the roll, aged 11 to 18 years, who had been placed there by 18 different local authorities; but only one child had been placed by a Welsh local authority. The view of the inspectors was that they constituted an extremely difficult and demanding group of pupils, most of whom had been placed at Hengwrt Hall because of the inability of previous schools to cope with their behaviour or the breakdown of residential or family support. A number of the children had little or no contact with their homes.

38.19 The inspectors found that few of the staff at Hengwrt Hall School on either the teaching or the care side had experience of special needs and that there was a high turnover amongst young and inexperienced care staff. Little had been done to improve the accommodation since a previous inspection in 1986 and many areas showed signs of neglect: the building was cold and in a generally poor state of repair and its general appearance was austere and depressing. Altogether the accommodation imposed severe limitations on both children and staff and made it difficult for pupils to be treated on an individual or family group basis. The school's poor state of repair, unsuitable scale and depressing decor were all in urgent need of review.

38.20 The inspectors were critical also of the school's educational provision. The educational experiences provided for pupils varied considerably in range and quality. Work was not generally well matched to pupils' level of development and there was little consistency or continuity in pupils' work. As for the quality of care, each child was allocated a key worker but some of them were not clear about this role and the part that they should play in planning a care programme for each child. Moreover, many of the reports supplied with pupils on admission were inadequate and referred to educational and social requirements "in a highly generalised way"; and SSDs or LEAs were represented at less than 50 per cent of the first reviews held usually six weeks after admission.

38.21 In relation to A, the inspectors noted that he was extremely aggressive and liable to react violently without prior warning. He had been subjected at Beech Tree House to an intensive behaviour modification programme to which he had responded from time to time but he was also used to a one to one teaching and caring situation on a 24 hour basis. He made inordinate demands upon the time and resources of the teacher and care staff: for parts of the day his needs could not be met and teaching staff admitted to being afraid of and unable to cope with his more violent outbursts.

38.22 The inspectors' conclusion was that it was unlikely that A's needs could currently "be well met within the present school situation". He required considerably more skilled individual attention than he was receiving. They were critical also of the Spastics Society's conduct in withdrawing A from the school without making alternative arrangements for him and without discussing with the Principal of Hengwrt Hall how best A's needs might be met.

38.23 Overall the opinion of the inspectors was that the school had a significant number of shortcomings, although pupils were not "at risk" in the sense that they were likely to be subjected to abuse or serious neglect. They did not comment upon the examples of ill-treatment referred to in the report presented by the Spastics Society the previous month. In the inspectors' view the quality of life provided for pupils and the amount of education and development planned on their behalf was inadequate. If the school were being considered for approval, it was unlikely that a positive recommendation would be made and the school had accepted pupils presenting difficulties that it did not have the staff and expertise to deal with.

38.24 There was some internal discussion within the Welsh Office about the appropriate response to this report before the decision to withdraw general approval under section 11(3)(a) of the Act of 1981 was taken. The parallel decision to grant omnibus individual consents under section 11(3)(b) of that Act was not, however, satisfactory, except (perhaps) as a stopgap measure, which should have been of specific limited duration. It did not face up to the problem referred to by the inspectors of pupils who should not have been accepted by the school. It appears that A, for example, was within this category, although Cheshire LEA expressed satisfaction with Hengwrt Hall School even after the Spastics Society's report; and A remained there for at least five years further, whilst general approval was still withheld by the

Secretary of State. In October 1989 21 pupils remained at the school. Their ages ranged from 13 to 18 years and they had been admitted between February 1981 and October 1988, the last being A on 3 October 1988. One only had been placed by a Welsh local authority (Mid Glamorgan).

38.25 The extraordinarily unsatisfactory situation was further highlighted in 1990 when it appears to have been recognised belatedly by the Welsh Office that, in respect of placements by English local authorities, it was the Secretary of State for Education and Science who had sole authority to approve, under section 11(3)(b), a specific placement. This was recognised when applications for further admissions to the school were made.

38.26 On 16 March 1989 Hengwrt Hall School was one of three schools featured in an edition of the "This Week" programme produced by Thames Television. The programme referred to the allegations made by the Spastics Society and to the subsequent Welsh Office inspection of the school. It referred to the profit being made by the proprietors and criticised alleged management failings, bad practice and the employment of inexperienced and insufficient staff but it did not suggest that ill-treatment was a problem, according to a Welsh Office note.

38.27 An unfortunate accident occurred at about 2.25 pm on 29 March 1989 when a 15 year old boy resident at the school (who was not in care) was run over by an ambulance on the main A494 in the vicinity of the school and sustained fatal injuries. Ten minutes or so earlier the boy had left a small group of residents who had assembled in a school building before being taken on a minibus trip to Dolgellau. It seems that the boy emerged from a recess in a gateway by the road, obscured by a wall, and ran, without looking to either side of him, into the path of the ambulance. A verdict of Accidental Death was recorded by the Coroner at the Inquest on 17 May 1989. The circumstances of the death were the subject of protracted subsequent correspondence involving the Member of Parliament for the constituency in which the boy's parents lived, the Rt Hon Paddy Ashdown, the Welsh Office and Care Concern International Ltd amongst others; and we do not know the outcome.

38.28 A was again the subject of a complaint in or about the Spring of 1990. He was taken with some other residents at that time to Bideford in Devon for a week's holiday in the care of four members of staff led by a Senior RCCO. It was alleged that, during this holiday, one of the staff (X, a male RCCO) had kicked A in the testicles or stomach. It was alleged also that X had kicked another child resident in the stomach and had thrown a rock at the head of yet another child. These allegations were reported at the end of the holiday by the Senior RCCO in charge of the group to her Team Leader, who gave oral evidence to the Tribunal about his dissatisfaction with the way in which the matter was subsequently dealt with.

38.29 John ap Iwan, the Team Leader in question, had been employed at Hengwrt Hall for ten years and had been a Team Leader since 14 May 1984. He told the Tribunal that he instructed the Senior RCCO to make a written report of what had happened and to take statements to accompany it from the two members of staff who had reported the allegations to her. An internal inquiry was then carried out by Vernon Jones and John Donovan, whom he described as directors. The alleged victims were not questioned, on the ostensible ground that "they might lie", and the two members of staff who had made statements were not asked to give oral evidence. The decision was that X should be severely reprimanded. No social worker or other outside representative of the children was informed of what had occurred.

38.30 Ap Iwan regarded these proceedings as a whitewash. He said that X had submitted his notice but then withdrew it on learning of the directors' decision. Ap Iwan had in mind that Donovan had dismissed a member of staff a year before for striking a child and on 20 June 1990 he wrote to the two directors querying both their decision and the procedure that had been followed. In response he was invited to meet them and, at that meeting, he was told that, if he remained dissatisfied he could seek employment elsewhere. Thereupon Ap Iwan gave notice on 19 July 1990 terminating his employment on 31 August 1990. He was then employed at Ynys Fechan for the following two years.

Surveillance by the Welsh Office

38.31 In the course of the history that we have summarised there were not less than nine visits to Hengwrt Hall School (later Aran Hall School) between January 1986 and February 1996 by HMIs and SWSO/SSIWs. During the same period there were inspections also by Gwynedd Fire Service and in August 1994 by the Inspection Unit of Gwynedd Social Services Department.

38.32 The two HMIs who carried out the inspections after general SEN approval had been withdrawn from the school were A R Large and J Griffiths; and the latter had been a party to the 1988 inspection prior to the decision to withdraw approval. Various SWSOs accompanied the HMIs and contributed to the reports between 1988 and 1993 but the last two reports were by the two HMIs only. Over the period from 1988 to 1996 the number of resident pupils declined from 31 to 13 (two from Wales). Of the 13 pupils (ten boys) resident in February 1996, four were about to leave, having attained the age of 19 years, but there were 11 inquiries for places under consideration at that time, of which eight were in respect of younger children, aged 14 years or less.

38.33 The reports submitted by the Inspectors were full and balanced but they make gloomy reading. We have summarised in paragraphs 38.19 and 38.20 the major criticisms made in the report of the 1988 inspection and progress subsequently to remedy these main defects was very slow. In 1991 the school was still relying upon an unsatisfactory water supply from a well. The demountable classrooms had not been replaced or refurbished adequately. The premises were still cold. Care staff were being paid less than local authority rates and none of them had professional qualifications. By 1993 a new water supply had been provided and fire safety requirements met but further work was needed on both the residential and classroom accommodation and there were still substantial improvements to be made in the education and care regimes to bring them up to acceptable standards. By January 1995 the school had effected significant improvements and the opinion of the inspectors then was that "the quality of teaching is at least satisfactory, and often good, across a range of lessons and activities". But there were still unsatisfactory features of the residential accommodation and site that affected the quality of life of pupils adversely. Moreover, priority needed to be given to developing and implementing the programme of in-service training and a proposed system for individual staff support and supervision.

38.34 In our judgment, on the basis of the reports that we have seen, the Secretary of State was fully justified in withholding general SEN approval from this school from 1989 to 1996. Furthermore, he would, in our view, have been justified also in refusing during this period to approve specific placements by Welsh local authorities under section 11(3)(b) of the Education Act 1981 and its successor provision. As it was, a degree of confusion reigned, at least for a period, after general approval had been withdrawn because the Secretary of State for Wales did not have jurisdiction to approve placements by non-Welsh local authorities. Some of his advisers were rightly apprehensive, therefore, about the possibility of an application for judicial review of the Secretary of State's decision made known on 3 April 1989 to give consent for existing placements to continue. Quite apart from the lack of jurisdiction we find it quite extraordinary that a regulatory authority should have purported to give blanket approval in this way for placements to continue indefinitely in an establishment considered to be unfit for general approval under the Act of 1981 on both educational and welfare grounds.

38.35 We do not criticise the Secretary of State for Wales' decision eventually to restore general SEN approval under the new statutory provision on 15 July 1996. It is to be noted, however, that an action plan was still necessary because some failings still had to be remedied after seven years of close scrutiny of the school.

Conclusions

38.36 Apart from the concerns expressed by the Spastics Society in 1988 and the allegations against X, about which we have not received any direct evidence, we are not aware of any suggestion that either physical or sexual abuse occurred at Hengwrt Hall School or its successor during the period under review.

38.37 There are aspects of these schools' history, however, which do give rise to considerable concern. A major anxiety is that the available provision for SEN pupils who require a high degree of care is so scarce that local authorities as far afield as Strathclyde and West Sussex should have considered it necessary and appropriate to place such children in a private school in Gwynedd so remote from their homes. Secondly, the division of responsibility for monitoring the performance of such a school is or may be so wide that the responsibility is not adequately shouldered by anyone. At times three Secretaries of State (for Wales, for Education and for Scotland) and up to 18 local authorities were responsible for satisfying themselves that Hengwrt Hall School was a safe and appropriate school at which to place or to continue to place specific pupils, but the only practical monitoring was carried out by the Welsh Office, which concerned itself mainly with the performance of the school as a whole rather than the extent to which the specific requirements of individual children were being met. However, it was only the complaint by the Spastics Society that brought about the withdrawal of the general SEN approval.

38.38 The evidence suggests that assessment prior to admission was often inadequate and that it was a matter of chance whether a child was placed by the education or social services authority: local authority staff played very little part in the reviews of pupils once they had been placed at Hengwrt Hall or latterly at Aran Hall. It was no doubt highly inconvenient for remote local authorities to send appropriately briefed and skilled representatives to such reviews but, in their absence, overall care planning for individual children was inevitably a theoretical exercise rather than a meaningful and practical process. Once a problem child had been placed at the school the problem was regarded as solved if the child could remain out of sight and almost out of mind until he/she reached the age of 19 years.

38.39 The unsatisfactory nature of this division of responsibility should have been pinpointed in 1988/1989 when it became apparent that Hengwrt Hall School had accepted, whilst having the benefit of general SEN approval, some pupils with whom it was not capable of dealing adequately. Instead, the problem was fudged[4], as we have described, and we are not aware that there was any critical re-appraisal of the needs of the misplaced pupils in order to find more suitable placements for them.

38.40 Outsiders who become aware of the large income received by private schools of this kind, derived almost wholly from public funds, frequently express dismay that the rein upon them is so light. In relation to Hengwrt Hall surprise may legitimately be expressed that it took so long, for example, to remedy obvious physical defects in the premises when the current income initially (that is, in 1989) was so high and the prospective income, with general SEN approval, was even higher. We do not think that it would be an unwarranted invasion of privacy to require a proprietor receiving public funds on this scale for such high risk services to disclose annual accounts and other relevant financial information to the regulatory authorities.

---

[4] See paras 38.24, 38.25 and 38.34.

The residential establishments of Paul Hett

Introduction

39.01 In paragraphs 5.10 to 5.13 of this report we have given a brief account of the three private residential homes and schools run by Paul Hett during the period under review. These were Ynys Fechan Hall, Dôl Rhyd School and Hengwrt House (otherwise known as Ysgol Hengwrt but not to be confused with Hengwrt Hall, referred to in the preceding chapter) and it is necessary in this chapter to give an expanded history of each of them.

39.02 Paul Hett, who was born at Shotton in Clwyd on 17 April 1941, entered the teaching profession in or about 1964 as a result of his marriage. On leaving school he had worked as a draughtsman and junior engineer at Hawarden Bridge Steelworks but he had then married a daughter of William Winston McGrail, the proprietor of a residential special school at Newnham-upon-Severn in Gloucestershire. This school was known as The Poplars. By chance, John Allen, who was the same age as Hett, also worked at Newnham-upon-Severn at about this time for the same organisation and moved in or about 1965 to Holywell in Clwyd under McGrail's auspices to run The Poplars Vocational Training Unit at the Talbot Hotel there[1]. There is no evidence, however, that John Allen played any part in Hett's Gwynedd activities or that Hett was involved in any way with the Bryn Alyn Community.

39.03 At McGrail's suggestion Hett took up an assistant teacher's post at The Poplars in Newnham-upon-Severn and he ran the schoolroom unit there from 1964 to 1969, whilst obtaining additional O and A levels at Gloucester College. After leaving The Poplars, Hett obtained the Certificate in Education after a three years course at Redland College, Bristol University, and then taught full time at a Bristol comprehensive school for two years.

39.04 It was in 1974 that Paul Hett moved to Wales and purchased **Ynys Fechan Hall** with the aid of a large mortgage and the help of McGrail. He retained that establishment for about 12 years, running a residential school there initially, until he sold it in September 1986 to Barry Young, who then operated it as a private children's home for up to 11 boys and girls.

39.05 **Dôl Rhyd School**, which occupied the premises of the former senior girls' house of Dr Williams' School for Girls at Dolgellau, was Hett's second acquisition on 1 December 1975. It operated as a school from January 1976 to July 1987. After it had been removed from the register of independent schools on 12 August 1987 it was re-opened by Hett's first wife and her sister as a unit for young adults with learning difficulties and registered as such with Gwynedd County Council.

---

[1] See para 21.02.

39.06 The third property purchased by Hett was **Hengwrt House,** which was bought in October 1980. It was run initially as a boarding facility for pupils attending Dôl Rhyd School but it was provisionally registered, in the name of Ysgol Hengwrt, as an independent school on 14 April 1986. It was removed from the register finally on 9 December 1991 but there was an earlier period in 1990 when it was removed from the register for six months. Thus, its effective life as a school was just over five years. An application to Gwynedd County Council for registration as a children's home was refused in October 1992 and an appeal against that decision was dismissed by the Registered Homes Tribunal in April 1993.

39.07 Paul Hett told the Tribunal that he was divorced from his first wife in 1982 or 1983 and that he married his second wife in 1984 or 1985. From 1989 he ran his remaining school, Ysgol Hengwrt, through a manager and staff whilst he attended Exeter University. He obtained the degree of Master of Education there in 1993. As we have said in paragraph 5.13, he described himself as "headmaster of a residential special school with no pupils since 1993".

Ynys Fechan Hall

39.08 This converted farmhouse, with six bedrooms and three reception rooms, the former home of a Midland businessman, was situated seven miles from Dolgellau, near the village of Arthog, overlooking the Mawddach estuary on its south side. It was set in pleasant grounds, including a spinney, and approached by a long private drive. There were also coachhouses and a stable suitable for conversion.

39.09 Ynys Fechan Hall opened as a private school on 28 June 1974 and was intended to provide a home for boys aged 11 to 14 years in need of long stay accommodation together with rehabilitation and education. According to Paul Hett, he and his first wife started by taking three pupils, after they had taken up residence with their own three children, but they were immediately inundated with further applications for places, including holiday placements. The Senior Officer (Children) of Gwynedd Social Services Department visited the premises as early as 26 July 1974 and found that 22 children were already in residence. Most of these were holiday placements but three of the children had been placed there by Dolgellau Area Office (the placements were said to be "of the remand type"). Bunk beds (20) had been installed but it was intended to reduce the intake to 15 and to charge fees of £40 to £45 per week. Apart from the Hetts themselves, the staff were "untrained, inexperienced and unqualified". After a further visit in the autumn of 1974 by the Senior Officer (Children), this time accompanied by the Assistant Director (Field Services), the Director of Social Services decided not to make any further use of the establishment and to advise other authorities of his decision.

39.10 The first Welsh Office inspection, by SWSO W F Brien, on 14 November 1974 resulted in a 20 page report. By that date there were 17 pupils, 16 (all subject to care orders) accommodated in the bunk beds and the other, a young man on probation, living in a caravan at the foot of the garden. Within the first five months of its existence 57 boys had either passed through or were still resident at the school (11 of whom had been from Gwynedd). Apart from the Hetts, there were six staff, three of whom were resident and none of whom were qualified.

39.11 The inspector's report contained many recommendations designed to enable the school to attain a minimum acceptable standard. He noted a number of points on the credit side, including the general frequency of supervisory visits to individual boys by care authorities and the tolerant regime. But paragraph 62 of the report summarised the problems facing the Hetts very effectively, as follows:

> "This private establishment, opened some 6 months ago, is a speculative venture by a young man who, though he has a University Certificate in Education, has limited experience and all the signs of limited capital resources. He and his wife, ambitious and undoubtedly hard-working, are faced with the demanding task of substantially up-grading the premises and surrounds; caring for difficult boys whom local authorities have failed to place in their own homes, and consolidating their financial ground so as to place the establishment, which is also their home, on a secure footing. Their difficulties are added to by the demands of their own three young children and by the need for constant support of remaining staff who, with the exception of a teacher/housemaster who holds a degree in criminology of an American university, are unqualified and inexperienced. The dangers of the situation are compounded by the isolation of the home and its freedom from frequent inspection by a locally based responsible body."

39.12 Considerable efforts were made by the Hetts to meet the requirements set out in the inspector's report, including the provision of central heating throughout the main house, the refurbishment of bedrooms and the recruitment of additional qualified staff. There were further visits by inspectors on 13 February and 28 May 1975 and the school was provisionally registered as an independent school before 21 April 1975, on which date a meeting took place at the Welsh Office between office members and specialists to discuss the future possible alternatives for Ynys Fechan Hall. A specific problem under consideration was whether an alternative status and purpose would be appropriate for the establishment if final registration as an independent school ought not to be granted.

39.13 In the event, Ynys Fechan Hall itself ceased to be registered as a school in February 1976. By that time Dôl Rhyd School had been purchased by the Hetts and provisional registration was granted to Dôl Rhyd/Ynys Fechan as an independent school on 12 October 1976 on the footing that Dôl Rhyd was the school and Ynys Fechan was merely a boarding house or dormitory of that school. Prior to this Ynys Fechan had been renting the former Arthog primary school for teaching purposes.

39.14 It appears that Ynys Fechan was used as a boarding house for older boys (13 years upwards) attending Dôl Rhyd School until 1980. Then in December 1980 Paul Hett bought Hengwrt House, which backed on to Dôl Rhyd School. From then on Hengwrt House took over Ynys Fechan's boarding function, but catered for the younger rather than older boys.

39.15 Ynys Fechan Hall had been unoccupied for several months when, in September 1981, it was destroyed by fire. It was rebuilt at a cost of £350,000 and then re-opened briefly in October 1984 as a school for dyslexic children. It closed finally as a school in May 1985, when the pupils were transferred to Dôl Rhyd School.

39.16 Ynys Fechan Hall was eventually sold in September 1986, for about a quarter of the rebuilding cost, to a member of the staff, Barry Young, who subsequently ran it as a private children's home for up to 11 resident boys and girls. This children's home was ultimately registered under the Children Act 1989 with Gwynedd County Council.

Dôl Rhyd School

39.17 Dôl Rhyd House, as it was formerly known, was a senior girls' residence, housing up to 50 girls and staff, when it formed part of Dr Williams' School for Girls at Dolgellau. It opened as Dôl Rhyd School on 5 January 1976 and, within a month, 30 boys were enrolled there, of whom 12 were resident at Ynys Fechan Hall.

39.18 On 4 February 1976 the school was visited by two representatives of the Wrexham branch of the Welsh Office Education Department (WOED) and Paul Hett wrote the same day to the WOED at Cardiff explaining the changes that had occurred. At Dôl Rhyd four rooms were being used as classroom accommodation and there were five members of the teaching staff. The school at Arthog was being re-decorated and it was intended to use it as a drama unit and as class accommodation for "small trial groups".

39.19 There were visits by Welsh Office HMIs on 11 March and 21 September 1976 (accompanied by a Medical Officer on the first occasion) before the school was provisionally registered[2]. The inspectors expressed misgivings about a number of matters, although they thought that there were no firm grounds on which registration could be refused, and eight major points of concern were raised, about which Hett was subsequently required to give written assurances.

39.20 There was a further visit by HMIs on 27 June 1978 before the school was finally registered on 15 February 1979 for up to 34 emotionally and behaviourally disturbed boys in the age range of 11 to 16 years, with Ynys Fechan Hall as a residential annexe.

39.21 In the eight years that followed its final registration there were recurring causes for concern. Some of these arose from complaints of abuse; others stemmed from local complaints about residents; and others were expressed by inspectors following visits to the school.

39.22 From the evidence before us, it appears that HMIs visited Dôl Rhyd School on 8 May 1980 (to discuss Hett's proposal to increase the intake to 50 pupils and to include girls); 28 October 1980; 11 November 1981 (without notice);

---

[2] See para 39.13.

19 May 1982; October 1982; 25 April 1983 (without notice); 11 October 1983 (to consider Hett's application for general approval to admit SEN pupils[3]); 6 November 1984 (for the same purpose); early in 1986; and February 1987.

39.23 We have not asked to see the full reports of all these visits because it has been unnecessary to do so. The proposals to expand the school and to admit girls were not pursued. The application for general SEN approval was refused in April 1984; it was still under re-consideration a year later when other events supervened. Some of the general anxieties about the school were set out in the reports by SWSO J K Fletcher of inspections on 19 May 1982 and 11 October 1983.

39.24 In the first of these reports the inspector drew attention to the conflict between Hett's expressed view that he was dealing with a criminal population with the major purpose of giving the boys a moral code and the statement in the school brochure that the school catered for exceptionally deprived and difficult boys of average and above average intelligence with the object of providing them with progressive remedial education. Sleeping accommodation at Dôl Rhyd was described as very poor and the regime as highly impersonal and institutional. Boys were not allowed personal possessions because, in Hett's view, they would inevitably be stolen. Only one member of the staff had any qualifications in residential child care and he did not impress as one making a professional approach to the treatment of difficult and disturbed boys. One other member of the staff had been there for three years but the average service of the remainder had been six months whereas the average stay of the 35 boys in residence was 18 months and five of them had been admitted before 1980.

39.25 Fletcher's summary was that the overall effect of Dôl Rhyd was "extremely depressing". The school was run on a shoestring and it was more institutional than anywhere he had seen for many years. It provided superb opportunities for leisure and outdoor activities of many kinds but very little to stimulate and enable social development. He concluded "If (Dôl Rhyd) were to express itself in terms of what it actually is, a long-stay outward bound centre with education, few local authorities would be interested at any price. It is therefore difficult to identify any starting point for discussion with the proprietor".

39.26 When Fletcher made his next visit in October 1983 some radical changes had been made. Hett appeared to have handed over management of the school to David Neil Edge[4], a qualified (CRCCYP) and experienced residential worker who had been the head of an Observation and Assessment Centre; and the only member of staff still in post from the earlier visit was the previously sole qualified care worker. Accommodation for the 18 boys in residence at Dôl Rhyd (only two from Wales) was being improved and Hengwrt House had been closed for extensive alterations. According to Edge, the school was looking to provide care for the youngster in trouble but not the serious offender: they were offering places to the "healthy delinquent" under the age of $14\frac{1}{2}$ years with the intention of providing a 12 month programme "to make the child safe".

---

[3] Under section 11(3)(a) of the Education Act 1981.
[4] He had previously been a "partner" briefly in running Clwyd Hall School: see para 23.06.

39.27 Despite the improvements Fletcher expressed understandable reservations about the viability of these plans and added:

> "The final question remains, irrespective of the nature and quality of the regime what relevance has a medium term residential unit in rural Wales to the needs of inner city boys especially if, as now appears to be the case, they are sought from among the "healthy" and not seriously delinquent."

39.28 The history of Dôl Rhyd School from the end of 1984 to its closure in July 1987 (before it was re-opened by Hett's first wife) is less clear than its earlier history. Following complaints by two members of the staff, all three senior members of the staff, that is, the Principal (Edge), Head of the School and the Head of Care (not the qualified care officer previously referred to) were dismissed in or about December 1984. This was a reason why re-consideration of the school's application for general SEN approval was deferred. Then, in May 1985 the WOED received proposals to establish separate schools for dyslexic pupils at Dôl Rhyd and for maladjusted pupils at Hengwrt House. These were the proposals that were considered by HMIs when they visited both establishments early in 1986. The two schools were judged to be making adequate provision for their pupils but it was thought that SEN approval for either would be premature. At the end of that year there were 16 pupils categorised as dyslexic at Dôl Rhyd School.

39.29 When an HMI accompanied by an SWSO visited Dôl Rhyd School in February 1987 they were highly critical of the care and education being provided for the reduced number of 12 dyslexic pupils and on 15 April 1987 the WOED wrote to Hett refusing SEN approval. The Department was then informed by Hett on 15 July 1987 that the school had closed and it was removed from the register of independent schools on 12 August 1987.

Hengwrt House (Ysgol Hengwrt, later called The Pioneer Centre)

39.30 This is a stone building standing in extensive grounds (with much woodland) in open countryside at Llanelltyd, a mile or so from Dolgellau and a similar distance from the head of the Mawddach estuary. The old and larger wing of the house provides an entrance hall, leisure room, dining room, staff room and kitchen on the ground floor with seven bedrooms (one double) and two bathrooms on the first floor. The new wing provides four more bedrooms (one double) and a bathroom. There is also a teaching block comprising two general classrooms, another teaching room and an office, together with store rooms.

39.31 These premises have had a chequered history since they were acquired by Paul Hett in October 1980. At first, they replaced Ynys Fechan Hall (before the fire there) as a boarding house for Dôl Rhyd, housing the younger pupils, but Hengwrt House closed for extensive alterations in 1983, by which time the number of pupils at Dôl Rhyd had fallen appreciably. In June 1984 Hett put forward his proposal to take dyslexic boys and girls at Dôl Rhyd/Ynys Fechan and early in 1985 the remaining non-dyslexic pupils at Dôl Rhyd were moved to Hengwrt House. According to Hett, there were eight pupils on the roll of

Hengwrt House in 1985, most of whom had come from Dôl Rhyd School. He then applied in or about May 1985[5] for Hengwrt House to be registered in the name of Ysgol Hengwrt as an independent school for up to 20 boys and girls aged 11 to 18 years; and provisional registration was granted on that basis on 14 April 1986, following an inspection by HMI on 21 January 1986.

39.32 Ysgol Hengwrt did not prosper and it was removed from the register first in March 1990. It was then provisionally restored to the register in September 1990 but finally removed on 9 December 1991. By February 1987, when it was again visited by two HMIs, accompanied by an SWSO, the pupil roll was down to four boys, although a new boy was expected the following week. Apart from this new admission, there had been only two new referrals since Ysgol Hengwrt opened.

39.33 At this time Paul Hett, having sold Ynys Fechan Hall, was seeking general SEN approval under section 11(3)(a) of the Education Act 1981 for both Dôl Rhyd School (dyslexic pupils) and Ysgol Hengwrt ("maladjusted" pupils). By July 1987, however, Dôl Rhyd School had closed so that a further inspection by two HMIs and an SWSO in October 1987 was limited to Ysgol Hengwrt, which was now being called "The Pioneer Centre".

39.34 In October 1987 the inspectors found that a number of important changes had occurred, of which the Welsh Office had not been notified. Paul Hett was no longer acting as head of the school and had delegated this responsibility to one of the teachers at the beginning of the autumn term. There were eight pupils on the roll, five boys and three girls, the girls having been admitted recently. All the pupils were of average intelligence and most could benefit from a full curriculum, although several (not statemented) had special educational needs. Seven had been placed by the social services departments of English metropolitan boroughs and one was a ward of court. The inspectors described them as follows:

> "They are in the main a difficult group of pupils, some of whom have disturbed home backgrounds, several have exhibited severe behavioural difficulties in former schools and a number comprise persistent offenders who have been the subject of court cases. Three of the school's pupils are currently the subject of a local court case accused of making false and malicious accusations against the proprietor."

39.35 The male teacher who was designated Head of Education had a Certificate of Education (main subjects, rural science and physical education). The female teacher, who had a first degree in education with honours, had read English as her main subject and was still a probationer, with previous experience at Dôl Rhyd School only. There was a head of care and five other care workers, four of whom were full-time, but none of them held a qualification in social work or in residential care. Moreover, it was not clear who was deemed to be in overall charge of the school and its general arrangements.

[5] See para 39.28.

39.36   The conclusion of the inspectors was that there were serious shortcomings in the work of the school. The organisation of educational arrangements was lax and not structured to meet the needs of all pupils; and there was also a lack of basic facilities for the teaching of many subjects. In a covering memorandum one of the HMIs, M W Stone, stressed the need for action to be taken and commented "If it were not for placements by social work departments without consultation with their education colleagues this school would not exist". He added in a further memorandum that, in his view, neither the proprietor nor the head of care was a suitable person for such a position because the latter had made false claims to professional qualifications on his own behalf and on behalf of another member of the care staff and the former had appointed them without satisfying himself about the authenticity of their qualifications or taking up proper references. The inspector pointed out also that the brochure issued by the school contained a number of misleading statements.

39.37   In the light of this 1987 report the Welsh Office started to draft a Notice of Complaint as a prelude to removing Ysgol Hengwrt from the register. However, the process of removal was very protracted. Inspectors visited the school in June 1988, in September and October 1989 and again on 31 January 1990. All their reports were critical of the school and the last of these visits took place shortly after the London Borough of Brent had removed six pupils that they had placed at the school, leaving only two pupils on the roll. But it was not until Hett wrote to the Welsh Office on 7 March 1990 referring to the "demise" of the school that the WOED felt able to remove it from the register on the basis that the school no longer existed.

39.38   The saga was not yet over, however, because on 12 July 1990 Hett informed the WOED that there were five pupils[6] at Ysgol Hengwrt once more and applied to be registered again as an independent school. The WOED concluded in September 1990 that this application had to be granted, by which time the number of pupils on the roll had risen to seven. There followed yet another inspection in December 1990, when there were eight pupils (six boys, two girls), aged 15 and 16 years, who had been placed there by the social services departments of English local authorities, primarily for social rather than educational reasons. All of them were described as having severe emotional and behavioural difficulties. By this time Hett was absent during the week, taking his full-time post-graduate course at Exeter and returning to Ysgol Hengwrt only at week-ends. There were three teachers, who had replaced others who had resigned in October 1990, and nine care assistants, none of whom had a professional qualification and eight of whom had been recruited from August 1990 onwards. The police had been involved on 15 occasions between 13 September and 8 December 1990 in matters affecting these pupils, including some visits to help staff to restore order.

39.39   The inspectors concluded that, although the accommodation was of a generally satisfactory standard, the staffing of the school was unsatisfactory, the curriculum was inadequately developed and the care arrangements did not

---

[6] A school with less than five pupils is not within the definition of an "independent school" contained in section 114(1) of the Education Act 1944.

ensure that pupils were adequately supervised. In their view individual teachers and care assistants made considerable efforts to teach the pupils and to deal with them with kindness and understanding but, as a whole, the school made unsatisfactory provision for the education and care of pupils.

39.40 Even this further adverse report did not result in the early removal of Ysgol Hengwrt from the register of independent schools. The WOED wrote to Hett on 10 April 1991 requiring him to carry out specified improvements within six months; and copies of that letter and the published HMI report were circulated to all authorities in England and Wales. A probable consequence of this adverse publicity was that, when HMI again visited the school in November 1991, there was only one pupil on the roll. Shortly after this visit Hett wrote to the WOED indicating that he proposed to seek registration of Ysgol Hengwrt with Gwynedd County Council as a community home with education[7]. Acting on this information Ysgol Hengwrt was finally removed from the register of independent schools on 9 December 1991 but the proprietor was reminded that, if five children or more were to receive full time education on the premises, it would again be necessary to register as an independent school.

Complaints of sexual abuse

39.41 We are not aware of any former resident of Ynys Fechan Hall who complains of sexual abuse during the Hett regime there.

39.42 One former resident of Dôl Rhyd School, who was there in 1983 and 1984 did complain of sexual abuse. He alleged that he was buggered against his will by another boy resident, who was older than him and a bully; but he did not make a complaint about it, as far as we know, until he made a statement to the police in March 1993. He said that he had consensual homosexual relationships with other boys whilst he was at the school from the age of 13 years. This complainant alleged further that he was indecently assaulted briefly by hand in his bedroom by a male member of the staff. He did not report the incident but the member of staff was dismissed within a week of its occurrence, apparently for other reasons.

39.43 It is to be noted also that HMIs who visited Dôl Rhyd School much earlier in November 1981 were informed that one of the care staff had been summarily dismissed following an allegation by a pupil of sexual interference.

39.44 Three former residents of Ysgol Hengwrt complained of sexual abuse by a member of the staff there but the alleged perpetrator was different in respect of each of them. Attempting to deal with them chronologically, the first was a girl (A) who arrived on 2 June 1987 from a children's home in Altrincham and who remained at Ysgol Hengwrt until 11 March 1988. A alleged that a senior member of the staff (X) befriended her initially and then forced her to have sexual intercourse on many occasions, sometimes once or twice per week, until she complained to another member of the staff, who came from Liverpool. That member of the staff put the allegation to X, who denied it, but eventually,

---

[7] See para 39.06 for the fate of that application.

after A had absconded several times, the Liverpool man and his wife helped her to escape. She subsequently made a written statement to the police in Manchester but was later told that "there was no evidence".

39.45 The second complainant was placed at Ysgol Hengwrt at the age of about 14 years, probably late 1986 or early in 1987, and he remained there until late in 1988. He alleged that during his period at Ysgol Hengwrt he was persistently indecently assaulted and buggered by a member of the staff. He did not make a complaint about this because he was threatened with an "unruly certificate"[8] if he did so. Eventually he ran away with two others and took a motor car, after which he was removed from Ysgol Hengwrt and went to live with his grandmother. He made a statement to the police in 1993 but a fellow resident who had been present when the alleged indecency began did not make any reference to it in his own statement.

39.46 The third complainant, B, whose evidence was read to the Tribunal, was at Ysgol Hengwrt in or about 1989, when she was 16 years old. B had previously been at the Bryn Alyn home in Shropshire known as Cotsbrook, where concern about her relationship with a female member of the staff, Y, had led to B's transfer to another residential home in Birkenhead. B's evidence was that she was moved on to Ysgol Hengwrt after just over six months in Birkenhead and was surprised on her arrival there to find that Y was on the staff. B alleged that Y resumed abusing her sexually until it was discovered after about two months that she and Y were again together in the same home. B was thereupon transferred to Gatewen Hall[9].

39.47 It appears from the evidence submitted by the Welsh Office that the complaints of A were reported to the Dolgellau Area Office of Gwynedd Social Services Department by the care worker from Liverpool already referred to and his girl friend on 11 March 1988, when they had been made redundant after only ten days' employment at Ysgol Hengwrt. Larry King[10] attended there and A was interviewed briefly about her complaints, as were the two care workers. The North Wales Police at Dolgellau, the Social Services Department (Trafford) responsible for A and the Welsh Office were all informed. Trafford agreed to collect A the same day in view of her refusal to return to Ysgol Hengwrt and the incident was reported to the Gwynedd Co-ordinating Committee. The member of staff accused denied A's allegations and said that they had been investigated (and dismissed) by Hett two months earlier. He was, however, the head of care referred to in paragraph 39.36, about whom his former employer had supplied a devastatingly critical report dated 5 October 1987; and he resigned in March 1988 following suspension in relation to A's allegations.

39.48 After investigating A's complaint, Trafford Metropolitan Borough withdrew three pupils from Ysgol Hengwrt in March 1988. The same month the Metropolitan Borough of Sefton withdrew their only pupil placed there for the same reason.

---

[8] See section 22(5) of the Children and Young Persons Act 1969 and the Certificates of Unruly Character (Conditions) Order 1977 SI 1977 No 1037.

[9] See para 21.05(d).

[10] Then Principal Officer (Child Protection).

39.49   Although the allegations at the Hett residential establishments between 1974 and 1991 were few in number, some of them were particularly grave. We do not have sufficient evidence before us to adjudicate firmly upon the allegations but, on the material that we do have, it is likely that most of them were true; and it is noteworthy that in most of the cases the complainant and the source of abuse were separated at quite an early stage. The response of Hett to the case of A, however, gave rise to justifiable misgivings about his ability to look after children in care and inspectors had drawn attention earlier to the potential vulnerability of girl pupils because of the layout of their accommodation at Ysgol Hengwrt.

Complaints of physical abuse

39.50   One of the many difficulties of investigating alleged abuse in the private residential establishments has been the fact that former residents of them are now very widely dispersed over the United Kingdom. Most of them were placed in North Wales from far afield with the result that they are difficult to trace now and many of them will be unaware of the existence of this Tribunal and its relevance to their experiences in care. We cannot be confident, therefore, that the picture that we have obtained of the extent of abuse in these homes is comprehensive.

39.51   In the event 16 former residents of the Hett establishments are known to have complained of physical abuse to the police and 15 of these have made allegations against identified members of the staff. However, comparatively few of these related to the Dôl Rhyd/Ynys Fechan period and most (ten) related to the period between 1986 and 1990 at Ysgol Hengwrt. We heard oral evidence, however, from only two witnesses about the earlier period and none about Ysgol Hengwrt.

39.52   All three known complainants from Ynys Fechan Hall and one of the three from Dôl Rhyd School alleged that they had been physically abused by Paul Hett and two of them complained about the other qualified social worker who was employed in the early years. The other complainant referred to two of the staff who were dismissed in December 1984[11].

39.53   All these complaints were of the use of excessive physical force in a variety of circumstances. The first of the "live" witnesses said that he was sent to Dôl Rhyd on 21 May 1976, when he was 12 years old, and that he remained there and at Ynys Fechan for four years. He was happy for the first two years but, when he grew older, he received beatings from Hett (he estimated four or five times in all). On one occasion when he was queuing at tea time, Hett just lashed out at him with his elbows and fists, hitting him in the mouth, with the result that his lip was cut, both inside and out, and his nose bled. There were three similar attacks on him by Hett later. On a couple of occasions other staff were present but he was not offered any assistance. He saw other children being struck similarly.

[11] See para 39.28.

39.54 The second "live witness" who was placed at Dôl Rhyd very shortly afterwards, on 1 June 1976, was 14 years old; he was transferred to Ynys Fechan and remained there until 25 May 1978 but he ran away 15 times. This witness complained of regular beatings by Hett, about once a week and starting after he had been at the school about ten months. Some of the assaults occurred in the sitting room in front of other children and staff whilst others took place in Hett's private study. Hett would "chin" him (hit him under the chin with Hett's elbow) and thump him in the stomach or chest and sometimes the face. If he fell to the floor, he would be kicked in the stomach. Hett would not say anything whilst administering these beatings but would pull funny faces and, after them, the witness would be left with red marks, which would last two or three days. This witness too saw other children suffering similar beatings. However, the situation improved after he was moved to Ynys Fechan. His complaint against the other member of staff was that the latter would punch him on the spots where he knew the complainant to be sensitive and that on one occasion he was picked up by his cheeks, leaving marks for a fortnight.

39.55 Two other former residents in the Dôl Rhyd/Ynys Fechan period who made statements to the police made similar complaints about Hett (one of them also alleged physical abuse by the other qualified social worker); and two of the ten complainants who were at Ysgol Hengwrt also complained to the police of serious physical assaults by Hett. There were complaints to the police also in 1993 of serious physical assaults by two other members of the staff at Ysgol Hengwrt in the late 1980s. None of these other complainants provided evidence to the Tribunal and at least one of them told the police that he became used to the way of life at Ynys Fechan, considering it to have been "a fairly good time" for him. It is necessary to mention these other complaints, however, because the Welsh Office itself received a number of similar complaints at the time of ill-treatment by Hett and other members of the staff, particularly in the first half of the 1980s.

39.56 In his written statement to the Tribunal the senior Welsh Office witness, John Lloyd, who was Director, Social Policy and Local Government within the Welsh Office from 1988, gave an account of these allegations of ill-treatment at the Hett establishments that were either made to or referred to the Welsh Office in the course of the 1980s. Thus, there was a complaint by an Islington parent in September 1980 that her son had been injured by Hett, which led to a visit by Gwynedd Social Services Department to Dôl Rhyd School on 22 September 1980. The conclusion by Gwynedd was that the injury had been inflicted accidentally in the course of restraint. But just over a year later, following the dismissal of two members of the care staff, 16 London boroughs that had placed children at the Hett establishments attended a meeting (at which Hett was present for part of the time) to discuss reports about conditions there. The decision of the meeting was to notify Hett of a number of requirements in writing including an explicit policy for the phasing out of corporal punishment and the introduction of a clear complaints procedure. The London boroughs resolved also to undertake reviews of all the children placed there for a period of months. Then, in March 1982, a local prospective Parliamentary candidate produced a bundle of statements from pupils, a care worker and a teacher alleging ill-treatment at Dôl Rhyd, mainly by Hett; and in late 1984 there were further allegations by a pupil alleging assaults by two teachers, which were investigated by the police (no prosecution ensued); and complaints by two members of the staff at Dôl Rhyd, who requested private interviews with HMI to express their concerns about the running of the school, including the harsh treatment of pupils, followed by the dismissals of three senior members of staff in December 1984[12].

39.57 Paul Hett denied all these allegations of assault when he gave oral evidence to the Tribunal. He said that the only corporal punishment used was the slipper and that was used very infrequently. Control of the children was exercised on "a family basis" and they tried to be caring and understanding. However, they were dealing with exceptionally disturbed children and he had to restrain residents throughout the years, which he had learnt how to do from his previous experience in a hospital, in a private approved school and, in particular, the care environment that he himself had developed. Some of the older and bigger pupils were violent and streetwise and had a tendency to go out to burgle and steal; he had to restore order in his school when violence occurred and there was no Welsh Office guidance on how to handle physical violence. Hett alleged also that at one stage from about 1989 Ysgol Hengwrt was receiving mainly 16 to 19 year olds because of the refusal of the Welsh Office to approve the admission of younger SEN children and Welsh Office warnings to local authorities intending to make placements, which had begun earlier.

39.58 It is impossible for us to reach a satisfactory conclusion about the extent of physical abuse at the Hett establishments or the allegations against Hett personally on the limited evidence before us. We accept that the staff had to deal with many very difficult and disturbed adolescents with whom various community homes had been unable to cope and that physical restraint had to be exercised quite frequently. Hett was, however, an unimpressive witness and we certainly do not accept that corporal punishment was limited to the use of the slipper. We have no doubt that excessive force was used to residents quite frequently by largely untrained staff in the absence of any clear guidelines but this was but one respect of many in which the quality of care provided fell below an acceptable standard.

Conclusions

39.59 The Hett establishments occupied the attention of the WOED and SWSO/SSIWs to an extraordinary extent for a period of 17 years during which only Dôl Rhyd of the three schools achieved full registration, and none of the three received general SEN approval but each was permitted to survive in turn until a sale or a transfer of registration or a reduction in numbers led to cancellation of its registration. The blame for this does not, in our view, rest upon the Inspectorates, who reported fully and frequently upon

---

[12] See para 39.28. Hett said in evidence that one reason for these dismissals was that the three had been "running down" the school with a view to purchasing it from him on favourable terms.

the deficiencies in management, staffing and organisation of the schools and who consistently pointed to their failure to achieve acceptable standards of care and education provision. In our judgment the fault lies, firstly, with the inadequate regulatory system and its over-elaborate procedures for de-registration and, secondly, with the Welsh Office for undue timidity and lack of grip in setting in train and implementing the Notice of Complaint procedure. Some blame must be attached also to the placement authorities but the history underlines the difficulties facing such authorities in monitoring adequately distant residential establishments. The evidence before us suggests that initially most of these authorities were conscientious in visiting Ynys Fechan Hall and Dôl Rhyd School but, almost inevitably as time passed, visits became irregular and pupils were only withdrawn after specific complaints had been received or a warning from the Welsh Office.

39.60 More generally, we accept the criticisms of Paul Hett and the successive schools made by the Inspectorates from time to time, which we have summarised. In our view the whole venture was ill-conceived and the gloomy forebodings of the inspector whose comments are cited in paragraph 39.11 of this report were abundantly fulfilled, to the serious detriment of many of the children and young persons who passed through the schools between 1974 and 1991.

Postscript on Ynys Fechan Hall

39.61 As we have said in paragraph 39.16, this establishment has been run as a private children's home for up to 11 resident boys and girls since late 1986; and it has been registered as such under the Children Act 1989 with Gwynedd County Council.

39.62 We have not received any complaints of abuse from present residents of Ynys Fechan Hall or from any former residents who lived there after September 1986 under the proprietorship of Barry Young. We did hear evidence, however, from John ap Iwan[13], who was employed there as a care worker from 1 September 1990 to 24 July 1992. He said that the home caters for children who have suffered abuse in the past and, when he was there, seven such children were in residence: although it is not a school, five of them were educated on the premises, one attended a local school and the other was undertaking a college catering course. There were four members of the staff and two handymen.

39.63 Ap Iwan made a number of allegations in his oral evidence to the Tribunal of physical abuse by Young to residents at Ynys Fechan Hall but he claimed to have witnessed only one such incident. Ap Iwan's allegation was that Young struck a boy on the left side of the head with his fist for no apparent reason. Ap Iwan's other allegations were made to the Social Services Department at Dolgellau Area Office early in 1991 and were based on alleged complaints made to him by three residents (two girls, one boy) six to eight weeks earlier. He met the Principal Officer (Children's Residential Services), Peter Hibbs, and two police officers on 1 February 1991 in relation to the complaints and an

---

[13] See paras 38.29 and 38.30 for his previous employment at Hengwrt Hall.

investigation followed (according to Hibbs it was already under way). The investigation did not result in any proceedings against Young.

39.64 A Salmon letter was served on Barry Young in respect of these allegations but no signed response was received from him, despite several reminders. However, we received a statement prepared on his behalf by solicitors in which he denied all the allegations made and reported by ap Iwan.

39.65 The Tribunal considers that ap Iwan was quite an impressive witness and we do not doubt that he saw the specific incident that he described but it is clear that, on the evidence as a whole, we cannot be satisfied that there has been any abuse at Ynys Fechan Hall since Young acquired it apart from that incident.

PART IX

ALLEGED ABUSE OF CHILDREN IN FOSTER HOMES IN GWYNEDD BETWEEN 1974 AND 1996

The overall provision of foster care in Gwynedd, 1974 to 1996

40.01 As we have said in paragraph 5.01, the balance in Gwynedd on 1 April 1974 between children in residential care and those boarded out/fostered was already heavily in favour of the latter (80 : 122). This was, of course, an inheritance from the predecessor counties, particularly the largest, Caernarvonshire. The number of "children in care" did not fluctuate very greatly in the following ten years above and below 300 (the extremes were 323 and 278), as Table B shows, but they began to decline quite steeply then to only 216 in 1989/1990. The table, for the period 1975 to 1990, was compiled by CIPFA and only those years for which the figures are incomplete have been omitted. It was not until the early 1980s that the percentage of children boarded out began to rise appreciably and the percentage of children in residential care declined. In terms of the actual numbers of children boarded out, the peak (181) was reached by 31 March 1986 but there was then a progressive decline to 137 by 31 March 1994 out of a total of 159 children in care (17 were in residential care).

40.02 In Wales as a whole the picture was broadly similar, as is shown by Table C, covering the whole period from 1975 to 1994. Ignoring a dubious figure for 1978/1979, the decline in the total number of "children in care" began in 1980/1981, when it was 4976, and the numbers progressed steadily downwards to 1970 by 31 March 1994, apart from a temporary increase between 1989 and 1991. The percentage of children boarded out rose steadily in the same period from 1980/1981, with only a few exceptions, from 34.7 to 81.3 by 31 March 1994.

40.03 During the first part of the period under review Area teams in Gwynedd were responsible for the recruitment, selection and preparation of foster parents as well as the placement and supervision of foster children. A senior social worker would be responsible for visiting and assessing prospective foster families. The Area's reports were then submitted to a Fostering Panel, which was responsible for making a recommendation. Foster parents were required to sign the undertakings prescribed in the Boarding Out Regulations. There was little guidance available to social workers involved in fostering, however, apart from supervision from senior staff, and there were considerable variations in practice.

TABLE B

CHILDREN IN CARE – GWYNEDD

Year	Population aged under 18	Children in Care	Rate per 1000 under 18	% in residential accommodation	% boarded out
1974 - 75	60,152	306	5.1	26.8	50.3
1975 - 76	60,626	323	5.3	27.6	47.7
1976 - 77	60,179	278	4.6	32.0	42.5
1977 - 78	59,601	308	5.2	26.6	38.0
1978 - 79	59,193	313	5.3	25.6	40.9
1979 - 80	59,348	315	5.3	21.3	45.7
1980 - 81	58,848	303	5.1	21.5	47.5
1981 - 82	57,975	289	5.0	15.4	58.7
1982 - 83	56,928	284	5.0	15.7	61.1
1983 - 84	55,727	301	5.4	15.9	59.5
1984 - 85	54,694	281	5.1	12.8	63.0
1985 - 86	53,957	263	4.9	10.3	68.8
1986 - 87	53,488	258	4.8	14.3	67.1
1989 - 90	52,924	216	4.1	14.8	75.0

TABLE C

ALL WELSH COUNTIES

Year	Population aged under 18	Children in Care	Rate per 1000 under 18	% in residential accommodation	% boarded out
1975 - 76	768,500	4884	6.4	38.1	32.9
1976 - 77	761,500	4952	6.5	36.9	31.3
1977 - 78	753,200	4841	6.4	36.1	31.9
1978 - 79	745,100	4184	5.6	33.8	32.7
1979 - 80	738,000	4832	6.5	31.6	34.8
1980 - 81	730,300	4976	6.8	28.6	34.7
1981 - 82	720,764	4659	6.5	28.6	39.4
1982 - 83	706,507	4442	6.3	26.6	41.5
1983 - 84	693,298	4058	5.9	29.1	44.3
1984 - 85	680,319	3756	5.5	26.4	47.9
1985 - 86	672,545	3588	5.3	23.4	52.8
1986 - 87	668,951	3506	5.2	24.1	54.8
1987 - 88	664,638	3248	4.9	29.4	71.4
1988 - 89	665,251	3033	4.6	23.4	60.3
1989 - 90	663,261	3307	5.0	21.6	64.6
1990 - 91	662,302	3195	4.8	19.2	51.7
1991 - 92	665,346	2477	3.7	25.0	75.0
1992 - 93	666,664	2430	3.6	23.0	77.0
1993 - 94	668,600	1970	2.9	18.7	81.3

40.04 During the early 1980s efforts were made by Area teams to improve and supplement selection methods by arranging meetings for applicants, by requiring them to attend "Parenting Plus" courses and by encouraging foster parents to meet each other.

40.05 We were told that increasing recognition of the complexity and specialist nature of foster care service led to the establishment in 1984 of a fostering unit at Cartref Bontnewydd[1]. At first this unit had only one member of staff but it expanded to a staff of four plus a clerical assistant. Under a partnership arrangement with Gwynedd County Council the unit assumed responsibility for the recruitment, selection, preparation, review and support of foster parents whilst the Areas retained responsibility for the placement and supervision of children in foster homes.

40.06 In the later part of the period under review, following the enactment of the Children Act 1989 and the Foster Placement Regulations 1991 made thereunder, Gwynedd procedures were governed by a Departmental Child Care Manual which set out details, amongst other things, of the planned and staged selection process in which applicants' group meetings were seen as an integral and essential part of the assessment. Detailed guidance in the Manual to residential carers was not, however, adapted for foster carers.

40.07 In the report of the Examination Team on Child Care Procedures and Practice in North Wales[2] Adrianne Jones drew attention[3] to the fact that both Clwyd and Gwynedd were then making considerably less use of residential care and had a higher proportion of children placed with foster carers than other authorities in England or Wales. In 1995 Gwynedd had access to 170 foster carers and this number included carers providing placement for children with disabilities. The report commented that Cartref Bontnewydd was a relatively small unit to bear responsibility for the support of so many carers spread over wide and difficult terrain as well as the responsibility for all recruitment and reviewing activity. It had been argued in 1991, when the Children Act 1989 was implemented, that additional resources were required and that a family placement officer ought to be established in each of the county's five areas, but that argument had not prevailed. A report in March 1994 by a Children Act Research Group of the University of Wales, Cardiff, which was commissioned by the Welsh Office Social Services Inspectorate, concluded, "The structure of the fostering service in Gwynedd, while properly underwritten by policy and procedures, has evident weaknesses that flow largely from the level of investment in staffing and the undeveloped management information system".

Complaints of abuse in foster homes in Gwynedd

40.08 One of the matters that attracted public attention in the course of the major investigation by North Wales Police was a reported suggestion in September 1992 that a file containing evidence of physical abuse of a foster child, including

---

[1] See para 37.02.
[2] Presented to Parliament on 17 June 1996.
[3] At para 4.95.

photographs, had remained in Gwynedd County Council's possession for eight years. This file, about a child hereafter called M, was in fact amongst documents to which the police had been given access but the report prompted the Chief Constable of North Wales Police to add his voice to those who were already calling for an inquiry into the conduct of the Social Services Departments of both North Wales counties.

40.09 In the event there was no public inquiry at that stage but the police did investigate M's allegations and brought charges against both foster parents and one of their sons. The foster mother was acquitted but her husband and son were both found guilty in the Crown Court at Mold of assault upon M (in the case of the foster father, of assault occasioning bodily harm).

40.10 It remained uncertain after these convictions whether or not the Secretary of State would order a public inquiry into the alleged abuse of children in care in North Wales generally. In 1994, therefore, in the light of the sentencing remarks made by the trial judge, His Honour Judge Gareth Edwards QC, Gwynedd County Council decided to commission an independent inquiry to review and report on the supervision by the County Council of M in the foster home between 1980 and 1986 and, in the light of that, to consider whether current child protection procedures and case management arrangements were adequate to avoid any further similar occurrences.

40.11 The report (referred to as the Walton report) of the three member inquiry team, including appendices, extended to 98 pages, and was presented in the autumn of 1995. It contained an exhaustive account of M's history and of his supervision during the relevant period and our summary account of the case in the next chapter of this report is based partly upon it.

40.12 Apart from the case of M, we are aware of seven foster parent households in which abuse of one kind or another is alleged to have occurred. In four of these the abuse is alleged to have been sexual. The relevant facts of these cases are, however, quite short and we deal with them in Chapters 42 and 43 of this report.

The case of M

Background

41.01 M, who was born on 7 March 1974, was the youngest of five children who were admitted into care on 11 January 1978 pursuant to a matrimonial care order[1] made by His Honour Judge Meurig Evans in divorce proceedings. M's mother lived at Holyhead and he was placed initially in Ucheldre Community Home at Llangefni before moving on to Y Gwyngyll at Llanfair PG on 19 January 1979[2]. He was first boarded out (separately from his half-brothers and half-sisters) with foster parents at Carreglefn in Anglesey on 5 October 1979 and he remained there until 11 November 1980, but the placement was not successful.

41.02 Speaking of this period in his life when making a statement to the police in March 1992, M said that his first recollection then was of Y Gwyngyll, about which he had no complaints to make: he was treated very well there. He said also that he had no complaints to make about the way in which he had been treated by his first foster parents.

41.03 M made a statement to representatives of the Tribunal in January 1997, in which he said that he was willing to give oral evidence to the Tribunal. However, when the time came for him to be called as a witness, he was not available and we admitted in evidence, therefore, his five statements to the police made in 1992 and his statement to the Tribunal.

41.04 M's second placement with foster parents lasted over five years, from 11 November 1980 to 11 April 1986, after which he returned to live with his natural mother on trial, with the intention that he should do so permanently. He was discharged from care on 10 June 1988, at the age of 14 years, when the care order was revoked.

41.05 M's second foster parents were Norman and Evelyn Roberts, who lived on a smallholding at Gwalchmai, in the centre of Anglesey. Norman Roberts was said to be a self-employed farm-worker, who also ran a mobile grocery business, although he described himself as a quarryman at his trial. Evelyn Roberts was a former SRN with two years' experience of nursing children (other than her own). They were approved as foster parents on 9 October 1978 and they were described as "most impressive" by the senior social worker who recommended them to the fostering panel.

41.06 Mr and Mrs Roberts had two sons and a daughter of their own aged in 1980 approximately 21, 17 and 16 years respectively. The two sons married in 1982 and left home. The daughter married in 1985.

---

[1] Under section 43 of the Matrimonial Causes Act 1973. A sixth child is referred to in para 41.24.
[2] See para 35.01.

41.07 During the period when M was fostered with them, Mr and Mrs Roberts had three other foster children staying with them. A boy (N) born on 15 February 1973 and his half-sister (O) had been placed with them briefly in 1979, and returned on a long term basis from 17 September 1981; and another girl (P), born on 15 November 1971, was placed with them on 25 May 1983.

41.08 When M was placed with Mr and Mrs Roberts the intention was that he should be fostered for a short period of nine to 12 months to provide him with individual attention, which (it was thought) would have an ameliorative effect on him. He remained with them from about early 1982, however, on a long term fostering basis.

The allegations of abuse

41.09 In his statement to the police made on 10 March 1992 M alleged that he had been treated cruelly, like a slave, throughout his period with Norman and Evelyn Roberts. He had been required to get up at 6 am daily to feed the animals in all weathers. False allegations of theft of food had been made against him and Norman Roberts had punished him by beating him across the hands with a bamboo type cane or by whipping him about the body with a horse whip. The whippings had occurred about three times a week and he had been made to have a cold bath after some of them.

41.10 M complained also of being undernourished throughout the period of his stay with the Roberts family. One type of punishment was to make him eat dry dog biscuits and this had occurred with similar frequency to the whippings.

41.11 Whilst M was fostered with the Roberts, he attended Gwalchmai Primary School and then latterly Bodedern School. He claimed that friends at the former saw marks of the whipping and that he showed marks later to two teachers at Bodedern School, who reported the matter to his social worker. He was too scared then to tell the latter what had happened but he was taken to hospital and a doctor photographed his injuries. Later, when his social worker and the Area Officer visited the foster home he said at first, in the presence of the foster parents, that a schoolboy was to blame; but he managed to speak to his social worker on her own just before she left and told her that it was his foster parents. He thought that she had then replied that it was "a bit too late to say that now". In the event nothing else happened: he continued to suffer the same treatment until his mother eventually managed to have him back home.

41.12 In further statements to the police in 1992 M said that two horse whips were used by Norman Roberts when whipping him and he identified the whips to the police. He said that he was always whipped on the bare skin and alleged that on occasions Ian Roberts (the elder son) would hold him upside down with his feet roped when Norman Roberts whipped him. But he was usually whipped when he was standing up. M also explained 14 photographs taken at the smallholding to illustrate findings there. He said that, on the occasion when he was taken to hospital, he had been whipped three or four days previously by Norman Roberts. At the school and at the hospital he had told different stories about what had happened and he had told the Area Officer, who took him to the hospital, that boys had caused the marks by hitting him with a ruler. This was because he was afraid of being whipped again by Norman Roberts if he told the truth. However, he did tell the Area Officer that Norman Roberts was responsible when they sat in a car park eating chips immediately after the visit to hospital.

41.13 M first alleged that Ian Roberts had whipped him in the last of his statements to the police, made on 27 November 1992, which was the occasion when the photographs were shown to him. In that statement he enlarged on aspects of the whipping and explained that the photographs had helped him to remember. M's allegation against Ian Roberts was that on some occasions he had used a small whip to hit M over his clothes on his back and on his bottom. On other occasions, when Norman Roberts had whipped M, Ian Roberts had held him hanging upside down (as previously said) over a beam.

41.14 Other allegations by M were that, when he wet the bed or soiled himself during the night, Norman Roberts would take him outside immediately, sometimes in the dark, and would hose him down over his pyjamas for about five minutes before ordering him upstairs to wash himself.

41.15 In relation to Evelyn Roberts, M made a number of separate allegations. A major complaint was that she gave him insufficient food to take to school to eat at dinner time so that he was forced to scavenge. He alleged also that food generally in the foster home was inadequate for him and that presents and clothes supplied for him by his mother were distributed by Evelyn Roberts amongst the other children without any authority or justification.

41.16 The charges laid in 1993 against Norman, Evelyn and Ian Roberts were based essentially on these statements of M and he gave evidence at their joint trial in June 1993 at Mold Crown Court. The two foster parents were charged with cruelty to M between 10 November 1980 and dates in 1985 and 1986 respectively. Norman Roberts was charged also with assault occasioning bodily harm on M in respect of the incident that led to the hospital visit, which was alleged to have occurred between 1 and 13 September 1985; and Ian Roberts was charged with common assault upon M between November 1980 and 31 August 1985 on the basis that he assisted his father in roping up M and suspending him for whipping. Both foster parents were acquitted of the cruelty charges on 1 July 1993 but Norman and Ian Roberts were found guilty of the assault charges.

41.17 When His Honour Judge Gareth Edwards QC sentenced Norman and Ian Roberts the following day he ordered that both of them should be conditionally discharged for a period of two years and that both should pay £1,000 towards the costs of the prosecution. The judge regarded the offences as grave but took into account the fact that they had occurred many years before, that the defendants were of previous good character and that they had to live with the disgrace brought upon them by the highly publicised case. He expressed the view also that an inquiry should follow the trial and that it should look "not only at the events of 1985, but at the period from 1980 to 1985".

41.18 In the course of the trial a considerable body of oral evidence was called and it has been neither necessary nor appropriate for that exercise to be repeated before this Tribunal. In addition to the evidence of M, there were numerous witnesses from his school and from the Social Services Department; the other foster children (of whom only P supported the evidence of M) and various friends and neighbours of the Roberts' were called; and the paediatrician who examined M on 13 September 1985, a consultant pathologist and a divisional police surgeon gave medical evidence. Finally, all three defendants gave evidence, repeating their previous denials to the police of any ill-treatment of M. One of the planks in the defence of Norman Roberts, in particular, was that the whip that he was alleged to have used to beat M in September 1985 had been purchased by him at the Royal Welsh Show in July 1986.

41.19 We received evidence from Norman, Evelyn and Ian Roberts in the form of written statements. These statements repeated the substance of what they had said at their trial in response to M's allegations. Norman Roberts said that he remembered being told by a social worker and the Area Officer about injuries to M's bottom in September 1985 but that he did not cause them and knew nothing about them until then. The only whip that he had in 1985 was a very long lungeing whip, which is not meant to strike anything with. Ian Roberts said that he was on holiday in Scotland between 8 and 11 September 1985, when M was alleged to have been injured. Evelyn Roberts dealt, in particular, with M's conduct and eating habits and difficulties that she experienced with P. She said that she had always regarded M as continuing to be a friend of the family and pointed out that, although N is now grown up, he still lives with the Roberts family and has chosen to make his home with them.

41.20 It is clear that the trial jury had much fuller oral evidence before them in the case of M than we ourselves have heard and we have not received any evidence that persuades us that the jury's verdicts were wrong. In order to avoid any misunderstanding, however, it is right to say that, on the basis of a question of law asked by the jury after they had retired to consider their verdicts, the trial judge inferred that they were not satisfied that Ian Roberts had played any part in whipping M, although they accepted that Ian Roberts had assaulted M by suspending him.

41.21 The activities of the Social Services Department in relation to M between 1978 and 1988 were subjected to minute scrutiny by the inquiry team who produced the Walton report and no useful public purpose would be served by repeating all the detail here. Bearing in mind our terms of reference and the trial jury's verdicts it is necessary, however, to consider the performance of Gwynedd Social Services Department in relation to M in three phases, namely, 1980 to 1985; September 1985 and the response to the evidence then; and 1986 to 1988.

Surveillance of M's placement between 1980 and 1985

41.22 We do not think that it is appropriate for us to criticise the original placement of M with Norman and Evelyn Roberts. In November 1980 they were held in high regard by the Social Services Department and we are not aware of any adverse reports at that time.

41.23 There is some confusion about the plan for M in November 1980. It is arguable that assessment in a residential home would have been appropriate for him on the breakdown of his first fostering placement but the Walton inquiry was told by an Assistant Director that there was no residential home in Gwynedd with appropriately qualified staff to make assessments at the time, a comment with which we agree. A six monthly review of M on 4 November 1980, a week before he was placed with the Roberts', is said (in the Walton report) to have assumed that a long term placement was in M's best interests but the initial plan seems to have been to work towards rehabilitation with his mother, following upon rehabilitation of his half-sisters. This plan was changed quite soon because of a combination of circumstances.

41.24 Without going into unnecessary detail it appears that M had developed a number of problems by 16 February 1981, when a further review of him took place. These problems (soiling, vomiting etc) were attributed by a child psychiatrist to M's contact with his mother and the upshot was that M had no further contact with her for the next year. Meanwhile, there were separate concerns about the mother's position and her ability to cope, following the birth of her sixth child (a boy) in 1981. In January 1982 it was said that the placement was to be considered long term fostering and the prohibition on contact with the mother continued, apart from a visit home by M on 8 March 1982. Yet the child psychiatrist did not attend a review until 17 January 1983. It was not until the mother had been seen by the psychiatrist in February 1983 that a pattern of two monthly access visits by the mother was established.

41.25 One of the causes of concern considered in the Walton report was the number of field social workers involved with M from time to time in this period and the pressure on the Area child care team, which increased from 1980 onwards because of the number of referrals. It was said by the Area Officer in February 1983 that "using the caseload weighting system as a guideline, the system indicates that only three-quarters of all child care cases are securing the attention that they should"; and he urged that the team establishment should be restored to its original 1979 figure of six and a half team members.

41.26 Between November 1981 and August 1985 three different field workers were allocated to the case of M in succession. The first was responsible until June 1982; the second took over after a gap of five months and was then responsible until September 1984, when she started maternity leave; and the third was an unqualified temporary member of the staff who took over in November 1984 until August 1985. There was then another gap before the fourth social worker took over: she was on leave when the September 1985 bruising was reported but appears to have taken over on her return from leave, when she visited the foster home with the Area Officer and saw M. The latter's comment in his Tribunal statement was that the fourth was "OK" but that the others did not help him at all.

41.27 The evidence suggests that there were some complaints or suspicions of physical abuse of M during this period prior to September 1985. M's mother alleged at Christmas 1980 that he had been sent home in "tatty clothes and covered in bruises". This allegation was made in a letter from the mother to the foster parents, who reported it to the Social Services Department. An emergency duty officer examined M, who did not know where or when he had suffered the two small bruises that were observable. M's social worker subsequently visited the foster home and M's mother, who agreed that the marks on M were consistent with a fall. Evelyn Roberts did take M to a doctor, who gave evidence at the trial, but there was no evidence of social worker contact about this.

41.28 At the Roberts' trial a retired school canteen lady at M's school alleged that on one occasion she had seen red marks on M's buttocks and that her finding had been reported via the cook to the Headmaster and thence to the Social Services Department. There was no documentary evidence, however, to substantiate this allegation.

41.29 There were indications in April and July 1983 that M was telling school friends that his foster parents were hitting him. These reports emanated, at least in part, from Evelyn Roberts, who said that M was seeking attention and pity. The social worker told Evelyn Roberts that she had heard this also from the police school liaison officer. It was assumed that M's allegations were lies or fantasy and no action was taken to investigate them.

41.30 The conclusions of the Walton report were critical of social work practice in the period 1980 to 1985 because there were no records on file of any six monthly reviews of M for two years between August 1984 and August 1986; and the reviews that were held before that appeared to have been carried out in a routine manner without reappraisal of M's long term future (they were preoccupied with narrow treatment of his behaviour problems and issues of access). They were critical also of the failure to visit M as regularly as the rules required and/or to record visits on the departmental forms. There was little evidence that, when M had been seen, his feelings and wishes on such matters as his long term future had been discussed; and there had been a major gap in the contact log, with no records of boarding out visits on file, between late 1984 and the autumn of 1985.

The response to the events of September 1985

41.31 It was the Deputy Headmistress of Bodedern School who reported on or about 11 September 1985 that M had disclosed bruises on his body to some of his schoolfellows, claiming that he had been hit on his bottom by his foster father. The school was told that there was no social worker for M but that his new social worker would be starting her duties the following Monday and would investigate; but the school requested an immediate investigation.

41.32 The Area Officer, who was the only member of the staff with knowledge of the case available, visited the foster home late that evening, on the return of Norman and Evelyn Roberts from a family celebration, and saw M in their presence. The Roberts' denied all knowledge of the bruising. M gave two different explanations for his bruises. The Area Officer did not examine them, but he asked the foster parents to make arrangements for M to see his general practitioner.

41.33 On 12 September 1985 the Area Officer visited Bodedern School and talked with M, who said that he had alleged that he had been pushed downstairs and hit by Norman Roberts in order to gain sympathy from his teachers. The Area Officer saw M's injuries and arranged for him to see the consultant paediatrician that evening at Ysbyty Gwynedd, the nearest major hospital. Two doctors examined M and took photographs for teaching purposes. They regarded the injuries as "classic": in their view they had been inflicted deliberately, probably seven or eight days earlier. M drew a picture of a leather horse strap with metal studs, claiming at one point that it was used by Norman Roberts to chastise him but later denying this, saying that he had fallen downstairs.

41.34 The Area Officer told the inquiry panel that he took M for fish and chips after the hospital visit but his account of the conversation differed from that of M, who alleged that he (M) told the Area Officer then that he had been whipped about three or four days previously. According to the Area Officer, M said that P had tried to blame his foster father for the injuries and that he wished to return to his foster home, where he was happy. The Area Officer had arranged a fall back place for M at Tŷ'r Felin and told M that he need not return to his foster home. On their return to Gwalchmai, the Area Officer told Mr and Mrs Roberts of the extent of the injuries. Norman Roberts admitted slapping M with a soft slipper but did not offer any other explanation of M's injuries.

41.35 The Area Officer sent a Notice of Accident form dated 17 September 1985 to the Director of Social Services, accompanied by the following memorandum:

"Your records will indicate that M is a boy in care fostered with Mr and Mrs Norman Roberts. Neither the boy, foster parents or school are able to identify the exact nature and cause of M receiving the blows to his buttocks. The two social workers supervising the children in this placement will, of course, monitor the situation. I will leave it to you as to whether you feel the police should be advised."

41.36 The Notice of Accident form described the injuries sustained by M as:

"Two or 3 strap marks about 6 inches long across both buttocks. Confirmed by Consultant Paediatrician as 3 successive blows to the buttocks with a hard object. Photographs have been taken."

41.37 There is a considerable conflict of evidence about the responsibility for the subsequent inaction by the Social Services Department with each senior officer blaming another. What is clear is that, whatever errors had occurred prior to 17 September 1985, there was a lamentable failure to take appropriate action from then onwards for which several senior officers must bear some of the blame. There were also, in our judgment, deliberate failures to inform the police and to report the facts fairly and accurately to the Chairman and members of the County Council's Children's Sub-Committee.

41.38 We do not propose to rehearse here every step that followed or all the allegations and counter-allegations that have been canvassed before the inquiry team and in evidence before the Tribunal, because to do so would be disproportionate to the original events in the context of our inquiry. It is sufficient to draw attention to the main sequence of what occurred.

41.39 The Notice of Accident Form and memorandum were sent to Gethin Evans, then a Principal Officer but who was to become Assistant Director (Children) from 30 September 1985. Gethin Evans passed them to Larry King, the Principal Officer responsible for child abuse, who signed the Notice of Accident Form and sent it to the County Treasurer. The latter then questioned on 26 September 1985 the relevance of the notice to the insurers and King responded with the following note:

> "Note: this is being dealt with by Area as non-accidental injury to be fully discussed shortly. Has already been (coord) tentatively informed so no urgency."

41.40 King's comments written on the Area Officer's memorandum of 17 September 1985 were:

(at the top)

> "Area have the option of dealing with this under CA procedures or taking up suitability of the FPs with social worker and Area Officer"

(at the bottom, on the question of reference to the police)

> "No, not required at this stage. Will visit to discuss."

King alleged in his evidence to the Tribunal that the original document had been torn across the bottom so that additional comments by him, to the effect that the police would be told "when we get the case conference" and that he was going to Area that day for a Co-ordinating Committee meeting at which the police would be present, were missing.

41.41 King did attend the Anglesey Co-ordinating Committee on Child Abuse, chaired by the Area Officer, on 17 September 1985 but the police were not represented because their representative was on holiday. The matter was apparently referred to under "Any other business" and, according to King, the photographs were shown around. The note of the meeting indicated that the Area Officer reported that "a child in care living with foster parents had received blows to the buttocks resulting in bruises. The department was working with foster parents and the school to identify the nature of the event".

41.42 An unaddressed note of the same date, signed by King, read:

> "long discussion with Area Office . . . injury most likely inflicted by foster parents accidentally . . . chastising him for some offence . . . the alternative is that some other boys have done this. Area Officer does not wish matter to be pursued further at this stage and is monitoring. He has made investigation himself and we must accept his judgment and decision (or question all of his decisions and his right to be Area Officer).
>
> Matter reported to Review Committee to leave in the hands of SSD and Area Officer who will report back if further investigation required."

41.43 In the event child protection procedures were not set in train. A case conference was not convened and the police were not informed. When the Area Officer and M's social worker visited the foster home on 16 October 1985 "the cause of injury was still not known", according to a note initialled by the Area Officer, and the reason for not instigating full child protection procedures was "to prevent endangering the placement of all the children".

41.44 This was stated to be the position despite the fact that, when a review of the other three foster children had been held on 23 September 1985, it had been said that a number of telephone calls had been received from local residents voicing concern that M was being allowed to remain in the foster home. On that occasion it had been said that police involvement was still awaiting a decision at headquarters. Then, the following day, there had been another telephone call from a local resident in which serious allegations against Norman Roberts had been made; and on 25 September the Deputy Head of M's school had telephoned to report that she had interviewed one of the boys alleged to have pushed M downstairs and that she was satisfied that it had not happened.

41.45 The decision to begin a programme to rehabilitate M with his mother was taken on a statutory review held on 12 November 1985 but it did not purport to be based on what had occurred two months earlier. The view of the psychiatrist previously had been that M's behavioural problems were attributable to his relationship with his mother rather than to his experiences in foster care and, as we have said, access to his own family had been prevented earlier on for a substantial period[3]. However, by November 1985 regular access had been renewed for over two years: M wanted to return home and it was believed by then that his mother would be able to care for him if he did so.

Developments between 1986 and 1988

41.46 Concern about M seems to have been deflected in December 1985 to consideration of his weight. He and N were found then to be underweight by the School Medical Officer, who reported that the boys' weight and height had not increased according to expectations since 1983. A case discussion followed, on 7 January 1986, between the SMO, the Area Officer, M's social worker, her Team Leader and a representative of the fostering unit at Cartref Bontnewydd. It was agreed that the two boys were not getting enough food and M's social worker expressed a variety of concerns about the quality of the placement. Amongst the many decisions taken were that the boys should be recommended for inclusion in the Child Protection Register, that all the Roberts' foster children should have school meals henceforth and that M's social worker should continue his preparation for placement at home on trial. A transfer of N to Gwynfa Residential Clinic was also to be considered.

41.47 This meeting led to a flurry of activity at headquarters. On 8 January 1986 Gethin Evans, the Assistant Director (Children), had a discussion with the Chairman of the Social Services Committee about the inclusion of the boys'

---

[3] See para 41.24.

names on the At Risk Register. Then, on 21 January 1986 the Anglesey Co-ordinating Committee (without authority to do so) agreed to place the names of M and N on the At Risk Register. According to the minutes, the stated reason for inclusion in the register was "neglect and failure to thrive"; and the boys' names were entered on 23 January 1986. Nomention was made of M's earlier injuries.

41.48 At the same time there were recriminations. On 21 January 1986 Gethin Evans wrote to the Area Officer expressing concern that headquarters had not been consulted earlier and that a case conference had not been convened. He questioned the conclusions reached and the line of action taken, particularly the timing; and he said that the last thing that they wanted to see was the total collapse of all four placements. He pointed out that placing the two boys on the Register obliged him to report the matter to the Children's Sub-Committee but that, before doing so, he had to examine the handling and oversight of the foster home since the four foster children had been placed there; and he said that he might start by asking King to examine relevant files.

41.49 Gethin Evans sent a memorandum to Lawrence King two days later requesting information about the social worker involved with the four foster children and details of the supervision, plans etc for each child prior to 1 January 1986. King, however, said that he never saw this memorandum at the time. If he had received it, he would have refused to do what was asked because he had no responsibility for foster care services. There was no response to the memorandum on the file.

41.50 A memorandum from the Area Officer in February 1986 stated that he had been advised that the Director of Social Services was requesting the Deputy Director, Glanville Owen, to investigate whether the Department was fulfilling its child care responsibilities in respect of M and hoped to involve an independent observer. The circumstances of the other children were to be investigated by Glanville Owen. In her response on 24 February 1986 the Director of Social Services said that she had asked Gethin Evans to conduct full statutory reviews on all the foster children.

41.51 Gethin Evans' report to the Children's Sub-Committee on 13 March 1986 was as follows:

> "During September 1985 M was found at school to have deep bruises on his buttocks. The boy said he had fallen. The matter was reported to the Area Co-ordinating Committee on Child Abuse.
>
> On 7 January 1986 a discussion was held about the two boys following the anxiety of medical personnel about their size and weight and conduct. It was decided that there was sufficient reason for anxiety about the two and they were placed on the Child Abuse Register which was confirmed by the established Committee later.
>
> Plans have been formulated for M to be reunited with his family. M's foster brother will remain with his sister. Overall situation is being monitored, but as a department the situation is unsatisfactory."

41.52 M returned home on trial on 11 April 1986 and his name was removed from the Register on 15 July 1986, by which time he had gained weight and height. The statutory review of all four foster children had been fixed for 16 April 1986 but did not take place because the social worker was off sick. On 18 April 1986, a meeting took place between Gethin Evans and the senior social worker responsible for M, who reported that M had been agitating to go home for some time and that this had caused stress in the foster home.

41.53 M presented behavioural problems at home and at school following his return home and was eventually admitted to a residential school on 22 June 1987, thereafter spending weekends and holidays at home until he left the school on 5 May 1990 (revocation of the care order having been granted by the Court on 29 June 1988). The other foster children remained with the foster parents.

41.54 The police only became aware of M's allegations of abuse in 1992, over six years after the event, when they interviewed M routinely as a potential complainant in the course of their major investigation. A large number of relevant witnesses in relation to M's complaints were then interviewed and a successful prosecution ensued despite the lapse of time.

Conclusions

41.55 The narrative of this single case has been so long that we have refrained from interspersing much comment in it. In the end the facts almost speak for themselves: there were so many obvious procedural breaches, errors of judgment and failures to act that the case stands as an indictment of the senior management of the Gwynedd Social Services Department who were or ought to have been involved.

41.56 Bearing in mind that this ground has already been traversed in considerable detail in the Walton report, we will confine ourselves to the main heads of criticism, which may be summarised as follows:

(1) There were serious gaps in the allocation of a social worker to M, in visits to him and in the recording of visits between 1980 and 1985[4].

(2) There was a failure to investigate adequately adverse reports such as that of the police school liaison officer[5].

(3) The initial investigation into M's complaints on 11 September 1985 took place in the presence of the foster parents and was inadequate as a whole (not even the injuries were inspected).

(4) The original arrangements for a medical examination by the foster parents' general practitioner were inappropriate.

(5) The other children in the foster home should have been interviewed and medically examined.

---

[4] See para 41.30.
[5] Ibid.

(6) The findings by the Consultant paediatrician and his opinion about them were given insufficient weight throughout[6].

(7) A case conference, attended by the police, should have been convened immediately.

(8) The procedure adopted of casual referral to the Co-ordinating Committee and de facto reliance upon the Area Officer's judgment as to whether further investigation should take place was wholly wrong, as King must have known. In particular, King must have known on the evidence that the matter should be reported to the police for investigation and the explanation of "accidental chastisement" was not based on Norman Roberts' admission of using a slipper or any other evidence[7].

(9) The stated reason for not invoking child protection procedures, namely, "to prevent endangering the placement of all the children" was most improper.

(10) The Department's duties under the Boarding Out Regulations to terminate boarding out if it appeared that it was no longer in the child's best interests[8] was not given adequate consideration.

(11) Headquarters appears to have let matters rest where they were without any inquiry for three months until the Senior Medical Officer raised a different issue.

(12) The procedure adopted for placing M and N on the At Risk Register was incorrect and circumvented the need to hold a child protection conference[9].

(13) Gethin Evans' response to this new development was inappropriate and wrong because he was more concerned about preserving the placements of the foster children and the adverse reflection upon the SSD of having two children in care registered as at risk than with the best interests of all four foster children[10].

(14) None of the arrangements mooted by the Director of Social Services and Gethin Evans for investigation and review of what had happened appear to have been followed through[11].

(15) Gethin Evans' report to the Children's Sub-Committee in March 1986 was inadequate and misleading in relation to what had occurred in September 1985[12].

---

[6] See para 41.33.
[7] See para 41.42.
[8] Regulation 4 of the Boarding Out Regulations 1955.
[9] See para 41.47.
[10] See para 41.48.
[11] See paras 41.48 to 41.50.
[12] See para 41.51.

41.57 It would not be profitable to spend time trying to weigh precisely the apportionment of blame amongst the senior officers for these shortcomings. A continuous thread emerges of preoccupation with preservation of the placements of all four foster children rather than rigorous investigation of the foster parents and the true cause of the marks on M's buttocks. There was also considerable confusion about the authority and responsibility of individuals. The Area Officer regarded himself as accountable in the matter to Gethin Evans as Assistant Director (Children). In discussion with the Walton Panel, he emphasised that any legal activity or any substantial change in circumstances, such as entering a child's name in the At Risk Register, or moving a child from a foster home needed approval from headquarters; and the instigation of an investigation involving the police required specific permission. Thus, the question of police involvement was put to Gethin Evans by the Area Officer in his memorandum of 17 September 1985.

41.58 The assumption of responsibility as between Gethin Evans and King was bedevilled by their poor personal relationship. As Principal Officers they had shared an office but Gethin Evans had won advancement and King, who did not speak Welsh, regarded himself as a victim of discrimination. Both bore responsibility for dealing promptly and properly with the alleged abuse of M; and it is of comparatively minor relevance that the Gwynedd child abuse procedures of the relevant date did not envisage the abuse of children in foster homes. King clearly should not have left a discretion as to further investigation with the Area Officer but Gethin Evans bore a direct and higher responsibility to ensure that a child protection conference was held and that the views of the Consultant paediatrician and other evidence were reported to the police. Furthermore, he was responsible for ensuring that the Department's duties under the Boarding Out Regulations were complied with. As it was, the Walton panel's findings were that the investigation was carried out by area office staff neither trained nor experienced in child abuse and that there was a reluctance to remove M because of the implications for the other foster children.

41.59 In their oral evidence to the Tribunal both Gethin Evans and King sought to justify their non-activity. King's defence essentially was that his role was advisory rather than executive. He said that he briefed the Deputy Director of Social Services, Glanville Owen, about the position before Gethin Evans wrote his memoranda in January 1986 and that Owen was very angry about the matter. King was not himself involved after that. Earlier he had been persuaded against his better judgment by the Area Officer that M's injuries could have been inflicted accidentally rather than intentionally by the foster parents giving M "a whack".

41.60 Gethin Evans said that it was for the Area Officer to inform the police and that King was responsible for the application of child abuse procedures, but he accepted that those procedures did not cover children in care and that King's role was advisory. Evans himself thought that the police would be informed through a case conference (which was never held). He accepted that he saw the photographs and that King might have discussed the matter with him but he told the Walton panel "I am sure that the information I internalised was that the accident did not take place in the foster home". In relation to his later activities he denied any disinclination to report complaints by children in care to the police or any intention to mislead the Children's Sub-Committee.

41.61 The evidence of the Deputy Director, Glanville Owen, was that his only involvement in M's case was when he was asked by the Director of Social Services to investigate what had happened: he did not play a part in the events as they occurred. When he investigated the matter he went to the Area Office, read the files and interviewed the Area Officer, the senior social worker and the social worker involved. He then wrote a report criticising the procedures that had been followed, stressing that headquarters should have been informed immediately and that a case conference should have been called. It is likely that he saw Gethin Evans' memorandum of 21 January 1986[13] but he was not aware of any suggestion that children in care should not be put on the At Risk Register.

41.62 Finally, the Director of Social Services, Lucille Hughes, said that she would have expected Glanville Owen to draw the matter to her attention when he found out about it. The case of M had come to her attention first when she was told that the names of M and N were to be put on the At Risk Register. She believes that she was told about the failure to thrive and that M had been involved in "some dubious corporal attack or punishment"; but she did not see the photographs until 1992. She agreed with the Walton panel's conclusions that the police should have been informed in September 1985 and that a full investigation should have taken place then. She agreed also that the proper course of action would have been to remove M, and possibly the other foster children, during the course of the investigation. She denied having had any wish for matters to be dealt with "in-house" in order to avoid publicity or to avoid the need for alternative placements for the foster children.

41.63 Having reviewed this evidence, our clear conclusion is that a major share of the blame for Gwynedd's failure in the case of M must rest upon Gethin Evans. Although the Area Officer did have a discretion himself to inform the police of suspected child abuse, it is clear that he sought guidance at the very least from Gethin Evans when he sent the Notice of Accident form to headquarters on 17 September 1985; and Gethin Evans should have taken charge of the matter, or at least should have monitored it closely, from then on. Moreover, even though he failed to do either, we are satisfied that he did see the photographs and that he knew both that a case conference had not been held and that the police had not been informed. King must also bear a share of the blame in view of his responsibilities for child protection, albeit in an advisory role, and his lack of direct authority over the Area Office does not excuse his failure to ensure that proper procedures were followed. Finally, the failure to inform either the Director or the Deputy Director at an early stage and their lack of close involvement throughout reflect badly on the administration of the Social Services Department generally, for which they must bear the ultimate responsibility.

---

[13] See para 41.48.

Alleged sexual abuse of children in foster homes in Gwynedd

Introduction

42.01 In this chapter we deal with alleged sexual abuse of children in care in four foster homes in Gwynedd. In the first two of these, however, Clwyd was the placement authority. Whilst Gwynedd agreed to undertake supervision in both cases the statutory responsibility for the care of the two relevant children remained with Clwyd County Council throughout.

42.02 The Tribunal has received in evidence statements from complainants in respect of only two of the foster homes but we have had access to the social services files, complainants' statements and Court records in respect of the other cases. For the sake of completeness, therefore, we have included all four cases but we do not make any findings against alleged abusers, except those who have been convicted of the relevant offences.

Malcolm Ian Scrugham

42.03 Foster child A was born in Clwyd on 29 July 1975 of a single mother and she was admitted to care at a very early age. Her mother married later and had two further children but she separated from her husband and all three of her children were in care. The NSPCC were involved with A early on and she was made the subject of a Place of Safety Order when she was ten months old, followed by an interim care order. Subsequently a supervision order for three years was substituted, with the unusual condition that she should remain in voluntary care; and she continued in voluntary care when the supervision order ended.

42.04 A was first fostered in Clwyd from August 1976 to October 1984 with a couple who lived at Old Colwyn. From about 1980, when it became clear that A's mother was unable to offer her a home, the aim was that she should be adopted by this couple but there were financial problems about this in the absence of an adoption allowances scheme. Although there had been some complaints about the foster home by others in the late 1970s, A seemed to be well settled there and the home was regarded as warm and caring. Then, in August 1984, the foster parents announced their intention to emigrate to South Africa without A; they said also that the foster mother was taking a college course and could not, therefore, cope with A. Their proposal was that A should be placed with their friends, Malcolm and Maria Scrugham, who had moved from Old Colwyn to Bala in 1982.

42.05 A was actually placed with the Scrughams by her first foster parents on 20 October 1984, without authority, and she remained in their household until April 1993, by which time she was pregnant by her boy friend and wished to move to her own accommodation. The Scrughams had two children of their own living with them: a boy born on 4 July 1979 and a girl born on 16 November 1981.

42.06 It was on 5 June 1992 that A's complaint of sexual abuse by Malcolm Scrugham first became known to a Clwyd family placement worker. A's allegation (initially made to two friends) was that she had been abused from the age of 11 to 14 years by Scrugham. Two months previously she had told the same social worker that Scrugham had been buying underwear for her.

42.07 The alleged child abuse was reported to the police and a full investigation ensued. A made four statements to the police, the first on 9 June 1992; and a Child Protection Case Conference was held on 24 June 1992 at Bala, at which A's status (in voluntary care) was clarified. She was interviewed also on 9 July 1992 by a Clwyd Child Care Manager, who saw her alone, despite Maria Scrugham's protest, and who made it clear to A that she was free to discharge herself from care and leave the foster home, if she wished to do so. By this time Maria Scrugham had petitioned for divorce and had said that she would never allow her husband, who was on police bail to an address in Somerset, to return to the home. A chose to remain with her.

42.08 In her statements to the police A alleged that Scrugham had begun to assault her sexually from about January 1987 and that she had been subjected to full sexual intercourse on a regular basis until she was 14 years old. She had then begun crying and resisting and there had been no sexual contact between them since. Intercourse had taken place mainly in Scrugham's car when he had taken her out in it after she had been punished by his wife. It had also occurred in the house on at least two occasions. Additional allegations were that Scrugham had forced A to perform oral sex with him regularly; that he had buggered her on one occasion; and that he had encouraged her to have sexual intercourse with two boy friends. She complained also of being given regular "hidings" by Scrugham as punishment for a variety of misdemeanours.

42.09 On 23 April 1993, in the Crown Court at Caernarvon, Scrugham was convicted of four sexual offences against A, namely, rape when she was 11 years old, rape when she was aged between 12 and 14 years, indecent assault and one offence of aiding and abetting a boy friend of A to have unlawful sexual intercourse with her. He was convicted also of an indecent assault on the boy friend. Scrugham was then sentenced to a total of ten years' imprisonment.

42.10 Whilst neither Clwyd nor Gwynedd social workers had any reason to suspect before June 1992 that A was being sexually abused by her foster father, there are grounds for substantial criticism of Clwyd and to a much lesser extent of their counterparts in Gwynedd.

42.11 Before A was left by the first foster parents with the Scrughams on 20 October 1984, A had become well known to the Scrughams because she had spent holidays with them during the preceding two years. The Scrughams' home was visited by a Gwynedd social worker on at least two occasions in August 1984 (once accompanied by a representative of the family placement unit). A report written by the social worker and dated 22 August 1984 expressed some concerns about conditions in the foster home. The Scrughams' general practitioner also had some reservations and declined to provide a reference. The report and other reports about the couple were supplied to Clwyd, making it clear that it was for Clwyd to decide whether or not to approve the foster parents for the placement of A. In the event, however, the Scrughams were never formally approved as foster parents, despite the fact that Clwyd purported to be "monitoring the situation closely". Gwynedd agreed in February 1985 to complete the standard Form F application form but in November 1985 the Dolgellau Area office was still seeking clarification from Clwyd of the Scrughams' status. Moreover, Clwyd took no steps to rationalise and secure A's own status (ostensibly in voluntary care) when they were aware of problems and knew that her mother could not be traced.

42.12 Although Gwynedd agreed to undertake supervision of A after her transfer to the Scrughams the arrangement appears to have faltered by 1987. Complaints of inappropriate punishment of A in October 1985 were properly investigated by Clwyd and Gwynedd social workers; and statutory review forms in 1986 were being submitted by Gwynedd to Clwyd for completion and signature. But it seems that there was a breakdown in visiting in the course of 1987. Thus, on 7 January 1988 Maria Scrugham told a Clwyd social worker who visited her that day that she had not seen a Gwynedd social worker since the former's previous visit in June 1987, despite a statement by him in the January 1988 review form that there had been visits by Gwynedd in July, August, October and December 1987.

42.13 In December 1988 Gwynedd wrote formally to Clwyd to confirm an earlier intimation that it was unable to continue supervising A because the responsible social worker was leaving (the child care team was fully stretched). This followed immediately upon a letter to Clwyd from the social worker reporting concerns expressed by a local general practitioner at Bala about conditions in the foster home and the presence there of a homeless young man. There is no evidence before us, that either Clwyd or Gwynedd investigated these concerns.

42.14 In 1989 the possibility of Clwyd assuming parental rights in respect of A was again mooted but it was not pursued because in July 1989 the Scrughams said that they wished to adopt A. At that stage it was agreed that adoption was in A's best interests and that a Clwyd family placement/adoption worker should hold the case pending adoption. It remained with her until June 1992, at which point a Rhyl Area social worker was about to be nominated to take over supervision of A. The proposed adoption had not proceeded, partly because of Scrugham's stroke and two heart attacks in 1991 but more importantly because of A's change of mind by February 1992.

42.15 On 1 June 1992 Malcolm Scrugham telephoned the Rhyl duty social worker to say that A had been absent overnight and it was on 5 June 1992 that it was reported that she had made allegations of sexual abuse by Scrugham. In her statements to the police A said that Scrugham had tried to stop her going out with her boy friend since February 1992.

42.16 This history demonstrates that there was a regrettable failure by Clwyd Social Services Department to grasp hold of A's case and make effective long term plans for her. They took no steps to secure A's legal position either when it first became apparent that her mother could not care for her or in the summer and autumn of 1984 when she was, in effect, abandoned by her first foster parents after eight years with them. The breakdown of this long standing placement, together with reservations about the suitability of the Scrughams' home and the concerns expressed subsequently in 1985 should have underlined the need for a thorough-going reassessment of A's needs leading to a long term plan for her future. Instead, the unsatisfactory placement with unregistered foster parents was allowed to continue, apparently without any positive decision making at an appropriate level.

42.17 It is noteworthy also that sexual abuse took place at a time when supervisory visits appear to have lapsed. Clwyd failed to take over close supervision when Gwynedd ceased to undertake it, even though the Clwyd social worker and her seniors identified what needed to be done and the responsibility for supervision rested upon Clwyd and not Gwynedd. It cannot be said with confidence that the sexual abuse would have been disclosed when it was occurring if the Boarding Out Regulations had been strictly complied with but the possibility of disclosure would have been greatly increased by such compliance.

42.18 It is pleasing to record that, despite A's misfortunes, she performed consistently well at school, both scholastically and socially, and was never in trouble with the police. She progressed to secretarial college and was then able to secure part-time employment.

Foster home B

42.19 The girl E, born on 27 December 1974, whose escapade at Butlins Holiday Camp on 2 September 1988 led to the Park House Inquiry that year[1], complained in her statement to the police made on 8 October 1992, which was read to the Tribunal, that she had been sexually abused by her male foster parent when boarded out with Mr and Mrs B between 1986 and 1987.

42.20 E had been admitted to care for a month or so at the age of nine years after complaining to the police that she had been sexually abused by a step-brother and the nervous breakdown of her mother. She and her mother had then stayed in Eire with E's grandmother before she was placed in 1984 at Park House, where her first stay lasted about two years. She was then boarded out by Clwyd County Council with Mr and Mrs B at Conwy in Gwynedd between 1986 and 1987; and Gwynedd agreed to supervise the placement.

42.21 In her statement to the Tribunal made on 4 November 1996 this witness added nothing to her 1992 police statement about her period in foster care with the Bs. We have before us, therefore, only her bare allegations that she left the Bs after a year as a result of being sexually abused by Mr B and that she complained to the police but believed that no action was taken because it was her word against his.

42.22 Detective Superintendent Ackerley of the North Wales Police, who was in charge of the major police investigation between 1991 and 1993, confirmed in his oral evidence to the Tribunal that E had complained in or about 1987 that she had been sexually abused by Mr B. From the sparse surviving

---

[1] See paras 17.79 to 17.87.

documentation he was able to say that the complaint had been investigated by the police: it appeared that no prosecution had followed in the absence of any corroboration.

42.23 The Tribunal received in evidence a statement from Mr B in which he vehemently denied E's allegations. He referred to E's persistent demands to return to Park House, where she had a particular friend, with whom she enjoyed dancing; and he quoted a social work report praising the progress E had made with the Bs. He gave an account also of what had happened on the day when E alleged that the sexual abuse had occurred: he had been detained by the police the following day and questioned for a considerable time before being released on bail. He was told later by his solicitor that the matter was closed.

42.24 We cannot usefully comment further on this matter save to say that:

    (a) there is no sufficient evidence before us to support a finding that Mr B did abuse E;

    (b) we have not seen or heard any evidence to justify criticising either Clwyd or Gwynedd Social Services Department in relation to this placement.

Foster home C

42.25 Four children were placed on 22 October 1979 with Mr and Mrs C as foster parents at Caernarvon. They had been received into care on 22 January 1979, on the breakdown of their parents' marriage, and were then aged from two years to nearly 11 years. Three of them went initially to Queens Park for a month but they then joined the oldest child at Y Gwyngyll, where they remained until they were fostered by the Cs. They were made the subject of care orders in matrimonial proceedings on 24 April 1980.

42.26 The foster child with whom we are principally concerned, C1, was the only daughter of her natural parents, born on 19 May 1970, and she remained with the Cs for four years until 14 October 1983. Mr and Mrs C had four other children living at their home during that period but their status is unclear.

42.27 C1 was a vulnerable girl who had received speech therapy for language difficulties. It emerged later that she and her brothers had been subjected to sexual abuse before they were admitted to care.

42.28 In her oral evidence to the Tribunal C1 alleged that she was sexually abused by the eldest of the other children in the foster home, X, who was a teenager. The abuse occurred over several months at the end of her placement with the Cs and began when X came to her bedroom when she was in her nightdress, put his hand over her mouth and told her to go to his bedroom. X had intercourse with her then in his room and this occurred on three occasions in all. C1 was frightened of X because he had previously "belted" her youngest brother and she thought that he might do the same to her. On the second occasion X said he would not "do it" again but the third time he was drunk.

42.29 C1 told two friends at school after the third occasion and they encouraged her to tell a teacher. Mrs C was then called to the school and she reported the complaint to Social Services late in the afternoon of 14 October 1983. A home visit was made that evening by a social worker, who also interviewed C, and X subsequently admitted that sexual intercourse had occurred. We have not been told who reported the matter to the police but a prosecution ensued and on 11 May 1984 X, who was then 19 years old, pleaded guilty to unlawful sexual intercourse with C1 when she was under 16 years old. He was fined £100.

42.30 C1 did not return to the foster home after complaining to the teacher, who accommodated her overnight. After spending the following two nights at Tŷ Newydd, she was placed in a second foster home before being reunited with her younger two brothers in February 1984 at Tŷ'r Felin, purportedly for assessment. The eldest brother had left foster home C on 25 January 1981. In all C1 was the subject of eight placements but she and her youngest brother were eventually adopted by their last foster mother just before C1's 18th birthday.

42.31 We heard other complaints about foster home C from C1 and her older two brothers, born in March 1968 and June 1969 respectively, whose statements were read to the Tribunal. Their complaints were directed mainly against another foster daughter in the household, Y, who was born in or about 1969. C1 and her two brothers complained of sexual assaults and indecent behaviour by Y as well as persistent bullying and cruelty by her. The younger of the two brothers complained also of bullying by X.

42.32 C1 did not allege that she made any complaint to the foster parents or to a social worker about Y's conduct. She did not feel that she had an opportunity to complain to the latter because she was only alone with the social worker during visits when Mrs C made tea. The eldest brother did complain of Y's bullying to his social worker, Peter Hibbs, after he had run away to Y Gwyngyll on 3 December 1980. The complaints were investigated by Hibbs, despite his view that the boy was an inveterate liar, but they were not supported by C1 or his younger brother and were denied by Y. Mr and Mrs C then said that his complaints were the last straw and asked that the eldest brother should be removed. They were persuaded to allow him to stay with them over the Christmas period and he moved to Tŷ'r Felin on 25 January 1981, where he remained until August of that year, when he was placed at a residential school in Cwmbran.

42.33 The younger of the two older brothers of C1 also alleged that he had complained to a social worker and that nothing was done about it, but he was unable to recall the latter's name and there is no documentary record to support his assertion. He said also that he had complained to Mr and Mrs C but that nobody took any notice.

42.34 The Tribunal were unable to trace Mr and Mrs C or X or Y.

42.35 It is clear, in our judgment, that C1 did suffer sexual abuse at the hands of X, as he admitted. It is likely also that all three complainants were subjected to bullying by Y but without fuller oral evidence we could not reach any satisfactory conclusion about the nature and extent of that abuse, bearing in mind her age at the time in relation to the ages of the complainants.

42.36 We have not seen sufficient documentary evidence to enable us to assess with confidence the quality of care provided by the Social Services Department during the period when C1 and her brothers were fostered with Mr and Mrs C but C1's file suggests that it was poor. It was difficult to determine from that file the actual frequency of visits to the foster home but recorded visits when C1 was reported to have been seen were at very irregular intervals. Moreover, there were complaints on the file from Alison Taylor about the lack of basic information provided to Tŷ Newydd on C1's admission and later by an SRCCO at Tŷ'r Felin about the unprofessional manner of her admission to that community home without any proper introduction by the social worker.

Foster child D

42.37 This foster child, who was born on 8 February 1974, was received into care on 3 January 1979. Her early history is not clear from the documents available to us, but she was the child of a broken home and her mother lived in Menai Bridge. At the age of about two years she was wrongly diagnosed as autistic but it was later inferred that she had suffered emotional damage when she was very young with the result that she was "slightly backward" at the age of nine years.

42.38 From 26 June 1980 onwards D's period in care was spent mainly with four successive pairs of foster parents until 6 September 1991, after which she went to approved supervised lodgings until she was discharged from care. There was, however, a break in the fostering of about two years, between 12 December 1984 and about December 1986, during which period she was placed at Tŷ Newydd community home in its last phase as such.

42.39 D alleged that she was subjected to sexual abuse in the first and last of her four foster homes (she alleged also one act of physical abuse by a male member of staff at Tŷ Newydd[2]). Her first foster placement was with a couple who lived in a small village in Anglesey, a few miles from Menai Bridge. She stayed with them from 26 June 1980 until 12 February 1982, leaving immediately after her eighth birthday. D's allegation was that she was sexually abused then by the eldest son of the family by indecent touching and by making her rub his penis and put it in her mouth. She said, however, that the boy neither hurt her nor penetrated her with his fingers or penis and that the abuse occurred when the foster parents were out.

42.40 This alleged abuse first came to light in December 1982 after D's second foster mother had become concerned that D was sexually disturbed and had questioned her. The foster mother reported the matter to D's social worker and the police were informed. D was interviewed by police officers on 10 and 15 December 1982, when she confirmed her allegations. There was difficulty in tracing the alleged abuser, who was by then 20 years old, but, when he was seen, he denied D's allegations emphatically. The view of the Woman Detective Constable who investigated the case was that D might have witnessed "perhaps

---

[2] She is referred to as the "third former girl resident" in para 34.09.

in vision only" some form of indecency but that, due to vigorous questioning by the second foster mother, the matter had been greatly exaggerated. No prosecution was instituted.

42.41 Two years later, in December 1984, D made another complaint of indecent assault or gross indecency but we have not been given details of the complaint or the person against whom it was made because D subsequently admitted that it was false and withdrew it formally. A case conference was held on 11 December 1984, at which it was decided that D required expert guidance and advice in a controlled environment. It was in pursuance of this decision that she was placed at Tŷ Newydd community home the following day.

42.42 D's fourth foster placement was from 10 August 1988 until 6 September 1991 with a couple who lived not far from Llanrwst, on the eastern boundary of Gwynedd. D's allegation that she had been sexually abused by her foster father there came to light on the latter date when a complaint by D was reported to the Arfon Area Office by the couple with whom D subsequently lodged at Llanberis. D claimed that the foster father had had full sexual intercourse with her over a period of years and had begun to abuse her sexually within a few months of her placement with him and his wife. D was moved to the lodgings at Llanberis forthwith on 6 September 1991 and did not return to the foster home. A joint investigation followed: the foster father was arrested but denied all D's allegations. He pointed out that D had previously accused him of touching her inappropriately but that she had retracted those allegations.

42.43 It is apparent from the documents before us that D had made allegations against the foster father within four months of her placement at this foster home. On that occasion D's allegations of indecent touching by the foster father had been reported by a teacher at her school via the Head of D's year to the Deputy Head; and this had led to a joint investigation by a social worker and a woman police officer. D had said that she did not want the foster parents to know what she had said because she was happy there and did not want to change schools. She retracted her allegations later and no action was taken.

42.44 A child protection case conference was convened on 12 November 1991, over which the Area Officer presided and at which a woman police officer represented the North Wales Police. At that stage the recommendation of the conference was that there should be no further involvement of the Social Services Department pending the outcome of the police investigations but that a service should be offered to the children and family "to help with coping with matters and consequences". No further placements were to be made with the foster parents whilst the police investigation continued. In the event there was no corroboration of D's allegations and the foster father was not prosecuted.

42.45 On the basis of this documentary material only we are unable to make any positive finding that D suffered sexual abuse and we see no reason to criticise the response by the relevant authorities to her successive complaints. D did not herself make any complaint to the Tribunal and we are not in a position to comment more generally upon the quality of care provided for her during her period of 13 years in care.

Conclusions

42.46 The number of known complaints of sexual abuse in foster homes in Gwynedd during the period under review is very small and two of the specific cases that we have discussed in this chapter were placements for which Clwyd Social Services Department bore the primary responsibility throughout. The first of those two cases, however, demonstrates a very alarming series of shortcomings in child care practice with dire results. We do not suggest that either Social Services Department had evidence on which those results should have been foreseen but, if good practice had been followed, they might have been avoided or halted earlier.

42.47 The other cases do highlight a number of important points in addition to the over-riding necessity of good quality practice in regular visits to (and recording of contact with) foster children. One is that a long series of short term or medium term foster placements may be even more damaging to a child in care than frequent changes of residential home. Secondly, the cases discussed illustrate the importance of school teachers (and possibly other members of the school staff) as potential recipients of information or complaints from abused children and the need for heads of schools to have clear guidance as to how to respond when relevant information reaches the staff. Finally, the danger of abuse within a foster home by persons other than the foster parents is such that social workers need to be vigilant about it constantly when making assessments and when discussing conditions in the home with the children for whom they are responsible.

Other allegations of abuse in Gwynedd foster homes

Introduction

43.01 In this chapter we discuss three foster homes in Gwynedd where forms of abuse other than sexual abuse are alleged to have occurred during the period under review. In the first of these foster homes, however, the placement authority was the City of Manchester, whereas Gwynedd Social Services Department agreed to supervise the placements on behalf of Manchester.

43.02 The second of the cases discussed differs from others with which we have dealt in this report because the complainants have not alleged that they were physically abused there in the usual sense. Their allegations relate to the general physical conditions under which they were compelled to live.

Foster home A

43.03 The four foster children in this case were three boys and a girl, who were the subject of a care order made on 22 May 1974 under which their care was committed to the City of Manchester Social Services Department. The three boys were born respectively on 7 March 1967, 8 October 1968 and 2 June 1972; and the girl was born in 1971. We have been concerned particularly with the youngest boy (A1) who gave oral evidence to the Tribunal and who is the only one of the four foster children to complain of abuse by Mr and Mrs A.

43.04 These children were removed from their parents in distressing circumstances under a Place of Safety Order on 2 January 1974, when their mother was terminally ill and their father was failing to provide satisfactory care for them. At first the two older children were placed in a children's home whilst the girl and A1 were placed in a residential nursery. The children's mother died in June 1974, very shortly after the care order was made, and the plan was to find a long term foster home for all four children together.

43.05 The foster parents, Mr and Mrs A, and their own children were also a Manchester family, who moved to Rhosneigr in Anglesey in 1975, shortly before the foster children were placed with them. They were in their early 30s and Mrs A was Mr A's second wife. They had responded to advertisements for foster parents that appeared in the local press in Manchester when they were planning their move to Anglesey and the children were boarded out with them on 21 December 1975. This had the effect of expanding their family to seven children because they already had with them three children of their own, namely, a teenage boy (of Mr A's first marriage), a second boy aged about five years and a baby daughter.

43.06 A1 remained in the foster home until 13 February 1987, by which time the family had moved to a large bungalow at Llanfaelog. He was charged with arson on the latter date, for starting a serious fire at the foster home, and granted bail on condition that he lived at Queens Park. On 8 July 1987 A1 was convicted of arson and ordered to be detained for five years under the provisions of section 53 (2) of the Children and Young Persons Act 1933. Under that order he was admitted to the special unit at Red Bank School, near Warrington, on 8 October 1987, after a period of assessment at Risley Remand Centre.

43.07 According to Mr A the other three foster children remained with Mr and Mrs A until they each reached the age of 17 years. The middle son, however, had special educational needs and attended Ysgol Talfryn[1] from the age of 14 years, spending his holidays at the foster home. All four children have remained in touch with Mr and Mrs A since they left the foster home. In particular, the As had attended A1's wedding and had gone on holiday with A1 and his family at his invitation. A planned further holiday as recently as April 1997 had been cancelled only because of the admission of A1's child to hospital.

43.08 Mr and Mrs A are active members of the Evangelical Free Church. Mr A is a qualified sewing machine mechanic and his wife is a trained teacher. Mrs A gave up teaching, however, whilst she was a foster parent and only undertook part time work, mainly in shops, during that period. Following the fire the As returned to Lancashire and Mr A has been employed as a school caretaker since 1990.

43.09 A1 told the Tribunal in his oral evidence that he was well looked after by Mr and Mrs A: the family lived in a nice, tidy house in a quiet area and both clothing and food were very adequate. His complaint was that things changed for him after about five years, which he put as in or about 1978, when the younger of his two older brothers began to get into trouble, "stealing all over the place", with the result that that brother was sent away to school. A1 said that Mr and Mrs A then began to "take it out on him" to try to ensure that he did not misbehave similarly as he became older.

43.10 One of A1's complaints was that, if he swore, the As would shove a piece of soap in his mouth and leave it in for a couple of hours or first Mr A and eventually Mrs A would start hitting him. His major complaint, however, was that Mr A began to hit him with a buckled belt after he and the As' young daughter had taken some refundable bottles from the back of a shop and had then returned them in order to obtain the refunds. According to A1, he was struck with the belt on that occasion by Mr A about ten times on the bottom of his bare back whereas the As' daughter was only smacked on the hand. As a result of the beating he had quite a few deep cuts, which he later showed to his schoolteacher. On another occasion Mr A administered similar punishment to him after the As' daughter had fallen off a wall with the result that she had had to have stitches. The beatings occurred also on "more than one occasion" for either swearing or for "just trying to be myself really, having fun with all the other kids". The beatings were always in private in the bedroom upstairs but Mrs A knew about them and told him after the shop incident that he "deserved it".

[1] See Chapter 19.

43.11 A1's additional allegations against Mrs A were that later, when he started getting into trouble with the police, Mrs A threw a golf club at him after he had been cautioned by the police for stealing. Before that she had smacked him across the face a couple of times but these were isolated actions on her part.

43.12 A1 said that his arson offence at the foster home was not triggered by any specific incident: his feelings had built up over the 12 years that he had been with the As and he was intending to pay them back for what they had done. He had not been able to share his feelings with his brothers or sister or his social worker but he had got on really well with his Gwynedd social worker, who had visited him regularly. She would talk to the foster parents for half an hour or so and would then spend ten or 15 minutes with the children in the presence of the foster parents. He could not recall any Manchester social worker visiting him. However, after he had been admitted to Queens Park following the arson offence, he told his social worker, in the course of working on his life story book, exactly what had happened when he was living with the As.

43.13 It is clear from the documentary evidence before us that bruising and weal marks on A1's back did give rise to concern at the end of June 1978, when he was just six years old. On 28 June 1978 his Headmaster telephoned the foster home and spoke to Mrs A about these marks: A1 had been showing his back to other children and the Headmaster was sending him home. This conversation took place just before A1's social worker called at the foster home to make an appointment and Mrs A reported the matter to her but Mrs A's explanation of what had occurred was far from satisfactory. Mr A's son had reported the marks to her that morning when he was getting A1 ready for school; she had not looked at the marks herself; she did not know what had caused them but attributed them to a nappy worn by A1 at night because of enuresis; and she was going to take A1 to see the general practitioner.

43.14 The social worker called at the foster home again the same evening. Mrs A then said that A1 had told the doctor that he had fallen backwards off his bicycle and had hit his back against a Tonka toy that had been left by the gate and that the doctor had accepted this explanation. A1 himself told the social worker that he had toppled backwards on to a Tonka toy. She noted that the bruising seemed to her to have been caused by contact with a solid mass such as a door or another solid piece of wood but that the scratches were very superficial.

43.15 Such records as we have seen do indicate that the social worker followed up this incident by talking to the Headmaster and a health visitor and a further visit to the foster home when Mrs A told her that the A's own son had confirmed that A1 had fallen off his bicycle. The upshot was that the social worker accepted the explanation given. When A1 was asked in evidence to comment on these records he said that they had been falsified to protect the As. He denied ever having told anyone that he had fallen over a Tonka toy: he did recall "a little meeting" with the social services about the incident but he was never told what the outcome of "his complaint" was. He had told the teacher that Mr A had hit him with a belt.

43.16 In his written statements to the Tribunal Mr A denied ever hitting A1 with a belt. Of the four foster children, the middle boy and A1 had been the naughtiest: they had stolen money from the As, a church and teachers and he had used a slipper to them from time to time as a reminder to the children about how to behave and to show them that the As would not put up with dishonesty. Apart from that both he and his wife had smacked the children from time to time but all the children in their home had been treated equally. Mr A emphasised also that he and his wife loved the foster children, did their very best for them and still kept in touch with all of them, including A1, whom he had recently taken for job interviews. He and his wife would have liked to adopt the foster children, if finances had permitted. They had always accepted that A1 did not intend to harm them when he started the fire in their home and they thought that it had been done to divert attention from the theft of money from Mrs A's purse.

43.17 In relation to the 1978 incident Mr A said that neither he nor his wife had been aware of A1's injuries until the headmaster telephoned. His recollection was that the Headmaster had reported that A1 had said that he had been hit with a stick by Mr A's son but the correct explanation had emerged when his wife had taken A1 to see the doctor. Neither he nor his wife had been asked to make a statement to the police arising from A1's complaints.

43.18 The eldest foster son of the As made a statement to the Tribunal in November 1996 confirming his earlier statement to the police in September 1992. He said that he had no complaints to make about the foster home, although he did not like the fact that the As were very strict and religious. He understood what they were trying to do for him and he regarded their treatment as fair. Punishment was usually a smack on the backside or legs. If he lied, his mouth would be washed out with soap or washing up liquid. This witness now lives in Manchester and he confirmed that he continues to telephone the As regularly.

43.19 A1 was seen by a consultant psychiatrist after his arson offence, on the advice of his Gwynedd social worker, in preparation for his appearance in Court. He told the psychiatrist that he had stolen money from the home and had been asked to recover it. His excuse for not doing so the next day was not believed and he determined to pay back his foster mother for this and many other "perceived injustices"; and he considered alternative schemes before deciding to set fire to the house. It became clear in the interview that his resentment was directed against Mrs A rather than Mr A. He said that he felt that she wanted the foster children as her own children and encouraged them to forget their origins. A1 took off his shirt in the course of the interview and showed the psychiatrist "extensive old scarring", which A1 claimed was the result of "belting" at the age of about eight years, and he referred also to the incident with a golf club. The view of the psychiatrist was that A1 was not suffering from any mental illness but that his personality development had been significantly impaired: his early experiences in Manchester had distorted his ability to relate and he seemed to have had no assistance in understanding his beginnings. The psychiatrist saw A1 as rootless, muddled and searching for a non-existent ideal family: it was essential that he should be helped immediately to find out about his background.

43.20 The allegations made by A1 to the psychiatrist were passed on to Gwynedd Social Services Department and investigated by them in 1987. An inter-agency meeting was held at the Anglesey Area Office at Llangefni on 27 May 1987 and a case discussion on 16 June 1987. At the first of these meetings it was decided that, in view of the lapse of time, the Social Services Department rather than the police should take up the matter with the As. A senior social worker and a social worker then visited the As but, unsurprisingly, their investigation did not reveal any significant new information.

43.21 Finally, Gwynedd Social Services Department was asked by the Welsh Office to look again into A1's allegations following the routine attendance of a social services inspector at a case conference at Red Bank School in relation to A1, as an offender detained under section 53(2) of the Act of 1933[2]. In consequence, a further Case Conference, presided over by Larry King[3], was held on 26 April 1988 at Bontnewydd Fostering Development Centre. Before this meeting, A1's sister, who had left the foster home in December 1987, had been seen by King and had said that she knew of no abuse taking place in the foster home (save that she did recall her eldest brother having his mouth washed out with soap when he had lied).

43.22 In reporting back to the Welsh Office on 28 April 1988, in a letter apparently drafted by King, the Director of Social Services (Lucille Hughes) said that the same allegations by A1 had been made by him to the consultant psychiatrist in May 1987 and had not been accepted as child abuse at the meeting of the local Review Committee on 16 June 1987. She said, however, that the following points had been agreed at the recent Bontnewydd meeting:

"(1) That if such a situation arose again, this Authority would not agree to supervise on any other Authority's behalf without a full contractual visiting arrangement by them being set up.

(2) That these parents were not properly prepared for the placement of 4 difficult and needy children.

(3) That the placement resulted in emotional and psychological disturbance both to these children and their own 3 children.

(4) There is no evidence that A1 was physically abused in this household. Medical and other evidence does not support this contention.

(5) However back in 1978/79 the matter should have been case conferenced in terms of well established Abuse procedures.

(6) The A family should be complimented for the efforts they made over many years with 3 difficult foster children, (and the girl who was not difficult)."

---

[2] See para 43.06.
[3] Principal Officer (Children).

43.23 In his statement to the police made on 24 September 1992 A1 referred to being struck across his back by Mr A over a period of several years until the fire but added "Although I've mentioned the punishments I've received at the hands of (Mr A), which I didn't agree with, I do not wish to make a formal complaint about it. I do not wish the police to investigate this matter. I have now moved from Rhosneigr and made a fresh start in my life".

43.24 It is impossible for us now, 11 years after the final Case Conference, to reach any different conclusion about the alleged physical abuse of A1. His recollection of the 1978 incident, when he was only just six years old, must now be very blurred and he was not able to give persuasive details of any other occasions when Mr A used a buckled belt to him, apart from the one when the As' daughter is said to have fallen off a wall. The As' regime was probably too strict and they may have resorted to inappropriate physical chastisement on occasions by the standards of many at the time but it would be wrong for us to hold that they were guilty of abuse, bearing in mind the views expressed by two of the other foster children and the difficulties that the As had to face in dealing with their three foster sons.

43.25 Nevertheless, there are many lessons to be learned from the case, as were noted at the 1988 Case Conference. It appears that there was little or no introduction of the foster children to the foster parents before the placement was made and the latter, who were not given any preparation for dealing with these potentially difficult foster children, had no prior experience of fostering. The placement was much too far from Manchester for any real supervision from there. Manchester Social Services Department played little or no part in the supervision once the placement had been made, despite its continuing statutory responsibility; and it was not even represented at the regular reviews that were held. Moreover, the placement was to be criticised on other grounds because it involved an attempt to weld one ready made family who had lost their mother with another close-knit family and the setting up, in effect, of a small group home of seven children without adequate financial and staff resources. Although the records suggest some effort was made in the very early stages to help the children understand their past, this was too little and too early for A1 whose need for active social work intervention aimed at helping him understand and come to terms with his history and current life situation was not addressed until the commission of a serious offence. In the event the As are to be congratulated on their continuing loyalty to the foster children and the response to that loyalty that they receive.

Foster home B

43.26 Mr and Mrs B, who were married on 1 July 1963, lived in a detached bungalow on the edge of an industrial estate just outside the town of Caernarvon. Mr B was 27 years old and his wife 16 months younger when they married. It was Mrs B's second marriage and she had custody of her two sons and a daughter by the first marriage, who were then aged six years, three years and seven and a half months respectively. Mr and Mrs B subsequently had a son, born on 3 August 1964, and a daughter, born on 8 August 1966.

43.27 The Bs were approved by Gwynedd County Council as foster parents for short and long term placements in 1977 and they fostered a large number of children subsequently. The two main complainants about this foster home were two sisters, B1 and B2, who were placed there from 9 September 1985 to 20 August 1986. By September 1985 Mr B, who had had a varied working history, had been unemployed for four years because of redundancy in his last employment and he did not expect to be successful in finding new work at his age of nearly 50 years. Of the five children of the family only two remained at home: they were the daughter of the first marriage, B3, and the Bs' son, B4.

43.28 There were two other members of the household, namely, a foster child and a former foster child, both male. The older was the former foster son, B5, born on 12 February 1964, who continued to live with the Bs at the age of 21 years; and the younger, B6, born on 2 October 1975, who had been fostered with the Bs when just under six months old and who was adopted by them on 2 July 1987.

43.29 Thus, there were eight in all in the household after B1 and B2 joined the Bs in September 1985. The bungalow itself had, according to the Cartref Bontnewydd Development Officer, four large bedrooms, two living rooms and a large kitchen, together with a lavatory and a bathroom. It was rather chaotic, however, because central heating was to be installed prior to complete re-decoration and there were two terriers to be accommodated as well.

43.30 The two complainants, B1 born on 17 April 1976 and B2 born on 26 August 1977, had had a disrupted life before they were placed with Mr and Mrs B. They had been removed from their own home as early as 28 February 1978, under a Place of Safety Order, following an alleged assault by their father on their half-brother. Their names were placed on the Child Protection Register at that time and a supervision order was made in matrimonial proceedings on 6 April 1978. It seems that they continued to live in North Wales until September 1980, when they moved with their mother to stay with the maternal grandparents in Birmingham until their mother obtained council accommodation there. The half-brother went to stay with other grandparents and did not figure in the subsequent relevant history.

43.31 It appears that the mother had an unstable way of life and, when she returned with the two girls to Bangor early in September 1985, she had no accommodation to go to. She spent a night or so with a friend who lived in the Maesgeirchen estate but B1 and B2 were taken from that address by the North Wales Police on a 14 day Place of Safety Order on 7 September 1985 and they were admitted to Tŷ'r Felin Community Home[4] for two nights. It was from Tŷ'r Felin that B1 and B2 went to the Bs on 9 September 1985 for short term fostering. The Place of Safety Order lapsed on 20 September 1985 but B1 and B2 were then received into voluntary care and remained with the foster parents on a boarding out basis.

---

[4] See Chapter 33.

43.32 Both B1 and B2 gave oral evidence to the Tribunal in which they made stringent criticisms of living conditions in the Bs' home during the period of nearly a year when they were living there. The two girls shared a bedroom, with separate beds, but a major complaint was that B2 frequently had to share her bed with B3, Mrs B's daughter of her first marriage, who was then 23 years old. At that time B3, who suffered from "mental instability" and incontinence, was spending most of her time as an in-patient at St Asaph Hospital, but was returning to the foster home at week-ends and for periods of a week at a time. On these occasions B2 had to share her bed with B3 and she complained of the wetness and B3's strange and insanitary behaviour, saying that she was frightened of B3 at the time because she did not understand why B3 acted as she did and that she would get over-excited on occasions. A further allegation was that sexual misconduct occurred in the bedroom between B3 and a member of the family who lived elsewhere.

43.33 This evidence was largely confirmed by B1 and a number of other complaints were common to them. They said, for example, that the bedroom was damp and cold and the bedding inadequate. It was particularly cold in winter and initially they had to use coats and curtains instead of blankets. There was no heating in the bedroom and no central heating had been installed. They bathed only once a week and there was insufficient hot water. There were complaints also of hair washing and hair cutting by Mrs B. The girls' clothes were second-hand or bought from Oxfam and the food that they were given was inadequate. Both of them alleged also that there were occasions when they had to eat snacks in the kitchen whilst the others had a cooked meal such as a roast dinner on a Sunday.

43.34 Some complaints were undoubtedly made on behalf of B1 and B2 in the course of their stay at foster home B. Their own evidence about this was that they complained to their social worker, telling her that they did not want to stay with the Bs, but that they did not say why because Mrs B was always present. They complained also to their mother, aunt and grandmother.

43.35 Social Services documents before us disclose that on 2 October 1985 Mrs B telephoned the social worker to complain that the mother of B1 and B2 was visiting them accompanied by "men" and that she was drunk on occasions. More pertinently, on 28 October 1985 a telephone message from the aunt and grandmother was recorded in which they made a number of complaints: they said that the house was cold and that no fire had been lit; that Mrs B had cut the hair of one of the girls herself and that both girls looked dishevelled; that they were not allowed to wear underwear in order to cut down the amount of laundry; that they said that they did not get enough to eat; and that Mrs B referred to them in an abusive way. The aunt and grandmother were said to regard Mrs B as totally unfit and they expressed disgust that a complaint by them to the Area six days earlier had not been looked into promptly. It appears also that B1 and B2 had been told at this time that they would have to remain in the foster home until their mother found accommodation and that they themselves had set their hearts on moving to Wakefield to stay with the aunt: this arrangement was made but was countermanded when the mother decided that she did not want the children to move so far away from her.

43.36 Other documents confirm that, before 28 October 1985, the aunt and grandmother had taken the children to headquarters, where they had been seen by Larry King[5]. The social worker's response (countersigned by her senior social worker) to the complaints was that she was satisfied that the children's welfare was adequate in the circumstances. In a statement to the police made in July 1992 the social worker said that she was responsible for supervising the placement of B1 and B2 until May 1986; she visited them at least once a month and used to speak to them alone. She said that the girls were not happy at the foster home because they wanted to be with their mother but she did not recall them ever complaining about conditions there.

43.37 This social worker did say that she was not satisfied with the conditions at the foster home but her only express reservation about it was that it was not kept as clean as it might have been: she referred specifically to visiting the bathroom on one occasion and being disgusted by the dirtiness of the lavatory. She did not recall ever visiting the bedroom but the statutory review form contained a question about this, and if she had done so, she would have noticed anything untoward. She added, however, that oversight of the foster homes was dealt with by Cartref Bontnewydd, which had the responsibility for examining them, and that the Social Services Department had limited influence over the Fostering Unit.

43.38 We have seen copies of the boarding out reviews that took place on 25 November 1985 and 3 April 1986. In both these the complaints were referred to but they were not specified. In the first it was said that they had been looked into and appeared to be unfounded. In the second (by the senior social worker) it was said:

> "As indicated in the Fieldworker's report there have been recent complaints made by members of the girls' extended family related to standards in this particular foster home. The review considered at length the substance of these allegations concluding quite categorically that the allegations were not substantiated in any way whatsoever. It was also clarified that the children's mother . . . has herself made no complaints whatsoever."

43.39 One other witness was fostered with the Bs shortly before B1 and B2. This was the witness A referred to in paragraphs 36.14 to 36.29 of this report, who was placed with Mr and Mrs B from 2 July to 30 September 1984 and again from 13 November 1984 to 10 April 1985, a period spanning his 15th birthday. When asked whether he had any complaint to make about his treatment in foster care, his reply was "Just I don't think they were suitable foster parents for anyone". He said that the house was dirty and that there was never any food in by the end of the week. He alleged also that B5 had "picked on him" from the day when he arrived. A particular complaint was that the Bs had bought for him blue bell-bottom trousers to wear to school from a second-hand shop when the correct school uniform was conventional black trousers. When cross-examined, A said that the Bs had treated him "alright", apart from the incident

---

[5] Principal Officer (Children).

with the school trousers, but he had left the first time because of B5's bullying and the second time because of the trousers. He had never tried to make a formal complaint but he had referred to the dirtiness of the kitchen and bedrooms, and to rats and flies, the lack of food and electric shocks from the sink in his statements to the police when asked about the condition of the foster home: the only room kept clean and tidy was the front room. A disagreed with a contemporary social work record, which stated that his placement was proving happy and stable and that the foster parents were willing to have him long term.

43.40 In their joint statements to the Tribunal Mr and Mrs B denied that the foster home was dirty and untidy but said that they were having considerable alterations carried out so that there were occasions when it was more like a building site than a family home. There was never any shortage of money and everyone had three big meals a day. They denied also that the house was cold, saying that it was centrally heated and that there were two coal fires and electric fires. The foster home was regularly inspected by social services and found to be satisfactory.

43.41 Dealing with other specific allegations, Mr and Mrs B said that A had refused to wear two pairs of trousers because he was going through a "punk rocker" phase and wanted to go to school in a leather jacket and jeans (but this was firmly refuted by A). They had received an affectionate letter from A shortly after he left them. Mr and Mrs B alleged also that B3 shared a bedroom with her own sister, rather than with B1 and B2; but that sister was shown to be already living away from home at Rhyl in March 1985 when the Bs' adoption application Form F in respect of B6 was made out. Conversely, they said that B5 had left the foster home when A was there, which he may have done at some earlier stage; but he was shown as living at home in March 1985 on the same Form F. Nevertheless, Mr and Mrs B denied all the allegations relating to B3 and B5 and maintained that B3's incontinence was a thing of the past by July 1984; they said also that all the beds were in perfect condition with quilts and blankets.

43.42 The social worker responsible for A whilst he was placed with the Bs told the police that she thought that the foster home was untidy but that it was a suitable placement for him. She did not recall him complaining about conditions there but she had a vague recollection of the dispute about trousers that led to him missing school.

43.43 Our conclusion is that, although there was probably some exaggeration by B1, B2 and A in their description of conditions in this foster home after the lapse of many years, those conditions were far from satisfactory in the period from 1984 to 1986. In favour of the Bs it must be said that they had a successful fostering record before this but, in our judgment, they were taking upon themselves excessive responsibilities by the mid 1980s at a time when (apparently) extensive work was about to be, or was being, carried out at the foster home. A troubling aspect of the case is that the records before us do not contain any account by a social worker of the position of B3 at this time or of the sleeping arrangements for B1 and B2 or of the condition of their bedroom;

and there appears to have been some confusion of responsibility for inspection of the foster home as between Cartref Bontnewydd Fostering Unit (in its early days) and the Social Services Department. There were also discrepancies in the accounts by Area and Fostering Unit social workers of the number of bedrooms and persons resident. We have no reason to doubt that B3 did share B2's bed when she stayed at the foster home but social workers appear to have been unaware of this and we are clear that it should not have been countenanced.

43.44 Apart from this serious specific criticism and its distressing consequences for B1 and B2, we are satisfied that general conditions in the foster home were low. It was over-crowded and Mr and Mrs B had many problems of their own to face. A placement there may have been just about adequate for a fairly robust teenage boy such as A but the foster home was unsuitable for two very young girls who had just been taken away from their mother in distressing circumstances. We have fully in mind that the Social Services Department were faced with an emergency in September 1985 and that it was hoped then that the placement would be of short duration but this household should not have been chosen. In the event, the placement was foreseeably prolonged, as was the girls' suffering in conditions that were, in our view, at least partly, intolerable.

Foster home C

43.45 The evidence about one other unidentified foster home was read to the Tribunal. The foster child in this case, C1, was a girl, born on 11 April 1980, who was in the care of Gwynedd County Council, together with her elder sister, for about four months from September 1983. The reason for the two girls' admission to care was that their father had allegedly chastised C1's sister excessively.

43.46 The two girls lived with their parents at Rhosybol in Anglesey and they were placed with Mr and Mrs C as foster parents at Llangefni. No complaint is made about either foster parent but C1 complained in a written statement to the Tribunal about the conduct of a female baby-sitter in their absence. According to C1 there was an occasion when she was unable to get into the lavatory at the foster home, because it was occupied, with the result that she soiled her pants. The response of the baby-sitter was to shout at her and to slap her across the bottom (she was wearing dungarees). C1 "screamed with pain and cried uncontrollably". The baby-sitter then cleaned her up and put her to bed.

43.47 C1 was unable to say whether Mr and Mrs C were told about this incident: she did not tell them herself. However, when she returned to her parents' home the following week-end, her father saw the outline of a hand mark on the right cheek of her bottom and she told him what had happened. Her father then made an official complaint to a Gwynedd duty social worker.

43.48 C1's father confirmed this complaint and said that he spoke later to someone he believed to be a supervisor. He was told in no uncertain terms that, if he pursued a complaint, it would be a retrograde step, if he wished to get his children back with him. As a result he did not pursue the matter but he remains embittered about the disparity between the way in which he was treated for chastising a child and the response to the baby-sitter's behaviour.

43.49 We have not been able to see any social services record of this matter and cannot, therefore, reach any satisfactory conclusion about it. We doubt whether C1 has any distinct recollection of it now, bearing in mind that she was less than four years old at the time. She has spoken now, in effect, with her father's voice because he is still resentful that his children were taken away from him, albeit for a short period. That does not mean that the allegations of slapping by the baby-sitter and of a nil response by headquarters to his complaint are untrue but we are unable to assess the other side of the case.

Conclusions

43.50 The evidence before us has not revealed any widespread physical abuse by foster parents in Gwynedd. On the contrary, the complaints that we have heard have been limited in their scope and there have been positive aspects of the fostering in both the cases that we have considered in detail, particularly that of Mr and Mrs A. Nevertheless, both cases have revealed serious defects in the management of fostering by Gwynedd Social Services Department and important lessons should be learned from them as we have indicated in paragraphs 43.22, 43.25, 43.43 and 43.44.

PART X

THE RESPONSIBILITY OF
HIGHER MANAGEMENT IN GWYNEDD

Management structures and responsibility for Gwynedd Social Services from 1974 to 1996

Introduction

44.01 In the first three paragraphs of Chapter 28 of this report we explained our approach in considering the responsibility of higher management in Clwyd. A similar approach is appropriate in relation to Gwynedd and it is unnecessary, therefore, to repeat here what we have said in paragraphs 28.01 to 28.03. We take as read also our account in Chapter 3 of this report of the legislative and administrative background to Gwynedd's assumption of responsibility for its large geographical area of about 960,000 acres (roughly 100 miles x 95 miles) on 1 April 1974.

44.02 In paragraph 3.22 we introduced the first Director of Social Services for the new county of Gwynedd, Thomas Edward Jones (always known as T E Jones), who held that office until September 1982, and it is convenient to begin this account of the management structures with that period.

The Social Services Department under T E Jones, 1974 to 1982

44.03 As we have said in paragraph 3.22, **T E Jones** was appointed as Director of Social Services for Gwynedd, at the age of 51 years, with effect from 6 July 1973, having served in the same capacity in Caernarvonshire for just over two years. He was brought up in Montgomeryshire and had no specific experience of child care work, except as clerk to a county council committee in 1951/1952. His background was in welfare work: he had served as County Welfare Officer in Merionethshire for 12 years from April 1952 and in the same office in Caernarvonshire for the following seven years; and he did not have any professional qualifications.

44.04 The first Deputy Director was **David Alan Parry**, who retained that post until 1983, after which he became Assistant Director (Special Duties) until 31 March 1987, when he accepted voluntary redundancy at the age of 51 years. At the time of his appointment as Deputy Director for Gwynedd he had been Director of Social Services for Anglesey for three years; and he was an applicant for the Director's post in Gwynedd but much younger than T E Jones. Unlike the latter, Parry had substantial experience in child care and, between 1964 and 1971, he had served successively as Deputy Children's Officer and Children's Officer for Anglesey. He had graduated at Aberystwyth in education and philosophy and had subsequently obtained diplomas in social science and in applied social studies at Swansea and Liverpool as well as the Home Office Letter of Recognition in Child Care. Parry had also attended several management courses, including a course for senior officers at Liverpool University and, in 1972, two short courses for Directors of Social Services at the Institute of Local Government Studies at Birmingham University.

44.05 Despite his background of experience, Parry was not given responsibility for children's services from the outset. Under the two senior officers, there were three Assistant Directors and the responsibility for children was divided between two of them, namely, the Assistant Director (Establishments) and the Assistant Director (Fieldwork). The former, Emyr Davies, was responsible for residential homes and had a Homes Officer (Elizabeth Hughes) reporting to him. The latter, G H Egerton, was responsible for the five Area Offices (based on the county districts) under an Area Controller; and, in a separate line of management, he had two Senior Officers and a Senior Assistant accountable to him, whose responsibilities were for children, for the elderly and handicapped and for the mentally disordered respectively. The Senior Officer (Children) in this structure from 1 August 1975 was Lawrence Reginald (Larry) King.

44.06 This initial structure, which was apparently devised by independent consultants, survived for less than two years for a number of reasons. According to T E Jones, Parry was incapable of performing the duties of Deputy. One of the latter's first duties had been to prepare a budget for the Social Services Department by October 1974 but he failed to do so and indicated that he was unable to carry out some of the duties outlined in his job specification. Parry was, therefore, relieved of the duties that had been intended for the Deputy, whilst continuing to hold that rank and title, and placed in charge of the Children's Section.

44.07 Additional difficulties, according to T E Jones, were that both Emyr Davies and Egerton were seriously ill: both were away for long periods and ultimately had to retire. T E Jones had, therefore, to shoulder not only many of the responsibilities of the Deputy Director but also those of two of the Assistant Directors.

44.08 The revised structure, approved with effect from 19 February 1976, introduced a new post of Principal Assistant Director of broadly similar status to that of the Deputy Director. This post was allocated to the third of the three original Assistant Directors, Lucille Margaret Hughes, who had been responsible for Development in the first management structure. Henceforth, she was to have the other two Assistant Directors, Emyr Davies and Egerton, working under her but their responsibilities were to be limited to the elderly (Emyr Davies) and mental health (Egerton). Parry, on the other hand, had a Senior (later Principal) Officer (Children), who was Larry King, working to him and, for at least part of the time, a Senior Assistant (Children), who was responsible for Intermediate Treatment but who left in May 1980.

44.09 It will have been seen that **Larry King** was prominent in the management structure in relation to children from 1 August 1975 and he was to remain so until he retired on 14 May 1988. Born in December 1926, he had served in the police in England, after army service, before transferring to the Colonial Police in Rhodesia, in which he served for 13 years and rose to the rank of Inspector. On returning to this country he had a brief spell as a housemaster at Bryn Estyn in 1964 but his continuous work in social services began in 1969 with Denbighshire County Council after he had qualified for the Home Office Letter of Recognition in Child Care by attending a course at Liverpool University. He was later a Senior Social Worker for Flintshire County Council and moved to the Llandudno Area Office in Gwynedd in 1974. His Senior Officer's post in Gwynedd from August 1975 was redesignated Principal Officer (Children) from 1 June 1979.

44.10 Not surprisingly, Parry gave a different account of the earliest years. He denied that he felt any personal hostility towards T E Jones or that he had been unable to work with him, but he did say that "the incorporation" of Anglesey Social Services Department into that of Gwynedd was not a happy one. There was, in his view, a substantial conflict of style between "the entrepreneurial staff of the Anglesey Department" and that of the rest of the new county. This cultural clash led to substantial differences of opinion and, to a degree, impaired working relationships. Parry said also that a seriously aggravating factor was the lack of resources for the children's section, a subject to which we will revert[1].

44.11 The changes made to the structure in 1976 were intended to be a temporary measure but they survived until July 1981, at which point responsibility for the children's section was transferred to the Principal Assistant Director, Lucille Hughes. This transfer coincided with the commissioning by the Chief Executive of an investigation by officials of Dyfed County Council into "complaints made by current and former members of staff of Gwynedd County Council" about the running of Y Gwyngyll Community Home.

44.12 We have dealt with the report of the Dyfed team, which covered also the administration of the children's section, in some detail in paragraphs 35.08 to 35.12 and it would be inappropriate to repeat those details here. It it necessary, however, to underline some points that are relevant to the management structure at this time. The most important of these is that, in or about 1980 Nefyn Dodd had assumed additional responsibility, that is, outside Tŷ'r Felin, for overseeing Y Gwyngyll and this responsibility was extended, probably late in 1981, to cover all the Gwynedd community homes. It was Parry who had initiated this in relation to Y Gwyngyll and it is clear that he was an uncritical admirer of Dodd. Thus, in discussion of various aspects of Gwynedd's child care services with SWSO Copleston on 11 January 1980[2] and, in particular, of Dodd's dominance (as chairman) of case conferences held at Tŷ'r Felin, Parry "seemed unwilling to consider the possibility that either Dodd's recommendations or his role might sometimes need to be questioned".

44.13 The Dyfed team's report commented critically also upon the fact that the Director of Social Services did not attend Sub-Committee meetings; and they expressed the view that there was "a complete lack of rapport and working relationship between the Director and the Deputy Director", observing that T E Jones took "little or no interest in the work of the Children's Section".

---

[1] See paras 46.36 to 46.44.
[2] See para 7 of Appendix 2 to SWSO Copleston's undated report of her visit to Y Gwyngyll.

44.14 The original reason why Dodd had been asked to take on additional responsibilities in 1978[3] was said to have been the prolonged absence on sick leave of the Homes Officer, Elizabeth Hughes. She was not shown in the diagrammatic representation of the 1976 management structure put before us but, according to Parry, the central staff of the Children's Section under him, comprised Larry King, who was responsible for fieldwork, the Homes Officer and a Fostering/Adoptions Senior Officer. However, the Homes Officer never returned after she had been absent for well over a year; and she was not replaced.

44.15 By the time that the Dyfed report was presented T E Jones was on the eve of retirement. He was well liked and respected generally and unsuccessful efforts were made to persuade the authors of the report to tone down their comments about him. He was not sufficiently well to give oral evidence to the Tribunal but he supplied us with a written statement and we have seen his contemporary written comments on the report. T E Jones repudiated particularly the suggestion that he took little or no interest in the Children's Section and he denied that Parry had been sidelined as the result of a personality clash between the two men. The former suggestion had not been put to him or to the Chief Executive by the Dyfed team and the Chief Executive had confirmed that he, the Director, had worried about the Children's Section and had spent much time involved with it. Moreover, Parry had been allocated to work within his expertise only after his failure to carry out the wider usual duties of a Deputy. In general, notwithstanding the financial constraints, resulting in a serious lack of social worker and supervisory posts, it was commendable that Gwynedd had provided the level of service that had been achieved, with comparatively few complaints of abuse.

44.16 At the time when the Dyfed team was preparing its report an investigation was carried out by Arthur Andersen and Company on behalf of the District Auditor into the administration of the rest of the Social Services Department. Two young consultants with Arthur Andersen and Company spent two weeks in the Department in September and October 1981 and their report was presented in March 1982. It is of limited relevance for our purposes, however, because (a) it excluded the Children's Section and (b) it recommended further detailed studies to develop and agree a revised structure (which was rejected by the Council in view of the expenditure that would have been required). However, the following comments and conclusions set out in the report are of some relevance:

(1) only in Merioneth was responsibility for establishments within its area delegated to the Area Office (in Dolgellau);

(2) only Anglesey had a permanent duty officer;

(3) there was inadequate documentation of departmental policy and only limited or out-of-date procedures and guidelines for case management;

---

[3] See para 33.22.

(4) as a consequence of (3), senior officers were required to provide guidance, and become involved, in too many day-to-day matters;

(5) the issue of accountability in individual cases was confused;

(6) reporting of the department's position to the various committees was performed orally and not from statements prepared and agreed in advance within the department;

(7) the Director and Principal Assistant Director were overloaded;

(8) the structure failed to provide effective line control between headquarters, area and establishment administration officers and staff.

44.17 As we have said, Parry ceased to have any responsibility for the Children's Section from July 1981 but he retained the status of Deputy Director until about May 1983. It is not clear what he did in the interim: he may have been suspended initially but he was "restored" before the Dyfed team reported. Then in 1982 he was involved in a motor car accident and was on sick leave for a long period. At that time his future was still being considered by a Disciplinary Panel appointed by the County Council, which had before it an undated report on the Dyfed team's findings, prepared in or about the Spring of 1982 by the Chief Personnel Officer and Management Services Officer, Lynn Ebsworth, who became Acting Director of Social Services on the retirement of T E Jones. Parry returned to work as Assistant Director (Special Duties) when he was fit again on some date after May 1983 but his position remained anomalous. The difficulty was only resolved ultimately in 1987, after negotiations with his professional association, by his acceptance of voluntary redundancy on 31 March 1987, with an enhanced pension.

44.18 The result of these various events was that the senior officer responsible, under the Director of Social Services, for children from July 1981 was **Lucille Margaret Hughes,** who was then nearly 47 years old. After graduating in English at what was then the University College of North Wales at Bangor, she had obtained the Certificate in Social Science at Liverpool University, qualifying her to receive the Home Office Letter of Recognition in Child Care. Hughes had then served in the Children's Departments of Caernarvonshire and Anglesey County Councils for 13 years, latterly as Children's Officer in both counties successively, before becoming Deputy Director of Social Services for Caernarvonshire in 1971. On the formation of Gwynedd County Council Hughes had become Assistant Director (Development) until 19 February 1976, when the first reorganisation took place and she was appointed Principal Assistant Director. In the latter capacity, however, her responsibilities until July 1981 were principally for the elderly and mental health.

44.19 One other headquarters officer who assumed responsibilities for children towards the end of the T E Jones regime was **Owain Gethin Evans,** another officer whose early career as a social worker had been with Caernarvonshire County Council. He had graduated in Social Administration at Manchester University in 1968 and had then obtained Diplomas in Education (1970), with distinction, at Cardiff and in Social Work Studies (1974) at the London School of Economics. Evans was a social worker in Caernarvonshire from 1971 for two years before his LSE course and he returned to Gwynedd in that capacity before becoming a Community Organiser for three years from 1975. His move to headquarters occurred in 1978 when he was appointed Senior Officer (General) with the main role of assisting Lucille Hughes in her development responsibilities but he became involved with children when he was appointed Principal Officer (Children). Initially this last appointment involved responsibility mainly for fostering and adoption and he did not have any responsibility for residential homes for children. However, on the transfer of duties to Lucille Hughes in July 1981, Evans was asked to assist her and his wider responsibilities were formally recognised in June 1982, when he became Head of Children's Services. He was to remain with Gwynedd until August 1995, when he was appointed Director of Social Services for the new Ceredigion County Council; and he was de facto Head of Gwynedd's Children's Services, under the Director, throughout the intervening period, apart from 1987 to 1992, when he was Assistant Director (Resources and Support). Evans was also an active member of Dwyfor District Council in Gwynedd from 1976 until 1986 and served as its chairman in the year 1983/1984.

The interregnum under Ebsworth (1982/1983)

44.20 It seems that T E Jones retired officially in September 1982 but he was absent on sick leave from May 1982. In his place **Lynn Ebsworth** was appointed Acting Director of Social Services, in addition to his duties as Chief Personnel Officer and Management Services Officer, and he served as such until a permanent successor, Lucille Hughes, was appointed with effect from 1 October 1983.

44.21 Ebsworth had been recruited by Gwynedd from industry in 1975, a year after re-organisation. In his original post he was responsible as Management Services Officer to Bowen Rees, who was then County Secretary, and as Chief Personnel Officer to Gwynedd's first Chief Executive, D Alun Jones. When Bowen Rees succeeded Alun Jones as Chief Executive in 1980, Ebsworth became accountable in both his capacities to Bowen Rees. He had no training or experience in any aspect of social services.

44.22 It was during Ebsworth's period as Acting Director of Social Services that the emerging roles of Gethin Evans and Nefyn Dodd[4] were defined. From June 1982 Evans retained the title Principal Officer (Children) but he became responsible for the management of the children's section, both field and residential, with Larry King and Nefyn Dodd accountable to him, although he had virtually no previous experience of working with children in care. One of Gethin Evans' early actions in his new role was to write a memorandum on 10 August 1982 emphasising that Dodd had full responsibility for all community homes[5]. That responsibility was said to be temporary but it was never revoked.

---

[4] For Dodd's background, see paras 10.148 to 10.150, 13.21, 13.22 and Chapter 33.
[5] See paras 33.23 and 33.24.

On the contrary, it was confirmed in a memorandum to all Officers-in-Charge in November 1983[6], in which Dodd was referred to as "Co-ordinator/Supervisor". He was later promoted to Principal Officer (Residential Care–Children).

44.23 When asked why Dodd had been assigned this role despite the criticisms made by the Dyfed team, Evans said that he was never shown the Dyfed report (he did not see it until two months before he gave evidence to this Tribunal) and that he simply accepted Dodd's role as it had already become when he took over responsibility for children's services.

44.24 This may be correct as an explanation of Dodd's occupancy of the role but it does not explain adequately Evans' long term acceptance of Dodd's dual position. He submitted a report to committee dated 6 August 1982 on the subject of residential work with children in which he spelt out the functions of a Supervisor/Co-ordinator in some detail[7]. This report was intended to provide an overall strategy for residential care in Gwynedd based on four units, namely, Tŷ'r Felin, Tŷ Newydd, Y Gwyngyll and 5 Queen's Park Close, each with specific roles, and it was agreed with Ebsworth, Lucille Hughes and Dodd before it was presented to (and accepted by) committee. Some of its detailed recommendations (for example, about staffing) were implemented but, as a blue print for differing functions for the four community homes, it was largely ignored.

The regime of Lucille Hughes, 1983 to 1996

44.25 The post of Director of Social Services was advertised nationally and Bowen Rees told the Tribunal that he had hoped that an appointment would be made from outside Gwynedd. In the event, it was decided to appoint the internal candidate, **Lucille Hughes**[8], who then served as Director of Social Services from 1 October 1983 until she retired on 31 March 1996, on the demise of Gwynedd County Council itself. Bowen Rees said that she performed admirably and better than he had expected.

44.26 Gwynedd County Council resolved that a new Deputy Director of Social Services should be appointed and **(David) Glanville Owen** was selected for the position, taking office with effect from 2 April 1984 (the other short-listed candidate was Gethin Evans). Glanville Owen had been brought up in Pwllheli and had become a trainee in the Children's Department of Liverpool Corporation in 1965, shortly after graduating in Economics at Liverpool University. He had subsequently obtained a Diploma in Applied Social Studies and the Home Office Letter of Recognition in Child Care after a year's course at Nottingham University ending in 1967. His experience encompassed four English local authorities and the National Children's Home; and he had risen quite rapidly in the 14 years preceding his Gwynedd appointment from Senior Social Worker with the National Children's Home to Assistant Director

---

[6] See para 33.25.

[7] In section 4 of that report.

[8] See para 44.18.

(Fieldwork) with Tameside Metropolitan Borough Council. At the time of his application for the Gwynedd post he was taking an advanced management course for local government at Birmingham University. He remained Deputy Director for Gwynedd until the reorganisation of local government and then served for 18 months as Head of the Policy Unit of the new Gwynedd County Council until September 1997, when his employment was terminated on the ground of redundancy.

44.27 Glanville Owen emphasised in his statement to the Tribunal that his experience throughout his career was in fieldwork and that he had never directly managed any community home for children nor worked within one, even when working as a senior social worker for the National Children's Home. He said also that during his period as Deputy Director he was remote from the residential section and did not have much contact with it: that was the province of the Director. In contrast, he visited Area Offices frequently, both formally and informally; he walked the corridors of those offices and conducted management meetings.

44.28 Despite what has been said in the preceding paragraph, Glanville Owen did take up with Gethin Evans, almost as soon as he arrived at Gwynedd, 12 points about the community homes for children that had been raised with him by the Chairman of the Children's Sub-Committee, including serious allegations about children visiting each others rooms at night and a member of staff smoking cannabis. The tone of the memorandum in response by Gethin Evans dated 2 June 1984 was both inappropriately complacent ("In looking back over the years at the management and regimes in our three Units I feel that I can now say that they are running at their optimum") and discourteously reproving. It was clearly intended to discourage intrusion by either the Deputy Director or the Sub-Committee Chairman.

44.29 When Lucille Hughes took office as Director of Social Services in October 1983 there was provision in the management structure for five Assistant Directors responsible to her through a Deputy Director. This included, however, Parry's anomalous post carrying responsibilities for "special duties" and a post of Assistant Director (Children), which was left unfilled. In 1985 the latter position was filled by the promotion of Gethin Evans, whose role as Head of Children's Services was thus formally recognised, from 30 September 1985; and the actual responsibilities that Dodd was shouldering were similarly recognised by his promotion from 1 October 1985 to Principal Officer (Residential Care—Children). Thus the Children's Section at headquarters had an Assistant Director with two Principals (King and Dodd) accountable to him but Dodd continued to be Officer-in-Charge of Tŷ'r Felin as well.

44.30 A major task undertaken by Glanville Owen soon after his appointment was to formulate proposals for the reorganisation of the Social Services Department. He did so in a closely typed eight page report, detailing a structure that he had devised in consultation with Lilian Hughes. A basic weakness of the existing structure identified in the report was that Area Officers did not have one line manager to relate to with the result that there was confusion about accountability and a weakening of the impact of headquarters management.

The solution proposed was that the county should be divided into two operational divisions, to be named Menai and Llyn/Eryri respectively, each with an Assistant Director responsible for it. Llyn/Eryri was to comprise three Areas, namely, Aberconwy, Dwyfor and Meirionnydd; and Menai was to comprise Arfon and Ynys Mon (Anglesey).

44.31 The proposed new structure provided for four Assistant Directors in all, including those for the two divisions but excluding Parry's obsolescent post. The Assistant Directors for Menai and Llyn/Eryri were to be accountable not only for the work of the Areas within each division but also for the line management of the headquarters based Principal Officers who would retain specialist responsibilities for particular client groups. In relation to children services, the Assistant Director (Menai) was to manage two Principal Officers responsible respectively for Children's Residential Services, including residential and day care establishments, and Children's Other Services (including Adoption). The two other Assistant Directors were to be an Assistant Director (Development) and an Assistant Director (Resources and Support). The latter post was to carry responsibility for the control of resources such as finance, manpower and the use of buildings but was also to involve responsibility for private and voluntary establishments (including the operation of the Registered Homes Act 1984) through a Principal Officer and an Administrative Officer. It is to be noted also that the allocation of responsibilities between the Principal Officers in the Children's Section did not incorporate the ideas that Gethin Evans had put forward, with the two divisions in mind, in a memorandum written in April 1983.

44.32 This new structure operated from April 1987 and remained in being until April 1992[9], but responsibility for the development of children's services was to be assigned to the Assistant Director (Resources and Support) rather than Assistant Director (Development). Gethin Evans was appointed to the former of these two posts.

44.33 The new Assistant Director (Menai) with responsibility for the Children's Section was Robert Evans, who had been Area Officer for Aberconwy since 5 November 1984 and who had to shoulder that responsibility for a further four or five months after taking up the post of Assistant Director. Robert Evans was a graduate in Social Sciences of Leicester University, who had obtained the CQSW in 1976. By 1984 he had had over ten years experience of social work in Northamptonshire and Dorset and had served as a Team Manager (with the pay of a Principal Officer) in the latter county. When restructuring took place in 1992, he became Assistant Director (Mental Health) and he held that position until he left local government on 31 March 1996, when he was about to become 45 years old. He was not a fluent Welsh speaker and he considered that his chances of obtaining a post in local government commensurate with his professional skills and experience were almost non-existent.

---

[9] This appears to be the correct date, although some of the witnesses said that it ended earlier.

44.34 The two Principal Officers accountable to Robert Evans in child care matters initially were Larry King[10] and Nefyn Dodd. King, who was designated Principal Officer (Child Protection), retired on 14 May 1988 and was succeeded by **Peter James Hibbs** from 1 August 1988. Hibbs had been brought up at Colwyn Bay until the age of 15 years, when he went to boarding school, and had graduated in 1973 in Sociology at the South Bank Polytechnic. After serving the Inner London Education Authority for four years as an Education Welfare Officer he had taken the CQSW course at the University College of North Wales, Bangor, where he obtained also a Diploma in Social Studies. Hibbs had then joined Gwynedd Social Services Department on 10 December 1979 as a member of the Child Care Team at the Anglesey Area Office and had been promoted to Senior Social Worker on 1 November 1985, after taking an O level in Welsh in 1984. When Dodd retired from his position as Principal Officer (Children's Residential Services) on 23 May 1990, Hibbs succeeded him and retained the post of Principal Officer until he himself retired on the ground of ill health on 8 January 1993. It seems, however, that he was responsible for residential services only briefly. As soon as he took over from Dodd the post was re-designated as Principal Officer (Adolescent Services), with responsibility for residential services, youth justice and leaving care; but Hibbs' wife died on 4 November 1990, after a long illness, and he was so badly affected by depression that he was found by the medical officer to be unable to carry on working after 1 December 1990. Hibbs estimates that he was only able to attend work for about eight months in all in the course of 1991 and 1992. Since November 1995 he has been a senior practitioner at a Family Centre based in Rhyl, which is run by the National Children's Homes.

44.35 It is unnecessary to go into other organisational details at any length because, with few isolated exceptions, the complaints that we have had to consider have related to events prior to 1992 and the major police investigation began in 1991. In the 1987 structure there was another Principal Officer with child responsibilities but his field was Community Support; and there were also officers responsible for Adoptions and for Children's Placement (Special Needs) but they did not play a part in the relevant history as far as we are concerned.

44.36 During the period when Robert Evans bore line management responsibility for the Children's Section his actual involvement in the work was comparatively slight because of the pressure of other work upon him. He told the Tribunal in his written statement that he was instructed very early on that, following a Health Advisory Service inspection of 1986, which was very critical of mental health services in the county, and in view of the need to plan for closure of large psychiatric hospitals, the development of mental health services must be seen as a priority. In Evans' view they achieved this so successfully that these services in the county were recognised as one of the leading community based services in Europe.

---

[10] See para 44.09.

44.37 In the event the new structure does not appear to have achieved the desired effect of clarifying and tightening line management. Hibbs, for example, said in his oral evidence that, on becoming a Principal Officer, he worked more directly to Gethin Evans than to Robert Evans, his line manager; and he had little contact with either the Deputy Director or the Director. His impression of the latter two was that they were remote and that they were occupied with other procedures. On the other hand, he saw Gethin Evans almost daily. As for Robert Evans, Hibbs saw him about once a week but Hibbs was uncertain whether he grasped child protection issues and regarded him as a mental health specialist. In 1988, Welsh Office SWSOs commented that the distribution of duties between these two Assistant Directors was not formally defined and said that they were puzzled as to how responsibilities were shared. They noted also that only one of the three relevant Principal Officer posts was filled at the time of their inspection.

44.38 Between 1988 and 1990 Hibbs spent a significant amount of his time dealing with child protection matters, as had King before him. He was not, therefore, directly concerned with the findings and recommendations of the SWSOs who visited Tŷ'r Felin and Queens Park in the autumn of 1988[11]. It is surprising, however, that he was not even shown a copy of the inspectors' report when he succeeded to Nefyn Dodd's responsibilities in respect of residential services in 1990 (he did not see it until it was shown to him by his Counsel in the course of the Tribunal's proceedings). His comments about it in his oral evidence were that he did not take issue with anything in it and that it gave a fair description of the position at that time.

44.39 Gethin Evans did not have direct line management responsibility for children's services in the period from 1987 to 1992; he was, however, responsible for the development of children's services, as we have said earlier. He must, therefore, have been closely involved in preparations for implementation of the Children Act 1989 from the moment when it was published as a Bill; and prior to that he must have been consulted quite frequently about child care matters as the recent Head of the Children's Section. He resumed direct line management responsibility for it in 1992.

44.40 The final major reorganisation of the Social Services Department implemented in April 1992 involved abandonment of line management arrangements based upon two divisions. The Area Officers became accountable again to the Deputy Director of Social Services and there was a headquarters team of five Assistant Directors responsible respectively for "specialist" fields such as mental health, mental handicap, and community care.

44.41 The new Assistant Director (Children), Gethin Evans, had a team of five (later four) working under him at headquarters and these included Hibbs (Adolescent Services) and an officer responsible for Child Protection. When Hibbs retired formally on 8 January 1993 he was replaced two months later by **Dafydd Ifans,** who had worked in the North Wales Probation Service for the preceding 10 years, after obtaining the CQSW at Cartrefle College and an

---

[11] See paras 33.52 to 33.55 and 36.48.

Open University degree. He had served for 15 years in the Army (rising to Sergeant), on leaving school at the age of 15 years to become an army apprentice; and he had then been an ASDA manager for two years before turning to social work. Ifans remained with Gwynedd until 31 December 1995 when he became Service Manager, Children and Family Services, for Conwy County Borough Council.

44.42 During his period of nearly three years as a Principal Officer with Gwynedd Ifans was the line manager responsible for the three remaining community homes for children, namely, Tŷ'r Felin, Queens Park and Cartref Bontnewydd. In addition he had an advisory role in relation to youth justice, leaving care and homeless young people. But he found that there were still line management problems involving the relationships between Area Managers (as they had become), the specialist Assistant Directors and the Deputy Director, despite an attempt by the Director of Social Services to clarify the position by a memorandum dated 29 July 1992. Following his arrival, Ifans himself submitted a memorandum to the Director on the role of Principal Officers, after discussing it with other Principal Officers in the team in which he was working, with the object of clarifying the relationship of Principal Officers to Area Managers and according some line manager responsibility to the former. This led to a meeting with the Director, who undertook to consider the matter further, but no action resulted before the counties were reorganised.

The role of the Chief Executive

44.43 Gwynedd County Council had three Chief Executives successively during the 22 years of its existence. They were David Evan Alun Jones (1974 to 1980), Ioan Bowen Rees (1980 to 1991) and Huw Vaughan Thomas (1991 to 1996).

44.44 **(David) Alun Jones,** a solicitor, came to Gwynedd with substantial local government experience in England and Wales, most recently as Deputy Clerk (1952 to 1961) and then Clerk of Denbighshire County Council for 13 years. After graduating in Law at the University College of Wales, Aberystwyth, he had served in various solicitor posts in Ilford, Southampton, Berkshire and Surrey before moving to Denbighshire; and he left Gwynedd to become the Commissioner for Local Administration in Wales for five years until his retirement in 1985.

44.45 In his written statement to the Tribunal Alun Jones emphasised the serious financial position of Gwynedd County Council from the outset, at a time when Gwynedd had the second highest number of low-income households of all county councils in England and Wales. The lack of financial resources was due partly to dilution of the "sparsity element" of the Rate Support Grant formula and partly to the lower than expected fund balances inherited from the predecessor authorities. Nevertheless, in 1974 Gwynedd was the third highest county in terms of expenditure per thousand population. The responsible panel concerned with the Council's resources considered that a substantial rise in the rate precept would be unacceptable, bearing in mind the marked poverty, high unemployment and high proportion of elderly people in the county. Moreover, the Government instructed local authorities to adopt a policy of nil growth in

1975/1976 and thereafter to reduce expenditure. Thus, throughout Alun Jones' period as Chief Executive, Gwynedd was unable to relax its belt tightening attitude over the whole field of its services; but he said that he had no reason to believe that the children's service was seriously underfunded, although the expenditure on social services as a whole was by no means generous, a plight shared by all the other services at the time.

44.46 The new County Council was launched with a staff that was 250 short of its establishment figure of 1178 and it was still 120 below strength at the end of 1974. Alun Jones described his position as that of a "free standing" Chief Officer without an executive department directly responsible to him. His staff, including a personal assistant and a secretary, totalled only four initially and was later reduced to three. He did not, as a rule, attend meetings of service committees or their sub-committees: they were attended by the County Secretary and Solicitor or by one of his Assistant Solicitors. As for the Social Services Department, the staffing structure was that recommended by management consultants and Alun Jones believes that it reflected, largely, the staff complements of the predecessor authorities at Area level.

44.47 During Alun Jones' period as Chief Executive, responsibility for formal performance reviews was assigned to the General Purposes Committee but they do not appear to have been carried out in his time. In his view monitoring of the functions of all service departments was the responsibility of the relevant committees before 1980 and he regarded the Social Services Committee as particularly well equipped in this respect because both its Chairman and its Vice-Chairman were highly competent and extremely hard working.

44.48 Alun Jones did not enlarge in his statement upon his view of the relationship between the Chief Executive and the Chief Officers of the various Departments. Such evidence as we have on the subject does not suggest that it was the practice of the Director of Social Services, T E Jones, to discuss problems relating to children or the community homes with Alun Jones; and we have no reason to think that the latter was aware of any complaints by residents. It is probable that T E Jones did complain to him from time to time about inadequate financial resources, as did all the other Chief Officers, but Alun Jones does not recall that children's services were ever pin-pointed as in special need.

44.49 Alun Jones was consulted by the Director of Social Services about the alleged failings of Parry as Deputy Director of Social Services in or about late 1974 and was involved in the subsequent discussions. After Ebsworth had investigated the matter, Alun Jones' own opinion was that Parry's services should be dispensed with but the view of the Chairman of the Social Services Committee (formerly of Anglesey County Council) that Parry should be made responsible for children's services prevailed.

44.50 **Ioan Bowen Rees** was County Secretary and Solicitor of Gwynedd County Council from its inception so that he was very familiar with its management structure and personalities when he succeeded Alun Jones as Chief Executive in 1980, at the age of 51 years. A native of Dolgellau, he had graduated in Modern History at Oxford after national service and had then served his articles with the Clerk of the Denbighshire County Council. Following his admission as a solicitor in March 1956, he had served in various capacities in local government in Lancashire, Cardiff and Pembrokeshire, latterly as Deputy Clerk of the County Council before reorganisation. In his later career Bowen Rees was very well known outside Gwynedd, serving on many public bodies, and he was regarded as an authority on local government: he was awarded the Haldane Medal by the Royal Institute of Public Administration in 1969 and an honorary LLD by the University of Wales in 1997, amongst other honours. He was also a mountaineer and author of several books. It is sad to record that he died early in May 1999.

44.51 Bowen Rees' terms of appointment referred to him as head of the Council's paid service, having "authority over all other Officers so far as this is necessary for the efficient management and execution of the Council's functions". He was also stated to be leader of the Officers' management team and, through the appropriate Committees, the Council's principal adviser on matters of general policy. In his oral evidence to the Tribunal, however, he agreed that Chief Officers were allowed their heads to run their own departments. He had no choice in the matter because it was the Council's choice: the Chairmen (that is, the admirable and the less admirable) and the Chief Officers, in combination, ran their departments. It was a federation, even a confederation, rather than a unified state.

44.52 In another passage of his evidence Bowen Rees explained that, in his view, Gwynedd was unique because there was no political party in power. It was a council of Independents in the main and the departmental committees were the important committees, with Chairmen tending to respect one another's fiefdom. Bowen Rees' difficulty as Chief Executive was that there was no Leader of the Council. There was a Policy and Resources Committee but it was not until a late stage that he had a Chairman of that Committee who was prepared to take a corporate lead. A Priorities Sub-Committee of the Policy and Resources Committee was set up in 1986 and by 1989 a Policy Unit had been established under the Chief Executive. But the financial situation throughout the 1980s caused a feeling of helplessness in the face of repeated losses of grant and left no room for manoeuvre.

44.53 During Bowen Rees' period the management team of ten heads of departments met once a month; and there were larger meetings once a quarter, attended by six other minor departmental heads, such as the County Valuer. Bowen Rees' feeling was that they were a team who got on well together and that they did share problems. He tried to give a lead on some matters but the departmental committee culture was a problem.

44.54 Despite the continuing difficulties that we have outlined very briefly, it appears that Bowen Rees was more interventionist in Social Services Department matters than his predecessor had been. Thus, he was told of the complaints about Y Gwyngyll in 1981; he asked Ebsworth and a senior solicitor to provide a report to him and he visited Y Gwyngyll, Tŷ'r Felin and Queens Park himself at the time. It was on his initiative that Dyfed County Council was asked to provide a team to inquire and report; and he played an active part in the decision making in relation to Parry after the report had been received, although the Council panel took a different view from him on Parry's future. Other matters in the report were left to the Social Services Department to deal with but he regarded the suggestion that T E Jones did not take any interest in children's services as unjustified to his own knowledge.

44.55 Bowen Rees was also aware in 1983/1984 of comments by the County Treasurer on the low funding for children's services but Bowen Rees satisfied himself that this was largely attributable to the Council's policy of boarding out children whenever it was possible to do so. Only ten per cent of the children being looked after were in children's homes and the boarding out policy saved a great deal of expenditure. He said that by 1989 Gwynedd had the highest proportion in Wales of children boarded out and the second highest in Great Britain. On the other hand, Gwynedd was spending more than any other county in Wales on elderly people.

44.56 Other Social Services Department matters in which Bowen Rees took particular interest subsequently were the police investigation arising from Alison Taylor's complaints and the 1987 restructuring of the Department. He told the Tribunal that he had very little recollection of the events surrounding the police investigation by the time that he gave evidence to us but that he had asked Lucille Hughes to get in touch with him when the inquiry was over. When she did so, she was "over the moon"; she told him that there were to be no proceedings and that there was no substance in the allegations. Bowen Rees wanted to know whether, irrespective of what the police did, there was a need for disciplinary proceedings; and he claimed to have satisfied himself about this, without further discussion with Lucille Hughes, by speaking to one or more senior police officers. In the event he issued statements (much criticised) to the press early in November 1986 to the effect that the police report had completely vindicated the decision by the County Council not to suspend any officer during the investigation[12]. He had not been fully aware of Nefyn Dodd's dual role at the time and he had been told that Alison Taylor was worse than a troublemaker.

44.57 Bowen Rees thought that Lucille Hughes was unfortunate in her Chairman during the mid 1980s, who was very wilful and tolerated only because of his war record. Hughes had not brought to him any management problems in relation to children as such but he had been involved in discussions about the restructuring of the Social Services Department into divisions with associated sub-committees. Bowen Rees opposed this proposal and was disappointed when the Council backed the Social Services Committee and not him.

44.58 **Huw Vaughan Thomas** came to Gwynedd as Chief Executive on 24 April 1991, at the age of 42 years, with a different background from his predecessors. Having spent his early years at Abertridwr in Mid Glamorgan, he graduated in Modern History at Durham University and then took a master's degree in Administrative Sciences at City University before entering the Civil Service. Thereafter he served in the Department of Employment or on bodies associated with that Department: he was Private Secretary to two successive

---

[12] See paras 2.12 to 2.17.

Ministers of Employment and then head of the Manpower Service Commission's employment rehabilitation programme for disabled people before moving to Wales in May 1988 as Director of the Training Agency, Wales. Since the further reorganisation of local government in Wales he has been the Chief Executive of Denbighshire County Council and he holds numerous other appointments on public bodies in Wales.

44.59 Thomas faced many difficulties during his comparatively short period of office as Chief Executive, not the least of these being the imminent reorganisation of local government, but he effected a number of important structural improvements; and his written evidence to the Tribunal was instructive. On his arrival he found that the resources available to him as Chief Executive were smaller than those available to other County Chief Executives and that management techniques such as appraisal and performance reviews were present only in a rudimentary form. There were no less than 15 Chief Officers and the relationship between Chief Executive and Chief Officers was still an out-dated version of "primus inter pares". Councillors were too involved in detailed aspects of staff management rather than broader policy and the allocation of resources owed much to history and political considerations rather than an assessment of need. The Council had an image of "fortress Gwynedd" with a single Welsh language agenda.

44.60 Thomas set about making such improvements as were practicable after extensive discussions. He restructured his own department to provide some broader strategic planning and gave priority to attempting to introduce more modern management techniques. He successfully recommended the establishment of a Sub-Committee of the Council's Policy Committee to vet departmental/committee proposals and to encourage re-distribution of resources alongside necessary budget reductions. This became in 1993 a standing Audit Sub-Committee. Thomas was anxious also to encourage participation by middle management in formulating the strategic agenda and to ensure that there were effective complaints procedures but, whereas middle managers were enthusiastic about these measures, the response of individual Chief Officers was variable. He found that within the Social Services Department there was an initial lack of readiness to consider whether changes were necessary to current procedures and practices and repeated approaches were often needed before a response was received.

44.61 Major difficulties during Thomas' period were that for most of the first three years a wide investigation by the police into the Gwynedd residential homes and ancillary matters was taking place and that, once the main part of the investigation had been completed, the shadow of local government reorganisation loomed very large. These developments restricted the Chief Executive's scope for action in relationship to the Social Services Department. Thus, for example, he received a letter from Alison Taylor in September 1991, shortly before the HTV television programme appeared on 26 September 1991[13], requesting a meeting to discuss allegations of ill-treatment of children

---

[13] See para 2.24.

in care. Having taken advice, Thomas replied to the effect that she should get in touch with him if she had any new matters not already investigated to report; but shortly afterwards Gwynedd asked the police to investigate the allegations made in the television programme. Alison Taylor did write again pressing for a meeting about the dossier that she had prepared but Thomas declined to meet her on the advice of the Council's legal officers and the Chief Constable. There were problems also due to the suspension of staff during the police investigation and civil actions brought against the Council by former children in care.

44.62 Nevertheless, relevant initiatives were taken when they were practicable. Thomas said in his statement that the inquiry into the case of M[14] was set up under Dr Ronald Walton only after repeated insistence by Thomas to the police and to the Welsh Office that Gwynedd had a responsibility to carry out its own inquiry, whatever other developments might take place. The result was that the report of the inquiry was presented to the Children's Sub-Committee on 26 June 1995. Somewhat similarly, an inquiry by O and K Associates was commissioned by the Director of Social Services in September 1994: that investigation was into the circumstances surrounding the theft of a diary belonging to a former resident of Tŷ'r Felin and into other allegations involving staff and residents at that community home[15]. The report was dated 14 February 1995 and was an important factor in the subsequent decision to close Tŷ'r Felin. Thomas said also that he wrote to the new Chairman of the Social Services Committee in August and September 1994 suggesting priorities for her in relation to performance review and finance for children's services in the light of a report by an internal working party on a County strategy for children's services.

Comments

44.63 Although we have outlined quite frequent organisational changes that were made during the period under review, it is clear that a very small headquarters team took active responsibility for child care matters on a day to day basis throughout. By early 1976 the effective Head of the Children's Section was Parry, who retained the title of Deputy Director, and under him the main figure was King as Senior (later Principal) Officer (Children). That remained the position until 1981 but, from 1978 onwards, Nefyn Dodd became a third figure in the hierarchy, initially replacing the Homes Officer on a temporary basis, but becoming in 1980/1981 Co-ordinator/Supervisor and placement officer in relation to all the surviving community homes. This development appears to have been the brainchild of Parry originally but it survived Parry's removal from child care matters, despite strong criticism by the Dyfed team in 1981.

44.64 The major changes in 1981 were the assignment of Parry to other duties and the emergence of Lucille Hughes and Gethin Evans as the leading officers responsible for children. Hughes, however, had a wide range of other duties as

---

[14] See paras 40.10, 40.11 and Chapter 41.
[15] See paras 33.126 to 33.130.

Principal Assistant Director and left day to day matters to Gethin Evans, who assumed increasing responsibilities that were formally recognised in June 1982 with his designation as Head of Children's Services. Hughes' active involvement was much the same as that of the first Director and it did not change to any material extent when she herself became the Director of Social Services from 1 October 1983. Moreover, it was Gethin Evans who underpinned Nefyn Dodd's position in the structure by emphasising the latter's role as line manager and discouraging direct access by Officers-in-Charge to headquarters. King, on the other hand, was largely side-lined in relation to the county's residential homes until his retirement in 1988, although he remained responsible for out of county placements and, more significantly, for child protection; and it was Dodd who became Principal Officer (Residential Care—Children) from October 1985. Glanville Owen was Deputy Director from April 1984 but his experience had been in fieldwork and he did not intervene in residential home matters unless specifically asked to do so.

44.65 The radical re-organisation that took place in 1987, when the county was divided into two divisions for operational purposes, was opposed by the Chief Executive at the time and proved to be unsuccessful. Under it lead responsibility for children's services was assigned to Robert Evans as Assistant Director (Menai) but Gethin Evans appears to have continued to act as adviser and consultant to the new Principal Officer, Hibbs, who succeeded King in 1988 and then Dodd in 1990, but who was only briefly effective because of his wife's fatal illness followed by his own breakdown.

44.66 In the final period from 1992 Gethin Evans was once more formally in charge of children's services as Assistant Director (Children) with a new Principal Officer responsible for children and adolescent services, Ifans, under him from March 1993. Ifans had no previous experience of children's homes but he was the line manager for the remaining three community homes, one of which (Tŷ'r Felin) closed in the autumn of 1995.

44.67 In our judgment the Children's Section was seriously undermanned for most of the period under review and there was no adequate supervision or monitoring of its performance. It may be said that these deficiencies were due, at least in part, to lack of resources and the prolonged illnesses of some senior officers and principal officers. These explanations do not, however, excuse the Social Services Department's failure to institute and maintain an effective system of line management for its community homes and effective arrangements for the care and protection of children. The enlarged role of Dodd was initially a makeshift measure but it was wrongly extended and enhanced, despite fully justified criticism, with the result that he was permitted to dominate residential homes for children and placements in the county for a decade, during which the county had no comprehensible strategy for residential services for children. Councillors and successive Directors of Social Services appear to have been pre-occupied with services for the elderly and the mentally handicapped at the expense of those for children in their care; and it was only in the late stages that coherent attempts were being made to put children's services on a sound footing.

The failure to eliminate abuse

Introduction

45.01 An important distinction between Gwynedd and Clwyd is that the evidence before us in relation to Gwynedd local authority community homes has not revealed the presence of any persistent sexual abuser on the scale of Howarth or Norris during the period of 24 years under review. We heard allegations of sexual abuse against nine identified members of staff but most of these were named by one complainant only and the complainant in respect of each of them was different. As for the others, one member of staff only was named by as many as six complainants but the allegations against him did not disclose any discernible pattern of sexual misconduct to lend them credibility and we are left in doubt about them.

45.02 A similar distinction has emerged in relation to the private residential establishments because it has not been suggested that any persistent sexual abuser was involved in the running of any of the private schools or homes that we have discussed. There were a few cases that we have outlined in Chapter 39[1] but Gwynedd Social Services Department was only involved in one of these and acted promptly and appropriately, as we have described in paragraph 39.48.

45.03 There were two cases in the period under review of proved sexual abuse in foster homes within Gwynedd[2]. In both these cases the offenders were prosecuted promptly after complaints had been made and we have discussed the relevant boarding out issues in relation to them in Chapter 42.

45.04 In these circumstances it is unnecessary to devote a separate chapter to consideration of the failure of Gwynedd Social Services Department to detect sexual abuse earlier or to prevent it from occurring. In general, the lessons that we have drawn in Chapter 29 in respect of Clwyd's experience of sexual abuse are equally relevant to local authorities within the former Gwynedd for the future but we do not suggest that there were particular failures by the former Gwynedd Social Services Department in relation to sexual abuse in the period under review as distinct from other forms of abuse. In particular, there is no evidence that their recruitment procedures failed to elicit relevant information about earlier sexual misconduct from any potential residential child care worker or potential foster parent.

45.05 In this chapter, therefore, we deal generally with Gwynedd's failure to eliminate abuse. Not surprisingly, the underlying reasons for this were broadly similar to those that we have found in Clwyd and they will be stated more shortly to avoid unnecessary repetition. But the pattern of abuse and the relevant line management in Gwynedd were different. About two-thirds of the

---

[1] See paras 39.43 to 39.48.
[2] See paras 42.03 to 42.17 and 42.25 to 42.29.

known complainants were former residents of Tŷ'r Felin during the period when Nefyn Dodd was Officer-in-Charge; and from 1981/1982 until November 1989, when he became unable to continue working, he was the line manager for all the community homes in Gwynedd. Much of the discussion in this chapter hinges, therefore, upon Nefyn Dodd's dominant role and his authoritarian personality.

The appointment and advancement of Nefyn Dodd

45.06 If Nefyn Dodd had not been appointed as Officer-in-Charge of Tŷ'r Felin with effect from January 1978, it is unlikely that there would have been any police investigation of Gwynedd homes in 1986/1987 or in 1991/1993 and Gwynedd would not have been included in the scope of this Tribunal's inquiry. There can be no doubt that his conduct at Tŷ'r Felin and the regime that he imposed there were the mainsprings of the complaints from children in care and that his methods affected the quality of residential care for children throughout Gwynedd.

45.07 With the benefit of hindsight it can be said confidently that Dodd's appointment to Tŷ'r Felin was a grave mistake. It is less easy to say so without that benefit but, in our judgment, it is very questionable whether he was a suitable person to appoint as head of an Observation and Assessment Centre, bearing in mind his limited credentials and even lesser experience. As it was, he had no trained staff to assist him in the relevant work and Tŷ'r Felin never functioned properly for the purposes for which it was designed.

45.08 We accept, however, that those responsible for Dodd's appointment could not have been expected to foresee at that time how his personality and practices would develop. The strongest criticism is that he was permitted to develop them, without any restraining influence, and then encouraged to extend his methods and authority, effectively without any close supervision and monitoring. The initial responsibility for these errors must rest upon the Deputy Director at the time, Parry, who had ample opportunity, as a frequent visitor to Tŷ'r Felin, to observe Dodd but seems to have been oblivious to his manifest failings, evidenced (for example) by his directions to members of staff in the log book[3].

45.09 In the event the advancement of Dodd to line management responsibility for the community homes was justly criticised by the Dyfed team in 1981 both on structural grounds and on the basis of Dodd's methods; but their views were ignored. Bowen Rees and Ebsworth were primarily concerned to protect T E Jones from what they regarded as unfair criticism and to use the inquiry to resolve the position in relation to Parry. Neither Lucille Hughes nor Gethin Evans was shown the report and the result was that Evans, who was a comparative newcomer, accepted Dodd's invitations to strengthen the latter's position by issuing memoranda to the Heads of Homes, emphasising that all communications by them to headquarters must be via Dodd[4].

---

[3] See para 33.43.
[4] See paras 33.23 to 33.25.

45.10 The inappropriate delegation of important headquarters responsibilities to a Head of Home reflected a wider penny-pinching attitude to child care matters in Gwynedd and Dodd's position became even more anomalous when he was advanced to Principal Officer (Residential Establishments—Children) whilst retaining his appointment as Officer-in-Charge of Tŷ'r Felin. The pattern of delegation without effective accountability in return was a feature of the Social Services Department throughout the period under review with the result that the interests of children in care were neglected at the highest level.

45.11 In practical terms the effect of these arrangements was that there was no meaningful channel of complaint, even for members of the residential care staff. At Tŷ'r Felin Nefyn Dodd was sole arbiter, reporting to himself; and for most of the period he had an ever present ally in his wife, June Dodd, who would carry to him swiftly news of any potentially embarrassing criticism, misbehaviour or rebellion. Alison Taylor's experiences, as we have recounted them in Chapters 33 and 34, illustrate very clearly the fate that was likely to befall any "whistleblower" who tried to by-pass Nefyn Dodd in order to gain the attention of higher authority; and it is noteworthy that her colleagues, working in the same oppressive regime, were willing to sign critical statements about her when she was disciplined for her actions. How much more oppressive must it have seemed to a child resident contemplating making a complaint and how unreal was the prospect of him/her doing so if the alleged abuser was (for example) Nefyn Dodd himself or John Roberts?

45.12 The denial of access to headquarters was not confined to residential care staff but extended to Area Officers and thence to field workers in respect of children in Gwynedd community homes. This was spelt out expressly in a memorandum dated 15 October 1984, which was drafted by Gethin Evans but signed by Lucille Hughes and addressed to all the Area Officers and Dodd. The purpose of the memorandum was stated to be "to clarify that area staff need not contact (headquarters) relating to problems concerning children in our own community homes". Moreover, it contained passages such as:

> "I would remind area staff that officers-in-charge are not expected to contact this office unless there is an absolute emergency when Mr Dodd cannot be found or contacted."

> "Area Officer and Co-ordinator/Supervisor should discuss together any acute problems which their staff cannot settle. Reference back to head office should not be necessary."

> "Head office staff should only become involved with youngsters in our homes when he or she is subject to transfer from a non-county establishment into our own homes, and where some element of interest needs to be retained."

45.13 This concentration of influence and authority in the hands of the Officer-in-Charge of one of the community homes and a person who did not even rank as a Principal Officer at the time must be very strongly criticised; and it is remarkable that the only reference in the memorandum to monitoring by headquarters was the statement that head office would "continue to monitor all out of county placements in liaison with area". The blame for these misconceived arrangements rests squarely upon Lucille Hughes and, under her, upon Gethin Evans and they are not excused by lack of knowledge of the Dyfed team strictures. The arrangements as such, detached from the personality of Nefyn Dodd, were bad structurally; and both Lucille Hughes and Gethin Evans had had ample opportunity by 1983/1984 to acquaint themselves with many of Nefyn Dodd's weaknesses and limitations. Unhappily, however, they provide strong evidence of Lucille Hughes' failure to involve herself actively in the management of children's services, despite her pre-1971 experience, and of Gethin Evans' disinclination to involve himself in the practical aspects of his responsibilities for the community homes.

The absence of complaints procedures

45.14 In the face of the arrangements that we have outlined in the preceding section, it is difficult to see how any conventional complaints procedure could have been effective but the reality was that no such procedure was available, even to staff, until the latest stages of the period under review. Furthermore, such documents as there were dealing with residential care practice were largely out of date until the late 1980s (at the earliest) and do not appear to have been readily available to residential care staff.

45.15 It would be wrong to give the impression that Gethin Evans was not a hard working man. On the contrary, the evidence before us is that he was very committed to his work; he arrived at his office very early and worked long hours, despite his additional responsibilities as a district councillor, but he was essentially an office man. Amongst his functions were the production and up-dating of departmental manuals but he said in evidence that there was no written complaints procedure until (he believed) 1990. Before that there were only "guidelines to do with complaints" that he had written "to the department around 1979/1980". When asked what he had expected to happen to a serious complaint by a resident, he replied that, between 1982 and 1987, he would have expected it to have reached him through Dodd.

45.16 We have referred earlier[5] to the pamphlet called "Handbook for Children in Residential Care", which was drafted by Nefyn Dodd and approved by Gethin Evans in 1988 and which contained a section on complaints. It is fair to say that it contained the outlines of a complaints procedure but it was already obsolescent when it was distributed to heads of homes on or about 28 October 1988, in view of the impending Children Act. It is very doubtful on the evidence before us that it was distributed to resident children generally and we have not been shown any up-dated version. Although it did envisage that a child might ring the Director of Social Services if dissatisfied, there was no change in the departmental procedure whereby all complaints by or through staff were to be channelled via Dodd; and only a very resolute child would have been likely to accept the invitation to complain to headquarters.

---

[5] See paras 33.116 and 33.117.

The incidence of, and response to, complaints

45.17 If any additional discouragement was needed for potential complainants, it was provided by the actual response of higher management to the few contemporary complaints that were pursued. We have illustrated this earlier in Chapters 33 and 34 in relation to complaints that arose at Tŷ'r Felin and Tŷ Newydd. Thus, the alleged assault on a boy by John Roberts on 24 May 1984 was reported by Alison Taylor to Lucille Hughes and Gethin Evans but no remedial action was taken; and June Dodd's reaction was to complain, "How could you let us down?"[6]. Again, a member of staff who wrote a report in 1984 in another boy's file when the latter complained that a visible lump on his head had been caused by John Roberts was told next day that the entry had been deleted[7]. Moreover, when Alison Taylor reported a complaint against June Dodd in February 1986 to the effect that she had thumped a boy on the shoulder in the office at Tŷ Newydd, Taylor was told by Gethin Evans, who investigated the matter, that she was creating trouble unnecessarily[8]. Yet again, Taylor's report to Dodd on 30 July 1985 about an incident in which X was alleged to have slapped a girl resident at Tŷ Newydd resulted in no action being taken by Gethin Evans on the ground that Evans believed X to have been under stress at the time[9].

45.18 These may be regarded as comparatively minor instances of alleged physical abuse (in the overall possible scale of such abuse) but the responses to them were symptomatic of a pervasive intention amongst senior officials from Nefyn Dodd upwards to suppress complaints when they were made, however serious they might be. A striking example of this was the response to the complaint by A of sexual abuse at Queens Park, which we have dealt with in detail in paragraphs 36.14 to 36.29. The evidence in relation to that incident indicates clearly that Lucille Hughes, Gethin Evans and Nefyn Dodd were all anxious to dispose of the matter quickly in the interest of the member of staff against whom the allegation had been made. No proper investigation took place and A's Area Officer was led to protest about the way in which the matter had been handled. It is clear also that Larry King, who had understood the need for a proper investigation, was left out of the matter after he had interviewed the alleged abuser, despite his responsibilities for Child Protection.

45.19 Another notable example of suppression was the response by headquarters to the allegations of physical abuse by the foster parent, Norman Roberts, in the case of M. We have traced the history of this in Chapter 41, in particular at paragraphs 41.31 to 41.45. It is abundantly clear from this evidence that a full investigation involving the police should have been set in train, having regard to the nature of the injuries and the available medical evidence; and the highly objectionable reason given for not doing so was "to prevent endangering the placement of all the children"[10]. In the event the prosecution of Norman

---

[6] See para 33.103.
[7] See para 33.120.
[8] See paras 33.90, 33.91 and 34.17(8).
[9] See paras 34.10 and 34.17(7).
[10] See para 41.43.

Roberts was delayed for over seven years because the police were not informed at the time and, in our judgment, Lucille Hughes, Glanville Owen, Gethin Evans and Larry King all bear a share of the responsibility for the failure to respond to the events appropriately. We underline also that Gethin Evans' report to the Children's Sub-Committee on 13 March 1986 was a gravely defective account of the relevant history[11].

45.20 In this climate any "whistleblower" was likely to receive short shrift and so events proved. Wholly independently of Alison Taylor, a former member of the staff at Tŷ'r Felin wrote to Glanville Owen in January 1985 listing a series of criticisms of Nefyn Dodd's management of that community home[12]. The response of Glanville Owen to this letter is related in paragraph 33.122 of this report. He saw the author of the letter to explain to him the seriousness of his complaints, asking him whether he wished to "stand by" them. Some were withdrawn, but not the allegations of physical abuse. According to Owen's evidence to the Tribunal, he then looked at the allegations as a whole rather than individually, whatever that may mean, after Nefyn Dodd had denied them and a dismissive letter was sent to the complainant in the name of the Director of Social Services. Owen's comment on the matter in his oral evidence was that, looking at the matter 12 years on, he was quite appalled by the allegations and the way that they were not investigated by him. It must be added that dismissal of the complaints was no doubt facilitated by Dodd's counter criticisms of the complainant's conduct and motivation. Dodd had refused to give the complainant a reference when the latter left Tŷ'r Felin and it appears to have been alleged that he, a married man with two children, had had an affair with a student at Tŷ'r Felin whereas the complainant's evidence was that the affair occurred after he left.

45.21 The responses to Alison Taylor's complaints were similar in quality and were classic illustrations of what is likely to happen to a "whistleblower". She was dubbed a "trouble maker" at an early stage and later the Chief Executive (Bowen Rees) was told that she was worse than that. It was particularly unfortunate also that the unsatisfactory Chairman of the Social Services Committee, criticised as such by Bowen Rees[13], should have been the person selected (or perhaps self-selected) to discuss with Alison Taylor her complaints and concerns in October 1986[14]. Again, we have no doubt that the police officer in charge of the 1986/1987 police investigation, Detective Chief Superintendent Gwynne Owen, was given a similar view of Taylor by senior officers of the Social Services Department at the outset of his investigation. Thus, a wall of disbelief was constructed before any of the individual allegations reported by Taylor was investigated and the ultimate decision not to prosecute anyone was accepted with inappropriate enthusiasm and without further scrutiny by the Social Services Department of the underlying evidence.

[11] See para 41.51.
[12] See para 33.121.
[13] See para 44.57.
[14] See para 34.23.

45.22 Any suggestion that Alison Taylor was a lone disaffected employee in her complaints about Nefyn Dodd is rebutted by the fact that the representative of social workers and child care officers in the Children's Section wrote a letter to Lucille Hughes on 24 January 1986, which was headed "Plea for Help— Open Letter". The following extracts from the letter, which was circulated to county councillors, speak for themselves:

> "It is with much regret that we have to bring to your notice of some of the problems that are the reason for the resignations, poor morale and the high level of sickness in this section.
>
> The staff are dissatisfied, misused and abused. The working conditions bear no resemblance to our conditions of service. We are discriminated against by having to work long hours up to 15 hours each Saturday and Sunday for which we receive no enhanced payments as do other sections. We have to work in an atmosphere of fear and put up with the obscene language of a very senior officer of this department. It is difficult at case conference to deal with this officer, very often to the detriment of the child in question . . .
>
> . . . Nothing will ever be right until an enquiry is conducted into this section. We are all being hoodwinked, manoeuvred, and degraded, we ask for your help in putting these matters right before it is too late."

45.23 Lucille Hughes said in evidence that she had difficulty in recollecting this letter but went on to refer to raising the question of bad language with Dodd subsequently at one of her regular meetings with him. She "would imagine" that the letter was looked at in committee, if it was circulated to county councillors, and she would have raised rota matters with the Assistant Director and staff officers.

Conclusions

45.24 To sum up, the organisation and management of the community homes in Gwynedd were such that a degree of child abuse was almost bound to occur and the only cause for relief is that it did not occur on a greater scale than has been disclosed by the evidence. Residential care staff were largely untrained and opportunities for in service training were very limited. There were no clear guidelines for staff and children with widely ranging needs were placed together in community homes without reference to any overall care strategy or individual care planning. Access to field workers was limited and, for most of the period, control of the community homes was vested in a single individual, without any adequate provision for monitoring and supervision by higher management. There was no recognised complaints procedure and direct contact with headquarters was actively discouraged. Moreover, the few contemporary complaints that did penetrate the system (including those in the fostering case of M) were treated dismissively by headquarters officers, who failed to investigate them fully and impartially.

45.25 For these failings the two main Directors of Social Services successively must bear major responsibility, together with the headquarters staff responsible for child care matters, to the extent that we have indicated, and Nefyn Dodd in his dual roles. Members of Gwynedd County Council and, in particular, the Social Services Children's Sub-Committee must also, however, bear a share of the responsibility for their failure to acquaint themselves adequately with conditions in the community homes and to monitor and control the operation of the Children's Section of the Social Services Department; and we will enlarge upon this comment in the next chapter.

Basic failings in the quality of care

Introduction

46.01 We have dealt with our approach to this subject in relation to Clwyd, in the context of our terms of reference, in the introductory section of Chapter 31 and we need not repeat what we said there. In Gwynedd, as in Clwyd, the major failings that we have identified were:

(a) The lack of adequate planning of each child's period in care.

(b) The absence of any strategic framework for the placement of children in residential care.

(c) Ineffective reviewing processes and lack of consultation with the child.

(d) Intermittent and inadequate surveillance by field social workers.

(e) Failure to establish any co-ordinated system for preparing residents for their discharge from care.

46.02 It will be necessary to say a few words in this chapter under each of these heads. We will deal also with three other matters of particular relevance to Gwynedd, namely, the response of the Social Services Department to various adverse reports during the period under review, the adequacy of the financial provision made for children's services and the responsibility of county councillors for failings in the quality of care that was provided.

The lack of adequate planning for each child in care

46.03 In paragraph 33.124 of this report we have listed six main defects in social work practice at Tŷ'r Felin affecting the quality of care provided and these defects permeated the whole of the residential care provision for children in Gwynedd for most of the period under review. A recurring refrain in the reports and evidence before us has been the absence of assessment or planning before the admission of a child into care. It has not been part of our task to assess the quality of preventive work undertaken before children were received into care but all too often, indeed in the vast majority of cases, children were received into the community homes as emergency cases without individual care plans.

46.04 As early as 4 March 1979 Nefyn Dodd, as Officer-in-Charge of Tŷ'r Felin, wrote to Parry, the Deputy Director, complaining of the unprofessional and haphazard way in which he was expected to admit children into that community home as an assessment centre. Yet, over nine years later, Welsh Office SWSOs found that recorded information showed very little evidence of detailed assessment prior to care. "There were no indications of probable outcomes of reception into care or committal to care; appropriate placement;

probable lengths of time or other salient indicators of the purpose of care. Reasons for reception into care were always expressed in terms of the situation the children were leaving rather than that to which they were going"[1].

46.05 Another recurring criticism was that the object of admission into care was often stated to be for assessment without any indication as to what was to be assessed or as to the purpose of the assessment. Thus, residential staff were not given clear guidance and assessment was too frequently seen as a means of providing a solution rather than as an aid to determining options for the child. Bearing in mind the lack of staff trained and experienced in assessment, the outcome of the process was unlikely to be satisfactory and the danger of drift resulting from admission into open-ended care was very real.

The absence of any strategic framework for placements

46.06 Despite the approval by the Children's Sub-Committee of the policy statement on this subject drafted by Gethin Evans in 1982[2], it appears to have been largely ignored and the remaining community homes became progressively less distinguishable from each other in terms of purpose. Dodd was the supreme arbiter in respect of placements in community homes within the county and his authority was reinforced by his practice of presiding over case conferences, at which his word prevailed. Moreover, in very many cases placements were determined by the availability of accommodation rather than the particular needs of the child.

46.07 This failure to implement any coherent placement strategy accentuated the risk of drift in care and inevitably diminished the quality of provision for individual children because each home had to provide for a wide range of conflicting behaviour and attitudes. Another adverse consequence was that some children were placed very many miles from their own homes (the distance could be as far as 85 miles), restricting severely the practicability of parental contact and a close relationship with a child's field social worker.

46.08 The Welsh Office SWSOs who visited Gwynedd in the autumn of 1988 found problems also in relation to boarding out placements, despite the partnership arrangement with the fostering unit at Cartref Bontnewydd, which had by then been in place for about four years[3]. There was divided responsibility and evidence of confusion and poor practice in the boarding out of children, especially from residential care. The SWSOs summarised their views on the boarding out arrangements in the following paragraph:

> "The evidence was of a placement policy and practice in need of major overhaul. We found hasty or ill-conceived introduction; poor preparation of foster home and child; an absence of agreed objectives and targets; long delays between solution and conclusion; little or no choice of family placement and placement at long distance and/or inappropriate locations."

[1] Report in late 1988 of SWSOs J K Fletcher and D Barker on 12 children at Tŷ'r Felin and Queens Park, at p.26.
[2] See para 44.24.
[3] See para 37.02.

The SWSOs concluded that the total amount of social work time committed to the development and support of fostering had almost certainly been reduced under the contractual arrangement rather than increased. These were truly alarming conclusions for a county that was placing heavy emphasis on boarding out as the preferred disposal for children in care.

46.09 Dafydd Ifans told the Tribunal that it was not until 1993 that guidelines for the selection of a placement were adopted; and it was he who set up an admissions panel to eliminate inappropriate admissions and to select placements. But he said that a consistent failure of the system was that up to 90 per cent of admissions were emergency receptions because of lack of planning in the field and the lack of resources to develop other initiatives so that inappropriate placements still occurred.

Ineffective reviewing processes and lack of consultation with the child

46.10 It is right to say that in 1988 the Welsh Office SWSOs reported favourably on some aspects of the reviewing process. They found that, at Tŷ'r Felin and Queens Park, reviews were carried out at regular intervals and were attended by a proper range of staff and representatives from other services such as health and education; and they praised the involvement of the children and their parents in the planning process. On the evidence that they saw "the planning process . . . produced realistic plans to which most of the participants could and did subscribe".

46.11 Nevertheless, according to the SWSOs, there were two inescapable problems about the process. The first was that it was very difficult to review, in the sense of evaluating success and progress, in the absence of a foundation assessment and care plan. Secondly, there was a lack of effective available resources to follow plans through. The family placement alternative to residential care was in practice repeatedly failing to meet the needs of some children. "Poor foster parent assessment and child matching, inadequate introduction to the foster parent and to the child, impossibly short introductory times and foster home breakdowns after a few months were the experience of many of the children"[4].

46.12 The criticisms that we heard of the reviewing process earlier in the period under review were much wider than these and were closely linked with the pressures on field social workers. Larry King was involved in monitoring statutory reviews for varied purposes and to a variable extent from 1975 to 1988 and he was critical of the Gwynedd practice in respect of these reviews for a number of reasons. It was not easy to elicit precise answers from him when he gave evidence but it appears that in the first half of his period (that is, when he was reporting to Parry) he visited Area Offices quite frequently to inspect children's files generally. Following Parry's departure, King's duties changed and he no longer bore responsibility for children in residential homes or who were boarded out, but he was responsible, in particular, for out of county placements and for child protection. In this latter phase it was his practice to visit Area Offices about twice per month: one visit would be for the purpose of

---

[4] See the report already cited in footnote 1, at p.30.

pursuing child protection issues and the other to inspect the files of those children who were not in Gwynedd community homes and not boarded out. Responsibility for monitoring statutory reviews of children in Gwynedd homes or boarded out rested with Gethin Evans from 1982. Those reviews took place in the community home or the foster home with Dodd usually presiding at reviews in the former and the relevant Team Manager from Area Office at a review in a foster home.

46.13 King's evidence, both in writing and orally, was that he complained frequently that statutory reviews were not being carried out on time. When asked to what period he was referring in relation to this criticism, he said that it was after he was "taken off the residential sector". Although he mentioned both Parry and Gethin Evans as recipients of his complaints, it appears that they were made mainly to Gethin Evans in the period between 1982 and 1987, that is, when he (King) was not directly responsible for children in residential care. King was in close touch with an administrative officer of many years' experience who held the Child Protection Register at that time and that officer pointed out to him that reviews of children in care were slipping badly, particularly in relation to boarded out children for whom the Anglesey Area office were responsible.

46.14 An underlying reason for this slippage was undoubtedly lack of financial resources, attested to by many senior officers, leading to recurring shortages of field social workers. There were various freezes on recruitment, the first in 1976 (according to King's recollection) and the position was aggravated by industrial action on several occasions. Thus, there were periods in 1980, 1985/1986 and again in 1987 when files were "stacked" and new children were not allocated to social workers. There were also periods of 'work to rule' when the casework of a previous postholder who had not been replaced would not be undertaken by any colleague. King's successor (Hibbs) found that there was difficulty about the allocation of field social workers to children. Up to 60 children were allocated to a single social worker; there were delays in allocation; and some children in residential care did not have a social worker allocated to them.

46.15 A separate but central criticism of the reviewing process during the period of almost ten years to 1988 when Dodd dominated the residential sector was that his views on the children in residential care almost invariably prevailed when they were in conflict with those of field workers. There were also inhibitions on the sharing of information about children: some details available in Area files were not disclosed to the community homes, apparently because it was thought that it might affect the attitudes of residential care staff to the children adversely; and, even after King left, Hibbs found that field social workers were not being afforded access to records in the home, having to rely instead on a summary from the head of the home. Hibbs' evidence was that the reports for reviews and the review documents themselves were "skeletal" but that they were the only planning documents in existence.

Intermittent and inadequate surveillance by field social workers

46.16 We have already mentioned in the preceding section of this chapter some of the difficulties that faced field social workers throughout the period under review in maintaining effective contact with, and surveillance of, the children for whom they were responsible. An additional factor for some of them, in respect of both community homes and some foster homes, was the long distance that it was necessary to travel to see a child; and their difficulties in this respect were aggravated by the imposition of mileage restrictions on the use of their own motor cars. Most seriously of all, Area staff understandably felt that they were being deliberately distanced from the children for whom they were responsible by a combination of organisational and procedural decisions and the overall attitude to them of Nefyn Dodd.

46.17 In the climate that we have outlined it was inevitable that the important link between field social worker and child in residential care should be weakened; and it is not surprising that the former preferred contact with a child when the latter was home on leave to visiting the child in a community or foster home. Such contact was not an adequate substitute, however, for regular visits in the community or foster home and time spent there alone with the child. The result in evidential terms has been that very few of the former residents of community homes and foster homes within Gwynedd have spoken of a meaningful relationship with their field workers; and the latter were of minimal value as a potential channel of complaint.

46.18 Headquarters staff were well aware of the unrest amongst Area Officers and their staff about the arrangements in place from 1982 onwards. They were aware also that field workers were not visiting children in the homes as frequently as they should. Both Parry and King gave evidence to this effect and King drew the attention of Areas and individual social workers to this both orally and in writing. Parry's evidence was that the only method of detecting whether a visit had taken place was by analysis by a member of the headquarters staff of the entries in the visitors' book; and Elaine Baxter's conclusion[5] was that either there had been a significant failure to visit the children or the visits had (wrongly) not been recorded.

46.19 Despite headquarters' knowledge of these failings, no effective action was taken to remedy the position. As we have indicated earlier, Gethin Evans spent the majority of his time in his office and his responsibilities, as Head of Children's Services, included the making of recommendations for action in the light of national and local reports and the production of Departmental Manuals. Gwynedd differed from Clwyd in that the former did produce detailed procedural manuals covering a wide range of activities but they bore little relevance to what occurred on a daily basis on the ground and Gethin Evans conceded that there was no mechanism in place to ensure that staff had access to and read (let alone understood) the manuals.

---

[5] In her appraisal for the Tribunal of social work practice in Gwynedd during the period under review.

46.20 The relevant manual was "Departmental Manual No.2. Child Care", which was revised several times in the course of the 1980s. We were invited to look, in particular, at the section in this manual dealing with Residential Care and the identification and functions of the "Primary Worker with Children in Care"[6]. We found it extremely difficult to interpret in practical terms; it seemed to be designed to secure observance of formal requirements rather than to meet children's needs; and Gethin Evans was forced to concede that a crucial paragraph defining the roles of field and residential social workers in relation to children newly admitted to care was "gobbledegook".

Failure to prepare residents for their discharge from care

46.21 The loosening of the tie between field social worker and child in residential care was likely to have particularly adverse consequences when the time came for a child to be discharged from care. Even more seriously, however, we have had little evidence of any coherent policy in Gwynedd for preparing children in care for independence.

46.22 In the earlier part of the period under review it seems that Tŷ Newydd was intended to play the central role in preparing adolescents for independence. It was opened in 1978 as a hostel for ten "boys" aged 16 to 21 years and was so described in the 1979 Regional Plan for Wales[7]; and it was envisaged that some of them, at least, would be in employment whilst living at Tŷ Newydd. This provision lasted only about three years, however, and the Dyfed team, who visited the hostel in July and August 1981, were appalled by its physical state[8].

46.23 When Tŷ Newydd re-opened as a community home in 1982, it was said to be intended to provide accommodation for children in a wide age range up to 18 years but the view expressed by Gethin Evans in his 1982 strategy document entitled "Residential Work with Children" was that Tŷ Newydd would provide for the younger age range of children; and this document was subsequently approved by the Children's Sub-Committee[9]. Tŷ Newydd was said to lack "private space", which was important for the adolescent. According to this document, all homes would seek to provide short term care primarily for the 12–17 age group with the objective that residents could either be re-integrated into their own families or, when this was not possible, integrated into the community, either on a permanent or semi-permanent basis, through a foster home, supervised lodging or private accommodation.

46.24 Within Gethin Evans' strategy the community home that would prepare adolescents for independent living was to be Y Gwyngyll, which had opened in 1979 and had accommodation for 16 boys and girls. This was to be the main focus of the unit and Gethin Evans had in mind that social links were to be forged with the careers' service, local employers and the private and public housing sectors with the assistance of field workers; and other Area staff were to be involved in group work with adolescents.

---

[6] Section 2.6.3.
[7] See para 34.02.
[8] Ibid.
[9] See paras 44.24 and 46.06.

46.25 This description of Y Gwyngyll's role was not in accord with the Regional Plan, which was already obsolete or obsolescent. More importantly, however, Y Gwyngyll never fulfilled that role, as far as we are aware. The design of the community home included bed-sitting accommodation for two school leavers but not even this was used for the purpose for which it was designed[10]. The home and its administration were robustly criticised by the Dyfed team in 1981 and it closed in 1986.

46.26 In the result we have found no evidence of a continuing strategy for adolescents leaving care in the 1980s. When eventually, towards the end of that decade, a "Handbook for Children in Residential Care" was produced[11], it did contain a short final section on "Leaving Care" but it was in bland general terms. On the subject of preparation, for example, it said:

> "Some (children) will grow up in a Community Home and one day move out and live by themselves. All young people need to learn how to manage cooking, money, shopping, simple household chores, repairs. Staff in the Community Home will be able to help you with these things, make sure that they do."

We have not received any evidence, of specific instructions to members of residential care staff on this subject or of any programme to prepare residents for independence.

46.27 The Welsh Office investigation in 1992 of outcomes for children leaving care in three Welsh counties[12] did not include Gwynedd so that we do not have before us the kind of detailed analysis that we have in respect of Clwyd. We are satisfied, however, that a similar investigation in Gwynedd at the time would have presented an equally bleak picture. Dafydd Ifans, the last Principal Officer with line management responsibility for the three remaining community homes from March 1993, recalled when giving evidence to the Tribunal that a researcher from the University of Wales, Swansea, was commissioned in 1994/1995 to interview a number of young people who had left care in Gwynedd in order to obtain their views on the service that they had received but we have not seen the report that she presented.

46.28 It was not until nearly the end of the period under review that Gwynedd's Departmental Manual No 2 included detailed guidance on the preparation of children for leaving care, drafted by Ifans in the light of the requirements of section 24 of the Children Act 1989 and the Welsh Office report on its Inspection of Outcomes for Children Leaving Care. Under the heading of Aftercare in the section dealing with Adolescent Services[13] a detailed procedure for the preparation of children was set out, including the completion by each child (with any necessary assistance) on reaching the age of 15 years, of answers to a comprehensive questionnaire. It included provision also for a compulsory

---

[10] See also para 35.35.
[11] See paras 33.116, 33.117 and 45.16.
[12] See para 31.30.
[13] Section 2.5.0.

Leaving Care Planning Meeting at that stage, attended by relevant family members and representatives of all the relevant services, including Housing, Careers and Benefit agencies.

The failure to heed adverse reports

46.29 A disquieting aspect of the history that we have related was the failure of Gwynedd Social Services Department to take appropriate remedial action in response to adverse reports; and the most striking example of this was their response to the report by the Dyfed inquiry team about the running of Y Gwyngyll and associated matters.

46.30 We have summarised in Chapter 35 of this report the matters that were considered by the Dyfed team and their more relevant findings[14]. It is unnecessary to repeat those details here but we emphasise that the team's criticisms were wide-ranging. Although they were critical, in different ways, of both T E Jones and Parry and the poor relationship between these two men, their report raised much broader issues that needed to be addressed urgently. There is no evidence, however, that these broader issues were ever discussed either by councillors or by appropriate senior officers. In effect, a protective veil was thrown around T E Jones and only a very small number of persons saw the report. It is not even clear that the full report was seen by members of the disciplinary panel who dealt with Parry. Attention was concentrated upon personal issues at the expense of broader questions of policy and practice and neither of the two officers to whom responsibility for children's services was transferred, Lucille Hughes and Gethin Evans, was shown a copy of the report or even given a summary of its relevant findings; and Glanville Owen was similarly ignorant of its contents after he had been appointed to Parry's former position as Deputy Director of Social Services.

46.31 The responsibility for the suppression of this report must rest primarily upon the Chief Executive, Bowen Rees, and the County Secretary, Lynn Ebsworth, who was to become Acting Director of Social Services for an interim period. But senior councillors cannot escape a share of the blame for failing either to insist upon full disclosure to at least some of them or to ensure that the policy issues were addressed, if any of them saw the full document. The result was that Dodd's position was confirmed and enhanced and that the organisational imbalance between Area staff and the residential care sector was permitted to worsen, with adverse impact on the children in residential care.

46.32 Another result of the failure to address the policy issues was that there was no adequate provision for independent monitoring and inspecting the community homes from then on throughout the 1980s. Whilst Parry and the Homes Officer, Elizabeth Hughes, had been regular visitors to these homes, Dodd became supreme when they had left and Gethin Evans' visits were infrequent. It was not until the 1990s that an independent inspection unit was established.

[14] See paras 35.08 to 35.12.

46.33 There was also a notable (although less startling) failure to respond adequately to the criticisms made by Welsh Office SWSOs in their report on 12 children in residential care in Gwynedd on 19 September 1988[15]. Part of the background to this was that there was still no effective strategy for residential child care in Gwynedd and the SWSOs had found that the children in Tŷ'r Felin and Queens Park were "interchangeable with reference to their ages and the kind of problems they presented"[16]. This was the situation despite further reports to the Children's Sub-Committee by Gethin Evans on 8 October 1985 and to the Llyn/Eryri Sub-Committee on 19 May 1988, purporting to follow up and re-state the principles outlined in his original 1982 strategy document. Nevertheless, the eight page response by Gethin Evans to the SWSOs' report, which was presented to the Social Services Committee on 5 September 1989, failed to address the problem of the use of the children's homes and other major problems highlighted in the report: the response was superficial and dismissive. The committee were told that the overall tenor of the report was generally positive and a tribute to the hard work done within the Homes and Area Offices; and the detailed criticisms made by the SWSOs were buried in defensive comment.

46.34 The following extract from the conclusions stated at the end of Gethin Evans' response illustrates the general limpness of the document:

"The department accepts the need to:–

    (a) Polish and refine its policy and practice (page 37 para 1)

    (b) To re-look at the way the department uses foster care and residential care (page 37 para 2)

    (c) Clarify objectives in all aspects of child care work so that there are clear and unequivocal statements of purpose and role (page 37 para 3)."

46.35 It appears that Gethin Evans himself disagreed with some of the criticisms in the SWSOs' report, which is not surprising, having regard to his own personal responsibility for children's services; but the Deputy Director of Social Services[17] conceded in cross-examination that Evans' response did not reflect the content of the report and he said that he did not agree with the response. However, both he and the Director, Lucille Hughes, left Gethin Evans to deal with the matter.

The lack of financial resources

46.36 For virtually the whole of the period under review local government expenditure was subject to increasingly strict central government control, backed by effective sanctions, and all the senior officers who gave evidence to the Tribunal stressed that children's services were handicapped by lack of

[15] See paras 33.52 to 33.55 and 46.10.
[16] See para 33.53.
[17] Glanville Owen.

financial resources. This can only be a comparatively minor explanation, however, of the failure of Gwynedd to make adequate provision for children in care for two main reasons.

46.37 The first of these reasons is that many of the failings stemmed from defects in the organisation of children's services and failures by the staff responsible for those services, as we have discussed in detail earlier in this report. The second is that it was Gwynedd County Council and, in particular, its Social Services Committee that was responsible for the low priority that was given to children's services in the allocation of priorities.

46.38 We have touched upon the latter subject earlier in discussing the role of the Chief Executive[18] but a broader account is necessary here. The evidence before us indicates that the allocation of expenditure to individual departments within the overall county budget remained substantially unchanged until the early 1990s, when Huw Thomas as Chief Executive introduced by stages the Audit Sub-Committee[19]. Until then it seems that cuts in expenditure were applied "across the board" as between departments because of the pervading federal culture and it was then left to individual departmental committees to decide how economies would be made. There was no effective mechanism to facilitate strategic planning or to enable the Council to re-consider priorities on a global basis. Moreover, there was no will on the part of councillors to achieve that objective because each department was regarded as a separate fiefdom. Thus, allocations between committees remained substantially unchanged from 1974 onwards, following broadly a pattern established by the three predecessor county councils.

46.39 It is questionable whether any substantial attempt was made at any time by the Social Services Committee to obtain an additional share of the overall county expenditure. The most prominent Chairman of that Committee during the period under review was Alwyn Roberts, who became Vice Principal of the University College of North Wales, Bangor and then in 1995 Pro Vice Chancellor of the re-named University of Wales, Bangor. He served on Gwynedd County Council for only seven years from 1974 to 1981, but he was Vice Chairman of the Social Services Committee for the first part of that period and then its Chairman from 1977 to 1981. His view generally, on the statistics available to him, was that expenditure in Gwynedd compared favourably with that of other Social Services Departments in rural Wales during his period on the County Council. In his oral evidence to the Tribunal he said that, at that time, decisions about competing claims for expenditure by the departments went to a small group of the Finance Committee, excluding Chairmen of the spending departmental committees. Budgets were built up on the basis of the previous year's expenditure, to which new committed growth was added, and the inner group then arbitrated between the departments in relation to the latter's lists of priorities. Roberts' contact was with the Chairman of the

[18] See paras 44.52, 44.53, 44.55, 44.59, 44.60.
[19] See para 44.60.

Finance Committee, who presided over this group, and he recollected two occasions in 1979 when increased allocations to the Social Services Department were obtained to improve the pay of residential staff.

46.40 Lucille Hughes' evidence was that there were many demands on Gwynedd's funds and that the social services were not a high priority, no matter how the Social Services Department tried over the years to turn them into a high priority. She added, "My ambition, when I became Director[20], was to have a really caring professional department giving a really high standard of service, second to none. I think we managed it by using resources and help from elsewhere in other sections of the clientele, but for the children I am afraid we failed".

46.41 We do not have sufficient statistical information to enable us to express a firm view about the level of expenditure by Gwynedd on social services during the period under review but we do have strong evidence to support Lucille Hughes' implicit opinion that the expenditure on children's services was inadequate. Lucille Hughes said that this imbalance was councillor driven and her view about this was supported by a member of the Social Services Committee and the Children's Sub-Committee, Harry Jones, who represented the Maesgeirchen Ward on the county council from 1979 to 1988. Gwynedd had an unusually high proportion of elderly residents and their needs were given priority. Opposition was particularly hostile to any proposed closure of a residential home for the elderly and when Lucille Hughes succeeded in gaining approval for one such closure, she was told by a number of councillors, "You will not do this again".

46.42 In this climate new additional expenditure by the Social Services Committee was mainly restricted to projects for which specific additional money was provided by central government, such as funding for mental handicap under the All Wales Strategy in the mid 1980s. As we have said earlier, the County Treasurer expressed some concern about the low expenditure on children's services in Gwynedd in 1983/1984[21] but his anxieties were allayed by the superficial explanation that the county's emphasis on fostering was reducing the cost of these services significantly[22]. The reality was that children's services in Gwynedd were seriously under-funded throughout the period of our review and that this was known to all the senior officers of the Social Services Department. Yet, such were the rigidity of the budgeting system and the commitment of councillors to services other than children's services, that Lucille Hughes conceded in evidence that she "did not make a huge fuss about it" during her long tenure as Director of Social Services.

46.43 Ten years after the County Treasurer had reported his concern, the District Audit Service presented a report to Gwynedd County Council entitled "Promoting the Well Being of Children and Young People", accompanying its

---

[20] On 1 October 1983.

[21] See para 44.55.

[22] 61.1 per cent of the children in care in Gwynedd were fostered/boarded out on 31 March 1983 as against 41.5 per cent for the whole of Wales.

audit of the Council's 1993/1994 accounts. The aim of the review on which the report was based was "to establish the extent to which children's services are being developed and managed by Gwynedd County Council in accordance with the Children Act and good practice guidelines". On the financial background, the report commented:

> "Children's services in Gwynedd receive fewer resources than in similar councils in other areas. This restricts the scope of services provided. Expenditure on children's services in Gwynedd is £29 per child under the age of 18. The average for similar councils is £40 per child. Budgeted expenditure for 1993/1994 was £1.8 million but it would be £2.4 million if Gwynedd spent the same as similar councils."

46.44 This under-funding had serious effects on the quality of care provided in many ways, some of which were reflected in contemporary reports. Inadequate staffing at headquarters; the use of Dodd in a dual role; acute shortages of field service staff; inadequate training opportunities, particularly for residential care staff; physical neglect of the community homes; economies even in food towards the end of the financial year: these were but some of the effects about which we have heard in the course of the evidence and they occurred despite the savings made by the closure eventually of all but three (and finally two) community homes. The lack of funding held back also the development of new services and affected individual children in care with special needs, whether educational or not. One boy, for example, was removed from his out of county placement with the Bryn Alyn Community after over five years there, without consultation with his Area Officer, and then placed at Tŷ'r Felin at the age of 15 years on the sole ground that his placement at Bryn Alyn did not justify the expenditure, despite the progress and the ties that he had made.

The input of councillors

46.45 Unhappily, the low financial priority given by councillors to children's services was part of a wider insensitivity to the needs of children in care. Two striking criticisms that we heard repeatedly were that attendance at meetings of the Children's Sub-Committee was almost invariably poor and that councillors persistently failed to fulfil their obligations to visit the community homes under a rota system despite repeated reminders and exhortations.

46.46 We have not heard any plausible excuses, or even mitigation, for these breaches of duty by councillors but a part explanation may be the geographical size of the county as a whole. In relation to visiting, it seems that the few councillors who did on occasions carry out their rota duties were uneasy about their roles and, particularly, about actual contact with the children in care; and their reports, usually mentioning only complaints by staff about housekeeping and maintenance matters, reflected their unease. By the late 1980s officers of the Social Services Department appear to have abandoned their fruitless attempts to persuade councillors to visit the homes but no alternative arrangement was found until an independent inspection unit was established in the 1990s.

46.47 There were one or two honourable exceptions to the general rule that councillors failed to fulfil their duty to visit the homes. Unfortunately, one of these, who made numerous visits to Tŷ'r Felin, in the final period before it closed, and some to the other homes in that period, misconceived her duties by visiting excessively and by acting as a disruptive influence, leading to critical comment in the report by O & K Associates dated 14 February 1995[23].

46.48 Apart from these specific individual failures by councillors to fulfil their obligations, there was a collective failure by the Children's Sub-Committee particularly to monitor and oversee adequately the provision of children's services. As the Dyfed team noted in 1981, the Sub-Committee relied far too often upon oral reports from attending officers; and the team recommended both that the Director of Social Services should attend Sub-Committee meetings and that written rather than oral reports should be presented at these meetings (after they had been approved by the Director), particularly when the reports dealt with major policy matters. One of the results of the non-disclosure of the Dyfed report was that these recommendations were ignored. Moreover, consequences of the reporting method were that councillors were unable to reflect upon issues in advance of a meeting and were likely to respond docilely to abbreviated oral summaries from which embarrassing detail had been omitted. Thus, the Children's Sub-Committee was not an effective monitor and its minutes disclose few examples of any thorough discussion of either principles or practice.

Conclusions

46.49 In this chapter we have sought to pinpoint the main relevant deficiencies in the quality of care provided by Gwynedd and the major contributory factors to those failures. Overall, we have been compelled to the conclusion that the County Council as a whole and its senior officers consigned children's services to a low place in its scale of priorities. A consequence of this was that children's services were chronically under-funded throughout the period under review. This was not the sole cause, however, of serious blemishes in the provision of child care. Another major factor was the authority's failure to establish, over many years, a fully effective senior management team. This was reflected in an inappropriate system of delegation of responsibility from the Social Services Committee downwards with the result that control rested in very few hands without adequate accompanying monitoring or accountability. Makeshift measures, such as the advancement of Dodd, were adopted, partly for financial reasons, and were then perpetuated; and informed criticism was suppressed or ignored. It was only under the impetus of the Children Act 1989 that important reforms began to be formulated and implemented; and responsibility was passed to the successor authorities before the reforms could be fully assessed.

---

[23] See paras 33.128 to 33.130.

PART XI

THE ROLE OF THE WELSH OFFICE

The position of the Welsh Office in the structure and its child care objectives

The establishment of the Welsh Office

47.01 The Welsh Office came into being in 1965, following the appointment in 1964 of the first Secretary of State for Wales, the Rt Hon James Griffiths, MP. Prior to that Welsh Affairs had been the responsibility from 1951 of successive Ministers for Welsh Affairs, who were members of the Cabinet but who held the Wales portfolio in addition to responsibility for another major Department of State. Thus, from 1951 to 1957, the Minister for Welsh Affairs was also the Home Secretary; and from 1957 to 1964 it was the Minister for Housing and Local Government who was also Minister for Welsh Affairs.

47.02 Although responsibility for health and welfare services was transferred to the Secretary of State for Wales on 1 April 1969, it was not until 1 January 1971 that responsibility for child care at central government level was transferred to him. Until the latter date the Home Secretary had borne the responsibility, giving general guidance with the assistance of an Advisory Council on Child Care. The transfer to the Welsh Office on 1 January 1971 included responsibility for the work of voluntary bodies in the field of child care and the employment of children of compulsory school age but it did not include responsibility for approved schools and remand homes, pending their integration under the system of community homes to be established under the Children and Young Persons Act 1969, or to youth treatment centres[1].

47.03 This transfer coincided with the commencement of the Act of 1969 and the disbandment of the former Children's Department of the Home Office; and from 1 January 1971 the former Home Office responsibilities for approved schools and remand homes and the new treatment centres together with responsibility for child care training were transferred to the Secretary of State for Social Services, heading the Department of Health and Social Security, which had been established on 1 November 1968, on the dissolution of the Ministry of Health and the Ministry of Social Security. In addition the Secretary of State for Social Services took over from the Home Office on 1 January 1971 responsibility in England alone for the child care functions and ancillary matters, referred to in the preceding paragraph, that in Wales were passed to the Welsh Office. The Home Secretary did, however, retain his responsibilities in respect of the functions of the courts, the police and the probation and after-care service in relation to children and young persons and the law on those matters. He remained for the time being responsible also for adoption, guardianship and legitimacy, pending the report of a Departmental Committee on Adoption.

---

[1] See section 64 and Part II of that Act.

47.04 Responsibility for the former approved schools and remand homes passed to the Welsh Office in 1973, by which time they had been assimilated into the community home system. The Secretary of State for Wales took over responsibility also for adoption services that year.

The administrative arrangements within the Welsh Office

47.05 It will have been understood from what we have already said in this chapter, that the Welsh Office was required to take over wide responsibilities in the child care field soon after it had been established as a Department of State and shortly before the period under review by this Tribunal began on 1 April 1974. At the same time the newly formed eight county councils in Wales were establishing their own service and administrative structures and policies. In particular, in the field with which we are concerned, these councils were required to implement the Local Authorities Social Services Act 1970, which provided the primary statutory code for the establishment and operation of local authority social services departments, combining responsibility for children, welfare and mental health.

47.06 It is unnecessary for the purposes of this report to go into great detail about the administrative arrangements made within the Welsh Office throughout the period under review. It is appropriate to emphasise, however, that, unlike the English Departments of State exercising parallel functions, the Welsh Office had a very wide range of responsibilities, covering almost the full spectrum of local authority services and some others; and they had limited staff with which to discharge those responsibilities. It was inevitable, therefore, that the Welsh Office would look, in particular, to the Department of Health and Social Security and the Department of Education and Science for leads in their respective fields of expertise.

47.07 In order to deal with its new responsibilities the Welsh Office set up a Community Health and Social Work Division, headed by an Assistant Secretary, within a larger Health and Social Work Group, led by an Under Secretary[2]. At the same time an integrated professional social work service was established at an address in Cathedral Road, Cardiff. This service was known as the Social Work Service and was directed by the Principal Social Work Service Officer. It comprised the former Home Office Children's Inspectors who had served Wales and the former Social Work Officers of the Welsh Office, forming a single group of SWSOs. Its role was said to be that envisaged by the Seebohm Committee for a body of the relevant central government department "to advise local authorities, to promote the achievement of aims and the maintenance of standards and to act as two way channels for information between central and local government"[3]. The remit of the Social Work Service was not, however, restricted to services for children because it was said to be "available to assist the Welsh Office, local authorities, hospital authorities and

---

[2] Welsh Office Circular 17/71 dated 3 February 1971.
[3] Report of The Committee on Local Authority and Allied Personal Social Services, Cmnd 3703, 1968, para 647(c).

voluntary bodies in Wales in all social work aspects of their functions"[4]. It was also to be available to the Department of Health and Social Security and the Home Office in relation to a limited number of relevant matters.

47.08 We can only give approximate numbers for the SWSOs forming the Social Work Service in Wales at its inception in 1971 but we were told that four were inherited from the Home Office. In the early 1970s there were 130 SWSOs in the Social Work Service for England and Wales, of whom 11 were serving in Wales. According to the detailed record from 1974 that was produced to us, there was a swift increase from a low of eight in 1974, of whom four were involved directly in services for children, to a peak of 18 in 1978 (including a Chief and two deputies) but the number reduced again and the usual establishment from 1982 onwards was ten or 11.

47.09 In 1985 the Social Work Service in England was re-designated as the Social Services Inspectorate and the Welsh Office followed suit, but not apparently until 1989, by re-naming its service the Social Services Inspectorate Wales (SSIW). This was said to be part of a policy of quality assurance and was intended to reflect the strengthening of commitment by the Welsh Office to providing independent mechanisms of such assurance. The intended role of the SSIW was described in this way:

> "The Social Services Inspectorate will continue, under existing statutory powers of the Secretary of State, to inspect personal social services. It is also proposed that it should play an important part in the Welsh Office's appraisal of authorities' social care plans. In addition, it is proposed that the SSI should advise and monitor the operation of the new registration and inspection units of the local authorities."[5]

47.10 Within the Welsh Office there was no separate Policy Division devoted solely to children's services. In 1974 a single Division was responsible for health and social services for the elderly, the physically handicapped, persons with mental disorder and children. This Division was one of four in a Group led by an Under Secretary. In a re-organisation in 1976 the Division's health responsibilities were transferred to another Division. The remaining part of the Division was re-named the Local Authority Social Services Division and it became responsible for all social services as well as the Welsh Office's dealings with the voluntary sector, but it stayed in the same Group as before. Its responsibilities continued to embrace the elderly, the physically handicapped and the mentally handicapped, persons suffering from mental illness and children. This structure remained in place for the next 11 years, except that the Division was re-named the Personal Social Services Division in 1985.

47.11 In 1987 more radical re-structuring took place. A Housing, Health and Social Services Policy Group was formed with three Divisions (1, 2 and 3), each responsible for aspects of Health and Social Services policy. Division 1's

---

[4] Welsh Office Circular 75/71 dated 19 May 1971.
[5] Caring for People, Cm 849, presented to Parliament in November 1989, para 11.43.

responsibilities initially were primary care, health promotion, public health and children but in 1991 its name was changed to Public Health and Family Division and its responsibilities were defined more extensively as:

> "Policy for health promotion, disease prevention, primary care and related services; Welsh Health Promotion Authority, drug misuse, tobacco, alcohol, prevention of HIV/AIDS and other infectious diseases, immunisation and vaccination programmes; child and family services, child health and child care, child protection and child abuse; maternity services, secure accommodation and intermediate treatment of offenders and adoption law."

47.12 Further changes occurred in 1994 and 1995 as part of a wider Departmental reorganisation. Responsibility for all health policy matters was merged with that for health management issues in the Welsh Office Health Department. The former Public Health and Family Division then became in 1994 the Child and Family Support Division; and it was merged in 1995 with another Division to become the Social Service Policy Division in the Local Government Group, under the present Permanent Under Secretary of State, who was then an Under Secretary[6]. Within the Social Services Policy Division, there was for the first time, from 1995, a Children and Families Unit[7] with responsibility for social services policy for children, young people and families; secure accommodation for young offenders; child protection; child abuse; and adoption law.

47.13 It will be seen from this brief account that there was relative stability in the organisational pattern for the first half of the period under review but that there was considerable upheaval in the second half with major changes on at least three occasions, that is, in 1987, 1991 and 1994/1995. These must have also involved changes of personnel. The Welsh Office was not able to give us accurate numbers of staff dealing with issues relating to children over the period, partly because, even at the time, work on children's matters was not separately quantified. However, John Lloyd, who was Director, Social Policy and Local Government Affairs within the Welsh Office from 1988, told us in evidence that there was a separate branch dealing with children in the Health and Social Services Policy Division from 1987. At first, the branch comprised a part-time Grade 7 with four support staff but this was increased progressively to the current complement of two Grade 7s and 11 support staff.

47.14 Devolution to Wales in education began in 1882 with the establishment of a Welsh Division of HM Inspectorate of Schools in England and Wales, which had itself been established in 1839. Then in 1907 the Welsh Department of the Board of Education was created, led by the first Chief Inspector of Schools in Wales, Sir Owen M Edwards. From 1907 to 1970, however, the Welsh Department of the Board of Education, including the Inspectorate in Wales, remained a branch of the central government's Education Ministry, which ultimately became the Department of Education and Science.

---

[6] J D Shortridge.
[7] See, however, the reference to a separate branch dealing with children in the next para.

47.15 In 1970 responsibility for the oversight of almost all educational matters in Wales was transferred to the Secretary of State for Wales. The Welsh Office Education Department (WOED) was established at the same time and the Inspectorate in Wales became part of it, although technically on loan to it until September 1992, when the Office of Her Majesty's Chief Inspector of Schools in Wales (OHMCI (Wales)) came into being as an independent, non-ministerial government department under powers conferred by the Education (Schools) Act 1992. The Department of Education and Science (now the Department for Education and Employment) retained responsibility for teachers' pay, conditions of service and superannuation throughout England and Wales and for the maintenance of "List 99", the list of persons considered unsuitable to be employed as teachers or as workers with children or young persons in schools or other educational settings.

47.16 The responsibilities of the WOED were extended to higher and further education in 1979 but its responsibilities for the education of children have remained largely unchanged since 1970. From 1979 the Department has had three Divisions, one of which dealt with schools, but this Schools Division was itself split in 1989 into a Schools Curriculum Division and a Schools Administration Division. The latter Division has a wide range of administrative and policy responsibilities, including general oversight of the provision of school education in Wales and of the implementation of government policies. It has a direct role in the administration of independent and grant maintained schools and other responsibilities include such matters as policy on the planning of school places, decisions on maintained school closures, school discipline, exclusions and provision for children with special educational needs. In 1997/1998 the Schools Administration Division had a staff of 30, of whom the equivalent of three full time staff had responsibility for SEN and independent schools.

47.17 The latest statistics provided for us by the OHMCI (Wales) show that in Wales there are about 2,000 LEA-maintained schools, of which 54 are special schools (40 per cent of which have residential provision). There are 17 grant-maintained schools and 62 independent schools. Ten of the independent schools cater wholly or mainly for pupils with special educational needs (SEN) and all but one of these ten are residential.

47.18 The statutory basis of the work of HMI from 1944 to 1992 was the Education Act 1944 and in 1974 its role was defined by the Welsh Office as undertaking "inspection of schools and education institutions other than universities, and advising local education authorities, governing bodies and teachers; advising the Secretary of State on educational matters in Wales". This role was restated in 1979 in slightly different terms but, more importantly, the Education (Schools) Act 1992 had major implications for HMI, as well as establishing the OHMCI. That Act imposed various duties and responsibilities on HMCI, as did other legislation in 1992 and 1993, but the relevant provisions were consolidated in the School Inspections Act 1996 whilst most other contemporary education legislation was consolidated in the Education Act 1996.

47.19 During the period under review by this Tribunal the number of HMI in Wales rose from about 47 to a peak of 59 in 1992. Following the establishment of the OHMCI (Wales), there was a rapid decline to 43 in 1996 and the latest figure that we have for the establishment (from 1 June 1997) is 35. Since 1993, however, OHMCI (Wales) has been funded to contract the inspection of individual schools to independent inspectors recruited and trained by OHMCI (Wales).

The Welsh Office's view of its role in respect of children's services

47.20 According to John Lloyd[8], the Welsh Office's main task in relation to children's services during the period under review by this Tribunal was to ensure effective implementation of legislation and develop good practice, jointly with developments in England. The statutory framework had placed the duty of caring for children on local authorities within a system subject to overall regulation and supervision by the Secretary of State, who had power to issue guidance to local authorities as well as to make statutory regulations. The emphasis of central government policy throughout the period, however, was upon giving local authority social service departments as wide a discretion as possible in the discharge of their statutory functions.

47.21 The Secretary of State's powers were eventually set out in Part XI of the Children Act 1989 but, in Lloyd's view, they were essentially the same throughout our relevant period. The main powers were:

(1) to make regulations amplifying the framework established by the primary legislation;

(2) to issue guidance to local authorities[9];

(3) to arrange inspections of children's homes and other premises in which children were accommodated;

(4) to register voluntary homes, to remove a voluntary home from the register and to close a community home;

(5) to provide grants for child care training, for local authority secure accommodation or for the provision and maintenance of homes for children who need special facilities;

(6) to require local authorities to submit returns;

(7) to undertake research;

(8) to cause inquiries to be held into some matters concerning children.

It was not until the National Health Service and Community Care Act 1990 was enacted that the Secretary of State was given general powers of direction in respect of local authority social services functions (by inserting a new section 7A into the Act of 1970).

---

[8] See para 47.13.
[9] See section 7 of the Local Authority Social Services Act 1970.

47.22　The list in the preceding paragraph does not include the powers and duties of the Secretary of State for Wales in relation to the registration and inspection of independent schools, including schools catering for children with special educational needs[10].

47.23　In the 1970s central government still intended to be involved in the planning and development of social services and to ensure that they were closely co-ordinated with health services. Thus, before local government reorganisation took effect, the Secretary of State for Wales called upon local authorities to submit ten year development plans for social services[11]. Authorities were provided with planning assumptions upon which they could assess their future needs, including those for children's services. The intention was that the resulting plans would provide the Welsh Office (and central government as a whole) with information on which to base national strategies and to make resource allocation decisions. An obvious absurdity about the timing of this, however, was that the first planning period was to run from 1 April 1973, a year before the changeover date, and that the plans would, therefore, be theoretical plans of the predecessor authorities, which had not been considered collectively by the shadow authorities, which did not come into being until that date. However, it was suggested that "authorities whose areas are to be joined following reorganisation should keep each other fully informed of their proposals and should seek to prepare plans which will reflect a joint approach to the development of Social Services in the new counties"[12]. Plans were to be submitted by 28 February 1973 and there was no requirement for up-dating but it was envisaged that a system of annual reviews would be developed.

47.24　In the event it was found that drawing up plans on a ten year basis was unrealistic and the requirement was changed from 1978 to one for three year plans, which were to be up-dated annually[13]. In the meantime, however, a standstill in local authority current expenditure had been called for by the Government in 1975[14]. Then, in 1979, the new Government announced its intention to "reduce substantially the number of bureaucratic controls over local government activities"[15]. The stated objective was to give local authorities more choice and flexibility and to allow them to become more efficient in their use of both money and manpower.

47.25　According to Lloyd, a new "climate of disengagement" was thus created in which the Government started to exercise more stringent control over the issue of circulars and papers to local government and reviewed the collection of local government statistical information. The Welsh Office continued to issue guidance on a number of matters in the 1980s, including the implementation of legislation, particularly the Children Acts 1975 and 1989 and the Adoption Act 1976, and collaborative arrangements for dealing with child abuse in

---

[10]　See Appendix 6, paras 36 to 42.

[11]　Welsh Office Circular 195/72.

[12]　Para 7 of the Circular.

[13]　Welsh Office Circular 99/77.

[14]　Welsh Office Circulars 142/75 and 228/75 and see the next section of this chapter.

[15]　Central Government Controls over Local Authorities (Cmnd 7634) presented to Parliament in September 1979, Department of the Environment, HMSO.

response to the findings of a number of public inquiries[16]. But Welsh Office circulars on the forward planning of social services were discontinued in 1987. We were not told expressly when the requirement of three year plans ended but the last circular on the subject was Welsh Office Circular 13/87 issued on 11 March 1987.

The Children's Regional Planning Committee for Wales

47.26   During the 1970s one particularly relevant aspect of forward planning, namely, for the provision of accommodation for children in the care of local authorities and for the equipment and maintenance of the accommodation, was undertaken by children's regional planning committees, established under Part II of the Children and Young Persons Act 1969. For this purpose Wales was designated as one region and the Children's Regional Planning Committee for Wales (CRPC) was established by the Welsh local authorities, pursuant to section 35(3) of the Act, in 1970 and then re-constructed, following local government reorganisation, on 31 May 1974. Welsh Office assessors attended its meetings as did an HMI from the WOED. SWSW also was invited to attend.

47.27   The CRPC employed no staff itself. Its principal professional social work adviser, secretary and treasurer were the appropriate chief officers of Mid Glamorgan, Clwyd and South Glamorgan County Councils respectively. The new staff engaged full time on CRPC functions were formally employed by Mid Glamorgan County Council.

47.28   The first regional plan had to be submitted to the Secretary of State for Wales by 31 December 1971. It had to contain proposals with regard to the nature and purpose of each community home for which it made provision; proposals were required also for the provision of facilities for observation of the physical and mental condition of children in care and for assessment of the most suitable accommodation and treatment for them[17]. The first plan was approved by the Secretary of State for Wales and came into effect on 1 April 1973.

47.29   The CRPC was also required to prepare an Intermediate Treatment Scheme for its region[18], that is, for community based schemes for the treatment of children who had committed offences rather than placement in residential institutions. The scheme came into operation on 30 January 1974.

47.30   The CRPC set up a number of Sub-Committees and Working Groups. The Community Homes Sub-Committee had responsibility for preparing the Regional Plan and dealt also with incidental matters such as capital buildings proposals and the Placement Information Liaison Service. Another Sub-Committee dealt with Intermediate Treatment similarly. There was a regional financial pooling arrangement and this was dealt with by the Finance and General Purposes Sub-Committee, which was advised by a Finance Working Group, comprised mainly of the County Treasurers.

---

[16] See eg "Working Together" Welsh Office Circular 26/88.
[17] Section 36 (4) of the Act of 1969.
[18] Section 19 of the Act of 1969.

47.31 The Placement Information Liaison Service was set up by the CRPC on 1 October 1975 and the Placement Information and Liaison Officer (PILO) was John Llewellyn Thomas[19], who began work four months earlier. The function of the PILO was not to make professional placement decisions but to provide a "clearing house" for vacancies and placements. He would record a considerable amount of information regarding each application and he circulated a monthly report to local authorities showing how the scheme was operating and the use being made of it.

47.32 There was a procedure also for monitoring placements out of Wales, which was agreed by the Regional Work Group, comprising all the Directors of Social Services of the Welsh County Councils.

47.33 In August 1977 the CRPCs in England and Wales were directed to submit revised regional plans by 1 April 1979. The new plans were to be in two sections, namely:

(1) a planning statement, to be revised at intervals of no more than three years, showing the situation of children in care of each local authority, the extent of available places, the assessment of need and the planning intentions, taking into account other facilities for children;

(2) a directory of residential accommodation for children in care in the region, including any firm planned provision for which government approval had been given, to be amended as changes occurred.

The revised Regional Plan for Wales came into operation on 1 April 1980, following approval by the Secretary of State.

47.34 This is not the place to give a full account of other aspects of the work of the CRPC for Wales during its comparatively short life. It must be said, however, that its working groups did visit some community homes in North Wales early on and that they concerned themselves with important matters such as assessment procedures, training and training facilities (noting the shortage of these in West and North Wales in 1975) and staffing.

47.35 The demise of the CRPCs appears to have been part of the development of the policy outlined in the 1979 White Paper[20]. Some criticisms had been made of them by the Association of Directors of Social Services, although Wales was excluded from the criticisms. More importantly, it was being asserted that local authorities had become self-sufficient in meeting residential needs for children in their care or nearly so. There was also increasing emphasis on placing children in community homes near their own homes and the use of boarding out/fostering instead of residential care had grown substantially.

47.36 The view of the Government was that section 4 of the Health and Social Services and Social Security Adjudications Act 1983 was in harmony with these changing circumstances. It abolished the statutory requirement for children's

---

[19] See para 28.25 for a summary of his career.
[20] See para 47.24.

regional planning and replaced it with a permissive power for local authorities to combine with others to meet their joint needs for new community homes[21]. The new statutory provision placed a duty on local authorities to make such arrangements as they thought appropriate for ensuring that community homes were available for children in their care and to widen the use to which community homes could be put to include use for children not in care but for whom local authorities had welfare responsibilities. It required local authorities also to place children in their care in accommodation near their homes.

47.37 Shortly before this, responsibility for producing Intermediate Treatment Schemes was transferred to local authorities, either on their own or in conjunction with other local authorities, with effect from 19 May 1983 under section 21 of the Criminal Justice Act 1982.

47.38 We were told that views were expressed in the Welsh Office questioning the advisability of abandoning the CRPC arrangements in Wales. This was not a matter to be decided by the Secretary of State, however, and in the absence of a statutory requirement for its activities the CRPC for Wales does not appear to have survived beyond the early months of 1984 (the PILO left in February 1984). Moreover, we have not received any evidence of combined local authority action to provide a new community home in Wales in the following years of the period under review.

The provision of financial resources

47.39 In the early years of the period under review local authorities continued to enjoy considerable discretion in their access to independent sources of revenue. Rates could be levied on residential and business premises at whatever level the authority considered appropriate. Central government made money available through rate support grant: the amount paid to each authority reflected its individual resource characteristics and a general view of its spending requirements and spending levels.

47.40 Following the announcement of the standstill in local government current expenditure in 1975, to which we have already referred[22], local authorities' sources of revenue and freedom to exploit them were increasingly constrained. A regime of penalties was introduced in 1980 and strengthened in 1982: grant monies were forfeited if individual authorities exceeded the level of expenditure the Government determined to be appropriate. In extreme cases "capping" was applied from 1985, a mechanism under which the Secretary of State could prescribe an authority's level of expenditure/rate level. Local authorities' ability to set the business rate in their area was removed in 1990 and replaced by the national non-domestic rate which is now set by central government and forms part of their grant distribution system.

---

[21] Replacing sections 31 to 34 of the Child Care Act 1980 with a new section 31 with effect from 1 January 1984.

[22] See para 47.24.

47.41 In Wales the current system, as explained to us by John Lloyd, is that the Secretary of State each year determines the amount that he considers it appropriate for local authorities to spend on revenue services (Total Standard Spending – TSS). This assessment is claimed to take account of the annual assessment of need to spend, including the effects of inflation and changes in responsibilities. The Secretary of State also takes a view of authorities' capacity for making savings and of what the country can afford.

47.42 Grant Related Expenditure Assessments (now Standard Spending Assessments) are the Government's assessment of an authority's relative need to spend within TSS. A specific amount for children's services is not identified in the SSAs for Wales, although it is in England. These assessments are the basis on which central government calculate their contribution in the form of Revenue Support Grant. The effect in 1997/1998 in Wales, according to Lloyd, was that central government support in the form of revenue support grant, national non-domestic rates and some specific grants represented approximately 88 per cent of TSS: the balance of 12 per cent was made up of council tax.

47.43 Figures produced by John Lloyd in his written evidence suggest that (at constant 1995/1996 prices) local authority expenditure in Wales on all local authority services remained very approximately level in the 1980s but rose by 13.5 per cent in the following five years (in terms of expenditure per 1,000 relevant population). Expenditure on personal social services in the 1980s on the same basis rose gradually by about 19 per cent. A very substantial increase then occurred, largely due to the progressive transfer of funds to local government to support its new responsibilities for the purchase of community care for the elderly and adults under the National Health Service and Community Care Act 1990.

47.44 Turning to child care, expenditure in Wales in the 1980s on all children in residential care or boarded out dipped in the mid 1980s but was about the same at the end of the decade as it had been at the beginning; and it rose by only 7.5 per cent in the following five years. Expenditure on residential care, however, dropped in real terms by about a third over the full 15 years, the steepest fall occurring in the early 1980s. Expenditure on boarding out/fostering in Wales, per 1,000 relevant population, almost quadrupled between 1979/1980 and 1994/1995, but the total cost of residential care for children still exceeded it by just over 25 per cent.

47.45 The figures for Clwyd in the same period, calculated again in terms of constant 1995/1996 prices, showed a substantial decline in expenditure on all local authority services, per 1,000 population, in the 1980s (18.4 per cent); and by 1994/1995 less than half of this "loss" had been recovered. In the same period the percentage of this expenditure directed to personal social services rose from seven to 20 but the major part of this increase (ten per cent) occurred in the five years to 1994/1995, reflecting the progressive transfer of community care funding to local government. Expenditure on residential care for children and boarding out/fostering rose by almost 30 per cent in the 1980s, despite dropping in the middle of the decade, and the rate was the same as for the whole of Wales in 1989/1990; but it then fell by 7.5 per cent in the following five years.

47.46 In Gwynedd expenditure on all local authority services per 1,000 population was appreciably higher (886 : 719) in 1979/1980 than the average for the whole of Wales, but it fell to a similar figure in the mid 1980s and ended the decade on about 3 per cent above the Welsh average. A major increase then occurred, raising it almost to its 1979/1980 level. Expenditure on personal social services increased slightly in the 1980s but doubled in the following five years, again largely as a result of the community care changes, both in real terms and as a percentage of its expenditure on all local authority services: the percentage in the end was the same as for Clwyd. Expenditure on residential care for children and boarding out/fostering was lower in Gwynedd, however, per 1,000 population, than in Clwyd and the whole of Wales throughout the whole period of 15 years. At its low point in 1984/1985 it was only half the figure for the whole of Wales. In 1989/1990 it was £24 against £40 for Clwyd and for the whole of Wales; and in 1994/1995, the comparable figures were £29 for Gwynedd against £37 for Clwyd and £43 for the whole of Wales. We do not place great emphasis on these figures because their reliability has not been tested before us and conditions across Wales varied considerably, but the general pattern is of interest and the figures do confirm that there was reason for concern about under-spending on children's services in Gwynedd over a long period.

The argument about the scope of the Welsh Office's duties

47.47 Major criticisms advanced to this Tribunal of the role played by the Welsh Office are that:

(a) it failed throughout the period under review to play a sufficiently interventionist part in the management and operation of county social services departments to ensure that appropriate standards were observed;

(b) as part of (a), it failed to plan the development of social services by setting clear aims and objectives and ensuring that they were understood;

(c) it failed to collect and disseminate adequate information about the services that were being provided on the one hand and the needs that ought to be met on the other;

(d) it failed to monitor adequately the performance of county social services departments in such a way as to promote the achievement of aims and the maintenance of standards;

(e) it failed to provide sufficient practical guidance to social services departments in a readily accessible form;

(f) it failed to provide adequate resources to enable those responsible in the Welsh Office itself and the county councils to discharge efficiently their respective wide and onerous duties in respect of children's services and, in particular, the protection of children in care.

47.48 These criticisms could be re-stated and elaborated in a variety of ways but we think that this list sufficiently indicates the broad spectrum of complaint about the Welsh Office's activities and alleged lack of activity during the period under review. Much of it is based on views about the overall practical effect of the recommendations made in the Seebohm report[23], on which much of the reorganisation of social services at the beginning of the 1970s was based.

47.49 Lady Scotland QC, on behalf of the Welsh Office, and Sir Louis Blom-Cooper QC, representing Voices from Care[24], submitted from their different standpoints that detailed criticisms of this kind are "fundamentally unsound" because they misinterpret the statutory functions of central government in the child care field. In effect, it is said, they elevate the philosophy and recommendations of the Seebohm report to an inappropriately exalted status, however meritorious the aspirations of that committee may have been. Seebohm was the guide but not the architect of the shape of social services over the following three decades.

47.50 According to this argument, the Children Act 1948, with its emphasis on "localism", foreshadowed the future of child care. It placed the duty on local authorities to provide a comprehensive service for the care of children deprived of the benefit of normal home life; a duty was imposed on local authorities to take those children into care who needed child care; a statutory preference for boarding out, rather than institutional care was declared; and local authorities were required to promote the best interests of the child and to provide them with the opportunity to develop their abilities. Although the Curtis Committee[25] had considered that central government ought to maintain standards and define the requirements of child care services through various powers, the Act of 1948 itself imposed upon central government a duty to give general guidance only: the exclusive responsibility for child care was placed upon local government rather than central government. The latter exercised control only indirectly, by financing local authorities and by its ability to influence policy and practice.

47.51 This remained the approach decreed by Parliament when the Local Authority Social Services Act 1970 was enacted. Section 7(1) of that Act, which remains in force, provides:

"Local authorities shall, in the exercise of their social services functions, including the exercise of any discretion conferred by any relevant enactment, act under the general guidance of the Secretary of State."

---

[23] Report of The Committee on Local Authority and Allied Personal Social Services (1968, Cmnd 3703).

[24] Formerly NAYPIC Cymru, an organisation for young people in Wales who are in care or who have left care but remain under local authority supervision.

[25] Report of the Care of Children Committee (1946, Cmnd 6922).

Thus, there is no duty upon the Secretary of State to give guidance; and a local authority is not bound to follow it in any particular circumstance[26], provided that it exercises its discretion properly.

47.52 It was not until 1 April 1991 that the Secretary of State was given power to issue directions to local authorities as to the exercise of their social services functions by the addition of a new section 7A to the Act of 1970[27], which provides:

> "(1) Without prejudice to section 7 of this Act, every local authority shall exercise their social services functions in accordance with such directions as may be given to them under this section by the Secretary of State.
>
> (2) Directions under this section -
>
>> (a) shall be given in writing; and
>>
>> (b) may be given to a particular authority, or authorities of a particular class, or to authorities generally."

Conclusions

47.53 We accept, in general terms, the (fuller) account of the legislative history on which the argument that we have just summarised is based but, in our judgment, it does not provide a complete answer to the criticisms of the Welsh Office formulated in paragraph 47.47. The Welsh Office forms part of central government and the latter cannot absolve itself of ultimate responsibility for the fate of children in care by referring to legislation that successive governments themselves initiated from time to time, whether or not with expert advice. Central government must bear responsibility for the arrangements that it makes, by legislation or otherwise, for a vulnerable section of the population placed in care under statutory provisions. It may be said also that this residual responsibility is particularly grave in respect of children, who are unlikely to be fully aware of their basic rights, within a system under which the High Court has only a very limited power to intervene because decision making has been vested by statute in local authorities, without any right of appeal[28].

47.54 It follows from what we have said that, in our judgment, central government could not shed or deny its responsibility for the general framework of arrangements for the care of the former children in North Wales with whom we are concerned, for the overall strategic planning of those arrangements, for monitoring them effectively and for informing itself about what was happening in practice. Even on the basis of John Lloyd's evidence[29], which did not go far enough, the Welsh Office's main task in relation to children's services was "to

---

[26] See De Falco v Crawley Borough Council (1980) QB 460; Laker Airways v Department of Trade (1977) QB 643; but see also R v Islington Borough Council, ex parte Rixon (1996) TLR 238.

[27] Section 50 of the National Health Service and Community Care Act 1990, brought into operation on 1 April 1991. The same section added section 7B to the Act of 1970, empowering the Secretary of State to order local authorities to establish complaints procedures. See also sections 7C and 7D dealing with the holding of inquiries and the Secretary of State's default powers, which were added at the same time.

[28] See A v Liverpool City Council (1982) AC 363.

[29] See paras 47.20 to 47.23.

ensure effective implementation of legislation and develop good practice", quite apart from the Secretary of State's powers later spelt out in Part XI of the Children Act 1989.

47.55 If further argument is needed to justify our conclusion, one has only to consider the flurry of central government activity and the major changes introduced at the end of the 1980s, with the enactment of the Children Act 1989 and the many new regulations made under it. Those events must rebut any suggestion that central government had neither the duty nor the power to act when it was thought to be appropriate to do so.

47.56 In considering the role played by the Welsh Office itself from 1974 onwards we have had very much in mind that it was new to child care responsibilities, as we have explained earlier in this chapter, and that it did not have the ultimate authority to decide what overall financial resources were allocated to it. Moreover, the evidence indicates that to a very large extent it followed the lead of the Department of Health and Social Security (later the Department of Health) in child care matters. These considerations cannot inhibit us from identifying what, in our judgment, went wrong during the period under review but we do not attempt to pin responsibility upon individuals for specific acts and omissions because it would be inappropriate to do so on the evidence before us, bearing in mind the very frequent changes in personnel and duties that occurred within the Welsh Office.

47.57 Three other general considerations need to be mentioned here. The first is that almost the whole of the sexual and physical abuse with which we have been concerned occurred in the period between 1974 and 1990 before the Children Act 1989 came into force. Secondly, it is clear that central government and local authorities did not have in mind that there was a significant possibility that children in residential care generally were being abused by staff until the second half of the 1980s. Moreover, on the basis of the evidence presented by the Welsh Office, it was not until September 1986 that the Welsh Office became aware, through an anonymous letter addressed to the Prime Minister, that there were allegations of mistreatment of children in social services establishments in Gwynedd; and it was in August 1990 that the Welsh Office was first told of alleged sexual abuse at Cartrefle in Clwyd[30], having heard before that only of an isolated case at Little Acton Assessment Centre in March 1978[31]. Thirdly, the evidence of the Inspectorates is that inspections are not a means by which either sexual or physical abuse is likely to be detected and the investigation of such abuse is not a purpose of them[32].

47.58 In our comments on the activities of the Welsh Office (and of central government) we do not forget that we have the obvious advantage of hindsight. Nevertheless, we have to consider why it was that widespread abuse occurred (and has been alleged to have occurred) within a comparatively short period

---

[30] See paras 15.05 to 15.18.
[31] See para 12.10.
[32] See paras 48.04, 48.05, 48.13 and also the comment of Sir William Utting quoted in para 48.29.

of 15 years or so following major reorganisation of local government and social services.

47.59 An inescapable conclusion must be that the scale of reorganisation at the beginning of the 1970s was too great in too short a time span. We have outlined in Chapter 3 of this report the legislative and administrative background to the period under review; and the Welsh Office's part in it is set out at the beginning of this chapter. Important consequences were that the Children's Department of the Home Office ceased to exist and that it was not replaced by any equivalent specialist section in the Welsh Office. At the same time local authority Children's Departments headed by a Children's Officer disappeared and the specialists within them were dispersed. The emphasis was on "generic" social work and the continuing need for specialists in the field of children's services was either overlooked or, at best, insufficiently heeded.

47.60 Defenders of the Seebohm report[33] will argue strenuously that this dissipation of expertise was not a necessary consequence of that Committee's recommendations[34]. The fact is, however, that it did occur and that it was aggravated by the radical reorganisation of local government that followed immediately after the creation of the new county Social Services Departments. At the same time effect had to be given to the many changes in responsibility for the residential care of children introduced by the Children and Young Persons Act 1969, most notably in the responsibility for the former approved schools and remand homes. The difficulties caused by the scale and timing of the changes were illustrated by the demand for ten year development plans addressed to the newly formed social services departments of obsolescent county councils before new shadow county councils were in place.

47.61 In the context of these changes we have been particularly dismayed by the absence of any clear guidance to either the old or the new county councils in relation to the conduct and management of the former approved schools. None of the relevant county councillors or officers had any experience of approved schools but Clwyd Social Services Department was required to take over responsibility (in effect, from the Home Office) for a substantial number of troubled boys at Bryn Estyn from all over Wales (and some from elsewhere); and the Department was expected to continue to run the home, with education on the premises, as a facility for the whole of Wales. In our judgment, the need for clear guidance and active development work to support Clwyd (and Denbighshire for a short period before that) ought clearly to have been foreseen. In their absence it was predictable that the Principal and staff would be left to decide the regime for themselves, despite the need for changes to adapt the former school to its new status and to meet the requirements of a wider range of children in care.

47.62 In the event Bryn Estyn became the worst centre of child abuse in North Wales over a period of ten years, undetected by outsiders; and it was closed shortly

---

[33] See footnote 23 to para 47.48.
[34] See, in particular, paras 161 to 164 of the Seebohm report.

after the demise of regional planning because of lack of demand for places rather than its own shortcomings.

47.63 A further compelling conclusion is that for over half the period under review children's services were given insufficient priority by central government and by the Welsh Office; and, in our judgment, it would not be an exaggeration to say that they were neglected. In the following two chapters of this report we look in detail at those activities of the Welsh Office that were specially relevant to residential care and boarding out, dealing with the Inspectorates in Chapter 48 and other activities in Chapter 49. It is necessary to stress here, however, the overall failure of the Welsh Office both to give an effective lead in the implementation of existing legislation and to inform itself adequately of what was happening on the ground, that is, in the individual county social services departments, in field social work practice and in the residential homes.

47.64 An illustration of the lack of leadership is the way in which forward planning was allowed to wither and die. It began inauspiciously with the demand for ten year plans from dying authorities and it appears that it became, at best, a flawed source of information rather than a coherent planning process with the result that it was abandoned in or about 1987. Rather similarly, regional planning was abandoned on the supposition that each county in Wales could provide for its own residential care needs but we have not been told of any audit by the Welsh Office to establish whether the overall provision of residential care was both adequate and available. Instead each county was left to pursue its own course in relation to residential care, despite their widely disparate needs, with the result that Gwynedd, for example, ended up with four homes that appeared to be indistinguishable in terms of their residents and purposes.

47.65 Another striking omission was the failure of central government to take any effective action before the Children Act 1989 to regulate private children's homes. Public concern about this matter was such that the Children's Homes Act 1982 was introduced as a Private Member's Bill. It made provision for the registration, regulation and inspection of private children's homes (including independent schools accommodating 50 children or less, if not approved under section 11(3)(a) of the Education Act 1981[35]); and it prohibited the placement by a local authority of a child in care in an unregistered private children's home. However, these provisions were never brought into force, in contrast to the provisions of the Registered Homes Act 1984 (governing private homes mainly for adults and elderly people), which were nearly all brought into effect on 1 January 1985. Instead, the provisions of the Act of 1982 were re-enacted, with some amendments, in the Children Act 1989 and did not come into effect until 14 October 1991.

47.66 Even more striking was the failure of central government to take steps to ensure that adequate facilities were made available for the training of residential child care workers. We deal with the training aspect of the Welsh Office's activities in Chapter 49, but its importance in relation to the quality of care provided in children's homes and the elimination of physical abuse cannot

---

[35] See Appendix 6, para 39.

be over-emphasised. Knowledge of the need for this training did not begin with reports such as that of the Wagner committee[36]. As long ago as 1967, the Williams report[37] recorded that the overwhelming majority of residential care staff were untrained (98 per cent in old people's homes and 82 per cent in children's homes).

47.67 Despite various initiatives and the very substantial decline in the number of children's homes, the position remained highly unsatisfactory in both England and Wales throughout the period under review. Sir William Utting reported in 1991[38] that only about 80 per cent of Officers-in-Charge of children's homes had a relevant professional qualification and about 44 per cent of assistant Officers-in-Charge. The percentage of other residential care staff in these homes with a professional qualification was 22. In Wales, in the same year, SSIW reported[39] a broadly similar picture: nearly three quarters of heads of children's homes and just over half of second tier managers had relevant social work qualifications; only a fifth of the other care staff were qualified.

47.68 A number of explanations have been advanced for the limited monitoring activities of the Welsh Office during the period under review. Thus, it was said by David Evans, the former Chief SWSO and then Chief SSIW, that frequent inspection of individual homes was thought to be inconsistent with the policy of the Local Authority Social Services Act 1970, which placed the responsibility for conduct of the homes upon local authorities together with a wide discretion. Limited resources within the Inspectorates and other Welsh Office departments was another explanation.

47.69 Commenting on SWSW inspection resources in the mid 1980s John Lloyd acknowledged that the level had been lower than senior officials "had felt comfortable with". In 1987 it had also been necessary to discontinue the previous arrangement under which individual inspectors had been assigned to maintain close liaison with particular social services departments. It was said also that the policy of "disengagement" was an additional reason for limiting monitoring activities in the interest of reducing bureaucracy. Yet another explanation was that emphasis was being placed on seeking alternatives to reception into care. These explanations do not, however, excuse the failure of the Welsh Office to acquaint itself adequately with the state of children's services in North Wales in order to ensure that the existing legislation was being effectively implemented and that children in care there were safe from harm in a wide sense.

47.70 Much of the relevant history of monitoring by the Welsh Office of Clwyd and Gwynedd Social Services Departments will be discussed in the next chapter of this report but its weakness is underlined by two specific examples that can usefully be referred to here. The first relates to Clwyd and Bryn Estyn, which

---

[36] Residential Care – A Positive Choice, 1988, HMSO.

[37] Caring for People – Staffing Residential Homes, 1967: the report of a committee of inquiry established by the National Council for Social Services and chaired by Lady Williams.

[38] Children in the Public Care, 1991, HMSO.

[39] Accommodating Children: a review of children's homes in Wales conducted by SSIW and Social Information Systems Ltd, November 1991.

was visited quite frequently by SWSOs, who gave priority to it as a former approved school that had previously been visited by Home Office inspectors. Despite the frequency of these visits, few significant improvements were made in the regime before it closed. An inspection of Bryn Estyn on 12 April 1978 revealed, according to the report, 28 incidents of absconding involving 27 boys in three months. David Evans said that this would have been discussed with Arnold but could not explain why the follow up letter to him of 20 April made no mention of it. We received no evidence that the matter was pursued in any other way. It is notable also that, when HMIs paid visits to Bryn Estyn at the instigation of the Parliamentary Under Secretary of State for Wales, they did not achieve the objective of securing effective involvement by Clwyd Education Authority in the provision of education at Bryn Estyn, despite its inadequacies[40].

47.71 The second example is provided by Gwynedd's record of expenditure on children's services. Despite the fact that, by 1984/1985, Gwynedd's rate of expenditure on residential care for children and boarding out/fostering was only half the comparable average rate of expenditure elsewhere in Wales, this disparity was never probed by the Welsh Office and was not investigated by SWSW. When an inspection did take place later (in 1988)[41], covering children in two of the four remaining community homes in Gwynedd, neither this disparity nor the complaints of Alison Taylor[42], of which the Welsh Office were aware, was within the scope of the inspection.

47.72 To sum up, in our judgment there were serious failings by the Welsh Office in providing the leadership, guidance and monitoring that were necessary to ensure effective implementation of the new legislation relating to children in care that came into force at the beginning of the 1970s and the development of good practice. At least some of those failings were attributable, in part, to wider government policies; and there were other aspects of personal social services policy, such as the All Wales Strategy for the Development of Services for Mentally Handicapped People, in which the Welsh Office gave a positive lead. For the future, however, the lesson must be that special attention will need to be given to the welfare of children in care in Wales by the Welsh Office and the Welsh Assembly[43] in the wake of further local government reorganisation; and the limited size and resources of the 22 new authorities will be important factors to be considered when a child care strategy is formulated.

---

[40] See paras 11.28 to 11.41.
[41] See paras 33.52 to 33.55 and 36.47.
[42] See paras 49.57 to 49.70.
[43] References to the Welsh Office (in the future) and to the Welsh Assembly are made in this report in this form for convenience. The full titles are the Wales Office and the National Assembly for Wales respectively.

The effectiveness of Welsh Office inspections

Introduction

48.01 In this chapter we deal with the work of two separate Inspectorates, namely:

(a) the Social Work Service for Wales (SWSW), employing SWSOs until it became belatedly the Social Services Inspectorate Wales (SSIW), staffed by SSIWs, in or about 1989[1];

(b) HMIs employed by the Welsh Office Education Department (WOED) until September 1992, when they became an independent body, OHMCI (Wales), under a Chief Inspector (HMCI)[2].

48.02 We heard oral evidence from David Evans, who became Chief SWSO in 1986 and then Chief SSIW on redesignation of the post. He provided also a voluminous statement about his Inspectorate's activities, extending to 325 pages (excluding annexes), which is so verbose that it has been difficult to extract relevant information from it. In that statement he said that a substantial shift of emphasis in the role of the Social Work Service occurred in the quarter of a century following its establishment on 1 January 1971. Evans said, in relation to its child care role, that it was established to provide professional advice on all aspects of child care policy and procedure. "The majority of its time was spent in dealing with queries about individual cases brought to the attention of the Welsh Office, studying reports on the role of local authorities and, in consultation with administrative colleagues, dealing with day to day work and longer term policy questions".

48.03 Evans stressed that SWSOs had no executive responsibility for children's services, either for policy or for practice. In his words they were "the Welsh Office's eyes and ears on local authority matters and the friends and advisers of local authorities". In relation to inspections the legal position was that section 58 of the Children and Young Persons Act 1969 (later section 74 of the Child Care Act 1980) conferred power upon the Secretary of State to "cause to be inspected" any premises at which one or more children in the care of a local authority were being accommodated and maintained as well as any community or voluntary home and premises at which one or more children were being boarded out or fostered, except premises (such as independent schools) subject to inspection by or under the authority of another government department. An inspector authorised by the Secretary of State to inspect a home or other premises under the section might inspect the children therein and make such examination into the state and management of the premises and the treatment of the children as he thought fit.

---

[1] See paras 47.07 to 47.09.
[2] See paras 47.15 to 47.19.

48.04 John Lloyd told us that in the earlier part of the period under review there was a heavier concentration in inspections on aspects such as the suitability of the fabric of the home rather than on case management issues. Later in his evidence he indicated that despite few references in inspection reports, it had become customary for inspectors to look at care plans and consult records in area offices.

48.05 The purpose of the inspection, as interpreted by SWSW, was described in Evans' statement as follows:

> "The emphasis and style of work involved building good networks and informal working relationships. As well as the supportive ethos which underpinned the relationship between central and local government, the small number of social services departments in Wales made it possible to develop a close working relationship between SWSW and the field authorities and frequent meetings were held at an all-Wales level between the Directors of Social Services and SWSW, which considered the development of services for children."[3]

48.06 The woolly description of the functions of SWSW given, for example, in an issues paper at the time of the Barclay report in 1982[4], which need not be quoted here, became more sharply focussed after it had been re-designated as the SSIW. The latter's Inspection Guide published in 1995, for example, defined the SSIW's objectives as:

> "● To provide Ministers and the Welsh Office with information about social services in Wales.
>
> ● To provide advice to enable the Welsh Office to develop policies which will lead to improvements in the quality, effectiveness and efficiency of the services and to enable the Department to carry out its statutory and other responsibilities relating to social services.
>
> ● To evaluate the effectiveness of social services in Wales and how well they work with other services.
>
> ● To promote improvements in the quality, effectiveness and efficiency of services amongst the agencies who provide services."

48.07 Part XI of the Children Act 1989 codified and extended a number of provisions governing the Secretary of State's supervisory functions and responsibilities, including financial support (amongst other things, for child care training), research and returns of information and default powers. Section 80 dealt with the inspection of children's homes: the powers of the Secretary of State to inspect premises where a child had been placed away from home were rationalised and extended, for example, to include placements for children under general health and welfare legislation and independent schools[5]; and powers to require information to be furnished and to inspect records were conferred.

---

[3] Para 3.3.10 of Evans' statement.

[4] Social Workers: Their Role and Tasks, published in May 1982 for the National Institute for Social Work.

[5] See also sections 85 to 87 of the Act and new sections 87A and 87B added from 1 January 1996 by the Deregulation and Contracting Out Act 1994.

48.08 Local authorities were directed by the Secretary of State to establish their own inspection units by April 1991 on the exercise of powers conferred by section 50 of the National Health Service and Community Care Act 1990[6].

48.09 The following table supplied by the Welsh Office indicates the relevant allocation of manpower resources within SWSW/SSIW during the last nine years of the period under review (the asterisk insertion is ours).

Allocation of Resources (SSI Equivalents)

Year	Children's Services	Services for adults	General Training/ Finance/ Research	Inspection*	All
1987/88	2.4	3.6	1.3	0.7	8
1988/89	2.5	6.0	1.0	1.5	11
1989/90	2.2	3.6	1.6	3.6	11
1990/91	2.4	4.1	2.3	2.2	11
1991/92	4.0	3.2	2.5	1.3	11
1992/93	3.0	4.0	1.6	2.4	11
1993/94	3.0	4.0	1.5	2.5	11
1994/95	1.7	2.2	1.5	4.4	11(sic)
1995/96	1.9	1.7	1.7	4.4	10

Note: Staffing figures include Chief Inspector & Deputies

*all services

48.10 We have given a brief account of the background and statutory basis of the work of HMIs in Wales in paragraphs 47.14 to 47.19 of this report. Prior to 1992 the statutory basis for inspections of educational establishments was contained in section 77 of the Education Act 1944, which required the Secretary of State to cause inspections to be made of primary, secondary, special and independent schools and certain other educational establishments. The inspections were to be at such intervals as appeared to the Minister to be appropriate and special inspections were to be made when the Minister considered them to be desirable. HMIs did not have any right to enter community homes, whether or not they provided education, because they were not within the definition of schools for the purposes of the Education Act 1944. However, very occasionally HMIs did join SWSOs/SSIWs at the latter's invitation in inspections of community homes such as Bryn Estyn in order to inspect the educational provision there. Similarly, SWSOs/SSIWs joined HMIs on some occasions in the inspection of residential schools.

---

[6] See footnote 27 to para 47.52.

48.11 Up to 1992 HMCI had no statutory powers apart from the inspection of schools by HMIs. The Education (Schools) Act 1992 gave the HMCI power to advise the Secretary of State on any matters connected with schools in Wales and to cause any school inspection (by Registered Inspectors and their teams from 1993) to be monitored by HMIs. Section 6(1) of the Act required HMCI to keep the Secretary of State informed about such matters as the quality of education provided by the schools, the educational standards achieved, the adequacy of their financial resources and various aspects of the development of the pupils. The Act also imposed other specific additional duties upon HMCI, including a duty to ensure that every school in Wales within the wide range of schools defined in section 9(2) was inspected on a five year cycle.

48.12 According to Susan Lewis, who has been HMCI in Wales since 1 June 1997, the purpose, aims and objectives of HMIs did not change significantly during the period under review, despite the legislative changes. Since September 1992 OHMCI (Wales) has defined its purpose as "to improve the quality of educational provision and the standards achieved by pupils and students". Its aims are:

"● to provide the Secretary of State for Wales, his officials and others with sound and timely information and advice, derived from inspection and reporting, on educational provisions, policies, trends or issues;

● to manage and monitor an efficient, effective and high quality system for the regular inspection of schools and of funded nursery provision;

● to raise awareness of the factors contributing to effectiveness and efficiency in education and thereby promote improvement in standards and quality at all levels of the system."

48.13 Lewis emphasised in her statement that HMIs were not, and are not, investigators; nor were they commissioned to enter schools in response to single-issue concerns such as an allegation of child abuse. In her view the responsibility and expertise for investigatory inspections rested with the local Social Services Department. HMIs would inquire into the arrangements made for pupils' welfare but much of this could only be done through indirect evidence such as policies, procedures and record-keeping.

48.14 The types of inspection have remained largely the same since the Act of 1992, as (in many aspects) have the principles and procedures guiding them, which are set out in a Handbook that is publicly available. The purposes of the inspections are said to be to assess quality and standards, to identify and disseminate good practice, to identify unsatisfactory/poor practice and bring it to the attention of those with responsibility for addressing it, to improve overall quality and standards and to enable HMI to advise the Secretary of State and others on the educational system.

The record of SWSW/SSIW inspections

48.15 The history of these inspections of local authority community homes conveniently divides into two because in or about 1985 there was a change of policy. In 1974 SWSW began to follow broadly, in relation to former approved schools, the earlier practice of Home Office Inspectors in making regular visits. Thus, Bryn Estyn was visited by SWSOs on no less than 18 occasions between May 1974 and July 1983; and 14 of these visits occurred prior to March 1979. In the same period of about nine years there were visits to two other community homes in the Wrexham area, namely, Little Acton Assessment Centre (seven, all but one before October 1976) and Bersham Hall (six, four of which were before March 1979). The only other inspections in Clwyd before 1985 were one of Cartrefle on 25 April 1977 and four of Tanllwyfan, an assisted community home with education, between September 1973 and April 1978.

48.16 In Gwynedd, there were four inspections of Tŷ'r Felin between July 1975 and November 1978 and one inspection of Y Gwyngyll on 9 October 1979, shortly after it opened as a community home. Tŷ'r Felin was also included in the agenda of a tour by a Minister, accompanied by an SWSO, on 4 July 1980.

48.17 The explanation for this unimpressive later record of inspections given by David Evans is that the "culture" of inspections inherited from the Home Office gradually changed. He said in his written statement[7]:

> "It began to appear increasingly out of step with our relationship with all other social services that these establishments in particular" (former approved schools and remand homes) "should be so closely monitored. They were no different in principle from any other local authority service and no less accountable to their controlling authority. And this pattern of inspection seemed also out of step with the new post-Seebohm relationship."

48.18 We have not been told who authorised the implementation of this change in inspectorial activity, but it appears that professionals working in the children's services in the early 1980s were dissatisfied with it. In an issues paper on the role of SWSW, drafted in 1984, Evans commented on the Barclay report in 1982[8] and the second report of the Select Committee on Social Services[9], both of which had favoured increased inspection to monitor practice in social work; but he was lukewarm and defensive about any extension of inspection, even though he recognised that it was likely to attract the strongest support from "those professionals working in the Children's Services". His account of the current position then was as follows:

> "In Wales, as in England, SWS has continued to exercise its inspectorial function mainly in relation to CHEs, secure accommodation and voluntary children's homes and, until the severe staff reduction in the last year, to a higher level than DHSS. It has not, however, been in a position

---

[7] Para 3.3.52.
[8] See footnote 4 to para 48.06.
[9] Session 1981/1982.

to review children's services provided as a whole by authorities, or those areas of services governed by regulations such as Boarding Out."

48.19 What eventually emerged was described as an "enhanced" inspection programme. In an explanatory internal departmental memorandum dated 17 January 1989 Evans said:

"The main features of the revised arrangements are:

(i) a detailed inspection programme together with related survey and development work is prepared annually for the forthcoming year and in outline for the subsequent two years. The draft programme is discussed with appropriate policy divisions in the light of their requirements for policy advice and with local authority social service departments in relation to the need to monitor the services they provide;

(ii) submitted formally to Ministers for approval;

(iii) submitted to the Welsh County Council's Committee (Social Services Sub-Committee) for consultation."

48.20 Although this memorandum was dated January 1989, the enhanced programme appears to have been started in 1987 and the memorandum referred to an increase in the time devoted to inspection work from 12 per cent of the Service's time in 1987/1988 to 25 per cent in 1989/1990. We have been supplied with what is called "Inspection Programme 1987–96"[10], which gives contrary (lower) figures for the number of SWSOs/SSIWs in post each year to those given in para 48.09. The list refers to the following inspections of aspects of children's services in North Wales:

1988/1990	Residential services for children in one county–Gwynedd[11].
1991/1992	A project in relation to child protection procedures in Clwyd was cancelled and one on fostering services in Gwynedd was postponed.
1992/1993	Children leaving care in Clwyd, Powys and South Glamorgan[12]. Children's services in Gwynedd, Dyfed and Mid Glamorgan.

In addition reports on the new county inspection units were published in 1992, 1994 and 1995. A table of inspections made between 1986 and 1996[13] suggests that there were three in Clwyd of, or related to, the client group "children" but the apparent discrepancy between it and Annex C is not explained.

---

[10] Annex C to Evans' statement.

[11] This was an examination of the care and careers of selected children in Tŷ'r Felin and Queens Park: see paras 33.52 to 33.55, 33.123, 33.125, 36.11, 36.12 and 36.48.

[12] See para 31.30.

[13] Annex D to Evans' statement.

48.21 Two further points need to be made about these later inspections. The first is that in the early months of 1994, in response to the Citizens Charter and following similar steps by the Department of Health, SSIW was divided into separate inspection and policy groups and lay people, including users and carers, were introduced into the process of inspection. A Deputy Chief Inspector was made responsible for inspection with four SSIWs as lead managers of inspection work; and thenceforth half of SSIW's time as a whole was to be dedicated to the inspection programme.

48.22 Secondly, from early in 1987 SSIW began to publish most of its reports. Before that there had been a division of opinion between those who regarded the reports as confidential, so that distribution of them should be limited to those "who needed to know", and others who thought that there should be greater openness, so that a wide range of persons with an interest might be informed and comment.

48.23 As we have indicated in paragraph 48.03, SWSW/SSIW had the power to inspect (but not otherwise to regulate) private residential establishments where children in care were accommodated under the Acts of 1969 and 1980; and section 80 of the Children Act 1989 rationalised and extended the list of premises that might be inspected, referring expressly to independent schools[14]. In relation to private establishments in Clwyd these powers were exercised almost wholly in relation to the Bryn Alyn Community and in conjunction with HMIs. Between 1975 and 1989 it seems that SWSOs visited the Bryn Alyn Community at approximately three year intervals and that there were at least three other visits in between (not less than nine in all)[15]. There was one visit also to Ystrad Hall School on 26 February 1975[16].

48.24 In Gwynedd the main focus of attention by SWSW/SSIW was upon Hengwrt Hall (later Aran Hall) School to which nine visits were paid between January 1986 and February 1996[17].

48.25 We have read a large number of the inspection reports prepared by SWSOs/SSIWs throughout the period under review on local authority and other establishments and on specific aspects of children's services in the second half of the period, and we have been provided with summaries of others. In general, we have been impressed by both the thoroughness and the high standards of these reports. What has emerged from the evidence before us and the reports themselves, however, is that SWSW/SSIW did not at any stage of the period under review provide an effective monitoring or supervisory service for residential care establishments for children in North Wales. Moreover, it was unlikely to play any significant role in the detection or elimination of physical or sexual abuse.

[14] See para 48.07.
[15] See references to some of these in paras 21.118 to 21.131.
[16] See para 22.29.
[17] See paras 38.31 to 38.33.

48.26 There were a number of reasons for this, some of which are quite obvious in the light of what we have already said. In the first place, although there has been some confusion about the number of officers/inspectors in post at any one time, it is clear that the establishment was insufficient to carry out regular inspections of the very many children's establishments requiring monitoring, quite apart from other social service establishments and services for children. Secondly, the small core of officers with Home Office experience of inspections of children's establishments dwindled rapidly. Thirdly, the view taken of the relationship between the Welsh Office and the county social services departments was such that the need for monitoring and inspection was not recognised by the Welsh Office until the second half of the 1980s; and the programme of inspection formulated then was directed, in general, to wider children's services issues than the standard of care in individual homes. Fourthly, awareness by central government and by social services professionals generally of the possibility of serious child abuse occurring in residential care establishments for children was a late development in the period under review.

48.27 Although there were apparently "numerous internal inquiries into the maltreatment of children in residential homes and schools in the years between 1945 and 1973"[18], and the Home Office register of offenders was established as early as 1952, it was not until the late 1980s that abuse of children being cared for in institutions became the subject of attention as the result of a series of reports of inquiries beginning with Leeways in 1985[19] and Kincora in 1986[20]. In June 1990 the Welsh Office issued a circular[21], to supplement advice and guidance in Working Together 1988[22], asking local authorities to review their policies and procedures relating to cases of actual or suspected abuse of a child within a residential school or other establishment accommodating children.

48.28 Even within the limited and vague purposes referred to in paragraph 48.05 above, however, there were deficiencies in the inspection system, particularly before the inspectors' reports began to be published in 1987. It was the practice of SWSOs to visit the Director of Social Services after inspecting a children's home to discuss their findings and any remedial action that they proposed to recommend. These were very informal meetings, however, and any follow up by SWSW to the recommendations was, at best, sporadic. Circulation of the reports was very limited and there were no guide lines for informing councillors, chief executives or even the relevant officers within the Social Services Department and the head of home. Thus, the dissemination of information about good practice was very uncertain and wider re-consideration of procedures was unlikely. It must be said also that SWSW/SSIW was rarely, if ever, informed of the results of other investigations

---

[18] Child Protection Practice, Private Risks and Public Remedies (1995) HMSO See Chapter 1, R Parker: A brief history of child protection.

[19] The Leeways Inquiry Report, London Borough of Lewisham.

[20] Report of the Committee of Inquiry into Children's Homes and Hostels, Belfast, HMSO.

[21] Welsh Office Circular 37/90: Child Protection.

[22] DHSS and Welsh Office, July 1988, HMSO: A guide to arrangements for inter agency co-operation for the protection of children from abuse.

commissioned by county social services departments, such as the Dyfed team inquiry into Y Gwyngyll[23], so that the two way exchange of information between central and local government envisaged by Seebohm was seriously flawed[24].

48.29   In his report "Children in the Public Care"[25], Sir William Utting described two types of inspection: regulatory inspections to check adherence to statute, regulations and guidance; and developmental inspections to provide empirical evidence against which progress in policy and practice can be monitored (the method now largely employed by SSI). He expressed the view that regulatory inspection less frequently than one substantial and one follow-up inspection each year is likely to be only marginally effective. He added:

> "Neither form of inspection is in any sense a substitute for the reasonable discharge of all the responsibilities of management. Both can assist management, applied separately or combined, by a dispassionate external scrutiny of the service (and, in the case of developmental work) by assisting in the preparation for future plans drawn up in accordance with national policies and standards. Neither can compensate for deficiencies of management: both provide additional safeguards for people living in residential homes; the best safeguard remains the commitment and competence of the body responsible for and the people running the home."

The record of HMI inspections

48.30   We can deal much more briefly with the inspections by HMI because they were directed, as we have explained, essentially to the educational provision at the establishments with which we are concerned.

48.31   In Clwyd, inspections by HMIs of local authority community homes and residential schools were confined to three at Bryn Estyn between 30 March 1976 and 12 June 1978, at approximately annual intervals[26]; and three visits to Ysgol Talfryn between 1988 and 1996[27]. There were visits also, however, to the Bryn Alyn Community and three other private residential schools. We are not sure that our records of the inspections of Bryn Alyn are complete but there were at least a dozen visits by HMIs between 1975 and June 1980; about half the number in the following ten years; and eight from December 1991, culminating in a full inspection from 28 to 31 October 1996[28]. Other inspections were of Ystrad Hall School (four, between 1974 and 1979[29]); Berwyn College for Girls (November 1984[30]); and Clwyd Hall School (four, between December 1977 and 1983[31]).

---

[23] See paras 35.08 to 35.12.
[24] See paras 47.07 and 49.85.
[25] Department of Health, 1991, HMSO: a review of residential care, at page 49.
[26] See paras 11.28 to 11.32.
[27] See paras 19.20 to 19.26.
[28] See paras 21.116 to 21.125.
[29] See paras 22.08 and 22.28 to 22.31.
[30] See paras 22.35, 22.37 and 22.38.
[31] See paras 23.08 to 23.14.

48.32 We have not been told of any visits by HMIs to local authority community homes in Gwynedd but they made numerous visits to Hengwrt Hall (later Aran Hall) School and to the Paul Hett establishments dealt with in Chapter 39 of this report. Between 1976 and 1996 there were not less than 15 visits to the former[32] and we calculate that HMIs visited the latter between March 1974 and November 1991 on about 20 occasions[33].

48.33 We have referred quite fully to the general purposes of inspections by HMI in paragraphs 48.13 and 48.14. However, the inspections of, and visits to, the establishments with which we have been concerned in Clwyd and Gwynedd were mainly occasioned by specific anxieties about the standard of education that was being provided. The visits to Bryn Estyn, for example, were made at the specific request of a Minister, who had expressed dissatisfaction with the use being made of the educational provision there[34]; and all the other visits were to residential schools catering, or intending to cater, for children with special needs but which had shortcomings that needed to be addressed.

48.34 We have no criticism to make of the assiduity of HMI in visiting and reporting upon these premises. On the contrary, we have been impressed by the frequency with which HMIs visited the private residential schools that we have discussed in detail in this report and the care with which their reports were prepared. The outcomes were less satisfactory but responsibility for this does not, in our view, rest with HMI. In the separate case of Bryn Estyn, a community home with education not within the definition of a school, Clwyd County Council was spurred to set up a working party to consider support by the Education Department to social service establishments providing education and the working party made helpful recommendations[35]; but it appears that few of them were implemented.

48.35 In the light of the accounts that we have given in Chapters 11, 21 to 23 and 38 and 39 of this report of the role played by HMI and the histories of Bersham Hall and Tŷ'r Felin[36], we consider that there were two main defects in the administrative arrangements during the period under review. The first was the exclusion of community homes with education from the requirements of inspection by HMI; and the second was that the arrangements for enforcing school closures on failure to remedy defects were too lax.

48.36 The first of these criticisms requires little elaboration in view of what we have said earlier in this report. The evidence indicates overwhelmingly that community homes with education were largely left to fend for themselves educationally, whether or not the local authority Education Department formally accepted responsibility for this part of the homes' activities. Individual teachers, often without any relevant previous experience, were left without guidance to deal with children of very disparate needs and there was

---

[32] See paras 38.31 to 38.35.
[33] See paras 39.18 to 39.40.
[34] See para 11.28.
[35] See para 11.32.
[36] See paras 13.67, 33.54 and 33.55.

no adequate monitoring of standards, despite the intention of SWSW to focus attention upon this type of home[37].

48.37 The second criticism draws together, in effect, what we have said earlier in Chapters 21 to 23, 38 and 39 about the outcomes of successive HMI inspections. We recognise fully the practical difficulties attendant upon the summary closure of a private residential school, affecting the proprietor, staff and pupils in varying degrees. But the delays in meeting their needs were crucial for the individual pupils affected, occurring as they did at times in the pupils' lives when opportunities lost were unlikely to recur. For them there was no time for prevarication or for vain hopes that adequate standards would be achieved eventually.

48.38 The opinion expressed by HMCI (Wales)[38] is that considerable improvements have been effected since 1992 in the follow up to inspections of schools that are judged to be unsatisfactory. She attributes these improvements to the Education (Schools) Act 1992 and the Education Act 1993. She describes the present position in this way:

> "Schools that have been judged to be failing and those judged to have significant shortcomings are monitored closely and regularly by HMI. The visits to them are included in the HMI Work Programme. They focus on the progress that the school is making in addressing the shortcomings identified by the inspection report. Of course, the visits can also identify new shortcomings. There is the usual feedback to the headteacher and, commonly, to the chair of the governing body or the proprietor, at the end of the day. The visits result in a NoV[39] and, in the case of failing schools, in a report to the Secretary of State. The NoV on independent schools are copied to WOED."

Nevertheless, in our judgment, the time scale of remedial action is all important and steely resolve on the part of WOED is necessary if paramount consideration is to be given to the best interests of the child.

Conclusions

48.39 To sum up, we have been impressed by the standard of reporting by SWSOs/SSIWs and by HMIs throughout the period under review but it is clear that neither form of inspection was designed to detect abuse of children in care and that the resources available to the Inspectorates were insufficient to enable them to provide regular monitoring of standards in individual residential establishments or to support the development of good practice. Such monitoring was only practicable in respect of private residential schools seeking general SEN approval, on which a disproportionate amount of time had to be expended.

[37] See para 48.18.
[38] See para 48.11.
[39] Note of Visit.

48.40 One of the results of the arrangements was that there was no adequate monitoring or inspection of community homes and similar residential establishments in Clwyd and Gwynedd until nearly the end of the period under review; and assessments of social services practice in the two counties were limited and sporadic. These deficiencies occurred despite the recognition from early in the 1980s by professionals that effective monitoring was needed. The "enhanced" inspection programme by SWSW from 1986 did not improve this situation significantly, although the surveys that ensued did provide helpful information on a limited number of practice matters.

48.41 There were also specific deficiencies in the monitoring and inspection of community homes with education because these homes were not defined as schools. The result was that they were not inspected by HMI, unless specifically asked to do so, even though SWSOs were not equipped to make expert assessments of the education provision. Thus, the overall regulatory and inspectorial systems that we have described were defective and the resources to support them inadequate.

48.42 Major lessons to be learnt are:

(a) the need for tighter and more continuous liaison between the two Inspectorates, particularly in relation to both private and local authority residential schools and children's homes that provide education on the premises, whether or not they are technically community homes with education or schools;

(b) the need to strengthen procedures for the follow up and dissemination of inspectors' reports and recommendations and to monitor the implementation of those procedures; and

(c) the importance of regular audits of field work practice to ensure compliance with statutory regulations.

In relation to (b), we regard it as very important that councillors and a wide range of relevant staff should be informed not only of the contents of the reports but also of the steps taken to implement recommendations.

Other relevant activities of the Welsh Office

Introduction

49.01 The evidence submitted to the Tribunal by the Welsh Office extends to several thousand pages and it covers a wide range of the Welsh Office's activities in relation to personal social services over the period of a quarter of a century on which it is neither necessary nor appropriate for us to comment. It must also be said that, within that evidence, in the field of children's services a high proportion of the material deals with recent activities, that is, in connection with the Children Act 1989 and since then. This disproportion was reflected in the final written submission of Counsel for the Welsh Office, of which not less than 81 (of 127) paragraphs were devoted to "Recent action by the Welsh Office".

49.02 The Tribunal itself is concerned essentially with the question "What went wrong in the period between 1974 and 1990, when the major abuse occurred?". Although sub-paragraph (d) of the terms of reference of our inquiry requires us to consider whether the relevant "caring agencies" are discharging their functions appropriately now, we take this to refer primarily (but not exclusively) to the successor local authorities. A review of national developments in law, procedure and practice since the abuse in North Wales occurred would be wholly impracticable for a Tribunal constituted, as we have been, with the major purpose of establishing disputed facts: neither our composition nor our method of investigation would be appropriate for a comprehensive audit of current practice and procedure and proposals for change that have been made even since the Tribunal was appointed.

49.03 When the setting up of this Tribunal was first announced the successor authorities had just taken over from the former two North Wales County Councils and, when our hearings ended, they had been in office for only two years. Moreover, before this inquiry was decided upon, Adrianne Jones had been appointed by the Secretary of State for Wales to undertake an examination of child care and other procedures related to the care and protection of children and the employment and management of staff in the Social Services Departments of Clwyd and Gwynedd and to assess the proposals for procedures and practice in the six successor authorities. Adrianne Jones submitted the report of her examination team in May 1996 and, since then, at the Tribunal's request, she has conducted an additional review, early in 1998, of the new authorities' current procedures and practice as disclosed in their evidence to the Tribunal. We shall refer later in this chapter to the Welsh Office's response to Adrianne Jones' report and in Chapter 54 to her evidence about her recent further review; but we emphasise that we do not attempt in this chapter to give a critical assessment of the Welsh Office's recent activities, except to the extent that they are directly relevant to our terms of reference.

49.04 The senior Welsh Office witness who dealt with policy, practice and procedures, John Lloyd[1], highlighted ten areas of its activities, namely, recruitment and staff selection; vetting; staff management; training; visiting; complaints procedures; control and discipline; regulation, registration and inspection; fostering; and the Adrianne Jones report. We have already dealt sufficiently with inspection and the associated topics of regulation and registration. Much of Lloyd's evidence on the other topics consisted of a recitation of the relevant legislation from time to time, which we have summarised in Appendix 6. However, we deal with these subjects in this chapter, adopting more helpful groupings.

49.05 The written evidence presented to us by David Evans, the former Chief SSWO/SSIW, dealt with historical matters that are covered, as far as is necessary, elsewhere in this report and with the history of inspections (including broader inspections of children's services), which we have outlined in the preceding chapter. In later sections of his statement, however, Evans went on to give an account of the allegations of abuse that had been brought to the attention of the Welsh Office, including the complaints made by Alison Taylor; and he referred to some training and development initiatives undertaken or sponsored by the Welsh Office and/or SSIW. We will deal also, therefore, with these subjects in this chapter.

Recruitment and management of staff

49.06 John Lloyd did not refer to any specific Welsh Office initiative in relation to the recruitment and selection of staff, which were the responsibility of local authorities and the voluntary and private organisations administering children's homes. The Community Homes Regulations 1972 did not lay down any requirements as to the manner of appointment of staff or as to their numbers and training. The Welsh Office guidance[2] did, however, stress the importance of appointing persons with suitable qualifications and experience and of taking up references with previous employers.

49.07 It cannot be said that the position has been significantly strengthened since then. Regulation 5 of the Community Homes Regulations 1991 provides that the responsible authority "shall ensure that the number of staff of each children's home and their experience and qualifications are adequate to ensure that the welfare of the children there is safeguarded and promoted at all times". However, the guidance issued under the Children Act 1989[3] makes it clear that it is for those responsible for running a children's home to decide what qualifications and experience are required for each post in it. It is said that, if the requirements cannot be achieved, the objectives of the home must be re-

---

[1] See para 47.13.
[2] Welsh Office Circular 64/72.
[3] Children Act 1989: Guidance and Regulations Vol 4.

considered or additional support provided from outside the home but, whilst opportunities for residential child care training remain scarce, this guidance is unlikely to be followed rigorously[4].

49.08 The practice of vetting by local authorities and other organisations for criminal convictions before making appointments to posts in residential care apparently dates back to 1964 when the Home Office issued a series of circulars addressed to local authorities, voluntary organisations and approved schools respectively[5]. The Home Office's Register of persons considered to be unsuitable for employment in community homes was transferred in 1971 to the Department of Health and Social Security, which continued to operate the service in Wales as well as England. The Department of Education and Science already had its own "List 99" by this time, covering teachers and others in education who were in regular contact with children and young people, and the service covered Wales similarly.

49.09 A joint review was carried out by the Home Office and the Department of Health in 1985 following a conviction for murder of a child. A Welsh Office Circular[6] followed the review and checking the possible criminal background of an applicant with local police forces was introduced. The procedures applied to local authority paid staff and volunteers engaged in the care of children and included registered childminders and foster parents.

49.10 Further circulars in 1988/1991[7] dealt with such matters as statements to be made by applicants on application forms and widening of the procedures to cover applicants for registration and managers of various types of home.

49.11 Although there has been much discussion of vetting procedures in the 1990s, a Home Office White Paper and several Welsh Office Circulars, the basic principles remained much the same during the period under review, save that the Voluntary Organisations Consultancy Service was added in 1994.

49.12 Guidance was issued by the Welsh Office in 1975, 1977, 1978 and 1994 on safeguards for children against offenders after their release from prison. This guidance dealt with arrangements for liaison between prison welfare officers and social services departments when relevant prisoners were due to be released and it was revised in 1994 to cover offenders irrespective of the location of their offences.

49.13 We have already drawn attention to the fact that it was not until June 1990 that the Welsh Office asked local authorities to review their policies and procedures in relation to actual or suspected child abuse to cover children accommodated in residential establishments such as a school[8]. This late response to the possibility of the abuse of such children is evidenced also by the absence of any

---

[4] See, however, the Code of Practice for the Employment of Residential Child Care Workers produced in 1995 by the Department of Health's Support Force for Children's Residential Care following the Warner report and see footnote 14 to para 49.18.

[5] Home Office Circulars 250/64, 251/64 and 252/64.

[6] Welsh Office Circular 28/86.

[7] Welsh Office Circulars 45/88 and 12/91.

[8] See para 48.27.

earlier reference to it in guidance on staff management or related topics. We find it surprising that complacency in this particular respect should have persisted so long, despite events that were occurring elsewhere and the concern, for example, that vetting procedures should be followed strictly in the recruitment of staff. However, even the Welsh Office Circular notifying local authorities and voluntary organisations of the coming into force of the Children's Homes (Control and Discipline) Regulations 1990 on 19 February 1990 was mainly in general terms. On the conduct of children's homes, it emphasised the need for "sound management, high standards of professional practice and care planning" and for "sound written policies for each home", but the possibility of abuse was not discussed.

49.14   Sir William Utting's report in 1991 of his review of residential child care in England[9] had sections on abuse by staff and abuse by residents. At paragraph 3.17 of that report he said:

> "However good the checks employed in the selection of staff there can be no guarantee that staff will not abuse children placed in their care. Consequently there must be management machinery in place which can detect abuse and be alert to the potential for abuse: for example, no child should be allowed to have an exclusive relationship with one member of staff. A climate needs to be created in which the possibility of abuse by staff is realistically acknowledged by children, staff, management and indeed the general public. Children must feel able to confide in trusted members of staff. Junior staff must feel able to report evidence which may implicate more senior staff."

49.15   At about the same time the Parliamentary Under-Secretary of State for Wales, Nicholas Bennett MP, instructed the SSIW to carry out a similar review of residential care in Wales, in the form of an audit of the quality of care being provided in Welsh children's homes. This followed the report of the Staffordshire "Pindown" inquiry[10] and allegations of abuse at Tŷ Mawr Community Home (a former approved school at Gilwern in Gwent) which were the subject of a separate inquiry[11]. The report of the SSIW review, entitled "Accommodating Children" was published by the Welsh Office in November 1991.

49.16   The authors of the report said that the review had not revealed examples of the causes of concern (abuse) that had given rise to it but that it had provided "the material on which to base an analysis of such incidents and to provide strategies for reducing their potential to a minimum". Their conclusion was that there was no evidence to suggest that sexual or systematic physical or emotional abuse occurred frequently in children's homes in Wales. In their view the risk of such abuse would be minimised by careful vetting of appointments, including the usual checks that we have already discussed, and

---

[9] Children in the Public Care, 1991, HMSO.

[10] The Pindown Experience and the Protection of Children: the Report of the Staffordshire Child Care Inquiry 1990 (Staffordshire County Council 1991).

[11] The Tŷ Mawr Community Home Inquiry 1992 by Gareth Williams QC (now Lord Williams of Mostyn) and John McCreadie.

by encouraging children and staff to talk to other staff, to line managers and other professionals inside and outside the home[12]. They added:

> "Because of its nature inspection, review, monitoring and spot checks are all equally ineffective as methods of finding or preventing" (abuse of this kind).

> "Attempts to ensure that this problem does not happen should certainly not drive the way we manage, monitor and inspect children's homes."[13]

49.17 The report made many critical findings and helpful recommendations, to some of which we will refer later in this chapter. It did not contain any separate section on staff management but it did refer specifically to the time spent by heads of homes and their deputies on managerial functions and commented later, "Management as a separate function with a different knowledge base from social work was not recognised by senior staff in the authorities as relevant to residential care".

49.18 According to John Lloyd, the Welsh Office, like the Department of Health, adopted the Warner recommendations[14] and they now set the standard for the recruitment and management of staff. The Welsh Office also accepted the recommendations of SSIW in the "Accommodating Children" report. Welsh Office Circular 34/93 set out a three year action plan for the implementation of the latter recommendations. A key element was the need for local authorities to establish, by the third year, an integrated plan for children's services, including the defined role of each children's home. A further circular, Welsh Office Circular 11/94, required production of Children's Service Plans by 31 March 1995, a year before local government reorganisation.

Control and discipline

49.19 We outline in Appendix 6 to this report, at paragraphs 21 to 24, the regulations that governed punishments in community homes, voluntary homes and private homes during the period under review.

49.20 Corporal punishment was not made unlawful in most homes until 1990, although it was outlawed in state-funded schools from 1987. It was abolished in community homes and voluntary homes by the Children's Homes (Control and Discipline) Regulations 1990, which came into force on 19 February 1990. In most private children's homes it remained lawful until Regulation 8 of the Children's Homes Regulations 1991 came into force on 14 October 1991. However, it had been prohibited in registered residential care homes[15] by the Residential Care Homes (Amendment) Regulations 1988, amending the 1984 Regulations made under the Registered Homes Act 1984.

---

[12] Cf Sir William Utting's comments on the same subject, quoted in para 49.14.

[13] Para 2.5 of the report.

[14] Choosing with Care: The report of the Committee of Inquiry into the Selection, Development and Management of Staff in Children's Homes, 1992, HMSO.

[15] See footnote 30 to para 49.44 for its limited application in relation to children.

49.21 The guidance given by the Welsh Office to local authorities on the subject of control and discipline prior to the coming into force of the Children Act 1989 had been contained in Welsh Office Circulars issued in 1972, 1988 and 1990[16]. The first of these was sent with the new Community Homes Regulations 1972. Unlike the earlier Administration of Homes Regulations 1951, which continued to apply to voluntary children's homes, the 1972 Regulations made no reference to corporal punishment. However, the memorandum of guidance with the 1972 Circular (applicable to community homes but not to voluntary children's homes or private homes) pointed out that it was for the responsible body to approve "such additional measures of control as may be necessary". On the subject of corporal punishment it said:

> "There has in recent years been a marked decline in the use of corporal punishment in all types of children's establishments including approved schools for boys (in approved schools for girls it has disappeared entirely) and it is hoped that this trend will continue. At the same time, however, it is recognised that it would be impracticable at this stage to prohibit the use of all forms of corporal punishment in every home. The regulations thus formally leave the matter to the discretion of the parties directly concerned. For all practical purposes, the use of corporal punishment will be confined to the circumstances envisaged in Regulation 10(2), that is, the measures and conditions under which they are employed must be approved in advance for each home by the local authority. . .who will thus be publicly accountable both for the measures approved by them and for the conditions of their use. It is hoped that they will authorise the use of corporal punishment sparingly and as a last resort and will consider at each annual review, in the light of experience, whether it is still needed."

49.22 In Welsh Office Circular 5/90 the statutory guidance given by the Secretary of State on permitted sanctions, again in respect of both community and voluntary children's homes, included the following:

> "It is recognised that some form of sanction will be necessary where there are instances of behaviour which would in any family or group environment reasonably be regarded as unacceptable. For example there is no intention to reduce the authority of staff in applying reasonable mealtime discipline or in the discretionary use of special treats. Where sanctions are felt to be necessary good professional practice indicates that these should be contemporaneous, relevant, and, above all, just. The responsible body should detail in writing the sanctions available to staff. . .Appropriate sanctions could be reparation, restitution, curtailment of leisure extras, additional house chores and use of increased supervision etc."

49.23 The 1990 regulations proscribed not only corporal punishment but also deprivation of food or drink, restriction or refusal of visits to and from parents or relatives (and certain other visits), requirements to wear distinctive or

---

[16] Welsh Office Circulars 64/72, 31/88 and 5/90.

inappropriate clothes and the use or withholding of medication or medical or dental treatments as punishments. Corporal punishment was not defined in the regulations but the guidance said that it should be taken to cover "any intentional application of force as punishment, including slapping, throwing missiles and rough handling". The guidance continued:

> "It does not prevent a person taking necessary physical action, where any other course of action would be likely to fail, to avert an immediate danger or personal injury to the child or another person or to avoid immediate danger to property. The use of 'holding' which is a commonly used, and often helpful, containing experience for a distressed child is not excluded. Intimate body searches of a teenager, as a punishment, after absconding, for example, would not be appropriate."

49.24 The provisions of the Children Act 1989 and the Children's Homes Regulations 1991 replaced these earlier regulations; the new provisions did not make any relevant change to the rules governing control and discipline in community and voluntary children's homes but the application of the rules was extended to private homes.

49.25 Further guidance on permissible forms of control in children's residential care was given by the Welsh Office in Circular 38/93 issued on 29 April 1993. This extended guidance given earlier in Volume 4 of the Children Act 1989 Guidance and Regulations: Residential Care. It stated that in recent years children placed in children's residential homes had tended to be older and more severely disturbed than their predecessors; and it was recognised that more positive advice about the control of often volatile young people was needed. Another major factor giving rise to the further guidance was said to be:

> "increasing concern by the Government and the wider public that we may have gone too far in stressing the rights of children at the expense of upholding the rights and responsibilities of parents and professionals in supervising them."

49.26 The guidance in 11 sections covered subjects such as the restriction of liberty, physical restraint, general principles governing interventions to maintain control, methods of care and control of children which fall short of physical restraint or the restriction of liberty, and training. On the subject of physical restraint it was stressed that staff should only use it if they had grounds for believing that immediate action was necessary to prevent injury or damage of specified kinds and should take steps in advance to avoid the necessity for it, if possible. It was stated further that only the minimum force necessary to prevent injury or damage should be applied and that the restraint should be an act of care and control, not punishment. The Welsh Office advised also that every effort should be made to secure the presence of other staff before applying restraint because they could act as assistants or witnesses.

Training

49.27 The non-departmental public body responsible for regulating and promoting social work training throughout the period under review was the Central Council for Education and Training in Social Work (CCETSW), established under section 11 of the Local Authority Social Services Act 1970. CCETSW assumed the functions of six bodies in all that had previously regulated different aspects of social work training, including the Council for Training in Social Work (CTSW) and the Central Training Council in Child Care. CCETSW inherited from CTSW the function of promoting training in social work by providing suitable facilities for training, approving suitable courses and attracting trainees; and the components of its function of promoting and developing training were re-stated in the Health and Social Services and Social Security Adjudications Act 1983. It is sponsored now by the Department of Health, the Scottish and Welsh Offices and the Department of Health and Social Services in Northern Ireland.

49.28 From its creation CCETSW became the awarding body of all the qualifications previously offered by its six predecessors. However, in the early 1970s these former qualifications were phased out and a single award for social workers, the Certificate of Qualification in Social Work (CQSW), was introduced. CCETSW introduced also an award for staff other than social workers, namely, the Certificate in Social Service (CSS). Then, in the late 1980s, these two awards were replaced by the Diploma in Social Work as a unified qualification. In 1987 CCETSW proposed that this new qualification should be based on a three year course (instead of two years for the CQSW). The annual additional cost would have been £40 million but the proposal was not accepted by the Government. The course was introduced as one of two years' study and supervised practice.

49.29 In addition, from 1975 onwards, CCETSW approved courses of post qualifying study and there were six such courses concerned with children's work. It was accredited to the National Council for Vocational Qualifications in 1989 as the awarding body in the care sector; and it now offers 46 vocational awards.

49.30 From September 1973 the cost of providing most training in local education authority colleges passed to local education authorities whereas the institutional costs of social work courses in universities were financed through the University Grants Committee. However, the student funding costs for post graduate students were met centrally by the Department of Health and Social Security, as it then was.

49.31 The Welsh Office acts as a sponsor in Wales of CCETSW and contributes to its funding, including its programmes; but CCETSW decides how to spend its resources.

49.32 The Seebohm report dealt with the questions of specialisation and training in particular kinds of social work[17]. The import of its discussion was that wider

---

[17] Report of The Committee on Local Authority and Allied Personal Social Services (1968, Cmnd 3703), see eg paras 524 to 527, 558 to 560 and its conclusions at paras 138, 140.

generic training was required and that specialisation would be necessary above the basic field level but that these specialisations would be likely to cluster differently from existing types of specialisation, with new types of specialisation emerging. At paragraph 527 the report stated:

> "There will undoubtedly be difficulties in the transitional period over welding numbers of specialist workers into members of a comprehensive single service. However, the kind of social worker we expect to emerge will be one who has had a generic training aimed at giving him competence, after experience, to cope with a whole range of special need, provided he has the support of adequate consultation and other resources."

49.33 A number of later reports of inquiries into child abuse cases noted the deficiency in child care training. Thus, the report into the case of Jasmine Beckford[18] concluded:

> "Social work training needs to produce a higher degree of proven competence in two ways:
>
> (a) in relation to particular "specialist" areas, like child care; and
>
> (b) in relation to the statutory duties imposed on social workers, in which the worker acts under mandate in a protective, inspectorial and controlling role."

49.34 CCETSW convened an expert group to draw up guidance on the qualifying training for residential child care workers and its report was published in the autumn of 1992. The report and a CCETSW guidance document on the knowledge and skills needed for work in residential child care were circulated to the bodies responsible for the Diploma in Social Work programmes.

49.35 Wagner (1988)[19], Pindown (1991)[20] and Warner (1992)[21] all emphasised the need for appropriate training of residential child care workers. Sir William Utting also[22] recommended that the Department of Health should give priority to residential care in its review of the adequacy of child care training and in its provision of grants. The Warner Committee considered that the range of knowledge and skills needed in residential child care could not be covered satisfactorily within the Diploma in Social Work course and recommended the introduction of a new Diploma as the professional qualification for staff working in residential child care. According to Lloyd, the recommendation "found almost no support from the field" and it was not accepted.

---

[18] A Child in Trust: The report of the panel of inquiry into the circumstances surrounding the death of Jasmine Beckford, 1985, London Borough of Brent.

[19] Residential Care—A Positive Choice, HMSO.

[20] See footnote 10 to para 49.15.

[21] See footnote 14 to para 49.18.

[22] See footnote 9 to para 49.14.

49.36 Financial support for training has been provided to local authorities in Wales by the Welsh Office since 1991 through the Training Support Programme (TSP), in which SSIW plays a leading role. TSP provides a 70 per cent contribution towards approved TSP-supported expenditure, local authorities being required to fund the balance. The annual grant covers all personal social services training and now exceeds £2 million. In the last two years of the period under review local authorities were required to pay special attention to the needs of staff in residential child care and this requirement continues. The Welsh Office requires that residential staff should receive "at least the share of training resources which their numbers in the workforce would suggest", according to David Evans, the former Chief Inspector, and this is checked before an application for grant is approved.

49.37 Welsh Office Circulars in 1993 and 1994 required local authorities also to complete an audit of staff skills and training together with a review of the numbers of staff employed in each home. This was to be the first stage of a three year action plan, in the second year of which plans were to be formulated to achieve correct staff numbers, to meet training needs and to prepare personal development contracts. These had reached only an early stage by 1996, however, and oversight of the implementation of the training recommendations in the Warner report is now being undertaken by the Adrianne Jones Report Implementation Group.

49.38 The problem of untrained residential care staff is unlikely to be solved by the provision of financial resources and opportunities for training alone. Whilst the status of residential child care work remains low, staff who gain a professional qualification will continue to seek transfer to broader social work and the turnover of staff, apart from this, will remain high. Sir William Utting found[23] that 43 per cent of the total care staff in children's homes in England had been in post for less than two years.

49.39 In his written evidence David Evans placed emphasis on what he described as the development and training activities of SWSW/SSIW during the period under review; and he annexed to his statement a summary of these activities headed "Development Programme 1970 to date". It does not, however, have much relevance to the issues with which we are concerned and the workshops and seminars to which he refers could not have had significant impact on practice in the residential care homes or in fostering. The list deals with the full range of personal social services and few (if any) of the workshops and seminars prior to 1988 were concerned with the treatment of children in care, except for a seminar on "Decisions in Child Care" in the period 1984/1986 and a workshop to "promote arrangements" for children in care in 1987/1988. The emphasis changed later to implementation of the Children Act 1989 and associated topics, including child protection generally, but the most relevant activity of SSIW was its participation in studies of such matters as secure care, outcomes for children leaving care, fostering services and of children's homes in Wales generally (for the Accommodating Children report).

---

[23] Children in the Public Care, Part 2 Appendix 6, 1991, HMSO.

Visiting

49.40 John Lloyd dealt with this subject in his written evidence but we do not know why he chose to highlight it because it is not an aspect of child care in respect of which the Welsh Office took any noteworthy action during the period under review. Lloyd recited the relevant provisions in successive regulations but made no comment on actual practice in Wales. The evidence before us does not suggest that the Welsh Office was aware of the failure of councillors, particularly in Gwynedd, to make rota visits to the community homes; nor is there any evidence that the problem of irregular visiting by field social workers was brought to its attention.

49.41 The Welsh Office did circulate to local authorities in 1984[24] a statutory code of guidance on access to children in care. This code had been prepared by the Secretaries of State for the Department of Health and Social Security and for Wales under the new section 12G of the Child Care Act 1980, inserted by Schedule 1, Part I, to the Health and Social Services and Social Security Adjudications Act 1983. The code itself contained wide guidance on matters such as the involvement, if possible, of parents in the admission process, the planning of access, inclusion of the wider family in the arrangements, the need to give due consideration to the child's wishes, the setting for visits and the procedures to be followed by managers of homes.

49.42 We have not heard any evidence about implementation of the provisions enabling independent visitors to children in care to be appointed when they had infrequent or no contact with their parents or guardians. The requirement upon local authorities to appoint such visitors in specified circumstances was contained in section 24(5) of the Children and Young Persons Act 1969, which was replaced by more elaborate provisions in the Children Act 1989[25] and the Definition of Independent Visitors (Children) Regulations 1991. The only comment made in Accommodating Children[26] about the actual practice of appointing such visitors in Wales was that "one authority had plans for an enhanced role for the independent visitor". Our firm impression is that little use was made of them. It is desirable, in our view, that the practice under the latest provisions should be assessed and that consideration should be given to revising the pre-conditions for appointing independent visitors, if it is thought that it would be beneficial to use them more widely[27].

Complaints procedures

49.43 The evidence indicates that neither the Department of Health nor the Welsh Office took any positive steps before 1989 to ensure that satisfactory complaints procedures were established in children's homes or for children in care who were boarded out. This broad statement is subject to the rider that a general code of practice called "Home Life" was circulated by both

---

[24] Welsh Office Circular 5/84.
[25] Schedule 2, para 17.
[26] See para 49.15. The comment is at para 8.1 of the report.
[27] For further comment on this, see para 54.18.

departments following the enactment of the Registered Homes Act 1984[28]. This code of practice, which had been prepared by a working party chaired by Kina, Lady Avebury[29], was distributed as guidance under section 7 of the Local Authority and Social Services Act 1970.

49.44 The relevance of this code of practice to children's homes was, however, very limited. It applied to private and voluntary residential care homes registered under the Act of 1984[30] but not to children's homes registered under the Child Care Act 1980, as amended in 1983. On the subject of children and young people, it said:

> "Most of the guidance in this code applicable to the care of adult residents applies also in relation to children. There are however emotional, psychological and developmental factors which are particular to child residents and which require different responses."

49.45 The section on children and young persons went on to deal with a number of specific matters relevant particularly to them, including planning goals, controls and sanctions and relationships with parents but said nothing about complaints procedures in the context of a child. The latter subject was dealt with in a section on general administration in the following terms:

> "Any infringement of this Code of Practice should normally be considered a legitimate cause for complaint. Other issues not covered in the Code may, of course, arise. All complaints should be treated seriously and recorded. They should never be dismissed automatically as without foundation because of the personal characteristics or mental capacity of the complainant. It follows that a resident should be able to bring complaints on any subject to the proprietor without fear of incurring disapproval, and if he is not satisfied with the outcome, he or someone on his behalf should be able to take the matter up with the registration authority."[31]

49.46 It is fair to say that this code of practice was never intended to meet the need for complaints procedures for children in care as a protection against the forms of abuse that we have had to consider in this report; and the accompanying Welsh Office Circular did not refer to the subject.

49.47 Section 26(3) of the Children Act 1989, which has been in force since 14 October 1991, was the first statutory provision to require local authorities to establish complaints procedures for children being looked after or in need, their parents, foster parents and other persons with a sufficient interest in such children's welfare. The procedures have to ensure that at least one person who

---

[28] Welsh Office Circular 40/84.

[29] The working party was appointed by the Centre for Policy on Ageing at the request of the Department of Health and Social Security and reported in 1983.

[30] "Any establishment which provides or is intended to provide, whether for reward or not, residential accommodation with both board and personal care for four or more persons in need of personal care by reason of old age, disablement, past or present dependence on alcohol or drugs or past or present mental disorder."

[31] Para 2.3.7.

is not a member or officer of the particular authority takes part in the consideration of any complaint and in any discussion held by the authority about any action to be taken in the light of that consideration.

49.48 The Representations Procedure (Children) Regulations 1991[32], which came into force the same day, make further detailed provisions about the procedure to be followed. They include requirements that representations received should be recorded and for an annual report on them to be prepared for monitoring purposes. The regulations apply also to voluntary organisations and to registered (private) children's homes; but independent schools and special schools not maintained out of public funds were exempted from the provisions from 1 January 1994[33].

49.49 Accommodating Children[34] noted the new statutory provisions, including those relating to independent visitors. By the date of its report[35] it seems that the introduction of formal complaints procedures by most local authorities was still at the planning stage. The children themselves knew little about formal or informal procedures for complaint. Some homes made a leaflet available; others provided a handbook; but a significant minority had no mechanism for informing children about complaints procedures. The authors of the report commented:

> "Children find it difficult to make complaints about staff. And staff find it difficult to deal with these complaints. Some staff told us how vulnerable they felt to malicious complaints. Each home needs to develop both informal and formal procedures to deal with complaints about staff. These must command the confidence of the children and the staff. Above all, the system must be able to deal with complaints against the head of the home."

49.50 The Warner Report in 1992[36] underlined the need for effective and robust complaints procedures and noted that inadequate procedures for complaints had been a common feature of children's homes prior to 1991. The Committee's recommendations included the provision of easily understood guidance, telephone helplines and an advocacy service, means for staff to be able to raise concerns outside the normal line management arrangements and widespread publicity for investigation procedures. It recommended also ways of improving the effectiveness of independent visitors. The Welsh Office asked local authorities to implement these recommendations by circulars issued in 1993 and 1994[37], the latter being in the form of statutory guidance.

---

[32] SI 1991/894.
[33] Regulation 11A inserted by SI 1993/3069, regulation 5; but the Children Act 1989 requirements do apply to some of them.
[34] See para 49.15 of this report and paras 8.1 to 8.3 and 14.1 to 14.4 of Accommodating Children.
[35] November 1991.
[36] See footnote 14 to para 49.18.
[37] Welsh Office Circulars 34/93 and 11/94.

49.51 Adrianne Jones' report[38] dealt with the progress made in Clwyd and Gwynedd in relation to complaints procedures by the time of re-organisation. She commented favourably on the steps taken in both counties to implement the new statutory provisions and added:

> "All the residential homes visited evidenced awareness of the complaints procedures and we were encouraged by the reference to this aspect of procedure and practice in all inspection reports. Foster carers in both Gwynedd and Clwyd had received clear information about complaints procedures and there is evidence on both file and in contact with foster carers that these were generally known.
>
> The understanding of parents and of those who had engaged with the complaints process was, inevitably, mixed. Some of the parents we interviewed in Gwynedd were vague on the procedure and its potential for use by them. In Clwyd, those whom we saw were clear that a procedure existed but less sure about the positive value, if any, of using it. Interestingly, one complainant viewed the benefit of being listened to and understood by the Complaints Officer as the only positive outcome. All felt that the system was bound to work in the favour of Council staff and were, therefore, cynical as to the benefit if it. However, all the parents considered that there should be a complaints system. Their view was for those servicing it to be more "independent" of the Council."[39]

Fostering

49.52 Appendix 6 to this report contains a summary of the successive Boarding Out Regulations governing both long term and short term placements during the period under review[40]. From the beginning of this period the statutory framework for the boarding out of children was provided by the Children Act 1948 and the Boarding Out of Children Regulations 1955. Moreover, boarding out was regarded as the preferred alternative to residential care for most children throughout the social services profession from 1948 onwards.

49.53 Guidance on this subject circulated by the Welsh Office during this period was directed mainly to practice matters. In 1976, for example, the Welsh Office distributed to all County Councils and relevant voluntary organisations what was, in effect, a code of fostering practice for social workers entitled "Foster Care—A Guide to Practice". This had been drawn up by the Working Party on Fostering Practice set up by the Secretary of State for Social Services in 1974. Similarly, a Handbook of Guidance was distributed before the Boarding Out of Children (Foster Placement) Regulations 1988 came into force on 1 June 1989; and comprehensive guidance was provided in Volume 3 (Family Placements) of the Children Act 1989 Guidance and Regulations.

---

[38] Report of the Examination Team on Child Care Procedures and Practice in North Wales, 1996, HMSO.
[39] Paras 6.18, 6.19 of the report.
[40] See paras 31 to 35.

49.54 Adrianne Jones[41] noted that, whereas in England and Wales as a whole, there had been no overall increase in the number of foster carers (despite the proportionate increase in foster care relative to residential care), there had been a real increase in both Clwyd and Gwynedd. Family placement had become not merely the placement of choice but, in practice, the placement in nearly all cases. Almost all young people in residential care had had a series of placements, including in many cases, several in foster care. Adrianne Jones commented that the use of foster care to a high level could hide considerable turbulence within the system that could impact adversely upon the lives of children and young people. She added:

> "It is not the fact of family placement, but the quality of that experience that is the key issue. All field social workers with whom we discussed this raised the problem of finding appropriate placements to meet the needs of individual children. They did not dispute that placements could be found, but instead took issue on occasions with their suitability either in terms of matching or geography."[42]

49.55 Amongst Adrianne Jones' recommendations were that:

(a) consideration should be given by the Welsh Office, in conjunction with the Department of Health, to establishing a review of the recruitment, selection and support of foster carers; and

(b) the Welsh Office should undertake an inspection of foster care services in the new unitary authorities of Gwynedd and Ynys Mon[43], in particular focussing upon the adequacy of resources allocated to support foster carers.

We were told by John Lloyd that (b) has been completed recently and that a report will be published.

49.56 The conviction of the foster carer Roger Saint in May 1997 for child abuse[44] gave rise to widespread concern. In consequence, the Children (Protection from Offenders) (Miscellaneous Amendments) Regulations 1997[45] were brought into force on 17 October 1997. They amended the Adoption Agencies Regulations 1983 and the Foster Placement (Children) Regulations 1991 in order to prohibit the approval by adoption agencies, local authorities or voluntary organisations of any person as a foster carer or adoptive parent where either that person or any adult member of the household is known to have been convicted of, or cautioned for, a specified offence (in relation to some offences the absolute prohibition only applies if the offender was 20 years old or more at the time of the offence). The regulations also require the relevant bodies (and managers of children's homes) to obtain information about any criminal convictions or cautions before an applicant is approved.

---

[41] See footnote 38 to para 49.51.
[42] See paras 4.102 and 4.103 of the report.
[43] Anglesey.
[44] See Chapter 25.
[45] SI 1997/2308.

The Welsh Office's responses to Alison Taylor

49.57　We have outlined in Chapter 2 of this report[46] the role played by Alison Taylor in the events leading up to this inquiry; and in Chapter 34 we dealt in greater detail with the history of her complaints whilst she was Officer-in-Charge of Tŷ Newydd between 1982 and 1987[47] that culminated in her suspension from duty at the end of 1986 and then her dismissal in November 1987. Her complaints to the Welsh Office began about the time of her suspension and continued until this inquiry was announced so that this part of her history conveniently supplements what has been said about her activities in Chapter 34.

49.58　The account given in his written statement by David Evans, the former Chief SWSO/SSIW, of Alison Taylor's representations to central government and other relevant persons and bodies between 1986 and 1996 extends to 44 pages, but only a brief summary is appropriate here. It seems that the Welsh Office first became aware of allegations of mistreatment of children in social services establishments in Gwynedd in September 1986 when an article appeared in the Daily Mail[48] referring to a police investigation into such allegations, and an anonymous letter from "concerned parents and residents in Gwynedd" addressed to the Prime Minister and mentioning the newspaper article was forwarded to the Welsh Office for attention. The first communication from Alison Taylor, however, which was also addressed to the Prime Minister and forwarded to the Welsh Office, was dated 2 December 1986, immediately after Taylor had been instructed to remain off duty[49]. Taylor enclosed with this letter a copy of a letter from her to the Commissioner for Local Administration in Wales bearing the same date.

49.59　By this time the initial police investigation by Detective Chief Superintendent Gwynne Owen of Taylor's allegations had been completed and both Bowen Rees, the Chief Executive of Gwynedd County Council, and the Chairman of the Social Services Committee had made statements to the press repudiating, in effect, Taylor's complaints.

49.60　Taylor's initial complaints were to the effect that she was being treated unjustly by Gwynedd County Council and that issues of public concern were not being investigated properly. The Commissioner for Local Administration, however, informed her that the matters that she had raised fell outside his jurisdiction. The Welsh Office wrote to her on 14 January 1987 stating that it could not intervene in matters that were for local determination and suggesting that she might wish to consider whether further action was necessary after the Social Services Department had "reported on her case".

49.61　It is clear from Evans' evidence that, in writing in those terms, the Welsh Office was substantially influenced by what it had been told by, or in the name of, the Director of Social Services for Gwynedd, Lucille Hughes. It had been told, for example, that Taylor was regarded as difficult to manage by the Social Services

---

[46] From para 2.08 onwards.
[47] From para 34.13 onwards.
[48] On 11 September 1986.
[49] See para 34.24.

Department of Gwynedd; that the outcome of the police investigation that she had initiated was that there was insufficient evidence to warrant criminal proceedings; that an internal inquiry by Gwynedd Social Services Department had also found nothing on which action could be taken; that the same department had taken the view that Taylor's behaviour had influenced "the breakdown in professional relations" and had adversely affected children in care and parents; and that the Director of Social Services was to submit a report to the Chief Executive and legal department of Gwynedd which would provide a basis on which to decide future action.

49.62 Contemporaneously at least two local Members of Parliament raised issues about the allegations investigated by the police with the Welsh Office and the Attorney-General. The Attorney-General considered the state of the evidence with the result that the police investigation was re-opened and further lines of enquiry were pursued until early in 1988. However, no prosecution ensued.

49.63 Following her initial rebuff, Alison Taylor persisted in her complaints to central government. Thus, she wrote again to the Prime Minister on 17 January and 3 March 1987, setting out a lengthy account of her history and her allegations of mistreatment of children in the first of these two letters. She wrote also at least two further letters to the Welsh Office directly. At the Welsh Office, the Minister of State, the Rt Hon Wyn Roberts MP (now Lord Roberts of Conwy), who happened also to be Taylor's constituency MP, dealt with the correspondence. After further internal discussion and consultation with Gwynedd Social Services Department, the Welsh Office sent replies that were again to the effect that it could not intervene in local matters of the kind that she had raised.

49.64 In the summer of 1987 Taylor invoked the assistance of the Children's Legal Centre and correspondence ensued between that Centre and the Department of Health and Social Security, although the latter had no jurisdiction in Wales. Taylor herself wrote also, in January 1988 to the Health Minister at the DHSS, referring to incidents of physical abuse that she and others had witnessed and making other allegations of misconduct by members of the Gwynedd staff. This letter was passed to the Welsh Office and appears to have been a factor in the decision to carry out an inspection or study of children in two community homes in Gwynedd later in 1988[50]. Taylor's complaints were not within the scope of the inspection, although she was eventually sent a copy of the inspectors' report on 19 June 1989.

49.65 In the following years, notwithstanding the successful outcome in August 1989 of her own proceedings against Gwynedd County Council for unfair dismissal[51], Alison Taylor continued to display remarkable tenacity in pressing for a fresh investigation of her allegations that children in care in Gwynedd had been abused. On 2 June 1991, for example, before the major police investigation had been initiated, she wrote very fully to the Secretary of State for Wales, presenting a complaint on behalf of a named child and listing 21

[50] See paras 33.52 to 33.55, 36.47 and 47.71.
[51] See para 34.26.

allegations; and copies of that letter were sent to the Prime Minister, the Secretary of State for Health and the junior Health Secretary, the Home Secretary, the Social Services Inspectorate of the Department of Health and to an MP and an MEP.

49.66 The reply, dated 12 July 1991, from the Minister of State for Wales on behalf of all the Government Ministers and officials to whom the letter of 2 June 1991 had been sent, stated that it must be concluded that allegations made prior to the police investigation and the SSIW inspection in 1988 had been properly investigated. Taylor was advised to consult her solicitor on how to proceed and was told to inform Gwynedd County Council of any new information and allegations of which she was aware. It was said also that the Minister would be pleased to pass on to officials copies of any documents relating to the period following the conclusion of the 1986/1988 police investigation.

49.67 The correspondence to which we have so far referred underlines the need for an independent agency to investigate complaints of the kind made by Taylor. However widely she spread her net, it was left to the Welsh Office to reply and the Welsh Office's response was invariably to the same effect, even though the mode of expressing it changed. It was unwilling to act in respect of "old" complaints and fresh complaints had to be addressed to Gwynedd County Council, despite the allegedly unsatisfactory manner in which the latter had dealt with the "old" complaints. It will no doubt be said that experience shows that a high percentage of persistent complainants who address their allegations to a range of government departments are eccentrics or persons with worn out axes to grind but not all are so, and severe recriminations are inevitable when it emerges in the end that the persistent complaints were well founded.

49.68 Quite apart from these general considerations, there is cause for grave disquiet about aspects of the correspondence that we have summarised. It was, of course, appropriate for the Welsh Office to consult Gwynedd Social Services Department about Taylor's allegations at the outset but we do not accept that it was right for the Welsh Office to accept so readily that she was a troublemaker, without any independent investigation of the background or circumstances. An enquiry of the police might have been fruitful, despite the views of the senior police officer conducting the investigation. It is perturbing also that Gwynedd alleged that it had conducted its own inquiry into the allegations but we have not received evidence of any process carried out that merits that description. It is also very unsatisfactory that it was wrongly suggested to Taylor that the 1988 inspection embraced the allegations that she put forward[52]. It is clear beyond argument from the evidence before us that the inspection did not do so and that the inspectors were only aware in a general way that there had been a police investigation of allegations of abuse made by Taylor.

49.69 This last point was taken up by solicitors acting for Taylor when they wrote to the Secretary of State for Wales on 24 March 1993 to express deep concern about the Welsh Office's continuing refusal to take action about her

---

[52] See para 49.64.

allegations. They pointed out that the inspectors' report of the 1988 inspection made no reference to the police investigation and that there was no basis on which the Minister should have been led to assume that the allegations made in Taylor's letter of 2 June 1991 had been properly investigated[53]. The solicitors' wide ranging letter accused the Welsh Office of persistently ignoring very serious allegations of child abuse and of failing to protect children in care: it alleged that the Welsh Office had been content to regard Alison Taylor as the source and extent of the problem.

49.70 It was not until three years later, following the further events that we have outlined in Chapter 2 and continuing pressure from Alison Taylor that a judicial inquiry was announced. The response of the Secretary of State in 1993 to the solicitors' letter was that any complaint about the police investigation should be pursued with the Chief Constable and, if necessary, the Home Office; and that complaints concerning Gwynedd County Council had to be taken up as a formal complaint, under the Children Act 1989, with that authority. Of the 1988 inspection, it was said that it was not an investigation but that, during the course of the inspection, the inspectors had held discussions with the youngsters in private in which they were given an opportunity to raise and discuss any issue in relation to the regimes and practices of the homes: no reference to abuse had emerged from those talks and, if it had, it would have been taken up "in the most appropriate manner with the relevant agency".

Other relevant information communicated to the Welsh Office

49.71 It appears from the evidence presented by the Welsh Office that they received only two "complaints" about relevant matters relating to local authority community homes in North Wales in the first 12 years of the period under review, that is, prior to September 1986.

49.72 The first of these related to the employment in 1976 at Tŷ'r Felin[54] of a gardener/handyman with a previous conviction for indecent exposure. The matter came to light when an applicant for another post recognised the man and mentioned his conviction. An SWSO was informed about this during a visit to Tŷ'r Felin on 18 March 1976 and it was not suggested that the man had committed any offence at Tŷ'r Felin. He resigned on 4 April 1976. A reference had been received from a former employer, the Warden of a charitable foundation, but no mention had been made of the conviction. Both the Director and Deputy Director of Social Services for Gwynedd were given appropriate guidance by SWSW about the need to follow the advice in Home Office Circular 250/64 about enquiries for information about potential employees and the need to report relevant incidents. It seems that the Deputy Director communicated with the charity and was assured that it would overhaul its procedure to prevent the repetition of such an omission.

---

[53] See paras 49.65 and 49.66.
[54] See Chapter 33.

49.73 The second "complaint" also came to light through a discussion with a responsible officer rather than through a communication from an abused person or a member of the general public. In March 1978 the Deputy Director of Social Services for Clwyd visited the Welsh Office for a general discussion with SWSW and disclosed the conviction of Leslie Wilson[55] when giving an account of the difficulties that had arisen at Little Acton Assessment Centre. On 16 March 1978 SWSW wrote to the Deputy Director enclosing a copy of Home Office Circular 250/64 and advising that Social Services Departments should (a) consult the DHSS register before appointing staff and (b) notify the Welsh Office of the particulars of any person who ceased to be employed by them on work connected with the care of children because of the commission of a criminal offence. There was some confusion subsequently because Clwyd supplied the particulars referred to in (b) to the DHSS and not to the Welsh Office; but it was agreed with the DHSS that the Welsh Office would be informed of all future notifications of convictions made to DHSS by Welsh local authorities.

49.74 It seems that the Welsh Office did not become aware of any other allegations of abuse in the Clwyd community homes until 1 August 1990, when the Director of Social Services for Clwyd wrote to the Chief Inspector of the SSIW advising him of the suspension of Stephen Norris on 18 June 1990[56]. Moreover, it was not until June 1991 that the Chief Inspector learnt from the Director, during a break in an SSIW meeting with Directors of Social Services, of allegations of abuse at Bryn Estyn.

49.75 The former Chief Inspector's account of SSIW's correspondence with Clwyd, mainly with the Director of Social Services, about Cartrefle, following the arrest of Stephen Norris, extends to 66 paragraphs and it makes dispiriting reading. From the outset in August 1990, the Chief Inspector pressed for "an internal management and ACPC review as under Part 9 of Working Together 1988". The Director, on the other hand, with the agreement of the County Council invited SSIW to carry out a full inspection of Cartrefle.

49.76 The correspondence continued for five years. SSIW refused to conduct an inspection and the Chief Inspector continued to urge a Part 9 review. The Director pointed out that there were four other matters, two involving foster parents, that merited consideration in a review of child care quality standards in Clwyd but the Chief Inspector recommended that it should be confined to incidents at Cartrefle.

49.77 Eventually, the initial review began in December 1990[57]. It comprised three reports by independent professionals, which were presented by June 1991; and these were then considered by an independent panel of five senior professionals, whose report was presented in February 1992.

[55] See para 12.10.
[56] See particularly, paras 15.05 to 15.18.
[57] See paras 15.42 and 32.24 to 32.34.

49.78 By the latter date events had moved on and the major police investigation into alleged abuse in children's homes in North Wales, particularly at Bryn Estyn, had been under weigh for several months. Moreover, both the chairman and another member of the independent panel had raised directly with SSIW concerns about the purpose of the review, its relationship to procedure under Part 9 of Working Together, the lapse of time since the incidents under investigation had occurred, how the panel should establish the facts and the desirability of publishing the panel's report. Furthermore, on 3 December 1991 the chairman of the panel had suggested to SSIW by telephone that, in view of recent events, it might be better to "ditch the report on Cartrefle" but the Chief Inspector had stressed the importance of finishing the work.

49.79 In the event the Chief Inspector did receive a copy of the panel's report for his personal attention only under cover of a letter from the Director of Social Services for Clwyd dated 4 September 1992. Then on 7 September 1992, the Parliamentary Secretary to the Welsh Office, Gwilym R Jones MP, stated that a public inquiry into allegations of abuse in North Wales would take place when the North Wales Police had completed their inquiries[58].

49.80 The panel's report was never published. The County Solicitor of Clwyd advised the Director of Social Services that it could not be published because (a) the relevant events had given rise to potential claims against the council, and that the Council's insurers were most anxious that the report should remain confidential and that any publication should not be construed as a waiver of public interest immunity; (b) the Crown Prosecution Service had vetoed publication because it might prejudice pending trials. However, on 6 January 1995 the Chief Inspector and the SSIW with responsibility for children and family matters met the Director of Social Services and members of the Social Services Department management team to discuss a series of issues raised by the panel's report and to identify matters that needed further attention, which were subsequently spelt out in a letter from the Chief Inspector to the Director dated 26 January 1995.

49.81 We have given a full account in paragraphs 32.35 to 32.63 of this report of the similar problems that arose in connection with the Jillings report. Following the initial intimation to the Chief Inspector by the Director of Social Services for Clwyd in June 1991 that there were allegations of abuse at Bryn Estyn, the Welsh Office was kept informed about the progress of the police investigations in Clwyd and then Gwynedd. The Chief Inspector was informed also on 12 January 1994 of the decision by Clwyd County Council to commission an internal inquiry[59] to find out what had gone wrong within its Social Services Department. The Welsh Office was subsequently involved in discussions with the Director of Social Services and the management team of the Social Services Department on 6 January 1995 and 25 July 1995 of issues arising out of the child abuse inquiries; but the Jillings inquiry does not appear to have been discussed at that stage. The Jillings report was not received by Clwyd County

---

[58] See para 2.36.
[59] See para 32.36 for the reasons for this decision.

Council until 22 February 1996 and it was in May 1996, after obtaining Treasury Counsel's advice, that the Welsh Office suggested that the County Council could publish an edited version of the report's recommendations[60].

49.82   In the course of the major police investigations and thereafter the Welsh Office became aware of four other cases of alleged abuse in what may be loosely called "the public sector" between July 1993 and March 1996: three of these related to children boarded out, the other to an employee at Gwynfa Residential Clinic, and all four cases have been dealt with in this report[61]. It is unnecessary, however, to elaborate the Welsh Office's late involvement in these cases.

49.83   In the private sector, the Welsh Office became aware from time to time from 1978 onwards of some allegations of abuse in residential establishments accommodating children. These involved the Bryn Alyn Community and Ystrad Hall in Clwyd, and Hengwrt Hall and the Paul Hett establishments in Gwynedd. We have dealt with the history of Welsh Office surveillance of each of these homes and schools in Chapters 21, 22, 38 and 39, however, and nothing need be added here.

49.84   The evidence discussed in this section confirms that, prior to the Cartrefle disclosure in June 1990, Alison Taylor was the only source of information to the Welsh Office about allegations of child abuse in local authority community homes in North Wales on any significant scale; and it appears that her allegations, from December 1986 onwards, were limited to Gwynedd until a much later stage.

49.85   David Evans referred more than once in his evidence to the importance of the SWSW/SSIW role as a two-way channel for information and consultation between central and local government[62]. It is regrettable to record, however, that the flow of information from both Clwyd and Gwynedd Social Services Departments was manifestly inadequate. Over and over again we were told that neither the Welsh Office administrators nor the Inspectorate was aware of inquiries held in particular homes: there was no notification of the holding of an inquiry, of the causes of concern that gave rise to it or of the outcome in the form of a report or recommendations. John Lloyd told the Tribunal that no specific indication was given to local authorities that they should send to the Welsh Office copies of reports of local authority internal inquiries. The belief of the Welsh Office that, in the light of the general spirit of co-operation with local authorities that it sought to foster, this would happen without an explicit request was plainly wrong. However, in respect of Alison Taylor, even when the Welsh Office was informed that an internal inquiry had taken place, no request was made for a copy of the report upon it[63]. In our judgment, therefore, it is clearly necessary that directions should be given to local authorities in Wales to ensure that the Welsh Office or the Welsh Assembly is in future supplied with details of all such inquiries together with copies of the reports upon them.

---

[60] See paras 32.51 and 32.52.
[61] See Chapters 25 and 41 and paras 20.18, 20.19 and 27.43 to 27.52.
[62] See the Seebohm report, footnote 17 to para 49.32, para 647 and Conclusion (190).
[63] See para 49.61.

49.86 The other point to be emphasised here is that the Welsh Office advice to the Director of Social Services for Clwyd about the nature of the inquiry that was necessary in the aftermath of the Cartrefle revelations was both confused and mistaken. The attempt to bring it within the procedure outlined in Part 9 of the 1988 edition of Working Together, which edition made no reference to abuse of children in a residential home,was misconceived and led to much confusion thereafter. Although the corresponding Part 8 of the 1991 edition of Working Together, under the Children Act 1989, does refer expressly to a child accommodated by a local authority in a residential setting or with foster carers[64], it is clear that the procedure is designed to deal with the case of an individual child who has been abused in a domestic setting. The urgency of action is stressed and the procedure is not appropriate for the independent investigation of wide ranging abuse in a children's home. In the result the procedure adopted was cumbersome, long drawn out and repetitive; and, although the analysis and recommendations, particularly those of John Banham, were excellent, the report was of limited benefit because it could not be published.

49.87 These events underline the need for clear guidelines to government departments and local authorities on the procedures to be followed when inquiries are deemed to be necessary into matters of public concern of this kind[65].

The response to the Adrianne Jones report[66]

49.88 Adrianne Jones made 41 recommendations in all for improvements in 11 areas of procedure and practice. Her terms of reference related to North Wales but the decision of the Welsh Office was to implement her recommendations throughout Wales. For this purpose a central development fund of £500,000 was allocated for the financial years 1996 to 1998, of which £440,000 has been made available to local authorities by means of a grant scheme.

49.89 The report itself was circulated to all local authority Chief Executives and Directors of Social Services in Wales on 4 July 1996 and was also drawn to the attention of health authorities. A schedule for implementation of the recommendations was enclosed and local authorities were asked for progress reports. A further circular was issued to local authorities in April 1997[67], informing them of the grant scheme and inviting each to submit plans for expenditure of up to £20,000 on one or more of six "themes", formulated in the light of the progress reports received and in consultation with the Child and Family Group of the Association of Directors of Social Services in Wales.

49.90 Those themes are:

(1) Reviews of inherited policies and procedures: defining and clarifying roles and responsibilities; and the development of new procedures, practice guidance and child care manuals.

---

[64] Para 8.1.
[65] See paras 32.61 to 32.63 for further discussion of this problem.
[66] See para 49.03.
[67] Welsh Office Circular 25/97.

(2) The implementation of the Warner recommendations[68].

(3) Department of Health "Looking after Children" materials[69] (for example, family and parental involvement in decision making; inter-agency working; involving education and/or health authorities).

(4) Planning, in particular, comprehensive placement strategies.

(5) Children's Rights (for example, involving young people in the planning, management and delivery of services).

(6) Complaints procedures.

49.91 An internal Welsh Office group, the Adrianne Jones Report Implementation Group, has been formed to spur, co-ordinate and monitor progress. According to John Lloyd, a key feature of the process is continuing dialogue with each local authority about its implementation of each recommendation.

Conclusions

49.92 Much of the material in this long chapter has been included because it is the Welsh Office's own account of its activities during the period under review. It confirms that, prior to the lead up to the Children Act 1989, the Welsh Office did not take any initiative of its own that was relevant to the possible occurrence generally of child abuse in either children's residential homes or foster homes. The few cases that came to its notice, mainly in private homes, were dealt with as isolated incidents and the Welsh Office limited itself to ensuring that appropriate disciplinary action was taken, including reporting to the relevant central authority. In relation to children's services generally the Welsh Office was content to follow the lead of the Department of Health and Social Security.

49.93 Alison Taylor's complaints to central government began at a time (December 1986) when it should have been becoming increasingly aware of the risk of abuse in children's homes, following reports about such homes as Leeways in 1985 and Kincora in 1986[70]. It is a matter for concern, therefore, that the response of the Welsh Office to Alison Taylor was so negative for at least five years until the major police investigation began. This negative response was reflected not only in the correspondence with her but also in the failure to ensure that the SSIWs who visited Gwynedd in 1988 were fully apprised of Taylor's allegations and required to consider any lessons to be drawn from them. It was reflected also in the failure to discuss the possibility of abuse in children's homes in the Welsh Office's guidance about control and discipline in 1990[71] and 1993[72].

---

[68] See footnote 4 to para 49.07.
[69] 1995, HMSO, following the report for the Department of Health of an independent working party on "Assessing Outcomes in Child Care", 1991, HMSO.
[70] See para 48.27.
[71] See paras 49.22 and 49.23.
[72] See paras 49.25 and 49.26.

49.94 It can fairly be said that, by the end of 1986, most of the major abuse that we have investigated had already occurred so that action by the Welsh Office then could not have prevented it. It must be added nevertheless that the response generally to the information available by the end of 1986 was lethargic, despite the gravity of the risk of abuse. It took over four years from then for the Government to take effective action, for example, to establish complaints procedures in community homes; and decisive action is still awaited in relation to the provision of residential child care training.

49.95 In the later part of the period under review children's services were given much greater attention by the Welsh Office, mainly in the implementation of the Children Act 1989. The findings of the Accommodating Children report were complacent in respect of the existence of child abuse in residential care but Part IV of the report emphasised the need for strategic planning based on an assessment of needs and the targeting of resources and for the development of a system of monitoring and evaluation. Moreover, the Adrianne Jones report has given further impetus to the planning process. We repeat[73], however, that further positive and firm leadership will be required from the Welsh Office and the Welsh Assembly if the safety of children in care in Wales is to be safeguarded adequately and the quality of care provided is to be improved.

---

[73] See para 47.72.

PART XII

THE POLICE INVESTIGATIONS IN CLWYD AND GWYNEDD

The general history of the police investigations and the nature of the criticisms

The North Wales Police

50.01 The North Wales Police assumed that title on 1 April 1974, the date when the new counties of Clwyd and Gwynedd came into existence. The force served the geographical areas of both the new counties as had its predecessor, the Gwynedd Police, which had been formed on 1 October 1967 by the merger of the former Flintshire, Denbighshire and Gwynedd Constabularies, the latter having been the police force for Caernarvonshire, Anglesey and Merionethshire.

50.02 The first Chief Constable of the North Wales Police was Sir Philip Myers, OBE, QPM, DL, who was brought up in Wrexham and who had been Deputy Chief Constable of the enlarged Gwynedd Police from 1968 to 1970 before becoming Chief Constable. He retired in 1982 to become one of HM Inspectors of Constabulary. Sir Philip was succeeded by David Owen CBE, QPM, who had been Chief Constable of Dorset from 1980 and who remained head of the North Wales Police until his retirement on 31 March 1994. Owen had had long experience in the Metropolitan Police, in which he had risen to Detective Chief Superintendent, and he had then served in senior positions in the Lincolnshire and Merseyside forces before his Dorset appointment. He served also as President of the Association of Chief Police Officers in 1990/1991. Owen's successor, Michael Argent, had a similar background to him and remains in office. After 25 years service in the Metropolitan Police, rising to Chief Superintendent, he became an Assistant Chief Constable in Merseyside for two years and then Deputy Chief Constable of Suffolk for a like period from 1992.

50.03 At the time of Owen's retirement there were 1,384 officers in the North Wales Police, of whom 120 were then in the CID.

Investigations 1974 to 1980

50.04 We have listed in paragraph 2.07(1) to (4) of this report five relevant convictions that occurred during this period, namely, those of Anthony David Taylor (Bryn Alyn, 1976), Leslie Wilson (Little Acton, 1977), Bryan Davies (Ystrad Hall, 1978), Gary Cooke and (Arthur) Graham Stevens (1980). There was also one other person, **Albert Frederick Tom Dyson,** then aged 40 years, who was convicted in 1980 of three offences of indecency against the boy identified as D in paragraphs 10.15 to 10.19 of this report, for which he was sentenced to 18 months' imprisonment. Dyson, who had befriended D's family, admitted to the Tribunal that he committed the offences at a time when D was in care and placed at Bryn Estyn, but he was not employed by Social Services at any time: he was then the owner of the 15/20 Club in Rhyl, which he disposed of in 1980, after owning it for 20 years.

50.05 In addition, the North Wales Police investigated allegations against a gardener/driver (Upper Downing, 1976)[1], Carl Evans (Little Acton, 1977)[2] and Paul Bicker Wilson (Bryn Estyn, 1977)[3], but no prosecution ensued at that time against any of these three men. According to the police evidence before us, there was also an investigation in 1980 of allegations against Huw Meurig Jones[4] but neither of the complainants in relation to that investigation (one is dead) gave evidence to the Tribunal and there was no prosecution.

50.06 We have not received any general criticism of these investigations by the police but it has been submitted that there was a paedophile ring in existence and that the investigations of Cooke, Stephens and Dyson[5] in 1980 should have gone further than they did. We deal with this subject in Chapter 52 of this report.

50.07 It has not been suggested that these ten investigations, all in Clwyd, were sufficient to trigger a wider investigation by the police of possible abuse of children in care in the county in the absence of other complaints brought to their attention. The allegations ought, however, to have given rise at least to anxiety in the Social Services Department and a corresponding determination to be vigilant. Unhappily, the climate of suppression was such that there was no general awareness of the potential problem and even co-operation with the police in cases such as that of Wilson seems to have been faint-hearted.

Investigations 1981 to 1989

50.08 During this period there were five further relevant convictions for sexual offences against children in care in Clwyd, as we have listed in paragraph 2.07(5) to (7) of this report. The five persons convicted were Iain Muir (Bryn Alyn, 1986), Jacqueline Elizabeth Thomas (Chevet Hey, 1986), David John Gillison (1987, a social worker who was not then employed in residential care)[6], William Gerry (1987, a former resident of Bryn Estyn) and Gary Cooke (1987, for further offences). It will be seen that only the first two of these were employed in children's residential establishments at the time when their offences were committed; and Thomas' conviction was for an offence against a 15 years old boy who was not in care at the time.

50.09 One other relevant person, namely, Huw Meurig Jones, was charged in 1981 with alleged sexual offences against a boy in care in Clwyd. Meurig Jones was then an unqualified social worker for Clwyd County Council but had not been employed in residential care in Clwyd, as far as we are aware, after March 1976[7]. He resigned on 28 July 1981 but it appears that the charges against him were not proceeded with.

---

[1] See paras 17.03 to 17.07.
[2] See paras 12.11 to 12.17.
[3] See paras 10.15 to 10.19.
[4] See paras 12.03, 12.29 to 12.35 and 14.05.
[5] We must record here that Dyson's evidence was that he first met Cooke in prison in 1980 and that we have not received any evidence that Dyson knew Stephens.
[6] See paras 14.32 to 14.40.
[7] See footnote 4 to para 50.05.

50.10 During this same period between 1981 and 1989 allegations against five other residential child care workers in Clwyd were investigated by the police but only one of the five was alleged to have committed sexual offences. The other four were Frederick Rutter (Bryn Estyn, 1983)[8], Paul Wilson (Chevet Hey, 1985)[9], Kenneth White junior (Bryn Alyn, 1988)[10] and Y (Ysgol Talfryn, 1989)[11]: each was alleged to have committed a physical assault or assaults on a boy in care but none of the four was prosecuted for reasons that have been stated in the cited passages of our report, where known to us.

50.11 The fifth person in Clwyd investigated by the police in this period but not prosecuted was David Evans, who was alleged to have indecently touched two girl residents at Park House in 1989[12]. In that case the Crown Prosecution Service advised that there was insufficient evidence to support a charge of indecent assault in respect of either girl.

50.12 Thus, 11 persons were investigated for alleged sexual or physical abuse in this period[13], of whom five were convicted. Of those investigated six were employed as residential care staff at the time of the alleged offences and one (Y) was employed as a teacher at a residential school.

50.13 Again, it must be said that we have not received any criticisms of these individual investigations, save for a submission that the further investigation of Gary Cooke (and possibly the investigations of Meurig Jones, Gillison and Gerry) should have been wider because of the alleged existence of a paedophile ring. As we have said earlier, we revert to this topic in Chapter 52.

50.14 Subject only to this point, the five proved cases of sexual abuse during this period did not, in our judgment, give rise to the need for a wider police investigation. The facts of the inter-linked cases of Gillison, Thomas and Gerry were, however, very perturbing and did call for an investigation in Clwyd on the lines directed by Mr Justice Mars-Jones. As we have said earlier, it is very regrettable that the response to this direction was both perfunctory and dilatory[14].

50.15 The first relevant police investigation in Gwynedd was into the alleged incident at Tŷ'r Felin on 24 May 1984 that we have related in paragraphs 33.102 and 33.103. The allegation, taken up by Alison Taylor, was that a boy, resident at Tŷ Newydd but who attended classes at Tŷ'r Felin, had been assaulted by John Roberts, who hit him, knocking his forehead against a desk. Roberts' evidence to the Tribunal was that he had asked the boy to sit down and put his hand on the boy's head, directing him towards his seat. We have not heard evidence as to who reported the matter to the police or the extent of the investigation by them. According to former Detective Chief Superintendent Robert Gwynne

---

[8] See paras 10.151 and 10.152.
[9] See paras 14.20 to 14.27.
[10] See para 21.99.
[11] See paras 19.08 to 19.15.
[12] See paras 17.43 and 17.88 to 17.91.
[13] See para 21.100 for one other investigation in 1989 of allegations at Bryn Alyn, of which we have not received direct evidence.
[14] See paras 32.18 to 32.21.

Owen, who was then head of the North Wales CID, the incident was not reported to the police until September 1984. There was then "an investigation by experienced officers, who, after consideration, decided that there should be no prosecution". The boy himself recollects making a statement to the police and thinks that Roberts was suspended from duty; but Roberts continued to teach at Tŷ'r Felin until July 1985.

50.16 It was in February 1986 that the first major police investigation into Alison Taylor's complaints began, following a meeting by Gwynne Owen with her and Councillor Marshall. According to Gwynne Owen, he had already instructed Detective Inspector Maldwyn Jones to investigate an allegation of unlawful sexual intercourse at Queens Park between a resident youth and a female social worker[15].

50.17 The course of this police investigation has already been outlined in paragraphs 2.12 to 2.15 and the history need not be repeated here. The first phase ended, subject only to minor further inquiries, in October 1986, when the initial decision not to prosecute anyone in respect of Alison Taylor's complaints was taken. It was then re-opened, in effect, because of fresh allegations against Nefyn Dodd by a former female resident of Tŷ'r Felin and the second phase of the investigation was not finally completed until April 1988, shortly before Gwynne Owen retired in July 1988, after 32 years police service.

50.18 This Gwynedd investigation has been heavily criticised and we discuss it in detail in the next chapter of this report. It is to be noted here that the initial decision not to prosecute anyone was closely followed by the decision of the Director of Social Services to suspend Alison Taylor from duty, purportedly for other reasons, on 1 December 1986. In the meantime Bowen Rees, the Chief Executive, had made an ill-considered statement to the press[16] about the effect of the decision not to prosecute. In this context there is a conflict of evidence between Gwynne Owen and the Director of Social Services, Lucille Hughes, about what he said to her at that time following his investigation, to which we will revert also in the next chapter.

50.19 There was one other investigation by the police in 1987 of an allegation of sexual abuse by a foster parent in Gwynedd but there was insufficient evidence to justify a prosecution and we are not aware of any criticism of that investigation[17]. It appears also that they were involved on a number of occasions in dealing with complaints at Paul Hett's establishments[18].

Investigations from 1990 to 1996

50.20 The first investigation in this period into sexual abuse in a children's home was into offences committed by Stephen Norris whilst Officer-in-Charge of Cartrefle[19]. The police were informed promptly on 17 June 1990 of the

---

[15] See paras 36.14 to 36.29.
[16] See para 2.14.
[17] See paras 42.21 to 42.23.
[18] See eg paras 39.44 and 39.56.
[19] See paras 15.07 to 15.09.

allegations that had been made by a boy to Henry Morton Stanley; and, in the course of the subsequent investigation led by Detective Inspector Donald Cronin, all ten current residents of Cartrefle, nine previous residents and 13 past and present members of the staff were interviewed. It revealed that six complainants alleged serious sexual abuse by Norris and on 5 October 1990, in the Crown Court at Chester, he pleaded guilty to five offences of indecent assault, involving three boy residents at Cartrefle. There were three other counts in the indictment against Norris involving the three other boys and an additional count alleging buggery with one of the first three boys but these were not proceeded with by the prosecution and not guilty verdicts were recorded by the Court in respect of three of them.

50.21 As appears from what we have said, the investigation of these offences was expeditious and the proceedings were completed in less than four months. The only criticism of the investigation of which we are aware is that it has been said that it should have been broadened to include Norris' previous activities at Bryn Estyn before his transfer to Cartrefle, having regard (amongst other things) to the repetitious nature of his sexual misconduct at Cartrefle. We consider this criticism in the next chapter of this report.

50.22 The other important police investigation before the county-wide investigation began was into the activities of Frederick Rutter as a foster parent and as Warden of a hostel at Connah's Quay[20]. This began on 3 April 1990 when a woman resident at the hostel complained to the police that Rutter had behaved improperly towards her and it culminated in his conviction on 30 July 1991, in the Crown Court at Chester, of four offences of rape and two offences of indecent assault involving three hostel residents and two girls who had lived in his household. We have not received any criticism of this investigation by the police.

50.23 The list before us of relevant police investigations is not comprehensive and it appears from the evidence that they were involved in at least one complaint of physical abuse at Gatewen Hall (Bryn Alyn Community) in 1990. They were involved also on many occasions towards the end of that year in resolving or investigating incidents arising at or stemming from Ysgol Hengwrt[21]. However, the next important event was the setting up of the major investigation into child abuse in Clwyd at the request of Clwyd County Council in July 1991. We have outlined the background to this request in paragraphs 2.22 and 2.23 of this report; and the investigation was broadened to include Gwynedd early in December 1991[22].

50.24 The Senior Investigating Officer in Charge of this investigation was Detective Superintendent Peter Ackerley, who became Detective Superintendent (Crime Operations) on 23 August 1991 and who was in his 21st year of police service. He remained in charge throughout but in August 1993, by which time the main part of the investigation was nearing completion, it was decided that there

---

[20] See para 2.07(8) and Chapter 26.
[21] See para 39.38.
[22] See para 2.24.

should be a reduction in the resources devoted to the inquiry and that Detective Inspector John Rowlands should take over the lead role under the supervision of Ackerley, who then resumed his general duties as Detective Superintendent (Crime Operations).

50.25 By December 1996 it is estimated that 3,860 statements had been obtained by the police from 2,719 witnesses (by September 1993, about 3,500 statements from 2,500 witnesses). Of these 2,719 witnesses about 1,700 had formerly been resident in children's homes in North Wales as children in care. About 500 of them alleged that they had themselves been subjected to sexual or physical abuse whilst in residential care at the hands of care workers or social workers (156 alleged sexual abuse). The remaining 1,200 former residents in care were either entirely 'negative' in relation to abuse or gave evidence or information about events or offences involving others. Many had been resident in more than one establishment and more than 36 establishments within North Wales were mentioned, excluding foster homes.

50.26 Allegations of varying strength against approximately 365 individuals were referred to the Crown Prosecution Service for decision. Some of them were the subject of more than one referral and police officers interviewed approximately 160 "suspects" under caution.

50.27 In the event eight persons were prosecuted, of whom six were convicted, as we have listed in paragraph 2.35 of this report. The two acquitted were the foster parent, Evelyn May Roberts and the residential care officer, David Gwyn Birch. The main culprits were Stephen Roderick Norris (for the second time), Peter Norman Howarth and John Ernest Allen, who were all convicted of grave sexual offences. The only person convicted of physical assaults in a community home, on his own pleas of guilty, was Paul Bicker Wilson.

50.28 There have been comparatively few criticisms of this major police investigation but we deal with them in the next chapter of this report.

Investigations from 1997 to date

50.29 Since the hearings by the Tribunal began in Janaury 1997 investigations by the police have continued and some of them have arisen from statements made to the Tribunal in connection with our inquiry. We have been kept informed by the North Wales Police in general terms of the progress of these inquiries. In order to avoid prejudicing the investigations we adopted the general policy that we would not hear evidence in support of complaints that were still under investigation by the police at the time when the evidence would otherwise have been heard by us. We regret that, to that extent, our investigation has been necessarily incomplete. We are satisfied, however, that the general accuracy of the history that we have given and our conclusions from it have not been significantly affected by these gaps in the evidence.

50.30 The best information that we have to date is that allegations by nine complainants in statements to the Tribunal have been under investigation by the police and complaints by some others not contained in Tribunal statements have also been investigated. The allegations have involved over a dozen members of staff at various homes, one of whom died in the course of the investigations and after our hearings had ended[23].

50.31 The following convictions and prosecutions since 1997 are relevant to our investigation:

(1) On 7 March 1997, in the Crown Court at Mold, **Roger Platres Saint** pleaded guilty to nine counts alleging indecent assaults upon a step-son, two pupils, a foster child and five adopted children; and he was sentenced on 23 May 1997 to six and a half years' imprisonment[24].

(2) On 14 March 1997, in the Crown Court at Mold, **Robert Martin Williams**, a former nursing auxilliary at Gwynfa Residential Unit, was convicted of two offences of rape of a girl patient, who was aged 16 years at the time of the offences and who is identified as P in paragraphs 20.12 and 20.13 of this report. Concurrent sentences of six years' imprisonment were imposed on him.

(3) On 4 July 1997, in the Crown Court at Chester, **Noel Ryan** pleaded guilty to 14 sexual offences (three of buggery, one attempted buggery and ten indecent assaults) against ten male residents under the age of 16 years at Clwyd Hall; and he asked for seven other offences of indecent assaults involving seven other boys to be taken into consideration. He was sentenced to 12 years' imprisonment[25].

(4) On 9 September 1998, in the Crown Court at Chester, **Mr B** pleaded guilty to three offences of rape and six indecent assaults upon B2 and four indecent assaults upon B1[26]. He was sentenced to a total of three years' imprisonment.

(5) **Richard Dafydd Vevar,** formerly a care worker employed by the Bryn Alyn Community, was charged in July 1998 with offences of buggery and indecent assault against the girl referred to in paragraph 21.55 of this report. On 23 June 1999 he was acquitted by a jury of the allegations of buggery but they were unable to reach verdicts on the other counts. At a later hearing the Judge entered verdicts of not guilty in respect of these other counts.

(6) **Richard Ernest Leake**[27], formerly Principal of Ystrad Hall School at Llangollen, has been charged with offences of indecent assaults on boys alleged to have been committed between 1972 and 1978. He denies all the charges and his trial has now been fixed for 8 November 1999.

---

[23] See para 21.52.
[24] See Chapter 25.
[25] See paras 23.17 to 23.27.
[26] See paras 27.20 to 27.28.
[27] See paras 22.07 and 22.15.

(7) **Richard Francis Groome**[28], formerly Warden of Tanllwyfan and then successively Head of Care and Principal at Clwyd Hall School, has been committed for trial on charges alleging sexual offences involving former boy residents at the latter school and at both these establishments and at others in Shropshire between 1981 and 1989. He has pleaded not guilty to all the charges and his trial is likely to take place early in 2000 at Mold.

50.32 It is necessary to mention also certain other recent criminal proceedings that are relevant to our inquiry, namely:

(1) **Roger Owen Griffiths** and his former wife, **Anthea Beatrice Roberts**, the proprietors of Gatewen Hall[29] residential school from 1977 to 1982, when the premises were sold to the Bryn Alyn Community, were convicted in the Crown Court at Chester on 3 and 4 August 1999. Griffiths was sentenced to a total of eight years' imprisonment for offences of buggery (one), attempted buggery (one), indecent assault (one) and cruelty (four) involving four boy residents at the school. Roberts was sentenced to two years' imprisonment for two offences of indecent assault on two other boy residents aged under 16 years.

(2) **Derek Brushett**, an SSIW employed by the Welsh Office, is currently suspended from duty whilst he awaits trial on numerous charges of sexual and other offences against boys alleged to have been committed in or about the 1970s, when Brushett was headmaster of Bryn-y-Don School (initially an approved school) in Dinas Powys. During his employment thereafter by the Welsh Office, Brushett took part in a few inspections in North Wales but there is no allegation of misconduct by him in that capacity, as far as we are aware.

Criticisms of police responses outside the main investigations

50.33 We deal in the next chapter with specific criticisms that have been made of the conduct by the North Wales Police of the three main investigations of alleged abuse in 1986/1988 (Gwynedd), 1990 (Cartrefle) and from 1991 onwards (North Wales generally); and in Chapter 52 we consider the allegation that they failed to investigate adequately an alleged paedophile ring. It is convenient here, however, to deal with more general criticisms, namely, that:

(a) they failed to respond to and investigate individual specific complaints by children in care who came to them; and

(b) they were insensitive in their dealings with absconders from children's homes and failed to probe sensibly the reasons for absconsions.

---

[28] See paras 18.06, 18.07, 18.21 to 18.26, 18.30, 23.06, 23.07 and 23.30.
[29] See para 21.05(d).

It is convenient also to deal with the allegation, canvassed by some in the press, that the thoroughness of the investigations generally was suspect because of the links of individuals with freemasonry.

50.34 In relation to both (a) and (b), it must be said that comparatively few of the complainants alleged that they made a complaint to the police of physical or sexual abuse whilst they were still in care. Of those who said that they did, most claimed to have done so when apprehended by the police as absconders, saying that they had told a police officer that the particular abuse had been the reason for their absconsion.

50.35 At this distance of time it is impossible for us to reach any confident conclusion about individual complaints of this kind in the absence of any supporting documentary evidence. It is likely, however, that there were a few complaints by children in care direct to the police other than in the course of absconding. We have no persuasive reason for disbelieving, for example, the evidence that a victim of Stephen Norris at Cartrefle went to the police station next door and alleged to an unidentified officer on duty that children were being abused, to be met with the response that the officer could do nothing without evidence[30]. Again, we heard evidence that a boy who was resident with the Bryn Alyn Community at Gatewen Hall reported several assaults by the staff there but the police were dissuaded from investigating the complaints and he was warned about wasting police time[31]. In another case, a social worker's report confirmed that a girl had gone to Prestatyn Police Station to complain of being picked on by Joan Glover but the police did not take any action beyond arranging for the girl's return to South Meadow[32].

50.36 According to the calculation by Counsel for the North Wales Police, about 50 per cent (134) of the former residents of children's homes and former foster children whose evidence is before us absconded at one time or another; and about 57 of these said that they came into contact with the police (not necessarily the North Wales Police) in the course of, or in connection with, absconding. We heard oral evidence from 49 of this group of 57 but only about ten in all (including three whose evidence was read) criticised the way in which they were dealt with as absconders.

50.37 Only one of these critics of the police alleged that he complained to them of being sexually abused in care. He was resident at Bersham Hall at the time and claimed to have been alone when he made his complaint at Corwen Police Station. Contemporary records, however, show that he was taken to that police station with two other absconders. That alone is not a sufficient reason for disbelieving him. We accept that he may have made a complaint and that it may have been brushed aside but we cannot be confident that that occurred.

50.38 Three of the other absconders alleged that they reported physical assaults to police officers who apprehended them but that they were disbelieved. Others complained that they were not asked their reasons for absconding, although

---

[30] See para 15.09.
[31] See paras 21.69 to 21.73.
[32] See para 17.32.

they did not volunteer the information: they were questioned, however, about any offences that they might have committed whilst "on the run" and one described being told off for absconding before being returned to the home from which he had escaped.

50.39 This evidence does not provide a firm basis for severe strictures on the North Wales Police about their response to individual complaints, bearing in mind the general lack of awareness of the risk of abuse in care for a substantial part of the period under review. It is also relevant that the obligation on a judge to warn a jury about the danger of convicting on the uncorroborated evidence of a complainant of sexual offences was not removed until 3 February 1995[33]. The limited complaints that we have heard do, however, underline the importance of both vigilance and sensitivity on the part of police officers when dealing with complaints by children in care, whether or not they are absconders and whether or not they have committed criminal offences or otherwise appear to be troublesome[34].

50.40 There was an occasion in 1981 or 1982 when John Allen's sexual activities might have come to the attention of the police. Police officers in Durham had become aware that a former resident with the Bryn Alyn Community was receiving substantial cheques from Allen. A police officer at Llay, near Wrexham, was asked to investigate the position and learnt from the Bryn Alyn accountant at that time that money was being paid to former residents. We heard the recollections of four witnesses about this matter but only one of them, Keith Allan Evans[35], claimed to have told the Llay police officer about rumours or banter in relation to residents who received gifts in return for "bending down" for Allen; and Evans himself did not believe what was being said about Allen. The Llay police officer, on the other hand, said that there was no suggestion by the Durham police or by the Bryn Alyn staff of blackmail. The officer said that blackmail was not the subject of investigation and that he was not told of any rumour of sexual abuse by Allen. In these circumstances we cannot be satisfied that anything was said to the North Wales Police at that time to put them on notice of allegations of sexual misconduct by Allen.

The alleged impact of freemasonry

50.41 Although this question was quite widely discussed in the press before the Tribunal's hearings began very few questions were asked about it during our inquiry and most of them were put by the Chairman of the Tribunal to give appropriate witnesses an opportunity to affirm or deny any connection with freemasonry.

50.42 The reason why freemasonry soon became a non-issue in the inquiry was that there was no evidence whatsoever that freemasonry had had any impact on any of the investigations with which we have been concerned. We have dealt with

---

[33] By section 32 of the Criminal Justice and Public Order Act 1994.

[34] See eg Appendix 3 at page 19 to "Missing from Care", the report of a working party chaired by Adrianne Jones CBE, published by the Local Government Association in 1997.

[35] See para 21.80.

this question earlier, in Chapter 9[36], because we understood it to be alleged specifically that Gordon Anglesea's membership of the Masons had led to a "cover up" of the allegations about him or to specially favourable treatment in consideration by the police of the strength of the evidence against him. There was also a suggestion that he had received special favour in being permitted to retire when he did.

50.43 It is inappropriate to repeat here our conclusions about the case of Gordon Anglesea, which are set out fully in Chapter 9. It is necessary, however, to repeat that:

(a) at the outset of the Inquiry Counsel for the North Wales Police stated, on the instructions of the Chief Constable, that none of the current or former senior officers from Assistant Chief Constable upwards during the period under review had been a freemason and that the same was true of the relevant Detective Chief Superintendents and Detective Superintendent Ackerley;

(b) a directive was issued by the Chief Constable in September 1984 warning existing Masons in the North Wales Police to "consider carefully how right it is to continue such membership" in view of the requirement that "openness must be seen by all", and the directive discouraged others from applying to join the Masons for the same reasons[37].

50.44 When Councillor Malcolm King[38] was asked about the alleged rumours of the involvement of freemasonry in either the alleged abuse or the investigation of it in North Wales, he said that there was speculation (he believed) that Lord Kenyon had asked for promotion for Gordon Anglesea. This was said by Councillor King to have been based on a conversation overheard at a police function; and the speculation was that Lord Kenyon had advocated Anglesea's promotion "for the purpose of covering up the fact that his son had been involved in child abuse activities".

50.45 We have received no evidence whatsoever in support of this allegation and it appears to have been merely a malicious rumour. In particular, there is no evidence that Lord Kenyon intervened at any time in any way on behalf of Anglesea. Both Lord Kenyon (the fifth Baron) and the son referred to (Thomas) are now dead. We deal in Chapter 52 with allegations about the latter and an alleged intervention by Lord Kenyon on his son's behalf. In relation to freemasonry, the only evidence about Lord Kenyon, who was Provincial Grand Master and a member of the North Wales Police Authority in the 1980s, was given by the Chief Constable at that time, David Owen. Owen's evidence was that, within a month following the publication of the directive referred to in paragraph 50.43(b), he met Lord Kenyon at Wrexham Police Station, at Lord Kenyon's request, when the latter put to him his concern as Provincial Grand Master about the contents of the directive. At this

---

[36] See paras 9.24, 9.37 and 9.38.
[37] See para 9.24.
[38] See paras 2.22 and 32.35.

meeting Lord Kenyon argued that the directive was totally misguided and asked that it should be withdrawn; and he mentioned that a police officer (unidentified, but not Anglesea) had been about to take the chair in a North Wales lodge but had declined to do so because of the directive.

50.46　Owen's evidence was that he told Lord Kenyon that he had no intention of withdrawing the directive. In response, Lord Kenyon argued that the Chief Constable knew nothing at all about freemasonry and suggested that it would be appropriate for him to join a lodge, such as the one at Denbigh, outside the area of his usual working activity; but this invitation was declined.

50.47　Nefyn Dodd was specifically asked whether he had ever been a Mason, in order that any suggestion of a "cover up" in his case on that ground should be probed. His answer was in the negative and he said that, to his knowledge, the only Mason known to him was Leonard Stritch[39]. The only other person figuring in this inquiry who is known to have been a Mason is John Ilton[40], who was for a time a member of the same lodge at Wrexham (the Berwyn lodge) as Gordon Anglesea. His evidence to the Tribunal was that he knew Anglesea by sight and vaguely remembered him as a member of the same lodge, but that he had never approached Anglesea.

---

[39] See paras 10.85 and 10.94 to 10.99.
[40] See paras 7.15, 7.24 and 10.109.

The three main police investigations

Gwynedd 1986/1988[1]

51.01 The decision to appoint Detective Chief Superintendent Gwynne Owen to conduct this investigation was made by the Chief Constable, apparently on the advice of an Assistant Chief Constable, at the end of February 1986. This was after Gwynne Owen had submitted a report, dated 21 February 1986, about the allegations made by Alison Taylor, in which he had said that the allegations of criminal offences merited police investigation. At that point he was aware that Taylor had referred to alleged assaults on seven children in care (one of whom was un-named) and to an alleged homosexual relationship between a male member of staff and a resident at Tŷ Newydd, as well as the alleged "theft" (his words) of two documents belonging to her and other alleged misconduct of a non-criminal kind.

51.02 The appointment of Gwynne Owen to head the investigation reflected its importance in the eyes of the Chief Constable but it was Gwynne Owen's decision to conduct the interviews himself with the assistance only of a woman detective constable. It was his decision also not to inform responsible officers of Gwynedd County Council that he was to conduct an investigation. His explanation for this was that he did not know at that time whether there was any substance in the allegations of dishonesty in investigation and suppression of evidence made by Taylor or who within social services might be involved. He did not believe, however, that his investigation would be hampered by the continued presence of Nefyn Dodd in post at Tŷ'r Felin because none of the alleged complainants was still resident there at the time.

51.03 Gwynne Owen gave us a detailed account in his evidence of the course of his inquiries. He began by obtaining a comprehensive statement from Alison Taylor on 26 March 1986. In that statement she listed assaults against the seven children previously mentioned which had allegedly been reported to her by that date. She did not claim to have witnessed any assault herself and she did not refer to any complaints made to her about Bryn Estyn. Beryl Condra[2] was mentioned as a potential source of information and she was seen by Gwynne Owen on 9 May 1986. Condra repeated allegations of frequent assaults by Nefyn Dodd on resident children but did not allege that she herself had witnessed any. According to Gwynne Owen, she did not provide any information additional to that already given by Taylor and a signed statement was not taken from her.

51.04 It appears that all but one of the complaints were investigated between May and September 1986, including the allegation of an homosexual relationship. One was not investigated on the ground that it had previously been

---

[1] See paras 2.12 to 2.15 and 50.15 to 50.17 for outlines of this investigation.
[2] See para 36.09.

investigated by the police in 1984[3]. Whilst the investigation was proceeding Alison Taylor reported alleged assaults on two other children and one other case came to Gwynne Owen's notice. Separately, a divisional investigation also took place into the allegations of A, which we have discussed in detail in Chapter 36[4]. Thus, the cases of 11 alleged victims were considered. Two of them did not substantiate the complaints that had been attributed to them and the boy alleged to have been involved in an homosexual relationship denied it; all three of them had left residential care by the date when they were interviewed. It must be said also that no admissible evidence was forthcoming to prove the alleged mistreatment of the unidentified child.

51.05 Gwynne Owen did not play any meaningful role in the investigation of A's complaint. This had been dealt with earlier, in or about February 1986, by a detective inspector, following a report by Beryl Condra to the police. Condra was seen by the detective inspector, who also interviewed the alleged abuser, X. According to Owen's report in September 1986, X denied the allegations emphatically and "because of the paucity of evidence and the absence of any form of corroboration, it was resolved that no further action would be taken by the police". Owen's report did not refer to any interview of A but he did refer to the investigating officer's strong suspicions about Condra's motivation. That officer investigated also, for reasons that are not clear, allegations of impropriety in the appointment of X as a temporary member of staff but, again, no action was recommended.

51.06 Of the other six complainants, three were still in residential care at the time of Owen's investigation, two were living in a probation hostel at Wrexham and the other, with severe learning difficulties, was living at home. No statement was taken from the last mentioned boy, in view of his disability, but the investigation did reveal that his alleged abuser, a temporary member of the care staff at Queens Park, who resigned on 6 July 1986, had been appointed to the post earlier that year by a panel who knew of his record of seven Court appearances between 1975 and 1980 for a variety of offences, mainly in relation to motor vehicles but including burglary.

51.07 This left five complainants (only one female) of variable quality as potential witnesses, all of whom made allegations of physical assault by members of staff. Three boys alleged assaults by Nefyn Dodd but one of them was not prepared to sign a statement to Owen or the detective constable to that effect. This complainant, who was by that time a resident at Y Gwyngyll, alleged that he had been assaulted by Nefyn Dodd and John Roberts at Tŷ'r Felin and by another person at Y Gwyngyll. The last mentioned assault had been reported by the complainant to the police at Menai Bridge on 19 March 1986 but he had signed a statement to the police the following day, in the presence of the Acting Officer-in-Charge of Y Gwyngyll, to the effect that the assault had also been reported to Social Services and that he did not wish the police to be involved.

[3] See paras 33.102, 33.103 and 50.15.
[4] See paras 36.14 to 36.29.

He did, however, make a witness statement to the police on 10 June 1986 giving details of the Y Gwyngyll incident, although he was only willing to give accounts orally of his allegations against Nefyn Dodd and John Roberts.

51.08 This complainant's refusals to make a signed statement about the latter allegations were repeated in further interviews on 19 June 1986. Six weeks later Alison Taylor informed Owen that the complainant, who had by then moved to Tŷ Newydd, wished to make a written statement to the police to prevent the same thing from happening to other children. However, on 30 July 1986 the detective constable who attended at Tŷ Newydd to take a statement from him was handed a typewritten document headed "Information taken from (the complainant) 29.07.86" and apparently signed by him. The detective constable then took a written statement from him, using the other document for reference purposes.

51.09 It is unnecessary to go into great detail about the further investigation of the complaints of the five referred to in paragraph 51.07. None of the cases was clear cut. In one there was no possible corroboration and two of the other lesser allegations had been the subject of investigation by the Gwynedd Social Services Department shortly after the event. It is not clear from the documentary evidence how far other potential witnesses were sought because Gwynne Owen's notes on this subject were defective and the answer cannot be found in his report. He confused the picture in his written evidence by producing a large number of statements taken by the police over five years later in the course of the major investigation; written statements from no more than about half a dozen witnesses (other than complainants, alleged abusers or Alison Taylor) made in 1986 were produced to us.

51.10 Each of the alleged abusers was interviewed, apart apparently from June Dodd, against whom there was only the allegation in relation to an incident at Tŷ Newydd on 2 February 1986[5]. Nefyn Dodd was interviewed under caution by Owen on 10 September 1986 at Tŷ'r Felin but we have no record of the interview, although the detective constable was present throughout. According to Owen, he interviewed Dodd "vigorously" and at length. Dodd made a statement under caution, in which he denied all the allegations against him. John Roberts was seen at his own home on 16 September 1986 but again we have no record of the interview. Owen told us that he spent just over an hour interviewing Roberts about alleged assaults, which Roberts denied; Roberts is said by Owen to have made a written statement but this was not produced to us. Owen did not refer to any other police officer as having been present.

51.11 Gwynne Owen submitted a report on the investigation to the Chief Constable later in September 1986. Before he did so a further telephone message was received from Alison Taylor to the effect that there were concerns about the treatment of a girl resident currently at Tŷ'r Felin. The detective constable was instructed to investigate the matter and did so promptly. The girl did not make any complaint of physical abuse and no criminal offence was revealed.

---

[5] See paras 33.90, 33.91 and 34.17(8).

51.12 Gwynne Owen was much criticised in cross-examination about the contents of his report, which extended to 97 pages. It was said that he expressed hostile and critical opinions about most of the complainants, if not all of them, without a sound basis for doing so, and defended social services staff inappropriately. He expressed strong criticism also of informants such as Alison Taylor and Beryl Condra and attributed demeaning motives to them on the basis of (at best) tittle-tattle amongst staff. Overall, ran the criticism, he failed to report on the investigation objectively, failed to display any sensitivity to the problems of vulnerable children in care and determined to prevent any prosecution arising from Alison Taylor's allegations.

51.13 There is undoubtedly much material in Owen's report to support criticism on the lines that we have indicated. A few examples will be sufficient to illustrate the point. Thus:

(a) it was said of one complaint that "the investigating officer is strongly of the opinion that . . . this was not a spontaneous complaint, but rather the case of a clever woman manipulating a malleable girl (probably with the reward of cigarettes)";

(b) of another, he said "It appears to be a case of a dull, wicked boy being manipulated, and given succour by a clever woman who 'used' him for her own purposes";

(c) "It is the investigating officer's opinion that many of the allegations were not spontaneous complaints made by child residents, but rather the result of a deliberate 'trawl' and subtle interrogation of children facilitated by some form of reward, eg cigarettes";

(d) "It is unfortunate that the myth of incompetency about the Social Services is being fostered by professionals within the service as well as by elected representatives. Such representatives may be reassured if they were to pay unannounced visits to Community Homes to observe the way they are run."

51.14 Gwynne Owen defended the opinions that he expressed in his report by saying that written guidelines issued by the Director of Public Prosecutions encouraged investigating officers to comment upon the reliability of particular witnesses, to refer to their previous convictions and to indicate, when evidence conflicted, which version was thought to be nearest to the truth. He added in his written statement to the Tribunal: "An officer is required in his conclusions to express his views on any of the issues, personalities or organisations involved, give an indication of any particular feeling in the local community or of local publicity about the matter. An officer is required to advance any other matters that might affect the decision to prosecute within his knowledge . . .". Of his impressions of Alison Taylor, he said that he could not now reconstruct precisely how they came to be formed but that they were "honestly formed on reasonable grounds".

51.15 Decisions whether or not to prosecute particular individuals are outside the terms of reference of this inquiry and we have not, therefore, investigated the decision making process in this particular case or, for example, considered the guidelines to which Owen referred. For the avoidance of any doubt, we should add that we do not dispute Owen's right to make observations on witnesses and issues in his report; and, in any event, we are not persuaded that Owen's comments had any significant impact on the eventual outcome of the investigation, bearing in mind the state of the evidence at that time. Nevertheless, we regard it as very regrettable that he expressed himself as he did. To an independent observer the report appears to have been very one-sided and gives the impression that he approached the investigation with a closed mind.

51.16 Another criticism of the investigation must be that there was no coherent liaison between Gwynne Owen and the Gwynedd Social Services Department. Owen's stated reason for this, to which we have already referred in paragraph 51.02, is understood but is not an adequate explanation. Co-operation from some employees of the Department was plainly necessary in the search for, and interviewing of, complainants and witnesses, many of whom were still in care; and examination of relevant records in an ordered way was equally necessary. In the event police officers did talk to quite a wide range of employees and had (unexplained) access to some records, as appears from Owen's statement and his report; but we can see no reason why the Chief Executive should not have been consulted at the outset and appropriate arrangements made for systematic scrutiny of the relevant documents, including personal files and logs. As it was, this aspect of the investigation was, at best, patchy and incomplete. Owen was unaware of the range of documents that existed. He did not see, for example, a copy of the adverse report on Tŷ'r Felin by a former staff member early in 1985[6]; and he thought that Dodd was only Officer-in-Charge of Tŷ'r Felin at the outset of the investigation.

51.17 In making this criticism, we have in mind that, in 1986, inter-agency co-operation between the police and social services in child abuse cases was still in an early stage of development but the foundations had already been laid and the North Wales Police had in post a senior police officer responsible for liaison with other services.

51.18 The conclusion of the Senior Crown Prosecutor, based at Colwyn Bay, after considering Owen's report and the file, was that prosecution proceedings would not be justified in 12 of the 13 cases covered by the report. In the case of the complainant referred to in paragraph 51.08, however, he advised that attempts should be made to trace two named witnesses who might provide corroborative evidence. They were subsequently found and made statements in February 1987 but the view of the Senior Crown Prosecutor then was that the evidence remained insufficient to justify prosecution.

51.19 There was a further investigation in 1987 arising from fresh allegations against Nefyn Dodd made by a woman who had been a resident at Tŷ'r Felin. The statement taken from her on 29 January 1987 alleged assaults by Dodd on five former residents of Tŷ'r Felin that she had witnessed and four former members of the staff at that home were named as potential supporting witnesses. Only

---

[6] See paras 33.120 and 33.121.

two of the alleged victims were still resident in Gwynedd; the others were living as far afield as Yorkshire (two) and Warrington. A sixth complainant, living in Birmingham, emerged during the investigation. All of them had been discharged from care.

51.20 This further investigation was completed by October 1987 when Gwynne Owen's file and his second report were sent to the Senior Crown Prosecutor. The four potential complainants outside Gwynedd were interviewed by local police officers on the basis of instructions that Owen transmitted to them. One of the six (living in Caernarvon) refused to co-operate at all and another made oral allegations of assault by Dodd but refused to sign a statement to that effect. The other four did allege assaults by Dodd but only one of them recalled the same incident as that seen by the woman referred to in the preceding paragraph[7]. As for the four corroborative witnesses named, one of them did say that she had seen three of the complainants slapped by Dodd but there were problems about linking what she recalled with their evidence; and the other three were seen but did not provide supporting evidence.

51.21 Nefyn Dodd was interviewed by Gwynne Owen on 5 October 1987, as before in the presence of the detective constable. We have not seen any record of the interview but he made a signed statement denying the allegations.

51.22 In his second report, addressed to the Assistant Chief Constable and dated 13 October 1987, Owen referred to the fact that the previous papers had been submitted to the Attorney-General's office, which had confirmed that criminal proceedings were not merited. He referred also to various events that had occurred since September 1986, including alleged or suspected activities of Alison Taylor, her husband and Beryl Condra, which he described as "the 'climate' prevailing" at the time when the fresh allegations were made. In the course of the report he said that his view of Taylor remained unchanged and that there was every likelihood that she would manipulate others in the future; but he did not refer to any established link between her and the woman who had made the fresh allegations or any of the six new complainants. Owen concluded his report:

> "It is the investigating officer's view that the paucity of evidence to support the allegations; the lapse of time since the alleged offences; coupled with the considered appreciation of public interest, dictate that this matter merits no further action and that the individuals primarily concerned be accordingly informed."

51.23 The response to the report of the Senior Crown Prosecutor on 5 January 1988 was that, although the complaints had to be treated seriously, there was insufficient evidence to give a reasonable prospect of conviction. He suggested that two other potential witnesses should be traced, if possible. Only one of the two was subsequently found and he denied seeing any assault (he denied even the existence of the goal posts) and the Senior Crown Prosecutor confirmed his advice against a prosecution on 5 April 1988.

---

[7] Throwing the boy over "the goalposts" cf para 33.76.

51.24 One other issue in relation to Gwynne Owen's investigations has to be mentioned. According to Owen, he saw Lucille Hughes, the Director of Social Services on three relevant occasions. His first meeting, which lasted two hours, was on 5 June 1986 at Hughes' office, when he outlined "the thrust of the allegations" and what was being said about Dodd. This followed a letter from Hughes to the Chief Constable, dated 21 May 1986, stating that the investigation had "come to (her) notice" and urging completion of the investigation with all possible speed. The second meeting took place on 23 October 1986, at the Imperial Hotel, Llandudno, when Owen briefed Hughes about the outcome of the investigation, following up a letter to her from the Deputy Chief Constable, dated three days earlier. Thirdly, there was a further discussion between them on 22 May 1987 at Police Headquarters, Colwyn Bay, when Hughes was attending a meeting there about juvenile crime. In this last discussion, Owen "apprised" Hughes of the further investigation into allegations against Dodd, of which she was already aware[8].

51.25 The conflict of evidence is about what Owen told Hughes on the second occasion. Owen's evidence to the Tribunal was that he gave her a detailed appraisal of the investigation that had taken place. He said that he stressed to Hughes the difficulties of such an investigation and that the decision not to prosecute did not mean that Dodd was entirely innocent of the allegations but reflected the lack of evidence to support a successful prosecution. His written statement continued "I did in fact inform Miss Hughes of my belief that Mr Dodd had physically assaulted some of the children and I left her in no doubt of my opinion of Dodd, who I saw as a vain, immature individual who, in my view, was unsuited to his position".

51.26 Owen gave oral evidence to the Tribunal to similar effect and added that he repeated his opinion about Dodd's unsuitability to Lucille Hughes at their meeting in May 1987. But under further cross-examination on behalf of Hughes, he conceded that he could not be certain that he did tell her that he considered Dodd to be unsuitable for his job. Lucille Hughes herself told us that she has no recollection that Owen expressed the opinion that Dodd was unsuitable. What she carried away from the Imperial Hotel meeting was that Dodd had "overstepped the mark on occasion in terms of his behaviour towards children". She regarded it as serious enough for her to take action as Director of Social Services and she spoke to Dodd about it subsequently, reminding him of the Council's policy in relation to corporal punishment. She received many reassurances from him about the future but she warned him that "if there was the slightest indication of anything like that again" he should expect to be disciplined and would be likely to lose his position.

51.27 We are satisfied on this evidence that Gwynne Owen did make some adverse comment to Lucille Hughes at their meeting in October 1986, despite the absence of any such comment in his first report on the investigation to the Chief Constable. We are equally clear, however, that he did not go as far as to suggest that Dodd was unfit for his job. Such a comment would have been remarkably

---

[8] Hughes had written to Owen on 3 March 1987 about the alleged activities of Alison Taylor's husband.

inconsistent with the tone of that first report. Moreover, it is almost unthinkable that a criticism of that gravity would not have been referred to directly, or at least obliquely, in the brief note of the points made (or to be made) to Hughes that Owen recorded in his own handwriting on a copy of the Deputy Chief Constable's letter to Hughes of 20 October 1986, which was produced in evidence.

51.28 Nefyn Dodd himself did not refer in his evidence to being given any warning by Lucille Hughes and it was not put to him in cross-examination because the evidence about it had not emerged at that stage. To complete the picture, it is appropriate to quote Gwynne Owen's assessment of Dodd, as recorded in his second report in October 1987, which was as follows:

> "Joseph Nefyn Dodd is, in the opinion of the investigating officer, a strict disciplinarian, jealously protective to maintain and be seen to maintain a well-run establishment. He displays varying attitudes and flexibility; of sternness and kindness. He is somewhat vain and immature in some respects, but he seems anxious to provide a secure and loving environment for unfortunate children . . .

> Many of the children accommodated (at Tŷ'r Felin) are already or potential offenders. It is essential to maintain an element of discipline and control in the interests of the public in general and of the children residing at the Centre . . . To achieve such control, it is a matter of common-sense that, on occasions, it may be necessary to chastise children. The investigating officer is of the opinion that Dodd did assault children within the strict definition of that term. However, such incidents are not considered to have amounted to gratuitous violence directed at individual children."

51.29 Sir Ronald Hadfield, assessor to the Tribunal in respect of police matters[9], was critical of many aspects of this Gwynedd investigation from 1986 to 1988. He was critical, for example, of the role that Gwynne Owen chose for himself and the size of his investigating team. He criticised also the decision not to involve the Director of Social Services from the beginning and the failure to seize all relevant documentation at the outset of the inquiry, despite the already established advantages of joint investigations in such cases. In Sir Ronald's view, Gwynne Owen ought to have had in mind that the evidence was likely to raise questions about Dodd's suitability for his post so that continuing contact between the investigating officer and the Director of Social Services was particularly necessary.

51.30 Paragraphs 2.4 to 2.9 of Sir Ronald's written advice to the Tribunal in Appendix 11 contain more detailed criticisms of both phases of this Gwynedd investigation, which need not be repeated here. He questions the thoroughness of both phases of the investigation and the speed of the second, commenting that the overwhelming impression of the latter was that it was "sluggish and shallow". In relation to method, he draws attention to the disadvantages of using junior officers of other police forces to make enquiries in circumstances

---

[9] See para 1.04 and Appendix 11.

of this kind and to the "startling" absence of contemporary notes of the interviews with Dodd, in breach of the requirements of the Police and Criminal Evidence Act 1984.

51.31 Commenting on the contents of Gwynne Owen's reports as investigating officer, Sir Ronald says[10]:

> "The police have always been encouraged to include in their reports their impressions of witnesses and any important or material issues bearing upon a prosecution which they feel will emerge should the matter go before a jury. However, in my experience, the comments made by Mr Owen in his report into the 1986 enquiry were thoroughly inappropriate and lacking in judgment. The fairness and objectivity called for in these circumstances was absent and his comments showed a lack of tolerance and understanding of the witnesses. Above all, very serious imputations appear to have been made about the character and motives of Alison Taylor and certain complainants . . . on the basis of little more than instinct."

51.32 Finally, Sir Ronald stresses the importance of the meeting between Gwynne Owen and Lucille Hughes on completion of the first investigation and is strongly critical of the absence of an agreed minute of that meeting or a letter from Owen confirming to the Director of Social Services what had been said.

51.33 In our judgment, all these criticisms are fully justified. Whether or not any criminal charges would have been brought if the defects referred to had not occurred is, of course, a matter of speculation and we have well in mind that the potential evidence in support of some of the allegations was either not forthcoming or very weak. A serious consequence of the way in which the investigations were conducted, however, was that seeds of distrust of the North Wales Police were sown amongst potential complainants, "whistleblowers" such as Alison Taylor, and some other interested persons, including politicians, which came to fruition when the wider police investigation was launched in 1991 and hampered that investigation to some extent.

Cartrefle, 1990

51.34 This investigation began on 17 June 1990 and was conducted from 25 June 1990 by Detective Inspector Donald James Cronin, who was responsible for the management of crime investigation in the Mold and Deeside Sub-Divisions and who returned from leave that day. During the intervening week Detective Sergeant Rees had been in charge of the investigation and there had been close co-operation with the Social Services Department through the Area Office at Hawarden. Although the established Child Protection procedures had not been followed in some important respects, there had been full discussion about arrangements for interviewing the resident children at Cartrefle, which began on 19 June 1990. There were four social workers in the team provided by the Social Services Department and Detective Sergeant Rees, who continued to

---

[10] See Appendix 11, para 2.8.

take part in the investigations, had two detective constables working with him. Norris was first arrested, interviewed and charged on 4 July 1990, after which he was released on bail. He was again arrested, interviewed and charged on 15 August 1990, from which date he was detained in custody.

51.35 We have outlined the history of this investigation in paragraphs 50.20 and 50.21 and little further detail is needed because the only substantial criticism of the North Wales Police in connection with it is that they failed to widen their enquiry into Norris' activities to include his period of service at Bryn Estyn. Cronin's evidence to the Tribunal about this was that he considered looking into Norris' background but that there was no pointer to earlier misconduct on his part. Raymond Bew[11], a former member of the Bryn Estyn staff, had been interviewed but he had proved to be a difficult witness and would not make any relevant criticism.

51.36 The police officers did not have access to headquarters files. Cronin said that he was and is satisfied that the social workers involved in the investigation worked with the police in good faith and provided all the necessary information to enable the police to trace former residents of Cartrefle and former staff there. Like the police officers, however, those social workers did not have access to the headquarters files. The police, had to rely upon "social services management through Mr Wyatt" to search those files and to communicate the information in them accurately. Cronin himself had direct contact with John Llewellyn Thomas[12] and Michael Barnes[13] as well as Geoffrey Wyatt[14]; and he understood that Wyatt had assumed personal responsibility for examining the relevant files. By the time that he gave evidence to us, Cronin had been informed that the Social Services files did contain information, at the time of the Cartrefle investigation, about Norris taking young boys from Bryn Estyn to his farm but he was not told about this when he was making the investigation. He said that, if the investigating team had had that information, they would have regarded it as "manna from heaven".

51.37 We have seen copies of some minutes of meetings of the internal Departmental Co-ordinating Group set up by Clwyd Social Services Department to deal with the problems arising from the Cartrefle disclosures. These minutes relate to meetings held on 3 and 17 August and 7 September 1990, at the second and third of which there was discussion of widening the investigation. The police were not represented at these meetings. On 17 August the question discussed was whether the police were going to widen their investigative trawl to include the full period of Norris' appointment. A social worker reported that the police were not keen to do so: if this was felt necessary, the Department would have to undertake their own enquiries. At the meeting on 7 September the same social worker reported that the police had decided that they did not wish to extend their enquiries further so that it was necessary to consider whether Social Services themselves wished to do so. Wyatt commented that there would be a

---

[11] See para 15.39.
[12] See para 15.45.
[13] See para 15.45.
[14] See paras 28.24 and 28.38.

danger (in extending the enquiries) that the matter would be forever investigated and never concluded. However, later in the meeting there was a consensus that an inquiry should be held but that Wyatt should discuss with the Welsh Office the appropriate form of inquiry.

51.38 Sir Ronald Hadfield's view[15] is that Detective Inspector Cronin took the investigation as far as could be expected at that time. A full indictment for serious offences was preferred against Norris; there were no complaints emanating from Bryn Estyn, which had been closed for six years; the Social Services Department gave no indication that Norris might have committed offences at Bryn Estyn; and the cost and delay of an extended inquiry, coupled with the desirability of a speedy prosecution in the interests of the known victims at Cartrefle, were factors that would have had to be considered before any decision in favour of such an extension could have been made.

51.39 Sir Ronald's conclusions are persuasive. His last reason was not mentioned by Cronin but it raises issues that would have had to be addressed at a high level if there had been a move to extend the investigation. The weak link was that the police did not have access themselves to headquarters files and that Wyatt was disinclined to probe further; but, on the evidence before us, those files would not, at that stage, have revealed sexual misconduct by Norris at Bryn Estyn or his practice of inviting young boys to his farm.

The major North Wales investigation, 1991 onwards

51.40 This was planned as a large scale investigation from the outset in response to the request made by the County Secretary on behalf of Clwyd County Council in his letter dated 17 July 1991, which was accompanied by several helpful lists, including lists of relevant persons convicted, of persons whose activities gave rise to suspicion and of others about whom there were queries. Detective Superintendent Peter Ackerley was appointed Senior Investigating Officer at the suggestion of the Chief Constable.

51.41 A separate investigation began in Gwynedd in October 1991, under Acting Detective Superintendent E G Jones, in response to a written request by Lucille Hughes dated 30 September 1991 that the North Wales Police should investigate allegations of abuse in children's homes in Gwynedd made in an HTV television broadcast of "Wales this Week" four days earlier.

51.42 The two investigations were merged from 2 December 1991 when it was agreed that both should be put on the HOLMES computer system[16]. By that date 54 statements from witnesses had been recorded in the Gwynedd inquiry. Thereafter, the merged investigation covering the whole of North Wales was managed by Ackerley with Detective Inspector John Rowlands as Deputy SIO; and, according to Ackerley, his inquiry team received full co-operation from both Clwyd and Gwynedd County Councils and their officers and staff.

---

[15] See Appendix 11, para 4.
[16] Home Office Large Major Enquiry System.

51.43 In December 1991 it was decided to tackle the Clwyd part of the investigation in four phases beginning with Bryn Estyn and ending with Clwyd County Council's queries list. For Gwynedd there were to be three phases covering Tŷ'r Felin, Queens Park and Y Gwyngyll successively. Initially it had been decided to record witness statements only from former residents who had complaints to make but on 16 December 1991 this policy was discontinued and thenceforth statements were taken from all persons interviewed, whether "negative" in content or not. By 19 December 1991, according to Ackerley, the broad outline of a major inquiry had been established and the necessary resourcing decisions had been made, including the identification and posting of the officers necessary to carry it out.

51.44 On 2 January 1992 a training and briefing meeting for the team members was held at Colwyn Bay. The object of this meeting was to bring together the full team, some of whom had already been involved in the investigation from its inception, to brief them fully on the background and to provide guidance and discussion on various aspects of the investigation. Of particular importance was the need for sensitivity in dealing with potential complainants and for special victim care; and directions were given as to the manner of interviewing witnesses and ancillary matters, including the need for liaison with other agencies.

51.45 In his written statement to the Tribunal, Ackerley provided a stage by stage account of the progress of the investigation from then on until June 1994 but it is unnecessary to repeat the details here in view of the limited number of criticisms of it that have been canvassed before us. The decision to scale down the inquiry was taken in August 1993 and Detective Inspector Rowlands took over the lead role from the beginning of the following month. The reduction in scale is illustrated by the fact that about 360 statements were taken in the following three years or so whereas about 3,500 statements had been recorded in the first two years.

51.46 Although various questions were raised in cross-examination of the senior police witnesses about the selection of officers for the investigating team and the adequacy of the initial briefing session, we do not think that any substantial criticism of this preparatory work by the North Wales Police is appropriate. We should add that we are satisfied, on the basis of all the evidence that we have heard in the course of 14 months' hearings, that this investigation was carried out both thoroughly and efficiently. We have received no evidence to justify any suggestion that there was a "cover-up" in respect of any part of it or to cast doubt upon the good faith of the police throughout the inquiry. On the contrary, confirmation of the reliability of the police investigation has been provided by the following facts:

(a) almost all the complainants who provided statements to the Tribunal attested that the complaints made in their statements to the police were true;

(b) few of them said that they had additional complaints to make against relevant individuals;

(c) despite the publicity given to the Tribunal and the Tribunal's own trawl for additional witnesses, we received few fresh complaints from witnesses who had not been seen by the police in the course of their investigation.

51.47 There were some critics of the method of approach to witnesses that was adopted in the investigation but such criticism was probably unavoidable, having regard to the nature of the inquiry. The decision taken was that potential complainants should be sought out and spoken to privately without prior warning; and the basic reasons for this were that, in most cases, the witnesses' personal circumstances were unknown to the police and that they were likely to be reluctant to talk about their experiences in care. It was envisaged that spouses, partners or others close to such witnesses might be unaware that they had been in care and were likely to be ignorant of any abuse, particularly sexual abuse, that they had experienced. Such knowledge could affect their current relationships radically and letters addressed to potential witnesses might have led to forced and embarrassing disclosures.

51.48 Sir Ronald Hadfield's view is that he too would have chosen to arrive unannounced in the circumstances of this inquiry. His only qualification to this statement is that "there must always be the case for an exception". Sir Ronald points out also the problems of written notification in an investigation of this kind, including the difficulty of obtaining accurate addresses and the real danger that a letter may be opened by someone other than the addressee.

51.49 In the event most of the complainants who were asked about the matter said that they were dealt with sensitively and properly by the police; and very many of them were interviewed on more than one occasion. Those who were likely to be called to give evidence in criminal trials agreed also that they were kept reasonably informed about the progress of the cases in which they were involved. An independent NSPCC telephone help line was established at the NSPCC office in Wrexham from 4 December 1991. This was intended initially to provide a confidential service for former residents of Bryn Estyn but the service was extended to cover all persons involved in the inquiry.

51.50 The difficulty of the investigation is illustrated by the fact that in respect of Bryn Estyn, for example, 28 potential witnesses were traced and seen but refused to make statements; and 30 traced persons failed to reply to repeated calls. Moreover, at least seven of the complainants who gave oral evidence to the Tribunal said, when cross-examined about their failure to make complaints of abuse to the police when first interviewed, either that they had been too scared or that they had been too embarrassed or that they just did not want to be involved.

51.51 The small number of complainants who did criticise the approach of individual police officers to them did so mainly to explain their failure to mention specific complaints. They said, for example, that "the police were only interested in sexual abuse", "I was not given the impression that they were interested in the actual physical abuse", and another alleged that the police had "brushed off" his complaint of being indecently assaulted. We did not find these explanations persuasive, however, and the more credible (and understandable) explanation is that they were reluctant to speak about these matters when interviewed and had pushed them to the back of their minds for a substantial period.

51.52 The most eloquent critic of the lack of prior warning of the approach by the police was a woman complainant who described it as hard hearted and insensitively carried out. She continued "After informing me that my name was taken at random, they systematically prodded me with names and places of which I had long since put into a place of safety in my mind, in order to get on with my life with some dignity". She ended her statement on this "To simply walk into a person's life, extract deeply intimate and painful memories with no concern for the consequences for that person was, in my opinion, outrageously insensitive, the cost for me was to have had the floodgates of these memories prised open for reasons unknown, without any support to put back the pieces of my life in order to feel safe once again".

51.53 We have sympathy with the witness' views and it may well be that, in her case, an alternative method of approach should have been adopted as soon as it became known that she was upset. She was, however, in a very small minority of persons who made such complaints and the response of the large majority was much more robust.

51.54 We deal finally under this head with more serious complaints that police officers were aggressive towards witnesses, put pressure upon them and, in some cases, that officers suggested that compensation would be available or recoverable if they complained that they had been abused. This last suggestion was a recurring one made particularly by or on behalf of some members of the staff of Bryn Estyn. Only about three actual witnesses endorsed it, however, and it was denied by the police officers to whom it was put.

51.55 The most persistent critic of the police was the witness referred to as B in Chapter 9 of this report[17]. As we have said in paragraph 9.33, B made many complaints about the way in which he was dealt with by police officers in the course of his interviews and on other occasions. In relation to the interviews, his allegations were levelled against three police officers and referred mainly to events shortly before and after his wife's death. He said, for example, that they were abrupt and abusive when his wife was ill, and that they refused to leave the house when he and even his wife asked them to do so. The most senior of the officers, a detective inspector, used particularly crude language also when questioning B. On a later occasion, when B's wife had died and he himself was living in the Midlands, officers called at his former house uninvited and refused to leave, when he spoke to them by telephone, until he had agreed to meet them later. On yet another occasion, B alleged, one of the three officers pinned him against a wall at the Colwyn Bay Police Headquarters and threatened him, apparently to deter B from complaining to senior officers about that officer's behaviour.

---

[17] See paras 9.05 and 9.32 to 9.34.

51.56 Other more general complaints made by B were that the police officers were only interested in allegations against the persons whom they named and that they would not allow him to give additional information. According to B, there were long discussions, which were not recorded, despite B's requests that they should be taped, and he "just signed statements to get them (the police) out of (his) hair". Moreover, he makes the specific allegation that six written statements made by him to the police in the full course of the investigation have not been produced in evidence by them.

51.57 There are many difficulties about this part of the evidence before the Tribunal. As we have explained in Chapter 9, the process of disclosure by B was exceptionally long drawn out and most of his allegations against the police in respect of his interviews appear to have been put forward by way of explanation (at least in part) for the lateness of some of his major allegations of physical and sexual abuse whilst in care. Another problem is that he did not make any written complaint to senior officers about his treatment by the police although he does say that he made repeated oral complaints about it whilst the investigation continued. His response to this criticism was that he was never asked to put his complaints in writing and was not handed a document on how to do so until after 1993, maybe as late as 1995.

51.58 B's allegations of mistreatment by police officers have all been denied by them and we are unable to make precise findings about what occurred between them and B in the absence of any independent evidence. As for the alleged missing statements, we accept Ackerley's evidence that two statements by B made before the major investigation (one at Bryn Estyn and another at Wrexham Police Station) were destroyed in accordance with the police force's normal destruction policy; but, in our judgment, B is mistaken in alleging that four others are missing and we can see no reason why the police should have suppressed them. On the other hand, we think (with the benefit of some hindsight) that it would have been wiser if B had been seen by police officers who were not known to him beforehand. It appears that at least one of the three police officers had had previous dealings with B and it is likely that this did affect their approach to him. He must have been known to be a difficult man and we accept that there was probably a degree of insensitivity in their approach to him, bearing in mind that they were unaware of the gravity of his wife's problems at the time. B said in evidence that he asked to be interviewed by a woman police officer and it may be that some of the difficulties about his evidence would have been avoided, if that request had been granted earlier than it was.

51.59 There is one other potential criticism of the investigation from 1991 onwards with which we should deal before concluding this section. It may be suggested that, if the investigation was truly thorough, it is surprising that the number of prosecutions that followed it was small in comparison with the volume of complaints. As we have already said more than once, scrutiny of decisions whether to prosecute named individuals is expressly excluded from the Tribunal's terms of reference. We should say, however, that in the course of the evidence presented by the North Wales Police to the Tribunal, we were shown lists (covering the period of the investigation to the end of November 1993) of individuals in respect of whom files were submitted to the Chief Prosecuting Solicitor. Those lists indicate the names of suspects in respect of whom recommendations to prosecute were made, those in respect of whom no recommendation either way was made and those against whom the police recommended that no proceedings should be taken. It is sufficient for us to say that there is nothing in these lists to cast doubt upon the thoroughness of the investigation or the willingness of the police to prosecute.

The demands for an investigation by an outside force

51.60 There were recurring demands during the final police investigation for another police force to be called in to take over the investigation and the Chief Constable at the time, David Owen, has been criticised for refusing to agree to this. It is necessary, therefore, that we should give a brief history of the demands and the reasons advanced for them from time to time.

51.61 There was no suggestion in the letter of 17 July 1991 from the County Secretary of Clwyd to the Chief Constable, which initiated the investigation, that it was necessary for, or desirable that, an independent police force should be called in to conduct it. However, on 26 July 1991 Councillor Dennis Parry, the leader of Clwyd County Council, referred to allegations of corruption within the North Wales Police at a meeting of the North Wales Police Authority. These allegations and other rumours mentioned on 20 July 1991 by Andrew Loveridge, then the Assistant County Secretary, to a senior police officer, which emanated from similar sources, did not involve any suggestion of child abuse. It transpired that the allegations referred to by Parry had been made by two former constables through another former constable and related to disciplinary issues rather than alleged criminality. They were investigated and subsequently withdrawn.

51.62 On 1 December 1991 the *Independent on Sunday* newspaper published an article on the child abuse investigation in North Wales[18]. In that article Councillor Parry was said to have accused the police of mounting a cover-up to conceal the failure of senior officers and social services executives to reveal the extent of abuse in the children's homes. He was quoted as saying: "I want to know why the police didn't uncover all the stuff that is coming out now". It appears also that at about the same time Dr John Marek, Member of Parliament for Wrexham, wrote to the Rt Hon Earl Ferrers, Minister of State at the Home Office, asking him to order an "independent inquiry" but we have not seen the request or the basis for it. Brief correspondence ensued between the Home Office and the Chief Constable but the request for an inquiry does not appear to have been pursued at that stage. The Home Office was told that the Crown Prosecution Service had advised against any prosecution on the basis of the earlier investigations in Gwynedd but that current enquiries were continuing and that the evidence would be referred to the Crown Prosecution Service. Parry was seen by Ackerley and Rowlands, the senior officers responsible for the current investigation, on 16 December 1991 and does not

---

[18] See paras 2.25 and 2.26.

appear to have pursued his allegation of a cover-up. He confirmed that he had never witnessed any offence against a child in care and that he was not in possession of any evidence of such an offence; he was told that the police investigation was confidential but that liaison with the County Secretary and the Director of Social Services would continue.

51.63 At this point, as we have made clear in Chapter 9, no witness had made a statement to the police alleging that he had been abused by former Superintendent Gordon Anglesea, who had retired in March 1991. The allegations against Anglesea began to emerge when the journalist Dean Nelson pursued his investigations in North Wales during 1992[19]. The first specific allegations of which we have heard were made by the deceased complainant referred to as A in Chapter 9[20] on or about 18 June 1992 to Nelson; and these were repeated to A's solicitors two months later. Very shortly after this, on 24 August 1992, B made his third written statement to the police in which he complained of being pestered by Nelson and said that "at no time did Gordon Anglesea ever sexually abuse me". It was not until September 1992 that B made allegations against Anglesea successively to John Jevons (2 September) Nelson (4 and 11 September) and the police (his fourth written statement, on 9 September).

51.64 At the end of August 1992 the *Observer* newspaper began a series of articles about the allegations of abuse in North Wales children's homes, which appeared in five successive issues from 30 August to 27 September 1992. In the article of 6 September reference was made to the naming of four police officers as suspects and the same article reported comments attributed to the Chairman of the North Wales Police Authority, a Gwynedd county councillor familiar with Alison Taylor's allegations, in which it was alleged that an inquiry into one Gwynedd home had been "deliberately killed". In the following article these allegations were widened: it was said that a former police chief had been named as a prime suspect[21] and that detectives believed half a dozen serving and retired police officers and more than 300 victims to be involved (the alleged number of police officers involved grew to 12, of whom three were still serving, by 27 September). Moreover, Councillor Dennis Parry and John Marek MP were reported to be calling for the investigation to be taken over by an outside force to restore confidence in the North Wales Police. By that time, on 7 September 1992, the Parliamentary Secretary to the Welsh Office had announced that a public inquiry into allegations of abuse in North Wales would take place when the North Wales Police had completed their inquiries[22].

51.65 It is necessary to explain here the reference to police officers other than Anglesea against whom allegations of abuse had been made. The evidence before us shows that there were three officers only against whom allegations of sexual abuse were made and that none of them had any known relevant

[19] See para 2.33.
[20] See para 9.29.
[21] See para 2.27.
[22] See para 2.36.

connection with Anglesea. We have not referred to the allegations against them earlier because none of their offences was alleged to have been committed against a child who was in care at that time.

51.66 All three of these police officers were serving in the Territorial Army and working as Instructors with Army Cadets when the alleged offences are said to have occurred. The complainant against two of the police officers, whom we will refer to as X and Y, was B, who was made the subject of a care order on 15 July 1977, when he was $14\frac{1}{2}$ years old. B had been encouraged by his father to join the Army Cadets and did so when he was about 11 years old. He remained a member until he was placed at Bersham Hall on 2 August 1977. He alleged that he suffered buggery and other forms of sexual assault at the hands of both X and Y in the course of his cadet service. These offences were committed separately by them; they occurred frequently in the cadet hut and on occasions in a police car.

51.67 B first alleged to the police that he had been abused by X (who was discharged from the police on medical grounds on 30 June 1990) when he was interviewed on 24 August 1992. In his written statement made that day he said that he had no complaint to make with regard to Y but he made a further statement to the police on 13 October 1992 in which he made detailed allegations of sexual abuse by Y. Both X and Y denied that they had abused B.

51.68 B did not make any allegations against the third police officer, Z, who was known to his family. The complainant against Z was another army cadet, who was not in care and who joined the Regular Army at the age of 16 years. He said that Z befriended him during his cadet service but that, on three occasions when he was about 15 years old, Z indecently assaulted him. This complainant never mentioned these incidents until the police got in touch with him in November 1992 and on 28 December 1992 he made a formal written statement recounting them. On 24 March 1993, when Z was no longer in the police force, he was given a written caution in respect of an offence of indecent assault against the boy, which he admitted.

51.69 The North Wales Police Authority considered the call for an investigation by an outside police force at its meeting on 14 September 1992, at which the Chief Constable made a statement in the course of which he said that allegations had been made against three serving officers and two former officers[23] but that there were no allegations of sexual abuse being made against any serving police officer. He affirmed the intention of the North Wales Police to leave no stone unturned "in further pursuing these allegations (of abuse), irrespective of the political, social or senior position of any person involved". The Chief Constable mentioned also that matters had already been referred to the Police Complaints Authority for them to consider whether they should supervise the inquiry: so far, they had not seen the necessity to supervise but there would be further discussions with them. The Police Authority resolved that the allegations of abuse should continue to be investigated "as an internal matter within the Force".

---

[23] We do not know of any allegations other than those we have referred to.

51.70 It seems that discussion about calling in an outside force rumbled on through the autumn of 1992 but petered out by the end of the year. In September 1992 Donald Elliott, one of HM Inspectors of Constabulary and the Inspector responsible for North Wales, expressed interest in the investigation because of the possible involvement of police officers as potential offenders but was not concerned about the overall inquiry[24]. Then on 1 October 1992 both Elliott and the Chief Constable attended a conference of the Association of Chief Police Officers (ACPO) and Elliott suggested informally to the Chief Constable that he should get in an outside force to deal with the investigation into child abuse. Elliott said that he had been thinking about the matter and felt that there were a lot of complications because of the interest of local politicians; if an outside force were to be invited to take over, it would resolve the issues.

51.71 The Chief Constable pointed out in his evidence that Elliott had not had any previous discussion with him or any briefing about the investigation before tendering this advice; and Elliott did not seek any briefing. The latter wrote subsequently to the North Wales Police Authority to seek their views but it was clear from the Clerk's reply, dated 16 October 1992, that the Authority did not consider it necessary at that time to call in an outside police force. This was not stated expressly and the author of the letter (Roger Davies[25]) appears to have forgotten the Authority's resolution on 14 September but he did refer to a full discussion of the issues that had taken place on 23 September 1992 between the Chairman, the Clerk and the Chief Constable.

51.72 Sir John Woodcock, HM Chief Inspector of Constabulary from 1 April 1990 to 30 June 1993 and a former Chief Constable of South Wales, visited the North Wales Police on 8 and 9 October 1992. It was a courtesy visit at a time when the Chief Constable was President of ACPO. In the course of that visit Sir John spent nearly two hours with the investigative team in the Major Incident Room that had been established in Colwyn Bay. In his written statement to the Tribunal he said that he was impressed by what he saw and heard that day and was delighted with the response that he received. He did not feel concerned about the conduct of the inquiry: it was obvious to him that the Chief Constable had a firm control on the inquiry and he wrote to the latter after his visit, saying how impressed he had been with the officers whom he had met.

51.73 On the subject of the advice given by Elliott, of which he was aware, Sir John said that he thought that it had been good advice and that he would probably have given the same advice but he added that he could not say so definitely. Sir John stressed that the decision whether or not to call in another force was a matter for the Chief Constable to decide: he was responsible and answerable for his own actions and was in the best position to make a professional judgment on the advice given.

---

[24] Letter from him to the Chief Constable dated 16 September 1992.
[25] See para 28.45.

51.74 Another visitor to the Major Incident Room was Mrs Causey, a member of the Police Complaints Authority; and Sir Leonard Peach, its chairman, also visited the North Wales Police at about this time. As Sir Ronald Hadfield, our assessor, has explained, however, all the serious allegations against police officers that we have discussed were outside the jurisdiction of the PCA so that supervision of the inquiry by that Authority was never a live possibility[26]. David Owen told us that he did refer "the matter" on a third occasion to the PCA following the allegation against Y in October 1992 but again received a negative response.

51.75 The Chief Constable told the Tribunal that he regarded it as unnecessary and impracticable to call in an outside force to take over the investigation in the autumn of 1992, which was the first and only time that it was mooted on a credible basis. By that time the investigation had reached an advanced stage; very many statements had been taken by the investigating team of approximately 51 officers; and prosecution had been recommended in about a dozen cases. If an outside force had been called in, the investigation would have been set back by a year and the cost of the exercise would have been unacceptable. The Chief Constable had full confidence in the reliability and professional capacity of the Senior Investigating Officer and, in the former's view, the progress and ultimate outcome of the investigation justified that confidence.

51.76 A further point made by the Chief Constable is that, although Gwynedd Social Services Committee joined in the call for an outside force in October 1992, the demands for this were otherwise restricted to a small group of people whose views had been publicised and he did not receive any correspondence from the general public in support of the demand. In an effort to assuage any anxiety felt by local politicians he arranged to meet Dr John Marek MP and Councillor Malcolm King with the Deputy Chief Constable in response to a suggestion of Earl Ferrers. At that meeting on 4 December 1992 the Chief Constable told them that, if they had a list of specific concerns, he would arrange for the responsible Assistant Chief Constable and Ackerley to meet them to try to resolve the issues. Accordingly, the further meeting took place on 17 December 1992 and it was continued on 26 February 1993, when Andrew Loveridge[27] attended in place of Dr Marek. We have seen what appear to be full notes of the subjects discussed at both of these later briefing meetings, most of which have been before this Tribunal. Our interpretation of the notes is that full and accurate information was given in response to the many questions that were raised.

51.77 Sir Ronald Hadfield said in his advice to the Tribunal[28] that he would only criticise the decision of the Chief Constable not to request that another police force should take over the investigation if it could have been shown to have been plainly wrong. In his view, there were many factors supporting that

---

[26] See Appendix 11, para 8.
[27] See para 51.61.
[28] See Appendix 11, para 7.

decision, as we have indicated in the preceding paragraph, and it follows that Sir Ronald does not criticise the way in which the Chief Constable exercised his discretion.

51.78 Our own view is that the Chief Constable made the correct decision on the right grounds in difficult circumstances. The earlier Gwynedd inquiry had given rise to justifiable criticism and lack of confidence in the determination of the North Wales Police to investigate the allegations of child abuse thoroughly and impartially. By the autumn of 1992, however, the Chief Constable had substantial grounds for confidence that the new comprehensive investigation was being carried out with integrity and professional efficiency; and replacement of the investigating team, with all the attendant confusion, delay and expense, could not be justified. We should add that, in our judgment also, a review of the investigation by an independent senior officer at that stage would not have served any useful practical purpose in relation to the investigation itself but it is arguable that such a review would have helped to assuage public concern[29].

Conclusions

51.79 To sum up, we consider that the first of the three police investigations that we have discussed in detail, namely, the investigation led by Detective Superintendent Gwynne Owen in Gwynedd between 1986 and 1988 was seriously defective for the reasons that we have indicated in paragraphs 51.29 to 51.32. As we have said there, it is a matter of speculation whether any criminal charges would have been brought if the investigation had been pursued more thoroughly and impartially by an adequate investigating team; and it is even less clear that such an investigation would have been widened to cover other children's homes. What is clear, however, is that the handling of the investigation did give rise to unease and dissatisfaction amongst a small but significant number of persons, including alleged victims of abuse, who had some knowledge of the circumstances. This in turn led to anxiety and adverse publicity about the North Wales Police when wider allegations of abuse came to be investigated about three years later.

51.80 We do not think that any substantial criticism is justified of the later two investigations, bearing in mind particularly the scale of the last. No doubt there were errors in the approach to some witnesses but the volume of complaints under this head of which we have heard has been notably small. Nevertheless, there are important lessons to be learnt from all three investigations. One is the importance of appropriate training in advance of a sizeable group of officers in each police force to equip them to carry out inquiries into abuse with appropriate sensitivity, however stale the allegations may be[30]. Another is the importance of close liaison between the police and other agencies, particularly social services departments. There will often be complications about this

---

[29] See also Sir Ronald Hadfield's comment on this: Appendix 11, para 9.
[30] Note also Sir Ronald Hadfield's comments on assistance from a psychologist: Appendix 11, para 6.4.

because allegations may impinge directly or indirectly on officers or staff of those agencies but a clear working relationship has to be established and access by the police to all relevant documents is of paramount importance.

51.81 It is common knowledge that, since this Tribunal was announced, there have been widespread investigations into the alleged abuse of children in care in several parts of the country on lines similar to that of the last North Wales investigation. It is strongly arguable, therefore, that the time has now arrived for a comprehensive inter-agency review of the conduct of such investigations, leading to the issue of appropriate guidelines, in the light of recent experience.

Was there a paedophile ring?

Introduction

52.01　The question whether a paedophile ring existed in North Wales was raised at the outset of the major police investigation in the letter of 17 July 1991 from the County Secretary of Clwyd to the Chief Constable. In that letter, after dealing with the four lists of persons that accompanied it, the County Secretary said:

> "I understand that when your officers investigated the case against (A) they were, at one stage, concerned as to the existence of a paedophile ring in North Wales.
>
> This question exercises my mind greatly and I believe it will be a matter of equal concern to you.
>
> A perusal of the contents of the list of individuals will immediately demonstrate that there are an overwhelming number of links back to the former approved school, later residential care home at Bryn Estyn which has now closed. It may, of course, be nothing more than coincidence but if it is coincidence then it appears to be an extremely high level of coincidence."

52.02　We have no doubt that the police did have this question firmly in mind throughout the investigation. There was, in reality, no danger that it would be forgotten because of its obvious importance and the fact that it was raised from time to time in newspaper articles and by individuals such as Councillor Malcolm King. The latter, for example, produced in July 1992 a list of the names of 11 boys alleged to have attended a party with nine male paedophiles and he raised questions touching upon an alleged paedophile ring at the meetings in December 1992 and February 1993, which are referred to in paragraph 51.75 of our report. Moreover, on 27 September 1992 the *Observer* newspaper published an article by a journalist, Brian Johnson Thomas, in which allegations were made about the existence of a paedophile ring that included several policemen.

52.03　Detective Superintendent Ackerley gave evidence to the Tribunal that all these allegations were investigated by the police as they arose but that no evidence of any substance could be obtained to support them. Most of the persons named by Councillor King were seen (six of the boys had already been seen and were re-interviewed) but the "overwhelming tenor" of the replies was that no party of the kind alleged had taken place; and that many of the persons on the list were not known to each other. Councillor King told the police that he had received the list from Dean Nelson, who in turn had allegedly received it in the form of a sworn affidavit from a former Bryn Estyn resident; but, when Nelson was asked about the matter on 22 December 1992, he told Ackerley that he had never received such information about a party attended by homosexuals. As for the author of the *Observer* article, he did not have any evidence to substantiate either the headline or the contents of the article.

52.04 Ackerley dealt also in his evidence with the suggestion that there was a paedophile ring at Bryn Estyn, pointing out that the alleged victims of Howarth and Norris were clearly distinct types in terms of their ages and other characteristics. His recollection was that only two complainants from that community home had alleged that more than one offender had been involved in a particular incident. With full particulars before him he could have added that no one alleged abuse by Howarth and Norris in each other's presence and only five out of 48 complaints of sexual abuse at Bryn Estyn alleged that they had been abused by both men. Ackerley concluded, therefore, that if the alleged paedophile ring involved victims being passed from one offender to another at Bryn Estyn, the evidence obtained by the police did not establish that that had occurred.

52.05 The difficulty about dealing with this question satisfactorily is that a paedophile ring may exist in many different forms and that the range of its possible activities is also wide. One cannot formulate easily, therefore, an umbrella definition that will withstand academic scrutiny and lay persons are likely to have widely varying concepts of the meaning of the phrase. Counsel for the North Wales Police, Andrew Moran QC, suggested that, for those who have continued to allege that such a ring existed in and around Wrexham in the 1970s and 1980s, an appropriate definition would be "a group of pederasts known to each other, who habitually exploit children for sexual gratification by passing information and the victims themselves around the group". Witness B[1], who was the principal source of allegations that such a ring existed, suggested a similar definition, namely, "a group of men who knew one another, who shared a common sexual interest in boys and who shared the boys they succeeded in abusing".

52.06 This is not the place for legal sophistry and we are content to accept these definitions as sufficient in the context of this particular case and to discuss the relevant evidence on that footing. There are, however, some wider matters of public concern, such as the recruitment of paedophiles, to which we will refer in the course of our discussion.

52.07 We should say at once that no evidence has been presented to the Tribunal or to the North Wales Police to establish that there was a wide-ranging conspiracy involving prominent persons and others with the objective of sexual activity with children in care. Equally, we are unaware of any evidence to establish that there was any coherent organisation of men with that objective. What we discuss hereafter in this chapter is whether there were groups of men, known to each other and associating informally, who did prey on children in care together and individually for sexual purposes during the period under review.

52.08 Bearing in mind that the main (but not sole) source of evidence on this subject before us has been witness B, this subject is most conveniently discussed under the following heads:

(a) Paedophile activity at and connected with Bryn Estyn and Cartrefle.

---

[1] See paras 9.05, 9.32 to 9.34 and 51.55.

(b) Recruitment generally.

(c) Paedophile activity in and around Wrexham town.

(d) The investigation of Gary Cooke in 1979.

(e) The Campaign for Homosexual Equality.

(f) Paedophile activity on the North Wales coast.

Paedophile activity at and connected with Bryn Estyn and Cartrefle

52.09 We have discussed the alleged sexual abuse at Bryn Estyn very fully in Chapters 8 and 9 of this report; and the allegations of sexual abuse at Cartrefle are dealt with similarly in Chapter 15[2]. We return to the subject here only for the purpose of considering whether there was any connecting thread or link between the proved offenders and whether there is any evidence that they shared victims or information about them.

52.10 The two main paedophiles who were active at Bryn Estyn in the period between 1974 and its closure in September 1984 undoubtedly were **Peter Howarth**, a bachelor, who became Deputy Principal in July 1976 and remained until 31 July 1984, and **Stephen Norris**, who was a houseparent at Cedar House for just over four and a half years (with his wife for the first three years) before becoming Senior Housemaster in charge of Clwyd House from about September 1978. Almost all the offences committed by Howarth took place in his flat at Bryn Estyn from 1974 onwards whereas Norris' known offences began when he assumed responsibility for Clwyd House and continued at Cartrefle from December 1984 until about June 1990. In his case the offences were committed in the shower blocks at both premises, in bedrooms there and on occasions when he took victims to his smallholding at Afonwen in Clwyd.

52.11 We have not heard any evidence of a significant association between Howarth and Norris, even though they were both members of the care staff at Bryn Estyn. On the contrary, the evidence has indicated that there was a mutual antipathy between them. There has been no suggestion, as far as we are aware, that Howarth knew of Norris' offences. As for Norris himself, he may have had suspicions about Howarth's activities, like some other members of the Bryn Estyn staff, but the evidence before us does not establish that he knew that Howarth was committing sexual offences against residents.

52.12 We have looked particularly for any evidence that other men (or women) were present when sexual offences are alleged to have been committed by either man. In the case of Howarth this was alleged by a small number of witnesses. One complainant, whose evidence was read to the Tribunal because he could not be traced, said that he was the victim of a serious joint indecent assault by Howarth and Paul Wilson in the former's flat whilst he was a resident at Bryn Estyn between March 1981 and June 1982; but both Howarth and Wilson were acquitted by a jury of this alleged offence on 8 July 1994.

---

[2] See particularly paras 15.07 to 15.14 and 15.22 to 15.24.

52.13 Another person who was alleged by complainants to have been present in Howarth's flat when offences were committed and to have participated in them is Gordon Anglesea. However, as we have explained in Chapter 9, a civil jury found (in effect) that he had not been involved in sexual misconduct at Bryn Estyn and we have not received persuasive evidence to justify us in reaching a different conclusion.

52.14 In relation to Norris there has been no acceptable evidence that anyone else participated in or witnessed any of his offences at Clwyd House or Cartrefle, nor has it been suggested that anyone else was present in the same place at the smallholding when he committed them. One complainant, however, whose evidence was read because he failed to appear several times to give oral evidence, did allege that on two occasions Norris took him to a very large house near Chester where he was sexually assaulted and buggered by both Norris and the occupier. This was alleged to have occurred when the complainant was resident at Bryn Estyn. He said also that, on another occasion, Norris arranged for him to be picked up by car after tea at Bryn Estyn and taken to a house in Chirk, where a big and strong man, aged 40 to 50 years, persistently assaulted him sexually, despite his attempts to resist. The man eventually gave up and made a telephone call, whereupon the complainant was driven back to Bryn Estyn by the driver who had picked him up earlier. On his return to Bryn Estyn, he was knocked unconscious by Wilson, by a punch to the face, because of his "behaviour with the man at Chirk". When he came to, he was taken to the secure unit.

52.15 There are obviously formidable difficulties about this evidence, not least the failure of the witness to face cross-examination about it. His allegations are wholly uncorroborated, the alleged "outside" abusers and their addresses are unidentified, and the allegation against Wilson is the only suggestion of complicity by him in sexual misconduct by Norris. Other allegations made by the witness against a substantial number of persons, including sexual abuse by John Allen at Bryn Estyn, are highly dubious and, in the circumstances, we cannot be satisfied that his account of the Chirk incident and its aftermath is true.

52.16 Similar difficulties arise about allegations made by witness B in a statement to the police, which he confirmed in part only when he gave oral evidence. The alleged abuser referred to by B, whom we will call X, has the surname of a well known and large non-Welsh family and he is said to be dead now. It has been suggested also (but not by B) that X was a friend or acquaintance of Howarth. According to B's statement to the police, X had several different motor cars and would wait for him at the bottom of Bryn Estyn Lane when he had a late pass. X would be accompanied by another paedophile now deceased and they would take B to various places. B alleged that he was buggered by X on four or five of these occasions, twice in the car in Moss Valley, once in the Crest Hotel at Wrexham and in the flat of Gary Cooke on the other occasions.

52.17 Witness B was, however, very reserved about these allegations when he gave oral evidence, saying that, after a particular press article had appeared, his house and his car had been destroyed and he had received numerous threats:

he was not taking any chances any more. He said, for example, that he knew the christian name of X but that he was unwilling to disclose it. His recollection in the witness box was that he had seen X three times, including once at the Crest Hotel. X had a young man who was his driver and this man liked people to think he was a member of X's family. B was unable to say who had told him X's name.

52.18 Both Detective Superintendent Ackerley and Dean Nelson, a journalist to whom X had been mentioned, were asked about any further enquiries that they made to establish his identity. Ackerley said that it was difficult to identify which member of the family was being referred to: he never had anything tangible to get hold of. Nelson was more outspoken. He said that the name was mentioned to him but he never received any proper allegation about X. He added: "So far as I was concerned the X thing was a distraction. I wasn't looking into X and I never heard anything that made me think I should".

52.19 Before leaving this subject, it is necessary to mention the evidence of one other complainant, although he was not a resident at either Bryn Estyn or Cartrefle. This witness, referred to as C in Chapter 21[3], was a resident with the Bryn Alyn Community in the Wrexham area between 1984 and 1986. In his oral evidence to the Tribunal he said that John Allen introduced him to two men with whom he had oral sex but that the identity of these men had not been established. However, he had purported earlier to identify one of them as a member of the X family by reference to a photocopied picture (one of four) produced to him by a journalist. His account had been that, whilst he was living at Gatewen Hall, he had been taken for a meal with John Allen and this man, who had paid for the meal with a gold credit card and who also had a Harrods account card. C had subsequently indicated, however, that he could not be one hundred per cent sure that his abuser was a member of the X family, and it is clear that he was referring to a different person from the man of whom B spoke.

52.20 It is obvious on this evidence that we cannot be satisfied that any member of the X family was involved in paedophile activity connected with either Bryn Estyn or Bryn Alyn and the name has not been mentioned in connection with residents of any other community home in North Wales.

52.21 We must add that two other names that have been linked with Bryn Estyn in connection with alleged paedophile ring activity are those of Gary Cooke and David Gillison but it will be more appropriate to discuss the evidence in relation to them later in this chapter.

Recruitment generally

52.22 Having regard to the number of former members of the staff of children's residential establishments in North Wales who have been convicted of sexual offences against children in care, a major concern in the forefront of our minds

---

[3] See paras 21.31 to 21.33.

throughout the hearings has been the question whether there is evidence of the systematic recruitment of paedophiles to the staff of all or any of these establishments.

52.23 It is convenient to discuss this question here because the circumstances in which both Howarth and Norris were selected for posts at Bryn Estyn have been a particular cause for anxiety. Those circumstances have already been outlined in this report at paragraphs 8.03 (Howarth), 8.23 and 8.24 (Norris); and it will have been seen from those accounts that the Principal, Granville Arnold, played a prominent role in the appointments of both men. Arnold had met Howarth at Ruskin College, Oxford, and later invited him to apply for posts at Axwell Park Approved School and then at Bryn Estyn. Arnold's part in the appointment of Norris to Bryn Estyn is less clear. According to the latter, it was Arnold who suggested that he and his wife should apply for vacant joint posts there, when they visited the home from Greystone Heath for other reasons. There are some grounds for doubting the complete accuracy of Norris' recollection of this[4] but we accept that Arnold did at least encourage Norris and his wife to move to Bryn Estyn.

52.24 We have not been able to probe Arnold's knowledge of Howarth and his reasons for encouraging Howarth to follow him to senior posts at Axwell Park and Bryn Estyn because both men died before the Tribunal was able to hear evidence from them. There is no other evidence before us, however, to suggest that Arnold had any sinister motive in encouraging Howarth to apply for the post of Deputy Principal at Bryn Estyn or to establish that he knew of Howarth's paedophile activities or tendencies at any stage whilst he was at Bryn Estyn. Our criticism of Arnold is that he was at fault in adopting such a defensive attitude in relation to Howarth and, in effect, shutting his eyes and ears to rumours about Howarth. In particular, in our view, it was a serious error of judgment on Arnold's part to condone Howarth's "flat list" practice[5].

52.25 We are in similar but less difficulty about Arnold's reasons for encouraging Norris to move to Bryn Estyn. There is no evidence before us to suggest that Arnold had any knowledge of Norris before then or that Norris had been guilty of any paedophile activity before he left Greystone Heath; and there is no evidence either that Arnold knew later of Norris' sexual misconduct at Bryn Estyn.

52.26 We have considered also other appointments to the staff of Bryn Estyn but there is nothing in the evidence before us that could support an inference that a paedophile ring was involved in recruitment there. The only other proved paedophile shown to have had some acquaintanceship with Arnold outside Bryn Estyn is John Allen and the evidence about this does not justify an adverse interpretation. Allen's evidence was that he first met Arnold at Axwell Park when he visited that school in the early 1970s in connection with the proposed placement of a youngster with the Bryn Alyn Community. Arnold subsequently invited himself to spend the night prior to his interview for the

---

[4] See para 8.23.
[5] See paras 8.12 to 8.16.

Bryn Estyn post at Allen's bungalow at Gresford, near Wrexham, which Allen occupied with his wife following their recent marriage. Subsequent contact between Allen and Arnold was limited to two visits by the former to Bryn Estyn, one in response to Arnold's invitation to "look around" and the other for a football match against a Bryn Estyn side.

52.27 We have looked carefully at the circumstances of the appointments of all the other proved and suspected paedophiles who were appointed to the other residential children's establishments (including private and voluntary establishments) discussed in this report but have not found any case in North Wales in the period under review in which a convicted paedophile was appointed to such a post. The nearest case in point was that of Gary Cooke[6], who was employed at Bersham Hall for two weeks before his services were dispensed with, probably shortly before the period under review began. Cooke was later employed in 1976/1977 by the Bryn Alyn Community for over a year but this employment was in Cheshire and then Shropshire. We have no evidence that Cooke's 1963 conviction was either disclosed or known to those who appointed him then. The only foster parent now known to have had a relevant previous conviction was Roger Saint, and that was not known at the time of his initial approval[7].

Paedophile activity in and around Wrexham town

52.28 The main witness about this activity in Wrexham, outside the community homes, was B[8], who was also the complainant who gave evidence about the investigation of Gary Cooke in 1979 and about the Campaign for Homosexual Equality, which are dealt with in the following sections of this chapter. B was in care from 15 July 1977 to 25 December 1980 and he alleges that, during this period, he was abused by no less than 20 men outside Bryn Estyn. His allegations against X and Gordon Anglesea have already been dealt with but it is necessary here to outline the circumstances in which, according to his evidence, he was abused by the other men.

52.29 During his period in care B was resident at Bersham Hall for assessment from 2 August to 27 September 1977 and then for 20 months at Bryn Estyn until 22 May 1979. In the following 14 months he lived at various places in the Wrexham and Chester areas but he was remanded in custody on 25 July 1980 to Risley Remand Centre and then placed at Neath Farm School[9] from 7 September 1980 until his discharge from care. On leaving Bryn Estyn he was in lodgings (aged 16 years) for just over two months and again in various lodgings for about six months the following year from 4 January 1980. In between these two periods in lodgings he spent 12 weeks at Chevet Hey followed by six weeks at Foston Hall Detention Centre, from which he was discharged to a hostel in Chester, where he stayed for nearly a month.

---

[6] See paras 52.40 and 52.41. There is a perturbing suggestion, outside the scope of our inquiry, that Cooke's paedophile inclinations were known to at least one senior probation officer when he was appointed later to be Assistant Warden of a Probation Hostel in Clwyd.

[7] See Chapter 25 and, particularly, paras 25.12 to 25.19.

[8] See footnote 17 to para 51.55.

[9] In West Glamorgan.

52.30 B's evidence about paedophile activity in and around Wrexham centred mainly on King Street, the Crest Hotel and various houses and flats, including some associated with the Lift Project. Prominent in many of his allegations were two convicted paedophiles, Gary Cooke[10] and Graham Stephens[11], and also Tom Kenyon[12], now deceased.

52.31 King Street was not said to be a place where actual paedophile misconduct occurred. The references in the evidence were mainly to a cafe in that street, near to public lavatories, where homosexuals, including some paedophiles, would call and where acquaintance could be made with boys or youths in care, who had a pass out or who had absconded from a community home.

52.32 The Crest Hotel was said to be a "motel" in Yorke Street, at which at least two traders attending the beast market in Wrexham on a Monday would stay and where some homosexuals would meet them on a Sunday evening.

52.33 The Lift Project was founded in 1972 by Owen Hardwicke, a Roman Catholic priest of over 40 years standing now, and described by him as his "brainchild". He was a parish priest for 15 years before qualifying for the CQSW in 1972 and he then became a lecturer at Cartrefle College from 1974 to 1980. The object of the Lift Project, as we understand it, was to provide accommodation for homeless persons in need; it was funded initially by private donations and later by an urban aid grant. The Project owned a number of premises from time to time but eventually had only one cottage left, in Haigh Road, Hightown.

52.34 B's evidence about Gary Cooke was that they met, before B was in care, when B was an army cadet and Cooke was an instructor based at Connah's Quay. Cooke abused him sexually on about half a dozen occasions before he went into care, at a time when he did not know what was right or wrong and when he felt that he could not tell anyone about it. Subsequently, he saw Cooke on many occasions when he was in care. Cooke would, for example, wait in a car for him in Bryn Estyn Lane when he had a pass out (often when he himself had not known in advance that he was to have a pass and had not asked for one) and it was Cooke who introduced him to numerous other paedophiles. Cooke was B's link with almost all the paedophiles whom he named, including the men who frequented the Crest Hotel on Sunday evenings and persons associated with the Lift Project.

52.35 It is unnecessary, and would be inappropriate, to list all the allegations made by B against the men whom he has named because the evidence is insufficient, in our judgment, to establish satisfactorily that particular named individuals committed specific offences on identified occasions. In summary, B's evidence was that he was buggered on many occasions and had oral sex on others. Some of the alleged offences occurred at Cooke's flat and at the premises of persons to whom he was introduced by Cooke, including the Haigh Road cottage

---

[10] See para 2.07(4) and (6).

[11] See para 2.07(4).

[12] Tom Kenyon had no previous conviction for a paedophile offence but was convicted at West London Magistrates' Court in September 1981 of persistently importuning for an immoral purpose in a public place and in September 1989 of committing an act of gross indecency with another male person unknown.

referred to in paragraph 52.33, where B stayed at Easter 1980. Others occurred in rooms at the Crest Hotel and some of the offences were committed in motor cars in which B was given a ride or lift. The alleged abusers included Cooke, Stephens and Tom Kenyon. B named also Huw Meurig Jones, whom B described as a friend of Cooke whom he had met at Bryn Estyn, when Meurig Jones was visiting there as a social worker, and later in King Street.

52.36 We heard oral evidence from 14 of the 18 "other men" referred to in paragraph 52.28, including Cooke, Stephens and Meurig Jones, and the evidence of one other was read to us. Of the other three, Kenyon is dead, one was identified only by his first name and is thought to be dead also and the other could not be traced. One of the 14 oral witnesses was a social worker, unconnected by evidence with any of the "other men", who was alleged by B to have committed a lesser indecent assault upon him; but the evidence given and produced by the witness was sufficient, in our view, to refute B's allegation. All the others whose evidence we received, with three exceptions, were proved or admitted homosexuals; but they all denied B's allegations vehemently and two denied that they even knew B. Meurig Jones was one of the three exceptions: he expressly denied when he gave evidence that he was a homosexual.

52.37 Another complainant, the witness referred to as C in Chapter 21 and in paragraph 52.19, alleged that he was the victim of abuse by Cooke. C alleged that he met Cooke in the King Street cafe, when C was living with the Bryn Alyn Community. C, who was about 16 years old at the time, was talking with friends or acquaintances when Cooke joined in the conversation: eventually C went with a friend to Cooke's flat in Brymbo, where he was indecently touched and buggered by Cooke. According to C, this happened on two occasions and on one of them another adult was present but he did not know that adult's name. If C was 16 years old when the offences were committed, the dates would have been between April 1984 and April 1985.

52.38 Two other witnesses who gave oral evidence spoke of being abused by Cooke. One of them was in care from 10 April 1973, when he was 16 years old, until the end of 1974. According to this witness, a friendship developed between them when he attended a youth club at Gresford, where Cooke was then a team leader (prior to the army cadets). On one occasion the witness absconded from Chevet Hey and stayed at the home of Cooke's parents. He subsequently stayed for some months in Leicester with Cooke, after breaking up with his girl friend, whilst undertaking an apprenticeship and still in care. Cooke started to abuse him within a week or two of their meeting and continued to do so until the witness told Cooke that it was not what he wanted, whereupon the relationship petered out. The witness alleged also that he was abused separately by Stephens, who may not have known Cooke then. Stephens took the witness to Denmark in December 1972 and the latter's mother, with two daughters went to live with Stephens, who started to have sex with him when he was living in Bersham Hall. In his view both Cooke and Stephens took advantage of him when he was in need of friendship but he did not allege that they introduced him to other paedophiles. In 1993 he withdrew the allegations against them that he had made to the police only a short time earlier but he re-affirmed them to the Tribunal.

52.39 The second of these other witnesses was a victim named in one of the four counts of buggery of which Cooke was convicted on 29 April 1987. This witness was 18 years old at the time of the offence in 1986 and was no longer in care, although he had been in care earlier from 1980 to 1983, at Bryn Estyn for three months in 1980 and then for nearly two years between 1981 and 1983, at Bersham Hall, where he was when he first met Cooke.

52.40 Gary Cooke, who was born on 7 January 1951, made three written statements to the Tribunal and was extensively cross-examined when he gave oral evidence to us. His first convictions for indecent assaults on a boy were on 12 September 1963, when he was only 12 years old; and he was subsequently convicted of paedophile offences in 1980, when he received five years' imprisonment, and in 1987, when he received seven years' imprisonment. His most recent convictions were in December 1995 when he received two years' imprisonment for two indecent assaults on a male aged 18 or 19 years. Most of his proved victims were not in care at the time of his offences but, according to the records before us, two of them in respect of whom he was convicted in 1987 were in care when offences of buggery and indecent assault of one and taking indecent photographs of the other occurred. One of the counts in the 1980 indictment, which alleged buggery with William Gerry[13], then aged 14/15 years and in care, was ordered to be left on the Court file on the usual terms[14].

52.41 Cooke has had a very varied employment career but much of it is irrelevant for our purposes and we have few reliable dates. It appears that at some point between 1972 and June 1974, after leaving the Army, he was employed for two weeks at Bersham Hall[15] but was then told by the Officer-in-Charge, Richard Leake, that his services were no longer required. He then moved to the Midlands for about two years, returning in or about 1976 to live with his mother in Llangollen. After a period of training as a nurse, during which he first became involved with the Army Cadet Corps, Cooke was employed as a care worker with the Bryn Alyn Community for over a year. He worked for a year at Marton's Camp in Cheshire until it closed (we believe in July 1977) and then at Cotsbrook Hall in Shropshire[16] for a few months but gave up the work (he says) because he found commuting from Llangollen, where he was again living with his mother, to be too much of a strain. His next known employment was as an Assistant Warden at a Probation Hostel for about six months, by which time he had moved to a flat in Napier Square, Wrexham. In 1978 he applied for a post as RCCO at Little Acton and the following year for a similar post at Chevet Hey but both applications were unsuccessful. There is evidence that he was engaged in some professional wrestling at about that time but he worked also as a taxi driver in Wrexham in or about 1978.

52.42 Cooke was detained in custody from 24 March 1980, when he was committed for trial by Wrexham Magistrates Court, and remained in prison until 23 November 1981, when he was released on parole. According to Meurig Jones,

---

[13] See para 2.07(6).
[14] Not to be proceeded with without the leave of the Crown Court or the Court of Appeal Criminal Division.
[15] See para 13.07.
[16] See para 4.23.

he became acquainted with Cooke in 1979/1980 when he, Meurig Jones, was taking the CQSW course at Cartrefle College, which he failed at the end of the first year. By the time that Cooke was released on this occasion B was no longer in care.

52.43 Most of the relevant evidence in relation to the alleged paedophile ring pre-dates B's discharge from care so that less detail is necessary about Cooke's later movements and employment. It is sufficient to say that he told the Tribunal that his main employment between November 1981 and his further arrest in December 1986 was as manager of a "sex shop" in Wrexham from 1982 to 1984 and that he lived successively in a cottage at Froncysyllte and a flat at Acrefair. Cooke lived then until his arrest in 1986 in a flat in Kent Road, Brymbo, where Meurig Jones stayed with him for about a month. On his release from his second long sentence on 19 June 1991, he lived for a time at Pentre Gwyn, Wrexham and at Llay with one of the "other persons" named by B, before moving to live on the Clwyd coast. Cooke's activities were the subject of additional police investigations in 1982, 1986 (when he was fined for gross indecency with a male) and 1992/1993.

52.44 Cooke denied all the allegations against him made by B and it is clear that there is now a very strong mutual antipathy between them. He said that he himself was sexually abused by adults when he was young and before and after his 1963 conviction; during his second prison term he underwent therapy and has benefited from it. He first met B when the latter was serving in the army cadets but there was no relationship between them. Later on, he and others observed that B would follow people into the King Street lavatories and make a bit of a nuisance of himself, usually with older men. This was at a time when B was living at Bryn Estyn. Cooke and two others approached B and told him not to do it. Cooke said that he and B did not speak to each other for a long time after this incident.

52.45 Cooke gave little evidence about B apart from this. He recalled one occasion, (on 4 July 1978, according to the Bryn Estyn log) when B had absconded from Bryn Estyn with others and Cooke returned the absconders in his car, whereupon they were put into pyjamas to discourage them from trying to do so again. Cooke described also the circumstances in which he invited B to stay in his Napier Square flat in the summer of 1979. According to Cooke, they had not spoken for a substantial time when he saw B one day in Wrexham looking unkempt, contrary to his usual smart appearance. B told Cooke that he had left care and was living in a boarding house where the landlady was giving him a bad time. They talked and B asked Cooke whether he knew of anywhere else that B could stay. Cooke was about to be away himself and was worried about his flat being empty so they agreed that B could stay there. This was the prelude to the events leading to Cooke's 1980 convictions, which are dealt with in the next section of this chapter. Cooke was bitter about the circumstances in which he came to be convicted and said that he never had any association with B after that. He described the suggestion that he had had a sexual relationship with B as "rubbish".

52.46 In answer to the allegations made by C, Cooke said that he did meet C in the King Street cafe but thought that C was the friend of another man. C subsequently visited Cooke's home at Brymbo but no sexual interchange occurred between them. Cooke only found out later that C was in care and, in later cross-examination, he said that C had displayed his homosexual nature openly. Of the witness referred to in paragraph 52.38, Cooke said that their sexual relationship did not begin until they moved to the Midlands and that he did not know at the time that the witness was in care. They had met as students in Wrexham and it was Cooke's first homosexual relationship.

52.47 Graham Stephens, who is 22 years older than Cooke and who was a coal miner and shotfirer until 1980, has been a close associate of Cooke at times in the past but they are now very antagonistic towards each other. Cooke alleges that they first met when Cooke was a boy and Stephens interfered with him sexually whereas Stephens said that they met in 1973, when Cooke would have been 22 years old. Stephens gave oral evidence to the Tribunal as a serving prisoner because he was sentenced on 16 May 1997 at Mold Crown Court to 21 months' imprisonment for inciting an act of gross indecency with a boy aged $11\frac{1}{2}$ years, who was not in care at the time. Before that he had appeared in Court on six occasions between 1955 and 1988, and had served five sentences of immediate imprisonment totalling nearly 12 years, for paedophile offences against boys; but he denied that any of his victims had been in care at the time, except for a 15 years old Bryn Estyn boy whom he assaulted indecently, for which he received a suspended sentence of imprisonment in August 1972 (he said that he only learnt later that the boy was in care).

52.48 According to Stephens, he lived in a house in Cefn Mawr, near Wrexham, where Cooke lodged with him for seven months from January 1974. Then, after a period in lodgings in Beechley Road in 1976/1977, he bought a house in Hightown, Wrexham, in June 1977, where he lived until his arrest on 11 August 1979 and where Cooke lived with him for about three months. He was sentenced with Cooke, but for separate offences from him in the same indictment, on 30 June 1980[17]. On that occasion he pleaded guilty to one offence of buggery (in the passive role) with one boy and to an indecent assault upon another boy, for which offences he received a total of three years' imprisonment. Another alleged offence against William Gerry[18] was left on the Court file on the usual terms[19]. A year or so after his release from prison following his 1980 sentence, Stephens went to live in Yorkshire, where he received shorter prison sentences in 1984 and 1988. His most recent convictions apparently stemmed from a visit to North Wales for Christmas 1995, at the invitation of a friend.

52.49 Stephens said that he "had sex" with Cooke on only one occasion, when Stephens was in lodgings (that is, in 1976/1977). They fell out later when he was living in Hightown because Cooke threatened to say that he (Stephens) was

---

[17] See para 2.07(4).

[18] See paras 52.52 to 52.56.

[19] Not to be proceeded with without the leave of the Crown Court or the Court of Appeal, Criminal Division.

"doing what he (Cooke) was doing to boys". Stephens arranged for Cooke to be "put out" of the house in Hightown and Cooke then acquired the council flat in Napier Square, Wrexham.

52.50 Stephens made many allegations of paedophile activity by Cooke in the years between 1974 and 1979 and he even kept a diary latterly in which he referred to these activities (apparently with writing a book about them in mind). In his oral evidence Stephens made specific allegations about Cooke's behaviour in the lodgings, in the house at Hightown and in the flat at Napier Square. In cross-examination by Counsel on behalf of B, Stephens said that he believed that Cooke had introduced B to him by a different surname and that the meeting had lasted only five minutes. Cooke had then taken B away. Stephens admitted that he and Cooke had both had sexual relations with four named boys (not apparently in care at the time) but he denied that he had had such relations with either B or William Gerry. Cooke told him that he (Cooke) had had sexual relations with B in the army cadets.

52.51 Cooke gave evidence to the Tribunal after Stephens. He said that he had had an "up and down" relationship with Stephens but that it had never been sexual; and he repudiated both Stephens' allegations against him and the incriminating entries in Stephens' diary that were put to him. What was striking about the evidence of both men, however, was the wide range of allegations that they made about the paedophile activities of other persons, some of whom were amongst the "other men" identified by B[20].

52.52 Before leaving this particular topic, it is necessary to refer to two other persons, namely, David John Gillison[21] and William Gerry[22]. Gillison, who was brought up in Wrexham, was employed as a temporary houseparent at Bryn Estyn from 1 August 1974 and again from 1 March 1976 (following absence due to a road accident) before being appointed to a permanent post there as a houseparent from 1 March 1977. He was suspended in April 1979 after he had informed the Principal that he had become Treasurer of the Chester branch of the Campaign for Homosexual Equality, an appointment that attracted some local newspaper publicity. Following various meetings and discussions he was then transferred to a post as craft instructor at a Wrexham day training centre from 30 May 1979 until he began the CQSW course at Manchester University in September 1981. After completing the course successfully in August 1983, he was employed as a social worker for the physically handicapped attached to the Rhuddlan area until his arrest in December 1985; and he has not been employed in social work since his release from prison in the Spring of 1988.

52.53 We heard only one allegation of sexual abuse that may have referred to Gillison during his Bryn Estyn period but the complainant could not remember the first name of his abuser and could only give the first three letters of his surname. The abuse was alleged to have been indecent touching in a tent in the course of a camping trip and it was first mentioned much later by the complainant to a

---

[20] See paras 52.28 and 52.36.
[21] See para 2.07(6).
[22] See para 2.07(6).

psychiatrist from whom he was still receiving treatment when he gave evidence. Gillison denied that any such incident had occurred and we cannot be sure about it in the uncertain state of the evidence.

52.54 Witness B said that he became friendly with Gillison when both were at Bryn Estyn whereas Gillison said in evidence that they became very friendly about a year after B left Bryn Estyn. Social services records show that there was some concern in December 1980, when B was about to be discharged from care, because he went to stay with Gillison instead of at a hostel that had been arranged for him. B does not allege, however, that he was ever abused by Gillison: their friendship continued until the early 1990s and Gillison said that he was the best man at B's wedding in 1988.

52.55 William Gerry, who was born on 28 May 1964, was a resident in all four of the main Wrexham community homes between 7 April 1978 and 2 March 1981 but his periods of admission were all short (the longest, involving three homes, was from 1 March to 21 September 1979). His last stay was for two months in Chevet Hey, ending on 2 March 1981. Prior to that he had made allegations of abuse in 1980 against Cooke, Stephens and Huw Meurig Jones. The allegation of buggery by Cooke and Stephens was a count in the 1980 indictment against both men and was ordered to be left on the file. Stephens alleged in his evidence to the Tribunal that he had seen Cooke in bed with Gerry in the flat at Napier Square but denied that he himself had had any sexual relationship with Gerry; and Cooke denied Stephens' allegation. A further allegation by Gerry and another boy of indecency by Huw Meurig Jones at the Lift cottage in Haigh Road was investigated by the police in December 1980 but no prosecution ensued. In his evidence to the Tribunal Meurig Jones denied any sexual relationship with either boy.

52.56 According to Gillison, he met Gerry in his chapel at Cefn-y-Bedd, near Wrexham, in 1981 and they became lovers later until they both went to prison. Gillison was living in Kinmel Bay from November 1983 and Gerry travelled there to and from Manchester but their relationship deteriorated progressively. As we have said earlier, Gerry committed suicide on 1 December 1997 and we did not receive a statement from him. He alleged to the police in 1992, however, that he had been buggered by an unidentified man whilst he was at Bryn Estyn.

52.57 The circumstances of the offences committed by Gillison and Gerry on 24 December 1985 at Jacqueline Thomas' flat at Gwersyllt have been sufficiently described in paragraphs 14.36 to 14.41 of this report and the details need not be repeated here. Of the two victims, one (G) was 16 years old and in care, living at Bersham Hall at the time; and the other (S), in respect of whom only Gerry was convicted, was about 15 years old[23].

52.58 Gerry was further sentenced on 28 February 1994, in the Crown Court at Chester, to four years' imprisonment for four offences of indecent assault on a male person. He received a concurrent sentence of six months' imprisonment for failing to surrender to bail.

---

[23] See para 14.35.

The investigation of Gary Cooke in 1979

52.59 This investigation is dealt with separately because witness B made a number of criticisms of police officers in connection with it.

52.60 The relevant events began on 1 August 1979, when Tom Kenyon complained to the police that a watch, a pair of jeans and some money had been stolen from him at Cooke's Napier Square flat. The following day Detective Sergeant Mon Williams saw B at the Crest Hotel and B admitted taking the articles, although he disputed the amount of the money. B was sentenced on 23 October 1979 at Wrexham Magistrates' Court to three months' detention for two offences of theft.

52.61 At the relevant time B was staying in Cooke's flat after leaving lodgings that had been found for him in Ruabon Road[24]. Whilst there he had come across some photographs, which, (he alleged) showed young boys with men in indecent sexual acts. There was considerable conflict in the evidence before us about the number of these photographs and the persons who were portrayed in them but it is clear that some were hidden in a hollowed out book. B alleged that others were under the carpet in the lounge. He said also that Cooke, Stephens and Kenyon were among the men shown in the photographs. He himself was in some of them and he named two of the other boys in the photographs. The majority had been taken in a house in Hightown owned by Stephens and in Cooke's flat.

52.62 B's recollection is that he handed some of these photographs to the Detective Sergeant, who later found others in the hollowed out book. Mon Williams' evidence, however, was that he went to the Napier Square flat with B and others in consequence of what B had told him and that the photographs were found there. The evidence about the events that day and subsequently is imperfect because Mon Williams had to rely almost entirely upon the notes that he made at the time. It is clear, however, that Kenyon told him that he had spent the night at the flat with B; although he prevaricated in his first interview about his relationship with B, he denied later that he had had sexual relations with B. The latter told Mon Williams that Kenyon had touched him on the knee, whereupon B had slapped him in the mouth; they had slept separately and B had told Kenyon to leave the next morning. A file was submitted to Mon Williams' supervisory officer, who advised against a prosecution of Kenyon for indecent assault on that evidence.

52.63 Extensive investigations followed into the photographs and the circumstances in which they had been taken. Both Cooke and Stephens made partial admissions and were successfully prosecuted the following year, as we have previously related. Cooke's explanation for his part in taking some of the photographs was that he had been asked to provide them for payment by a man whom he had met in a sauna bath in Wrexham, who had a restaurant in Epsom.

---

[24] See para 52.45.

52.64 B's criticisms in this context have been directed mainly against Mon Williams. His first allegation is that he had previously been called a liar by this officer in 1978, when he was interviewed by the police as a potential witness in connection with the allegation against Paul Wilson that led to a boy (D) being transferred from Bryn Estyn to Neath Farm School[25]. B denied having seen the alleged assault but said that he began to tell Mon Williams of the abuse at Bryn Estyn, going into minor details, but the officer just told him that he was a liar. On a later occasion, when he was still at Bryn Estyn, he had begun to give the same officer more details of the abuse, but the latter had called him a lying bastard and pinned him up against the wall, saying "If you are telling me the truth, you get me the proof. You get me the evidence".

52.65 The difficulty about these allegations is that Mon Williams is adamant that he met B first on 2 August 1979, after B had left Bryn Estyn, when Kenyon identified B to him at the Crest Hotel. Moreover, such documentary records as are still available tend to confirm that Mon Williams was not involved in the investigation of the allegation against Wilson in 1978 because it was other officers who took statements from the potential witnesses. Mon Williams said in evidence that he saw B on several occasions about the events of August 1979 and developed an amicable relationship with him. There was never any occasion when he called B a liar or pinned him against the wall.

52.66 B's other criticisms are that (a) the investigation in 1979 was insufficiently wide and that others should have been prosecuted about the activities disclosed in the photographs and (b) fresh inquiries should have been made into them later in the course of the major police investigation when additional evidence became available. It seems that B is particularly bitter that Cooke (and possibly Stephens also) were not prosecuted for offences against him.

52.67 We have not been persuaded that any of these criticisms by B can be upheld. It seems clear that his allegations against Mon Williams are misdirected, if there is any substance in the suggestion that he tried in 1978 to tell a police officer of abuse at Bryn Estyn. As for the 1979 investigation, Cooke and Stephens were prosecuted for a reasonably wide range of grave offences, for which they received substantial sentences of imprisonment. The evidence that B appeared in any of the photographs is disputed, although one police officer said that he did, and an additional charge in respect of B would not have added significant weight to the case. Moreover, there is nothing tangible before us to show that Kenyon or anyone else was named as an additional photographer or depicted as an abuser in the photographs. It must be added that there was nothing in the evidence then to lead on to an investigation of abuse within Bryn Estyn itself and B does not allege that he referred to it in the course of the 1979 investigation.

52.68 Finally on the subject of B's criticisms, Detective Superintendent Ackerley said that, in the course of the major investigation that began in 1991, the North Wales Police were unable to get hold of the file relating to the 1979 prosecution. They were unclear as to what specific matters had been proceeded with and

[25] See paras 10.15 to 10.19.

what other matters had been left on the file. It was not until the end of October 1992 that it was realised that B was making fresh allegations. Ackerley did not believe that it would be fruitful to question Cooke about B's later allegations because Cooke would not make any admissions and a prosecution could not be sustained on B's evidence alone. On the other hand, observations on and information about Cooke in 1986 had produced abundant further evidence against him, resulting in convictions in April 1987 for very serious offences, including buggery and indecent assault of a boy, aged 12 years and in care, who had been picked up by Cooke in a Wrexham cafe, and indecent photographing of another boy in care, who had met Cooke in the same way. There was a further investigation into Cooke's contemporary activities, which resulted in his convictions in 1995. Sir Ronald Hadfield, our assessor on police matters, said in evidence that he did not detect any flaw in anything that Ackerley did in pursuing inquiries into these matters.

52.69 One other matter needs to be mentioned in the context of the 1979 investigation. Cooke's evidence was that he met Tom Kenyon only once, although another witness (not B) said that he met Kenyon through Cooke. According to Cooke, his meeting with Kenyon took place at the Crest Hotel, after he (Cooke) had been arrested and charged. Kenyon came over to him and gave him a note. In that note Kenyon apologised for what had happened but said also that, if Cooke agreed "not to say anything", he would have a word with his father[26] to ensure that things went better for Cooke in Court. Cooke told the journalist, Dean Nelson, about this letter and said that he handed the letter subsequently to the police: he sought to link it with (what he claimed to be) his early release on parole in 1981.

52.70 The police officers who dealt with Cooke at that time deny that any such letter was handed to them. Moreover, Cooke is mistaken in his belief that he served only 18 months in custody because he was detained for the full relevant third of his total sentence, namely 20 months. It is clear also that Lord Kenyon was not in a position to influence the course of the prosecution or the decisions of the sentencing judge or the Parole Board. It appears that, if the letter was written, which remains in considerable doubt, it was an aberration of Tom Kenyon only in his embarrassing situation.

The Campaign for Homosexual Equality

52.71 Some former officers and members of this organisation were amongst the "other men" referred to by B, some of whom were from the Wrexham area. It is a national organisation but we refer only to its Chester branch, which was set up in or about 1973, and nothing that we say in this report about "CHE" carries any imputation against the wider organisation.

52.72 The evidence that we heard about CHE relates to the first eight years or so of its existence and we were told by one founding member that it has not existed since the 1980s. It established an office in the Bridge Street Rows and a "help line" telephone; and a witness claimed that, at one time, it had the largest

---

[26] See para 50.45.

membership (300) of any branch in the country. Former officers of CHE in this period and some others closely involved with it said that the organisation, including the help line, was strictly controlled and that anyone who sought to use it as a means of "picking up" under-age boys was immediately proscribed. A small number of witnesses, on the other hand, voiced strong criticism of CHE. Cooke, for example, described it in his evidence as "the most vile organisation ever thought of" and told Dean Nelson that the whole of CHE was a "pick up thing". He alleged that he threatened one of the "other men", who was a committee member of CHE, and had a physical confrontation with him because he used it to abuse a young man called David. Another Wrexham witness said that he walked away from the organisation because it was being abused by those who wanted to have sexual relations with youngsters.

52.73 We heard some linked evidence also about clubs in Chester frequented by members of the gay community from time to time during the same period. The particular relevance of these clubs was that B alleged that he was taken along by Cooke to CHE and to the clubs, where he was introduced to several paedophiles. This led in turn to invitations to gay parties and, in at least one instance, to an invitation to stay in Cheshire.

52.74 B's evidence to the Tribunal about the circumstances in which he went to live in a bungalow at Mickle Trafford in Cheshire owned by a member of CHE was that the accommodation was arranged for him by social services and that he was taken there by his social worker[27]. He added that everyone in the care system, including every member of the staff that he had mentioned in his evidence up to that point, assumed that he was gay ("queer") and that that was how he was treated. On his arrival at the bungalow he was sat down in the lounge and the social worker actually gave him a copy of a newspaper called Gay News to read, saying "I suggest you read that: that might help you". B went on to say that, during his stay at the bungalow, he suffered sexual abuse involving oral and anal sex from five of the named "other men"[28] and two other partly identified men. The abuse occurred mainly at the bungalow and B referred to a big party there one night, which he described as an "orgy", but he was also taken to two of the abusers' own homes and oral sex also occurred in a motor car.

52.75 A preliminary difficulty about these allegations is that B did allege (for example, in his statement to the police on 8 February 1993) that he went to the Mickle Trafford bungalow after leaving Neath Farm School in December 1980, which was six months after the relevant social worker left the employ of Clwyd County Council. It is now clear from the documents and, in particular, the detailed typed record kept by the social worker, that B went to stay at the bungalow on 4 January 1980. The social worker's record covers the full period from 2 August 1977, when he "received the case", to 6 June 1980; and we have seen also a copy of the statutory review of B in or about February 1980.

---

[27] The social worker referred to in para 52.36.
[28] See paras 52.35 and 52.36.

52.76 We are satisfied from the documents and the social worker's evidence that social services staff were concerned about B from August 1979 (at the latest) onwards because they thought that B was in moral danger. On 7 December 1979 B was collected by the social worker on his discharge from Foston Hall Detention Centre and taken to an After Care hostel in Watergate Street, Chester, where accommodation had been arranged for him; and he obtained employment as a commis chef at Chester Steakhouse, beginning on 18 December 1979, which his social worker had helped to arrange. However, he left the hostel on or about 4 January 1980 and reported to his social worker four days later that he had moved to the Mickle Trafford bungalow, where he was visited by the social worker on 14 January 1980.

52.77 B was admitted to Chester City hospital on 26 January 1980 following an "overdose", where he was visited by the social worker on 28 January 1980. B would not discuss the reasons for his overdose. On the latter date he was discharged, after being referred to the psychiatric out-patient clinic at Chester Royal Infirmary. The review stated that this was for "treatment to help him accept his possible homosexual nature".

52.78 It seems that B obtained lodgings in Acrefair, near Wrexham, on his discharge from hospital but a report by a senior social worker in the Delyn Area team for Mold Crown Court in September 1980 stated:

> "From this point (that is, his discharge from hospital) B started an almost nomadic existence, moving from one lodging to another in Chester, Wrexham, Rhyl and Flint areas, often staying for just a few days, and making repeated appeals to his Social Worker for help in finding accommodation and for money to pay for lodgings. It was very difficult to keep track of his movements and to find him accommodation. B consistently refused offers to return to residential care and would not co-operate in the efforts that were made to establish him in a stable job and accommodation. He made extreme demands on the time and energies of his Social Worker and other social services staff."

52.79 In the light of this evidence we are satisfied that B's allegation that his social worker arranged for him to stay at the Mickle Trafford bungalow is incorrect. We have no difficulty in accepting, however, that he was subjected to sexual abuse repeatedly by several persons during his stay there, despite the denials of those whom he named as his abusers. It is clear also, in our view, that that abuse was, at least, a major cause of the overdose that he took on 26 January 1980.

Paedophile activity on the North Wales coast

52.80 We heard only a small amount of evidence about this and it was less obviously linked with young persons in care at the time, but it merits a mention here.

52.81 The main focus of such evidence as we received was upon the 15/20 Club, owned by Albert Dyson[29], a native of Rhyl, from about 1960 to 1980. It was described by several witnesses as a gay club and Dyson himself told the Tribunal that it was a gay venue on Saturday nights, organised by a Rhyl group, during the last 18 months to two years of its existence.

52.82 Dyson befriended the family of the boy referred to as D in paragraphs 10.15 to 10.19 of this report and was convicted in June 1980 of three offences of indecency against him committed when he was in care and living at Bryn Estyn. Dyson used to collect D from Bryn Estyn for week-end leaves and the latter worked at the club at times in the late 1970s. Dyson said that there was only one offence and that it occurred early on during D's period at Bryn Estyn, that is, in late 1978.

52.83 Amongst visitors to the 15/20 Club on occasions were David Gillison, Huw Meurig Jones and a prominent one time officer of CHE but we have not received any evidence of paedophile activities in the Club. Both Gillison and Cooke were questioned closely about their activities in the Rhyl area in more recent years but both denied knowingly associating with any persons in care.

Conclusions

52.84 Although much of the evidence that we have heard about the existence of a paedophile ring has been tarnished in one way or another and the evidence of B has been demonstrated to be incorrect in some respects, the cumulative effect of all the evidence has been to satisfy us that, during the period under review, a significant number of individual male persons in the Wrexham and Chester areas were engaged in paedophile activities of the kind described by B. Whilst we have no reason to doubt the evidence given to us by some office holders of the Chester CHE that precautions had been taken to prevent abuse of the organisation, it is clear to us that some of its less reputable members or habitués saw it as a useful agency for identifying and contacting potential victims. These and other individuals were targeting young males in their middle teens and it was inevitable that some young persons in care should be caught in their web. The evidence does not establish that they were solely or mainly interested in persons in care but such youngsters were particularly vulnerable to their approaches for emotional and other reasons; and the abusers were quite prepared to prey on such victims, despite the risks involved.

52.85 Many, but not all, of these paedophiles were known to each other and some of them met together frequently, although there were strong antagonisms between individuals from time to time. Inevitably, some information about likely candidates for paedophile activities was shared, expressly and implicitly, and there were occasions when sexual activity occurred in a group. We accept that B himself was one of the victims of these activities as a whole. As he said in his oral evidence to the Tribunal "The way I see it, I was a slave; I was sold. Yes, I was given money; yes, I was given things".

---

[29] See para 50.04.

52.86   We have concentrated our attention on evidence relating to children who were in care at the time, having regard to our terms of reference, but we have necessarily heard some evidence about others who were on the fringe of the care system, that is, children who were later committed to care and youths who had recently been discharged from care. In our judgment, the perils for such persons are as great in this respect as for those actually in care and our findings emphasise the importance of continuing support by social services for those who are discharged from care.

52.87   We draw the attention of Parliament also to the abuse suffered by B between the ages of 16 years and 18 years, in circumstances which appear to have made him question his own sexuality for a period. Much of the later abuse was not inflicted by persons in a position of trust in relation to him and there can be no doubt that he was significantly corrupted and damaged by what occurred.

52.88   To the extent that we have indicated we accept that there was an active paedophile ring operating in the Chester and Wrexham areas for much of the period under review. The evidence does not establish, however, that there was a conspiracy to recruit paedophiles to children's residential establishments or to infiltrate them in some other way. Although there have been one or two allegations that individual members of residential staff arranged for a child to be provided to an outsider for sexual purposes, the evidence in support of these allegations has been far from satisfactory and we cannot be sure that they are true.

52.89   Counsel for B invited us to infer that a senior member or senior members of Bryn Estyn staff knowingly allowed him to be abused by paedophiles, particularly Cooke. This inference was to be drawn, Counsel said, mainly from the circumstances in which B was granted passes freely and Cooke would be waiting in the lane to meet him[30]; but we do not consider that that inference can safely be drawn.

52.90   In reaching our conclusions we are conscious of the difficulty of prosecuting individuals for specific paedophile offences alleged to have occurred many years ago on the testimony of the complainant alone or with the aid of only vulnerable corroborative evidence. It is for this reason that we have not named the "other men" referred to by B but we are firm in our own conclusions.

[30] See para 52.34.

PART XIII

THE SUCCESSOR AUTHORITIES

The new structures and resources

Introduction

53.01 The statements in this chapter are based on the written evidence of the successor authorities to the former Clwyd and Gwynedd County Councils submitted to the Tribunal in December 1997 and some figures which were supplied by them early in 1998. We emphasise that some of the information is subject to frequent change and we have given relevant dates wherever possible.

53.02 Under the provisions of section 1 of the Local Government (Wales) Act 1994 and Schedule 1 to that Act six new principal areas of local government were established in North Wales on 1 April 1996. These were the four counties of Caernarfonshire and Merionethshire (which adopted the single name of Gwynedd on 2 April 1996), Anglesey, Denbighshire and Flintshire and the two county boroughs of Aberconwy and Colwyn (subsequently called, singly, Conwy) and Wrexham.

53.03 The relative approximate sizes and resources of the new areas and councils in April 1996 are summarised in the following table:

Council	Population	Area (hectares)	Size of Council	Total net budget (£000s)	Percentage expenditure on Social Services
Anglesey	68,500	71,500	40	62,580*	17.2
Conwy	110,700	113,000	60	79,000	20.4
Gwynedd	118,000	255,000	83	107,000	18.4
Denbighshire	89,000†	84,000	48	83,500	18.4
Flintshire	145,000	43,700	72	117,800	21.5
Wrexham	123,500	49,900	52	101,422	19.5

* This is the budget for 1997/1998 because we were not given the figures for the previous year.

† Denbighshire lost the area of Llangollen Rural (population about 1,800) in April 1997 to Wrexham. The population and area given exclude Llangollen Rural.

Broadly speaking, the first three areas replaced the former county of Gwynedd and the latter three replaced the former county of Clwyd but Conwy includes parts of Clwyd.

53.04 Five of the six new councils appointed a Director of Social Services from the senior or departmental management team of their former county (in Conwy, the new Director was from the former Gwynedd). Wrexham, however, brought together Housing and Social Services under a Director of Personal Services, with a Chief Social Services Officer as one of three officers directly under him.

Anglesey

53.05 The Social Services Committee is one of eight service committees. It does not have a Children's Sub-Committee but has various panels and boards working under it.

53.06 The Council has appointed a Children's Services Manager as the senior child care specialist, who is not a member of the Departmental Management Team. She is responsible to the Assistant Director (Client Services), who is one of two Assistant Directors working immediately under the Director. Children's services were formerly provided in the short term by a generic duty team and in the long term by a dedicated children's team. There are now two dedicated children's teams, one dealing with short term and the other with long term services. The children's services management team, which meets "on a three week cycle", comprises the Assistant Director (Client Services), the Children's Services Manager, the Reviewing and Development Officer (Clients) and five Team Leaders, covering such areas as family support, hospital services and learning and physical disabilities as well as the children's teams. A child care consultancy service has been set up using the services of the former Area Manager.

53.07 According to the Council's evidence to the Tribunal, it has also responded to Adrianne Jones' recommendations by increasing significantly the level of expenditure on children's services. The Council says, for example, that its disaggregated purchasing budget for these services from the former Gwynedd was £514K but this was increased to an actual figure of £654K for 1996/1997. The Council estimates that the apportionment of the Social Services budget for children's services has risen from under five per cent to a current figure of about ten per cent (including an element of disability budgets).

53.08 The age group 0 to 18 years represents about 23 per cent (15,800) of Anglesey's population (the percentage aged 65 years and upwards is probably now about 20). On 15 January 1998 the county had 61 looked after children, of whom 21 were the subject of full or interim care orders. Only four of these children were placed in Anglesey's sole community home, Queens Park[1]. The other 57 children were fostered, six of them outside the county; and Anglesey has 60 approved foster carers. It follows that none of the children were placed in residential homes or similar establishments outside the county. At the time when the county's Children's Services Plan was written there were seven children in residential care, of whom three were placed outside the county.

53.09 According to the Director of Social Services, Queens Park is a four bedded unit for adolescents aged between 13 and 16 years. It does not provide emergency placements and is available only where foster placements are unsuitable. The future of the unit is said to be under review. It is intended that Anglesey should enter into an agreement with Gwynedd for the joint management of children's residential services for both authorities.

[1] See Chapter 36.

53.10 Anglesey has established a contingency fund of £100,000 to meet unexpected and expensive placements in addition to a revenue budget of £41,000. When the Director's evidence was submitted to us in 1998 there had been no such placements for two years but guidelines for the use of them were being developed jointly with Gwynedd.

53.11 Anglesey has already developed a number of relevant joint arrangements with Gwynedd. Thus, from 1 September 1997 Gwynedd has provided a contracted inspection unit for Anglesey, absorbing the staff that previously served Anglesey's own inspection unit, which was formed after re-organisation. The inspection unit applies the same standards in the local authority sector as it does to private and voluntary establishments. It has representation from the independent residential sector on its advisory committee and lay assessors work with the inspection teams.

53.12 Other joint ventures are in the out-of-hours emergency service and fostering. The former is with Conwy and Gwynedd, Conwy acting as lead authority: a duty team based at Conwy co-ordinates the response by social services to any emergency occurring after 5 pm or at weekends. In relation to fostering, there is a joint agency agreement with Cartref Bontnewydd Fostering Services Unit[2] and Gwynedd. The Unit has responsibility for recruiting, assessing and supporting foster carers and currently employs four staff with one other from each of the two counties. In 1997 it was involved in the placement of 110 children (77 in Gwynedd and 30 in Anglesey). Anglesey also participates with the other five North Wales counties in the North Wales Child Protection Forum and the joint guardian ad litem service.

53.13 Anglesey's Fostering Panel is presided over by the Children's Services Manager. It meets monthly to consider all applications for approval and to review foster carers. The Children's Service Manager chairs also the Adoption Panel, which includes an elected member, three social workers and three independent members. Inter-authority adoptions are arranged through a specialist agency, the Catholic Children and Family Care Society (Wales).

53.14 The evidence of the Director of Social Services is that members of the Council (presumably, that is, of the Social Services Committee) are expected to assess the quality of care provided for children in residential care and to monitor the implementation of the county's policies on their statutory visits. The members have practice guidelines and training in respect of these duties.

Conwy

53.15 The Social Services Committee is comprised of 30 members of the Council (that is, half the total membership). It has three sub-committees, one of which is the Services for Children and Families Sub-Committee, with 15 members.

53.16 The management structure within the Social Services Department was modified in 1997 because of financial constraints. From 1 October 1997 there were three Assistant Directors immediately under the Director, of whom one

---

[2] See paras 40.05 to 40.07.

was the Assistant Director (Children and Families), a member of the Directorate Group, which itself met weekly and with certain elected members monthly. There was also a Departmental Management Group, including Service Managers, which met monthly. Similar arrangements continue but since 1 April 1998 the number of Assistant Directors has been reduced to two, one for Adult Services and the other for Children and Support Services. The latter is now supported by two (instead of one) Service Managers.

53.17 The Social Services budget for Conwy was increased by £1,160K between 1996/1997 and 1997/1998 and the increase in the Child and Families component in this was £216,000, raising its percentage of the Social Services budget to 14 (the percentage allocated to services for older people was 48.3).

53.18 The Registrar General's mid year estimates of population in 1995 for the areas now within Conwy indicate that about 26 per cent of the total (29,000) were within the 0 to 18 years group, whereas about 33.5 per cent were beyond the standard retirement age of 65 years. Welsh Office migration figures showed net migration into Conwy of about 4,000 in the preceding four years, one of the highest in Wales in terms of the number and as a proportion of the total population.

53.19 On 15 January 1998 Conwy had 105 looked after children, of whom 47 were subject to full or interim care orders. Of the total of 105, 97 children were boarded out, including six placed outside the county; and the number of approved foster carers within the county was 78. There were only two children placed in a community home in Conwy: they were at Llwyn Onn, Rhos on Sea[3], which had maximum accommodation for three. Conwy, however, uses also a plan, piloted in some inner cities, under which accommodation is provided by local authorities and housing associations to enable a family or a young person to live under the supervision of a "live-in" social worker and with appropriate support. At the time when the Council's evidence was submitted in 1998 there were three such houses, each accommodating one young person. At least one of the balance of three looked after children was placed out of county with Corvedale Care in Shropshire because there was no suitable resource within Conwy.

53.20 Conwy had inherited two residential units, Llwyn Onn and Belgrave Road[4] at Colwyn Bay, from Clwyd. However, it employed external consultants to review its residential services in 1996. As a result of the review both the former units were closed and Llwyn Onn was re-opened to fulfil the earlier function of Belgrave Road, providing semi-independent accommodation for three young persons with a staff group formed into a Leaving Care Team. The remaining part of Llwyn Onn was developed into an education unit (jointly resourced with the Education Department) providing education for six pupils who had been excluded from full time education. A joint strategic planning panel has been formed of representatives of both departments for the development of further projects as well as planning joint responses to individual cases.

---

[3] See para 4.30(11).
[4] See para 4.30(24).

53.21 Like Anglesey, Conwy County Borough Council sets aside a contingency fund of £100,000 for out of county placements. The revenue funding in 1997/1998 was insufficient to meet the cost of such placements (we have been told of five for varying periods between 1 March 1997 and 24 March 1998), even though they are exceptional and the county policy is to keep children within or as close as possible to their own communities.

53.22 As we have said in paragraph 53.12, Conwy is the lead authority in the joint out-of-hours emergency service. It is not involved in other joint arrangements, except the North Wales Child Protection Forum and the joint guardian ad litem service, both of which embrace all six new unitary authorities. Conwy has its own Registration and Inspection Unit with three full time and two part time Registration and Inspection Officers working under the head of the unit, who is also the Departmental Complaints Officer. There are eight lay assessors, who attend inspections, and an Advisory Panel established in line with Welsh Office guidance[5].

53.23 Conwy decided to manage its own fostering service and formed a Family Placement Team. It consists of four qualified social workers and it has reviewed all the foster carers inherited from the former County Councils under the supervision of the Team Manager. A major recruitment campaign has also been undertaken. The Fostering and Adoption Panels are presided over by the Service Manager and include some councillors and a representative of a voluntary organisation. Recommendations for approval of foster carers are made to the Director, who is responsible for the decision.

53.24 Members of the Social Services Committee resolved in April 1997 that members of the Children's Sub-committee should take the lead in visiting children's residential facilities on a monthly basis, but without excluding other members of the committee from doing so, if they wished. Seminar training is given to members, who are provided with a pro forma for visits, which are monitored. The focus is on the quality of the residential provision and an annual report to the Social Services Committee, based on members' returns, is prepared. As a back up to this, a senior manager visits the establishments monthly and completes the statutory checks.

Gwynedd

53.25 The Social Services Committee is one of six service committees. The Council's committee structure includes also five corporate committees, three Area Committees and four boards responsible respectively for particular services such as civil engineering and environmental services. There is no Children's Sub-Committee (three statutory panels of marginal relevance report to the Social Services Committee). The Area Committees are responsible for areas

---

[5] Welsh Office Circular 68/94.

co-terminous with the old district boundaries of Arfon, Dwyfor and Meirionydd. In relation to Social Services the functions delegated to Area Committees are:

(a) monitoring the standards of service delivery;

(b) identifying and examining local service needs for the area;

(c) examining the scheme for care in the community;

(d) considering any inspection reports with particular regard to the area; and

(e) making appropriate recommendations to the Social Services Committee in the light of (a) to (d).

53.26 The Departmental Management Team is the principal planning group and is comprised of the Director, his Executive Officer, three Area Directors, the Head of the Policy Unit and the Finance Manager. It is the Area Director for Arfon who has the lead responsibility for children's services. Initially, there were only two Children's Services Managers provided for in the management structure but Adrianne Jones drew attention to the potential weakness of this provision and there are now four such managers. One has responsibility for operational management in Arfon; another has the same responsibility for the two other areas; the third is responsible for the operational management of Cartref Bontnewydd as a community home and also, by agreement with Anglesey, for Queens Park (she is also responsible for policy and development for children looked after); and the fourth is responsible for policy and development in the field of child protection and family support. Four additional full time social workers and three administrators (two part time) have been appointed in response to Adrianne Jones' recommendations.

53.27 According to the figures presented to the Tribunal by the Director of Social Services, the social services budget for Gwynedd was increased by £2,447K in 1997/1998, of which £446K was in respect of children's services, an increase of about 28 per cent in the latter. It is noteworthy, however, that the budget for children's services in 1996/1997 was one of the lowest in Wales and only just over half the Welsh average[6]. The increase in the Department's total net expenditure was due to the transfer of All Wales Strategy funds to the Revenue Support Grant. Expenditure on services for the elderly was reduced by 2.7 per cent to 47.7 per cent.

53.28 The Registrar General has estimated that in mid 1996 24.7 per cent of Gwynedd's population were under 19 years of age and 24.5 per cent were aged over 60 years. On 15 January 1998 there were 67 children being looked after, of whom 23 were subject to full or interim care orders. The number of children being boarded out was 60, of whom nine were placed outside the county; and there were 69 approved foster carers in Gwynedd. Of the remaining seven

---

[6] Report of SSIW on Inspection of Child Care Procedures and Practice in North Wales, August 1998.

children, five were in residential care at Cartref Bontnewydd[7], which has accommodation for seven adolescents aged between 12 and 18 years and is Gwynedd's only community home.

53.29 Gwynedd, like Anglesey, had no out of county placements in residential care between 1 April 1996 and 31 March 1998. However, it too has established a contingency fund of £150,000 for the purpose and has increased the annual budget provision to £50,000.

53.30 Gwynedd's joint agency arrangements are those outlined in paragraphs 53.11 and 53.12 in the section of this chapter on Anglesey. It has Fostering and Adoption Panels chaired by the Children's Services Manager and the Area Director for Arfon respectively. The joint inspection unit has been operative since 1 September 1997: in effect, it is the Gwynedd Inspection Unit that undertakes the role of inspection unit on behalf of Anglesey. It comprises a Head of Unit, three inspectors, a review officer, an administrator and a clerk. Gwynedd has also appointed ten lay assessors to accompany the inspectors during the formal annual inspections of residential homes for the elderly and for children.

53.31 The Director of Social Services said in his written evidence to the Tribunal that his Department recognises the vital role of elected members as "responsible parents" for children in the authority's care. The provision of information to members is being enhanced progressively and has been facilitated by the formation of local children's service groups from April 1997. The Arfon Area Director has formulated guidelines for members on their role and responsibilities as visitors to residential homes, which were approved in June 1997. Seminars for members have also been arranged.

53.32 Cartref Bontnewydd is visited regularly by the Arfon Area Director (bi-monthly) and the senior Children's Services Manager.

Denbighshire

53.33 The Social Services Committee, one of five service committees, has 28 members. It has established 12 panels, eight of which relate to children. There is also a Children and Families Sub-Committee of 12 members, the minutes of which go to the Social Services Committee and thence to the full Council for confirmation. Inspection reports on children's homes go to this Sub-Committee.

53.34 The Social Services Directorate is one of six directorates (the other five combine several related functions). The designated senior manager of services for children is the Head of Client Services, who is a member of the Departmental Management Team (with the Director, the Head of Strategic Planning and Support Services and all Services Managers), which meets every three weeks.

---

[7] See Chapter 37.

53.35 Under the Head of Client Services, are five managers, one of whom is the Children's Services Manager, who in turn is responsible for five units or teams as well as the two residential units and a finance officer. Two units are concerned with child protection, there are two child care teams and, finally, a resources team.

53.36 In response to the Adrianne Jones report, Denbighshire has established a Child Care Planning and Operations Management Group, chaired by the Head of Client Services, the main functions of which include identification of the need for revised policies and procedures, monitoring the implementation of key tasks identified in the Children's Services Plan and consideration of strategic issues within children's services. We have not been told the composition of this Group. There is also a separate Denbighshire Strategic Planning Forum for Children, involving senior officers from the Health Service, Education and Social Services, which meets monthly.

53.37 The Social Services net budget for Denbighshire of £15.7m for 1996/1997 was increased by £1,270K for 1997/1998 whereas the increase in the overall budget was only £889K. The amount allocated to Children and Family Services rose from £2,187K (13.9 per cent) to £2,289K (13.5 per cent).

53.38 Following the transfer of Llangollen Rural area to Wrexham, it was estimated that 18,900 (21.3 per cent) of the total population were under 18 years of age (26.6 per cent were over 60 years). On 15 January 1998 there were 70 looked after children in this county of whom 28 were the subject of full or interim care orders. Of the 70 children, 54 were boarded out, including one only placed outside the county; and Denbighshire had then 76 approved foster carers. Six of the other children were placed in community homes within the county, of which there are two, and six others were placed in residential care outside the county.

53.39 The residential children's homes in Denbighshire in 1997/1998 were Medea Drive, Rhyl[8], which provides placements for two children, and 8 Llys Garmon, Llanarmon yn Ial[9], which accommodates four children of the same family. We were told that it was intended to rehabilitate the latter four children with a member of their family and to replace the two residential units during 1998/1999 by a more flexible single unit provided by NCH Action for Children with accommodation for a maximum of four children.

53.40 The out of county placements by Denbighshire were almost wholly in North Wales. One boy was with Corvedale Care in Shropshire, following the breakdown of foster placements, but four were at private establishments in the Wrexham area[10] and one at Ynys Fechan Hall[11]. The county does not have a contingency fund for such placements and finances them out of revenue.

---

[8] See para 4.30(26).
[9] See para 4.30(25).
[10] Wilderness Mill Farm and Prospects: see paras 4.24 and 13.03.
[11] See paras 5.10 and 5.12.

53.41 The North East Wales Registration and Inspection Unit, which serves Denbighshire, Flintshire and Wrexham under a formal service delivery contract, was set up in April 1996; and it is accountable to a joint management board comprising of the Chairman of the Social Services Committee and the Director of Social Services for each of the three counties. The Head of the Unit is line managed by the Director for Denbighshire, who provides managerial support. The former was responsible in his previous appointment for the inspection of children's homes and his team includes an inspector responsible for children's services, who is responsible to a senior inspector with wide experience of children's services. The Unit has a team of lay assessors and a joint advisory panel; and the Head of Unit presents an annual report to each Social Services Committee. An independent auditor appointed by the three Chief Executives audits the work of the Unit. The same standards are applied to local authority, private and voluntary homes. The county also participates in the North Wales Child Protection Forum and the guardian ad litem service for all six authorities.

53.42 Denbighshire has its own Adoption and Fostering Panel, which decides whether an applicant is suitable. The Panel includes three elected members. Final approval is given by the Director of Social Services. A programme of post approval training is offered to foster carers.

53.43 Members of the Social Services Committee undertake rota visits. A progress report on these visits was presented on 1 April 1997, following which a number of improvements were introduced. The Children's Society was commissioned to review these visits from the perspective of children and young people and further improvements followed. A seminar with elected members, led by the Children's Society, to focus on children's rights issues has been arranged.

Flintshire

53.44 The Social Services Committee, with 36 members, is one of 13 Council Committees. There is no sub-committee structure: the policy is "to appoint *ad hoc* or standing consultative bodies of varying membership to permit wide consultation into the policy formulation and services delivery" of each committee. One such body is the County Task Group for Children and Young People. There are also an Early Years Forum (planning service delivery to children aged under five years) and three panels, two of which are appeals panels.

53.45 The Director of Social Services applied for early retirement in July 1997, only 15 months after the Department had taken over its responsibilities, and this was approved with effect from 30 November 1997. At the time when the Tribunal's hearings were concluded no suitable replacement had been found and the Senior Assistant Director was continuing to perform the duties of the Director.

53.46 The designated senior manager of children's services is the Assistant Director (Children's Services), who is one of only two Assistant Directors immediately under the Director. The other is the Senior Assistant Director, who is responsible for Adult and Corporate Services. Under the Assistant Director

(Children's Services) the structure provides for two managers and a co-ordinator, responsible respectively for Children's Social Work (field social work services), Children's Planning and Support Services (including Adoption and Fostering and Residential Services) and Child Protection. It is perturbing to record that, when the Council's evidence was presented to the Tribunal none of these three posts was filled: one was to be advertised early in 1998 and two were to be re-advertised. The post of Team Manager (Adoption and Fostering) was also vacant.

53.47 The Directorate Management Team, which meets weekly, comprises the Director, the two Assistant Directors, three operational service managers and five senior managers from finance, planning and corporate services. There are also monthly meetings of all Directorate managers.

53.48 The Social Services net budget for 1996/1997, after reductions as the result of a mid-year review, was £17,977K (a reduction of £292K). Of this amount £2,541K (14.1 per cent) was allocated to children's services, excluding components of the Community Care and the All Wales Strategy budgets. The Social Services budget was increased by £653K for 1997/1998 and the allocation for children's services by £69K, reducing the percentage to 12.65. The comparison in percentage terms is distorted, however, by a change in the treatment of a special grant provision for mental handicap and illness, which gave rise to an apparent rise of £1.51 million in the allocation for learning disability. We were told that 36.3 per cent of the children's services net budget for 1996/1997 was used to support children accommodated away from their home in foster care or residential care.

53.49 According to mid 1996 estimates, 23.2 per cent of Flintshire's population were then under the age of 17 years and only 14.7 per cent were aged over 65 years. On 15 January 1998 91 children were being looked after, of whom 59 were the subject of full or interim care orders. It is difficult to reconcile the various figures put forward in the Council's evidence[12] but we were told that, on 15 January 1998, 83 of these children were fostered within the county and the other eight fostered outside the county.

53.50 Flintshire has no "traditional" residential homes for children but it does provide respite care and family support in three units, namely:

(1) Cornel Clyd, Connah's Quay, for children with substantial disabilities, which can accommodate three children;

(2) Clivedon Road, Connah's Quay, for difficult to manage young persons, with accommodation for two;

(3) New Parade, Greenfield, for one child at a time preparing for alternative family care.

---

[12] In paras 7.4.1 and 7.4.2 of the statement.

The county's written evidence stated that 34 children received a respite/shared care service under Flintshire Family Link Scheme for children with a disability and three children with emotional and behavioural difficulty were the subjects of shared care packages with their families.

53.51 Flintshire has entered into a service level agreement with NCH Action for Children for the provision of residential services at these three homes from about 1 April 1998.

53.52 There is still a need for out of county placements for some of the children looked after and we have been supplied with a list of out of county placements by Flintshire in 1997 and 1998, supplementing the list of five such placements in their written statement[13]. It appears that three children were placed with their extended families in Cheshire and Liverpool and four children of one family were placed with or by the North West Foster Care Association in Oldham. At least six other children were placed in private residential homes in Cheshire, Shropshire, Lancashire, Derbyshire and Staffordshire; and one 15 year old child was placed in secure accommodation in County Durham.

53.53 We were not informed of any contingency fund set aside by Flintshire to fund out of county placements.

53.54 Flintshire participates in the North East Wales Registration and Inspection Unit with Denbighshire and Wrexham[14] and the North Wales Child Protection Forum and the guardian ad litem service with all five other authorities. Like Denbighshire, it has its own Fostering and Adoption Panel, which receives all applications and makes recommendations to the Director of Social Services. The Department's adoption agency operates independently of the county's family placement service and is staffed by 15 social workers.

53.55 Six seminars were organised for members of the Social Services Committee covering all aspects of the Department's activities and we are told that 36 reports on child care matters had been presented to the Committee by the date[15] when the Council's evidence was submitted. Members of the Committee undertake monthly visits to the three homes listed in paragraph 53.50. Following a decision made on 3 December 1996, a pool of 12 elected members has been established to undertake visits to all of the Council's residential and day care facilities; and a training programme was provided for them in June 1997.

Wrexham

53.56 The Council has a structure of nine committees and the Corporate Policy and Resources Committee has five sub-committees. The Chairman of the Social Services Committee is Councillor Malcolm King, the former Chairman of Clwyd's Social Services Committee.

---

[13] In para 7.3.3.
[14] See para 53.40.
[15] December 1997.

53.57 The Director of Personal Services (one of five Directors) is responsible for two Departments, namely, (a) Social Services and (b) Housing and Building Maintenance, each with its own Chief Officer. The Director of Personal Services, however, has the statutory role of Director of Social Services. The Director, the two Chief Officers and the Resources Manager meet weekly as a Directorate Management Team. The Resources Group provides development and support services and a Planning and Development Team, which includes two posts specialising in children's services.

53.58 The Chief Social Services Officer has a Social Services Management Team comprising four Senior Managers, including the Senior Manager (Children and Family Services) and the Performance Review Officer. The Senior Manager (Children and Family Services) took up her appointment as the senior children's officer on 5 January 1998.

53.59 Delivery of social services has now been planned on the basis of three localities, Wrexham Town, Wrexham North and Wrexham South, each with a "Locality Team". However, the structure depicted in the Council's evidence[16] shows four Team Managers, the Child Protection Co-ordinator and the Reviewing Officer directly under the Senior Manager (Children and Family Services) and responsible to her. One of these Team Managers is responsible for children looked after, residential care, fostering, adoption and leaving care.

53.60 The Social Services net budget for 1996/1997 was £19,422K, which rose to £21,893K (20.83 per cent of the net total) in 1997/1998, but the increase was accounted for by changes in the treatment of Government grants. The Council had to absorb substantial cuts in both years and the savings found in social services were £585K in 1996/1997 and £1,068K in 1997/1998. Wrexham did not supply us with a breakdown of Social Services expenditure in these two years but it appears that 19.8 per cent was allocated to children and families in 1996/1997. The Council stated that a specific provision of £100K was made in 1997/1998 to strengthen children's services and that an additional £130K was planned for this purpose in 1998/1999.

53.61 The population figure for Wrexham of 123,500 given in the table in paragraph 53.03 appears to be the estimated figure in 1994 rather than mid 1996 and does not include the population of 1,800 in the Llangollen Rural area, which was added to the county borough in April 1997. Of the 1994 total, 24,600 (19.9 per cent) was the estimated number of children aged under 15 years (24 per cent are now said to be under 18 years[17]) and 20,200 (16.4 per cent) were aged 65 years and upwards.

53.62 On 15 January 1998 Wrexham had 107 looked after children of whom 47 were the subject of full or interim care orders. We were informed that on that date 73 children were placed with foster parents, including three placed outside the county borough; and 11 children were in residential care within the county borough. We were told also that four children were in residential care in

---

[16] See para 4.6.3.
[17] Report by SSIW on Inspection of Child Care Procedures and Practice in North Wales, para 9.1, issued in August 1988.

England but an amended list refers to seven such children, two of whom were in a secure unit for "offending behaviour" and another at Aycliffe Young Persons Centre for the same reason. Two were at schools, which were regarded as the most suitable placement; another was undergoing drug rehabilitation; and the seventh was on remand.

53.63 Wrexham has four residential homes for children, but one (Tan-y-Dre in Wrexham) is temporary, having been opened in November 1997 to provide care and accommodation for three young children from one family who could not be placed with foster parents at that time because of severe behavioural difficulties following the breakdown of their family. The other three are Cherry Hill[18], 15 Norfolk Road and 21 Daleside Avenue[19]. Cherry Hill can accommodate up to six young persons and the other two homes two children each. Cherry Hill is for young persons in the age range of 14 to 17 years who cannot be placed in families and whose behaviour will often be challenging. The other two homes are for children with disabilities, Norfolk Road providing long term care and Daleside Avenue short term care.

53.64 Wrexham does not have a contingency fund to provide for out of county placements. It states, however, that "where there is a decision that a residential placement out of county best suits the needs of the individual, two or three way agreements are made between the Social Services Department, the Education Department and the Health Authority". It says also that recently a joint panel for the education of children looked after has been set up and that this will provide a formal mechanism for reaching decisions about the educational placements of children looked after. It is intended that the panel will be incorporated into a Joint Children's Services Planning Framework drawn from senior management of all the main statutory agencies and voluntary organisations, which was launched in April 1997.

53.65 Wrexham participates in the North East Wales Registration and Inspection Unit described in paragraph 53.41. The Chief Social Services Officer has the responsibility to act in response to the Unit's recommendations but the Director of Personal Services, who is a member of the Unit's joint management board, oversees the implementation of action plans and reports to members of the Social Services Committee.

53.66 The Council is also a member of the North Wales Regional Child Protection Forum; and the guardian ad litem service is provided jointly with the five other North Wales Councils. Revised child protection procedures have been developed jointly with Flintshire and Denbighshire.

53.67 The recommendations of Wrexham's Adoption and Fostering Panel go to the Chief Social Services Officer, who is responsible for making all decisions in consultation with the Chairman of the Social Services Committee.

---

[18] See para 4.30(6) and Chapter 16.
[19] See para 4.30(10).

53.68 A panel of six members of the Social Services Committee has been appointed to fulfil the statutory duty of elected members to visit the Council's children's homes. The visits are monthly and written reports on them are submitted to the Chief Social Services Officer. The Director of Personal Services meets the latter together with the Chairman and Vice-Chairman of the Social Services Committee fortnightly and issues arising from the rota visits are discussed at these meetings. Summary reports on rota visits are presented to the Social Services Committee. Members of the Committee serve also on four members' panels dealing with such matters as appeals, representations and complaints.

Some continuing concerns

Introduction

54.01 Sub-paragraph (d) of the Tribunal's terms of reference requires us "to consider whether the relevant caring and investigative agencies discharged their functions appropriately and, in the case of the caring agencies, whether they are doing so now". However, the format and composition of a Tribunal of Inquiry of this kind are not designed to enable it to carry out an audit of social work practice and that task was, in effect, assigned to Adrianne Jones' Examination Team on Child Care Procedures and Practice in North Wales shortly before we were appointed. Since then Adrianne Jones has considered, at our request, the written evidence supplied to this Tribunal by the successor authorities and we summarise her views upon it, given in oral and written evidence, in the next section of this chapter; but it would be inappropriate for us to attempt to traverse the same ground in detail.

54.02 It is relevant also that the Welsh Office itself established the Adrianne Jones Report Implementation Group[1]; and the Social Services Inspectorate for Wales carried out an inspection in October 1997 to assess the progress made by the six North Wales Social Services Departments in implementing the recommendations of the Adrianne Jones Examination Team. The report on that inspection was issued in August 1998 and was based on the facts as they were over halfway through the Tribunal's hearings. In these circumstances we will confine our comments in this chapter, after referring to Adrianne Jones' evidence, to matters of specific continuing concern that are of particular relevance to the central purposes of our inquiry.

The responses of the successor authorities to Adrianne Jones

54.03 The 41 recommendations in the Adrianne Jones' report covered 11 areas of concern, namely, strategic planning, child protection, child care planning, residential care, foster care, management, personnel and employment, staff development and training, inspection, complaints and children's rights. Much of the written evidence submitted by the six successor authorities to the Tribunal referred directly or indirectly to their responses to those recommendations; and Adrianne Jones told us that, in assessing the responses, she approached her task primarily from the perspective of keeping children safe.

54.04 In her oral evidence Adrianne Jones said that there were two main and recurrent themes in the responses by way of explanation for any delays that had occurred in implementing her recommendations: these were lack of financial resources and pressure on staff time. All the written responses referred to the issue of finance for children's services in the context of enforced overall cuts in

---

[1] See paras 49.88 to 49.91.

social services; despite having had to make reductions elsewhere, most of the authorities had allocated additional sums to the children's budget for specific purposes. All of them, however, spoke of identified needs that cannot be met in the current financial situation.

54.05 The position in relation to overall staffing is less clear, although Flintshire's difficulties at the end of 1997 in filling senior positions[2] were both striking and highly perturbing. The evidence in general has been that the successor authorities have not found difficulty in recruiting new staff, except for residential care staff because of the poor pay structure and, possibly, the impact of this Tribunal's hearings. Exceptions to the favourable staff recruitment picture, however, were Anglesey, which referred to a shortage of staff with the necessary bi-lingual ability, and Gwynedd, which has found a dearth of experienced social workers. Wrexham too wrote of a lack of quality in applicants for managerial posts and field social workers at level three. As Adrianne Jones herself said, the lack of staff time is not attributable solely to financial constraints: it involves also questions of priorities and the experience and training of existing staff.

54.06 One of Adrianne Jones' main recommendations[3] was that Directors of Social Services should ensure that there was one designated person with overall policy and service responsibility for children's services within each social services senior management team; and it was implicit that this "Children's Officer"[4] should be at Assistant Director level or the equivalent. This recommendation was intended to be part of a package designed to achieve "clarity of purpose, delegation and accountability".

54.07 The response by the individual successor authorities has been outlined in Chapter 53. Each does now have such a designated person but there are considerable variations in the structures that have been adopted. Adrianne Jones' view is that they have borne the recommendation in mind but that she cannot say unequivocally that they have all achieved what she would like to see, namely, a very clean structure with the head of children's services sitting on the senior management team. The issues are whether the children's service manager is sufficiently senior to take responsibility for and influence what is happening at the most senior level and to have responsibility "at the strategic level" for developing children's services and providing resources so as to ensure that they match needs. We strongly endorse these views, which are of particular importance in relation to authorities with insufficient resources to permit the appointment of an exclusive Children's Services Manager as a member of the senior management team; and the paramount need is to ensure that appropriate priority is given to children's services.

---

[2] See paras 53.45 and 53.46.
[3] Recommendation 24.
[4] We refer back to the pre-1974 arrangements.

54.08 It is notable that, because of geographical considerations, Gwynedd has developed an Area structure of management[5], not dissimilar to the earlier Divisional structure adopted by the former Gwynedd between 1987 and 1992[6], which did not prove to be successful. The Arfon Area Director now carries "lead responsibility" for children's services but does not have line management responsibility for all those services and each Area Director carries responsibility for at least some aspects of them. Moreover, Gwynedd acknowledges that the work load of the Arfon Area Director is such that there is a need "to strengthen the management structure to allow her the capacity to address children's services issues appropriately".

54.09 The Adrianne Jones report contained a number of recommendations for combined action by the successor authorities in the fields of child protection and residential care and the authorities have taken such action in relation to inspection on their own initiative. As we have said in the previous chapter, the North Wales Child Protection Forum, covering all six authorities and supporting the work of the Area Child Protection Committees, continues to exist and has replaced the former Co-ordinating Committee, which had similar purposes. Adrianne Jones' view was that there was a need also for a North Wales forum "for residential care managers (including the independent sector) to share information about good practice and consider specialist issues affecting their day to day work". The responses to the report indicate that there is wide support for the proposed North Wales Residential Forum and that draft plans for establishing it have reached a reasonably advanced stage. In her oral evidence, Adrianne Jones suggested that it should have a wider remit to encourage cross-boundary co-operation, such as the provision by one local authority of services to another, and to assist in the strategic planning of services; and part of the recommendation is that the Forum should have the support of the SSIW. One local authority suggested that the Forum should consider issues relating to accommodation for children and young people generally and not only the provision of residential care.

54.10 There are now three inspection units covering different parts of North Wales and only Conwy has opted to establish its own inspection unit. However, in its responses to Adrianne Jones, Conwy welcomed the proposal (supported by the Association of Directors of Social Services) for the establishment of a National Unit as well as the introduction of "National Benchmark Standards, to be locally applied and discharged".

54.11 There was a varied reaction by the other successor authorities to the idea of a National Unit for inspection but the general view is that inspection units should be locally based. There is wide support for two inspection units, covering North West and North East Wales, whether they be self-contained or parts of an overall North Wales Inspection Unit. It appears that there is a degree of co-operation at present between Conwy's inspection unit and the Gwynedd unit that provides inspection services for Anglesey but we have not been persuaded that these separate units are preferable to a joint North West

---

[5] See paras 53.25 and 53.26.
[6] See paras 44.30 to 44.36.

Wales inspection unit covering all three of the areas (in Conwy there were 101 residential establishments to be inspected and in Gwynedd and Anglesey 96). We should add that there is general support also for the establishment of the inspection units as wholly independent entities from the local authorities whose services they inspect.

54.12 A wide range of other matters was discussed in the course of Adrianne Jones' evidence and we touch upon the most relevant of them here. According to the responses provided by the successor authorities, there are very few children looked after in North Wales to whom a social worker is not allocated at any particular time and any gaps in the allocation are short term only because of illness or a similar reason. It is said also that the children are visited by social workers regularly, at the least in accordance with statutory requirements, and they are instructed that they are expected to see a child alone in the course of a visit. It appears that, in general, there has been significant improvement in complying with good practice requirements, including the recording of visits but Anglesey, for example, was criticised in an SSIW report on its audit of fostering practice in the county and Flintshire has not fully complied with the statutory requirements for the timing and scheduling of reviews under the Foster Placements (Children) Regulations 1991. Regular monitoring by senior managers is not yet standard practice but the need for it is acknowledged.

54.13 All six of the successor authorities are experiencing difficulties in recruiting foster carers, particularly for children with special needs, but these difficulties are occurring nationwide. The emergence of an increased number of private fostering agencies in competition with local authorities and willing to pay higher rates is one of the factors affecting the supply. The response to advertising tends to be poor and Adrianne Jones emphasises the need for local authorities to offer a "whole package" to prospective carers, involving training to enable them to develop the necessary skills and continuing support as well as remuneration reflecting the needs of the child.

54.14 The evidence submitted by the new authorities is to the effect that the necessary checks on applicants for employment and prospective foster carer and adopters are now being carried out vigorously, although two authorities were shown to have been omitting checks with the Department of Health until this was brought to their attention. The speed of response to inquiries has been improved but the need for a central repository of information is stressed by many of the authorities. This need should now be met when the provisions of the Protection of Children Act 1999 are fully implemented.

54.15 Most children in foster care or in residential care now receive information about the complaints procedures applicable to them when they are admitted to such care. The information is usually set out in a leaflet or a similarly accessible document, which is handed to each child, and there are continuing efforts to make them more "user-friendly"[7]. Flintshire and Wrexham supply the Children's Rights Service with particulars of all accommodated children (in Wrexham all children being looked after over the age of 11 years) and that

---

[7] See in this connection paras 49.47 to 49.51.

Service itself circulates appropriate information to the children. Less progress, however, has been made in relation to whistleblowing procedures, which we consider to be of at least equal importance. At the time when the evidence was submitted to us, only Flintshire had formally approved such a procedure. Denbighshire had issued an instruction to staff but had not formulated its policy and Gwynedd was merely planning to develop a policy (staff are "encouraged" to raise matters of concern about colleagues). In the other three authorities the policies were either in draft form and/or in the process of being considered by committees. In the light of our findings about the discouragement of the small number of whistleblowers in both the former North Wales counties, we attach great importance to the conscientious implementation of these policies in the future and close independent monitoring will be essential.

54.16 In the closing stages of our hearings the Tribunal heard some disquieting evidence of dissatisfaction amongst professional staff in Flintshire about the response to staff complaints before the county's present whistleblowing procedures were approved. Part of the evidence, in the form of an agreed statement, dealt with serious breaches of child protection procedures and record keeping in five separate cases. Complaints were made by four social workers about different aspects of these cases but they were dealt with inadequately at a high level. It was said that the absence of a whistleblowing procedure led to an atmosphere of personal hostility between various members of staff. Three senior officers subsequently apologised for their respective roles in these events but one of the complainants[8] decided to take early retirement in view of his disillusionment with the service. The rest of the evidence dealt with the response to allegations of physical abuse of a child at Cornel Clyd and revealed management failings that were aggravated by the lack of a whistleblowing procedure. The Tribunal referred these events to the Welsh Office for investigation.

54.17 We commented in paragraph 49.42 of this report upon the absence of evidence about the appointment of independent visitors under the former regimes in North Wales. Adrianne Jones sought specific information about this from the successor authorities. The responses disclosed that Conwy only has appointed such a visitor: two children were identified as in need of the service and had been provided with visitors "via the North Wales GALRO service". It was intended by Conwy to develop by 1 June 1998 a combined service provided by the Children's Society, embracing a children's rights advocacy service and independent visiting. A number of other children in Conwy met the criteria for the appointment of an independent visitor but they had rejected the offer. All but one of the other authorities reported that there were children in need of independent visitors (Anglesey 2, Gwynedd 1, Denbighshire 1, Wrexham 9) but that none had yet been appointed.

---

[8] Jeffrey Douglas, who is referred to in paras 17.58 to 17.78 of this report.

54.18 In her comment upon these responses, Adrianne Jones drew attention to the statutory duty imposed upon local authorities in this respect under paragraph 17(1) of Schedule 2 to the Children Act 1989 and to Sir William Utting's comments on this subject[9]. She added that the responses raise the questions whether all children who might be befriended by an independent visitor are being considered for such assistance and whether it would be available, having regard to the lack of developed schemes and problems with the recruitment of suitable persons. These responses reinforce our view that a wider review of the practice under the statutory provision is desirable and that consideration should be given to revising the pre-conditions for appointing independent visitors.

The overall provision of residential care

54.19 The figures that we have quoted in Chapter 53 showing where children were accommodated on 15 January 1998 are brought together in the following table:

County	Children looked after	Residential Care		Foster Care	
		In County	Out of County	In County	Out of County
Anglesey	61	4	0	51	6
Conwy	105	2 + 3	1	91	6
Gwynedd	67	5	0	51	9
Denbighshire	70	6	6	53	1
Flintshire	91	0	0	83	8
Wrexham	107	11	7	70	3
Totals	501	31	14	399	33

We cannot vouch for the accuracy of these figures but they give an adequate picture of the way in which children looked after were accommodated in North Wales almost two years after the successor authorities came into being, except possibly in relation to the use of out of county facilities for residential care.

54.20 The table shows that only ten per cent of the children looked after are in residential care and only six per cent are accommodated in residential homes within their own local authority area. Moreover, there were only nine local authority children's homes available in North Wales for use as such with maximum accommodation for 33 children, excluding the three Flintshire homes used for respite care and the three houses in Conwy used to prepare one person in each for independence; and the provision of at least two of the nine children's homes is regarded as temporary.

54.21 We regard it as strongly arguable that this provision for residential child care in North Wales as a whole is inadequate and that the extent of reliance upon out of North Wales placements (both actual and potential) is unacceptable. There is wide agreement that such placements are disadvantageous to children

---

[9] See People Like Us, 1997, The Stationery Office, paras 10.13 to 10.16 for his most recent views.

for numerous reasons that need not be catalogued here; but the language and cultural problems for a child brought up in North Wales may be particularly severe. The range of needs of children for whom suitable foster placements are unavailable is certainly not met by the existing children's homes and it is likely that co-operative action will be necessary to find a solution. There is no enthusiasm amongst the successor authorities for revival of the former Regional Plan mechanisms but the need for concerted action is recognised and, in our view, active Welsh Office participation in the process will be essential.

54.22 It is important that any such review should include the private and voluntary children's homes in North Wales and similar private residential establishments for children, including schools that cater for special needs. The information supplied to us on this subject is very incomplete and a full analysis is overdue. Any review should include those homes presently accommodating fewer than four children that are excluded from the requirement of registration under current legislation. Much dissatisfaction with this exclusion has been expressed to us and, in our view, it should now be re-considered within the full framework of the provision of residential care.

The monitoring of foster placements

54.23 The proportion of children looked after by North Wales authorities who are fostered fell by about one per cent in the two years following reorganisation but the actual number increased from 329 to 405 because of a 20 per cent rise in the number of children looked after. It appears that there have been progressive improvements in the allocation of social workers to individual children and in the frequency of social workers' visits, which are encouraging; and we are not aware of any specific contemporary complaints by foster children. The responsibility of monitoring the availability of placements and the quality of fostering services over a wide area is, however, onerous and we are not persuaded that there is any effective mechanism for this in place. Specific inspections, for example, by the SSIW from time to time can play a useful role but more continuous appraisal is needed and, as in the case of inspection units, it is likely to be more sensitive and responsive if it is locally based.

54.24 This need for effective independent monitoring of foster placements is closely linked with the problem of adequate residential care provision. Whilst the continuing bias in favour of foster care is understood and accepted, it does not provide a universal solution: the need for a range of alternative placements remains and the suitability of individual foster placements needs to be kept under continuous review, particularly in respect of children with special needs or who otherwise present special problems.

54.25 There is a particular need to keep under overall review the resort to multiple foster placements for children looked after. The evidence before the Tribunal has disclosed that, during the period under review, many of the complainants were subjected to numerous changes of foster placements as well as changes from one community home to another. We accept that this may be unavoidable in the case of some disturbed children but multiple foster placements are likely to be highly damaging and may indicate a serious weakness in fostering practice. It is important, therefore, not only to scrutinise the causes of breakdown in individual cases but also to ensure that comprehensive records of the success or failure of placements are maintained and readily accessible.

54.26 The relatively low number of complaints against former foster parents received by the North Wales Police and the Tribunal does not, in our view, justify complacency about the risk of abuse in foster care. As we have said earlier, the constraints upon a foster child in making such complaints tend to be even greater than they are upon children in residential homes and this has been illustrated by some of the cases that we have discussed. Moreover, some of the cases that have been reported to us have been particularly grave. Vigilance by everyone who has contact with the children is all important, therefore, and it is particularly necessary that teachers, members of the medical profession and police officers, who are likely to or may have such contact, should be informed about and responsive to signs of abuse.

The supervision of children leaving care

54.27 The requirements of section 24 of the Children Act 1989 and some recent SSIW inspections have done much to focus the attention of the successor authorities upon the needs of young persons leaving care; and all these authorities now use the relevant Department of Health "Looking After Children" material in preparing children for leaving care. We are satisfied that the commitment exists but the practical implementation of policies such as those modelled on the former Clwyd's Leaving Care Strategy (published in May 1995) will again require continuous monitoring. The problems facing former foster children may well be as severe as those for children leaving residential care; and the forms of assistance that may be needed are wide ranging. In their final submissions to the Tribunal, the successor authorities supported Sir William Utting's recommendation[10] that section 24 of the Act of 1989 should be amended to extend the duties of local authorities to include helping foster carers to continue providing support to their former charges on leaving care.

Financial provision generally

54.28 In explaining the financial provision that they have made for children's services since April 1996, the successor authorities point out that the budgets for social services (and for children's services as part of them) for each new authority derived from the budgets of the former County Councils did not take into account any additional expenditure that might be necessary to provide appropriately skilled higher management of those services. This is but one aspect, in their submission, of the failure of central government to match financial resources and actual needs; and subsequent imposed savings, enforced by capping, made it extremely difficult even to maintain the level of children's services.

---

[10] People Like Us, 1997, para 8.64.

54.29 The force of these submissions is compelling and, in our judgment, there is a strong case for a fresh assessment of the needs of children's services on an all-Wales basis. Such a re-assessment would be particularly timely following the implementation of the Children Act 1989 and the reorganisation of both central and local government in Wales. It would be able to take into account the special needs of the more numerous and smaller unitary authorities, including the opportunities for co-ordinated provision or action by them; and it would provide an opportunity for re-assessment of priorities in the social services, giving due weight to the parental responsibility of local authorities towards every child in its care.

Conclusions

54.30 The evidence presented by the successor authorities has been reassuring in some respects and has demonstrated awareness of most of the problems that have still to be faced. The size and financial resources of the new authorities, however, are such that they will need considerable help and guidance from the Welsh Office/Welsh Assembly in order to achieve effective provision of children's services and discharge of their parental responsibilities throughout North Wales. The continuing work of the Adrianne Jones Report Implementation Group will be of importance in monitoring practice standards for the time being but we do not envisage that it will provide a satisfactory permanent mechanism. As we have indicated in this chapter, concerted action by the authorities in a number of fields is highly desirable and Welsh Office/Welsh Assembly participation in this, at least by way of supervision, is likely to be necessary. Moreover, the financial support for children's services and the degree of priority to be given to them are matters that will have to be addressed on a nationwide basis.

54.31 Amongst our recommendations is one identifying the need for management training of senior managers (first, second and third tier) in Social Services Departments. One of many factors giving rise to this need is that reorganisation of the Social Services Department in North Wales was effected from within the former two counties at senior management level[11] with the result that there has been little opportunity for cross-fertilisation of ideas and practice from outside. Moreover, the size of the authorities and the need for competence in Welsh speaking will inevitably limit to some extent the opportunities for recruitment from outside Wales in the future. The need to keep managers up to date with rapidly developing practices in many fields is, therefore, of special importance.

---

[11] See para 53.04.

PART XIV

CONCLUSIONS
AND
RECOMMENDATIONS

Conclusions

Introduction

55.01 A major benefit of this Inquiry has been that the evidence of 259 complainants, of whom 129 gave oral testimony, has been heard in public. For the vast majority of them this was the first opportunity for their accounts of their periods in care to be publicised and very many of them have expressed satisfaction that this has now been achieved. We are very conscious of the burden that giving evidence, in whichever form, imposed upon these witnesses; and that burden was generally most obvious when some of them were subjected to necessarily severe cross-examination by Counsel for those against whom they made specific allegations. We believe, however, that the satisfaction in their minds of knowing that they have been listened to will substantially outweigh the disadvantages of providing that evidence[1].

55.02 For the "Salmon letter" recipients the Inquiry has been a particularly anxious time: that has been unavoidable, given the nature of the allegations against them. The anxiety has been mitigated, as far as it was permissible for us to do so, by the Tribunal's anonymity ruling for the period of our hearings in respect of any person against whom an allegation of physical or sexual abuse had been or was likely to be made[2]. For reasons that we have explained in paragraph 6.14 of this report, that ruling could not properly be applied to the report itself but, we have exercised restraint in "naming names" and have done so only where we have considered it to be necessary in order to fulfil the purposes of this public inquiry.

55.03 Particular burdens upon the "Salmon letter" recipients (other than those against whom the allegations were limited to abuse) and Counsel who represented them were the wide range of matters with which they had to deal and the scale of the documentation involved. Whereas in conventional litigation between parties the issues are narrowed by statements of each party's case and there is ample time to study relevant documents, the ambit of our inquiry and the necessary timetable of our hearings did not permit these refinements. We acknowledge the additional strains that were imposed by the inquiry on those "Salmon letter" recipients and their Counsel and are grateful to them for their co-operation in accepting them. They are factors that we have borne in mind in reaching our conclusions.

55.04 We have outlined our approach to the evidence submitted to us in Chapter 6 of this report, in which we referred to the special difficulty of investigating a very wide range of events, most of which occurred many years ago[3]. Although it may be obvious, it is necessary to stress also that an inquiry of this kind cannot emulate, for example, an investigation by the police. The resources of

---

[1] See Appendix 5 for the report of the Witness Support Team.
[2] See paras 1.08 to 1.10.
[3] See paras 6.01 and 6.02.

the Tribunal and its mechanisms inevitably limit its ability to seek out new witnesses and to interrogate them. Thus, in the course of probing the existence of an alleged paedophile ring, we have been unable to do more than hear what the relevant witnesses known to us have been prepared to say on the subject and there has been very little documentary evidence to assist us. These limitations, as well as the lapse of time, should be borne in mind when the report is read because they are reasons for the lack of specificity in some of our conclusions.

55.05 At the beginning of the period under review, 1 April 1974, there were 542 children in care in Clwyd and 290 children in care in Gwynedd. At that date, 203 of the Clwyd children were in residential care and 212 were boarded out whereas in Gwynedd about 80 were in residential care compared with 122 boarded out. The period under review ended on 31 March 1996 and the latest (1995) figures that we have show that the children in Clwyd now described as looked after children had been halved, to 244, of whom 190 were fostered. In Gwynedd the changes had also been substantial, if less dramatic, because by 31 July 1995 the number of children looked after was 157, of whom 18 were in residential care and all the rest were fostered.

55.06 Our inquiry has focussed upon the children's homes and foster placements that were the main subject of complaints by former residents. The comparatively few other complaints have not been investigated for a variety of reasons such as lack of identification of the abuser, the fact that the alleged abuse occurred outside the period under review, closure of the home early in that period and/or the fact that the complaint was an isolated one unsupported by any significant body of other complaints in relation to the same home.

55.07 The result has been that we have examined in detail the histories of nine local authority homes in Clwyd[4] (of 23 that existed from time to time) and one voluntary children's home[5] (of four). We have also investigated complaints emanating from a local authority residential school and a National Health Service residential clinic[6]. In the private sector we have examined residential homes/schools in Clwyd run by three organisations[7], namely, the Bryn Alyn Community, Care Concern International and Clwyd Hall for Child Welfare, embracing not less than eight establishments on different sites. Thus, the detailed Inquiry has covered 20 residential establishments in Clwyd over substantial periods as well as the investigation of complaints about seven foster homes[8].

55.08 On the same principle we have examined the histories of five local authority homes in Gwynedd[9] (of ten that existed from time to time). The only other establishments that required investigation in the light of the complaints were

---

[4] See Chapters 7 to 17.
[5] See Chapter 18.
[6] See Chapters 19 and 20.
[7] See Chapters 21 to 23.
[8] See Chapters 25 to 27.
[9] See Chapters 33 to 37.

in the private sector and we examined particularly one that belonged to Care Concern International and three run by Paul Hett[10]. Thus, the Inquiry covered nine residential establishments in Gwynedd and eight foster homes[11].

55.09 It is our hope that, despite its length, this report will be read fully and widely by policy makers, members of the social services profession, administrators and all others who have responsibility for the welfare of looked after children. We draw attention specifically to the fact that many of the children in the residential establishments that we have discussed and in North Wales foster homes were placed there by English authorities. The accounts that we have given of the residential establishments reveal not only how sexual and physical abuse of children can arise and fester but also the extent to which many of these establishments have failed to provide an acceptable minimum standard of care for children in dire need of good quality parenting. The report discloses also widespread shortcomings in practice and administrative failings in the provision of children's services, including failure to apply basic safeguards provided for by regulation, which must be addressed if local authorities are to discharge adequately the parental responsibilities imposed upon them in respect of looked after children. The Children Act 1989 has provided a springboard for many improvements in children's services but the need for vigilance and further positive action remains if the ever present risk of abuse is to be minimised.

Summary of our conclusions

55.10 The following is a summary of the major conclusions that we have reached, as indicated earlier in this report:

Clwyd

Sexual abuse

(1) Widespread sexual abuse of boys occurred in children's residential establishments in Clwyd between 1974 and 1990. There were some incidents of sexual abuse of girl residents in these establishments but they were comparatively rare.

Local authority homes

(2) The local authority community homes most affected by this abuse were (a) Bryn Estyn, where two senior officers, Peter Norman Howarth[12] and Stephen Roderick Norris, sexually assaulted and buggered many boys persistently over a period of ten years from 1974 in the case of Howarth (paras 8.03 to 8.22) and about six years from 1978 in the case of Norris (paras 8.23 to 8.34) and (b) Cartrefle, where Norris[13] continued, as Officer-in-Charge, to abuse boys similarly from 1984 until he was arrested in June 1990 (paras 15.05 to 15.18).

---

[10] See Chapters 38 and 39.

[11] See Chapters 41 to 43.

[12] Sentenced to 10 years' imprisonment in July 1994 and died on 24 April 1997.

[13] Sentenced to 3½ years' imprisonment in June 1990 for indecent assaults at Cartrefle and to 7 years' imprisonment in November 1993 for buggery and lesser offences at Bryn Estyn.

(3) The Tribunal heard all the relevant and admissible evidence known to be available in respect of the allegation that Police Superintendent Gordon Anglesea committed serious sexual misconduct at Bryn Estyn but we were not persuaded by this evidence that the jury's verdict in his favour on this issue in his libel actions was wrong (para 2.31 and Chapter 9).

(4) In addition to the abuse referred to in (2) there were other grave incidents of sexual abuse of boy residents by male and female members of the residential care staff between 1973 and 1990 at five local authority homes in Clwyd, namely, Little Acton Assessment Centre (para 12.10), Bersham Hall (paras 13.14 to 13.20), Chevet Hey (paras 14.32 to 14.45), Cartrefle (paras 15.21 to 15.25) and Upper Downing (paras 17.08 to 17.14).

Private establishments

(5) There was widespread sexual abuse, including buggery, of boy residents in private residential establishments for children in Clwyd throughout the period under review. Sexual abuse of girl residents also occurred to an alarming extent.

(6) The most persistent offender in the Bryn Alyn Community was the original proprietor himself, John Ernest Allen, who was the subject of complaint by 28 former male residents and who was sentenced to six years' imprisonment in February 1995 for indecent assault on six former residents (paras 21.23 to 21.47). One other member of the staff was convicted in 1976 of sexual assaults on boys (paras 21.48 and 21.49) and another was under police investigation for alleged sexual abuse during the Tribunal's hearings and until his death in August 1998 (paras 21.52 and 21.53). The Deputy Headteacher of the Community's school was also convicted in July 1986 of unlawful sexual intercourse with a girl resident under 16 years and sentenced to 6 months' imprisonment (paras 21.50 and 21.51).

(7) Richard Ernest Leake, formerly of Bersham Hall, who was the first Principal of Care Concern's Ystrad Hall School from 1 July 1974 and later Director of the organisation, is awaiting trial on 8 November 1999 on charges of indecent assault on boys between 1972 and 1978 (paras 22.07 and 50.31(6)). The Tribunal is aware of 16 male former residents of Ystrad Hall School who have complained of sexual abuse by members of the staff (six have been named). The Deputy Principal, Bryan Davies, was convicted in September 1978 of three offences of indecent assault against two boys and placed on probation[14] (paras 22.10 to 22.14). We were unable to hear the evidence in respect of Leake because of the continuing police investigation and the evidence that we heard in respect of other members of the staff was insufficient to justify a finding, except in respect of Davies (paras 22.15 to 22.19).

---

[14] See para 2.07(3) for the full order of the Court.

(8) There was persistent sexual abuse, including buggery, of not less than 17 boy residents at Clwyd Hall School between 1970 and 1981 by a houseparent, Noel Ryan, for which he was sentenced in July 1997 to 12 years' imprisonment (paras 23.17 to 23.27). Richard Francis Groome, the former Officer-in-Charge of Tanllwyfan, who was Head of Care and then Principal at Clwyd Hall School between November 1982 and July 1984, has been committed for trial on charges of sexual offences against boys, some of which relate to former boy residents at these establishments. His trial will take place early in 2000.

(9) There was yet again persistent sexual abuse of boy residents of Gatewen Hall, which was a private residential school prior to its sale to the Bryn Alyn Community in 1982[15]. The abusers were the two proprietors from 1977 to 1982, Roger Owen Griffiths and his then wife, now Anthea Beatrice Roberts, who were convicted on 4 and 5 August 1999 in the Crown Court at Chester. Griffiths was sentenced to eight years' imprisonment and Roberts to two years' imprisonment[16].

Voluntary homes

(10) There were complaints of sexual abuse from six former boy residents of the only voluntary home that we investigated, namely, Tanllwyfan. They were directed against a former care assistant at the home, Kenneth Scott, who was there from 1974 to 1976 and who was sentenced in February 1986 to eight years' imprisonment for buggery and other offences against boys committed in Leicestershire between 1982 and 1985. We have no reason to doubt the accuracy of the two complainants who gave evidence of indecent assaults on them by Scott during his period at Tanllwyfan (paras 18.12 to 18.16). There is one charge against Richard Francis Groome in respect of his period as Officer-in-Charge of Tanllwyfan (para 18.30).

Gwynfa

(11) Allegations of sexual abuse during the period under review at Gwynfa Residential Unit or Clinic, an NHS psychiatric hospital for children, were made by ten former residents to the police and involved four members of the staff. One former member of staff was convicted in March 1997 of two offences of rape of a girl aged 16 years committed in 1991, when she was a resident but not in care (paras 20.12 and 20.13). Allegations against another member of staff, Z, were being investigated by the police in the course of the Tribunal's hearings and some of them were made by former children in care but the decision has now been taken that Z should not be prosecuted (paras 20.16 and 20.19 to 20.24). We have not attempted to reach detailed conclusions in relation to Gwynfa for reasons that we explain (para 20.28).

[15] See para 21.05(d).
[16] See para 50.32(1).

Physical Abuse

(12) Physical abuse in the sense of the unacceptable use of force in disciplining and excessive force in restraining residents occurred at not less than six of the local authority community homes in Clwyd, despite the fact that it was the policy of Clwyd County Council throughout the period under review that no member of staff should inflict corporal punishment on any child or young person in any circumstances (para 30.04). It occurred also at most of the other residential establishments for children that we have examined.

Local authority homes

(13) Such abuse was most oppressive at Bryn Estyn, where Paul Bicker Wilson was the worst offender. There was a climate of violence at the home in which other members of the staff resorted to the use of impermissible force from time to time without being disciplined for it. Bullying of residents by their peers was condoned and even encouraged on occasions as a means of exercising control (Chapter 10).

(14) Physical abuse was less prominent in the five other community homes referred to in (12), namely, Little Acton, Bersham Hall, Chevet Hey, Cartrefle and South Meadow, but was sufficiently frequent to affect a significant number of residents adversely. The use of force was often condoned and its effects were aggravated by the fact that some Officers-in-Charge from time to time, such as Peter Bird, Frederick Marshall Jones and Joan Glover, were themselves the perpetrators (Chapters 12 to 15 and paras 17.17 to 17.40).

Ysgol Talfryn and Gwynfa

(15) Physical abuse occurred also from time to time at a local authority residential school, Ysgol Talfryn, and at the NHS residential clinic for children, Gwynfa (paras 19.04 to 19.19 and 19.27; 20.10 to 20.28).

Private establishments

(16) Physical abuse was prevalent in the residential schools/homes of the Bryn Alyn Community in its early years and to a lesser extent at Care Concern's Ystrad Hall School. John Ernest Allen himself was a prominent offender in this respect at the former but impermissible force was used by other members of the staff quite frequently (paras 21.59, 21.60, 21.61 to 21.106 and 21.133; 22.20 to 22.27 and 22.32).

Abuse in foster homes

(17) There were comparatively few complaints of abuse in foster homes in Clwyd but the evidence before the Tribunal disclosed major sexual abuse in five such homes, in respect of which there were convictions in four of the cases (the fifth offender hanged himself before his trial) (Chapters 25 and 26, paras 27.20 to 27.35 and 27.43 to 27.52).

Failings in practice etc

(18) It was a serious defect nationally that complaints procedures were not introduced generally until the late 1980s. In Clwyd, there were no complaints procedures in any of the residential establishments that we have examined in detail between 1974 and 1991 when the major incidents of abuse occurred (paras 29.49 and 29.50).

(19) Few resident children made complaints of abuse (except at Park House, where long term residents felt freer to do so). Those who did complain were generally discouraged from pursuing complaints and recording of complaints was grossly defective (paras 30.15 and 30.31 to 30.35). It was, however, the complaint of a boy resident at Cartrefle to a sensitive member of staff that led to the first convictions of Stephen Roderick Norris (paras 15.12, 15.14 and 29.27).

(20) There were no procedures in any of the establishments to enable members of staff to voice matters of concern and, in many of them, complaints by staff were strongly discouraged.

(21) The worst exemplar of the "cult of silence" on the part of staff was Bryn Estyn, where there were grounds for suspicion and gossip about Howarth's "flat list" activities for many years but the Principal, Arnold, threatened staff with dismissal if they gave currency to the rumours. Arnold was responsible also for covering up the true circumstances in which a resident had been injured and both he and Howarth were seriously at fault in failing to deal with Wilson's oppressive conduct (paras 8.11 to 8.22, 11.02 to 11.06 and 29.51 to 29.57).

The quality of care

(22) The quality of care provided in all the local authority homes and private residential establishments examined was below an acceptable standard throughout the period under review and in most cases far below the required standard. Those well below the standard were Bryn Estyn (paras 11.49 to 11.58), Little Acton (para 12.51), Bersham Hall (paras 13.66 and 13.69), Chevet Hey (paras 14.80 to 14.83), Cartrefle (paras 15.39 to 15.50), Park House (para 17.95), the Bryn Alyn Community (paras 21.107 to 21.132) and Clwyd Hall School (paras 23.11 to 23.14 and 23.31). The quality of care was also well below standard at Ysgol Talfryn by 1993 (para 19.25).

Secure units

(23) There was misuse of the secure units provided (but not approved for use as such) at Bryn Estyn (paras 11.07 to 11.25) and Bersham Hall (paras 13.61 to 13.65).

Education

(24) The provision of education was inadequate in all the local authority community homes with educational facilities (paras 11.26 to 11.41, 12.46 to 12.48, 13.67) and in the private residential schools at Bryn Alyn (paras 21.116 to 21.125) and Clwyd Hall (paras 23.11 to 23.14).

| | (25) | There were many breaches of approved practice in the appointment of residential care staff, most notably at Bryn Estyn, where several members of the staff were recruited informally without references and without any adequate investigation of their past records (paras 30.09 to 30.14). |

Recruitment (25) There were many breaches of approved practice in the appointment of residential care staff, most notably at Bryn Estyn, where several members of the staff were recruited informally without references and without any adequate investigation of their past records (paras 30.09 to 30.14).

(26) Manifestly unsuitable residential care staff were appointed to some vacant senior posts in community homes without any adequate assessment of their suitability for those posts. This was most blatant at Cartrefle with the successive appointments of Stephen Roderick Norris and Frederick Marshall Jones (paras 29.14, 29.15, 14.19, 15.51 and 30.27 to 30.29).

Police checks (27) Checks upon the records of potential employees and foster parents held by the police, the Department of Health and the Department of Education were not made routinely before appointments were confirmed. In the particular case of the foster parent Roger Saint the North Wales Police were at fault in failing to explain to the Social Services Department the narrow limits of their check on Roger Saint's record of convictions in August 1978; and the Department itself was at fault subsequently in failing to make a further check in 1982 at the request of Tower Hamlets and in failing to take any appropriate action when informed of his conviction in 1988 (paras 10.43, 10.63, 10.66, 10.68, 10.125, 24.08, 25.15 to 25.18, 25.75 and 25.77).

Training (28) Training opportunities and practice guidance for residential care staff were grossly inadequate and no instruction was given to them in proper measures of physical restraint (paras 30.06 and 30.37 to 30.42).

Recording (29) The recording of events within residential establishments was frequently of poor quality and on occasions knowingly false (paras 30.31 to 30.36).

Visiting (30) Visiting by field social workers was in too many cases both irregular and infrequent and recording standards were very variable; in general, the quality of contact was poor (paras 29.60 to 29.64 and 31.16 to 31.21).

Care planning (31) There were deficiencies in care planning and in the statutory review process for each child on a similar scale. Too often reviews were paper exercises carried out without the involvement of the child and much later than they should have been (paras 31.04 to 31.06 and 31.11 to 31.16).

Leaving care (32) There were no adequate arrangements for preparing children for leaving care (paras 31.22 to 31.30).

Supervision by other authorities (33) The supervision of children from outside Clwyd by the placing authorities, whether in a residential establishment or in a foster home, was generally inadequate (paras 21.124, 21.131, 25.47 to 25.74 and 25.78).

Management

(34) The arrangements for the oversight of the operation of the Social Services Department at the most senior levels in the County Council were inadequate (paras 28.50 to 28.54).

Leadership

(35) The Social Services Department failed to provide at the most senior level effective and positive leadership to ensure that, in relation to decisions affecting each child in their care, first consideration was given to the welfare of the child and to foster a climate in which that principle was followed (paras 28.55 to 28.62 and 31.31 to 31.32).

Structure

(36) The senior management of the Social Services Department in relation to children's services was subjected to frequent changes and remained confused and defective without adequate expertise at the highest level and clear lines of responsibility and accountability (paras 28.56 to 28.62).

Planning

(37) The Social Services Department failed to establish any strategic plan for the provision of residential placements following the demise of the Regional Plan for Wales (paras 31.07 to 31.10).

Inspection and monitoring

(38) There were no coherent arrangements by Clwyd Social Services Department for the management, support and monitoring of the authority's community homes and for supervision and performance appraisal of residential care staff for most of the period under review. This grave defect had its most serious impact on Bryn Estyn where, despite the existence of a management committee charged with responsibility for it and two other Wrexham community homes, the Principal was left to run the home without any effective supervision or guidance (paras 29.65 to 29.85 and 29.88).

Complaints and discipline

(39) The response by senior management, particularly by Geoffrey Wyatt, to complaints was discouraging and frequently inappropriate; and the implementation of disciplinary procedures was fundamentally flawed (paras 30.15 to 30.30).

Response to reports

(40) The Social Services Department failed to respond positively to successive adverse reports on individual community homes, most of which were of county-wide relevance in relation to the management of the residential sector and the state of the community homes (paras 12.06 to 12.08, 15.42 to 15.50, 17.46 to 17.52 and 17.79 to 17.87 and 32.04 to 32.34).

Information to the SSC

(41) The information supplied to members of the Social Services Committee by officers, including the contents of reports on inquiries, was inadequate and, on occasions, positively misleading (paras 32.09, 32.12, 32.20, 32.21, 32.23, 32.24 and 32.27).

The role of councillors

(42) Members of the Social Services Committee prior to 1990 failed to discharge their parental responsibilities to the children in their care by informing themselves adequately about the state of children's

services in the county and insisting that officers supplied appropriate information to them about matters of concern (paras 32.01, 32.02 and Chapters 29 to 32 generally).

Visits by councillors etc

(43) Visits to community homes by councillors and headquarters' officers were grossly inadequate for most of the period under review (paras 29.65 to 29.85).

The Cartrefle and Jillings reports

(44) Clwyd County Council cannot fairly be blamed for failing to publish the Cartrefle and Jillings reports before it ceased to exist, having regard to the continuing police investigation at that time and its contractual duty to its insurers; but it is desirable that the Law Commission should consider the legal issues that arise in relation to the conduct of inquiries of a similar kind initiated by local authorities or other public bodies and publication of the reports of such inquiries (paras 32.24 to 32.63).

Gwynedd

The reason for the inquiry

(45) Without Alison Taylor's complaints about Nefyn Dodd there would not have been any public inquiry into the alleged abuse of children in care in Gwynedd (paras 45.06 and 49.57 to 49.70). In general terms, she has been vindicated.

Complaints generally

(46) Of about 120 complainants to the police who were former residents of one or more of the five local authority community homes in Gwynedd that we have investigated, about half (58) made complaints that they had been abused by Nefyn Dodd; and all but six of the latter alleged abuse by him at Tŷ'r Felin.

Sexual abuse

Local authority homes

(47) We have not received acceptable evidence of any persistent sexual abuse in any of the local authority homes in Gwynedd (paras 33.56 to 33.59, 34.08, 35.18, 35.19, 36.13 and 37.05). We did, however, hear perturbing evidence of incidents of alleged sexual abuse at different times by two women members of the staff (X and Y) at Queens Park community home involving one (different) resident only in respect of each. The allegations against X were inadequately and inappropriately investigated and, in effect, suppressed. The allegations against Y were not made until 1996. In the absence now of any supporting evidence in respect of either set of allegations we are unable to find that they have been proved (paras 36.14 to 36.39).

Private establishments

(48) There were some isolated incidents of sexual abuse at two of Paul Hett's establishments, namely, Dôl Rhyd School and Ysgol Hengwrt. The five alleged abusers were all male members of the staff involved with one victim each; three of the victims were boys and two were girls. Four of the abusers left the staff shortly after

complaints had been made but the fifth was not the subject of complaint until 1993, over four years after the victim had run away (paras 39.42 to 39.49).

Physical abuse

Local authority homes

(49) Physical abuse in the sense that we have defined it in (12) occurred frequently at Tŷ'r Felin during the regime of Nefyn Dodd as Officer-in-Charge between 1978 and 1990 but was less frequent in the last three or four years of that period. There were 75 complainants to the police who alleged physical abuse there. The worst offenders were Nefyn Dodd himself (paras 33.60 to 33.85) and John Roberts (paras 33.93 to 33.108). We have not been persuaded that either June Dodd or Mari Thomas was guilty of physically abusing residents (paras 33.87 to 33.92 and 33.109 to 33.113).

(50) There was no persistent physical abuse at any of the four other local authority community homes in Gwynedd that we have investigated and comparatively few complaints of such abuse were made to the police about Tŷ Newydd (paras 34.08 to 34.12), Queens Park (paras 36.42 to 36.46) and Cartref Bontnewydd (paras 37.05 to 37.10). There were more (11) complainants to the police who alleged that they had been physically abused by a named abuser at Y Gwyngyll and four of them named Nefyn Dodd; but any incidents of physical abuse that occurred were isolated and were not the subject of complaint until many years afterwards. We accept, however, that Nefyn Dodd did use excessive force to residents at Y Gwyngyll on a limited number of occasions (paras 35.18 and 35.20 to 35.28).

Private establishments

(51) We did not receive any complaint of physical abuse at Hengwrt Hall School but there were complaints by the Spastics Society in 1988 and by a Senior RCCO in 1990 of incidents of alleged abuse, which gave rise to concern (paras 38.14 to 38.30).

(52) 15 former residents of Paul Hett's establishments complained of physical abuse by identified members of the staff but most of their complaints related to Ysgol Hengwrt between 1986 and 1990. We have no doubt that excessive force was used to residents quite frequently by largely untrained staff in the absence of any clear guidelines (paras 39.51 to 39.58).

Other abuse

Nefyn Dodd

(53) The regime imposed by Nefyn Dodd and, to a lesser extent, John Roberts upon staff and children at Tŷ'r Felin was autocratic, oppressive and contrary to the best interests of the residents (paras 33.30 to 33.49 and 33.132).

Abuse in foster homes

(54) Both sexual and physical abuse of children in care occurred in a small number of foster homes in Gwynedd during the period under review.

(55) Complaints of sexual abuse were made by four foster children placed in Gwynedd, but two of them were placed there by Clwyd Social Services Department. One of the foster parents of a Clwyd child (Malcolm Ian Scrugham) was sentenced to ten years' imprisonment in April 1993 for rape and other offences against the foster child (paras 42.03 to 42.17). Gwynedd foster child C1 was sexually abused by the eldest other child in her foster home, for which he was fined in 1984 (paras 42.25 to 42.29). We are not satisfied that the two other foster children were sexually abused (paras 42.19 to 42.24 and 42.37 to 42.45).

(56) Two foster children placed by Gwynedd were subjected to physical abuse in their foster homes. In the case of M, the foster father and one of his two sons were eventually convicted in July 1993 of assaults many years after they occurred; but there were many breaches of good practice by the Social Services Department earlier in dealing with M's complaints (paras 41.09 to 41.63). It is likely also that C1 and her two brothers were subjected to bullying in the foster home (paras 42.30 to 42.35).

Failings in practice etc

Similarities to Clwyd

(57) Although the extent of abuse of children in care in Gwynedd was much less than it was in Clwyd the failings in practice were of a similar order or degree.

(58) The following failings in practice mirrored those in Clwyd:

Complaints

(i) There were no complaints procedures in any of the residential establishments between 1974 and 1991 (paras 45.14 to 45.16).

(ii) The few residents who complained were discouraged and their complaints generally suppressed (paras 41.31 to 41.54 and 45.17 to 45.19).

(iii) There were no procedures for staff to voice matters of concern and complaints by staff were strongly discouraged (paras 33.120 to 33.122 and 45.20 to 45.23).

The quality of care

(iv) Quite apart from the oppressive nature of Nefyn Dodd's regime at Tŷ'r Felin referred to in conclusion (53), the quality of care provided in all the local authority community homes was below an acceptable standard (paras 33.115 to 33.125, 34.06, 35.29 to 35.35, 36.47 to 36.50 and 37.11 to 37.13).

Education

(v) The provision of education at Tŷ'r Felin was inadequate (paras 33.54 and 33.55).

Visiting

(vi) Visiting by field social workers was in too many cases both irregular and infrequent and the quality of contact was poor (paras 46.16 to 46.20).

Care planning

(vii) There were serious and persistent deficiencies in care planning and in the statutory review process (paras 46.03 to 46.05 and 46.10 to 46.15).

Leaving care

(viii) There were no adequate arrangements for preparing children for leaving care (paras 46.21 to 46.28).

Supervision by other authorities

(ix) The supervision of children from outside Gwynedd by the placing authorities, whether in a residential establishment or in a foster home, was generally inadequate (paras 38.37 to 38.39, 42.05, 42.10 to 42.17 and 43.25).

(59) Monitoring by social workers of the quality of individual boarding out placements was inadequate and there was confusion of responsibility for this (paras 43.37, 43.39, 43.43, 43.44 and 46.08).

(60) The child protection procedures and the provisions of the Boarding Out Regulations 1955 were not used for that purpose in some cases (paras 41.56, 41.63 and 43.22).

Management

Retention and advancement of Nefyn Dodd

(61) Major causes of Gwynedd's failure to eliminate abuse in its residential homes for children were the failure to recognise Nefyn Dodd's shortcomings as Officer-in-Charge of Tŷ'r Felin and his advancement to a position of control over all the county's community homes (paras 33.22 to 33.50 and 45.06 to 45.13).

(62) As in Clwyd:

Leadership

(i) The Social Services Department failed to provide at the most senior level effective and positive leadership in the provision and monitoring of children's services (paras 44.67, 45.24 and 46.49).

Structure

(ii) The senior management structure of the Social Services Department in relation to children's services was subjected to frequent changes and was confused and defective without adequate expertise at the highest level and clear lines of responsibility and accountability (paras 44.63 to 44.67).

Planning

(iii) The Social Services Department failed to establish any strategic plan for the provision of residential placements (paras 46.06 to 46.09).

Inspecting and monitoring

(iv) There were no coherent arrangements for inspecting community homes and for monitoring the performance of residential care staff for most of the period under review. The effect of this was to leave Nefyn Dodd in sole control, accountable to himself alone (paras 45.09 to 45.16 and 46.32).

Response to complaints	(v) The response by senior management to complaints, in particular to those made by Alison Taylor, was discouraging and generally inappropriate (paras 45.17 to 45.23).
Response to reports	(vi) The Social Services Department failed to respond to successive adverse reports on the community homes, most of which were of county-wide relevance in relation to the residential sector and the state of the homes (paras 46.29 and 46.30).
Information to the SSC	(vii) The information supplied to members of the Social Services Committee by officers was inadequate and, on occasions, positively misleading (paras 46.31 and 46.35).
The role of councillors	(viii) Members of the Social Services Committee failed to discharge their parental responsibilities to the children in their care by informing themselves adequately about the state of children's services in the county and insisting that officers supplied appropriate information to them (paras 46.31 to 46.35 and 46.45 to 46.49).
Visits by councillors	(ix) Visits to community homes by councillors were grossly inadequate (paras 46.45 to 46.47).
Financial allocation to children's services	(63) Inadequate financial resources were allocated by Gwynedd County Council to children's services throughout the period under review and the adequacy of the allocation was never re-appraised by reference to children's needs (paras 44.55, 44.60 and 46.36 to 46.44).
Leadership	(64) Prior to 1991 the managerial arrangements at the most senior levels in the County Council were outdated and failed to provide an adequate oversight of the operation and performance of the Social Services Department in relation to children's services (paras 44.46 to 44.48, 44.51, 44.53 and 44.59).

The Welsh Office and Central Government

Legislation	(65) Too many changes were imposed in the organisation of local government in Wales and of social services in too short a time span (paras 47.59 and 47.60).
Leadership and guidance	(66) At a time of major upheaval in local government in Wales and in the organisation of social services, the Welsh Office failed to provide leadership and guidance to ensure that the provision and administration of social services were given appropriate priority and failed to inform itself adequately about what was happening in relation to those services in North Wales (paras 47.63 and 47.64, 47.68 to 47.71 and 48.42).

Bryn Estyn's change of status and control

(67) The Welsh Office failed to give Clwyd County Council (or its predecessor, the then Denbighshire County Council) any guidance in relation to the management, administration, supervision and running of Bryn Estyn Community Home following its change of status from an approved school controlled by the Home Office (paras 47.61 and 47.62).

Staffing

(68) The policy and inspectorate branches of the Welsh Office were inadequately staffed with officials of sufficient experience in children's services to support and monitor the provision of those services by local authorities in Wales effectively (paras 47.13, 47.69, 48.09, 48.39 to 48.42).

Strategic planning

(69) Following the demise of regional planning in 1984, the Welsh Office failed to ensure that there were adequate strategies for the provision of residential accommodation for children in care in North Wales (including placements outside Wales) and that such strategies were implemented (paras 47.32, 47.38 and 47.64).

Private children's homes

(70) Central government failed to take any action before the Children Act 1989 to regulate private children's homes despite the provision for this in the Children's Homes Act 1982 on the initiative of a Member of Parliament (para 47.65).

Regulation and inspection of residential establishments for children

(71) The regulatory and inspectorial regimes for community homes and for private residential schools were defective and the findings of inspectors were insufficiently publicised (paras 48.39 to 48.42).

Training

(72) Insufficient priority was given to the need for appropriate training for residential care staff (including guidance on appropriate methods of physical restraint), despite a succession of reports drawing attention to the need for such training (paras 47.66 and 47.67).

Alison Taylor's complaints

(73) Although the Welsh Office did not become aware of allegations of mistreatment of children in care in Gwynedd until September 1986 and of persistent sexual abuse in a Clwyd community home[17] until August 1990, its response to Alison Taylor's complaints was inappropriately negative and inadequate (paras 49.57 to 49.70).

The North Wales Police

Investigations generally

(74) Save for the investigations in Gwynedd from 1986 to 1988 of Alison Taylor's complaints, there was no significant omission by the North Wales Police in investigating the complaints of abuse to children in

---

[17] Cartrefle: see Chapter 15.

care that were reported to them prior to 1990 (paras 50.06, 50.07 and 50.13). This finding includes the investigation of Gary Cooke (and Graham Stephens) in 1979 (paras 52.66 and 52.67).

(75) The evidence before the Tribunal does not justify severe strictures on the police for their response to individual alleged complaints by children in care, including absconders, but it does underline the need for vigilance and sensitivity by police officers when dealing with such complaints (para 50.33).

1986/1988 investigations in Gwynedd

(76) The investigations in Gwynedd between 1986 and 1988 of Alison Taylor's complaints were defective in many respects and may fairly be described as "sluggish and shallow". The role played by Detective Superintendent Gwynne Owen was inappropriate and the size of the investigating team inadequate. There was no liaison with the Social Services Department and relevant documents were not seized. The reports on the investigation were one-sided and regrettable in tone; and the oral report to the Director of Social Services was inadequate (paras 51.29 to 51.33 and 51.79).

The Cartrefle investigation

(77) The investigation of sexual abuse at Cartrefle in 1990 led by Detective Inspector Cronin was thorough and he pursued it as far as could reasonably be expected on the basis of the information before him; but the mode of access to social services files afforded to the police was unsatisfactory (paras 51.35 to 51.39).

The major investigation from 1991

(78) The major police investigation of child abuse in Clwyd from 1991 onwards was carried out thoroughly (para 51.59). It was also carried out sensitively according to most of the complainants, although a small number were critical of the method of approach to them (paras 51.47 to 51.58).

An outside force

(79) The decision by the Chief Constable not to request that an outside police force should take over the major police investigation was justified (paras 51.60 to 51.78).

Re-opening the Cooke 1979 investigation

(80) The decision of the senior investigating officer not to re-open the 1979 investigation of Gary Cooke (and Graham Stephens) was also justified (para 52.68).

Freemasonry

(81) Freemasonry had no impact on any of the police investigations and was not relevant to any other issue arising from our terms of reference (paras 9.24 and 50.41 to 50.47).

Inter-agency review of major police investigations

(82) It would be timely now to arrange a comprehensive inter-agency review of the conduct of major police investigations into the alleged abuse of looked after children (para 51.81).

Paedophile ring

(83) During the period under review there was a paedophile ring in the Wrexham and Chester areas in the sense that there were a number of male persons, many of them known to each other, who were

engaged in paedophile activities and were targeting young males in their middle teens. The evidence does not establish that they were solely or mainly interested in persons in care but such youngsters were particularly vulnerable to their approaches (paras 52.84 to 52.90).

The Successor Authorities

Need for co-ordinated action

(84) The number and size of the new local authorities responsible for social services in North Wales give rise to special problems, some of which can only be solved by co-ordinated action (paras 54.09 and 54.30).

New management structures

(85) The new management structures for social services in some counties do not all provide a single officer at senior management level who is both dedicated to and responsible for children's services and who is of sufficient seniority to influence adequately the allocation of resources to those services (paras 54.06 and 54.07).

Financial resources

(86) There is cause for continuing concern about the adequacy of financial resources allocated to children's services. A fresh assessment of the needs of these services on an All Wales basis is highly desirable (paras 54.04, 54.28 and 54.29).

Recruitment at managerial level

(87) Difficulties are being experienced by some authorities in recruiting officers of appropriate ability and experience in child care services at senior and middle management level and there has been little cross-fertilisation of ideas and practice (paras 53.04, 53.45, 53.46 and 54.05). Provision for appropriate management training is required (para 54.31).

Recruitment of residential care staff

(88) The recruitment of suitable residential care staff for children is a widespread problem that needs to be addressed urgently (para 54.05).

Residential care establishments

(89) The provision of residential care establishments in North Wales is inadequate and needs to be reviewed, together with the use of out of county and private establishments, with a view to co-operative action (paras 54.19 to 54.22).

Fostering

(90) There is a shortage of foster parents with requisite skills and a similar review of the availability and quality of fostering services is needed (paras 54.13 and 54.23 to 54.25).

Inspection

(91) The present organisation of inspection units needs revision. Any National Unit should have a local base within North Wales (paras 54.10 and 54.11). Inspection should include also the provision and quality of fostering services (paras 54.23 to 54.25).

Whistleblowing

(92) There is real danger that the discouragement of "whistleblowing" may persist and positive action is required to ensure that the new procedures are implemented conscientiously and that any fear of reprisals is eliminated (para 54.16).

Independent visitors

(93) The need for independent visitors requires re-assessment, as do the pre-conditions for their appointment (paras 54.17 and 54.18).

Awareness of signs of abuse

(94) Vigilance by everyone who has contact with looked after children is of great importance and this applies particularly to teachers, members of the medical profession and police officers (para 54.26).

Leaving care

(95) The problems for children leaving foster care may well be as severe as those facing children leaving residential care and the forms of assistance that they need may be wide ranging. The implementation of leaving care strategies will need continuous monitoring (para 54.27).

Postscript

55.11 This inquiry has revealed that many of the aspirations of policy makers in the 1960s in relation to children's services were not realised in the following two decades. Reorganisation of local government and social services led to a dissipation of specialist skills and knowledge in child care, which were not replaced. Moreover, the intention of the Children and Young Persons Act 1969 that delinquent children, whose misbehaviour was seen as a consequence of deprivation and disturbance, should receive the same programme of care and treatment as children who had suffered similarly but who had not offended was not effectively implemented.

55.12 It must also be said that, in terms of crime prevention, the care system in Clwyd and Gwynedd was notably unsuccessful. From the records available to us in respect of all but two of the 129 complainants who gave oral evidence to the Tribunal, it appears that 52 had convictions before they entered care but 85 were convicted of offences whilst they were in care and 85 are known to have been convicted after they left care; and the figures for both counties were proportionately broadly similar. It would be a mistake to attach great importance to unanalysed statistics of this kind but they do underline the gravity of the problems that local authorities face.

55.13 One of the many explanations for this sorry record may be that delinquent children saw themselves as being more severely punished than their predecessors because they were now subject to orders that could continue up to the age of 18 years instead of orders for shorter specified periods. On the other hand, some children who had not offended before were introduced to delinquency and to harsh regimes in which they were treated by some staff as "little criminals". Neither category of child received a service that could be described as remedial or therapeutic and some regimes encouraged absconsion and increased offending. It is not surprising in the circumstances that many regarded themselves as lost in care.

55.14 Despite what we have said, however, a significant number of children regarded life in care, even at Bryn Estyn, as distinctly better than life at home and did not want to return to their family of origin. They were fed and clothed regularly and preferred a more predictable life to the unstable and sometimes dangerous one that they had known. We do not subscribe, therefore, to the view that children should be kept out of care at all costs, even though radical improvements in children's services may take some years to achieve.

Recommendations

Introduction

56.01 Formulating the Tribunal's recommendations has been an especially difficult task because there have been so many relevant developments since the events that we have described occurred and even since the Tribunal was appointed. The Children Act 1989 and the regulations made under it introduced major changes in the practice of child care but they did not come into effect until two years later, close to the end of our period under review, and little of the evidence before us has provided reliable guidance as to the effectiveness of the changes in preventing child abuse and detecting it when it occurs. A separate problem has been that, since the mid-1980s, there has been a continuous flow of other initiatives in the form of reports, consultation documents, legislation and statements of government intention touching directly upon the protection of children and the quality of child care. Such initiatives continued throughout our hearings and whilst this report was being prepared.

56.02 We welcome these initiatives unreservedly but they pose for us a problem of selection when setting out our recommendations. It would, for example, be otiose for us to recommend changes that have already been embodied in legislation, even if that legislation has not yet come into effect. We received many submissions in favour of a "one stop shop" for information about persons who may become involved in the care of children and statutory status for the Department of Health's Consultancy Service Index but we make no recommendation about these matters because they have already been dealt with in the Protection of Children Act 1999. More difficult questions of selection have arisen in relation to reports already published and statements of government intention. Some of these may require legislation but many of them are matters requiring only administrative and practical action to put them into effect and there is only patchy evidence before us, at best, to indicate the extent to which this has already been carried out.

56.03 A further problem is that we have inevitably received evidence and submissions touching upon a wide range of child care issues, not all of which can be said to impinge directly upon prevention of the abuse of children in care. At the conclusion of our hearings we received helpful submissions about our recommendations from Counsel on behalf of all the parties who appeared before us and Counsel to the Tribunal, for which we express our great gratitude. As we have said earlier, we had the benefit also of hearing the views of a representative panel of experts in the course of a two day seminar, to whom we are also very grateful. In the end, however, our recommendations have to be directed to our specific terms of reference and based upon the evidence that we have received, including some helpful suggestions by witnesses themselves.

56.04 In the light of these introductory comments our recommendations are focussed upon what we regard as continuing areas of concern and the measures necessary to deal with them, whether or not a particular recommendation has already been made in an earlier report and whether or not it has been endorsed by central government. In our judgment this is the only way in which we can present a relevant body of recommendations in response to our terms of reference. In relation to such matters as recruitment and training, which have previously been considered in great detail, the form of our recommendations takes account of this.

The Tribunal's recommendations

56.05 The Tribunal make the following recommendations:

RECOMMENDATION	Source[1]

The detection of, and response to, abuse

Children's Commissioner   (1) An independent Children's Commissioner for Wales should be appointed. — **1 to 21 45 to 58**

  (2) The duties of the Commissioner should include:

    (a) ensuring that children's rights are respected through the monitoring and oversight of the operation of complaints and whistleblowing procedures and the arrangements for children's advocacy;

    (b) examining the handling of individual cases brought to the Commissioner's attention (including making recommendations on the merits) when he considers it necessary and appropriate to do so;

    (c) publishing reports, including an annual report to the National Assembly for Wales.

Children's Complaints Officer   (3) Every social services authority should be required to appoint an appropriately qualified or experienced Children's Complaints Officer, who should not be the line manager of residential or other staff who may be the subject of children's complaints or complaints relating to children. — **18 to 21 58(i) to (iii)**

  (4) Amongst the duties of the Children's Complaints Officer should be:

    (a) to act in the best interests of the child;

    (b) on receiving a complaint, to see the affected child and the complainant, if it is not the affected child;

---

[1] Where the source is stated to be a plain number in the range of 1 to 95 it is a Conclusion set out in para 55.10 of the report. Other sources cited are paragraphs in the report.

RECOMMENDATION

    (c) thereafter to notify and consult with appropriate line managers about the further handling of the complaint, including:

        (i) any necessary interim action in relation to the affected child, the complainant and the person who is the subject of complaint, including informal resolution of the complaint, if that is appropriate;

        (ii) consideration of the established procedures to be implemented, such as child protection and disciplinary procedures and including any necessary involvement of the police and/or other agencies;

    (d) to ensure that recourse to an independent advocacy service is available to any complainant or affected child who wishes to have it;

    (e) to keep a complete record of all complaints received and how they are dealt with, including the ultimate outcome;

    (f) to report periodically to the Director of Social Services on complaints received, how they have been dealt with and the results.

Response to complaints

(5) Any decision about the future of a child who is alleged to have been abused should be made in that child's best interests. In particular, the child should not be transferred to another placement unless it is in the child's best interests to be transferred.

19, 58(ii)

Complaints procedures

(6) Every local authority should promote vigorously awareness by children and staff of its complaints procedures for looked after children and the importance of applying them conscientiously without any threat or fear of reprisals in any form.

(7) Such complaints procedures should:

    (a) be neither too prescriptive nor too restrictive in categorising what constitutes a complaint;

    (b) encompass a wide variety of channels through which complaints by or relating to looked after children may be made or referred to the Children's Complaints Officer including

RECOMMENDATION	Source

teachers, doctors, nurses, police officers and elected members as well as residential care staff and social workers;

(c) ensure that any person who is the subject of complaint will not be involved in the handling of the complaint.

Whistleblowing (8) Every local authority should establish and implement
procedures conscientiously clear whistleblowing procedures enabling members of staff to make complaints and raise matters of concern affecting the treatment or welfare of looked after children without threats or fear of reprisals in any form. Such procedures should embody the principles indicated in recommendation (7) and the action to be taken should follow, as far as may be appropriate, that set out in recommendation (4).

20, 58(iii), 62(v)

Duty to (9) Consideration should be given to requiring failure by a
report abuse member of staff to report actual or suspected physical or sexual abuse of a child by another member of staff or other person having contact with the child to be made an explicit disciplinary offence.

Field social (10) An appropriate[2] field social worker should be assigned
workers to every looked after child throughout the period that the child remains in care and for an appropriate period following the child's discharge from care.

(11) Field social workers should be required by regulation to visit any looked after child for whom they are responsible not less than once every eight weeks[3]. In the case of older children, they should be required also to see the child alone and at intervals away from their residential or foster home.

30, 58(vi)

(12) Any arrangements made for the provision of residential care or fostering services should expressly safeguard the field social worker's continuing responsibilities for supervision of the placement and care planning.

59

Awareness (13) Area Child Protection Committees should arrange
of abuse training in sexual abuse awareness for social services staff and for those from other departments, agencies and organisations in their area.

---

[2] "Appropriate" in this recommendation and in succeeding recommendations means a social worker with specific training in working with looked after children.
[3] See Sir William Utting, People Like Us, 1997, The Stationery Office at para 3.46 in relation to visits to foster homes.

	RECOMMENDATION	**Source**

(14) Steps should be taken through training and professional and other channels periodically to remind persons outside social services departments who are or may be in regular contact with looked after children, such as teachers, medical practitioners, nurses and police officers, of their potential role in identifying and reporting abuse, the importance of that role and the procedures available to them.

Police log (15) A log of all incidents, disturbances, reports, complaints and absconsions at a children's home should be kept at an appropriate nearby police station and made accessible, when required, to officers of the Social Services Department.   **19, 29**

Absconders (16) Police officers should be reminded periodically that an absconder from a residential care or foster home may have been motivated to abscond by abuse in the home. They should be advised that, when apprehended, an absconder should be encouraged to explain his reasons for absconding and that the absconder should not automatically be returned to the home from which he absconded without consultation with his field social worker.   **75**

(17) It should be a rule of practice that any absconsion should be reported as soon as possible to the absconder's field social worker and that the absconder should be seen on his return by that social worker or by another appropriate person who is independent of the home.

Strategy on investigation of complaint (18) When a complaint alleges serious misbehaviour by a member of staff, the Director of Social Services should appoint a senior officer to formulate an overall strategy for dealing with the complaint, including such matters as liaison with the police in relation to investigation and with other agencies as appropriate, the impact on the child and other residents, any links with other establishments, the handling of any disciplinary proceedings, treatment of any looked after children who are or may become abusers themselves, the management of information for children and parents, staff, elected members and the public.   **Paras 15.15 to 15.18, 16.06 to 16.19**

Liaison with police (19) Whenever a police investigation follows upon a complaint of abuse of a looked after child, the senior officer referred to in recommendation (18) or another senior officer assigned for the specific purpose should establish and maintain close liaison with the senior   **76, 77**

RECOMMENDATION   Source

investigating officer appointed by the police for that investigation and the local authority's officer should be kept informed of the progress of the investigation.

Disciplinary proceedings   (20) Any disciplinary proceedings that are necessary following a complaint of abuse to a child should be conducted with the greatest possible expedition and should not automatically await the outcome of parallel investigations by the police or the report on any other investigation. In this context it should be emphasised to personnel departments and other persons responsible for the conduct of disciplinary proceedings within local authorities that:

    (a) police or any other independent investigation does not determine disciplinary issues;

    (b) disciplinary proceedings may well involve wider issues than whether a crime has been committed;

    (c) the standard of proof in disciplinary proceedings is different from that in criminal proceedings; and

    (d) statements made to the police by potential witnesses in disciplinary proceedings, including statements by a complainant, can and should be made available to local authorities for use in such proceedings, if consent to this is given by the maker of the statement.

  (21) Personnel departments and other persons responsible for disciplinary proceedings within local authorities should be reminded that:

    (a) in deciding whether or not a member of staff should be suspended following an allegation of abuse to a looked after child, first consideration should be given to the best interests of the child;

    (b) suspension is a neutral act in relation to guilt or innocence;

    (c) long periods of suspension are contrary to the public interest and should be avoided whenever practicable;

    (d) depending upon the gravity of the allegation of abuse, the employment of a member of staff in another capacity not involving contact with children or other vulnerable persons may be an

The source column value for recommendation (20): **21, 39, 62(v)**

RECOMMENDATION	Source

appropriate decision at the time of suspending or finally, having regard to the importance of protecting looked after children from abuse.

Review of procedures in major investigations and guidance

(22) In the light of the recent experience gained in both England and Wales in major investigations of alleged wide ranging abuse of children in care/looked after children, an inter-agency review of the procedures followed and personnel employed in those investigations should now be arranged with a view to issuing practical procedural guidance for the future. In any event guidance is required to social services departments and police forces now in relation to:

82

(a) the safeguarding and preservation of social services files;

(b) the safeguarding and preservation of police records of major investigations, including statements and the policy file;

(c) access by the police to social services files;

(d) the supply of information about alleged and suspected abusers by the police following an investigation; and

(e) the sharing of information generally for criminal investigation and child protection purposes.

The prevention of abuse

Recruitment of staff

(23) Social Services Departments should be reminded periodically that they must exercise vigilance in the recruitment and management of their staff in strict accordance with the detailed recommendations of the Warner committee[4]; and compliance with them by individual local authorities should be audited from time to time.

25 to 27

Approval of foster parents

(24) Similar vigilance should be mandatory in relation to all applications for approval as foster parents. In particular, any application to foster by a member of a local authority's child care staff should be stringently vetted by a social worker who is not known to the applicant.

27
Paras 26.05 to 26.15

[4] Choosing with care, 1992, HMSO.

	RECOMMENDATION	Source
Induction training	(25) Social Services Departments should ensure that appropriate and timely induction training is provided for all newly recruited residential child care staff.	28
Training generally	(26) The Tribunal endorses all five of the most recent recommendations of Sir William Utting in "People Like Us"[5] in relation to the content and provision of training for staff in children's homes and the care units of residential special schools and recommends that they should be implemented as expeditiously as possible.	
	(27) It should be a requirement that senior staff of children's homes (including private and voluntary homes) must be qualified social workers or, if that is not practicable before appointment, that it should be a condition of their appointment that they undertake qualifying training within a specified period.	26
	(28) Central government should take the initiative to promote and validate training in safe methods of restraint with a view to making such training readily available for residential child care staff and foster parents.	12, 28, 49
	(29) Suitable specialist training in child care at post-qualifying level should be made widely available and, in particular, to the senior residential care staff of children's homes and to field social workers.	
Attracting suitable staff	(30) There should be a national review of the pay, status and career development of residential child care staff and field social workers to ensure as far as possible that there is a sufficient supply of candidates for such posts of appropriate calibre.	

The quality of care

Assessment	(31) Whenever it is possible to do so, an appropriate social worker should carry out a comprehensive assessment of a child's needs and family situation before that child is admitted to care.	31, 58(vii)
	(32) All emergency admissions should be provisional and should be followed, within a prescribed short period, by a comprehensive assessment of the child's needs and family situation.	37, 62(iii)

[5] Sir William Utting, op cit, at paras 12.22, 12.28, 12.31, 12,34 and 12.37.

	RECOMMENDATION	Source

Care planning (33) The comprehensive assessment referred to in recommendations (31) and (32) should form the basis for the preparation of a care plan in consultation with and for the child within a prescribed short period after the child's admission to care.

31, 58(vii)

(34) An appropriate social worker should be designated as the person responsible for the implementation of the care plan and supervision of the looked after child.

Foster carers (35) Foster carers should receive continuing support and have access as necessary to specialist services. In this context we endorse the recommendations of Sir William Utting in relation to training in "People Like Us"[6].

Leaving care (36) The daily regime in residential establishments and foster homes should encourage and provide facilities for the acquisition of skills necessary for independent living.

32, 58(viii)

(37) A leaving care plan should be prepared for each looked after child, in consultation with that child, a year in advance of the event and should be reviewed periodically thereafter until the child ceases to require or be eligible for further support.

58(viii)

(38) The duty upon local authorities under section 24(1) of the Children Act 1989 to advise, assist and befriend a child with a view to promoting his welfare when he ceases to be looked after by them should be extended so as to ensure that placing authorities provide the level of support to be expected of good parents, including (where appropriate) help to foster parents to provide continuing support[7].

Fostering breakdowns (39) Every local authority's fostering service, whether provided directly or by another agency, should monitor breakdowns in placements with a view to analysing the causes and remedying any faults in the service and should report upon them periodically to the Director of Social Services.

Para 49.54

Compliance with safeguards (40) Appropriate key indicators of compliance with safeguards for looked after children should be developed, covering particularly:

34, 62(i)

(a) the allocation of a designated social worker to each looked after child;

---

[6] Sir William Utting, op cit, at paras 12.23 and 12.34.
[7] Sir William Utting, op cit, at para 8.64.

RECOMMENDATION

Source

   (b) compliance with fostering and placement regulations;

   (c) statutory review requirements; and

   (d) rota visits by elected members.

Private children's homes and residential schools

Registration of homes (41) All private children's homes should be required to register with the independent agency referred to in recommendation (47). 71

Governing body (42) The owner of a private children's home and the owner of a private residential school approved generally for SEN children or receiving SEN children with the consent of the Secretary of State should be required, if the establishment is above a size to be determined, to appoint an appropriately constituted governing body under arrangements approved by the relevant regulatory authority, to include representation from the local social services and education authorities (as appropriate) and the local community. 71

Accounts etc (43) The accounts and other relevant financial information relating to private children's homes and private residential schools approved generally for SEN children or receiving SEN children with the consent of the Secretary of State should be disclosed to the relevant regulatory authorities. 71

Regulation of schools (44) There should be an urgent review of the legislation governing the regulation of private residential schools to include particularly: 71

   (a) approvals and consents under section 347 of the Education Act 1996[8] and for provisional registration of schools,

   (b) the Notice of Complaints provisions and the procedures for the withdrawal of approvals generally, and

   (c) the interaction with the provisions for registration of private children's homes,

with a view to establishing a stricter and more readily enforceable regulatory regime.

---

[8] Previously section 11(3) of the Education Act 1981.

<table>
<tr><td></td><td align="center">**RECOMMENDATION**</td><td align="right">**Source**</td></tr>
</table>

Assessment   (45)   Any placement of a child by a local education department or by a social services department in a residential school should be preceded by:

> (a) consultation between the departments as to whether an assessment by an appropriate social worker of the child's needs and family situation is needed as well as an educational assessment; and

> (b) in the light of (a) and any subsequent assessment, a decision about the need for (and extent of) any further involvement of the social services department with the child to ensure continuity of planning for the child's long term welfare and protection of the child's rights.

Emergency admissions   (46)   Emergency admissions should not be made to private residential schools.

Inspection

Inspection agency   (47)   Without prejudice to the continuing role generally of the Social Services Inspectorate for Wales, an independent regulatory agency for children's services in Wales should be established, with a local base or local bases in North Wales, and charged with the responsibility of inspecting: **38, 62(iv), 68**

> (a) all local authority, voluntary and private children's homes;

> (b) the welfare provision in residential schools;

> (c) fostering services; and

> (d) the other components of children's services.

(48)   When inspections are made by the agency of homes, schools or services mentioned in recommendation (47) at least one of the inspectors should have substantial experience of child care.

Joint inspection of SEN schools   (49)   The agencies responsible for educational and welfare inspections of private residential schools accommodating children with SEN pursuant to section 347 of the Education Act 1996 should be required to agree joint programmes of inspection and reporting.   **71**

Common standards   (50)   A common set of standards should be applied to the local authority, voluntary and private sectors in relation to residential provision and other services for looked after children.

	RECOMMENDATION	**Source**

Reports (51) Copies of the reports of inspections of local authorities' children's homes and services should be sent to the Chief Executives as well as the Directors of Social Services. — **40, 62(vi)**

(52) Copies of reports of inspections of private and voluntary children's homes and of private residential schools should be sent to the Director of Social Services of any placing authority with a child at the school and of the authority in whose area the establishment is located.

(53) The agency referred to in recommendation (47) should present an annual report on all aspects of its work, including any constraints upon that work and any shortfall in fulfilling its obligations.

Senior management

Structure (54) There should be at least one full member of a local authority's social services department management team with child care expertise and experience. — **35, 36, 62(i)(ii)**

(55) The responsibility for policy and service development and for oversight of the delivery of a local authority's children's services should be assigned to one member of the social services department management team of at least Assistant Director status. — **36, 62(ii)**

(56) Staffing resources at intermediate management level for a local authority's children's services should be sufficient in number and quality to enable positive and close supervision and support to be given to residential establishments and the fostering service. — **38, 62(iv)**

Training (57) Local authorities in Wales should review their current arrangements for management training and development for senior managers, including social services managers, giving particular attention to the development of skills in strategic planning, policy implementation and performance appraisal. — **34 to 38, 62(i) to (iv), 64**

Elected members

Responsibilities (58) Elected members should from time to time be advised about and reminded of their responsibilities to develop policy and to oversee and monitor the discharge by the local authority of its parental obligations towards looked after children. — **42, 62(viii)**

Reports by Director of Social Services (59) It should be the explicit duty of the Director of Social Services to assist and support elected members in discharging those responsibilities and, in particular: — **40 to 42, 62(vi) to (viii), 63**

RECOMMENDATION **Source**

    (a) to inform elected members of all matters of concern touching upon children's services, including reports upon them, whether adverse or favourable;

    (b) to provide information on comparative spending on children's services by local authorities in Wales and an analysis of that information;

    (c) to submit an annual report to the Social Services Committee on the department's performance in relation to children's services including its record of compliance with required safeguards for looked after children.

Guidance about visits   (60) The purpose and scope of visits to children's homes, whether by councillors or by senior and intermediate managers, should be clearly defined and made known to all such visitors.

Rota visits   (61) The willingness of councillors to visit children's homes should be a pre-condition of appointment to the committee responsible for the homes and the importance of fulfilling the duty to visit and to report on visits conscientiously should be emphasised to them. Elected members should be provided with appropriate guidance, including reference to the need to be vigilant in protecting the interests of the child residents as well as to be supportive of the staff.   **43, 62(ix)**

Strategic issues

Advisory Council   (62) An Advisory Council for Children's Services in Wales comprised of members covering a wide range of expertise in children's services, including practice, research, management and training, should be established in order to strengthen the provision of children's services in Wales and to ensure that they are accorded the priority that they deserve.   **65 to 72**

    (63) The functions of the Advisory Council should include:

    (a) advising on government policy and legislation with regard to their likely impact on children and young people;

    (b) commissioning research;

    (c) disseminating information and making recommendations.

RECOMMENDATION		Source
Nationwide review of children's services	(64) There should be a nationwide review of the needs and costs of children's services based on local authorities' development plans and leading to a comprehensive and costed strategy for those services, including any necessary education and health elements.	**35, 37, 42, 62(i)(iii)(viii), 63, 66, 69. Paras 54.28 to 54.30**
Local authority plans	(65) Local authorities, in collaboration with voluntary and other relevant organisations and acting together with other local authorities where appropriate, should prepare costed development plans for children's services as a prelude to the proposed nationwide review, such plans to ensure (amongst other things) that:	**37, 62(iii)**
	(a) there is an adequate range of residential care provision of appropriate quality, including secure provision, within reasonable reach of a child's family or other relevant roots;	**Para 54.21**
	(b) such residential provision includes safe places where children can recover when relationships break down;	
	(c) as in (a), there is an adequate range of fostering facilities available of similar quality and accessibility;	**Para 54.23**
	(d) all residential placements are designed to be developmental and therapeutic rather than merely custodial;	
	(e) full educational opportunities are available for looked after children, including remedial education.	**24, 58(v)**
Use of residential schools	(66) Central government should examine the extent to which residential schools are being used as a substitute for social services care and support, and identify the implications for children's long term welfare.	**89**
Availability of placements	(67) Provision should be made for repeated monitoring at appropriate intervals of the availability and quality of residential placements and fostering services on a nationwide basis.	**Para 54.24**
Management training	(68) Consideration should be given at national level to the need for, and provision of, training and management development for senior managers in local authorities in Wales, including the availability of such facilities for social services managers[9].	**34 to 38, 62(i) to (iv), 64**

---

[9] See also Recommendation (57).

	RECOMMENDATION	Source

Resources at national level (69) Adequate resources should be provided to ensure that the departments in Wales responsible at national level for children's services are sufficiently and appropriately staffed to support and monitor the provision of these services in Wales.   **68**

Statistics (70) The national statistics services in Wales should be strengthened to provide a comprehensive management information system.

Supplementary matters

Law Commission (71) The Law Commission should be invited to consider the legal issues that arose in relation to the publication of the Jillings report and the associated problems, as explained in Chapter 32 of this report.   **44**

Guidance on inquiries (72) Subject to the preceding recommendation, guidance to local authorities on the setting up and conduct of inquiries and the dissemination of reports thereon should be up-dated and re-issued[10].   **44**

---

[10] See Ad Hoc Inquiries in Local Government (1980) published jointly by the Society of Local Authority Chief Executives and the Royal Insititute of Public Administration.

APPENDICES

Acknowledgements

1   The Tribunal wishes to express its gratitude to everyone who has contributed to its work, including Flintshire County Council, which provided us with a convenient and well equipped venue for our work.

2   We were very fortunate to be served by staff of high quality and excellent temperament, who were willing to work very long hours without complaint in order to keep up with a demanding time-table. Counsel to the Tribunal provided outstanding leadership in gathering and presenting the evidence and we are grateful to them for advising us soundly throughout. The Treasury Solicitor's team and the administrative staff also were indefatigable and ensured the smooth running of our hearings in the face of many difficulties.

3   We would not have been able to hear and assimilate such a large volume of evidence in 195 working days without the highly professional and unstinted assistance of Counsel and solicitors acting for all the parties.

4   The production of the Tribunal's report has been an arduous task lasting well over a year. In that work we have been helped by a small but very efficient team led by Fiona Walkingshaw and administered by Richard Groves. We mention particularly Colin Salters, who has undertaken much analysis and research for us, Helen Burke and Maureen Griffiths, who have been responsible for processing the whole of it, and David Norbury, our Press Officer, who has performed his duties with great courtesy and tact.

The Tribunal and its staff

The Tribunal

The Honourable Sir Ronald Waterhouse (Chairman)

Margaret Clough

Morris le Fleming DL

Assessor in respect of police matters
Sir Ronald Hadfield QPM DL

Clerk to the Tribunal
Fiona Walkingshaw

The Tribunal's legal team

Counsel to the Tribunal
Gerard Elias QC
Ernest Ryder QC (QC–April 1997)
Gregory Treverton-Jones

Solicitor to the Tribunal
Brian McHenry–until December 1997
Stuart Howard–from December 1997

Assistant Solicitors
Stuart Howard–until December 1997
Sara Rees–(14.11.96–11.12.97)
Ian Philliskirk–(09.09.96–15.11.96)
Christopher Allen–(04.02.97–31.10.97)
Virginia Dewhurst–(13.03.97–07.06.97)
Julia Steele–(26.06.97–15.05.98)

Trainee Solicitors
Grace Martins Waring
Kirsten Mackay
Paralegal support
Provided by 39 legal assistants
from time to time

Witness Interviewing Team : Reginald Briggs assisted by eight retired detective officers

Administrative support to the Tribunal

Chief Administrative Officer
Evan Hughes assisted by eight administrative staff including his deputy, Richard Groves

Press Officer
David Norbury

Tribunal Usher
John Price

Representation

*The reference in brackets is to the first paragraph of the report
in which reference is made to the witness*

Client	Counsel	Instructing Solicitor
45 complainants including OCEAN[1]	Timothy King QC Margaret de Haas (QC–April 1998) Stephen Bedford	Marron Dodds
61 complainants	Timothy King QC Margaret de Haas Stephen Bedford	The Wales and Chester Group comprising the following firms of solicitors: Capper & Jones Cross Solicitors Hywel Davies & Co Freed Kemp Rapport Hugh James, Jones & Jenkins Gwilym Hughes & Partners Elwyn Jones & Co Jewels & Kydney Lindsay Ford Loosemores Martyn Prowel Edwards & Davies North & Nam Palmer Hart Paul Ross & Co Shirley Garnett Williams & Co Swayne Johnson & Wight
14 complainants	Timothy King QC Margaret de Haas Stephen Bedford	Counsel instructed by the following firms of solicitors: Clement Jones Cuddy Woods & Cochrane S R Dew Protheroe & Williams Earl Galpin J Charles Hughes & Co Kaufman Copitch Norman Jones Grayston Oliver & Co P Lloyd Jones & Co Roberts Moore Nicholas Jones Tudor Williams & Co
19 complainants including NORWAS[2]	Nick Booth	Pannone and Partners

[1] OCEAN: Official Campaign for Ending Abuse Nationwide.
[2] NORWAS: North Wales Abuse Survivors.

Client		Counsel	Instructing Solicitor
Michael Barnes	(12.21)	Anna Pauffley QC	Counsel were instructed by the
Peter John Bird	(12.02)	Rachel Langdale	following firms of solicitors:
Beryl Anne Condra	(36.09)		Arthur Boulton & Son
Reginald Gareth (Gary) Cooke			Carter Vincent Jones Davis
	(2.07(4))		T R Evans, Hughes & Co
Paula Dean	(15.34)		Gersten & Nixon
Jeffrey Douglas	(17.58)		Hains & Lewis
Carl Johnson Evans	(12.04)		Hopley Pierce & Bird
Elizabeth (Liz) Evans	(10.68)		John Hughes, Foulkes & Reeves
(Joseph) Emlyn Evans	(3.20)		Jacobs & Co
Keith Allan Evans	(21.80)		James, James & Hatch
Owain Gethin Evans	(44.19)		P Lloyd Jones & Co
Peter Gadd	(34.05)		Poole Alcock & Co
Joan Glover	(17.20)		Pritchard Edwards
Janet Handley	(30.12)		Walker, Smith & Way
Owen Hardwick	(52.33)		Whittle Robinson
John Patrick Harvey	(35.14)		
Peter James Hibbs	(44.34)		
David Bayley Hughes	(33.13)		
Lucille Margaret Hughes	(44.18)		
Andrew Humphriss	(14.77)		
John Leslie Jeffreys	(21.92)		
Frederick Marshall Jones	(13.26)		
Huw Meurig Jones	(12.03)		
Robert Jones	(10.66)		
T E Jones	(3.22)		
Heather Patricia Lynn	(15.21)		
Phillip Murray	(10.59)		
(David) Glanville Owen	(44.26)		
Raymond Powell	(28.09)		
Walter Gordon Ramsay	(28.09)		
Emma Rogers	(36.10)		
Kenneth Andrew Scott	(18.12)		
Henry Morton Stanley	(15.26)		
Peter Steen	(21.61)		
Michael Taylor	(13.08)		
Christopher Ian Thomas	(12.22)		
Iorwerth Thomas	(28.09)		
John Llewellyn Thomas	(28.24)		
Mari Thomas	(33.109)		
Richard Dafydd Vevar	(50.31)		
Christopher Williamson	(22.20)		
Geoffrey Wyatt	(28.10)		
and 61 other witnesses			

Client		Counsel	Instructing Solicitor
Mervyn Hugh Phillips	(28.45)	Alistair Webster QC	E H McClorry
Roger Davies	(28.45)	Suzanne Goddard	Walker, Smith & Way
John Jevons	(28.23)		Jacobs & Co
Andrew Loveridge	(32.35)		
David Alan Parry	(3.23)		
Huw Vaughan Thomas	(44.58)		
and 3 other witnesses			

Client		Counsel	Instructing Solicitor
David Gwyn Birch	(2.35)	Theresa Pepper	Chris Saltrese
John Cunningham	(10.133)		
Enoch Ellis Edwards	(14.03)		
David John Gillison	(2.07(6))		
and 4 other witnesses			
Paul Bicker Wilson	(2.35(3))	John Lever	John Hughes, Foulkes & Reeves
John Ernest Allen	(2.35(6))		Quinn Melville
Richard Ernest Leake	(13.07)	Charles Gratwicke	Hallett & Co
Gordon Anglesea	(2.27)	Andrew Caldecott QC	Russell Jones & Walker
		Benjamin Hinchliff	
David Cheesbrough	(10.87)	Barrie Searle	Russell Jones & Walker
John Ilton	(10.85)		
Maurice (Matt) Matthews	(10.83)		
John Roberts	(33.93)		
and 3 other witnesses			
Peter Norman Howarth	(2.35(3))	Anthony Jennings	Bindman & Partners
Frederick Rutter	(2.07(8))	Stephen Bevan	Bobbets Mackan
Tom Davies	(10.124)	David Knifton	Chris Saltrese
(Joseph) Nefyn Dodd	(10.148)		(also represents BESSG)[3]
June Dodd	(33.05)		Walker, Smith & Way
(Gwyneira) Gwen Hurst	(10.86)		
Anthony Nicholls	(10.63)		
Jacqueline Elizabeth Thomas			
	(2.07(5))		
and 5 other witnesses			
Stephen Roderick Norris	(2.07(7))	Jodie Swallow	Llewellyn Jones, Morris & Ashton
		Nick Parry	
		(Solicitor Advocate)	
A former police officer		David Potter	A W Brown & Lloyd
Roger Platres Saint	(24.07)	Steven Crossley	Chadwick Lawrence
(Daniel) Gledwyn Jones	(3.21)	Colin Samuel	Morgan Bruce
David Alan Challinor	(21.88)	Stephen Warburton	Tudor Williams & Co
Kenneth Henry White (senior)		(Solicitor)	
	(21.08)		
and 1 other witness			
Ioan Bowen Rees	(44.50)	J Tudur Owen	Tudor Owen Roberts
Evelyn May Roberts	(2.35(1))	(Solicitor Advocate)	Glynne & Co
Ian Malcolm Roberts	(2.35(1))		
Norman Brade Roberts	(2.35(1))		
and 4 other witnesses			

[3] BESSG: Bryn Estyn Staff Support Group.

Client		Counsel	Instructing Solicitor
Voices from Care[4]		Sir Louis Blom-Cooper QC	Stephens Innocent
Alison Taylor	(2.08)	Rhodri Davies & Co (Solicitor Advocate)	
Dean Nelson	(2.25)	Robin Oppenheim	Stephens Innocent
Councillor Malcolm King	(32.35)	William Birtles	William Jones & Talog Davies
Councillor Dennis Parry	(32.35)		
Welsh Office		Lady Scotland QC Dermot Main Thompson	Diana Babar
North Wales Police		Andrew Moran QC Peter Cowan	J A Trigger
Crown Prosecution Service[5]		Jerry Hyde (Solicitor Advocate)	
Municipal Mutual Insurance Limited		John Golding QC Kathryn Thirlwall (QC–April 1998)	Browne Jacobson
North Wales Health Authority Clwydian Community Care NHS Trust Gwynedd Community Care NHS Trust		Peter Gregory	Hill Dickinson
Successor local authorities: Isle of Anglesey County Council Flintshire County Council Denbighshire County Council Gwynedd Council Wrexham County Borough Council Conwy County Borough Council		Merfyn Hughes QC Joan Butler (QC–April 1998)	Ronald Evans on behalf of all six authorities
London Borough of Tower Hamlets		Bryan McGuire	Russell Power

NOTE:

The Tribunal also received written submissions from:

— Association of Directors of Social Services

— District Judges of the Wales and Chester Circuit

— The National Youth Advocacy Service

— Gwen James, Director of Voice for the Child in Care

— Peter Newell, Co-ordinator EPOCH (End Physical Punishment of Children)

[4] This organisation was represented for the purposes of making submissions and recommendations only.
[5] The CPS was represented for the purpose of making submissions only.

Note by the Chairman of the Tribunal on its procedures

Preparations for the hearings

1   Leading Counsel to the Tribunal, Gerard Elias QC, made his opening speech on 21 and 22 January 1997, seven months after the setting up of the Tribunal had first been announced by the Secretary of State for Wales and just under five months after the members of the Tribunal had been formally appointed. This was the very minimum period required for preparation, having regard to the large number of potential witnesses to be seen, the enormous number of documents to be inspected and the widespread dispersal of both documents and sources of information that had occurred on local government reorganisation with effect from 1 April 1996.

2   All three Counsel to the Tribunal were fully engaged in the preparations from early in September 1996 onwards. By that time the Treasury Solicitor had appointed a small team of lawyers, led by Brian McHenry (who had wide experience of public inquiries) as Solicitor to the Tribunal, to instruct Counsel and supervise a large group of up to 30 (from time to time) paralegals and two trainee solicitors in the preliminary work. This involved at first the examination of some 9,500 unsorted children's files, numerous staff files and 3,500 statements made to the police as well as the records of both former County Councils and of about 85 children's homes. In the end 12,000 documents were scanned into the Tribunal's database, including documents extracted from the large number of files submitted by the Welsh Office.

3   A Chief Administrative Officer to the Tribunal, Evan Hughes, was seconded from the staff of the Welsh Office and he had a team of eight working under him to provide administrative and financial support. He was responsible, under the Welsh Office budget holder, for authorising expenditure and dealt with all the ancillary services as well as the processing of bills. There was a memorandum of understanding with the Welsh Office.

4   We were fortunate to secure about half of the former but new headquarters of the Alyn and Deeside District Council at Ewloe in Flintshire, near major road junctions, as the venue for our hearings and as the office for the Tribunal and the main part of its staff. It was necessary, however, to obtain separate accommodation at the Shire Hall, Mold, for the purpose of housing many of the documents and carrying out the initial trawl through them. The former Council Chamber at Ewloe was specially adapted for the hearings with convenient working space for Counsel and solicitors and seating accommodation for the public.

5   Preliminary matters that had to be negotiated under the leadership of the Welsh Office and with the guidance of its legal adviser, David Lambert, included the appointment of a witness interviewing team (WIT) comprised of former detective officers of the South Wales Police and adjacent forces, the engagement of a witness support service (The Bridge Child Care Development Service[1]), including a detailed specification of the service to be provided, and the provision of a Live Note transcript service by Sellars Imago, including document imaging. A Press Officer, David Norbury, was appointed in January 1997.

6   Inspection of the statements to the police disclosed that about 650 former children in care had made complaints of abuse of varying gravity. The Tribunal itself advertised its proceedings widely with a request that complainants should make themselves known and about 100 persons responded to this request. In addition, the Tribunal's legal team selected at random as potential witnesses 600 former residents of children's homes in North Wales (about ten per cent) who were not known to have made any complaint. The members of the WIT were eventually able to interview 400 widely dispersed witnesses and travelled over 80,000 miles.

7   The Tribunal decided that, as a general rule, we would receive evidence of abuse only from complainants who could be traced and who were willing to make a statement to the Tribunal. This involved, for most of them, making a statement to a member of the Tribunal's WIT, who was provided with a proforma containing guidance as to how the interview should be conducted; and complainants were informed that they could have their solicitor present at the interview, if they wished, and of the availability of the support service, if they required it.

8   Two major problems intensified the work of the Tribunal's legal team throughout the preparation for the hearings and the subsequent proceedings. The first of these was the need to draft "Salmon letters" to all those who were alleged to have been guilty of abuse and to those who were likely to be the subject of other criticism, giving adequate particulars of what was said against them. In the case of alleged abusers, the problem was mainly one of timing because the evidence of the complainants had to be obtained before the letters could be drafted. Most of the alleged abusers had been interviewed by the police so that they had at least a general recollection of what might be alleged but the Salmon letters had to be based on the available up to date evidence, which, in some cases, included new allegations. To our great regret many Salmon letters had to be posted for this reason during the pre-Christmas period because of the urgent need to begin the hearings.

---

[1] See Appendix 5 for the report by The Bridge on its work.

9   The Salmon letters addressed to administrators and some others presented the different problem of diffuseness. They had to be drafted before the Tribunal's legal team had received any clear evidence of divisions of responsibility within the two former social services departments and the Welsh Office; and, even if the legal team had received some preliminary evidence about this, it would still have been necessary for the Salmon letters to have been drafted in wide terms, covering a broad range of issues. The result was that some Salmon letter recipients had to undertake considerable work, referring to forgotten files, in order to deal with the matters raised in the letters. Moreover, it was inevitable that informal interrogatories had to be addressed to some of the recipients, after their statements had been received in order to remedy omissions or clarify matters that remained unclear.

10   I confess that I have not been able to devise a practical solution to the problem of over-diffuse Salmon letters. If matters of potential criticism are omitted, the Tribunal is open to the criticism of unfairness unless it grants an appropriate adjournment; and successive adjournments would cause major difficulties for everyone involved. A form of preliminary hearing or investigation could take place before each Salmon letter in this category was sent out, but that would also lengthen the hearings considerably in any complex case; and the procedure would not necessarily lead to a more concise statement of issues unless the relevant lines and areas of responsibility were clear cut. It may be that our own procedure was the only practicable one open to us, having regard to the fact that we had to investigate nearly a quarter of a century of administrative and other activity.

11   The other main problem was that of disclosure of documents to the interested parties. Public interest immunity from disclosure was claimed by the successor authorities as a matter of principle in respect of a large proportion of the two former social services departments' documents, particularly the children's files and staff personal records. In the event, we adopted a procedure whereby the initial selection of relevant documents for each witness was made on a broad basis by the paralegal team under supervision; a narrower selection was then made on the basis of relevance by the Tribunal's legal team; and the final choice was made by me after weighing the public interest issue. The result was that all relevant documents, as far as the Tribunal was aware of them, were disclosed. In the case of police documents (other than statements to the police) they were divided, by agreement between the Tribunal's Counsel and Counsel for the North Wales Police, into two categories, namely, documents that could be copied by the parties and those that could be inspected but not copied. Inspection of documents and disclosure were made subject to appropriate undertakings limiting the use of information or documents to the purposes of the Tribunal. Parties were at liberty to apply for disclosure of any specific documents that had been withheld.

12   On the basis of these procedures, core bundles containing all the main relevant documents were formed. These were, however, too large and unwieldy for repeated reference to in the course of a witness' evidence. A relevant smaller bundle was therefore prepared by the Tribunal's legal team for each witness; any other documents required by any of the parties were added to it; and the witness was then able to read and cope with the selected bundle before and in the course of giving evidence.

13   On the whole, the procedure for disclosure of documents worked quite well with the co-operation of Counsel and solicitors but the volume of documentation to be absorbed in a short time undoubtedly imposed considerable strain on those most closely involved, including some witnesses. There were comparatively few complaints of being taken by surprise and short adjournments were granted whenever asked for on the ground of late disclosure. The Tribunal itself was assisted greatly in assimilating and dealing with the documents and in all other respects by its Clerk, Fiona Walkingshaw, a solicitor who joined us full time in December 1996, after secondment by the Welsh Office to the European Commission in Brussels, and who remained as de facto Secretary to the Tribunal until the presentation of our report.

Preliminary hearings

14   It was necessary for the Tribunal to hold four preliminary hearings at intervals of five or six weeks beginning on 10 September 1996, mainly to deal with questions of representation. Before our first hearing HM Attorney-General authorised the Tribunal to say that anything any witness said in evidence before the inquiry would not be used in evidence against him or her in any criminal proceedings, except in relation to any offence of perjury or perverting the course of justice.

15   We decided at the first preliminary hearing to grant anonymity to complainants of physical or sexual abuse and to persons against whom such an allegation was or was likely to be made, in the terms set out in paragraph 1.08 of our report and for the reasons given in the following paragraph of the report. On 11 and 12 February 1997 an application was made by Leading Counsel on behalf of the British Broadcasting Corporation, the *Liverpool Daily Post* and the *Western Mail* that we should set aside this "direction". The application was refused and the Tribunal's reasons for rejecting it, as explained by me on 12 February 1997, are annexed to this Appendix together with the revised notice given to the press and media after the application.

16   We indicated at the first preliminary hearing that any complainant who made a written statement to the Tribunal would be granted representation by Counsel and solicitor, if he/she wished to be represented. We did so on the grounds that it was necessary in the public interest that their views on a range of issues should be put to the Tribunal with professional assistance. It was necessary also that persons against whom they made allegations should be

cross-examined on their behalf and that they should have the protection of legal representation when dealing with any counter-allegations that might be made against them.

17   The obvious problem was that a wide range of solicitors had already been consulted by complainants, some in connection with civil claims and other firms because of their known experience of inquiries into child abuse of a similar kind. Without going into unnecessary details, it became possible by agreement for one silk and two juniors to represent 119 of the complainants and for a separate junior Counsel to represent 18 other complainants. One firm of solicitors acted for 45 of the complainants and another for 18 whilst 61 were represented by 16 firms, forming a Wales and Chester Group led by Gwilym Hughes and Partners for the purpose of joint representation by Counsel[2]. The other 14 complainants were represented by 11 firms of solicitors. In this way nearly all the complainants who gave oral evidence to the Tribunal were legally represented as well as a small number of those who gave written statements but who were not called.

18   A similar approach to the problem of representation of Salmon letter recipients was adopted as a result of very helpful co-operation by them and by their solicitors. In the event 103 of these recipients were represented by Anna Pauffley QC and Rachel Langdale. The 103 were mainly former residential care workers, including Officers-in-Charge, but some were former senior officers of the Social Services Departments. Representation of other Salmon letter recipients was more diffuse but some former teachers at Bryn Estyn, for example, were jointly represented.

19   An early objection to these arrangements when they were at the discussion stage was that there were potential conflicts of interest between clients within the same group. A similar problem in more acute form had been faced and overcome, however, in the course of the Aberfan Tribunal's hearings despite wide joint representation, and we considered that the range of experienced Counsel instructed on behalf of the various parties was sufficient to enable any conflict to be accommodated without professional embarrassment. In the event we are not aware that any difficulty arose and we are satisfied that each of the "parties" who required legal representation was fully and fairly represented.

20   In any prolonged inquiry of this kind the question of legal representation is inextricably linked with the issue of costs, which, in other forms of litigation, would be dealt with separately. In the present inquiry few of the "parties" had sufficient means to meet the cost of their own legal representation. On the other hand the Tribunal itself had no power to make any order for costs: it could only make a recommendation to the Secretary of State for Wales, who had set up the inquiry, that the costs of a particular party should be met out of public funds.

---

[2] See Appendix 3 for the details of representation.

21   Guidance on this subject was given by HM Attorney-General in answer to a Parliamentary question on 29 January 1990[3] in the following terms:

> "Tribunals and Public Inquiries can be set up in a variety of ways. So far as ad hoc tribunals and inquiries are concerned the Government already pays the administrative costs. So far as the costs of legal representation of parties to any inquiry are concerned, where the Government have a discretion they always take careful account of the recommendations on costs of the Tribunal or inquiry concerned. In general, the Government accept the need to pay out of public funds the reasonable costs of any necessary party to the inquiry who would be prejudiced in seeking representation were he in any doubt about funds becoming available. The Government do not accept that the costs of substantial bodies should be met from public funds unless there are special circumstances."

22   Since the Tribunal's hearings ended the Treasury Solicitor's Department has issued a memorandum[4] containing further guidance on the payment of costs, dealing with such matters as the basis of representation, the control of costs and the process of assessment, including provision for appeals.

23   A particular problem that arose in this inquiry was that several of the Salmon letter recipients were members or former members of trades unions which had a discretion, usually to be exercised by the union's executive committee, as to whether or not the member or former member should be given support in the form of legal aid in defending himself/herself against allegations in relation to the performance of his/her duties whilst still a member. It is not surprising that, with varying degrees of hesitation, all but two of the relevant trades unions decided against giving legal support in this inquiry and we do not know of any means by which that decision could be challenged successfully. In these circumstances the Tribunal felt bound to recommend that the costs of the past and present members of the unions that had made that decision should be met out of public funds in the light of the Attorney-General's guidance.

24   The other two trades unions declined to make a decision either way before the Tribunal made its own decision on the costs issue; and Counsel representing the seven Salmon letter recipients affected by this refusal renewed his application that the Tribunal should recommend that his clients' costs be paid out of public funds on the penultimate day of our sittings. Faced with this situation, we agreed to make the recommendation to the Secretary of State for Wales that was sought but to inform him of the background circumstances in which it was made. The Tribunal's dilemma on this issue highlights a real difficulty about the Attorney-General's statement in 1990. Underlying that difficulty is the question whether a "party" whose union agrees to provide legal support is less meritorious than one whose union refuses to do so.

---

[3] Hansard, 29 January 1990, Col 26.

[4] Guidance on payment of legal costs to parties represented at public expense in public inquiries, June 1998.

The Tribunal's hearings

25 As we have said in paragraph 1.11 of the report, we sat on 201 days between 21 January 1997 and 7 April 1998 to hear evidence and submissions. In all 264 witnesses gave oral evidence and we received the written evidence of 311 further witnesses. Evidence was read for a wide variety of reasons, including the deaths of some witnesses, but the range of reasons need not be canvassed here. No important evidence on an abuse issue was read in the face of objections to it. The contents of much of the written evidence that was read were not agreed but it was possible to agree a number of substantial written statements.

26 Counsel for the various "parties" were invited to make opening statements on their clients' behalf at the conclusion of the opening address by Leading Counsel to the Tribunal.

27 For convenience, the evidence was divided into successive phases. In Phase 1 we heard the main evidence of alleged abuse (including evidence from alleged abusers), dealing with the various categories of residential establishments in Clwyd and Gwynedd in turn. In Phase 2 we heard the evidence of senior staff and officers from Officer-in-Charge of residential homes upwards to Directors of Social Services. Phase 3 comprised the evidence of the Welsh Office and Phase 4 that of the North Wales Police. In Phase 5 we dealt with Chief Executives and Councillors whilst Phase 6 covered the role of the insurers and Phase 7 the evidence of the six successor authorities.

28 This division into phases was helpful for a number of reasons. The most important was that it enabled the Tribunal's legal team to formulate an orderly time-table for serving Salmon letters on higher officials and for their responses. Another benefit was that Counsel to the Tribunal were able to present opening statements at the beginning of each phase, clarifying the issues in the light of evidence that had already been given and the Salmon letter responses as well as inter-party discussions in the course of the hearings. Counsel for some of the "parties" chose to make opening statements at the beginning of the phase affecting them.

29 In view of the distances those involved in the hearings had to travel, the length of the Inquiry, the number of clients to be seen and the documentation, the Tribunal sat for four days each week from 2 pm on Mondays to 1 pm on Fridays, daily from 10.30 am to 1 pm and from 2 pm to 4.30 pm. We sat in sessions of about six weeks with short breaks in between to enable the preparatory work for each session to be completed in the intervals.

30 Although there are some advocates of wholly inquisitorial proceedings in investigations of this kind, in which the questioning is conducted almost exclusively by the Tribunal itself or Counsel on its behalf, I reached the firm conclusion that such a procedure would be inappropriate in this inquiry. It was

essential, in my view, that complainants should be given a full opportunity to put relevant matters based on their own special knowledge to persons against whom they made allegations. Conversely, it was equally important that alleged abusers should have their cases put as they wished to the complainants who made allegations against them. This adversarial factor in the proceedings was inescapable, having regard to the nature of the allegations that the Tribunal had to consider.

31 In the event Counsel for the many parties exercised proper restraint in questioning the witnesses and there were comparatively few occasions when I had to intervene because of the nature or manner of cross-examination. There were a small number of regrettable incidents and some complainants resented "being put in the dock" as they would describe it but most of them recognised that it was inevitable that their allegations would be challenged by close questioning. It must be said also that Counsel were economical in their cross-examinations with the result that no witness was detained for an excessive time.

32 In order to save time the written statements to the Tribunal by complainants called to give evidence and any earlier statements to the police that they confirmed were taken as read and formed part of their evidence. Complainants were called by Counsel for the Tribunal and then cross-examined and re-examined in an agreed order. All other witnesses were witnesses of the Tribunal but Salmon letter recipients were led in evidence initially by their own Counsel in order to introduce themselves and to amplify or clarify any matters in their written statements to the Tribunal that they wished to before they were cross-examined.

33 At the conclusion of the evidence on 12 March 1998, Counsel and solicitors were given time to prepare full written submissions, including any recommendations that their clients wished to make. The Tribunal read these submissions before convening again on 31 March 1998 for a week to hear final oral submissions, limited to 30 minutes for each "party" or group of "parties". Leading Counsel to the Tribunal then made concluding oral submissions supplemented by detailed written submissions.

34 We held a well attended seminar on 6 and 7 May 1998 to discuss possible recommendations that the Tribunal might make. The expert panel at this seminar comprised Sir William Utting CB, Sir Ronald Hadfield QPM, DL, Adrianne Jones CBE, Brian Briscoe, and Dr Anthony Baker[5]. Questions were addressed to the panel by Counsel to the Tribunal and by other Counsel and solicitors on behalf of the "parties", supplemented by questions from members of the Tribunal.

---

[5] See para 1.12 of the report.

Anonymity

12 February 1997

Giving the Tribunal's reasons, the Chairman of the Tribunal, Sir Ronald Waterhouse, said

"I must say, first of all, that this is not a ruling in any meaningful legal sense. It is an explanation of action taken by the Tribunal, given as a matter of courtesy in response to submissions made on behalf of the BBC and some newspapers. In giving the explanation I should say that, in so far as I touch on matters of law, they represent my view, but so far as questions of general assessment are concerned, they are the view of the Tribunal collectively.

I accept that this Tribunal has no power to make an order affecting the press, apart from statute, and I make clear that no order has been made by the Tribunal under either section 4 or section 11 of the Contempt of Court Act 1981. The word 'direction' that appears in the material guidance is, at least partly, a misnomer. The word was used only in the sense of a practice direction explaining procedure and was intended to be an indication to the parties involved in the Inquiry as to how the Tribunal was intending to proceed, coupled with an intimation to the press as to the view that the Tribunal would take, and in particular, the action I would take as Chairman, if the identity of any person in the 'anonymous' categories referred to in the document was to be disclosed in a publication.

The background to the action we have taken is that the Tribunal has received requests from virtually all the potential witnesses who are complainants of abuse and from the persons against whom allegations of abuse are made that they should be granted anonymity in the proceedings. We have been given information about the impact of the Inquiry and the gathering of evidence upon potential witnesses and we have reached the firm conclusion that there is substantial risk that the course of justice and the proceedings of the Tribunal would be seriously impeded and prejudiced if there were to be general publication of the identity of the abusers and persons against whom allegations of abuse are made. For that reason we regard it as necessary that anonymity should be conferred as far as possible upon the witnesses referred to in order to avoid the risk of serious prejudice of the kind that was discussed in the House of Lords in the case of *Attorney-General versus Leveller Magazine* reported in 1979, as well as that specified in the Contempt of Court Act 1981.

In considering what we should do, we have had a large number of considerations in mind. These include the terms of reference which we have to follow, the background to the setting up of the Inquiry and the need for full disclosure by witnesses to avoid any continuing suggestion of cover-up. By 'full disclosure' I mean the interviewing of every available potential witness and the objective that those witnesses shall give as full and true an account as they can of the facts within their knowledge both in their written statements and in their oral testimony if and when they are called to give evidence.

We have had in mind also that, in the context of the first paragraph of our terms of reference, the identities of particular complainants or persons against whom allegations are made is of much less importance than the question whether the alleged abuse occurred and the circumstances in which it is alleged to have happened. We have obviously had regard also to the provisions of the Sexual Offences (Amendment) Act 1992 to the extent that they are relevant.

These are all matters that we have had in mind in making our assessment that the course of justice in these proceedings is likely to be seriously impeded if anonymity is not conferred upon the potential witnesses in the first part of our inquiry.

The difficulty that we had to face, however, is that, despite the need for anonymity, there is no practical means of conducting the actual hearing within the Tribunal Chamber by adopting a series of symbols for witnesses; neither a numerical nor an alphabetical system would be readily comprehensible, bearing in mind the large number of persons involved.

The problem is not confined to intelligent Counsel and solicitors steeped in the case, but extends, of course, to witnesses and the transcribers of the evidence. The prospect of a witness, probably ill-educated because of circumstances beyond his control, being faced with the problem of not naming persons to whom he wishes to refer, but identifying them by a code set in front of him in the witness box, is too appalling to contemplate. The length of the proceedings and the extra public expense involved in that procedure would be intolerable, and the ultimate report of the Tribunal might be delayed by many months.

An alternative possible procedure would be for the Tribunal to sit 'in camera' but that would defeat one of the major objects of the setting up of the Tribunal, namely, to assuage public anxiety about what has occurred in the past. It could lead to unjustified suggestions of a cover-up and we have rejected it, bearing in mind what was said by the Salmon Commission about the need for hearings to be in public.

Taking fully into account that guidance, we have decided that it is necessary for the hearings to take place in public and for names to be given in the course of the hearings. In the event the prejudice to the witnesses is likely to be, and has proved to be, minimal because attendance at the Inquiry by the general public has been very limited. The proceedings have been entirely open, but attendance has been largely confined to persons who have a direct interest in the subject matter of the Inquiry, most of whom are legally represented or who are at least potentially witnesses.

Thus, the result of names being given in the hearings involves only a minor breach of the anonymity which we wish to confer upon the witnesses to whom we have referred. Most of the people who hear names in the course of the hearing would be entitled to know the names because of their position in relation to the Inquiry and would not therefore be covered by the anonymity rule.

Having considered all the difficulties, and not least the exchanges that occurred in Parliament when the announcement was made that the Inquiry would take place, we decided to proceed as we have done but to indicate to the press in clear terms that in our view the publication of material enabling the public to identify witnesses who are either complainants of abuse or persons against whom allegations of abuse are made would seriously impede and prejudice the course of the hearings of this Inquiry. It would do so because it would tend very strongly to dissuade witnesses of either category from coming forward and telling the full truth, and such a disincentive would affect also such independent witnesses who were either residents at the relevant care homes or present there as employees or in some official other capacity from giving honest evidence.

In giving that express intimation, we believe that we were following the guidance given, in particular, by Lord Edmund Davies in the Leveller case and the spirit of what was said by Lord Diplock in his opinion. In our view, there can be no misunderstanding of that intimation to the media.

I stress that the consequences of any publication of the identity of a witness of the prohibited kind would have to be considered on its merits if and when it occurred. If that event were to happen, there would have to be a complaint about the matter and the Tribunal would have to consider it. I would have to decide whether in the circumstances it was appropriate to certify the matter in accordance with section 1(2) of the Tribunals of Inquiry (Evidence) Act 1921 to the High Court, and ultimately it would be a matter for the High Court to consider.

It is for that reason that it would be inappropriate to call this explanation a ruling. But it is proper for me to say that, as a matter of law, I regard it as highly doubtful whether an editor could rely on the defence provided by section 4(1) of the Contempt of Court Act 1981 if a publication that did seriously prejudice the course of justice in these proceedings were to be published now, despite the intimation given by this Tribunal, supported by senior counsel on all sides, who are fully acquainted with the nature of the evidence and the circumstances in which it has been obtained.

Apart from the argument as to whether the particular publication did offend the strict liability rule defined in the Act of 1981, there would be the question whether the material was published in good faith. I will say only that it would surprise me if a court were to hold that publication in the face of an express warning was 'in good faith'. But that would be an issue to be decided upon the facts of the particular case rather than as a theoretical question.

Finally, I should say that our intimation applies only to witnesses in the first stage of this Inquiry. The intimation is without time limit, subject to the provisions of the legislation, but it applies only to witnesses who are either complainants of abuse or the subject of allegations of abuse and witnesses who give evidence touching upon those allegations. Different considerations entirely will arise when we pass at a later stage to administrative matters relating to the children in care.

We will keep under review the question of the application of the anonymity principle. We have already excepted persons whose names are already in the public domain, namely, those who have been convicted of offences forming part of our Inquiry and one of the complainants who is well known through the press as a potential witness in these proceedings[6]. But, if any particular question arises in relation to a specific witness, we will consider it and our Press Officer is always available to advise the press and the media if there is any matter left in doubt."

---

[6] This witness subsequently applied for and was granted anonymity.

North Wales Tribunal of Inquiry
Important information for the Assistance of
the Press and Media

1   The Tribunal wishes to indicate that it will regard the following as prima facie evidence of a contempt of court:

>   publication of any material in a written publication (as defined in section 6(1) of the 1992 Act) available to the public (whether on paper or in electronic form), or in a television or radio programme for reception in England and Wales, which is likely to identify any living person as a person by whom or against whom an allegation of physical or sexual abuse has been or is likely to be made in proceedings before the Tribunal, with the exception of those who have been convicted of criminal offences of physical or sexual abuse of children in care.

2   The Tribunal considers that such publication is likely to create a substantial risk that the course of justice in the proceedings of the Tribunal would be seriously prejudiced or impeded, not least because in the event of such publication, potential witnesses may be deterred from testifying, or from testifying fully, to the Tribunal. In the event of such publication, the Chairman would be minded, subject to any representations made to him at that time, to refer the matter to the Attorney General, and/or to the High Court, under the Contempt of Court Act 1981, and the Tribunals of Inquiry (Evidence) Act 1921.

3   This is a general intimation. It is open to the Tribunal to give a different intimation in relation to any specific witness. The intimation will be subject to continuous review both during the proceedings of the Tribunal, and at the time of publication of the Tribunal's report.

Report of the Witness Support Team

Introduction

Six weeks before the start of the Tribunal, The Bridge[1] was asked to set up a witness support programme for people who were to give evidence. Witnesses included those who had suffered abuse in residential or foster care as well as those who were alleged to have abused children or young people looked after by local authorities.

The Bridge had no idea in advance how many witnesses there would be, how many of them would need a service or how many would be located in North Wales or elsewhere.

It was clear from the outset that The Bridge was setting up a programme to support witnesses and not to counsel them because the latter would require long-term arrangements which the Tribunal was not in a position to make or finance.

The agreement was that the programme would offer support on a number of levels:

— providing two days training for staff who were running the Tribunal Helpline, which had been set up for witnesses who wanted to talk about giving evidence;

— providing back-up support to the Tribunal Helpline before the start of the formal hearings;

— supporting witnesses before and after they gave oral evidence;

— supporting witnesses on the day(s) that they gave evidence; and

— where a witness needed and asked for longer term counselling or therapy, negotiating local arrangements to meet the request.

Setting up the programme

The Bridge had to identify a core team with the equivalent of three full-time staff. They were required to have professional qualifications laid down in a protocol between the Tribunal and The Bridge. In addition, it was agreed that staff used in the programme would come from outside North Wales and should not have worked in residential care in the area covered by the Tribunal. The team appointed was made up of six part-time staff, a mixture of social workers, social work managers and counsellors. Some of the staff were employed directly by The Bridge, others came on secondment from other agencies (Barnardos, Victim Support and the City of York Social Services), whose help was greatly appreciated.

---

[1] The Bridge Child Care Development Service.

The team was completed by a full-time administrator, who played a key part in ensuring that the systems were maintained and information co-ordinated. Organisational support was provided from The Bridge centrally, which found and equipped an office base in Holywell.

As the work of the Tribunal unfolded, it became necessary to identify a range of professionals (in addition to the core team) who could offer support to witnesses living away from North Wales. These professionals were a mixture of social workers, counsellors and psychologists and were based across the United Kingdom stretching from Scotland to Devon. This was not easy to achieve, but a number of agencies showed a desire to help. In the case of the core team and other professionals special arrangements had to be made for police checks to be undertaken.

Despite the shortage of time in setting up the programme, The Bridge did manage to have two staff in place by the time the Tribunal opened.

The Task

The first task for the staff was to listen to witnesses on the telephone. The levels of distress being experienced by those individuals, even up to 20 years on from the experience, was clear from the outset. Yet very few had received counselling or therapy to help with the impact of abuse on their mental health. At this stage the task was very much to listen. From the beginning the team had to be clear that in whatever way help was given it should not contaminate the evidence the witness was to give to a Tribunal with judicial powers.

The team had to provide services to those who had been abused as well as those who it was alleged had abused children or young people. It was important to ensure that an even-handed service was delivered to both complainants and alleged abusers and discussions took place within the team to ensure that this happened.

In some instances staff spent a great deal of time with individual witnesses to help them decide whether or not they wished to make contact with the Tribunal in order to give evidence. This included helping an individual to focus on the impact that giving evidence would have on them and on their partners, families and communities.

Once the Tribunal hearings started The Bridge had two team members present at the Tribunal every day, plus an additional team member to answer The Bridge Helpline, which was set up to offer support.

On the days when the Tribunal was sitting the team members helping witnesses would typically:

— be available when the witness arrived;

— show them where the witness waiting room and other facilities were;

— explain the function of The Bridge team members;

— explain how the day would run;

— show them where they would be giving evidence from;

— show them who would be sitting where in the Tribunal room and explain their part in the proceedings and the difference between these proceedings and a court;

— point out the visible "technology" e.g. large computers for displaying documents and statements;

— point out where The Bridge team member would be whilst the witness gave evidence;

— show the witness where they should go after they had given evidence or when an adjournment occurred;

— ensure they were able to have a drink and, at lunch time, sandwiches;

— if family members were there as well, to show them where they could sit or to stay with them if they did not wish to hear the evidence;

— to help witnesses deal with their anxieties and the frequently long wait to give evidence; this was aimed at helping them to be able to cope with giving evidence and to give of their best;

— offer advice on how to cope with the stress of being in the Tribunal room, for example not being afraid to ask for a break, responding directly to the Tribunal Chairman, remembering that it was their personal experience that was important for the Tribunal members to hear;

— liaise with legal representatives where required; and

— ensure that where a group of witnesses were waiting to give evidence, those who wanted to talk to a Bridge staff member could do so whilst those who wished to wait in a quiet environment could do so as well.

Once a witness had given evidence the same team member would be available to listen, support or advise for as long as this was necessary; this was particularly important bearing in mind that many witnesses had to drive themselves home safely after what had been an emotional experience. The accounts given to the team in the waiting room often went way beyond the formal evidence given in the Tribunal.

Once a witness had given evidence they were reminded that The Bridge could offer medium-term support which they could use if they so chose; alternatively, they could be offered support from a professional in their own area if they lived away from North Wales.

As the months went by those witnesses who clearly needed more than could be offered by the witness support service were gradually introduced to long-term services in their area.

These were in the main, but not exclusively, adult mental health services.

The Witnesses' Experience

The way in which witnesses made use of the witness support service ranged from no contact at all, to the occasional telephone call, to regular face to face contact. In setting up the programme The Bridge wanted to ensure that it was the witnesses who determined how the service was used and to be clear that it was alright if witnesses chose not to use the service.

Throughout the hearings it was indeed the witnesses who determined how much or how little support was required. For example, one small self-help group requested that The Bridge team did not provide support at the hearings whilst others asked for consistent longer term help.

Ultimately 121 witnesses, of whom 106 were people who had been abused in care, made use of the service outside the hearings in one form or another. Of these, 56 lived in North Wales and 65 in other parts of Britain, ranging from Lothian to Devon. Twenty nine were female and 92 were male.

In total, outside Tribunal hearings 1,087 hours of support were provided to the 121 witnesses.

The statistics, however, do not tell the real story. The whole Tribunal process was concerned with the excruciating suffering that so many witnesses had experienced. Day after day witnesses told their story in the witness box; for many this meant reliving the horror of the abuse from which they suffered; some had been helpless onlookers unable to affect the situation they saw; a few experienced remorse for abuse inflicted.

Set out below are some of the individual stories:

— One young person burst into tears in the witness room and spent $1\frac{1}{2}$ hours with a team member before feeling able to face their family who had come to give moral support.

— Another, who had arrived apparently confident, afterwards sat with one of the team struggling to make sense of the day's events. They had thought they had moved on from the abuse in care but the painful memories came flooding back.

— A witness who for 20 years had successfully held down a good job felt unable to return to work for several weeks and needed the supportive help of the witness support service, friends and GP.

— One witness was very distressed and described giving evidence as like being abused all over again; the witness very much needed contact with the team for several weeks.

— A parent recently reunited with their adult child sat and listened to the account of the abuse that had been suffered in care. The team member recalls the intensity of the feelings—pain, guilt, anger, sadness and remorse.

— A young adult now running a business and employing others decided to tell the full story of the abuse for the first time at the Tribunal. Previously there had been fears of the impact on the business of giving evidence and the effect on the people employed learning about the past. The decision to put these fears to one side was motivated by the determination to stop other children being abused in care (this was often cited by people as a reason for agreeing to give evidence at the Tribunal).

— From a Helpline call, a parent who remembered insisting that their child return to care from home leave despite protests, asked "why didn't someone tell me what was happening there?"

A very small number of witnesses required an emergency admission to psychiatric hospital. Others came from prison to give evidence; it proved more difficult, though just as important, to find longer term help for those individuals.

For others who were already feeling vulnerable before attending the Tribunal, or who were already undergoing counselling or therapy, our task was to ensure the support they needed continued.

On other occasions external but major things needed our attention such as helping a parent tell an adult child that they were terminally ill.

Other witnesses found the experience to have some form of cathartic effect and some examples are set out below.

— One young adult had used our service to develop the confidence to give evidence and attending the hearing was part of the moving on process.

— A young adult gave evidence with a partner and child sitting in the public gallery so that they could hear the story, it was seen as "my day in court". Although feeling a little distressed the family left holding on to each other as though leaving something negative behind.

— One witness told The Bridge Helpline he came away feeling much more positive than they had in ages— "like a human being again".

— Another witness wrote "The process returned some of my dignity".

— Another wrote "Thank you for all your help over the last few months".

Sometimes it was what seemed to us the simple things that helped a witness most. For example, a team member helped one young adult access their social services file, where the only photograph was found of the witness as a child.

The Tribunal has been about the experience of witnesses and so has the witness support service. As one of the team put it "nothing could have prepared you for this experience". Sharing the witnesses' experience in a very small way by listening again and again as they repeatedly told their stories was a deeply humbling experience and has affected all team members in a way that will ensure their practice will never be the same again. As this is being written we are reminded of how difficult it is to convey a picture of the pain, the long-term suffering and the negative consequences for so many people.

What can we learn about witness support in such circumstances?

1 Recognising that for many people giving evidence of abuse and rape in any setting means emotionally reliving the experience and that in itself can traumatise them or undermine their abilities to cope.

2 The importance of involving a support service from the early stages, at the point a witness makes a written statement or makes telephone contact.

3 The value of a service which was separate from the Tribunal itself, outside the internal machinery, and used staff who had not worked in the geographical area where the abuse had occurred.

4 The importance of having clear operational protocols to ensure:

      (i) evidence is not contaminated;

      (ii) service is consistent.

5 Recognising that witness support in Tribunals can mean something different for each witness and the service needs to be flexible enough to be able to respond to the individual needs.

6 Recognising that witnesses have a right not to use the service.

7 The desperate need that exists for long-term counselling and therapy services nationally which can be accessed much more speedily by young adults in need.

Perhaps the most important lesson that was learnt through The Bridge's work at the Tribunal was the fact that so few of the complainant witnesses had received any counselling or therapeutic help to deal with the pain of the abuse they had suffered. The witnesses were adults who had not received appropriate help for anything up to 20 years after the event.

The Bridge's experience in other settings is that only in a handful of situations do children abused in the community or residential care receive any formal therapy or counselling. If the pain and suffering that The Bridge has witnessed is to be eased, if children, young people and adults are to be helped to recover, then a radical change in mental health service provision is needed.

Main statutory regulation from 1974 until the Children Act 1989 came into force on 14 October 1991

1   The main legislative changes affecting the child care system that were a prelude to the period under review have been discussed in Chapter 3 of this report. The powers and duties of local authorities thereafter in relation to children were detailed and complex. In this appendix we outline only those provisions that are most relevant to our report and, in doing so, we use terminology current at the time.

Modes of entry to care

2   In the 1970s and 1980s there was a wide variety of routes by which a child might enter into care. However, those most relevant to the large majority of children whose histories and complaints we have considered were:

(a) Reception into care by voluntary agreement[1].

This could be followed by the assumption of parental rights by the local authority in defined circumstances[2].

(b) Committal to the care of the local authority by the courts in care proceedings[3].

Care orders replaced, from 1971, the former approved school orders and fit person orders. Under care orders parental rights were transferred to the local authority, which was given full discretion as to the placement of children made subject to such orders.

(c) Committal to the care of the local authority by the courts in matrimonial proceedings in specified circumstances[4].

The powers of local authorities in such cases were similar to those in (b) but there were some limitations on their discretion.

The duties of a local authority

3   The general duty of a local authority in reaching a decision relating to any child in its care was:

(a) so to exercise its powers with respect to the child as to further the child's best interests and afford the child the opportunity for the proper development of his/her character and abilities; and

---

[1] Section 1 of the Children Act 1948 and section 2 of the Child Care Act 1980.
[2] Section 2 of the Act of 1948 and section 3 of the Act of 1980.
[3] Section 1 of the Children and Young Persons Act 1969.
[4] Section 2(1)(e) of the Matrimonial Proceedings (Magistrates' Courts) Act 1960, replaced from 1 February 1981 by section 10 of the Domestic Proceedings Magistrates' Court Act 1978; and section 43(1) of the Matrimonial Causes Act 1973.

(b) to make such use of facilities and services available for children in the care of their own parents as appeared to the local authority reasonable in each child's case[5].

4   With the effect from 1 January 1971 local authorities' powers and duties were enlarged (a) to add an obligation to receive a child committed into its care and (b) to confer on them the same powers and duties as a parent or guardian would have had apart from the order, including (but subject to regulations) the power to restrict the child's liberty[6].

5   On 1 January 1976, the general duty was significantly amended by the Children Act 1975. The amended duty was re-stated in the same form by the Child Care Act 1980 as follows:

(a) to give first consideration to the need to safeguard and promote the child's welfare throughout his childhood; and

(b) so far as practicable to ascertain the wishes and feelings of the child regarding any decision relating to that child and to give due consideration to them having regard to the child's age and understanding.

6   The local authority was obliged to discharge its duty to accommodate and maintain a child in its care by[7]:

(a) boarding the child out (state approved fostering) in accordance with the regulations made by the Secretary of State[8]; or

(b) maintaining the child in a home provided by the local authority or in a voluntary home; or

(c) making such other arrangements as seemed appropriate to the local authority (including the power to allow a child to be under the charge and control of a parent, guardian, relative or friend).

7   The Act of 1948 required local authorities to consider boarding out in preference to placement in a residential home but this duty was not re-enacted in the Act of 1969. The new duty gave local authorities the discretion to make arrangements for accommodation and maintenance as they saw fit. However, a high percentage of children boarded out continued to be seen as an indicator of good practice.

Ways of accommodating children

8   Both the Children and Young Persons Act 1969 and the Child Care Act 1980 imposed a duty upon local authorities to provide community homes within overall arrangements for the regional planning of accommodation. Until the 1 January 1984 the duty upon a local authority was to provide, manage, equip

---

[5] Section 12 of the Children Act 1948.

[6] Section 24 of the Children and Young Persons Act 1969.

[7] Sections 13 and 14 of the Children Act 1948 as amended and substituted by section 49 of the Children and Young Persons Act 1969.

[8] Pursuant to section 14 of the Children Act 1948.

and maintain such community homes as were included in the regional plan approved by the Secretary of State. The plan had to contain proposals with regard to the nature and purpose of each home and for the provision of facilities for observing the physical and mental condition of children in care and for assessing the most suitable accommodation and treatment for them.

9   In 1984 the regional plan arrangements were discontinued. From then on, local authorities, acting alone or jointly, were required to make arrangements by themselves or with voluntary organisations to provide for the accommodation needs of children in care; and this requirement included a duty to ensure that community homes were available for the accommodation and maintenance of such children. In making such arrangements local authorities had to have regard to the need to ensure that accommodation of different descriptions was available and suitable to meet the varying requirements of children.

Statutory reviews

10   It was the duty of the local authority (under section 27(4) of the Children and Young Persons Act 1969) to review the case of every child in its care every six months and, if he was the subject of a care order, to consider upon the review whether to apply to discharge the order.

11   The Children Act 1975 made provision for the duty to be defined further by regulations to be made by the Secretary of State, which could include the manner, the times and the matters to be reviewed. Despite the importance of the potential effect of such regulations on the quality of child care provision and the enactment of a like provision in section 20 of the Child Care Act 1980, neither provision was ever brought into force.

12   Regulations eventually appeared as the Review of Children's Cases Regulations 1991[9]. These regulations require a first review within four weeks of the date upon which a child begins to be looked after or provided with accommodation by a responsible authority, a second review not more than three months after the first and subsequent reviews at not more than six months intervals.

The regulation of children's homes

13   Local authority community homes were not required to be registered during the period under review. They were, however, regulated by the Community Homes Regulations 1972, with effect from 1 April 1972, until those regulations were superseded by the Children's Homes Regulations 1991, made under the Children Act 1989. The latter regulations did not come into force until 14 October 1991.

14   Voluntary children's homes have been required to be registered since the Children Act 1948[10]. Sections 15 and 31 of that Act authorised the Secretary of State to make regulations for the conduct of both local authority and voluntary

---

[9] Made under section 26 of the Children Act 1989.
[10] Section 29.

homes; and, until 1 April 1972, both categories of home were governed by the Administration of Homes Regulations 1951. From April 1972, however, the regulatory provisions diverged: the 1951 regulations continued to apply to voluntary homes until they too were superseded by the Children's Homes Regulations 1991[11].

15   Private children's homes were not required to be registered until they were brought into a common framework with voluntary homes when section 63 of the Children Act 1989 came into force on 14 October 1991; and there were no regulations prior to the 1991 regulations governing the conduct of private children's homes. Provision for the registration of private children's homes had been made in the Children's Homes Act 1982 but the relevant provisions were never brought into force. Thus, there were quite glaring gaps and inconsistencies in the regulatory framework for residential establishments for children.

16   The Community Homes Regulations 1972, which applied to controlled community homes and assisted community homes as well as local authority homes, required the local authority (or the defined body responsible for other community homes) to arrange for the community home under their charge "to be conducted so as to make proper provision for the care, treatment and control of the children who are accommodated therein"[12]. There were requirements also for monthly visits and reports on local authority homes by such persons as the local authority considered appropriate (and by a manager in the case of other community homes); for the provision of suitable facilities for visits by parents, guardians, relatives and friends of the children accommodated in the homes; and for the person in charge of the home to provide information and access to records to persons entitled to inspect it under section 58 of the Act of 1969. Other matters dealt with in the regulations were control and secure accommodation, which are referred to in paragraphs 22 to 26 of this Appendix.

17   The Administration of Homes Regulations 1951, which governed voluntary homes until October 1991, required the administering authority to make arrangements for every home provided or carried on by them to be conducted "in such a manner and on such principles as are calculated to secure the well-being of the children in the home"[13]. Again, there were provisions for monthly visits and reporting by a person (on behalf of the administering authority) who had to satisfy himself whether the home was being conducted in the interests of the well-being of the children and in relation to facilities for visiting by parents and guardians, as well as detailed provisions about other matters, (which need not be quoted here) such as the keeping of records, religious instruction, health and fire precautions. The Children Act 1948 also laid a duty

---

[11] An exception to this was that Regulation 11 of the 1951 regulations governing punishment was replaced by the Children's Homes (Control and Discipline) Regulations 1990 with effect from 19 February 1990.

[12] Regulation 3(1).

[13] Regulation 1.

upon local authorities to arrange visits from time to time to children in voluntary homes in their area in the interests of the well-being of the children, whether or not the children there were in their care.

18 Section 63 of the Children Act 1989, as amended in 1991 and 1993, now provides that no child shall be cared for and provided with accommodation in a children's home unless the home is registered under Part VIII of the Act with the local authority for its area. For this purpose "children's home" is defined as follows:

> "(a) means a home which provides (or usually provides or is intended to provide) care and accommodation wholly or mainly for more than three children at any one time; but
>
> (b) does not include a home which is exempted by or under any of the following provisions of this section or by regulations made for the purposes of this subsection by the Secretary of State."

19 Establishments falling outside this definition include community homes, voluntary homes, health service hospitals and schools. However, an independent school is a children's home at any time if at that time accommodation is provided for more than three of the children at that school, or under arrangements made by the proprietor of the school, for more than 295 days in that year or it is intended to do so, unless the school is approved by the Secretary of State[14]. Voluntary children's homes have to be registered by the Secretary of State under section 60 of the Act of 1989.

20 The Children Act 1989 and the 1991 regulations contain additional provisions governing the welfare of children in private children's homes, annual reviews of the registration and the duties of local authorities in respect of the homes.

Control and punishment

21 Corporal punishment was not banned in community homes and voluntary children's homes until 19 February 1990 when the Children's Homes (Control and Discipline) Regulations 1990 came in to force[15]. The ban was extended to registered private children's homes by Regulation 9 of the Children's Homes Regulations 1991.

22 Until 1 April 1972 punishment in both community homes and voluntary homes was governed by Regulation 11 of the Administration of Children's Homes Regulations 1951, which continued to apply thereafter to voluntary homes only until 19 February 1990. Regulation 11 dealt with the subject in some detail as follows:

> "(1) No corporal punishment except that authorised by paragraph (3) of this regulation shall be administered by any person except the person in charge of the home or in his illness or absence his duly authorised deputy.

---

[14] Under (now) section 347 of the Education Act 1996 (originally section 11 of the Education Act 1981) as a school catering for "statemented" pupils with special educational needs.

[15] It was banned in state schools from 1987 by section 47 of the Education (No 2) Act 1986.

(2) No corporal punishment shall be administered to a girl who has attained the age of ten years or to a boy who has attained the age at which he is no longer required by law to attend school (hereafter referred to as 'school leaving age').

(3) No corporal punishment shall be administered to a child under ten years of age except by smacking his hands with the bare hand of the person administering the punishment.

(4) No corporal punishment shall be administered to a boy who has attained the age of ten years but has not attained school leaving age except the caning of the posterior of the boy with a cane of a type approved by the Secretary of State applied over the boy's clothing to the extent of six strokes or less.

(5) No caning shall be administered in the presence of another child.

(6) No corporal punishment shall be administered, without the sanction of the medical officer of the home, to any child known to have any physical or mental disability."

23 From 1 April 1972 the relevant regulation governing community homes (until 19 February 1990) was Regulation 10 of the Community Homes Regulations 1972, which did not make any express reference to corporal punishment. Sub-paragraph (1) required the control of a community home to be maintained on the basis of "good personal and professional relationships between the staff and the children resident therein". Sub-paragraph (2) permitted undefined "additional measures" for the maintenance of control to be taken but such measures and the conditions under which they were to be taken had to be approved in respect of each home by the local authority or other responsible body. The approval had to be reviewed every 12 months and a permanent record of any use of the measures, including the circumstances in which they were used, had to be kept by the Officer-in-Charge.

24 Regulation 2(2) of the Children's Homes (Control and Discipline) Regulations 1990 prohibited a number of specified sanctions as well as any form of corporal punishment. These were deprivation of food and drink; any restriction or refusal of any facility to receive visits or communications from specified persons, including a solicitor; any restriction or refusal of any facility to make visits to parents or guardian or relatives; requiring a child to wear distinctive or inappropriate clothes; and the use, or withholding, of medication or medical or dental treatment. The list of prohibitions was re-enacted in Regulation 8 of the 1991 Regulations and extended by the addition of intentional deprivation of sleep, the imposition of fines (except by way of reparation) and any intimate physical examination of the child. These prohibitions apply to registered children's homes as well as community homes and voluntary homes.

Secure accommodation

25 By section 24(2) of the Act of 1969 a local authority was given the power to restrict a child's liberty to such extent as it thought appropriate. However, by

section 43(2)(c) of the same Act, the Secretary of State was given power to make regulations regarding the conduct of community homes, including power to require his approval for the use of secure accommodation and to impose requirements as to the placement of children.

26 The Secretary of State exercised these powers in Regulations 11 to 14 of the Community Homes Regulations 1972. Secure accommodation had to be expressly approved by the Secretary of State, who could and did impose conditions, and strict time limits were imposed: the maximum continuous period, in general, to be authorised by the local authority was 28 days and the maximum period with the authority of the Officer-in-Charge was one continuous period of 24 hours or a total of 48 hours in a consecutive period of seven days. An extension could be granted by the responsible body (local authority or voluntary organisation), subject to review every three months.

27 A new scheme was implemented from 1 January 1984 by the insertion of section 21A into the Child Care Act 1980[16]. Thereafter no child in the care of a local authority could be placed or kept in accommodation provided for the purpose of restricting liberty unless one or more of the following criteria was met:

(a) he had a history of absconding and was likely to abscond from any other description of accommodation; and

(b) if he absconded, it was likely that his physical, mental or moral welfare would be at risk; or

(c) if he was kept in any other description of accommodation he was likely to injure himself or other persons.

28 The new scheme, to which there were limited exceptions, was a marked improvement because it imposed a requirement that a local authority had to apply to the court for any extension beyond an initial specified period. New Secure Accommodation Regulations in 1983 and 1986 replaced the relevant provisions of Community Homes Regulations 1972 and the discretion of the officer in charge to detain a child in specified circumstances was increased to a consecutive period of 72 hours (or 72 hours in aggregate in a consecutive period of 28 days). Separate guidance[17] indicated that single secure rooms in community homes would no longer be approved. It stated also, however, that "control imposed or applied by staff or other responsible adults will not be considered to constitute the restriction of liberty, though control should always be applied in a manner consistent with good child care practice".

Powers of inspection

29 Before leaving this account of the legislation affecting community homes it is appropriate to emphasise that throughout the period under review comprehensive powers to inspect all forms of premises in which children in care

---

[16] Section 25(1) of the Criminal Justice Act 1982 and Sch 2 para 50 of the Health and Social Services and Social Security Adjudications Act 1983.

[17] At para 4 of Annex B to Welsh Office Circular 63/83.

were accommodated were vested in the Secretary of State. These powers of inspection[18] extended to private children's homes and to premises where children had been boarded out by a voluntary organisation and where foster children and protected children were being accommodated and maintained. The person authorised by the Secretary of State to conduct the inspection could be an officer of a local authority but only with the consent of that authority.

Independent visitors

30   An additional statutory safeguard was a local authority's duty to appoint an independent visitor for any child over the age of five years accommodated by the local authority in a community home or other establishment who had not been allowed to leave in the preceding three months to attend school or work and where it appeared to the authority that communication between him and his parents or guardian had been so infrequent that it was appropriate to appoint a visitor for him. Moreover, if the child had not been visited by either parent or a guardian in the previous 12 months, the local authority had to appoint a person independent of the authority and unconnected with the community home to be the child's visitor. The role of the independent visitor was to befriend the child and to advise him and he had the power to apply for the child's discharge from care[19]. The duty applies now in respect of a child looked after by a local authority whether or not he is in compulsory care and where family contact in the previous 12 months has merely been infrequent, provided that the child agrees to the appointment.

The boarding out of children in care

31   The boarding out of children in care with foster parents was governed throughout the period under review by successive Boarding Out Regulations. The 1955 Regulations remained in force largely unchanged until they were superseded by the 1988 Regulations in June 1989. Thus, it was the 1955 Regulations and the accompanying Home Office memorandum[20] that governed practice in this field during almost the whole of the period in which the abuse that we have investigated occurred. We set out below only the main provisions of those regulations that related to long term placements by a local authority. The 1988 Regulations were a re-statement and refinement of the earlier version but they were soon replaced in October 1991 by new regulations made under the Children Act 1989.

32   The 1955 regulations provided quite a comprehensive framework of regulation for boarding out, including provision for the vetting of prospective foster parents. Regulation 17 required a written assessment to be made, prior to

---

[18] Under section 58 of the Children and Young Persons Act 1969 and subsequently section 74 of the Child Care Act 1980.

[19] The intention of the provisions in section 24(5) of the Act of 1969 and section 11 of the Act of 1980 has been carried forward and extended by the Children Act 1989.

[20] HMSO 1955.

placement, of the suitability of both the home and the foster parents and their ability to meet the needs of a particular child. The supervisory regime included the following responsibilities:

— to ensure that a visitor should see the child and visit the foster homes at specified minimum intervals and forthwith after the receipt of a complaint by or concerning the child unless it appeared that action upon it was unnecessary;

— to consider the welfare, health, conduct and progress of the child and any complaint concerning the child whenever the visitor saw the child and to make a written report;

— to compile and keep case records;

— to keep registers of all children boarded out in the area;

— in the light of the visitors' reports to review the welfare, health, conduct and progress of every child within three months of placement and thereafter no less often than once every six months[21];

— to ensure that children were medically examined before and throughout placement.

33   It was the duty of the placing local authority to terminate boarding out if it appeared that the boarding out was no longer in the child's best interests. Moreover, the regulations conferred a power for the supervising visitor to remove a child from the foster home forthwith if the visitor considered that the conditions in which the child was boarded out endangered the latter's health, safety or morals. An undertaking in a form specified in the schedule to the regulations was required to be signed by foster parents: the undertaking covered such matters as permitting visits, access to the child and permitting removal of the child from the foster home when requested by the local authority.

34   The Foster Placement (Children) Regulations 1991 came into force from 14 October 1991. The main changes under these regulations are that:

— approval is of the foster parents rather than the household in which the child is to live;

— foster parents may be approved by only one local authority or voluntary organisation at any one time;

— an emergency placement may be made with any approved foster parent for up to 24 hours;

— an immediate placement may be made with a relative or friend for up to six weeks;

---

[21] cf para 10 of this Appendix.

— local authority responsibilities towards children placed by voluntary organisations are increased;

— foster parents now have to undertake in writing not to administer corporal punishment to any child placed with them.

35   These regulations came into force contemporaneously with a number of other regulations made under the Children Act 1989, notably:

        Arrangements for Placement of Children (General) Regulations 1991;

        Placement of Children with Parents etc Regulations 1991;

        Disqualification for Caring for Children Regulations 1991.

Registration and inspection of independent schools

36   The legislative framework governing the registration and inspection of independent schools remained substantially unchanged throughout the period of our review. An independent school was defined by the Education Act 1944 (and now by the Education Act 1996) as an establishment where full time education is provided for five or more pupils of compulsory school age and which is neither maintained by a local education authority nor a non-maintained special school nor a grant maintained school. Independent schools account for three per cent of all schools in Wales and they must be registered by the Secretary of State for Wales. The process of registration is governed by the Education (Particulars of Independent Schools) Regulations 1982, as amended in 1994, and it is an offence to conduct an independent school that has not been registered.

37   Once certain required information has been provided by the proprietor an applicant school is automatically granted provisional registration pending inspection by HMI. Full registration is only granted on the recommendation of HMI, after one or more inspections. The standards expected for final registration are set out in Welsh Office guidance to proprietors. HMI have to have regard to the suitability of the premises and accommodation, staffing, the curriculum, standards of teaching and welfare arrangements. According to the evidence submitted by the Welsh Office, many independent schools remain provisionally registered for several years.

38   Some independent schools are specifically approved to take pupils with statements of special educational needs (SEN). Approval as an independent special school can only be granted after or with approval as an independent school. Independent special schools came into existence under the provisions of the Education Act 1981 following the report of the Warnock Committee three years earlier. In place of earlier categories of disability the Act referred to children with learning disabilities and those with special educational needs. Local education authorities were required to assess children and prepare a statement of their special needs where these could not be met by local mainstream schools.

39   The Education Act 1981 introduced approval and consent procedures for independent special schools and the placement of children in them, which were subsequently embodied in specific regulations in 1991[22]. Section 11(3) of that Act provided that:

> "(3) Where a local education authority maintain a statement for a child under section 7 they shall not make arrangements for the provision of education for that child at an independent school unless—
>
> > (a) the school is for the time being approved by the Secretary of State as suitable for the admission of children for whom statements are maintained under section 7; or
> >
> > (b) the Secretary of State consents to the child being there."

Thus, if an independent school was refused approval by the Secretary of State under section 11(a), the Secretary of State could still consent under section 11(b) to the placement of a specific child there by a local education authority. Moreover, a Social Services Department could place an SEN child at an unapproved independent school without the Secretary of State's consent if the placement was wholly funded by the Social Services Department. However, the Children Act 1989 introduced provisions to ensure the exchange of information between Education and Social Services Departments and central government guidance encourages close collaboration between them before the placement in a school of an SEN child who is looked after by the local authority[23]. In January 1996 110 children with SEN statements provided by Welsh local education authorities were placed in independent schools.

40   Until 1993 schools were inspected by HMIs who were part of the Welsh Office. In 1992 a separate government department, the Office of Her Majesty's Chief Inspector in Wales (OHMCI(Wales)) was established. Independent schools with SEN approval under section 11(3)(a) of the Act of 1981 are now inspected by OHMCI(Wales) registered inspectors under a five year cycle of inspections prescribed by the Chief Inspector for Wales under section 9(2) of the Education (Schools) Act 1992. In addition to these full inspections, independent special schools are subject to annual visits, except in years when a full inspection takes place. For other independent schools the Secretary of State requires an annual visit by registered inspectors to all those that are provisionally registered whereas fully registered schools are visited by HMIs once in every four or five years (at the rate of ten per year).

41   There are various provisions enabling the Secretary of State to remove an independent school from the register. It may be removed if the number of children on the roll falls below five and there is a clear intention by the proprietor to discontinue the school or if the proprietor, a teacher or other member of staff is on the Department of Education's List 99. Otherwise, the Secretary of State has had power since the Education Act 1944 to serve a Notice of Complaint specifying his full grounds of concern and the measures

---

[22] Now the Education (SEN)(Approval of Independent Schools) Regulations 1994.
[23] See sections 28 and 85 and Welsh Office Circular 56/94.

considered necessary to remedy them within a specified timescale of not less than six months. If the notice is not complied with, the school may be struck off the register, subject to a right of appeal to an Independent Schools Tribunal[24].

42   We have referred at paragraph 19 to the introduction of dual registration (ie as independent schools and children's homes) for independent schools in the Children Act 1989. This Act contains a number of measures designed to promote and safeguard the welfare of children at independent boarding schools, including powers for inspections and action by a Social Services Department and the Secretary of State if there is concern about the welfare of accommodated children. The Act also requires proprietors of independent boarding schools to safeguard and promote children's welfare and the Social Services Department for the area has to take reasonable practicable steps to determine whether the proprietor is complying with this duty. This gives power to Social Services Departments to inspect the welfare provision at all independent schools providing accommodation for children within the definition cited in paragraphs 18 and 19 above. Copies of the reports on such inspections are sent to the Welsh Office Education Department and Social Services Departments have to notify the Secretary of State formally if they are of the opinion that a child's welfare is not being safeguarded.

Statutes and statutory instruments

43   A list of statutes and statutory instruments relevant to the period and matters under review in this report is at Appendix 7.

---

[24] The relevant provisions are now contained in the Education Act 1996, having been earlier amended in the Children Act 1989.

Statutes and Statutory Instruments cited in the report

Tribunals of Inquiry (Evidence) Act	1921	Chapter 7
The Approved School Rules	1933	No 744
Children and Young Persons Act	1933	Chapter 12
Education Act	1944	Chapter 31
National Assistance Act	1948	Chapter 29
Children Act	1948	Chapter 43
The Approved School Rules	1949	1949 No 2052
The Administration of Children's Homes Regulations	1951	SI 1951 No 1217
Defamation Act	1952	Chapter 66
The Boarding-Out of Children Regulations	1955	SI 1955 No 1377
Matrimonial Proceedings (Magistrates' Courts) Act	1960	Chapter 48
Children and Young Persons Act	1963	Chapter 37
Children and Young Persons Act	1969	Chapter 54
Local Authority Social Services Act	1970	Chapter 42
Local Government Act	1972	Chapter 70
Community Homes Regulations	1972	SI 1972 No 319
Local Employment Act	1972	Chapter 5
Matrimonial Causes Act	1973	Chapter 18
Children Act	1975	Chapter 72
Adoption Act	1976	Chapter 36

Certificates of Unruly Character (Conditions) Order	1977	SI 1977 No 1037
Domestic Proceedings and Magistrates' Courts Act	1978	Chapter 22
Child Care Act	1980	Chapter 5
Education Act	1981	Chapter 60
Children's Homes Act	1982	Chapter 20
Criminal Justice Act	1982	Chapter 48
The Education (Particulars of Independent Schools) Regulations	1982	SI 1982 No 1730
Health and Social Services and Social Security Adjudications Act	1983	Chapter 41
The Secure Accommodation Regulations	1983	SI 1983 No 652
Secure Accommodation (No 2) Regulations	1983	SI 1983 No 1808
The Education (Special Educational Needs) Regulations	1983	SI 1983 No 29
The Adoption Agencies Regulations	1983	SI 1983 No 1964
Police and Criminal Evidence Act	1984	Chapter 60
Registered Homes Act	1984	Chapter 23
The Adoption Rules	1984	SI 1984 No 265
Education (No 2) Act	1986	Chapter 61
Secure Accommodation (No 2) (Amendment) Regulations	1986	SI 1986 No 1591
Residential Care Homes (Amendment) Regulations	1988	SI 1988 No 1192
The Boarding-Out of Children (Foster Placement) Regulations	1988	SI 1988 No 2184
Children Act	1989	Chapter 41

National Health Service and Community Care Act	1990	Chapter 19
The Children's Homes (Control and Discipline) Regulations	1990	SI 1990 No 87
Arrangements for Placement of Children (General) Regulations	1991	SI 1991 No 890
Definition of Independent Visitors (Children) Regulations	1991	SI 1991 No 892
Placement of Children with Parents etc Regulations	1991	SI 1991 No 893
Representations Procedure (Children) Regulations	1991	SI 1991 No 894
Review of Children's Cases Regulations	1991	SI 1991 No 895
Foster Placement (Children) Regulations	1991	SI 1991 No 910
Children's Homes Regulations	1991	SI 1991 No 1506
Disqualification for Caring for Children Regulations	1991	SI 1991 No 2094
Sexual Offences (Amendment) Act	1992	Chapter 34
Education (Schools) Act	1992	Chapter 38
Education Act	1993	Chapter 35
Criminal Justice and Public Order Act	1994	Chapter 33
Deregulation and Contracting Out Act	1994	Chapter 40
Local Government (Wales) Act	1994	Chapter 19
The Education (Special Educational Needs) (Approval of Independent Schools) Regulations	1994	SI 1994 No 651
Education Act	1996	Chapter 56
School Inspections Act	1996	Chapter 57
Sex Offenders Act	1997	Chapter 51
The Children (Protection from Offenders) (Miscellaneous Amendments) Regulations	1997	SI 1997 No 2308
Protection of Children Act	1999	Chapter 14

List of main relevant publications

1	Curtis, Myra CBE: Report of the Care of Children Committee	September 1946, Cmnd 6922, HMSO, London
2	The Child, The Family and The Young Offender	August 1965, Home Office, HMSO, London
3	Royal Commission on Tribunals of Inquiry Report of the Commission under the Chairmanship of the, Rt Hon Lord Justice Salmon	November 1966, Cmnd 3121, HMSO, London
4	Williams, Professor Lady Gertrude CBE: Caring for People - Staffing Residential Homes: Report of a Committee of Enquiry set up by the National Council of Social Service	1967, George Allen and Unwin, London
5	Children in Trouble	April 1968, Home Office, Cmnd 3601, HMSO, London
6	Seebohm, Frederic: Report of The Committee on Local Authority and Allied Personal Social Services	July 1968, Cmnd 3703, HMSO, London
7	Home Office Advisory Council on Child Care: Care and treatment in a planned environment. A Report on the Community Homes Project	1970, HMSO, London
8	Clark, R V G and Martin, D N: Absconding from Approved Schools	Home Office Research Unit Report, HMSO, London
9	Advisory Council on Child Care, Department of Health and Social Security: Community Homes Design Guide	1971, HMSO, London
10	Intermediate Treatment: A guide for the Regional Planning of new forms of treatment for children in trouble	January 1972, HMSO, London

11	Residential Task in Child Care: The Castle Priory Report	November 1972, Belmont Press, Northampton
12	The Act on Trial: The non-implementation of the Children and Young Persons' Act 1969	May 1975, MIND Report 14, London
13	Kennedy, P J M, QC: Report of the Committee of Inquiry into the Provision and Co-ordination of Services to the Family of John George Auckland	September 1975, Department of Health and Social Security, HMSO, London
14	Children and Young Persons Act 1969 - Observations on the Eleventh Report from the Expenditure Committee	May 1976, Home Office, Welsh Office, Department of Health and Social Security, Department of Education and Science, Cmnd 6494, HMSO, London.
15	Marre, Sir Alan: Ad Hoc Inquiries in Local Government. A Solace/RIPA Project	1978, Society of Local Authority Chief Executives, Paxman Press Ltd
16	Department of the Environment: Central Government Controls over Local Authorities	September 1979, Cmnd 7634, HMSO, London
17	Ad Hoc Inquiries in Local Government	August 1980, Local Authorities Associations
18	Utting, W B: Control and Discipline in Community Homes. Report of a Working Party	January 1981, Department of Health and Social Security, HMSO, London
19	Legal and professional aspects of the use of secure accommodation for children in care. Report of a DHSS Internal Working Party	February 1981

20	Barclay, Peter M: Social Workers - Their Role & Tasks	May 1982, National Institute for Social Work, Bedford Square Press
21	Philpott, Terry (ed): A New Direction For Social Work? The Barclay report and its implications	1982, IPC Business Press
22	Child Abuse: A Study of Inquiry Reports 1973 - 1981	1982, Department of Health and Social Security, HMSO, London
23	Kina, Lady Avebury: Home life: Code of Practice for Residential Care	1984, Centre for Policy on Ageing, Henry Ling Ltd, The Dorset Press
24	House of Commons Second Report from the Social Services Committee, Session 1983 - 1984. Children in Care Volume 1. Report together with the Proceedings of the Committee	28 March 1984, HMSO, London
25	Social Services Inspectorate of the Department of Health and Social Security: Inspection of Community Homes	September 1985, Department of Health and Social Security
26	Social Work Decisions In Child Care: Recent Research Findings and their Implications	1985, Department of Health and Social Security, HMSO, London
27	Blom-Cooper, Louis QC (Chair): A Child in Trust: the Report of the Panel of Inquiry into the circumstances surrounding the death of Jasmine Beckford	1985, London Borough of Brent
28	Report of the Committee of Inquiry into Children's Homes and Hostels	1986, HMSO, Belfast
29	The Law on Child Care and Family Services	January 1987, Cm 62, HMSO, London
30	Butler-Sloss, Right Honourable Lord Justice, DBE: Report of the Inquiry into Child Abuse in Cleveland 1987	Cmnd 412, HMSO, London

31	The Law Commission: Family Law Review of Child Law Guardianship and Custody	25 July 1988, Law Com No 172, HMSO, London
32	Wagner, Gillian, OBE, PhD: Residential Care - A Positive Choice. Report of the Independent Review of Residential Care	1988, National Institute for Social Work, HMSO, London
33	Working Together. A guide to arrangements for inter-agency co-operation for the protection of children from abuse	1988, Department of Health and the Welsh Office, HMSO, London
34	The Boarding-Out of Children (Foster Placement) Regulations 1988. Handbook of Guidance	1989, Department of Health, Welsh Office
35	Seebohm, Frederic: Seebohm Twenty Years on: Three Stages in the Development of the Personal Social Services	1989, Policy Studies Institute
36	Robbins, Diana: Child Care Policy: Putting it in Writing - A Review of English Local Authorities' Child Care Policy Statements	1990, Department of Health Social Services Inspectorate, HMSO, London
37	Protecting Children: A Guide for Social Workers undertaking a Comprehensive Assessment	1990, Department of Health, HMSO, London
38	Child Abuse: A Study of Inquiry Reports 1980 - 1989	1991, Department of Health, HMSO, London
39	Accommodating Children - A Review of Children's Homes in Wales. Volumes 1 and 2	November 1991, Welsh Office
40	Westcott, Helen L: Institutional Abuse of Children. From Research to Policy: A review	December 1991, NSPCC
41	Utting, Sir William: Children in the Public Care. A Review of Residential Child Care	1991, HMSO, London
42	Looking after Children: Assessing Outcomes in Child Care. The Report of an Independent Working Party established by the Department of Health	1991, HMSO

43	Pattern and Outcomes in Child Placement: Messages from current research and their implications	1991, Department of Health, HMSO, London
44	Levy, Allan, QC, and Kahan, Barbara: The Pindown Experience and the Protection of Children: The Report of the Staffordshire Child Care Inquiry 1990	1991, Staffordshire County Council
45	Working Together Under the Children Act 1989 - A guide to arrangements for inter-agency co-operation for the protection of children from abuse	1991, Home Office, Department of Health, Department of Education and Science, Welsh Office, HMSO, London
46	The Report of the Inquiry into the Removal of Children from Orkney in February 1991	27 October 1992, HMSO, Edinburgh
47	Smith, Janet, QC: Report of the Scotforth House Inquiry	November 1992, Lancashire County Council
48	Inspection of Outcomes for Children Leaving Care. Report of an Inspection	November and December 1992. Welsh Office - Social Services Inspectorate
49	Another Kind of Home - a review of residential child care	1992, Scottish Office, The Social Work Services Inspectorate for Scotland, HMSO, Edinburgh
50	Warner, Norman: Choosing with Care: The Report of the Committee of Inquiry into the Selection, Development and Management of Staff in Children's Homes	1992, Department of Health, HMSO, London

51   Lady Howe: The Quality of Care. Report of the   1992,
      Residential Staffs Inquiry   The Local
                                                            Government
                                                            Management Board
                                                            on behalf of The
                                                            National Joint
                                                            Council for Local
                                                            Authorities'
                                                            Administrative,
                                                            Professional,
                                                            Technical & Clerical
                                                            Services

52   Finlayson, Alan F, OBE, MA, LLB: Reporters to   1992,
      Children's Panels. Their Role, Function and   The Scottish Office,
      Accountability   Social Work Services
                                                            Group

53   Williams, Gareth, QC and McCreadie, John. M.Ed: 1992,
      Tŷ Mawr Community Home Inquiry   Gwent County
                                                            Council

54   Kirkwood, Andrew, QC: The Leicestershire Inquiry   February 1993,
      1992: The Report of an Inquiry into aspects of the   Leicestershire County
      Management of Children's Homes in Leicestershire   Council
      between 1973 and 1986

55   Corporate Parents: Inspection of Residential Child   Department of Health.
      Care Services in 11 Local Authorities November   Social Services
      1992 to March 1993   Inspectorate

56   Smith, David R: Safe from Harm. Voluntary   1993,
      Organisations - A Code of Practice for   Home Office,
      Safeguarding the Welfare of Children in Voluntary   Department of Health,
      Organisations in England and Wales   Department of
                                                            Education,
                                                            Welsh Office

57   All Wales Review: Local Authority Fostering   March 1994,
      Services in Wales   Welsh Office - Social
                                                            Services Inspectorate

58   Support Force for Children's Residential Care: October 1994,
      A Strategic Planning Framework - Part I -   Department of Health
      Analysing Need

59	Mead, Deryk: Protecting Children in Public and Private Institutions	2 December 1994, Gloucestershire Social Services Department
60	Welsh Office Social Services Inspectorate - Inspection Guide	1994, Welsh Office Social Services Inspectorate
61	Support Force for Children's Residential Care: Out of Authority Placements: Checklist of Information to be Obtained	January 1995, Department of Health
62	Quality Care in Children's Homes in Wales. A report of an inspection focusing on the role of local authorityinspection units and key findings of their inspection reports	March 1995, Welsh Office Social Services Inspectorate
63	Support Force for Children's Residential Care: Staff Supervision in Children's Homes	April 1995, Department of Health
64	Support Force for Children's Residential Care: A Strategic Planning Framework - Part II - Implementing Change	April 1995, Department of Health
65	Support Force for Children's Residential Care: Code of Practice for the employment of residential child care workers	June 1995, Department of Health
66	Support Force for Children's Residential Care: Specialising in Residential Child Care - A Discussion Paper by Keith Bilton	September 1995, Department of Health
67	Support Force for Children's Residential Care: Contracting for Children's Residential Care Parts 1 and 2	October 1995, Department on Health
68	Support Force for Children's Residential Care: Unit Costing and Financial Management in Children's Residential Care Parts 1 and 2	October 1995, Department of Health
69	Support Force for Children's Residential Care: Residential Care for Children and Young People - A Positive Choice? Final Report to Secretary of State for Health	October 1995, Department of Health
70	Support Force for Children's Residential Care: Good Care Matters - Ways of Enhancing Good Practice in Residential Child Care	November 1995, Department of Health

71	Support Force for Children's Residential Care: The Use and Development of Databases of Residential Child Care Resources	November 1995, Department of Health
72	The Challenge of Partnership in Child Protection: Practice Guide	1995, Department of Health, HMSO, London
73	Jones, Adrianne, CBE: Report of the Examination Team on Child Care Procedures and Practice in North Wales	17 June 1996, HMSO, London
74	Burgner, Tom: The Regulation and Inspection of Social Services	July 1996, Department of Health and Welsh Office
75	Accreditation for social workers in child care. Report on a consultation exercise of Social Services Departments in England and Wales	October 1996, The Association of Directors of Social Services
76	The Obligations of Care. A Consultation Paper on the setting of Conduct and Practice Standards for Social Services staff	October 1996, The UK Health Departments
77	The Annual Report of the Council on Tribunals for 1995/96	17 December 1996, The Stationery Office, London
78	The Foster Carer Market - A National Perspective	Association of Directors of Social Services, Children and Families Committee Report
79	Lord Williams of Mostyn (Chairman): Childhood Matters. Report of the National Commission of Inquiry into the Prevention of Child Abuse	1996, NSPCC The Stationery Office, London
80	Child Protection: Messages from Research	Department of Health, HMSO, London
81	Hodgkin Rachel, and Newell, Peter: Effective government structures for children. Report of a Gulbenkian Foundation Inquiry	1996, Calouste Gulbenkian Foundation, London

82   "In Care Contacts" - The West Case. The Report of a Review of Over 2,000 files of Young People in Residential Care
    1996,
The Bridge Child Care Development Service and Gloucestershire Social Services

83   Inspection of Local Authority Fostering 1995 - 96 National Summary Report
    Social Services Inspectorate, Department of Health

84   Listening to Children - The Issues
    1996,
The Bridge Child Care Development Service

85   Neglect - A Fifty year Search for Answers
    1996,
The Bridge Child Care Development Service and Islington Area Child Protection Committee

86   Dartington Social Research Unit in conjunction with the Support Force for Children's Residential Care: Matching Needs and Services. The Audit and Planning of Provisions for Children looked after by Local Authorities
    Dartington Social Research Unit

87   Support Force for Children's Residential Care: Towards Better Selection of Children's Residential Staff - Key Messages from two case studies
    1996,
The Local Government Management Board

88   Support Force for Children's Residential Care: Towards Better Selection of Children's Residential Staff - A practical guide to monitoring and validating your selection processes
    1996,
The Local Government Management Board

89   Private Fostering - Development of policy and practice in three English local authorities. A report of a study undertaken by the African Family Advisory Service
    January 1997,
Save the Children

90   Interface or Interference. The first line management of residential care for children and young people. Report of a Departmental Workshop run jointly by the Support Force for Children's Residential Care, The Social Services Inspectorate and The National Children's Bureau, Children Residential Care Unit held on 24 - 25 April 1995
    February 1997,
Department of Health

913

91	"......When leaving home is also leaving care......" An Inspection of Services for Young People Leaving Care	February 1997, Social Services Inspectorate, Department of Health
92	Social Services. Achievement and Challenge	March 1997, Cm 3588, Department of Health and Welsh Office, The Stationery Office, London
93	Waterhouse, Suzette: The Organisation of Foster Services: A study of the arrangements for delivery of fostering services by local authorities in England	March 1997, National Foster Care Association
94	The BEST for Special Education. A Welsh Office Green Paper on Special Educational Needs	October 1997, Welsh Office, The Stationery Office
95	Review of the Functions of the Central Council for Education and Training in Social Work. A Report to UK Sponsoring Ministers	December 1997. Department of Health, Welsh Office, Scottish Office, DHSS Northern Ireland
96	Kent, Roger: Children's Safeguards Review	1997, The Scottish Office, Social Work Services Inspectorate for Scotland, The Stationery Office
97	The Howard League Troubleshooter Project. Lessons for Policy and Practice on 15 Year Olds in Prison. A Report by the Howard League	1997
98	Berridge, David: Foster Care - A Research Review	1997, The Stationery Office, London
99	Foster Care in Crisis - A call to professionalise the forgotten service	1997, National Foster Care Association

914

100   Utting, Sir William: People Like Us. The Report Of   1997,
The Review Of The Safeguards For Children Living   The Department of
Away From Home   Health, The Welsh
Office, HMSO,
Norwich

101   Missing from care: procedures and practices in   1997,
caring for missing children   Local Government
Association

102   Working Together to Safeguard Children: New   February 1998,
Government proposals for inter-agency co-   Children's Services
operation. Consultation Paper   Branch Department of
Health

103   Inspection of Child Care Procedures and Practice in   August 1998,
North Wales (Implementation of Examination   Social Services
Team Recommendations)   Inspectorate for Wales

Welsh Office and other departmental Circulars cited in the report

Memorandum on the Boarding-Out of Children Regulations 1955	September 1955, Home Office
Ministry of Education - The Use of Independent Schools for Handicapped Pupils	27 March 1961, Circular 4/61
Appointment of Persons to Employment involving the Care of Children	27 October 1964, Home Office Circular 250/1964
Appointment of Persons to Employment involving the Care of Children	27 October 1964, Home Office Circular 251/1964
Appointment of persons to employment connected with the residential care of children	27 October 1964, Home Office Circular 252/1964
Ministerial Responsibility for the Personal Social Services— Secretary of State for Wales	3 February 1971, WOC 17/71
The Social Work Service in Wales including Monmouthshire	19 May 1971, WOC 75/71
Children and Young Persons Act 1969 The Community Homes Regulations 1972	10 March 1972, WOC 64/72
Local Authority Social Services Ten Year Development Plans 1973-1983	31 August 1972, WOC 195/72
Children and Young Persons Act 1969 The Community Homes Regulations 1972 Secure Accommodation	15 March 1973, WOC 69/73
Children and Young Persons Act 1969— Arrangements for Education in Community Homes	31 August 1973, WOC 194/73
Children and Young Persons Act 1969 The Community Homes Regulations 1972 Secure Accommodation	13 March 1974, WOC 55/74
Secure Accommodation in Community Homes	28 February 1975, WOC 39/75

Local Authority Expenditure in 1976/77 - Forward Planning   3 September 1975,
WOC 142/75

Rate Support Grant Settlement 1976/77   31 December 1975,
WOC 228/75

Forward Planning of Local Authority Personal Social Services   16 December 1977,
WOC 99/77

Criminal Justice Act 1982 Section 25—Restriction of Liberty   12 May 1983,
The Secure Accommodation Regulations 1983   WOC 30/83

Health and Social Services and Social Security Adjudications   19 December 1983,
Act 1983, Schedule 2 Paragraph 50—Restriction of Liberty   WOC 63/83
The Secure Accommodation (No 2) Regulations 1983

Health and Social Services and Social Security   10 January 1984,
Act 1983: Access to Children in Care   WOC 5/84

Registration of Residential Homes and   4 September 1984,
Homes Tribunals   WOC 40/84

Protection of Children: Disclosure of Criminal Background of   17 July 1986,
with Access to Children   WOC 86/28

Forward Planning of Local Authority Personal Social Services   11 March 1987,
WOC 13/87

Working Together for the Protection of Children From Abuse   6 July 1988,
WOC 26/88

Registration of Residential Homes   27 July 1988,
WOC 31/88

Protection of Children: Disclosure of Criminal Background of   9 December 1988,
with Access to Children   WOC 45/88

Conduct of Community and Voluntary Children's Homes—   9 February 1990,
Homes (Control and Discipline)   WOC 5/90
Regulations 1990

Child Protection   29 June 1990,
WOC 37/90

Disclosure of Criminal Background: Proprietors and   March 1991,
Managers of Residential Care Homes and Nursing Homes   WOC 12/91

"Accommodating Children"—A Review of Children's Homes Wales	16 April 1993, WOC 34/93
Guidance on Permissible Forms of Control in Residential Care	29 April 1993, WOC 38/93
Plans for Children's Services: Second Phase of Report Implementation	20 July 1994, WOC 11/94
Citizen's Charter: Inspecting Social Services in Wales	12 September 1994, WOC 68/94
The Education of Children with Emotional and Difficulties	December 1994, WOC 56/94
Implementation of the Adrianne Jones Report: from the Secretary of State's Development Fund	4 April 1997, WOC 25/97

Anatomy of a weekend

The weekend really started on Thursday evening when Mr Norris discovered that a bed had been set on fire in one of the Clwyd dormitories. Mr Matthews reported this to me at home at about 11.30 on Thursday evening. The matter was left to Friday with Mr Wood staying on a waking watch in Clwyd. Friday morning Mr Stritch took over and referred the matter to Fire Service and Police. Mr Norris continued his investigations both within Clwyd and at the Police Station. Late on Friday afternoon Mr Norris established beyond doubt that resident A had deliberately started the fire in resident B's bed as an act of revenge for a fight he had had earlier with B and out of which he had come badly. I agreed with Mr Norris's premise that we were faced with two choices (a) to seek the instant removal of resident A either to a place beyond Bryn Estyn or to transfer him to Main School, (b) to work this out with the Clwyd boys and establish with them a rapport and climate into which resident A could fit aided by them, seeming (sic) their forbearance and co-operation in enabling resident A to come to terms with the group and his traumatic removal from Fifeshire and home. I supported Mr Norris in this more risky yet purposeful endeavour although Mr Norris would be away for the weekend and promised to support the Clwyd staff throughout Friday night and the weekend. Friday night was again a disturbed night for A and Mr Wood, since one of A's cries of distress is to suffer asthma attacks or feel very ill in the early hours of the morning. A does suffer from asthma - but to our untutored eyes not as dramatically as he would portray. Saturday found that A was still at an ill peace with his group and I again discussed with Mrs Bew whether I should remove him. With support he managed to survive Saturday and slept slightly better. The whole situation is still risky since we have no certainty that A at a minute's notice will not disappear and recommence his arson. Thus against A's undoubted needs, there has to be placed as an equal factor the safety of the other fourteen boys in this group, not to mention the expensive building and its equipment. As of Sunday evening the situation is 'holding' and during meals I have observed that A seems a little less fraught and more at ease with the group. He is also avidly seeking their attention and staff attention, giving them his food and asking staff for favours.

Within the main school Friday evening was quiet, somewhat fraught by a noticeable banding together of residents C, D, E, F and G. The pressure became more tense when Miss Evans brought back D from the Youth Club, after a minor disagreement there when he refused to accept Miss Evans's authority. He sat with C discussing absconding but presumably the thunderstorm put them off. A party went with Mr Martin plus other staff to the Open Day at the Fire Station, marred only by the fact that residents H and I failed to return with the party. It was assumed incorrectly that they would be chasing around Wrexham after girls and accordingly I waited until six o'clock to notify the police. They had still not returned by late Sunday evening and presumably are farther afield than Wrexham.

Miss Evans phoned from the Rugby Club around six, that she had seen four boys on the Club's property and we found that C, D, F and G had left the School through the upstairs fire escape. Mr McLeod and Mr Martin went in the school bus, to seek these four, I drove down Cefn Road on the same errand. Later I met Mr McLeod with D in the school bus returning to the school. He told me that Mr Martin was still in pursuit of three boys. We both independently searched again down Cefn Road, but failed to see either boys or Mr Martin. We returned to the school, to see Mr Martin returning with C and F. D was with Mr Green in the office, in a belligerent mood, and after Mr Martin reported that C, actively encouraged by G, had threatened him with a knife (albeit a table knife), I decided to remove all boys and Mr Green with me to the Secure Unit. The main purpose of this was less to use the security afforded in locked cells, than to have a place removed from the gawping crowd of boys to whom had permeated the more dramatic details, and anxiously sought to be involved in the discussion. We separated D and C into a cell each, saw F who agreed to the absconding, witnessed the knife threats, and had actively co-operated with Mr Martin in disarming C and bringing him back to the school. G's imprecations and abuse, together with his wild demeanour had led Mr Martin to abandon pursuit of him and return with the two boys he had with him. It must be appreciated that Mr Martin was on his own, some mile from the school, and could have been in a precarious position if all three boys had chosen to band against him, that he behaved with excellence and brought a highly charged situation under control, with a two-thirds satisfactory conclusion.

Within the Secure Unit, both C and D had calmed considerably and separately had talked of their fears and worries. C accepted that his particular action was highly dangerous, and if it were officially reported would lead to some severe action from Magistrates in his forthcoming court case. Both boys were taken out of their dirty wet clothes and bathed, dressed in dressing-gowns and settled to watch television. At this point, Mr Rees brought through to us J who had been sniffing glue with K. He was closely followed by K, who was in his usual post glue condition of uncaring and belligerence. We bathed these two also, and then left them also watching T.V. I went for a meal and returned to the group. Again I went through the problems they complained of with each boy and for what it is worth extracted some degree of contact from them. I do not rate these contacts as other than ephemeral, with no lasting consistency. They were put to bed in their dormitories at normal bed-time, except for K who I isolated in an empty dormitory since he would have spent much of the early night retailing his stories to the others, and it seemed pointless to allow this.

I left the school at 12.15, having checked with the night staff that they were settled, and asking them to inform me if they needed help or there were any other problems. At that time, G, H and I were still missing and I reiterated this to Police Control.

On Sunday morning I was phoned at home by Mrs Williams, who had returned home on Saturday evening towards midnight and found G with a neighbour. It seems he had been there some two hours or so. She ascertained that he was indeed missing, phoned the police and cancelled him as an absconder and kept him for the night. She offered to keep him for the remainder of Sunday, but I asked her to bring him in to the school and she brought him at 11.30 am as requested. I saw him briefly but since he had discussed most of his immediate worries with Mrs Williams, it seemed pointless to cover the same ground. I reminded him of his share in the scene with Mr

Martin and advised him of the difficulties he now faced. He agreed with this and there I left the matter, returning him to the main group. He quickly was surrounded by his friends and seemed to enjoy telling them of his escapade and return. I note that his right wrist was marked, but not lacerated, where he tells me he had used a bottle on his wrist. He seemed unnaturally elated throughout the day, asking for fresh favours and seeming mildly surprised when his requests were not immediately granted.

Sunday evening, I, with the staff on duty, closed down very firmly at around 7.30, video films were provided by Mr Martin and the large majority of boys settled to watch these. Interestingly enough, G again wanted to do something different, could he play pool. C and B were not enthusiastic at having to stay in one place but seemed to settle to it. From staff comments, D was a little subdued from his previous night's experience, but C is still talking of absconding. He had a visit from his foster parents on Sunday afternoon, but was reluctant initially to see them. He seems committed to the idea that he is on his way to a custodial sentence and there is little point in settling.

GBA/CH

20 July, 1982

Statement of Sir Ronald Hadfield, assessor to the Tribunal in respect of police matters

1 I address below the principal issues which have arisen during the evidence concerning the response of the North Wales Police to complaints of abuse made by or on behalf of children in care between 1974 and 1996. The comments set out below are made solely from a policing perspective.

2 **The 1986/1987 investigation of DCS Gwynne Owen**

   2.1 There were a number of features of this investigation which were, in my experience, very unusual:

   2.1.1 the decision to ask the head of the CID to conduct an enquiry personally.

   2.1.2 the decision to undertake such extensive enquiries with a team of two, one of whom was head of the CID.

   2.1.3 the fact that Mr Owen carried out the actual interviews of some witnesses and alleged offenders.

   2.1.4 the decision not to involve the Director of Social Services in the investigation, together with the decision not to seize all available documentation, at the outset.

   2.2 The concept of joint investigations was not a new one at that time and in not consulting the Director, DCS Owen denied himself access to the files and other documents held by the Department. He also denied the Department the opportunity of addressing the position of Mr Dodd. In my experience, the primary action necessary if collusion is feared, is the rapid seizure of evidence and the taking of important statements. Yet this did not happen in the 1986/1987 investigation: I can see no advantage, and significant disadvantage, in DCS Owen's method of proceeding.

   2.3 Moreover, Mr Owen ought to have been aware from the outset that the evidence he was gathering would bring into question not only the criminal liability of Mr Dodd but also could raise questions as to his suitability for the post he held. I therefore find it inexplicable that there was such limited contact between him and Lucille Hughes [the Director of Social Services].

   Thoroughness of the 1986 investigation

   2.4 In carrying out his investigation, DCS Owen was under an obligation to do so with a high degree of thoroughness, particularly in the light of the fact that, as head of the CID, he had been selected to carry it out. Whether he discharged that obligation is essentially a matter for the Tribunal in the light of the evidence which it has heard, but in my view the following are some of the more important issues which require to be considered:

2.4.1 was any consideration given to the existence of documentary material in the possession of the Social Services Department, particularly at the commencement of the investigation, and, if not, why not?

2.4.2 was the allegation of assault by Nefyn Dodd upon (a boy at the tea-table)[1] properly investigated in the light of the number of potential witnesses to that event?

2.4.3 why did DCS Owen's team fail to find the 2 witnesses to (another) complaint[2] prior to submitting his 1986 report to the Chief Constable?

Urgency and thoroughness of the 1987 investigation

2.5 The 1987 enquiry commenced in December 1986 and was not completed until May 1988. In support of her statement (the former resident of Tŷ'r Felin)[3] offered the names of members of staff who would support her contentions. These witnesses were not all interviewed until the 21 March 1987. Bearing in mind the limited number of statements taken during the 1987 investigation, the overwhelming impression is of a sluggish and shallow investigation.

2.6 I would draw attention to the decision to delegate a number of the enquiries to surrounding police forces and in some cases to distant forces. These enquiries were conducted by junior officers who were briefed only by the covering letter. I am aware that to request a force to make enquiries on behalf of another was not unusual but I would suggest that in these circumstances it was unwise. The disadvantages of using officers from another force are obvious: they cannot have adequate local knowledge; they are unlikely to be sufficiently familiar with what other parties may have said, and may not be able to eliminate ambiguity and uncertainty; it may be seen by complainants as demonstrating a lack of commitment to them; and, in the particular circumstances of this investigation, there may be language difficulties. The cost involved in using North Wales Police officers would have been minimal.

The interviews with Nefyn Dodd: non-compliance with the provisions of the Police and Criminal Evidence Act 1984

2.7 The requirements of the Police and Criminal Evidence Act, which sets out the manner in which interviews will be conducted, were not complied with. No contemporaneous notes were taken. In my view, this is a startling omission, particularly in the light of the seniority

---

[1] See para 33.76 of the report.
[2] See paras 51.08 and 51.18 of the report.
[3] See para 51.19 of the report.

of the investigating officer. Whether DCS Owen gave Mr Dodd "a hard time" during these interviews, or whether he simply permitted Dodd to dictate his own version of events, is a matter for the Tribunal to determine, but, if the latter, may reflect upon the question of the officer's commitment to the investigation.

The reports to the Director of Public Prosecutions

2.8 The police have always been encouraged to include in their reports their impressions of witnesses and any important or material issues bearing upon a prosecution which they feel will emerge should the matter go before a jury. However, in my experience, the comments made by Mr Owen in his report into the 1986 enquiry were thoroughly inappropriate and lacking in judgment. The fairness and objectivity called for in these circumstances was absent and his comments showed a lack of tolerance and understanding of the witnesses. Above all, very serious imputations appear to have been made about the character and motives of Alison Taylor and certain complainants[4] on the basis of little more than instinct.

Feedback to the Director of Social Services

2.9 It is my opinion that the meeting between DCS Owen and the Director of Social Services [Lucille Hughes] in the Imperial Hotel, Llandudno, was not only essential but should have been supported by an agreed minute or letter confirming the content of the meeting. Whether DCS Owen did express the view then or at any time that Nefyn Dodd was unsuited to his position is a matter of evidence for the Tribunal. Similarly, the 1987 investigation revealed a considerable amount of further evidence against Dodd, and should have resulted in a detailed briefing of Ms Hughes by DCS Owen.

3 I should stress that in considering the adequacy of the 1986/1987 investigation, I have been mindful that practices have changed since the mid-eighties particularly in relation to allegations of child abuse, and have sought to put to one side the advantages of hindsight.

4 **The 1990 investigation**

4.1 It is my opinion that the officer in charge of the enquiry Detective Chief Inspector Cronin took that enquiry as far as I would have expected at that time, and I would not criticise him for not going back to explore Norris's earlier time at Bryn Estyn.

4.1.1 the investigating team obtained a clear and coherent case from its interviews with past and present staff and residents of Cartrefle, sufficient to found a multi-count indictment alleging serious offences against Norris.

4.1.2 there were no complaints from or indicators towards Bryn Estyn, a home which had closed some 6 years earlier.

---

[4] See para 51.13 of the report.

4.1.3 this was a "working together" investigation: DI Cronin gave evidence that he asked the Social Services Department for all relevant information about Norris, and was in regular contact with Geoffrey Wyatt. According to his evidence, there was no indication from the Department that Norris may have committed offences while at Bryn Estyn.

4.1.4 before any decision to extend the enquiry to Bryn Estyn was taken, consideration would be given to the cost and delay: the complainants in the Cartrefle prosecution were young and extremely vulnerable. In reality, if the investigation was to be extended to Bryn Estyn, the police would have had to carry out an investigation similar to that mounted in 1991/1992, ie would have sought to trace and interview all, or a large proportion, of former residents who passed through Cedar House and Clwyd House during Norris' time there.

5 The 1991/1992 enquiry

5.1 This was a complex and widespread enquiry, carried out against a background of considerable interest by the media and local politicians. The linking of the lines of enquiry, the tracing of victims, and the arrest of suspects, were all conducted appropriately. Indeed, in the light of the scale and complexity of the investigation, I consider that it was conducted thoroughly and impressively. There are, nevertheless, a number of issues which were canvassed in evidence, upon which I would comment as follows.

6 Adequacy of training of officers and briefing of those officers

Interviews of complainants by trained officers

6.1 It is clear from the evidence that the North Wales Police had a number of officers trained in interviewing possible victims of child abuse. The practices and procedures of interviewing vulnerable witnesses have improved dramatically over the past 20 years. Awareness of the difficulties in this form of enquiry had grown by 1992 and it is clear that the police were trying to ensure that the witnesses they were about to interview were properly cared for and considered. Training has improved further since 1992.

6.2 Taking into account the number of witnesses and severely traumatised witnesses the North Wales Police interviewed, and the comparatively small number of complaints of their treatment by the Police made by witnesses before the Tribunal, I do not consider that the force should be criticised for the manner of its treatment of witnesses generally. The Tribunal may find there to have been exceptions in individual cases, but, overall, the treatment of witnesses appears to have been satisfactory.

Proportion of female officers

6.3 According to the evidence, at the time of this enquiry the force had about 10 per cent female officers and a number of them were trained as interviewers of victims of abuse. There were five such officers in the enquiry team and the remainder had to remain on division to continue normal enquiries. I do not consider that unreasonable, and I would not criticise the breakdown of the teams by sex of the officers concerned.

Assistance from a psychologist

6.4 There may be a need, and perhaps this will be considered in another session in this Tribunal, for a national index to be maintained of suitably qualified instructors for this purpose who are available for such a task. The question of relevant experience and clearly defined purpose is important. It has been my experience that there are experts who offer their services during many types of police enquiries, but their value to the police investigation can be questionable.

Prior knowledge

6.5 I have experience of an enquiry in which prior knowledge of the witness by the police officer was used deliberately as a criterion for selecting the interviewing officer. Obviously, prior meetings which have been confrontational and negative are hardly likely to be conducive to a sensitive disclosure of abuse. This issue will always need to be addressed in each case by the senior investigating officer.

Statement-taking outside the North Wales Police's own geographical area

6.6 I commend the practice adopted of statement-taking by North Wales officers irrespective of the address of the witness. The commitment this shows, the local awareness and above all the avoidance of the witness being confronted by a total stranger from the area he has now chosen as a home, is in my view very important.

Arriving unannounced to see witnesses

6.7 This policy was explored in detail in evidence. In the circumstances of this enquiry, I personally would have chosen to arrive unannounced. The only additional comment I would make and a slight variation on the policy chosen by the North Wales Police, is that there must always be the case for an exception. Written advance notification is an alternative approach but the absence of available counselling, the difficulty in obtaining accurate addresses, and the possibility that others apart from the addressee may open or read the letter are but three of the problems which inevitably would have produced subsequent complaints if such methods had been adopted.

7 Calling in an outside force

7.1 There were at various times calls for an outside force to be brought in to take over or supervise the major enquiry:

At the outset of the enquiry

7.2 When the 1991 enquiry was launched there was only one force to carry it out, and to have requested any other force to do so would have been unusual in the extreme. There were no grounds for employment of an outside force at that stage and it should not be forgotten that the then complainants, the Clwyd County Council referred the matter to the North Wales Police. The allegations of corruption in the CID and the suppression of evidence which were made at the very outset were explored by the police and were shown to be with foundation.

December 1991: the Independent on Sunday *article*

7.3 Although there were calls for an outside force following publication of the article, as at that time there had in fact been no allegations of sexual abuse by serving or former police officers, and it is possible to see upon what rational basis the Chief Constable could have called in another force.

August 1992: allegations against Anglesea, X and Y[5]

7.4 Once police officers became involved in the allegations from August 1992 onwards the debate took a new twist. The reasons why it was not practicable to call in an outside force were rehearsed at length in evidence. Plainly, the Chief Constable had to exercise a discretion in the matter, and I would only criticise his decision if it could be shown to have been clearly wrong at the time. In reality, there were many factors supporting his decision. Above all, the major inquiry was very well advanced; the prime suspects had long since been arrested; the allegations against serving and former officers were closely linked to those against at least one of the suspects (Howarth); and a very large number of complainants had already been interviewed by the North Wales Police.

8 Supervision by the Police Complaints Authority

8.1 The purpose of supervision by the PCA is to ensure that allegations against serving police officers are investigated thoroughly and impartially. In the event, supervision of the 1991/1992 inquiry was never a live possibility, as all of the serious allegations against serving and former police officers fell outside the purview of the PCA. X and Gordon Anglesea had already retired from the police at the time that allegations were made against them; Z[6] was a former

---

[5] See paras 51.66 and 51.67 of the report.
[6] See para 51.68 of the report.

special constable, to whom the statutory provisions governing the PCA did not apply; and although Y was a serving officer, the allegations against him pre-dated those statutory provisions.

9 A review

9.1 A review of the enquiry as it was being conducted may have been one option to answer the perceived need in some quarters to question the independence of the North Wales Police, but such a review would have been an entirely new phenomenum. In 1991/1992 such reviews were confined to reviews of eg a murder enquiry in which no arrest had been made in the first 28 days or so in order that the investigating officer had the benefit of a second opinion to confirm that he had forgotten or omitted nothing. They were not intended as a means of reassuring the public or sections of it that an enquiry was being conducted thoroughly and impartially.

Sir Ronald Hadfield

GLOSSARY

OF

ABBREVIATIONS

Glossary of Abbreviations

ACPC	Area Child Protection Committee
ACPO	Area Child Protection Officer
ACPO	Association of Chief Police Officers
BAAF	British Association of Adoption and Fostering
CCETSW	Central Council for Education and Training in Social Work
CHE	Community Home with Education on the premises
CIPFA	Chartered Institute of Public Finance and Accountancy
COMT	Chief Officers Management Team
CPS	Crown Prosecution Service
CQSW	Certificate of Qualification in Social Work
CRCC	Certificate in the Residential Care of Children
CRCCYP	Certificate in the Residential Care of Children and Young People
CRPC	Children's Regional Planning Committee for Wales
CSE	Certificate in Secondary Education
CSS	Certificate in Social Services
CTSW	Council for Training in Social Work
DES	Department of Education and Science
DHSS	Department of Health and Social Security
EBD	Emotional and Behavioural Difficulties
ESN(s)	Educationally Sub-normal (severe)
GALRO	Guardian ad Litem Reporting Officer

GCE	General Certificate of Education
GRE	Grant Related Expenditure
HAS	Hospital (Health) Advisory Service
HMCI(Wales)	Her Majesty's Chief Inspector of Schools (Wales)
HMI	Her Majesty's Inspector of Schools
HOLMES	Home Office Large Major Enquiry System
ISCSC	In-Service Course in Social Care
LEA	Local Education Authority
LSE	London School of Economics
MMI	Municipal Mutual Insurance Ltd
NAI	Non Accidental Injury
NALGO	National Association of Local Government Officers
NoV	Note of Visit
OHMCI(Wales)	Office of Her Majesty's Chief Inspector of Schools (Wales)
PCA	Police Complaints Authority
PCSC	Preliminary Certificate in Social Care
PILO	Placement Information and Liaison Officer
PPIAS	Parent to Parent Information on Adoption Service
RAMC	Royal Army Medical Corps
RCCO	Residential Child Care Officer
RDCO	Residential and Day Care Officer
SEN	Special Educational Needs
SI	Staff Inspector (part of HMI)
SLR	Salmon letter recipient